SOME FAMOUS CITIZENS OF HARRISON COUNTY.

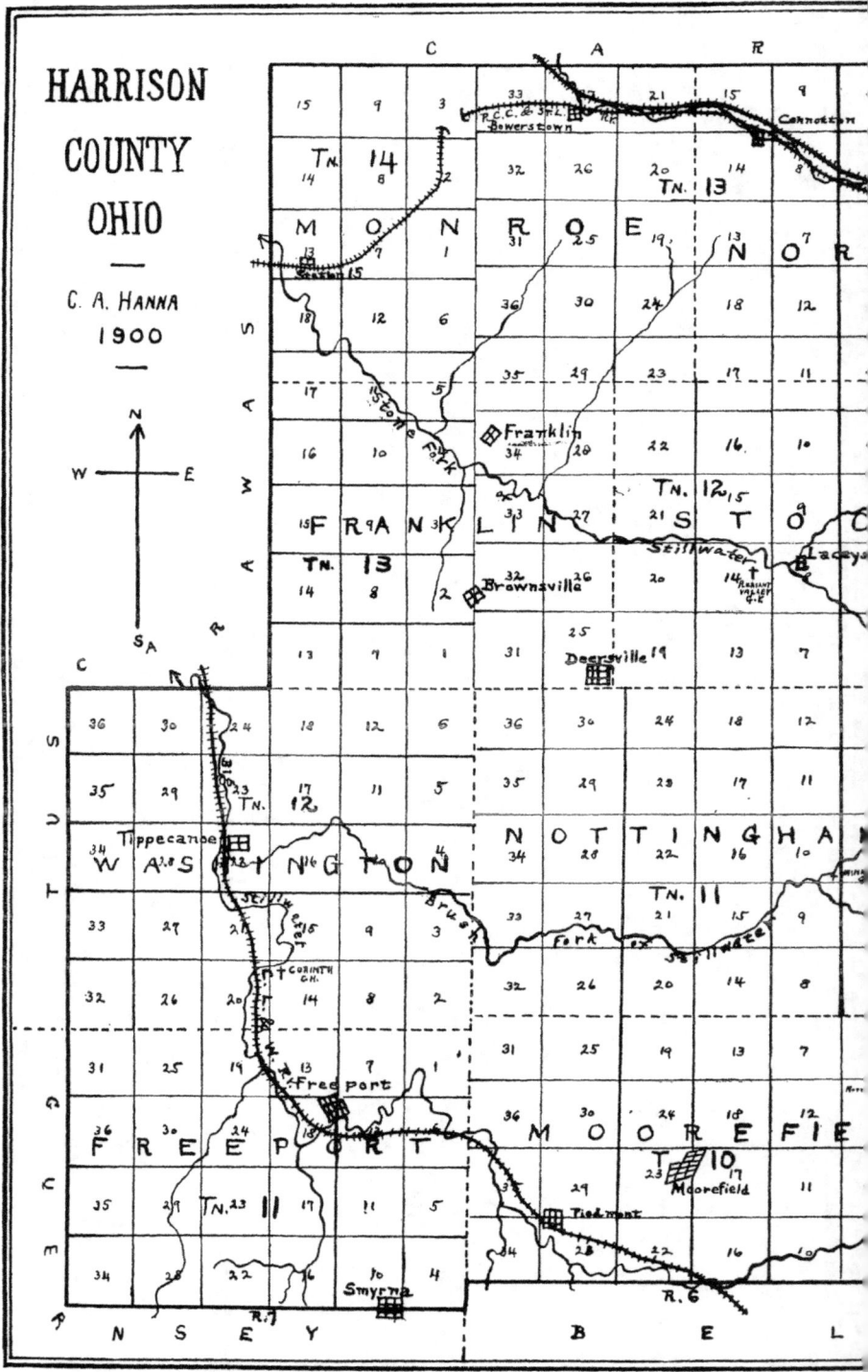

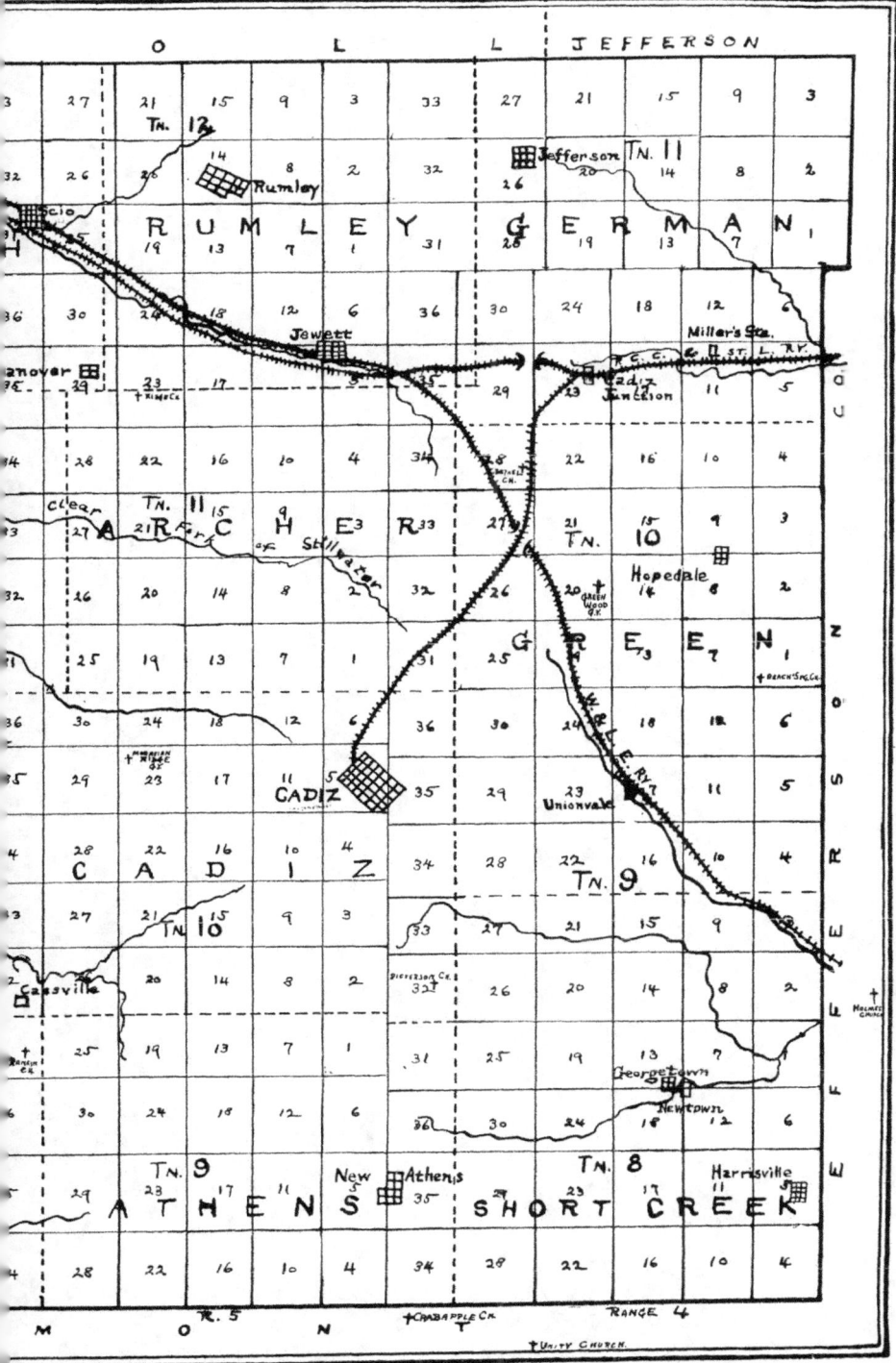

Historical Collections of
Harrison County
in the State of Ohio

with Lists of the First Land-Owners, Early
Marriages (to 1841), Will Records (to 1861),
Burial Records of the Early Settlements,
and Numerous Genealogies

Charles A. Hanna

HERITAGE BOOKS
2010

HERITAGE BOOKS
AN IMPRINT OF HERITAGE BOOKS, INC.

Books, CDs, and more—Worldwide

For our listing of thousands of titles see our website
at
www.HeritageBooks.com

A Facsimile Reprint
Published 2010 by
HERITAGE BOOKS, INC.
Publishing Division
100 Railroad Ave. #104
Westminster, Maryland 21157

Copyright © 1900 Charles A. Hanna

— Publisher's Notice —
In reprints such as this, it is often not possible to remove blemishes from the original. We feel the contents of this book warrant its reissue despite these blemishes and hope you will agree and read it with pleasure.

International Standard Book Numbers
Paperbound: 978-0-7884-1811-2
Clothbound: 9978-0-7884-8508-4

PREFACE.

The writer has long felt the need of a history of his native county, and in common with many citizens of that part of Ohio, has come to the conclusion that the lack of a suitable history has been due not so much to the dearth of interesting material as to the absence of a diligent collector sufficiently interested in the subject to gather the material up. While the present volume is concerned chiefly with the record of names and events connected with the first thirty years of the century, it will be found that the pioneer annals of Harrison county embrace by no means the least interesting portion of the county's history. So far as it goes, therefore, this book is offered as an attempt to supply a deficiency, the existence of which must be realized by all who have tried to learn something of the history of Harrison county.

Two or three of the sketches given in these Collections were printed in an abbreviated form during the year 1898 in the Cadiz "Republican." These have since been re-written and largely added to, and a number of others have been prepared, with a view to giving the reader as extensive a record of early Harrison county history as may be contained within the limits of one volume.

The second part of the book will be found to contain a very large amount of invaluable material for the student of the county's pioneer history, being made up of much of the county's land, marriage, burial, and will records. In the preparation of these records for printing, where such a vast number of names and dates have to be gone over, copied, re-copied, and arranged in order, it is very difficult to escape occasional errors in the spelling of a name or the transcribing of a date. While the utmost pains have been taken to prevent such errors, it is impossible to eliminate them all.

Following is a list of the principal sources of information regarding the history of Harrison county and Eastern Ohio to which the writer has had access:

Records of the Probate, Recorder's, Comissioners', Sheriff's, Clerk's, Auditor's, and Surveyor's offices of Harrison county.
Records of the Ohio State Adjutant General's office.
Records of the Presbytery of the Ohio.
Records of Steubenville Presbytery.

Records of the United States Interior Department.
Annual volumes of the Ohio Archaeological and Historical Society.
History of the County of Ayr, by James Patterson: Ayr, 1847.
History of Belmont and Jefferson counties, by J. A. Caldwell: Wheeling, 1880.
Historical Sketch of Bethel Methodist Episcopal Church, 1811-1894, by J. Fletcher Birney: Cadiz, 1894.
Travels in Holland, the United Provinces, England, Scotland, and Ireland, by Sir William Brereton: The Chetham Society, 1844.
Historical Sermon Preached in the First United Presbyterian Church of Cadiz, Ohio, August 26, 1876, by Rev. W. T. Meloy, Steubenille, 1876.
Historical Sketch of the First Presbyterian Church of Cadiz, by Rev. W. P. Shrom: The Cadiz "Republican" for August 28, 1884.
Memorial Dedication of Dickerson M. E. Church: Columbus, 1888.
History of Dumfries and Galloway, by Sir Herbert Maxwell: Edinburgh, 1896.
History of Fayette county, Penna., by Franklin Ellis: Philadelphia, 1882.
Autobiography of Rev. James B. Finley: Cincinnati, 1853.
Historical Address of Dr. Andrew Finley Ross at the Semi-Centennial Anniversary of the Founding of Franklin College, New Athens, June 23, 1875.
Lands and Their Owners in Galloway, by P. H. McKerlie: Edinburgh, 1877.
The Hamilton Manuscripts: Belfast, 1867.
Atlas of Harrison county, by J. A. Caldwell: Condit, Ohio, 1875.
Historical Sketches of Harrison County, by Rev. R. M. Coulter: The Cadiz "Republican," during 1898 and 1899.
Biographical Record of Harrison and Carroll Counties: Chicago, 1891.
A Brief History of Harrison County, by Dr. S. B. McGavran: Cadiz, 1894.
The Pathfinders of Jefferson County, by W. H. Hunter: Columbus, 1899.
Diary of David McClure: New York, 1899.
The Diary of Richard Lee Mason: The Chicago "Daily Record" for January 1st, 2d, 3d, and 4th, 1897.
The Montgomery Manuscripts: Belfast, 1869.
Forty Years' Pastorate [at Nottingham Church] and Reminiscences, by Rev. T. R. Crawford, D. D.: Wheeling, 1887.
Historical Collections of Ohio, by Henry Howe: Norwalk, 1896.
History of the Backwoods; or, The Region of the Ohio, by A. W. Patterson: Pittsburg, 1843.
Pennsylvania Archives: Philadelphia, 1852-55, Harrisburgh, 1874-1900.
American Pioneer, vol. ii.: Cincinnati, 1843.
Southern Quakers and Slavery, by Stephen B. Weeks: Baltimore, 1896.
Red-Men's Roads, by Archer Butler Hulbert: Columbus, 1900.
Old Redstone [Presbytery], by Joseph Smith, D. D.: Philadelphia, 1854.

Anniversary Discourse Delivered in the Ridge Church by Rev. Robert Herron, D. D., Dec. 13, 1873: Uhrichsville, 1874.
History of the Presbytery of St Clairsville, by T. R. Crawford and Robert Alexander: Washington, Pa., 1888.
History of the Presbytery of Steubenville, 1819-1887: Wooster, 1888.
The Scot in Ulster, by John Harrison: Edinburgh, 1888.
The Scottish Nation, by William Anderson: Edinburgh, 1870.
Annual volumes of the Scotch-Irish Society of America, 1889 to 1896.
Historic Events in the Tuscarawas and Muskingum Valleys, by C. H. Mitchener: Dayton, 1876.
Chronicles of Border Warfare, by Alexander S. Withers: Clarksburg, Va., 1831.
History of Washington County, Penna., by Boyd Crumrine: Philadelphia, 1882.
History of the Presbytery of Washington, by Rev. W. F. Hamilton and others: Philadelphia, 1889.
Sketches of Western Adventure, by John A. McClung: Dayton, 1854.
History of the Pan-Handle of Western Virginia, by J. H. Newton and J. A. Caldwell: Wheeling, 1884.
Notes on the Settlement and Indian Wars of the Western Parts of Virginia and Pennsylvania, by Rev. Joseph Doddridge: Wellsburg, Va., 1824.
Indian Wars of Western Virginia, by Wills DeHass: Wheeling, 1851.
History of Westmoreland County, Penna., by G. D. Albert, Philadelphia, 1882.
History of York County, Penna., by John Gibson: Chicago, 1886.

New York, July 1, 1900.

TYPICAL HARRISON COUNTY CITIZENS.

CONTENTS.

CHAPTER I.
THE SCOTCH-IRISH IN HARRISON COUNTY 1

CHAPTER II.
THE FRIENDS, OR QUAKERS, IN HARRISON COUNTY . . 22

CHAPTER III.
THE GERMANS AND VIRGINIANS IN HARRISON COUNTY . 34

CHAPTER IV.
THE FIRST SETTLERS IN EASTERN OHIO 43

CHAPTER V.
HARRISON COUNTY PIONEERS 54

CHAPTER VI.
EARLY DAYS IN CADIZ 75

CHAPTER VII.
BEECH SPRING CHURCH 92

CHAPTER VIII.
HARRISON COUNTY IN 1813 101

CHAPTER IX.
HARRISON COUNTY SETTLERS IN 1813 116

CHAPTER X.
CRABAPPLE AND UNITY CHURCHES 128

CHAPTER XI.
THE EARLY CHURCHES OF CADIZ 139

CHAPTER XII.
THE EARLY CHURCHES OF CADIZ—Continued . . . 156

CHAPTER XIII.
NOTTINGHAM AND FREEPORT CHURCHES 166

CHAPTER XIV.
DICKERSON, BETHEL, AND RANKIN CHURCHES . . . 175

CHAPTER XV.
THE RIDGE CHURCH 183

PART SECOND.

FIRST LAND OWNERS OF HARRISON COUNTY . . . 195

EARLY MARRIAGES IN HARRISON COUNTY—1813-1840 . . 238

GRAVEYARD RECORDS OF HARRISON COUNTY . . . 313

WILL ABSTRACTS OF HARRISON COUNTY—1813-1860 . . 401

HISTORICAL COLLECTIONS OF HARRISON COUNTY.

CHAPTER I.

THE SCOTCH-IRISH IN HARRISON COUNTY.

There is, perhaps, no one subject taught in our schools and institutions of learning to-day on which more misinformation has been imparted to the students than that of American history; and probably there is no part of that subject concerning which American people are more in ignorance than the part relating to their own racial origin.

Good Americans, generally, approved of the spirit of Mark Twain's rejoinder to Max O'Rell, when, in the course of a recent international exchange of compliments between the French and the Missouri humorists, the latter, to the charge that the average American did not usually know the name of his own grandfather, allowed that such might be the truth; but thought that Brother Jonathan was more apt to be sure of the name of his own father than were some others. The oft-repeated story of the observation made by a successful American gentleman traveling in Europe, who, when shown by an English lord the pictures of the latter's illustrious ancestors for some hundreds of years back, admitted that he had nothing of the kind at his home in America, because he was an illustrious ancestor himself,—is a characteristic illustration of the spirit in which, until quite recently, matters of race and family history have generally been regarded by the busy American workers of the present day.

Nevertheless, there is one class of our fellow citizens which has never been negligent in preserving the traditions and histories of their fathers; and never backward in letting America and the world at large know all about their merits and accomplishments. These are the people of New England—a people who, from the time of their first settlement in America, have preserved written records of most of their communities, and of almost every member living in and making a part of those communities; so that, as a consequence, there are few persons of New England descent living in the United States to-day, but who can find pages and volumes of history and eulogy in print as perpetual monuments to the virtues of one or several of their more or less remote progenitors.

Another and much more important consequence of this habit of committing to writing the history of men and communities in New England, is, that nearly all of our so-called histories of America have been written by New England men, are based chiefly upon New England records and examples, and have necessarily had to pass over in silence, or in a cursory way, the history of those other portions of our country and our citizens, of whom none of these written records have been preserved.

It is not strange, therefore, that in most of our schools to-day, and, I venture to say, in the public schools of Harrison county, American history is taught chiefly from books written by New England men, or their descendants; is viewed in these books from the conventional New England stand-point; and is based largely upon New England traditions, prejudices, and, in some cases, misrepresentations.

The chief misrepresentation to which attention may be called at this time, is the one so repeatedly made in certain of the newspapers and reviews, and by certain orators, and after-dinner speakers, that all the progress made by America since it was first colonized, and all the glorious history of which Americans are so proud, has been made because its people are of the Anglo-Saxon race, and in their progress are only continuing in the new world what their English forefathers had begun in the old.

Now, as a matter of fact, no such thing is the case. And while there should be no just praise withheld from the descendants of Englishmen for what their forefathers have done for America, it would be as great a wrong to them if we were to say that they had done nothing whatever, as it is to other Americans, of non-English origin, for the descendants of Englishmen to claim that the English have done it all.

How can these claims that the great men of American history are of exclusively English origin be considered in face of the fact that, of Washington's hundred generals, more or less, not half of them were of English blood; or, that of the great generals of the civil war on both sides, but little more than one-third were of English extraction; or, that of our twenty-four presidents, less than half the number have been of that stock; or, that of our great editors, three-fourths have been non-English in origin; or, that of our great judges, less than half have been English; or, that of American inventors of world-wide fame, about three out of every four have been of another race than English; or, that of the great leaders in the National congress, not half of them have been English by descent; or, that in our population to-day, nearly one-half are of other races than English. Yet these facts are all capable of ready demonstration, and can be verified by any one who will take the trouble to consult any standard biographical and statistical dictionary.

In the State of Ohio, for instance, if the English are to have the sole credit for all the good that has come to America, what would become of the fame of Arthur St. Clair, of Jeremiah Morrow, of Allen Trimble, of Duncan McArthur, of Joseph Vance, of Wilson Shannon, of Mordecai Bartley, of Reuben Wood, of Rutherford B. Hayes, of Seabury Ford, of William Medill, of James E. Campbell, of Thomas L. Young, of Joseph B. Foraker, of Charles Foster, of William McKinley, and of some few others who have been governors of the State? Or, of Presidents Grant, Hayes, Garfield, and McKinley? Or, of certain supreme court judges, such as Jacob Burnet, John McLean, Joseph R. Swan, John C. Wright, Thomas W. Bartley, W. B. Caldwell, William Kennon, Hocking H. Hunter, George W. McIlvaine, W. J. Gilmore, Rufus P. Ranney, Josiah Scott, John Clark, W. W. Johnson, and John H. Doyle? Or, of certain well-known journalists, such as Whitelaw Reid, W. L. Brown, John A. Cockerill, Joseph Medill, Samuel Medary, W. W. Armstrong, the Farans and McLeans, and Richard Smith? Or, of Bishop Simpson, of John A. Bingham, and of Salmon P. Chase? Or, of William Dean Howells and of John Q. A. Ward? Or, of Generals U. S. Grant, Phil Sheridan, Quincy A. Gilmore, James B. Steadman, Irvin McDowell, John Beatty, O. M. Mitchell, James B. McPherson, Henry W. Lawton, and the fighting families of the McCooks?

No, the truth of the matter is, that a vast proportion of American people, sometimes classed by the historians as British, have had their hard-earned laurels transferred to the brows of the so-called Anglo-Saxons, or English; and very much of the honor and glory which are so frequently claimed for the English in this country, really belong to the people of another, and a distinctly different race.

These people are the Scotch-Irish, as they have come to be called, who have done vastly more in the settlement and development of the central and southern portions of our country than the English, and yet a people who have been too busy making history to spare the time to write it; and one whose early annals, for this reason, have been, until recent years, so far neglected as to be well-nigh forgotten. This is the race to which belong, with the exception of those of Howells, Garfield, and Sheridan, probably all of the names given above; and to the same race, also, belong, it is safe to say, at least seventy-five per cent. of the sturdy farmers and substantial citizens of Harrison county.

It is needless to ask in addition, therefore, what would become of the fair name and fame of Harrison county, if the English were the only people who have made America what it is to-day.

Nevertheless, the Scotch-Irish communities and people of Harrison county, as a rule, have few traditions or remembered history back of the time when settlements were first begun there, in the early years of the present century. These people know in a general way that their respective fathers or grandfathers came from the East—from Pennsylvania usually—and in most cases from the territory originally included in the counties of Washington, Westmoreland, Cumberland, York, or Chester. The majority of them know that they are of Scotch-Irish descent; without understanding clearly what that term, in its American sense, signifies, some having the impression that it means the descendants of a married couple, of whom one parent is Scotch, and the other Irish. It may be that this feeling of belonging to a mixed nationality deters them from making any inquiries as to what are the real sources of the Scotch-Irish blood.

If the facts are ascertained, however, they will find that they have a race history than which no other nation or people can boast one more proud, whether it be English or German, Roman or Castillian. The Scotch-Irish are not, nor have they ever been, of Irish blood—using the latter word in its racial sense; but are purely Scottish. Their emigrant ancestors in this country, to whom the name was first applied, were people of unmixed Scotch descent, who came to America from their Scottish communities in the North of Ireland; and all the glorious history and ancestral traditions of their Scottish forefathers belong to their descendants in Harrison county to-day, just as much as the history and ancestral traditions of the English belong to people of early New England stock.

And, truly, it is a noble heritage, and one that will not suffer a whit by comparison with that of the English. It begins in the time of Agricola, the Roman general, who, when he had conquered all the present territory of England, and carried his victorious banners north to the Grampian hills in Scotland, found there a foe who could effectually hinder his further advance, and cause him for the first time to acknowledge that here was at last an unknown and unconquerable race beyond his own conquered ULTIMA THULE. It continues in the plundering forays and invasions of the Scots and Picts, who carried their dreaded arms from one end of the island to the other, unchecked; and, later, in the piratical incursions of the Vikings, who came westward from their safe retreats within the Norwegian fiords, to fight, to plunder, to destroy, and eventually to settle, among the sea-girt islands and peninsulas of western Scotland. Its dark and bloody deeds are instanced by the tragic history of Macbeth; and its bright and chivalrous actions are shown by incidents like that of the Battle of Otterburn, so spiritedly set forth in the glowing pages of Froissart, who says of it, that "of all the battles that have been described in my history, great and small, this was the best fought, and the most severe." Scotland's early glory came in the days of William Wallace and Robert Bruce, when its independence was won from the English by the sword; and continued through the two centuries following, because kept fresh by the blood of opposing Scots and English shed on more than two hundred battlefields. Its high ideal of freedom was realized first in the days of Knox and of Melville, when those men bid defiance to tyrants, and dared declare that rulers were amenable to law, and could be punished by law; and was again vindicated in the days of their successors, the Scots clergy, who, "when the light grew dim, and flickered on the altar, . . . trimmed the lamp, and fed the sacred flame," and kept alive for themselves, for their children, and for all mankind, the precious heritage of human liberty.

The Scotsman is of composite race. The forefathers of three-fourths of the Scotch-Irish in Harrison county lived in the western Lowlands of Scotland, and their blood was of various strains, blended into what finally became that of the Scottish race. The basis of the race was the Romanized Briton (and from this line the Lowland Scot gets his Celtic blood, and not from Ireland), with more or less marked departures, occasioned by intermarriages, first with the Picts and Scots, then with the Angles, the Danes, and the Norsemen. From the last-named stock comes most of the Teutonic blood of the western Scot; while the Angles occupied and largely peopled the east coast. After the eleventh century, the Normans came into Scotland in large numbers, and occupied much of the land; so that many families can claim Norman descent. Long before the seventeenth century, when the emigration to Ireland began, the various race groups had become fused into one composite whole, having the attributes of the Celt, the Norse, the Angle, and the Norman; thus typifying many centuries ago the identical race which we are beginning to recognize here as the American—a combination of the Teuton and the Celt. Let us hope the type may include all the virtues of both without the defects of either.

The real history of the forefathers of that part of the American people who live in Harrison county, therefore—with a few individual exceptions—is not to be found in the pages of the historians and writers of England; but of those of Scotland. Their lives and spirits have been not unworthily portrayed by the wizard hand of Scott, and their joys and sorrows have been divinely sung in the inspired notes of Burns. And it is in the heart-touching stories of MacLaren, and Barrie, and Stevenson, that we find the true prototypes and the doubles of ourselves and our friends in Harrison county.

The history of Scotland as a country, and of Scottish men and institutions, however, is as a sealed book to ninety-nine out of every hundred students in most of our high-schools and colleges; and it is partly because of the entire absence of any information to the contrary in the ordinary historical text-books, that the erroneous impression has gained ground in so many places outside of New England, that our American colonies and American institutions are almost entirely of English origin.

Now, to bring the matter nearer home to the readers of this history, let us take a few of the family names that are so well known in Harrison county, and see how many of them are English, and how many are Scotch.

In 1898, Mr. Orville Dewey contributed some interesting articles to the Cadiz Republican, giving an account of the early history of his own family, and from this we learn that the Deweys came from Connecticut. They were English, although there were many of the early Scotch-Irish who settled in New England. The Hollingsworths were originally Pennsylvania Quakers, tracing back through the North of Ireland to England. The Browns were also English; likewise, the Scotts, Arnolds, Laceys, Hearns, Woods, and others. But the early representatives of nearly all of these families having intermarried with the Harrison county Scotch-Irish, their descendants living there to-day are more Scotch than English. Other originally English families from the North of Ireland may be mentioned, of whom were the Hammonds, the Phillipses, and the Haverfields; but their forefathers lived and intermarried amongst the Scotch for so long a time before coming to America that their descendants in Harrison county to-day can hardly be said to retain more than a trace of the English blood, or traits, or anything else English but the names.

The Cunningham family originated in the district of Cunningham, in Ayrshire; as did likewise the Carrick and Kyle families in the other two districts of that county.

Other Ayrshire family names represented in Harrison county are those of Aiken, Alexander, Allison, Anderson, Barclay, Blair, Boggs, Boyd, Caldwell, Cannon, Clark, Cochran, Collins, Coulter, Crawford, Culbertson, Dunlap, Ervin, Ferguson, Fullerton, Fulton, Hamilton, Hunter, Jackson, Jamison, Kennedy, Logan, McCready, Mitchell, Montgomery, Moore, Morrison, Patton, Porter, Rankin, Rea, Richey, Rogers, Simpson, Thompson, Vance, Wallace, Watson, Welch, Wiley, Wilson, and a great many more besides.

The McFaddens are first mentioned in history in connection with their residence on the Island of Mull, off the coast of and belonging to Argyleshire. All the "Macs" living in Harrison county, it may be safely said, are of Scottish descent, and usually Celtic or Highland Scots. The prefix "Mac" (meaning "son of"), is of Celtic origin, and in early times it was rarely found in connection with the names of the Lowland clans, except in the cases of McCulloch and McClellan, and a few other ancient Galloway families. Later in Scotland's history, however, the "Macs" were carried pretty much all over the country, and into Northern Ireland, as the clans continued to migrate and to intermarry with the Lowlanders. The name, McConnell, is corrupted from McDonald, or McDonnell, at one time the largest and most powerful of the Highland clans.

From the counties of Wigtonshire and Kirkcudbrightshire (once forming the ancient principality of Galloway, and from whence come the Galloway cattle,) besides the McCullochs and the McClellans, come also the Agnews, Boyles', Douglasses, Carnahans, Carsons, Glendennings, Gordons, Hannas, Herrons, Kerrs, McCreas, McBrides, McMaths, McMychens, McMillans, Maxwells, Ramseys, Stewarts, and others.

James Hogg, the "Ettrick Shepherd," and poet, was from Selkirkshire, and the name also occurs in Perthshire.

From Fifeshire come the Bealls, the Hendersons, and also some of the Gillespie families.

From Dumbartonshire, just north of Glasgow, come the Calhouns and the Macfarlands.

From Elginshire come the Birnies.

From Inverness, in the Highlands, come the McBeans, McKinleys, and Finlays, (all septs of the once powerful Clan Chattan, of whom the chiefs were McIntoshes and McPhersons); also the Davidsons and Grants.

From Lanarkshire, the Biggars.

From Forfarshire, the Lyons and the Ogilvies.

From Stirlingshire, the Buchanans, Forsythes, and Pattersons.

From Edinburghshire, the Craigs, Kerrs, Gilmores, Ramseys, and Waddells.

From Sutherland, in the northern Highlands, the McKays, McCoys, McKees, etc., many of whom are also found in Galloway.

From Dumfriesshire, south of Glasgow, the Carothers', Elliotts, Dicksons (and, possibly, also the Dickersons), the Johnstons, and the Kirkpatricks.

From Caithness, the most northern county of Scotland, the McRaes (and, possibly, also the Raes, Reas, or Rays, although many of this name lived in Galloway and Ayrshire).

From Renfrewshire, the Knoxes.

Nearly all the Scotch who settled in the North of Ireland at the time of the first plantation of Ulster (1606 to 1625), came from the western Lowland counties of Scotland, lying on the opposite coast and less than thirty miles distant from county Down. The greater part of them came from Ayrshire and Galloway, and those two districts in Scotland were the nesting-places of the early Scottish ancestors of the majority of the people living in Harrison county to-day. The scene of Scott's "Guy Mannering" is laid in Wigtonshire (the western half of Galloway), as is also that of much of S. R. Crockett's "Galloway Herd." All readers of Burns, and of Stevenson's "Master of Ballantrae," are familiar with Ayrshire. The places and people of these districts are also well known to those who have read of the persecutions and sufferings of the early Scottish Covenanters.

The story of the Scottish emigration to Ulster may be outlined in a few paragraphs. It begins near the close of the year 1602, when Con McNeale O'Neale, of Castlereagh, got into serious trouble, by reason of not having his wine-casks full at the time when he had invited some of his relatives to have a "wee drop" with him. Con ruled the Upper Clannaboye, the north half of County Down; and happened to be holding high state in his halls of Castlereagh with his brothers, and cousins, and relatives of near degree. They were all "proper" men—to use a Celtic term of respect—and quite naturally drank Con's cellar dry; whereupon he despatched retainers to Belfast, two miles distant, for a fresh supply of wine. There his servants had a quarrel with certain soldiers of Queen Elizabeth, who were stationed at Belfast Castle, and they came back to their master without the "drink." This naturally roused Con to fury, and he threatened dire vengeance on his clansmen if they did not return to the fight, punish the English, and recover the wine. The second encounter proved more serious than the first; an English soldier was killed, and the Irish Government took the matter up. Con was charged with "levying war against the Queen," and thrown into the Castle as a prisoner, from whence he seemed likely to escape only by the loss of his head. In this extremity, Con's wife appealed for help to Hugh Montgomery, Laird of Braidstane, in Ayrshire, whose home lay on the Scottish coast, across the Irish channel. Montgomery, for a "consideration," agreed to help Con to escape; and to that purpose immediately sent his relative, Thomas Montgomery of Blackston, who was the owner of a trading-sloop, to Carrickfergus Castle. Arriving there, the canny Thomas, without loss of time, proceeded to make love to the keeper's daughter; and to such good effect, that having been admitted to the Castle, he contrived to get the prison-guard to drink a very large quantity of what was possibly some of the same wine over which the fight had arisen. Con was then furnished with a rope, by which he let himself out of a window, found Thomas Montgomery's sloop waiting for him in the Lough, and was across to Braidstane and safety within a few hours. Here, Con entered into an agreement with Hugh Montgomery, by which he agreed to cede to him half his lands in Clannaboye (the proportion afterwards being increased to two-thirds), on condition that the latter should procure him a free pardon from King James for all his offences, and get Con admitted to the King's presence, and allowed to kiss the King's hand. Through the assistance of Mr. James Hamilton, an influential courtier, this pardon was later obtained, and Con admitted to His Majesty's presence; and two-thirds of Con's estates were in due time confirmed to Hamilton (who also required a "consideration") and Montgomery by the Crown.

As soon as the patents were issued by the Irish Council, Con's beneficiaries crossed into Scotland again, to call upon their whole kith and kin to aid them in the plantation of their estates, it having been a condition imposed by the King, in confirming the grant, that the lands were to be "planted" with English and Scottish colonists; and to be granted only to those of English and Scottish blood, "and not to any of the mere Irish." To Hamilton fell the western portion of North Down, to Montgomery, the eastern; and both seem to have added to their estates, as Con O'Neale was forced to sell the third which he had reserved for himself. Both were Ayrshire men, and both from the northern division of the county. Hamilton was of the Hamilton family of Dunlop; and Montgomery was from near Beith. The former founded the towns of Bangor and Killyleagh, and raised churches in each of the six parishes embraced in his estate—Bangor, Killinchy, Holywood, Ballyhalbert, Dundonald, and Killyleagh. Montgomery's estate embraced the country around Newton and Donaghadee known as the Great Ards. He belonged to a family having numerous connections throughout North Ayrshire and Renfrewshire, and to them he turned for assistance. His principal supporters were his kinsmen, Thomas Montgomery. his brother-in-law, John Shaw, son of the laird of Wester Greenock, and Colonel David Boyd, of the noble house of Kilmarnock. With their help he seems to have persuaded many others of high and low degree to join in trying their fortunes in Ireland, among them being the Montgomeries, Calderwoods, Agnews, Adairs, Cunninghams, Shaws, Muirs, Maxwells, Boyles, Harvies, and many others with good west-country surnames.

The success of this settlement made by Hamilton and Montgomery was immediate; for four years after the foundation of the colony—in 1610—Montgomery alone was able to bring before "the King's mustermaster a thousand able fighting men to serve, when out of them a militia should be raised." Four years after this time, in a letter written from North Down by the Earl of Abercorn to John Murray, King James's secretary of state, he says, in referring to the same colonists: "They have above 2,000 habile Scottis men well armit heir, rady for his Majestie's service as thai sall be commandit." This muster of 2,000 men able to bear arms, represented an emigration of at least 10,000 persons.

Meantime, across the river Lagan, in county Antrim, a plantation had been made by Sir Arthur Chichester, then Lord Deputy of Ireland. This, though not at first peculiarly Scottish, was soon to become so. In 1603, Chichester obtained a grant of the Castle of Belfast, and around this fortress a village soon sprang up. The Commissioners' Survey, taken in the year 1611, reports that "the town of Belfast is plotted out in a good forme, wherein are many famelyes of English, Scotch, and some Manksmen already inhabitinge, and ane inn with very good lodging." The Settlement Commissioners passed along the north shore of Belfast Lough, finding everywhere houses springing up, and in every part of the Lord Deputy's lands, "many English famelies, some Scottes, and dyvers cyvill Irish planted." While South Antrim was thus "planted," mainly by English settlers, the northern half of the county was opened up for settlement, without the violent transference of land from Irish to Briton, which was carried out in other parts of Ulster. The northeast corner of Ireland had been long held by the MacDonnells (the Highland pronunciation of this name is MacConnell), a clan which also peopled the island of Jura, and Cantyre on the mainland of Scotland. The chief of these Scoto-Irishmen, Randall MacDonnell, after the Earl of Tyrone's rebellion, resolved to throw in his lot with the Government, and turn loyal subject. This he did, and as reward received a grant of the northern half of county Antrim, from Larne to Portrush, and the honor of knighthood. He set himself to the improvement of his lands, letting out to the natives on the coast, and also to the Scottish settlers, such arable portions of his lands as had been depopulated by the war, for terms varying from twenty-one to 301 years. These leases seem to have been largely taken advantage of by the Scottish settlers, who allowed the natives to keep the "Glynnes," or Glens, and themselves took possession of the rich land along the river Bann, from Lough Neagh to the town of Coleraine, near its mouth. Thus, in time, county Antrim, from north to south, became nearly as Scottish as the portion of county Down lying north of the Mourne mountains.

The plantations in counties Down and Antrim, however, were limited in scope in comparison with the "Great Plantation in Ulster," for which James I.'s reign will be forever remembered in Ireland.

About the year 1607, O'Neill, Earl of Tyrone, and MacDonnell, Earl of Tyrconnel, with a number of the lesser Irish chiefs, having rebelled against the King and been proclaimed traitors, their lands were confiscated by the Crown; and all of northern Ireland—Londonderry, Donegal, Tyrone, Cavan, Armagh, and Fermanagh—passed into the hands of the King.

The plan adopted by James for the colonization of these six "escheated" counties, was to take possession of the finest portions of this great tract of country (amounting in all to nearly four millions of acres); to divide it into small estates, none larger than two thousand acres; and to grant these to men of known wealth and substance. Those who accepted grants were bound to live on their lands themselves, to bring with them English and Scottish settlers, and to build for themselves and for their tenants fortified places for defence, houses to live in, and churches in which to worship. The native Irish were assigned to the poorer lands and less accessible districts; while the allotments to the English and Scots were kept together, so that they might form communities, and not mix or intermarry with the Irish. The purpose was not only to transfer the ownership of the land from Irish to Briton, but to introduce a British population in place of an Irish one.

James seems to have seen that the parts of Scotland nearest Ireland, and which had most intercourse with it, were most likely to yield proper colonists. He resolved, therefore, to enlist the assistance of the great families of the southwest, trusting that their feudal power would enable them to bring with them bodies of colonists. Thus, grants were made to Ludovick Stewart, Duke of Lennox, who had great power in Dumbartonshire; to James Hamilton, Earl of Abercorn, and his brothers, who represented the power of the Hamiltons in Renfrewshire. North Ayrshire had been already largely drawn on by Hamilton and Montgomery, but one of the sons of Lord Kilmarnock, Sir Thomas Boyd, received a grant; while from South Ayrshire came the Cunninghams and Crawfords, and Andrew Stewart (Lord Ochiltree) and his son. But it was on Galloway men that the greatest grants were bestowed. Almost all the great houses of the time are represented—Sir Robert MacLellan, Laird Bomby, as he is called, who afterwards became Lord Kirkcudbright; John Murray of Broughton, one of the secretaries of state; Vans (Vance) of Barnbarroch; Sir Patrick McKie of Laerg; Dunbar of Mochrum; one of the Stewarts of Garlies, from whom Newtown Stewart takes its name. With the recipient of 2,000 acres, the agreement was that he was to bring "forty-eight able men of the age of eighteen or upwards, being born in England or the inward [i. e., southern] parts of Scotland." The progress of the colonies in the different counties is very accurately described in a series of reports by Government inspectors, at various periods between the years 1610 to 1620, and in the letters of Chichester himself, which are to be found in the Calendar of State Papers for Ireland, and in the Carew Papers (both published by the British Government).

The most interesting of these reports are those regarding "undertakers" (as the grantees were called), who took possession in the year 1610, made up their minds to remain and to thrive in Ulster, and who founded families whose names were afterwards to be well known in Ireland. In Donegal, on Lough Swilly, will be found on the map the names of two villages, Manor Cunningham and Newtown Cunningham. The men who introduced so Scottish a name into so Irish a county are thus noticed in the report of 1611: "Sir James Cunningham, Knight, Laird Glangarnoth, 2,000 acres, took possession, but returned into Scotland. Three families of British residents preparing to build . . . John Cunningham of Cranfield, 1,000 acres, resident with one family of British . . . Cuthbert Cunningham, 1,000 acres, resident with two families of British; built an Irish house of coples, and prepared materials to re-edify the Castle of Coole-McEtreen." In county Tyrone, "The Earl of Abercorn, chief undertaker in the precinct in the county of Tyrone, has taken possession, resident with lady and family, and built for the present near the town of Strabane some large timber houses . . . His followers and tenants have since May last built twenty-eight houses of fair coples, and before May by his tenants, who are all Scottish men, the number of thirty-two houses of like goodness." "The Lo. Uchelrie [Lord Ochiltree] 3,000 acres in the county of Tyrone, being stayed by contrary winds in Scotland, arrived in Ireland at the time of our being in Armagh, upon our return home, accompanied with thirty-two followers, gent. of sort, a minister, some tenants, freeholders, and artificers."

In 1618, the Irish Government instructed Captain Nicholas Pynnar to inspect every allotment in the six "escheated" counties, and to report on each one, whether held by "natives" or "foreign planters." Pynnar's report (published in the Irish State Papers), presents a very exact picture of what had been done by the settlers in the counties inspected— Londonderry, Donegal, Tyrone, Armagh, Cavan, and Fermanagh. He states that, "there are upon occasion 8,000 men of British birth and descent for defence, though a fourth part of the lands is not fully inhabited." Of these, fully three-fourths must have been Scots; and if there be added the great colonies in Down and Antrim, there must have been an immigration from Scotland of between 30,000 and 40,000 in these ten years.

The only county in which the Scottish settlers failed to take firm root was Fermanagh, for there, in 1618, when Pynnar reported, a large number of the Scottish proportions had been sold, and were held by Englishmen. The result is seen in the small number of Presbyterians in comparison to Episcopalians to be found at the present day in county Fermanagh.

The most exact account of the emigration to Ulster is contained in a book of travels in Scotland and Ireland, by Sir William Brereton, of Cheshire, England. He states that he came to Irvine, in Ayrshire, on July 1st, 1635, and was hospitably entertained by Mr. James Blair, and that his host informed him that "above ten thousand persons have within two years last past left this country wherein they lived, which was betwixt Áberdine and Enuerness [Inverness], and are gone for Ireland; they have come by one hundred in company through this town, and three hundred have gone hence together, shipped for Ireland at one tide. None of them can give a reason why they leave the country; only some of them who make a better use of God's hand upon them have acknowledged to mine host in these words, 'that it was a just judgment of God to spew them out of the land for their unthankfulness.' One of them I met withal and discoursed with at large, who could give no good reason, but pretended the landlords increasing their rents; but their swarming in Ireland is so much taken notice of and disliked, as that the Deputy has sent out a warrant to stay the landing of any of these Scotch that come without a certification."

The closing sentence of the foregoing extract gives us a brief and characteristic description of Scottish motives and methods in the colonization and settlement of a new country, that may well be applied to every one of their successive migrations, or "swarmings," from that day to this. It was the spirit of unrest, the thirst for adventure, and, chiefly, the desire to better their worldly condition, that led them into the Land of Promise in that day, and at numerous periods since. They came without regard to the jealous forebodings of the governing few, already on the ground, who feared they themselves would be outnumbered by the strangers; they likewise paid no regard to the official restrictions by which the rulers of Ireland at that time, and the Councils of American colonies a century later, sought to prevent their entry.

The emigration from Ireland to America of the grandchildren and great-grandchildren of these Scottish colonists of the sixteenth century began soon after 1700; and for more than three-quarters of a century afterwards, Ulster poured into America a continuous stream, sometimes reaching the dimensions of a flood, of people of Scottish birth or descent. In 1718, several hundred of them came together from the Valley of the Bann, south of the town of Coleraine, in county Londonderry, landing at Boston. Here, they were not permitted by the Puritans to remain, but were obliged to go out to the frontiers, forming colonies along the coast of Maine, at Londonderry, in New Hampshire, and at Worcester, in Massachusetts. In the latter place, they built a church, and contemplated having Presbyterian services, after the manner of their fathers; but the bigoted Puritans, then in the majority, tore down the building in the night; forced them to abandon the project, and taxed them to support their own State Church. Many of these settlers were thus obliged to move further out towards the frontier, where they founded the towns of Pelham and Coleraine, in Massachusetts.

A great many Scotch and Scotch-Irish also emigrated to New York, to New Jersey, and to Maryland, Virginia, and the Carolinas. But it was to Pennsylvania, the Quaker Colony, that the great bulk of the Ulster migration came. They began to reach there before 1710; and before 1720, thousands had come into the colony by way of Newcastle, Del. (then included in Pennsylvania). At first, they generally settled near the disputed Maryland boundary line. Before 1730, they had occupied much of the lower lands in the townships of East and West Nottingham, Cecil county, Maryland, and Mill Creek and White Clay Creek in Newcastle county, Delaware. In Pennsylvania they settled in the townships of London Britain, New London, Londonderry, London Grove, East and West Nottingham, Upper and Lower Oxford, East and West Fallowfield, Sadsbury, East and West Caln, and the newer townships between, in Chester county; Little Britain, Colerain, Bart, Sadsbury, Salisbury, Drumore, Martic, and Donegal in Lancaster county; and Derry, Paxtang, and Hanover, in Dauphin county. They had also gone into Bucks county in large numbers, settling in Warwick and Warminster townships, along Neshaminy creek; and in Northampton county, in Allen and Hanover townships.

James Logan, then secretary of the province, and himself a Scotch-Irish Quaker, writing of them to the Penns in 1724, states that they had generally taken up the southern lands (towards the Maryland line), and as they rarely approached him with proposals of purchase, he calls them "bold and indigent strangers, saying as their excuse, when challenged for titles, that we had solicited for colonists and they had come accordingly." They were, however, understood to be a tolerated class, exempt from quit-rents by an ordinance of 1720, in consideration of their being a frontier people, and forming a cordon of defence about the non-fighting Quakers. They thus served to protect them, if need be—and the necessity often arose—from the murderous incursions of the Indians, and from Maryland and Virginia invaders who claimed part of the land as within the bounds of their own colonies.

In 1729, Logan expresses himself as pleased to find that Parliament is about to take measures to prevent the too free emigration from Ulster to America. "It looks," he writes, "as if Ireland is to send all its inhabitants hither, for last week not less than six ships arrived, and every day, two or three arrive also. The common fear is that if they thus continue to come they will make themselves proprietors of the Province. It is strange that they thus crowd where they are not wanted. . . The Indians themselves are alarmed at the swarms of strangers, and we are afraid of a breach between them—for the [Scotch-] Irish are very rough to them." In 1730, he writes and complains of the Irish as having in an "audacious and disorderly manner" possessed themselves about that time of the whole of Conestoga Manor, a tract of about 15,000 acres, which had been reserved by the Penns for themselves, as it contained some of the best land in the Province. In taking this land by force, he says, they alleged that "it was against the laws of God and nature, that so much land should be idle while so many Christians wanted it to labor on, and to raise their bread." This same spirit on the part of the Scotch-Irish led them in after years (1745-50) to settle in the Tuscarora and Path Valleys, where their cabins were burned by the provincial authorities, and later (1763-8), along Redstone creek in what is now Fayette county, where they were warned off by the Quaker Assembly, "under pain of death;" and later still (1779 and 1784-7) along and near Short creek, in what is now the territory of Jefferson, Belmont, and Harrison counties, Ohio, where they were repeatedly driven off by United States troops, their cabins burned, and their improvements destroyed; but to which localities they as persistently returned and rebuilt, and remained on the land, improving it, until the Territory was thrown open for settlement.

In another letter written by Logan, about the same time (1730), he says: "I must own, from my own experience in the land-office, that the settlement of five families from Ireland gives me more trouble than fifty of any other people. Before we were broke in upon, ancient Friends and first settlers lived happily; but now the case is quite altered."

Logan's successor, Richard Peters, had a somewhat similar experience with the Scotch-Irish emigrants of his day. In a letter written by him in 1743, he states that he went to the Manor of Maske, to warn off and dispossess the squatter settlers. This was another choice tract of upwards of 40,000 acres, located in the wilderness by the Penns as a reservation, lying on both sides of Marsh creek, then in Lancaster, now in Adams county, being the site of Gettysburg, and including the bottom lands southward to the Maryland line. On that occasion, the people who were settled there, to the number of about seventy, assembled and forbade Penn's surveyors to proceed. On the latter persisting, the settlers broke the surveyors' chain, and compelled them to retire. Peters had with him at the time a sheriff and a magistrate; and many of the settlers were afterwards indicted; but a compromise was effected, by which the squatters were permitted to lease and purchase the Penn titles for a comparatively insignificant consideration; and they were left in possession.

The reasons for the emigration of the Scotch from Ulster to America are in part the same as those given to Brereton by the emigrant from Scotland to Ireland in 1635, which are noted above. But there was another and more cogent reason in addition. In Ireland, notwithstanding the fact that they had saved that country to Protestantism and to the Crown in the revolution of 1688, the Scots were grievously and unjustly discriminated against in the matter of their religion, which was, of course, generally of the Presbyterian form. These discriminations took the form of certain enactments by the Bishop's party in the Irish Parliament (which was then entirely ruled by the ecclesiastics of the Episcopal or State Church). These enactments deprived Presbyterians of the right to hold office in Ireland, required them to pay tithes in support of the Episcopal clergy, prohibited marriages from being performed by any but a Bishop-ordained priest, either of the Roman or Episcopal Church; and annulled marriages theretofore performed by Presbyterian ministers, declaring illegitimate the children of such marriages. Adding to these the economic causes arising from a discriminating tariff levied against Irish woollens and linens, in favor of the English manufacturers, and the raising of rents by the landlords, to whom a great majority of the Ulster Scotch-Irish were but tenants, and we have a sufficient explanation of the reasons for the exodus which took place from Ireland to America during the eighteenth century. Archbishop Boulter, Primate of Ireland, writing to the Bishop of London in 1728 concerning the emigration to America, says:

Dublin, March 13, 1728.

My Lord—As we have had reports here that the Irish gentlemen in London would have the great burthen of tithes thought one of the chief grievances that occasion such numbers of the people of the north going to America, I have for some time designed to write to your lordship on that subject.

But a memorial lately delivered in here by the Dissenting ministers of this place, containing the causes of this desertion, as represented to them by the letters of their brethren in the north, (which memorial we have lately sent over to my lord lieutenant), mentioning the oppression of the ecclesiastical courts about tithes as one of their great grievances. I found myself under a necessity of troubling your lordship on this occasion with a true state of that affair, and of desiring your lordship to discourse with the ministry about it.

The gentlemen of this country have, ever since I came hither, been talking to others, and persuading their tenants, who complained of the excessiveness of their rents, that it was not the paying too much rent, but too much tithes that impoverished them; and the notion soon took among the Scotch Presbyterians, as a great part of the Protestants in the north are, who it may easily be supposed do not pay tithes with great cheerfulness. And indeed I make no doubt but the landlords in England might with great ease raise a cry amongst their tenants of the great oppression they lay under by paying tithes.

What the gentlemen want to be at is, that they may go on raising their rents, and that the clergy should still receive their old payments for their tithes. But as things have happened otherwise, and they are very angry with the clergy, without considering that it could not happen otherwise than it has, since if a clergyman saw a farm raised in its rent, e. g., from 10 to 20 l. per annum, he might be sure his tithe was certainly worth double what he formerly took for it. Not that I believe the clergy have made a proportionable advancement in their composition for their tithes to what the gentlemen have made in their rents. And yet it is upon this rise of the value of the tithes that they would persuade the people to throw their distress.

In a conference I had with the Dissenting ministers here some weeks ago, they mentioned the raising the value of the tithes beyond what had been formerly paid, that a proof that the people were oppressed in the article of tithes. To which I told them, that the value of tithes did not prove any oppression, except it were proved that that value was greater than they were really worth, and that even then, the farmer had his remedy by letting the clergy take it in kind.

And there is the less in this argument, because the fact is, that about the years 1694 and 1695, the lands here were almost waste and unsettled, and the clergy in the last distress for tenants for their tithes, when great numbers of them were glad to let their tithes at a very low value, and that during incumbency, for few would take them on other terms; and as the country has since settled and improved, as those incumbents have dropped off, the tithe of those parties has been considerably advanced without the least oppression, but I believe your lordship will think not without some grumbling. The same, no doubt, has happened where there have been careless or needy incumbents, and others of a different character that have succeeded them.

I need not mention to your lordship that I have been forced to talk to several here, that if a landlord takes too great a portion of the profits of a farm for his share by way of rent (as the tithe will light on the tenant's share), the tenant will be impoverished; but then it is not the tithe but the increased rent that undoes the farmer. And indeed, in this country, where I fear the tenant hardly ever has more than one-third of the profit he makes of his farm for his share, and too often but a fourth or perhaps a fifth part, as the tenant's share is charged with the tithe, his case is no doubt hard, but it is plain from what side the hardship arises.

Another thing they complain of in their memorial is, the trouble that has been given them about their marriages and their school-masters. As to this I told them, that for some time they had not been molested about their marriages; and that as to their school-masters, I was sure they had met with very little trouble on that head, since I had never heard any such grievance so much as mentioned till I saw it in their memorial.

Another matter complained of is, the sacramental test, in relation to which I told them the laws were the same in England.

As for other grievances they mention, such as raising the rents unreasonably, the oppression of justices of the peace, seneschals, and other officers in the country, as they are of no ways of an ecclesiastical nature, I shall not trouble your lordship with an account of them, but must desire your lordship to talk with the ministry on the subject I have now wrote about, and endeavor to prevent their being prepossessed with an unjust opinion of the clergy, or being disposed, if any attempt should be made from hence, to suffer us to be stript of our just rights.

The spirit of emigration—fostered no doubt by the accounts sent home by their countrymen who had preceded them—seized these people to such an extent that it threatened almost a total depopulation. Such multitudes of husbandmen, laborers, and manufacturers flocked to the other side of the Atlantic, that the landlords began to be alarmed, and to present ways and means for preventing the growing evil. Scarce a ship sailed for the colonies that was not crowded with men, women, and children. It is stated by Proud, in his history of Pennsylvania, that by the year 1729, six thousand Scotch-Irish had come to that colony, and that before the middle of the century, nearly twelve thousand arrived annually for several years. In September, 1736, alone, one thousand families sailed from Belfast, on account of the difficulty of renewing their leases.

The first extensive emigration took place from about the year 1718 to the middle of the century. A second emigration occurred from about 1771 to 1773, although there was a continuous current westward between these two periods.

The cause of this second emigration was somewhat similar to the first. It is well known that a greater portion of the lands in Ireland are owned by a comparatively small number of proprietors, who rent them to the farming classes on long leases. In 1771, the leases on the estate of the Marquis of Donegal having expired, the rents were so largely advanced that many of the tenants could not comply with the demands, and were deprived of the farms they had occupied. This roused a spirit of resentment to the oppression of the large landed proprietors, and an immediate and extensive emigration to America was the result. From 1771 to 1773, there sailed from the ports in the north of Ireland, nearly one hundred vessels, carrying upwards of 25,000 passengers, nearly all of whom were Presbyterians. This was shortly before the breaking out of the Revolutionary War, and, as has been often remarked, these people, leaving the old world in such a temper, became a powerful contribution to the cause of liberty, and to the Independence of the colonies.

The Scotch-Irish emigrants landed principally at Newcastle and Philadelphia, and thence found their way northward and westward into the eastern and middle counties of Pennsylvania. From thence, one stream followed the Cumberland and Virginia valleys into Virginia and North and South Carolina, and from these colonies, passed on into and settled Tennessee and Kentucky. Another powerful body went into western Pennsylvania, and settling on the head waters of the Ohio, became famous, both in civil and ecclesiastical history.

The Pennsylvania Scotch-Irish began to settle west of the Blue Ridge mountains before 1750, where up to that time the Indians held undisputed sway. Fear of an Indian outbreak led the Penns in that year to send the justices of Cumberland county over the mountains into the Tuscarora, Aughwick, and Path Valleys, where the settlers were dispossessed, their cabins burned, and their bonds taken that they should return to the older settlements. Some of them did return for a brief period, but soon went back, while others hid themselves away in the woods, and after the justices had departed, built themselves new cabins, and continued to improve their "claims." Before 1760, small settlements were made by members of this hardy and adventurous race around the the military posts of Forts Bedford, Redstone, and Ligonier; and in 1768,

Rev. John Steel and others were sent by the Provincial authorities to warn off the settlers at Redstone (in Fayette county) and Turkey Foot (in Somerset county). In 1769, however, the land having been ceded by the Indians, all of southwestern Pennsylvania was thrown open to settlement, and within the next ten years more than 25,000 people were living in the territory now comprising the counties of Westmoreland, Allegheny, Fayette, and Washington. In 1790, the population of these four counties amounted to upwards of 63,000, Washington county alone containing nearly 24,000 inhabitants.

In his "Introductory Memoir to the Journal of Braddock's Expedition," Winthrop Sargent gives an estimate of the character of the Scotch-Irish, which, although properly objected to by some as exaggerated, is not an unfavorable description of many of the early pioneers of Pennsylvania:

They were a hardy, brave, hot-headed race, excitable in temper, unrestrainable in passion, invincible in prejudice. Their hand opened as impetuously to a friend as it clinched against an enemy. They loathed the Pope as sincerely as they venerated Calvin and Knox; and they did not particularly respect the Quakers. If often rude and lawless it was partly the fault of their position. They hated the Indian while they despised him, and it does not seem, in their dealings with this race, as though there were any sentiments of honor or magnanimity in their bosoms that could hold way against the furious tide of passionate, blind resentment. Impatient of restraint, rebellious against everything that in their eyes bore the semblance of injustice, we find these men readiest among the ready on the battle-fields of the Revolution. If they had faults, a lack of patriotism or of courage was not among the number.

CHAPTER II.

THE FRIENDS, OR QUAKERS, IN HARRISON COUNTY.

The founder of the society of Friends was George Fox, who was born at Drayton in the Clay, in Liecestershire, England, in July, 1624. His father was a Puritan weaver, and the son, originally intended for the church, was apprenticed to a shoemaker and dealer in wool. "In 1643," he says, "I left my relations, and broke off all familiarity with young or old." For the next few years, he was in spiritual darkness, and groped after the light. He dates the beginning of his Society from Liecestershire, in 1644. The course of Quakerism was at first toward the north of England. It appeared in Warwickshire in 1645; in Nottinghamshire in 1646; in Derby in 1647; in the adjacent counties in 1648, 1649, and 1650. It reached Yorkshire in 1651; Lancaster and Westmoreland, 1652; Cumberland, Durham, and Northumberland, 1653; London, and most other parts of England, Scotland, and Ireland, in 1654. In 1655, Friends went beyond sea, "where truth also sprung up," and in 1656 "it broke forth in America, and many other places." (Fox's Journal, II., 442.)

The Society of Friends was not organized by the establishment of meetings to inspect the affairs of the church until some years after Fox began preaching, and then a prominent part of the business of these meetings was to aid those Friends who were in prison, for persecution followed hard upon their increase in numbers. In 1661, 500 were in prison in London alone; there were 4,000 in jail in all England; and the Act of Indulgence liberated 1,200 Quakers in 1673. But Quakerism flourished under persecution. They showed a firmness which has been seen nowhere else in the annals of religious history. Other Dissenters might temporize, plot against the Government, or hold meetings in secret; the Quakers, never. They scorned these things. They received the brutal violence of the Government in meekness; they met openly, and in defiance of its orders; they wearied it by their very persistence. Nevertheless, the simplicity, the earnestness, the devotion, and the practical nature of this system of theology, when contrasted with the dry husk of Episcopacy, and the jangling creeds of the Dissenters, won them adherents by the thousands. They came mostly from the lower ranks of society, but from all sects.

Quakerism is distinctively the creed of the seventeenth century. Seekers were in revolt against the established order. It gave these seekers what they were looking for. In theology, it was un-Puritan; but in cultus, modes, and forms, it was more than Puritan. The Quaker was the Puritan of the Puritans. He was an extremist, and this brought him into conflict with the established order. He believed that Quakerism was primitive Christianity revived. He recognized no distinction between the clergy and the laity; he refused to swear, for Christ had said, swear not at all; he refused to fight, for the religion of Christ is a religion of love, not of war; he would pay no tithes, for Christ had said, ye have freely received, freely give; he called no man master, for he thought the terms, Rabbi, Your Holiness, and Right Reverend connoted the same idea. He rejected the dogmas of water baptism and the Puritan Sabbath, and in addition to these, claimed that inspiration is not limited to the writers of the Old and New Testaments, but is the gift of Jehovah to all men who will accept it, and to interpret the Scriptures, men must be guided by the Spirit that guided its authors. Here was the cardinal doctrine of their creed, and the point where they differed radically from other Dissenters. Add to this the doctrine of the Inner Light, the heavenly guide given directly to inform or illuminate the individual conscience, and we have the corner-stones of their system.

In July, 1656, Ann Austin and Mary Fisher, the vanguard of a Quaker army, appeared in Boston from Barbadoes. They were the first Quakers to arrive in America. They were imprisoned and shipped back. In October of the same year, a law was passed, which provided a fine for the shipmaster who knowingly brought in Quakers, and obliged him to carry them out again. The Quaker was to be whipped, and committed to the house of correction. Any person importing books, "or writings concerning their devilish opinions," or defending their "heretical opinions," was to be fined, and, for the third offense, banished. Nor was any person to revile the magistrates and ministry, "as is usual with the

Quakers." The law of October, 1657, imposed a fine for entertaining a Quaker. If a Quaker returned after being sent away once, he was to lose one ear; if he returned the second time, the other ear; and the third offense was punished by boring the tongue. The law of October, 1658, banished both resident and foreign Quakers, under pain of death. In Massachusetts, Quakers had their ears cut off; they were branded; they were tied to the cart-tail and whipped through the streets; women were shamefully exposed to public gaze; and in 1659-60, three men and one woman were hanged on Boston Common. Such was the welcome of the first Quakers to American soil.

Pennsylvania, the Quaker Colony, was founded by William Penn, in 1681, under a patent granted by Charles II. on March 4th of that year. The first colony left England in August, 1681, in three ships, the John and Sarah, from London, the Amity, from London, and the Factor, from Bristol. The John and Sarah is said to have landed first; the Amity was carried by a gale to the West Indies; and the Factor, having proceeded up the Delaware as far as the present town of Chester, was, on December 11th, frozen up in the channel, and its passengers obliged to pass the winter there. William Penn had sent his cousin, Captain William Markham, with the colonists, as deputy governor, and did not emigrate himself until the month of August, 1682, when he embarked on the Welcome. After a passage of some two months, during which smallpox broke out among the emigrants, and carried off one-third of their number, Penn and his fellow colonists landed at Newcastle, Del., on October 27th. Of the history of Penn's colony, and of the Quaker government during the next ninety-three years, and until it was finally overthrown in 1776 by the Revolutionary Scotch-Irish, it is not necessary here to speak. Much of this is familiar history to every school-boy. But the influence of the Quakers in the settlement and growth of the states south of Pennsylsylvania, has never been sufficiently recognized; and as it was from these states that most of the Quaker emigrants to Harrison and adjoining counties came, it will be appropriate to inquire into the history of the Quaker in the South. "They appeared in Virginia," says Dr. Stephen B. Weeks (from whose work on Southern Quakers and Slavery much of this sketch is condensed), "soon after their organization; they were in the Carolinas almost with the first settlers; they were considerable in number and substance; they were well-behaved and law-abiding; they maintained friendly relations with the Indians; they were industrious and frugal; they were zealous missionaries; and through their earnest and faithful preaching became, toward the close of the seventeenth century, the largest and only organized body of Dissenters in these colonies.

"They have always been zealous supporters of religious freedom. They bore witness to their faith under bodily persecution in Virginia; under disfranchisement and tithes in the Carolinas and Georgia. By reason of their organization and numbers, they were bold and aggressive in North Carolina, in the struggle against the Established Church. They took the lead in this struggle for religious freedom in the first half of the eighteenth century, as the Presbyterians did in the latter half. They continued an important element in the life of these states until about 1800, when their protest against slavery took the form of migration. They left their old homes in the South by thousands, and removed to the free Northwest, particularly Ohio and Indiana. These emigrants composed the middle and lower ranks of society, who had few or no slaves, and who could not come into economic competition with slavery. They were accompanied by many who were not Quakers, but who were driven to emigration by the same economic cause, and so great was this emigration that in 1850, one-third of the population of Indiana is said to have been made up of native North Carolinians and their children.

"Soon after 1800, Quakers disappeared entirely from the political and religious life of South Carolina and Georgia. They now number only a few hundred in Virginia. They are now relatively less important in North Carolina than in colonial days, but are still an important factor in the making of that state."

Under the Ordinance of 1787, passed by Congress for the government of the Northwest Territory, neither slavery nor involuntary servitude, except for crime, was to be allowed in any part of this territory; and with a legal guarantee in the organic law of the territory, it became a fit home for men who found themselves driven to migration by the institution of slavery in the South.

When we come to study these Quaker migrations in detail, there is little to differentiate those of one state from those of another. They went in substantially the same way, but owing to difference in location, pursued different routes. At first, North Carolina Quakers went very largely to Tennessee, while Virginia Quakers, being nearer, went directly to Ohio. In this way, Virginia Quakers took possession of Ohio, while North Carolina Quakers pressed on to Indiana.

The first settlers going West, after the opening of the Northwest

Territory to settlement, stopped naturally in Ohio. As there were then no Friends' meetings in that territory, Quaker emigrants left their certificates at Redstone (in Fayette county) and Westland (in Washington county), Pennsylvania. The first certificate to Westland meeting is dated June 24, 1785. Most of the certificates to Westland and Redstone came from Virginia meetings. The migrations of Carolina Friends to this part of the West were few, until after the establishment of the Ohio meetings. After 1785, certificates from Virginia monthly meetings to Redstone and Westland became numerous; about half of them represent families, some of them being young couples who turned to the West for their fortunes. Those Friends who took certificates to Redstone and Westland were but the advance guard of the western migration which set in about the year 1800. They continued to go to these meetings for a year or two longer; thus South River sent twelve to Westland in 1801, and the southern Goose Creek sent fifteen in 1801 and 1802, of which thirteen were families, besides a considerable number sent before the beginning of the present century. Meetings were soon established within the Northwest Territory, and then Westland soon disappears as a stopping-place. Thus, in 1802, we find certificates from South River to "Concord Monthly Meeting, Northwest Territory;" but this name almost immediately gives place to "Concord Monthly Meeting, State of Ohio," and the migrations at once become very numerous. Mr. Williams' very full account of the emigration of his own family from North Carolina to Concord settlement (in Colerain township, Belmont county) will be found in the Chapter on Harrison County Pioneers. During the first ten years of the century, most of the emigrants from Virginia went from Crooked Run, Hopewell, South River, and the two Goose Creek Monthly Meetings; during the second decade they went from Hopewell, South River, and the southern Goose Creek Monthly Meetings. The migration from the northern Goose Creek and Hopewell became active again about 1825, and continued so until 1836. The meetings in Virginia which belonged to Baltimore Yearly Meeting were the first to send out settlers, for they were nearer the western country, and had less to hold them in the way of local associations. From 1812-16, there was a considerable migration from the lower meetings of the Virginia Yearly Meeting. Of the meetings belonging to this Yearly Meeting, South River furnished the greater number of emigrants. From this meeting there went eighty-six families, and forty-three single persons, their removal covering the forty years from 1801 to 1840. In the same way, migrations from the southern Goose Creek began with the century, were to Westland first, and then to Ohio. These removals sapped the life of the Meeting, and it was laid down in 1814. In 1811, the movement began among all the lower meetings. Emigrants from Virginia went largely to Ohio. Those who took certificates to the Indiana meetings belong to the later period.

The first migration from North Carolina to the West was made directly over the Allegheny mountains, by the adventurers who laid the foundations of Tennessee. The first considerable movement of Friends from North Carolina to the Northwest was made from the Contentnea Quarter. It was emphatic and sweeping in its character. It was literally a migration. A letter written from Concord, Belmont county, Ohio, (the Quaker settlement a few miles southeast of New Athens), by Borden Stanton, one of the leaders of this migration, to Friends at Wrightsborough, Ga., who were also thinking of going West, and who did so at a later date, has fortunately been preserved. It reveals to us the motives, the troubles, and the trials of these modern pilgrims to an unknown land. It is dated 25th of 5th month, 1802, and reads as follows:

Dear Friends—Having understood by William Patten and William Hogan, from your parts, that a number among you have had some thoughts and turnings of mind respecting a removal to this country; and . . . as it has been the lot of a number of us to undertake the work a little before you, I thought a true statement (for your information) of some of our strugglings and reasonings concerning the propriety of our moving . . .

I may begin thus, and say, that for several years Friends had some distant view of moving out of that oppressive part of the land, but did not know where, until the year 1799, when we had an aceptable visit from some traveling Friends of the western part of Pennsylvania. They thought proper to propose to Friends for consideration, whether it would not be agreeable to best wisdom for us unitedly to remove northwest to the Ohio river,—to a place where there were no slaves held, being a free country. This proposal made a deep impression on our minds . . .

Nevertheless, although we had had a prospect of something of the kind, it was at first very crossing to my natural inclination; being well settled as to the outward. So I strove against the thoughts of moving for some time . . . as it seemed likely to break up our Monthly Meeting, which I had reason to believe was set up in the wisdom of Truth. Thus, I was concerned many times to weigh the matter as in the balance of the sanctuary; till at length, I considered that there was no prospect of our number being increased by convincement, on account of the oppression that abounded in that land . . .

Under a view of these things, I was made sensible, beyond doubting, that it was in the ordering of wisdom for us to remove; and that the Lord was opening a way for our enlargement, if found worthy. Friends generally feeling something of the same, there were three of them who went to view the country, and one worthy public Friend. They traveled on till they came to this part of the western country, where they were stopped in their minds, believing it was the place for Friends to settle. So they returned back, and informed us of the same in a solemn meeting; in which dear Joseph Dew, the public Friend, intimated that he saw the seed of God sown in abundance, which extended far northwestward. This information, in the way it was delivered to us, much tendered our spirits, and strengthened us in the belief that it was right. So we undertook the work, and found the Lord to be a present helper in every needful time, as he was sought unto; yea, to be as "a pillar of cloud by day and the pillar of fire by night;" and thus we were led safely along until we arrived here.

The story of their departure from their old homes can be given substantially in their own words (records of Contentnea Quarterly Meeting):

It appears by a copy of the minutes of a monthy meeting on Trent river, in Jones county, N. C. held in the ninth and tenth months, 1799, that the weighty subject of the members thereof being about to remove unitedly to the territory northwestward of the Ohio river, was and had been before that time deliberately under their consideration. And the same proposal was solemnly laid before their Quarterly Meeting, held at Contentnea on the ninth of the tenth month; which, on weighing the matter and its circumstances, concluded to leave said Friends at their liberty to proceed therein, as way might be opened for them; yet the subject was continued till their next Quarter. And they having (before the said Monthly Meeting ceased) agreed that certificates be signed therein for the members, to convey their rights respectively to the Monthly Meeting nearest to the place of their intended settlement, showing them to be members whilst they resided there; such certificates for each other mutually were signed in their last Monthly Meeting, held at Trent aforesaid, in the first month, 1800; which was then solemnly and finally adjourned and concluded, and their privilege of holding it, together with the records of it, were delivered up to their Quarterly Meeting, held the 18th of the same month, 1800.

They stopped first at the settlements of Friends on the Monongahela river, in Fayette and Washington counties, Penna., to prepare for their new settlement over the Ohio. They brought their certificates with them, laid their circumstances, with extracts from the minutes of their former monthly and quarterly meetings in Carolina, before Redstone Quarterly meeting, and received the advice and assistance of Friends there.

Thus they proceeded, and made their settlement in the year 1800; and were remarkably favored with an opportunity to be accommodated with a quantity of valuable land at the place which was chosen for their settlement by the Friends who went to view the country, before the office was opened for granting lands in that territory.

Borden Stanton continues (Friends' Miscellany, XII., 216-223):

> The first of us moved west of the Ohio in the ninth month, 1800; and none of us had a house at our command, to meet in, to worship the Almighty Being. So we met in the woods, until houses were built, which was but a short time. In less than one year, Friends so increased that two preparative meetings were settled; and in last twelfth month a monthly meeting, called Concord, also was opened, which is now large. Another preparative meeting is requested, and, also, another first and week-day meeting. Four are already granted in the territory, and three meeting-houses are built. Way appears to be opening for another Monthly Meeting; and, I think, a Quarterly Meeting. . . .
>
> I may say that as to the outward [i. e., worldly possessions], we have been sufficiently provided for, though in a new country. Friends are settling fast, and seem, I hope, likely to do well.

This seems to have been the first considerable migration from North Carolina to the West. It seems also to have been the only case on record where a whole meeting went in a body. But it was not the only case of removal from Contentnea Quarter. Removals from this Quarter either to the West, or to upper meetings of the same Quarter, continued until Carteret, Beaufort, Hyde, Craven, and Jones counties were depopulated of Quakers, and the meetings there laid down. Friends in these counties now reported to Core Sound Monthly Meeting, in Carteret county. Migration from Core Sound began in 1799, when Horton Howard, secretary of the monthly meeting, took a certificate to Westland. Josiah Bundy and Joseph Bishop also removed to Westland that year. In 1802, ten parties asked for certificates; no destination was given, but we are justified in assuming that it was Westland or Concord. In 1802-04, the movement was to Concord, Northwest Territory. There was then no more emigration from there until 1831. Migrations began from Contentnea Monthly Meeting in 1800. Between 1800 and 1815, we find thirty-six certificates issued. Two were to Redstone, one to Indiana, and all the rest to Ohio, most of them to Concord.

In the following list, an attempt has been made to give the names of those families which were the leaders in the westward migration, or which furnished the most recruits to it, from the various monthly meetings in the East. The names of the meetings to which the particular families went have also been given, with an approximation of the date:

Hopewell Monthly Meeting, Va., sent to Concord (1803-05), members of the families of Lupton, Piggot, Jenkins, Pickering, Miller, Ellis, Steer, Bevin; to various other monthly meetings in Ohio (1804-   ): McPherson, George, Walter, Wickersham, White, Walton, Wilson, Allen, Adams, Branson, Cope, Crampton, Faucett, Hackney, Janney, Lloyd, Little, Lupton, Pickering, Steer, Smith, Swayne, Townsend, Taylor.

Fairfax Monthly Meeting, Va.— To Short Creek, Harrison county (1803-22): Lacy, Ball, Hague, Rattekir, Wood, Schuley; to other Ohio meetings (1807-44): Wright, Richardson, Connard, Wilkinson, Wood, Swayne, Janney, John, Myers, Wilson.

Goose Creek (northern) Monthly Meeting, Va.—To Concord (1805-08): Evans, Pancoast, Sinclair, Spencer, Gregg, White, Whiteacre, Canby, Dillon, Smith; to other meetings, nearly all in Ohio (1820-54): Talbott, Buchanan, Rose, Hampton, Hughes, Nichols, Bradfield, Trehern, Mead, Wilson, Birdsall, Brown, Shoemaker, Taylor; to Salem, Columbiana county (1806-07): Craig, Smith, Canby, Janney, Gilbert.

Crooked Run Monthly Meeting, Va.—To Concord (1803-06): Faucett, Pickering, Wright, Lupton, Piggott, Holloway, Branson, Como, Smith, Wright, Sharp.

Goose Creek (southern) Monthly Meeting, Va.—To Concord (1802-06): McPherson, Bond, Coffee, Broomhall, Pidgeon.

South River Monthly Meeting, Va.—To Concord (1802-05): Pidgeon, Gregg, Bloxom, Wildman; to Salem, (1805-07): Stanton, Carle, Macy, Gurrell, Fisher; to other meetings, mostly in Ohio: Redder, Milliner, Holloway, Fisher, Ferrell, Early, Moorman, Stratton, Johnson, Preston, Burgess, Ballard, Terrell, Lea, Cox, Cadwalader, Butler, Morgan, Bailey, Lynch.

Cedar Creek Monthly Meeting, Va.—To Salem (1812-23): Stanley, Blackburn; to Short Creek (1813-41): Moorman, Terrell, Maddox, Hargrave, Creek.

White Oak Swamp Monthly Meeting, Va.—To Ohio meetings, not specified (1811-36): Ratcliff, Crew, Ladd, Harrison, Bates, Hockaday, Hargrave, Terrill, Andrews, Binford, Johnson, Ricks. Most of these went to Short Creek.

Western Branch Monthly Meeting, Va.—To Concord (1805-33):
Bond, Morlan, Curl, Johnson, Anthony, Lewis, Larow, Moorland, Perdue, Howell, Powell, Butler, Stanton, James, Draper, Ricks, Chapel, Hunnicutt, Trotter, Lawrence.

Mount Pleasant Monthly Meeting, Va.—To Concord (1805): Vimon, Davis, Bundy, Woods; to other Ohio meetings (1804-24): Thomas, Lundy, Bond, Ballard, Sumner, Beek, Pierce, Stalker, Scooly, Green, Gray, Williams, Robinson, Pierson, Wildman, Ward, Johnson, Pike, Lewis, Cary, Hunt, Anthony, Hiatt, Betts, Bundy, Jones, Chew, Davis.

Piney Grove Monthly Meeting, S. C.—To Ohio meetings (1805-12): Stafford, Mendenhall, Beauchamp, Thomas, Marine, Moorman, Harris, Morris, Lingagar, Almond.

Piney Woods Monthly Meeting, N. C.—To Ohio (1806-28): Goodwin, Smith, Harrel, Bamb, Elliott, Thornton, Bogue, Moore, Newby.

Rich Square Monthly Meeting, N. C.—To Short Creek (1805-11): Patterson, Maremoon (or Moreman), Taylor; to other Ohio meetings (1805-12): Patterson, Maremoon, Hicks, Crew, Reams.

Contentnea Monthly Meeting, N. C.—To Concord (1802-05): Hall, Edgerton, Outland, Doudna, Albertson, Dodd, Bailey, Morris; to other meetings in Ohio (1805-34): Copeland, Bundy, Collier, Cox, Price, Hollowell, Hobson, Spivy, Thomas, Peele, Hall, Jinnett.

Bush River Monthly Meeting, S. C.—To Ohio meetings, not specified (1805-): Galbreath, Marmaduke, Mendenhall.

Wrightsborough Monthly Meeting, Ga.—To Ohio meetings, not specified: Butler, Hollingsworth, Moore, Jay, Pearson, Killey, Henderson, Williams, Brooks.

Gravelly Run Monthly Meeting, Va.—To meetings chiefly in Ohio (1822-30): Butler, Thomas, Peebles, Binford, Wrenn, Johnson, Hunnicutt, Sems, Watkins.

Core Sound Monthly Meeting, N. C.—To Concord (1802-04): Harris, Thomas, Scott, Williams, Mace.

Cane Creek Monthly Meeting, N. C.—To Ohio meetings, not specified (1805-09): Stanton, Haydock, Cox, Hadly, Baker, Clark, Hussey, Hasket, Moffit, Hale, Ratcliff.

New Garden Monthly Meeting, N. C.—To Ohio meetings, not specified (1803-31): Hines, Hodgson, Perkins, Starbuck, Williams, Thornburgh, Flanner, Macy, Bunker, Low, Brown, McMuir, James, Jenkins, Russell, Knight, Swain, Blizzard, Jessop, Coffin, Hunt.

Springfield Monthly Meeting, N. C.—To Ohio meetings, not specified (1803-32): Pidgeon, Reece, Newby, Kersey, Bundy, Tomlinson, Mendenhall, Wright, Kellum, Beard, Harlan, Millikan, Spears, Spencer, Hoggatt.

Deep River Monthly Meeting, N. C.—To Ohio meetings, not specified (1811-37): Pike, Pegg, Cook, Jones, Stafford, Hubbard.

Many of the first comers to Concord and Short Creek, Ohio, emigrating before those meetings were definitely established, left their certificates with the nearest meetings in Pennsylvania, being those of Westland, in Washington county, and Redstone, in Fayette county. The following families came to one or both of these places: From Hopewell, Va. (1786-1803): Faulkner, Perviance, Townsend, Sidwell, Berry, Mills, Blackburn, Branson, Hodge, Lewis, Brock, White, Bailey, Smith, Roberts, Wells, Morris, Finch, Antrim. From Fairfax, Va. (1785-1833): Smith, Stokes, Wharton, Davis, Hough, Ward, Mitchner, Plumber, Shine. From Crooked Run, Va. (1787-1803): Cadwalader, Reyley, Hank, Russel, Berry, Wright, Hunt, Richards, Mullen, Updegraff, Lupton, Wood, Evans, Cleaver, Yarnell, Painter, Dillhorn, Taylor, Holloway, Penrose, Miller. From Goose Creek (southern), Va. (1801-03): Oliphant, Erwin, Lewis, Morlan, Richards, Whitaker, Pidgeon, Schooley, Wright, Parsons, Sinclair. From South River, Va. (1801-02): James, Hanna, Baugham, Harris, Holloway, Terrell, Stratton, Ferrall, Carle, Via, Tellus. From Core Sound, N. C. (1799-1802): Howard, Bundy, Bishop, Dew, Ward, Mace, Stanton, Williams. From Contentnea, S. C. (1800): Thomas Arnold. From Mt. Pleasant, Va. (1802): Bradford. From Bush River, S. C. (1802-03): Pugh, Jay, Kelly, O'Neal, Mills, Peaty, Horner, Wright.

The locations of the various monthly meetings named in the foregoing list are as follows:

Bush River.—Newberry county, S. C., eight miles northwest from Newberry.

Cane Creek.—Alamance county, N. C., fourteen miles south from Graham.

Cedar Creek.—Hanover county, Va.

Contentnea.—Wayne county, N. C., fifteen miles north from Goldsboro.

Core Sound—Carteret county, N. C., six miles north from Beaufort.

Crooked Run.—Warren county, Va., nine miles south from Winchester.

Deep River.—Guilford county, N. C., twelve miles southwest from Greensboro.

THE FRIENDS, OR QUAKERS

Fairfax.—Loudoun county, Va., seven miles west of north from Leesburg.

Goose Creek (northern).—Lincoln, Loudoun county, Va.

Goose Creek (southern).—Bedford county, Va., ten miles southeast from Bedford City.

Gravelly Run.—Dinwiddie county, Va., about four miles east from Dinwiddie.

Hopewell.—Frederick county, Va., six miles north from Winchester.

Mount Pleasant.—Frederick county, Va., nine miles southwest from Winchester.

New Garden.—Guilford county, N. C.

Piney Grove—Marlborough county, S. C., nine miles north from Bennettsville.

Piney Woods.—Davidson county, N. C., twelve miles north of east from Lexington.

Rich Square.—Northampton county, N. C.

South River.—Campbell county, Va., near Lynchburg (?).

Springfield.——Guilford county, N. C., near High Point.

Western Branch.—Isle of Wight county, Va., seven miles, nearly southeast from Isle of Wight Court House.

White Oak Swamp.—Henrico county, Va.

Wrightsborough.—McDuffie county, Ga., thirty-six miles northwest from Augusta.

CHAPTER III.

THE GERMANS AND THE VIRGINIANS IN HARRISON COUNTY.

That industrious, thrifty, patriotic, and generally intelligent portion of the population of Harrison county, familiarly known as the

PENNSYLVANIA DUTCH,

but more properly the Germans, are descendants of those hardy pioneer settlers who immigrated to Pennsylvania and Maryland from various German states, commencing as early, at least, as the year 1683. Perhaps there is no people who were more frequently the subject of remark in the early history of Pennsylvania, and during the last century, than these Germans, whose numerous descendants are now to be found in every State west and south of Pennsylvania.

Though more than twenty-five thousand names of German immigrants are recorded in the Pennsylvania Archives from 1725 to 1775, few of those are recorded who arrived in Pennsylvania prior to 1700. In volume seventeen of the Archives, Second Series, may be found the names of all who took the oath of allegiance between 1727 and 1775, comprising about thirty thousand names, with the names of the vessels in which they came to America, ports from which they sailed, and dates of departure. Probably four-fifths of the Germans living in Harrison county to-day can find the names and dates of arrival of their emigrant ancestors in that volume.

In 1683, some Germans arrived in Pennsylvania, and commenced a settlement at what is now Germantown. Among these, were Pastorious, Hartsfelder, Schietz, Spehagel, Vandewall, Uberfeld, Strauss, Lorentz, Tellner, and others. About the year 1684 or 1685, a land company was formed at Frankfort-on-the-Main, which bought 25,000 acres from William Penn. Those who left their Fatherland from 1700 to 1720, the Palatines, so-called, because they came principally from the Palatinate States, along the Rhine, whither many had been forced to flee from their homes in France, and other parts of Europe, endured many privations before they reached the Western Continent.

In 1708 and 1709, upwards of 10,000, many of them very poor, arrived in England, and were there for some time, in a starving, miserable condition, lodged in warehouses, with no subsistence beyond what they got by begging on the streets; until some sort of provision was made for them by Queen Anne. In 1709, 3,000 of them were sent to Ireland, but of this number many returned to England, on account of insufficient provision having been made for them by the Royal Commissary. In the summer of 1710, several thousand of these Palatinates, who had been maintained at the Queen's expense in England (and for sometime afterwards in America), were shipped to New York; and of these, many came to Pennsylvania. Among these German emigrants were Mennonites, Dunkards, German Reformed, and Lutherans. Their number was so great, that James Logan, Secretary of the Province of Pennsylvania, wrote in 1717, "We have, of late, a great number of Palatines poured in upon us without any recommendation or notice, which gives the country some uneasiness, for foreigners do not so well among us as our own English people."

Those who arrived between 1700 and 1720, settled in the lower parts of Montgomery, Bucks, Berks, and Lancaster counties. In 1719, Jonathan Dickinson wrote, "We are daily expecting ships from London, which bring over Palatines, in number about six or seven thousand. We had a parcel who came out about five years ago, who purchased land about sixty miles west of Philadelphia [the Pequea settlement, in Lancaster county], and prove quiet and industrious. Some few came from Ireland lately, and more are expected thence."

From 1720 to 1730, several thousand landed at Philadelphia, and others came by land, from the province of New York. The latter settled in Tulpehocken, having left New York because they had been ill-treated by the authorities of that province. The influx now became so great as to cause some alarm. It was feared by some that the numbers from Germany, at the rate they were coming in during the last three years of this decade, would soon produce a German colony here, and perhaps such a one as Britain once received from Saxon-land, in the fifth century. Jonathan Dickinson went so far as to state, that it was apprehended Sir William Keith, a former governor, with two of his friends, had sinister projects of forming an independent province in the West, towards the Ohio, to be peopled by his friends among the Palatines. In 1727, six vessels arrived at Philadelphia with Germans; three in 1728; three in 1729; and three in 1730.

From 1730 to 1740, about sixty-five vessels, filled with Germans, arrived at Philadelphia, bringing with them ministers and schoolmasters to instruct their children. A large number of these remained in Philadelphia; others removed seventy to eighty miles from that city—some settling in Lebanon county, and others west of the Susquehanna, in York county.

From 1740 to 1755, upwards of one hundred vessels arrived with Germans; in some of them, though small ships, there were from 500 to 600 passengers. In the summer and fall of 1749, not less than twenty vessels, with German passengers to the number of twelve thousand, arrived.

At first, the immigration of Germans into Pennsylvania was confined to the Sectaries, the Quietists, and the other religious denominations, who, on account of their extremity in doctrines and practice, found it difficult to get along with their more conservative Protestant brethren. The Labadists, for instance, were followed by the Mennonites, who took up much land, and formed many communities in the counties of York, Lancaster, and Adams; by the Seventh Day Baptists, the followers of Spener, who established their monastery at Ephrata; by the Voltists, and the Cocceians; and by the hundred other sects of the day. But after these Sectaries came the Deluge. The Germans had found out that there was a land of peace on the other side of the Atlantic; and they knew by sad experience that their own country was a land of war. A man was deprived, practically, not only of the enjoyment of his own religion; but he was also robbed incessantly of the fruits of his labor. This was a state of things which he naturally rebelled against, and emigration afforded him the only relief.

The religious fanaticism of Louis XIV., which so long desolated the low countries, and which, when he revoked the edict of Nantes, deprived that monarch of his best and most thrifty subjects, broke in upon the Palatine in the shape of one of the most desolating wars of which there is any record in history. Turrenne, Saxe, Vendome, Villars, Villeroy, Taillard, Marsin, Berwick, Noailles, and Luxembourg, each in his turn, helped to desolate the Palatine, and to contribute immigrants to the colonies. The homeless and ravished peoples of Germany sought and found homes in the new land of peace and plenty. At one time the immigration of German Palatines into Pennsylvania and Maryland was in excess of all other immigration. Many hundreds thus came into Maryland, many thousands into Pennsylvania. They came chiefly from the harried Palatinate, but also from Alsace, Suabia, Saxony, and Switzerland. There were Wittenbergers, and people from Darmstadt, Nassau, Hesse, Eisenberg, Franconia, Hamburg, Mannheim—all classed as "Palatines."

In 1700, there were nearly 145,000 Germans in Pennsylvania, the total population then not exceeding 435,000. These included the Sectaries above referred to, the Dunkards, and the Hessian soldiers, who had been taken prisoners by Washington's army, and preferred not to be exchanged after the Revolution. A great proportion of this latter class settled in Somerset county, Pennsylvania, from whence many have come into Harrison county. These German subsidiary troops were bought in Brunswick, Hanau, Anspach, Waldeck, Hesse-Cassel, Hesse-Darmstadt, Brandenberg, etc., in large numbers. They cost George III. the sum of $8,-100,000, and 11,000 of them died, or perished in battle. The other immigrants were German Calvinists, Moravians, Schwenkenfelders, Omishites, Dunkards, Mennonites, and Separatists (or Seventh Day Baptists).

Up to about 1760, the Germans in Maryland were supplied from these plentiful sources, by way of Pennsylvania. A good many Palatines came in by direct consignment to Chesapeake Bay, but the great majority of the Germans drifted down from York and Lancaster counties, Pennsylvania, and occupied the land along Antietam creek, and about Hagerstown and Frederick in Maryland, and the lower Shenandoah Valley in Virginia.

THE VIRGINIANS.

The first settlers of the Virginia Panhandle were mainly of the Cavalier class, many of them coming from the northern and eastern counties east of the mountains, and a few from the Virginia valley, the latter usually being of Scotch-Irish descent. In later years, when the Scotch-Irish occupied Washington county, many of them crossed the line and settled in Ohio (now Brooke) county, Virginia, in the vicinity of Wellsburg. Some of the early settlers in Harrison county were from that section; and not a few were of the old tide-water, horse-racing, gambling, and cock-fighting class, which before the middle of the century, formed the aristocracy and much of the middle-class population of Virginia. Dr.

Joseph Doddridge, although himself born in Bedford county, Penna., belonged to this latter class, his father, originally from Maryland, having settled near West Middletown, in Washington county, about 1773. The son became first a Methodist, and later, an Episcopalian clergyman, and settled at Wellsburg, where he died in 1826. Two years before his death, he wrote a book, called "Notes on the Settlement and Indian Wars of the Western Parts of Virginia and Pennsylvania, from 1763 to 1783," which contains the best written account we have of the early customs, habits of life, and occupations of those pioneers, many of whom were the forefathers of Harrison county citizens of the present day. In reading Doddridge's account, it must be borne in mind that he wrote of two very different classes of settlers, that class amongst which he spent his life being for the most part of the cavalier type—the jolly, rollicking, careless, lawless, and often shiftless character so long associated with the development of the slave-holding South. The other class was the Scotch-Irish —sometimes erroneously called the Puritans of the South, sober-minded, God-fearing, Psalm-singing Presbyterians, for the most part, whose only relaxation after a week of hard toil in the forest or field was to ride or walk from one to fifteen miles to meeting of a Sabbath, there to listen to a series of dry theological dissertations, lasting from morning until night, with but a brief intermission for lunch. Some unfriendly and untruthful writers about the Scotch-Irish, have sought to apply Doddridge's description of the least law-abiding of his fellow pioneers as a general condemnation of this race; maliciously misrepresenting the facts as to the class about whom the description was written. A direct testimonial as to the character of the two classes, given by an eye-witness more than a century ago, has but recently come to light, being an extract from the Diary of Rev. David McClure, published in 1899. David McClure was the first Presbyterian minister to labor in the settlements west of the Alleghenies, having come out as a missionary in 1772, traveled among the Indians of Ohio as far west as Coshocton, and ministered to the scattered settlers of Western Pennsylvania for a period of six months or more. Under date of December 17, 1772, Mr. McClure writes:

Attended a marriage, where the guests were all Virginians. It was a scene of wild and confused merriment. The log-house, which was large, was filled. They were dancing to the music of a fiddle. They took little or no notice of me, on my entrance. After setting awhile at the fire, I arose and desired the music and dancing to cease, and requested the bride and bridegroom to come forward. They came snickering and very merry. I desired the company, who still appeared to be mirthful and noisy, to attend with becoming seriousness, the solemnity.

As soon as the ceremony was over, the music struck up, and the dancing was renewed. While I sat wondering at their wild merriment, the lady of a Mr. Stevenson sent her husband to me, with her compliments, requesting me to dance a minuet with her. My declining the honor, on the principle that I was unacquainted with it, was scarcely accepted. He still politely urged, until I totally refused. After supper, I rode about three miles, to the house of a friend.

The manners of the people of Virginia, who have removed into these parts [Fayette county, Penn.], are different from those of the Presbyterians and Germans. They are much addicted to drinking parties, gambling, horse-race, and fighting. They are hospitable and prodigal. Several of them have run through their property in the old settlements, and have sought an asylum in this wilderness.

Doddridge states that the first settlements along the Monongahela were commenced in 1772. In 1773, they extended to the Ohio. The first settlers came mostly from Maryland and Virginia, and generally traveled by way of Braddock's route. Some from Pennsylvania came by the military road, passing through Bedford and Ligonier. Their removals were generally on horses with pack-saddles. Settlement entitled the settler to 400 acres of land, free. Their claims were usually located by means of the tomahawk, with which they blazed the trees marking their boundary lines. Hence, such claims came to be called "Tomahawk Rights." They usually chose ground in a hollow or depression, for their houses and barns; so that whatever came to the house might come down hill.

Generally, the male members of the prospective settler's family came over the mountains in the spring, and after clearing a plot of ground, planting a small patch of corn, and sometimes erecting a rough log cabin, they went back for their families, and brought them out in the fall. They depended much upon lean venison, wild turkeys, and the flesh of the bear at times, for food. They awaited with much anxiety for the first growth of the potatoes, pumpkins, corn, etc., and when the young corn came, it was made a time of jubilee, and the green ears were roasted for a feast. When the corn hardened and was gathered in the fall, it was customary to provide meal for the family Johnny-cake ("journey-cake," it was then called) by grating the ears on a tin-grater.

The original settlers were usually their own mechanics, and each man made everything needed by himself, that could not be conveniently brought along from the older settlements. The hominy-block and hand-mills were found in most of their houses. The block was hollowed out at the top by burning, and the play of the pestle ground the corn. Sometimes a sixteen-foot sweep was used to lessen the toil, in pounding corn into meal for mush or cakes. The hand-mill was another and a better contrivance, made of two circular stones, the under being the bed-stone, and the upper, the runner. These were enclosed in a wide hoop, or band, having a spout to discharge the meal. The "runner" was moved by a long staff, or pole, passing through an upright fixed in the stone. Such mills are still used in the Holy Land, as they were in the time of Christ.

Their water-mills were tub-mills, readily made, and at small expense. This mill consisted of an upright shaft, at the lower end of which a water-wheel, four or five feet in diameter was attached, the upper end of the shaft passing through the bed-stone, and carrying the runner, secured to its top. Sifters were used in lieu of bolting cloths, made of deer-skin parchment, stretched over a hoop, and pierced with small holes, by means of a hot wire.

The material for their clothing, aside from deer-skins, was spun by the women of the household. Almost every pioneer woman could weave linsey-woolsey cloth, and make the family clothing. Every family tanned its own leather. The tan-vat was a large trough, sunk in the ground; bark was shaved and pounded; wood-ashes were used in lieu of lime, for removing the hair; bear's grease, hog's lard, and tallow served for dressing the leather, instead of fish-oil; the currying was done with a drawing-knife; the blacking made of hog's lard and soot. Most families contained their own tailors and shoemakers. Those who could not make shoes, easily learned to make shoe-packs, which were made, like moccasins, of a single piece of leather, fitted to and removed from the foot by means of a cord gathering. In cold weather, these moccasins were stuffed with dried grass, deer's hair, or dried leaves, to keep the feet warm. Plows were made of wood; harrows, with wooden teeth; and cooper-ware of staves.

Fights were of frequent occurrence among the younger male members of the community; and the method of fighting was very dangerous to the participants. Although no weapons were used, fists, teeth, and feet were employed at will; and the favorite mode of disabling an antagonist was to gouge out one of his eyes.

The furniture for the tables, for several years after the settlement of the country, consisted of a few pewter dishes, plates, and spoons, but chiefly of wooden bowls, trenchers, and noggins. If these last were scarce, gourds and hard-shelled squashes made up the deficiency. The iron pots, knives, and forks, were brought from east of the mountains, with the salt and iron, on pack-horses.

For a long time after the first settlement of the country, the inhabitants married young. There was no distinction of rank, and very little of fortune; on this account, first love usually resulted in marriage; and a family establishment cost but a little labor, and nothing more. Marriages were celebrated at the house of the bride, and the announcement of a prospective wedding created a general sensation; it was looked upon by young and old as an occasion for frolic, feasting, and fun; and was more efficacious in gathering a crowd of people together than even a log-rolling, house-raising, or hunting expedition. The groom usually started early from his father's house so as to reach the home of the bride by noon, the hour generally set for the ceremony—as it was always followed by a bountiful dinner. The assembled company were all pioneers, and there being no store, tailor, or dress-maker within a hundred miles of the trans-Allegheny settlements, they all came dressed in home-made garments. The men wore shoe-packs or moccasins, leather breeches, usually made of buck-skin, linsey hunting shirts, and leggins. The women dressed in linsey petticoats, and linsey or linen bed-gowns, coarse shoes, stockings, kerchiefs, and buckskin gloves, if any. The horses were caparisoned with old saddles, old bridles or halters, and pack-saddles, with a bag or blanket thrown over them; a rope or cord formed the usual girth. The wedding procession, on such occasions, marched in double file, where the horse-paths permitted—for they had no roads. Such paths were sometimes barred by fallen trees, and sometimes barred with mischief aforethought, by interlocking grapevines and saplings, to intercept the progress of the procession. Sometimes a party of neighbors would wait in ambush, and when the procession came up, fire a blank charge from their rifles, which covered the party with clouds of smoke, created surprise and shrieks amongst the ladies, and chivalrous bluster on the part of their escorts. As the procession neared the house of the bride, it sometimes occurred that two or more young men would start for the domicile on horseback, full tilt, to win the bottle of whiskey, which it was previously understood would be hung out from the entrance to the cabin as a prize for the first arrival. The start of the race was announced by an Indian-like yell; and the more the route was encumbered by fallen logs, brush, and muddy hollows, the better opportunity it gave the rival swains to show their horsemanship. The bottle gained, the winner returned to the party, first handing it to the groom, and thence it went from one rider to another, in the manner of a loving cup, each taking a draught, the ladies included.

For the wedding dinner, the table, made of a large slab of timber, hewn out with a broad ax and set on four sticks, was spread with beef, pork, fowl, and sometimes deer and bear steak. Sometimes, there were a few old pewter dishes and plates, but the majority of the guests ate from wooden bowls and trenchers. A few pewter spoons were generally to be seen, but the most of them were made of horn. If knives were scarce, the men used their scalping-knives, or hunting knives, which they always carried in the belts of their hunting-shirts.

After dinner was over, dancing commenced, and it usually lasted until the following morning. The figures danced were reels, quadrilles, and jigs. The dance always commenced with a quadrille, which was followed by a jig; none were allowed to steal away for sleep and if the girls became tired, they were expected (as chairs were very scarce) to sit upon the knees of the gentlemen.

About nine or ten o'clock at night, some of the young ladies would steal away with the bride, and see her safely tucked in bed. The bridal chamber was frequently a loft or attic, above the dancers, to which access was gained by climbing a ladder, and such a chamber was floored with clap-boards, lying loose, and without nails. Some of the young men, in the meantime, would lead away the groom, and send him up the ladder to join his bride; followed later in the evening by refreshments, of which the chief constituent was a huge flash of whiskey, called by the frolickers, "Black Betty."

These entertainments sometimes lasted for several days, none desisting until the party was thoroughly fagged out. If any of the bride's neighbors felt themselves slighted by not being bidden to the festivities, it sometimes occurred that they would show their resentment by cutting off the manes, foretops, and even tails of the horses belonging to the wedding-party.

CHAPTER IV.

THE FIRST SETTLERS IN EASTERN OHIO.

In 1888, there was held in the city of Marietta a Centennial celebration, to commemorate what was said to be the first settlement of the territory northwest of the Ohio. Properly speaking, it was the first settlement only in the sense of being the first authorized by the United States Government. This settlement was made in 1788 by a colony of New England families from Connecticut and Massachusetts, mostly officers or participants in the War of the Revolution; and no colony in America was ever planted by a more liberal and estimable body of men and women than were these Marietta colonists. They included the Meigs', the Putnams, the Cutlers, the Danas, the Sproats, the Whipples, and many other famous New England families. Their purchase embraced about 1,500,000 acres of land lying along the Ohio River from Marietta, west, and including Meigs, much of Athens, and portions of Washington and Gallia counties.

The first settlements in the territory west of the Ohio river were made by families from Pennsylvania and Virginia, nearly ten years before 1788; and there were more white settlers living in eastern Ohio as early as 1785 than the whole number comprised in the Marietta colony of 1788. These pioneer settlers had established two or more towns, and set up courts of justice before 1785, and, although some of them were occasionally driven off their lands by soldiers sent out by Congress for that purpose, the majority seem to have continued as permanent settlers, and in some instances their descendants are living in the same localities today.

In 1902-3 it is proposed to hold another Centennial in Ohio, in commemoration of the admission of the State into the Union; and the year 1904 will witness the hundreth anniversary of the laying out of the town of Cadiz. The Centennial of the settlement of Harrison county would nominally be about 1900,—1800 being the year in which the land office was opened at Steubenville for the sale of lands in the territory now included in Harrison. The records of that office during the five years following that date show, among others, entries of land titles in what is now Harrison county by the following named settlers: James Arnold, Arthur Barrett, Thomas Barrett, James Black, Robert Braden, George Brown, George Carnahan, John Carnahan, Samuel Carnahan, Joseph Clark, Robert Cochran, John Craig, Thomas Dickerson, Samuel Dunlap, James Finney, Samuel Gilmore, Eleazer Huff, John Huff, Joseph Huff, William Huff, James Hanna, James Haverfield, Thomas Hitchcock, Joseph Holmes, William Ingles, John Jamison, Joel Johnson, Joseph Johnson, William Johnson, Absalom Kent, George Layport, John Love, John Lyons, William McClary, John McConnell, Robert McCullough, William McCullough, John McFadden, Joseph McFadden, Samuel McFadden, John Maholm, Samuel Maholm, Robert Maxwell, Thomas Maxwell, William Moore, Samuel Osburn, Baldwin Parsons, John Pugh, Rev. John Rea, John Ross, Jacob Shepler, Samuel Smith, Martin Snyder, John Taggart, Thomas Taylor, Hugh Teas, Robert Vincent, Thomas Vincent, John Wallace, Michael Waxler, Daniel Welch, James Wilkin, Thomas Wilson.

Of these, it is known that the McFaddens, Craigs, Jamisons, Gilmores, Hannas, Reas, Welches, Moores, and Lyons' came from Washington county, Pennsylvania; the Arnolds, Dunlaps, Dickersons, and Maholms, from Fayette county; and most of the others were without doubt from the same districts. The probability is that many of these settlers were in Harrison county before 1800; as the date of their recorded title is not necessarily the date of their first settlement on the land; and it was the custom of that day, as it is in the western states to-day, to make improvements, and to reside on pre-empted land for some months or years before acquiring title from the Government. It is reasonably certain that Alexander Henderson occupied the land near Cadiz, until recently known as the Walter Jamison farm, as early as April, 1799; having removed from Washington county, Pennsylvania, with his family, about that time; and that Daniel Peterson then resided with his family at the forks of Short creek.

In an article printed in the Cadiz Republican, Oct. 31st, 1895, Rev.

R. M. Coulter stated that the first white child born within the present limits of Harrison county was Jesse DeLong, born in what is now Short Creek township, about 1776; he died at the age of 106, leaving descendants who are still residents of Tuscarawas county.

The following letter, from one of these descendants, will be found interesting in this connection:

Midvale, Ohio, May 20, 1898.

Charles A. Hanna, Chicago:

Dear Sir—I am in receipt of your letter sent to me at Station Fifteen, Ohio. I have moved from Harrison county, April 1st, 1897.

In regard to the DeLongs as early pioneers of that county, I will give you all the information I am in the knowledge of, which is not very much; but am willing to state the facts as far as I know.

Solomon DeLong, the father of Jesse, comes of French descent, having emigrated from France to Maryland, near Baltimore, from thence to Pennsylvania, near Philadelphia; from there they went to West Virginia, before Wheeling was built, there being nothing there but a block-house where Wheeling now stands. They crossed the Ohio river and built their cabin on Short creek, where Bridgeport now stands. At that time, there being no other white families on the Ohio side of the Ohio river, they were quite frequently driven back to the block-house for refuge from the hostile Indians.

His wife's maiden name was Lamasters. To their union quite a family was born, the exact number is not known, but Jesse was the fifth child in order of birth.

The DeLong family have always been noted as warriors. Solomon and his brothers, as well as his older sons, took part in the Revolutionary War, and also the War of 1812. He settled at Bridgeport, on Short creek, about the year 1775. His son, Jesse, was born there the first of May, 1776. The length of time they lived there is not exactly known. From there they came to Little Stillwater about two miles east of Dennison, and entered a tract of land of 160 acres—that, at the present time, is owned by Mr. Kinsey—that being the place of his death; the date I do not know. After his death, the widow went back into Harrison county to live, near Franklin, or Tappan.

Their pioneer life in Harrison county was before the counties were divided as they now are. Jesse DeLong was a pioneer of Tuscarawas county, being one of its first settlers. He entered the land east of Dennison, now Thornwood Park. He was accidentally shot in a bear hunt by Dan Iler, in Harrison county, on the land now owned by William McCauley, near Station Fifteen. By that, he was crippled for life, became quite an invalid in his old days, dying May 8, 1882, at the age of 106 years. His mother also lived to near the age of 100 years. The DeLong family in politics were Whigs, and Republicans of the staunchest kind, and were also strong believers in Methodism. He was united in marriage with

Nancy Wagner. To them twelve children were born, and of that number there are but two now living. One son, Jesse-William, of Oreana, Macon county, Ill., and Espy, who was a resident of Harrison county for twenty-five years. I purchased a farm and moved on it the first of April, 1872, and left April 1, 1897, and have lived in Midvale since that time.

I believe that the DeLong family would be termed pioneers of Tuscarawas, more than of Harrison county.

I have given about all I can think of at present. Hope this will be satisfactory, and of some good to you in your work. Yours,

ESPY DELONG.

From this letter, it would appear that Jesse DeLong was not born in Harrison county at all. It may also be remarked, that, if he was born on Short creek, he could not, as his son states, have been born at the site of Bridgeport, in Belmont county; for Short creek runs through Warren township, Jefferson county, and enters the Ohio at Warrentown. If he was born as early as 1776, it would seem very improbable that he could have been born in Ohio at all, unless it was during the temporary sojourn of his parents west of the river. Two or three years later than 1776, however, a number of settlements had been made in Ohio.

There are traditions in Harrison county of early settlements along Stillwater creek; but whether these have ever been verified or not, the writer does not know. However, there are good reasons for believing that in the territory now composing the counties of Mahoning, Columbiana, Jefferson, Stark, Carroll, Harrison, Belmont, Guernsey, and Monroe, were scattered cabins of pioneer settlers as early as the Revolutionary War. What these reasons are may here be presented:

To the Salt Springs in the present county of Trumbull, white hunters had resorted as early as 1754, and salt was made there by Pennsylvanians some twenty years later.

From the old settlement of Wheeling and its vicinity a number of adventurers crossed the river from time to time and erected cabins. A number who came out with General McIntosh to Fort Laurens in 1778, as axemen, scouts, hunters, etc., are supposed to have remained and built homes on several of the branches of the Ohio and the Muskingum.

The first attempt to drive out the squatters northwest of the Ohio was made in October, 1779, when Captain Clark, of a Pennsylvania regiment, with sixty soldiers, was sent to Wheeling by Colonel Brodhead, then in command of Fort Pitt, with orders to cross the river and apprehend some of the principal trespassers, and destroy their huts. Captain Clark did not succeed in finding any of the trespassers, but destroyed several huts, and reported that many improvements had been made along the Ohio from the mouth of the Muskingum to Fort McIntosh (Beaver, Pa.) and thirty miles up some of its branches.

General Brodhead's report of this expedition will be found in two of his letters printed in volume twelve of the Pennsylvania Archives (First Series), pp. 176-177, which read as follows:

Pittsburgh, Oct. 26th, 1779.

To His Excellency, John Jay, Esq.:

Sir—Since I did myself the honor to address you by a former letter, some of the inhabitants from Youghagenia and Ohio counties [the western portion of Washington county, Pennsylvania, and the Panhandle of West Virginia], have been hardy enough to cross the Ohio river, and make small improvements on the Indian lands, from the river Muskingum to Fort McIntosh, and thirty miles up some of the branches of the Ohio river. As soon as I received information of the trespass I detached a party of sixty men under command of Captain Clarke, to apprehend the trespassers and destroy their huts, which they have in a great measure effected, and likewise dispatched a runner to the chiefs of the Delawares, at Cooshocking, to prevent their attacking the innocent inhabitants, but as yet have received no answer from them. Capt. Clarke informs me that the trespassers had returned, and that the trespass appeared to have been committed upwards of a month ago.

It is hard to determine what effect this imprudent conduct may have on the minds of the Delaware chiefs and warriors, but I hope a favorable answer to the speech I sent them. I presume a line from your Excellency to the Governor and Council of Virginia, will tend to prevent a further trespass and the murder of many innocent families on this frontier.

I have the honor to be, with perfect respect, your Excellency's most obed't and most humble servant,

D. BRODHEAD, Col. Commanding.

Pittsburgh, Oct. 26th, 1779.

To His Excellency, General Washington:

Dear Gen'l—Immediately after I had closed my last (of the 9th of this instant), I received a letter from Colonel Shepherd, Lieutenant of Ohio county, informing me that a certain Decker, Cox, and Company, with Indians, had crossed the Ohio river, and committed trespasses on the Indians' lands; wherefore, I ordered sixty rank and file to be equipped, and Capt. Clark, of the 8th Pennsylvania Regiment, proceeded with this party to Wheeling, with orders to cross the river at that part, and to apprehend some of the principal trespassers and destroy the huts. He returned without finding any of the trespassers, but destroyed some huts. He informs me some of the inhabitants have made small improvements, all the way from the Muskingum river to Fort McIntosh, and thirty miles up some of the branches. I sent a runner to the Delaware Council at Coochoching, to inform them of the trespass, and assure them it was committed by some foolish people, and requested them to rely on my doing them justice, and punishing the offenders, but as yet have not received an answer.

I have the honor to be, with perfect regard and esteem, your Excellency's most Obed't Humble Servant, D. BRODHEAD.

After the treaty of Fort McIntosh, it was feared that there would be such a rush of squatters into that portion of the territory bordering on Pennsylvania and Virginia, that evil results would ensue, and, accordingly, means were taken both to drive out the intruders already there and prevent the entrance of others. June 15, 1785, Congress ordered the following proclamation published and circulated in the territory:

Whereas, it has been represented to the United States, in Congress assembled, that several disorderly persons have crossed the Ohio, and settled upon the unappropriated lands; and, whereas, it is their intention, as soon as it shall be surveyed, to open offices for the sale of a considerable part thereof, in such proportions and under such regulations as may suit the convenience of all the citizens of the United States, and others who may wish to become purchasers of the same; and, as such conduct tends to defeat the object they have in view, is in direct opposition to the ordinances and resolutions of Congress, and is highly disrespectful to the federal authority, they have heretofore thought fit, and do hereby issue this proclamation, forbidding all such unwarrantable intrusions, and enjoining all those who have settled thereon to depart with their families and effects, without loss of time, as they shall answer the same at their peril.

The intrusion was confined principally to the territory now forming the counties of Columbiana, Jefferson, Stark, Carroll, Harrison, Belmont, Guernsey, and Monroe, and the names of the intruders in 1785, were as follows: George Atchison, Jonas Amspoker, Albertus Bailey, William Bailey, John Buchanan, Henry Cassil, Walter Cain, Jacob Clark, James Clark, John Castleman, Charles Chambers, William Carpenter, Henry Conrad, John Custer, Thomas Dawson, Nicholas Decker, Solomon DeLong, Daniel Duff, Zepaniah Dunn, Hanamet Davis, Jesse Edgerton, John Fitzpatrick, Henry Froggs, John Goddard, Joseph Goddard, Archibald Harbson, Robert Hill, Adam House, Wiland Hoagland, Thomas Johnson, William Kerr, Frederick Lamb,

Jacob Light, John McDonald, Thomas McDonald, William McNees, William Mann, Jonathan Mapins, Daniel Menser, Daniel Matthews, John Nixon, John Nowles, John Noyes, James Paul, Haines Piley, Jesse Parremore, Nathaniel Parremore, John Platt, Michael Rawlins, Joseph Reburn, Benjamin Reed, George Reno, John Rigdon, Joseph Ross, William Shiff, John Tilton, Thomas Tilton, William Wallace, Charles Ward, James Watson, James Williams.

In March, 1785, Colonel Harmar, commandant at Fort McIntosh, had sent out troops to dispossess the squatter settlers whose names are given above. The squatters actually banded together to resist the United States troops; but a compromise was effected, whereby they were allowed to prepare temporary houses on the Virginia side before leaving their homes in the Northwest Territory. Some of them retired from the Ohio country, temporarily, but subsequently most of them returned, and their descendants are now numerous in Eastern Ohio and in the valleys of the Tuscarawas and the Muskingum.

The extent and location of these settlements at that early period within the limits of what was then Jefferson county (including Belmont) are shown by the report of Ensign Armstrong, who was sent by Colonel Harmar down the Ohio river from Fort McIntosh, with a detachment of soldiers, for the purpose of enforcing the Government's orders; and, also, by the Journal of General Richard Butler, one of the Commissioners appointed by Congress to treat with the western Indians. Ensign Armstrong's report is as follows:

Fort McIntosh, 12th April, 1785.

Sir:—Agreeable to your orders, I proceeded with my party, on the 31st of March, down the river. On the first instant we crossed Little Beaver, and dispossessed a family. Four miles from there, we found three families living in sheds, but, they having no rafts to transport their effects, I thought it proper to give them until the 31st inst., at which time they promised to demolish their sheds and remove to the east side of the river.

At Yellow creek [south of the site of Wellsville], I dispossessed two families and destroyed their building. The 2d inst., being stormy, nothing was done. The 3d, we dispossessed eight families. The 4th we arrived at Mingo Bottom, or Old Town [Mingo, Jefferson county]. I read my instructions to the prisoner, [Joseph] Ross, who declared they never came from Congress, for he had late accounts from that honorable body, who, he was convinced, gave no such instructions to the Commissioners. Neither did he care from whom they came, for he was determined to hold possession, and if I destroyed his house he would build six more within a week. He also cast many reflections on the honorable the Congress, the Commissioners, and the commanding officer. I conceived him to be a dangerous man, and sent him under guard to Wheeling. Finding that most of the settlers at this place were tenants under the prisoner, I gave them a few days, at which time they promised to move to the east side of the Ohio river, and to demolish their buildings. On the evening of the 4th, Charles Norris, with a party of armed men, came to my quarters in a hostile manner, and demanded my instructions. After conversing with them some time, and showing my instructions, the warmth with which they first expressed themselves began to abate, and for some motive lodged their arms with me till morning. I learned from the conversation of the party that at Norris' Town (by them so called), eleven miles farther down the river, [probably the site of the present village of Warrentown, at the mouth of Short creek], a party of seventy or eighty men were assembled with a determination to oppose me. Finding Norris to be a man of influence in that country, I conceived it to my interest to make use of him as an instrument, which I effected by informing him it was my intention to treat any armed parties I met as enemies of my country, and would fire on them if they did not disperse.

On the 5th, when I arrived within two miles of the town, or place where I expected to meet with opposition, I ordered my men to load their arms in the presence of Norris, and then desired him to go to the party and inform them of my intentions. I then proceeded on with caution, but had not gone far when paper No. 1 was handed me by one of the party, to which I replied, that I would treat with no party, but intended to execute my orders. When I arrived at the town there were about forty men assembled, who had deposited their arms. After I had read to them my instructions, they agreed to move off by the 19th inst. This indulgence I thought proper to grant, the weather being too severe to turn them out of doors. The 6th I proceeded to Hoglin's, or Mercer's Town [Martin's Ferry], where I was presented with paper No. 2, and, from the humble disposition of the people, and the impossibility of their moving, I gave them to the 19th, and I believe they generally left the settlement at that time. At that place I was informed that Charles Norris and John Carpenter had been elected Justices of the Peace; that they had, I found, precepts, and had decided thereon. I then proceeded on till opposite Wheeling, where I dispossessed one family and destroyed their buildings. I hope, sir, that the indulgences granted some of the inhabitants will meet your approbation. The paper No. 2 is a copy of an advertisement, which is posted up in almost every settlement on the western side of the Ohio. Three of my party being landed, I left them about forty miles from this place under care of a corporal. The remainder I have ordered to their respective companies, and the prisoner I have delivered to the prison guard. I am, sir, with great respect, your obedient servant, JOHN ARMSTRONG, Ensign.

This record shows that a number of white settlements existed on the west side of the Ohio river in 1785; that some of them were quite populous, over sixty names of the principal settlers of Mercertown alone being given; and that they had so far advanced in setting up a civil government as to have elected two Justices of the Peace, who had already decided cases tried before them. Armstrong failed to break up the settlement, and met with such bitter opposition that he compromised with them, giving them a certain length of time, at the end of which they agreed to leave, if the Government did not rescind the order. Few of them left, however. The Journal of General Richard Butler, who was appointed by Congress, in 1785, as one of the Commissioners to treat with the Indians, shows the subsequent action of the Government and the settlers in the matter.

General Butler started on his mission in the fall of 1785. He left Fort Pitt September 26, 1785, accompanied by General Samuel H. Parsons, Colonel James Monroe (afterwards President of the United States), and others. He arrived at Fort McIntosh, at the mouth of Beaver creek, where Colonel Harmar still commanded, and where a detachment of troops was furnished to accompany the Commissioners. The party set off in boats from Fort McIntosh on September 30th, and General Butler kept a diary of the events of the expedition, from which it will be seen that a portion of his duties was to warn off the settlers that were located on the west bank of the Ohio river. In his Journal, under date of September 30th, he speaks of meeting the United States surveyors at the Pennsylvania state line, who were then just making a beginning for the survey of the first seven ranges of land within the Northwest Territory. The following extracts are from his entires for the succeeding days:

October 1st.—Passed Yellow creek and found several improvements on both sides of the river. Put in at one Jesse Penniman's, on the north side, five miles below Yellow creek; warned him off. Called on one, Pry. who I warned off, also; this appears to be a shrewd, sensible man. He assured me that he would go off; that he would go to Kentucky. . . . He seemed not well pleased, though he promised submission.

At this Pry's house, we met one William McCullum, from the Illinois; he says he passed General Clark at the Falls. . . . Passed on to the Mingo towns, where we found a number of people, among whom one Ross [the same who had been made a prisoner, and carried to Fort McIntosh by Ensign Armstrong six months before]; seems to be the principal man on the north [west] side of that place. I conversed with him and warned him and the others away. He said he and his neighbors were misrepresented to Congress; that he was going to Congress to inform them that himself and neighbors were determined to be obedient to their ordinances.

Passed on to near Cross Creek, eight miles below the Mingo towns.

Cross Creek, Sunday, October 2d.—Capt. O'Hara had a fine cow killed for the troops, who arrived at nine o'clock; had the men served with provisions, who were set to cooking, while some loaded flour and corn for the use of the troops and cattle, and all was got ready and started at one o'clock. The people of this country appear to be much imposed upon by a religious sect called Methodists, and are become great fanatics. They say they have paid taxes which were too heavy.

Called at the settlement of Charles Norris, whose house has been pulled down, and he has rebuilt it. At this place found one Walter Kean, who seems but a middling character, and rather of the dissentious cast. Warned all these off, and requested they would inform their neighbors, which they promised to do. . . .

Called at the settlement of one Capt. Hoglan, whom we also warned off. His house had also been torn down and rebuilt. We informed him of the impropriety of his conduct, which he acknowledged, and seemed very submissive, and promised to remove, and to warn his neighbors off, also. Come on very well to Wheeling, where we stayed all night. This is a fine settlement, and belongs to one Zane.

These records are sufficient to show, therefore, that the first white settlements in Ohio were not made at Marietta, in Washington county, but were made in the present townships of Steubenville, Wells, and Warren, in Jefferson county, and Pease, in Belmont county; and, as Mr. William H. Hunter, in his admirable history of the Pathfinders of Jefferson County, points out, "These people were real settlers, in the sense that they had built cabins and block-houses, and cultivated crops for subsistence. They possessed horses; for we know that John Carpenter, after making a clearing in 1781, on the site of Portland [in Jefferson county], took two horses to Fort Pitt, with which to convey salt; we know that a son of John Tilton's was killed by Indians while up Short creek after his father's cows. We know they had houses. . . . They were a religious people, . . . so religious, in fact, were these settlers on the bottom lands of Jefferson county—Mingo Bottoms, extending from what is now Mingo Junction, to the present southern line of the county—that Colonel Butler reported that they were great fanatics. We know, also, that Rev. George Callahan held the first Methodist Episcopal services in the Northwest Territory, in 1787, at Carpenter's Fort." Carpenter's Fort was located on Short creek, not far above its mouth, and near the present Portland station, on the Cleveland and Pittsburgh railway. See an article on "The Holmes Family," in the Lancaster (Ohio) Gazette, July 15, 1899.

We get another glimpse of the Norristown (now Warrentown) settlement as it was in the summer of 1787, during the progress of the survey of the Seven Ranges, by referring to the diary of John Mathews, a nephew of General Putnam, who came out from Massachusetts to assist in the survey. On August 5th, 1787, he was at Esquire McMahan's house, a few miles south of Mingo Island, on the Virginia side of the Ohio river, whence his Journal proceeds as follows:

6th. At 9 o'clock A. M. embarked on board of a boat for Muskingum, in company of Captain Mills, Lieutenant Spear, and Doctor Scott. Twelve o'clock, stopped one mile above Short creek, on the northwest side of the river [Warrenton]. At this place are about ten families collected, and are determined to stand it out against all opposition, either from the Indians or the troops. After a drink of good punch, proceeded on our way. At six, arrived at Wheeling, and tarried all night.

Interesting as it is to trace the footsteps of these early pioneers, however, we can find but little information of them on the records during the next ten years; and it was not until after the year 1800 that extensive settlements began to be made in Harrison county. Settlers had come into the county in considerable numbers before 1805, and taken up much of the choicest lands along the streams. The best means we have of determining their centres of settlement is to examine the history of the early churches of the county. It was characteristic of that race of people which chiefly settled Harrison county that its pioneers usually established a church or preaching station, even if it were no more than a "tent," as soon as they became seated with their families in a new country. We find, accordingly, that two of these stations were erected to accommodate the worshippers who lived in what is now Harrison county, as early as 1803, one at Daniel Welch's (Beech Spring, or Unionvale), and the other a short distance south of the present village of New Athens, (Crabapple). The next year, occasional preaching services began to be held on the site of the present town of Cadiz.

CHAPTER V.

HARRISON COUNTY PIONEERS.

The first white settlers in Harrison county came here before any roads were built, and it is reasonable to suppose, before it was possible to bring with them any wheeled vehicles. Their household furnishings, salt, and flour or meal, were brought by pack-horses; and the first avenues of travel in the county were probably old Indian trails or paths, following the courses of the streams, or piercing the seemingly endless forest along the tops of the high ridges, or "divides." The first to come were the Indian fighters, scouts, and hunters, of whom a number lived along the Ohio river frontier, contemporaries and neighbors of the Wetzel brothers, of Adam and Andrew Poe, of Captain Samuel Brady, and of Major McCulloch. Among these, Jacob Holmes, Robert Maxwell, and Joseph and William Huff settled along Indian Short creek, as it was then called, the Huffs locating near the site of Georgetown. In a letter from Curtis Wilkin, a relative of Joseph Huff, published by Mr. Hunter in his history of the Pathfinders of Jefferson County, the writer states that Joseph Huff did not settle on Short creek before 1796; and that his house was the frontier house in that vicinity for upwards of three years. William Huff shot an Indian near where Georgetown now stands, about the year 1800, because he had boasted in Huff's presence of the number of white men's scalps he had taken. Of Jacob Holmes, Mr. Curtis Wilkin, of Kenton, Ohio, in a letter to the Steubenville Gazette, written March 6, 1899, says:

Jacob Holmes was my grandfather, and my information is derived from Jacob Holmes himself, from his wife, and from my mother. John Huff, my grandmother's brother, married Sallie Johnson, a sister of

John and Henry Johnson, who were captured by the Indians [in Warren township, Jefferson county, in 1793], killed their captors, and returned home. John Huff settled at Columbia, on the Ohio river, a few miles above Cincinnati, at about the close of the last century, and lived to be an aged man, dying there something over fifty years ago. Besides his sister (my grandmother), he had a brother, Eleazer Huff, and a son in the vicinity of my father's farm in Highland county.

Jacob Holmes was born December 8, 1768, in Rockingham county, Va. While Jacob was a small boy, his father moved to Bedford county, Pa., and a few years later to Washington county, Pa., near Catfish, now Washington; then a few years later to what is now Brooke county, W. Va., and settled on Buffalo creek, not far from the Ohio river. Here our subject grew to manhood, and in 1791 was married to Elizabeth, daughter of Michael and Hannah Doddridge Huff. Shortly after his marriage he was employed by the United States Government as an Indian scout, and, in company with his brother-in-law, Kinsey Dickerson, and a man named Washburn, was thus employed for three years. For his services he received a tract of land on Short creek, a few miles north of where Mt. Pleasant now stands. To this place he moved his family in the spring of 1796, my mother being but six months old. He resided on this farm some twenty-five years, when he sold to a man named Comley, and removed to the northern part of Harrison county. The farm on which he then located is now in Carroll county. He resided here until 1832, when he again sold out and removed to Fairfield township, Highland county. In the summer of 1838, he again sold out, and bought a farm one mile north of Kenton, Hardin county, to which he moved in the spring of 1839, and there he died October 14, 1841.

In another letter Mr. Wilkin writes:

Joseph Huff was the brother of my grandmother, the wife of Jacob Holmes. My grandfather, Michael Huff, had the following sons: Michael, who was killed by the Indians on the Mississippi river, in the early settlement of Illinois; Joseph, who I think died in Harrison county many years ago, not far from where his father settled in Jefferson (now Harrison) county, and near Georgetown; William, who died near the same place; John, who died at Columbia, a short distance above Cincinnati, about 1842; Samuel, who died in Highland county about 1846; Eleazer, who died in Highland county about 1833. The old Huff Bible, that contains the record of all the Huff family, is now in possession of David C. Holmes, of Kenton, a grandson of Jacob Holmes.

Henry Howe, in his history of Ohio, written in 1847, states that in April, 1799, Alexander Henderson and family, from Washington county, Pennsylvania, "squatted" on the southwest corner of the section of land on which Cadiz stands; and at this time Daniel Peterson resided at the forks of Short creek, with his family, the only one within the present limits of Harrison county. If this statement be true, then Joseph Huff could not have settled in Harrison county much before 1800.

Major Erkuries Beatty, father of the late Dr. Charles C. Beatty of Sterbenville, who was paymaster of the western army, came to the Ohio country in 1786 and 1787, in the discharge of his official duties, and kept a diary of his tours and transactions. On the 31st of July, 1786, Major Beatty set out from Pittsburgh to descend the Ohio river. On the second day afterwards, he made the following entry in his diary:

August 2. Started early, stopped opposite the mouth of Little Beaver and breakfasted with the surveyor, who is waiting for troops. Arrived at Mingo Bottom 3 o'clock, where Capt. Hamtramck's, McCurdy's, and Mercer's companies encamped, and had just been mustered and inspected by Major North. Showers of rain to-day. The troops encamped on the bank of the river opposite the lower end of a small island.

August 3. Waiting for Major North, who is going with me to Muskingum. About 2 o'clock two detachments from Capt. Mercer's company, one commanded by Lt. Kersy, the other by Ensign Rigart, marched to destroy some improvements on the river ten or fifteen miles up Short creek.

"Ten or fifteen miles up Short creek" would locate this settlement which the soldiers were about to destroy, at somewhere between Adena and Georgetown, and if Major Beatty's information was exact, it would indicate that some of the hardy pioneers of that day had penetrated the wilderness and made improvements in Short Creek township as early as 1786.

The first survey of the public lands northwest of the Ohio river was that of the Seven Ranges, made in pursuance of an act of Congress of May 20, 1785. In July, 1786, the surveyors, under the direction of Thomas Hutchins, who had been appointed geographer of the United States, assembled at Pittsburgh. John Mathews, a nephew of General Rufus Putnam, one of the surveyors, came on from Massachusetts to assist in the survey, arriving at Pittsburgh July 26, 1786. His diary, kept during the progress of the survey, has been published. He spent the early part of September, 1787, at the house of Esquire McMahan, in Ohio (now Brooke) county, West Virginia. On the 20th, a small party proposed to cross the Ohio and go out into the woods for a few days to dig ginseng. In those early times, when the plant was plentiful, it was a source of profit to the frontier inhabitants, who had few articles to give in exchange for money, or the more valuable articles of merchandise brought out by the traders. This proved to be rather a hazardous trip, as the Indians were hostile, and killed all the white men they found encroaching on their hunting grounds. Mathews' journal proceeds:

September 20th, 1787. A little before sunset the Squire and myself crossed the Ohio, and went about two miles, and tarried all night at a house which was left by the inhabitants [who had probably fled, from fear of the hostile Indians then in the vicinity].

September 21st.—Four men joined us, and we set off by Williamson's Trail a little before sunset. We encamped half a mile beyond the Big Lick, on the head waters of Short creek, in the ninth township of the fourth range.

The ninth township of the fourth range comprises the north half of the present township of Short Creek and the south half of Green, in Harison county; and the "Big Lick" may have been the spring near which some twelve or thirteen years later Daniel Welch established his horsemill—in his day known as Beech Spring, from which the first church erected in Harrison county took its name.

The ginseng diggers proceeded westward along the ridge dividing the waters of Short creek and the Stillwater, and dug ginseng four days. Mathews says: "It grew here in great abundance. Men accustomed to the work could dig from forty to sixty pounds a day."

September 28. Collected our horses and prepared to start for the river. At 1 o'clock completed their loading. At sunset, encamped within about sixteen miles of the Ohio.

29th. Arrived at the river about three o'clock P. M. We were much surprised to hear that three men had been killed and one taken prisoner by the Indians, about ten miles up Cross creek, who were out after ginseng on Sunday last. Two of the party made their escape. They had also killed a family the week following, up Wheeling creek, and done considerable other damage. While we were out we were very careless and came on their trail, but very fortunate they did not fall in with us. I feel very happy that I have reached my old quarters, and will give them liberty to take my scalp if they find me out after ginseng again this year.

October 12th. This evening McMahan returned from over the river, where he had been with a party of men in pursuit of some Indians, who yesterday morning killed an old man near Fort Steuben. He did not discover them, but by the signs thought them to be seven or eight in number.

Nov. 30th. A part of this month I have been on the west side of the Ohio, with Mr. Simpson and Colonel Martin, assisting them in the survey of the lands they bought at public sales in New York.

Dr. Thomas R. Crawford, for forty years pastor of Nottingham Church, in his book of "Reminiscences," published at Wheeling in 1887, gives the following account of an Indian fight which took place within the present boundaries of Harrison county more than a hundred years ago:

> The earliest visit of white men of which we have any account, into the territory of which this county was ultimately formed, was in the fall of 1793, when Capt. William Boggs, Robert Maxwell, Joseph Daniels, —— Johnson, and —— Miller were sent out from the old blockhouse [Fort Henry], located on the ground afterwards occupied by the city of Wheeling, West Va. These men were Indian scouts and spies. They made their excursion from the mouth of Wheeling creek up to the dividing ridge, and crossed over on the evening of the second day after they left the river, to the headwaters of Stillwater, venturing rather far into the interior with so small a force. This little band of daring men struck up a fire and camped at a spring on the banks of a stream, near to the place where the old Crawford brick house now stands. The party prepared and ate their supper, and being much fatigued with the journey of two days through an unbroken wilderness, they lay down to rest around the burning embers of a camp fire, not expecting an enemy near, for they had seen no recent traces of the red man from the time they left the Fort. Soon they were wrapped in sleep, only to be awakened and startled by the hideous yell of Indians, followed by the report of firearms. A ball took effect in the knee of Captain Boggs, which so crippled him that he was unable to flee. He called to his companions, "Make your escape, if possible, and leave me to my fate," which they did, leaving their brave leader to perish at the hands of a terrible and cruel foe. Three out of the four that fled arrived safely at the block-house, and reported the disaster that befell their expedition. Measures were immediately taken, and a company of men was sent out in a short time to seek for the remains of Mr. Boggs. After much precaution in travel, the party found the place where the spies had encamped on that fatal night, and soon discovered the mutilated body of their captain; took up the remains and buried them a few rods northeast from the above-named spring, on one of the tributary streams of Big Stillwater, which ever after has been called "Boggs' Fork," from the name of this adventuring but unfortunate man. It is to be regretted that all traces of the grave of this brave and trustworthy soldier have disappeared.

Some knowledge of the hardships and privations of the early settlers of Harrison county may be gathered from a biographical account, published in 1891, of Robert Cochran, who was born in what is now Dauphin county, Pennsylvania, in 1771. He came to Allegheny county with his father's family, when eighteen years of age. Shortly after the year 1803, he emigrated to Ohio, and bought eighty acres of land in what is now Harrison county, paying $200 for the same. Here he built himself a cabin of poles, daubed inside and out with mud, having a stick chimney, puncheon floor, clap-board roof, and clap-board door. Here, in winter seasons, he was joined by John Maholm, an old friend from Pennsylvania, and together they lived in Mr. Maholm's cabin, eating supper and breakfast in company, and each working on his own " clearing " during the day.

During the fall and winter of 1804-5, Mr. Cochran secured the services of a man to do his cooking, hired a mill-wright and several axemen, and erected a two-story grist-mill, worked by horse-power. No iron was used in its construction, except some strengthening bands around the trundle head and spindle; wheels and parts were all made of wood, and all hand-made, as saw-mills were unknown in the county at that day. The mill-stones were brought down the Ohio to Steubenville and hauled across the country, the trip occupying four days. Unwieldy as it was, the mill was kept constantly going, day and night, Sundays excepted, the farmers coming for miles around to have their grinding done. It was a common sight to see men occupying the time, while waiting their turn for grinding, in throwing the tomahawk at marks attached to trees. As time passed on, this mill was superseded by water-mills, but in dry seasons, when water failed, the neighbors were obliged to return again to Cochran's horse-mill. It was the first mill erected west of that of Daniel Welch, at Beech Spring, and in early days was of great benefit to the pioneers. The land on which Mr. Cochran settled lies about half a mile north of Cadiz, and is now occupied by his descendants.

The early pioneers came to Harrison county from Pennsylvania, Virginia, and Maryland, but chiefly from Washington county, Pennsylvania. The journeys from localities east of the mountains were sometimes long and full of danger. The paths across the mountains were rough and difficult. Pack-horses were at first the only means of transportation; on some, the pioneers packed the stores and rude agricultural implements, and on others, the furniture, bedding, and cooking utensils, and again, on others, their wives and children. Horses which carried small children were each provided with a pack-saddle and two large creels made of hickory withes, in the fashion of a crate, one over each side, in which were stowed clothes and bedding. In the center of each would sometimes be tucked a child or two, the top being well secured by lacing, so as to keep the youngsters in their places. The roads, frequently, were barely passable; sometimes lying along the brink of precipices; frequently overflown in places by swollen streams, all of which had to be forded; horses slipping, falling, and carried away, both women and children were often in great danger.

The creels would sometimes break and send the children rolling over the ground in great confusion. It was no uncommon thing for mother and child to be separated from each other for hours whilst on the journey to their new homes, in a wild forest, amidst beasts, and exposed to attacks by the Indians. When the pioneer reached his destination, he usually put up a brush shelter, until he could build his cabin. The latter was made of rough logs, without nail, board, or window-pane. He then turned his attention to clearing a small plot of ground on which to raise such food as was needed for the support of his family.

The food question was the all-important one with the settlers. Their hard labor resulted in giving them keen appetites, and much account was taken of the feasts, merry-making parties, and public gatherings. The quality of the food was not so much regarded as the quantity. Times were when the providential appearance of a deer averted starvation, and the fortunate catching of a fish, or the trapping of game, eked out a scanty subsistence. Journeys of many miles were made for a few pounds of flour or meal.

Their cabins contained little or no furniture; beds with no mattresses, springs, or even bed-cords—the couches being spread upon the floor, and sleeping apartments separated by hanging blankets. About the fireplace were found hooks and trammel, the bake-pan and the kettle. Sometimes chairs were represented by sections of a tree of the required height. Upon the shelves were spoons of pewter, blue-edged plates, cups and saucers, and the black earthen tea-pot; and later, perhaps, one corner of the room was occupied by a tall clock, while in another corner stood an old-fashioned, high-post, corded bedstead, covered with an "Irish chain" quilt—a marvel of patchwork ingenuity and laborious sewing.

The following extracts from a letter written by Robert Van Horn in 1895, furnish an interesting account of the incidents of an early trip over the Allegheny mountains, made by one of the pioneer families in Harrison county. Mr. Van Horn was born at New Athens in 1812, the son of Edward and Margaret Hamilton Van Horn. He writes:

My grandmother's maiden name was Martha McMillan, and she had a sister, Jane, married to John Perry. My first certain knowledge of them finds Grandmother living in Nottingham township, Chester county, Pennsylvania, and Uncle John Perry near by, on the Susquehanna river, running a herring fishery.

The country, though near Philadelphia, was new, and covered largely with pine forests, and the ground was strewed with the resinous knots of decayed trees, like the bones of dead animals. These knots were gathered by the poor, and laid by, to burn in the winter, instead of candles, and many an armful my mother carried home to her humble dwelling.

Part of my mother's time, when a girl, was spent in the family of her uncle, John Perry, and part of her occupation was to hunt the cows in the woods, morning and evening. Rising early, she would stick a herring in the hot ashes to roast, and when done she would take it for a morning lunch, and hie away to the woods, as blithe and merry as a lark, her ears alert for the tinkling of the cow-bell.

How long the families remained there, I do not know; but Uncle Perry resolved to seek a better country, if not a heavenly one; and, like Abraham of old, he gathered up his substance, and, with his family, which was quite numerous, and my grandmother and her family, making together quite a respectable caravan, he started for the far West, a distance of some three hundred miles. Their goods seem to have been drawn by a single train, of four or six horses. There may have been more, but tradition does not say so. Perhaps the children, if not the mothers, " walked afoot." The only incident of the journey which I can recall was as follows:

On reaching the top of one of the mountains, they found the western slope, which was quite long and steep, covered with a solid sheet of ice from top to bottom, making the descent extremely perilous. A consultation was held, and, as on all similar occasions, advice was plenty, and my grandmother contributed her share in true womanly style. She wanted him to cut down a great big sapling, and tie it to the hind end of the wagon, TO HOLD IT BACK ! And old Uncle Perry, in true masculine style, after listening to this and other suggestions equally wise, went and did just as he had a mind to. He did not cut down the sapling, nor anything of the kind; but by rough-locking and careful driving, reached the foot of the perilous descent in safety. On reaching the bottom of the hill, he stopped the team, took off his hat, and, wiping his brow, said that he had had that hill on his mind ever since he left home.

On reaching their destination, they located in the extreme western part of Washington county, near West Middletown. Just how long they remained there, I do not know, but it must have been a number of years, for there several of the Hamilton children married and three of them died.

My father and mother removed to Harrison county in 1807, with their three oldest children. And some years before, the Perrys, Gastons, Alexander Morrison, and Grandmother Hamilton, had all settled near Morristown, in Belmont county.

On Saturday, May 5th, 1900, the writer paid a visit to a native of Harrison county, who was born near Cadiz, November 5, 1800, nearly one hundred years ago. This was Thomas West, who lives on a farm near Lafayette, in Coshocton county, Ohio. He was born a few miles north of Cadiz, the son of William and Sarah Boyd West, and grandson of Morris West. His parents came to Harrison county before 1800, and settled on the farm where he was born. There they died in 1830. He was married to Eliza Tipton, of Cadiz, niece of Rev. William Tipton, in 1831; and they removed to Coshocton county about 1844.

Thomas West stated that his father went from Steubenville into what was then the backwoods of Jefferson (now Harrison) county, and built himself a log-cabin, afterwards returning for his father (Morris West), who accompanied the family to their frontier home. At that time, and for some years afterwards, there were no roads in the county, and the settlers found their way from place to place by means of blazed trees, or trees from which a small portion of the bark had been chopped off, so as to leave a mark. Thomas West had as a schoolmate one Philip Kail, and some of his neighbors were Samuel Maholm, Nathan and Lemuel Green, and James Forbes. He went three miles to school, making his way through the forest by means of the blazings, and could not remain for the afternoon sessions, as he had to return home before evenings in order to avoid the wolves. The United States spelling book was the principal book used in his school days. The school-houses which he attended were all log buildings, and the light was let in by means of a square hole cut out between two logs, the opening being covered with greased paper. The boys were warned by the teacher against punching holes through the windows with their quill pens, and suffered severe punishment if caught in such an act.

The first religious meetings were held in private houses, traveling circuit riders occasionally visiting the settlement and preaching for them. When a log church was afterwards erected (now Bethel church), the services were attended by many in the neighborhood, but the attendants usually wore their every-day suits and dresses, as few of the pioneers possessed clothing that could be called "Sunday best." Man and wife usually rode to meeting together, on the back of the same horse.

Clothing was generally made of coarse linen. For winter wear, it was customary to weave the cloth with two "shots" of wool alternating with every two "shots" of tow thread. The pioneers had plenty to eat and live on, though it was a rough diet. After the first few years, they had plenty of meat and potatoes, turnips, milk, and butter—"hog and hominy, milk and butter," as Mr. West expressed it. When a small boy, his principal occupation was to pick up brush, following the men, whose labor for many years after settlement was chiefly devoted to making clearings here and there in the forest, upon which they might plant crops. One of Mr. West's earliest recollections was that of an adventure the family had with a bear. When still a small boy, his father had cleared sufficient of his land to give him a space for two fields, and had constructed a fence between, which ran from the cabin to the timber line. While this fence was building, one day when the men had come in for their supper, an occasion arose for using the family ax, and it was found that it had been left out in the clearing, at the end of the fence. Thomas was sent out to fetch it, and ran down the field alongside the fence to where it lay. As he ran, he noticed that the family pig was running down the field on the other side of the fence, as if expecting to receive some food from the hands of the boy, as was its wont. As Thomas reached the ax, and stooped down to pick it up, he heard the pig set up a terrific squealing, and saw it held tightly between the forelegs of a large black animal, which stood up on its hind legs, and seemed to have conceived a wonderful affection for Tommie's pet piggie. At the same time, his father began to shout and to clap his hands vigorously, and by so doing succeeded in starting the bear back to the woods, where it dropped the hog between the forked limbs of a low tree, and then departed. The men got down a gun, and started into the woods, but failed to find the bear. They brought back the hog, however, but its life had been crushed out, and its back broken in three places by the bear's tight squeeze.

Pork was the chief animal food of the Harrison county pioneer. In the early days, the salted meat was packed in a trough, which was set deep in the ground near the front of the cabin door, and a clap-board top staked down over the trough, to keep wolves and other beasts from getting at its contents. Mr. West said that when he had grown to be a man, he bought salted pork from Edward Healey, a neighbor, who told him that he hadn't seen the bottom of his meat hogshead for seven years, "and it was as good meat as ever went into a man's mouth," said Mr. West. "Salt was salt in those days. It is not so good now, and it is difficult to get it of sufficient strength to keep the meat from souring."

"The ploughs were all made of wood," he proceeded, "excepting a coulter to split the ground, and a small share-point. Threshing was done with a flail. I have whipped out hundreds of bushels of wheat on the puncheon floor of a log-barn. Johnny-cake was a staple article of diet. It was baked by putting it on a smooth board and setting it before a fire, with a stone before it, to keep it from falling down. When one side was done, we turned it over, and baked the other side. Wheat bread was baked by making a hole in the earthen fire-hearth, into which the loaves were placed, the hole covered with a flat stone, and live coals heaped on the stone. Sometimes the wheat was so rank, that it made you sick to eat bread made from it, and even made the hogs sick. This may have come from poisonous herbs being ground up with the flour, but it was usually thought to be due to the wheat having too much shade while growing. In the early days, the crops were planted in small patches, wherever clearings had been made, and the patches were surrounded on all sides by the tall trees of the forest. I remember one day a distant female relative came to visit at our house at a time when the wheat was too rank to make wholesome bread. My mother had to serve corn-bread, or Johnny-cake, and explained the reason for doing so by saying that the wheat that year was unfit for bread. Our visitor was inclined to turn up her nose at Johnny-cake, and thought my mother had invented the excuse about the wheat bread, merely to hide her poverty; so she stated that she was very fond of bread made from wheat grown on new soil, and liked no other kind so well. This nettled my mother some, as she could see from the manner of her visitor that her own hospitality was questioned; and she resolved to give her all that she desired. So my mother made up some of the new wheat flour into bread, and at the next meal let her visitor eat her fill. The result was, a very sick woman, and no doubt a wiser one. We used to go two miles to the house of a neighbor to get our grinding done. He had a hand-mill, and sometimes it was necessary to wait for hours before our turn would come to take the mill. Later, when Bower's mill was set up [at the site of Bowerstown], I often rode horseback through the woods to that mill, with a bag of corn or wheat behind, had it ground, and carried the meal or flour home. One afternoon, while returning from the mill, I noticed a number of wild animals, like large dogs, which followed the horse, and one of them, once or twice snapped at my feet. But I was a small boy then, and my feet did not reach down very far; so I did not become uneasy. When

I reached home, my parents told me that the animals which followed me were wolves, and they marvelled at my escape without injury. I had never seen wolves before, and when I found out what had chased me, became very much frightened at my experience.

"In the early days in Harrison county, fist fights were of very frequent occurrence, and public gatherings of all kinds usually ended with a fight between one or more pairs of fighters. While I was still a little boy, my uncle, Augustus West, was forced into a fight with a bully, during the time of a camp-meeting which was held in the woods near our house. This occurred one day after the services had been held. My uncle was standing on the grounds, talking with some of his friends, when a big, swaggering fellow came along, elbowing people out of his way, and looking and walking very much like a big Brahma rooster that is spoiling for a fight. 'I am the best man that walks the road,' he said, when he reached the place where my uncle was standing with his friends. Now, my uncle was not naturally a fighting man, and I think if he had been choosing a place for a fight he would not have picked on the grounds of a camp-meeting. But he hated a bully, and when the fellow repeated his brag, my uncle said to him in a quiet tone, 'Stranger, untried.' This was enough to egg on the bully, and he struck my uncle. Then the fight began. Uncle Augustus was a short and heavy-set man, built like a Dutchman's horse, and he could parry the blows of his antagonist until he finally succeeded in 'cutting his wind.' Then he sailed into him, and very soon had him with his back on the ground.

"General musters were often held at Cadiz, and in the country near there, and I attended many of these when a young man, although not myself a member of the militia, on account of my defective hearing. One day, at muster, I saw two men fight for three-quarters of an hour. Their names were Salsman and Watson. Salsman stripped for the fight, and prepared himself for it better. Watson was dressed up, and as he was something of a dandy, would not take off his coat, nor even his stock and necktie. The kind of neckties they wore in those days were very large and cumbersome, and I do not see how Watson could have fought as he did with that cloth wound around his neck. After the fight was over, Salsman had to keep his bed for three weeks. Watson was able to get around again in a few days; and probably would not have had a scratch if he had prepared himself for the fight as the other man did.

"About the time I was married, wheat sold in Harrison county for forty cents a bushel. A day's wages for a reaper was fifty cents, or sometimes a bushel of wheat was given for a day's work. I hired out to work one summer for a bushel of wheat a day. In the fall, when pay-day came, the price of wheat had risen to $1.00. My employer then wanted to pay me in money on the basis of the value of wheat when I began working; but of course, I could not agree to that.

"When I started for myself, the first sheep I bought cost me seventy-five cents each. At that time a good big four year old steer fetched ten dollars. Before that time, a farm laborer's wages was generally not much over twenty-five cents per day. My son-in-law has some men hired on this place where we are to-day, and pays them as much for a day's wage as men used to get for working a week and a day.

"I used to go to Cadiz to do my trading, generally dealt with Kilgore and Lyons, and knew the Olmsteads, the Pritchards, the Maholms, and McFaddens, most of whom were engaged in business in that town. One day a neighbor and myself went to Cadiz, and after doing our trading, and getting what provisions we had come for, the store-keeper (I am not sure, but it may have been Mr. Kilgore), asked us if we were going back home without taking out new calico dresses for our wives. We told him that we had no money with which to buy calico dresses, that it took all our surplus earnings, beyond what went to improving our farms, to buy such necessaries as we could not raise ourselves. He told us that we could buy the dresses without paying for them then, that he would trust us for the price, and we could pay for them at another time. This was my first experience in buying on credit, and it seemed so complimentary to my neighbor and myself that the store-keeper should trust us, that we both bought some of his calico, and our wives had fine new dresses. And we afterwards paid for them, too. Men were not trusted in those days unless it was pretty certain that they would pay. Credit then was not so free or general as it is to-day."

John S. Williams, who edited the American Pioneer, published at Cincinnati in 1843, wrote a series of articles on his knowledge and experience of pioneer life, which are of especial interest to Harrison county readers, as he was an early settler in the Concord settlement in Colerain township, Belmont county, south of Mt. Pleasant, and not far from the southeastern corner of Harrison county. In the spring of 1800, with his mother, sister, and brother, he emigrated from Beaufort, North Carolina, to what was then a part of Jefferson county, in the Northwest Territory. Some of his pioneer experiences were recounted, as follows:

In April, 1800, we sailed from Beaufort for Alexandria (Va.), in company with seventy other emigrants, large and small, say twelve families. We had one storm, and were once becalmed in Core sound, and had to wait about two weeks at Currituc inlet for a wind to take us to sea. From thence to Alexandria we had a fine run, especially up the Potomac bay.

At Alexandria we remained several days before we got wagons to bring us out. Here everything was weighed. My weight was just seventy-five pounds. We stopped near two weeks on what I think was called Goose creek, in Virginia, before we could be supplied with a wagon to cross the mountains, in place of the one we occupied, which belonged there.

The mountain roads, (if roads they could be called, for pack-horses were still on them), were of the most dangerous and difficult character. I have heard an old mountain tavern-keeper say that, although the taverns were less than ten miles apart in years after we came, he had known many emigrant families that stopped a night at every tavern on the mountains. I recollect but few of our night stands distinctly—say, Dinah Besor's, Goose Creek, Old Crock's, near the South Branch; Tomlinson's, Beesontown [Uniontown], and Simpkins', and Merrittstown, Our company consisted of Joseph Dew, Levina Hall, and Jonas Small, with their families. [For a further account of these emigrants, see Chapter II., which relates to the emigration of Southern Quakers to Harrison county.]

After a tedious journey, we all arrived safely at Fredericktown, Washington county, Pa., where we stopped to await the opening of the land office at Steubenville, Ohio. Here, we found Horton Howard and family, who had come on the season previous. Here, also, the children had the whooping-cough. Those whom we left at Alexandria came to Redstone Old Fort [Brownsville], ten miles below Fredericktown, where they sojourned for the same purpose; and although, as we thought, unfortunately detained, they were the first at their resting place.

Jonas Small, Francis Mace, and several other families from Redstone returned to Carolina, dissatisfied with the hills, vales, and mud of the Northwest, little dreaming of the level and open plains of this valley. Horton Howard and family started first from Fredericktown; Joseph Dew, Levina Hall, and ourselves, made another start in September, or early in October. We started in the afternoon, and lay at Benjamin Townsend's on Fishpot Run; we lay also at the Blue Ball, near Washington, at Rice's, on the Buffalo, and at Warren [at the mouth of Short creek], on the Ohio. These are all the night stands that I recollect in fifty-five miles. We arrived safe at John Leaf's, in what is now called Concord settlement. From Warren, Joseph Dew and Mrs. Hall proceeded up Little Short creek, and stopped near where Mt. Pleasant now is. In what is now called Concord settlement, four or five years previously, five or six persons had squatted and made small improvements. The Friends, chiefly from Carolina, had taken the land at a clear sweep.

Mr. Leaf lived on a tract bought by Horton Howard, since owned by Samuel Potts, and subsequently by William Millhouse. Horton Howard had turned in on Mr. Leaf, and we turned in on both.

If anyone has an idea of the appearance of the remnant of a town that has been nearly destroyed by fire, and the homeless inhabitants turned in upon those who were left, they can form some idea of the squatters' cabins that fall. It was a real harvest for them, however, for they received the rhino for the privileges granted and work done, as well in aid of the emigrants in getting cabins up as for their improvements. This settlement is in Belmont county, on Glenn's Run, about six miles northwest of Wheeling, and as much northeast of St. Clairsville.

Emigrants poured in from different posts, cabins were put up in every direction, and women, children, and goods tumbled into them. The tide of emigration flowed like water through the breach in a milldam. Everything was bustle and confusion, and all at work that could work. In the midst of all this, the mumps, and perhaps one or two other diseases prevailed, and gave us a seasoning. Our cabin had been raised, covered, part of the cracks chinked, and part of the floor laid when we moved in, on Christmas day. There had not been a stick cut except in building the cabin. We had intended an inside chimney, for we thought the chimney ought to be in the house. We had a log put across the whole width of the cabin for a mantel, but when the floor was in we found it so low as not to answer, and removed it. Here was a great change for my mother and sister, as well as the rest, but particularly my mother. She was raised in the most delicate manner, in and near London, and lived most of the time in affluence, and always comfortable. She was now in the wilderness, surrounded by wild beasts, in a cabin with about half a floor, no door, no ceiling overhead, not even a tolerable sign for a fireplace; the light of day and the chilling winds of night passing between every two logs, the cabin so high from the ground that a bear, wolf, panther, or any animal less in size than a cow, could enter without even a squeeze. Such was our situation on Thursday and Thursday night, December 25th, 1800, and which was bettered but by very slow degrees. We got the rest of the floor laid in a few days; the chinking of the cracks went on slowly, but the daubing could not proceed until the weather was more suitable, which happened in a few days; doorways were sawed out and steps made of the logs, and the back of the chimney was raised up to the mantel, but the funnel of sticks and clay was delayed until spring.

In building our cabin, it was set to front the north and south, my brother using my father's pocket compass on the occasion. We had no idea of living in a house that did not stand square with the earth itself. This argued our ignorance of the comforts and conveniences of a pioneer life. The position of the house, end to the hill, necessarily elevated the lower end, and the determination to have both a north and a south door added much to the airiness of the domicile, particularly after the green ash puncheons had shrunk so as to leave cracks in the floor and doors from one to two inches. At both the doors we had high, unsteady, and sometimes icy steps, made by piling up the logs cut out of the wall. We had a window, if it could be called a window, when, perhaps, it was the largest spot in the top, bottom, or sides of the cabin at which the wind could not enter. It was made by sawing out a log, placing sticks across, and then, by pasting an old newspaper over the holes, and applying some hog's lard, we had a kind of a glazing which shed a most beautiful and mellow light across the cabin when the sun shone upon it. All other light entered at the doors, cracks, and chimney.

Our cabin was twenty-four by eighteen. The west end was occupied by two beds, the center of each side by a door, and here our symmetry had to stop, for on the side opposite the window, made of clap-boards, supported by pins driven into the logs, were our shelves. Upon these shelves my sister displayed, in ample order, a host of pewter plates, basins, and dishes, and spoons, scoured and bright. It was none of your new-fangled pewter, made of lead, but the best of London pewter, which our father himself bought of Townsend, the manufacturer. These were the plates upon which you could hold your meat so as to cut it without slipping and without dulling your knife. But, alas! the days of pewter plates and sharp dinner knives have passed away, never to return. To return to our internal arrangements. A ladder of five rounds occupied the corner near the window. By this, when we got a floor above, we could ascend. Our chimney occupied most of the east end; pots and kettles opposite the window under the shelves, a gun on hooks over the north door, four split-bottom chairs, three three-legged stools, and a small eight by ten looking-glass sloped from the wall over a large towel and comb-case. These, with a clumsy shovel and a pair of tongs, made in Frederick, with one shank straight, as the best manufacturer of pinches and blood-blisters, completed our furniture, except a spinning-wheel, and such things as were necessary to work with. It was absolutely necessary to have three-legged stools, as four legs of anything could not all touch the floor at the same time.

The completion of our cabin went on slowly. The season was inclement; we were weak-handed and weak-pocketed—in fact, laborers were not to be had. We got one chimney up breast-high as soon as we could, and got our cabin daubed as high as the joists outside. It never was daubed on the inside, for my sister, who was very nice, could not consent to "live right next to the mud." My impression now is, that the window was not constructed till spring, for until the sticks and clay were put on the chimney we could possibly have no need for a window; for the flood of light which always poured into the cabin from the fireplace would have extinguished our window, and rendered it as useless as the moon at noon-day. We got a floor laid overhead as soon as possible, perhaps in a month; but, when it was laid, the reader can readily conceive of its imperviousness to wind or weather, when we mention that it was laid of loose clap-boards, split from a red-oak. That tree grew in the night, and so twisting that each board laid on two diagonally opposite corners, and a cat might have shook every board on our ceiling.

It may be well to inform the unlearned reader that clap-boards are such lumber as pioneers split with a frow, and resemble barrel staves before they are shaved, but are split longer, wider, and thinner; of such our roof and ceiling were composed. Puncheons were planks made by splitting logs to about two and a half or three inches in thickness and hewing them on one or both sides with a broad-axe. Of such our floor, doors, tables, and stools were manufactured.

The monotony of the time for several of the first years was broken and enlivened by the howl of wild beasts. The wolves howling around us seemed to moan their inability to drive us from their long undisputed domain. The bears, panthers, and deer seemingly got miffed at our approach, or the partiality of the hunters, and but seldom troubled us. We did not hunt for them. The wild-cat, raccoon, 'possum, hornet, yellow-jacket, rattlesnake, copperhead, nettle, and a host of small things, which seemed in part to balance the amount of pioneer happiness, held on to their rights until driven out gradually by the united efforts of the pioneers, who like a band of brothers usually aided each other in the great work. These things, as well as getting their bread, kept them too busy for law-suits, quarrels, crimes, and speculations, and made them happy.

When spring was fully come, and our little patch of corn—three acres—put in among the beech roots, which at every step contended with the shovel-plough for the right of soil, and held it, too, we enlarged our stock of conveniences. As soon as bark would run (i. e., peel off), we could make ropes and bark boxes. These we stood in great need of, as such things as bureaus, stands, wardrobes, or even barrels, were not to be had. The manner of making ropes of linn-bark was to cut the bark in strips of convenient length, and water-rot it in the same manner as rotting flax or hemp. When this was done, the inside bark would peel off and split up so fine as to make a pretty considerably rough and good-for-but-little kind of a rope. Of this, however, we were very glad, and let no ship-owner with his grass ropes laugh at us. We made two kinds of boxes for furniture. One kind was of hickory bark, with the outside shaved off. This we would take off all around the tree, the size of which would determine the caliber of our box. Into one end we would place a flat piece of bark or puncheon, cut round to fit in the bark, which stood on end the same as when on the tree. There was little need of hooping, as the strength of the bark would keep that all right enough. Its shrinkage would make the top unsightly in a parlor now-a-days, but then they were considered quite an addition to the furniture. A much finer article was made of slippery-elm bark, shaved smooth, and with the inside out, bent round and sewed together where the ends of the hoop or main bark lapped over. The length of the bark was around the box, and inside out. A bottom was made of a piece of the same bark, dried flat, and a lid, like that of a common band-box, made in the same way. This was the finest furniture in a lady's dressing-room, and then, as now, with the finest furniture, the lapped or sewed side was turned to the wall, and the prettiest part to the spectator. They were easily made oval, and while the bark was green, were easily ornamented with drawings of birds, trees, &c., agreeably to the taste and skill of the fair manufacturer. As we belonged to the Society of Friends, it may be fairly presumed that our band-boxes were not thus ornamented.

To the above store of bark ropes and bark boxes must be added a few gums before the farmer considered himself comfortably fixed. It may be well to inform the unlearned reader that gums are hollow trees cut off, with puncheons pinned on, or fitted into one end, to answer in the place of barrels.

The privations of a pioneer life contract the wants of man almost to total extinction, and allow him means of charity and benevolence. Sufferings ennoble his feelings, and the frequent necessity for united efforts at house-raisings, log-rollings, corn-huskings, &c., produced in him habitual charity, almost unknown in these days.

We settled on beech land, which took much trouble to clear. We could do no other way than clear out the smaller stuff and burn the brush around the beeches, which, in spite of all the burning and girdling we could do to them, would leaf out the first year, and often a little the second. The land, however, was very rich, and would bring better corn than might be expected. We had to tend it principally with the hoe, that is, to chop down the nettles, the water-weed, and the touch-me-not. Grass, careless, lambs-quarter, and Spanish needles were reserved for the better prepared farmers. We cleared a small turnip patch, which we got in about the 10th of August. We sowed in timothy seed, which took well, and the next year we had a little hay besides. The tops and blades of the corn were also carefully saved for our horse, cow, and the sheep. The turnips were sweet and good, and in the fall we took care to gather walnuts and hickory nuts, which were very abundant. These, with the turnips, which we scraped, supplied the place of fruit. I have always been partial to scraped turnips, and could now beat any three dandies at scraping them. Johnny-cake, also, when we had meal to make it of, helped to make up our evening's repast. The Sunday morning biscuit had all evaporated, but the loss was partially supplied by the nuts and turnips. Our regular supper was mush and milk, and by the time we had shelled our corn, stemmed tobacco, and plaited straw to make hats, &c., &c., the mush and milk had seemingly decamped from the neighborhood of our ribs. To relieve this difficulty, my brother and I would make a thin Johnny-cake, part of which we would eat, and leave the rest until morning. At daylight we would eat the balance, as we walked from the house to work.

To get grinding done was often a great difficulty, by reason of the scarcity of mills, the freezes in winter, and the droughts in summer. We had often to manufacture meal (when we had corn) in any way we could get the corn to pieces. We soaked and pounded it, we shaved it, we planed it, and, at a proper season, we grated it. When one of our neighbors got a hand-mill, it was thought quite an acquisition to the neighborhood. In after years, when in time of freezing or drought, we could get grinding by waiting for our turn no more than one day and a night at a horse-mill, we thought ourselves happy.

To save meal we often made pumpkin bread, in which, when meal was scarce, the pumpkin would so predominate as to render it almost impossible to tell our bread from that article, either by taste, looks, or the amount of nutriment it contained. To rise from the table with a good appetite is said to be healthy, and with some is said to be fashionable. What then does it signify to be hungry for a month at a time, when it is not only healthy, but fashionable? Besides all this, the sight of a bag of meal, when it was scarce, made the family feel more glad and thankful to Heaven then, than a whole boat-load would at the present time.

Salt was five dollars per bushel, and we used none in our corn-bread, which we soon liked as well without it. What meat we had at first was fresh, and but little of that; for had we been hunters, we had no time to practice it.

We had no candles, and cared little for them, except for summer use. In Carolina we had the real fat light-wood—not merely pine-knots, but the fat, straight pine. This, from the brilliancy of our parlor of winter evenings, might be supposed to put not only candles, lamps, camphine, Greenough's chemical oil, but even gas itself to the blush. In the West we had not this, but my business was to ramble the woods every evening for seasoned sticks, or the bark of the shelly hickory, for light. 'Tis true that our light was not so good as even candles, but we got along without fretting, for we depended more upon the goodness of our eyes than we did upon the brilliancy of the light.

One of my employments on winter evenings, after we raised flax, was the spinning of rope yarn, from the coarsest swingling tow, to make bed-cords for sale. "Swingling tow" is a corruption of "singling tow," as "swingle-tree" is of "single-tree." The manner of spinning rope yarn was by means of a drum, which turned on a horizontal shaft driven into a hole in one of the cabin logs near the fire. The yarn was hitched to a nail on one side of the circumference next to me. By taking an oblique direction, and keeping up a regular jerking, or pulling of the thread, the drum was kept in constant motion, and thus the twisting and pulling out went on regularly and simultaneously, until the length of the walk was taken up. Then, by winding the yarn first on my forearm, and from that on the drum, I was ready to spin another thread.

The unlearned reader might inquire what we did with the finer kinds of tow. It is well enough to apprise him that next to rope yarn in fineness was filling for trousers and aprons; next finer, warp for the same, and filling for shirts and frocks; next finer, of tow thread, warp for sheets and frocks, unless some of the higher grades of society would use flax thread. Linen shirts, especially seven hundred, was counted the very top of the pot, and he who wore an eight hundred linen shirt was counted a dandy. He was not called a dandy, for the word was unknown, as well as the refined animal which bears that name. Pioneers found it to their advantage to wear tow linen and eat skim milk, and sell their flax, linen, and butter.

Frocks were a short kind of shirt worn over the trousers. We saved our shirts by pulling them off in warm weather, and by wearing nothing in the day-time but our hats, made of straw, our frocks and our trousers. It will be thus perceived that these things took place before the days of suspenders, when everyone's trousers lacked about two inches of reaching up to where the waistcoat reached down. Suspenders soon became a part of the clothing, and were a real improvement in dress.

The girls had forms without bustles, and rosy cheeks without paint. Those who are thin, lean, and colorless, from becoming slaves to idleness or fashion, are, to some extent, excusable for endeavoring to be artificially what the pioneer girls were naturally; who, had they needed lacing, might have used tow strings, and if bran were used for bustles might have curtailed their suppers. Those circumstances which frequently occasioned the bran to be eaten after the flour was gone, laced tight enough without silk cord or bone-sets, and prevented that state of things which sometimes makes it necessary to eat both flour and bran together as a medicine, and requires bran or straw outside to make the shape respectable.

Not only about the farm, but also to meeting, the younger part of the families, and even men went barefoot in summer. The young women carried their shoes and stockings, if they had them, in their hands, until they got in sight of the meeting-house, where, sitting on a log, they shod themselves for meeting, and at the same place, after meeting, they unshod themselves for a walk home, perhaps one or two miles. Whether shoes, stockings, or even bonnets, were to be had or not, meeting must be attended.

Turnips, walnuts, and hickory-nuts supplied the place of fruit till peaches were raised. In five or six years, millions of peaches rotted on the ground. Previous to our raising apples, we sometimes went to Martin's Ferry, on the Ohio, to pick peaches for the owner, who had them distilled. We got a bushel of apples for each day's work in picking peaches. These were kept for particular eating, as if they had contained seeds of gold. Their extreme scarcity made them seem valuable, and stand next to the short biscuit that were so valued in times gone by. Paw-paws were eaten in their season. When we got an abundance of apples, they seemed to lose their flavor and relish.

Pasturage was abundant in summer, being composed mostly of nettles, waist high, which made us fine greens, and thus served for both the cow and her owner, and yet, like everything else on earth, seemed to balance the account by stinging us at every turn. Even the good pasturage of this new country, considered as pasture, had its balancing properties; for the same rich soil from which spring nettles and pasture in such abundance, brought forth also the ramps, or wild garlic, which, springing first, was devoured by the cows. Cows could not be confined, for want of fences, nor dared we neglect milking, lest they might go dry; and so for two or three weeks cows were milked, in pails, and the milk thrown out and given to the hogs. We never milked on the ground, as it seemed a pity, and some said it was bad luck.

Our axe-handles were straight and egg-shaped. Whether the oval form and the crooked bulbous ends of the present day is an improvement or not is immaterial here to inquire; but had we used the present form then, I should at times have been fixed to the axe. The hand that holds this pen had, before it felt the cold of twelve winters, been so benumbed by chopping in the cold as to have the fingers set to the handle, making it necessary to slip them off at the end, which could not have been done were they of the present shape. After the fingers were off, a little rubbing and stretching from the other hand would restore them, but would not dry up the blood nor heal the chaps with which they were covered.

These, and kindred things, are well calculated to make one, by contrast, appreciate the blessings of leisure and ease; until they become too common, when we lose our relish of them, and the gratitude we ought to feel for time even to think.

Note.—Morris West, grandfather of the centenarian, Thomas West, whose reminiscences appear in the foregoing chapter, seems to have settled in the southeastern corner of Archer township, about a mile and a half east of north from Cadiz. His name does not appear on the list of original grantees of land by the United States. Neither does that of his son, William West, the father of Thomas. On July 8, 1809, Bazaleel Wells, the original patentee, deeded a portion of section 31, township 10, range 4, being the southeastern section in Archer township, to Morris West. Some mention of Morris West may also be found in the sketch of the history of Bethel Church.

CHAPTER VI.

EARLY DAYS IN CADIZ.

The land upon which Cadiz was built was granted to Zaccheus Beatty by the United States Government, April 29, 1804, and was by him conveyed to Zaccheus Biggs, October 16, 1805. Biggs was the first receiver of the Land Office at Steubenville, having been appointed July 1, 1800. He was also one of the surveyors in 1805, of Short Creek, Athens, and Moorefield townships; and doubtless in that way became acquainted with the resources and richness of soil of the country now included within the bounds of Harrison county.

A portion of the site of Cadiz is said to have been occupied by one Garret Glazener, for a blacksmith shop, about the year 1800; but this statement rests mainly on tradition, and is open to confirmation. The first horse path, or trail, reaching this point from the East without doubt led to Wellsburg (or Charlestown, as it was first called), and probably entered the present limits of the county at a point nearly east of Beech Spring Church. Another path left the Ohio at Warrentown, and followed Short creek to its head-waters, and from thence to a connection with the Charlestown road. As soon as the land office was opened at Steubenville (1800), and probably before that date, a third route, following the old Indian trails, was opened between the site of Cadiz and the river, later continued on to what is now the town of Cambridge, in Guernsey county, and since then known as the Steubenville and Cambridge road. The opening of this road was no doubt occasioned by the fact that most of the emigrants into the Northwest Territory, wherever they crossed the Ohio, had to proceed to Steubenville to make their filings in the land office before taking up their lands; and many, whose destination was west of the sources of Short creek, would naturally proceed by the shortest route to regain the main traveled road through this latitude, which led west from what is now Wellsburg. The intersection of these two roads was at the site of Cadiz.

In Mr. Archer Butler Hulbert's monograph on "The Indian Thoroughfares of Ohio," published in the January (1900) Quarterly of the Ohio State Archaeological and Historical Society, and since issued in book form, the author defines the route of an early Indian trail which passed through Harrison county, and which he designates by the name of the Mingo Trail. This lead from the Mingo Bottoms (Steubenville), on the Ohio, to Will's Town (now Duncan's Falls, a short distance below Zanesville, in Muskingum county), on the Muskingum. If a straight line be drawn on the map of Ohio, connecting these two points, it will be found to pass through Harrison county a short distance south of Cadiz. Mr. Hulbert states that this Trail passed "across the highlands of Noble, Guernsey, Harrison, and Jefferson counties. This route is identical with that denominated the "Federal Trail" in Dr. Robertson's History of Morgan county, Ohio (p. 126). Undoubtedly, it is practically the route of the present Steubenville and Cambridge road, which was first known as the Steubenville and Zanesville road.

In speaking of Indian trails, Mr. Hulbert says: "It is possible to believe, that in the earliest times, the Indians traveled only on rivers and lakes. When they turned inland, we can be practically sure that they found, ready-made and deeply worn, the very routes of travel which have since born their name. For the beginning of the history of road-making in this central west, we must go back two centuries, when the buffalo, urged by his need of change of climate, newer feeding grounds, and fresh salt-licks, first found his way through the forests. Even if the first thoroughfares were made by the mastodon and the mound-builder, they first came to white man's knowledge as buffalo "traces," and later became Indian trails. . . One who has any conception of the west as it was a century and a half ago, who can see the river valleys filled with the immemorial plunder of the river floods, can realize that there was but one practicable passage-way across the land for either beast or man, and that on the summit of the hills. Here on the hilltops, mounting on the longest ascending ridges, lay the tawny paths of the buffalo and Indians. They were not only highways, they were the highest ways, and chosen for the best reasons: 1. The hilltops offered the driest courses. 2. The hilltops were windswept. 3. The hilltops were coigns of vantage for outlook and signalling. . . .

"An interesting proof of the use made of Indian trails by the white man is found in the blazed trees which line them. There is not an important trail in Ohio which is not blazed, and it is well known that the red men were not in the habit of blazing their trails. . . . Upon the high summits of the long ranges of hills one may to-day see upon the aged tree trunks savage gashes made not less than a century ago, as the writer has ascertained by a study of the blazes made in Washington county on roads laid out by the surveyors of the Ohio Company, 1795-1800."

While there was no wagon road in Harrison county before 1800, it is reasonable to suppose that both the paths above referred to were widened and made passable for vehicles soon after that date; for the emigration that followed the opening of the Steubenville land office poured in like a hugh wave. In fact, large numbers of people had come into the adjoining counties in Pennsylvania and Virginia, months before the opening of the land office, to be on the ground and ready to get in early, and have their pick of the choicest land; just as a few years ago was the case in the Indian Territory, when Oklahoma was opened for settlement. It may be readily understood, therefore, that when the bars were first let down, the settlers came in with a rush; and during the next three or four years many of the best sections in the present townships of Green, Short Creek, Cadiz, and Athens had been pre-empted.

The town of Cadiz was laid out by Zaccheus A. Beatty and Zaccheus Biggs, the plat being acknowledged by Z. A. Beatty, one of the proprietors, before Benjamin Hough, Justice of the Peace, October 29, 1804, and recorded the same day at Steubenville, Jefferson county. The lots were numbered, 1 to 141. The streets were South, Warren, Market, Spring, North, Muskingum, Steubenville (now Main), Ohio, and Wheeling (now Buffalo).

The first deed for a lot was made by Zaccheus Biggs and wife, Eliza Biggs, to John Finney, the consideration being $20. The date of the deed was February 28, 1806; recorded March 4, 1806; Lot No. 4. From that date to the time of the organization of Harrison county (February 1, 1813), the following lots were sold, some of the deeds for the same appearing on the records of Jefferson county only:

John Finney, February 28, 1806, Lot 4; consideration, $20.

Phineas Ash, March, 1806, Lot 88; consideration, $44.

John Perry, March 22, 1806, Lot 22; consideration, $13.

James McMillen, April 9, 1806, Lots 74 and 75; consideration, $36.

John Pritchard, of Fayette county, Pa., April 9, 1806, Lot 87; consideration, $27.

Martin Snyder, Aug. 11, 1806, Lot 86.

Andrew McNeely, Aug. 12, 1806 Lots 112 and 129; consideration, $70.

William Foster, before Dec. 31, 1806, Lot 13.

Sarah Young, Dec. 31, 1806, Lot 13.

John Maholm, October, 1806 (?), Lot 70; consideration, $30.

Jacob Browne, of Brooke county, Va., Oct. 9, 1806, Lots 110 and 111; consideration, $137.

Robert H. Johnson, Oct. 20, 1806, Lots 105 and 106.

Samuel Boyd, Nov. 7, 1806, Lot 91.

John Pugh, of Frederick county, Va., Dec. 8, 1806, Lot 14; consideration, $30.

Joseph Harris, Dec. 31, 1806, Lot 108.

Jacob Arnold, June 17, 1806, Lot 109; consideration $65.75.

Peter Wilson, June 25, 1807, Lot 31.

John L. Baker, Aug. 17, 1807, Lot 130; consideration, $12.

Zaccheus A. Beatty, Oct. 7, 1808, Lot 79.

Rebecca Paul, of Philadelphia, Oct. 17, 1808, Lot 69; consideration, $30.

Rudolph Hines, July 24, 1809, Lot 82.

John Ourant, of New Lisbon, July 24, 1809, Lot 102; consideration, $30.

John McGaughy, before Sept. 22, 1809, Lot 77.

William Orr, before Nov. 14, 1809, Lot 89.

John McCray, June 12, 1810, Lot 55; consideration, $40.

William Grimes, March 26, 1810, Lot 99; consideration, $30.

John Sherrard, Aug. 4, 1811, Lot 130.

James Simpson, Dec. 5, 1810, Lot 100; consideration, $30.

William Sherrard, Aug. 4, 1811, Lot 130; consideration, $14.56.

Isaac Meek, Sept. 14, 1811, Lot 103.

Adam Snyder, Dec. 18, 1811, Lot 144.

Samuel Jackson, Jan. 13, 1812, Lot 145.

Thomas Dickerson, Feb. 28, 1812, Lot 113; consideration, $50.

Robert Stephens, of Fayette county, Pa., Feb. 14, 1812, two acres adjoining the northwest corner of Cadiz; consideration, $46.

William Vaughn, March 7, 1812, Lot 149.
John McClintock, April 16, 1812, Lot 117; consideration, $30.
Easter Tingley, April 15, 1812, Lot 101.
John Pugh, Jr., April 15, 1812, Lot 14.
George McFadden, April 15, 1812, Lot 83.
Charles Chapman, April 15, 1812, Lot 92.

John McFadden, Samuel Carnahan, John Craig, William Hamilton, and John Jamison, "trustees, appointed by the Associate Reformed Congregation of Cadiz," April 15, 1812, Lots 58, 59, and 60 (the site of the old Union church, now occupied as a residence by Mr. A. H. Carnahan); consideration, $20.

Robert Cochran, April 16, 1812, Lot 30.

Nathan Adams, April 17, 1812, certain lands "on the waters of Short creek, in the town of Cadiz, being Lots 122 and 138"; consideration, $75.50.

Robert Kelly, April 18, 1812, Lot 4; consideration, $13.

Job Gatchel, Oct. 7, 1812, Lot 54.

John Baxter, before Oct. 7, 1812, Lot 54.

Henry Pepper, Nov. 25, 1812, Lot 114.

Henry Howe's description of Cadiz in 1807, published in his Historical Collections in 1847-48, is no doubt familiar to most of the readers of this volume; and as it was taken by Mr. Howe from the lips of some of the original settlers, it gives us the most direct account we have of the establishment of the village. While a comparison of this description with the foregoing list of lot-owners, shows that Mr. Howe's informants did not include all the first settlers in their account, the latter is especially valuable as giving us an idea of the business and occupation of many of the early fathers. Howe's description is as follows:

Cadiz, the county seat, is a remarkably well-built and city-like town [this was in 1847], four miles southeasterly from the center of the county, 115 easterly from Columbus, twenty-four westerly from Steubenville, and twenty-four northerly from Wheeling. It contains one Presbyterian, one Methodist Episcopal, one Associate (Seceder), and one Associate Reformed church. It also contains two printing presses, twelve dry-goods, seven grocery, and two drug-stores, and had, in 1840, 1,028 inhabitants.

Cadiz was laid out in 1803, or 1804, by Messrs Biggs and Beatty. Its site was then, like most of the surrounding country, a forest, and its location was induced by the junction there of the road from Pittsburg, by Steubenville, with the road from Washington, Pa., by Wellsburg, Va., from where the two united, passed by Cambridge to Zanesville; and previous to the construction of the national road through Ohio [built in 1825-27], was traveled, more, perhaps, than any other road northwest of the Ohio river. In April, 1807, it contained the following named persons, with their families: Jacob Arnold, inn-keeper; Andrew McNeeley, hatter and justice of the peace; Joseph Harris, merchant; John Jamison, tanner; John McCrea, wheel-wright; Robert Wilkin, brick-maker; Connell Abdill, shoemaker; Jacob Myers, carpenter; John Pritchard, blacksmith; Nathan Adams, tailor; James Simpson, reed-maker; William Tingley, school-teacher; and old Granny [Sarah] Young, midwife and baker, who was subsequently elected (by the citizens of the township in a fit of hilarity) to the office of justice of the peace; but females not being eligible to office in Ohio, the old lady was obliged to forego the pleasure of serving her constituents.

The first celebration of Independence in Cadiz was on the 4th of July, 1806, when the people generally, of the town and country for miles around, attended, and partook of a fine repast of venison, wild turkey, bear meat, and such vegetables as the country afforded; while for a drink, rye whiskey was used. There was much hilarity and good feeling.

Mr. Howe's list contains the names of but thirteen families; but the list of first lot-owners shows the names of at least twenty persons who had purchased lots or were residents of Cadiz before 1808.

It will be not without interest to locate these earliest lot-owners, so that we may be able to form some idea of the appearance of the village in 1807. It is not probable that all of the lots sold up to that time were built upon; and those on which houses stood were doubtless surrounded by forest trees, or the stumps of trees. The houses, of course, were of the rudest description, small log cabins, containing one, two, or three rooms, similar to those of which a few are still to be seen in parts of Harrison county, although by no means so well-made. Some of these log cabins are still standing in Cadiz, without a doubt, covered up and disguised by the more modern weather-boarding, and with additions and extensions built on since the days of the pioneers, but with the same eighteen inch thick walls, of oak or walnut timber, as when their sites were first built upon.

Beginning at what was then the eastern extremity of Market street, at the intersection of the present Buffalo street (then called Wheeling street, and forming the southeastern boundary of the village), and proceeding thence to the northwest, we find the first corner lot on the right was owned by John Finney. The lots, it should be observed, were originally all sixty-six feet wide; the most of them on the main streets have been since subdivided into narrower and more numerous lots. At that time, three lots constituted a quarter of a block (the lots being 198 feet in depth, or three times their width). The lot next to John Finney's was bought by John Pugh. Directly across the street (late the residence of John Rea) and the adjoining ground stood the domicile of Sarah Young, then, as in recent years, the site of a bakery. Adjoining her lot was that of John Perry, which extended to the alley (later occupied by the residence of Tunis Hilligas); across the alley, on the opposite side of the street, Peter Wilson bought; and there were no more houses between his and Ohio street. Crossing Market street again, and proceeding further up the hill, we come to John Maholm's place (now occupied in part by the residence of Wilson Houser). On top of the hill, turning to the right, and into Steubenville (now Main) street, the second lot from the corner (now occupied in part by the post-office building), belonged to Martin Snyder; and next to him, reaching to the alley, was the lot on which stood John Pritchard's story and a half log-house.. Beyond him was Phineas Ash; while Robert H. Johnson owned the two lots directly across Main street from Pritchard and Ash. Half a block down the street from Phineas Ash, on the further corner of Spring and Main streets, was the lot of Samuel Boyd. On the corner now occupied by the Farmers' and Mechanics' National Bank stood the house of Joseph Harris, his lot extending along Market street back to the alley (now occupied by the Bank, Opera House, and the buildings between). Below him, in the middle of the next quarter-block, Andrew McNeely owned the second lot above Muskingum street, the street which then formed the northwestern boundary of the village, being the lot recently occupied by the Smiley family. Directly opposite Andrew McNeely's was John Baker, who bought in 1807. Passing around the front of the Public Square, and down Main street towards Warren, the first house was Jacob Arnold's tavern, which stood on the site of F. J. Wagner's bakery. The remaining two lots in that quarter-block (now occupied by the old Music Hall and the Swan House) belonged to Jacob Brown. The lot since occupied by the United Presbyterian church then belonged to Andrew McNeely, and it is probable that his cabin stood on that spot; although, as stated above, he also owned the lot nearly opposite the Presbyterian church, above the present residence of Dr. S. B. McGavran. The two lots on the opposite side of South Main street, between the Presbyterian parsonage and the Hearn residence, belonged to James McMillan.

This completes the list of lot owners whose deeds bear dates prior to 1808, seventeen in all; but in addition to the names of some of those given above, Henry Howe mentions seven more, as living in Cadiz in 1807. These seven did not obtain titles to lots until a later period; and in most cases there is no way of determining where they lived in the meantime. Perhaps some of them may have been inmates with some of the house-holders, and it is not unnatural to presume, that Mine Host Jacob Arnold, had permanent acommodations for at least a few "regular boarders," until they could better provide for themselves. Again, some then classed as citizens of Cadiz may have had their homes on their farms outside of the village, as it is certain a number of those whose names appear as lot-owners were also extensive land-owners in the county. The nearest that can be done towards locating the remaining seven residents mentioned by Howe, is to give the location of the property first purchased by each one of them, which was as follows: Connel Abdill, in 1832, bought the lot on Market street now occupied in part by the K. W. Kinsey homestead. John Jamison lived on his farm near Cadiz. John McCrea, in 1810, bought the lot at the corner of Market and Ohio streets, since occupied in part by James Bullock's residence. Jacob Myers appears to have been a tenant. James Simpson, in 1810, bought the lot across the alley from and southwest of the home of Frederick J. Wagner; and the lot next to James Simpson's was purchased in 1812 by Easter Tingley, William Tingley not acquiring any titles until 1825. Robert Wilkin, brick-maker, may have lived out of town, or bought his lot at second-hand.

A complete list of the original owners of each lot in Cadiz, and additions thereto, is given herewith:

Connel Abdil, before May 18, 1832, Lot 39, (see Thomas Lee).

Nathan Adams, Nov. 14, 1809, Lot 89, (deeded by William Orr); July 24, 1811, Lot 107; before March 20, 1815, Lot 93, (see Jacob Snediker); April 7, 1812, Lots 122 and 138, "on the waters of Short creek, in the town of Cadiz;" March 25, 1813, Lots 148 and 150, (deeded by Jacob Arnold; before Feb. 4, 1815, Lot 171, (see Benjamin Bennett); before Aug. 20, 1816, Lot 174, (see Jacob Holmes); before Dec. 18, 1818, Lots 172 and 173, (see Hines Mechan and David McGyre); before Sep. 12, 1831, Lots 175 and 176, (see James Knox); before Dec. 20, 1837, Lots 169 and 170, (see Daniel Morris).

Isaac Allen, before Aug. 7, 1829, Lots 187, 188, 190, (see Reuben Allen).

James Allen, Aug. 3, 1836, Lot 195, (deeded by Philip Trine).

Reuben Allen, Aug. 7, 1829, Lots 187, 188, 190, (deeded by Isaac Allen).

Jacob Arnold, July 17, 1806, Lot 109; before Dec. 18, 1811, Lot 144, (see Adam Snider); before Jan. 13, 1812, Lot 145, (see Samuel Jackson); before March 7, 1812, Lot 149, (see William Vaughn); before May 13, 1812, Lots 142 and 143, (see John Braden); March 6, 1813, Lot 21, (deeded by Francis Mitchell); before March 25, 1813, Lots 148 and 150, (see Nathan Adams).

James Arnold, before March 24, 1819, Lots 191 and 192, (see Thomas Bradford and John McIntire); before March 29, 1819, Lot 193, (see James McElroy); before June 12, 1819, Lots 186 and 189, (see Robert Clark and Zebedee Cox).

Rezin Arnold, March 13, 1818, Lot 178, (deeded by Andrew McNeely).

Phineas Ash, March —, 1806, Lot 88.

John L. Baker, Aug. 17, 1807, Lot 130.

John Baxter, before Oct. 7, 1812, Lot 54, (see John Gatchel).

Zaccheus A. Beatty, Oct. 7, 1808, Lot 79; Oct. 22, 1814, Lots 90 and 116; Oct. 24, 1814, Lot 63.

Walter B. Beebe, May 24, 1813, Lots 145, 155, and 156; Dec. 6, 1819, Lots 159, 162, and 163.

Benjamin Bennett, Feb. 4, 1815, Lot 171, (deeded by Nathan Adams).

George Bohrer, before March 25, 1814, Lot 40, (see John Stoakes).

Samuel Boyd, Nov. 7, 1806, Lot 91.

John Braden, May 13, 1812, Lots 142 and 143, (deeded by Jacob Arnold).

David Bradford, June 27, 1814, Lot 158.

Thomas Bradford, March 24, 1819, Lot 191, (deeded by James Arnold).

Jacob Brown, of Brooke county, Va., April 9, 1806, Lot 111; July 19, 1806, Lot 110.

Joseph Burnell, March 29, 1825, Lot 81, (deeded by William Henderson).

John Burns, May 27, 1815, Lot 160.

Kins Cahill, before May 24, 1814, Lot 147, (see John Sullers).

Samuel Carnahan, April 16, 1812, (see John McFadden).

Charles Chapman, April 15, 1812, Lot 92; March 24, 1815, Lot 104, (deeded by John Forney).

Robert Clark, June 12, 1819, Lot 189, (deeded by James Arnold).
Robert Cochran, April 16, 1812, Lot 30.
Zebedee Cox, June 12, 1819, Lot 186, (deeded by James Arnold).
John Craig, April 16, 1812, (see John McFadden).
James Crossan, April 2, 1850, Lot 197, (deeded by William Knox).
Robert Croskey, June 18, 1814, Lot 84, (deeded by Thomas Stoakes).
Thomas Dickerson, Feb. 28, 1812, Lot 113.

John Finney, Feb 12, 1806, Lot 4, (the first lot sold in Cadiz; deeded again by Zaccheus Biggs to Robert Kelly, April 18, 1812).

John Forney, before March 24, 1815, Lot 104, (see Charles Chapman).

William Foster, before Dec. 31, 1806, Lot 13, (see Sarah Young).
Job Gatchel, Oct. 7, 1812, Lot 54, (deeded by John Baxter).

William Gilmore, before Feb. 29, 1848, Lot 153, (see James Matthews).

William Grimes, March 26, 1810, Lot 99; Sept. 14, 1811, Lot 131; April 1, 1815, Lot 120, (deeded by Thomas Henderson).

William Hamilton, April 16, 1812, (see John McFadden).
A. F. Hanna, before July 1, 1837, Lot 199, (see School Directors).
John Hanna, April 21, 1814, Lots 161 and 164.
Joseph Harris, Dec. 31, 1806, Lot 108.

Thomas Henderson, before April 1, 1815, Lot 120, (see William Grimes).

William Henderson, before March 29, 1825, Lot 81, (see Joseph Burnell).

Rudolph Hines, July 24, 1809, Lot 82.
Eleazer Huff, Feb. 15, 1814, Lots 45 and 115.
William Huff, Oct. 8, 1814, Lot 46.
Jacob Holmes, Aug. 20, 1816, Lot 174, (deeded by Nathan Adams).
John Hover, Sr., before June 22, 1816, Lot 165, (see John Hover, Jr.).

John Hover, Jr., June 22, 1816, Lot 165, (deeded by John Hover, Sr.).

Samuel Jackson, Jan. 13, 1812, Lot 145, (deeded by Jacob Arnold).
John Jamison, April 16, 1812, (see John McFadden).
Robert H. Johnson, Oct. 20, 1806, Lots 105 and 106.
Robert Johnson, May 5, 1814, Lot 112, (deeded by Andrew McNeely).
Robert Kelly, April 16, 1812, Lot 4, (see John Finney); May 14, 1814, Lot 70, (decded by Samuel Williams).

James Knox, Sept. 12, 1831, Lots 175 and 176, (deeded by Nathan Adams).

William Knox, before Aug. 6, 1833, Lot 194, (see George White); before June 23, 1837, Lot 196, (see Samuel McCormick); before Jan. 13, 1838, Lot 198, (see Robert McCullough); before April 2, 1850, Lot 197, (see James Crossan).

Thomas Lee, May 18, 1832, Lot 39, (deeded by Connel Abdil).

John McClintock, April 16, 1812, Lot 117.

Samuel McCormick, June 23, 1837, Lot 196, (deeded by William Knox).

John McCray, March 12, 1810, Lot 55.

Robert McCullough, Jan. 13, 1838, Lot 198, (deeded by William Knox).

James McElroy, March 29, 1819, Lot 193, (deeded by James Arnold).

George McFadden, April 15, 1812, Lot 83.

John McFadden, Samuel Carnahan, John Craig, William Hamilton, and John Jamison, "trustees appointed by the Associate Reformed Congregation of Cadiz," April 16, 1812, Lots 58, 59, 60.

James McC. Galbraith, May 2, 1815, Lot 181, (deeded by Andrew McNeely.

John McGaughy, Sept. 22, 1809, Lot 77; before Feb. 21, 1814, Lot 76, (see John Marshall).

David McGyre, Dec. 28, 1818, Lot 173, (deeded by Nathan Adams).

John McIntire, March 24, 1819, Lot 192, (deeded by James Arnold).

Andrew McKee, June 30, 1819, Lot 185, (deeded by Andrew McNeely).

James McMillan, April 9, 1806, Lots 74 and 75.

Alexander McNary, May 24, 1814, Lot 157.

Andrew McNeely, Aug. 12, 1806, Lot 129; before May 5, 1814, Lot 112, (see Robert Johnson); before May 2, 1815, Lots 181 and 182, (see James McC. Galbraith and Stephen Perry); before Sept. 11, 1816, Lot 184, (see James Moore); before March 13, 1818, Lot 178, (see Rezin Arnold); before Sept. 5, 1818, Lot 177, (see William R. Slemmons).

John Maholm, Aug.-Oct., 1806, Lot 70, (see Robert Kelly and Samuel Williams; also, Pritchard, Maholm, and Harris).

John Marshall, Feb. 21, 1814, Lot 76, (deeded by John McGaughy).

James Matthews, Feb. 29, 1848, Lot 153, (deeded by William Gilmore).

Hines Mechan, Dec. 28, 1818, Lot 172, (deeded by Nathan Adams).

Isaac Meek, Sept. 14, 1811, Lot 103.

Isaac Miller, June 1, 1813, Lots 166 and 167.

Francis Mitchell, before March 6, 1813, Lot 21, (see Jacob Arnold).

James Moore, Sept. 11, 1816, Lot 184, (deeded by Andrew McNeely).

Daniel Morris, Dec. 20, 1837, Lots 169 and 170, (deeded by Nathan Adams).

William Orr, before Nov 14, 1809, Lot 89, (see Nathan Adams).

Isaac Osburn, Sept. 17, 1814, Lot 53, (deeded by Eward Wood).

Samuel Osburn, June 5, 1813, Lot 146, (deeded by Jesse Sparks).

John Ourant, July 24, 1809, Lot 102.

Leonard Parrish, before Jan. 23, 1826, Lot 168, (see Mordecai Parrish).

Mordecai Parrish, Jan. 23, 1826, Lot 168, (deeded by Leonard Parrish.

Rebecca Paul, of Philadelphia, Oct. 17, 1808, Lot 69.

Henry Pepper, Nov. 25, 1812, Lot 114; July 4, 1815, Lots 32, 38, 47.

John Perry (or Parry), March 22, 1806, Lot 22.

Stephen Perry May 2, 1815, Lot 182, (deeded by Andrew McNeely).

John Pritchard, of Fayette county, Pa., April 9, 1806, Lot 87; Oct. 17, 1808, Lot 85; Dec. 5, 1810, 5.74 acres adjoining the plat of Cadiz, and the land of Abraham Forney; July 13, 1815, Lots 65 and 68.

John Pritchard, John Maholm, and Joseph Harris, April 16, 1812, Lots 1, 2, 3, 6, 7, 8, 9, 10, 11, 12, 16, 17, 18, 19, 20, 21, 22, 23, 24, 25, 26, 27, 28, 29, 34, 35, 36, 41, 42, 43, 44, 49, 50, 51, 56, 57, 60, 61, 62, 66, 67, 71, 72, 73, 94, 95, 96, 97, 98, 118, 119, 121, 123, 124, 125, 126, 127, 128, 132, 133, 134, 135, 136, 139, 140, 141.

John Pugh, of Frederick county, Va., Dec. 8, 1806, Lot 14; April 14, 1808, Lots 64 and 74; Nov. 24, 1809, Lot 75 and 78.

John Rankin and Samuel Rankin, June 5, 1813, Lots 33, 37, 48, 52, (deeded by Daniel Workman).

School Directors, June 1, 1837, Lot 199, (deeded by A. F. Hanna).

John Sherrard, Aug. 4, 1811, Lot 130, (originally deeded to John L. Baker).

William Sherrard, April 4, 1811, Lot 137.

Short Creek School House, April 15, 1812, Lot 15.

James Simpson, Dec. 5, 1810, Lot 100.

Sarah Simpson, April 22, 1816, Lots 151 and 152.

William R. Slemmons, Sept. 5, 1818, Lot 177, (deeded by Andrew McNeely).

EARLY DAYS IN CADIZ

Jacob Snediker, March 20, 1815, Lot 93.
Adam Snider, Dec. 18, 1811, Lot 144, (deeded by Jacob Arnold).
Martin Snyder, Aug. 11, 1806, Lot 86.
Jesse Sparks, before June 5, 1836, Lot 146, (see Samuel Osburn).
Robert Stephens, of Fayette county, Pa., Feb. 4, 1812, two acres adjoining the northwest corner of Cadiz.
John Stoakes, March 25, 1814, Lot 34, (deeded by George Bohrer).
Thomas Stoakes, before June 18, 1814, Lot 84, (see Robert Croskey).
Henry Stubbins, Oct. 20, 1827, Lot 179, (deeded by Andrew McNeely).
John Sullers, May 24, 1814, Lot 147, (deeded by Kins Cahill).
Abraham Timmons, May 18, 1822, Lot 5.
Benjamin Timmons, May 10, 1849, Lot 180, (deeded by William Timmons).
William Timmons, before May 10, 1849, Lot 180, (see Benjamin Timmons).
Easter Tingley, April 15, 1812, Lot 101.
Philip Trine, before Aug. 3, 1836, Lot 195, (see James Allen).
William Vaughn, March 7, 1812, Lot 149, (deeded by Jacob Arnold).
John Ward, Aug. 15, 1815, Lot 80, (deeded by Daniel Workman).
George White, Aug. 6, 1833, Lot 194, (deeded by William Knox).
Samuel Williams, before May 14, 1814, Lot 70, (see Robert Kelly and John Maholm).
Peter Wilson, June 25, 1807, Lot 31.
Edward Wood, before Sept. 17, 1814, Lot 53, (see Isaac Osburn).
Daniel Workman, before June 5, 1813, Lots 33, 37, 48, 52, (see John and Samuel Rankin); before Aug. 15, Lot 80, (see John Ward).
Sarah Young, Dec. 31, 1806, Lot 13, (deeded by William Foster).

In the foregoing list it will be observed that on April 16, 1812, all the lots remaining unsold in the original plat were conveyed to Pritchard, Maholm, and Harris. Joseph Harris transferred his interest in these lots to John Pritchard and John Maholm, who later conveyed them as follows:

John Burn·, Lot 97, May 27, 1815.
James McC. Galbraith, Lots 66 and 67, Sept. 3, 1817.
William Grimes, Lot 136, May 24, 1814.
John Hanna, Lots 125, 126, and 141, June 29, 1814.
Conrad Hilligas, Lots 28, 42, and 43, June 18, 1814.
Phineas Inskeep, Lots 1, 2, 16, 17, 18, 19, June 10, 1814.

William Jamison, Lots 118, 133, and 134, July 25, 1814.
Robert Kelley, Lots 8, 10, 25, 26, 27, May 14, 1814.
Jacob Kidwiler, Lot 50, April 4, 1817.
Samuel McFadden, Lot 73, June 18, 1819.
Andrew McNeely, Lots 119, 132, and 135, May 27, 1814.
James Means, Lot 121, Aug. 17, 1816; Lots 94, 95, and 96, Aug. 29, 1818.
Trustees Methodist Episcopal Church, Lot 3, April 20, 1816.
John Pugh, Lots 57 and 61, Jan. 20, 1815.
Zachariah Pumphrey, Lot 12, June 10, 1814; Lots 56 and 62, before Aug. 31, 1816, (see Michael Swagler); Lot 71, Jan. 6, 1817; Lot 6, March 7, 1817; Lot 23, before March 27, 1817, (see Joseph White).
John and Samuel Rankin, Lots 34, 35, 36, June 14, 1814.
John Rea, Lots 29, 41, and 44; May 3, 1817.
Philip Riley, Lot 98, April 22, 1816.
Thomas Shaw, Lot 72, July 25, 1814.
Sarah Simpson, Lots 128 and 139, April 22, 1816.
John Speer, Lot 51, Jan. 28, 1824.
Michael Swagler, Lots 56 and 62, Aug. 31, 1816, (deeded by Zachariah Pumphrey).
John Timmons, Lot 20, Jan. 31, 1824.
Moses Urquehart, Lot 49, Jan. 27, 1824.
William Waddle, Lots 124, 127, and 140, Feb. 23, 1814.
Joseph White, Lot 23, March 27, 1817, (deeded by Zachariah Pumphrey).

The total number of lots in the original plat of Cadiz, as laid out by Biggs and Beatty in 1804, was 141. The first addition to the village was platted about 1812 by Jacob Arnold, who kept tavern in a log-cabin standing on the lot now occupied by Mr. F. J. Wagner. Arnold's addition consisted of nine lots, numbered from 142 to 150. These are the lots on the southwest side of Market street ("Gimlet Hill"), lying between Buffalo street and the alley opposite the old home of the Boggs family. The deed for the first one of these lots sold bore date May 13, 1812. A second addition was platted by Messrs. Pritchard and Maholm on May 24, 1813, containing seventeen lots, numbered from 151 to 167, forming the irregular block lying between Market, Buffalo, and Spring streets, and the Cemetery avenue. A fourth addition was platted by Nathan Adams, containing nine lots, numbered from 168 to 176, from which the first lot was sold Feb. 4, 1815. These lots lie along the southwest side of Bingham avenue. Another addition, also containing nine lots, was platted by Andrew McNeely May 1, 1815, the lots numbering from 177 to 185. These lie along the northeast side of Spring street, southeast of Buffalo. Another addition, comprising lots 186 to 193, laid out by James Arnold March, 15, 1815, extend along the southwest side of South street, between Main and Ohio, now occupied in part by the residence of Mr. Garret Shank. Lots 194 to 198 were platted by William Knox May 25, 1836, and extend from Muskingum street down the northeast side of Market, to the beginning of Lincoln avenue. Lot 199 was platted by Andrew P. Hanna June 1, 1837, when he deeded it to the school directors. It is now partly occupied by the residence of Melford J. Brown, Jr.*

Besides the above, Messrs. Pritchard and Maholm platted a second addition to Cadiz, which was filed May 24, 1813, consisting of a dozen lots, which were sold to the following purchasers:

John Braden, Lot 13, May 8, 1818.
Rowland Craig, Lot 12, July 4, 1816.
John Hanna, Lot 5, Dec. 2, 1818.
Thomas Hogg, Lot 11, May 8, 1846.
John Maholm, Lots 7, 8, and 9, June 29, 1824.
James Means, Lots 1, 2, 3, and 4, before June 2, 1825, (see William Tingley).
Matthew Simpson, Lot 6, April 22, 1816.
William Tingley, Lots 1, 2, 3, and 4, June 2, 1825, (deeded by James Means).

Another addition to Cadiz, containing eight lots, was platted by Jacob Arnold, and the plat filed March 30, 1816, which was some two years after all the lots had been sold. The purchasers of these lots were as follows:

Nathan Adams, Lot 7, March 25, 1813.
Daniel Arnold, Lot 8, May 15, 1812.
Benjamin Bennett, Lot 5, Sept. 18, 1813.
James Boyd, Lots 2 and 3, Nov. 26, 1812.
John Braden, Lot 1, Jan. 1, 1813.
Phineas Inskeep, Lot 6, Nov. 28, 1812.
William Vaughn, Lot 4, March 7, 1812.

In Brown's "Western Gazetteer, or Emigrant's Directory, published by Samuel R. Brown, at Auburn, N. Y., in 1817, may be found a brief description of the counties and towns of Ohio. Mr. Brown states that "Harrison county is settled chiefly by emigrants from Pennsylvania.

Cadiz, a small village of twenty houses, is situated on a hill, twenty-six miles west of Steubenville, on the Zanesville road. This county has four or five other villages, mostly new and small."

The following extracts from the diary of Dr. Richard Lee Mason will not be without interest in connection with the history of Harrison county before 1820. In the fall of 1819, he emigrated from Maryland to Illinois. His diary is now in possession of his daughter, who resides in Jacksonville, Ill.; and it was printed by the Chicago Record in the daily issues of that paper during the early part of January, 1897. Dr. Mason, with his friend, Dr Hall, left Philadelphia for the West on Monday, October 4, 1819. They reached Pittsburg on October 12th. From there, the journal proceeds:

Oct. 15. Left Pittsburgh at seven o'clock. Traveled over a poor and hilly country for thirty-six miles. Passed a few travelers bound to Ohio. . . . Crossed the Ohio river after night at Steubenville. Stopped at Jenkinson's, an intelligent, gentlemanly, hospitable man. Visited the market. Beef, good, six and a quarter cents a pound.

Oct. 16. . . . . Rainy day, fatigued by broken country, determined to spend this day in Steubenville, a busy little village on the bank of the Ohio. Purchased a plain Jersey wagon and harness for $60.

Oct. 18. Myself and friend proceeded on our journey. We arat Siers' [Sears'], a distance of thirty miles, at dusk, much relieved by the change from our horses to the wagon. The roads were muddy, the weather drizzly, and the country hilly. Buildings indifferent. The land was fertile and black. Trees uncommonly tall. Passed the little village of Cadiz. In this country, a store, a smith shop, and two or three cabins make a town. Passed ten or fifteen travelers. Great contrast between the quality of the land from Chambersburg to Pittsburg, and that which we have already traveled over from Steubenville, in Ohio.

Oct. 19. Left Siers' at six o'clock a. m. The morning fair and cold. Roads extremely rough. Country fertile, but hilly. Log cabins, ugly women, and tall timber. Passed a little flourishing village called Freeport, settled by foreigners, Yankee Quakers, and mechanics. Remarkable, with two taverns in the village, there was nothing fit to drink, not even good water. The corn-fields in the woods, among dead trees, and the corn very fine. We arrived at Adair's, a distance of twenty-seven miles, at six o'clock p. m. Passed some peddlers and a few travelers. Value of land from Steubenville to Adair's, $2 to $30 per acre. Lots in Freeport, eighteen months old, from $30 to $100. . . . .

Oct. 20. Left Adair's at six o'clock, a. m. The country extremely hilly, and not quite so fertile. Independent people, in log cabins. They make their own clothes, sugar, and salt; and paint their own signs. They picture a lion like a dove, a cat like a terrapin, and General Washington like a bird's nest. Salt wells and sugar orchards are common in this country. Steep hills, frightful precipices, little or no water, and even a scarcity of new whiskey. Ragged and ignorant children, and but little appearance of industry. Met a number of travelers, inclining to the East, and overtook a larger number than usual, bound to the Land of Promise. The evening being rainy, the roads soon became muddy. We arrived at Silver's Travelers' Rest, at six o'clock. Distance, twenty-nine miles. Passed a little village called Cambridge.

If good Dr. Mason could return to Harrison county now, and ride again over the road between Steubenville and Cambridge, doubtless he would find the trees not so tall, and certainly the women not ugly; but it is to be feared that the happy days of old will never return again to Harrison county, when it can be said of it that water there is scarcer than new whiskey.

CHAPTER VII.

BEECH SPRING CHURCH.

While it becomes necessary, in outlining the history of the early settlement of Harrison county, to make frequent and extended references to the organizations of the Presbyterian and United Presbyterian churches in the county, it should be understood that such reference is made solely for the purpose of enabling us to gain what light we may from such occasional facts as are preserved upon their records; and, while these records are sadly lacking in detail and continuity, and at best give us but occasional glimpses of the real life and growth of the communities with which they are concerned, they are practically all we now have left in the way of contemporary data; and constitute the chief source of information in regard to Harrison county during the time its territory was still a part of Jefferson.

The most valuable and least appreciated of these early records are the old tomb-stones in the church graveyards. Taken together, they afford a more nearly complete roll of the early membership of the church and the settlement than we can now obtain from any other source. Much valuable information is also furnished by the sessional records of the churches, where such have been kept, and the books preserved. It is much to be regretted that the session book of the Presbyterian church at Cadiz, which had been in use for, perhaps, more than half a century, was lost or mislaid a few years ago, and has never been recovered.

The writer is fortunate in being able to present to the reader of these sketches a brief account of the beginnings of the early churches in Harrison county, written by the man who founded them, thus being in the nature of a contemporary document. This consists of an outline sketch of the history of the congregations of Rev. John Rea, the pioneer preacher of Harrison county; and it was written as a part of his farewell sermon delivered to the Beech Spring congregation in January, 1851.

Before presenting Mr. Rea's sketch, let us survey his field of labor, and the conditions under which he entered it.

The first Presbytery organized west of the Allegheny mountains was that of Redstone, erected by the Synod of New York and Philadelphia in May, 1781. Its territory embraced the present counties of Westmoreland, Fayette, Armstrong, Indiana, Allegheny, Beaver, Washington, and Greene, in Pennsylvania, and adjacent tertory, including the Panhandle of western Virginia. Its membership at the time of organization consisted of but four ministers, viz., Revs. James Power, John McMillan, Thaddeus Dodd, and Joseph Smith. Within the next three years Revs. James Dunlap, John Clark, and James Finley were added to the Presbytery; and this organization continued to provide for the spiritual needs of the greater portion of the population west of the mountains until 1793. In that year, the Presbytery of Redstone was divided, and that of the Ohio formed,—those ministers whose charges were nearest the river being detached from the parent body, and erected into the new Presbytery. They were John McMillan, John Clark, Joseph Patterson, James Hughes, and John Brice.

The bounds of the Ohio Presbytery first extended to the Scioto, or beyond; and nearly all of these original members of the Presbytery made missionary tours into Jefferson county before any churches were organized in what is now the county of Harrison. The first regularly installed minister to preach to congregations, composed, at least, in part, of Harrison county people, was Rev. Joseph Anderson, who was also the first minister installed by the Ohio Presbytery in what is now the State of Ohio. He was licensed by the Presbytery on October 17, 1798, and engaged at once in missionary work in the Western Territory, where he succeeded in gathering congregations at several points. On August 20, 1800, he was installed as pastor of the three churches of Richland (now St. Clairsville, Short Creek (now Mount Pleasant), and Cross Roads (now Crabapple). If this congregation of Crabapple was the same as that now known by the name, and it probably was, then the latter must claim priority in organization over that of Beech Spring; although the year of its erection is usually given as 1804. From the fact that Mr. Anderson gave up the charge of Crabapple in 1802, however, it is possible that the people there were not sufficiently strong numerically to sustain a minister, even for one-third of his time, and that its permanent organization was accordingly deferred until after Mr. Rea was settled at Beech Spring. Robert McCullough represented Crabapple Church, as an elder, at a meeting of the Presbytery in 1801.

Mr. Anderson was ordained by Rev. John McMillan, at Crabapple, but his principal congregation was that now known as Mount Pleasant; and there can be no reasonable doubt that many of the then residents of Short Creek township who were inclined to be church-going people were members of the congregation, and some of them communicants, of the church of Mount Pleasant. The first ruling elders of that church were Richard McKibben, Thomas McCune, James Clark, and James Eagleson.

It was not until the years 1802 and 1803 that the settlers began to come in large numbers to that part of the county now comprising the townships of Short Creek, Green, Cadiz, and Athens. A year later (1804), John Rea was licensed by the Presbytery of Ohio, and entered this field as a supply for the people of Beech Spring and Crabapple.

Rev. John Rea was born in Tully, Ireland, in 1772, the son of Joseph and Isabel Rea. About the year 1790 he emigrated to America, and first resided in Philadelphia for a short time. He left there, on foot, and started for the west, traveling usually without company; and, after crossing the mountains, located in Washington county, where, in 1793, he married Elizabeth Christy. He made his home for a time in the house of James Dinsmore, then a ruling elder of Upper Buffalo church, by whom he was encouraged and assisted in his attempts to gain an education. A few years later, he entered Jefferson College, and was graduated in 1802, being one of the members of the first class graduated at that institution. On August 22, 1805, having been duly called by the congregations which he had served as supply, Mr. Rea was ordained and installed as pastor of Beech Spring and Crabapple. In April, 1810, he was released from Crabapple, and thenceforth gave all his time to Beech Spring, where he continued in active charge until 1848, although not finally severing his connection with that church until some three years later. He died February 12, 1855.

The work of Dr. Rea has been summed up in a few words by Rev. W. F. Hamilton, in his History of the Presbytery of Washington, who says:

Dr. Rea was in an eminent sense a pioneer minister. His early labors were largely evangelistic. Several churches now exist on the territory once wholly occupied by him. It may safely be said that no man exerted a greater influence than did he in forming the religious character of the early inhabitants of a large section of Eastern Ohio.

In the words of Dr. Crawford, "the early history, not only of this vicinity [Nottingham], but of the Presbyterian Church in Eastern Ohio, is closely connected with the biography of Dr. Rea. In the early part of his public work he was remote from his clerical brethren. In the whole region that now embraces the territory of four Presbyteries, in the eastern part of this state, there were but six Presbyterian ministers, where there are now [1888] over one hundred; and not more than twelve or fifteen churches, where there are now one hundred and eighty-five. Such a man as Dr. Rea was destined to make and leave an impression behind him—an impression not easily erased from the minds of those multitudes acquainted with his early self-denial and successful labors."

He is quoted by Dr. Crawford as saying near the close of his life: "My early toils and dreary travels were on horseback, through the bounds of your present charge, as also through a large district of country, mostly traversing paths through an unbroken wilderness; and wherever an early settler was found, and, more especially, wherever and whenever I heard of one in our communion, him I visited, by day and by night, at all seasons of the year."

An examination of the records of the Presbytery of the Ohio, now in possession of Dr. W. J. Holland, of the Carnegie Museum at Pittsburgh, shows an application for supplies for the people of Indian Short Creek to have been made on October 19th, 1802, the Presbytery then being in session at West Liberty. On Wednesday, October 20th, Mr. James Hughes was appointed to supply "at Daniel Welsh's on Short Creek, the third Sabbath of December, and Mr. [George M.] Scott on the first Sabbath of April." The Presbytery met at Washington, Pa., again in January, 1803, and on Wednesday, the 19th, Jacob Lindley was appointed to supply at "Welch's, on Indian Short Creek, on the second Sabbath of March." In June, 1803, Presbytery met at Ten Mile, and on Wednesday, the 29th, applications for supplies were received from the "heads of Indian Wheelin [Crabapple] and Short Creek." Rev. Joseph Anderson was appointed to preach at head of Indian Wheeling creek on the first Sabbath in August; and Rev. James Snodgrass, at Welch's, on the second Sabbath of July. At Montour's, on Wednesday, Oct. 19, 1803, the Presbytery received an application for supplies from "Welsh's on Indian Short Creek," and Mr. Hughes was appointed for the first Sabbath in

April, 1804. At Ten Mile, on Wednesday, Dec. 14, 1803, Mr. Nicholas Pittinger was appointed to supply at "Crabapple on the third Sabbath of January, and at Beech Spring on the fourth Sabbath of January." This is the first time these two congregations appear on the records of Presbytery under the names by which they have since been known. On Tuesday, April 17th, 1804, Presbytery having met at Cross Roads (in Washington county, Pa.), applications for supplies were again received from Crabapple and Beech Spring; and on the 19th, Rev. Samuel Ralston was directed to preach at Crabapple one Sabbath at discretion, and Rev. Joseph Anderson at Beech Spring on the third Sabbath of May, and at Crabapple one Sabbath at discretion.

At the meeting of Presbytery held at Cross Creek, Washington county, Pa., on Wednesday, June 27th, 1804, John Rea, as the name appears on the records, was licensed to preach. On the following day, Mr. Rea was appointed to preach at Beech Spring on the first Sabbath in August, at Crabapple on the second Sabbath in August, at "Stillwater" (this may have been Nottingham or Cadiz), on the fourth Sabbath of September, and at Crabapple again on the fifth Sabbath of September. On the same day, Rev. William McMillan (afterwards president of Franklin College), was appointed to supply at Beech Spring on the third Sabbath of September. At the meeting of Presbytery at Raccoon, on October 16, 1804, applications for further supplies were received from Beech Spring and Crabapple. On Thursday, the 18th, Rev. Joseph Patterson and Rev. Elisha Macurdy were appointed to preach at Beech Spring on the second Sabbath of November, and to administer the Lord's Supper. Mr. Anderson was also appointed to preach there on the fourth Sabbath of November, and at Crabapple, on the first Sabbath of the following April. Mr. John Brice was appointed to preach at Crabapple on the third Sabbath of November. "Mr. Rea, being appointed by Synod to itinerate as a missionary, no appointments are to be made him prior to next meeting of Presbytery." The next meeting was held at Cross Creek on Christmas Day, 1804, and Mr. Rea was appointed to supply at Beech Spring on the first and third Sabbaths of February, and at Crabapple on the second and fourth Sabbaths of the same month.

Presbytery met at West Liberty again in April, 1805, and on the 16th instant, "a call was presented for Mr. Rea from the united congregations of Crabapple and Beech Spring, which being read, was put into his hands for consideration." Mr. Rea having signified his acceptance of the call, the Presbytery, on Thursday, April 18th, "agreed to proceed to the ordination of Mr. Rea in August next, provided the way be clear, and appointed him to prepare and deliver a sermon on Isaiah, lv., 7, as part of trial. Mr. Brice was appointed to preach the ordination sermon, and Mr. Macurdy to preside and give the charge." The Presbytery met at Crabapple on Tuesday, August 20th, 1805, and on the 22d of the same month, "the Presbytery proceeded to the ordination of Mr. Rea, and did with fasting and prayer, and the laying on of the hands of the Presbytery, solemnly ordain him to the holy office of the Gospel ministry, and installed him as pastor of the united congregations of Crabapple and Beech Spring. Mr. Brice preached on the occasion, and Mr. Macurdy presided and gave the charge."

The size of Mr. Rea's congregation at the time of his installation, and for some years thereafter, may be very closely approximated from the reports preserved in the records of Ohio Presbytery. On April 16th, 1806, less than eight months after the beginning of his pastorate, the Presbytery, having met at Upper Buffalo, "called on each member to report the number of existing communicants in the congregation, and the number of persons baptized." Mr. Rea reported that Beech Spring and Crabapple had 131 communicants, and that ten infants had been baptized by him since the beginning of his ministry. The next report, under date of Dec. 20th, 1808, shows but 109 members in communion, fifteen having been added during the past year, and thirty-five infants baptized. On January 9th, 1810, the total communicants were 191, fourteen having been added during the past year, and twenty-five infants baptized. At this meeting of Presbytery, Mr. Rea reported that the congregation of Crabapple was in debt to him in the sum of sixty dollars, which became due on the 16th instant. On October 17th, of the same year, the report shows 146 communicants, fifteen having been added since last report, and eighteen infants baptized. On April 21st, 1812, there were 119 communicants, twenty-seven having been added during the year, and one adult and twenty-nine infants baptized. April 19th, 1814, the number of communicants was 185, twenty-five having been added, and four adults and thirty-two infants baptized. April 18th, 1815, there were 201 members, sixteen having been added, and twenty-three infants baptized. On April 16th, 1816, the total number of members was 222, of whom thirty-three had been added during the year, and fifty-five infants baptized. April 15th, 1817, the report showed a total communion of 239, thirty-three having been added during the year, and three adults and thirty-three infants having been baptized.

7

The following is a part of the farewell sermon delivered by Rev. John Rea, at Beech Spring Church, in January, 1851:

I have come here to-day, in somewhat feeble health, to discharge what I deem a solemn duty; to take my leave of, and bid a final adieu to a church that has been under our care, and where we have lived and labored for nearly half a century—a church where we have lived to see one generation pass all away, and another rise in its room.

That justice, in some measure, may be done thereto, reference must be had to her early history, and to some of the changes that have shaped her destiny thus far.

To prevent being tedious, we shall do little more than outline it.

This church was organized some time in the fall of the year 1803, by two Rev. Fathers, Patterson and Macurdy, who are now no more. Three persons were chosen, and set apart at the time as ruling elders, and a communion followed. This appears to have been the beginning, the morning of the existence of what has since been called Beech Spring, a name said to have been given to it by Mr. [Daniel] Welch, and took its rise from a group of beech trees that enclosed a large spring of water on a lot of five acres he had generously donated for the use of the church, on the west corner of his section.

The year following another young man and myself, of the first class of students that graduated at Jefferson College, having finished a course of Theological studies under the direction of Rev. Dr. McMillan, were licensed to preach the Gospel by the Presbytery of Ohio, June, 1804. After a tour of three months through the interior of this State, and another up the Allegheny towards the Lakes, the winter following I supplied here, and at Crabapple, by order of Presbytery. In April, a joint call was prepared by these two congregations, then in union, and forwarded to Presbytery signed by the following persons, viz: John Miller, S. Dunlap, W. Watt, Henry Ferguson, Jesse Edgington, D. Welch, Esq., and William Harvey. You will readily excuse me in the mentioning of these names, when it is remembered that these were the men who founded the Church of Beech Spring; these were the men who called me, who first gave me the hand of fellowship, and welcomed me to these woods; most of whom I remember with affection, and would gladly visit were they living; but they are no more; the last died the other day. This call being accepted, I was accordingly ordained and installed pastor of the united congregation of Crabapple and Beech Spring by the Presbytery of Ohio, August, 1805. [The first elders of Crabapple were Robert McCullough, William McCullough, and David Merritt.]

The field covered by these two societies, at the time of our settlement, was very extensive, and the labor proportionably great. Crabapple claimed as being within her bounds, the whole extent of country between the south fork of Short creek and the farthermost part of Nottingham. Beech Spring was equally, if not still more extensive, including the entire region of country from the Piney Fork and the Flats, on west to Stillwater. All passed under the general name of Beech Spring. There was no Smithfield, nor Bloomfield, nor any other field, whereby to fix our limits. All was Jefferson county, and Steubenville, the seat of Justice.

Over all this extensive field, claimed by both churches, we had to travel. Wherever one was found, or whenever we heard of one in our connection, him we must visit; day and night, summer and winter, all seasons of the year, without a road in most places, save the mark of an axe or the bark of a tree, or the trail of an early Indian. No man that now comes in among us at this distant day, and highly improved state of the country, can so much as conjecture the labor and fatigue of the primitive pioneers of the Ohio forests, out of which the savage had just begun to recede, but continued still in large encampments in some places, near the skirtings of little societies, where the few came together to worship under the shade of a green tree.

The two churches under our care lay nearly twelve miles apart. Many Sabbath mornings, in the dead of winter, I had to travel ten miles to the place of meeting in Crabapple, having no road but a cow-path, and the underwood bent with snow over me all the way. Worn down by fatigue, and frequently in ill-health, I was more than once brought near the confines of the grave.

In all the region around, there were but two clerical brethren who could afford me any assistance, where now there are two Presbyteries and well-nigh thirty preachers. Notwithstanding all this, I must say of these early times, as Jehovah once said of Israel, eight hundred years after, "I remember thee, the kindness of thy youth, the love of thy espousals, when thou wentest after me in the wilderness, in a land that was not sown." Those were the best times, and that generation, that Israel, as a nation, ever saw. During the first years of these two congregations, a great and good Providence was evidently seen over them. They prospered exceedingly. Their increase was unprecedented; within our knowledge, we have seen nothing like it; without anything very special that could be called a revival (though something of the effects of the great western revival still remained, and appeared at times in our meetings), yet so rapid was their growth, that in less than five years each became able to support a minister all his time.

Accordingly, in April, 1810, the union existing between these churches was by mutual consent dissolved, and the way opened for each to employ a pastor. Shortly after, a call was prepared by this congregation for the whole of our time, and received through the same Presbytery as before. About this time there were several small societies forming at some distance from us, and appeared to be promising. From one of these societies an earnest request was forwarded to the session at Beech Spring, that some part of their pastor's time might be granted them. With this request the congregation complied, and for some years the fourth of our time was spent in laying the foundation of what has since become a numerous and respectable congregation, known by the name of the Ridge.

After the division of Jefferson county had taken place, and a new county formed out of it, Cadiz, then a small village, became the Seat of Justice of Harrison county. This village lay within our limits, and was considered a part of our congregation. Here we organized a church, at the request of the villagers, and labored a part of our time for three years; since which our ministry has been chiefly confined to this place alone.

For several years after, this church continued still more to increase, until she became, as was generally supposed, the largest in the State of Ohio. Out of this congregation, at different periods, there have been formed not less than six contiguous organized churches. Still, she continued to maintain her standing entire, until April, 1848, when age and infirmity made it necessary that I should resign, and the pastoral relation of forty-three years was at length dissolved.

Having thus briefly outlined the history of this church,—for

"Why should the wonders He has wrought,
Be lost in silence and forgot."

some notice is due to its officers.

In the Presbyterian Church the membership of elder is recognized in all her courts. The interest this class of men take, or the course of conduct pursued by them, will go far in shaping the destiny, the well-being, or ill-being of any church. In the organizing of this church at first I had no concern; it took place before my settlement. But in the course of years, as the congregation increased, frequent additions had to be made, until at one time we had not less than ten members in session. All were chosen by the people, and ordained by myself, with the exception of three, viz: James Kerr, Sr., John McCullough, Esq., and Dr. Thomas Vincent. These were valuable men, and useful members of the session. They obtained their ordination elsewhere, and were received as such here.

CHAPTER VIII.

HARRISON COUNTY IN 1813.

Harrison county was erected from parts of Jefferson and Tuscarawas. As at first constituted, the county included the southern portion of Carroll county; while the western half of Franklin and nearly all of Monroe townships were retained by Tuscarawas county. Carroll county was erected in 1832, from parts of Jefferson, Harrison, Columbiana, Stark, and Tuscarawas, which left the northern boundary of Harrison as it is to-day. The original townships of Jefferson county, which covered nearly all of the present territory of Harrison, were Short Creek and Archer. As organized in 1803, Short Creek township included all the present townships of Nottingham, Moorfield, Cadiz, Athens, Short Creek, and the south three-sevenths of Green, besides three tiers of sections in Jefferson county; while Archer included the eastern halves of Monroe and Franklin, all of North, Stock, Rumley, Archer, and German, and the north four-sevenths of Green, besides the southern tier of sections in Carroll and the northwestern portion of Jefferson counties.

Harrison county was organized under an act of the Legislature passed January 2, 1813, to take effect January 1, 1814. On January 12, 1813, the Legislature amended the act, making it take effect February 1, 1813, which, accordingly, is the date of erection of the county. On January 14, 1813, the Legislature appointed three commissioners, to locate the county-seat for the new county, and named Messrs. Jacob Myers, Joseph Richardson, and Robert Speer for this purpose. On the fifteenth of the following April, these commissioners made their report to the common-pleas court for Jefferson county, naming the village of Cadiz as the county-seat.

While Harrison county was still included within the territory of Jefferson, the second war with Great Britain broke out. Jefferson county furnished at least one full regiment, consisting of thirteen companies and 1065 men, and contributed to the formation of others. The officers of the regiment were as follows:

Lieutenant-Colonel, John Andrew; majors, Thomas Glenn, James Campbell, George Darrow, Jacob Frederick; adjutant, Mordecai Bartley; surgeon, Thomas Campbell; quartermaster, Jacob Van Horn; sergeant-major, John B. Dowden; quartermaster-major, John Patterson; drum-major, John McClintock; fife major, John Niel; captains, (1) Aaron Allen, (2) Thomas Latta, (3) John Alexander, (4) John Allen Scroggs, (5) James Alexander (6) Nicholas Murray, (7) William Faulk, (8) Jacob Gilbert, (9) Joseph Holmes, (10) James Downing, (11) Joseph Zimmerman, (12) David Meek, (13) William Stoakes; lieutenants (in same relative order with captains, as to their companies, (1) John Vantillburg, (2) Hugh Christy, (3) ——————, (4) John Ramsey, (5) Henry Bayless, (6) Nathan Wintringer, (7) John Berkdell, (8) John Teeton, (9) William Thorn and John Ramsay, (10) Peter Jackson, (11) James Kerr, (12) Joseph Davis, (13) Thomas Orr; ensigns (in same relative order with captains and lieutenants, as to their companies), (1) William Mills, (2) William Pritchard, (3) David Jackson, (4) John Caldwell, (5) John Myers, (6) John Carroll, (7) Jacob Crauss, (8) Abraham Fox and Conrad Myers, (9) Gavin Mitchell, (10) Thomas Smith, (11) Conrad Myers, (12) Jacob Sheffer, (13) John Caldwell.

Of the companies enumerated in the foregoing list, at least three were enlisted wholly or in part within the territory of Harrison county. The first was that of Captain Joseph Holmes. Following is a muster-roll of this Company, taken from the records of the Adjutant-General's office at Columbus, under date of August 26, 1812:

Captain, Joseph Holmes; lieutenants, William Thorn and John Ramsey; ensign, Gavin Mitchell; sergeants, Francis Popham, James Gilmore, Alexander Smith, John McCully; corporals, Edward Van Horne, John Pollock, Thomas McBride, Joseph Hagerman; drummers, John McClintock, James Robb; privates (enlisted to serve from Aug. 26, 1812, to Feb. 28, 1813), Rezin Arnold, James Arnold, Samuel Arnold, Anthony Asher, William Barcus, James Belch, James Brown, George Brokaw, John Brottle (also written Brittel), David Briggs, George Carpender, Philip

Cahill, James Chaffin, Findley Elliott, Thomas Elliott, Isaac Edgington, John Ferguson, Thomas Ferguson, Benjamin Foster, Thomas Glass, Samuel Gilpin, John Guttery, William Harper, Isaac Henry, Joseph Hughes, John Harriman, John Hawthorne, Rhesa Kendall, Matthew Kelly, Samuel Kerr, William Kyle, Jacob Lanning, Richard Logan, John Leach, James Long, Benjamin McClery (also written McClay), James Minnis, George McElroy, Patrick H. Madden, James McCullough, Charles McMillan, Robert Maxwell, Thomas McDonald, James Moore, William McClintock, John McCormick, Thomas McFadden, Jacob Meek, Jacob Osburn, Jacob Osler, John Parks, Hugh Porter, Richard Ross, Jeremiah Roach, Ebenezer Roach, Isaac Skeels, Charles Smith, James Sankey, Henry Snider, Joseph Strahl, George Sullivan, David Stevens, Luke Tipton, William Tipton, Jonathan Tipton, Isaac Van Bibber, Joseph White. Most of these privates re-enlisted for the spring campaign of 1813, as well as the following in addition (enlisted to serve from Jan. 1, to April 13, 1813): David Potts, Johnston Rollins, John Robertson, Charles Robertson; (enlisted to serve from Jan. 1, to Feb. 28, 1813): John Scholes, Jonathan Wist (or West), Edward Yealdhall.

Captain Aaron Allen's company was also largely recruited in Harrison county, and the adjoining townships of Jefferson and Belmont, the most of the company enlisting for six months' service, from September, 1812, to March, 1813. The roll of this company is as follows:

Captain, Aaron Allen; lieutenant, John Vantilburg; ensign, William Mills; sergeants, James Clare, John Farquer, Richard Shaw, Thomas Henderson; corporals, Christopher Abel, Hugh Livingston, James Johnston, David Workman; privates, Philip Ault, James Ayres, Samuel Avery, Anthony Asher, Benjamin Abel, John Barr, Robert Bay, Frederick Burchfield, Adam Beamer, Nehemiah Brown, Emery Burris, William Brown, Obadiah Barnes (or Burns), Lewis Corbet, Ryan Carter, Alexander Campbell, John Close, Alexander Conn (or Cann), Alexander Crawford, John Carson, Samuel Carson, Joseph Caughey, Henry Davis, John Degoir, Thomas Duvall, Anthony Doyell, James Ellison, David Freet, Abram Flecker, Frederick Fisher, John Fisher, Michael Fivecoats, John George, Thomas Graden, Martin Grim, Joseph Gibson, Michael Gladman, John Hitchcock, John Hardenbrook, James Hill, Jerome Hardenbrook, James Hukill, Samuel Holley, Joseph Haverfield, Jacob Haning, William Hill, John Harriman, John Haye, John Hickory, Nathaniel Jinnings, John James, James Kean, Samuel Kerr, John Lyons, John Logue, John Lyon, Samuel Lane. Samuel Lees, Robert Lisle, Emanuel

Myers, John Moody, James Mays, William McCloud, Thomas Mays, Joseph Mallen, William Montgomery, James Moorehead, Jacob Myers, Thomas McNiles, William McColly, Samuel Main, Robert McClerg, Felix McClelland, David McCaskey, William McClintock, Jacob Miller, Isaac Pugh, Thomas Packman, George Palmer, John Peterson, John Quinn, Adam Quillen, William Rutledge, Robert Ralston, Robert Russel, Mathew Richeson (or Richardson), Daniel Rickey, Caleb Reynolds, James Ray, Job Ruysel, Benjamin Ritter, Joseph Ralston, James Stuart, Philip Shaffer, Jacob Shover (or Shawber), Allen Speed (or Speedy), John Stoakes, John Smith, Adam Simmons, Daniel Steven, Benjamin Sessions, John Skelton, William Skelton, Samuel Smith, John Shepherd, John Taylor, Moses Thompson, Nicholas Wheeler, Daniel Welch, Jr., John Willits.

A third company was that of Captain Allen Scroggs, enlisted September 21, 1812, to serve until November 30, 1812. The roll of this company is as follows:

Captain, John Allen Scroggs; lieutenant, John Ramsey; ensign, John Caldwell; sergeants, William Wilkin, William Dunlap, William Holson, William Robertson; corporals, Samuel Avery, Joseph Haverfield, John Conoway, John Wallace; privates, Benjamin Abbott, Peter Bebout, John Brokaw, Farrington Barricklow, Adam Beamer, Homeny Buris, William Brokaw, Horace Belknap, Michael Conoway, James F. Carr, Archibald Fletcher, James Francis, Benjamin Foster, Michael Fivecoats, Michael Gladmore, Abraham Henary, John Hitchcock, Samuel Holly, William Hill, Edward Jack, Henry Johnson, Ebenezer Gray, Duber Lawrence, John Dewalt, David Finley, Samuel Lees, John McClay, John McCormick, Thomas McGonigle, James Moffit, Thomas McFadden, William McKain, Robert Mintier, Jacob Myers, William McCally, Charles Parson, Peter Pittenger, Alexander Porter, Stephen Perry, John Reed, John Reed, Jr., Samuel Reed, Charles Robertson, Moses Robb, Nicholas Shale, John Scholes, Samuel Smith, Charles Tenet, Moses Thompson, John Welch, Archibald Wilkins, Edward Yielhall.

It will be observed that many of these names are repeated on the rolls of two or three of the companies given above. This may have been caused by the transference from one company to the other, or by a tour of service in each one of the companies.

Another Company was organized in Harrison county, before its separation from Jefferson, and took the field against Great Britain. This was the Company of Captain Baruch Dickerson, in service in 1814.

Before giving its muster-roll, the following account of its organization and record may be repeated, the same having been dictated by the aged Joshua Dickerson, in two interviews had with him in the fall of 1896. Mr. Dickerson spoke as follows:

"I was but six years old, or thereabouts, when the Indians living along Lake Erie made frequent marauding excursions through this part of the State. This was about the year 1810 or 1811. There were no incidents of cruelty in this immediate neighborhood, but apprehending well the danger that might be, the settlers sought to prevent further trouble. Although I was but a child, I remember well the occurrences; perhaps my memory of this is strengthened somewhat by having heard my father relate the matter repeatedly.

"David Barrett, a Quaker, came to my father, and asked what he advised doing, to prevent trouble with the Indians. Father said, 'in time of peace, prepare for war,' and on election day a Militia Company was formed. After the election, the Company numbered sixty, and in a short time reached a hundred. David Barrett having organized the Company, was chosen its first captain; Samuel Gilmore, first lieutenant; John Jamison, second lieutenant. Two years later, Baruch Dickerson, having succeeded David Barrett as captain, the Company was called out to serve against the British.

"The Company was to serve nine months, but was out only six. They went from Cadiz, first, to Steubenville, then north to Sandusky. During the whole six months there was no actual engagement; only on two or three occasions were any shots fired. The camp life was very disagreeable. At Sandusky, they camped in a swamp, where they were obliged to cut down cedar trees, roll the logs together, and cover them with cedar branches. These cedar branches formed their bed, and covering.

"Samuel Gilmore was sick when they started home. He lived where Samuel Cochran now lives; he was a broad-shouldered, well-made man, of about forty years, and had three or more children. Gilmore, two days before his discharge, being on the way back to Cadiz, took the fever, and not at that time having a horse, was in bad condition; and refusing assistance from his comrades, walked thirty miles. Then the officers contributed sufficient money to purchase a horse, and Gilmore rode the remainder of the way to Cadiz, for the last two days of his march being held on the horse by his companions. The Company reached Cadiz on a Saturday, where a large assemblage was waiting to welcome their return.

Gilmore was able to recognize only his wife among the crowd; was at once conveyed to his home south of the village; and during the following week [Sept. 8, 1814], he died."

The roll of Captain Baruch Dickerson's Company, as shown on the records of the Adjutant-General's office at Columbus, is given below, the Company forming a part of Lieutenant-Colonel William Cotgreve's (or Colgrove's) Second Regiment of Ohio Militia. It will be observed that the titles of some of the officers differ from those given in Mr. Dickerson's account. This may possibly be accounted for by the fact that it was customary for the militia companies of that day to elect new officers every year or so. The Company as made up to fight the British numbered but thirty-six men, and was enlisted March 12, 1814, for service until September 12, 1814, as follows:

Captain, Baruch Dickerson; lieutenant, John Jamison; ensign, Samuel Gilmore; sergeants, William Haverfield, Charles Holmes, Laken Wells; musicians, James Robb, David Young; privates, Samuel Browning, Ezekiel Chambers, Samuel Carson, John Carson, Joseph Craig, Andrew Foster, Moses Foster, Michael Fivecoats, Isaac Hitchcock, James Haverfield, John Hurless, John Hovey, Samuel Holmes, Elsy Holmes, James McConkey, Samuel McConkey, Aaron Mecham, Benjamin Nelson, Joseph Parrish, John Richison, Francis Smith, David Scott, Bazaleel Steel, Francis Warpenboy, Nathaniel West, John Walraven, Henry Welday, George Young.

While on the subject of the war with Great Britain, it will not be out of place to record in this place the names of some of the surviving soldiers of the Revolutionary War, who afterwards located and lived in Harrison county. So far as known there are no printed records of these veterans in existence, save the names of those who were pensioners, and as such enrolled on the pension lists of the Government. The first of these pension rolls was published by Congress about 1820, in volume four of Executive Papers, No. 55, first session of the Sixteenth Congress. In this roll, which is very lengthy, the pensioners are classified as to residence only by States, and it is not possible to determine to what counties they then belonged. In 1835, a second roll was printed by Congress, showing the pensioners then living, or whose heirs were drawing pensions, with their place of residence, and age. To Harrison county at that time were credited the following:

John Brannon, of the Pennsylvania Line, age, 89 years.
Timothy Boyles, of the Delaware Line, age, 96 years.

Thomas Haley, of the Maryland Line, age, 74 years.

Thomas Johns, of the Virginia Line, age, 92 years.

James Larkins, of the Pennsylvania Line, died July 13, 1828, aged 70 years.

Neal Peacock, of the Maryland Line, died Aug. 17, 1827, aged 74 years.

John Parker, of the Pennsylvania Line, age, 68 years.

Henry Rankin, of the Pennsylvania Line, age, 72 years.

In the Government Census for 1840, a list of pensioners was prepared, and printed in the Census Report. This gave the names of all then drawing pensions for Revolutionary, or other military service, which included pensioners of the War of 1812 and of the various Indian Wars. Harrison county then contained the following pensioned veterans:

In Rumley township, George Dickerson, aged 94.

In Washington township, John Parker, aged 81.

In Cadiz village, William Boggs.

In Cadiz township, Robert Alexander, aged 45; Charles D. Wells, aged 82.

In Hanover village, Charles Conaway, aged 88.

In North township, Mordecai Ames, aged 90.

In Stock township, Frederick Walters, aged 80.

In Nottingham township, William Todd, aged 84; Isaac Suddith, aged 80.

The following letter, written by Walter B. Beebe, then a young lawyer, who had but recently emigrated to the West from his home in Massachusetts, gives an interesting description of the settlers and conditions which he found in the newly organized county, where he had determined to seek his fortune. It will be observed the letter bears a date scarcely two weeks later than the date of organization of the county:

Cadiz, County of Harrison, State of Ohio,
February 14, 1813.

Honored Parents:—I take this opportunity to inform you that I am well and in good spirits. Since I left home, I have become tolerably well acquainted with the science of traveling. I started from St. Clairsville (the place from which I wrote you), on or about the 1st of December, and took a convenient route through the middle section of this State, a route of about 500 miles. The more I get acquainted with this part of the country, the better I like it. It is certainly the best land I ever beheld. Judge Ruggles went with me to Chillicothe, the seat of Government, at which place the Legislature was then sitting. I got acquainted with Governor Meigs, and many of the members, who all appear to be very friendly to young men emigrating to this part of the country. Governor Meigs is a Yankee, from Middletown, Connecticut. At Chillicothe, I was examined by the Judges of the Supreme Court of this State, and admitted to practice as an attorney and counsellor at law in the several courts of record in this Staate. I found a good many counties in my route, which I thought would be good places for an attorney, but was induced to settle in this, the county-seat of Harrison county, from the following considerations, to-wit: Notwithstanding this county was set off and organized when I was in Chillicothe, yet it is an old settlement, and the settlers are generally rich. The inhabitants of this county, and counties adjoining, have but few Yankee settlers, but settled by Virginians, Pennsylvanians, Germans, Scotch, and Irish, who are more litigious and quarrelsome than the Yankees are, and pay their money more freely. There is no lawyer in this county, and I have the assurance of being appointed State's attorney, which will be worth eighty a year, and will be attended with but very little trouble and very little inconvenience to other business, being only barred in criminal prosecution from appearing against the State of Ohio.

This county is so situated that there are five other counties within one day's ride of it, and it is the practice in this State for lawyers to practice in adjoining counties. It is the healthiest part of the State, and the water is good. These, together with other considerations, have induced me, after having been a bird of voyage for three months, to pitch on this place for my permanent home.

This town is about twenty miles from the Ohio river, about seventy miles from Pittsburgh, and sixteen miles west of St. Clairsville. It is the shire-town of the county, and will soon be a populous town. I think my prospects are as good as a young man can reasonably expect, and I have no fear, if I have my health.

I am in a land abounding in very many of the good things of this life. I have seen good pot-turkeys, weighing twenty pounds, sell for twenty-five cents; hens and chickens, six cents. Money is very plentiful in this State, probably more plentiful than usual, owing to its being near the N. W. army. I remain, your dutiful son,

To Capt. Stewart Beebe,   WALTER B. BEEBE,
  Wilbraham, Hampden Co., Mass.

It is to be regretted that some of our eastern writers of American history, who have never been west of the Allegheny mountains, cannot have the advantage of a visit to Ohio, and learn as General Beebe did, that Yankees were exceedingly scarce there, outside of the Marietta and Western Reserve settlements.

The first courts of Harrison county were held at the houses of Thomas Stokes and William Grimes. At a meeting of the county commissioners held April 12, 1813, they entered into an agreement with the trustees of the Associate Reformed congregation of Cadiz, leasing the meeting-house belonging to that society for the term of three years, for the purpose of holding the courts of the county. On October 24, 1815, this lease was extended for a second term of three years, or until the newly begun court-house of the county should be completed. The first term of court was held in the house of Thomas Stokes on May 3, 1813. Very little business was transacted at this term. The second term was held August 24-26, 1813. Judges Benjamin Ruggles, President, and James Roberts, Samuel Boyd, and Ephraim Sears, Associates, occupied the bench. The court appointed Walter B. Beebe as prosecuting attorney for Harrison county, and allowed him the sum of $33.33, as salary for his services during the August term. The first grand jury was composed of Andrew McNeely, foreman, William Smith, Zachary Baker, William Mercer, William Hamilton, Samuel Gilmore, William Moore, Thomas Hitchcock, John McConnell, William Conwell, Richard McKibben, and John Taggart. On motion of Mr. Beebe, Rev. William Knox, a minister of the Methodist Episcopal Church, was licensed to officiate at marriages within the State of Ohio. The Court also licensed John Adams to keep a tavern at his place of residence in Nottingham township, for the term of one year; and likewise, William Grimes and Messrs. Middie, Niel and Maholm, to keep taverns in the village of Cadiz. The first empanelled jury was composed of Messrs. John Paxton, Samuel Osburn, Jonathan Seers, Robert Croskey, Samuel Dunlap, James McMillan, Samuel Huff, David Barrett, John Clark, Andrew Richey, James Porter, and Benjamin Johnson. The grand jury returned one indictment for larceny, four for riot, and seven for assault and battery; thus apparently vindicating Lawyer Beebe's judgment as to the quarrelsome character of some of the Ohio pioneers.

The following named persons served on the judicial bench of Harrison county prior to 1851:

President Judges—Benjamin Ruggles (1810 to 1814), George Tod (1814 to 1816), Benjamin Tappan (1816 to 1823), Jeremiah H. Hallock (1823 to 1836), George W. Belden (1837 to 1839), William Kennon (1840 to 1846), Benjamin Cowan (1847 to 1852).

Associate Judges—James Roberts (1813 to 1819), Samuel Boyd (1813 to 1819), Ephraim Sears (1813 to 1818), Matthew Simpson (1818 to 1819), Alexander Henderson (1819 to 1827), John McCullough (1820 to 1834), John McCurdy (1820 to 1825), Thomas Bingham (1825 to 1839),

David Campbell (1827 to 1829), John McBean (1829 to 1836), Robert Maxwell (1834 to 1841), Alexander Patterson (1836 to 1841), John Hanna (1840 to 1846), Samuel Moorehead (1841 to 1848), Thomas Lee (1841 to 1848), James Maxwell (1846 to 1852), William McFarland (1848 to 1852), William Boggs (1848 to 1852). Judges after 1851: Thomas L. Jewett (1852 to 1854), Thomas Means (1854 to 1855), Samuel W. Bostwick (1855 to 1861), George W. McIlvaine (1862 to 1870), John H. Miller (1870 to 1877), James Patrick (1877 to 1882), Joseph C. Hance (1882 to 1884, and 1889 to 1891), John S. Pearce (1884 to 1889), John Mansfield (1892 to ———), Walter G. Shotwell (1899 to ———).

Following is a list of the Senators and Representatives in the State Legislature, who served from and were residents of Harrison county:

Senators—Daniel Welch (1811, then from Jefferson county), Samuel Dunlap (1814 to 1815), Matthew Simpson (1816 to 1820, and 1822 to 1828), James Roberts (1820 to 1822), Daniel Kilgore (1828 to 1832), Joseph Holmes (1832 to 1834), Thomas C. Vincent (1834 to 1838), Chauncey Dewey (1841 to 1842), Samuel G. Peppard (1852 to 1854), Charles Warfell (1856 to 1858), Marshall McCall (1860 to 1862), John C. Jamison (1864 to 1866), James B. Jamison (1868 to 1872), Samuel Knox (1872 to 1878), David A. Hollingsworth (1880 to 1884), George W. Glover (1888 to 1890), Charles M. Hogg (1892 to 1896).

Representatives—Samuel Dunlap (1803 to 1808, and 1810 to 1813, from Jefferson county), Stephen Ford (1808 to 1810, and 1813 to 1818, from Jefferson county, prior to 1813), Andrew McNeely (1810, 1814, and 1815, from Jefferson county in 1810), William Moore (1816 to 1819), John Patterson (1819 to 1820, 1821 to 1822, 1823 to 1824, and 1826 to 1830), Ephraim Sears (1820 to 1821), William Wiley (1822 to 1823, and 1824 to 1826), Walter B. Beebe (1830 to 1831), Joseph Rea (1831 to 1833, and 1838 to 1840), Samuel W. Bostwick (1833 to 1836), John Gruber (1836 to 1838, and 1842 to 1843), Josiah Scott (1840 to 1842), William McFarland (1843 to 1844), Jacob Lemmon (1844 to 1846), Samuel A. Russell (1846 to 1848), John Hammond (1849 to 1850), Marshall McCall (1850 to 1854), Reynolds K. Price (1854 to 1856), Ephraim Clark (1856 to 1858), James Day (1858 to 1860), William H. McGavran (1860 to 1862), Smith R. Watson (1862 to 1866), Ingram Clark (1866 to 1868), Lewis Lewton (1868 to 1870), Anderson P. Lacey (1870 to 1872), David Cunningham (1872 to 1874), Samuel Herron (1874 to 1876), A. C. Nixon (1876 to 1878), Jesse Forsythe (1878 to 1880), Oliver G. Cope (1880 to 1882), Samuel B. McGavran (1882 to 1884), Jasper N. Lantz (1884 to

1886, and 1888 to 1890), George M. Patton (1886 to 1888), Wesley B. Hearn (1890 to 1892), Samuel K. McLaughlin (1894 to 1898), Samuel S. Hamill (1898 to 1900).

Other names on the Civil List of Harrison county are as follows:

Probate Judges—Brice W. Viers (1852 to 1854), Allen C. Turner (1854 to 1867), Amon Lemmon (1867 to 1894), Elias B. McNamee (1894 to 1900), John B. Worley (1900 to ——).

Auditors (the title of the first three was "Clerk of Commissioners")—Walter B. Beebe (1813 to 1816), Lared Stinson (1816 to 1817), James L. Hanna (1817 to 1820), John Hanna, clerk and first auditor, (1820 to 1822), Joseph Harris (1822 to 1832), Joseph Meek (1832 to 1833), James Miller (1833 to 1837), Charles Patterson (1837 to 1840), Zephamiah Bayless (1840 to 1843), John Sharp (1843 to 1845), Robert Edney (1845 to 1849), Reynolds K. Price (1849 to 1853), John Sloan (1853 to 1854), Will-S. Granfell (1855 to 1856), Kersey W. Kinsey (1856 to 1860), Samuel Knox (1860 to 1864), William H. McCoy (1864 to 1869), Reuben A. McCormick (1869 to 1871), William O. Potts (1871 to 1875), Thomas W. Giles (1875 to 1880), James M. Scott (1880 to 1883), Henry Spence (1883 to 1884), James C. Carver, deputy for Henry Spence, (1883 to 1884), George A. Crew (1884 to 1891), Henry G. Forker (1891 to 1896), Harvey B. Law (1896 to ——).

Treasurers—Samuel Osburn (1813 to 1828), John S. Lacey (1828 to 1836), James McNutt (1836 to 1840), William Milligan (1840 to 1844), Zephamiah Bayless (1844 to 1848), Ralph Barcroft (1848 to 1852), David Hilbert (1852 to 1854), J. J. Johnson (1854 to 1858), John Russell (1858 to 1860), Thomas Richey (1860 to 1862), Frank Grace (1862 to 1864), Wesley S. Poulson (1864 to 1866), Elias Foust (1866 to 1870), George A. Haverfield (1870 to 1876), Harvey L. Thompson (1876 to 1878), Nimrod B. Pumphrey (1878 to 1882), Albert J. Harrison (1882 to 1886), Samuel A. Moore (1886 to 1890), Nathaniel E. Clendennin (1890 to 1894), Robert Stewart (1894 to 1899), Joseph J. Sears (1900 to ——).

Prosecuting Attorneys—Walter B. Beebe (1813 to 1834), Josiah Scott (1834 to 1838), Edwin M. Stanton (1838 to 1839), Samuel W. Bostwick (1839 to 1844), Thomas L. Jewett (1844 to 1848), Samuel G. Peppard (1848 to 1851), Allen C. Turner (1851 to 1853), Lewis Lewton (1854 to 1856), Jesse H. McMath (1856 to 1861), Amon Lemmon (1861 to 1863), William P. Hayes (1863 to 1866), David Cunningham (1866 to 1869), John S. Pearce (1869 to 1875), David A. Hollingsworth (1875 to 1877), John C. Given (1878 to 1881), John M. Garvin (1882 to 1887), Walter G.

Shotwell (1888 to 1894), William T. Perry (1894 to 1900), Barkley W. Rowland (1900 to ——).

Recorders—William Tingley (1814 to 1829), Joseph Harris (1829 to 1832), William Johnson (1832), Samuel M. McCormick (1832 to 1838), Matthew M. Sloan (1838 to 1844), William Boyce (1844 to 1850), Lancelot Hearn (1850 to 1857), William A. Hearn (1857 to 1858), Joseph Rea (1859 to 1868), George Woodborne (1868 to 1874), John Graybill (1874 to 1880), Landon B. Grimes (1880 to 1886), Albert B. Hines (1886 to 1892), Thomas Arbaugh (1892 to 1898), S. Edwin Thompson (1898 to ——).

Sheriffs—Elescondo Henderson (1814 to 1816), James Boswell (1816 to 1817), John Stokes (1817 to 1821), Rezin Arnold (1821 to 1824), Baruch Dickerson (1824), John S. Lacey (1824 to 1826), Matthew McCoy (1826 to 1832), James McNutt (1832 to 1835), William Mulligan (1836 to 1839), William Cady (1840 to 1842), William Barrett (1842 to 1846), John McCormick (1846 to 1848), David Hilbert (1848 to 1853), James Boyd (1853 to 1855), Alexander Barger (1855 to 1858), Edwin S. Woodborne (1858 to 1861), Stephen R. McGee (1862 to 1866), John E. McPeck (1866 to 1870), James Moore (1870 to 1872), Samuel S. Hamill (1872 to 1876), Elisha Hargrave (1876 to 1878), Emanuel Howard (1878 to 1880), James C. Carver (1880 to 1886), Jefferson C. Glover (1886 to 1888), Albert Quigley (1888 to 1892), David P. Host (1892 to 1896), Samuel B. Moore (1896 to 1900), Davis Garvin (1900 to ——).

Clerks of Court—Joseph Harris (1813 to 1815), William Tingley (1815 to 1838), Thomas Vincent (1838 to 1845), Samuel McCormick (1845 to 1851), Charles Patterson (1852 to 1854), Thomas C. Rowles (1855 to 1860), R. M. Lyons (1861 to 1863), John Fogle (1863 to 1867), John Garvin (1867 to 1875), Allen W. Scott (1875 to 1882), Elias B. McNamee (1882 to 1888), Martin J. McCoy (1888 to 1894), E. B. Kirby (1894 to ——).

Commissioners—John Pugh (1813), James Cobean (1813 to 1814), Eleazer Huff (1813), William Phillips (1813 to 1816), William Wiley (1813 to 1821), John Craig (1814 to 1820, and 1824 to 1825), Robert Maxwell (1816 to 1828), William Henderson (1820 to 1826), Joseph Holmes (1820 to 1824), David Thompson (1825 to 1833), Thomas Martin (1826 to 1832), Brice W. Viers (1828 to 1831), John Caldwell (1831 to 1834), Henry Ford (1832 to 1838), John Ramage (1833 to 1836), Samuel Colvin (1834 to 1840), Jesse Merrill (1836 to 1839), John Sharp (1838 to 1841), Andrew Richey (1839 to 1842), James P. Beall (1840 to 1843), Thomas Day (1841

HARRISON COUNTY IN 1813

to 1842), John Downing (1842 to 1845), James Hogland (1843 to 1846), Samuel Hitchcock (1845 to 1851), Samuel Richey (1846 to 1852), Luther Rowley (1847 to 1853), John Carrick (1851 to 1852), John Yost (1852 to 1857), Elijah Carver (1852 to 1855), Joseph Masters (1854 to 1856), Jacob Cramblett (1855 to 1861), Jackson Croskey (1856 to 1863), Charles Wells (1860 to 1866), James J. Billingsley (1861 to 1867), Walter Craig (1863 to 1865), Andrew Jamison (1865 to 1871), Levi Snyder (1866 to 1872), William Evans (1867 to 1873), James Patton (1871 to 1877), John Sloan (1872 to 1874), Alexander Henderson (1873 to 1879), John Latham (1874 to 1878), Thomas McMillen (1877 to 1883), Enoch W. Phillips (1878 to 1881), George Love (1879 to 1882), Lindley M. Branson (1882), Jackson Rea (1882 to 1884), John Miller (1882 to 1886), Michael B. Firebaugh (1883 to 1890), Robert B. Moore (1884 to 1891), Andrew Smith (1886 to 1891), John W. Spiker (1890 to 1896), William C. Adams (1891 to 1897), Thomas H. Ryder (1892 to 1898), John H. Pittis (1896 to ——), John C. Patton (1897 to ——), Henry P. Worstel (1897 to ——).

Surveyors—James McMillan (1820 to 1825), Abner Hixon (1825 to 1830, and 1834 to 1837), Curtis W. Scoles (1833 to 1834), Daniel Morris (1837 to 1840), Samuel McCormick (1840 to 1847), Daniel Spencer (1847 to 1849), Samuel Bell (1849), Jacob Jarvis (1849 to 1894), Benjamin J. Green (1894 to ——).

Congressmen—Daniel Kilgore (1834 to 1838), John A. Bingham (1855 to 1863, and 1865 to 1873).

Members State Board of Equalization—Walter Jamison (1850), Carleton A. Skinner (1890).

Members of Constitutional Conventions.—Samuel Moorehead (1850-51), Josiah Scott (1850-51), William G. Waddle (1872-73).

Prominent Attorneys, who have been or are now members of the Harrison County Bar—Walter B. Beebe, Edwin M. Stanton, Chauncey Dewey, Thomas L. Jewett, Samuel W. Bostwick, Samuel A. Russell, Samuel G. Peppard, Josiah Scott, Joseph Sharon, Jesse H. McMath, Lewis Lewton, Josiah M. Estep, David Cunningham, David A. Hollingsworth, John S. Pearce, Walter G. Shotwell.

Natives or residents of Harrison county who have attained a National reputation—Edwin M. Stanton, Bishop Matthew Simpson, General George A. Custer, John A. Bingham, Thomas L. Jewett, Frank Hatton.

The towns and villages of Harrison county were organized as follows: Bowerstown (first called Bowersville) was platted by David Bowers,

Henry Hoover, and Nathaniel Bowers, Aug. 21, 1852; plat filed, Aug. 22, 1852.

Brownsville was platted by Absalom Kent, Jr., Dec. 20, 1815; plat filed Dec. 22, 1815.

Cadiz was platted by Zaccheus A. Beatty and Zaccheus Biggs, Oct. 29, 1804; plat filed in Jefferson county, Oct. 29, 1804; in Harrison county, May 24, 1813.

Deersville was platted by John Cramblett, Nov. 25, 1815; plat filed, Dec. 19, 1815.

Fairview (Jewett) was platted by John Stahl, Dec. 5, 1851; plat filed, Jan. 9, 1852.

Franklin was platted by John Marshall, March 4, 1837; plat filed, March 7, 1837.

Freeport was platted by William Melton, Daniel Easly, and Jonathan Bogue; plat filed in Tuscarawas county, March 7, 1810, in Harrison county, 185 (Mason's Journal, quoted on another page, states that Freeport was laid out some eighteen months before his visit there, which was made in October, 1819).

Georgetown was platted by George Riggle; plat filed, Sept. 3, 1814.

Harrisville was platted by John Wells, Thomas Gray, Store Hutchinson, and Robert Dutton, Oct. 19, 1814; plat filed, Jan. 9, 1815.

Hopedale was platted by Cyrus McNeely, Oct. 15, 1849; plat filed, July, 30 1851.

Jefferson was platted by Frederick Zollers, December, 1815; plat filed, Jan. 3, 1816.

Jewett, see Fairview.

Masterville was platted by G. W. Holmes in 1851.

Moorefield was platted by Michael Moore and Gabriel Cane, Dec. 15, 1815; plat filed, Dec. 27, 1815.

New Athens was platted by Rev. John Walker and John McConnell, Feb. 10, 1817; plat filed, Feb. 10, 1817.

New Hanover was platted by John Fisher, Aug. 13, 1812; plat filed, July 25, 1834.

New Market (Scio) was platted March 30, 1852.

New Rumley was platted by Jacob Custer; plat filed, Aug. 16, 1813.

Pennsville was platted by Joseph H. Penn, Oct. 30, 1851; plat filed, Jan. 8, 1852.

Scio, see New Market.

Smyrna was platted by Samuel Burrows, Aug. 4, 1817; plat filed, Aug. 4, 1817.

Tippecanoe was platted by Alfred Heacock, Dec. 8, 1840; plat filed, Dec. 22, 1840.

CHAPTER IX.

HARRISON COUNTY SETTLERS IN 1813.

Following are the names of some of the early settlers and non-resident land-owners of Harrison county (outside of Cadiz village) up to and including the year 1813. This was the year in which Harrison county was erected, its territory before that time being comprised in Jefferson county. This list includes the names of all those who had land patents issued by the United States Government before 1815; and it is from the dates of these that many of the dates in the list are taken. Nearly all of these patents were issued after 1804; although, as a matter of fact, in almost every case, settlement and improvements had been made on the land by the patentee or his assignor, from one to five years before. The first lands sold in Harrison county after the opening of the land office in Steubenville were under a credit system, which gave the purchaser four years' time after the date of his entry to make his payments; and patents were not issued until the payments had been completed. In some cases time of payment was extended for some years beyond the original period, so that the patent may have been dated several years after settlement was begun. A full list of all Harrison county land patents issued by the United States will be found in the latter part of this volume. Several dates in the following list are taken from the old township book of Short Creek township, an abstract of which was prepared by Mr. Oliver Cope, and printed in the Cadiz Republican near the close of the year 1895. Other dates, particularly those prior to 1804, are taken from family histories and records, and not to be relied upon absolutely. In this regard the list is not so full or correct as could be desired, and the

HARRISON COUNTY SETTLERS IN 1813

writer regrets that the data at his command does not include more of the early settlers of Harrison county.

In Archer Township before 1814.—Samuel Amspoker, 1803; William Anderson, 1811; Comfort Arnold, 1810, from Pennsylvania; Daniel Blair, 1812, from Somerset county, Pa.; William Barnhill, 1811; John P. Pond, 1811; Samuel Boyd, 1812; John Busby, before 1812, from Maryland; Zebediah Cox, 1810; Alexander Crawford, 1808, from Brooke county, (West) Va.; Edward Crawford, 1806, from Brooke county, (West) Va.; James Devore, 1811; Andrew Endsley, 1810; David Endsley, 1808; John Endsley, 1810; Andrew Farrier, 1808; Samuel Ferguson, 1812; George Fisher, 1811, from Washington county, Pa.; James Fisher, 1811; Isabella Haggerty, 1811; George Harriman, 1811, from Washington county, Pa; Thomas Hitchcock, before 1809, from Maryland; Gabriel Holland, before 1812, from Maryland; Peter Kail, 1810; Isaac Lemasters, 1813, from western Virginia; William Lisle, 1811; Joseph McClair, 1812, from Westmoreland county, Pa.; William McCreery, 1811, from Westmoreland county, Pa.; Robert McKee, before 1811, from Fayette county, Pa.; Alexander McKittrick, 1813, from Washington county, Pa.; Robert Meeks, 1812; David Moody, 1813; Hugh Orr, 1812, from Westmoreland county, Pa.; Isaac Osburn, 1809; Charles Porter, 1813; Arthur Reed, 1810, from Pennsylvania; John Roush, 1812; James Steward, 1813, from Washington county, Pa.; William Wartembe, 1807, from Brooke county, (West) Va.; John Welch, about 1804, from Pennsylvania; Thomas Williams, 1812, from Brooke county, (West) Va.

In Athens Township before 1814.—Simpson Bethel, 1806, from Loudoun county, Va.; Stacy Bevan, 1811; Jacob Black, Sr., 1808, from Fayette county, Pa.; James Cooke, before 1810, from Washington county, Pa.; Joseph Covert, 1813, from Fayette county, Pa.; William Crawford, 1809; David Cunningham, 1811, from Fayette county, Pa.; Joshua Dickerson, 1811, from Fayette county, Pa.; David Drake, 1806; Adam Dunlap, before 1809, from Fayette county, Pa.; John Dunlap, 1812, from Fayette county, Pa.; William Dunlap, 1806, from Fayette county, Pa.; John Fagley, 1810; Samuel Foster, 1813, from Allegheny county, Pa.; Thomas Gordon, 1811; Samuel Hanna, 1805, from Washington county, Pa.; Joseph Hollaway, 1810; Samuel Hutchison, 1810, from Chester county, Pa.; Robert Innis, 1812, from Westmoreland county, Pa.; Samuel Jumpes, 1812; Samuel Knight, 1808; Job Lewis, 1811; John Loney, 1812; John Love, 1808, from Washington county, Pa.; John McAdams, 1811, from Washington county, Pa.; George McConnell, 1805, from Washington county, Pa.; John McConnell, 1806, from Washington county, Pa.; John McCoy, 1806, from Washington county, Pa.; Thomas McCoy, before 1810, from western Virginia; Robert McCracken, 1805, from Washington county, Pa.; James McDowell, 1806, from Fayette county, Pa; John McDowell, 1809, from Fayette county, Pa.; Samuel McDowell, Jr., 1806, from Fayette county, Pa.; John Maholm, 1812; Alexander Moore, 1813; Nathaniel Parramour, 1811; Caleb Pumphrey, 1808; John Reed, 1812; Nathan Shepherd, 1807, from Brooke county, (West) Va.; Roger Toothaker, 1811; Jacob Webb, 1806, from Fayette county, Pa.

In Cadiz township before 1814 (Exclusive of Cadiz Village.)—John Agnew, 1807, from Washington county, Pa.; Reuben Allen, 1812, from Maryland; James Allison, about 1810; George Barricklow, 1812, from Fayette county, Pa.; Henry Barricklow, 1809, from Fayette county, Pa.; Valentine Barriger, 1813, from Adams county, Pa.; Arthur Barrett, 1808, from Frederick county, Va.; John Baxter, 1812, from Allegheny county, Pa.; Zaccheus A. Beatty, 1804; Zaccheus Biggs, of Steubenville, 1806; John Blair, before 1810; Rannel Blair, 1809, from Brooke county, (West) Va.; Thomas Burkhead, 1812; Samuel Carnahan, 1806; Joshua Cecil, 1813; Nathan Chaney, 1805, from Virginia; Robert Cochran, before 1805, from Allegheny county, Pa.; Samuel Dunlap, 1805, from Fayette county, Pa.; John Eagleson, 1813, from Maryland; Abraham Furney, before 1805, from Germany; John Gilchrist, 1811, from Fayette county, Pa.; Francis Gilmore, 1808; Samuel Gilmore, before 1805, from Hopewell township, Washington county, Pa.; William Grimes, 1813; Jesse Haines, 1811; James Haverfield, before 1810, from Huntingdon county, Pa.; Samuel Heavlin, 1812; Samuel Hedges, before 1810, from Virginia; Alexander Henderson, 1813, from Pennsylvania; John Jamison, before 1805, from Hopewell township, Washington county; Absolom Kent, 1805, from Fayette county, Pa.; George Leporth, 1806; Samuel McDowell, 1811; John McFadden, before 1805, from Hopewell township, Washington county, Pa.; Joseph McFadden, before 1805, from Hopewell township, Washington county, Pa.; John McMillan, 1807; Andrew McNeely, before 1805, from Berks county, Pa.; James Mahon, 1812; Arthur Martin, 1813, from Lancaster county, Pa.; Matthew Mitchell, 1806, from Washington county, Pa.; John Morris, 1813, from western Virginia; John Oglevee, before 1805, from Fayette county, Pa.; John Perry, 1813; James Porter, before 1805, from Washington county, Pa.; Samuel Porter, before 1805, from Washington county,

Pa.; Joseph Rogers, 1808, from Maryland; William Rogers, 1811, from Maryland; Adam Ross, 1804, from York county, Pa.; John Ross, 1804, from Pennsylvania; Joseph Steer, 1805; James Stewart, 1812; David Thompson, about 1814, from county Tyrone, Ireland; Elizabeth Toole, 1810; Bazaleel Wells, of Steubenville, 1806; Charles D. Wells, 1813; Robert Wilkin, before 1802, from Pennsylvania; Thomas Wilson, 1812, from Brooke county, (West) Va.

In Franklin Township before 1814.—Walter Craig, 1809; William Craig, 1809, from Washington county, Pa.; Benjamin Johnson, 1812, from Brooke county (West) Va.; Joel Johnson, 1812, from Brooke county, (West) Va.; Joseph Johnson, 1811, from Brooke county, (West) Va.; Benjamin Price, before 1805, from New Jersey; Jonathan West, 1811, from Pennsylvania.

In Freeport Township before 1814.—Isaac Cadwallader, 1811, from Fayette county, Pa.; Samuel Colvin, 1812, from Washington county, Pa.; Daniel Easley, 1810, from Halifax county, Va.; John Gilmore, 1810, from New York; John Hollett, about 1806, from Maryland; Berriman McLaughlin, 1808; William Milton, 1812, from Washington county, Pa.; James, John, Richard, Thomas, and William Reeves, 1813; Henry Stevens, 1808.

In German Township before 1814.—George Abel, from Loudoun county, Va.; John Abrams, 1811; George Atkinson, 1804, from Brooke county (West) Va.; Jacob Beckley, 1812; Robert Birney, 1807, from Chester county, Pa.; Stephen Ford, 1807; William Gallaher, 1809, from Fayette county, Pa.; David Gibson, 1809, from Brooke county, (West) Va.; Nicholas Gutshall, 1806, from Washington county, Pa.; James Hanna, 1810, from Washington county, Pa.; George Hartford, 1809, Brooke county, (West) Va.; James Hazlett, 1812, from Fayette county, Pa.; Henry Heisler, 1806, from Northumberland county, Pa.; Peter Hesser, 1807; Francis Holmes, 1811; Nathan Johnson, 1812; Jacob Kail, before 1806, from Pennsylvania; John Kail, before 1810, from Pennsylvania; James Kelly, 1809; Robert Kelly, 1811, from Brooke county, (West) Va.; William Kelly, 1812, from Brooke county, (West) Va.; James B. Magrew, 1806, from Westmoreland county, Pa.; Peter Markley, 1811, from Washington county, Pa.; Benjamin Menyard, 1811; David Miller, 1812; William Nichols, 1813; George Pfautz, 1805, from Cumberland county, Pa.; Frederick Reed, 1807; John Riddle, 1812, from Allegheny county, Pa.; Jacob Sadler, 1806; George Shultz, 1810, from Loudoun county, Va.; Jacob Smyer, 1810; Joseph Sprott, 1806, from

Fayette county, Pa.; Jacob Stees, 1812; Matthias Stohl, 1806; William Wallace, 1809, from Brooke county, (West) Va.; Benjamin Wheeler, 1806, from Baltimore county, Md.; Nicholas Wheeler, before 1810, from Maryland; John Winnance, 1812.

In Green Township before 1814.—John Baker, before 1805, from Pennsylvania; Henry Barriger, 1813, from Adams county, Pa.; William Birney, 1813; James Black, 1806, from Adams county, Pa.; Anthony Bricker, 1804; George Brokaw, before 1805, from Pennsylvania; John Caldwell, 1808, from Fayette county, Pa.; Alexander Cassil, 1806, from Washington county, Pa.; Joseph Clark, 1806, from Westmoreland county, Pa.; John Craig, 1803, from Donegal township, Washington county, Pa.; John Croskey, before 1805, from New Jersey; Robert Croskey, before 1805, from Pennsylvania; Robert Davidson, before 1805, from Pennsylvania; Philip Deleny, 1806; Henry Ferguson, 1806, from Washington county, Pa.; Archibald Fletcher, 1813, from Adams county, Pa.; James Ford, 1808, from Brooke county, (West) Va.; John Fowler, before 1810, from Maryland; John Fulton, 1806, from Fayette county, Pa.; John Gardner, 1810, from Washington county, Pa.; Hugh Gwynn, 1813; William Hanna, 1805, from Pennsylvania; William Hogg, 1804, from Fayette county, Pa.; William Holmes, before 1804, from Pennsylvania; Joseph Kent, 1806, from Washington county, Pa.; John Laughlin, before 1806, from Pennsylvania; Caleb Merryman, 1807, from Baltimore county, Md.; Jane Milligan, 1811, from Adams county, Pa.; Mark Milliken, before 1812, from Pennsylvania; William Moore, before 1805, from Hopewell township, Washington county, Pa.; John Nicodemus, before 1805; John Oldshoe, before 1806; Robert Orr, before 1805, from Westmoreland county, Pa.; William Orr, 1812; Joseph Pumphrey, 1806; William Pumphrey, 1806; John Ramsey, before 1805, from Washington county, Pa.; Thomas Rankin, 1807; Rev. John Rea, 1804, from Washington county, Pa.; John Shepherd, 1807; Jacob Shepler, 806, from Westmoreland county, Pa.; Martin Snyder, before 1805; John Stapler, 1806, from Bucks county, Pa.; Galbreath Stewart, 1805, from West Middletown, Washington county, Pa.; John Taggart, before 1805, from Washington county, Pa.; Hugh Tease, 1806; Edmund Tipton, about 1814; John Wallace, 1804, from York county, Pa.; William Watt, before 1804, from Washington county, Pa., Pa.; Bazaleel Wells, of Steubenville, 1805; Daniel Welch, before 1803, from Cecil township, Washington county, Pa.; John Wilson, 1806, from Washington county, Pa.; John Young, 1814, from Anne Arundel county, Md.

In Monroe Township before 1814.—William Baun, 1801; Bernard Bower, 1812; John Bower, 1809; William Constable, 1801; Jacob Easterday, 1811; John Fry, 1813.

In Moorefield Township before 1814.—Robert Baxter, 1812; Robert Bell, 1811; John Cadwallader, Jr., 1812; Thomas Crabtree, 1812; Robert Hurton, 1811, from Ohio county, (West) Va.; Henry Johnson, 1812, from Allegany county, Md.; Joseph and Lemuel Johnson, 1812; William Johnson, 1810, from Allegany county, Md.; John Kennedy, 1811, from Washington county, Pa.; Matthew Kennedy, 1811, from Scotland and the District of Columbia; John Knight, 1812; Edward Lafferty, 1810, from Washington county, Pa.; James Lamb, 1810; John Lamb, 1806, from Washington county, Pa.; Peter John Lance, 1812; Anne Mifflin, of Philadelphia, 1807; William Ramage, 1808; Thomas Rankin, 1805, from Mt. Pleasant township, Washington county, Pa.; Rachel Titus, 1812; Alexander Wilson, before 1810; Israel Wilson, 1811; James Wilson, 1812; Jonathan Wright, 1811.

In North Township before 1814.—Jacob Albert, 1811; Martin Boghart, 1812, from Somerset county, Pa.; Christian Canaga, 1807, from Somerset county, Pa.; Jacob Canaga, 1807; Philip Creplever, 1812, from Washington county, Pa.; James English, 1812, from Fayette county, Pa.; John and Philip Firebaugh, 1812, from Somerset county, Pa.; Nancy Forney, 1812, from Westmoreland county, Pa.; Peter Forney, 1810, from Somerset county, Pa.; Joseph Gundy, 1812, from Somerset county, Pa.; Joseph Keiser, 1812; Henry Miser, 1811; Peter Smith, 1812, from Somerset county, Pa.; Thomas Yarnell, 1811, from Washington county, Pa.

In Nottingham Township before 1814.—William Arnst, 1811; James Caldwell, 1813; George Carothers, 1811, from Washington county, Pa.; John Carson, before 1812, from Maryland; Peter Crabtree, 1812, from western Pennsylvania; William Grist, of West Nottingham township, Chester township, Pa., 1809; Isaac Haines, 1812; Thomas Haines, 1807; John Hines, before 1810, from Westmoreland county, Va.; Benjamin Johnson, 1810, from Allegany county, Md.; John Johnson, 1810; John McCorkle, 1812; William Phillips, of West Nottingham township, Chester township, Pa., 1809; John Pugh, 1807, from Chester county, Pa.; John Richardson, 1813; John Riley, 1812; Jonathan Sayes, 1811.

In Rumley Township before 1814.—Samuel Buchanan, 1806, from Washington county, Pa.; David Custer, 1811; Emanuel Custer, 1812, from Allegany county, Md.; George Custer, 1804, from Fayette county, Pa.; Andrew Hendricks, 1812, from Allegany county, Md.; John and

Joseph Hendricks, 1813, from Somerset county, Pa.; Adam Kimmel, 1813; Leonard Kimmel, 1807, from Somerset county, Pa.; John Lowmiller, 1808, from Pennsylvania; Joseph McLain, 1812, from Westmoreland county, Pa.; John Miller, 1806, from Frederick county, Md.; Abraham Noffsker, 1806; Abraham Pittenger, 1813, from New Jersey; John Rough, 1812; Jacob Turney, 1813.

In Short Creek Township before 1814.—John Adams, 1805, from the North of Ireland; Thomas Anderson, before 1805; Joseph Applegate, 1805, from Brooke county, (West) Va.; James Beatty, 1803; John Beatty, 1803; David Belknap, 1807; Robert Braden, 1802, from Washington county, Pa.; William Brown, 1805, from Brooke county, (West) Va.; James Carrick, 1812, from Adams county, Pa.; Sarah Chambers, 1806, from Brooke county, (West) Va.; Joshua Clark, 1808, from Fayette county, Pa.; John Cope, 1813, from Frederick county, Va.; Thomas Crumley, 1812, from Virginia; Robert Culbertson, 1811, from the North of Ireland; Thomas Dickerson, before 1805, from Fayette county, Pa.; James Ervin, 1812, from Maryland; James Finney, 1806, from Fayette county, Pa.; John Fuller, 1806; Joseph Gill, 1806; Samuel Hanna, before 1806, from Washington county, Pa.; Simpkins Harryman, 1802, from Maryland; Samuel Haund, 1801; Robert Hill, 1807; Isaac Holmes, about 1800, from Brooke county, (West) Va.; Joseph Holmes, about 1800; Ellis Hoopes, 1812; Nathan Hoopes, 1809; Joseph Huff, before 1800, from Brooke county, (West) Va.; John Hurford, before 1810, from Culpepper county, Va.; Abner Hutton, 1805; Jonathan Jessop, 1806; John Johnson, 1807, Westmoreland county; William Johnson, about 1804, from Pennsylvania; Enoch Jones, 1806; James Kerr, 1807, from Adams and Westmoreland counties, Pa.; James McBride, 1809, from Washington county, Pa.; Vincent Metcalf, before 1804; Baldwin Parsons, 1803; Samuel Primes, 1806; Andrew Ritchey, Jr., before 1805, from York and Washington counties, Pa.; Charles Richey, 1805, from Washington county, Pa.; John Ritchey, about 1807, from York and Washington counties, Pa.; Richard Ridgway, 1803; James Roberts, before 1806; Hugh Rogers, 1806, from Washington county, Pa.; William Rouse, 1805; William Sherrod, 1804; John Singer, about 1808, from Virginia; William Smith, 1812; Benjamin Stanton, 1803; Silas Stephen, about 1810; Jacob Styers, 1812; Jonathan Taylor, 1813; Bradway Thompson, 1804, from Washington county, Pa.; Isaac Thomas, 1812; Thomas and William Thorn, 1806; Joseph Townsend, about 1812, from Bucks county, Pa.; Nathan Updegraff, 1806; Thomas Vanbuskirk, 1804;

Joseph Vanlaw, 1805, from Burlington county, N. J.; William Walraven, before 1805; John Wells, 1806; Ezra Wharton, 1806, from Bucks county, Pa.; William Wiley, 1804, from Washington county, Pa.; Michael Yost, 1806, from Frederick county, Va.; Charles Young, 1805, from Washington county, Pa.

In Stock Township before 1814.—Michael Conaway, before 1810; James Hoagland, 1811; Isaac Johnson, 1812; William Johnson, 1812; Hugh McDonough, 1812; Alexander Moore, 1811; Charles Prather, of Brooke county, Va., 1811; John Simpson, before 1810, from Washington county, Pa.; Aquila Tipton, before 1812; George Venamon, 1809, from Washington county, Pa.

In Washington Township before 1814.—John Henry Carver, 1812, from Germany; John Cooper, 1813; Lewis Davidson, 1809, from Fayette county, Pa.; Nathaniel Gilmore, 1811; Jesse Huff, 1811; John Huff, 1812; William Huff, 1810; Robert Parks, 1810.

Besides the names given above, a list of the first lot-owners in the town of Cadiz will be found in connection with the account of its early settlement; and, as stated before, a complete list of the Government land patents issued for lands in Harrison county, is given in another portion of this book. There were many early settlers in the county, however, who did not get their land directly from the Government, but bought it at second-hand from the original pre-emptors. The names of some of these are given in the following supplementary list, covering the period from 1814 to 1829, inclusive. This list is very incomplete; and it is a matter of regret that more records are not available to the writer. But such as have been obtained are here given; although many families will find the names of their pioneer ancestors missing, when they properly deserve a place in such a list as this:

John Adams, Freeport, before 1812, from Erie county, Pa; Thomas Adams, Cadiz, 1815, from Pennsylvania; George Addleman, Monroe, 1820, from Greene county, Pa.; James Aiken, German, 1826, from Washington county, Pa.; John Alexander, Freeport, 1828, from county Antrim, Ireland; John Arbaugh, Rumley, about 1820, from Maryland; John Archbold, Archer, 1814, from Westmoreland county, Pa.; David Barclay, Moorefield, about 1826, from county Derry, Ireland; James Barnes, Athens, 1824; Zenas Bartow, North, 1819, from Washington county, N. Y.; Samuel P. Baxter, Green, 1821, from Fayette county, Pa.; James P. Beall, Nottingham, before 1825, from Pennsylvania; Sampson Beatty, Archer, before 1826, from the North of Ireland; Samuel Beck, Freeport,

1814; Peter Barger, Cadiz, 1818; Joseph Bernhard, Short Creek, 1814, from Chester county, Pa.; Hugh Birney, Green, before 1820, from the North of Ireland and Chester county, Pa.; Samuel Borland, North, 1819, from Westmoreland county, Pa.; James Bradford, Cadiz, before 1821, from Washington county, Pa.; Benjamin Brindley, Archer, 1825, from Harford county, Md.; John Cadwallader, Freeport, 1814; Joseph Cadwallader, Freeport, 1814; John Cady, Cadiz, 1824, from county Tyrone, Ireland; John Campbell, Green, before 1822, from Pennsylvania; Erasmus Cannon, Athens, 1815, from Harford county, Md.; John Cecil, Moorefield, 1819; Philip Cecil, Franklin, before 1823, from Maryland; Robert Christy, Archer, before 1830, from Scotland; Robert Clark, Cadiz, before 1830; James Clements, Cadiz, before 1820, from Maryland; Jacob Condo, German, 1814, from York county, Pa.; Hiram Conwell, Cadiz, before 1816, from Virginia; Caleb and Imla Cooper, Washington, 1814; William Cooper, Washington, 1814; James Copeland, Green, 1816; Thomas Copeland, Green, about 1814; William Coultrap, Stock, 1815, from western Virginia; Nathaniel Crawford, Moorefield, 1814; John Creal, North, 1820, from Maryland; Valentine Creamer, Freeport, 1814; James Cree, Freeport, about 1818, from Pennsylvania; James Cummings, Monroe, before 1820, from Kent county Del.; Samuel Curry, Archer, 1821; Jacob Custer, Rumley, before 1816, from Anne Arundel county, Md.; Jacob Dennis, Green, before 1830, from New Jersey; Chauncey Dewey, Cadiz, 1821, from Norwich, Conn.; Henry Dillon, Archer, 1814; James Endsley, Archer, 1817, from Lancaster county, Pa.; David Firebaugh, North, before 1817, from Pennsylvania; John Firebaugh, North, before 1825, from Pennsylvania; John Ford, Nottingham, before 1820, from Fayette county, Pa.; William Foreman, German, 1818; Jesse Forsythe, Washington, 1825, from Fayette county, Pa.; Alexander Foster, German, 1815; George Foster, 1816, from England; John Fowler, North, before 1820, from Pennsylvania; John Fulton, Green, 1816, from Harford county, Md.; Philip Fulton, Nottingham, before 1820, from Maryland; James McC. Galbraith, German, 1814, from Cumberland county, Pa.; Abram Gaudy, before 1810, from Maryland; Hezekiah Garner, Nottingham, 1818, from Maryland; John Green, Freeport, 1825, from the North of Ireland; Robert Guttry, Moorefield, 1814; William Guttery, Athens, 1815; Elijah Guyton, Nottingham, about 1826, from Maryland; Edward Hagan, Short Creek, 1815, from Adams county, Pa.; W. P. Hall, Archer, about 1815; Samuel W. Hamill, Monroe, 1828, from the North of Ireland; Francis H. Hamilton, Cadiz, 1820, from the North of Ireland; Joshua Hamilton, Cadiz, before 1825, from Pennsylvania; James Hanna, German, about 1816, from Washington county, Pa.; John Hanna, Cadiz, 1814, from Westmoreland county, Pa.; Robert Hanna, Green, 1814; Hezekiah Harrison, Green, 1820, from Maryland; John Harrison, North, 1816, from Yorkshire, England; Christopher Hartley, North, about 1820, from England; John Haverfield, Cadiz, 1817; Joseph Haverfield, Cadiz, 1817; James Hawthorne, Short Creek, before 1830, from the North of Ireland; John Heberling, Short Creek, 1823, from Berkeley county, Va.; John Hefling, Washington, 1821; Henry Hemry, Archer, 1815; John Henderson, Rumley, 1816, from Indiana county, Pa.; Jacob Hendricks, Rumley, 1814; Thomas Hidey, Rumley, 1830; Leonard Hilton, 1826, from Maryland; Rudolph Hines, 1814, from Germany; Samuel Hitchcock, 1808; Robert Holliday, Freeport, 1815, from the North of Ireland and Westmoreland county, Pa.; Henry Houser, Cadiz, before 1825; Edward Huston, Moorefield, before 1830, from Pennsylvania; Solomon Insley, Franklin, 1816, from Maryland; Andrew Jamison, Green, before 1825, from Pennsylvania; William Jenkins, Washington, 1814, from Nova Scotia; Alexander Johnson, German, 1814; from county Tyrone, Ireland, and Pennsylvania; Derrick Johnson, Moorefield, 1814; Samuel R. Johnson, Monroe, 1824, from Maryland and South Carolina; Daniel Kilgore, Cadiz, before 1815, from Pennsylvania; John Kimmel, North, 1814; Charles Kinsey, Cadiz, before 1820, from Bucks county, Pa.; Hugh Kirkpatrick, Athens, 1818; James Kirkpatrick, Athens, 1821, from Cecil county, Md. and Washington county, Pa.; William Knox, Cadiz, before 1813, from the North of Ireland and Maryland; John S. Lacey, Cadiz, 1816, from Sussex county, Del.; Samuel Lafferty, Moorefield, 1814, from Washington county, Pa.; James Laughridge, North, before 1820, from the North of Ireland; John Law, Monroe, 1826, from the North of Ireland; George Lewis, Rumley, about 1818, from England; Jacob Long, Moorefield, 1816; Robert Lyons, Cadiz, 1819, from Pennsylvania; George McAdams, Moorefield, 1815; James McAfee, Rumley, 1823, from Washington county, Pa.; James McAfee, North, 1828, from Westmoreland county, Pa.; Joseph McBeth, Monroe, 1829, from Westmoreland county, Pa.; John McClery, Green, 1814; John McClintock, Nottingham, 1830; Robert McConnell, Washington, 1814, from Pennsylvania; James McDivitt, North, 1820, from Pennsylvania; Samuel McFadden, Cadiz, 1815; Robert McFarland, Athens, before 1824; John McMillan, Nottingham, 1818, from Pennsylvania; Thomas Maddox, Short Creek, 1825, from Virginia;

Joseph Maholm, Cadiz, 1814; Emanuel Mallernee, Nottingham, 1829, from Maryland; Allen Manly, Green, before 1817; Thomas Marquis, Athens, before 1823; Arthur Martin, Archer, before 1817, from the North of Ireland, and Lancaster county, Pa.; Peter Martin, Green, 1823, from Virginia; Abraham Mattern, Green, before 1830, from Westmoreland county, Pa.; John Megaw, North, 1816, from Westmoreland county, Pa.; Micajah Merryman, Cadiz, before 1820, from Maryland; Alexander Millekin, Cadiz, 1815; John Mitchell, Archer, before 1816, from Maryland; John Mitchell, Cadiz, before 1828, from Washington county, Pa.; Ezekiel O'Bryan, Moorefield, 1814; Alexander Osburn, Athens, 1815, from Westmoreland county, Pa.; Jane Pattison, Moorefield, 1816; Joseph Patterson, Archer, before 1820, from the North of Ireland; James Patton, Short Creek, 1816, from Pennsylvania; Joseph Patton, Rumley, 1816, from Fayette county, Pa.; Thomas Patton, Green, 1816; Thomas Perry, Moorefield, 1815; John Phillips, Cadiz, before 1828, from West Nottingham township, Chester county, Pa.; Richard Phillips, Washington, 1815, from Pennsylvania; Thomas Phillips, Cadiz, before 1826, from West Nottingham township, Chester county, Pa.; John Pollock, Green, 1814, from Fayette county, Pa.; Joshua Quillan, Freeport, 1815; John Ramsouer, Rumley, before 1820; James Rankin, Athens, 1815; Robert Rankin, Cadiz, 1818; Thomas Richey, Cadiz, 1817; Robert Roberts, German, 1817, from Brooke county, Va.; Robert Robertson, Cadiz, before 1826, from Loudoun county, Va.; John Robison, Franklin, about 1826, from Virginia; William Ross, Archer, 1817; John Rowland, Moorefield, 1815, from York county, Pa.; John Sampson, Stock, 1827, from county Tyrone, Ireland; Adam Sawvel, Rumley, 1815, from Pennsylvania; Matthias Schilds, Monroe, 1814; James Scott, Cadiz, 1819, from Yorkshire, England; Thomas Scott, Athens, about 1822, from county Down, Ireland; William Scott, Archer, 1817; Peter Sewell, 1828, from Delaware; George Shambaugh, Rumley, 1817, from Perry county, Pa.; John Sharp, Cadiz, before 1830; John Shivers, Cadiz, before 1816, from Pennsylvania; Hugh Shotwell, Washington, 1814, from New Jersey and Pennsylvania; John Shotwell, Washington, 1814, from Fayette county, Pa.; James Simpson, Green, 1829, from Washington county, Pa.; Samuel Skinner, Moorefield, about 1820, from the Shenandoah valley, Virginia; Andrew Smith, Archer, 1814; Daniel Smith, Stock, 1821; from Huntingdon county, Pa; John Smith, Nottingham, 1818, from the North of Ireland; David Smylie, Cadiz, 1815, from Washington county, Pa.; John Sneddeker, German, 1816, from Washington county, Pa.; John

Snider, North, before 1824; Eli Sparrow, Green, before 1820, from Maryland; Thomas Sproul, about 1820, from the North of Ireland; Jacob Stahl, Rumley, 1816, from Charles county, Md.; Basil Steel, Washington, 1815, from Berkeley county, Va., and Pennsylvania; Robert Steel, Moorefield, 1816; Archibald Stewart, Cadiz, 1816, from Pennsylvania; Matthew Templeton, Athens, 1815; Andrew Thomson, Moorefield, 1815, from Washington county, Pa.; Samuel Thompson, 1813, from Franklin and Westmoreland counties, Pa.; Thomas Thompson, Green, 1816, from Centre county, Pa.; Thomas Thompson, Freeport, 1820, from the North of Ireland; Charles Timmons, Cadiz, 1817, from Berkeley county, Va.; Eli Town, Jr., Freeport, 1814, from Washington county, Pa.; Alexander Urquhart, 1813, from Scotland; Henry Utterback, Cadiz, 1820, from Virginia; Joseph Walker, Stock, 1822, from county Derry, Ireland; John Wallace, Moorefield, 1822, from York county, Pa.; Samuel Welsh, Archer, 1814; John Weyandt, Monroe, about 1817, from Washington county, Md., and Somerset county, Pa.; John Whan, 1815, from Chester, Northumberland, and Washington counties, Pa.; Ezra Wharton, Short Creek, 1818, from Bucks county, Pa.; Isaac Wheldon, Freeport, 1814; Joseph White, Nottingham, about 1818, from Maryland; Archibald Wilkin, Washington, before 1818, from Pennsylvania; Isaac Wood, Archer, 1814; Jonathan Worrall, Short Creek, 1815; **David Wortman, North, 1825**; John Wylie, German, before 1818.

CHAPTER X.

CRABAPPLE AND UNITY CHURCHES.

While Beech Spring was the first Presbyterian church organized within the present limits of Harrison county, the congregation of

CRABAPPLE,

composed largely of Harrison county people, and for five years united with Beech Spring under the same pastoral charge, was gathered some three or four yyears before that of the latter.

Crabapple church is situated in Wheeling township, Belmont county, about two miles south of New Athens, and a short distance north from Uniontown. Near here, at the beginning of the present century, the settlers were perhaps more numerous than in any other part of the county. The most of them had come from Washington and Fayette counties, Pennsylvania; and for some years before 1800 the Presbytery of the Ohio, whose members were then chiefly stationed in Washington county, had sent nearly every one of their number on missionary tours to the new settlements in the Western Territory, as Ohio was then called. Among these ministers were Rev. John McMillan, Joseph Patterson, and Elisha Macurdy, the first named being one of the earliest Presbyterian ministers to settle west of the Allegheny mountains, and at that time perhaps the most prominent.

On October 17, 1898, Rev. Joseph Anderson was licensed by this Presbytery, and at the same time appointed to visit the settlements west of the Ohio river, and to preach at "Indian Wheelin Creek" (St. Clairsville), on the fourth Sabbath of October, and at "Indian Short Creek" (Mt. Pleasant), on the first Sabbath of November. He continued to supply these churches occasionally, and on October 15, 1799, at a request of a committee from these churches, the Presbytery appointed Mr. Anderson as a stated supply for one year. On April 15th of the following year, however, a call from the united congregations of Indian Wheeling Creek (now first called Richland, and later, St. Clairsville), Short Creek (Mt. Pleasant), and Cross Roads (Crabapple), was made for the pastoral services of Mr. Anderson, and accepted by him. His ordination took place at Cross Roads, Western Territory, on August 20, 1800, Presbytery having met at that place the day before. This is sometimes erroneously stated to have been the first ordination of a Presbyterian minister in what is now the State of Ohio; but such is not the case, Rev. James Kemper having been ordained and installed, at Cincinnati, by the Presbytery of Transylvania, as early as October 23, 1792. It was, however, the first ordination by the Presbytery of Ohio within the present limits of that state.

Mr. Anderson was a member of the church of Upper Buffalo, in Hopewell township, Washington county, Pennsylvania, and probably pursued his studies in part at the Canonsburg Academy. He was a man of deep and abounding zeal, a faithful and devoted laborer, and in an eminent sense, a pioneer. Within two years after his installation, Cross Roads (Crabapple) ceased to be a part of his charge, owing, doubtless, to increased labors resulting from his rapidly growing congregations. In April, 1813, his pastoral relation to Short Creek (Mt. Pleasant) was dissolved; but in 1820, Short Creek is again coupled with Richland in Presbytery's report to Synod. In 1827, Richland is first reported as St. Clairsville, and in 1829, is reported as his sole pastoral charge. He was released October 3, 1830; and in June, 1835, he was dismissed to the Presbytery of St. Charles. His death occurred at Monticello, Mo., in 1847, in the eightieth year of his age. Mr. Anderson's wife was a daughter of Rev. Joseph Smith, first pastor of Cross Creek and Upper Buffalo churches, in Washington county, Pennsylvania.

Robert McCullough and William McCullough were the first ruling elders in Crabapple church. In this capacity, Robert McCullough represented the infant congregation in a meeting of the Synod of Virginia held at Washington, Pennsylvania, in 1800; and he also attended the meeting of the Presbytery of Ohio in the following year. The organization of the church, nevertheless, seems to have become dormant in 1802, and so continued for a year or more. In the spring of 1804, however, in union with the newly organized congregation of Beech Spring, Crabapple presented a call to Rev. John Rea, whose acceptance of the same, and subsequent labors in this field, have already been related in connection with the former sketch of the history of Beech Spring Church.

A somewhat different account from the above, of the permanent erection of Crabapple congregation is given by Mr. J. A. Caldwell, in his "History of Belmont and Jefferson counties." Mr. Caldwell says:

> In the year 1803, Robert and William McCullough sent to Georgetown, Harrison [then Jefferson] county, Ohio, for Samuel Hanna, to "come up and help" them to form a "praying society." He came, and from this germ planted in the wilderness, sprang Crabapple Presbyterian Church, the first and largest church organization in Wheeling township, Belmont county, Ohio. The first sermon was preached by the Rev. John Rea, and the church organized with forty members, in 1804, by Rev. Joseph Anderson and Dr. [Samuel] Ralston, a committee sent by the Presbytery of Ohio. The early records are lost, but the following families were among the first members: The McCulloughs, McKibbons, Campbells, Snedekers, Brokaws, and Merritts. The first bench of elders was composed of William McCullough, Robert McCullough, and Daniel [David] Merritt.

While the account is probably correct, so far as it goes, yet, undoubtedly it refers to the second organization of the church. Rev. Joseph Anderson had certainly gathered the nucleus of the congregation here as early as 1799, and it seems to have continued as one of his preaching stations for two or three years afterwards. The records of the Presbytery of Ohio show a meeting of Presbytery at Cross Roads, Western Territory, as Crabapple was then called, on Aug. 19, 1800, as stated above. At this meeting were present, Revs. John McMillan, James Hughes, John Brice, and Thomas Marquis, all well-known ministers of Washington county, Pennsylvania, and elders, Samuel Dunlap and John Irwin. On Wednesday, August 20th, "Presbytery proceeded to the ordination of Mr. Joseph Anderson, and by fasting and prayer, and with the laying on of the hands of the Presbytery, solemnly ordained him to the holy office of the gospel ministry, and installed him pastor of the united churches of Richland, Short Creek, and Cross Roads, W. T." Dr. McMillan preached on this occasion, from 2d Corinthians, v. 20; and Rev. John Brice gave the charge.

Mr. Anderson relinquished the charge of Crabapple in 1802, as stated above; and in August, 1805, was succeeded by Rev. John Rea. An account of Mr. Rea's five years' ministration here has been given in the sketch of Beech Spring Church, which during that period was united with Crabapple as one pastoral charge. At the end of five years (in April, 1810), he withdrew from Crabapple, that he might give all his labors to the Beech Spring congregation. The Crabapple division of his charge had become too laborious for him, spreading over a district of nearly fourteen miles square; for the territory of the future churches of New Athens, Morristown, and Nottingham was within its bounds. The latter was then a mission station, under the care of the pastor and elders of Crabapple.

The following extracts from the records of the Presbytery of Ohio will give us an idea of the strict orthodoxy of the early fathers of Crabapple congregation; and it is possible they may also furnish one of the reasons for Mr. Rea's withdrawal from the charge of this congregation.

The Presbytery met at Cross Roads, in Washington county, Pa., on October 10th, 1808. On Friday, October 21st, "Samuel Hannah, a member of Crabapple congregation, appeared in the Presbytery with the following charge:

"The Reverend John Rea is hereby charged with preaching and circulating heterodox sentiments at the following places, viz., at Crabapple, the Sabbath on or about the 20th of April last, and on Monday at Samuel Hannah's, at an examination: That the Covenant of Grace was not made with Christ, but with man only, and that man promises faith and repentance on his part; and maintains, that if the Covenant of Grace was made with Christ, he could not be the Mediator of it.

"The Presbytery agreed to take up the charge, and ordered the parties to appear before them at their next meeting, prepared to have the matters brought to an issue."

Upper Buffalo, December 21st, 1808. "The Presbytery proceeded to the consideration of the charge which was at the last meeting brought by Samuel Hannah against the Revd. John Rea. The charge being read, Mr. Rea denied that ever he had taught as stated in the charge." Witnesses were accordingly sworn and examined, William and Robert McCulloch on that day, and Andrew Ackelson and William Wylie on the day following. Presbytery then "ordered Mr. Rea to prepare a written explanation of his sentiments." On the 23d, "Mr. Rea brought in a written explanation of his sentiments, which being read and considered, the Presbytery proceeded to consider the several items in the charge; and judged that they were not supported by the testimony."

Rev. Thomas B. Clark, a licentiate of the Presbytery of Hartford, was ordained and installed pastor of Crabapple in 1811, preaching one-fourth of his time at the Nottingham mission station; and continued until 1818, when his relation to this charge was dissolved.

The third pastor was Rev. Samuel Cowles, who was installed in 1819, and continued seven years. After Mr. Cowles, there occurred a vacancy of several years, supplied from various sources; and then Mr. Jacob Coon, a licentiate of the Presbytery of Washington, preached as a candidate for settlement, received and accepted a call, and in 1834 was ordained and installed. He remained four years.

Rev. Moses Allen was the fifth pastor of the church. He studied theology under his father-in-law, Dr. John McMillan, and was licensed to preach by the Presbytery of Ohio in 1807. He remained for thirty years in the bounds of that Presbytery, and then removed to the state of Ohio, where he was installed as pastor of Crabapple church in 1839. He continued in this relation from that time until his death, a period of seven years.

In June, 1847, Rev. McKnight Williamson was installed pastor of this church, and remained for five years and nine months. He was succeeded by Rev. William R. Vincent, who served for thirteen years. Mr. Vincent was followed in succession by John P. Caldwell (1869-1872), T. J. Milford (1874-1882), and George S. Hackett (1883).

The first structure used by Crabapple Church as a place of worship was a so-called "tent," being nothing more than a rude pulpit, erected in the forest, possibly built against the side of a tree, and with a small projecting roof or hood of clap-boards, designed to protect the minister and his bible from the sun and rain. His congregation usually stood around in groups, or seated themselves on the grass, or on fallen logs. Soon afterwards, a log house was built, which later was succeeded by a brick building, and this in turn gave place to a frame structure, which has continued in use since its erection.

About the year 1835, under the ministrations of Rev. Jacob Coon, Crabapple church seems to have reached the flood-tide of its prosperity. Its communicants then numbered over three hundred, with a Sabbath school of some two hundred members. Revs. William M. Grimes, Thomas R. Crawford, James Grimes, Robert Armstrong, Robert Tannehill, and Joseph Lyle were reared in this church, and received their early religious training in its Sabbath school.

UNITY CHURCH.

The first sermon preached to the families of this congregation was delivered by Rev. Joseph Scroggs, about the year 1812-13. As Dr. Scroggs was not licensed by his Presbytery until October, 1813, it is possible the date of his visit may not have been until after that event. The church was regularly organized as an Associate Presbyterian congregation by Rev. John Walker, in 1814, and at that time consisted perhaps of no more than eight families, whose heads were as follows: John Trimble, James Cook, Robert McCracken, Alexander McCall, Robert Hammond, John Love, Thomas Love, and John McCaskey. The first bench of elders was composed of Messrs. John Trimble, Robert McCracken, Alexander McCall, and Robert Hammond.

Of the first minister of this congregation, more than a passing notice is required; as few men have had a greater or more beneficial influence upon the moral welfare of the county, than John Walker. He was born in 1786, in Washington county, Pennsylvania; was educated at Jefferson College, and studied Theology with Dr. John Anderson, at Service, Pa.; was licensed in the summer of 1809 by the Presbytery of Ohio, and ordained July 11, 1811, by the same; served as pastor of Mercer and connections in Pennsylvania, until September 14, 1814; was installed over Unity, Mt. Pleasant, and Cadiz, in the summer of 1815. As his congregations increased, he resigned Cadiz in 1818, but retained the others until his death, which occurred March 8, 1845, from erysipelas. He was not distinguished for scholarship, but possessed an exceedingly enthusiastic temperament, which made him very energetic and active in his labors. He was a pioneer in the temperance cause, even to total abstinence; was very decided in his opposition to Free Masonry; and was intensely bitter in his hostility to slavery. He was always ready, even anxious, to defend his views, and oppose what he regarded as error. Hence, he was engaged in a number of public discussions, the most memorable of which was that with Alexander Campbell, the founder of the Campbellite Baptists. Mr. Walker desired to establish a classical school in Harrison county, and as none of the villages would take hold of the matter, he, in connection with a neighbor, laid out a town upon the adjacent portions of their farms, which they named New Athens. Here he started a classical school, and rested not until he succeeded in getting from the Legislature the charter of Franklin College. He studied medicine in his youth, and practiced more or less in an amateur way during his whole ministry. In later years he felt a necessity to open a regular practice. The burning of his house, together with a boundless hospitality, and a general financial mismanagement, made him very poor. For some time before securing the charter for his college, he conducted it as an academy in New Athens, under the name of the "Alma Mater," in active rivalry with a similar institution carried on by Rev. Donald McIntosh, in Cadiz. In the archives of Franklin College is found the record of a single meeting of the trustees of that academy, held on September 28, 1824, the names of the trustees being: Rev. Salmon Cowles (president), John McCracken (secretary), Rev. John Walker, John Whan, John Wylie, Alexander Hammond, Alexander McNary, Daniel Brokaw, and John Trimble. At this time, the project for a charter for the academy at Cadiz was being agitated; but by the superior activity and tact of Mr. Walker, the charter was obtained for the academy at New Athens, under the name of "Alma College." This name was changed at the next meeting of the Legislature to that of Franklin College. The charter is dated January 22, 1825, and the original incorporators were Revs. John Rea, Salmon Cowles, and John Walker, and Messrs. David Jennings, William Hamilton, John McCracken, John Wylie, James Campbell, David Campbell, John Trimble, John Whan, Daniel Brokaw, Alexander McNary, and Alexander Hammond. To these were added by election, at the first meeting of the trustees under this charter, held April 5, 1825, Rev. Thomas Hanna, John McGlaughlin, Stephen Caldwell, Joseph Grimes, and Matthew Simpson. At this same meeting of the trustees, the Rev. William McMillan (a nephew of Dr. John McMillan), of Canonsburg, Penna., was elected President, with John Armstrong, of Pittsburg, as Professor of Mathematics; and on June 8th of the same year, the college was formally organized.

At the Semi-Centennial Celebration of the organization of Franklin College, held at New Athens, June 23, 1875, Dr. Andrew Finley Ross, then president of the institution, sketched the history of the school from its organization; and from his address on that occasion, the following account has been condensed.

The leading spirit in the enterprise was Rev. John Walker, a minister of the Secession church. Mr. Walker was a fit son of that particular branch of the church; a church characterized by its zealous orthodoxy and sturdy theology. He was a man of deep conviction upon the subject of equal rights. Hence, he entered into the anti-slavery contest with all the ardor of his impetuous nature, and during that long controversy, was one of the leading anti-slavery spirits of the West. By the superior tact

UNITY CHURCH

and energy of Rev. John Walker, the charter of Franklin College was obtained. Dr. William McMillan was elected President, and John Armstrong, Professor of Mathematics. Dr. McMillan was the nephew of Dr. John McMillan, the original founder of Jefferson College at Canonsburg, Penna., of which institution he had been for some time president. He had thus been associated with and reared under the tuition of that noble band of men, the Smiths, Powers, McMillans, and Ralstons, who were so instrumental in planting the seeds of Presbyterianism and sound learning in the country west of the Alleghenies. John Armstrong was the mathematical oracle of western Pennsylvania. He made all the almanacs, and solved all the mathematical propositions. Learned societies in Europe recognized his attainments by admitting him to their fellowships. What are the results? In this small college, with its two professors, were educated such men as the Hon. John Welsh, of the Supreme Court of Ohio; the Hon. William Kennon, a member of Congress during Jackson's administration, a friend and adviser of the President; Wilson Shannon, a former governor of Ohio; Dr. Joseph Ray, the well-known mathematical writer, whose works have maintained a longer popularity and gained a wider circulation than perhaps any other mathematical works ever written; besides giving to the church such men as Drs. Johnson, Bruce, Henderson, Walkinshaw. Surely, this is harvest enough for less than seven years. Dr. McMillan died in 1832. [He was followed, in succession, by Revs. Richard Campbell and Johnson Welsh] In 1837, the Board appointed as president, Dr. Joseph Smith, then pastor of a church in St. Clairsville, the grandson of Rev. Joseph Smith and Dr. James Power, both noted pioneers of Presbyterianism in western Pennsylvania. He was thus from the same stock, and reared under the same tuition with Dr. McMillan.

The anti-slavery agitation was becoming more and more intense. The people who attended the ministrations of Rev. John Walker were almost to a man strongly anti-slavery. The Presbyterian General Assembly was divided. The congregation of Crabapple was divided, although Rev. Jacob Coon, the pastor, was strongly anti-slavery. Dr. Smith opposed agitation of the question. Mr. Coon left Crabapple, removed to New Athens, and organized a Presbyterian church. Dr. Smith resigned the presidency, and Mr. Coon was elected in his stead. The majority of the Board was composed of anti-slavery men, but it was not their intention to commit the college to this principle. Coon was succeeded in a year, by Rev. William Burnett, an Associate Reformed minister, from near Pittsburgh, but born in South Carolina, and conservative on the slavery question. He resigned within a twelve-month, followed by Professor Armstrong.

In 1840, the Board appointed Rev. Edwin H. Nevin, President; George K. Jenkins, Professor of Mathematics; and Rev. Andrew Black, Professor of Languages. The members of the Board then resolved to throw themselves entirely upon the side of the anti-slavery sentiment of the country. The place had already come to be regarded as the hot-bed of Abolitionism in eastern Ohio; and Mr. Nevin's eloquent denunciation of the monster iniquity, aided by the hot shot of Rev. John Walker, soon began to tell upon the community.

The college had become involved in debt, and the creditors sued for their claims. The anti-slavery men, then in control, were unable to meet these claims, for various reasons, and in consequence, the property of the college was taken in execution, and sold by the sheriff. Thus Franklin College, after her long struggles, found herself without a home. But this was not all. The college edifice, with its appurtenances, was purchased by the colonization, or pro-slavery party, and under the name of "Providence College," they succeeded in establishing a rival institution. The anti-slavery men, however, were adequate to the crisis, and notwithstanding the demands that had already been made upon their liberality, they at once raised funds for the erection of a building for the accommodation of Franklin College. To secure it from the claims of the old creditors, yet unliquidated, and for the satisfaction of which their property had been sacrificed, they located their edifice upon their church lot, thus vesting their title in the trustees of the church; and so Franklin College was accommodated with a home. The popular qualities of President Nevin and his associates in the faculty attracted at once all the students that resorted to the place, and Providence College, after a feeble effort to gain a hold upon the public patronage, was abandoned. The anti-slavery men had now fairly won the field. President Nevin, in having the bell cast for the new college, placed upon it the words: "Proclaim Liberty Through all the Land."

Dr. Nevin was succeeded in 1845 by Rev. Alexander D. Clark, who remained until 1861.

The sons of Franklin College are found occupying high positions all over the land. She has given to the Senate of the United States a Cowan, a Fowler, and a Sharon; and to the House of Representatives, a Kennon, a Bingham, and a Lawrence. She is represented in the halls of medical science by an Armor; on the Supreme Bench of Ohio, by a Welsh; on that of Alabama, by a Bruce; and in the theological seminaries of the country, by a Bruce, a Clark, and a Henderson. Seventy-five per cent. of her graduates have entered the Christian ministry, and some of the most distinguished and useful men who adorn the pulpit are found among them.

In his "Pathfinders of Jefferson County," Mr. William H. Hunter has recorded considerable of the once forgotten history of the Abolition movement in Ohio, and in referring to that part of the subject connected with Harrison county, he says: "The Short Creek valley, from Cadiz to Mt. Pleasant, and including the region about New Athens and Crabapple church, just over the divide, on the head waters of Wheeling creek, was noted for its warmth of abolition sentiment, from 1820 down to the close of the irrepressible conflict—abolition of slavery, pure and simple; the hard-headed, austere Seceders, the followers of Dr. John Walker, and other ministers of his kind, would tolerate no compromise, and they looked upon Benjamin Lundy's colonization schemes with almost the same disrespect that they would consider any half-way measure proposed by the pro-slavery advocates. Franklin College, founded by John Walker, was long recognized as the fountain-head of the abolition sentiment of eastern Ohio, and it is but natural that the people first to drink of the stream were powerfully influenced; and further, it was in accordance with the eternal fitness of things, that numerous 'underground stations,' so-called because slaves were surreptitiously conveyed along certain routes, kept hid during the day, and hurried during the night season from one station to another, on their way to Canada, should be established in this valley.

"Of course, there were stations at the mouth of Short creek, one kept by George Craig, and one by William Hogg. One was kept by Joseph Medill, on Warren Ridge, near Hopewell M. E. Church. There were many in Mt. Pleasant, the slaves being kept during daylight in any of the houses in the village, and there is authority for the statement that one good Friend kept a number of strong negroes on his farm from cornplanting until after harvest. The house of Rev. Benjamin Mitchell was a noted station, there being a trap-door in the kitchen floor, through which runaway slaves reached a large hole in the ground when slave-hunters were searching the premises. The Updegraff house, a mile west of Mt. Pleasant, and that of David Robinson, west of Trenton, were also well known to the slave on his way to liberty. The Bracken house in Mt.

Pleasant was so constructed that the negroes could enter an attic by means of a trap-door in the roof, after climbing a ladder. Benjamin Ladd, the Quaker philanthropist, kept the Smithfield station. The one at Lloydstown, named for Jesse and Isaac Lloyd, was kept by Eli Nichols; one at Unity, kept by Rev. John Walker, the courageous Seceder minister; at Hammond's Cross Roads, by Alexander and John Hammond —John Hammond, Jr., and Joseph Rodgers, now of Cadiz, being conductors between this point and Hopedale; one at the house of James Hanna (brother of Rev. Thomas Hanna), near Georgetown; one at the house of Cyrus McNeely (founder of Hopedale College), between Hopedale and Unionvale; one at the house of Judge Thomas Lee, near Cadiz; one at Miller's Station, by David Ward; one at Richmond, by James and William Ladd; and from here, the negroes were conducted to the home of Judge Thomas George, on Yellow creek, and then to Salem, in Columbiana county, from which point they had comparatively safe passage into British possessions."

Those who harbored fugitive slaves in those days ran great risks, the penalty being $1,000 fine, and imprisonment.

John Walker was succeeded at Unity by Rev. William Wishart, who began his ministry in September, 1847, and served until April, 1868. He was followed, November 30, 1869, by Rev. William G. Waddle.

The first meeting-house of Unity congregation was built in 1815, on the site of the present graveyard. The structure was built of round logs, and was twenty-five feet in size. It had a clap-board roof, and the whole of one end of the house was occupied by the fire-place. This building was very primitive in construction, and defective in ventilation; so that the congregation, in order to avoid the smoke, which filled the room when a fire was burning, worshipped on the outside during the winter season, whenever the weather was sufficiently mild. The second building, made this time of hewn logs, was erected in 1820. and was entered through three different door-ways. This house was built under the direction of Rev. John Walker, near the site of the present building, and was occupied by the congregation until 1833, when a third building, of brick, was erected in its stead. The brick house was fifty-five by sixty-five feet in dimensions, and it is said to have accommodated 500 worshippers. It stood until 1875, when the present frame structure was erected.

The congregation reached its greatest period of prosperity about the year 1841, under the ministrations of Rev. John Walker. At that time the membership numbered nearly two hundred and fifty persons, more than twice its present size.

CHAPTER XI.

THE EARLY CHURCHES OF CADIZ.

In taking up the history of the early churches of Cadiz, we find that some years elapsed after the town was established before any church organization was made. The Presbyterian worshippers of the community were then included in the congregation of Beech Spring, and ministered to by Rev. John Rea, who undoubtedly preached in Cadiz at private dwellings before 1810. Most of the first settlers who took up lands in the vicinity of Cadiz seem to have been of the Associate Reformed Presbyterian faith, among them being the large families of the McFaddens, Gilmores, Jamisons, and Craigs, from Washington county, Pennsylvania. The membership of this church in America is made up chiefly from descendants of the Scotch-Irish immigrants who came to America from Ulster after the close of the Revolutionary War. More than ninety per cent. of the pre-Revolutionary emigration from Ireland consisted of Presbyterians of the Old School. The later emigrants, on first coming to Pennsylvania, where their relations or friends had settled many years before, found much of the best lands taken in these older settlements. Though at first they settled in the western counties of the Keystone State, they were not satisfied with their condition, but usually took up with the earliest opportunity of bettering it. This came to them with the opening to settlement of the lands in the Northwest Territory; and it was not many months after the land office was opened at Steubenville before many of the choicest tracts in the vicinity of Cadiz were occupied by these Washington county Scotch-Irish. During the time between their removal to Harrison county, and the organization of the Associate Reformed Presbyterian Church at Cadiz, it is hardly reasonable to suppose that they were without occasional religious services. The present United Presbyterian Church of Cadiz, as of other churches of that denomination throughout the country, was formed in 1858, by the union of the two former congregations known as the Associate Presbyterian and the Associate Reformed Presbyterian churches. Prior to the formation of the Second Ohio Associate Reformed Presbytery, in 1824, Cadiz was included in the territory of the Presbytery of Monongahela, and as such was doubtless often visited and preached to by ministers belonging to that Presbytery who were residents of Washington county. And it is reasonable to assume that many of them came as missionaries before the formal organization of the congregation in 1810. The writer, not having the minutes of Monongahela Presbytery before him, is unable to give any details as to the number or frequency of these early "supplies"; but that they were provided and paid for, there is no reason to doubt. It is also very probable that a small log church building may have been erected in Cadiz township by this congregation some years before the erection of their meeting-house in Cadiz village.

We find from the records of Harrison county, that Lots numbered 58, 59, and 60 in the town of Cadiz (the present residence of Mr. A. H. Carnahan), were deeded on April 16, 1812, to "John McFadden, Samuel Carnahan, John Craig, William Hamilton, and John Jamison, trustees appointed by the Associate Reformed congregation of Cadiz," for the purpose of a meeting-house for public worship. We can therefore determine positively that prior to the date here given, this congregation was fully organized and able and ready to sustain a minister. An historical sermon was delivered by Rev. W. T. Meloy, D. D., then pastor of the United Presbyterian Church at Cadiz, on August 26, 1876, giving the history of the congregation from the time of the organization of the Associate Reformed church. This history is so full of interest, and contains so much information regarding the subject to which it relates, as to be in every way worthy of permanent preservation; and the historical part of Dr. Meloy's discourse is therefore given here in full:

THE UNITED PRESBYTERIAN CHURCH.

The Associate Reformed Presbyterian Church of Cadiz was one of the earliest mission stations west of Pennsylvania. As early as October 10th, 1810, we find them petitioning the Monongahela Presbytery for supplies. Rev. Buchanan was appointed to preach in Cadiz the 2d and 3d Sabbaths of March, 1811. Supplies were afterwards frequently sent them. June 23d, 1813, an application was made to have the Lord's Supper dispensed; Mr. Buchanan was appointed for that service, and to preside at an election of ruling elders in that society. Rev. Buchanan reported to Presbytery, the following September, that Joseph McFadden, George McFadden, William Hamilton, and Robert Orr, had been elected ruling elders. At the same meeting Revs. Riddell and Buchanan were appointed to dispense the supper at Cadiz on the fifth Sabbath of October, 1813, and to attend to the ordination of elders the preceding Friday. On the 30th of October, 1813, Joseph McFadden and Robert Orr were ordained and installed to the eldership. George McFadden declined accepting the office, and William Hamilton was absent.

November 10th, 1813, application was made for the moderation of a call by Cadiz, and Upper Wheeling, a society near Uniontown. There was, however, a connection existing between it and Lower Wheeling and Short Creek. Discretionary power was then given to Mr. Buchanan, who was, in general, to be guided by the resolution—"that, provided Lower Wheeling and Short Creek shall satisfy the member who shall be appointed to moderate, that they willingly relinquish the connection existing between them and Upper Wheeling, then, and in that case, he shall proceed to this business." The minutes of the two subsequent meetings of Presbytery were lost, and the Clerk records such business as he could recall. He forgot to record the report of Mr. Buchanan. The result, however, was, that Mr. Buchanan proceeded to moderate, and Mr. William Taggart was elected Pastor.

The first house of worship used by this congregation was a log building, erected on grounds purchased from Zachariah Biggs, situated on the corner of South and Ohio streets. The purchase price was $20. The deed for these lots is on record in Jefferson county. The log building was torn down and a substantial brick erected in 1828. This house was occupied by the congregation until 1870. Its cost cannot now be determined. It was not completed till 1833, when the pews were sold to pay for its completion. The total value of sixty-six pews was $1,812, the lowest being appraised at $10, and the highest at $40. Nearly all the pews were sold, as the amount received was $1,740.67.

The Trustees were incorporated by act of Legislature, Feb. 18, 1830, and were John McFadden, Thomas Patton, William Hamilton, David Thompson, and Thomas Bingham. William Haverfield was elected the same year, in place of Thomas Patton, deceased. The building committee were John McFadden, David Thompson, and Thomas Bingham. Mr. Bingham very often advanced money, and generally settled by taking the even hundreds and deducting the odd dollars and cents, for which, doubtless, the congregation felt duly grateful, although no record is made of their expressing it.

The building was no doubt one of the best in Cadiz, and was esteemed at the time most eligibly located. Yet why our fathers persisted in erecting store rooms and hotels on front streets and churches out of town, or on back streets, it is difficult to tell. They certainly did not advocate the penance of wading unnecessarily through the rich mud of Harrison county, on scriptural or sanitary grounds. It was the custom of the time to spend most of the Sabbath in and about the Church. The forest trees had been cleared away, where the old graveyard now is, but on every side the chestnut and oak and maple afforded a pleasant shade under which to hitch the horses, eat the Sabbath biscuit and discuss the sermon. It is even hinted that in those days there were worldly men, who talked about stock and politics, and women who discussed their neighbors' dresses, and gay young people who arranged for week night meetings that were not strictly ecclesiastical. And to that old grave-yard, now so sadly neglected, the mourner went, Bible in hand, and read over the verses on the new gray sand-stone, now fallen and broken, dropped a flower on the grave where now the briers and old ivy twine together, and with wet eyes turned again to the house of God to hear a reverend pastor tell of a Savior who is "the Resurrection and the Life." But the mourner and the mourned have met together, the grave encloses both.

As already noticed, the first pastor elected was Mr. William Taggart. He, together with Mr. Samuel Findley, had been taken under care of Presbytery as students, on Sept. 5th, 1809. He was licensed Sept. 1st, 1813. He delivered his ordination trials at Cadiz, Nov. 9, 1814. Rev. Findley preached the ordination sermon from 2d Corinthians, ii., 16, "And who is sufficient for these things;" after which Mr. Taggart was ordained to the office of the holy ministry;" and installed pastor of the united congregations of Cadiz and Upper Wheeling. He was about thirty-two years old when he began his labors here, and fifty-five when he was released. He gave to this field the years of his vigor. He was a man of very fine reasoning power. He spoke slowly, and at times with apparent hesitation, but when the discourse was completed, antecedent and consequent, premise and conclusion, were bound together by a chain that could not be broken.

It must, however, be confessed that Mr. Taggart took ample time for the elucidation of his text. His discourse never fell short of an hour, and frequently reached twice that length. The order in public worship then was to have, after the invocation prayer, the reading and explanation of the psalm. This exercise was as long as a modern sermon, and as it proceeded, more and more of the hidden beauties of Divine truth were displayed. Each thought of God is a deep, and the pastor loved to bring up its treasures, that the people might sing with full hearts. The precentor then gave out, and the people sang one line at a time. It was something of a departure to mingle bass with the air, but this was occasionally done. On communion Sabbaths, there were long debarrances made, that seemed to shut out the very elect from the table. Tokens of admission to the table were distributed on Saturday, and were brought on Sabbath to the table, where an elder received them. The male portion of the congregation carried the leaden token in the vest pocket, and the female, carefully tied up in the corner of a snow white 'kerchief, Seated upon rude slabs, the rustic sofa of the early times, Mr. Taggart spoke to the people all the words of this life. Socially he was a man of courteous though dignified demeanor, and was greatly beloved.

We must not, however, take the salary paid, or rather promised him, as the measure of the people's affection. Nominally it was $180 for half his time; yet there is a record in the full, clear hand of Thomas Patton, Clerk, that on the 11th of September, 1830, there was owing to the pastor $663.60. That is, the congregation was less than four years in arrears. On the 2d of June, 1836, we find the following record: "After a careful investigation it was found that there was a balance yet due Mr. Taggart of $1,122." On the 27th of May, 1837, this amount was reduced to $350.50. An excuse for this tardiness that was somewhat amusing, though it might be a terror to rich fathers-in-law, was, that Mr. Taggart had stock in a St. Clairsville bank and had married a rich wife. The Uniontown church took all of Mr. Taggart's time, and he removed there in 1838. On September 6th, 1865, Rev. William Taggart ceased from his labors. His body rests in the grave at St. Clairsville. This old and honored servant of God was not called to his reward until the eighty-fourth year of his age. To him the shadows had grown very long, and the rest of the evening time was sweet.

In 1838, Rev. Thomas Speer was elected pastor, but declined the call. Two hundred and fifty dollars a year was appropriated for the payment of supplies, and raised by a levy on the pews.

On the twenty-seventh of September, 1839, Rev. Parks moderated in a call which was made in favor of Rev. Alexander Wilson, his salary being fixed at $500. His labors began November 1st, 1839. Rev. William Burnett preached the sermon on this occasion, and a copy was requested by the congregation for publication.

The women of the church were not in those days supposed to have much to do with its management, as we notice that on January 25th, 1841, it was announced from the pulpit that the "male members" would detain to attend to congregational business. Possibly this may account, in part, for imperfect management, as we certainly would fail to-day without the help and counsel of our sisters. We were not surprised, therefore, to find that the congregation, six months later, appointed a committee to wait upon Mr. Wilson and inquire of him whether he would be willing to accept of $400 as his salary or stipend, after the present year. Charles Warfel, one of the members of that committee, refused to serve, and if he were living I would commend him for it. During the years 1841-42, the male members frequently met and attempted to doctor the salary, which was falling constantly behind. The arrearages were, in '41, $36.76; '42, $93.31, '43, $116.67. At last the collectors, seemingly in utter despair, resigned, and new ones were appointed. It was then resolved, November 23d, 1844, that these arrearages be assessed on the pews. To this plan there must have been serious objections, for on January 27th, 1845, this resolution was repealed.

The male members met in October, 1845, and reported the following arrearages: 1842, $93.31; '43, $109.67; '44, $181.50; '45, $384.00. A report on this subject was presented by S. McFadden, C. Warfel, and M. H. Urquhart.

Joseph Braden, Moses Urquhart, John Mitchell, James Patton, Samuel Carnahan, and David Carnahan were chosen singers, and two of them were allowed to rise at one time. The worldly business in which Mr. Wilson was constantly engaged, was some excuse for a low salary, and might have justified a petition for his release, but it was no excuse whatever for neglecting to pay a debt when it fell due.

At this time the number of families in this congregation was seventy-seven, and of communicants, 144.

In December, 1850, Mr. Wilson tendered his resignation. The congregation adopted the following, which may seem very strange, so far as the connection between the statement and resolution is concerned:

> Whereas, it is the duty of every congregation to support the pastor, and: Whereas, the said congregation has withheld from the said Alexander Wilson that support which a faithful pastor merits; therefore:
>
> Resolved, That no objections be made by the congregation to the prayer of said Petition to Presbytery.

The congregation then attempted to settle with him on the basis of $300 a year. Mr. Wilson claimed fifty dollars more, and after appealing to Presbytery, his claim was paid, and for once the congregation was free from debt.

It would indeed be difficult to tell how a pastorate, involved in such constant and harassing troubles, could be successful. The services of Mr. Wilson were doubtless rendered ineffective by them, and yet the congregation maintained its position and even advanced during his pastorate.

Two candidates were again before the congregation December 6th, 1851, some twenty-five of the "male members" being present. Rev. Thomas Cunningham received 17 votes, and James Forsythe, 8. Rev. Lorimer moderated in this call, February 24th, 1852. Rev. Cunningham having declined to be a candidate, the blank was filled by inserting the name of Rev. James C. Forsythe. He was installed October 27th, 1852. His salary was at first fixed at $500, but was afterwards raised to $600.

A meeting was called October 31st, 1857, to regulate the singing of the congregation, at which the clerk was directed to stand at the pulpit rather than in the center of the house, the vote being 40 to 25. It was also decided, by a vote of 50 to 15, that the psalm should be sung without lining out. Gradually the old land marks that had arisen with the necessities of the time, faded away; they filled their purpose; and while these customs were dear to many, they yielded to the claims of the present, and were willing to give up all but the principles which as a church they had maintained. The pastorate of Rev. Forsythe was brief. He resigned April, 1858.

The congregation enjoyed considerable prosperity under his ministry; and with the union of the two churches, the Associate Reformed Congregation of Cadiz ceased to exist.

We now return to the other branch of this church.

THE ASSOCIATE CONGREGATION OF CADIZ

was organized A. D. 1813. Its first place of worship was a "tent," which had been pitched a short distance north-west of the present depot of the P., C. & St. L. R. R. This tent was a house of worship for the pastor alone. It was about six or eight feet square, was reached by high steps, was under a roof that fell off to each side, and was boarded up in front to about the height of the pastor's waist. The congregation sat outside on logs, and benches made of split timbers, under the shade of the trees. If it did not rain or storm they experienced no inconvenience. A slight rain did not spoil our mothers' bonnets. In the winter, services were held in the court house or in private houses of members. The location of the tent was finally changed to a part of Mr. Grimes' farm, nearer town, where afterwards a brick church was erected. It does not appear that there was entire unanimity about the new church. The first resolution in regard to it was adopted May 7th, 1827, at a meeting of which John Miller was chairman, and James Lee, clerk.

> Resolved, That this congregation take up a subscription to build a brick meeting-house, sixty feet long and forty feet wide.

The following January a motion was lost that the ground then occupied be sold and the house built on a lot owned by George Craig. It was, however, ordered, that "the trustees have discretionary power as to the size of the meeting house, according to the funds subscribed." A second resolution was "to see what additional funds could be raised, provided the house would be built on George Craig's lot;" an expedient which, resorted to some forty years later, secured the present location of our church. At a subsequent meeting it was determined not to build on Craig's lot, not to build a house in connection with the Union congregation, and that the house should be one story.

On the first of January, 1830, the fifty-eight pews were appraised, the values ranging from $2.25 to $7.50, the whole value, $275.50. The largest subscriber was to have the first choice. No pew was to be sold for less than its appraised value. No person could purchase more than two pews nor less than one. The minister's salary was to be assessed by a regular per centum on the pews so sold. In case any one refused or neglected to pay his assessment, three months grace was to be given him, and if not paid at that time, the pew was to be offered for sale to make up the deficiency. In case it did not sell, the pew was to become the property of the congregation. It was further made the duty of the trustees to raise what money they could from those not purchasing pews, in order to lighten the assessment on purchasers, until all the congregation, or those subscribing, shall have obtained pews. It will readily appear how, under such financial management, this congregation would be kept out of debt. There is nothing in the records to show that they were ever seriously troubled. Occasionally they got in arrears, but prompt measures were taken to remedy this. How much more the Word preached would profit under such circumstances. There was no action taken but such as was based on principles of fairness and honor. A good financial pilot was at the helm. Shrewd business ideas prevailed then as now. In a slip torn from a will which had been written at that time and was used to mark the page in the congregational book, I find the following bequest of Mr. W———, of Bloomfield: "I will and bequeath my big brass clock to whichever of my sons-in-law will give the most for it." But as that was only a book-mark of the clerk, it would not be fair to hold the congregation responsible for it.

This church was not well located. The site was low, much lower at that time than is indicated now. Arrangements for ventilation were not much cared for in those days, and had not been needed when worshipping at the tent. Many a good sermon has been spoiled by bad air. In June, 1847, a new and violent form of disease suddenly appeared among the flock. From what we can learn from the symptoms of this fatal disease, it was the typhoid fever. No such name was then known, and, as it was at first confined entirely to members of this congregation, it was universally called the "Seceder fever." Many of the members died from it, among whom was the amiable wife of the pastor. This disease spread throughout the country, and showed equal violence when preying on the members of other churches and upon heretics. Many of those attacked died. The physicians, ignorant of its nature, in some cases, resorted to that old foe of human life—the lancet, and aided the disease in quickly reducing the sufferer. The angel of death brooded over many homes, and the mourners were often met on the streets. It is impossible to tell certainly the cause of this malady. It was asserted that a stranger who had contracted the disease abroad, was that Sabbath a worshipper, and that there was a pool of water under the church. This was denied. Some light is gained by a bill which I find for digging the earth from about the church. Impure air must have given rise to the disease, and this may have resulted from a full house with too limited a supply of fresh air and too much of what had been de-oxodyzed a score of times. The miasmatic influence was in the air, and may have arisen from physical causes not even guessed at, as has often been the case since. The house was blamed, and whether guilty or not, it was well that suspicion attached to it. It never had been comfortable. Members of the congregation attended services as usual, but strangers sought some other place of worship. It was therefore resolved soon after to build a new meeting house, forty-five by fifty-five feet, and a committee was appointed to select a site. A committee was also appointed to find how much more funds could be raised to build in town than on the present lot. Lot numbered 103, on Steubenville street, was purchased from William Reid for $200, and a frame house, yet standing, was erected thereon. Part of the material of the old church was put in the foundation of this building. This house was occupied until the time of the union of the churches, when it was sold to Mrs. Hatcher, for $1,400.

This congregation was organized about 1813, though occasional sermons had been preached here before. The first record is Oct. 1st, 1814. "The Rev. John Walker accepted the call of and took charge of said congregation." He was installed sometime between the 24th of May and the 4th of July, 1815, and was at the time twenty-nine years of age. His time was divided between Mt. Pleasant, Unity, and Cadiz. The installation occurred at Unity. Revs. French and Allison were appointed to this duty, but Mr. Allison was prevented from attending. Thomas Maxwell was ruling elder. The winter following, William Braden was installed, and Joseph Braden ordained to that office. The roll of the congregation rapidly increased under Mr. Walker's labors. But, alas! poor human nature. Discipline soon had to be exercised against offenders. Greater and lesser offences were strangely combined in the early discipline of the church. The first offence was intoxication. The offender was rebuked, and notification given to the congregation. The friends of the next accused, will pardon me for naming her—"Mrs. Agnes Crossen confessed her sorrow for violating the laws of the church and breaking her own vows, in that she was married without publication." She was accordingly admonished—possibly not to fall into the same offence again, which she was not likely to do while her husband lived—and then restored to church privileges. The musters of the time were fruitful causes of offence, also the huskings and choppings. Any one who sets up the claim that there was no drunkenness at that time, need only read over the session records.

Rev. John Walker, the first pastor of this church, was, in many respects, a remarkable man, and was esteemed a preacher of great ability. His utterances were easy and rapid. With a quickness of perception, he knew well to say the right thing in the right place. His manners outside the pulpit were agreeable and easy. Outside of his profession he was shrewd and active. He was instrumental in securing the location of Franklin College at New Athens, and would have gone forty miles on horse or foot to secure a student for that institution. He was a good physician, and had an extensive practice; and, as he looked after both the souls and bodies of his hearers without receiving much pecuniary compensation, he became very popular, and was widely known. He conformed to the custom of his time and preached sermons of immoderate length.

To this day there are some who delight to tell how long the services were at the Tent. This was signally so on Communion Sabbath, when there was the most minute examination of heart and life. The offences of the time were most severely denounced, and the man who had tossed a copper, marked the ashes with a stick, or resorted to any similar form of divination, did not go unwarned. The weightiest matters, too, were not neglected. Persons who grew tired of sitting, rested themselves by standing. The Sabbath evening examination on the shorter catechism properly belonged to exercises of the day. To criticise a sermon, or comment on the dress, manners, or bearing of the minister, would have been esteemed a serious offence. The people carried their Bibles, and committed the text, and the older members of the family were questioned about the introduction, divisions, and application. Dr. Walker was released about 1820, and gave his entire time to Unity. He died March 8th, 1845, in the sixtieth year of his age, and thirty-sixth of his ministry. His body rests in the cemetery at Unity, and on his tombstone are the words: "Remember ye not, that when I was yet with you I told you these things!"

Mr. Thomas Hanna accepted a call to Cadiz, Piney Fork, and Wills Creek, and was ordained as pastor, December 16th, 1821. The number of families in the Cadiz church at this time was forty-one, in Piney Fork, thirty-eight, and in Wills Creek, fourteen. He was soon after released from the Wills Creek branch. In 1835 his whole time was given to Cadiz.

At the time of Mr. Hanna's settlement, the session consisted of Robert, Henry, and Thomas Maxwell, James Alexander, William Henderson, and James and Thomas Lee. William Miller and Richard Hammond were ordained, and James Hanna installed June 19th, 1834. Francis Grove was installed, and Matthew Clark was ordained and installed, May 11th, 1837. Dr. Hanna was not a fine pulpit orator, nor was he regarded as a profound theologian. He was, however, a very instructive preacher. His sermons were often so systematically and minutely divided that one who took away the divisions carried the whole sermon. He had a very kind heart and was eminently sympathetic. It became convenient for him to live in Washington, Pa., owing to his marriage with Miss Foster, then, and for many years after, the honored Principal of the Washington Female Seminary. He was released April 24th, 1849. Dr. Hanna took charge of the church in Washington in May, 1850, and continued as pastor until physical prostration compelled him to give up the field. He died February 9th, 1864, in the sixty fourth year of his age, and the forty-third of his ministry. His memory is fondly cherished by his people.

There were many offenders against the law and order of the church during his pastorate, and there was not one meeting of the session in six that did not have one or more persons arraigned. Intemperance was doubtless the prevailing evil. But it was often the case that persons felt encouraged in carrying complaints to the session, just as children do to a parent or teacher. One man, when riding to Cadiz, had boasted with an oath, that he could ride down all the Whig horses in the county; occasional hearing; marrying without publication; shooting **for pennies**; dancing; neglect of ordinances; unfair dealing; cutting bee trees; teaching on fast days; with an occasional sin of a graver nature, occupied most of the session's time. The cases seemed to grow the more they were dealt with, until the 7th of April, 1848, the following committees were appointed: Robert Maxwell and Thomas Lee were appointed a committee to confer with three persons, whose names I withhold, for occasional hearing; James Hanna, a committee to confer with three others about attending a ball; William Henderson, a committee to confer with W. W—— and wife, for neglect of ordinances; and Matthew Clark, a committee to confer with J. D. B—— for the same offence. A large amount of business, truly, for one day. The church militant was rapidly earning the title of the church litigant. Discipline, however, in most cases was effective, and the erring were brought back. The membership of the church constantly increased, and its spiritual condition was healthy.

On the 5th of June, 1839, Thomas Lee presented the following:

> Resolved, That all members of the Secession Church who approve of a resolution passed at a political meeting, held in Cadiz on the 15th day of May, A. D., 1839, approving of the course pursued by the State and National Administration on the subject of abolition, are guilty of a breach of the moral law, and the principles of the Secession Church.

The vote on this resolution stood, ayes four, noes four. The moderator asked time to decide. A month later he cast his vote in the negative. A month later the vote was reconsidered, and the resolution adopted. An appeal from this was taken by Robert Maxwell. The whole matter was finally referred to Synod. The Church had already seen the "impending crisis," and was preparing for the noble stand she afterwards took and maintained on the day of our nation's trial.

The Solemn Covenant engagement to duties is also recorded, although the date is not given. It was about 1840. There are but seven persons members of this church at the present time who joined in it. The scene must have been one of deep solemnity when the congregation, with uplifted hands, swore to live for Christ. A single sentence of this lengthy engagement will suffice: "We do, with our hands lifted up to the Most High God, hereby confess, and before God, angels, and men, solemnly declare, that we desire to give glory to the Lord by believing with the heart; confessing with the mouth; and subscribing with the hand, that in Him we have righteousness and strength."

The congregation was vacant about a year, when Rev. J. R. Doig was called, and became pastor in May, 1850. He was never installed, owing to a neglect on the part of Presbytery. He had supplied the congregation during the preceding winter, in the absence of Dr. Hanna, who was most of his time in Washington with his new wife. When, therefore, Dr. Hanna resigned in the spring, Mr. Doig was ready to take his place. He was at that time a professor in Franklin College, and continued to reside in Athens. His work, therefore, could not have been so effective as it otherwise would have been.

Mr. Doig, in the fall of '51, was taken ill, and remained so during the entire year. This, together with the death of his partner, induced him to resign, after having held a last communion with his people.

Rev. Samuel Patton was the next pastor. He was ordained and installed December, 1853. His relations with the people are said to have been pleasant, although he was not here long enough for his labors to be deeply impressed on the minds of the people, or to gain a lasting place in their memories and hearts. Two causes may have led to his early removal. He married in the congregation, and possibly imagined that what is true of a prophet is also true of his wife. He had preached at Detroit before settling at Cadiz, and the people there desiring his return, he accepted their call, and was released July 12th, 1854. His pastorate lasted only a little over six months. He labored but a short time in Detroit, when the Master called him home to an early reward.

For about two years the congregation depended on supplies, and but few records were kept to show either its spiritual or financial condition. Mr. J. S. McCready was ordained and installed as pastor, August 7th, 1856. He soon gained a deep hold on the affections of his people. He was kind and unobstrusive in his manners, courteous in his bearing, yet firm as a rock in his convictions. His preaching largely partook of these characteristics, and was of a kind to set forth the truth in both its attractiveness and strength. He had early imbibed an abhorrence of oppression, and showed by his conduct the sincerity of his faith. The religious instruction of the colored children of Cadiz had been neglected. He organized, and during his ministry superintended, their Sabbath School.

The Universalists had for some years gained a foot-hold in Cadiz. In 1857, Mr. McCready was challenged to discuss the question by an able debater named Emmet, who had often been engaged in discussions of this kind. The debate began Tuesday morning, and closed Friday evening. A writer who was familiar with the debate, says: "The truth was not only vindicated, but rendered triumphant. The Universalists were repelled, routed, and overcome."

They have not had a single sermon in Cadiz since.

Meantime, the two churches, whose separate history we have been tracing, were growing more closely together. Unkind words and acts had been hidden away under the sacred mantle of charity. It was even hinted that the churches were already one—one in worship and in heart, and so nearly one in faith that but few were able to tell the difference between them. There were over-cautious ones who deprecated union, over-timid ones who deplored it. God's time had come. The two streams were to flow in one, and to be so commingled that the separate source of either could not be traced. The Associate Synod was meeting in Pittsburgh, and the Associate Reformed in Allegheny City, on the 26th of May, 1858. The vote on union had carried in the Union Synod. Great anxiety was felt about the result in the Seceder Synod. It was also carried there. The union was complete. A few discontented spirits still sought to maintain the Associate Church, but they had not the force of head or heart of a Marshall or a Clarkson, and no recruits could now come from over the water. Their numbers, small at first, are now less than 1,200. The United Presbyterian Church, pledged to maintain the truth and forbear in love, continued to bear forward the history of the illustrious ones whose bans had been proclaimed.

This cause in Cadiz found itself now with two congregations, two houses of worship, and one pastor, Rev. Forsythe having resigned. A basis of union between the two congregations was agreed upon. Each congregation was to choose three of its members, who were to constitute the Board of Trustees. The church was to be called the "First United Presbyterian Congregation of Cadiz." The trustees of the Associate congregation were to transfer all their property to the new Board. The United Church was to occupy the brick house, and the pews in it were to be forever free. Each congregation was to have an equal number of elders. The United Congregation was to meet on the last Saturday of March to ask for the moderation of a call. These conditions were signed by Andrew Jamison and John McFadden, on the part of the Union Church, February 20th, 1859, and by Martin Wilson and John Carnahan, on the part of the Seceder Church, February 26, 1859. In accordance with these propositions, the Seceder church building was sold to Eliza Hatcher for $1,400, and the congregation worshipped in the old Union Church. The elders of the Seceder Church were Alexander Haverfield, William Miller, John Carnahan, Daniel Mitchell, and Thomas Jamison —five. Those of the Union Church were Joshua Hamilton, Robert Davidson, and Charles Warfel—three. Andrew Jamison and James C. Love were elected to make the number equal. Mr. Love was installed, but Mr. Jamison declined to serve.

Rev. McCready demitted his charge April 19th, 1859. On the 3d of the following May a call was unanimously made for his services by the First U. P. Congregation of Cadiz. This call was accepted on the 14th of the following June. The congregation seemed now to enter on a career of unbounded prosperity. But already the dark shadow of civil war was beginning to fall on our country. The aggressions of the slave power were felt. This church had always, in the branches from which it came, denounced slavery. But now, alas! its extension became largely a political issue. On this subject our church gave no uncertain sound. Rev. McCready had not waited to be an abolitionist until slavery was overthrown. He was not one of those braves who stab the dead Percy. He was a patriot; and was willing to seal with his blood the testimony of his lips. He entered the Union army, August 14th, 1862, as Captain of Company H, 126th O. V. I. Two months later he wrote to his congregation: "Your pulpit was not silent in regard to those sins which have convulsed the land. Nor did it give an uncertain, non-committal sound, taking its cue from the dictation of party politics. It was 'known and read of all men.' Seven years ago, when thousands of statesmen and divines who are now with it, were against it, it preached what it preaches today, and what all the pulpits are coming rapidly to preach. It had not to be impelled by divine judgments. To these truths, which I have preached to you, dear brethren, if I fall in this struggle, I am a martyr. But for their influence, I had not been here. My home was as dear, my life as sweet, my congregation as near to me as others are to them. As for official promotion, I was stepping down. As for money, I am probably losing. Besides, what is money, compared with life and home comforts?

"But you and I had raised up a standard for God's truth. We stood up for its divinity. We had talked—the time came to act. God demanded sacrifice in its behalf. The clergy of the South had shown how much they were willing to dare for this error—this great self-evident lie—this blot upon civilization—this outrage upon all religion, and all virtue. God put the question to us: Were we willing to do and dare as much for truth, for liberty, for country? What could I reply? I may fall! your beloved sons and brothers may fall! Be it so. Our testimony in behalf of God's truth is not lost. You will reap the benefit of it in future years."

As such letters from the absent soldier pastor were read, feeling in the congregation ran high, and some refused to hear them at all. Others, who had sons and brothers and husbands with him, were indignant at this, and for a time the peace of the congregation was much disturbed. C. L. Vallandingham was nominated for Governor of Ohio in 1863, by the Democratic party. He was at the time banished for disloyalty, and was stopping at the Clifton House, in Canada. The following resolutions were passed by the Session:

Resolved, That it is utterly inconsistent with the principles of the United Presbyterian Church to vote for C. L. Vallandingham for Governor of Ohio.

Resolved, That we consider that voting for that candidate involves a great moral question, and that no member of the United Presbyterian Church can vote for him without ignoring his principles on slavery and countenancing and encouraging disloyalty.

These resolutions were read on the 27th of September. Rev. McCready obtained leave of absence and came home soon after. He moderated the Session, and dispensed the Supper Oct. 17th, 1863. It would have been strange if he, fresh from the field of battle, where his brave boys then were (save those who had fallen), could have been silent. He was not wont to conceal his convictions of the truth. Thirteen families and a large number of adherents withdrew from the church. A few of these never formed any ecclesiastical connection, but most of them were received into the communion of the Presbyterian church of Cadiz. It was my privilege to meet Mr. McCready after his return from the army.

He talked of the field at home but spoke no words of bitterness. Doubtless he would have suffered more had it not been a time when such mighty emotions were swaying the hearts of men. In the army, Captain McCready was the same in modesty, candor, firmness, bravery, and courtesy, that he was at home. His company, brave as any in the army, united with him in daily prayers to the God of battles. On the 6th day of May, 1864, Mr. McCready was wounded in the left arm during one of the terrible battles of the Wilderness. He was carried from the field, taken to Washington, and finally died in Baltimore, at the house of Mr. Carson, Sept. 7th. His end was peace.

The church was draped in mourning. All classes wept for him. Even those who had spoken harshly, now spoke with broken utterance. But no sincerer mourners gathered about his bier than the colored men whose constant friend he had been. He, of all the ministers who served this church, is the only one who died while its pastor.

On the night of the 31st of December, 1864, your present pastor arrived in Cadiz to fill, by arrangement, the appointment of Rev. Mr. McKenzie. Another brother had been secured to preach, but generously refused when he heard that I was present. But as he was paid the regular per diem for listening to me, I did not feel that he was greatly injured.

The appearance of the house was not in the least prepossessing. The arched ceiling had been painted blue, and an occasional board had partly broken loose from its fastenings and threatened to drop, like the famous sword of Damocles. The pulpit had come down from its original height, but was still reached by a flight of stairs—about eight in number. An ill-fitting window was directly at the back of the little pulpit-box, and an occasional blast of wind from the north reminded me that there was a broken pane in it. The day was unpleasant and the congregation small. A slight survey of the audience convinced me that there were many earnest and intelligent men and women among them.

I preached twice afterwards, and in the early spring was elected pastor. The entire congregation united in the call. My regular labors began the third Sabbath of May, 1865. I was ordained and installed June 23d, 1865, by the Presbytery of Wheeling. Rev. Campbell preached the sermon from 2d Cor. v., 20.

The congregation was at the time somewhat discouraged. Withdrawals had been frequent. The salary promised was $800. It was, after six years, generously raised to $1,200. It was still the custom to preach two sermons on Sabbath, with a half hour's interval. Changes, however, had been made. The word "male" had disappeared from the record of our proceedings, and the singing was led by a choir, most of whom were ladies. The excuse for this was that the young men of the congregation had generally gone to the army. The Sabbath School was re-organized, and Charles Warfel elected Superintendent. The Session consisted of Joshua Hamilton, Daniel Mitchell, Alexander Haverfield, John

Carnahan, and Charles Warfel. Robert Paxton and Alexander Campbell were ordained and installed May 11th, 1866; J. D. Osburn and Samuel Kyle, May 22d, 1868, at which time Ebenezer McKitrick was installed. T. C. Grove and James Megaw were ordained and installed Nov. 8th, 1873.

The propriety of erecting a new church had been considered for some time. The first meeting was held in 1867. The proposition was discussed at some length, and with considerable warmth, and was voted down by an overwhelming majority. Subsequent meetings were held, at which it was argued that the church was needing repairs; that in a few years a new one must be built; that the present one could not be made comfortable; that it was located at such a distance from the main street that it would not be possible to keep a good pavement to it; that money was plenty, and the congregation abundantly able to build. It was argued on the other hand that the old church could be repaired at a very slight cost; that although money was plenty, building materials were high; and that the present location was eligible, affording ample hitching room for the horses. The advocates of the new church constantly gained in number, until finally in the fall of 1868, a committee to solicit subscriptions was appointed. The congregation subscribed liberally. About $7,000 was raised, and there was nearly $2,000 in the treasury remaining from the sale of the Associate church. It was finally determined to build on a lot adjoining the church property on Steubenville street. This lot was purchased and additional subscriptions taken. Many of the congregation, however, had talked about the present location. But Mrs. McNutt still occupied rooms in the old hotel located on it, and was, in her infirmity of mind and body, unwilling to remove. She died about this time (January, 1869). A meeting of the congregation was called. The matter was left in the hands of a committee, and $4,000 additional was subscribed on condition that the new church be located on the McNutt lot. This lot was purchased for $3,200. The congregation had now six lots, and the jest was made that they were going into the real estate business. The transaction, however, was carefully managed. The old church property was sold for $2,500, and the lot first purchased, at an advance of $100. The old buildings were also sold, and work on the new church commenced. As it progressed, changes were made in the original plan. The ladies had joined in the work and raised a considerable sum with which to carpet and cushion the house. The children also helped. The people had a mind to the work. Comfortable stalls were erected for the horses.

The basement of the church was occupied in the spring of 1870. As the work neared completion, a proposal was made to sell the pews and stalls. To this there was earnest opposition. An effort was made to raise the balance, but failed. The pews were then appraised. The lowest valued at $10 and the highest at $100. The total appraised value was $2,700. The pews were all sold, and also the stalls.

The building committee consisted of John C. Jamison, Walter Craig,

W. L. Hamilton, Andrew Jamison, William Hamilton, Sr., and David Cunningham. Their work was done to the entire satisfaction of the congregation, and was a standing evidence of fine business management. The Ladies' Mite Society contributed $2,000. The church was dedicated on Thursday, Nov. 24th, 1870 (Thanksgiving Day).

The congregation has suffered heavily from removals. Joshua Hamilton, one of the oldest members of Session, removed to Springfield. His loss was deeply felt, as also the removal of the younger members, Alexander Campbell and Samuel Kyle. Death, too, has greatly thinned our roll. Dr. Wilson, a man who had been eminently useful in the church, who had been a power in its meetings for prayer, was gathered home January 10th, 1872, aged 87 years. Our hearts were again made sad by the sudden death, from typhoid fever, of Elder C. Warfel, whose name had often appeared on our records. He was at the time a ruling elder and trustee, and had long and efficiently superintended the Sabbath School. He died February 2, 1871. His remains were taken to the church, which was thronged with the congregation and friends, among whom were many colored people, to whom he had been a constant friend.

Alexander Haverfield was, after a few months' illness, released from earthly labors January 24th, 1875. His death made a breach in the Session which could not be easily filled. He had long been a devoted friend to the congregation, and was a man of large religious information.

On the 11th of August, 1876, Daniel Mitchell died. He was one of the oldest members of the Session, and a man of irreproachable character. He was conscientiously regular in the observance of religious ordinances.

Of the history of our church in Cadiz no one need be ashamed, while all her true children may rejoice in it. I have neither sought to magnify the virtues nor palliate the faults of our fathers. One loved pastor fell in the great struggle for the life of our country and the freedom of a race. From her communion there went forth as heralds of the Gospel such men as Hans W. Lee, Thomas B. Hanna, and John B. Clark, who, though early called from earth, held places second to none in the churches, and in the affections of the people. A daughter of one of the early and earnest men of this church is pointing the sisters in Egypt to the Lamb of Calvary.

CHAPTER XII.

THE EARLY CHURCHES OF CADIZ.—Continued.

While the Associate Reformed congregation was doubtless the first regularly organized religious society in Cadiz, it is probable the citizens were first ministered to by the Presbyterian minister at Beech Spring—Rev. John Rea. He is said to have preached his first sermon in Cadiz in 1804, standing under the shade of a large forest tree, which stood on the site of the present court-house. At this time, it is thought, there were but two buildings in the village, namely, Garret Glazener's blacksmith shop, and a log dwelling-house.

THE PRESBYTERIAN CHURCH.

The first mention of Cadiz, as a separate congregation on the records of the Presbytery of Ohio, appears under date of Wednesday, June 11th, 1816. The Presbytery having met at Raccoon, in Washington county, Pa., applications for supplies were made from Cadiz and Freeport. Mr. Joseph Stevenson was appointed to preach at Cadiz on the second Sabbath of July, and Elisha Macurdy one Sabbath at his discretion. Rev. John Rea was appointed to supply at Freeport on the first Sabbath of July. The Presbytery met again at the same place on October 15th, 1816, and applications for supplies were again received from Cadiz and from Freeport. On the following day, " Mr. [John] Munson, a licentiate from Presbytery of Hartford [Ohio], was granted leave to itinerate, and ordered to supply Cadiz the fourth Sabbath of October, and Freeport, the first Sabbath of January." Rev. Moses Allen was directed to preach at Cadiz on the second Sabbath of December, and John Rea, one Sabbath at discretion. Rev. Joseph Anderson was likewise appointed to preach at Freeport on the third Sabbath of November; and Andrew Gwinn, at Cadiz, on the second Sabbath of November. From this time on, supplies seem to have been sent as frequently as Presbytery could furnish them, until the installation of a regular minister.

The following account of this church is taken from an historical sermon delivered by Dr. W. P. Shrom at Cadiz, on August 21st, 1884:

If the records to which we have had access are correct, there was but one white family living within the limits of what is now Harrison county previous to the year 1799. This was the family of Mr. Daniel Peterson, and his place of residence was at the forks of Short creek. During the year 1799, Mr. Alexander Henderson and his family moved into this vicinity from Washington county, Pennsylvania. In the following year immigration set in, chiefly from western Pennsylvania, and the ancestors of a large portion of the present inhabitants made this region their home—the names of Craig, Jamison, McFadden, and others being almost as familiar then as now.

The immigration was evidently very rapid, for in 1820 the population of the county is given at 14,345, and in 1830 at 20,920, while the population as given in the census of 1880 is only 20,455, being less than that given in 1830 by 465.

The county was organized in 1813 from portions being struck off from Tuscarawas and Jefferson counties. The town of Cadiz was laid out in 1803 or 1804, by Messrs. Biggs and Beatty. The present ground was then covered by a heavy forest, and inhabited by the Indian and such wild animals as abounded in this region. The town was laid out at this precise point because of its being the junction of two roads— the one from Pittsburg via Steubenville, and the other from Washington, Pennsylvania, via Wellsburg, leading to Zanesville. Before the building of the National Pike, this was the chief thoroughfare through the State from east to west. Very early in the history of the settlement of this county, attention was given to the organization and building of churches. The first church built in this region was what is still familiarly known as Beech Spring Church, one mile west of the eastern boundary line of this county. Its first building was a small log structure which was destroyed by fire. This was succeeded by a larger one, holding 1,000 people, and was the center to which all Presbyterians tended from a wide range of country. It was at one period the largest Presbyterian church in this State, numbering upwards of 400 members. The Rev. John Rea became pastor of this church in 1804, at which time what is now Cadiz, was regarded as in the central portion of his parish. His first sermon in this immediate vicinity was preached in 1805 in a private house. As was then the custom, he continued to preach at different points in his large parish, and this region became one of these preaching points. The services were generally held on Sabbath afternoons or evenings in private houses or in the log school-house, as was most convenient. This continued until the spring of 1817, when, under the direction of the Presbytery of Ohio, with Mr. Rea as chairman of the committee, the Presbyterian Church of Cadiz was organized.

In his historic sketches, Mr. Rea says: "I first saw the ground on which Cadiz is now located, in 1804, when the place now occupied by the court-house and other public buildings, was a forest of oak, walnut, and sugar trees." Mr. Rea continued to preach after the organization of the church, as stated supply until 1820. The history of the church from its organization is a little more difficult to trace, from the fact that the early records of the church have been lost. The earliest sessional record we have been able to find is June 18, 1831—so that fourteen years of the most valuable records are wanting.

The church was organized under Ohio Presbytery, and was for a time under its care. Then in 1819 the Presbytery of Steubenville was struck off by order of the synod of Pittsburg, and this church then belonged to that Presbytery until 1839, when the Presbytery of St. Clairsville was organized, under whose care the church is at this time.

In Steubenville records of 1820, Cadiz church appears with several others—the last on the list as "vacant, not able." The same record occurs in 1821, with the addition that Obediah Jennings, of Steubenville First Church, was appointed to preach at Cadiz. At a meeting of the Presbytery, held April 16, 1822, at Two Ridges, Matthew McCoy appeared before Presbytery, and presented a call for the pastoral services of Mr. Donald McIntosh, and was granted permission to prosecute the call before the Presbytery of Ohio, of which he was then a licentiate. The call was accepted, and Mr. McIntosh was ordained and installed pastor of this church, October 17th, 1822, Rev. Obediah Jennings preaching the sermon, and Rev. John Rea delivering the charge (whether to people or pastor is not stated).

Rev. Donald McIntosh was the first pastor that served this church. He was born in Aberdeen, Scotland, but came to this country early in life, and graduated in his collegiate course at Jefferson College, in the year 1817, and was licensed to preach the gospel by the Presbytery of Ohio.

He continued to serve the church as pastor until 1826, when the pastoral relation was dissolved on account of ill-health. Mr. McIntosh then returned to the State of New York, and from there he went to Florida, in 1828, where he died in 1830. Thus early in life the first pastor passed away to his eternal rest and reward.

The second pastor was the Rev. John McArthur. He was born March 25, 1803, in Argyle, Washington county, N. Y. He removed to Ohio in 1819, took the degree of A. B. at Jefferson College in September, 1825, and was licensed to preach by the Presbytery of Hartford, October 3, 1827, then in session at New Lisbon, and was ordained and installed pastor of the united charge of the Ridge and Cadiz churches—in the former Nov. 19, and in the latter Nov. 20, 1828, and continued until October 3d, 1837, when his relation was dissolved by the Presbytery of Steubenville. Mr. McArthur then removed to Miami University, and entered upon the duties of a Professorship in the Greek language, to which he had been elected, and for twelve years he taught in this university, and preached to a small congregation until his death, which occurred in 1849.

The third pastor was Rev. James Kerr. He was born Dec. 23, 1805, in the county of Wigton, Scotland. He emigrated to America in 1832. He finished his education at the University of Glasgow, was licensed to preach by the Presbytery of Baltimore, April 27, 1836, and was ordained as an evangelist by the Presbytery of Winchester, April 22d, 1837, and labored in Hampshire county, Virginia, until July 15th, 1838, and being invited he visited the Church of Cadiz as a candidate, and in due time received a call and was installed pastor, May 6th, 1839, by the Presbytery of St. Clairsville, and remained sixteen years the incumbent of said office until his death, which occurred April 19, 1855.

The fourth pastor was the Rev. William M. Grimes, who was born at Crabapple, Belmont county, Ohio, September 15th, 1821. He took the degree of A. B. at Franklin College in September, 1844, was licensed to preach the gospel by the Presbytery of St. Clairsville on the 18th day of April, 1850, and was ordained and installed pastor by the same Presbytery in the Church of Concord, November 20th, and in the Church of Beallsville—the one-half of his time in each place—and remained in this field of labor about six years. A call from the Church of Cadiz, Ohio, was presented in the Presbytery of St. Clairsville for the ministerial labor of the Rev. William Grimes, and after considerable discussion, the pastoral relation between Mr. Grimes and the Churches of Concord and Beallsville was dissolved on June 17th, 1856, with a view of his accepting the call from Cadiz, and he was installed pastor of this church in October, 1856, by the Presbytery of St. Clairsville. A call from the First Church of Steubenville, Ohio, was presented before the Presbytery of St. Clairsville for the ministerial labors of the Rev. William M. Grimes, and the pastoral relation between the Rev. William M. Grimes and the First Church of Cadiz was dissolved on January 25th, 1876, after a pastorate of over nineteen years. Very much might in truth and justice be said about each of these pastoral relations, but especially the last. Its unusually happy relations of pastor and people—the unusual results—all would be sufficient reason for continued remark. But we deem it best to leave this for future occasion, your own familiarity with this portion of the pastoral history making this the less necessary.

The fifth pastor was the Rev. Robert Dickson, called September 18, 1876. Mr. Dickson was born in County Down, Ireland, in 1818, and was educated at Belfast Royal College. The first nine years of his ministry were spent in Ireland. He came to the United States in 1850, and continued his ministry in Pennsylvania and Ohio. He served a term during the war, as Chaplain of the 100th Pennsylvania Regiment. He was called from the Second Presbyterian Church of New Albany, to take the pastoral charge of the church in Cadiz, and continued at this place until 1881, when he was called to Clifton, Ohio. The church was without a regular pastor for about two years following.

Your recent pastor is the sixth in order. The installment took place on the 14th day of June, 1883. What the results will be remain to be seen.

There have been since the organization of the church thirty elders elected, of whom ten are now living, and constitute the present session. The first were Matthew McCoy, John Hanna, and William Ramsay, who seemed to have been elected at the time of organizing the church. [Among other early elders were Robert McCullough, John Megaw, and Peter Barger]. Most of these have been men who have left a good record, and whose influence is seen and felt to this day in the church and in the community.

I have not been able to secure either the names or the number of those who composed the church at the time of its organization, except three elders already named. But previous to the pastorate of Mr. Kerr, there had been 323 identified with the church. During his pastorate, 279 were added. During the pastorate of Dr. William M. Grimes 664 were added. During the pastorate of Dr. Dickson, 146. Since the dissolution of his pastorate, 52 have been added, making a total membership of 1,464, of whom far the larger part have passed from the church militant to the church triumphant, and we trust uniting with the former pastors in praising God in the upper sanctuary—464 remain, while many are scattered to every quarter and some are holding places of responsibility and trust in other churches. Two at least are preaching the Gospel to other churches.

The ground on which the present church building stands was purchased from Daniel Kilgore for a consideration of $150.

There have been two church buildings on the ground. The first was built about 1831 or 1832. It was a large building for the time, with galleries on three sides, and was built at a cost of about $5,000 or $6,000. The money was raised for building by subscription, and paid partly in money and partly in labor. The brick work was done by John Pepper, and the wood work by Mr. Robinson. Before the erection of this building the services were held in the Court House and in private houses, and also in the Associate Reformed Church.

With the building of the present church you are all too familiar to need any word from me. It was dedicated May 25th, 1871, the sermon being preached by Dr. S. J. Wilson, of Allegheny Seminary, the house costing about $40,000.

The method of ministerial support in those early times was quite liberal, as compared with the cost of living. Subscriptions were sometimes made partly in money and partly in produce.

EARLY CHURCHES OF CADIZ 161

At its organization in 1820, the church had to receive support from the committee of Domestic Missions, which then composed the present board of Home Missions.

It has not in the past been forgetful of and will not in the future forget its debt of gratitude to this agency of the church, for helping new and growing churches in the days of their infancy and necessary financial weakness. The church has had two seasons of special revival, —one in 1840 under the ministry of Rev. James Kerr, when many were awakened and converted, and another beginning in 1865 and continuing for two years, during which time 120 persons united with the church. This was under the ministry of Dr. Grimes.

THE METHODIST EPISCOPAL CHURCH*

was established in Harrison county as early as the year 1801. The first Methodist emigrants settled on the south branch of Short creek, and consisted of Joseph Holmes, Samuel Humes, William Walraven, Isaac Buskirk, and others. Soon after, Thomas Dickerson came from Redstone, Fayette county, Pennsylvania, and cleared some land and built a cabin near the settlement. Through his labors and influence a Class was formed, prayer meetings were established, and the people instructed in religion. Following the labors and progress of this good man, came the itinerant minister—Asa Shinn—and the first M. E. church of the county was erected and named "Dickerson." In the year 1802, the first seed was planted by Henry Johnson, who penetrated the forest to that place, and gathered to him after awhile a Methodist class. As early as 1814, there were societies organized at Rankin, Deersville, Bethel, Morris West's, two miles northeast of Cadiz, and at Cadiz. In the years 1807-8, Rev. James B. Finley traveled through this region and organized a number of classes in the western part of the county. He preached with such power as to impress himself and his message upon the minds of the people, so that neither were ever forgotten. Rev. Finley has given us in a book of his life, an account of his work during these years and a description of his circuit as it had been formed by the Rev. James Watt. It was called "Wills Creek Circuit," and was not less than seventy-five miles in extent. "Beginning at Zanesville and running east, it embraced all the settlements on the Wheeling road, on to Salt Creek and Buffalo fork of Wills creek, thence down to Cambridge and Leatherwood, on Stillwater, including all the settlements on its various branches to the mouth, thence up the Tuscarawas through New Philadelphia, thence up Sandy View to Canton, and on to Carter's, thence up Sandy to Sugar

* This sketch was prepared by Mr. William M. McConnell.

creek and down said creek to the mouth, thence down the Tuscarawas to William Butts, thence down to the mouth of White Woman, thence after crossing the river, and including all the settlements of the Wapatomica, down to Zanesville, the place of beginning."

About this time the societies and the classes in the territory of Harrison county were placed in West Wheeling Circuit. This circuit was composed of three counties, Harrison, Belmont, and Jefferson, and belonged to the Baltimore Conference. While in the Baltimore Conference, Thornton Fleming was presiding elder, and R. R. Roberts preacher in charge. At a conference held in 1808, the West Wheeling Circuit was transferred to the Western Conference, with James Quinn, presiding elder; Jacob Young, preacher in charge; and James Wilson, James Watts, and Thomas Church, assistants. Together with these brethren were others, named, Revs. Michael Ellis, Caleb Humphrey, and Archibald McElroy, the latter at that time a vigorous local preacher, and afterwards a regular itinerant for years.

The early history of the church scarcely furnishes a more singular character than that of McElroy. He was without advantages in his youth, and of very limited education. But endowed with good sense, great natural and moral courage, and withal an honest man, he enjoyed the confidence of all who knew him. Possessed of stout frame, manly bearing, and open and frank countenance, and being absolutely "fearless in pursuit of the right, he won the respect of all, even those of the baser sort." At a time when the traffic in intoxicating liquors was some part of almost every man's business, and when scarcely a man was to be found, either in the pulpit or out of it, to open his mouth upon the subject, McElroy came forward with lance and trumpet—an unpolished lance, but a trumpet with no uncertain sound—and made war with the beast. He delivered hundreds of temperance lectures, the most electrifying ever heard in the State of Ohio. Without any temperance organizations, or newspapers to support him, with many of the clergy opposed to him, and very few to encourage him, alone in those pioneer times, he lifted up his standard. As a preacher he was earnest, enthusiastic, and successful. It is said that at one of his quarterly meetings the church could not hold the congregation, and they resorted to a grove in the neighborhood. The master of a dancing school in the place and some of his pupils went to the church late, and finding it vacated, danced awhile, when the master said: "Now let us go to the church and get converted." When they reached the ground the preacher, Rev. Swayze, was closing his sermon with a thrilling exhortation. The master listened for a few minutes, and fell to the ground crying aloud for mercy. McElroy was on hand, and when he saw the dancing master down, he improvised an altar and cried: "All hands to, here's a bull in the net, here's a man who taught the people to serve the devil by rule, and I pray God to break his fiddle, convert his soul, and turn his heart to sing his praise." Rev. J. B. Finley says in his Autobiography that this occurred at St. Clairsville, but Alfred Brownson insists that it took place at Cadiz.

In those years, when churches were very small, and when the settlers lived in cabins, and many of them in rude huts, the people sought the groves, and camp meetings were of wonderful interest and success to the new and restless church. We have accounts of these meetings being held within the bounds of West Wheeling Circuit as early as 1808. In that year there was one held at St. Clairsville, under the management of James Quinn and Isaac Young, at which, with very little ministerial assistance, more than one hundred were added to the church.

A camp meeting was held near Cadiz in 1812, which was attended by many of the leading preachers of the Conference. Bishop Asbury came from a meeting at Uniontown, Pennsylvania, to attend the meeting at Cadiz. Jacob Gruber, then presiding elder of the Ohio District of the Baltimore Conference, accompanied him. Rev. William Lambden, who was probably in charge of West Wheeling Circuit, was present, with the able support of such men as Rev. J. B. Finley, Rev. Michael Ellis, and Rev. Archibald McElroy. The order at the meetings was generally good; but a slight interruption occurred on Saturday night. On that occasion Bishop Asbury took the stand at midnight, and after saying some kind things, told the rabble that the Methodists were not all sanctified, and if they perssted in disobeying the rules of the meeting they would find that out. The Bishop preached during the meeting. The ministrations were all able, and much good was done.

Just when the Methodists of Cadiz commenced their worship is not known. As early as 1806 or 1807, a few families met together from time to time, going from house to house with prayer and religious services. More frequently, than at any other place, these services were held at Brother James Simpson's, the father of the renowned Bishop Simpson. The services continued until about 1815, when the society was organized, and a Board of Trustees chosen for the purpose of erecting a house of worship. This Board consisted of Matthew Simpson, the Bishop's uncle, William Tipton, Joseph Tingley, and Thomas Inskeep. On April 20,

1816, they purchased the lot at the south corner of Spring and Buffalo streets, and erected thereon a small church. In this church the Methodists of Cadiz worshipped without pride or ostentation, and without preserving much history, for twenty years.

In this building, which is still standing, although now much dilapidated and used for a tenement house, the renowned Bishop Simpson preached many of his most powerful sermons. In fact, he was at this time sent as an associate pastor to the church, and made his home there.

Being of very progressive views, he suggested to the church the advantages of having a Sabbath School. The older and wiser brethren shook their heads and said it would not do to bring the children into the church with their dirty faces on Sabbath, that they had hard work enough to keep the house clean and in order as it was. The young preacher finally succeeded in the organization of a Sabbath School in the house, upon the condition that he would give the house an extra sweeping after Sabbath School. This is reputed to be the first Methodist Sabbath School established, and the only one existing in the entire county for many years.

Before the removal of Mr. Simpson, measures were introduced with a view to the incorporation of the Society, and to replace the old church with a more commodious and better structure. In December, 1835, the Legislature of Ohio passed an act of incorporation, and Matthew Simpson, Edward Tipton, William Tingley, Robert McKee, James Poulson, Phillip Trine, John Davis, George White, and Elijah Laizure are named in the act as trustees. The Matthew Simpson named at the head of the list was an uncle to the Matthew who afterward became Bishop Simpson.

When this church was incorporated, Cadiz was the chief appointment of the then St. Clairsville Circuit. The other appointments were Dickerson's, New Athens, Stiers, Uniontown, Eaton's, Wesley Chapel, Bates', Neff's, Weige's, Crozier's, Mt. Glenn or Cross Road, Scott's, Bridgeport, Martin's Ferry, Crose's, and Harrisville; two preachers on the circuit. The first record of names of preachers is Rev. I. C. Taylor, pastor in charge when the second church was built, and James Drummond, his colleague, the latter having been received on trial at the conference the spring previous.

Cadiz remained on this circuit until 1866, when it became a regular station. The lot upon which the second church was built, and upon which now stands the third commodious structure, was deeded to the congregation by William Tingley and wife. Mr. Tingley was permitted to live many years afterward, and was one of the church's most ready and willing workers. Among other names as members appear Edmond Tipton and wife, Robert McKee and wife, Michael McConnell and wife, Charles Chapman, wife and daughters, Judge Turner, Mrs. Major Lacy, Thomas Thompson, Matthew White, Mrs. William Arnold, and Mrs. Dr. McBean. All of them have been called from the church militant to the church triumphant. The second church building was commenced in 1835, but was not completed until 1836. The dedicatory sermon was preached by Rev. Wesley Browning, of Wheeling. Bishop Simpson, who was stationed then in Monongahela City, preached at night.

The present beautiful church building was erected in 1876.

CHAPTER XIII.

NOTTINGHAM AND FREEPORT CHURCHES.

For several years after the beginning of the present century, the territory comprising Nottingham congregation, together with the region where Cadiz and Freeport are now located, as well as many other points in eastern Ohio, were mission fields, sustained in part by the Synodical Home Mission Fund of the Presbyterian Church, which had its officers and headquarters in Pittsburgh. For nearly sixteen years there was only a mission station in the vicinity where Nottingham Church now stands; and all was connected with the pastorate of Crabapple. So far as known, Rev. John Rea, pastor of Beech Spring and Crabapple, preached the first sermon in this region, on the second Sabbath of June, in the year 1806, on the old Cunningham homestead. The history of

NOTTINGHAM CHURCH

has been made familiar to many residents of Harrison county, through the sketches published in 1886, in the "Reminiscences" of Dr. Thomas Crawford, for forty years the pastor of this congregation, and though the good Doctor's form is now missed from its accustomed place in the church, it is to be hoped the remembrance of his genial, helpful, kindly presence will live forever in the hearts and minds of his congregation and their posterity. In detailing the history of this church, we will follow Dr. Crawford's own words:

In this sketch we propose some historical reminiscences of the Presbyterian Church of Nottingham—its pioneers, pastors, progressive work, and historical incidents. In the preparation of this narrative I was governed by my diary, old records, and, in some instances, by the recollections of the oldest citizens.

For several years the territory of this congregation was considered within the limits of Crabapple and Cadiz churches. Although eight to nine miles distant, it was traveled by our forefathers, in hot and cold weather, and often on foot, more regularly than do some of us who live but two or three miles distant from the house of public worship. To remedy this inconvenience and exposure, a preaching point was established in this vicinity, and the first sermon ever preached by a Presbyterian minister in this part of Harrison county was by the Rev. John Rea, D. D., in the summer of 1806, at the root of a large chestnut tree, standing on the eastern slope of the hill, near where the barn now stands on the Cunningham farm, and about one-half mile from this house.

The same element that settled Western Pennsylvania settled Southeastern Ohio, and gave to it, as to the former, the Presbyterianism which both possess to a very large extent. Those pioneers came into an unbroken wilderness, which required hard labor and much self-denial to gain a subsistence, and for a time many of them lived in rude and uncomfortable cabins, but were not disposed to leave their religion behind them, as is too frequently the case with many emigrating to a new country, for no sooner had they found a home for themselves in the western wilderness, than they sought a place where they might worship the Lord our God.

Ninety-five years ago this whole region was an unbroken forest, and over these hills and through these valleys roamed the wild beast of the wood, and the more savage men, with their implements of death. Near to this site passed the Indian trail to their hunting grounds in the Muskingum and Scioto countries. At the close of the Revolutionary War, peace was declared, but only established between Great Britain and the United States.

The Indians still continued hostilities on our frontier settlements, partly owing to the deceptions and frauds imposed upon them by the early traders. Scenes, however, began to change for the better, which opened up the way for a daring and enterprising population to come into the Northwest Territory and to settle in companies, even before Congress declared Ohio to be regularly constituted a State.

But those emigrating so early not only encountered the common hardships of a frontier life, but for a few years were continually exposed to attacks from savage warriors, under such cruel leaders as the renegade "Simon Girty," "Old Cross-fire," and "Red Jacket," who, with their Indian forces, infested this whole region, and continued more or less for several years after the white population began to locate in communities near some garrison or block-house, into which they were often compelled to flee in times of alarm, both for defense and safety.

The first settlements in this vicinity were made from 1798 to 1803. Abraham Brokaw, John Glenn, William Ingles, George Laport, Thomas

Wilson, Arthur Barrett, —— Jones, and —— Moffitt, and perhaps others. These were but the advance of a great mass of people that in a few years scattered over a large tract of country. So, as by magic, the Northwest Territory was settled, and signs of civilization were evident, by subdued forests, newly erected dwellings, followed by the school house and church building.

So far as we can learn, the first families that came into the bounds, and identified themselves with the congregation of Nottingham, were those of Abraham Brokaw, John Glenn, Richard Baxter, Adam Dunlap, Samuel Lafferty, and John Price. These were the pioneers of Presbyterianism in this region, and amid many trials and discouragements labored earnestly to establish a nucleus of a church, in which they finally succeeded.

When peace was ratified with the Indians, and Ohio admitted into the Union of States, the tide of emigration began to flow strongly in this direction. In 1802, the great western thoroughfare passed not more than three-quarters of a mile from Nottingham Church, which was the route from Pittsburgh by the way of Steubenville, and from central Pennsylvania by the way of Charleston (now Wellsburg), forming a junction in this county, which induced the location of Cadiz; then running west nine or ten miles, forked on the lands of William Ingles (now owned by James Roland). The right branch of this road passed through the "White Eye" plains, and on by "Fort Defiance," into the Sandusky region; the left branch running by the way of Zanesville into the Scioto and Miami valleys. Howe, in his "Historical Collections" of this State, says, "that previous to the construction of the National Road through Ohio, this road was perhaps traveled more than any other route west of the Ohio river."

Mr. Ingles, then residing at the junction of the western division of this road, found it necessary to keep a public house, for the accommodation of the unexpected rush of emigration into this and other settlements further west. In the spring of 1802, he erected a large double log cabin, considered in those days a magnificent house; and supposed to be the first "Hotel" ever kept in the bounds of this county. A part of the remains of this old tavern was still to be seen, until quite recently, as a monument of the past, though vacated long since, and in a retired and lonely spot, less than one mile north of this place, but deserted both by residents and roads.

Some award to our county seat the first public-house erected in the territory of Harrison county, which, according to history, is incorrect. Cadiz was laid out in 1804, by Messr. Biggs and Beaty. In 1806, is the first record we have of a hotel kept in that town, by Jacob Arnold.

At this day of comparative ease and plenty, we know but little of the self-denial, privations and hardships endured by the early settlers who came into the wilderness to find a home. They mostly emigrated from New Jersey, Delaware, Maryland, Pennsylvania, and some of them soon sought for a place where they might worship God according to the dictates of conscience, and after the order of their Puritan fathers. But few of the first inhabitants were religiously educated, and especially in the Presbyterian faith; and that few were necessitated for a time to travel some distance to worship in the church of their choice. In 1804, the church was organized at Crabapple, by the Presbytery of Ohio, under the direction of Drs. McMillan and Ralston, nine miles distant from our present house of worship. A committee was appointed to confer with Rev. John Rea, D. D., and the elders of Crabapple church, as to the propriety of establishing a mission station in the "Ball-Lick" settlement. It was thought better, for the time being, that all in this vicinity should form a connection with that congregation, until further developments of divine Providence, which soon indicated a change, because of the distance and inconvenience of travel, constraining those in this region to have a place for public service nearer home.

In 1806, a stand was erected in the forest at the base of a large tree (before noted), where Dr. Rea preached his first sermon in this part of the county. Six weeks after, he returned and held religious services in the same place, encouraged by a much larger attendance than on the former occasion. A council was held by a few, in connection with the preacher, as to the propriety of an organization at this point; but on more mature reflection it was thought advisable to make this an outpost for missionary work, tributary to Crabapple church, and that their pastor should continue to labor here part of his time, preaching and administering the sealing ordinances of the church to such as desired them, to which all parties agreed. Although there was no formal organization of this church until several years after, yet it was virtually organized under the ministry of Dr. Rea, who continued for five years to preach occasionally at this point, a part of the time in a private house, and in suitable weather, in the grove.

In 1808, a tent was erected on the south side of the graveyard, by Abraham Brokaw, Robert Baxter, John Glenn, and Adam Dunlap. This tent was occupied in the summer season for eight or ten years, and the house of Robert Baxter in the winter or stormy days.

In the call that was made out in 1805 by the church of Crabapple and vicinity for the labors of Rev. John Rea the one-half of his time, the representatives of Nottingham interest signed said call with the express understanding that a part of the pastor's services would be employed in this region, if desired. Fifty pounds per annum was the sum specified in the call, one-half in cash and the other half in produce; the latter to be delivered at a certain flouring mill near the mouth of Big Short creek. In keeping with these conditions, the supplies of grain increased rapidly, at such prices as 20 to 25 cents a bushel for wheat, and 12 to 25 cents for corn and rye. It soon became necessary for the minister to have his large stock of produce manufactured and put into market, that he might procure some funds wherewith to replenish his library, and supply the wants of his household. When a sufficient number of barrels and lading were ready to fill a flat boat, a man of approved character and ability was employed to take the oversight of the cargo, and ship it down the Ohio and Mississippi rivers to some southern port, make sale, and bring back the returns, which, after paying expenses, were often quite small.

Mr. Rea was the first minister of the gospel of Christ to gather a group of worshippers in the western part of Harrison county, and amid great difficulties and much self-denial, continued his mission to this people until the Beech Spring congregation presented a call for the whole of his time, with a salary of one hundred pounds sterling, payable semi-annually, which he was constrained to accept in 1810, and immediately occupied all his time in that church.

Mr. Rea established the Nottingham Mission, in 1806, and served it at stated times from the beginning, until 1810, when all his labors were required at Beech Springs, where his pastorate continued forty-five years, and during all this time, he was much beloved and appreciated by the people. The older members of the congregation were enthusiastically attached to him, both as a preacher and spiritual adviser, and well they might be, for he was untiring in his exertions for their well-being.

Thomas B. Clark, a licentiate of the Presbytery of Hartford, Ohio, came into this vicinity in the spring of 1811, and supplied the Mission Station every fourth Sabbath for six years; for there was no formal organization of a church here then, though often considered and desired by the scattered families of the "Ball Lick" settlement, but from some cause unknown to us, it was still postponed, perhaps from the pretext that regular preaching, and the sealing ordinances were enjoyed at this place, as an outpost of Crabapple.

Mr. Clark was ordained and installed at Crabapple by the Presbytery of Ohio, June, 1811, and continued to preach there, and fill this appointment until he was dismissed in 1818. He had the credit of being quite punctual in his engagements, and rarely failed to meet his contracts for public worship, although his labors were abundant, for his pastorate covered a territory of about fourteen miles square.

When coming to this place, his road passed a flouring mill, on a branch of Stillwater. Being a conscientious and zealous man, he was exceedingly annoyed by the running of this mill on the Sabbath, and was in the habit of reproving the miller (Mr. Logan) for his desecration of the Lord's day. On one occasion, when coming to his preaching place at the "Old Tent," as he passed on Sunday morning, near the hour of public service, discovering that the mill was in motion, he stopped his horse, paused for a moment, as if reflecting on what was his duty, at length dismounted and tied up his bridle-strap, went into the mill to dissuade, if possible, his reckless friend from a continued violation of civil and divine law. But Mr. Logan evaded the minister, for, going out at the rear door, he locked it after him, and coming round he secured the other door, "making," as he said, "a prisoner of the parson," and keeping him confined until the hour of public worship had expired.

Then Mr. Clark, for a few moments, directed his discourse to the transgressor, and kindly remonstrated with him on what was his duty in reference to the claims of God and the commonwealth, and in view of his family and himself in future. His exhortations were not lost, for the Lord succeeded these efforts to the reformation of Mr. Logan, who became the warm friend of Mr. Clark, changed his course of life, and in a few months made a profession of religion under his ministry.

In the spring of 1821, Rev. William Wallace, an evangelist, under the direction of Steubenville Presbytery, came into this neighborhood, and after preaching here and elsewhere for about six months, he made application to Presbytery, by request of the people, for an organization of a church at the "Tent."

The request was granted, and Mr. Wallace was chairman of a committee that organized the Church of Nottingham, November 17, 1822, with twenty-two names on the roll, as follows: Archibald Todd, Nancy Todd, Thomas Morrow, Jane Morrow, William Crawford, Adam Dunlap, Abraham Brokaw, Margaret Brokaw, Elizabeth Lafferty, Samuel Lafferty, John Glenn, Nancy Glenn, John Price, Mrs. Price, William Hamilton, Elizabeth Hamilton, John Reed, Ann Reed, Robert Baxter, Margaret Baxter, Mary W. Wallace, and Sarah McKibbon.

The following persons were elected ruling elders, and immediately ordained and installed, namely: Archibald Todd, William Crawford, and Thomas Morrow.

Rev. William Wallace, a member of the Presbytery of Steubenville, having spent a few months in this and other missionary points in the western part of the county, a call for one-half of his labors was made out by the congregation of Nottingham, March 18, 1822, signed by Archibald Todd, Robert Baxter, and fourteen others, moderated by Rev. John Rea, and carried up to the April meeting of the Presbytery and put into the hands of Mr. Wallace, who, signifying his acceptance, was duly installed pastor.

The stipend was to be paid quarterly, one-fourth in cash and three-fourths in produce. Money was scarce, and little to sell with which to procure it. The products of the ground were few, until the wilderness was subdued and turned into cultivated fields; and after a supply of grain was had, the markets were so distant, the labor of shipping so tedious and costly, that when the expenses were paid the agriculturist had little left.

The whole amount of salary promised Mr. Wallace was but three hundred dollars per annum, paid equally by this and the Freeport Church. To us this appears like short allowance for the preacher, as it surely was. Yet it would go as far in those days toward supporting a family as more than double the amount would do with the prices of these times.

Rev. William Wallace, son of John and Margaret (Anderson) Wallace, was born in Chester county, Pa., March 17, 1787. He finished his academic education at Jefferson College, Pa,; studied Theology under the direction of James Hervey, D. D., and was licensed to preach the Gospel by the Presbytery of Steubenville in the spring of 1821. He entered the service of his Divine Master as a domestic missionary, going through the new settlements of eastern Ohio, and hunting up families of the Presbyterian order, and when finding one or more such families in any destitute place, he would publish a notice for preaching at some convenient point, and in this way was instrumental in gathering up and forming nuclei from which have arisen some of our most prominent congregations.

After reporting progress to Presbytery, he was appointed chairman of a committee that organized several churches in this territory, and among them the Churches of Nottingham and Freeport, and to each of the last named places he gave one-half of his labors for eighteen years, until his health so failed that he was compelled to resign his charge in 1839, and after two years of increasing infirmities, he died of heart disease, December 18, 1841, in the fifty-fifth year of his age, having spent twenty years in the work of the ministry.

Rev. Gilbert M. Hair was then in charge of this congregation two years. Mr. Hair graduated at Washington College, Pa., in 1838, studied Theology (while teaching an academy in Martinsburg, Ohio), with Henry Hervey, D. D., and was licensed to preach the Gospel by the Presbytery of Richland, October, 1840. He received a call from the congregation of Nottingham, and was ordained and installed pastor of this church in the Spring of 1841, by the Presbytery of St. Clairsville, and continued in this relation two years. Another opening offering itself more to his mind, he then asked and received a dismission in April, 1843, to the church at Wellsburg, W. Va. Mr. Hair, after laboring successfully in fourteen different charges, died June 5, 1884, at Elyria, New York.

Thomas R. Crawford, a licentiate of the Presbytery of Steubenville, immediately received a call from the church of Nottingham. He began his ministerial work October 19th, 1846, and in due time was ordained and installed pastor, continuing in this office forty years. He graduated at Franklin College, Ohio, in 1844, and on the same day was chosen Professor of Mathematics in said College; and during the time of his teaching there, he read Hebrew under the President, Rev. A. D. Clark, D. D., and Theology under Dr. Rea. He soon left college for the purpose of completing his studies; and was licensed to preach the Gospel by the Presbytery of Steubenville, October 6th, 1846.

He was born near New Athens, Ohio, March 8th, 1821, and when but a few months old, his parents and family removed to Jefferson county, near Steubenville, Ohio. At the age of fourteen, he began his academic studies, preparatory to entering college. In the eighteenth year of his age, he united with the church under the ministry of Rev. Jacob Coon, of New Athens, during a revival of religion that occurred among the students in 1840.

After he received authority to preach, he took a traveling certificate to the Presbyterian church and Presbytery of Marion, but never reached the place; for when ready to start, Dr. Rea insisted on him filling an appointment at the Church of Nottingham, which was vacant, and at once he received a call, and returning his traveling certificate to the Presbytery of Steubenville, was regularly dismissed to the Presbytery of St. Clairsville, and in due time was ordained and installed pastor of said church, for two-thirds of his time; and the one-third at Deersville, as stated supply for nine years, from October, 1846, when he was called to spend all his time and labors at the Church of Nottingham.

At the time of my installation as pastor, the Board of Elders consisted of Archibald Todd, Nathan Tanneyhill, Alexander Russell, Alexander Beall, William Kirkpatrick, and John W. Milligan. Shortly after, Joseph Rea and Allen Wallace were added to the Session; but one of the former is still living and quite infirm, being far advanced in years. All those men were reliable and trustworthy in counsel. In 1863, A. J. Rea and Samuel M. Wallace were introduced into the Session. In 1870, John W. Hilton, Jacob Compher, and William Scott were added to the Board of Elders.

The first house of worship erected by this congregation was a log-cabin, which stood a short distance above the "Old Tent," and was built in 1821 by Abraham Brokaw, Thomas Morrow, Archibald Todd, Adam Dunlap, and Samuel Lafferty. The last two named men having good teams, were requested to draw in the logs, whilst the balance of the labor was divided according to choice. The ladies, by personal efforts, procured the nails and glass. It was a rude structure, but answered the purposes for the time being. In the winter season, a pile of logs was built on an earthen platform in the center of the building, and fired up to warm the auditory, whilst the smoke escaped as best it could from the roof. This house corresponded in the main with the improvements of those days, and was equal in architecture to the dwellings of the worshippers. There were no Boards of Home Missions and Church Erection in those times to aid young and feeble congregations to build houses or sustain preaching in their midst. There was, however, a Synodical Fund for the purpose of aiding mission stations. Money was scarce and hard to be got; and had there been convenient markets, there was not grain to sell, for the land was not yet cleared out, but crops were produced abundantly in proportion to the ground brought under cultivation.

The second house of worship was a brick building, fifty by forty feet, and began to be constructed in 1828, but was not completed until 1833. The congregation worshiped in this edifice twenty-nine years, until it became rather small for the people that desired to attend church, to be comfortably seated. It was deemed necessary to call a meeting to consider the propriety of erecting a larger house for the accommodation of the increased attendance on the preaching of the Word.

According to previous notice, the people met in the month of August, 1859, to confer upon the subject, in relation to building a third house of worship. The books were opened at said meeting, and about one-half of the whole amount of money necessary to complete the structure was subscribed on sight, in less than thirty minutes. Duplicate papers were prepared and sent around to the absentees, and in due time returned with the required money pledged. A building committee was appointed at a meeting held February 3, 1860, and directed to erect a house seventy-three by fifty feet in the out, with gallery in front, twenty-feet story in audience room, and tower one hundred and six feet high.

The committee, after receiving sealed proposals on a certain day, let out the contract to Mr. John McGraw, of Wheeling, W. Va., who undertook and finished the entire building ready for occupancy, in a satisfactory and workman-like manner. And this house was dedicated, free from debt, to the worship of Almighty God, April 18th, A. D. 1861, and continues to this time.

FREEPORT PRESBYTERIAN CHURCH.

This church was organized in 1821, by the Presbytery of Steubenville. Messrs. Holliday, Leaper, and Kincade were ordained and installed ruling elders. For five years before that date the congregation had received occasional supplies from Presbytery, some account of them already having been given in connection with the sketch of the Presbyterian Church of Cadiz. The first pastor was Rev. William Wallace, who divided his services equally between Nottingham and Freeport. He supplied both pulpits until the spring of 1839, when he was compelled to resign, on account of failing health. He died of heart failure, Dec. 18, 1841. Mr. Wallace was a man of ardent piety and practical worth. The Freeport church attained a larger membership and greater efficiency under his pastorate than it has ever enjoyed since.

Rev. John Hattery, an evangelist from Washington Presbytery, became stated supply at Freeport in 1843, for two-thirds of his labors, and remained until 1847. He was succeeded by Rev. Samuel Mahaffey, who served as stated supply for something over eight years. From 1857 to 1859, occasional supplies were sent by Presbytery; and in the latter year Rev. John B. Graham became stated supply, giving Freeport a portion of his time, and remained until 1865, when he was dismissed to the Presbytery of Washington. After his departure, Rev. Samuel Mahaffey was again invited to supply Freeport for one-half his time, and served the congregation from 1867 to 1873. He was succeeded, three years later, by Rev. H. R. McDonald, who remained until 1881.

CHAPTER XIV.

DICKERSON, BETHEL, AND RANKIN CHURCHES.

The following Historical Address, giving an account of the early history of Dickerson Church, was delivered by Mr. Joseph Holmes, one of the trustees, at the dedication of the new building, near Cadiz, on October 7, 1888:

The history of the Dickerson Society commences early in the present century. As early as March, 1801, Joseph Holmes moved to the farm on which he lived and died. Soon after, the following settlers came into the neighborhood: Joseph Huff, William Walraven, Thomas Dickerson, Eli Dickerson, William Scoles, James and Thomas Worley, Abraham Holmes, and William Welling. In the Fall of 1802, Thomas Dickerson settled on the farm on which Dickerson Church is located. He was a man of strong religious convictions, and during the same Fall, he succeeded in the organization of a prayer-meeting circle, at which he gave religious instruction to those who attended the meetings. The meetings were held weekly, from house to house in the neighborhood, and they increased in numbers and interest from time to time, under the supervision of Thomas Dickerson. In 1804, a Society of Methodists was organized, with Thomas Dickerson duly appointed class-leader.

Among the first members of the society were: Thomas Dickerson and wife, Joseph Holmes and wife, William Walraven and wife, William Scoles and wife, James Worley and wife, Abraham Holmes and wife, Eli Dickerson and wife, William Welling and wife, and James Jones and wife. Preaching was held like the prayer-meetings, from house to house. In those days, sermons were like angel's visits, "few and far between." The first quarterly meeting was held on the farm of Joseph Holmes in the summer of 1805. This meeting was conducted by the Rev. Asa Shinn. Methodists and others from beyond and about Wellsburg, on the Ohio river, and from the Holmes Church, on Short creek, came to the meeting, not only to renew the friendship of other years, but to aid in pushing forward the cause of Christ.

It may seem strange to those of modern times, when we describe the arrangements for holding this first quarterly meeting. The meeting was held in the grove. The seats were made of rails, logs, and puncheons. A few puncheons were used for a platform. In each of two trees, standing about six feet apart, a notch was cut, and in those notches was placed a puncheon about sixteen inches wide, and on this the preacher laid his Bible, and this was the make-up of the preacher's pulpit. The meeting was one of great spiritual power, and several persons united with the church.

The second quarterly meeting was held on the farm of Thomas Dickerson in 1807, with the same arrangements, and like results. In 1813, a quarterly meeting was held in the barn of Thomas Dickerson, conducted by Rev. James B. Finley. From 1807, preaching services became more frequent. Asa Shinn, James B. Finley, Bishop Roberts, and the Rev. McElroy, were some of the early itinerate ministers who have preached in our community.

The first church was built in 1817; although the selection of a site for a church had been made in 1806. The first burial in the cemetery was in 1807. The ground was conveyed by Thomas Dickerson and wife to Joseph Holmes, William Scoles, William Welling, James Worley, and Abraham Holmes, as trustees of the M. E. Church.

The organization of the Dickerson Church is clearly traceable to the labors of Bishop Asbury and Bishop McKendree, from the fact that the first members of the church came from Virginia and Pennsylvania, direct from the fields of labor of these great and good men. But directly to Thomas Dickerson, more than to any other, belongs the honor of the organization of the church at this place. He was blessed with a fine social nature, and a vigorous constitution. His piety was deep and uniform. . . . From 1817 to 1828, the church moved steadily forward. In 1828, Thomas Hudson and S. R. Brockunier were appointed to the West Wheeling Circuit, and this circuit included the Dickerson appointment. During this year, there were some accessions to the church, and the membership was greatly revived. But the year 1829 is especially remarkable for its great spiritual prosperity at Dickerson's. During this year, Thomas Hudson and William Tipton were travelling the circuit and Joshua Monroe, Presiding Elder.

At the first meeting of the Quarterly Conference that year, a resolution was passed to hold a camp-meeting on the farm of Thomas Dickerson. The meeting was appointed, and was largely attended. In the "Life and Times of Rev. Thomas M. Hudson," he says, as the meeting progressed, the work of revival greatly increased, awakenings becoming more general, and conversions more frequent every day. . . . He tells us, that among the numerous subjects of that great revival that he received into the church at Cadiz, were many interesting young men,

DICKERSON CHURCH

five of whom became ministers of the Gospel. Bishop Simpson was one of them.

Some weeks after the close of the camp-meeting, Hudson determined to hold a meeting at the Dickerson appointment. As a result of this meeting, over sixty persons professed conversion. . . . This revival included to a greater or less extent the families of the entire neighborhood, and bore its fruit for many years.

From 1829 to 1835 the church was in a prosperous condition. But during 1835 and 1836 many members of the Dickerson appointment removed their membership to New Athens. The number of members thus removing was about twenty-five. This greatly weakened the Dickerson Society. This removal of membership was caused by a new church being built at New Athens. But those remaining still adhered to the Society with a strong faith. In 1839, the second camp-meeting was held, on the old camp ground. . . . As a result of this meeting, several persons united with the Society.

From 1840 to 1850, the membership remained about the same. There were several additions to the church during 1851 and 1852, but during the winter of 1853, a revival meeting was held by Rev. D. P. Mitchell and Rev. J. D. Knox. . . . This was the last protracted effort ever held in the old church building. . . .

It was the opinion of many and the desire of others, that as soon as Thomas Dickerson was gone, the old church should be abandoned, and that the members of the Society should either go to Cadiz or New Athens—but those persons were much mistaken. Thomas Dickerson died. The workman fell, but still the work went on. The mantle of Thomas Dickerson was resting on the shoulders of his son, Joseph Dickerson. By much labor of his own, with such help as he could secure, the second church was built, in 1854. The dedicatory sermon was preached by Dr. Nesbitt. After the building of the new church, the Society received new life. The membership increased from sixty-five in 1856, to ninety-three in 1858. For the next two years after, the membership remained about the same.

The next four years were years of war, and while the Society and community were loyal to the church, they were also loyal to the Government. In proof of this, twenty-eight of the young men that were either members or patrons of the Society gave their services to their country. Within a circle of one and one-fourth miles from the church, thirty-eight of our best and bravest young men left for the seat of war. It is not saying too much when we declare, that the Dickerson neighborhood furnished more soldiers to the square inch than any other country-place in the county.

The first Sabbath school was organized in 1825, with Joseph Dickerson as superintendent.

This history would be deficient without the names of its class-leaders from its organization to the present. They are as follows: Thomas

Dickerson was leader for forty-eight years. During the latter part of his life, he had an assistant. The next, in order, were Joseph Dickerson, Joshua Dickerson, A. H. Thomas, William Perry, Washington Soule, Joseph Holmes, Abraham Holmes, R. B. Green, S. M. Dickerson, and G. B. Holmes. From 1804 to 1855, there was but one class. In the latter year, it was divided into three classes, and a leader appointed for each class.

Time has removed nearly all who were born before the building of the first church. Only three remain with us [in 1888]. They are, Asa and Mary Holmes, and (Knob) Joshua Dickerson. Only seven persons now hold their membership with us who were members of the Society when the second church was built. The others have either died or removed to other places. Joshua Dickerson's membership—now the oldest —dates from 1837.

In the history of the Society, we deem it necessary to briefly refer to others who have gone from our midst, and were either members of the church or Sabbath school.

From the family of William Scoles, two young men went forth to preach the Gospel. The family of James and Susan Jones furnished five Methodist preachers. A. H. Thomas died when he was Presiding Elder. During the last decade, O. W. Holmes and W. H. Dickerson have entered the ministry from this Society; also, David Porter, who was a member of the Sabbath school.

There are others who have taken high positions in life. From a class of twelve young men in the Sabbath school, which I had the pleasure of teaching, were Capt. Joseph Dickerson, Capt. Thomas McElravy, Capt. John Finley Oglevee, ex-auditor of the State of Ohio, Col, J. T. Holmes, of Columbus, Abraham Thomas, a minister of the North Ohio Conference, Dr. Hamline Welling, of Columbus, Capt. William McElravy, of Iowa, William Oglevee, of Illinois, Rev. D. S. Porter, David Harrison of Kansas, James Oglevee of the 126th O. V. I., now resting in the cemetery at this place, and Robert McElravy, who was killed in the capture of Richmond.

BETHEL CHURCH.

The following sketch of Bethel Church was written by Mr. J. Fletcher Birney, of Means, Ohio, and printed by him in 1894:

Rev. James B. Finley, the pioneer of Ohio Methodism, organized the first class in this vicinity, at what is now the home of Joseph L. Thompson, one mile north of Cadiz, in the year 1811.

It consisted of nine members, as follows: Morris West, leader; John Baker, Sr., and Margaret Baker; William Foreman, Sr., and Sarah Foreman; Zebedee Baker and Cassandra Baker; Joseph Kent, and Elizabeth Chaney.

In 1814, when John Birney, Sr., from Ireland, and his brothers,

BETHEL AND RANKIN CHURCHES

Hugh and William, with their families, from Pennsylvania, arrived here, two other classes were formed, one at the Baker farm, one mile west of the church, on the Cadiz and Jefferson road; the other at what is now the home of Mrs. Samuel Pittinger, one-half mile south of Jewett. Hugh Birney, Sr., and John Baker, Sr., led the classes alternately. Robert McKee and Richael McKee, and Nancy Moore (Foreman), joined soon after.

The three classes continued until 1818, when Bethel Society was formed. In March of that year, one acre of land was purchased of Robert Orr, for which twenty dollars was paid. It was deeded to John Baker and others. On this lot the old log church was built. It was about thirty feet square, and stood about twenty-five feet west of and parallel with the present building. The door was in the center of the east end. The pulpit was in the west end, with a window on each side of it. The seats were split logs, with legs in them. In the rear part of the house, they were placed north and south; and in the fore part, east and west.

The preaching then, was at noon on Thursdays.

Rev. Jacob Young followed Rev. Finley as circuit preacher.

From the building of the church, to 1830, the following persons united with the organization: Hugh and Jane Brown, Robert and Margaret Birney, Mrs. Keziah Wheeler, Mrs. Nancy (Foreman) Moore, Mrs. Mary Ralston, Abraham and Deborah Busby, Rebecca Busby, William Kent, Sr., and his wife.

From 1830 to 1840: Samuel Foreman, Lemuel and Mary Green, Ellen Gallagher, Otho and Mary Baker, Evan Baker, John and Leucintha Ralston, Charles Conaway and wife, Lydia Ryan, John Brindley, Sr., and wife, James McKee, Hamilton and Hugh Birney, Jane Scarlot, Abram and Mary Mattern, Mary, wife of George Lease, Sr., Cassandra Fife, Jacob and Rebecca Dennis, Jacob Lewis, Sr.

Of the above named persons, but four are now [1894] living (Hamilton Birney, John Brindley, Sr., Jane Lease, and Deborah Maxwell). The rest have gone to their reward. Most of their bodies rest in Bethel cemetery.

The present church is about forty by fifty feet. It was begun in 1839—Rev. Pardon Cook the preacher in charge. Its seating capacity is about 300. The brick was made near where the church stands, by James Means, of Cadiz; the mason work was done by Andrew and James Jelly; the carpentering, by T. W. Wells, who lived near the church. The pulpit, at first, was one of the upper story kind, as it took three high steps to get into it; and the preacher had to stand up to see over the top. The seats were high-backed, and closed at the bottom. The building cost $1,600. . . . It was dedicated by Revs. Edward Smith and A. J. Rich, entirely free from debt, in 1840.

Following were the preachers who ministered to Bethel congregation from 1825 to 1860 (Cross Creek Circuit): William Tipton and W. Hank, 1825-26; J. Monroe and S. Adams, 1826-27; J. Monroe and J.

Graham, 1827-28; J. Graham and E. H. Taylor, 1828-29; W. Knox and E. H. Taylor, 1829-30; W. Knox and D. C. Merryman, 1830-31; S. R. Brockunier and D. C. Merryman, 1831-32; Simon Lauck and Walter Athey, 1832-33; Simon Lauck and P. Green, 1833-34; E. H. Taylor and W. Athey, 1834-35; J. P. Kent and H. Wharton, 1835-36; T. Jamison and Job Wilson, 1836-37; J. W. Minor and P. K. McCue, 1837-38; C. Thorn and Alexander Scott, 1838-39; Pardon Cook and J. Hammett, 1839-40; Edward Smith and A. J. Rich, 1840-41; James C. Taylor and W. F. Lauck, 1841-42; Wesley Smith and J. L. Clark, 1842-43; Wesley Smith and T. McCleary, 1843-44; Ebenezer Hays and B. F. Sawhill, 1844-46; Charles Thorn and David S. Welling, 1846-47; J. C. Merryman and J. Henderson, 1847-48; J. C. Merryman and J. W. Shirer, 1848-49; John J. Moffit and C. A. Holmes, 1849-51; D. P. Mitchell and George Crook, 1851-52; D. P. Mitchell and J. D. Knox, 1852-53; S. F. Minor and L. Pettay, 1853-55; S. P. Wolf and Hiram Sinsabaugh, 1855-57; John J. Moffitt and E. W. Brady, 1857-58; John J. Moffit and W. B. Watkins, 1858-59; J. M. Bray and H. M. Close, 1859; J. M. Bray and James Day, 1860; Alexander Scott and J. W. Shearer, 1860; Alexander Scott and T. J. Scott, 1860-62.

Bethel appointment was first in the bounds of Knox Circuit, Muskingum District, Western Conference, with James Quinn Presiding Elder. The Conference for that year (1811) was held at New Chapel, Shelby county, Kentucky, on November 1st, 1810. In 1813, it fell into the Ohio Conference, and in 1825, into the Pittsburgh Conference. The Circuit then bore the name of Cross Creek, which it retained until 1834, when it was changed to Richmond. In 1838, the Conference was held at Cadiz, Bishop Enoch George presiding. Bethel was then joined to Cadiz Circuit, which had been formed the year previous. In 1847, the Circuit was composed of the following appointments: Cadiz, Bethel, Athens, and Harrisville. Stiers was added in 1850, and Jefferson in 1852 (formed in 1847, by David Welling), Rumley and Hanover (the latter formed by C. Thorn and W. Devinney), in August, 1853, and Jewett (formed in 1847), in December, 1853. The same year, Harrisville, Athens, Stiers, and Dickerson's were joined to other Circuits, leaving five appointments. In 1854, Rumley was dropped. In 1864, Cadiz and Dickerson's were joined, leaving Bethel, Jefferson, Jewett, and Hanover. The Circuit was then named Bethel Circuit, which name was retained until 1887, when it was changed to Jewett. After the formation of the Society at Howard Chapel (Cadiz Junction), in 1892, a new Circuit was formed, consisting of Bethel, Howard Chapel, Mount Hope, and Asbury Chapel, and named Bethel Circuit, which name it still retains.

The District bore the following names: West Wheeling, 1825-26; Barnesville, 1826-32; Steubenville, 1832-36; Wheeling, 1836-40; Steubenville, 1840-47; Cambridge, 1847-76; New Philadelphia, 1876-94.

Presiding Elders, to 1860: Rev. W. Lambdin, 1825-28; Rev. D. Limerick, 1828-29; Rev. J. Monroe, 1829-32; Rev. W. Browning, 1832-

36; Rev. S. R. Brockunier, 1836-40; Rev. R. Hopkins, 1840-44; Rev. H. Gilmore, 1844-46; Rev. S. R. Brockunier, 1846-48; Rev. J. C. Taylor, 1848-52; Rev. W. Cox, 1852-55; Rev. John J. Moffiitt, 1855-56; Rev. W. F. Lauck, 1856-60; Rev. W. A. Davidson, D. D., 1860-63.

The cemetery was laid out when the old church was built, the lots in rows, about ten feet wide, running north and south, and were taken by families as follows, beginning at the west end: First row, Holland, Webster, Devore; second row, Tipton, Hatton, Rutledge; third row, Busby, Auckerman, Braden, Young; fourth row, Busby, Pittinger, Adams; fifth row, Pittinger, Lemasters, Fife, Maxwell; sixth row, Ralston, Rankin, Knox, Ryan; seventh row, McKee, Brindley; eighth row, Foreman; ninth row, Thompson, Campbell; tenth row, Baker; eleventh row, Beaty, Brown, Green, Dennis; twelfth row, Hugh Birney, John Birney, Sr.; thirteenth row, Lewis, Kent, Robert Birney, Sr.; fourteenth row, George Lease, Wheeler; fifteenth row, Norman, Bargar; sixteenth row, Mehollin, Speer; seventeenth row, H. Thompson, Busby. In 1858, the cemetery was enlarged by the purchase of fifty-four perches of ground; and again, in 1881, by the addition of two acres. Hugh Brown's head-stone is dated 1822; and those of Margaret, wife of John Baker, Sr., and Margaret, daughter of John Birney, Sr., are both dated 1829. Many headstones have crumbled, until the dates are lost.

Deceased members, with year of death: Cash Adams, 1892; Maggie C. Ault, 1891; John Baker, Sr., 1847; Margaret Baker, 1829; Otho Baker, 1855; Mary Baker, 1870; Evan Baker, 18—; John Baker, Jr., 1879; Rezin Baker, 1876; Sarah T. Baker, 1892; William Baker, 1890; Laura B. Baker, 1886; Mollie Baker, 1889; Mary Jane Baker, 1863; John Birney, Sr., 1854; Rebecca B. Birney, 1843; Hugh Birney, Sr., 1861; Elizabeth B. Birney, 1828; Nancy C. Birney, 1854; Robert Birney, Sr., 1871; Margaret Birney, 1866; John N. Birney, 1876; Hugh Birney, 1880; Robert Birney, 1884; Rachel M. Birney, 1886; Nelson Birney, 1867; Samuel F. Birney, 1894; Isabel Birney, 1863; Hester M. Birney, 1888; Elias Benedict, 18—; Hugh Brown, 1822; Jane Brown, 1884; William Brown, 1874; Lizzie Brown, 1887; John Brown, 1873; Sarah Boals, 18—; Ann B. Brindley, 1889; Wesley Brindley, 1876; Albert Brindley, 1869; Mary Ann Bradford, 1882; Abraham Busby, 1855; Deborah Busby, 1884; Rebecca Busby, 1892; Shird Busby, 1884; May A. Crawford, 18—; Charles Conaway, 18—; Fanny Conaway, 18—; John Campbell, 18—; Margaret Copeland, 1861; Ankrim Caldwell, 1881; Arthur Chaney, 1884; Elizabeth Chaney, 18—; Jacob Dennis, Sr., 1880; Jacob Dennis, Jr., 1890; Rebecca Dennis, 1883; Aaron Dennis, 1866; Cassandra Fife, 18—; William Foreman, Sr., 1845; Sarah Foreman, 1864; Jennie R. Ford, 1893; John Folks, 18—; Lemuel Green, 1860; Lizzie Green, 18—; Mary T. Green, 1879; Cordelia Gallaher, 1865; Rebecca Gutshall, 1881; Thomas Healy, 18—; Phebe J. Hines, 1884; Lewis Hall, 18—; Hiram Harriman, 18—; S. O. Howell, 1880; Rachel Jenkins, 1886; William Kent, Sr., 1872; Katie Kent, 1882; W. W. Kent, 1886; Asbury Kent,

18—; Susan C. Kent, 1886; Zachariah Kent, 18—; Kennedy Kent, 1883; Joseph Kent, Sr., 18—; Joseph Lewis, 1853; Mary Lewis, 1850; Elizabeth Lewis, 18—; Josiah Lewis, 18—; William Lemasters, 1878; Jacob Lewis, Sr., 1882; Abram Mattern, 1889; Mary B. Mattern, 1890; Hugh Mattern, 1876; Robert McKee, Sr., 1851; Rachel McKee, 1847; Hannah McKee, 18—; James McKee, Sr., 18—; Catharine McKee, 1861; Ann B. McDivitt, 1863; Martha A. Norman, 1890; James Roberts, 18—; John Ralston, 1881; Leusintha A. Ralston, 1846; Ella Rutledge, 1884; Jane Scarlot, 1868; Rebecca Snyder, 1882; Ruth A. Snyder, 1892; Catharine Speer, 1883; Margaret Speer, 1886; Sophia Speer, 1849; John Thompson, 1892; Elizabeth Thompson, 1858; Hugh T. Thompson, 1878; Mary Ann Thompson, 1880; Harry Thompson, 1891; Thomas Thompson, Sr., 1875; Rebecca Thompson, 1854; Mary Thompson, Sr., 1860; Thomas Tumbleson, 18—; Keziah Wheeler, 1876; Morris West, 18—; Molinda Young, 18—.

RANKIN CHURCH.

This church was organized about the year 1814, by Rev. James Roberts and Thomas Dickerson. Services were held for some five years in the log-cabin of Thomas Rankin, during which time, among others, the following members were enrolled: Thomas Rankin, Mary Rankin, James and Hester Rankin, William Johnson and wife, Joshua Dickerson, John Early and wife, Jonathan Early and wife, Margaret Early, Arthur Barrett, Isaac Barrett, William Jones, Rachel Jones.

In 1819, Thomas Rankin donated an acre of ground to the Society on Section 31, in Moorefield township, for the site of a church, and burying ground. Soon after, a log building was erected, and the membership of the church materially increased. At one time, it numbered over 100 members. Four ministers were sent out from this church, namely, Benjamin Johnson, Baruch D. Jones, John Moffit, and Allan Moffit. Before 1850, the membership began to decrease, and at one time the roll was reduced to thirteen members. In 1870, a new building was erected; and since that time, the congregation has regained much of its former prosperity.

CHAPTER XV.

THE RIDGE CHURCH.

This church is the oldest religious organization in Archer township, and one of the oldest Presbyterian churches in Harrison county. The congregation has had four different preaching places or building sites since the church was set off from that of Beech Spring. The first of these was at the house of William Barnhill, then standing on section four. The second location, and site of the first church building, was on the northwest quarter of section eight; the third, on the southwest quarter of section seventeen; and the present building, on the southwest quarter of section twenty-three, near the village of Hanover.

The following history of Ridge Church is condensed from an Anniversary Discourse, delivered by its pastor, Rev. Robert Herron, D. D., at the church on December 13, 1873 (printed at Uhrichsville, Ohio, 1874):

The importance of having a continuous history of this church on record engaged the attention of the session early in the present pastorate. The importance of this was the more manifest from the fact that all the first records, both of the session and the congregation, were lost or mislaid, so that they could not be reached. This solicitude on the part of the session led to the adoption of the following resolution, which is taken from the records of the session of Ridge Church, Sept. 26, 1851:

> The Moderator was appointed to collect the facts, and write out a history of the church from its organization to the present time.

> The Moderator in due time submitted the following report to the session, which was accepted and approved by that body:

> "According to the foregoing action of the Session, I have taken considerable pains to collect and arrange, in a historical form, all the facts relating to this church. I regret, however, that after having written to the Stated

Clerks of the Presbyteries of Ohio and Steubenville, I am unable to ascertain how many persons were organized into a church here, or who were the ruling elders at the time of its organization."

The report was then presented, containing a historical sketch of this church, drawn from such information as could be gleaned from tradition, in the memory of a few of the older persons yet living among us; from congregational records commencing with the year 1835, and from sessional records commencing in the year 1842, which will be made the basis of our historical sketch, until the commencement of the present pastorate.

The Ridge Church, under the direction of Divine Providence, owes its existence to the following circumstances: The boundary of Beech Spring on the west extended for a considerable distance down the valleys of Stillwater and Connotton creeks. Hence, those members of this church found that their regular attendance upon the means of grace dispensed in the church where they worshipped was attended with great inconvenience. This fact induced them to ask the congregation to give their consent for their pastor, Rev. Dr. John Rea, to come and preach stately among them a portion of the time. To this request the congregation readily assented. The pastor, with a self denial and zeal in his Master's service, by which his long ministerial life was characterized, cheerfully came to break unto them the bread of life eternal. The extent of this self denial can be learned, partially, it is true, by reflecting on the fact that every time he visited this part of his charge, he travelled from home a distance of from ten to twelve miles, over roads new and poorly made, in a broken country. Dr. Rea's labors commenced in this way in the spring of 1810, and continued until the spring of 1817, a period of seven years. The proportion of time which Dr. Rea spent in this manner cannot be satisfactorily ascertained; but it is judged to have been about one-fourth of it, during this period.

He commenced his labors by preaching in the house of Mr. William Barnhill, on the farm now owned by Mr. John Reed, on the road leading from Smithfield to the road leading from Cadiz to Congress Furnace, and four miles from the point of intersection with it where the church now stands. He preached and administered the ordinances of religion, alternating this place occasionally with other dwelling-houses for a few years, when it was deemed advisable by the parent congregation to settle upon some place for holding their public services. Accordingly, a location was selected on the New Rumley and Cadiz road, on the farm now owned by Mr. John Lisle, three miles north of Cadiz. There they erected a house of worship, in which they were accustomed to assemble during the remainder of Dr. Rea's ministrations among them. This building—a log-cabin—was, doubtless, of small proportions, and of humble pretensions, yet it would sustain a favorable comparison with the dwellings of those who assembled there to worship the Most High; for they did not dwell in ceiled houses. . . .

The Providence of God appeared to indicate in the spring of 1817, that this society should be left without the stated means of grace, by Dr. Rea's withdrawal from them. Dr. Rea proposed to the people, now respectable in numbers, that they should covenant with God, and with one another, that they would remain united together, whatever should befall. This agreement was made by the whole body holding up their right hands. Thus ended Dr. Rea's official connection with the germ of the Ridge Church. . . .

A Presbyterian church was now about to be organized in Cadiz, and it was believed that if this society should continue to assemble in its present place of worship, it would stand in the way of that church's progress. This consideration prompted removal from this spot to another, on the northeast corner of the farm of John Endsley, Sr., now owned by his grandson, John E. McPeck. Here a tent was set up, and around it the people were accustomed to assemble for Divine worship.

The society now felt the necessity of assuming an organized form, as a Presbyterian church. In order to do this, they presented a petition to the Presbytery of Ohio, whose boundary extended thus far westward. This petition was favorably regarded by the Presbytery, and a committee, consisting of Revs. Messrs. Snodgrass and Clark was appointed to visit the field, and organize a church if the way were found to be clear. The committee discharged their duty, and organized the Ridge Presbyterian church, on the 17th day of October, 1818.

The Synod of Pittsburgh ordered the organization of the Presbytery of Steubenville previously to this committee's reporting to the Presbytery of Ohio, as to their action in the premises. This resulted in placing the name of the Ridge church on the roll of the churches of the Presbytery of Steubenville, without its being found on the roll of churches of the Presbytery of Ohio.

The organization continued to worship in this vicinity, occupying private houses and barns for two years, when they removed their place of worship to the village of Hanover, where they erected a tent for preaching purposes, north of where the Methodist church now stands. They met here, and in adjacent dwelling houses, for devotional purposes until February, 1823. But not finding this an eligible site on which to build a permanent house of worship, they secured, by purchase, two acres of ground from Mr. George Hospelhorn. One of these was used for building purposes, and the other was appropriated to burial uses.

At a meeting of the congregation held March 15th, 1823, it was resolved to proceed at once to erect a house of worship, and a tent. The house was for use on inclement Sabbaths, and the tent was to be occupied in favorable weather. The house was to be built fifty feet long by thirty wide, with a story twelve feet high. The tent was to be built eight feet long and six feet wide, and be weatherboarded.

Messrs. Samuel Buchanan, John Archibold, and Samuel Welsh were appointed a committee to carry out this action of the congregation.

This church building was completed and occupied by the congregation in the latter part of the following year. No doubt the work went forward as rapidly as the means of the people could drive it onward, as their number was small, and their resources limited.

This church now became united with the church of Cadiz as one pastoral charge. They unitedly called Rev. Donald McIntosh to become their pastor, giving to each part one-half his ministerial labors. The salary promised him from this branch of his charge was two hundred dollars: one-half cash, and the other half in produce, at the following rates—wheat, fifty cents per bushel; rye and corn, each thirty-three cents per bushel. The grain was to be delivered to Mr. Matthew McCoy, Cadiz, Ohio, with whom Mr. McIntosh boarded, being an unmarried man. The writer of this paper has in his possession a book, in which the following note is inscribed, by Mr. John Morrison Forsythe: "The Reverend Donald McIntosh, this 9th day of February, 1823, began his heavy labors in Archer township. It shall be said of this man, and that one, that he was born there." Mr. McIntosh was regularly installed pastor over this united charge; and from a communication sent to the trustees of this congregation, it appears that he also had charge of an academy for two years, when he resigned it, in order that he might devote himself entirely to his ministerial work.

Mr. McIntosh's care of this charge continued until 1826, when failing health required his resignation, in order to admit his travelling southward. Mr. McIntosh is remembered as an accomplished scholar and an instructive preacher. He died soon after in East India.

Rev. John McArthur became pastor of the same united charge in the year 1828. Mr. McArthur was regarded by his co-presbyters as a thorough scholar, and well-skilled in the doctrines of the holy Scriptures; a faithful expositor of God's word, and an acceptable and instructive preacher.

Mr. McArthur was born in Washington county, New York, March 25th, 1803. He graduated in Jefferson College, at Canonsburg, Pa., in 1825; studied theology under the Presbytery of New Lisbon, and was licensed by them in the fall of 1827; married Miss Christina Ann Robertson, daughter of Rev. James Robertson, of Carrollton, Ohio, in the winter of 1829, by whom he had six sons and one daughter. Two sons died in infancy. His wife survived him about seven years.

Mr. McArthur continued in this relation until 1836, when his time was entirely devoted to the Cadiz branch of his charge. The memory of Mr. McArthur was ever carefully cherished by all who were under his pastoral care. He is believed to have been the instrument in the hand of God in moulding this church in the pattern of sound doctrine and good government.

It was at his instance, and through his influence that the congregation obtained a charter as an incorporated body in the year 1835, by act of the Legislature of Ohio. The incorporators in this act were, "Walter McClintock, Jacob Richey, Samuel Buchanan, Ralph Atkinson, Jacob Vasbinder, Thomas Day, James L. McLane, James Megaw, John Lyons, George McPeck, John Welsh, Jr., William Lisle, Thomas Albertson, William Miller, and James McClintock."

He afterwards became professor of languages in Miami University, at Oxford, Ohio, and died at Indianapolis, Ind., in July, 1849.

Rev. William Doane McCartney became pastor of this church, devoting his entire labors to it, in 1838, and sustained this relation to it until 1842, when, at his request, the pastoral relation was dissolved.

Mr. McCartney was born in Montrose county, Pa., January 20th, 1806. He made a profession of religion in the Presbyterian church of Derry, Pa., September, 1822; graduated at Washington College, Pa., 1832, and immediately commenced the study of theology in the Western Theological Seminary. He was licensed to preach the gospel by the Presbytery of Washington, April, 1833; and by the same Presbytery he was ordained to the whole work of the ministry, June 27th, 1836.

Mr. McCartney and Miss Maria Jane Stewart, of Washington county, Pa., were united in marriage, April 25th, 1837. The result of this marriage was four children. One of these, the wife of Mr. D. S. Noble, ruling elder in Wellsville church, survives him, Mrs. McCartney and his other children having preceded him to their heavenly home.

He was called to bear severe afflictions near the close of his life, but the full vigor of his mental powers, and the sustaining grace of the Lord Jesus Christ were with him to the end, and that end was peace. He fell asleep in Jesus near Wellsville, Ohio, July 27th, 1863, and his mortal remains repose in Bethel churchyard, awaiting the resurrection of the just.

Rev. James Cameron became pastor of this church in the year 1844, and sustained that relation until the year 1847, when, at his own request, the pastoral relation was dissolved.

Mr. Cameron was born in the city of Pittsburgh, Pa., June 1st, 1813. He obtained his primary education in the place of his nativity, and graduated at the Jefferson College, Pa., in the year 1839. Soon after he entered the Western Theological Seminary, where he completed the prescribed course of study, and was licensed to preach the gospel by the Presbytery of Ohio, in the year 1842.

He received and accepted a call from this church to become its pastor, and in the year 1844 the Presbytery of Steubenville ordained and installed him pastor over this church. Two-thirds of his labor were to be given to this church, and the remaining one-third to Centre Unity. His record here is that of an industrious and efficient pastor, who did what he could to extend the interests of this part of the kingdom of the Lord Jesus Christ.

Mr. Cameron's wife was Miss Isabella Richey, of Pittsburgh, Pa., by whom he had four children—three sons and one daughter—all of whom, with their mother, survive him. His death occurred May 1st, 1866, in Brunswick, Ill., and was the result of paralysis.

The following records are found amongst the papers of Mr. Samuel Buchanan, deceased:

"Messrs. Walter McClintock and Jacob Richey were ordained Ruling Elders for the Ridge congregation, by Rev. Mr. Clark, August 21st, 1819.

"Messrs. Ralph Atkinson and Jacob Vasbinder were ordained Ruling Elders for the Ridge congregation, by Rev. Mr. McIntosh, August 22d, 1823.

"Messrs. William Patterson and Samuel Buchanan were ordained Ruling Elders for the Ridge congregation, by Rev. Mr. Rutherford, April 29th, 1827."

An election was held for Ruling Elders, by the congregation, it is believed, in the year 1834, which resulted in the choice of Messrs. James Megaw, Thomas Day, James L. McLane, and John Lyons. They accepted the office, and were ordained and installed by Rev. Mr. McArthur.

On the 20th day of August, 1844, Messrs. Alexander Osburn, Hugh McIlravy, and George McKinney were elected Ruling Elders by this congregation. Mr. Osburn had formerly been a Ruling Elder in Crabapple church, and therefore only required installation in this church. The other Elders elect were ordained and installed by Rev. Mr. Cameron.

Messrs. Robert Scott, Samuel Adams, and Samuel Osburn were elected Deacons by the congregation, August 20th, 1844, and were ordained and installed in their office by Rev. Mr. Cameron a few weeks afterwards. Of these, Messrs. Adams and Osburn remain in the discharge of their duties amongst us; but Mr. Scott has fallen asleep, as we believe, in Jesus, and was fully ripe for eternal glory, through the saving grace of the Lord Jesus Christ.

Thus far we have traced the way along which the Lord led this church in paths which are known to us only as revealed by the pen of the historian, or handed down by tradition. From this time forward we are enabled to speak of things which we ourselves have seen.

The present pastor formed a slight acquaintance with this congregation in the fall of 1847, while preaching a few Sabbaths to relieve a sick friend, Rev. Ephraim Ogden, then temporarily in charge of the congregation. The congregation becoming vacant, he was invited by the congregation at a meeting held June 20th, 1848, to visit them, and if he and they were mutually satisfied, to become their pastor. This invitation was accepted, and his labor in this way commenced on the fifth day of the succeeding July. His ministrations being regarded as satisfactory, a meeting of the congregation was held on the 20th day of September, next, for the purpose of taking the sense of the congregation on that subject, and on the vote being taken, it was unanimously in favor of the candidate's election as pastor, and a call was accordingly made out for two-thirds of his ministerial services, promising him a salary of three hundred dollars a year in half yearly payments. He being a licentiate, under the care of the Presbytery of Washington, the Presbytery of Steubenville gave the congregation permission to prosecute the call before that body. The Presbytery of Washington placed the call in his hands, and it was by him accepted October 14th, 1848, whereupon he was dismissed to the Presbytery of Steubenville. . . . Presbytery ordered that the ordination take place at Corinth on the 17th day of the approaching November, and assigned to him Hebrews, xii., 1. . . . The ordination took place according to the order of Presbytery, Rev. Dr. Beatty presiding, asking the constitutional questions, and leading in the prayer of ordination.

Presbytery directed that the installation of the pastor elect take place on the 13th of the approaching December, and appointed Rev. Joseph H. Chambers to preside, preach the sermon, and propose the constitutional questions, and Rev. Dr. Brown to deliver the charges to the pastor and people. The installation services took place as directed by Presbytery, according to the stipulations of the call.

A careful canvass of the church was now made by the session of the church, in order to ascertain the strength of its membership. The result of this investigation showed that at that time there were seventy-two persons in full communion in the church. Several of these were aged and infirm, so that the active working force of the church may be set down as sixty.

Officers in the church, 1848:

Ruling Elders—Samuel Buchanan, Thomas Day, John Lyons, Alexander Osburn, Hugh McIlravy, George McKinney, and James Megaw.

Deacons—Robert Scott, Samuel Adams, and Samuel Osburn.

Trustees—George Fisher, John Lyons, John Welch, Jr., Hugh McIlravy, Joseph Buchanan, and Thomas Day.

Treasurer—George McPeck.

Clerk of the Congregation—William Smiley.

Precentors—(Who stood before the people, gave out the lines of the hymn, pitched the tune, and led in singing it)—John Welch, Jr., Hugh McIlravy, George McKinney, and Samuel Osburn.

Additions to the church officers to 1873:

Moses Cole and Isaac Pratt were elected to the office of Ruling Elder, and ordained and installed February 10th, 1853.

Samuel Herron and John E. McPeck were elected to this office, and ordained and installed October 13th, 1860.

Robert Anderson, formerly a Ruling Elder in New Hagerstown church, was elected and installed in this office, February 3d, 1862.

Samuel Osburn was elected to this office, and ordained and installed January 18th, 1867.

John E. McPeck, having withdrawn from the membership of the church, owing to a change of residence, and having now returned to us, he was elected and installed in this office, October 28th, 1870.

Present Church Officers [1874]:

Ruling Elders—John Lyons, Samuel Herron, Robert Anderson, Samuel Osburn, and John E. McPeck.

Deacons—Samuel Adams and Samuel Osburn.

Trustees of the Congregation—David Patton, Robert Anderson, Samuel Currey, John S. Adams, Eli Cavin, and John Atkinson.

Congregation's Clerk—G. M. McPeck.

Treasurer—George McPeck.

It is proper that in this place there should be given a brief resume of the pastor's labors and successes during the quarter of a century just now closing.

The labors of this time were commenced by giving two-thirds of my time to this church, and the remaining one-third to Centre Unity. This arrangement continued until January 1st, 1864, a period of fifteen years, when this congregation began to occupy my entire time, until the present. The reported number of sermons, of members received, and of baptisms administered, will cover only those pertaining to this congregation.

I have preached twelve hundred sermons in the interest of the Ridge church, in discharging my pastoral duty to it.

I have received into full communion in the Ridge church three hundred members. Some of these persons have come to this church on letters of dismissal from other churches of our own order; and a proportion of them have come from other denominations; but much the larger part of these additions have been made on examination.

I have administered the ordinance of baptism, in the interest of this congregation, to twenty-seven adult persons, and to two hundred and seventy-five infants.

I have solemnized the marriage of one hundred and twenty-nine couples, that being, in some instances, of the parents and the offspring.

It has been my lot to be present and officiate, wholly or in part, at the funerals of one hundred and eighty-five persons. These have, however, not all been in connection with this congregation, nor even with the Presbyterian church.

Nearly two generations of men have passed away since the organization of this church. It is not known that any one of the original members is now living.

If we limit our range of vision by the horizon of the last twenty-five years, we find, to-day, in the session of this church but a single member, Mr. John Lyons, Sr., who was in it at that time. Two others, Messrs. Hugh McIlravy and George McKinney, are believed to be yet living, in other localities.

To-day, there are but fifteen living members in connection with us, who were members of this church at the commencement of the present pastorate, and who have retained their membership in it until the present time.

The condition of the church is specially encouraging. During the present year she has sent forth a colony of thirty persons to form a church in the neighboring village of Fairview, on the P., C. & St. L. Railway, called Buchanan Chapel. And still are left one hundred and fifty active workers in the cause of Christ, besides a few fathers and mothers in Israel, who linger among us to bless us with their counsels and prayers.

The congregation is free of debt, and owns a substantial and convenient brick house of worship.

PART SECOND.

HARRISON COUNTY LAND PATENTS, EARLY MARRIAGES, BURIAL RECORDS, AND WILL ABSTRACTS.

PART SECOND.

FIRST LANDOWNERS IN HARRISON COUNTY.

The first measure providing for the establishment and maintenance of government by the United States in the territory northwest of the Ohio river, was an ordinance passed by Congress on April 23, 1784. The ordinance was reported by a committee of which Thomas Jefferson was chairman, and contained a clause prohibiting slavery in the territory after the year 1800. This provision, however, was stricken out before the ordinance was finally passed. The only important result accomplished under the first ordinance was the beginning of the survey of the territorial lands.

Congress, having purchased from the Indians at the treaty of Fort Stanwix, October 27, 1784, whatever title the Six Nations had to lands in the valley of the Ohio, now sought to provide for the survey and disposal of the same; and on May 20, 1785, was passed, "An Ordinance for Ascertaining the Mode of Disposing of Lands in the Western Territory." This ordinance provided that a surveyor should be appointed from each State.

On May 27th Congress chose as surveyors: Nathaniel Adams, New Hampshire; Rufus Putnam, Massachusetts; Caleb Harris, Rhode Island; William Morris, New York; Adam Hoopes, Pennsylvania; James Simpson, Maryland; Alexander Parker, Virginia; Absalom Tatum, North Carolina; William Tate, South Carolina; and on July 18th, Isaac Sherman, Connecticut. Benjamin Tupper was appointed instead of Rufus Putnam from Massachusetts, as the latter was then surveying lands in Maine, and could not serve. Caleb Harris and Nathaniel Adams having resigned, Col. Ebenezer Sproat and Winthrop Sargent were chosen in their places.

The surveyors were to divide the territory into townships, six miles square. The first north and south line was to begin on the Ohio river, at a point due north from the western terminus of a line that had been run at the southern boundary of Pennsylvania; and the first east and west line was also to begin at the same point.

It was provided that as soon as seven ranges of townships had been surveyed, the Geographer should transmit the plats of the same to the Board of the Treasury. The Secretary was then to take by lot a number of townships and fractional townships, both of those to be sold entire and of those to be sold in lots, such as would be equal to one-seventh part of the whole seven ranges, for the use of officers and soldiers of the Continental army.

The survey was begun in July, 1786, under the management of Thomas Hutchins, the Geographer of the United States. He started on the Pennsylvania line at the north bank of the Ohio river, and first ran a line west through Columbiana and Carroll counties, now known as the "Geographer's Line," a distance of forty-two miles, setting a post each mile. Every six miles was a township corner, and from these corners the south lines were run to the Ohio river, and the north lines to the southern boundary of the Connecticut, or Western Reserve. Hutchins began numbering sections at the southeast corner of the township, which was called section 1, thence north to the northeast corner, which was section 6. Section 7 began at the bottom again, west of section 1, and the numbers were carried up to section 36, which was in the northwest corner. In Charles Whittlesey's tract on the "Surveys of the Public Lands in Ohio," it is stated that this is the first application in the history of land surveys, of the rectangular system of lots in squares of one mile, with meridian lines and corner posts at each mile, where the number of the section, town, and range was put on the witness trees in letters and figures. This system of numbering was followed in the survey of the Ohio Company's lands about Marietta, and in the Symmes Purchase. It was changed to the present system in 1799, by which the numbering of the sections begins in the northeast corner of the township, and proceeds alternately from east to west, and thence west to east.

The plan originally adopted by Congress for the sale of the lands in the Northwest Territory, proposed to sell it in tracts of two million acres; the second ordinance, in smaller tracts, of one million. Under the last ordinance, the contract of the Ohio Company, on the Muskingum, and that of Judge Symmes and his associates, between the Miamis, were made, the former for two millions, the latter for one million acres. By a subsequent ordinance, passed in May, 1785, seven ranges of townships, each six miles square, were surveyed westward from the Ohio river and the Pennsylvania line, which were divided and offered for sale, in quarter townships; first at Pittsburgh, and afterwards in Philadelphia. Harrison county lies between the western lines of Ranges three and seven, its townships thus being included in the four western ranges.

In May, 1796, an act was passed by Congress, directing the Surveyor General to cause the public lands to be divided into townships of six miles square; and one-half of these townships, taking them alternately to be divided into sections of one mile square, and the residue into quarter townships of three miles square. In the year 1800, another law was passed, ordering a portion of these lands to be subdivided, and sold in half sections, of three hundred and twenty acres. When this law came into operation, land offices were established at Cincinnati, Chillicothe, Marietta, and Steubenville, and a large quantity of the richest and most productive soil was brought into the market.

Before that time, the tracts of land offered for sale by the Government were so large that men of limited means were unable to purchase. The smallest tract that could be bought was a section, containing six hundred and forty acres. Under this arrangement, most of the lands in the present townships of Short Creek, Athens, Green, and Cadiz were entered by the section; thus indicating that the first comers were men of more than ordinary means or enterprise. Although the later provision for the accommodation of the settler of limited means was of much importance, yet it was not sufficiently so as to advance the settlement of the Territory with much rapidity. But an act passed at a subsequent session of Congress which ordered the sections and half sections to be subdivided and offered for sale in quarter sections (160 acres), at two dollars per acre, on a credit of four years, was of vastly more importance; as it enabled thousands to become landowners who otherwise must have remained tenants; and it thus encouraged and increased emigration to the western country.

The Act of May 18, 1796, (First Statute at Large, 464), and the Act of May 10, 1800 (Second Statutes at Large, 72), provide, in substance, for the sale of public lands to the highest bidder, one-fourth of the purchase money to be paid at the time of sale, one-fourth within two years, one-fourth within three years, and the remaining one-fourth within four years from date of sale. The Act of March 2, 1821 (Third Statutes at Large, 612) provides for the relief of purchasers of the public land, where the purchase was made prior to July 1, 1820, and they had been unable to comply with the provisions of the previous act.

In all credit sales patented prior to the passage of this relief act, it is safe to assume that the purchase was made within the four or five years preceding the patent. Cash entries, as a rule, were made from six months to two years prior to the date of patenting, although in the case of a few suspended entries, this rule would not apply.

Hence, as a general rule, all patents issued for lands in Harrison county prior to 1821 (and many during the next four or five years after 1821), bear a date from four to five years later than the date of the original entry and settlement of the land.

In the descriptions of lands given in the following list, the words, "section," "township," and "range" have been omitted, and are to be understood as following the three numbers describing the location of the respective tracts. For instance, "all 6.9.4" means "all of section 6, township 9, range 4," which would locate the tract as section number 6 in Short Creek township. "W½ SW 6.9.4 means, "the west half of the southwest quarter of section 6, township 9, range 4," which would locate the tract as eighty acres of section number 6 in Short Creek township. A section of land comprises 640 acres, the common subdivisions of which are half sections (containing 320 acres), of which there may be the north half, the west half, the south half, or the east half; quarter sections, or "quarters" (containing 160 acres), of which there may be the northeast (NE) quarter, the northwest (NW) quarter, the southwest (SW) quarter, and the southeast (SE) quarter, as well as adjoining halves of two adjoining quarters; eighth sections, or "eighties" (containing eighty acres), of which there may be the north half of the northeast quarter (N½ NE), west half of the northeast quarter (W½ NE), etc., east half of the northwest quarter (E½ NW), etc., east half of the southwest quarter (E½ SW), etc., south half of the southeast quarter (S½ SE), etc., as well as any two adjoining or cornering half-eighties; and sixteenth-sections, or "forties" (containing forty acres), of which there may be the northwest quarter of the northeast quarter (NW NE), etc., and so on through sixteen different descriptions, as well as any two adjoining or cornering twenty acre tracts which taken together comprise forty acres. It will be remembered that there are thirty-six sections in a township, the numbering beginning with the section in the southeast corner, which is numbered one, and proceeding thence north to the section in the northeast corner of the township, which is numbered six, thence beginning again on the south line of the township with the section adjoining number one on the west, which is numbered seven, and proceeding north to section twelve; and so on; the section in the northwest corner of each numerical township being numbered thirty-six. The different numerical townships and ranges of Harrison county correspond with the geographical names of the different townships as follows:

Township 8, Range 4: Sections 4, 5, 6, 10, 11, 12, 16, 17, 18, 22, 23, 24, 28, 29, and 30 form the south half of Short Creek township.

Sections 34, 35, and 36, form part of the east one-sixth of Athens township.

Sections 1, 2, and 3, 7, 8, 9, 13, 14, 15, 19, 20, 21, 25, 26, 27, 31, 32, and 33 form the east three-fourths of Wheeling township, Belmont county (adjoining Short Creek township, Harrison county, on the south), in which are located Crabapple and Unity churches.

Township 9, Range 4: Sections 1, 2, 3, 7, 8, 9, 13, 14, 15, 19, 20, 21, 25, 26, and 27 form the north half of Short Creek township.

Sections 4, 5, 6, 10, 11, 12, 16, 17, 18, 22, 23, 24, 28, 29, and 30 form the south three-sevenths of Green township.

Section 31 forms the northeast corner section of Athens township.

Sections 32, 33, 34, 35, and 36 form the east one-seventh of Cadiz township.

Township 10, Range 4: Sections 1, 2, 3, 4, 7, 8, 9, 10, 13, 14, 15, 16, 19,

20, 21, 22, 25, 26, 27, and 28 form the north four-sevenths of Green township.

Sections 5, 6, 11, 12, 17, 18, 23, 24, 29 (excepting the northwest eighty acres), and 30 (excepting the west 160 acres) form the south two-fifths of German township.

Sections 33, 34, and the south half of 35 form part of the east one-sixth of Archer township.

Section 26, the north half of 35, the west 160 acres of section 30, and the northwest 80 acres of section 29 form part of the southeast corner of Rumley township.

Township 11, Range 4: Sections 1, 2, 3, 7, 8, 9, 13, 14, 15, 19, 20, 21, 25, 26, and 27 form the north three-fifths of German township.

Sections 31, 32, and 33 form part of the east one-fifth of Rumley township.

The remainder of township 11-4 lies in Jefferson and Carroll counties.

Township 9, Range 5: Sections 4, 5, 6, 10, 11, 12, 16, 17, 18, 22, 23, 24, 28, 29, and 30 form the south three-fourths of Athens township.

Sections 34, 35, and 36 form part of the east one-seventh of Moorefield township.

Sections 1, 2, 3, 7, 8, and 9 form the west fourth of Wheeling township, Belmont county.

Sections 13, 14, 15, 19, 20, 21, 25, 26, 27, 31, 32, and 33 form the east two-fifths of Flushing township, Belmont county.

Township 10, Range 5: Sections 1, 7, 13, 19, and 25 form the north fourth of Athens township.

Section 31 forms the northeast corner section of Moorefield township.

Sections 2, 3, 4, 5, 6, 8, 9, 10, 11, 12, 14, 15, 16, 17, 18, 20, 21, 22, 23, 24, 26, 27, 28, 29, 30, 32, 33, 34, 35, and 36 form the west six-sevenths of Cadiz township.

Township 11, Range 5: Sections 1, 2, 3, 4, 7, 8, 9, 10, 13, 14, 15, 16, 19, 20, 21, 22, the south half of sections 5, 11, 17, and 23, and the east two-thirds of sections 25, 26, 27, 28, and of the south half of 29 form the township of Rumley.

Sections 6, 12, 18, 24, the north half of sections 5, 11, 17, and

23, and east fourth of section 30 and of north half of 29 form part of the south one-third of Rumley township.

Township 12, Range 5: Sections 1, 2, 3, 7, 8, 9, 13, 14, 15, 19, 20, 21, and the east fourth of sections 25, 26, and 27 form part of the north two-thirds of Rumley township.

The remainder of township 12.5 lies in Carroll county.

Township 10, Range 6: Sections 4, 5, 6, 10, 11, 12, 16, 17, 18, 22, 23, 24, 28, 29, 30, 34, 35, and 36 form part of the south three-fourths of Moorefield township.

Sections 1, 2, 3, 7, 8, 9, 13, 14, 15, 19, 20, 21, 25, 26, 27, 31, 32, and 33 are in Belmont county.

Township 11, Range 6: Sections 1, 7, 13, 19, 25, and 31 form part of the north one-fourth of Moorefield township.

Sections 2, 3, 4, 5, 6, 8, 9, 10, 11, 12, 14, 15, 16, 17, 18, 20, 21, 22, 23, 24, 26, 27, 28, 29, 30, 32, 33, 34, 35, and 36 form all of Nottingham township.

Township 12, Range 6: Sections 1, 2, 3, 4, 7, 8, 9, 10, 13, 14, 15, 16, 19, 20, 21, and 22 and the south portion of sections 5, 11, 17, and 23 form the west eight-elevenths of Stock township.

Sections 6, 12, 18, and the north portion of sections 5, 11, and 17 form part of the southwest quarter of North township.

Sections 25, 26, 27, 28, 31, 32, 33, 34, and the south portion of sections 29 and 35 form the east two-fifths of Franklin township.

Sections 24, 30, 36, and the north portion of sections 23, 29, and 35 form part of the southwest corner of Monroe township.

Township 13, Range 6: Sections 1, 2, 3, 7, 8, 9, 13, 14, and 15 form the northwest portion of North township.

Sections 19, 20, 21, 25, 26, 27, 31, 32, and 33 form the northeast portion of Monroe township.

The remainder of township 13.6 lies in Carroll county.

Township 11, Range 7: Sections 4, 5, 6, 10, 11, 12, 16, 17, 18, 22, 23, 24, 28, 29, 30, 34, 35, and 36 form the south three-fourths of Freeport township.

Sections 1, 2, 3, 7, 8, 9, 13, 14, 15, 19, 20, 21, 25, 26, 27, 31, 32, and 33 are in Guernsey county.

Township 12, Range 7: Sections 1, 7, 13, 19, 25, and 31 form the north one-fourth of Freeport township.

Sections 2, 3, 4, 5, 6, 8, 9, 10, 11, 12, 14, 15, 16, 17, 18, 20, 21, 22, 23, 24, 26, 27, 28, 29, 30, 32, 33, 34, 35, and 36 form all of Washington township.

Township 13, Range 7: Sections 1, 2, 3, 4, 7, 8, 9, 10, 13, 14, 15, 16, and the south portion of sections 5, 11, and 17 form the west three-fifths of Franklin township.

Sections 6, 12, and 18, and the north portion of sections 5, 11, and 17 form part of southwestern portion of Monroe township.

The remainder of township 13.7 lies in Tuscarawas county.

Township 14, Range 7: Sections 1, 2, 3, 7, 8, 9, 13, 14, and 15 form the northwest portion of Monroe township.

The remainder of township 14·7 lies in Carroll and Tuscarawas counties.

LIST OF HARRISON COUNTY LAND PATENTS.

George Abel, Loudoun county, Va., SE 15.11.4, June 19, 1813.
George Abel, Loudoun county, Va., NW 21.11.4, Nov. 26, 1813.
John Abrams, assignee of Philip Everhart, dec'd, SW 8.11.4, Nov. 30, 1811.
John Adams, Harrison county, NE 4.11.7, Feb. 14, 1817.
William Adams, Jefferson county, SW 21.11.5, March 7, 1818.
John Agnew, Washington county, Pa., all 11.10.5, Feb. 10, 1807.
Jacob Albert, Jefferson county, SE 2.13.6, Dec. 30, 1811.
Esther Alexander, Harrison county, W½ NW 36.11.6, July 1, 1831.
Isaac Alexander, assignee of Jacob Manback, E½ NW 13.13.6, Aug. 10, 1827.
John Alexander, Harrison county, W½ NW 24.12.6, Nov. 1, 1830.
Reuben Allen, Harrison county, E½ 32.11.6, Aug. 18, 1817.
Isaac Allen, Harrison county, NE 31.11.6, Aug. 18, 1817.
Oliver Allis, W½ SW and N½ SE 22.10.6, Jan. 23, 1822.
Oliver Allis, Harrison county, E½ SW 22.10.6, Sept. 10, 1823.
Oliver Allis, Jefferson county, NW 22.10.6, Aug. 19, 1824.
Asa Anderson, Belmont county, SW 24.10.6, May 29, 1818.
Isaac Anderson, Jefferson county, W½ NW and SE SW 22.12.6, Sept. 10, 1834.
James Anderson, Fayette county, Pa., SW 35.11.6, Aug. 30, 1816.
William Andreson, Jefferson county, NE 13.11.5, Nov. 10, 1811.
Joseph Applegate, Charlestown, all 1.9.4, July 22, 1805.
Daniel Arbaugh, Harrison county, NE 3.13.6, May 22, 1827.
John Arbaugh, assignee of David Custard, NE 6.11.5, July 29, 1819.
John Archbold, Westmoreland county, Pa., NW 17.11.5, Aug. 4, 1814.

John Archbold, Harrison county, NE 28.11.5, Aug. 3, 1818.
John Archbold, Harrison county, E½ NE 34.11.5, Nov. 13, 1822.
George Atkinson, Brooke county, Va., all 27.11.4, Aug. 18, 1804.
James Atkinson, Washington county, Pa., NE 15.11.5, Aug. 1, 1819.
John Atkinson, Harrison county, W½ NE 21.12.6, April 30, 1822.
John Auld, Union county, Pa., NW 35.11.6, Jan. 21, 1819.
Samuel Auld, Northumberland county, Pa., NE 33.11.6, June 26, 1820.
Samuel Auld, Jr., Harrison county, W½ NW 34.11.6, Nov. 13, 1822.
Samuel Auld, Jr., Harrison county, W½ SE 5 and W½ SE 6.12.7, April 20, 1827.
Samuel Auld, Harrison county, W½ NE 4.12.7, Nov. 18, 1833.
William Auld,Northumberland county, Pa., NE 28.11.6, June 26, 1820.
Thomas Ayres, assignee of James Kendal and Thomas Mills, NW 8.12.5, Aug. 19, 1824.
George Badger, Washington county, Pa., NW SE 28.12.7, Dec. 8, 1835.
Emmor Baily, assignee of Charles Lownes, SW 10.12.7, Dec. 29, 1818.
Daniel Bair, Somerset ccounty, Pa., SE 6.11.5, May 23, 1810.
Daniel Bair, Somerset county, Pa., NE 5.11.5, June 8, 1812.
Daniel Bair, Harrison county, NW 35.10.4, Aug. 4, 1814.
George Baker, Harrison county, W½ SE 30.12.7, Nov. 12, 1832.
John Baker, Harrison county, SE 25.13.6, March 7, 1817.
Otho Baker, Harrison county, W½ NE 36.12.6 and E½ NW 25.13.6, Nov 1, 1830.
Nathan Ball, Carroll county, NW SW 9.14.7, April 1, 1837.
Cornelius Barber, Harrison county, E½ SW 4.11.7, Dec. 6, 1831.
Barger, see Barriger and Berger.
John Barkhurst, Jefferson county, W½ SW 33.12.7, Jan. 1, 1833.
James Barnes, assignee of Horton Howard, Belmont county, E½ SW and W½ SW 22.9.5, Aug. 19, 1824.
William Barnhill, assignee of Samuel Osburn, SE 4.11.5, May 10, 1811.
William Barnhill, Harrison county, NW 3.11.5, Dec. 18, 1816.
William Barnhill, Harrison county, E½ NE 29.12.6, May 20, 1826.
John Barr, Washington county, Pa., SW 29.10.5, Nov. 24, 1814.
Arthur Barrett, Sr., Frederick county, Va., all 26.10.5, Jan. 20, 1808.
Arthur Barrett Sr., Jefferson county, NW 33.10.5, Jan. 20, 1812.
Arthur Barrett, Sr., Jefferson county, NE 33.10.5, Aug.19, 1812.
George Barricklow, Fayette county, Pa., SW 15,10.5, July 30, 1812.
Henry Barricklow, assignee of William Welling, NW 13.10.5, Jan. 20, 1809.
Henry Barricklow, Jefferson county, SW 36.9.5, Dec. 9, 1815.
Barriger, see also Berger.
Henry Barriger, Adams county Pa., NW 21.10.4, Aug. 10, 1813.
Valentine Barriger, Adams county, Pa., NE 21. 10.5, Aug. 4, 1814.
Xopherius Bartholome, Harrison county, NE SE 14.14.7, April 1, 1837.
David Barton, Washington county, Pa., all 13.8.4, Dec. 20, 1808.
George Barton, Harrison county, E½ NE 6.12.6, Nov. 1, 1830.
George Bartow, Harrison county, NE 5.12.6, Dec. 29, 1818.

George Bartow, Harrison county, W½ SW 18.12.6, March 21, 1832.
William Baun and William Constable, assignees of Arnold Henry Dorhn, all of Town. 13, Range 7, May 15, 1801.
John Baxter, Allegheny county, Pa., NE 28.10.5, Dec. 15, 1812.
Robert Baxter, assignee of John Maholm, SE 6.10.6, Dec. 15, 1812.
Alexander Beall, Harrison county, W½ SE 21.11.6, April 8, 1828.
Colmore Beall, Washington county, Pa., SE 22.11.6, March 7, 1818.
Colmore Beall, Washington county, Pa., NE 21.11.6, Nov. 13, 1822.
Colmore Beall, Washington county, Pa., W½ NW 21.11.6, Nov. 1, 1830.
Dory Beall, Harrison county, E½ SW 4.12.6, Oct. 2, 1821.
James P. Beall, Harrison county, W½ NE 22.11.6, Dec. 10, 1827.
John Beall Harrison county, E½ NW 21.11.16, Dec. 10, 1827.
Alexander Beard, Belmont county, W½ NW 26.12.7, July 1, 1831.
Sampson Bealy, Harrison county, E½ NW 30.12.7, Nov. 18, 1833.
William Beatty, Harrison county, W½ SW 21.12.5, May 6, 1824.
Zaccheus A. Beatty, Steubenville, all 5.10.5 (the site of Cadiz), April 20, 1804.
Samuel Beck, Harrison county, NE 11.11.7, Sept. 29, 1814.
Jacob Beckley, assignee of Stephen Ford, NE 15.11.4, July 30, 1812.
Walter B. Beebe, Harrison county, NE 19.12.5, Aug. 19, 1818.
Walter Butler Beebe, Cadiz, W½ SW 4.12.6, Dec. 2, 1832.
Harvey Beens, Washington county, Pa., W½ NW 34.11.7, Nov. 1, 1830.
George Beer, Frederick county, Md., NW 9.12.5, Oct. 20, 1819.
David Belknap, assignee of Thomas Hayne, all 2.9.4, Feb. 2, 1807.
Robert Bell, Belmont county, NE 11.10.6, Aug. 10, 1811.
James Cummings Bennett, Tuscarawas county, W½ SE 7.14.7, Dec. 6, 1831.
Berger, see also Barriger.
Peter Berger, Harrison county, NE 22.10.5, Aug. 3, 1818.
Valentine Berger, Adams county, Pa., SE 21.10.5, Aug. 6, 1813.
Valentine Berger, Adams county, Pa., NW 22.10.4, Aug. 18, 1817.
Heirs and legal Representatives of James Best, dec'd, Westmoreland county, Pa., E½ NW 22.11.5, May 25, 1825.
Simpson Bethel, Harrison county, SE 31.9.5, Aug. 19, 1824.
Thompson Bethel, Harrison county, E½ SW 35.10.6, May 20, 1826.
Stacy Bevan, Belmont county, NW 29.9.5, Aug. 10, 1811.
Zaccheus Biggs, Steubenville, all 10.10.5, May 20, 1806.
Zaccheus Biggs, assignee of Zaccheus Beatty, all 33.9.4, Aug. 27, 1807.
William Billingsley, Belmont county, W½ SE 11.12.7, June 23, 1826.
Hugh Birney, Harrison county, E½ SW 36.12.6, May 20, 1826.
Hugh Birney, Harrison county, W½ SW 36.12.6, May 30, 1826.
John Birney and William Birney, Harrison county NW 17.10.4, Oct. 20, 1824.
William Birney, Steubenville, NE 22.10.4, March 20, 1813.
William Birney, Harrison county, E½ NW 36.12.6, Oct. 6, 1826.
William Birney, Harrison county, E½ SE 30.12.7, April 20, 1827.
John Bishop, Harrison county, E½ NE 18.10.4, Sept. 10, 1823.

Daniel Black, assignee of Frederick Erfort, NE 33.13.6, Dec. 27, 1822.
Jacob Black, Sr., Fayette county, Pa., all 12.9.5, Jan. 20, 1808.
James Black, assignee of Benjamin Hough, all 4.10.4, March 1, 1810.
Archibald Blair, Bedford county, Pa., E½ 36.11.6, March 7, 1818.
Rannel Blair, Brooke county, Va., all 23.10.5, Jan. 20, 1809.
Edward Bleakney, Harrison county, E½ NW 18.12.6, March 21, 1832.
Kesiah Bliss, Columbiana county, NE 31.12.6, Aug. 19, 1824.
Zadok Bliss, Harrison county, W½ SE 32.12.6, July 1, 1831.
Martin Boghart, Somerset county, Pa., SW 9.13.6, Jan. 20, 1812.
Jonathan Bogne, Tuscarawas county, SW 7.12.7, Dec. 26, 1815.
Samuel Bolen, Harrison county, E½ SW 22.11.6, Nov. 1, 1830.
James Boles Harrison county, E½ NE 21.12.7, April 17, 1828.
James Boles, Harrison county, W½ NE 21.12.7, Nov. 1, 1830.
William Boling, assignee of Barton Hooper, E½ SW 14.11.6, May 25, 1825.
John P. Bond, Brooke county, Va., NE 32.10.4, Nov. 30, 1811.
John Booth, assignee of William Rouse, NW 3.14.7, Nov. 2, 1829.
John Borland, Westmoreland county, Pa., NE 15.13.6, March 7, 1818.
Samuel Boreland, Westmoreland county, Pa., SE 9.13.6, Jan. 27, 1819.
Samuel Borland, Harrison county, E½ NE 20.12.6, Dec. 6, 1831.
Bernard Bower, Jefferson county, SE 27.13.6, July 30, 1812.
Bernard Bower, Tuscarawas county, SW 27.13.6, Nov. 13, 1822.
Bernard Bower, Tuscarawas county, SW 21.13.6, Aug. 19, 1824.
Bernard Bower, Tuscarawas county, W½ NE 32.13.6, June 23, 1827.
David Bower, Sr., Tuscarawas county, E½ NE 32.13.6, June 23, 1827.
David Bower, Tuscarawas county, W½ NW 13.13.6, Nov. 1, 1830.
David Bower, Tuscarawas county, E½ SW 26.13.6, Dec. 2, 1830.
David Bower, Tuscarawas county, E½ NE 19.13.6, March 21, 1832.
Henry Bower, Tuscarawas county, SW 32.13.6, Dec. 2, 1830.
Jacob Bowers,Tuscarawas county, W½ NW 31.13.6, Nov. 1, 1830.
Jacob Bowers, E½ NE 1.14.7, Nov. 1, 1830.
John Bower, Jefferson county, NW 27.13.6, Jan. 20, 1809.
John Bower, Harrison county, E½ NW 24.12.6, Aug. 10, 1827.
John Bower, Harrison county, E½ SW 30.12.6, April 17, 1828.
Madelena Bower, Tuscarawas county, W½ SE 26.13.6, Dec. 2, 1830.
John Boyd, assignee of John Dixon, NE 25.12.7, Nov. 6, 1815.
John Boyd, Jefferson county, NW 20.12.7, June 5, 1816.
Samuel Boyd, Brooke county, Va., all 12.10.5, Sept. 8, 1806.
Samuel Boyd, assignee of Zaccheus Beatty, SW 7.11.5, June 8, 1812.
Jeremiah Bradley, Westmoreland county, Pa., SW 29.11.5, Aug. 19, 1824.
John Branson, Stafford county, Va., SW 15.9.5, March 16, 1815.
Rees Branson, Frederick county, Va., SW 27.9.5, Feb. 1, 1814.
Bricker, see also Pricker.
Anthony Bricker, assignee of Zaccheus Beatty, all 24.9.4, Aug. 18, 1804.
George S. Brock, Belmont county, NW 5.10.6, July 8, 1818.

Jesse Brock, Stafford county, Va., NW 27.9.5, Dec. 15, 1811.
George Brokaw, Jefferson county, NE 15.9.5, June 8, 1812.
James Brown, assignee of John Brown, NW 30.10.6, June 26, 1820.
John Brown, assignee of David Custard, SE 7.12.5, July 29, 1819.
John Brown, Jr., assignee of John Brown, NW 25.11.6, June 26, 1820.
John Brown, Harrison county, E½ SE 33.12.7, Dec. 6, 1831.
Michael Brown, Harrison county, W½ NE 22.12.7, Sept. 1, 1823.
William Brown, Brooke county, Va., all 13.9.4, Aug. 27, 1805.
William Brown, Washington county, Pa., E½ SW 15.12.5, Sept. 10, 1823.
William Brown, Washington county, Pa., E½ SE 29.11.5, April 2, 1829.
William Brown, Harrison county, E½ NW 27.12.7, Dec. 6, 1831.
Ezekiel Orrick Bryan, Prince George county, Md., N½ 28.10.6, July 2, 1814.
Samuel Buchanan, Washington county, Pa., NW 11.11.5, May 8, 1806.
Nathaniel Buck, Harrison county, SW 8.12.7, March 28, 1820.
John Burkhead, Harrison county, NW 36.10.5, Aug. 26, 1815.
Thomas Burkhead, Jefferson county, SW 17.10.5, July 30, 1812.
Thomas Burkhead, Harrison county, NE 36.10.5, Aug. 19, 1824.
William Burns, Harrison county, E½ NW 30.12.6, July 1, 1831.
Benjamin Burrows, Brooke county, Va., SW 36.10.6, May 5, 1821.
Samuel Burrows, Harrison county, W½ SW 4.11.7, Nov. 13, 1822.
Joseph Burt, Washington county, Pa., SW 34.11.7, Nov. 26, 1819.
Thomas Burton, Jefferson county, NE 5.11.6, Aug. 10, 1827.
Abraham Busby, Baltimore county, Md., SW 35.10.4, Jan. 27, 1819.
Abraham Busby, Harrison county, E½ SW 5.11.5, Sept. 15, 1823.
Isaac Cadwalader, Fayette county, Pa., NE 6.11.7, Dec. 30, 1811.
John Cadwallader, Jr., Tuscarawas county, SW 1.11.6, July 30, 1812.
John Cadwallader, Fayette county, Pa., NE 12.11.7, March 16, 1814.
John Cadwallader, Jr., Tuscarawas county, SE 12.11.7, March 16, 1814.
John Cadwallader, Tuscarawas county, SW 1.12.7, Aug. 4, 1814.
Joseph Cadwallader, Harrison county, NE 2.12.7, Aug. 4, 1814.
Griffith Cahill, assignee of George Bohrer, SE 33.10.5, March 9, 1815.
Alexander Calderhead, Jefferson county, SE 3.8.4, April 15, 1812.
William Calderhead, Jefferson county, NE 3.8.4, April 10, 1812.
James Caldwell, St. Clairsville, NW 32.11.6, May 22, 1813.
David Campbell, Washington county, Pa., SW 21.8.4, Oct. 9, 1812.
James Campbell, Westmoreland county, Pa., W½ SE 7.12.6, Feb. 20, 1827.
John Campbell, Washington county, Pa., all 26.8.4, Feb. 26, 1806.
Christian Knagy (Canaga), Somerset county Pa., SW 26.12.5, March 10, 1807.
Christian Kanagy (Canaga), Somerset county, Pa., E½ 26.12.5, Jan. 30, 1810.
Christian Kanagy (Canaga), Jefferson county, NW 25.12.5, Oct. 1, 1811.
Jacob Kanagy (Canaga), SW 32.12.5, March 10, 1807.
Jacob Kanagy (Canaga), Jefferson county, NW 32.12.5, Nov. 1, 1811.
Joshua Carens, Harrison county, W½ NE 20.12.6, Dec. 2, 1830.
Samuel Kernaghan (Carnahan), Jefferson county, all 6.10.5, Sept. 15, 1806.

Samuel Kernaghan (Carnahan), Jefferson county, Northwest Territory, all 9.10.5, Dec. 1, 1809.
George Carothers, Washington county, Pa., SW 8.11.6, Dec. 30, 1811.
George Carothers, Washington county, Pa., SE 14.11.6, Aug. 26, 1815.
George Carothers, Harrison county, SW 31.11.6, Sept. 10, 1831.
James Caruthers, Harrison county, NE SE 5.12.7, Nov. 18, 1833.
Jesse Caruthers, Harrison county, E½ SE 6.12.7, Nov. 18, 1833.
John Caruthers, Harrison county, NW SE 35.11.6, Nov. 18, 1833.
Samuel Caruthers, Belmont county, NE 5.12.7, Aug. 10, 1827.
Elizabeth Carr, Washington county, Pa., W½ SW 15.12.5, Sept. 15, 1823.
Elizabeth Carr, Harrison county, W½ SE 15.12.5, Nov. 1, 1830.
James Carr, Jefferson county, W½ NW 27.12.7, Oct. 10, 1831.
John Carson, Harrison county, NE 4.11.6, March 7, 1817.
John Carson, Harrison county, W½ NW 15.12.6, May 6, 1824.
Evan Carter, Jefferson county, SE NW 26.12.7, Dec. 11, 1839.
Henry Carter, Tuscarawas county, W½ NE 15.14.7, Dec. 10, 1827.
Henry Carver, Jefferson county, SE 27.9-5, June 23, 1810.
Henry Carver, Belmont county, SE 14.12.7, Aug. 19, 1812.
Henry Carver, Harrison county, NE 13.12.7, May 29, 1818.
Ninian Cash, Harrison county, E½ SE 21.11.6, Sept. 1, 1823.
Alexander Cassil, Washington county, Pa., all 23.9.4, Sept. 10, 1806.
John Castell, Jr., Harrison county, SW 19.12.6, Nov. 1, 1830.
Michael Castner, assignee of William R. Dickinson, NE 33.12.5, May 3, 1822.
Michael Castner, Jefferson county, NW 27.12.5, Aug. 10, 1827.
Wilson Cawood, Harrison county, NE 25.12.6, May 21, 1819.
Hazle Cecil, Harrison county, SW 6.11.6, Oct. 21, 1816.
John Cecil, SE 35.9.5, April 22, 1819.
Joshua Cecil, assignee of John McMillan, SW 20.10.5, July 30, 1813.
Sarah Chambers, Brooke county, Va., all 30.8.4, Feb. 18, 1806.
Eli Chandler, Belmont county, SE 34.10.6, Aug. 19, 1824.
Enoch Chandler, Belmont county, W½ SW 34.10.6, Oct. 10, 1831.
William Chaney, Harrison county, NE 9.14.7, Aug. 19, 1824.
Daniel Chicken, Kent county, Del., NE 24.11.7, July 27, 1814.
George Christy, Jefferson county, SW 19.11.5, July 30, 1812.
Alexander Clark, Ohio, E½ NW 34.11.7, Jan. 22, 1822.
Alexander Clarke, Harrison county, E½ SE 5.11.7, July 1, 1831.
John Clark, Belmont county, assignee of James Stevens, NW 15.8.4, June 6, 1814.
Joseph Clark, assignee of Richard Noble, Sr., all 18.9.4, Oct. 10, 1806.
Robert Clark, Sr., assignee of Asa Engle, SE 30.10.6, Jan. 10, 1820.
Robert Clarke, Jefferson county, W½ NW 29.12.7, Oct. 24, 1826.
Thomas and Mathew Clarke, Jefferson county, E½ NE 35.12.7, Oct. 24, 1826.
Thomas Clarke and Matthew Clarke, Harrison county, SW 30.12.7, Sept. 10, 1834.

Samuel Clifford, Brooke county, Va., SW 33.10.5, Oct. 10, 1815.
Charles Cole, Jefferson county, E½ SW 18.10.4, May 30, 1826.
John Coleman, Jefferson county, Northwest Territory, all 1.8.4, Feb. 1, 1810.
John Coleman, Harrison county, W½ NW 28.11.6, April 2, 1829.
William Coltrap, Jefferson county, NW 19.12.6, Nov. 1, 1818.
Samuel Colvin, Washington county, Pa., NW 18.11.7, July 30, 1812.
William Calvin, Fayette county, NE 3.12.7, June 24, 1815.
William Colvin, Fayette county, Pa., NE 35.11.7, July 1, 1816.
William Colvin, Fayette county, NE 32.12.7, March 7, 1817.
William Compher, Harrison county, NE 22.10.6, March 7, 1818.
Eli Conoway, Harrison county, E½ SW 34.11.5, Jan. 1, 1833.
Michael Conoway, Harrison county, W½ SW 33.11.5, Nov. 1, 1830.
James Conel, Jefferson county, SW 20.12.6, Nov. 21, 1820.
Joseph Cook, Jefferson county, NW 23 and NE 29.11.7, March 7, 1818.
Joseph Cook, Jefferson county, SW 23.11.7, Sept. 10, 1831.
William John Cook, Harrison county, SE SW 17.11.7, Dec. 10, 1839.
John Coope, assignee of Thomas Johnson, NE 21.9.4, Jan. 23, 1813.
Caleb and Imla Cooper, Harrison county, NW 8.12.7, Aug. 4, 1814.
Caleb Cooper, Harrison county, W½ SE 15 and E½ 15.12.7, June 23, 1827.
John Cooper, Fayette county, Pa., SW 14.12.7, March 20, 1813.
William and John Cooper, Jr., Harrison county, SW 9.12.7, Aug. 4, 1814.
David Copeland, Jefferson county, W½ SE 23.12.6, Dec. 2, 1832.
James Copeland, Harrison county, NE 21.10.4, July 5, 1816.
James Copeland, Jefferson county, E½ NE 34.12.7, Nov. 1, 1850 (?).
John Cousins, Jefferson county, NE SE 23.12.6, Sept. 10, 1834.
Elijah Covington, Harrison county, NE NW 26.12.7, Jan. 1, 1833.
Zebediah Cox, Jefferson county, S½ 20.11.5, Nov. 1, 1810.
Zebediah Cox, Jefferson county, NW 19.11.5, Jan. 1, 1811,
Zebediah Cox, Jefferson county, SE 19.11.5, May 10, 1811.
Zebediah Cox, Jefferson county, NW 1.11.6, Nov. 10, 1811.
Cornelius and Gabriel Crabtree, Harrison county, SW 29.11.6, May 25, 1825.
Peter Crabtree, Harrison county, SW 17.11.6, July 16, 1819.
Thomas Crabtree, Jefferson county, NW 19.11.6, Aug. 19, 1812.
John Craig, Washington county, Pa., all 29.9.4, Sept. 15, 1806.
Stokely Craig, Greene county, Pa., W½ SE and E½ SW 35.12.7, Sept. 15, 1823.
Walter Craig, Washington county, Pa., SE 27.12.6, Oct. 1, 1811.
William Craig, Washington county, Pa., SW 27.12.6, Oct. 30, 1809.
William Craig, Washington county, Pa., NE 33 and SW 34.12.6, Oct. 1, 1811.
John Cramblit, Jefferson county, SE 25.12.6, Dec. 9, 1819.
John Cramblett, Jefferson county, W½ SW 22.12.6, Dec. 1, 1830.
Robert Craven, assignee of William Davis, SW 10.12.5, Dec. 22, 1819.
Alexander Crawford, Brooke county, Va., NE 25.11.5, March 1, 1808.
Alexander Crawford, assignee of John Henderson, SW 19.12.5, June 23, 1827.
Edward Crawford, Brooke county, Va., NW 13.11.5, Sept. 7, 1812.

John Crawford, Harrison county, W½ NW 17.12.6, Nov. 1, 1830.
Nathaniel Crawford, Jefferson county, SW 5.10.6, Oct. 8, 1814.
William Crawford, Belmont county, SE 29.9.5, Feb. 10, 1809.
Joseph Creal, Steubenville, SW 27.12.5, Nov. 13, 1822.
Valentine Creamer, Harrison county, NW 31.12.7, Jan. 15, 1814.
Philip Creplever, Washington county, Pa., SW 8.13.6, Jan. 20, 1812.
John Crom, Harrison county, SE 15.13.6, April 22, 1819.
Robert Crosson, Harrison county, E½ NW 20.11.5, Aug. 10, 1827.
John Crumrine, Tuscarawas county, E½ NE 2.14.7, Sept. 10, 1823.
John Crumrine, Tuscarawas county, W½ SW 1 and E½ SE 2.14.7, Dec. 2, 1830.
Thomas Cummings, Tuscarawas county, E½ NW 14.14.7, Oct. 10, 1831.
Thomas Cummings, Tuscarawas county, W½ SW 15.14.7, Dec. 6, 1831.
Thomas Cummings, Tuscarawas county, W½ SE 15.14.7, Nov. 12, 1832.
Robert Cummings, assignee of William Henderson, NE 18.11.5, May 21, 1819.
David Cunningham, assignee of James Dougherty, NW 36.9.5, Nov. 10, 1811.
David Cunningham, Harrison county, NE 5.10.6, March 16, 1814.
Samuel Curry, Westmoreland county, Pa., NW 28.11.5, April 27, 1821.
John W. Curtis, Harrison county, E½ SW 24.11.6, Dec. 1, 1830.
David Custard, Jefferson county, NE 7.12.5, Oct. 1, 1811.
Emmanuel Custer, Allegany county, Md., NE 14.12.5, Oct. 7, 1812.
George Custard, Fayette county, Pa., all 36.10.4, March 20, 1804.
Jacob Custer, assignee of Emmanuel Custer, SE 14.12.5, Aug. 10, 1815.
James Darrah, assignee of Archibald Jones, NE 18.11.6, April 17, 1820.
Daniel David, assignee of Robert Thompson, SW 6.11.7, Jan. 30, 1816.
Henry David, Harrison county, SE 17.11.7, Feb. 14, 1817.
Henry David, assignee of Thomas Gray, SE 23.11.7, March 7, 1817.
James David, Jefferson county, NE 23.11.6, Aug. 10, 1827.
Jesse Davidson, Harrison county, E½ NW 28.11.7, April 20, 1827.
John Davidson, Allegany county, Md., SW 34.12.7, Aug. 19, 1824.
John Davidson, Harrison county, E½ NW 34.12.7, June 23, 1827.
Lewis Davidson, Tuscarawas county, SE 29.11.7, Nov. 6, 1815.
Lewis Davidson, Harrison county, W½ NE 27.12.7, Nov. 12, 1832.
Samuel Davidson, Allegany county, Md., SE 27.12.7, Aug. 4, 1814.
Thomas Davidson, Allegany county, Md., NW 29.11.7, Nov. 13, 1822.
Thomas Davidson, Harrison county, E½ SW 29.11.7, Oct. 10, 1831.
William Davis, Harrison county, W½ SE 31.13.6, March 2, 1831.
Samuel Dearmon, Columbia (?) county, E½ SE 22.12.7, Jan. 30, 1827.
Philip Deleny, assignee of John Miller, all 9.10.4, Sept. 10, 1806.
Abraham DeLong, Tuscarawas county, E½ SE 14.14.7, Dec. 2, 1830.
William Denning, Jefferson county, NW 30.11.7, Nov. 2, 1829.
James Derry, Harrison county, W½ SW 7.12.6, Nov. 1, 1830.
Jesse Desellems, Belmont county, NW 21.9.5, March 7, 1818.
James Devore, Jefferson county, SE 9.11.5, Aug. 10, 1811.
John Dever, Brooke county, Va., all 13.9.5, July 1, 1807.

John Dewitt, Harrison county, W½ NE 26.11.6, March 20, 1828.
Joshua Dickerson, assignee of Robert Latta, NE 19.10.5, Jan. 14, 1811.
Thomas Dickerson, Fayette county, Pa., all 32.9.4, Sept. 10, 1806.
John Dicks, assignee of Nathaniel Buck, Harrison county, SE 8.12.7, Aug. 19, 1824.
John Dicks, Harrison county, W½ NW 24.12.7, March 10, 1825.
Henry Dillin, Washington county, Pa., NE 2.11.5, Dec. 19, 1814.
William Disart, Washington county, Pa., SE 15.8.4, Aug. 10, 1813.
John Dixon, Allegany county, Md., NW 19.12.7, May 21, 1819.
James Dodds, assignee of John Beall, SE 18.11.6, Feb. 20, 1827.
James Donaghey, Allegheny county, Pa., NW 12.12.7, Feb. 28, 1821.
James Donaghey, Allegheny county, Pa., NE 18.12.7, May 25, 1825.
John Donaghey, Harrison county, E½ NW 18.12.7, April 20, 1827.
James Dougherty, Washington county, Pa., W½ NE 22.11.7, July 1, 1831.
David Drake, Jefferson county, all 11.9.5, Oct. 1, 1806.
Jefferson Drake, Washington county, Pa., W½ SW 29.11.7, April 2, 1829.
Thomas Drummond, Jefferson county, SE 31.12.6, Aug. 19, 1824.
Nathaniel Dunham, Harrison county, E½ SW 26.12.6, Oct. 2, 1821.
William Dunham, Jefferson county, SE 26.12.6, May 10, 1820.
Adam Dunlap, Fayette county, Pa., assignee of William R. Dickerson, SW 13.10.5, Feb. 16, 1809.
John Dunlap, Jefferson county, NW 23.9.5, April 20, 1812.
Samuel Dunlap, Fayette county, Pa., SE 20.10.5, Dec. 10, 1805.
William Dunlap, assignee of Roger Toothaker, NW 19.10.5, Nov. 15, 1809.
William Dunlap, Fayette county, Pa., SE 36.9.5, Oct. 8, 1818.
Jeremiah Dutton, assignee of Jesse Clark, W½ SW 20.13.6, May 25, 1825.
Daniel Easely, Halifax county, Va., SE 18.11.7, June 23, 1810.
Daniel Easley, Halifax county, Va., NE 17.11.7, Dec. 15, 1810.
Daniel Easley, Halifax county, Va., SE 19.12.7, Dec. 15, 1810.
Daniel Easley, assignee of Berriman McLaughlin, NW 13.12.7, Aug. 30, 1816.
Daniel Easley, Harrison county, NW 11.11.7, March 7, 1818.
Jacob Easterday, Jefferson county, NE 27.13.6, Aug. 10, 1811.
James Edwards, Belmont county, E½ NE 26.11.6, Oct. 24, 1826.
John Edwards, Tuscarawas county, W½ SW 7.14.7, May 20, 1826.
Thomas Elder, assignee of James Edie, W½ NE 20.11.5, May 25, 1825.
Jonathan Ellis, Belmont county, all 3.9.5, Aug. 15, 1807.
Theodore Ellis, Frederick county, Va., NW 33.9.5, Feb. 16, 1809.
Theodore Ellis, assignee of Stacy Bevan, SW 33.9.5, June 1, 1815.
Endsley, see also Insley.
Andrew Andsley, assignee of Henry Hemery, SE 5.11.5, Dec. 23, 1811.
David Endslay, Jefferson county, NE 4.11.5, Aug. 26, 1808.
John Endsley, assignee of Isaac Osburn, SW 17.11.5, Aug. 22, 1810.
James English, Harrison county, NE 12.12.6, Aug. 18, 1817.
James English, Harrison county, E½ NW 5.12.6, June 23, 1827.

James English, Harrison county, E½ NW 12.12.6, Nov. 1, 1830.
Erwin, see also Irwin.
Andrew Erwin, Harrison county, W½ SW 33.12.6, Oct. 10, 1831.
James Ervin, assignee of Philip Spiker, NW 31.12.6, May 25, 1825.
Jane Erwin, Harrison county, W½ NW 14.12.6, Aug. 10, 1825.
Joshua Erwin, assignee of Robert Irwin, W½ SE 15.12.6, Aug. 10, 1827.
Robert Erwin, Harrison county, SE NW 32.12.6, Nov. 18, 1833.
Robert Erwin, Harrison county, NE NW 32.12.6, Sept. 10, 1834.
Asher Evans, Harrison county, W½ NE 15.12.7, Dec. 1, 1830.
James Evans, Harrison county, E½ SE 5.12.6, Dec. 1, 1830.
William Evans, Harrison county, W½ SE 4.12.6, Dec. 2, 1832.
John Everhardt, Harrison county, NW 1.12.5, Jan. 21, 1819.
Jacob Fadley, Loudoun county, Va., NW 15.12.5, Aug. 19, 1818.
Jonas Fagley, Jefferson county, Ohio, assignee of Josiah Wickersham, NW 28.9.5, June 19, 1813.
Henry Ferguson, Washington county, Pa., all 3.10.4, June 6, 1806.
Samuel Ferguson, Washington county, Pa., SE 13.11.5, July 30, 1812.
James Ferrell, Harrison county, E½ NW 15.11.5, April 5, 1822.
James Ferrell, Harrison county, W½ NW 15.11.5, April 30, 1822.
James Ferrell, Harrison county, E½ NE 22.11.5, April 20, 1825.
James Ferrell, assignee of Robert Thompson, W½ NE 22.11.5, Aug. 10, 1827.
Andrew Farrier, Jefferson county, NW 27.11.5, Oct. 5, 1808.
Andrew Ferrier, assignee of Thomas Archbold, S½ 23.11.5, April 20, 1812.
Andrew Farrier, Harrison county, SE 26.11.5, Oct. 8, 1814.
James Finney, Fayette county, Pa., all 27.9.4, Sept. 15, 1806.
David Firebaugh, Harrison county, NE 20.13.6, Oct. 18, 1826.
John Firebaugh, assignee of Elizabeth Forney, SE 14.13.6, June 8, 1812.
John Firebough, Tuscarawas county, NE 13.13.6, Nov. 6, 1815.
Heirs of Philip Firebaugh, dec'd, of Allegany county, Md., SW 33.12.5, Sept. 7, 1812.
Philip Firebaugh, Somerset county, Pa., NW 14.13.6, Nov. 17, 1812.
Philip Firebaugh, Tuscarawas county, SW 15.13.6, March 28, 1820.
George Fisher, Washington county, Pa., NW 10.11.5, Dec. 30, 1811.
George Fisher, assignee of William Barnhill, Harrison county, NW 23.11.5, Aug. 19, 1824.
George Fisher, Harrison county, W½ SW 24.11.5, July 1, 1831.
James Fisher, assignee of Samuel Osburn, NW 4.11.5, June 10, 1811.
James Fisher, assignee of Samuel Osburn, SW 4.11.5, Dec. 30, 1811.
James Fisher, Harrison county, SE 8.14.7, Sept. 1, 1819.
James Fisher, Tuscarawas county, W½ SW 2.14.7, ———— 15, 1823.
James Fisher, Tuscarawas county, W½ NE 7.14.7, May 30, 1826.
James Fisher, Tuscarawas county, SE NE 8.14.7, Nov. 18, 1833.
John Fisher, assignee of Dory Beall, W½ NE 6.12.6, May 25, 1825.
John Fisher, Harrison county, E½ SW 6.12.6, July 1, 1831.

John Fisher, Harrison county, W½ SE 1.13.6, Dec. 2, 1832.
Thomas Fisher, Jefferson county, NE 29.11.5, June 5, 1816.
John Fissal, Harrison county, E½ NW 30.11.5, Jan. 10, 1820.
Thomas Fitzgerald, Harrison county, SW SE 35.11.6, Dec. 8, 1835.
Archibald Fletcher, Adams county, Pa., SW 21.10.4, July 30, 1813.
Henry Ford, Harrison county, E½ NE 36.11.5, Nov. 1, 1830.
Isaac Ford, assignee of Lewis Ford, Harrison county, NW 29.11.6, Nov. 13, 1822.
James Ford, Brooke county, Va., all 34.9.4, Oct. 5, 1808.
James Ford, Harrison county, SE 36.10.6, June 5, 1816.
John Ford, Harrison county, E½ SE 35.11.6, Aug. 10, 1827.
Lewis Ford, Fayette county, Pa., SW 5.11.6, Oct. 8, 1818.
Stephen Ford and Peter Hesser, executors of Nicholas France, all 1.11.4, Aug. 1, 1807.
Stephen Ford, assignee of John Cook, all 31.11.4, Oct. 1, 1811.
Stephen Ford, assignee of John Schwartz, NW 31.12.5, Sept. 9, 1817.
Thomas Ford, Harrison county, E½ SE 32.12.5, Nov. 1, 1830.
John Fordyce, Tuscarawas county, E½ NW 33.12.7. Oct. 10, 1831.
Samuel Fordyce, Fayette county, Pa., W½ NW 35.12.7, May 20, 1826.
William Foreman, Harrison county, SE 17.10.4, Dec. 29, 1818.
Nancy Forney, Westmoreland county, Pa., NW 7.13.6, Jan. 1, 1812.
Peter Forney, Somerset county, Pa., NW 8.13.6, Sept. 21, 1810.
Alexander Foster, assignee of Henry Emes, NW 6.10, 4, March 30, 1815.
Samuel Foster, Allegheny county, Pa., SW 29.9.5, Sept. 3, 1813.
John Fowler, Harrison county, SE 36.11.5, March 7, 1818.
John Fowler, Harrison county, W½ NW 23.12.6, May 20, 1826.
John Fowler, Jr., W½ SE 30.12.6, Nov. 1, 1830.
John Fowler, Harrison county, W½ NE 20.12.6, July 1, 1831.
France, see Stephen Ford, executor.
George Fresh, Jefferson county, SE 21.8.4, April 15, 1813.
John Fry, Jefferson county, NW 20.13.6, Aug. 10, 1813.
John Fuller, assignee of Jacob Myers, all 10.8.4, April 5, 1806.
John Fulton, Fayette county, Pa., all 35.9.4, Sept. 15, 1806.
William Fulton, Harrison county, W½ SE 23.12.7, Aug. 10, 1825.
William Fulton, assignee of Isaac Webb, E½ SE 23.12.7, Aug. 25, 1825.
James McC. Galbraith, Cumberland county, Pa., NE 23.10.4, March 18, 1814.
William Gallaher, Fayette county, Pa., NE 17.10.4, Feb. 20, 1809.
George Gamble, Tuscarawas county, E½ SW and W½ SE 9.14.7, Nov. 1, 1830.
William Gamble, Jefferson county NE 3.14.7, May 21, 1819.
William Gamble, Tuscarawas county, W½ SE 32.13.6, Nov. 1, 1830.
William Gamble, Jr., assignee of William Gamble, W½ NW 33.13.6, Feb. 20, 1827.
John Gardner, Washington county, Pa., E½ 22.9.4, Nov. 1, 1810.
John Gardner, Washington county, Pa., SW 22.10.4, May 15, 1811.
John Gardner, Washington county, Pa., SE 22.10.4, Oct. 7, 1812.

HARRISON COUNTY LAND PATENTS 213

Mahlon Gardner and other heirs at law of Samuel Gardner, dec'd, NW 22.11.6, Nov. 10, 1827.
Samuel Gardner, assignee of William Bush, NW 23.11.6, March 5, 1818.
Samuel Gardner, Berkeley county, Va., SW 23.11.6, March 5, 1818.
William Garmier, Greene county, Pa., SW 3.14.7, Aug. 25, 1825.
Hezekiah Garner, assignee of John Johnson, Sr., SW 28.11.6, Aug. 19, 1818.
Casparus Garretson, Jefferson county, NE 23.11.7, March 18, 1814.
Jacob Gatchel, Harrison county, SW 28.10.5, Jan. 27, 1819.
Christian Geabeler, Harrison county, SW 2.12.5, Aug. 10, 1827.
William Geary, Allegheny county, Pa., SW 20.11.6, May 10, 1820.
William Gervis, Harrison county, W½ NE 23.11.5, April 5, 1822.
David Gibson, Brooke county, Va., SW 17.10.4, Feb. 20, 1809.
Joseph Gilbert, Harrison county, W½ NE 11.11.6, Nov. 1, 1830.
John Gilchrist, Fayette county, Pa., SW 14.10.5, Jan. 1, 1811.
Archibald Gilkison, assignee of James Steel, admr. of James Turbet, dec'd, NE 34.11.6, May 5, 1821.
Joseph Gill, assignee of David Lupton, all 23.8.4, June 3, 1806.
William Gillespie, Jr., Jefferson county, SW 32.11.6, Aug. 3, 1818.
Francis Gilmore, Jefferson county, NW 14.10.5, Dec. 29,1808.
Francis Gilmore, Jefferson county, NE 19.11.5, Feb. 1, 1810.
Francis Gilmore, Jefferson county, NE 25.10.5, Sept. 7, 1812.
Gordon R. Gilmore, assignee of Nathaniel Gilmer, Harrison county, E½ SW 29.12.7, Aug. 19, 1824.
John Gilmore, New York, SW 13.12.7, Jan. 1, 1810.
Nathaniel Gillmor, assignee of James Wright, SE 24.12.7, Jan. 1, 1811.
Nathaniel Gilmer, assignee of James Wright, assignee of David Moody, E½ NE 17.12.7, Aug. 19, 1824.
Samuel Gilmore, Washington county, Pa., all 3.10.5, Feb. 10, 1807.
Robert Given, assignee of James Boyd, SW 10.12.6, April 10, 1827.
Mathias Glass, Tuscarawas county, SW NW 9.14.7, Jan. 1, 1833.
Mathias Glass, Harrison county, NW NW 9.14.7, April 1, 1837.
Peter Goodman, Washington county, Pa., W½ NW 22 11.7, Sept. 1, 1826.
John Gordon, Washington county, Pa., W½ SE 29.11.5, Oct. 6, 1826.
Thomas Gordon, assignee of Robert Guttray, SW 25.10.5, Oct. 1, 1811.
John Gutschall, Cumberland county, Pa., SW 6.11.5, July 5, 1819.
Jonas Gotshall, Perry county, Pa., NW 21.12.5, Sept. 25, 1823.
Joseph Gotshall, Harrison county, NE 15.12.5, Sept. 20, 1823.
Margaret Gotschall, Harrison county, NE 12.10.4, June 23, 1827.
Nicholas Gutshall, Washington county, Pa., all 17.11.4, May 8, 1806.
Francis Grace, Harrison county, W½ SW 11.12.6, Oct. 20, 1824.
Francis Grace, Harrison county, E½ SE 17.12.6, Dec. 1, 1830.
Francis Grace, Harrison county, SE NW 11.12.6, Jan. 1, 1833.
John Grace, Harrison county, W½ SE 36.12.6, April 2, 1829.
John Grace, Harrison county, E½ SE 36.12.6, Nov. 1, 1830.

William Gracey, Jefferson county, NW 32.12.7, Dec. 29, 1818.
Ebenezer Atherton Gray, Harrison county, W½ SE 34.12.7, Sept. 10, 1834.
Henry Green, Harrison county, E½ NE 27.12.6, April 20, 1827.
Abraham Grein, assignee of Jesse Edgington, NW 23.10.4, May 5, 1820 (cancelled).
Jonathan Grewell, Harrison county, W½ SW 27.12.7, Dec. 6, 1831.
Moses Griffin, Belmont county, NE 26.9.5, Aug. 15, 1808.
William Griffith, Harrison county, W½ SW 6.12.7, Nov. 1, 1830.
Abraham Grim, assignee of Jesse Edgington, NW 23.10.4, Feb. 21, 1821.
William Grimes, assignee of Alexander Millikan, NW 15.10.5, July 30, 1813.
William Grist and William Philips, assignee of Benjamin Stanton, SW 9.11.6, Dec. 1, 1809.
Abraham Grove, Greene county, Pa., W½ NE 35.12.7, May 6, 1824.
John L. Grubb, Brooke county, Va., SE 24.11.7, May 25, 1825.
Benjamin Gudgeon, Harrison county, SE 4.11.7, Oct. 8, 1818.
Joseph Gundy, Somerset county, Pa., NE 14.13.6, Jan. 10, 1812.
Joseph Gunty, Harrison county, SW 14.13.6, July 10, 1817.
Joseph Gundy, Harrison county, W½ NW 1.13.6, May 20, 1826.
Josiah Guttry, Harrison county, SE SE — 12.7, Nov. 18, 1833.
Robert Guttry, Jefferson county, NW 35.9.5, Aug. 4, 1814.
William Guttery and Matthew Templeton, assignees of Thomas Henderson S½ 30.9.5, Oct. 10, 1815.
Elisha Guyton, Tuscarawas county, E½ NE 4.12.7, Oct. 6, 1826.
Elisha Guyton, Tuscarawas county, E½ NW 34.11.6, Oct. 6, 1826.
Hugh Gwynn, Jefferson county, SW 22.9.4, Aug. 6, 1813.
Abraham Hagey, Franklin county, Pa., SW 3.12.5, July 5, 1816.
Isaac Haines, Jefferson county, SE 4.11.6, July 30, 1812.
Jesse Haines, assignee of Thomas Barrett, NE 27.10.5, Oct. 1, 1811.
Samuel and Israel Haynes, and other heirs of John Haynes, NW 10.11.7, Nov. 2, 1829.
Thomas Haines, assignee of David Barrett, NW 9.11.6, March 10, 1807.
Isabella Haggerty, Jefferson county, SW 3.11.5, May 10, 1811.
John Hamble, Jefferson county, SW 12.11.6, Feb. 17, 1820.
William Hamilton, assignee of Samuel Pickering, NE 32.9.5, Aug. 15, 1811.
Fiet Handel, Jefferson county, W½ SW 18.10.4, Oct. 20, 1824.
Robert Hanlin, Jefferson county, W½ SW 12.12.6, Jan. 1, 1833.
James Hanna, Washington county, Pa., S½ 29.10.4, March 1, 1810.
Robert Hanna, assignee of Charles Wilson, NW 28.10.4, Oct. 8, 1814.
Samuel Hanna, Washington county, Pa., all 10.9.5, Aug. 27, 1805.
Samuel Hanna, Washington county, Pa., all 24.8.4, Sept. 15, 1806.
John Harding, Harrison county, SE 28.12.6, Dec. 1, 1830.
Jacob Harman, Harrison county, E½ NW 3.13.6, April 2, 1829.
Michael Harmon, Harrison county, NW 21.13.6, May 29, 1818.
Michael Harmon, Harrison county, SE 21.13.6, Jan. 27, 1819.

HARRISON COUNTY LAND PATENTS 215

Michael Harmon and Joseph Bartholomew, Tuscarawas county, NW 26.13.6 May 25, 1825.
George Harrimon, Washington county, Pa., NE 14.11.5, May 15, 1811.
Jeremiah Harris, Jefferson county, SW 31.9.5, July 10, 1821.
Joseph Harris, Harrison county, W½ SW 3.12.7, Nov. 13, 1822.
John Harrison, Steubenville, W½ SE 33.12.5, Aug. 19, 1824.
Joseph Harrison, Harrison county, E½ SE 33.12.5, Aug. 10, 1828.
George Hartford, Brooke county, Va., NE 6.10.4, Feb. 1, 1809.
James Harvey, Jefferson county, SE 18.10.6, Feb. 14, 1817.
William Hatfield, Belmont county, SE 5.11.6, Sept. 1, 1819.
Abraham Havmer, Chester county, Pa., SE 26.9.5, April 5, 1806.
John Haverfield, Harrison county, SE 22.10.5, March 7, 1817.
Joseph Haverfield, Harrison county, NW 22.10.5, May 20, 1817.
David Hazen, assignee of John Bower, SW 32.12.7, Feb. 14, 1817.
James Hazlett, Fayette county, Pa., NW 18.10.4, Jan. 20, 1812.
James Hazlett, Jefferson county, W½ NE 18.10.4, Sept. 25, 1823.
Thomas Hazlett, Steubenville, NW 6.11.6, Feb. 14, 1817.
John Histand, Somerset county, Pa., SE 20.13.6, Aug. 10, 1827.
John Heastand, Tuscarawas county, W½ NE 19.13.6, July 1, 1831.
Edward Heath, Jefferson county, E½ NW 21.12.6, April 30, 1822.
Edward Heath, Jefferson county, W½ NW 21.12.6, Sept. 10, 1823.
Adam Heavilin, Harrison county, W½ SE 2.12.6, Aug. 19, 1827.
Samuel Heavilin, Jefferson county Pa. (?), NE 30.10.5, Jan. 1, 1812.
Samuel Heavilin, Harrison county, SE 25.11.5, Jan. 27, 1819.
Samuel Hedges, assignee of John Caldwell, who was assignee of Robert Mc-
    Laughlin, admr. of James McLaughlin, dec'd, SW 30.10.5, May 15, 1822.
Fielding Hefling, Harrison county, E½ SW 6.12.7, Nov. 1, 1830.
John Hefling, Belmont county, NW 6.12.7, March 2, 1821.
John Hefling, Belmont county, NE 12.12.7, Aug. 19, 1824.
Henry Heisler, Northumberland county, Pa., all 9.11.4, Feb. 17, 1806.
Charles Henderson, assignee of Gavin Allison, SE 10.10.6, ——————.
John Henderson, assignee of John Young, all 27.8.4, June 6, 1806.
William Henderson, Jefferson county, NE 17.10.5, April 10, 1812.
William Henderson, Harrison county, SW 3.13.6, Aug. 10, 1827.
Andrew Hendricks, Allegany county, Md., NE 35.10.4, Dec. 12, 1812.
Andrew Hendricks, Harrison county, NW 3.12.5, Aug. 4, 1814.
Andrew Hendricks, Harrison county, NW 12.11.5, Oct. 8, 1814.
Andrew Hendricks, Harrison county, W½ NE 12.11.5, Aug. 25, 1825.
Emanuel Hendricks, Harrison county, E½ NE 32.12.5, Dec. 10, 1827.
Jacob Hendricks, Harrison county, NE 3.12.5, Aug. 4, 1814.
Jacob Hendricks, Harrison county, SE 19.12.5, May 21, 1819.
Jacob Hendricks, Harrison county, W½ NE 32.12.5, Dec. 10, 1827.
John Hendricks, Somerset county, Pa., NE 21.11.4, March 20, 1813.

John Hendricks, Somerset county, Pa., SE 20.12.5, Oct. 25, 1813.
John Hendricks, Sr., assignee of Timothy Spencer, Jr., SW 13.12.5, Aug. 19, 1818.
Joseph Hendricks, Somerset county, Pa., NE 20.12.5, March 20, 1813.
Henry Hemry, Harrison county, NW 32.10.4, March 30, 1815.
James Henry, Westmoreland county, Pa., SW 11.11.5 and SE 32.11.5, Sept. 1, 1819.
Robert Henry, Westmoreland county, Pa., NW 4.12.6, April 27, 1821.
William Henry, assignee of Anthony Sell, Harrison county, SE 13.12.5, Nov. 13, 1822.
Heirs of Christian Herr, SE 8.13.6, June 10, 1811.
James Hicks, assignee of William Newsam, NE 2.12.5, July 25, 1820.
Thomas Hidey, W½ NE 21.12.5, Nov. 1, 1830.
Anthony Hiller, Greene county, Pa., E½ SE 32.13.6, Dec. 1, 1829.
John Hines, Harrison county, SW 36.10.5, Aug. 19, 1824.
Joseph Hines, Harrison county, W½ SE 30.11.6, Nov 1, 1830.
James Hoagland, Jefferson county, Pa., NE 33.11.5, Oct. 1, 1811.
James Hoagland, Harrison county, E½ SE 33.11.5, Oct. 10, 1831.
Thomas Hougland, Harrison county, E½ SE 7.12.6, April 2, 1829.
Francis Hobson, assignee of Joseph Pugh, SE 11.11.6, Jan. 20, 1817.
Mary Hoff, Harrison county, W½ SW 19.13.6, Nov. 1, 1830.
Richard Hoff, Harrison county, E½ SE 26.13.6, April 8, 1828.
Robert Hogge, Washington county, Pa., SE 26.12.7, Jan. 21, 1819.
William Hogg, Fayette county, Pa., all 11.9.4, Nov. 27. 1804.
John Hollet, Jefferson county, SE 11.11.7, March 5, 1818.
John Hollett, Jefferson county, W½ SW 5.11.7, May 11, 1824.
Robert Holliday, Jefferson county, NE 30.11.7, Jan. 20, 1817.
David Hollingsworth, E½ NW 5.12.7, April 20, 1827.
Aaron Holloway, Stafford county, Va., NW 32.9. 5, Jan. 2, 1810.
Asa Holloway, Sr., Belmont county, NE 27.9.5, Jan. 20, 1812.
Daniel Holloway, Belmont county, SW 11.12.7, Feb. 14, 1817.
Jacob Holloway, assignee of Horton Howard and Isaac Parker, S½ 21.9.5, July 16, 1819.
Jacob Holloway, Belmont county, E½ 22.9.5, April 20, 1825.
Jacob Holloway, assignee of Horton Howard, NE 21.9.5, Feb. 6, 1826.
James Holloway, Harrison county, W½ NW 5.12.7, June 23, 1826.
Jonas Halloway, Harrison county, W½ SW 5.12.7, Dec. 2, 1830.
Jonas Holloway, Harrison county, E½ NE 10.12.7, Dec. 6, 1831.
Joseph Holloway, Belmont county, SE 23.9.5, Nov. 15, 1810.
Robert Holloway, assignee of John Porter, NW ?1.9.5, March 2, 1821.
Francis Holmes, Jefferson county, SW 11.10.4, Oct. 1, 1811.
Heirs of Isaac Holmes, dec'd, assignees of Daniel McMillan, W½ SW 14.14.7, Oct. 18. 1826.
Joseph Holmes, Jefferson county, Northwest Territory, all 25.9.4, Jan. 22, 1806.

HARRISON COUNTY LAND PATENTS

John Hoobley, Harrison county, E½ SE 27.12.5, Nov. 2, 1829.
Ellis Hoopes, Jefferson county, SE 15.9.4, Oct. 7, 1812.
Nathan Hoopes, Jefferson county, NW 15.9.4, Dec. 4, 1809.
John Hoover, Jefferson county, E½ NW 35.12.6, March 2, 1831.
Horton Howard, assignee of James Pollock, NW 15.9.5, Aug. 26, 1815.
Abel Howell, Belmont county, SW 23.9.5, May 12, 1815.
Abel Howell, Belmont county, E½ SE 17.10.6, Oct. 10, 1831.
John Howell, Belmont county, SE 25.9.5, Jan. 20, 1812.
Seth Howell, Pittsburgh, SE 29.10.6, Dec. 9, 1819.
Benjamin Howse, Jefferson county, SE 6.11.6, April 22, 1819.
Francis House, Jefferson county, SE 32.10.5, Dec. 26, 1815.
William House, Harrison county, E½ SE 20.12.6, Dec. 2, 1830.
Benjamin Hudson, Harrison county, E½ NW 24.11.7, Aug. 19, 1824.
Eli Hudson, Harrison county, W½ NW 24.11.7, April 2, 1829.
Jesse Huff, Jefferson county, NW 14.12.7, Dec. 15, 1811.
John Huff, Jefferson county, NE 20.12.7, Nov. 17, 1812.
Joseph Huff, Jefferson county, all 36.8.4, Sept. 10, 1806.
William Huff, Jefferson county, SE 4.12.7, Feb. 1, 1810.
James Huntsman, Belmont county, W½ NE 10.12.7, Nov. 12, 1832.
William Humphreys, Harrison county, E½ SE 4.12.6, Dec. 1, 1830.
William Humphreys, Harison county, W½ SW 34.11.5, Dec. 1, 1830.
Isaac Herless, Harrison county, E½ NE 18.12.6, Nov. 1, 1830.
Samuel Hurleass, Harrison county, E½ SW 18.12.6, Oct. 10, 1831.
Samuel Harless, Harrison county, NW SE 18.12.6, Sept. 10, 1834.
Robert Hurton, Ohio county, Va., NW 17.10.6, Aug. 10, 1811.
John Hutchinson, York county, Pa., NW 3.8.4, June 7, 1808.
Samuel Hutchinson, Chester county, Pa., NE 13.10.5, June 23, 1810.
Heirs of Samuel Hutchinson, Chester county, Pa., NE 13.10.5, Feb. 28, 1816.
William Hutchinson, Jefferson county, SW 3.8.4, Jan. 20, 1812.
Samuel Hyde, Harrison county, E½ NW 31.13.6, Sept. 15, 1823.
Robert Innis, Westmoreland county, Pa., SE 28.9.5, Nov. 16, 1812.
Insley, see also Endlsey.
Micajah Insley, assignee of William Sherron, E½ SE 19.12.6, Aug. 10, 1827.
Micajah Insley, Stark county, Ohio, W½ SE 19.12.6, Nov. 1, 1830.
James Irons, Allegany county, Md., NE 29.12.7, Feb. 17, 1820.
Thomas Irons, Allegany county, Md., SE 28.12.7, May 25, 1825.
Thomas Irons, Harrison county, E½ SE 28.12.7, Nov. 1, 1830.
Irwin, see also Erwin.
Robert Irwin, SW 31.12.6, Sept. 19, 1817.
Joseph Janney, Loudoun county, Va., all 2.9.5, Aug. 27, 1805.
John Jeffries, Harrison county, W½ NW 19.13.6, April 2, 1829.
Catherine Jeffries, Harrison county, E½ NW 19.13.6, April 2, 1829.
Michael Jenkins, Hampshire county, Va., all 20.8.4, Oct. 10, 1806.
Michael Jenkins, Belmont county, all 19.9.5, July 30, 1812.

Jonathan Jessop, assignee of Josiah Updegraff, all 31.9.4, April 30, 1806.
Amon Shannon Johnson, Harrison county, NE NE 29.11.5, Dec. 8, 1835.
Andrew Johnson, Harrison county, E½ NE 15.12.6, April 2, 1829.
Benjamin Johnson, Allegany county, Md., SW 10.11.6, May 23, 1810.
Benjamin Johnson, Brooke county, Va., NW 27.12.6, April 20, 1812.
Benjamin Johnson, Brooke county, Va., W½ NE 27.12.6, Aug. 10, 1827.
Derrick Johnson, Jefferson county, SE 31.11.6, March 18, 1814.
Elijah Johnson, Harrison county, W½ SW 21.11.6, Sept. 1, 1823.
Enoch Johnson, in his own right, and assignee of Benjamin Johnson, NW 10.11.6, Aug. 25, 1825.
Henry Johnson, Allegheny county, NE 24.10.6, June 8, 1812.
Isaac Johnson, assignee of Abel Johnson, Brooke county, Va., NW 34.12.6, Oct. 7, 1812.
James Johnson, Sr., Tuscarawas county, NW 23.12.7, June 1, 1815.
Joel Johnson, Brooke county, Va., SW 28.12.6, April 10, 1812.
John Johnson, assignee of Samuel Dannell, all 29.8.4, Aug. 27, 1807.
John Johnson, Jefferson county, NW 27.11.6, May 23, 1810.
John Johnson, Sr., Harrison county, SW 30.11.6, Oct. 3, 1816.
John P. Johnson, Harrison county, SW 25.12.6, May 21, 1819.
John Johnson, Tuscarawas county, W½ NE 31.13.6, Dec. 10, 1827.
Joseph Johnson, Brooke county, Va., NW 28.12.6, Dec. 25, 1811.
Joseph and Lemuel Johnson, Tuscarawas county, SE 24.10.6, Aug. 19, 1812.
Joseph Johnson, Steubenville, NE 28.12.6, March 7, 1817.
Joseph Johnson, Harrison county, NE 34.12.6, Aug. 3, 1818.
Joseph Johnson, assignee of Abraham Lance, NE 30.10.6, May 21, 1819.
Joseph Johnston, Harrison county, SE 24.11.5, Sept. 1, 1819.
Josiah Johnson, Harrison county, SW 29.12.6, Nov. 2, 1829.
Nathan Johnson, Jefferson county, NW 11.10.4, April 10, 1812.
Nathan Johnson, Harrison county, NW 30.11.6, May 21, 1819.
Nimrod Johnson, E½ SE 33.12.6, Aug. 19, 1824.
Samuel R. Johnston, Steubenville, SE and SW 20.12.6, Oct. 20, 1824.
Thomas Johnson, Tuscarawas county, W½ NE 30.11.6, Nov. 1, 1830.
Thomas Johnson, Harrison county, W½ NE 15.12.6, Oct. 10, 1831.
William Johnson, Allegany county, Md., NW 18.10.6, May 23, 1810.
William Johnson, assignee of Joel Johnson, SE 34.12.6, Jan. 1, 1812.
William Johnson (of James) Jefferson county, NE 23.12.7, July 30, 1812.
William Johnson, Harrison county, E½ NE 35.9.5, May 25, 1825.
Malachi Jolly, Harrison county, E½ SE 1.13.6, Oct. 10, 1831.
Edward Jones, Harrison county, NW 30.10.5, July 29, 1819.
Elijah Jones, assignee of Richard McKibben, Belmont county, SW 17.10.6, Aug. 19, 1824.
Henry Jones, Harrison county, E½ NW 1.13.6, Dec. 1, 1830.
Isaac Jones, Harrison county, E½ NE 15.12.7, May 20, 1826.
John Jones, Harrison county, E½ SW 11.11.6, Aug. 19, 1824.

HARRISON COUNTY LAND PATENTS

John Jones, Harrison county, W½ SW 36.12.7, May 20, 1826.
John Jones, Harrison county, W½ NW 30.12.7, April 2, 1829.
William Jones, Belmont county, W½ NE 35.9.5, April 20, 1825.
William Jones, Belmont county, W½ SE 17.10.6, April 20, 1825.
Zachariah Jones and James Hutson, Harrison county, SE 28.10.6, June 20, 1820.
Samuel Jumpes, Jefferson county, SW 24.9.5, Nov. 17, 1812.
Jacob Kail, Harrison county, W½ SE 18.10.4, Dec. 2, 1830.
Peter Kail, Jefferson county, NW 18.11.5, May 23, 1810.
Peter Kail, Jefferson county, SE 18.11.5, Oct. 7, 1813.
John Karr, Harrison county, E½ NE 23.11.5, Aug. 19, 1824.
James Keep, Allegheny county, Pa., NW 2.12.5, Aug. 19, 1824.
Benjamin Keeran, Harrison county, E½ NE 32.11.6, Oct. 20, 1824.
Joseph Keiser, Harrison county, NE 2.13.6, Sept. 3, 1813.
Thomas Kells, Steubenville, NW 26.11.5, Aug. 3, 1818.
James Kelly, Washington county, Ohio (?), all 3.11.4, Feb. 1, 1809.
Robert Kelly, Brooke county, Va., NE 29.10.4, Nov. 10, 1811.
William Kelly, Brooke county, Va., SE 23.10.4, Jan. 20, 1812.
Amanda Kemp, Harrison county, W½ SW 5.11.5, March 10, 1825.
Citizen James Kennedy, Harrison county, E½ NE 30.11.6. Dec. 1, 1830.
John Kennedy, Washington county, Pa., NW 6.10.6, Dec. 15, 1811.
Matthew Kennedy, Harrison county, NW 13.11.6, March 7, 1817.
Matthew Kennedy, Harrison county, SW 13.11.6, Nov. 2, 1829.
Absalom Kent, Fayette county, Pa., all 1.12.6, Aug. 27, 1805.
Absalom Kent, Jefferson county, N½ 24.10.5, Aug. 27, 1805.
Absalom Kent, Jefferson county, SE 29.10.5, Aug. 27, 1805.
Absalom Kent, Fayette county, Pa., all 31.11.5, Feb. 1, 1809.
Absalom Kent, Jefferson county, SE 9.12.6, Dec. 25, 1811.
Absalom Kent, Jefferson county, NE 7.12.6, Jan. 20, 1812.
Absalom Kent, Harrison county, SW 32.12.6, Jan. 21, 1819.
Absalom Kent, Sr., assignee of James Darrow, SW 18.12.7, Aug. 10, 1827.
Joseph Kent, Washington county, Pa., all 27.10.4, July 14, 1806.
William Kent, Harrison county, E½ NE 36.12.6, Nov. 1, 1830.
James Kerr, assignee of Zaccheus A. Beatty, all 8.9.4, Feb. 1, 1810.
Josiah Kidwell, assignee of Leonard Barnes, NE 1.11.6, March 28, 1820.
John Kiggen, assignee of Zaccheus A. Beatty, NE 34.10.6. Jan. 26, 1809.
James Kimble, Pennsylvania, W½ SW 22.11.6, Jan. 26, 1822.
Adam Kimmel and Jacob Turney, Harrison county, SE 2.12.5, April 15, 1813.
Adam Kimel, Harrison county, NE 1.12.5, July 1, 1816.
John Kimel, Jefferson county, SW 20.12.5, March 16, 1814.
John Kimel, Harrison county, NW 19.12.5, July 1, 1816.
John Kimel, Jefferson county, SW 7.12.5, July 1, 1816.
John Kimmel, Harrison county, E½ NE 25.12.5, Nov. 1, 1830.
Leonard Kimel, Sr., NW 20.12.5, July 1, 1816.
William King, Harrison county, E½ NE 22.12.6, May 6, 1824.

William King, York county, Pa., E½ NW 8.14.7, Aug. 12, 1826.
Christopher Kinsey, Harrison county, SE 2.12.7, July 16, 1819.
Richard Kinsey, assignee of Daniel Johnson, NW 6.11.7, June 5, 1816.
Stephen Kinsey, Jefferson county, NE 33.9.5, Jan. 20, 1812.
Benjamin Kirk, Belmont county, SE 15.9.5, Dec. 22, 1812.
Hugh Kirkpatrick, assignee of John Wallace, of Ohio, NW 25.10.5, March 7, 1818.
Israel R. Kirkpatrick, assignee of Jesse Updegraff, who was assignee of Daniel Hoobler, E½ NE 27.12.5, Aug. 25, 1825.
Israel Kirkpatrick, Harrison county, E½ SW 24.11.5, April 2, 1831.
George Kitt, Harrison county, NE 35.12.6, April 8, 1828.
John Knight, Jefferson county, NE 18.10.6, Oct. 7, 1812.
John Knight, Tuscarawas county, NW 3.11.6, March 16, 1815.
Heirs of John Knight, dec'd, Tuscarawas county, SW 18.10.6, Sept. 19, 1817.
John Knight, Harrison county, E½ NW 28.11.6, April 2, 1829.
Samuel Knight, Somerset county, Pa., all 7.10.5, Dec. 20, 1808.
Jacob Kuhn, Washington county, Pa., all 14.8.4, Aug. 27, 1805.
Benjamin W. Ladd and Henry Crew, in trust for the use of certain persons of color, emancipated, E½ NE 21.12.6, Jan. 26, 1822.
Benjamin W. Ladd, E½ NW 22.12.6, April 2, 1829.
Edward Laferty, Washington county, Pa., NE 10.10.6, Jan. 1, 1810.
Samuel Lafferty, Washington county, Pa., SW 10.10.6, Oct. 8, 1814.
Samuel Laffarty, Harrison county, NW 10.10.6, Jan. 27, 1819.
Jonathan Lazer, Harrison county, NW 8.11.6, May 25, 1825.
William Laizure, Harrison county, W½ SW 11.11.6, Nov. 1, 1830.
John M. Lakin, Bedford county, Pa., W½ SE 22.12.7, Feb. 20, 1827.
Thomas Lakin, Sr., Bedford county, Pa., SW 36.11.7, March 7, 1818.
Thomas Lakin, Jr., Bedford county, Pa., NW 36.11.7, Jan. 10, 1820.
Thomas Lakin, Sr., Harison county, E½ SW 22.12.7, Feb. 20, 1827.
Isaac Lamasters, Harrison county, SE 11.11.5, March 20, 1813.
John Lamb, assignee of John Williams, NW 11.10.6, Sept. 10, 1806.
John Lamb, assignee of John Williams, SW 12.10.6, June 1, 1810.
John Lance, Jefferson county, SW 19.11.6, Dec. 12, 1815.
Peter John Lance, assignee of Thomas Johnson, NW 24.10.6, Dec. 14, 1812.
Matthew Lane, Harrison county, NE SW 22.12.6, Jan. 1, 1833.
Adam Lauver, Tuscarawas county, E½ NW 33.13.6, Oct. 20, 1824.
John Lavely, assignee of Robert Laughlin, NW 29.10.5, May 25, 1825.
John Law, Harison county, W½ SW 25.13.6, Dec. 2, 1830.
John Law, Harrison county, E½ SW 25.13.6, Dec. 2, 1830.
John Law, Harrison county, E½ SE 31.13.6, Dec. 2, 1830.
John Law, Harrison county, E½ NE 31.13.6, Dec. 2, 1830.
Matthew Law, Harrison county, W½ SE 34.11.5, July 30, 1828.
Matthew Law, Harrison county, W½ NE 22.12.6, Oct. 10, 1831.
James Leeper, assignee of Henry Dillin, E½ 3.11.5, Oct. 3, 1816.

HARRISON COUNTY LAND PATENTS

John Leeper, Harrison county, NW 10.12.6, May 6, 1824.
Jacob Lemmon, Pickaway county, NW 7.12.7, May 5, 1821.
Samuel Leonard, Washington county, Pa., W½ SW 22.11.7, May 6, 1824.
Abraham Leeport, Harrison county, E½ NW 14.12.6, Nov. 13, 1822.
George Leporth, Jefferson county, all 18.10.5, May 8, 1806.
George Leporth, Jefferson county, NE 14.12.6, June 8, 1812.
Job Lewis, Belmont county, NE 28.9.5, July 12, 1811.
William Linsley, Jefferson county, W½ SW 21.12.6, Sept. 10, 1823.
Amasa Lipsey, assignee of John Cadwalader, SW 12.11.7, Dec. 15, 1812.
George Lisator, Steubenville, assignee of Charles Wilson, SW 30.11.7, March 7, 1818.
William Lisle, Jefferson county, NW 8.11.5, Jan. 13, 1811.
John Liston, Harrison county, E½ NW 26.12.5, Dec. 2, 1830.
Heirs of Adam Little, Allegany county, Md., E½ NW 15.13.6, Aug. 10, 1827.
Samuel Little, assignee of Nathaniel Gillmer, SW 12.12.7, May 5, 1821.
Abel Lloyd, Jefferson county, NE 2.11.6, July 1, 1816.
John Loney, Jefferson county, NE 30.9.5, July 30, 1812.
Adam Long, Westmoreland county, Pa., SW 34.11.6, Aug. 19, 1824.
Charles Long, Washington county, Pa., SW 9.14.7, Sept. 10, 1834.
Esther Long, Washington county, Pa., NW 9.13.6, March 2, 1821.
Jacob Long, Westmoreland county, Pa., NW 36.10.6, Aug. 30, 1816.
Jacob Long, Westmoreland county, Pa., E½ 1.12.7, July 25, 1820.
Jacob Long, Westmoreland county, Pa., SE 10.127, May 25, 1825.
Jacob Long, Westmoreland county, Pa., SW 36.11.6, Feb. 20, 1827.
Samuel Long, Harrison county, W½ SW 12.11.5, May 12, 1828.
Jonathan Longshore, Greene county, Pa., SW 25.12.7, Sept. 9, 1817.
Robert Longshore, Greene county, Pa., E½ SW 27.12.7, Nov. 13, 1822.
Solomon Longworth, assignee of Elisha Nelson, NW 18.11.6, Nov. 26, 1820.
Edward Laughridge, Jefferson county, SE 12.12.6, Aug. 19, 1824.
Edward Laughridge, Harrison county, E½ SW 12.12.6, Aug. 10, 1828.
Edward Loughridge, Jefferson county, W½ NE 17.12.6, April 2, 1829.
James Laughridge, Harrison county, W½ NW 3.13.6, Nov. 1, 1830.
Joseph Loughridge, Harrison county, NW 5.12.6, Dec. 10, 1839.
Matthew Loughridge, Harrison county, W½ SW 6.12.6, July 20, 1828.
William Loughridge, Harrison county, E½ SE 18.12.6, July 1, 1831.
George Love, Jefferson county, SW 15.8.4, Oct. 25, 1813.
James Lowery, assignee of Peter Crabtree, of Harison county, W½ SE 23.11.6, Nov. 13, 1822.
John Lawrey, Cadiz, SE 17.11.6, Feb. 17, 1820.
James Lyon, Guernsey county, E½ NE 32.11.5, arch 21, 1832.
John Lyons, assignee of Jacob Rymor and Aaron Morris, NE 9.12.7, May 25, 1825.
George McAdams, Harrison county, SW 6.10.6, June 1, 1815.
John McAdams, Washington county, Pa., NW 24.9.5, Nov. 1, 1811.

John McBeath, Harrison county, W½ NW 25.13.6, April 2, 1831.
William McBeath, Harrison county, W½ SW 30.12.6, July 1, 1831.
James McBride, Washington county, Pa., SW 21.9.4, July 1, 1809.
James McBride, Washington county, Pa., NW 21.9.4, Dec. 23, 1815.
Alexander McCall, Washington county, Pa., all 33.8.4, Jan. 26, 1809.
William McCarroll, Harrison county, E½ SW 11.12.6, Jan. 1, 1833.
Joseph McClain, Westmoreland county, Pa., NE 17.11.5, June 8, 1812.
Joseph McClean, Westmoreland county, Pa., SE 25.12.5, Jan. 15, 1814.
Joseph McClean, Westmoreland county, Pa., S½ 30.11.5, June 26, 1815.
William McClean, Washington county, Pa., NE 7.13.6, Feb. 14, 1817.
John McClery, Jefferson county, assignee of Isaac Osburn, SE 21.10.4, Jan. 15, 1814.
John McClintock, E½ SE 30.12.6, Dec. 2, 1830.
Kerr McClintock, assignee of Robert McClintock, SW 3.12.6, Aug. 10, 1827.
Noble W. McClintock, Steubenville, E½ SW and W½ SE 33.11.5, Aug. 10, 1825.
John McCollum, Harrison county, W½ NW 8.14.7, Sept. 10, 1834.
William McCombs, Columbiana county, E½ NE 30.12.6, April 2, 1831.
John McConkey, Harrison county, SW 10.11.5, Aug. 25, 1825.
Alexander McConnell, Washington county, Pa., all 7.8.4, Oct. 21, 1805.
Alexander McConnell, Belmont county, SE 12.12.7, Jan. 10, 1820.
George McConnell, Washington county, Pa., all of 4.9.5, Dec. 20, 1805.
James McConnell, Jefferson county, W½ NE 18.12.6, July 1, 1831.
John McConnell, Washington county, Pa., all 5.9.5, April 20, 1804.
John McConnell, Washington county, Pa., all 34.8.4, July 14, 1806.
John McConnell, assignee of George Cox, SE 5.10.6, March 7, 1817.
Robert McConnell, Belmont county, NW 11.12.7, Oct. 8, 1818.
Francis McCord, Harrison county, SW 5.12.6, Sept. 10, 1834.
John McCorkle, SE 3.11.6, June 8, 1812.
John McCoy, Washington county, Pa., all 1.10.5, Feb. 26, 1806.
William McCreery, Westmoreland county, Pa., NE 24.11.5, May 10, 1811.
Alexander McCullough, Harrison county, E½ NE 15.11.6, Sept. 1, 1823.
James McCullough, Harrison county, SE 17.12.7, May 25, 1825.
Richard McCullough, Jefferson county, NW 32.11.5, Aug. 19, 1824.
William McCullough, Guernsey county, NW 14.11.6, May 10, 1820.
Daniel McCurdy, assignee of Richard Kinsey, SE 33.9.5, Nov. 16, 1812.
Joseph McDannell, Tuscarawas county, SE 9.14.7, Sept. 10, 1834.
Charles McDivit, Harrison county, SE 23.12.6, Jan. 1, 1833.
Charles McDivit, Harrison county, NW SW 17.12.6, Nov. 18, 1833.
George McDivit, Fayette county, Pa., NW 35.11.5, Oct. 8, 1818.
George McDevit, Jr., assignee of George Fisher, W½ NE 11.12.6, March 6, 1827.
George McDevit, Harrison county, W½ NE 36.11.5, Dec. 1, 1830.
George McDivit, Harrison county, W½ NW 11.12.6, Dec. 6, 1831.
George McDivit, Harrison county, NE NW 11.12.6, Nov.18, 1833.
George McDivit, Jr., Harrison county, E½ NE 11.12.6, Dec. 2, 1832.

HARRISON COUNTY LAND PATENTS

John McDivit, Harrison county, W½ SE 11.12.6, April 2, 1829.
Samuel McDivit, Tuscarawas county, E½ NW 17.12.6, Dec. 2, 1832.
Alexander MacDonald, assignee of Thomas Christy, SE 30.10.5, May 30, 1826.
Robert McDonald, Harrison county, E½ SW 33.12.7, Nov. 13, 1822.
Hugh McDonough, Jefferson county, NE 4.12.6, Nov. 17, 1812.
John McDounaugh, assignee of Zenas Barton, SE 6.12.6, July 10, 1821.
John McDanaugh, assignee of William Mimons, SW 1.13.6, May 25, 1825.
James McDowell, Fayette county, Pa., SE 24.9.5, Feb. 18, 1806.
John McDowell, Fayette county, Pa., NE 24.9.5, Feb. 16, 1809.
John McDowell, Fayette county, Pa., NE 23.9.5, Jan. 1, 1811.
John McDowell, Fayette county, Pa., NE 36.9.5, Jan. 1, 1811.
Samuel McDowell, Jr., Fayette county, Pa., all 18.9.5, Dec. 31, 1806.
Samuel McDowell, Jefferson county, NE 20.10.5, Jan. 1, 1811.
James McElwee, Jefferson county, SE NE 17.12.6, Dec. 8, 1835.
John McFadon, Washington county, Pa., all 4.10.5, May 8, 1806.
John McFadon, Jefferson county, SE 13.10.5, July 1, 1809.
Samuel McFadin, Jefferson county, SE 25.10.5, Oct. 7, 1812.
Samuel McFadin, Harrison county, SW 22.10.5, June 1, 1815.
George McGee, assignee of Asa Engle, NW 29.10.6, Jan. 10, 1820.
Hugh McGee, Harrison county, SW 13.12.6, Jan. 21, 1819.
Heirs of James McGinnes, dec'd, assignee of James Means, NE 13.12.5, Aug. 3, 1818.
James McKein, Harrison county, SW 18.12.6, Jan. 1, 1833.
Alexander McKeown, Belmont county, NW 35.11.7, March 6, 1827.
Richard McKibben, Harrison county, SW 11.10.6, Aug. 3, 1818.
Alexander McKitrick and James Steward, Washington county, Pa., SW 15.11.5, March 20, 1813.
Berriman McLaughlin, Jefferson county, NE 19.12.7, Dec. 22, 1808.
David McMath, Harrison county, W½ NW 26.11.6, March 6, 1827.
Daniel McMillan, Tuscarawas county, NW 7.14.7, March 15, 1815.
Daniel McMillan, Tuscarawas county, NE 13.14.7, Dec. 29, 1818.
Daniel McMillan, Tuscarawas county, E½ SW 8.14.7, May 20, 1826.
Daniel McMillan, Tuscarawas county, W½ NW 13.14.7, Aug. 12, 1826.
John McMillan, assignee of Jonathan Jessop, all 2.10.5, Aug. 24, 1807.
Patrick McMullin, Tuscarawas county, E½ NE 25.13.6, Sept. 20, 1823.
Patrick McMillan, Tuscarawas county, W½ NE 25.13.6, Nov. 1, 1830.
Patrick McMillan, Tuscarawas county, W½ NW 30.12.6, Dec. 2, 1830.
Robert McMillen, Jefferson county, NE 20.11.6, Feb. 28, 1821.
James B. Magrew, Westmoreland county, Pa., all 13.11.4, Feb. 18, 1806.
John Maholm, Jefferson county, N½ 31.10.5, July 30, 1812.
Joseph Maholm, Jefferson county, SE 28.10.5, Jan. 15, 1814.
James Mahon, Jefferson county, SE 17.10.5, Aug. 19, 1812.
Jacob Mambeck, Harrison county, assignee of George Brown, SW 1.12.5, July 10, 1821.

Benjamin Manbeck, Harrison county, W½ SE 27.12.5, April 8, 1828.
Robert Manley, Tuscarawas county, E½ SE 19.13.6, July 30, 1828.
Thomas Mansfield, assignee of John Johnson, NW 25.12.6, Jan. 10, 1820.
William Markey, Harrison county, NE 24.12.7, March 30, 1815.
Daniel Marckley, Harrison county, E½ SE 15.12.5, Sept. 20, 1823.
Peter Markly, Washington county, Pa., assignee of John Roush, NW 29.10.4, Dec. 15, 1811.
Thomas Marquis, Washington county, Pa., all 7.9.5, Nov. 15, 1807.
Daniel Marrit, Washington county, Pa., all 31.8.4, Aug. 27, 1805.
John N. Marsh, Jefferson county, W½ NW 36.12.7, April 20, 1827.
John Marshall, Jefferson county, E½ SW 15.12.6, Nov. 13, 1822.
Arthur Martin, Lancaster county, Pa., SW 24.10.5, Nov. 26, 1813.
Joel Martin, Harrison county, NW 20.11.6, Aug. 19, 1818.
Samuel Martin, Washington county, Pa., SE 34.11.7, Sept. 1, 1823.
Samuel Martin, Washington county, Pa., W½ SE 22.11.7, Sept. 10, 1823.
William Mathers, Belmont county, E½ SE 35.12.7, Dec. 8, 1835.
Jonathan Maxson, assignee of the executors of James Robinson, deceased, SW 19.12.7, Dec. 29, 1818.
Henry Maxwell, Harrison county, W½ NW 20.11.5, Nov. 1, 1830.
Robert Maxwell, Harrison county, SW 26.11.5, Aug. 19, 1824.
Robert Maxwell, Harrison county, E½ NE 27.11.5, Nov. 1, 1830.
William Maxwell, Harrison county, NW 14.11.5, Feb. 14, 1817.
George May, Fayette county, Pa., SE 29.12.7, Nov. 1, 1830.
George May, Fayette county, Pa., SW 28.12.7, Nov. 1, 1837.
James Means, Jr., assignee of Thomas McFaddin, Harrison county, SW 26.11.6, Nov. 13, 1822.
Robert Meeks, Sr., assignee of Benjamin Johnson, SW 9.11.5, Nov. 17, 1812.
John Megaw, Westmoreland county, Pa., NE 30.11.5, Nov. 24, 1814.
Henry Miser, assignee of John Funk, NE 31.12.5, May 15, 1811.
Henry Meiser, Jefferson county, W½ SE 32.12.5, Aug. 19, 1824.
William Meldrum, Jefferson county, SE 18.12.7, Dec. 2, 1832.
Barnabas Melone, SW 28.11.7, April 2, 1829.
William Melton, Tuscarawas county, SE 13.12.7, Jan. 30, 1816.
Benjamin Menyard, assignee of Stephen Ford, NW 15.11.4, Oct. 1, 1811.
Caleb Merryman, Baltimore county, Md., all 25.10.4, Nov. 15, 1807.
Benjamin Michener, Jefferson county, E½ NE 11.11.6, Aug. 19, 1824.
William Middleton, Tuscarawas county, E½ NW 9.14.7, Dec. 2, 1830.
Anne Mifflin, Philadelphia, SW 29.10.6, Jan. 3, 1807.
Asa and Eli Miller, Harrison county, NW 15.12.7, Nov. 1, 1830.
David Miller, assignee of Obediah Jennings, SE 8.11.4, Oct. 7, 1812.
David Miller, Jr., Pittsburgh, SE 2111.5, March 5, 1818.
David Miller, Harrison county, E½ NE 8.12.5, Oct. 20, 1824.
John Miller and Francis Dever, Rockingham county, Va., Trustees of colored persons emancipated by Ruth Davis, W½ NW 36.11.5, Sept. 28, 1826.

HARRISON COUNTY LAND PATENTS

Mason Miller, Jefferson county, NW 1.12.7, March 15, 1815.
Heirs of Peter Miller, Somerset county, Pa., SE 8.12.5, Aug. 19, 1824.
Alexander Milliken, Harrison county, SW 21.10.5, June 1, 1815.
Alexander Milliken, Harrison county, NW 21.10.5, July 30, 1816.
Jane Millegan, Adams county, Pa., SW 15.10.4, Dec. 30, 1811.
John Milliken, assignee of Alexander Milliken, NW 34.10.5, May 9, 1818.
William Millison, assignee of Henry Carver, SW 31.12.7, Aug. 18, 1817.
William Milton, Washington county, Ohio (?), NE 18.11.7, Jan. 30, 1812.
John Minart, Harrison county, NE 1.13.6, Aug. 25, 1825.
John Minnick, Tuscarawas county, NE 9.13.6, Dec. 26, 1815.
Matthew Mitchell, Washington county, Pa., NE 32.10.5, Sept. 10, 1806.
James Molesworth, Jefferson county, NE 35.11.6, April 27, 1821.
David Moody, assignee of Peter Pettinger, NW 9.11.5, June 19, 1813.
David Moody, Harrison county, assignee of Jesse Young, SE 15.11.5, Oct. 3, 1816.
Alexander Moore, Jefferson county, SW 25.11.5, June 10, 1811.
Alexander Moore, Jefferson county, SW 31.10.5, March 20, 1813.
Alexander Moore, Harrison county, NE 35.10.5, Oct. 9, 1813.
Alexander Moore, Jr., Harrison county, SW 18.11.6, Aug. 19, 1824.
Ammi Moore, Harrison county, NE 7.11.6, Aug. 19, 1824.
James Moore, Harrison county, SE 27.11.6, Aug. 19, 1824.
Maurice Moore, Tuscarawas county, W½ SW 31.13.6, May 6, 1824.
Michael Moore, Jefferson county, NE 23.10.6, March 7, 1818.
Michael Moore, assignee of William Harris and John Fate, NW 23.10.6, Aug. 19, 1824.
Robert Moore, Jefferson county, SE 13.11.6, Aug. 24, 1816.
Robert Moore, Harrison county, W½ NW 2.11.6, Feb. 20, 1827.
William Moore, Jefferson county, NW 15.14.7, Sept. 10, 1823.
William Moore, Harrison county, E½ SE 14.12.6, Nov. 1, 1830.
John Morton, Jr., Jefferson county, W½ NW 5.11.6, Nov. 13, 1822.
Benjamin Murphy, assignee of John J. Moore and Gabriel Cain, SW 23.10.6, Nov. 2, 1829.
Samuel Myers, Tuscarawas county, W½ NW 18.12.7, Nov. 1, 1830.
John Nace, Baltimore county, Md., NE 28.11.7, Dec. 26, 1815.
Abraham Naffsker, all 32.11.4, July 23, 1806.
Jacob Naffster, Harrison county, E½ NW 12.10.4, April 8, 1828.
John Nauftzger, SE 31.12.5, May 3, 1814.
William Neel Belmont county, NW 9.12.7, May 25, 1825.
Elisha Nelson, E½ SE 21.12.6, April 5, 1822.
William Nelson, Harrison county, NW 9.12.6, Aug. 10, 1827.
Isaac and Thomas Nevett, assignees of James W. Right, Jr., NW 10.12.7, May 25, 1825.
William Nichols, Steubenville, assignee of Alexander Holmes, NE 8.11.4, Oct. 25, 1813.

William Nichels, Belmont county, E½ SE 22.10.6, April 30, 1822.
Samuel Nickle, Harrison county, assignee of William Nickle, E½ NE 22.11.7, March 21, 1832.
Thomas Nickle, Guernsey county, E½ NW 22.11.7, Oct. 10, 1831.
John Nichodemus, Frederick county, Md., assignee of Thomas McCausten, all 2.10.4, May 21, 1805.
John Nixon, assignee of Joseph McDannal, SE 17.11.5, Nov. 1, 1818.
Joseph Norrick, Harrison county, W½ SE 19.13.6, Nov. 1, 1830.
Charles Norris, Frederick county, Md., W½ NW 33.12.7, Nov. 1, 1830.
James Brown Norris, Harrison county, E½ NW 22.12.7, Aug. 10, 1827.
Jeremiah Norris, Harrison county, SW SE 28.12.7, April 1, 1837.
Sarah Norris, Greene county, Pa., E½ NW 29.12.7, April 2, 1829.
Samuel Oatley, Washington county, Pa., E½ NW 26.11.6, May 25, 1825.
Thomas Ogden, Frederick county, E½ NW 36.12.7, April 2, 1829.
William Oglevee, Harrison county, NW 17.11.7, Oct. 10, 1831.
John Oldshoe, of Fayette county, Pa., all 28.9.4, June 3, 1806.
Joseph O'Neal, Bedford county, Pa., SE 23.10.6, Feb. 14, 1817.
John O'Rourke, assignee of Peter Marckley, SE 3.12.5, Jan. 27, 1819.
Hugh Orr, Westmoreland county, Pa., NW 24.11.5, Jan. 1, 1812.
John Orr, Jr., Harrison county, E½ NW 24.11.6, April 17, 1828.
William Orr, assignee of John Williams, NE 28.10.4, July 30, 1812.
William Orr, Harrison county, W½ NW 24.11.6, Nov. 1, 1830.
Isaac Osburn, Jefferson county, NE 10.11.5, March 20, 1809.
Daniel Palmer, Chester county, Pa., SW 11.11.7, Nov. 13, 1822.
James Palmer, Tuscarawas county, W½ SE 14.14.7, Oct. 10, 1831.
John Palmer, Harrison county, E½ SE 29.11.6, Oct. 10, 1831.
Lerick Palmer, Harrison county, NE 26.12.7, Sept. 19, 1817.
James Parkenson, assignee of Nathaniel Wells, NE 17.11.6, Dec. 12, 1822.
John Parker, Harrison county, W½ NE 17.12.7, Dec. 6, 1831.
David Parks, Belmont county, SW 35.10.6, Nov. 18, 1833.
David Parks, Belmont county, NW SW 35.10.6, Sept. 10, 1834.
Robert Parks, Jefferson county, SE 3.12.7, May 23, 1810.
Robert Parks, Harrison county, E½ SW 3.12.7, Aug. 12, 1826.
Nathaniel Parramour, Jefferson county, SW 19.10.5, Jan. 13, 1811.
Mordecai Parrish, Jr., assignee of John Johnson, SE 1.14.7, Oct. 3, 1816.
Joseph Patten, Jr., assignee of Henderson and Mills, NW 13.12.5, Aug. 18, 1817.
Andrew Patterson, Washington county, Pa., all 2.8.4, Dec. 16, 1806.
Arthur Patterson, Allegheny county, Pa., NE 26.11.5, Feb. 17, 1820.
Samuel Patterson, Harrison county, E½ SW 31.13.6, Dec. 10, 1827.
William Patterson, Harrison county, E½ NW 1.14.7, Nov. 1, 1830.
Jane Pattison, assignee of Farrington Barricklow, SW 35 9.5, June 5, 1816.
Thomas Patton, assignee of David Moody, SW 28.10.4, July 5, 1816.
John Paxton, Belmont county, NE 14.10.5, Aug. 20, 1806.
Eli Peacock, Harrison county, W½ SW 14.11.6, Dec. 10, 1827.

HARRISON COUNTY LAND PATENTS

Thomas Peairs, assignee of Joseph Cook, NE 13.11.6, Aug. 18, 1817.
Hugh Peasley, Harrison county, NE 10.11.7, Dec. 12, 1815.
Samuel Peoples, Harrison county, SW 9.12.5, Aug. 10, 1827.
Jonathan Perrin, Harrison county, NE 19.11.6, March 16, 1815.
John Perry, Jefferson county, SW 34.10.5, July 30, 1813.
Thomas Perry, assignee of Levi Engle, Sr., SE 12.10.6, Feb. 1, 1815.
Leroy Petty, Harrison county, E½ NW 15,12.6, Dec. 2, 1830.
Rodern Petty, Harrison county, E½ NW 11.11.6, Nov. 1, 1830.
George Pfautz, Cumberland county, Pa., all 14.11.4, Oct. 26, 1805.
George Pfautz, Cumberland county, Pa., all 19.11.4, Oct. 26, 1805.
George Pfautz, Cumberland county, Pa., all 33.11.4, Dec. 1, 1807.
Jacob Pfautz, Harrison county, W½ SW 13.13.6, Nov. 1, 1830.
John Pfautz, Harrison county, W½ NE 23.12.6, April 2, 1829.
Jonathan Pfauts, Harrison county, E½ NE 23.12.6, May 22, 1827.
Michael Pfoutz, Harrison county, E½ SW 13.13.6, Oct. 20, 1824.
Michael Pfoutz, Tuscarawas county, E½ SW 20.13.6, July 1, 1831.
Joseph Phillips, Jefferson county, W½ NW 21.12.7, April 2, 1829.
Richard Phillips, Jefferson county, SW 21.12.7, June 1, 1815.
Richard Phillips, Harrison county, SW 20.12.7, Oct. 3, 1816.
Richard Phillips, Harrison county, NE 33.12.7, May 24, 1817.
Richard Phillips, Harrison county, E½ NW 21.12.7, Nov. 1, 1830.
William Philips and William Grist, assignees of Benjamin Stanton, SW 9.11.3, Dec. 1, 1809.
Alexander Picken, Harrison county, W½ SE 35.11.5, April 1, 1837.
Matthew Picken, Harrison county, assignee of James Boyd, SW 35.11.5, May 12, 1815.
Matthew Picken, assignee of Michael Pfoutz, SW 7.13.6, April 10, 1827.
Matthew Picken, Harrison county, E½ NW 34.11.5, Nov. 1, 1830.
Matthew Picken, Harrison county, E½ SE 35.11.5, July 1, 1831.
Matthew Picken, Harrison county, W½ NW 34.11.5, Dec. 2, 1832.
Enos Pickering, Belmont county, NE 25.9.5, Nov. 2, 1829.
Hiram Pickering, Harrison county, NW SE 5.11.7, Sept. 10, 1834.
John Pickering, Belmont county, SW 26.9.5, Dec. 3, 1808.
Jonathan Pickering, Belmont county, E½ SE 11.12.7, June 23, 1826.
Jonas Pickering, Belmont county, all 20.9.5, July 20, 1808.
John Piggott, assignee of Joel Gilbert, NW 26.9.5, Aug.3, 1810.
Abraham Pittinger, assignee of John Roush, NE 11.11.5, Oct. 9, 1813.
Robert Pittis, Tuscarawas county, E½ NE 32.12.6, March 6, 1827.
Elias Polen, Harrison county, SE NE 14.14.7, Sept. 10, 1834.
Nathaniel Poler, Jefferson county, SE 12.10.4, Aug. 19, 1824.
Nathaniel Polen, Harrison county, W½ SW 12.10.4, Aug. 10, 1827.
John Pollock, Fayette county, Pa., SE 15.10.4, March 6, 1814.
John Pollock, Jefferson county, SE 10.11.5, March 18, 1814.
John Pollock, Jr., Harrison county, NW 15.10.4, Dec. 19, 1814.

Charles Porter, assignee of Thomas Hazlet, SE 27.11.5, Jan. 23, 1813.
Charles Porter, Steubenville, SW 25.12.5, Jan. 15, 1814.
Charles Porter, Steubenville, NW 6.12.6, Jan. 21, 1819.
Charles Porter, Steubenville, SW 36.11.5, Jan. 21, 1819.
Samuel Porter, assignee of Samuel Holmes, all 8.10.5, Aug 27, 1807.
John Poulson, devisee of James Poulson, SE 36.10.5, July 5, 1816.
John Poulson, Frederick county, Md., W½ NW 15.11.6, Sept. 1, 1823.
John Poulson, Frederick county, Md., W½ NE 15.11.6, Sept. 1, 1823.
Nelson Poulson, Harrison county, E½ NW 15.11.6, June 23, 1827.
John Prather, Harrison county, W½ SE 14.12.6, Sept. 10, 1823.
John Prather, assignee of Robert Carson, Harrison county, NE 13.12.6, Aug. 19, 1824.
Charles Prather, Brooke county, Va., all 8.12.6, Feb. 2, 1804.
Charles Prather, Brooke county, Va., SW 9.12.6, May 8, 1806.
Anthony Pricker (Bricker?), assignee of Peter Kail, all 24.10.4, July 1, 1807.
Samuel Primes, Jefferson county, all 12.8.4, Nov. 3, 1806.
Provines, see also Purviance.
Matthew Provines, Washington county, Pa., SW 14.12.6, Jan. 20, 1817.
John Pugh, Chester county, Pa., NE 3.11.6, March 10, 1807.
John Pugh, Chester county, Pa., NE 9.11.6, March 10, 1807.
John Pugh, Chester county, Pa., SE 10.11.6, March 10, 1807.
John Pugh, Frederick county, Va., NW 33.11.6, Dec. 1, 1807.
John Pugh, Chester county, Pa., NE 10.11.6, June 1, 1810.
John Pugh, Jefferson county, SW 2.11.6, Jan. 10, 1811.
John Pugh, Frederick county, Va., SW 33.11.6, Aug. 19, 1812.
Thomas Pugh, assignee of Benjamin Tappan and John C. Wright, of Steubenille, SW 4.11.6, Nov. 13, 1820.
William Pugh, Harrison county, SE 9.11.6, Nov. 21, 1820.
Caleb Pumphrey, Jefferson county, all 17.9.5, Oct. 19, 1808.
John Pumphrey, Harrison county, E½ SW 34.10.6. May 30, 1826.
Joseph Pumphrey, Jefferson county, all 13.10.4, July 18, 1806.
Joseph Pumphrey, assignee of Thomas McMillan, Jefferson county, W½ SE 33.12.7, Aug. 19, 1824.
Reason Pumphrey, Brooke county, Va., W½ NW 33.12.6, Aug. 10, 1827.
Reason Pumphrey, Brooke county, Va., E½ NE and W½ SE 13.14.7, Dec. 10, 1827.
Reason Pumphrey, Tuscarawas county, E½ NW 33.12.6, Oct. 10, 1831.
Reason Pumphrey, Tuscarawas county, W½ SE 33.12.6, Oct. 10, 1831.
William Pumphrey, Brooke county, Va., all 4.9.4, Oct. 1, 1806.
Purviance, see also Provines.
Thomas Purviance, Jefferson county, W½ SE 28.11.7, Nov. 13, 1822.
Harlan Pyle, Washington county, Pa., NE 35.10.6, July 5, 1816.
Adam Quillan, Jefferson county, NE 31.12.7, March 7, 1818.
Elihu Quillan, Harrison county, W½ SE 32.12.7, Dec. 10, 1827.

Joshua Quillin, Jefferson county, SE 25.12.7, May 12, 1815.
William Ramage, Belmont county, all 4.10.6, March 21, 1808.
Obadiah Ramsbottom, Harrison county, E½ SE 21.12.5, Sept. 25, 1823.
John Ramsower, assignee of John Barr, Harrison county, W½ NE 8.12.5, Nov. 13, 1822.
James Rankin, Jefferson county, NW 30.9.5, Oct. 10, 1815.
Robert Rankin, assignee of John Gibson, of Pennsylvania, SE 15.10.5, March 7, 1818.
Thomas Rankin, Jefferson county, all 30.9.4, Feb. 10, 1807.
Thomas Rankin, assignee of Abraham Pittinger, SE 31.10.5, Aug. 10, 1813.
William Rankin, Harrison county, SE 35.11.7, Nov. 26, 1819.
John Rea, assignee of Eli Chandler, Fayette county, Pa., SW 30.10.6, Aug. 19, 1824.
Frederick Reed, Belmont county, all 30.10.4, Feb. 10, 1807.
John Reed, Jefferson county, NE 29.9.5, June 8, 1812.
John Reeves, Harrison county, SE 7.12.7, March 20, 1813.
Jacob Reigal, Harrison county, E½ NW 29.12.6, Dec. 2, 1830.
Caleb Reynolds, Jefferson county, W½ SE 5.12.6, April 22, 1819.
John Richardson, Chester county, Pa., NE 8.11.6, July 30, 1813.
Philip J. Richardson, assignee of William Grigory, NW 32.10.5, July 8, 1818.
Andrew Ritchey, Jr., Washington county, Pa., all 28.8.4, Sept. 15, 1806.
Jacob Ritchie, Jr., Washington county, Pa., NE 9.11.5, May 24, 1817.
Thomas Ritchey, Harrison county, NE 15.10.5, March 7, 1817.
John Riddle, Allegheny county, Pa., SW 23.10.4, July 30, 1812.
Richard Ridgway, all 11.8.4, Nov. 3, 1803.
Richard Ridgway, all 4.8.4, Nov.3, 1803.
Timothy Ridgeway, Greene county, Pa., SW 2.12.7, Nov. 6, 1815.
John Riley, Jefferson county, SW 27.11.6, Jan. 20, 1812.
John Riley, Harrison county, SE 36.12.7, July 5, 1819.
Moses Riley, Harrison county, E½ SW 36.12.7, Aug. 12, 1826.
Daniel Rineker, assignee of John Brown, SE 9.12.5, Sept. 1, 1819.
John Ripley, Belmont county, NE 36.11.7, March 30, 1815.
John Ripley, Harrison county, SE 36.11.7, April 27, 1821.
James Roberts, Fayette county, Pa., all 13.9.4, Sept. 10, 1806.
Aaron Robinson, Harrison county, E½ NW 5.11.6, April 2, 1829.
Job Robinson, Harrison county, E½ NW 36.11.6, April 2, 1829.
William Robinson, Harrison county, W½ SW 27.11.5, Jan. 1, 1833.
Joseph Roby, Jefferson county, W½ NW 1.14.7, Dec. 2, 1832.
Leonard Roby, Tuscarawas county, E½ SE 7.14.7, Dec. 2, 1832.
William Roby, Harrison county, E½ SW 35.12.6, Dec. 2, 1832.
Hugh Rogers, Washington county, Pa., all 19.9.4, May 20, 1806.
Joseph Rogers, Harrison county, NW 4.11.6, Aug. 10, 1827.
William Rogers, assignee of Thomas Rogers, NW 28.10.5, June 10, 1811.
William Rogers, Jefferson county, SE 34.10.5, June 10, 1811.

John Roland, assignee of James H. Ball, SE 12.11.6, May 9, 1818.
Moses Romans, Chester county, Pa., SE 10.11.7, Aug. 3, 1818.
Robert Rose, Harrison county, W½ SE 28.11.6, Oct. 24, 1826.
Adam Ross, York county, Pa., SE 24.10.5, June 8, 1812.
William Ross, Harrison county, SE 22.11.5, July 10, 1817.
William Ross, Harrison county, E½ NE 21.11.5, Oct. 20, 1824.
Elizabeth Roush, Harrison county, NW 6.11.5, March 28, 1820.
John Roush, Jefferson county, SE 12.11.5, April 20, 1812.
Hugh and Thomas Rowland, Allegheny county, Pa., S½ 15.11.6, July 29, 1819.
Edward Rubey, Jefferson county, SE 7.11.6, Dec. 26. 1815.
John Rubey, Jr., Allegany county, Md., SE 2.11.6, Feb. 17, 1820.
John Rule, Harrison county, W½ NW 35.12.6, Oct. 2, 1821.
Alexander Russell, Belmont county, E½ SW 21.11.6, Aug. 10, 1827.
Ann Russell, Tuscarawas county, W½ NW 14.14.7, Dec. 2, 1830.
Patrick Russell, Allegheny county, Pa., SE 34.11.6, May 25, 1825.
Daniel Rutan, Harrison county, E½ NE 21.12.5, Dec. 2, 1830.
John Rymmerfield, Harrison county, NE SW 17.11.7, Dec. 10, 1839.
Jacob Sadler, Washington county, Pa., all 26.11.4, July 14, 1806.
John Sampson, Harrison county, SE 22.12.6, Dec. 10, 1827.
Jonathan Sayes, Jefferson county, assignee of William James, NE 27.11.6, May 10, 1811.
Jacob Schunck, Jefferson county, NW 14.12.5, Nov. 6, 1815.
Matthias Schilds, Greene county, Pa., SW 33.13.6, June 4, 1814.
George Schultz, Loudoun county, Va., NW 8.11.4, May 23, 1810.
Charles Scott, Jefferson county, W½ NE 32.12.6, Oct. 10, 1831.
John Scott, Harrison county, W½ NW 32.12.6, July 1, 1831.
Thomas Scott, Washington county, Pa., E½ SW 15.14.7, April 2, 1829.
Thomas Scott, Washington county, Pa., E½ NE 15.14.7, April 2, 1829.
William Scott, Harrison county, NW 7.11.5, March 7, 1817.
Enoch Sears, Tuscarawas county, E½ NW 28.12.7, Oct. 24, 1826.
Adam Seebert, Frederick county, Va., all 9.8.4, Dec. 28, 1807.
Nicholas Selbey, assignee of Caleb Selby, NW 35.10.5, June 20, 1820.
John Senter, Westmoreland county, Pa., NW 35.10.6, March 2, 1821.
Edward Settle, Jr., Culpepper county, Va., NW 7.12.6, March 6, 1829.
Elijah Seward and Stephen Miller, Harrison county, E½ SW 5.11.7, Nov. 1, 1830.
Elijah Seward, Harrison county, SW SE 5.11.7, Sept. 10, 1834.
Andrew Sewell, Jefferson county, W½ NE 30.12.7, Aug. 10, 1827.
Andrew Sewell, Tuscarawas county, E½ NE 30.12.7, Dec. 6, 1831.
George Shambach, Harrison county, NW 7.12.5, July 10, 1817.
Joseph Sharpe, Washington county, Pa., all 32.8.4, Feb. 18, 1806.
Thomas Sharp, Washington county, Pa., all 9.9.5, May 8, 1806.
Joseph Shearer, assignee of William D. Mefendish, NE 9.12.5, March 28, 1820.
John Shepherd, assignee of Jeremiah Burran, all 10.9.4, Dec. 20, 1807.

HARRISON COUNTY LAND PATENTS

Nathan Shepherd, Brooke county, Va., all 35.8.4, Aug. 15, 1807.
Nathan Shepherd, Jefferson county, NW 21.8.4, Nov. 16, 1812.
Nathan Shepherd, Jefferson county, SE 22.8.4, Dec. 12, 1812.
Nathan Shepherd, Jefferson county, NE 21.8.4, Oct. 25, 1813.
Heirs of Ezekiel Shimer, dec'd, NE 6.11.6, May 25, 1825.
Jacob Shipler, Westmoreland county, Pa., all 14.10.4, April 7, 1806.
William Shipton, Harrison county, E½ NE 20.11.5, April 8, 1828.
Benjamin Shreeve, assignee of Charles Wilson, SW 32.11.5, May 25, 1825.
Hugh Shotwell, Fayette county, Pa., NE 14.12.7, July 2, 1814.
Hugh Shotwell, Fayette county, NE 8.12.7, July 5, 1816.
Hugh Shotwell, Fayette county, Pa., SE 9.12.7, July 5, 1816.
Hugh Shotwell, Harrison county, NW 27.10.5, July 10, 1817.
Hugh Shotwell, Harrison county, E½ SE 15.12.7, Nov. 1, 1830.
John Shotwell, Fayette county, Pa., SE 21.12.7, July 2, 1814.
John Shotwell, Fayette county, W½ SW 15.12.7, Sept. 1, 1823.
Alexander Simpson, Harrison county, W½ NE 10.12.6, Oct. 10, 1831.
Alexander Simpson, Harrison county, NE 17.12.6, Jan. 1, 1833.
John Simpson, Harrison county, SE 10.12.6, Jan. 21, 1819.
Matthew Simpson, Harrison county, NW 29.11.5, Jan. 10, 1820.
Robert Simpson, Harrison county, W½ NW 36.12.6, Nov. 1, 1830.
Robert Simpson, Harrison county, W½ NE 9.12.6, Dec. 2, 1830.
Robert Simpson, Harrison county, E½ SE 15.12.6, Dec. 6, 1831.
Joseph Sims, assignee of David Mathews, NW 25.11.5, Sept. 10, 1831.
Thompson Sinclair, Belmont county, W½ NW 4.12.7, Nov. 12, 1832.
Joseph James Slemmons, assignee of William Glumer, NW 34.10.6, May 5, 1821.
Alexander Smith and Frederick Schilds, Greene county, Pa., NE 26.13.6, March 6, 1818.
Alexander Smith, Harrison county, E½ SE 32.12.7, Nov. 13, 1822.
Andrew Smith, Jefferson county, NE 8.11.5, June 6, 1814.
Daniel Smith, Huntingdon county, Pa., SE 3.12.6, Aug. 19, 1824.
Daniel Smith, Harrison county, W½ SW 15.12.6, April 20, 1825.
Daniel Smith, Huntingdon county, Pa., NE 2.12.6, May 25, 1825.
Daniel Smith, Harrison county, E½ SW 13.14.7, Dec. 10, 1827.
Ely Smith, Harrison county, E½ NE 11.12.7, Jan. 30, 1827.
George Smith, Guernsey county, SW 10.11.7, Aug. 19, 1824.
George Smith, Harrison county, W½ NE 27.12.5, Nov. 1, 1830.
James Smith, Harrison county, W½ NE 11.12.7, April 5, 1822.
John Smith, Jefferson county, SW 18.11.7, Nov. 1, 1818.
John Smith, assignee of Thomas Scoles, SE 24.11.6, March 6, 1827.
Peter Smith, Somerset county, Pa., NW 2.13.6, Oct. 7, 1812.
Peter Smith, assignee of David Moody, NE 8.13.6, July 30, 1816.
Peter Smith, Harrison county, NE 21.13.6, Aug. 19, 1824.
Robert Smith, Harrison county, W½ NW 15.13.6, Nov. 1, 1830.
Robert Smith, W½ NE 30.12.6, Dec. 6, 1831.

Samuel Smith, Harrison county, NW 2.12.6, Jan. 27, 1819.
William Smith, Brooke county, Va., W½ 22.8.4, July 30, 1812.
William Smith, Jefferson county, NW 3.12.7, Nov. 17, 1812.
William Smith, Pittsburg, Pa., E½ SE 12.10.4, Nov. 1, 1830.
William Smith, Harrison county, E½ SW 17.12.6, March 21, 1832.
Jacob Smyer, Adams county, Pa., SW 6.10.4, June 1, 1810.
Garret Snedeker, Brooke county, Va., all 1.9.5, Sept. 10, 1806.
David Snyder, Washington county, Pa., NE SE 8.14.7, Dec. 8, 1835.
John Snider, Harrison county, SE 13.13.6, Sept. 1, 1819.
John Snider, Harrison county, W½ NW 18.12.6, July 1, 1831.
Lawrence Snyder, Harrison county, SE 1.12.5, Nov. 13. 1822.
Samuel Snyder, Harrison county, W½ NE 24.12.6, Jan. 30, 1827.
Samuel Snyder, Harrison county, W½ NW 29.12.6, April 8, 1828.
Christian Spiker, Jefferson county, NW 20.12.6, Jan. 15, 1814.
Isaac Spiker, assignee of William Bush, NE 24.11.6, Dec. 29, 1818.
Isaac Spiker, assignee of Jacob Vasbenner, SW 2.12.6, Aug. 10, 1827.
Isaac Spiker, Harrison county, E½ NW 23.12.6, Dec. 2, 1832.
Henry Spiker, Allegheny county, Pa., NE 26.12.6, May 29, 1818.
Frederick Spring, assignee of John Rowland, NE 29.10.6, March 7, 1818.
John Springer, Harrison county, W½ SW 35.12.6, Nov. 1, 1830.
Joseph Sprott, Fayette county, Pa., all 2.11.4, Oct. 1, 1806.
Hugh Sproul, Washington county, Pa., NE 36.10.6, Aug. 18, 1817.
Hugh Sproul, Washington county, Pa., NW 31.11.6, July 25, 1820.
John Sproul, Washington county, Pa., SE 25.11.6, July 16, 1819.
John Sprowl, Harrison county, W½ NW 12.12.6, Dec. 1, 1830.
William Sproul, Harrison county, E½ NW 36.11.5, July 1, 1831.
Elijah Staats, Fayette county, Pa., NW 4.11.7, Dec. 29, 1818.
Benjamin Stanton, all 9.9.4, Nov. 3, 1803.
Benjamin Stanton, Jefferson county, all 5.8.4, April 5, 1806.
John Stapler, Bucks county, Pa., all 5.9.4, May 20, 1806.
David Starling, Tuscarawas county, E½ SW 1.14.7, Dec. 2, 1830.
Jacob Stees, Jefferson county, SW 15.11.4, Dec. 12, 1812.
Bezaleel Steel, Jefferson county, SW 26.12.7, June 26, 1820.
Robert Steel, Jefferson county, NE 6.10.6, Jan. 30, 1816.
Joseph Steer, Jefferson county, SE 27.10.5, Oct. 23, 1805.
Joseph Steer, assignee of John Lemasters, SE 33.11.6, Nov. 15, 1810.
Henry Stevens, assignee of Rimrod (Nimrod) Ferguson, SE 6.11.7, July 20, 1808.
Archibald Stewart, assignee of William Griffith, assignee of James Harman, assignee of Joseph Whitney, NE 6.12.7, Nov. 2, 1829.
Galbreath Stewart, Middletown, Pa., all 12.9.4, Dec. 20, 1805.
Galbreath Stewart, Washington county, Pa., all 17.9.4, Dec. 20, 1805.
James Stewart, assignee of John Pugh, SW 27.10.5, April 20, 1812.
James Stewart and Rowet Kerr, Harrison county, NE 34.11.7, May 24, 1817.

HARRISON COUNTY LAND PATENTS

John Stockdale, Jr., Guernsey county, E½ NE 31.11.7, June 12, 1828.
Matthias Stohl, Jefferson county, all 20.11.4, May 8, 1806.
Samuel Stokely, Steubenville, W½ SW 29.12.7, April 20, 1827.
Samuel Stokely, Steubenville, E½ NW 35.12.7, June 23, 1827.
Samuel Stokely, Steubenville, W½ SW 35.12.7, Aug. 10, 1827.
Samuel Stokely, Steubenville, E½ SW 5.12.7, Oct. 10, 1831.
Samuel Stokely, Steubenville, E½ SE 34.12.7, Oct. 10, 1831.
Samuel Stokely, Steubenville, W½ SW 22.12.7, Oct. 10, 1831.
Samuel Stokely, Steubenville, W½ NW 28.12.7, Oct. 10, 1831.
Samuel Stokely, Steubenville, E½ SW 14.14.7, Dec. 6, 1831.
Samuel Stokely, Steubenville, E½ 7.14.7, Dec. 6, 1831.
Samuel Stokely, Steubenville, W½ SE and E½ SE 30.11.7, Dec. 6, 1831.
Samuel Stokely, Steubenville, E½ NW 4.12.7, March 21, 1832.
Samuel Stokely, Steubenville, W½ NW 22.12.7, Nov. 12, 1832.
Samuel Stokely, Steubenville, E½ SW 33.12.6, Nov. 12, 1832.
Samuel Stokely, Steubenville, W½ NE 34.12.7, Nov. 17, 1833.
Samuel Stokely, Steubenville, E½ NE 22.12.7, Sept. 10, 1834.
Samuel Stokely, Steubenville, W½ SW 8.14.7, Sept. 10, 1834.
Samuel Stokely, Steubenville, W½ SE 14.14.7, April 1, 1837.
Samuel Stokely, Steubenville, E½ SE 15.14.7, April 1, 1837.
William Stringer, assignee of Joseph Scott, NW 3.12.6, Jan. 21, 1819.
Hugh Strong, Jefferson county, SW 4.12.7, Jan. 27, 1819.
John Christian Stroub, York county, Pa., W½ NE 8.14.7, Aug. 12, 1826.
Jacob Styers, Jefferson county, NE 22.8.4, Dec. 12, 1812.
John Sullivan, assignee of Basil Moreland, E½ SW 7.12.6, Aug. 10, 1827.
John Swim, Jefferson county, SW 28.10.6, Jan. 21, 1819.
Magdalene Swinehart, Washington county, Pa., SE 3.13.6, March 2, 1821.
James Tarbert, assignee of Edward Rubee, NW 7.11.6, Sept. 19, 1817.
Alexander Tayler, Harrison county, E½ NE 9.12.6, Dec. 6, 1831.
Jonathan Taylor, Jefferson county, NE 15.9.4, March 20, 1813.
Hugh Tease, Jefferson county, all 7.10.4, Feb. 26, 1806.
John Tennar, Baltimore county, Md., SE 29.12.6, July 5, 1819.
Isaac Thomas, Jefferson county, SE 21.9.4, April 10, 1812.
Ann Thompson, Harrison county, E½ SE 11.12.6, Dec. 2, 1832.
Bradway Thompson, Washington county, Pa., all 18.8.4, Feb. 2, 1804.
John Thompson, Harrison county, E½ NE 10.12.6, Sept. 15, 1823.
Thomas Thompson, assignee of Caleb Reynolds, NW 25.12.7, Jan. 21, 1819.
Andrew Thomson, Washington county, Pa., assignee of George Bohrer, NE 12.10.6, Aug. 9, 1815.
William Thorn and Thomas Thorn, trustees of heirs of Isaac Thorn, dec'd, all 14.9.4, April 3, 1806.
William Tingley, Harrison county, E½ SE 23.11.6, March 10, 1825.
William Tingley, Cadiz, E½ SE 30.11.6, Oct. 10, 1831.
Aquila Tipton, Jefferson county, NE 19.12.6, Feb. 1, 1815.

Samuel Tipton, Harrison county, NW 13.12.6, March 6, 1827.
Samuel Tipton, Harrison county, W½ SE 20.12.6, Nov. 1, 1837.
Sylvester Tipton, Harrison county, E½ SE 18.10.4, Sept. 20, 1823.
Rachel Titus, assignee of William R. Dickinson, SE 1.11.6, Aug. 19, 1812.
Rachel Titus, Harrison county, E½ SE 28.11.6, Dec. 6, 1831.
William Todd, Washington county, Pa., assignee of Thomas Peairs, NE 14.11.6, Aug. 19, 1818.
Thomas Thomlinson, Harrison county, W½ NW 26.12.5, Oct. 10, 1831.
Elizabeth Toole, Sr., assignee of Levi Cecil, NW 20.10.5, Aug. 3, 1810.
Roger Toothaker, Jefferson county, SE 19.10.5, Jan. 1, 1811.
Matthew Torrence, Allegheny county, Pa., NW 33.12.5, March 7, 1818.
Eli Towne, Jr., Washington county, Pa., SE 31.12.7, May 3, 1814.
Joseph Tripp, Washington county, Pa., E½ SW 22.11.7, Sept. 1, 1823.
William Turner, Tuscarawas county, E½ NE 27.12.7, Nov. 1, 1830.
John Turnpaugh, Jefferson county, SW 32.10.5, July 30, 1812.
Robert Twigg, Harrison county, NE 36.12.7, March 7, 1818.
Thomas Underhill, Harrison county, E½ SE 35.12.6, Dec. 2, 1830.
Thomas Underhill, Harrison county, W½ SE 35.12.6, Oct. 10, 1831.
Nathan Updegraff, Jefferson county, all 26.9.4, Oct. 10, 1806.
George Venamon, Washington county, Pa., NE 3.12.6, June 20, 1809.
George Vaneman, Washington county, Pa., SW 13.11.5, April 21, 1810.
George Vaneman, Washington county, Pa., NW 33.11.5, April 21, 1810.
Joseph Vanlaw, Burlington county, N. J., assignee of Samuel Haines, all 17.8.4, March 18, 1805.
Isaac Vanordstrand, assignee of Peter Vanordstrand, SW 31.12.5, Jan. 27, 1819.
William Vaughan, Tuscarawas county, SW 14.12.5, March 7, 1818.
Jonathan Veasy, assignee of Joshua Buckingham, W½ SW 24.11.6, Aug. 10, 1827.
John Vickers, Jefferson county, E½ NW 26.12.6, Sept. 10, 1823.
John Vickers, Jefferson county, W½ NW 26.12.6, Dec. 2, 1830.
Archibald Virtue, assignee of Dory Beall, E½ SW 5.12.6, April 27, 1821.
Archibald Virtue, Harrison county, W½ SW 5.12.6, March 2, 1831.
John Wagers, Harrison county, E½ SW 23.12.6, Nov. 1, 1830,
Richard Wagers, Harison county, W½ SW 23.12.6, Nov. 1, 1830.
Joseph Wagstaff, Harrison county, W½ NE 21.11.5, April 2, 1829.
William Wagstaff, Allegheny county, Pa., SE 14.11.5, June 1, 1815.
James Walker, Washington county, E½ NW 2.11.6, Nov. 13, 1822.
James Walker, Harrison county, W½ NE 32.11.5, April 2, 1829.
John Walker, assignee of James Rieves, SW 35.11.7, Aug. 10, 1827.
Robert Walker, Harrison county, NW 17.11.6, April 10, 1827.
David Wallace, assignee of Samuel Grimes, all 8.8.4, Dec. 30, 1807.
David and Agnes Wallace, Belmont county, NE 15.8.4, Jan. 15, 1814.
William Wallace, Brooke county, Va., NE 11.10.4, Feb. 10, 1809.
Henry Walters, Harford county, Md., SE 35.10.5, Dec. 12, 1815.

HARRISON COUNTY LAND PATENTS

Abraham Warner, assignee of Michael Lawber, SE 3.14.7, May 25, 1825.
Abraham Warner, Tuscarawas county, NW 32.13.6, Nov. 2, 1829.
John Warner, Tuscarawas county, W½ SE 2.14.7, Dec. 2, 1832.
William Wartembe, Brooke county, Va., all 33.10.4, July 1, 1807.
William Watkins, NE SE 9.14.7, Jan. 1, 1833.
Matthew Watson, Columbiana county, E½ SW 19.13.6, Dec. 2, 1830.
William Watt, Washington county, Pa., all 10.10.4, July 14, 1806.
William Watt, assignee of Joseph Patterson, NE 15.10.4, Jan. 30, 1816.
Allen Watters, Harrison county, E½ NW 24.12.6, Dec. 2, 1830.
Heirs of Henry Waters, dec'd, Harrison county, NE 34.10.5, Aug. 10, 1827.
William Waters, Harford county, Md., SW 3.11.6, May 20, 1817.
John B. Way, Columbiana county, W½ NE 12.20.7, Aug. 10, 1827.
Jacob Webb, Fayette county, Pa., all 6.9.5, Feb. 18, 1806.
Heirs of John Webster, Harrison county, E½ SW 12.11.5, Aug. 19, 1824.
Welch, see also Welsh.
Daniel Welch, Washington county, Pa., all 1.10.4, March 10, 1807.
Daniel Welch, Washington county, Pa., all 6.9.4, March 10, 1807.
Henry Welday, Jefferson county, SE 7.13.6, Aug. 19, 1824.
David Welling, Harrison county, SW 23.9.5, Aug. 18, 1817.
Bezaleel Wells, Steubenville, all 20.9.4, March 6, 1806.
Bezaleel Wells, Steubenville, all 36. 9.4, March 6, 1806.
Bezaleel Wells, Steubenville, all 31.10.4, April 5, 1806.
Bezaleel Wells, assignee of Thomas Holmes, all 19.10.4, June 6, 1806.
Bezaleel Wells, Steubenville, all 1.11.5, Aug. 20, 1808.
Bezaleel Wells, Steubenville, SW 32.10.4, Aug. 10, 1811.
Bezaleel Wells, Steubenville, SW 2.11.5, July 30, 1812.
Bezaleel Wells, Steubenville, NE 7.11.5, July 30, 1812.
Bezaleel Wells, Steubenville, SE 7.11.5, July 30, 1812.
Bezaleel Wells, Steubenville, SE 2.11.5, July 30, 1812.
Bezaleel Wells, assignee of Zaccheus Beatty, all 34.10.4, July 30, 1812.
Bezaleel Wells, assignee of Zaccheus A. Beatty, SW 8.11.5, Sept. 7, 1812.
Bezaleel Wells, assignee of Zaccheus A. Beatty, SE 8.11.5, Sept. 7, 1812.
Bezaleel Wells, Steubenville, SE 32.10.4, Sept. 7, 1812.
Bezaleel Wells, Steubenville, NW 5.11.5, Aug. 6, 1813.
Charles D. Wells, Harrison county, SW 35.10.5, Oct. 9, 1813.
Isaiah Wells, Harrison county, SW 24.12.7, March 16, 1815.
Welsh, see also Welch.
John Welsh, Washington county, Pa., NW 21.11.5, April 5, 1822.
Samuel Welsh, Harrison county, SE 28.11.5, July 2, 1814.
Samuel Welsh, Harrison county, E½ SW 22.11.5, April 30, 1822.
Samuel Welsh, Harrison county, W½ NE 27.11.5, Sept. 15, 1823.
Samuel Welsh, Harrison county, E½ SW 27.11.5, Oct. 20, 1824.
Samuel Welch, Harrison county, SW 28.11.5, Dec. 10, 1827.
Samuel Welsh, Harrison county, W½ SE 22.11.5, July 1, 1831.

John Wert, Harrison county, W½ SE 31.12.5, Oct. 20, 1824.
John Wert, Harrison county, E½ SW 21.12.5, Oct. 20, 1824.
John Wert, Harrison county, E½ NE 12.11.5, July 30, 1828.
John Weyandt, Tuscarawas county, W½ SW 26.13.6, Jan. 30, 1827.
John Weyandt, Tuscarawas county, E½ SW and E½ NW 2.14.7, Dec. 10, 1827.
John Weyandt, Tuscarawas county, W½ NW 2.14.7, Dec. 2, 1830.
John Weyandt, Tuscarawas county, W½ NE 2.14.7, Jan. 1, 1833.
Ezra Wharton, Bucks county, Pa., all 6.8.4, May 20, 1806.
Benjamin Wheeler, Sr., Baltimore county, Md., all 5.10.4, June 6, 1806.
Benjamin Wheeler, Jr., assignee of Anthony Beck, SE 6.10.4, Jan. 7, 1808.
Isaac Wheldon, Tuscarawas county, NE 7.12.7, June 6, 1814.
Levi Wherry, Washington county, Pa., NE 25.11.6, Dec. 29, 1818.
Charles White, Harrison county, W½ NW 11.11.6, Dec. 10, 1827.
Elijah White, Fayette county, Pa., W½ NW 28.11.7, Dec. 10, 1827.
James Whittaker, Harrison county, NE 35.11.5, Oct. 8, 1818.
James Whittaker, Harrison county, W½ NW 30.11.5, April 2, 1829.
William Whitten, Jefferson county, W½ SW 26.12.6, April 8, 1828.
William Whitten, Harrison county, E½ SE 32.12.6, Oct. 10, 1831.
William Whittenton, Harrison county, E½ SE 22.11.7, May 6, 1824.
George Wible, Harrison county, E½ SE 34.11.5, March 21, 1831.
George Wible, Harrison county, W½ NE 34.11.5, Dec. 6, 1831.
Thomas Williams, Brooke county, Va., SW 14.11.5, Nov. 17, 1812.
Thomas Williams, Washington county, Pa., SW 25.11.6, Feb. 1, 1815.
John Williamson, Harrison county, NE 17.10.6, March 7, 1817.
Charles Willison, Harrison county, SE 19.11.6, Jan. 27, 1819.
Charles Wilson, Steubenville, NW 24.12.7, Aug. 3, 1818.
Hans Wilson, Steubenville, NW 17.12.7, Jan. 30, 1816.
Hans Wilson, Steubenville, SW 17.12.7, July 30, 1816.
Hans Wilson, Steubenville, E½ NE 7.14.7, Dec. 2, 1832.
Israel Wilson, Tuscarawas county, SE 35.10.6, Oct. 1, 1811.
Israel Wilson, assignee of Dudley Milner, NE 5.11.7, Nov. 16, 1812.
Israel Wilson, Tuscarawas county, SE 20.12.7, Dec. 12, 1815.
Israel Wilson, Harrison county, NW 5.11.7, Jan. 27, 1819.
James Wilson, Jefferson county, NW 12.10.6, Oct. 7, 1812.
James Wilson, Jr., assignee of James Wilson, SW 7.11.6, Aug. 24, 1816.
John Wilson, Jefferson county, W½ NW 12.10.4, Oct. 20, 1824.
Thomas Wilson, Brooke county, Va., NW 17.10.5, June 10, 1812.
James Winder, NW 12.11.7, Feb. 10, 1809.
James Winders, Fayette county, Pa., NW 2.12.7, July 1, 1816.
John Winnance, Jefferson county, SE 21.11.4, Jan. 20, 1812.
John Winance, Jefferson county SW 21.11.7, Dec. 12, 1812.
John Wynants, Jefferson county, SW 8.12.5, July 30, 1813.
John Winte, Wheeling, Va., all 19.8.4, Feb. 11, 1806.
John Winter, Wheeling, all 25.8.4, April 10, 1804.

Isaac Wood, Jefferson county, SW 18.11.5, May 3, 1814.
John Wood, Harrison county, E½ SE 28.11.7, Dec. 6, 1831.
John Wood, Harrison county, W½ SW 17.11.7, Nov. 12, 1832.
Jonathan Worrall, Jefferson county, SW 15.9.4, March 16, 1815.
David Wortman, Jefferson county, W½ NE 25.12.5, March 10, 1825.
Jacob Wright, Harrison county, E½ SE 2.12.6, Feb. 20, 1827.
James Wright, Belmont county, SE 32.9.5, Aug. 15, 1811.
James Wright, Belmont county, NW 25.9.5, Feb. 17, 1820.
James Wright, Belmont county, NE 31.9.5, Nov. 13, 1822.
James Wright, Jefferson county, W½ NE 29.11.6, Nov. 13, 1822.
John C. Wright, Steubenville, SE 8.11.6, Oct. 20, 1819.
Jonathan Wright, Belmont county, SE 11.10.6, May 18, 1813.
Moses Wright, Harrison county, SW 24.11.7, Jan. 10, 1820.
Thomas Washington Wright, Harrison county, SE NE 29.11.6, Nov. 18, 1833.
William Wright, Belmont county, SW 32.9.5, March 5, 1818.
William Wright, Harrison county, E½ SW 21.12.6, April 5, 1822.
William Wright, Harrison county, W½ SE 21.12.6, April 30, 1822.
William Wright, Jefferson county, SW SE 29.11.6, Sept. 10, 1832.
William Wright, Jefferson county, NW SE 29.11.6, Nov. 18, 1833.
Peter Wicoff, Brooke county, Va., NE 12.11.6, June 24, 1815.
Peter Wicoff, Brooke county, Va., NW 12.11.6, Feb. 28, 1821.
William Wyckoff, Tuscarawas county, SE 26.11.6, Feb. 14, 1817.
Heirs of John Wylie, dec'd, SE 11.10.4, May 9, 1818.
Jesse Young, Harrison county, SE 13.12.6, April 17, 1820.
John Young, Anne Arundel county, Md., NW 22.9.4, Jan. 29, 1814.

MARRIAGES IN HARRISON COUNTY.

1813 to 1840, Inclusive.

Adam Abel and Rachel Wagner, Aug. 11, 1829, by John Gruber, J. P.
John Abel and Elizabeth Shick, June 10, 1827, by John Wagner, J. P.
John Abel and Sarah Ann Abel, Oct. 29, 1837, by John Wagner, J. P.
Elias Ackerman and Elizabeth Shades, Dec. 1, 1830, by Rev. John Crom.
Baldwin Adams and Eleanor Brock, Jan. 18, 1820, by Desberry Johnson, Esq.
George Adams and Milly Hitchcock, Dec. 24, 1835, by John McArthur, V. D. M.
James Adams and Elizabeth Cope, Dec. 16, 1824, by Phineas Inskeep, J. P.
James Adams and Nancy McDowell, Nov. 30, 1826, by William Wallace, V. D. M.
Joshua Adams and Jane Brown, Dec. 14, 1835, by Rev. James C. Taylor.
Samuel Adams and Jane Stewart, Aug. 30, 1833, by John McArthur, V. D. M.
William Adams and Elizabeth Clark, March 7, 1825, by Rev. James Roberts.
William H. Ady and Rebecca Ady, Aug. 13, 1828, by John Heberling, J. P.
George Albaugh and Betsy Ammons, Sept. 10, 1829, by John C. Huston, J. P.
Solomon Albaugh and Presila Makisan, Nov. 4, 1817, by Martin Guilinger, J. P.
William Albaugh and Sarah Thompson, Sept. 18, 1823, by B. W. Veirs, J. P.
Thomas Alberson and Fanny Campbell, Jan. 22, 1820, by Robert Maxwell, J. P.
Isaac Alexander and Nancy Hurless, Aug. 20, 1822, by John Hurless, J. P.
Robert Alexander and Elizabeth Carothers, Dec. 1, 1834, by Richard Campbell.
Thomas Alexander and Esther Miller, Nov. 6, 1821, by John Rea, V. D. M.
James Allen and Mary Knox, Jan. 9, 1834, by Rev. William Tipton.
Ruton Allensworth and Eliza Barnhouse, May, 23, 1838, by John Wagner, J. P.
James Allison and Margaret Hervey, Oct. 12, 1815, by John Rea, V. D. M.
Ephraim Allwood and Elizabeth Salsbury, July 15, 1824, by John Wagner, J. P.
Peolia Alwood, and Mary Ann Salsbury, June 20, 1826, by Rev. Jacob Winter.
Daniel Amies and Mary Thornburg, Feb. 11, 1826, by John Wagner, J. P.
Philip N. Amiss and Edna Basyn, July 19, 1830, by Thomas Phillips, J. P.
William Aims and Precilla Shultz, Aug. 26, 1828, by John Wagner, J. P.
Alexander Amspoker and Mary Lyons, Jan. 27, 1831, by John Rea, V. D. M.
John Amspoker and Catherine Bay, Oct. 4, 1827, by John Rea, V. D. M.
Samuel Amspoker and Ellen Bell, May 5, 1840, by Rev. Alexander Wilson.
Benjamin Anderson and Agnes Love, Aug. 31, 1826, by John Walker, J. P.
George W. Anderson and Jane Pritchard, Oct. 8, 1840, by James Kerr, V. D. M.
Grafton Anderson and Mary Henry, April 24, 1832, by Silvanus Lamb, J. P.
Harmon Anderson and Mary Ann White, July 25, 1839, by Samuel Lewis, J. P.
Jacob Anderson and Lavina Field, May 7, 1835, by William Arnold, J. P.
James Anderson and Lavina Carrick, Feb. 21, 1822, by John Rea, V. D. M.
James T. Anderson and Mariah Lindsley, Nov. 6, 1838, by James Evans, J. P.
John Anderson and Maria Young, Sept. 17, 1822, by Phineas Inskeep, J. P.

EARLY MARRIAGES

John W. Anderson and Rachel Grubb, Nov. 16, 1826, by Joseph Fry, J. P.
Samuel W. Anderson and Matilda Tipton, Feb. 20, 1837, by David Finnicum, J. P.
William Anderson and Jane Frier, Feb. 18, 1834, by Thomas Phillips, J. P.
William Anderson and Matilda Wagstaff, Nov. 28, 1837, by William Taggart, V. D. M.
Barton Andrews and Rachel Barrett, April 2, 1815, by Rev. James Roberts.
Charles Andrews and Jane Glasgow, Sept. 8, 1831, by Thomas Phillips, J. P.
David Andrews and Mary Ramsey, Dec. 20, 1820, by John Rea, V. D. M.
Hazel Andrews and Martha Archbole, March 21, 1816, by Thomas Fisher, J. P.
Jeremiah Andrews and Libby Archbold, Aug. 5, 1813, by William Barnhill, J. P.
Charles Angel and Eva Muntz, May 19, 1822, by John Wagner, J. P.
Israel Angel and Nancy Hardner, Feb. 1, 1818, by John Rinehart.
John Anguis and Sarah Cook, Nov. 14, 1820, by Joseph Fry, J. P.
Benjamin Ankrim and Nancy Race, March 22, 1832, by Robert Pittis, J. P.
James Ankrum and Susanna Auld, Nov. 3, 1836, by William Wallace, V. D. M.
John W. Ankrim and Margaret Hamilton, Nov. 25, 1830, by William Wallace, V. D. M.
Benjamin Antrim and Elizabeth Merit, April 12, 1825, by Silvanus Lamb, J. P.
David Arbaugh and Susanna Long, Feb. 19, 1837, by Rev. Abraham Keller.
James Arbuthnot and Eliza Armstrong, Dec. 29, 1823, by Salmon Cowles, V. D. M.
Thomas Archbold and Phebe Valentine, Dec. 3, 1835, by John McArthur, V. D. M.
Thomas Armstrong and Elizabeth Patterson, Oct. 29, 1833, by Rev. Jacob Coon.
Jacob Arnda and Caty Miller, Feb. 8, 1818, by Martin Guilinger.
James Arndt and Sarah McClintock, Nov. 20, 1817, by Rev. John Rea.
George Arnold and Rachel Walker, March 11, 1840, by William Boggs, J. P.
John W. Arnold and Elizabeth Davis, Oct. 3, 1834, by William Arnold, J. P.
John Arnold and Nancy Galbraith, June 17, 1836, by William Arnold, J. P.
Solomon Arnold and Barbara Stonebrook, Oct. 29, 1820, by Jacob Tope, J. P.
William Arnold and Miss Jane Hoyt, May 17, 1831, by Rev. William Tipton.
Daniel Ashbaugh and Christence Ann Little, Sept. 20, 1838, by George Shaffer, J. P.
Anthony Asher and Milly Barks, Aug. 8, 1816, by William Wyckoff, J. P.
Richard Askin and Cynthia Dorsey, Dec. 5, 1837, by Rev. Benjamin Wood.
John Askren and Julianna Lee, June 5, 1825, by Rev. James Roberts.
Samuel Askren and Eliza Worley, Oct 13, 1822, by Rev. James Roberts.
David M. Atherton and Eliza Nevitt, Nov. 1, 1821, by Joseph Fry, J. P.
Barten Atkison and Margaret Hendricks, Aug. 29, 1839, by William D. McCartney, V. D. M.
David B. Atkinson and Nancy Amanda McCollough, Feb. 22, 1837, by Rev. Jacob Coon.
John Atkinson and Mary F. Ritchey, Dec. 27, 1831, by Rev. Thomas Hanna.
John Atkinson and Ann Ross, Feb. 4, 1836, by Rev. Thomas Hanna.
Samuel Atkinson and Rebecca Kyle, Dec. 20, 1840, by Joseph Clokey, V. D. M.
William Atkinson and Mary Kyle, Jan. 4, 1838, by Rev. Joseph Clokey.
Daniel Auld and Jane Auld, March 22, 1839, by Andrew Isaacs.
James Auld and Helena Alexander, May 20, 1839, by Andrew Isaacs.
John G. Auld and Hannah Marinda Ankrum, Sept. 3, 1835, by William Wallace, V. D. M.

John L. Auld and Jane Hanna, May 23, 1837, by M. B. Lukins, J. P.
Stewart Auld and Sarah Connel, Sept. 30, 1819, by Joseph Johnson, J. P.
Stewart M. Auld and Martha Matilda Ankrum, April 18, 1839, by William Wallace, V. D. M.
William Auld and Mary McAdow, Sept. 25, 1817, by Thomas B. Clark, J. P.
William Auld and Elizabeth Todd, June 11, 1822, by John Russel, J. P.
William Auld and Elizabeth Alexander, Aug. 5, 1829, by John Walker, V. D. M.
George Ayres and Leah Flory, Jan. 22, 1833, by Thomas Ford.
Jacob Ayres and Polly Petty, June 7, 1832, by Rev. Jacob Lemmon.
John Bain and Polly Taylor, Nov. 21, 1825, by Thomas Hanna, V. D. M.
Daniel Bair and Elizabeth Manbeck, Sept. 22, 1831, by Thomas Day, J. P.
George Bair and Hannah Robinson, Aug. 9, 1838, by David G. McGuire, J. P.
John Bear and Mary Turner, March 6, 1827, by George Brown, J. P.
Andrew Baker and Ann Young, Dec. 9, 1840, by John Knox, J. P.
Eli Baker and Polly Easlick, Dec. 16, 1823, by Robert Maxwell, J. P.
George Baker and Jane Birney, Oct. 12, 1825, by Rev. William Tipton.
Iven Baker and Belinda Cox, Jan. 22, 1823, by John Busby, J. P.
John Baker and Nancy Thompson, March 6, 1832, by Rev. William Knox.
John Baker and Elizabeth Foreman, Nov. 6, 1834, by Rev. Edward H. Taylor.
Nathaniel Baker and Balinda Busby, Nov. 11, 1819, by Rev. Elijah C. Stone
Otto Baker and Mary Cox, March 29, 1811, by Rev. Elijah C. Stone.
Otho Baker and Nancy Buchannan, Sept. 7, 1837, by Rev. James L. Russell.
Rezin Baker and Sarah Thompson, Feb. 13, 1834, by Rev. Aurora Callender.
Samuel Baker and Mary McCombs, Oct. 28, 1830, by John McArthur, V. M. D.
Samuel Baker and Betsey Orr, Feb. 3, 1836, by William Taggart V. D. M.
William Baker and Mary Waters, Feb. 1, 1827, by Robert Orr, J. P.
William Baker and Ann Barnhouse, Sept. 10, 1829, by Jacob Tope, J. P.
Zachariah Baker and Ede Busby, Feb. 3, 1825, by Rev. Elijah C. Stone.
Mordica Balderson and Ann Kirby, Nov. 15, 1839, by Joseph Clokey, V. D. M.
Colmore Ball and Mary Lance, Oct. 2, 1838, by Rev. Pardon Cook.
James H. Ball and Terry Andrews, Aug. 15, 1815, by Rev. James Roberts.
James Banister and Caty Woods, Aug. 24, 1815, by Henry Ford, J. P.
James Barber and Betsey Jane Martin, July 16, 1835, by Thomas Phillips, J. P.
Cornelius Barber and Prudence Ford, Oct. 29, 1817, by William Wyckoff, J. P.
John Barber and Lucinda Dewell, Feb. 15, 1827, by Samuel Dunlap, J. P.
John Barcroft and Anna Stone, Oct. 25, 1827, by John Rea, V. D. M.
Ralph L. Barcroft and Margaret Guinn, May 27, 1819, by H. H. Leavitt.
Abraham Barger and Mary Welch, May 21, 1840, by M. D. McCartney, V. D. M.
Alexander Barger and Elizabeth Lafferty, Feb. 21, 1837, by William Wallace, V. D. M.
George Barger and Deborah Pugh, March 8, 1838, by Richard Hammond, J. P.
John Barger and Eliza Ann Gatchel, May 28, 1835, by John McArthur, V. D. M.
John Barger and Isabella Day, Oct. 27, 1836, by John McArthur, V. D. M.
Peter Barger and Ruth Ann Crawford, April 11, 1834, by Rev. William Tipton.
Arnold Barker and Isabella Rutan, Nov. 24, 1831, by Rev. John McArthur.
Joseph Barker and Anne Manchester, March 31, 1825, by J. R. Kirkpatrick.
Matthew Barker and Rachel Duel, June 30, 1825, by Samuel Dunlap, J. P.
Charles Barkhurst and Ellen Davis, Feb. 9, 1837, by Rev. Jas. C. Taylor.
Charles Barkhurst and Mary Booth, April 18, 1839, by Rev. John Wilson.
Daniel Barkhurst and Mary Wallraven, Dec. 26, 1833, by Rev. J. Waddell.

EARLY MARRIAGES

Isaac Barkhurst and Isabel Moore, May 29, 1833, by Thomas Parkinson, J. P.
James Barkhurst and Elizabeth C. Welling, July 29, 1830, by William Tipton.
John Barkhurst and Rebeckah Belch, April 16, 1816, by Paul Preston.
Thomas Barkhurst and Susanna Davis, July 13, 1837, by Rev. James C. Taylor.
William Barkhurst and Drusilla Tipton, March 12, 1834, by Rev. Aurora Callender.
Elisha S. Barlow and Sarah Harris, Jan. 13, 1837, by John Chalfan, J. P.
James A. Barnes and Betsy Barnett, Nov. 12, 1815, by Charles Chapman, J. P.
John P. Barns and Aby Barnett, Dec. 23, 1820, by William Haverfield, J. P.
Levi Barnes and Susan Rogers, April 10, 1823, by Hugh Shotwell, J. P.
Richard H. Barnes and Susan J. Dorsey, Oct. 10, 1839, by Rev. J. H. Miller.
Jacob Barnhart and Sophia Turner, Feb. 3, 1825, by Alex. Moore, J. P.
Hugh Barnhill and Maria Finnicum, Dec. 2, 1830, by Van Brown, J. P.
John Barnhill and Mary Thompson, March 16, 1837, by John McArthur, V. D. M.
Francis Barnhouse and Nancy Kelly, Oct. 28, 1828, by Robert Orr, J. P.
Jacob Barnhouse and Elizabeth Cane, May 9, 1839, by James Endsley J. P.
John Barnhouse and Ann Kail, Sept. 29, 1831, by John H. Huston, J. P.
Peter Barnhouse and Susanna Beckley, June 19, 1825, by John Wagner, J. P.
William Barnhouse and Eleanor Holmes, Dec. 28, 1827, by John Rea. V. D. M.
William Barnhouse and Mary Graham, Dec. 23, 1830, by Michael Conaway, J. P.
William Barnhouse and Sarah Kelly, Nov. 8, 1838, by John Caldwell, J. P.
Henry Barnet and Elizabeth Maxwell, March 13, 1824, by Hugh Shotwell, J. P.
Henry Barnett and Jane Haverfield, March 13, 1831, by William Taggart, V. D. M.
James Barnett and Mary M. Lacy, May 28, 1834, by William Arnold, J. P.
John Barnett and Ceney Merryman, March 14, 1833, by J. Staneart, J. P.
Joseph Barr and Marjery Hall, Feb. 27, 1833, by J. Staneart, J. P.
Thomas Barr and Emily Fincer, Jan. 19, 1826, by Michael Conaway, J. P.
Arthur Barrett and Hannah Sears, March 2, 1837, by Thomas P. Jenkins, J. P.
Erasmus Barrett and Susannah Rogers, June 11, 1836, by Thomas Phillips, J. P.
Isaac Barret and Rachel Cannon, Feb. 7, 1813, by Rev. David McMasters.
Thomas Barrett and Susan Perry, Jan. 22, 1835, by Thomas Phillips, J. P.
William Barrett and Phebe McKeever, Sept. 24, 1829, by Rev. William Knox.
John Barricklow and Rachel Watson, March 24, 1836, by Rev. Jacob Coon.
Edward Barrister and Milly Crabtree, July 31, 1815, by William Knox.
John M. Bartholow and Sarah Sears, Feb. 14, 1839, by Rev. Jacob Lemmon.
William Bartholow and Mary Miller, Feb. 22, 1838, by Rev. Jacob Lemmon.
Charles Bartlet and Ursula Wyckoff, July 5, 1822, by Benjamin S. Cowan, J. P.
John Bartlett and Margaret Lamb, Aug. 10, 1818, by John Crawford, J. P.
Absolom Bartley and Susanna Springer, Sept. 16, 1817, by David Custer, J. P.
Charles Bartley and Hannah Mulford, Jan. 27, 1840, by Thomas Finnicum, J. P.
Francis Bartow and Mary Lisle, Aug. 31, 1837, by Rev. Thomas Hanna.
George Bartow and Matilda Pickin, March 30, 1820, by Michael Conaway, J. P.
Zenus Bartow and Mary Boyce, June 7, 1814, by Thomas Dickerson, J. P.
Martin Bash and Catherine Noffzgar, March 16, 1837, by Rev. Adam Hetsler.
Wiatt Basye and Jane Wilson, March 8, 1823, by Silvanus Lamb, J. P.
Jesse Batten and Mary Ann Rosenberger, Sept. 22, 1831, by Edward Talbotz, J. P.
Thomas Batten and Mary Steel, Sept. 6, 1827, by Thomas Lakin.
John Baxter and Lucinda Suddith, Jan. 8, 1828, by Samuel Hitchcock, J. P.

Thomas Baxter and Nancy Suddeth, March 1, 1834, by Rev. Benjamin Wood.
William Baxter and Sarah Paulson, March 4, 1830, by Rev. Jacob Lemmon.
Hugh Bay and Rebecca Donel, April 23, 1835, by John McArthur, V. D. M.
Zephemiah Bayless and Jane Dickey, June 11, 1832, by John McArthur, V. D. M.
George Beall and Margaret Elliot, March 28, 1839, by Rev. Benjamin Wood.
Isaac Beal and Jane Neel, Oct. 14, 1830, by William N. Smith.
John Beal and Provy Davis, Nov. 19, 1819, by Charles Chapman, J. P.
James P. Bealle and Minerva Huff, Dec. 9, 1819, by Abriam Johnson, J. P.
James Beall and Mary Garner, Sept. 21, 1837, by M. B. Lukins, J. P.
Samuel Beal and Mary Ann Leard, June 11, 1835, by John L. Layport, J. P.
Harman M. Beans and Sarah Broadhurst, Dec. 2, 1830, by Edward Talbott, J. P.
Joseph Beans and Abigail Rankin, June 7, 1838, by Samuel Lewis, J. P.
Thomas Beard and Eliza France, Oct. 24, 1833, by Thomas Hunt.
Abram Beatty and Ruth Hall, June 7, 1814, by Thomas Dickinson, J. P.
Sampson Beatty and Rachel Johnson, April 15, 1826, by Rev. William Tipton.
Samuel Beatty and Margaret Wilson, Feb. 6, 1827, by William Taggart, V. D. M.
William Beatty and Maria Hendricks, Nov. 13, 1823, by Michael Conaway
William Beatty and Mary Black, Sept. 4, 1832, by John Rea, V. D. M.
William Beatty and Mary Wilkins, Nov. 9, 1837, by Samuel Skinner, J. P.
Isaac Beaver and Betsey Trusal, Nov. 20, 1832, by Lot Deming, J. P.
George Beck and Delila Miller, Dec. 26, 1839, by John Knox, J. P.
James Beck and Nancy Turnpaugh, Nov. 10, 1825, by George Brown, J. P.
Levi Beck and Rachel Dutton, May 15, 1839, by Thomas Phillips, J. P.
Michael Beck and Eve Bair, April 19, 1831, by John Gruber, J. P.
Presley Beck and Sarah Boyles, Dec. 16, 1827, by T. P. Jenkins, J. P.
Henry Beckley and Ann McGee, March 22, 1832, by John Wagner, J. P.
Jacob Beckley and Susanna Shulty, July 12, 1818, by John Wagner, J. P.
John D. Bedwell and Polly Foster, Nov. 5, 1829, by Rev. Benjamin Wood.
Horace Belknap and Saloma Winders, March 16, 1826, by Daniel Limerick, Elder M. E. Church.
Dary Bell and Cassa Moore, June 18, 1840, by William Arnold, J. P.
George W. Bell and Jane Heavlin, Feb. 2, 1826, by Alexander Moore, J. P.
Graft Bell and Margaret Leeper, April 3, 1832, by Michael Conaway, J. P.
Graft Bell and Margaret McClintick, April 11, 1840, by Aaron Conaway, J. P.
John Bell and Betsey Turner, Aug. 26, 1825, by Silvanus Lamb, J. P.
John Bell and Catherine Grimes, July 31, 1832, by William Tipton,
Robert Bell and Charlotte Blanchard, Sept. 26, 1821, by William Taggart, V. D. M.
Robert H. Bell and Jane Simpson, July 31, 1823, by William Taggart, V. D. M.
Robert H. Bell and Margaret Richards, March 25, 1840, by Aaron Conaway, J. P.
Samuel Bell and Rachel Croskey, Dec. 28, 1826, by James Phillips, V. D. M.
Walter Bell and Sarah Hovey, Jan. 18, 1816, by Charles Chapman, J. P.
Walter Bell and Anne Parker, Sept. 1, 1835, by John McArthur, V. D. M.
William Bell and Martha Hooper, March 29, 1838, by William Wallace, V. D. M.
John Beltz and Martha Stuffy, May 26, 1830, by John Wagner, J. P.
John Bendue and Ann Hibbs, July 16, 1839, by Samuel Skinner, J. P.
Philip Benedict and Sarah Harmon, Nov. 4, 1830, by John Gruber, J. P.
Jarret Bennett and Mary Turner, Oct. 29, 1829, by Joseph Rea, J. P.
Valentine Berger and Elizabeth Wable, Jan. 11, 1827, by Samuel Ramsey, J. P.

EARLY MARRIAGES

Daniel Berry and Isabella Hayes, Feb. 26, 1835, by John Rea, V. D. M.
Jesse Berry and Hariett Walker, Jan. 15, 1828, by William Taggart, V. D. M.
Samuel Berry and Jane Hays, Feb. 11, 1836, by John Rea, V. D. M.
Barnet Bethel and Anne Chandler, Jan. 24, 1823, by George Brown, J. P.
John Bethel and Elizabeth Oglevee, March 7, 1827, by Joseph Rea J, P.
Jacob Betz and Christena Feltenberger, Dec. 22, 1836, by John Wagner, J P.
Philip Bidinger and Sarah Hartman, April 5, 1821, by John Graham.
Alexander Biddle and Mary Knossker, May 17, 1832, by Rev. Adam Hetsler.
Joshua Biddle and Sally Notsker, July 12, 1838, by James McGaw, J. P.
James Bigger and Polly Bigger, April 4, 1817, by William Taggart, V. D. M.
James J. Billingsley and Jane Meldrum, Feb. 1, 1838, by Rev. Jacob Lemmon.
Wesley Binas and Anna Haver, Nov. 12, 1833, by James Smith, J. P.
Michael Binger and Elizabeth Zollars, Oct. 12, 1828, by John Gruber, J. P.
Jacob Bingham and Katherine Kennard, Aug. 16, 1832, by Silvanus Lamb, J. P.
Joseph Bingham and Rachel Bernhard, April 14, 1825, by Silvanus Lamb, J. P.
Stephen N. Bingham and Sarah Townsend, April 5, 1821, by Rev. James Roberts.
Hamilton Birney and Rachel McKee, Sept. 23, 1839, by Rev. Parden Cook.
Israel Birney and Martha Hedge, Aug. 23, 1837, by John McArthur, V. D. M.
John Birney and Hannah McKee, Nov. 28, 1833, by Rev. Aurora Callender.
Letchworth Birney and Nancy Forsyth, Nov. 14, 1839, by Rev. Lewis Janney.
Robert Birney and Elizabeth Law, Feb. 2, 1836, by Rev. Job Wilson.
William Birney and Nancy Moore, March 2, 1830, by John McArthur, V. D. M.
John Bishop and Naomi Blue, Aug. 16, 1817, by Henry Kail, J. P.
Thomas Bishop and Susanna Gutshall, Feb. 17, 1831, by Thomas Day, J. P.
Daniel Black and Mary Fulton, Oct. 2, 1823, by William Holmes, J. P.
Zigismond M. Black and Ruth Ann Peterson, Oct. 18, 1837, by Rev. William Knox.
Samuel Blackford and Sarah Williams, Nov. 2, 1819, by Thomas Dickerson, J. P
Samuel Blackstone and Rachel Rowlands, Jan. 10, 1839, by Samuel Skinner, J. P.
Adam Blair and Elizabeth Scoles, Dec. 22, 1829, by Thomas M. Hudson, J. P.
Archibald Blair and Susanna Orr, Feb. 6, 1824, by James McMahon
Daniel Blair and Susanna Haverfield, Nov. 2, 1819, by William Anderson, J. P.
John Blair and Eleanor Haverfield, Dec. 28, 1826, by Samuel Hitchcock, J. P.
John Blair and Isabella Oliver, Aug. 1, 1827, by Rev. William Knox.
John Blair and Jane Brokaw, Nov. 19, 1830, by Rev. William McMillan.
Randel Blair and Sarah Barnett, July 11, 1820, by Rev. William Haverfield, J. P.
William Blair and Sarah Day, Dec. 14, 1826, by Alexander Moore, J. P.
John Bleeks and Darcus Maholm, Nov. 20, 1823, by Donald McIntosh, V. D. M.
James Boals and Margaret Clifford, Feb. 12, 1837, by John McArthur, V. D. M.
James Bowles and Martha Hanna, Oct. 17, 1839, by Joseph Clokey, V. D. M.
Robert Boals and Catherine Manly, Oct. 25, 1822, by John Rea, V. D. M.
William Boggs and Martha Beatty, Sept. 6, 1827, by Rev. Salmon Cowles.
William Boggs and Martha Simeral, June 19, 1838, by John Rea, V. D. M.
Joshua Bond and Ruth Cole, Dec. 21, 1815, by John Roberts.
Alexander Bonham and Susannah Yarnel, Nov. 21, 1833, by Rev. Benjamin Wood.
Evan Bonham and Mary Worley, May 1, 1828, by Rev. Benjamin Wood.

Smith Bonham and Julian Worley, Jan. 4, 1827, by Rev. Benjamin Wood.
Michael Boop and Elizabeth Winings, June 29, 1823, by Rev. Daniel Rahauser.
Jacob Boothe and Mary Barkhurst, Dec. 26, 1833, by Rev. G. Waddell.
Jeremiah Booth and Elizabeth Ann Carner, Sept. 26, 1838, by William Arnold, J. P.
Isaac Boothe and Leah Arbuckle, Dec. 7, 1824, by Salmon Cowles, V. D. M.
John Bothe and Mary Cox, Aug. 20, 1818, by James Roberts.
John Booth and Mary Ann Aikins, April 21, 1831, by Rev. John Secrest.
John Boothe and Elender Ann McKee, April 11, 1833, by Edward Talbott J. P.
Samuel Borland and Mary Little, April 20, 1820, by John Hurless, J. P.
Samuel Boreland and Elizabeth Heavlin, Oct. 4, 1827, by Rev. Sewel C. Briggs.
Jacob Bosley and Elizabeth N. Kail, June 25, 1835, by John Wagner, J. P.
Medad Bostick and Mary N. Craig, Oct. 1, 1819, by Desberry Johnson, J. P.
Elias Bowers and Forilla McDonald, April 13, 1818, by Rev. M. Cole.
William Bowers and Crilly Barnes, Feb. 3, 1818, by Charles Chapman, J. P.
William Bower and Sarah Tanner, June 16, 1836, by David Bower, J. P.
David Bowersock and Margaret Shick, April 8, 1827, by James Manning.
Abraham Boyce and Elizabeth Cram, April 20, 1816, by Thomas Dickerson, J. P.
William Boyce and Sarah Reynolds. Jan. 7, 1825, by Michael Conaway, J. P.
James F. Boyles and Mary Ann Heck, June 2, 1837, by B. W. Viers, J. P.
Albert Boyd and Rachel Ann J. Eaton, Dec. 20, 1836, by M. B. Lukins, J. P.
James Boyd and Maria Barger, Nov. 4, 1830, by John McArthur, V. D. M.
John Boyd and Caty Henry, Sept. 24, 1829, by Henry Ford, J. P.
John Boyd and Mary Barnett, Oct. 22, 1832, by Thomas Phillips, J. P.
John Boyd and Karenhappuck Parrish, June 30, 1835, by William Taggart, V. D. M.
Samuel Boyd and Eliza Christy, Dec. 23, 1828, by Samuel Hitchcock, J. P.
Samuel Boyd and Nancy Allen, Feb. 16, 1838, by John M. Brown, J. P.
Thomas Boyd and Catherine Kent, March 6, 1832, by John McArthur, V. D. M.
William Boyd and Anna White, March 13, 1823, by John Graham.
William Boyd and Margaret Boles, April 3, 1824, by Joseph Fry, J. P.
Joseph B. Braden and Isabella Sharp, Oct. 23, 1839, by Rev. William Taggart, V. D. M.
Walter Braden and Esther Long, May 6, 1824, by Thomas Hanna, V. D. M.
Walter Braden and Eliza Graham, April 2, 1840, by James Kerr, V. D. M.
Thomas Bradford and Mary Ann Palmer, Sept. 6, 1821, by John Rea, V. D. M.
Jesse Bradinburgh and Matilda Turner, May 19, 1818, by Desberry Johnson, J. P.
Thomas Bradley and Rachel Scott, March 17, 1836, by John McArthur, V. D. M.
William Breidenthal and Catherine Timmons, March 20, 1828, by Rev. James Moore.
James B. Brennan and Esther Matson, April 19, 1820, by Thomas Parkinson, J. P.
John Brannon and Nancy McLaughlin, Jan. 7, 1823, by Thomas Patton, J. P.
Richard Brewer and Mary Mercer, Aug. 3, 1837, by John Chalfan, J. P.
Henry Bricker and Lydia Miser, Shortcreek, April 20, 1813, by Samuel Dunlap, J. P.
John Bricker and Anna Busby, Feb. 14, 1833, by William Arnold, J. P.
John Brindley and Ann Brown, April 8, 1830, by Rev. William Knox.
William Brindley and Mary Little, July 2, 1840, by James Evans, J. P.

EARLY MARRIAGES

Joseph Broadhurst and Rachel Carver, May 9, 1816, by Paul Preston.
Reuben Brock and Elizabeth Riley, Dec. 30, 1824, by Phineas Inskeep, J. P.
Thomas Brock and Delila Fagley, Jan. 11, 1820, by Desberry Johnson, Esq.
Thomas Brock and Mary Smith, Jan. 7, 1823, by Archibald McElroy.
Abraham Brokaw and Mary Guthrie, June 3, 1840, by Rev. Moses Allen.
Benjamin Brokaw and Martha Kidwell, Sept. 23, 1830, by Philip Fulton, J. P.
George Brokaw and Eliza Hamilton, Aug. 13, 1827, by William Wallace, V. D. M.
Peter Brokaw and Sarah Grant, Sept. 20, 1825, by Isaac Allen, J. P.
John Brooks and Mary Faucet, Feb. 27, 1822, by Elias Crane, D. C.
Thomas Brooks and Mary Grace, May 15, 1828, by Rev. William Knox.
Clark Brown and Rachel Poulson, March 22, 1832, by Rev. William Knox.
Daniel Brown and Susanna Updegraff, April 1, 1828, by Rev. Joseph Anderson.
Elisha Brown and Margaret Ann Vanhorn, July 25, 1839, by Richard Hammond.
George Brown and Nancy Lamb, March 27, 1818, by William Wyckoff, J. P.
George Brown and Sarah Tipton, Nov. 9, 1820, by William Anderson, J. P.
George Brown and Susanna Kidwell, Jan. 24, 1839, by Charles Thorn.
Grigsby Brown and Sarah Rubel, Sept. 19, 1837, by Thomas P. Jenkins, J. P.
Jacob Brown and Eleanor Tipton, April 16, 1840, by Robert Caldwell, J. P.
James Brown and Mary Dryden, Feb. 11, 1836, by Andrew Isaac.
Jefferson Brown and Mary Gass, March 27, 1832, by John McArthur, V. D. M.
Joel Brown and Leah Hister, May 8, 1823, by David McMasters.
John R. Brown and Mary Beek, Sept. 10, 1818, by Peter Johnson, J. P.
John Brown and Sarah Davis, Dec. 23, 1824, by Rev. John Watterman.
John Brown and Martha Williams, Nov. 8, 1827, by Michael Conaway, J. P.
John Brown and Hannah Beck, Aug. 20, 1829, by Thomas P. Jenkins, J. P.
John Brown and Elizabeth Kirkwood, April 20, 1831, by Van Brown, J. P.
John M. Brown and Eliza Jane Norris, Jan. 2, 1834, by John L. Grubb, J. P.

Joseph Brown and Mary Meek, April 2, 1825, by Rev. John McMahon.
Joseph Brown and Eliza Robinson, Sept. 23, 1830, by John McArthur, V. D. M.
Joshua Brown and Sally Barnes, Feb. 16, 1826, by James Clements.
William Brown and Lena Dawson, Jan. 11, 1823, by William Wallace.
William Brown and Margaret Culbertson, Feb. 14, 1839, by Rev. Jacob Coon.
William Brownin and Hannah Barr, Feb. 28, 1818, by Desberry Johnson, J. P.
James Brownlee and Elizabeth Sheridan, July 6, 1830, by Rev. John Moffit.
Samuel Brumley and Lydia Wyne, April 17, 1828, by Rev. Jacob Lemmon.
Alexander Buchanan and Rosanna Gilmore, May 3, 1832, by Thomas Philips, J. P.
George A. Buchanan and Elizabeth Ferris, Nov. 4, 1838, by Charles Thorn.
John Buchanan and Mary Pittinger, Dec. 4, 1832, by John McArthur, V. D. M.
Joseph Buchanan and Elizabeth Hynes, Feb. 8, 1838, by Rev. John Knox.
Abraham Buck and Eleanor Chicken, Jan. 26, 1828, by Rev. Jacob Lemmon.
William Buck and Corander Smith, April 5, 1814, by Rev. James Roberts.
Nathaniel Buck and Nancy David, Oct. 13, 1815, by William Wyckoff, J. P.
Jesse Buffington and Fanny Wallace, Nov. 3, 1835, by Samuel Skinner, J. P.
John Buger and Rachel Markley, May 22, 1814, by George Pfautz, J. P.
John Burch and Elizabeth Pasley, Dec. 5, 1816, by John Crawford, J. P.
Resin Burdett and Rachel Martin, March 17, 1833, by John Barry, J. P.
Daniel Burger and Caty Albough, Dec. 23, 1818, by Martin Guilinger, J. P.
James Burk and Elizabeth Smoot, Sept. 5, 1826, by James Clements, J. P.

Matthias Burkhart and Elizabeth Kail, Feb. 24, 1829, by John Wagner, J. P.
William Burkhart and Fanny Arnold, May 6, 1823, by John Wagner, J. P.
Abraham Burkhead and Anna Burkhead, Nov. 31, 1826, by Samuel Hitchcock, J. P.
Joshua Burkhead and Maria Turnpaugh, May 23, 1827, by Samuel Hitchcock, J. P.
Joshua Burkhead and Elizabeth Cox, Sept. 19, 1839, by Thomas Phillips, J. P.
Mahalaleel Burkhead and Sarah Blair, Aug. 19, 1824, by Isaac Allen, J. P.
Nathan Burkhead and Susanna Rogers, Feb. 5, 1831, by Peter Barger; J. P.
Thomas Burkhead and Sarah Ann Gordon, June 15, 1837, by Richard Hammond, J. P.
John Burns and Rachel Lott, Feb. 25, 1817, by John Crawford, J. P.
John M. Burns and Elizabeth Hilbert, Jan. 4, 1839, by Andrew Lynch, J. P.
William Burns and Rachel Randolph, April 29, 1830, by John McArthur, V .D. M.
Robert Burnside and Margaret McAdam, March 12, 1840, by Hugh Parks. V. D. M.
Benedict Burrass and Elizabeth Creder, Dec. 30, 1823, by Rev. William Wallace.
Jacob Burrier and Catherine Hendricks, Sept. 3, 1833, by David Finnicum, J. P.
Lee S. Burton and Hannah Stone, July 28, 1831, by John Rea, V. D. M.
Joseph Burwell and Mary Scott, Jan. 13, 1824, by Rev. William Wallace.
William Burwell and Nancy Morris, Feb. 2, 1832, by William L. Robison, J. P.
Robert Busby and Amanda Kemp, March 10, 1825, by James Phillips.
Joshua Bush and Ruth Ann Peterson, Jan. 9, 1823, by Rev. James Roberts.
William B. Bush and Sarah McCleary, Dec. 25, 1832, by Edward Talbott, J. P.
James Bushfield and Mary Garnee, April 8, 1824, by Jesse Hooper, J. P.
John Butler and Sarah Jane Lowrey Buchanan, May 3, 1838, by George Atkinson, J. P.
John Butterfield and Emma Shepherd, June 14, 1832, by Rev. Jacob Cozad.
Thomas Butterfield and Mary Minnick, Oct. 7, 1832, by Lot Deming, J. P.
William Cady and Rachel Barnett, March 29, 1836, by John McArthur, V. D. M.
David Cahill and Eleanor Capper, Jan. 8, 1829, by John C. Huston, J. P.
Griffith Cahill and Mary McQueen, March 22, 1821, by B. W. Veirs, J. P.
William Cahill and Rebeckah Barrett, March 16, 1815, by William Knox.
Thomas Calahan and Nancy Bennington, Oct. 28, 1824, by Jacob Tope, J. P.
Alfred Calvert and Cassa Browning, Dec. 24, 1841, by John Hastings.
John Caldwell and Sarah Reed, Jan. 7, 1819, by John Rea, V. D. M.
John Caldwell and Elizabeth Granfell, Sept. 5, 1839, by Rev. L. D. Kinnear.
Joseph Caldwell and Nancy Gillespie, May 18, 1837, by John McArthur, V. D. M.
Thomas P. Caldwell and Catherine Crabb, April 25, 1839, by William Taggart, V. D. M.
Levi Caldwell and Catherine Smith, Oct. 29, 1833, by J. Staneart, J. P.
Abram Camp and Nancy Nance, Aug. 24, 1837, by George Nickels.
Archibald Campbell and Catherine Hauk, June 17, 1830, by John Rea, V. D. M.
James Campbell and Sarah Foster, Nov. 14, 1830, by Rev. Benjamin Wood.
John Campbell and Elizabeth Flickinger, Feb. 7, 1828, by John Huston, J. P.
John Campbell and Lucinda Plowman, April 6, 1837, by David Bower, J. P.
Robert Campbell and Margaret Archbold, June 10, 1824, by Michael Conaway, J. P.
William Campbell and Mary Kerr, June 15, 1837, by John Rea, V. D. M.
Jacob Canagey and Sarah Fisher, Dec. 17, 1835, by Rev. Adam Webster.

EARLY MARRIAGES

Canaga, see also Kenagey.
Moses Cannon and Rachel Turner, Oct. 14, 1819, by William Wyckoff, J. P.
Thomas Cantwell and Arey Buckingham, March 30, 1820, by Rev. William Knox.
David Capper and Mary Elliott, Jan. 3, 1828, by Rev. William Knox.
John Capper and Susanna Morrisson, April 28, 1831, by John Graham.
Meredith Capper and Eliza Carter, Feb. 5, 1822, by B. W. Veirs, J. P.
Samuel Carnahan, and Sarah McFadden, Sept. 21, 1829, by William Taggart, V. D. M.
Carnahan, see also Kernaghan.
John Carnes and Eliza Nelson, June 9, 1831, by Joseph Johnson, J. P.
Thomas Carrens and Elizabeth Harding, Nov. 7, 1838, by M. B. Lukins, J. P.
William Carnes and Susan Riggle, March 16, 1832, by Joseph Johnson, J. P.
George Carlisle and Hannah McCurdy, Aug. 14, 1832, by John Huston, J P.
James Carlile and Nancy McDowell, Oct. 9, 1830, by Jacob Tope, J. P.
Philip Caroll and Maria Feltbarger, Sept. 13, 1832, by Van Brown, J. P.
George Carothers and Anne Burnes, Sept. 12, 1815, by John Rea, V. D. M.
George Carothers and Ann Black, March 24, 1828, by Jesse Hooper, J. P.
James Carothers and Elizabeth Wilson, Sept. 22, 1831, by Samuel Skinner.
John Carothers and Susanna Burges, Dec. 30, 1830, by Robert Pittis, J. P.
Lemmuel Carruthers and Margaret Phillips, Feb. 21, 1833, by Rev. Jacob Lemmon.
Uriah Caruthers and Rebecca Denning, April 19, 1832, by Thomas P. Jenkins, J. P.
William Caruthers and Elizabeth McClintack, April 28, 1814, by John Rea, V. D. M.
Aaron Carpenter and Priscilla Cornelius, Jan. 1, 1828, by Thomas P. Jenkins, J. P.
George Carpenter and Rebeckah Clow, April 6, 1816, by Paul Preston.
Elijah Carson and Margaret Mehaffy, Jan. 12, 1832, by Thomas Phillips, J. P.
Samuel Carson and Elizabeth Willoughby, Jan. 4, 1815, by Charles Chapman, J. P.
Walter Carson and Harriet Lewis, June 25, 1837, by Richard Hammond, J. P.
William Carson and Elizabeth Wells, Oct. 25, 1840, by Rev. G. D. Skinner.
Dr. John Carter and Mary Jane Johnson, Oct. 4, 1840, by James Love.
Abner Carver and Eliza Norris, Aug. 5, 1830, by Rev. Jacob Lemmon.
Elijah Carver and Nancy Boals, Nov. 26, 1835, by Mark Hogge, J. P.
Thomas Carver and Tomson Gray, Feb. 12, 1818, by James Roberts.
John Carwood and Jane McDonald, March 21, 1826, by Michael Conaway, J. P.
Elias Case and Lorana Sparrow, July 3, 1838, by John Caldwell, J. P.
Lloyd Case and Susanna Cope, Aug. 12, 1830, by John Wilson.
John Casel and Elizabeth Boothe, Oct. 23, 1823, by Phineas Inskeep, J. P.
William Cash and Lydia Carson, Dec. 5, 1833, by Rev. Robert Cook.
William Cash and Rachel Pugh, Sept. 9, 1838, by Thomas Phillips, J. P.
Abraham Cass and Peggy Barkhurst, Nov. 24, 1815, by James Roberts.
Charles Cave and Mary Ann Castell, May 30, 1833, by John C. Auld, J. P.
Aden Cecil and Rachel Wright, Dec. 17, 1840, by Rev. Jacob Lemmon.
Hazel Cecil and Sarah Heavlin, March 6, 1828, by John Carson, J. P.
Jeremiah Cissel and Elizabeth McClintick, July 12, 1839, by R. Brown.
Jesse Cecil and Elizabeth Goddard, Jan. 4, 1838, by M. B. Lukins, J. P.

John Cecil and Phebe Ann Davis, Jan. 8, 1824, by James McMahon.
Samuel Chamberlin and Hannah Hillhouse, Dec. 15, 1825, by George Brown, J. P.
David Chambers and Elizabeth Barnes, Nov. 27, 1838, by John M. Broclair, J. P.
William Chambers and Lydia Croxen, Dec. 14, 1815, by Martin Guilinger, J. P.
William Chambers and Jane Vincent, Jan. 20, 1820, by John Rea, V. D. M.
William Chambers and Jane Miller, Jan. 21, 1833, by John McArthur, V. D. M.
Aaron Chance and Jane Beal, March 25, 1840, by Richard Hammond, J. P.
Benjamin Chance and Sarah Falin, March 19, 1820, by Thomas Parkinson, J. P.
Curtis Chance and Violet Stephens, March 11, 1824, by Thomas Robinson, J. P.
Enoch Chandler and Sarah Knock, June 10, 1830, by Rev. Jacob Lemmon.
Elsey Chaney, and Dolly Cursy, Nov. 23, 1817, by Robert McKee, J. P.
Jane Cheney and Polly Coozer, Feb. 8, 1816, by Thomas Dickerson.
John Chaney and Martha Clark, Jan. 26, 1832, by William Arnold, J. P.
John Cheney and Rebecca Crawford, June 15, 1837, by Rev. Z. Ragan.
Joshua Chaney and Betsey Aimes, March 8, 1821, by William Carothers, J. P.
Thomas Chaney and Hannah Gardner, Feb. 11, 1830, by George Brown, J. P.
Thomas Chaney and Elizabeth Clark, Sept. 27, 1836, by William Arnold, J. P.
William Chaney and Elizabeth Alberson, Feb. 24, 1824, by William Holmes, J. P.
William Chaney and Sarah Steel, June 13, 1824, by George Brown, J. P.
William Chaney and Rachel Lyon, March 15, 1836, by William Arnold, J. P.
William Chaney and Elizabeth Millhorn, March 31, 1839, by Samuel Lewis, J. P.
Daniel D. Chicken and Charlotte Norris, Sept. 6, 1832, by Rev. Jacob Lemmon.
John Chicken and Elizabeth Boothe, Nov. 15, 1832, by Joseph Fry, J. P.
Daniel M. Christian and Milla Smith, Nov. 28, 1827, by Joseph Johnson, J. P.
Herod Henry Christian and Henrietta Peterson, April 12, 1832, by George W. Bell, J. P.
David Christy and Sarah Wilkins, Jan. 4, 1825, by Thomas Hanna, V. D. M.
John Cristy and Effie Mariah Eaton, Oct. 28, 1840, by John Knox, J. P.
Richard D. Cristy and Sarah Porter, Nov. 5, 1840, by James Kerr, V. D. M.
Robert Christy and Jane McCleary, Dec. 15, 1831, by Rev. John McArthur.
William Christy and Martha Harper, May 10, 1821, by William Taggart, V. D. M.
William Christy and Maria Peoples, Sept. 22, 1835, by Samuel Lewis, J. P.
Joseph Clabough and Lavina Louisa Stephens, Nov. 23, 1839, by Thomas Beck.
Abisha Clark and Sarah McAdow, Oct. 8, 1834, by William Wallace, V. D. M.
Alexander Clark and Rachel Adams, Nov. 9, 1823, by John Russell, J. P.
Alexander Clark and Elizabeth Morrison, Aug. 15, 1840, by John Rea, V. D. M.
Andrew Clark and Mary Reed, Nov. 17, 1836, by John McArthur, J. P.
Francis Clark and Nancy Wilken, June 18, 1818, by John Rea, V. D. M.
George Clark and Elizabeth Penn, Jan. 3, 1839, by Thomas Phillips, J. P.
Hezekiah G. Clark and Jane Abraham, May 22, 1832, by Robert Pittis, J. P.
James J. Clark and Mariah Courtney, Feb. 28, 1828, by Ezekiel Paramer, E. C. C.
James Clark and Eleanor Chaney, March 17, 1831, by Thomas Phillips, J. P.
John Clark and Matilda Hows, June 3, 1819, by James McMahon.
John Clark and Henrietta Murrey, Dec. 23, 1824, by Rev. James Roberts.
Joseph Clark and Jane Haverfield, Feb. 17, 1831, by Rev. Thomas Hanna.
Moses Clark and Elizabeth King, July 17, 1823, by John Conaway, J. P.
Robert Clerk and Margaret Moore, Sept. 18, 1817, by John Rea, V. D. M.

EARLY MARRIAGES

Samuel Clark and Jane Hawthorn, Jan. 12, 1832, by William Taggart, V. D. M.
Thomas Clark and Mary Stiers, Jan. 27 1824, by John Walker, J. P.
Thomas W. Clark and Anna Turner, Dec. 19, 1833, by Rev. Elijah C. Stone.
William Clark and Rachel Lock, Nov. 28, 1824, by Rev. Jacob Lemmon.
William Clark and Margaret Anderson, Jan. 3, 1839, by Rev. Thomas Hanna.
William Clark and Jane McCoy, Jan. 2, 1840, by William Arnold, J. P.
William Clawson and Levena Myers, Dec. 7, 1837, by James M. Piper.
Guian Clements and Mary Rogers, Oct. 4, 1831, by John Rea, V. D. M.
Hezekiah Clement and Betsey Wood, June 19, 1828, by Rev. Benjamin Wood.
Jeremiah Clemens and Charlotte M. Smith, July 20, 1834, by Samuel Skinner, J. P.
Joseph Clemens and Rebecca Arrison, May 23, 1832, by John McArthur, V. D. M.
William Clemens and Catherine Harrison, April 8, 1824, by John Hurless, J. P.
William Clendenen and Elizabeth Birney, Dec. 19, 1833, by Rev. Jacob Lemmon.
John Clevinger and Matilda Barrister, Sept. 21, 1815, by William Wyckoff, J. P.
Samuel Clickner and Mary Ann Hilbert, Oct. 8, 1835, by John Gruber, J. P.
Benjamin Clifford and Jane Milliken, April 18, 1837, by John McArthur, V. D. M.
Edward Clifford and Rebecca Dunlap Feb. 10, 1830, by William Wallace, V. D. M.
James Cobean and Louisa McNeely, May 27, 1830, by John Rea, V. D. M.
Samuel Cobean and Nancy Kerr, Jan. 1, 1835, by John Rea, V. D. M.
William Cobb and Mary Copeland, March 24, 1836, by John McArthur, V. D. M.
Rice Cochron and Rachel Quillen, July 8, 1834, by Rev. Robert Cook.
Samuel Cochran and Sarah Jane Hedges, Oct. 10, 1839, by James Rea, V. D. M.
Charles Cole and Emma Hardsock, Nov. 14, 1838, by Andrew Lynch, J. P.
Ezekial Cole and Mariah Jane Smith, Feb. 3, 1837, by William Argo.
Joseph Cole and Mary Eagleson, April 24, 1835, by James McCoy.
Thomas Cole and Catherine Hardsock, March 30, 1826, by John Wagner, J. P.
Thomas Cole and Sarah Salsbury, April 16, 1832, by Rev. Elijah Stone.
Aaron Coleman and Salome Foreman, Aug. 10, 1828, by John Graham.
Charles Coleman and Elizabeth Fuller, Aug. 15, 1816, by James Roberts.
John Coleman and Hannah McConnell, Nov. 4, 1821, by Joseph Fry, J. P.
John Coleman and Esther Belveal, Nov. 6, 1823, by Rev. James Roberts.
Thomas Coleman and Jane Johnson, Feb. 14, 1828, by Robert Orr, J. P.
William Coleman and Sarah Huff, May 3, 1827, by David Winder, J. P.
Elijah Combs and Deborah Murry, Feb. 16, 1836, by James McCoy.
James Comston and Nancy Early, Nov. 28, 1835, by John Bethel, J. P.
Aaron Conaway and Darcus Busby, March 28, 1833, by Thomas Phillips, J. P.
Charles Conaway and Fanny Arnold, Dec. 17, 1819, by William Anderson, J. P.
Jeremia Condo and Lydia Stall, May 1, 1836, by John Gruber, J. P.
James Connel and Jane Auld, Aug. 15, 1831, by William Wallace, V. D. M.
John Conel and Margaret Lewis, Oct. 25, 1827, by Joseph Johnson, J. P.
William Conner and Catherine Dunlap, Oct. 11, 1838, by Nathan Tannehill, J. P.
Joseph Conrad and Eva Stonebrook, May 12, 1823, by Rev. John Crom.
Hiram Conwell and Mary Cady, Oct. 26, 1817, by William Knox.
Jeremiah D. Conwell and Christean Caruthers, Oct. 13, 1835, by Rev. Moses Scott.
Louis Conwell and Prudence McConnell, Dec. 17, 1833, by James Smith, J. P.
David Cook and Amelia E. Smith, Aug. 28, 1832, by George W. Bell, J. P.

George Cook and Nancy Anderson, Aug. 29, 1824, by Robert Maxwell, J. P.
Jesse Cook and Mary Vansickel, Feb. 20, 1827, by Rev. James Roberts.
John Cook and Jane Guttery, Feb. 25, 1817, by Thomas B. Clark.
John Cook and Mary Bradley, Dec. 3, 1835, by B. W. Viers, J. P.
Joshua Cook and Betsey Larkin, Jan. 18, 1827, by John Hagey, J. P.
Roswell Cook and Mary Houser, June 11, 1833, by Thomas Phillips, J. P.
William Cook and Rebecca Moore, July 15, 1814, by Samuel G. Barnhill, J. P.
Harris Cool and Martha McGlaughlin, Oct. 9, 1832, by Van Brown, J. P.
Imla Cooper and Susanna Dawson, Jan. 22, 1822, by Joseph Fry, J. P.
James Cooper and Julian Johnson, Dec. 19, 1828, by Rev. Thomas J. Taylor.
Rezin Cooper and Mary Jane Smith, Dec. 18, 1840, by Thomas McClintock, J. P.
William Cooper and Nancy Holiday, Feb. 27, 1817, by Peter Johnson, J. P.
William Cooper and Maria M. Miller, Dec 25, 1831, by Robert Pittis, J. P.
Ellis Cope and Rachel Cecil, Nov. 7, 1837, by William Taggart, V. D. M.
Isaac Cope and Abigal Cope, March 7, 1839, by Thomas Phillips, J. P.
James Cope and Eleanor Harrison, April 8, 1830, by John McArthur, V. D. M.
John Cope and Eliza Singer, Aug. 16, 1832, by Silvanus Lamb, J. P.
Joshua Cope and Mary Chambers, Aug. 20, 1835, by John McArthur, V. D. M.
Thomas Cope and Mary Ann Gwyn, July 15, 1838, by William Arnold, J. P.
William Cope and Sarah C. Dungan, Nov. 22, 1827, by John Heberling, J. P.
William Cope and Anne Cope, May 12, 1835, by Thomas Phillips, J. P.
James Copeland and Christena Croskey, April 14, 1825, by James Phillips, V. D. M.
James Copeland and Mary Ann Walters, Nov. 21, 1837, by Levi Peddycoart, J. P.
Thomas Copeland and Nancy Shepler, Feb. 7, 1814, by John Rea, V. D. M.
Abraham Corbin and Jane Gulick, Sept 18, 1830, by Thomas Phillips, J. P.
Elija Covington and Elizabeth Carver, Dec. 4, 1817, by Daniel David, J. P.
Robert Cosgrove and Hannah Cook, Jan. 15, 1824, by Rev. William Wallace.
William Cotton and Polly Derry, July 31, 1817, by Daniel David, J. P.
Benjamin C. Couchman and Mary C. Timberlake, Nov. 8, 1840, by George Atkinson, J. P.
John Cowlson and Mary Matson, Jan. 9, 1817, by James Roberts.
John Coulson and Alcinda Huston, Sept. 2, 1838, by Samuel Skinner, J. P.
Benjamin Coulter and Polly Nash, Sept. 6, 1832, by Peter Barger, J. P.
Henry Coultrap and Elizabeth Cramblet, Oct. 19, 1820, by Rev. William Knox.
James Courtwright and Rebecca Sneary, March 22, 1825, by J. R. Kirkpatrick, J. P.
James H. Coventry and Pricilla Barthelow, July 24, 1831, by Thomas Lakin.
Joseph Covert and Nancy Bohier, Aug. 17, 1813, by James B. Finley.
Morris Covert and Jane Wright, Nov. 29, 1838, by Charles Thoms.
Joshua F. Covey and Rhoda Fordyce, Aug. 27, 1837, by Rev. Jacob Lemmon.
James Cowan and Margaret Beaty, March 5, 1834, by Rev. Jacob Coon.
Abraham Cox and Jane Atkinson, Sept. 13, 1831, by John Busby, J. P.
Elisha Cox and Elizabeth Ann Green, May 13, 1830, by Samuel Hitchcock, J. P.
Elisha Cox and Ruth Merryman, Nov. 22, 1832, by Michael Conaway, J. P.
Hiram Cox and Hannah Hall, April 22, 1834, by John McArthur, V. D. M.
Jacob Cox and Agnes Baker, Sept. 22, 1829, by John Busby, J. P.
Jacob Cox and Mary Randal, Dec. 29, 1836, by Rev. William Knox.

EARLY MARRIAGES

Nicholas Cox and Mary Huff, Jan. 3, 1833, by Michael Conaway, J. P.
Sheridan Cox and Betsey Laughlin, July 6. 1824, by John Busby, J. P.
William Cox and Mary Carver, March 6, 1828, by David Winder, J. P.
William Cox and Sarah Maxwell, Nov. 27, 1834, by Joseph Johnson, J. P.
Zebadiah Cox and Charlotta Busby, Feb. 11, 1822, by Rev. Elijah C. Stone.
Zebadiah Cox and Elizabeth Ryan, March 11, 1832, by Rev. Elias C. Stone.
Andrew Coyl and Susanna Hull, Jan. 31, 1833, by John Gruber, J. P.
Elias Cozad and Jane Lyons, March 24, 1831, by Rev. Jacob Cozad.
Washington Crabb and Anne Mahood, Jan. 5, 1836, by William Taggart, V. D. M.
Gabriel Crabtree and Rebecca Moore, June 19, 1820, by Abriam Johnson, J. P.
James Crabtree and Jane Cahill, July 31, 1815, by William Wyckoff, J. P.
Lewis Crabtree and Margaret McMillan, Oct. 19, 1826, by Philip Fulton, J. P.
Thomas Crabtree and Eleanor Davis, June 15, 1820, by William Wyckoff, J. P.
William Crabtree and Sarah Delaney, Dec. 25, 1823, by Joseph Fry, J. P.
John Craig and Mary Osburn, Sept. 27, 1827, by William Taggart, V. D. M.
Johnson Craig and Martha Thompson, July 10, 1834, by John McArthur, V. D. M.
Samuel Craig and Margaret McFadden, May 29, 1838, by William Taggart, V. D. M.
Samuel Cram and Rhoda Burkhead, March 28, 1816, by Thomas Dickerson, J. P.
Andrew Cramblet and Charlotte Young, Feb. 11, 1830, by Thomas McCleary.
Daniel Cramblet and Elizabeth Lukens, May 21, 1829, by Deacon John W. Minor.
John T. Cramblitt and Caroline Castel, Aug. 22, 1839, by M. B. Lukens, J. P.
William Cramblett and Rachel Moore, Jan. 20, 1820, by William Wyckoff. J. P.
Benjamin Cramer and Anne Speck, March 12, 1817, by Peter Johnson, J. P.
Joseph M. Cramer and Nancy Adams, Dec. 23, 1830, by Rev. John Crom.
Joseph M. Cramer and Sarah Lants, March 19, 1840, by Rev. Jacob Keips.
Hiram Craven and Mary Barkhurst, April 6, 1820, by Rev. James Roberts.
Hiram Craven and Hannah Walker, Jan. 15, 1831, by Moses Wright, J. P.
Alexander Crawford and Ziporah Cox, Aug. 28, 1828, by John Busby, J. P.
Arnold Crawford and Ann Culbertson, Aug. 11, 1836, by Rev. Jacob Coon.
Ephraim Crawford and Mary Ann Birney, Sept. 18, 1834, by Walter Athey.
John Crawford and Catherine Grace, May 22, 1832, by W. C. Henderson.
Joseph Crawford and Rebecca Hester, April 8, 1823, by James McMahon.
Joseph R. Crawford and Myra McMillan, May 6, 1834, by John McArthur, V. D. M.
Josiah Crawford and Eleanor Farel, Aug. 27, 1829, by John McArthur, V. D. M.
Thomas Crawford and Jane Kelly, Nov. 26, 1829, by William Taggart, V. D. M.
Thomas Crawford and Eleanor Forbis, March 5, 1839, by Richard Brown.
William Crawford and Louisa Foot, April 2, 1840, by Samuel Skinner, J. P.
Elias Crea and Martha Cochran, July 3, 1827, by John Walker, V. D. M.
Elihu L. Crane and Accions Chaney, April 17, 1816, by Thomas Fisher, J. **P.**
David Cripleever and Caty Smith, March 6, 1817, by Martin Guilinger, J. P.
John Crochran and Mary Wiant, April 28, 1831, by John C. Huston, J. P.
Jesse Croghan and Elizabeth Giles, Aug. 6, 1840, by Rev. Benjamin Wood.
Jacob Crom and Anne Overholt, April 17, 1825, by Rev. John Crom.
William Cromey and Hetty Shields, Dec. 27, 1831, by Rev. James Robertson.
Jackson Croskey and Elizabeth Ann Baker, Jan. 5, 1837, by John Rea, V. D. M.
John Croskey and Esther Davidson, Oct. 24, 1827, by William Taggart, V. D. M.

John Croskey and Elizabeth Long, March 18, 1839, by Rev. William Haden.
Michael Croskey and Rachel Lewis, March 17, 1831, by Rev. William Tipton.
Samuel Croskey and Grazella Scroggs, July 6, 1815, by John Rea, V. D. M.
William Croskey and Susanna Baxter, Jan. 16, 1840, by Cyrus McNeely.
William Cross and Sarah Cole, April 27, 1833, by Thomas Phillips, J. P.
Alexander Crossen and Eliza Atkinson, Sept. 30, 1834, by Henry Maxwell, J. P.
James Crossan and Elizabeth Mullin, March 9, 1826, by Donald McIntosh, V. D. M.
Robert Crossen and Jane Crossen, June 6, 1820, by Robert Maxwell, J. P.
Samuel Crossan and Harriet Ricketts, March 12, 1833, by James McCoy.
Henry Crouch and Rachel Hoover, Dec. 29, 1840, by John Gruber, J. P.
Joseph Crouch and Margaret Robinson, April 16, 1840, by Cyrus McNeely.
Robert Crouch and Ann Gray, Sept. 23, 1823, by John Rea, V. D. M.
William Crouch and Elizabeth Fulton, April 1, 1830, by John McArthur, V. D. M.
William Crow and Elenor Leslie, Dec. 25, 1825, by John C. Huston, J. P.
Thomas Crozier and Libby Buhart, Oct. 5, 1830, by John C. Huston, J. P.
Abram Crum and Jane McIlroy, March 23, 1820, by Rev. Elijah C. Stone.
Peter Crum and Phebe Ann Brown, June 30, 1840, by Aaron Conaway, J. P.
Ira Crumley and Jane Dickerson, Jan. 30, 1840, by Rev. Parden Cook.
Samuel Crumley and Betsey Dickerson, Sept. 4, 1823, by Rev. James Roberts.
Thomas Crumley and Elizabeth Davis, Aug 31, 1830, by Rev. Jacob Lemmon.
Henry Crumrine and Ldyia Montz, April 25, 1839, by D. Rothacker.
Benjamin Culbertson and Nancy Moore, Nov. 20, 1830, by William Wallace, V. D. M.
George Culbertson and Sarah Crawford, Nov. 24, 1836, by John McArthur, V. D. M.
Hugh Culbertson and Mary Lindsey, Feb. 12, 1835, by Rev. Jacob Coon.
William T. Cullen and Sarah Humpress, Nov. 6, 1817, by Daniel David, J. P.
William T. Cullen and Mary Holliday, Aug. 24, 1829, by Thomas P. Jenkins.
Elias Cullison and Polly Gridgen, Dec. 29, 1821, by Rev. Curtis Goddard.
Lemuel Culver and Mary Parmer, Sept. 10, 1839, by John Rea, V. D. M.
John Cummins and Susanna Lett, Nov. 25, 1818, by James Roberts.
Joseph Cummings and Jane Foster, Feb. 7, 1839, by Rev. John Willinor.
George Cunningham and Mary Ann Humphrey, Nov. 17, 1831, by Rev. Thomas Hanna.
James Cunningham and Anna Ekins, April 16, 1835, by John Rea, V. D. M.
John Cunningham and Nancy Sharp, Feb. 3, 1829, by William Taggart, V. D. M.
Stephen Cunningham and Margaret Ward, June 19, 1832, by John McArthur, V. D. M.
John Curry and Elizabeth Shirey, Jan. 20, 1840, by Joseph W. Spencer, J. P.
John W. Curtis and Sarah Palmer, March 28, 1827, by Rev. Samuel Adams.
Emanuel Custer and Matilda Veirs, Aug. 7, 1828, by John Rea, V. D. M.
Emanuel H. Custer and Maria Kirkpatrick, Feb. 23, 1836, by John McArthur, V. D. M.
Jacob Custer and Catherine Gutshall, Oct. 20, 1836, by David McGuire, J. P.
George Damm and Elizabeth McCardle, Sept 26, 1839, by Rev. Robert E. Carrothers.
George Dancer and Rachel Holland, Aug. 12, 1823, by John Hurless, J. P.
John Dancer and Margaret Boyce, July 10, 1823, by John Hurless, J. P.

EARLY MARRIAGES

Samuel Daniel and Nancy Maple, Dec. 4, 1825, by Van Brown, J. P.
Charles Darby and Eliza Ann Star, Jan. 1, 1833, by Rev. Jacob Coon.
Rufus Darby and Belinda B. White, March 12, 1835, by Rev. Jacob Coon.
Joseph Darling and Elizabeth Bedwell, Aug. 25, 1833, by Rev. Jacob Coon.
John Darr and Rachel Waters, June 16, 1831, by John Wagner, J. P.
James Derrough and Polly Barr, Nov. 25, 1830, by George W. Bell, J. P.
William Darrow and Bettsy ———, Dec. 12, 1816, by Robert Erwin, J. P.
William Darrow and Namoi Lukens, Oct. 25, 1827, by Michael Conaway, J. P.
Jesse Davidson and Nancy Dinning, April 10, 1821, by Joseph Fry, J. P.
Jesse Davidson and Eleanor Carey, March 31, 1836, by Thomas P. Jenkins, J. P.
Jonah Davidson and Sally Joice, Dec. 3, 1829, by Thomas P. Jenkins, J. P.
Lewis Davidson and Polly Longshore, Nov. 28, 1826, by Joseph Fry, J. P.
Lewis H. Davidson and Lucinda Latham, Jan. 7, 1830, by Moses Wright, J. P.
Thomas L. Davidson and Rebecca Walker, Oct. 22, 1837, by John Knox, J. P.
David Davis and Mary McCuinor, Dec. 24, 1819, by Desberry Johnson, J. P.
Evan Davis and Sarah Reed, Sept. 6, 1832, by John C. Huston, J. P.
Ezekiel Davis and Elizabeth Wiley, Nov. 7, 1833, by John Rea, V. D. M.
Ezekiel Davis and Catherine Norris, Sept. 7, 1837, by Rev. Thomas Foster.
Francis A. Davis and Lucy Smith, Feb. 1, 1833, by Joseph Fry, J. P.
Guian Davis and Priscilla West, Sept. 5, 1839, by James Kerr, V. D. M.
James Davis and Nancy Baker, Jan. 18, 1838, by George W. Bell, J. P.
Jesse Davis and Mary Ann Wallcutt, Oct. 26, 1830, by George Waddell.
John Davis and Elizabeth Knox, Sept. 11, 1819, by William Wyckoff, J. P.
John Davis and Nancy Walker, Dec. 14, 1838, by L. G. Walker.
Thomas Davis and Susan Spring, March 30, 1820, by John Russell, J. P.
Thomas Davis and Eliza McClenighan, March 6, 1828, by Joseph Johnson, J. P.
John Davy and Sarah Snider, Nov. 21, 1826, by John Wagner, J. P.
Isaac Dawson and Martha Daly, Dec. 22, 1836, by Samuel Moorhead, J. P.
William Dawson and Ann Porter, Nov. 6, 1832, by Lot Deming, J. P.
John Day and Margaret Wilkins, Nov. 10, 1829, by William Taggart, V. D. M.
Uriah Day and Luesia Keesey, June 3, 1831, by Peter Barger, J. P.
Uriah Day and Prudence Jones, Feb. 6, 1834, by Peter Barger, J. P.
John Deary and Polly MacCurdy, June 15, 1816, by John Rea, V. D. M.
Ephraim Deavenbaugh and Rebecca Redden, June 2, 1825, by J. R. Kirkpatrick, J. P.
Abraham Deens and Sarah Shouse, May 20, 1832, by John Chaffant, J. P.
David Dehuff and Margaret Phillips, Oct. 9, 1828, by Morris Allbaugh, J. P.
John Dahuff and Hannah Hasfilhorn, Jan. 7, 1819, by William Anderson J. P.
Samuel Delany and Albina McNeely, June 21, 1826, by John Rea, V. D. M.
Aaron Dell and Isabella Conaway, Dec. 13, 1832, by John McArthur, V. D. M.
Peter Dell and Margaret Walsh, Nov 30, 1830, by John Gruber, J. P.
Thomas Dell and Jane A. Waller, June 23, 1836, by Rev. James C. Taylor.
Isaac Delong and Sarah Dickerson, Jan. 16, 1823, by Joseph Johnson, J. P.
Jesse Delong and Elizabeth Middleton, May 18, 1833, by John W. Iler, J. P.
John Delong and Demaris Delong, Dec. 2, 1838, by Levi Peddycoart, J. P..
George Deming and Eliza Conrad, Feb. 6, 1823, by Elias Cran, D. C.
Treat Deming and Catherine Lyons, Nov. 28, 1837, by Rev. Richard Brown.
Jacob Dennis and Rebecca Lyon, Jan. 11, 1827, by Robert Orr, J. P.
John Dennis and Mary Herrel, April 26, 1840, by John Brown, J. P.
Jacob Devon and Elizabeth Jones, May 16, 1816, by David Custer, J. P.

John Derry and Elizabeth Orr, March 1, 1832, by George W. Bell, J. P.
John Derry and Berthia Warton, Dec. 19, 1839, by Joseph Fry, J. P.
George Denser and Sarah Little, June 27, 1826, by Henry Ford, J. P.
Samuel Deusenberry and Susan Swallow, Jan. 17, 1840, by Rev. Parden Cook.
Moses Devore and Polly West, January 14, 1836, by William Arnold, J. P.
John Dew and Winifred Kirby, March 6, 1840, by William Arnold, J. P.
John Dewalt and Rachel McLovedy, Dec. 18, 1823, by Robert Orr, J. P.
William Dewalt and Hannah Strausbaugh, June 28, 1830, by John Patterson, J. P.
Solomon Dewel and Patience Potts, June 1, 1815, by Martin Gullinger, J. P.
John Dewell and Phebe Jolly, Jan. 30, 1828, by Van Brown, J. P.
Samuel Dewell and Mary Vanhorn, June 22, 1826, by Samuel Dunlap, J. P.
Chauncey Dewey and Nancy Prichard, Feb. 11, 1823, by John Rea, V. D. M.
George Dewit and Sarah Britt, Sept. 2, 1828, by Jesse Hooper, J. P.
John Dewit and Mary Ruble, Jan. 19, 1832, by Thomas P. Jenkins, J. P.
Lyle Dewitt and Nancy Simpson, March 29, 1831, by John Graham.
Robert Dick and Elizabeth Dick, April 23, 1829, by Rev. William McMillan.
Samuel Dick and Martha Clark, May 13, 1836, by Thomas P. Jenkins J. P.
William Dick and Sarah Biggart, Dec. 16, 1828, by William Taggart, V. D. M.
Asa Dickerson and Jane Dunlap, April 27, 1836, by John McArthur, V. D. M.
Eli Dickerson and Sarah Crumley, Sept. 12, 1822, by Rev. James Roberts.
Hiram Dickerson and Mary Crumley, Jan. 14, 1830, by Thomas M. Hudson.
John Dickerson and Eliza McFadden, Feb. 23, 1832, by William Taggart, V. D. M.
Joshua Dickerson and Nancy Glasener, Sept. 21, 1820, by Thomas Dickerson, J. P.
Joshua Dickerson and Belijah Lafferty, Jan. 28, 1830, by William Wallace, V. D M.
Joshua Dickerson and Elizabeth Crumley, May 2, 1833, by Rev. William Tipton.
Levi Dickerson and Margaret Hanna, Dec. 20, 1823, by Salmon Cowles, V. D. M.
Thomas Dickerson and Mary Chew, May 6, 1819, by Rev. James B. Finley.
William Dickerson and Elizabeth Holmes, Jan. 7, 1818, by James Roberts.
William Dickerson and Jane Lafferty, March 8, 1838, by William Wallace, V. D. M.
William W. Dickerson and Susan Ann McCoy, Oct. 17, 1839, by James H. White.
Benjamin Dickey and Nancy Watson, Oct. 29, 1840, by M. F. Burkhead, J. P.
Joseph Dicks and Anna Smith, Jan. 2, 1826, by James Smith, J. P.
James Dillon and Rachel McQueen, Jan. 6, 1825, by John Hurless, J. P.
George Dinger and Mary Heisler, March 11, 1821, by John Wagner, J. P.
Alexander Dinning and Margaret Couch, Sept. 18, 1834, by Rev. Robert Cook.
William Dinning and Margaret Hinton, June 8, 1826, by Joseph Fry, J. P.
Samuel Dixon and Delila Figley, Jan. 3, 1839, by Samuel Skinner, J. P.
Stacy Doan and Elizabeth Wells, Aug. 8, 1826, by Silvanus Lamb, J. P .
David Dobbins and Martha Smith, Oct. 23, 1828, by William Wallace, V. D. M.
John Dobbins and Ann McCullouch, April 8, 1819, by John Rea, V. D. M.
Matthew Dobbins and Eliza McKibbin, Feb. 3, 1820, by John Rea, V. D. M.
James Donaghey and Ruth Loudon, Jan. 9, 1835, by Mark Hogge, J. P.
John Donaghey and Sarah Picken, Dec. 11, 1823, by Michael Conaway, J. P.
Philip Donaghey and Eleanor Auld, April 12, 1821, by Abriam Johnson, J. P.
Benjamin Doney and Elizabeth Summers, Jan. 15, 1839, by Matthew Phillips, J. P.

EARLY MARRIAGES

Samuel Doney and Mary Covert, Jan. 15, 1828, by George Brown, J. P.
Samuel Douglas and Isabella Pritchard, March 23, 1827, by John McArthur.
David Dougherty and Mary Davidson, March 6, 1834, by John L. Grubb, J. P.
James Dougherty and Sarah Lucy, Sept. 22, 1831, by Elder George Lucy.
Michael A. Dowden and Ruth Greenland, Feb. 18, 1820, by Rev. Elijah C. Stone.
Merriam Downey and Jemima Vanhorn, April 3, 1826, by Rev. Salmon Cowles.
Bazel Downing and Eliza Rees, Oct. 4, 1824, by Rev. Samuel Cowles.
Richard Downes and Elizabeth McKinney, April 5, 1821, by Joseph Johnson, J. P.
David Drak and Nancy Drummond, Dec. 6, 1838, by Samuel Skinner, J. P.
George Drake and Rachel Johnson, March 1, 1820, by Abraham Johnson.
Joseph Drake and Actions Greer, Sept. 23, 1827, by Samuel Dunlap, J. P.
Samuel Drake and Susan McCarthy, June 24, 1835, by William Arnold J. P.
Thomas Drake and Hannah Browning, Jan. 25, 1837, by Samuel Skinner, J. P.
James Drummond and Fanny Phillips, Nov. 26, 1818, by William Taggart.
James Drummond and Lydia Ann Hutchison, Feb. 25, 1824, by William Tipton.
Rev. James Drummond and Catherine Taggart, July 29, 1840, by Rev. William Knox.
John Drummond and Sarah Leinerd, Jan. 6, 1818, by Charles Chapman J. P.
Samuel Drummond and Anna Bird, April 1, 1821, by Charles Chapman, J. P.
David Duff and Jane Carr, July 11, 1815, by John Rea, V. D. M.
William Dugan and Esther Gilmore, Jan. 23, 1834, by Samuel Ramsey, J. P.
Maxon Duly and Lydia Dawson, July 8, 1817, by Daniel David, J. P.
Joseph Dunbar and Eleanor Welch, Feb. 14, 1839, by William D. McCartney, V. D. M.
Archibald Duncan and Mary Williamson, April 21, 1831, by William Wallace, V. D. M.
James Duncan and Margaret Williamson, Nov. 25, 1834, by William Wallace, V. D. M.
Nicholas Dunfee and Rebecca Shaeffer, March 26, 1834, by Lot Deming, J. P.
Jesse Dungan and Margaret Grisell, May 1, 1823, by Rev. James Roberts.
Abel Dunham and Rachel Harding, Aug. 13, 1839, by Rev. G. D. Kinnear.
Lewis Dunham and Sarah Ann Nelson, Nov. 5, 1824, by Rev. John Crom.
Adam Dunlap and Jane Patterson, Oct. 2, 1817, by Thomas B. Clark, J. P.
John Dunlap and Ann Vanhorn, Nov. 2, 1815, by Martin Guilinger, J. P.
John Dunlap and Betsey Berger, Oct. 4, 1819, by William Haverfield, J. P.
Joseph Dunlap and Sarah Gilmore, May 18, 1819, by John Rea, V. D. M.
Joseph Dunlap and Mary Ann Roberts, Nov. 3, 1840, by Jacob Coon.
Mathew Dunlap and Ann Greer, July 1, 1813, by Alexander Lee, J. P.
Robert Dunlap and Polly Patterson, April 29, 1819, by Thomas B. Clark, V. D. M.
Samuel Dunlap and Hannah Greer, May 10, 1821, by Robert McLaughlin, J. P.
William Dunlap and Mariah Ramage, Sept. 12, 1839, by William Wallace, V. D. M.
Thomas Dunn and Sarah Dorsey, March 3, 1836, by Rev. Cornelius D. Battelle.
Jacob Dunmire and Rebecca Snediker, May 9, 1828, by John Wagner, J. P.
John Duvall and Rachel Jones, Nov. 22, 1834, by Joseph Fry, J. P.
Nicholas Durbin and Margaret Oliver, May 21, 1823, by Thomas Parkinson.
Thomas Durban and Miram Groves, Oct. 9, 1837, by James McCoy.
Cyrenius Dusenberry and Isabella McConkey, Nov. 3, 1836, by R. H. Sedwick, V. D. M.

David Dutton and Hulda Strade, Aug. 8, 1839, by Thomas Phillip, J. P.
William Eagleson and Jane Gourley, March 17, 1830, by John Rea, V. D. M.
William Eagleson and Matilda Biggart, April 7, 1831, by William Taggart, V. D. M.
John J. Eager and Ann Forbes, May 26, 1836, by Richard Brown.
James Eakins and Elizabeth Foster, Jan. 24, 1830, by John Rea, V. D. M.
Samuel Eakins and Mary Eagleson, May 27, 1840, by John Rea, V. D. M.
William Eakins and Martha Osburn, May 10, 1836, by John McArthur, V. D. M.
Aaron Earley and Rebecca Joy, Sept. 21, 1826, by James Clements, J. P.
Aaron Earley and Elizabeth Conner, July 26, 1831, by Rev. Benjamin Wood.
Alexander Earley and Nancy Davis, Dec. 18, 1822, by John Russel, J. P.
Ira Earley and Eliza Eicher, March 11, 1840, by Charles Thorn.
John Earley and Nancy Rankin, Dec. 10, 1835, by Rev. Cornelius D. Battelle.
Jonathan Earley and Matilda Ruby, Sept. 27, 1825, by Philip Fulton, J. P.
Richard Easley and Elizabeth Valentine, June 11, 1827, by Rev. James Roberts.
Isaac Easley and Mary Norris, April 8, 1830, by Rev. Jacob Lemmon.
James Easter and Sarah Maholm, Oct. 10, 1839, by Rev. William Taggart, V. D. M.
Martin Easterday and Peggy Shaber, Jan. 31, 1818, by John Rinehart.
Joseph Eastland and Mary Ann Norris, Dec. 24, 1835, by Joseph Masters, J. P.
David P. Eaton and Eliza Jane Marshall, Feb. 28, 1839, by Rev. Robert Cook.
Johiel E. Eaton and Sarah Coalman, March 26, 1840, by Rev. J. D. Kinnear.
Joseph E. Eaton and Peggy Anna Ankrim, Feb. 16, 1832, by William Wallace, V. D. M.
Jacob Ebert and Nancy Vandolah, April 6, 1812, by Donald McIntosh, V. D. M.
Joshua Edie and Rachel Hall, Aug. 7, 1821, by Rev. James Roberts.
William Edgar and Betsey Kirkpatrick, Dec. 28, 1820, by Thomas B. Carter, J. P.
Harvey Edwards and Edith Voshel, Oct. 22, 1839, by David Bowers, J. P.
John Edwards and Eliza Moore, June 25, 1833, by Cornelius Crabtree, J. P.
Joseph Edwards and Sarah Barkhurst, March 20, 1834, by Rev. Moses Scott.
John Eicher and Nancy Davis, Feb. 16, 1831, by William McMillin.
Samuel Eimes and Eleanor Robinson, May 5, 1831, by John Wagner, J. P.
William Elgar and Nancy Watson, Nov. 2, 1830, by John Gruber, J. P.
John Elliott and Susan Kendal, March 24, 1830, by Alexander Simpson, J. P.
Martin Elliott and Mary Hawkins, Dec. 17, 1840, by Elias Gatchel.
Berin Ellis and Mary Ann Moffet, March 17, 1831, by Lentulus Kirk, J. P.
Jonathan Ellis and Margaret Lister, Feb. 17, 1820, by John Russel, J. P.
Nathan Ellis and Margaret Brian, March 26, 1835, by Rev. Jacob Lemmon.
Washington Ellison and Sarah Kent, Jan. 29, 1834, by Samuel Ramsey, J. P.
George Ely and Sarah Girt, March 27, 1823, by Thomas Patton, J. P.
Thomas Ely and Barbara Ann Moore, Nov. 8, 1827, by Michael Conaway, J. P.
William Emmons and Catherine Bussler, Feb. 11, 1832, by John C. Huston, J. P.
Simon Emory and Rebecca Minick, June 3, 1840, by E. Greenwold.
Thomas Endsley and Matilda Kerr, March 4, 1824, by Thomas Hanna, V. D. M.
James Endsley and Christian Baker, Oct. 29, 1829, by John McArthur, V. D. M.
Asa Engle and Mary Ripley, July 9, 1818, by William Wyckoff, J. P.
John English and Rebecca Miller, Dec. 30, 1817, by Thomas Dickerson.
John English and Elizabeth Baker, May 28, 1835, by William Arnold, J. P.
Matthew English and Melila Anderson, March 14, 1839, by Thomas Phillips, J. P.

Patrick English and Susanna Dickerson, Feb. 3, 1818, by Thomas Dickerson, J. P.
Thomas English and Susanna Walraven, Oct. 28, 1820, by Thomas Dickerson, J. P.
Jacob Ensminger and Elizabeth Huff, Nov. 17, 1825, by James Smith, J. P.
William Erskine and Rachel Barber, Feb. 20, 1838, by Rev. James Drummond.
Barney Ervin and Mary Fisher, Jan. 15, 1833, by John Chalfan, J. P.
Henry Ervin and Elizabeth Wheeler, Nov. 27, 1838, by M. B. Lukins, J. P.
John Ervin and Nancy Carson, Dec. 8, 1833, by Thomas M. Granfel, J. P.
William Ervin and Anna Hardin, July 27, 1837, by Thomas M. Granfel, J. P.
Erwin, see also Irwin.
Andrew Erwin and Esther McIlroy, March 6, 1821, by Rev. William Knox.
James Erwin and Martha Dunham, Feb. 19, 1829, by Joseph Johnson, J. P.
Joshua Erwin and Nancy Hyret, May 23, 1825, by Michael Conaway, J. P.
William Erwin and Sarah Dunham, Aug. 1, 1825, by Rev. John Crom.
George Eschaltot and Nancy Hanna, Sept. 26, 1829, by Robert Pittis, J. P.
Benoni Evans and Elizabeth Bradley, Sept. 23, 1819, by William Wyckoff, J. P.
Ezekiel Evans and Mary Simpson, Sept. 3, 1818, by Rev. William Knox.
George W. Evans and Elizabeth Spiker, April 15, 1838, by Rev. Jacob Lemmon.
James Evans and Elizabeth Simpson, Feb. 13, 1821, by John Graham.
James Evans and Willimenah Rigel, May 10, 1832, by Silvanus Lamb, J. P.
Mordicai M. Evans and Lydia Dillon, Sept. 26, 1825, by Silvanus Lamb, J. P.
Robert Evans and Amanda McGrew, July 11, 1839, by Samuel Lewis, J. P.
Barnabas Everhart and Rachel Hofane, Aug. 3, 1813, by George Pfautz, J. P.
David Everheart and Rachel Hicks, Nov. 13, 1819, by Rev. John Rinehart.
John Everhardt and Cerrillah Shaw, June 20, 1832, by Charles Fawcett, J. P.
Peter Everhart and Polly Fry, Feb. 27, 1816, by Martin Guilinger.
Philip Everhart and Polly Carpenter, March 23, 1830, by John Gruber, J. P.
Thomas Everhart and Mary Wheeler, Nov. 13, 1817, by Rev. M. Cole.
John Fairchild and Lenday Welch, April 20, 1824, by Thomas Parkinson, J. P.
William Faris and Elizabeth Riley, Feb. 13, 1831, by Thomas Phillips, J. P.
Alexander Fawcett and Elizabeth Brooks, Aug. 16, 1826, by Josiah Foster.
Charles Faucet and Marjery Brooks, Jan. 25, 1820, by John Graham.
Jonathan Faucett and Caroline McGibbons, March 21, 1839, by Matthew H. Phillips, J. P.
George Faulknor and Mary Hidey, Aug. 22, 1825, by Morris Albaugh, J. P.
John Faulkner and Ellen Miller, Sept. 18, 1817, by David Custer, J. P.
Jonas Fayley and Nancy Johnson, March 28, 1814, by Henry Barricklow.
William Feinery and Mary Smith, Feb. 18, 1813, by Rev. Thomas B. Clark.
Charles Feister and Margaret Thompson, July 3, 1827, by Jesse Hooper, J. P.
Robert Feister and Mary Crabtree, Oct. 13, 1828, by C. E. Weirich.
Joseph Fell and Sarah Peck, Aug. 26, 1815, by James Roberts.
Thomas Fell and Willy Ann Gray, Feb. 15, 1827, by Rev. William B. Evans.
Henry Feltenbarger and Susan Stonebrook, Dec. 28, 1838, by John Graber, J. P.
Benjamin Ferguson and Cynthia Haskings, Nov. 17, 1833, by Rev. Benjamin Wood.
Hugh Furgeson and Margaret Sharp, June 12, 1832, by John McArthur, V. D. M
Macomb Ferguson and Mary Patton, June 19, 1840, by John Walker.
Rezin Ferguson and Martha Ann Andrews, Oct. 29, 1832, by John Chalfan.

Vincent Ferguson and Mary Amspoker, March 19, 1835, by John McArthur, V. D. M.
William Ferguson and Rebecca Walker, Aug. 18, 1831, by John Gruber, J. P.
Benjamin Ferrell and Sarah Ann McNamee, Nov. 5, 1840, by John Knox, J. P.
James Ferrell and Peggy Ann Cook, Aug. 18, 1836, by William Arnold, J. P.
John Ferrell and Jane McGoogan, Sept. 30, 1824, by Thomas Hanna, V. D. M.
David Ferrier and Susan Hendricks, Nov. 23, 1820, by Robert Maxwell, J. P.
John Fife and Cassander Lyon, Dec. 23, 1828, by Robert Orr, J. P.
Jacob Figley and Maria Shannon, July 10, 1834, by William Wallace V. D. M.
William Figley and Margaret Chord, Aug. 11, 1823, by Rev. Curtis Goddard.
John Finney and Betsey Cannon, Dec. 10, 1816, by William Taggart, V. D. M.
David Finnicum and Elizabeth Lowmiller, June 29, 1828, by John Gruber, J. P.
William S. Finnicum and Maria Richards, Sept. 28, 1822, by Robert McLaughlin.
Daniel Firebaugh and Caty Little, March 30, 1827, by Henry Ford, J. P.
Jacob Firebaugh and Catherine McCarroll, Dec. 30, 1835, by Thomas Foster.
Barak Fisher and Jane Pickering, Nov. 14, 1822, by George Brown, J. P.
Boanaparte N. Fisher and Lydia Canagey, Feb. 17, 1836, by Rev. Alexander Biddle.
Eli Fisher and Elizabeth Maxwell, Feb. 26, 1831, by Rev. Thomas Hanna.
Garret Fisher and Ann Hamilton, Oct. 31, 1816, by James Roberts.
George Fisher and Susanna Johnson, Dec. 24, 1818, by Thomas Dickerson, J. P.
George Fisher and Elizabeth Burkhead, Dec. 23, 1823, by Isaac Allen, J. P.
George M. Fisher and Anna L. Brown, Dec. 21, 1830, by John Gruber, J. P.
George Fisher and Mary Welch, Sept. 4, 1833, by John McArthur, V. D. M.
George Fisher and Sarah Lisle, Oct. 17, 1839, by Rev. William Taggart.
James Fisher and Ann Harrison, Oct. 13, 1815, by James Roberts.
John Fisher and Mary Fowler, Oct. 27, 1825, by Rev. Elijah C. Stone.
John R. Fisher and Sarah Early, Oct. 21, 1830, by John Russel, J. P.
John Fisher and Eliza Edwards, Jan. 4, 1838, by David Bowers, J. P.
Samuel Fisher and Elenor Marshall, Nov. 4, 1824, by Michael Conaway, J. P.
Thomas Fisher and Elizabeth Picken, Oct. 5, 1815, by Charles Chapman, J. P.
Thomas Fisher and Elizabeth Holtzman, Nov. 5, 1829, by Morris Allbough, J. P.
Michael Fivecoats and Nancy Cheney, Aug. 31, 1815, by Charles Chapman, J. P.
Nathan Fivecoats and Eleanor Steel, Oct. 30, 1837, by Thomas Phillips, J. P.
Absalom Flemming and Sarah Wright, March 10, 1821, by John Russel, J. P.
Robert Fletcher and Martha Moorehead, Aug. 21, 1832, by John Rea, V. D. M.
Abraham Flory and Catherine Hagney, Sept. 3, 1821, by John Hurless, J. P.
Joseph Fogle and Sabra Cochran, March 27, 1836, by Thomas P. Jenkins, J. P.
Frederick Foltz and Anna S. Williams, Oct. 11, 1832, by Rev. Jacob Lemmon.
James Force and Mary Williams, June 1, 1821, by John Graham.
James Ford and Susan Delany, June 16, 1833, by John L. Grubb, J. P.
Lewis Ford and Rebecca Dodd, April 15, 1819, by William Wyckoff, J. P.
Richard Ford and Darkey Pierce, April 4, 1821, by Phineas Inskeep, J. P.
Stephen Ford and Elizabeth Thompson, Feb. 4, 1838, by David G. McGuire, J. P.
Thomas Ford and Catherine Polen, Dec. 13, 1821, by Williamson Carrothers, J. P.
David D. Fordyce and Margaret Feister, June 28, 1831, by Rev. Jacob Lemmon.
John Fordyce and Lydia Ann Parkes, Nov. 28, 1826, by Joseph Fry, J. P.
Henry L. Foreman and Jane Cosgrove, April 25, 1833, by Thomas Lakin.

Levi Foreman and Elizabeth Amanda Jones, March 24, 1836, by Rev. Benjamin Wood.
William Foreman and Susanna Cummins, Sept. 5, 1839, by John Graham.
Joseph Forker and Mary Conwell, Oct. 16, 1834, by William Taggart, V. D. M.
Peter Forney and Fanny Gundy, March 20, 1823, by Rev. John Crom.
John B. Forsythe and Christena Burkhart, June 2, 1831, by John Gruber, J. P
Abraham Foster and Lucinda Coleman, Dec. 25, 1823, by William Holmes, J. P.
Alansin Foster and Mary Ann Prouf, Nov. 16, 1839, by Samuel Ramsey, J. P.
David Foster and Jane Johnston, Feb. 24, 1831, by John Rea, V. D. M.
Eli Foster and Sarah H. Edie, Jan. 3, 1828, by Rev. William B. Evans.
George Foster and Jane Davis, May 24, 1837, by David G. McGuire, J. P.
John Foster and Fanny Hendrickson, Feb 14, 1822, by Joseph Fry, J. P.
Josiah Foster and Rebecca Johnson, May 24, 1831, by Robert Pittis, J. P.
Moses Foster and Hannah Randels, March 14, 1819, by Charles Chapman, J. P.
Samuel Foster and Sarah Young, May 9, 1815, by Charles Chapman, J. P.
Samuel Foster and Mary Moore, March 18, 1824, by Isaac Allen, J. P.
Samuel Foster and Anne Johnson, Jan. 27, 1831, by Robert Pittis, J. P.
Andrew Fowler and Betsy Martin, April 26, 1821, by William Carrothers, J. F.
Francis Fowler and Mary Giles. Nov. 4, 1830, by Rev. Elijah C. Stone.
Garret Fowler and Hannah Eagleson, April 3, 1819, by Rev. Elijah C. Stone
Harrison Fowler and Elizabeth Bridgeman, Oct. 7, 1839, by M. B. LuKens, J. F.
James Fowler and Mary Gifford, Feb. 11, 1830, by Rev. John Crom.
Joel Fowler and Esther Fisher April 20, 1836, by Rev. Elijah C. Stone.
John Fowler and Cassander Keepers, April 10, 1822, by Rev. Elijah C. Stone.
John Fowler and Amanda Burchfield, Dec. 24, 1835, by Thomas Foster.
Thomas Fox and Sarah Hartley, June 28, 1838, by George Shaffer, J. P.
James Francis and Amelia Selby, May 21, 1813, by Rachel Hall.
James Fransis and Nancy Boals, Aug. 11, 1835, by William Taggart, V. D. M.
James Frasure and Rebecca Erwin, June 20, 1833, by George W. Bell, J. P.
Daniel Frester and Rachel Ann Darling, July 10, 1831, by Rev. Jacob Lemmon.
Ludwig Frietsh and Catherine Manbeck, Feb. 21, 1832, by Rev. Adam Hetzler.
Robert Fryer and Susanna Oram, Aug. 30, 1836, by Rev. Thomas Hanna.
David Furby and Fanny Luke, Dec. 16, 1838, by Samuel Lewis, J. P.
James Furbay and Beulah Stephen, May 8, 1838, by George Atkinson, J. P.
Thomas Furbay and Margaret White, Sept. 15, 1825, by Rev. James Roberts.
Alexander Fulton and Sarah Ramsey, Nov. 2, 1826, by Joseph Rea, J. P.
William Fulton and Polly Moore, Oct. 28, 1823, by Donald McIntosh, V. D. M.
William Fulton and Elizabeth Pugh, May 3, 1832, by James Miller, J. P.
James M. Galbreath and Caty Delany, Nov. 10, 1819, by Elijah C. Stone.
Robert Galbraith and Lydia Yarnell, Nov. 27, 1820, by John Rea, V. D. M.
Samuel Galbraith and Rebecca Able, Oct. 24, 1839, by John Gruber, J. P.
Henry Galentine and Ellen Treacle, March 5, 1838, by Mark Hogge, J. P.
John Gallaher and Levina Young, May 10, 1832, by William Arnold, J. P.
Patrick Gallaher and Sarah Gibson, May 15, 1819, by Phineas Inskeep.
Patrick Gallaher and Martha Bevard, Aug. 25, 1837, by Rev. William Knox.
Thomas B. Gallaher and Jane Farmer, Feb. 15, 1838, by Rev. Joseph Clokey.
William C. Galaher and Eleanor Green, Dec. 5, 1839, by Rev. Parden Cook.
John Gamble and Sarah Heck, Dec. 29, 1839, by B. W. Veirs, J. P.
Joshua Gamble and Elizabeth Heck, March 27, 1834, by William Arnold, J. P.
John Gant and Elizabeth Cellar, Oct. 9, 1828, by Salmon Cowles, V. D. M.

Joseph Gant and Sarah McClish, June 2, 1836, by W. B. Lukins, J. P.
Andrew Gardner and Elizabeth Riddlemoser, Nov. 20, 1834, by George Brown, J. P.
George Gardner and Sarah Wright, May 9, 1826, by Alexander Moore, J. P.
Isaac Gardner and Nancy Rose, May 12, 1818, by Rev. Samuel Hamilton.
Lemuel Gardner and Mary Derault, Feb. 10, 1831, by Robert Orr, J. P.
John Garner and Sarah Cusick, May 6, 1830, by Jesse Hooper, J. P.
Edward B. Garrett and Catherine Suddith, March 29, 1831, by Rev. Benjamin Wood.
John Garret and Margaret Haines, Jan. 13, 1820, by Phineas Inskeep, J. P.
Joseph W. Garretson and Jane N. Poor, Dec. 15, 1836, by Rev. Jacob Coon.
John Garvin and Hannah Whan, March 11, 1819, by Thomas Dickerson, J. P.
John Garvin and Agness Rankin, Jan. 25, 1838, by Rev. Jacob Coon.
Charles Gassuch and Matilda Roberts, July 17, 1828, by Rev. James Moore.
Amor Gatchel and Almira Moore, April 16, 1835, by John McArthur, V. D. M.
Amos Getchell and Elizabeth Burger, June 22, 1826, by John McArthur, V. D. M.
Elias Gatchel and Mary Sudduth, Nov. 8, 1825, by Donald McIntosh, V. D .M.
Elijah Getchell and Harriett Drake, July 29, 1827, by Philip Fulton, J. P.
Job W. Gatchel and Francis Clemens, Aug. 7, 1835, by William Wallace, V. D. M.
Henry Gayer and Betsey McAfee, Nov. 21, 1833, by B. W. Viers, J. P.
Anderson Geary and Catherine Vanhorn, Nov. 2, 1820, by Rev. Thomas B. Clark.
Matthew Geary and Drusilla Johnson, May 1, 1817, by John Crawford, J. P.
James Gearwood and Mary McCleary, Oct. 19, 1824, by John Hurless, J. P.
Barnhart Geasy and Juliann Ruble, Oct. 6, 1839, by Joseph Fry, J. P.
Hezekiah Geddes and Tamer Yarnell, Oct. 17, 1828, by Ezekiel Paramer, E. C. C.
John Geddes and Julian Geddes, July 24, 1831, by Edward Talbott, J. P.
George B. George and Mary Warfel, March 13, 1834, by William Taggart, V. D. M.
Edward Gibbins and Emily E. White, June 30, 1836, by Rev. C. D. Battell.
Henry Gibbins and Ann Wilson, Nov. 17, 1836, by Rev. Jacob Coon.
David Gibny and Rebecca Henry, Dec. 23, 1830, by Thomas Phillips, J. P.
James B. Gibson and Polly Ann Maxwell, Jan. 29, 1829, by Rev. Thomas Hanna.
Robert Gibson and Elizabeth S. Maxwell, Nov. 8, 1827, by Thomas Hanna, V. D. M.
Robert Gilbreath and Mary Beeman, June 5, 1828, by Michael Conaway, J. P.
Thomas C. Gilcrest and Eleanor Guttery, May 26, 1835, by John McArthur, V. D. M.
James Giles and Lettice Gordon, Jan. 28, 1838, by Rev. Henry Wharton.
John Gill and Caroline Richards, Dec. 18, 1832, by Joseph Wolff, J. P.
Charles Gillaspie and Margaret Himebaugh, Dec. 27, 1832, by Dewalt Rothacker.
James Gillespie and Susan Catherine Painter, June 7, 1832, by Rev. David C. Merryman.
John Gillespie and Tama Biggart, Jan. 16, 1835, by Rev. Jacob Coon.
Moses Gillespie and Catherine Turner, April 16, 1836, by David Finnicum, J. P.
Thompson Gillespie and Hetty Chapman, Dec. 17, 1826, by Daniel Limerick, E. of M. E. C.
Cyrus Gilmore and Hannah Moore, Oct. 23, 1834, by John McArthur, V. D. M.
Francis Gilmore and Elizabeth Shimer, Feb. 1, 1833, by John McArthur, V. D. M.

Francis Gilmore and Mary Ann Patterson, Aug. 29, 1839, by M. F. Burkhead, J. P.
Nathaniel Gilmore and Mary Craig, March 25, 1828, by William Taggart, V. D. M.
William Gilmore and Polly Simson, Dec. 28, 1819, by Desberry Johnson, Esq.
William Gilmore and Esther McMullan, March 20, 1834, by Samuel Ramsey, J. P.
William Gilmore and Phebe West, Nov. 26, 1834, by John McArthur, V. D. M.
George Gibson and Mary Johnson, Nov. 27, 1823, by Joseph Fry, J. P.
Thomas Girt and Sally Jeffers, Aug. 10, 1820, by Williamson Carrothers, J. P.
Mathew Givin and Sally Smith, May 18, 1815, by Rev. Thomas B. Clark, V. D. M.
James Glandon and Agnes Carnahan, Sept. 15, 1840, by Rev. Alexander Wilson.
Absalom Glasener and Elizabeth Pierce, Feb. 25, 1830, by Rev. Thomas W. Hudson
Eli Glasener and Hannah Crumley, April 17, 1838, by Rev. James Drummond.
Garret Glasner and Anne Maholm, Oct. 5, 1820, by Rev. Elijah C. Stone.
Jacob Glasner and Rebecca Craig, March 6, 1823, by Thomas B. Carter, J. P.
John Glasner and Mary Holmes, April 22, 1819, by Rev. James Roberts.
James Glasgow and Sarah Boyd, Feb. 11, 1838, by M. F. Burkhead, J. P.
William C. Glasgow and Jane Hitchcock, June 17, 1830, by John McArthur, V. D. M.
Joseph Glenn and Anna Moore, Oct. 12, 1826, by William Wallace, V. D. M.
William Goben and Elizabeth Snider, April 13, 1823, by Rev. John Crom.
William Goben and Elizabeth Knox, Feb. 1, 1835, by Lot Deming, J. P.
Joseph Goff and Sarah Stone, Jan. 14, 1830, by Morris Allbaugh, J. P.
Enoch Golden and Sarah Richards, Oct. 23, 1823, by Joseph Fry, J. P.
Harlan Gomery and Mary Clark, April 30, 1829, by Rev. William B. Evans.
Lewis Goodwin and Mirnirva Webb, March 17, 1836, by George Atkinson, J. P.
Samuel Gooden and Martha R. Luke, Sept. 6, 1832, by Silvanus Lamb, J. P.
Wilson Goodwin and Abigail Wharton, Feb. 9, 1837, by Samuel Lewis, J. P.
David Gordon and Libby Archbold, June 22, 1820, by Michael Conaway, J. P.
Samuel Gordon and Betty Archbold, Aug. 29, 1816, by William Slemmons, J. P.
James Gould and Nellie Brannon, Dec. 26, 1839, by Matthew H. Phillips, J. P.
Michael Grable and Susan Fulton, Dec. 27, 1832, by John Rea, V. D. M.
John Grace and Letitia Faucett, Nov. 22, 1831, by John C. Huston, J. P.
Robert Gracey and Sarah Barnett, Jan. 21, 1818, by Charles Chapman, J. P.
Thomas Graden and Chrissa Ann Speedy, July 7, 1840, by Rev. John Knox.
George Graham and Elizabeth Kitt, April 16, 1838, by William Arnold, J. P.
James Graham and Polly Browin, April 11, 1826, by George Brown, J. P.
Samuel Graham and Sarah Butterfield, Oct. 16, 1821, by Rev. Elias Crane.
William Granfell and Jane McMannis, Aug. 27, 1819, by B. W. Veirs, J. P.
William Granfell and Sarah Ann Delong, March 8, 1840, by M. B. Lukins, J. P
Ebenezer Gray and Eliza Boland, Feb. 23, 1832, by Rev. Thomas Lakin.
Elijah Gray and Charlotte Davis, Aug. 25, 1825, by Thomas Parkinson, J. P.
John Gray and Mary Moore, April 7, 1835, by John McArthur, V. D. M.
John P. Gray and Eliza Thompson, Feb. 20, 1839, by John Rea, V. D. M.
Jonathan Gray and Maria Thompson, Sept. 13, 1837, by John Rea, V. D. M.
Robert Gray and Ann Turner, Aug. 17, 1830, by John McArthur, V. D. M.
Jacob Green and Mary Chicken, March 10, 1831, by Moses Wright, J. P.

Nathan Green and Rebecca Perregay, Sept. 5, 1839, by Rev. Parden Cook.
William M. Greeneltch and Jane Garrett, Sept. 1, 1836, by Rev. Robert Cook.
George Greer and Sarah Lee, Nov. 15, 1827, by Jacob Tope, J. P.
Presley Gregg and Sarah Barricklow, Feb. 5, 1824, by Hugh Shotwell, J. P.
William Gregg and Nancy Clark, Dec. 20, 1822, by Rev. James Roberts.
David Gregary and Leetha Cecil, April 15, 1828, by Samuel Ramsey, J. P.
John Gregory and Sarah Cash, Aug. 8, 1833, by Rev. William Knox.
William Gregory and Ann McClelland, Nov. 12, 1832, by Philip Fulton, J. P.
Ezekiel Grewell and Ruhameh M. Covington, March 22, 1838, by Rev. Jacob Lemmon.
John Grewell and Nancy Farsons, Nov. 18, 1819, by Joseph Fry, J. P.
Jonathan Grewell and Mary Dennis, Oct. 31, 1833, by Joseph Fry, J. P.
Thomas Grewell and Elizabeth Sawyer, Aug. 27, 1835, by Mark Hogg, J. P.
William Gray and Susanna Van'ibber, June 20, 1832, by James McCoy.
Thomas W. Griffin and Mary Wilson, Sept. 29, 1830, by Joseph Wolff, J. P.
Thomas H Griffith and Milly Jane Wright, March 27, 1838, by John McKinney, J. P.
William Griffith and Deborah Moore, May 22, 1832, by Lot Deming, J. P.
William M. Griffith and Lavinia Garretson, April 3, 1835, by George Brown, J. P.
Zadok Griffith and Catherine Petty, Aug. 24, 1832, by George W. Bell, J. P.
Daniel Grim and Mary Shuman, May 6, 1823, by J. Wagenhals.
Jacob Grim and Rachel Shultz, Feb. 28, 1828, by Rev. John Hilligas.
Joseph Grimes and Martha McCullough, Nov. 2, 1820, by Joseph Anderson, J. P.
Thomas D. Grimes and Margaret Lafferty, Jan. 29, 1835, by William Wallace, V. D. M.
William A. Griphey and Margaret Hucal, Jan. 23, 1839, by David G. McGuire, J. P.
Robert Grooms and Polly Smith, May 21, 1829, by George W. Bell, J. P.
John Gruber and Margaret Tedrow, March 15, 1827, by James Manning.
Samuel Gruber and Rachel Lower, June 4, 1823, by Robert Orr, J. P.
Henry Grumrine and Mary Given, Sept. 20, 1838, by Rev. Adam Heiltz [Hetzler?].
Samuel Gudgeon and Catherine Heffling, July 19, 1829, by Rev. Jacob Lemmon.
John Gundy and Sarah Ann Huston, Sept. 14, 1837, by Adam Hetsler.
William Gundy and Susanna Cutshell, May 4, 1838, by Rev. Adam Hetsler.
David Guttery and Mary Ann Kirkpatrick, March 7, 1820, by Desberry Johnson.
James C. Guttery and Elizabeth Auld, Aug. 2, 1821, by John Russel, J. P.
Samuel Gutrey and Susannah Kimmel, Feb. 7, 1819, by Martin Guilinger.
Daniel Guttshall and Mary Hosplehorn, March 6, 1817, by William Slemmons, J. P.
George Gutshall and Anna Albaugh, Sept. 12, 1822, by B. W. Veirs, J. P.
George Gutshall and Elizabeth Gutshall, June 25, 1833, by Dewalt Rothacker.
Jacob Gutshall and Ruth Ann Matthias, April 19, 1838, by David G. McGuire.
John Gutshall and Mary Polend, March 20, 1817, by Mordecai Cob.
John Gutshall and Elizabeth Reeser, Nov. 4, 1830, by Dewalt Rhodocker.
Joseph Gutshall and Mary Ann Hosterman, July 1, 1836, by John Gruber, J. P.
Michael Gutshall and Mary Gutshall, Aug. 8, 1834, by Richard Lyons, J. P.
Samuel Gutshall and Caty Fisher, May 7, 1818, by William Anderson, J. P.
John Gutty and Margaret Cunningham, Oct. 10, 1815, by Henry Barricklow, J. P.

EARLY MARRIAGES

Amos Gye and Anna Caliman, Jan. 16, 1831, by George Brown, J. P.
Lloyd Guy and Margaret Caloman, March 16, 1826, by George Brown, J. P.
Henry Guyer and Rebecca Dewell, Jan. 2, 1823, by Robert McLaughlin, J. P.
John Guyton and Amanda Fitzgerald, May 24, 1838, by Rev. Jacob Lemmon.
Jesse Gwynn and Mary Ady, June 28, 1826, by Silvanus Lamb, J. P.
Jesse Gwynn and Nancy Mullin, Nov. 24, 1835, by Thomas Phillips, J. P.
John Guinn and Edith McMillan, Sept. 16, 1819, by Rev. James Roberts.
John Gwynn and Gule Elma Marie McMillan, Feb. 11, 1830, by Thomas Phillips, J. P.
James Hagerty and Eleanor Crawford, Jan. 9, 1817, by John Rea, V. D. M.
Abraham Hagey and Susan Harner, Dec. 17, 1829, by John Gruber, J. P.
Thomas R. Hague and Louisa Johnson, Jan. 16, 1838, by Samuel G. J. Worthington.
John Haley and Catherine Shuck, Sept. 16, 1832, by Charles Fawcett, J. P.
Joseph Haley and Rebeckah Sharrin, March 15, 1816, by Elijah C. Stone.
Hiram Haines and Mary Mastin, Nov. 9, 1820, by Thomas B. Carter, J. P.
Jesse Haines and Nancy Milliken, April 24, 1832, by James Miller, J. P.
John Hains and Margaret Pears, Feb. 10, 1818, by William Wyckoff, J. P.
Joshua Haines and Mary Hillis, July 17, 1838, by Rev. Robert Cook.
Nathan Haines and Phebe Morris, Nov. 28, 1839, by John Huntsman.
Timothy Haines and Hannah Tomlinson, Oct. 1, 1829, by Rev. William B. Evans.
Christopher S. Hall and Hannah Styres, Dec. 15, 1831, by Rev. William Knox.
William Hall and Hannah Tipton, July 27, 1820, by Thomas Patton, J. P.
Eli Hamilton and Mary Hilton, Dec. 24, 1840, by William Wallace, V. D. M.
John Hamilton and Jane Lafferty, Jan. 1, 1829, by William Wallace, V. D. M.
John Hamilton and Elizabeth Amspoker, May 12, 1831, by Rev. Elijah C. Stone.
Robert Hamilton and Alfreda Baily, Nov. 4, 1817, by Rev. John Rea.
Thomas Hamilton and Effy Gourley, March 24, 1840, by John Rea, V. D. M.
William Hamilton and Mary McFadden, March 4, 1840, by Rev. Alexander Wilson.
Isaac Hammel and Jane Scott, Aug. 15, 1837, by Rev. Z. Ragan.
Charles Hammell and Sarah Rowland, Dec. 8, 1825, by Alexander Moore, J. P.
George W. Hammond and Elizabeth Ann Thompson, Feb. 20, 1837, by M. B. Lukins, J. P.
Thomas Hammond and Sarah Bernard, Nov. 25, 1832, by Edward Talbott, J. P.
William Hammond and Jane Garrett, March 29, 1836, by William Taggart, V. D. M.
John Hanby and Mary Poland, Dec. 16, 1824, by Rev. James Roberts.
William Hanlin and Catherine Banister, April 16, 1835, by Robert P. Simpson, J. P.
Andrew F. Hanna and Susanna Craig, Jan. 13, 1835, by John McArthur, V. D. M.
James Hanna and Mary McCreary, Dec. 12, 1816, by John Rea, V. D. M.
James L. Hanna and Mary H. Craig, June 28, 1819, by H. H. Leavitt, J. P.
James Hanna and Margaret Fulton, June 22, 1824, by Donald McIntosh, V. D. M.
James Hanna and Margaret Rankin, Nov. 13, 1827, by Thomas Hanna, V. D. M.
John Hanna and Margaret Wiley, May 20, 1819, by Rev. Elijah C. Stone.
John E. Hanna and Susan Robertson, June 8, 1826, by Rev. David McMasters.
John Hanna and Rachel Fulton, Dec. 7, 1826, by Rev. Salmon Cowles.
John Hanna and Louise Perry, Dec. 26, 1839, by John Rea, V. D. M.

Matthew Hanna and Mary Ann Orr, April 21, 1828, by William Taggart, V. D. M.
Robert Hanna and Mary Hanna, Sept. 23, 1823, by John Walker, V. D. M.
Robert Hanna and Jane Cobean, March 14, 1826, by John Rea, V. D. M.
William Hanna and Jane Caldwell, March 16, 1837, by Rev. Richard Brown.
Davis Hannon and Ann Hannon, Feb. 25, 1823, by Charles Chapman, J. P.
Elias Harbin and Sarah Hibbs, July 12, 1834, by Samuel Skinner, J. P.
Pollard Hardgrove and Mary Ervin, Sept. 14, 1826, by George Brown, J. P.
James Harding and Prdudence Herron, March 11, 1834, by William Wallace, V. D. M.
Henry Hardy and Sarah Freeman, Feb. 10, 1825, by James Phillips.
Andrew Harmon and Jane Wilson, March 5, 1827, by Van Brown, J. P.
George Harmon and Judy Whitmore, July 10, 1817, by Henry Kail, J. P.
George Harmon and Louisa Richard, Jan. 15, 1829, by Van Brown, J. P.
George Harmon and Mary Ann Glasgo Belsher, May 22, 1831, by John Gruber, J. P.
Jacob Harmon and Elizabeth Stephen, Dec. 28, 1819, by B. W. Veirs, J. P.
Jacob Harmon and Elizabeth Clark, Feb. 8, 1821, by Robert Laughlin, J. P.
Michael Harmon and Catherine Flickinger, Jan. 27, 1825, by John Wagner, J. P.
Joseph Harner and Rebecca Salmon, March 12, 1835, by David Finnicum, J. P.
Rachel Harner and John Taylor, Dec. 2, 1819, by John Rea, V. D. M.
James Harper and Polly Crawford, Jan. 18, 1821, by William Taggart, V. D. M.
Samuel Harper and Cassandra Cox, Nov. 1, 1821, by Rev. Elijah C. Stone.
Alexander Harrah and Margaret Taggart, Nov. 14, 1832, by John Rea, V. D. M.
Charles Harrah and Rachel Sharp, March 13, 1832, by John McArthur, V. D. M.
John Harrah and Jane Taggart, April 17, 1839, by John Rea, V. D. M.
William N. Harrah, and Deborah Delany, Nov. 25, 1830, by John Graham.
Daniel Harriman and Mary Fulton, Sept. 7, 1821, by Phineas, Inskeep, J. P.
Isaac Harimon and Mary Young, Sept. 2, 1826, by Rev. James Roberts.
Robert Harriman and Ruth Cox, May 4, 1820, by Joseph Johnson, J. P.
Joseph Harris and Nancy Johnson, Oct. 26, 1837, by Samuel Lewis, J. P.
Samuel Harris and Hannah Millison, May 17, 1836, by Mark Hogge, J. P.
David Harrison and Louisa Haines, Dec. 27, 1832, by John Chalfan, J. P.
Elisha Harrison and Mary Harrison, Aug. 29, 1816, by Thomas Dickerson, J. P.
Hezekiah Harrison and Lydia Hilbert, March 25, 1834, by John McArthur, V. D. M.
John Harrison and Margaret Dysart, May 12, 1819, by Thomas Dickerson, J. P.
John Harrison and Rosanna Crosby, Oct. 8, 1829, by Rev. John McArthur, V. D. M.
William J. Harrison and Lydia Capper, Sept. 5, 1820, by John Hurless, J. P.
William Harrison and Elizabeth Morgan, Oct. 20, 1825, by J. R. Kirkpatrick, J. P.
Benjamin Hart and Matilda Hibbard,, Dec. 29, 1835, by Rev. Jacob Lemmon.
Jesse Hart and Drusilla Cash, April 5, 1838, by Rev. Jacob Lemmon.
Lawrence Hartnedd and Mary Burton, Dec. 13, 1820, by Joseph Hurless, J. P.
Samuel Harvey and Mary Johnson, Dec. 20, 1821, by George Brown, J. P.
Seth Harvey and Mary Ann Townsend, Nov. 26, 1839, by Rev. Thomas Hanna.
Marcus Haskins and Isabel A. Tracy, Sept. 3, 1835, by James C. Taylor.
Samuel Hass and Jane Hines, April 5, 1838, by Rev. Thomas Jameson.

EARLY MARRIAGES

James Hastings and Elizabeth Cope, Oct. 22, 1840, by Charles Thorn.
John Hastings and Jane Knox, Aug. 30, 1826, by William Wallace, V. D. M.
James Hatton and Sarah Fuller, Dec. 14, 1815, by James Roberts.
Robert Haughey and Hannah Wyckoff, March 13, 1817, by Thomas B. Clark.
Jacob Haun and Sarah Stull, March 18, 1828, by Rev. John Hilligas.
Robert Hauncher and Catherine Brokaw, Dec. 24, 1839, by Rev. Pardon Cook.
Domnic Havner and Elizabeth Jeffers, Nov. 13, 1823, by Robert Orr, J. P.
James Havener and Rachel Cox, Aug. 12, 1824, by Robert Orr, J. P.
Alexander Haverfield and Catherine Shimer, Sept. 10, 1833, by Rev. Thomas Hanna.
James Haverfield and Mary Richey, Nov. 8, 1825, by William Taggart, V. D. M.
John Haverfield and Nancy Ritchey, Nov. 9, 1835, by William Taggart, V. D. M.
Edward Hawthorn and Nancy Wabel, Feb. 13, 1834, by Samuel Ramsey, J. P.
Hugh B. Hawthorn and Grisey Ann Richey, May 21, 1840, by Jacob Coon.
William Hawthorn and Mary Ann Lemmon, April 29, 1840, by Joseph Clokey, V. D. M.
John Hay and Jane Lysle, Sept. 6, 1832, by John Gruber, J. P.
Joseph Hays and Sarah Buffington, April 8, 1830, by Thomas P. Jenkins, J. P.
Samuel W. Hayes and Matilda Johnson, June 4, 1835, by Rev. Robert Cook.
Frederick Hayles and Selina Castell, Sept. 4, 1831, by Robert Pittis, J. P.
Jesse Haynes and Phebe Doney, Aug. 16, 1839, by Thomas Phillips, J. P.
Samuel Haynes and Anna Merrill, Dec. 18, 1823, by Joseph Frey, J. P.
George Haslett and Catherine Gray, July 31, 1828, by Rev. W. P. Evans.
James Haslett and Margaret Miller, March 9, 1836, by John Gruber, J. P.
John Hazlett and Mary Wiles, Jan. 25, 1827, by John Wagner, J. P.
John Heacock and Mary Bowers, March 15, 1832, by Silvanus Lamb, J. P.
John Healea and Eleanor Thompson, Feb. 1, 1837, by Rev. James C. Taylor.
Thomas Healea and Rebeckah Crom, Aug. 13, 1821, by Rev. Elijah C. Stone.
Thomas Healea and Eleanor Conwell, April 2, 1839, by William Taggart, J. P.
Lancelot Hearn and Barbara Urquehart, Jan. 17, 1822, by James McMahon.
Jacob Heastant and Catherine Forney, June 17, 1824, by Rev. John Crom.
John Heasten and Mary Hines, July 4, 1833, by Walter Athey.
Edward Heath and Hannah Johnson, Dec. 29, 1825, by William Johnson, J. P.
John Heath and Betsey Wright, July 21, 1825, by Alexander Moore, J. P.
Abraham Heavlin and Josephine Simms, Oct. 6, 1840, by Rev. Robert Cook.
Adam Hevlin and Lucinda McCain, Aug. 20, 1818, by William Anderson, J. P.
Daniel Heavlin and Mary Gamble, Nov. 5, 1840, by William D. McCartney, V. D. M.
Jacob Heavlin and Susannah Jones, Jan. 2, 1834, by William Arnold, J. P.
John Heavilin and Jemima Petty, Nov. 18, 1830, by George Bell, J. P.
Samuel D. Heavlin and Margaret Bemon, Sept. 25, 1827, by Michael Conaway.
Samuel W. Heavelin and Charlotte Ann Simes, Jan. 28, 1834, by George W. Bell, J. P.
Stephen W. Heavlin and Penelope Marshall, April 7, 1825, by Michael Conaway, J. P.
George Heberling and Matilda Spurrier, July 16, 1835, by Thomas Phillips, J. P.
Henry Heberling and Hannah Lewis, June 3, 1835, by Samuel Lewis J. P.
Hiram Heberling and Catherine Dickerson, Jan. 2, 1834, by William Arnold, J. P.
Samuel Hedge and Hannah Lewis, Oct. 12, 1826, by Samuel Hitchcock, J. P.

Samuel Hedge and Ann Gregory, Aug. 5, 1831, by Rev. William Knox.
John Heffling and Elizabeth Robinson, Nov. 23, 1826, by David Winder, J. P.
Noah Hefling and Martha Herron, Nov. 12, 1839, by Rev. Robert Cook.
Wesley Heffling and Sarah Eaton, Nov. 17, 1831, by Rev. Jacob Lemmon.
Henry B. Hellyer and Mary Weyant, Dec. 7, 1837, by Rev. Adam Hetsler.
John Hellyer and Margaret Gamble, April 27, 1837, by John McArthur, V. D. M.
Isaac Hemery and Nancy McCollough, Feb. 26, 1829, by John C. Huston.
John Hemery and Ellen Capper, Dec. 7, 1820, by Jacob Tope, J. P.
Lewis W. Henbener and Nancy McNeal, Oct. 10, 1839, by Thomas Phillips, J. P.
John Hendershot and Elizabeth Pickering, Jan. 6, 1825, by George Brown, J. P.
Charles Henderson and Margaret Moodey, Jan. 21, 1823, by John Hurless, J. P.
George Henderson and Sarah Wilson, Oct. 24, 1831, by Joseph Wolff, J. P.
James Henderson and Mary Henderson, May 4, 1837, by Joseph Masters, J. P.
James Henderson and Susan McClintock, Oct. 16, 1838, by Rev. Robert Brown.
John Henderson and Rebecca Adams, March 18, 1819, by John Crawford, J. P.
Samuel Henderson and Lettice Moody, July 11, 1822, by John Hurless, J. P.
Thomas Henderson and Darus Russel, May 9, 1822, by Benjamin S. Cowen, J. P.
William L. Henderson and Phebe Patterson, Oct. 7, 1823, by Thomas Hanna, V. D. M.
William Henderson and Jane Anderson, Dec. 19, 1839, by Rev. James Drummond.
Andrew Hendricks and Betsey Rouck, Dec. 19, 1816, by Martin Guilinger, J. P.
Bazell Hendricks and Catherine Gutshall, March 25, 1840, by C. H. Custer, J. P.
Emanuel Hendricks and Eliza Thompson, Nov. 6, 1828, by Morris Allbaugh, J. P.
James Hendricks and Lenea Richerson, Jan. 6, 1818, by Martin Guilinger, J. P.
Peter Hendricks and Caty Webster, Sept. 21, 1820, by William Anderson, J. P.
Thomas Hendricks and Lydia Reniker, Aug. 21, 1834, by Rev. D. Rothacker.
Benjamin Hennis and Edith Cornwell, March 20, 1817, by S. G. Berryhill, J. P.
Abraham Henery and Caty Shuman, Feb. 15, 1818, by Martin Guilinger, J. P.
James Henry and Mary Williams, March 28, 1822, by Thomas Hanna, V. D. M.
James Henry and Catherine Hendricks, May 14, 1836, by John McKinney, J. P.
Robert Henry and Mary Ann Chaney, Feb. 2, 1837, by Rev. Adam Hetsler.
Samuel Henry and Margaret Corbett, Feb. 18, 1835, by John McArthur, V. D. M.
Smith Henry and Mary Thompson, Dec. 27, 1836, by Rev. James C. Taylor.
William Henry and Sarah Derry, Nov. 14, 1822, by Joseph Fry, J. P.
Jesse Herril and Nancy Guy, April 18, 1822, by Rev. James Roberts.
David A. Hervey and Margaret M. Christy, May 13, 1836, by William Taggart, V. D. M.
George Hesford and Charity Bartow, Sept. 20, 1835, by Joseph Masters, J. P.
Daniel Hess and Betsey Walters, Dec. 30, 1824, by Rev. John Wagenhals.
Adam Hetsler and Christena Noffsgar, March 13, 1827, by Rev. John Crom.
William Hibbs and Sarah Hollett, Aug. 22, 1822, by Joseph Fry, J. P.
Jacob Hicks and Harriet Shoves, Jan. 13, 1837, by Rev. Jacob Coon.
John Hicks and Caty Shoover, Oct. 18, 1819, by Rev. John Rinehart.
Wilson Hicks and Mary West, Nov. 14, 1839, by Levi Peddycoart, J. P.
Jacob Hidey and Milly Koontz, Aug. 14, 1828, by Morris Allbaugh, J. P.
John Hidey, Jr., and Nancy Koonts, Dec. 26, 1822, by B. W. Veirs, J. P.
Thomas Hidey and Susanna Manbeck, July 30, 1833, by Thomas Day, J. P.

Eli Hill and Mary Penn, Aug. 23, 1839, by Thomas Phillips, J. P.
James Hill and Esther Clements, Sept. 16, 1823, by John Rea, V. D. M.
John Hill and Sarah Cook, Dec. 1, 1836, by Henry Maxwell, J. P.
Samuel Hill and Sarah McGovarn, May 21, 1818, by Robert McLaughlin, J. P.
Wesley Hill and Mary Ann Buck, May 26, 1830, by Thomas P. Jenkins, J. P.
John Hillhouse and Margaret Chamberlin, July 29, 1830, by Thomas Phillips, J. P.
William Hilligas and Jane Sparrow, Dec. 28, 1839, by Thomas Phillips, J. P.
Tunis Hilligas and Nancy T. Lacey, Oct. 4, 1832, by Thomas Phillips, J. P.
Abraham Hillis and Mary Milliken, March 27, 1827, by Samuel Ramsey, J. P.
Greenberry Hilton and Mary Carpenter, Dec. 19, 1840, by M. B. Lukins, J. P.
Joseph Hinds and Ann Poulson, Jan. 10, 1817, by William Dixon.
Abraham Hines and Hannah Carson, Feb. 15, 1831, by Thomas Phillips, J. P.
Christopher Hines and Rebecca Heastand, Nov. 19, 1835, by Joseph Masters, J. P.
Daniel Hines and Sarah Treacle, Nov. 27, 1834, by Richard Hammond, J. P.
Isaac F. Hines and Susan Gutshall, Oct. 25, 1838, by John Selby, J. P.
James Hines and Hannah Mehaffy, Sept. 13, 1832, by William Tipton.
Joseph W. Hines and Prudence Green, Oct. 22, 1840, by Rev. G. D. Skinner.
William Hines and Eliza Hitchcock, March 11, 1833, by Rev. William Tipton.
William Hines and Isabella Hitchcock, Feb. 15, 1827, by Samuel Hitchcock, J. P.
Thomas Hinton and Elizabeth Johnson, July 19, 1823, by Joseph Fry, J. P.
William Hinton and Hannah Twigg, June 22, 1822, by Joseph Fry, J. P.
David Hirschfield and Elizabeth Beckley, Dec. 17, 1821, by John Wagner, J. P.
John Hiseler and Polly Bair, April 13, 1826, by John Wagner, J. P.
John Hitchcock and Sarah Kelly, Jan. 8, 1835, by Rev. John Taggart.
Thomas Hitchcock and Margaret Barnes, Dec. 22, 1829, by Samuel Hitchcock, J. P.
James Hixon and Elizabeth Dougherty, June 16, 1831, by William Wallace, V. D. M.
John Hixon and Keziah Monroe, Jan. 10, 1836, by B. W. Viers, J. P.
Henry Hogeland and Ruth Lyons, Oct. 11, 1832, by George W. Bell, J. P.
James Hoagland and Harriett Smith, Feb. 24, 1825, by Michael Conaway, J. P.
James Hoagland and Nancy Keeper, June 15, 1826, by Michael Conaway, J. P.
Lemuel Hobbs and Julian Leek, June 24, 1827, by George Brown, J. P.
James Hogge and Hannah Conner, Oct. 16, 1828, by Thomas J. Jenkins, J. P.
Mark Hogge and Elizabeth Cree, Dec. 20, 1838, by William Wallace, V. D. M.
Matthew Hogge and Jane Steel, Dec. 14, 1819, by Joseph Fry, J. P.
John Holland and Esther West, May 14, 1840, by William Arnold, J. P.
Nimrod Holland and Mary Ann Banford, June 24, 1830, by Rev. William Knox.
James Hollensworth and Sarah Howel, Jan. 13, 1835, by Thomas Parkinson, J. P.
Joseph Hollett and Elizabeth Jones, Oct. 5, 1837, by John Knox, J. P.
Israel Holliday and Susan Palmer, April 14, 1833, by Joseph Fry, J. P.
Robert Holliday and Eliza White, March 30, 1821, by Rev. Elijah C. Stone.
Robert F. Holliday and Anna Dick, Sept. 18, 1834, by William Wallace, V. D. M.
Abraham Holmes and Mary Marshall, Jan. 20, 1820, by Rev. William Knox.
Asa Holmes and Mary McCoy, Feb. 1, 1837, by Rev. James C. Taylor.
Charles Holmes and Elizabeth Chance, July 1, 1813, by Elias Crane, Deacon.

George Holmes and Hannah Lynn, Jan. 3, 1822, by James McMahon.
George Holmes and Mary Clipliver, Jan. 19, 1837, by Rev. Henry Wharton.
Isaac Holmes and Jane Vincent, March 20, 1834, by John Rea, V. D. M.
Henry Holmes and Jane Bennett, Nov. 26, 1837, by David Bower, J. P.
Thomas Holmes and Jemina Hennis, June 28, 1829, by Rev. William B. Evans.
Jonas Holloway and Lydia Jones, Aug. 24, 1826, by James Smith, J. P.
Jonas Hollaway and Caroline M. Jones, Oct. 10, 1838, by Rev. Jacob Lemmon.
Owen Holt and Lydia Corbin, May 7, 1835, by Thomas Phillips, J. P.
Samuel Holt and Sarah Matson, Feb. 18, 1830, by Edward Talbott, J. P.
Andrew Hobler and Jane Carpenter, Jan. 18, 1838, by M. B. Lukins, J. P.
David Hoobler and Mary Lisle, Dec. 13, 1832, by Joseph Walters, J. P.
Jacob Hoobler and Polly Shawver, June 3, 1824, by Rev. Daniel Rahauser.
Michael Hubler and Catherina Shultz, Oct. 26, 1813, by George Pfautz, J. P.
Daniel Hook and Frances Kelly, Aug. 16, 1832, by John C. Huston, J. P.
James Hook and Sarah Lyle, Feb. 7, 1828, by John Huston, J. P.
Clement Hooper and Rachel Armstrong, Oct. 26, 1837, by James M. Piper.
Jesse Hooper and Abagail Shannon, Nov. 11, 1832, by Cornelius Crabtree, J. P.
John Hooper and Jane Lazure, July 21, 1825, by Robert Fulton, J. P.
Joseph Hoops and Abagail Cope, Nov. 2, 1821, by Phineas Inskeep, J. P.
Charles Hoover and Martha Rogers, Sept. 30, 1834, by Rev. James Robertson.
John Hoover and Margaret Poland, June 19, 1834, by John Wagner, J. P.
Rev. Hope and Mary Reid, Dec. 22, 1831, by John Rea, V. D. M.
James Horn and Eleanor Davidson, Dec. 23, 1830, by Rev. Thomas P. Jenkins.
John Horn and Hannah Phillips, April 18, 1837, by Rev. Jacob Lemmon.
Moses Horn and Vilinda Ann Grear, Jan. 11, 1838, by Samuel Skinner, J. P.
Noah Horn and Rebecca Tucker, May 2, 1839, by Rev. Jacob Lemmon.
Thomas Horn and Lucinda Davidson, April 3, 1834, by James McCullough, J. P.
Henry Hornbaker and Catherine Lightner, Feb. 4, 1830, by Rev. William Tipton.
Lewis Horseman and Isabella Murphey, Aug. 30, 1821, by George Brown, J. P.
John Hosey and Mary Moore, April 18, 1816, by Charles Chapman, J. P.
Jacob Hospelhorn and Rebecca Wilson, Sept. 26, 1816, by William Slemmons, J. P.
John Hosterman and Polly Hoobler, Oct. 13, 1825, by John Wagner, J. P.
Peter Hosterman and Elizabeth Lisle, Aug. 16, 1831, by John Wagner, J. P.
Jacob Hough and Agnes Campbell, Sept. 29, 1829, by Lot Deming.
Hillary Howse and Rachel Crabtree, Dec. 30, 1820, by Rev. Joseph Casper.
John House and Mary Wroland, Nov. 30, 1819, by William Wyckoff, J. P.
Nathan House and Sophia Johnson, Dec. 11, 1823, by James McMahon.
Samuel House and Betsey Eaton, July 15, 1817, by William Haverfield, J. P.
William House and Matilda Cox, Feb. 28, 1833, by George W. Bell, J. P.
Gasaway Houser and Lydia Walker, May 17, 1826, by William Taggart, V. D. M.
William Houser and Martha McCarrol, Nov. 21, 1839, by Rev. P. K. McCue.
William H. Houston and Eliza Pritchard Feb. 4, 1829, by W. Millan, V. D. M.
James R. Howard and Tabathia Ann Covington, May 1, 1839, by Rev. John Wilson.
John C. Howard and Anna Cadwallader, Jan. 3, 1825, by Joseph Fry, J. P.
Joshua D. Howard and Harriett Warfel, Nov. 6, 1834, by William Taggart, V. D. M.
Joseph Howell and Mary Perry, April 12, 1838, by Samuel Moorehead, J. P.

EARLY MARRIAGES

William Howell and Jane Ellen Fraisure, Jan. 18, 1838, by John Caldwell, J. P.
Caleb Huff and Madelena Welch, April 25, 1839, by David Ruggles, J. P.
Jacob Huff and Rebecca Gladden, Sept. 20, 1830, by William Arnold, J. P.
Joseph Huff and Hester Webb, Nov. 22, 1821, by Elder William Cunningham
Reuben Huff and Letty McAdow, Feb. 11, 1830, by Thomas P. Jenkins, J. P
Zacheus B. Huff and Margaret Donahy, Feb. 23, 1820, by Abriam Johnson, J. P.
Benjamin Hughes and Elizabeth Barrett, Aug. 7, 1834, by Thomas Phillips, J. P.
Samuel Hughes and Jane Galbraith, April 6, 1836, by Rev. Thomas Hanna.
John Hull and Elizabeth Christy, Oct. 12, 1830, by Robert Orr, J. P.
John S. Hull and Clarissa Pritchard, March 23, 1837, by John McArthur, V. D. M.
Joseph Hull and Sarah Kail, Nov. 18, 1830, by Thomas Day, J. P.
George Humphrey and Eliza Gutridge, Dec. 31, 1820, by Rev. Joseph Casper.
Christopher Humphreys and Catherine Noble, Nov. 20, 1834, by William Wallace, V. D. M.
William Humphreys and Jane Law, April 11, 1834, by Rev. David C. Merriman.
Joseph H. Hunter and Ann Walker, Feb. 14, 1839, by Rev. Jacob Lemmon.
Thomas Hunter and Amelia Crist, Jan. 23, 1827, by James Roberts.
Michael Huntsman and Hannah Anderson, Nov. 6, 1828, by Edward Talbott, J. P.
Michael Huntsman and Maria Burges, Sept. 2, 1839, by Cornelius Crabtree, J. P.
William Huntsman and Mary Aderson, Feb. 29, 1820, by Phineas Inskeep, J. P.
Isaac Hurless and Caty Stillwell, June 3, 1830, by Lot Deming, J. P.
Isaac Hurless and Amma Jones, June 5, 1834, by George W. Bell, J. P.
John Hurless and Christine Morgan, April 10, 1821, by Robert Maxwell, J. P.
Samuel Hurless and Susanna Snider, March 24, 1818, by Joseph Johnson, J. P.
Samuel Hurless and Hannah Curry, Feb. 27, 1834, by B. W. Veirs, J. P.
Alexander Hueston and Margaret Crabtree, Nov. 21, 1821, by John Russel, J. P.
Benjamin Hughston and Rachel Johnson, Dec. 4, 1821, by John Russel, J. P.
Edward Hughston and Catherine Lamb, Aug. 10, 1818, by John Crawford, J. P.
Michael Hughston and Charlotte Keller, March 10, 1818, by John Crawford, J. P.
James R. Hutchison and Anne Culbertson, Sept. 16, 1833, by Rev. Jacob Conn.
James Hutchison and Mary Jamison, Oct. 4, 1838, by William Taggart, V. D. M.
John Hutchinson and Mary Foot, Dec. 5, 1822, by George Brown, J. P.
William Hutchinson and Elizabeth Leslie, June 28, 1835, by George Atkinson, J. P.
Benjamin Hutson and Ann Butterfield, Sept. 5, 1822, by Elias Crane, D. C.
Samuel Icenoggle and Elizabeth Kendal, May 28, 1835, by John Wagner, J. P.
Micajah Indsley and Clarissa Hous, March 31, 1825, by John Russel, J. P.
James Irons and Jane Titus, Dec. 27, 1838, by Rev. Jacob Lemmon.
Thomas Irons and Mary Davidson, Jan. 13, 1825, by Joseph Fry, J. P.
Francis Irvin and Hannah Gatchel, Aug. 9, 1838, by Rev. Dyer Neal.
John Irwin and Lena Hearn, June 15, 1826, by Thomas Parkinson, J. P.
Robert Irwin and Mary Auld, Aug. 13, 1818, by Thomas B. Clark, J. P.
Robert Irwin and Rebecca Law, Sept. 12, 1838, by C. C. Wierock.
William Irwin and Mary Carnine, Nov. 24, 1818, by Thomas B. Clark, J. P.
Robert Israel and Julian Heggins, Jan. 27, 1818, by David McMasters.
John Jackson and Mary Crawford, March 19, 1818, by Thomas B. Clark, V. D. M.

Israel James and Lydia Ann Harrison, Dec. 7, 1837, by Samuel Lewis, J. P.
John James and Rebecca Johnson, Sept. 30, 1830, by John Hebling, J. P.
Robert James and Mary Webb, July 2, 1829, by George Brown, J. P.
Samuel James and Lany Hall, June 3, 1829, by William Arnold, J. P.
Scott James and Harriet Arnold, July 27, 1820, by Thomas B. Carder, J. P.
David Jemison and Mary Jane McKnight, Dec. 30, 1824, by William Taggart, V. D. M.
David Jemison and Esther Bishop, Dec. 2, 1837, by John Wagner, J. P.
James Jemison and Barbara Layport, March 6, 1834, by John McArthur, V. D. M.
Walter Jamison and Martha Beaty, Jan. 24, 1828, by Salmon Cowles, V. D. M.
Walter Jamison and Mary Snider, July 13, 1837, by John McArthur, V. D. M.
Joseph Jeffers and Barbara Moore, June 20, 1826, by Thomas Hanna, V. D. M.
Joseph Jeffers and Elizabeth McCombs, March 25, 1830, by Robert Orr, J. P.
Joseph Jeffrey and Sarrah Ann Talbot, May 9, 1837, by George W. Pollard.
James Jelly and Margaret Rebecca Simpson, Jan. 30, 1840, by John Rea, V. D. M.
Samuel Jelly and Lydia Davidson, Feb. 6, 1840, by Rev. Alexander Wilson.
John Jenkins and Catherine Johnson, Dec. 27, 1822, by Joseph Fry, J. P.
John Jenkins and Mary Chalfan, Feb. 14, 1838, by Samuel Skinner, J. P.
John Jewel and Margaret Killer, March 7, 1826, by Rev. Benjamin Wood.
John Jobe and Ann Miser, Feb. 26, 1839, by Rev. Harvey Bradshaw.
Aaron Johnson and Hannah Feistor, Feb. 8, 1838, by Samuel G. J. Worthington.
Aaron Johnson and Rebecca Early, June 1, 1838, by Nathan Tannehill, J. P.
Abel Johnson and Mary Heath, May 10, 1832, by Robert Pittis, J. P.
Abel Johnson and Margaret Gillaspie, Feb. 26, 1833, by George W. Bell, J. P.
Abriam Johnson and Lydia Turner, Aug. 5, 1819, by William Wyckoff, J. P.
Abraham Johnson and Mary Newhouse, Sept. 14, 1824, by Donald McIntosh, V. D. M.
Adam Johnson and Rebecca Ridgeway, Oct. 2, 1823, by Joseph Fry, J. P.
Alexander Johnson and Sarah Lathram, Dec. 20, 1838, by Richard Hammond, J. P.
Andrew Johnson and Margaret Humphries, Oct. 24, 1833, by Rev. D. C. Merryman.
Benjamin Johnson and Eurith Davis, Feb. 17, 1825, by John Russel, J. P.
Benjamin Johnson and Sarah Crabtree, April 12, 1832, by Rev. Jacob Lemmon.
Benjamin Johnson and Rache: Shannon, June 28, 1838, by Rev. Jacob Lemmon.
Benjamin Johnson and Elizabeth Gillespie, Oct. 15, 1840, by Rev. Lewis Jenny.
Charles Johnson and Elizabeth Coaltrap, May 16, 1822, by Joseph Johnson, J. P.
Charles M. Johnson and Hanna A. Gray, Dec. 13, 1832, by Edward Talbott, J. P.
Cyrus Johnson and Maria Johnson, Feb. 21, 1834, by James McCollough, J. P.
Davis Johnston and Rachel Caldwell, Jan. 15, 1839, by Levi Peddycoart, J. P.
Disbury Johnson and Mary Cooper, June 29, 1817, by William Slemmons, J. P.
Elias Johnson and Eliza Hide, March 23, 1819, by Joseph Johnson, J. P.
Elias Johnson and Anna Harvey, Dec. 23, 1831, by John Chaffan, J. P.
Emon Johnson and Louisa Burgess, Dec. 23, 1835, by Rev. James C. Taylor.
Gabriel Johnston and Nancy Suddeth, Dec. 31, 1819, by Charles Chapman, J. P.
George Johnston and Jane Grace, Sept. 29, 1839, by Thomas Thompson.
Griffin Johnson and Mariah Groves, Oct. 28, 1838, by Rev. Jacob Lemmon.
Henry Johnson and Margaret Gibson, May 6, 1824, by James Smith, J. P.

Hosier Johnson and Jane Simonton, April 23, 1835, by John McArthur, V. D. M.
Isaac Johnson and Nancy Johnson, Feb. 8, 1825, by James Smith, J. P.
Jacob Johnson and Mary McMillen, Feb. 16, 1832, by Rev. Jacob Lemmon.
James Johnson and Jane Gordon, July 29, 1813, by William Barnhill, J. P.
James Johnson and Jamima Griffin, Aug. 22, 1816, by William Wyckoff, J. P.
James Johnson and Eleanor Mowder, March 29, 1820, by John Russel, J. P.
James Johnson and Jane Carr, April 4, 1822, by Robert McLaughlin, J. P.
James P. Johnson and Rosetta Smith, March 2, 1824, by Donald McIntosh, V. D. M.
James Johnson and Nancy Bedwell, June 14, 1827, by Thomas P. Jenkins, J. P.
James P. Johnson and Hannah Jane Boyd, Dec. 8, 1836, by John McArthur, V. D. M.
John Johnson and Rebecca Johnson, March 28, 1816, by Rev. M. Cole.
John Johnson and Susan Asher, Aug. 15, 1816, by Peter Johnson, J. P.
John B. Johnson and Sarah Bruce, April 29, 1828, by William McMillan, V. D. M.
Joseph Johnson and Betsey Eliott, Oct. 19, 1815, by James Roberts.
Joseph P. Johnson and Jane Long, Oct. 19, 1837, by Rev. Robert Cook.
Joseph Johnson and Isabel Vasbinder, Dec. 6, 1838, by William Taggart, J. P.
Lewis Johnson and Elizabeth Vanhorn, Dec. 25, 1839, by Rev. Robert Cook.
Matthew Johnson and Nancy Welch, Dec. 17, 1840, by William D. McCartney, V. D. M.
Nathan Johnson and Jane Maria Auld, Dec. 10, 1818, by William Taggart.
Robert Johnson and Margaret Bell, March 22, 1832, by George W. Bell, J. P.
Samuel Johnston and Elizabeth Milliken, Feb. 8, 1825, by Robert Maxwell, J. P.
Samuel R. Johnston and Rebecca Barnhill, July 20, 1826, by William Wallace. V. D. M.
Samuel B. Johnson and Eleanor Thompson, Feb. 19, 1829, by William McMillan, V. D. M.
Samuel Johnson and Rachel Clark, Feb. 21, 1833, by Samuel Skinner, J. P.
Samuel Johnson and Jane Wells, Jan. 10, 1836, by William Taggart, V. D. M.
Thomas Johnson and Jane Gilmore, July 9, 1835, by John Layport, J. P.
Thomas Johnson and Rebecca Marshall, April 19, 1838, by Samuel Skinner, J. P.
Thomas Johnson and Rhoda Crabtree, Aug. 27, 1840, by Rev. Robert Cook.
William Johnson and Sarah Ruby, Sept. 3, 1818, by William Wyckoff, J. P.
William C. Johnson and Jane McFadden, Jan. 25, 1836, by William Taggart, J. P.
Zachariah Johnson and Susan Lindsey, Aug. 5, 1830, by Thomas Phillips, J. P.
Daniel Jolby and Mary Mapel, April 10, 1823, by Robert McLaughlin, J. P.
John Jonas and Betsey Sawvell, Sept. 25, 1834, by Rev. D. Rothacker.
Calvin Jones and Rachel Kysinger, Nov. 13, 1834, by John McArthur, V. D. M.
Daniel Jones and Amelia Downing, March 25, 1830, by Rev. Thomas S. Taylor.
George Jones and Susan Turner, Jan. 28, 1818, by John Crawford, J. P.
Henry Jones and Rebecca Ann Huston, Nov. 16, 1834, by Rev. Jacob Lemmon.
Isaac Jones and Hannah Knight, Dec. 10, 1840, by Thomas Phillips, J. P.
Israel Jones and Christena Ann Huston, Dec. 18, 1836, by Samuel Skinner, J. P.
Jacob Jones and Mary Creal, March 2, 1837, by Rev. Henry Wharton.
James Jones and Susanna Dickerson, March 23, 1820, by Jacob Young.
James Jones and Charlotte Christian, March 7, 1823, by Joseph Johnson, J. P.
James Jones and Lucy Hefling, Jan. 14, 1836, by Rev. Jacob Lemmon.
John D. Jones and Anna Cecil, Feb. 2, 1832, by Philip Fulton, J. P.

Perry Jones and Margaret Clark, Oct. 23, 1823, by John Russel, J. P.
Peter Jones and Catherine Shivers, Sept. 9, 1827, by John Carson, J. P.
Rees Jones and Ann Moreland, April 1, 1825, by Arch. McGrew, J. P.
Samuel Jones and Margaret Rankin, Feb. 25, 1836, by John Bethel, J. P.
Samuel Jones and Sydney Musgrove, May 25, 1840, by Joseph Fry, J. P.
Thomas Jones and Susanna Edwards, April 12, 1836, by Jesse Merrill, J. P.
Thompson Jones and Mary Merryman, Nov. 26, 1840, by Aaron Conaway, J. P.
Wesley Jones and Maria Medley, March 26, 1833, by Rev. Benjamin Wood.
William Jones and Peggy Case, Jan. 2, 1833, by Rev. Benjamin Wood.
George Joy and Elizabeth Early, March 30, 1826, by Rev. William B. Evans.
Adam Junkins and Archra Burkhead, Jan. 8, 1818, by William Haverfield, J. P.
Daniel Justice and Polly Daly, May 21, 1828, by John Secrest.
Abraham Kail and Polly Traner, June 15, 1819, by Martin Guilinger, J. P.
Adam Kail and Elizabeth Wiands, Nov. 1, 1827, by John C. Huston, J. P.
Frederick Kail and Elizabeth Wilson, Aug. 11, 1834, by William Arnold, J. P.
Gabriel Kail and Betsy Devore, July 13, 1815, by Martin Guilinger, J. P.
John Kail and Sally Arnold, Sept. 5, 1816, by Henry Kail, J. P.
Daniel Keeser and Polly Springer, Nov. 28, 1816, by Thomas Fisher, J. P.
Henry Keesey and Margaret Layport, May 24, 1838, by Aaron Conaway, J. P.
Alfred M. Kelly and Velleriah E. Dunn, March 8, 1838, by John Rea, V. D. M.
Justice Kelly and Rebecca Courtright, Oct. 22, 1840, by George Atkinson, J. P.
Philip Kelly and Mary Barnhouse, Jan. 17, 1828, by Robert Orr, J. P.
Robert Kelly and Sarah Rutledge, May 23, 1833, by Robert Orr, J. P.
Thomas Kelly and Almeda Campbell, March 19, 1833, by Rev. James Robertson
John G. Kemp and Margaret Bricker, March 13, 1829, by William Arnold, J. P.
Joseph Kenagy and Nancy Mowrey, April 19, 1831, by Rev. William Knox.
Levi Kenagey and Rachel Berger, June 24, 1831, by Rev. George Lucy.
Ahio H. Kennedy and Elizabeth Harvey, Dec. 26, 1833, by Samuel Skinner, J. P.
Carvill G. Kennedy and Mary Latham, Dec. 1, 1836, by Samuel Skinner, J. P.
Henry Kennedy and Mary Spring, Dec. 27, 1832, by John Chalfan, J. P.
James Kennedy and Maria Johnson, Jan. 16, 1823, by Joseph Fry, J. P.
Napoleon B. Kennedy and Mary Gilmore, Oct. 24, 1826, by William Taggart, V. D. M.
Return Matthew Kennedy and Jane Moore, Feb. 19, 1824, by Joseph Fry, J. P.
William Kenneday and Sarah Wyckoff, Feb. 4, 1819, by James McMahon.
Abner Kent and Dianna Heavlin, May 26, 1829, by Michael Conaway, J. P.
Absalom Kent and Isabella Worth, Oct. 4, 1821, by Thomas Patton, J. P.
Absalom Kent and Mary Walker, Dec. 5, 1833, by John McArthur, V. D. M.
William Kent and Catherine Baker, June 22, 1820, by William Carrothers, J. P.
Samuel Kernaghan and Betsey Williams, Aug. 13, 1832, by William Taggart, V. D. M.
Edward Kerr and Lucinda Fletcher, July 23, 1823, by John Russel, J. P.
John Karr and Catherine A. Gossone, Dec. 31, 1829, by John McArthur, V. D. M.
John Kerr and Martha Wiley, Nov. 28, 1833, by John Rea, V. D. M.
Robert Karr and Mary Endsley, April 7, 1825, by Donald McIntosh, V. D. M.
Thomas Kerr and Nancy Cobean, Feb. 13, 1834, by John Rea, V. D. M.
Andrew Keys and Minerva Young, Jan. 21, 1830, by John Gruber, J. P.
George Kidwell and Elizabeth Gatchel, Jan. 13, 1825, by Isaac Allen, J. P.
Daniel Kilgore and Mary Pritchard, April 14, 1816, by Walter B. Beebe, J. P.
Robert S. Kimber and Rachel Scole, May 25, 1823, by Rev. Samuel Brockunier.

EARLY MARRIAGES

Frederick Kimmel and Elizabeth Yingling, Jan. 12, 1826, by Henry Ford, J. P.
Henry Kimmel and Christena Geddinger, June 27, 1813, by Rev. John Rinehart.
Henry Kimmel and Sarah Nop, Feb. 20, 1840, by Thomas Finnicum, J. P.
John Kimmel and Eve Tanney, Aug. 6, 1813, by Rev. John Rinehart.
Jonathan Kimmel and Maria Nop, Jan. 31, 1837, by William Arnold, J. P.
Hamilton King and Sarah Easlick, Dec. 22, 1831, by Rev. John McArthur.
John King and Sarah Ann Ellis, June 7, 1833, by John Rea, V. D. M.
Charles Kinsey and Tabitha Gutshall, Sept. 20, 1827, by John Carson, J. P.
John Kinsey and Mary Burrows, Jan. 10, 1828, by Thomas P. Jenkins, J. P.
Thomas B. Kinsey and Sarah Kerr, Dec. 17, 1832, by David C. Merriman.
Ephram Kirby and Elizabeth Bair, May 17, 1832, by Lot Deming, J. P.
Isaac Kirby and Elizabeth Waters, Dec. 14, 1824, by J. R. Kirkpatrick, J. P.
James Kirby and Christiann Hester, April 18, 1830, by Rev. John Wilson.
John Kerby and Maria McMillan, Aug. 30, 1835, by Samuel Lewis, J. P.
Erastus U. Kirk and Mary Ann Price, Sept. 15, 1831, by Thomas P. Jenkins, J. P.
Joshua Kirk and Hannah Moffit, April 7, 1832, by George Brown, J. P.
Samuel Kirk and Polly Hukill, Nov. 17, 1830, by John McArthur, V. D. M.
Israel Kirkpatrick and Mariah Ward, Jan. 8, 1823, by B. W. Veirs.
James Kirpatrick and Catherine Clifford, Feb. 19, 1829, by William Wallace, V. D. M.
James Kirkpatrick and Eliza Mahafey, Sept. 9, 1831, by William Wallace, V. D. M.
John Kirkpatrick and Hannah Fulton, Feb. 19, 1835, by William Wallace, V. D. M.
James Kirkwood and Polly Sheeley, Feb. 1, 1827, by Samuel Dunlap, J. P.
Jacob Kitch and Mary Winnings, June 18, 1818, by John Wagner, J. P.
John Klinger and Sabina Brown, Nov. 13, 1838, by John Knox, J. P.
Immer Knight and Rachel Ross, Jan. 8, 1838, by Richard Hammond, J. P.
Daniel C. Knock and Phebe Easley, April 19, 1831, by Thomas P. Jenkins, J. P.
William Knock and Maria Stanley, April 17, 1834, by John L. Grubb, J. P.
John Knox and Mary Davis, Oct. 12, 1819, by Jacob Young.
Thomas Knox and Eleanor Simpson, May 28, 1829, by William Wallace, V. D. M.
William Kyle and Jane Slemmons, April 16, 1839, by W. D. McCartney, V. D. M.
Amos Lacy and Catherine Ridgway, April 8, 1824, by Joseph Fry, J. P.
John H. Lacy and Juliann Hicks, July 10, 1817, by Elias Crane.
John S. Lacey and Ann Janette Hoyt, Dec. 31, 1820, by Rev. William Knox.
John M. Lacy, and Anne Wallace, June 1, 1835, by William Arnold, J. P.
Thomas S. Lacey and Patty Ward, Feb. 13, 1830, by Morris Allbaugh, J. P.
Edward Lafferty and Margaret McFadden, Oct. 14, 1813, by Thomas B. Clark, V. D. M.
Edward Lafferty and Susanna Dickerson, Dec. 24, 1835, by William Wallace V. D. M.
James Lafferty and Mary Patterson, Dec. 15, 1831, by Rev. Jacob Coon.
Samuel Lafferty and Elizabeth Mansfield, Dec. 30, 1824, by Rev. William Wallace.
John M. Laird and Eleanor Martin, Jan. 12, 1830, by William Taggart, V. D. M.
Michael Leard and Ann Hitchcock, Oct. 16, 1817, by Robert McKee.
Amos Laizure and Martha McCullough, Jan. 1, 1827, by William Wallace, V. D. M.

Elijah Laisure and Louisa Chapman, Jan. 1, 1835, by Rev. D. C. Merryman.
Elijah Laisure and Elizabeth Moore, Jan. 31, 1837, by Rev. James C. Taylor.
William Laizure and Jane McCullough, Nov. 7, 1822, by Joseph Anderson.
William Laizure and Ann Chinneth, March 19, 1840, by William Cobb, J. P.
Jacob Lamb and Elizabeth Adams, April 16, 1819, by John Crawford, J. P.
Jacob Lamb and Mary Ann Williams, Feb. 2, 1832, by Samuel Skinner, J. P.
John Lamb and Nancy Knight, Nov. 21, 1817, by John Crawford, J. P.
Lawrence Lamb and Matty Burtch, Nov. 3, 1815, by William Wyckoff, J. P.
Sylvanus Lamb and Isabella ———, Nov. 3, 1819, by Rev. James Roberts.
Timothy Lamb and Darkey Robinett, Aug. 14, 1817, by William Wyckoff, J. P.
John Lanning and Susan Woodward, Dec. 30, 1830, by Edward Talbott, J. P.
John Lannum and Polly Havenner, May 13, 1819, by John Rea, V. D. M.
Walter Lannum and Ann Ellen Havener, Aug. 3, 1820, by Rev. Elijah C. Stone.
John Lantz and Elijah Fulton, Dec. 6, 1837, by Rev. Thomas Foster.
William Lance and Susan Glandon, Oct. 2, 1838, by Rev. Parden Cook.
Thomas Lakin and Margaret Staats, April 10, 1832, by Rev. Jacob Lemmon.
Thomas N. Lakin and Mary Ann Pepper, Oct. 31, 1836, by Thomas Phillips, J. P.
William Lakin and Luesa Packer, Jan. 19, 1836, by Thomas P. Jenkins, J. P.
James Larkins and Rebecca Sharp, Sept. 1, 1831, by Thomas Day, J. P.
Townsend T. Larkin and Rebecca Boothe, Dec. 30, 1830, by Edward Talbott, J. P.
Washington Larkin and Martha Dillen, May 16, 1822, by B. W. Veirs, J. P.
Warner J. Larimore and Rachel Hollet, April 26, 1838, by John Knox, J. P.
Robert Lathan and Susanna Davidson, March 24, 1831, by Moses Wright, J. P.
Benjamin Latimer and Elizabeth Miller, March 24, 1835, by Rev. James Robertson.
David Laughlin and Eleanor Cox, April 20, 1831, by John Busby, J. P.
James W. Laughlin and Sarah Kerr, Feb. 8, 1837, by John Rea, V. D. M.
Henry Law and Elizabeth McMillan, Dec. 18, 1839, by Richard Brown.
Matthew Law and Rebecca Birney, March 30, 1836, by Rev. John P. Kent.
John Lawrence and Elizabeth Kerr, Dec. 19, 1822, by Thomas Hanna, V. D. M.
Stephen Lawrence and Elizabeth Smith, Nov. 22, 1834, by Joseph Johnson, J. P.
Michael Lawver and Mary Brown, Dec. 26, 1837, by David Bowers, J. P.
Solomon Lawver and Sarah McDaniel, Oct. 22, 1833, by Rev. Alexander Biddle.
Abraham Layport and Nancy Christy, Oct. 9, 1828, by John Carson, J. P.
Charles D. Layport and Sarah Wallace, May 17, 1832, by John McArthur, V. D. M.
George Layport and June Leeper, July 8, 1824, by Michael Conaway, J. P.
George Layport and Ann Johnson, Feb. 12, 1829, by Joseph Johnson, J. P.
Isaac Layport and Margaret Hitchcock, Sept. 21, 1830, by Peter Barger, J. P.
John L. Layport and Verlinda Harrison, March 16, 1826, by Alexander Moore, J. P.
Samuel Layport and Nancy Mowder, Sept. 17, 1826, by Samuel Hitchcock, J. P.
William Layport and Hannah Milliken, Dec. 31, 1833, by Rev. Robert Cook.
Jonathan Leass and Martha Medley, June 15, 1837, by Rev. Jacob Lemmon.
David Lee and Julian Dobbins, April 8, 1827, by Van Brown, J. P.
James Lee and Jane Martin, Dec. 23, 1819, by John Walker, V. D. M.
John Lee and Margaret Kail, Nov. 7, 1835, by James Endsley, J. P.
Martin Lee and Sarah McClelland, June 19, 1828, by John Carson, J. P.
Thomas H. Lee and Ann Bockias, May 5, 1831, by Joseph Wolf, J. P.

EARLY MARRIAGES

William Lee and Maria Pritchard, March 23, 1824, by Donald McIntosh, V. D. M.
William Lee and Mary Dickerson, Feb. 18, 1839, by William Wallace, V. D. M.
James Leech and Anna Teets, Sept. 22, 1835, by Samuel Ramsey, J. P.
John Leech and Fanny Boals, June 6, 1822, by John Rea, V. D. M.
James Leeper and Hannah Wright, Dec. 26, 1833, by Rev. David Wortman.
Moses Leeper and Rachel Keer, Nov. 12, 1840, by Rev. Thomas Hanna.
Samuel Leeper and Lavina Connell, Nov. 24, 1833, by Thomas M. Cranfel, J. P.
William Leeper and Rebecca Johnson, March 28, 1826, by Robert Orr, J. P.
Jesse Legget and Elizabeth Jane Robey, Dec. 24, 1835, by Rev. Moses Scott.
John Ligget and Rachel McAfee, June 22, 1837, by David G. McGuire, J. P.
Joseph Leggit and Mary Nelson, Jan. 8, 1818, by William Anderson, J. P.
Samuel Legget and Jane Stackhouse, July 28, 1831, by John Watson, J. P.
Thomas Ligget and Rebecca Gillis, May 29, 1828, by Rev. Thomas Hunt.
Henry Leinard and Margaret Moore, Feb. 24, 1825, by Rev. William Wallace.
Jacob Leinard and Esther Ruby, May 8, 1838, by Samuel G. J. Worthington.
John Leinard and Sally Dugan, Dec. 24, 1818, by Charles Chapman, J. P.
Samuel Leinard and Rebecca Reed, July 3, 1833, by William Arnold, J. P.
Abraham Lemaster and Nancy Barnes, Jan. 8, 1824, by Hugh Shotwell, J. P.
Ebenezer Lomaster and Rebecca D. Nixon, Aug. 27, 1840, by Thomas Phillips.
John Lemasters and Mercy Johnson, March 21, 1833, by Rev. Jacob Lemmon.
William Lemaster and Elizabeth Busby, Nov. 28, 1839, by Thomas Phillips, J. P.
Griffith Lemmon and Margaret Lemmon, Oct. 21, 1835, by B. Mitchell, V. D. M.
Abraham Lett and Eleanor Beard, Feb. 2, 1821, by Phineas Inskeep.
Elizas Lett and Elizabeth Calliman, April 26, 1821, by Thomas Dickerson, J. P.
Mesheck Lett and Amelinza Wallace, May 21, 1821, by Thomas Dickerson, J. P.
Samuel Lett and Jane Bull, Nov. 25, 1818, by James Roberts.
Curtis Lewis and Ellen Runnells, Nov. 14, 1836, by James C. Turner.
Davis Lewis and Mary Ann Ames, March 23, 1836, by Thomas Parkinson, J. P.
Elias M. Lewis and Mary Dickerson, Sept. 1, 1836, by George Atkinson, J. P.
Ephraim Lewis and Elizabeth Likes, Jan. 20, 1820, by Desberry Johnson, Esq.
Ira Lewis and Sarah Wilson, Jan. 10, 1833, by Edward Talbott, J. P.
Isaac Lewis and Lydia Gummere, Nov. 16, 1836, by Samuel Lewis, J. P.
James Lewis and Rebecca Gregory, Aug. 8, 1833, by Rev. William Knox.
Jesse Lewis and Catherine Kent, Sept. 12, 1839, by William Arnold, J. P.
Morgan Lewis and Sarah Lewis, July 14, 1835, by Samuel Lewis, J. P.
Pinkney Lewis and Jane Anne Adams, Dec. 22, 1829, by John McArthur, V. D. M.
Samuel Lewis and Sarah Moore, Sept. 1, 1825, by John Graham.
Samuel Lewis and Susanna Cash, Dec. 14, 1833, by Thomas Phillips, J. P.
Syra Lewis and Sarah Ann Grizel, March 14, 1839, by Samuel Lewis, J. P.
Thomas Lewis and Rebecca Heberling, March 16, 1837, by George Atkinson, J. P.
William Lewis and Nancy Crawford, Oct. 1, 1829, by John McArthur, V. D. M.
Zedekiah Lewis and Isabel Connel, July 22, 1829, by Robert Pittis, J. P.
George Licester and Margaret Norris, June 21, 1838, by John M. Brown, J. P.
James Likes and Mary Cunningham, Feb. 27, 1817, by Charles Chapman, J. P.
Samuel Licks and Sarah Speck, March 28, 1816, by Richard Price, J. P.
Simon Linder and Milly Christian, Sept. 11, 1834, by Joseph Johnson, J. P.

David Lindsey and Martha Orr, Jan. 30, 1823, by William Taggart, V. D. M.
John Lindsey and Anne Biggart, Feb. 17, 1831, by Thomas Phillips, J. P.
Samuel Lippencott and Elizabeth Givens, Dec. 15, 1821, by Joseph Fry, J. P.
Job Lisiter and Mary Blackiston, Feb. 28, 1833, by T. P. Jenkins, J. P.
John Lyle and Susanna Slemmons, Oct. 29, 1829, by John McArthur, V. D. M.
John Lisle and Eliza Ann Johnston, April 4, 1831, by John Rea, V. D. M.
Robert Lisle and Polly Slemmons, March 10, 1818, by John Rea, V. D. M.
Robert Lisle and Elizabeth Campbell, Nov. 15, 1837, by Samuel Moorehead. J. P.
Samuel Lisle and Jane Fosbinder, Sept. 14, 1824, by Donald McIntosh, V. D. M.
John Lissler and Susanna Markley, April 26, 1821, by B. W. Veirs, J. P.
John Lister and Catherine Springer, Sept. 11, 1827, by Robert Orr, J. P.
David Little and Christina Shaffer, Nov. 25, 1824, by Rev. John Wagenhals.
James Little and Lydia Swigert, Nov. 29, 1826, by Joshua Munroe.
John Little and Rachel Williamson, Sept. 4, 1838, by William Waller, V. D. M.
Manuel Little and Margaret Fulmer, July 15, 1833, by Rev. Adam Hetzler.
Robert Little and Elizabeth Fissel, Sept. 27, 1827, by Michael Conaway, J. P.
Solomon Little and Sarah Richard, Sept. 27, 1829, by Rev. John Secrest.
William Little and Charlotte Burger, July 12, 1826, by Henry Ford.
Jacob Livergood and Catherine Miller, Feb. 28, 1837, by Rev. Abraham Keller.
Cyrus M. Livingston and Catherine Bosley, Sept. 5, 1837, by John Wagner, J. P.
John Lock and Agness Maxwell, Oct. 4, 1827, by John Busby, J. P.
William Logan and Margaret Figley, Nov. 18, 1834, by John W. Iler, J. P.
Richard Loney and Rebecca Kirkpatrick, Aug. 31, 1824, by Isaac Allen, J. P.
Andrew Long and Rebecca Little, Dec. 29, 1827, by John Hagey, J. P.
John Long and Susannah Shearer, Jan. 20, 1839, by Abraham Keller.
William Long and Elizabeth Braden, Feb. 3, 1825, by Thomas Hanna, V. D. M.
John Longeley and Mary Wood, Nov. 8, 1826, by Rev. Benjamin Wood.
John Loos and Ketherine Lowmiller, July 7, 1816, by Rev. John Rinehart.
Joseph Loper and Sarah Ann Summers, April 1, 1834, by Samuel Lewis, J. P.
John Lovall and Pemby Parsons, July 13, 1815, by Rev. James Roberts.
John Losey and Mary Martin, April 17, 1834, by James McCollough, J. P.
Robert Loudon and Polly Shroyer, Sept. 28, 1825, by David Winders, J. P.
Edward Loughrige and Margery McConnell, Feb. 10, 1824, by John Conaway, J. P.
James Laughridge and Anne Henderson, Dec. 20, 1836, by David G. McGuire, J. P.
Matthew Loughrige and Nancy Hendricks, Aug. 28, 1834, by Lot Deming, J. P.
Moses Louthan and Rachel McGoogan, Dec. 31, 1829, by John McArthur, V. D. M.
James Love and Jane McFadden, April 11, 1839, by William Taggart, J. P.
George R. Lovett and Mary Ann Vanhorn, Dec. 19, 1838, by Charles Thorn.
David Lower and Rachel Reed, May 25, 1820, by Thomas Patton, J. P.
Henry Lowmiller and Eve Hagey, Aug. 18, 1825, by Rev. John Wagenhals.
Joshua Lowmiller and Mary Snider, Aug. 29, 1839, by Andrew Lynch, J. P.
Dennis Lowry and Dianna Spiker, Jan. 6, 1825, by John Conaway, J. P.
Harrison Lawrey and Comfort Twigg, Aug. 17, 1826, by Isaac Fordyce, Esq.
George Lukens and Nancy Tipton, Dec. 4, 1828, by Michael Conaway, J. P.
Jacob C. Lukens and Sarah C. Bliss, May 27, 1830, by Thomas McCleary.
Merican Lukens and Mary Hanna, Jan. 8, 1832, by Robert Pittis, J. P.

Andrew Lynch and Nancy Peoples, Dec. 12, 1832, by Rev. James Robertson.
Charles Lyon and Mary Salmon, Oct. 31, 1839, by John Gruber, J. P.
James Lyons and Nancy Ramsey, Oct. 2, 1817, by John Rea, V. D. M.
James Lyons and Ruth Walters, May 12, 1831, by Michael Conaway J. P.
John Lyons and Mary Miles, Dec. 4, 1817, by Rev. John Rea.
John Lyons and Margaret Reed, March 5, 1822, by John Rea, V. D. M.
John Lyons and Susanna Forbus, May 21, 1835, by Rev. James Robertson.
Richard Lyons and Nancy Veirs, May 27, 1830, by John McArthur, V. D. M.
Robert Lyons and Anne Bowland, Aug. 7, 1832, by John McArthur, V. D. M.
Samuel Lyon and Lydia Stone, May 12, 1832, by Rev. Eliza C. Stone.
William Lyons and Hannah Robb, Jan. 1, 1829, by William Wallace, V. D. M.
George McAdams and Ann Jane Moore, Jan. 22, 1840, by Hugh Parker, V. D. M.
James McAdams and Catherine Simmons, Aug. 28, 1830, by Lot Deming, J. P.
John McAdams and Susan Dunlap, March 12, 1829, by William Wallace, V. D. M.
Hugh McAdoo and Cady Hyde, Dec. 31, 1819, by Abram Scott, V. D. M.
James McAfee and Lettice Gorden, June 2, 1840, by Joseph W. Spencer, J. P.
Hamilton McAlhanney and Sarah Reaves, Feb. 20, 1834, by Rev. Jacob Lemmon.
Samuel McBarnes and Mary Maxwell, Nov. 8, 1838, by Samuel Ramsey, J. P.
John McBean and Belinda Johnson, March 8, 1829, by Rev. Thomas T. Taylor.
James McBeath and Martha Burns, Nov. 22, 1831, by Joseph Johnson, J. P.
John McBeth and Mary Webster, April 18, 1833, by Rev. Jacob Cozad.
Alexander McBride and Emily Medley, March 29, 1838, by Rev. Benjamin Wood.
Robert McBride and Agnes Harriman, Dec. 24, 1833, by Thomas McCall, J. P.
George McCalester and Lucy Shuck, Aug. 7, 1817, by Martin Guilinger, J. P.
John McCall and Elizabeth Atkinson, May 9, 1833, by John Walker, V. D. M.
John McCamis and Mary Morrison, June 18, 1833, by Rev. Jacob Robertson.
John McCandless and Mary Ann Neel, Oct. 9, 1828, by Rev. Benjamin Wood.
Allen C. McCardy and Rebecca Mercer, Sept. 3, 1840, by James Kerr, V. D. M.
John McCarroll and Jane Laughridge, Aug. 21, 1834, by Rev. David C. Merryman.
Enoch McCartney and Elizabeth Matson, Jan. 7, 1834, by Rev. Robert Cook.
John McCarty and Abagail Howard, Nov. 16, 1837, by William Arnold, J. P.
William McCaslin and Jane McClery, July 8, 1813, by John Rea, V. D. M.
Matthew McClarren and Sarah Wilkisson, April 4, 1820, by John Wagner, J. P.
Matthew McClarren and Catherine Gilmore, March 4, 1830, by Rev. George Lucy.
Josiah McClenagan and Phebe Erwin, Aug. 15, 1833, by Thomas M. Cranfel, J. P.
James McClintock and Elizabeth Johnson, Oct. 12, 1820, by John Rea, V. D. M.
John McClintock and Eva Ann Snider, Jan. 27, 1825, by J. R. Kirkpatrick, J. P.
Kerr McClintock ad Margaret Delong, Sept. 15, 1825, by Donald McIntosh, V. D. M.
Thomas McClintick and Elizabeth Fisher, May 19, 1814, by John Rea, V. D. M.
William McClintock and Susan Dewey, Dec. 2, 1840, by James Kerr, V. D. M.
Abraham McColloms and Ruth Tipton, June 1, 1837, by Rev. James C. Taylor.
Archibald McCombs and Catherine Jeffers, Feb. 9, 1820, by William Carrothers. J. P.

Hugh McComb and Jane Burtch, June 10, 1818, by John Crawford, J. P.
David McCombs and Isabella Ferrell, Feb. 7, 1828, by Samuel Hitchcock, J. P.
James McCombs and Hannah Atkinson, June 26, 1838, by Rev. Jacob Coon.
John McCombs and Mary Ann Busby, Dec. 23, 1834, by William Arnold, J. P.
Joseph McComb and Jane Tipton, Sept. 11, 1837, by William Arnold, J. P.
David McConkey and Lucinda Kail, Sept. 22, 1837, by B. W. Veirs, J. P.
Joseph McConkey and Maria Kent, March 11, 1830, by Robert Orr, J. P.
Samuel McConkey and Jane Moodey, April 4, 1816, by Thomas Fisher, J. P.
Samuel McConkey and Elizabeth McDonough, Aug. 15, 1831, by George W. Bell, J. P.
William McConkey and Mary Atkinson, Jan. 27, 1835, by John McArthur, V. D. M.
John McConnell and Jane Robinson, Oct. 23, 1823, by Archibald McGrew, J. P.
John P. McConnell and Catherine Medley, March 28, 1833, by Rev. Benjamin Wood.
John C. McConnell and Jane Bowles, March 3, 1836, by Mark Hogg, J. P.
Michael McConnell and Susan Gallagher, March 26, 1826, by Rev. Simon Lauck.
Robert McConnell and Abigail Burwell, Aug. 11, 1825, by Rev. William Wallace.
William McConnell and Mary McCollough, April 22, 1830, by James McCollough, J. P.
John McCormick and Hester Allen, June 29, 1837, by M. B. Lukins, J. P.
James McCourt and Ann Faucett, Jan. 9, 1821, by Rev. Elias Crane.
Jacob McCoy and Elizabeth Condon, July 9, 1840, by William Arnold, J. P.
John McCoy and Eliza Walker, May 28, 1839, by William Boggs, J. P.
Thomas McCue and Mary Barnett, April 2, 1830, by Rev. William Tipton.
Alexander McCollough and Elizabeth Smith, March 30, 1815, by Rev. Thomas B. Clark, V. D. M.
Alexander McCullouch and Elizabeth McCullouch, Feb. 11, 1819, by John Rea, V. D. M.
Alexander McCullough and Eleanor McCullough, March 8, 1836, by John Graham.
George McCollough and Hetty Simpson, Jan. 29, 1829, by Rev. William Knox.
George McCollough and Sarah Whan, June 11, 1829, by Salmon Cowles, V. D. M.
Hugh McCullough and Margaret Kerr, March 9, 1836, by Andrew Isaac.
James McCullough and Rebecca Smith, Feb. 13, 1816, by Thomas B. Clark. V. D. M.
James McCollough and Mary Strong, April 22, 1829, by John Russel, J. P.
John McCullough and Rebecca Templeton, April 7, 1831, by Rev. Jacob Lemmon.
Joseph McCullough and Sarah Lyons, May 5, 1817, by John Rea, V. D. M.
Thomas McCulloch and Mary Neil, July 14, 1831, by Anderson Isaac.
William McCullough and Juliann Lazure, March 9, 1821, by Abriam Johnson, J. P.
William McCullough and Anne Wells, Jan. 6, 1837, by Rev. William Knox.
William McCollough and Betsey Edgar, Dec. 22, 1837, by William Wallace, V. D. M.
William McCollough and Nancy Jamison, Dec. 17, 1840, by William Wallace, V. D. M.
Hugh McCune and Betsey Simpson, Sept. 1, 1831, by George Brown, J. P.

Ebenezer McCurdy and Anna Vincent. Dec. 30, 1834, by John Rea, V. D. M.
George McDaniel and Mary Dunlap, March 15, 1832, by Joseph Wolff, J. P.
George McDavitt and Rachel Moodey. Dec. 15, 1831, by Thomas Ford, J. P.
Andrew McDivitt and Jane Moodey, Nov. 16, 1831, by Thomas Ford, J. P.
Andrew McDivitt and Eliza Corkhill, April 28, 1837, by Charles Evans, J. P.
Charles McDivitt and Fanny Fisher, Sept. 18, 1823, by Michael Conaway, J. P.
George McDivitt and Mary Johnston, Oct. 23, 1817, by Thomas Fisher, J. P.
George McDivitt, Jr., and Mary Fisher, Oct. 10, 1820, by John Hurless, J. P.
James McDivitt and Anne Birney, Dec. 15, 1831, by Rev. David Merryman.
John McDivitt and Susanna Simpson, Dec. 18, 1827, by Michael Conaway, J. P.
Elza McDonald and Mary Mustard, May 13, 1840, by Rev. Richard Brown.
John McDonnal and Catherine Miles, Jan. 6, 1819, by Robert McKee, J. P.
Thomas McDonnall and Mary Byers, Jan. 1, 1823, by William Taggart, V. D. M.
John McDonnah and Masey Hoglin, May 18, 1813, by William Barnhill, J. P.
John McDowell and Nancy Clements, April 19, 1832, by William Wallace, V. D. M.
Samuel McDowell and Jane Watson, Oct. 9, 1828, by William Wallace, V. D. M.
Robert McElravy and Harriett Atkinson, May 3, 1832, by John McArthur, V. D. M.
James McElwee and Lucy Smith, Dec. 20, 1834, by Pleasant Underwood.
Benjamin McFadden and Mary Wilson, Sept. 4, 1821, by William Taggart, V. D. M.
George McFadden and Elizabeth Kelly, Dec. 18, 1821, by William Taggart, V. D. M.
Hamilton McFadden and Susanna Picken, Sept. 27, 1827, by Michael Conaway, J. P.
John McFadden and Mary Dunlap, March 4, 1815, by Rev. Thomas B. Clark
John McFadden and Elizabeth Stringer, June 27, 1819, by William Anderson, J. P.
Joseph McFadden and Polly Thompson, Dec. 28, 1826, by William Taggart, V. D. M.
Nathaniel McFadden and Elizabeth Green, Dec. 15, 1833, by Jacob L. Grubb, J. P.
Samuel B. McFadden and Sarah McFadden, Dec. 7, 1836, by William Taggart, V. D. M.
William McFadden and Elizabeth Thompson, June 28, 1825, by William Taggart, V. D. M.
Wilson McFadden and Tabitha Cumi English, Dec. 8, 1831, by Michael Conaway, J. P.
Fielden McFee and Sally Thompson, Nov. 25, 1830, by Edward Talbott, J. P.
John McGare and Nancy Ann House, Nov. 18, 1828, by Rev. James Moore.
Andrew McGee and Lydia Beckley, March 17, 1836, by John Wagner, J. P.
Hugh McGee and Sarah Wilson, Aug. 1, 1830, by Samuel Hitchcock, J. P.
William McGee and Rachel Beckley, Aug. 3, 1826, by John Wagner, J. P.
William McGiffin and Lydia Butterfield, Oct. 27, 1825, by Rev. Elias Crane.
Thomas McGill and Rebecca Baxter, Oct. 8, 1833, by Samuel Ramsey, J. P.
James McConigle and Margaret Turner, March 31, 1831, by William Taggart, V. D. M.
Joseph McGonagle and Elizabeth Crawford, Nov. 25, 1834, by John McArthur, V. D. M.

McCaslin McGonagle and Louiza Cummins, March 24, 1836, by John McArthur, V. D. M.
Robert McGonagle and Eliza McFadden, Nov. 15, 1827, by Samuel Hitchcock, J. P.
Thomas McGonigal and Mary Thompson, Dec. 12, 1833, by John McArthur, V. D. M.
David G. McGuire and Anna Roush, Aug. 17, 1819, by Robert McKee, J. P.
George McGrew and Margaret Bricker, Feb. 28, 1838, by Rev. Thomas Hanna.
John McHaines and Nancy Peppers, Dec. 29, 1833, by Samuel Ramsey, J. P.
Charles McHugh and Jane McCamis, Jan. 24, 1833, by Rev. James Robertson.
George McIlroy and Nancy Eschallot, Nov. 4, 1832, by Thomas M. Granfell, J. P.
James McElroy and Cassy Baker, Nov. 21, 1816, by William Anderson.
John McIlroy and Jerusa Ann Murphy, April 24, 1832, by Thomas P. Jenkins, J. P.
Robert McIlroy and Mary McFadden, May 21, 1818, by William Anderson, J. P.
Archibald McIntire and Rachel Haley, Feb. 28, 1817, by Charles Chapman, J. P.
James McKee and Sarah Lewis, Nov. 4, 1834, by John McArthur, V. D. M.
Rev. Joseph McKee and Sarah E. Crocker, Nov. 20, 1839, by Rev. Thomas Hanna.
George McKibbon and Eleanor Morrison, Jan. 19, 1836, by Rev. Jacob Coon.
Matthew McKibbon and Jane Eagleson, Oct. 11, 1832, by Rev. Jacob Coon.
Ebenezer McKinnie and Jane Williams, Feb. 15, 1832, by Rev. Thomas Hanna.
Friar McKinnie and Emeline Bell, Nov. 11, 1830, by George W. Bell, J. P.
George McKinney and Elizabeth Conaway, Oct. 10, 1828, by Joseph Johnson, J. P.
James McKinney and Mary Orr, Feb. 3, 1831, by George W. Bell, J. P.
John McKinney and Nancy Campbell, June 19, 1820, by Abriam Johnson, J. P.
John McKisson and Elizabeth Packer, Oct. 20, 1830, by Edward Talbott.
James McKiterick and Nancy Walker, April 2, 1834, by Rev. Thomas Hanna.
James McLaughlin and Mary Bair, March 2, 1820, by B. W. Veirs, J. P.
Robert McLaughlin and Rachel Merryman, April 10, 1834, by George W. Bell, J. P.
James McLean and Sarah Endsley, Aug. 5, 1824, by Donald McIntosh, V. D. M.
David McMath and Charity Mowders, March 21, 1822, by John Russel, J. P.
Harland McMath and Julian Mitchell, Aug. 7, 1835, by Joseph Fry, J. P.
Simeon McMath and Hannah Adams, Jan. 16, 1836, by Samuel Skinner, J. P.
Amos McMillan and Jane Porter, Jan. 4, 1821, by Thomas B. Carter, J. P.
Asa McMillan and Mary Kelly, May 8, 1827, by William Wallace.
John McMillan and Alice Bernhard, Dec. 28, 1820, by Thomas B. Carter, J. P.
John McMillan and Elizabeth Peacock, Oct. 17, 1822, by Benjamin S. Cowan, J. P.
Robert McMillen and Margaret Ann Moore, Dec. 6, 1838, by William Wallace, V. D. M.
Samuel McMillan and Clarissa Milligan, April 16, 1840, by Rev. Thomas Thompson.
William McMillan and Jane Downey, July 13, 1830, by Van Brown, J. P.
James McMullen and Isabella Todd, Oct. 19, 1830, by William Wallace, V. D. M.
John McMullin and Fanny Law, Dec. 24, 1835, by Joseph Masters, J. P.
Barnabas McNamee and Elizabeth Brannon, March 6, 1840, by Matthew Phillips, J. P.

EARLY MARRIAGES

Ruben McNamee and Pricilla Humphres, Oct. 13, 1825, by Joseph Fry, J. P.
William McNamee and Margaret Fisher, Aug. 29, 1826, by Michael Conaway, J. P.
Joseph McNutt and Nancy Yates, Dec. 20, 1832, by John McArthur, V. D. M.
James McNary and Amelia Grove, Feb. 2, 1836, by Rev. Thomas Hanna.
John McNary and Margaret Hawthorn, Nov. 6, 1838, by Rev. Thomas Hanna.
Elisha McOrr and Sarah Kail, March 17, 1824, by Robert Orr, J. P.
George McPeck and Jane Endsley, Oct. 6, 1831, by Rev. John McArthur.
George W. McPherson and Harriet Johnson, July 14, 1836, by Rev. C. D. Battell.
Edward McPheter, and Rachel Hitchcock, Feb. 26, 1839, by Charles Thorn.
Elisha McQueen and Elizabeth Tope, July 1, 1827, by John C. Huston, J. P
John McQueen and Mary Crozier, Nov. 15, 1821, by Rev. Elias Crane.
Samuel McQueen and Barbara Whiteman, April 22, 1827, by John C. Huston, J. P.
Matthew McShanks and Elizabeth E. Nicholason, Jan. 31, 1826, by Rev. John Crom.
Asa McVaigh and Nancy Wilson, Sept. 19, 1816, by John Crawford, J. P.
Stacey McVeigh and Mary Fencer, April 18, 1819, by William Wyckoff, J. P.
Daniel McWilliams and Jane Braden, Sept. 20, 1836, by William Taggart, V. D. M.
Thomas Mackey and Anne Ely, April 5, 1838, by Rev. James Drummond.
Zenas Macomber and Hannah McKee, June 16, 1833, by Edward Talbott, J. P.
John Madens and Mary Ann Light, June 22, 1818, by Charles Chapman, J. P.
James Madison and Sarah Melaung, Aug. 3, 1815, by Charles Chapman, J. P.
Samuel Magoogan and Sarah Patton, Dec. 1, 1831, by Rev. John McArthur.
Joseph Mehaffey and Letitia Wells, July 31, 1832, by Peter Barger, J. P.
William Mahaffey and Harriett Ourant, Dec. 30, 1830, by Peter Barger, J. P.
John Maholm and Martha Bolen, April 4, 1822, by William Taggart, V. D. M.
Joseph Meholin and Margaret McFadden, June 24, 1816, by William Taggart, V. D. M.
Samuel Maholm and Hetty Delany, Aug. 16, 1821, by Rev. Elijah C. Stone.
Joseph Mahan and Rebecca Brown, Nov. 12, 1835, by Rev. Moses Scott.
Thomas Mahon and Anne Ferrell, April 8, 1830, by Samuel Hitchcock, J. P.
William Mairs and Elizabeth Gamble, April 8, 1837, by John McKinney, J. P.
John Major and Edith Webb, Jan. 8, 1826, by Rev. James Roberts.
Emanuel Malernee and Hannah Eaton, July 9, 1829, by Rev. Jacob Lemmon.
John Z. Mallanee and Sarah Hayes, April 28, 1831, by Rev. Thomas J. Taylor.
Levi Mallernee and Eleanor Johnson, Dec. 6, 1838, by Rev. Robert Cook.
Matthew F. Mallanee and Catherine Hoyt, Jan. 30, 1838, by Thomas Phillips, J. P.
John Manbeck and Elizabeth Gutshall, Oct. 14, 1824, by Rev. John Crom.
Peter Manbeck and Margaret Stall, Sept. 15, 1829, by John Gruber, J. P.
William Mann and Elizabeth Covert, Feb. 19, 1829, by George Brown, J. P.
John G. Mannie and Eliza L. Ankrum, Nov. 15, 1832, by Salmon Cowles, V. D. M.
James W. Manro and Sally Fisher, March 9, 1826, by Alexander Moore, J. P.
Ransom Manrow and Prudence Hanna, March 27, 1838, by John Rea, V. D. M.
John Mansfield and Rhoda Welch, June 5, 1828, by John Rea, V. D. M.
John Mansfield and Mary Cave, June 4, 1840, by Samuel Skinner, J. P.

Richard Mansfield and Elizabeth Shimer, Nov. 3, 1831, by William Arnold, J. P.
Thomas Mansfield and Elizabeth Fisher, Dec. 14, 1829, by John Carson, J. P.
William Mansfield and Margaret Ann Bell, July 11, 1838, by William Taggart, V. D. M.
David Maple and Mary Farmer, March 1, 1816, by Alexander Lee, J. P.
Joseph Maple and Elizabeth Rider, Dec. 13, 1831, by Joseph Wolf, J. P.
Thomas Mapel and Mary Rider, May 23, 1827, by Van Brown, J. P.
James Markee [Marquis?] and Rhoda Nevitt, June 18, 1829, by Rev. William Tipton.
James Markee and Eliza Ellen Hilton, Oct. 22, 1839, by M. F. Burkhead, J. P.
Joseph Markey and Mary Fordyce, April 18, 1830, by Thomas McCleary.
William Markee and Hannah Norris, Jan. 14, 1830, by Thomas McCleary.
William Markey and Miranda Ann Johnson, July 16, 1835, by John M. Brown, J. P.
Daniel Markley and Caty Everhart, Sept. 20, 1817, by Martin Guilinger, J. P.
Jonathan Markley and Anna Stine, Jan. 5, 1832, by Maurris Albaugh, J. P.
Jonathan Markley and Mary Ann Hartley, May 25, 1837, by B. W. Veirs, J. P.
Joseph Markley and Sevilla Wallace, July 24, 1828, by Morris Allbaugh, J. P.
Moses Markley and Elizabeth Everhart, Feb. 26, 1822, by B. W. Veirs, J. P.
Moses Markley and Sarah Shaeffer, March 31, 1825, by John Wagner, J. P.
Robert Markley and Leah Kooken, March 6, 1834, by Richard Lyons, J. P.
James E. Marquis and Harriet Johnston, Nov. 21, 1823, by Salmon Cowles, V. D. M.
Jacob Marshal and Martha Laughlin, May 2, 1839, by William Arnold, J. P.
Jarret Marshell and Margaret Marshall, June 7, 1832, by Michael Conaway, J. P.
Jarett Marshall and Ruth Harding, March 20, 1838, by M. B. Lukins, J. P.
John Marshall and Zipora Cox, June 16, 1814, by John Busby, J. P.
John Marshall and Margaret McKinny, June 10, 1824, by Michael Conaway, J. P.
Joseph M. Marshall and Jane McFadden, Nov. 6, 1834, by John McArthur, V. D. M.
Samuel Marshall and Nancy Layport, Jan. 1, 1835, by George W. Bell, J. P.
Andrew Martin and Jane Gibson, May 30, 1831, by Thomas P. Jenkins, J. P.
Edward Martin and Elizabeth Haverfield, Sept. 24, 1839, by Rev. William Taggart.
Hugh Martin and Anne Wiley, March 3, 1831, by William McMillan.
James Martin and Ann Tewalt, March 16, 1816, by Walter B. Beebe, J. P.
James Martin and Jane Devine, May 29, 1823, by Archibald McGrew, J. P.
James Martin and Elizabeth Dewalt, Jan. 12, 1838, by John Caldwell, J. P.
James Martin and Louisa Grove, Feb. 27, 1840, by John M. Branen, J. P.
John Martin and Harriet Hitchcock, March 13, 1840, by Richard Brown.
Joseph H. Martin and Rebecca Sawville, June 26, 1837, by B. W. Viers, J. P.
Luther Martin and Jane Clark, Dec. 9, 1830, by John Rea, V. D. M.
Marshall Martin and Melinda Skinner, March 24, 1836, by Rev. Cornelius D. Battelle.
Samuel Martin and Susanna Worley, Aug. 15, 1822, by William Cunningham.
Samuel H. Martin and Rebecca Mercer, March 7, 1838, by John Chalfan, J. P.
William Martin and Sarah Lewis, Aug. 27, 1835, by George Atkinson, J. P.
Daniel Matron and Sarah Lee, Jan. 25, 1816, by John Roberts.

Benjamin Matson and Rebecca Simpkins, June 26, 1836, by Samuel Lewis, J. P.
Enoch Matson and Mary Turner, Sept. 25, 1817, by James Roberts.
John Matson and Elizabeth Spurrier, Aug. 17, 1837, by Thomas Phillips, J. P.
Nehemiah Matson and Mary Townsend, Dec. 9, 1818, by James Roberts.
Nehemiah Matson and Mary Anderson, June 23, 1836, by Samuel Lewis, J. P.
Nicholas Matson and Olivia Myers, May 22, 1831, by Edward Talbott, J. P.
Uriah Matson and Jane McKee, April 22, 1830, by John Heberling, J. P.
Washington Matson and Elizabeth Talbott, May 15, 1836, by Samuel Lewis, J. P.
Abraham Mattern and Mary Brown, April 4, 1833, by Rev. —— Tipton.
John Mattern and Margaret Griffin, Jan. 1, 1833, by John Caldwell, J. P.
Henry C. Matthews and Nancy Rankin, Oct. 16, 1820, by William Wyckoff, J. P.
James Matthews and Jane Thompson, Jan. 11, 1830, by John Hebling, J. P.
Thomas Matthews and Martha Ridgway, July 20, 1826, by Joseph Fry, J. P.
Thomas Matthews and Julian Kindle, July 23, 1828, by John Wagner, J. P.
Arthur May and Elizabeth Sisler, Dec. 31, 1825, by J. R. Kirkpatrick, J. P.
Henry May and Henrietta Gardner, March 7, 1839, by Rev. Jacob Lemmon.
John May and Mary Dempsey, April 12, 1832, by Rev. Jacob Lemmon.
Joseph Mays and Rebecca Work, Sept. 14, 1824, by John Rea, V. D. M.
William Mayhugh and Sarah Spurrier, Dec. 14, 1829, by Thomas Parkinson, J. P.
Nathan Maxon and Susanna Dicks, July 18, 1815, by Richard Prue, J. P.
William Maxon and Delilah Bowland, Jan. 26, 1832, by Rev. Jacob Lemmon.
Alexander E. Maxwell and Sarah A. Keepers, Jan. 12, 1832, by Rev. John Moffit.
Alexander Maxwell and Elizabeth Plummer, Oct. 12, 1839, by Aaron Conaway, J. P.
Henry Maxwell and Esther Orr, Jan. 30, 1823, by William Taggart, V. D. M.
James Maxwell and Jane Maxwell, Aug. 12, 1824, by Thomas Hanna, V. D. M.
John Maxwell and Jane Orr, Feb. 9, 1826, by William Taggart, V. D. M.
Robert Maxwell and Elizabeth Fisher, Dec. 21, 1821, by William Anderson, J. P.
Robert Maxwell and Jemima Keepers, Dec. 20, 1838, by William D. McCartney, V. D. M.
Walter Maxwell and Hannah Hawthorn, April 1, 1830, by Rev. Joseph Clokey.
William Maxwell and Sarah McGaw, Dec. 31, 1840, by James Kerr, V. D. M.
James Means and Jane Drummond, Aug. 24, 1824, by Isaac Allen, J. P.
George Mecasky and Elizabeth Kelly, Jan. 17, 1827, by Rev. Thomas Hunt.
Robert Mecaskey and Sarah McCausland, May 21, 1831, by James Robertson, A. M.
George Mecausland and Mary Kelly, Sept. 2, 1823, by Rev. Thomas Hunt.
Elisha Medcalf and Elizabeth McDaniel, Feb. 2, 1834, by Rev. David C. Merriman.
Rezin Medley and Milly Jones, Sept. 20, 1815, by William Wyckoff, J. P.
Richard Medley and Margaret Browning, Dec. 28, 1826, by George Brown, J. P.
Isaac Meek and Margaret Heady, Feb. 17, 1831, by Rev. Nathaniel Callender.
Peter Meek and Margaret Guier, Oct. 8, 1829, by Samuel Dunlap, J. P.
Samuel Megaw and Jane McCombs, Nov. 13, 1834, by John McArthur, V. D. M.
Thomas Meldrum and Matilda Phillips, Nov. 30, 1837, by Rev. Jacob Lemmon.
William Mellor and Sarah Fell, June 17, 1832, by Edward Talbott, J. P.
Moses Melton and Ann Hockins, Aug. 12, 1819, by William Wyckoff, J. P.
Aaron Mercer and Polly Cecil, June 30, 1831, by George Brown, J. P.

Elias Mercer and Polly Randels, June 29, 1820, by Rev. James Roberts.
Ellis Mercer and Nancy Bush, Dec. 18, 1817, by Rev. James Roberts.
John M. Meredith and Delila Jones, Aug. 29, 1839, by Joseph Fry, J. P.
Amos Merrick and Catherine Bonecutter, May 23, 1816, by Paul Preston.
David Merrill and Jane Knock, Nov. 14, 1831, by Joseph Fry, J. P.
John Merrill and Margaret Guttery, Sept. 24, 1835, by William Wallace, V. D. M.
John Meryman and Margaret Eliza Ray, Dec. 12, 1839, by M. F. Burkhead, J. P.
Nicholas Meryman and Amma Moore, June 18, 1840, by William Arnold, J. P.
Sheridan Merryman and Sarah Ann Wible, April 30, 1840, by William Arnold, J. P.
Adonijah Messenger and Rachel Burgess, Sept. 9, 1821, by Joseph Fry, J. P.
Barr Mewherter and Mary Reed, Jan. 30, 1821, by John Wagner, J. P.
James Mewherter and Lydia Reed, June 18, 1818, by Martin Guilinger, J. P.
Samuel Micklederry and Sarah Elder, April 7, 1831, by Rev. John Donaldson.
David Middleton and Hester House, Nov. 1, 1832, by Rev. Jacob Lemmon.
John Midleton and Martha Earley, Oct. 6, 1836, by Rev. Jacob Lemmon.
Leonard Middleton and Susan Turnpaugh, March 19, 1835, by Rev. Jacob Lemmon.
Andrew Mikesell and Mary Lowmiller, May 19, 1840, by Rev. Benjamin Pope.
George Mikesell and Barbara Guthrie, April 13, 1836, by John Gruber, J. P.
Jacob Mikesell and Sally Shoos, Jan. 27, 1831, by John Gruber, J. P.
Charles H. Mildred and Nancy Botkin, May 6, 1824, by Jacob Tope, J. P.
Abner Miller and Rachel Beck, April 27, 1820, by Joseph Fry, J. P.
Daniel Miller and Susanna Lowmiller, Dec. 27, 1815, by Henry Kail, J. P.
Harrison Miller and Mary Ann Wheeler, Oct. 24, 1839, by John Gruber, J. P.
Harrison Miller and Elizabeth Gibler, Dec. 24, 1839, by Thomas Finnicum, J. P.
John Miller and Rebecca Lowmiller, May 26, 1825, by John Wagner, J. P.
John Miller and Leah Brokaw, Jan. 16, 1839, by Charles Thorn.
Joseph Miller and Isabel McClintock, Dec. 18, 1835, by John McArthur, V. D. M.
Levi Miller and July Ann Riley, April 18, 1839, by Rev. Robert Cook.
Nathan Miller and Amy Jones, Nov. 17, 1831, by Thomas P. Jenkins, J. P.
Richard J. Miller and Ann Barrett, Aug. 23, 1832, by Rev. Jacob Lemmon.
Rozel D. Miller and Jane Curry, Dec. 17, 1834, by John McArthur, V. D. M.
Samuel Miller and Sally Miller, March 13, 1822, by Thomas Hanna, V. D. M.
Thomas Miller and Margaret R. Henderson, Oct. 21, 1822, by Thomas Hanna, V. D. M.
Thomas Miller and Mary Cramblet, Aug. 24, 1837, by Rev. Jacob Lemmon.
Thomas Miller and Mary Johnson, Sept. 13, 1838, by Samuel Skinner, J. P.
William Miller and Polly Haun, Jan. 9, 1823, by Rev. Salmon Cowles.
William Miller and Lydia Barthelow, Oct. 13, 1836, by Rev. Jacob Lemmon.
Alexander Milligan and Margaret Richey, Dec. 10, 1816, by William Taggart V. D. M.
Joseph Milligan and Isabella Wallace, May 12, 1825, by Thomas Hanna, V. D. M.
Thomas Milligan and Sarah Bennett, Nov. 17, 1825, by Donald McIntosh, V. D. M.
Thomas Milligan and Martha Vincent, Feb. 3, 1827, by John Rea, V. D. M.
William Milligan and Lydia Miller, Nov. 6, 1823, by Thomas Hanna, V. D. M.
John Milliken and Jemima Haines, Oct. 18, 1834, by Thomas McClintock, J. P.
Michael Milliken and Charity Day, Jan. 9, 1838, by John Selby, J. P.
Elias Mills and Isabella Glendon, Dec. 29, 1836, by Samuel Skinner, J. P.

John Mills and Sarah Arnold, Feb. 15, 1816, by Charles Chapman, J. P.
Nathan Mills and Susan Condon, May 10, 1838, by Samuel G. J. Worthington.
William Mills and Margaret Markee, July 9, 1816, by John Graham.
Henry Minick and Mary Trushel, Oct. 28, 1823, by Rev. J. Wagenhals.
Henry Minor and Catherine Bowers, May 3, 1838, by David Bowers, J. P.
John Minteer and Catherine Simmons, April 22, 1821, by Thomas Dickerson, J. P.
Daniel Miser and Mary Hay, July 7, 1825, by John Wagner, J. P.
George Miser and Caty Markley, Aug. 28, 1816, by Martin Guilinger, J. P.
Henry Misor and Hannah Need, July 20, 1817, by Henry Kail, J. P.
John Miser and Mary Stone, Feb. 12, 1815, by Rev. John Rinehart.
John Miser and Angeline Stonesifer, May 17, 1838, by John Wagner, J. P.
Philip Miser and Peggy Shultz, Sept. 9, 1821, by John Wagner, J. P.
Daniel Mitchell and Elizabeth Kerr, Feb. 9, 1832, by Rev. Thomas Hanna.
Hugh Mitchell and Elizabeth Ferrall, Jan. 30, 1834, by Rev. Thomas Hanna.
Ira Mitchell and Elizabeth Harden, Jan. 26, 1836, by Joseph Fry, J. P.
James Mitchell and Martha Timmons, March 24, 1825, by Donald McIntosh, V. D. M.
William Mitchell and Mary Ann Atkinson, Oct. 18, 1838, by Rev. Thomas Hanna.
Allen S. Moffit and Rebecca Jones, Feb. 11, 1836, by Rev. Cornelius D. Battelle.
Henry Moffit and Mary Lewis, April 23, 1815, by Charles Chapman.
Henry Moffet and Ann Johnson, Jan. 7, 1819, by Charles Chapman, J. P.
Rev. John Moffet and Julian Norris, June 23, 1830, by John Graham.
William Moffit and Rebecca Kelly, Nov. 11, 1819, by John Rea, V. D. M.
James Moles and Betsey Connel, Sept. 21, 1820, by Rev. William Knox.
Augustus Molesworth and Mary Ann Smith, March 19, 1840, by Rev. J. D. Kinnear.
Thomas Moncrief and Isabella Walker, March 15, 1822, by John Rea, V. D. M.
James Moodey and Nancy Giles, April 9, 1833, by Thomas Ford, J. P.
Thomas Moody and Rachel Hutchinson, Feb. 25, 1836, by B. W. Viers, J. P.
William Moody and Elenor McDonaugh, June 2, 1814, by John Busby, J. P.
Aaron Moore and Mary Ellen Hilton, Nov. 23, 1837, by Rev. Robert Cook.
Abraham Moore and Elizabeth Hagey, Oct. 2, 1831, by Joseph Walters, J. P.
Alexander Moore and Catherine McIntire, June 13, 1826, by Alexander Moore, J. P.
Alexander Moore and Mary Baxter, March 12, 1829, by William Wallace, V. D. M.
David Moore and Elizabeth King, Dec. 5, 1817, by Henry Kail, J. P.
David Moore and Sarah Cidwell, April 15, 1824, by Hugh Shotwell, J. P.
David Moore and Sarah Dunlap, Aug. 28, 1838, by William Waller, V. D. M.
David Moore and Minerva Wright, Aug. 6, 1840, by Rev. Robert Cook.
Edward Moore and Catherine Spiker, May 6, 1819, by Joseph Johnson, J. P.
George R. Moore and Deborah Hutchinson, Dec. 7, 1826, by Silvanus Lamb. J. P.
Henry Moore and Elizabeth Finley, Aug. 21, 1828, by Salmon Cowles, V. D. M.
Henry R. Moore and Lydia Ann Burson, May 16, 1832, by Samuel Skinner, J. P.
Hilery Moore and Albina West, March 11, 1837, by William Arnold, J. P.
Hugh Moore and Elizabeth Jones, Feb. 27, 1817, by William Slemmons, J. P.
Ire Moore and Prudence B. Ford, April 25, 1839, by M. B. Lukins, J. P.

Isaac Moore and Elizabeth Cook, July 3, 1834, by Lot Deming, J. P.
Isaac Moore and Eliza Coleman Feb. 23, 1840, by M. B. Lukins, J. P.
Isaiah Moore and Rachel Tipton, Oct. 12, 1837, by William Arnold, J. P.
James Moore and Elizabeth Rowland, Jan. 8, 1829, by Philip Fulton, J. P.
James Moore and Rebecca Cook, Sept. 7, 1836, by Robert P. Simpson, J. P.
James Moore and Mary Moore, Nov. 26, 1839, by Hugh Parks, Jr., V. D. M.
Jesse Moore and Ruth Atkinson, Sept. 7, 1814, by William Knox.
John Moore and Nancy Foreman, Oct. 27, 1822, by Rev. William Knox.
John Moore and Mary Ann House, Dec. 4, 1832, by Rev. John Moffet.
John Moore and Alsy Johnson, Dec. 25, 1834, by William Wyckoff, J. P.
John Moore and Elizabeth Williamson, March 12, 1835, by William Wallace, V. D. M.
John Moore and Elizabeth McCullough, May 24, 1836, by John Rea, V. D. M.
John Moore and Sarah Mansfield, May 4, 1837, by Samuel Skinner, J. P.
Peter Y. Moore and Mary Rickets, June 30, 1836, by Robert Scott.
Peter Moore and Sally Johnson, June 24, 1838, by William Wyckoff, J. P.
Robert A. Moore and Mary Peacock, March 31, 1831, by William Wyckoff, J. P.
Samuel Moore and Polly Riggle, June 18, 1818, by James Roberts.
Sylvanus Moore and Isabella Muncy, April 23, 1829, by Rev. W. B. Evans.
Sylvanus Moore and Alcinda Smith, Oct. 17, 1838, by Rev. Benjamin Wood.
Thomas Moore to Susan Cook, June 6, 1840, by E. Greenwold.
William Moore and Jane Boales, March 14, 1833, by Rev. Thomas Hanna.
William Moore and Ruth Harvey, April 30, 1835, by Samuel Skinner, J. P.
William Moore and Lydia Delany, March 15, 1838, by Thomas Phillips, J. P.
Samuel Moorhead and Sarah Holmes, Aug. 27, 1824, by John Rea, V. D. M.
Thomas Moorehead and Polly Hill, June 4, 1821, by Robert W. Laughlin, J. P.
Benjamin Morgan and Margaret Thompson, Dec. 12, 1816, by William Anderson.
Elias Morgan and Nancy Harman, Dec. 30, 1824, by John Wagner, J. P.
George Morgan and Elizabeth Shuck, May 31, 1825, by Rev. John Crom.
John Morgan and Polly Kirby, July 14, 1829, by Rev. John Crom.
John Morgan and Jemima Merrill, March 5, 1833, by J.. Staneart, J. P.
Michael Morgan and Eleanor Whann, Feb. 6, 1838, by Rev. Jacob Coon.
Thomas Morgan and Betsey Harmon, July 28, 1831, by Thomas Ford, J. P.
Edward Morris and Catherine Susan Matson, Sept. 15, 1831, by Edward Talbott, J. P.
John Morris and Charlotte Huff, Jan. 28, 1817, by Thomas Dickerson..
John Morris and Margaret Shepherd, Dec. 28, 1826, by Jesse Hooper, J. P.
John Morris and Maria Burson, July 9, 1829, by John Heberling, J. P.
John Morris and Charlotte Dickerson, Jan. 20, 1839, by Samuel Lewis, J. P.
Jonathan Morris and Mary Ann Parker, Feb. 22, 1827, by William B. Evans.
John Morrison and Peggy Martin, Dec. 22, 1821, by George Brown, J. P.
John Morrison and Mary Norris, Feb. 25, 1828, by Rev. William Knox.
Thomas Morrison and Jane Gilmore, Oct. 17, 1815, by Henry Barricklow, J. P.
William Morrison and Eleanor McCraney, Dec. 28, 1819, by Rev. James Roberts.
Alexander Morrow and Hetty Fletcher, April 19, 1832, by John Rea, V. D. M.
George B. Morrow and Eliza Guthrie, Dec. 30, 1840, by Rev. Moses Allen.
Thomas Morrow and Jane Brokaw, Dec. 13, 1813, by Thomas B. Clark, V D. M.
William Morrow and Margaret Fogle, Nov. 29, 1838, by Thomas P. Jenkins, J. P.
William Mortimer and Mary Butler, Dec. 8, 1825, by Silvanus Lamb, J. P.

EARLY MARRIAGES

Samuel Morton and Jane McKee, Feb. 5, 1826, by John Busby, J. P.
Conrad Mortz and Sarah Hines, Sept. 12, 1838, by Rev. John W. Minor.
Henry Moseworth and Margaret Strong, Dec. 29, 1836, by Rev. Richard Brown.
Conrad Mowder and Mary Mowder, Jan. 13, 1830, by Rev. William Tipton.
Jacob Mowder and Sarah White, Feb. 12, 1835, by Samuel Lewis, J. P.
John L. Mowder and Catherine Toland, Dec. 2, 1830, by Edward Talbott, J. P.
Joshua Mowder and Mary Brewer, Sept. 5, 1832, by William Wyckoff, J. P.
William Mowder and Sally Turner, May 4, 1822, by Joseph Fry, J. P.
Jacob Mowry and Peggy Zimmerman, Nov. 15, 1819, by John Hurless, J. P.
Michael Mowry and Eve Giddinger, Sept. 7, 1823, by John Hurless, J. P.
Joel Moxly and Nancy Ring, Aug. 29, 1829, by Joseph Clokey.
John Mull and Elizabeth Cotton, March 27, 1840, by Joseph Fry, J. P.
Charles Mullen and Phebe Merit, April 17, 1828, by Rev. James Roberts..
Alexander Mummy and Nancy Coultrap, Sept. 12, 1838, by C. E. Weirick.
Charles Mummy and Rebecca Hedge, Jan. 11, 1821, by William Haverfield.
George Munson and Emily Bliss, Jan. 5, 1832, by Robert Pittis, J. P.
John Murdock and Henrietta Darling, Feb. 16, 1837, by Rev. Jacob Lemmon.
William Murdock and Nancy Thompson, Feb. 20, 1823, by Michael Conaway, J. P.
Arnold Murphy and Ann Richardson, Oct. 7, 1823, by John Wagner, J. P.
John Murphy and Mary Auld, May 8, 1838, by William Wallace, V. D. M.
Patrick W. Murphy and Maria Kimber, Dec. 14, 1826, by Daniel Limerick, Elder of M. E. Church.
John P. Murry and Mary Musgrove, Dec. 7, 1839, by Joseph Fry, J. P.
Washington Murry and Mary Abdil, July 1, 1824, by Donald McIntosh, V. D. M.
Pearson Mustard and Jane Carson, Jan. 26, 1837, by Jesse Marrell, J. P.
David Myers and Sally Binger, Nov. 17, 1831, by Morris Albaugh, J. P.
Eli Myers and Eliza Pinkerton, Nov. 23, 1831, by Charles Faucett, J. P.
George Myers and Hannah Riggle, Feb. 27, 1820, by John Wagner, J. P.
Jacob Myers and Rhoda Case, Oct. 24, 1830, by George Waddle.
John Myers and Fanny Lowmiller, March 15, 1818, by Martin Guilinger, J. P.
Joseph Myers and Ellen Hardin, Oct. 17, 1839, by C. H. Custer, J. P.
Lewis Myres and Nancy Sager, April 1, 1823, by B. W. Veirs, J. P.
Michael Myers and Sarah Markee, Oct. 31, 1822, by Rev. Curtis Goddard.
Patrick Myers and Nancy Darr, March 9, 1830, by Thomas Phillips, J. P.
Phillip Miers and Catherine Fordice, Nov. 18, 1824, by Joseph Fry, J. P.
Samuel Myers and Mary Connel, Nov. 2, 1830, by Robert Pittis, J. P.
William Myres and Nancy Pinkerton, May 29, 1828, by Jacob Tope, J. P.
George Mynart and Susanna Smith, Sept. 9, 1819, by Rev. John Crom.
John Minard and Barbary Shaeffer, Nov. 11, 1824, Rev. John Wagenhals.
Daniel Naragong and Eliza Hosterman, March 27, 1831, by John Wagner, J. P.
Nicholas Narragong and Polly Wilson, May 4, 1832, by John Wagner, J. P.
Samuel Noragong and Hester Ann Dean, Jan. 18, 1838, by John Wagner.
William Narragong and Nancy Ann Watters, Jan. 1, 1835, by John Wagner, J. P.
George Need and Sarah Miser, Nov. 10, 1816, by Nancy Kail, J. P.
James Neel and Temperance Johnson, March 17, 1829, by Salmon Cowles, V. D. M.
Lyas Neal and Mary Ann Barrett, Aug. 7, 1839, by Charles Thorn.
William Neil and Nancy Armstrong, Oct. 12, 1824, by Thomas Hanna, V. D. M.

Hugh Nelson and Betsy Wilson, Sept. 15, 1815, by Charles Chapman, J. P.
John Nelson and Hannah Moody, March 5, 1816, by Robert Orr, J. P.
Samuel Neson and Sally Preston, July 8, 1819, by William Anderson, J. P.
Joseph Nevil and Maria Starkey, Dec. 1, 1832, by Rev. Jacob Coon.
Isaac Nevitt and Rhoda Johnson, May 13, 1819, by Thomas Dickerson, J. P.
James Newell and Sarah White, Jan. 16, 1840, by William Arnold, J. P.
John Nibloch and Sarah Grewell, Aug. 20, 1829, by Thomas P. Jenkins, J. P.
John Niblock and Matilda Haun, Sept. 23, 1840, by Mark Hogge, J. P.
Henry Nicebaum and Lydia Holtzman, Dec. 25, 1832, by Dewalt Rothacker.
Samuel Nicholas and Sarah Ann Medley, Nov. 20, 1837, by William Arnold, J. P.
William M. Nicolason and Jane McGowan, March 11, 1824, by Rev. Daniel Rahauser.
William Nixon and Agnes Campbell, Dec. 20, 1827, by Joshua Monroe.
James Noah and Cassey Ann Madden, Sept. 10, 1829, by John Heberling, J. P.
James Noble and Martha Davis, Sept. 6, 1822, by James McCollough.
William H. Noble and Mary Bosley, June 13, 1839, by Andrew Lynch, J. P.
Jacob Noftsker and Susanna Gutshall, Nov. 12, 1840, by John Gruber, J. P.
Samuel Nossker and Polly Foos, March 31, 1825, by John Wagner, J. P.
George Norman and Nancy Sparrow, Aug. 30, 1832, by Silvanus Lamb, J. P.
George Norman and Susan Wallcut, June 9, 1836, by Samuel Lewis, J. P.
Daniel Narrick and Betsey Winkfield, April 3, 1816, by Martin Guilinger.
Jacob Norrick and Emily Houser, Dec. 24, 1838, by Robert P. Simpson, J. P.
Alexander Norris and Christena Spiker, Oct. 14, 1838, by Rev. Jacob Lemmon.
John Norris and Sarah McMillan, Feb. 15, 1827, by William Wallace, V .D. M.
John T. Norris and Elizabeth Davis, Dec. 19, 1830, by Rev. Aurora Callender.
Jacob Norvick and Mary Hurless Feb. 22, 1820, by John Hurless, J. P.
James Nowells and Sarah Jones, June 1, 1825, by Isaac Allen, J. P.
James Null and Rebecca Wilken, Sept. 8, 1831, by Andrew Lee.
Joshua Null and Sarah Brown, Sept. 7, 1837, by Thomas Phillips, J. P.
William O'Brien and Susanna Johnston, Feb. 9, 1816, by William Wyckoff, J. P.
William Oden and Kitty A. Ellis, Jan. 15, 1835, by Rev. Jacob Lemmon.
Mordicai Ogle and Betsy Waninto, Jan. 4, 1815, by Alexander Lee, J. P.
Baruch Oglevee and Rachel Dunlap, March 6, 1823, by Rev. Salmon Cowles.
Hugh Oglevee and Elizabeth M. Russell, Feb. 4, 1830, by William Wallace, V. D. M.
John Ohler and Sophia Shook, July 28, 1829, by Lot Deming.
John Oldfield and Sarah Ann Brown, Nov. 12, 1837, by John Caldwell, J. P.
Henry Olen and Mary Staples, April 11, 1840, by Rev. Adam Hetzler.
Henry Olmstead and Martha Bingham, Sept. 20, 1832, by John McArthur, V. D. M.
Walter O'Nail and Ann Jones, Aug. 24, 1815, by William Haverfield, J. P.
Zachariah Oram and Nancy Davis, May 16, 1822, by Jesse Hooper, J. P.
George Orr and Jane Wilkin, Nov. 24, 1829, by William Taggart, V. D. M.
John Or and Sarah Ayres, Feb. 10, 1819, by Thomas Parkinson, J. P.
John Orr and Arey Moore, Sept. 8, 1831, by Joseph Johnson, J. P.
Thomas Orr and Margaret Newhouse, June 24, 1819, by Rev. James Roberts.
Thomas Orr and Elizabeth Keepers, Dec. 11, 1828, by Michael Conaway, J. P.
Thomas Orr and Caroline Sudduth, April 4, 1837, by Thomas Phillips, J. P.
William Orr and Anne Darrah, Aug. 9, 1832, by Joseph Johnson, J. P.

EARLY MARRIAGES

Alexander Osbourn and Margaret Leeper, Nov. 6, 1837, by James Evans, J. P.
Isaac Osbun and Nancy Mansfield, May 17, 1829, by Rev. Benjamin Wood.
John Osburn and Sarah Amspoker, Nov. 24, 1836, by John McArthur, V. D. M.
Samuel Osburn and Elizabeth Welch, Sept. 3, 1835, by John McArthur, V. D. M.
William B. Osburn and Rebecca Rankin, Oct. 2, 1828, by William Taggart, V. D. M.
John Oswalt and Hannah Neill, Jan. 29, 1818, by Robert McLaughlin, Esq.
Washington Ourant and Mary Martin, Jan. 27, 1830, by John Carson, J. P.
Joseph Overholt and Franah Forney, Dec. 5, 1824, by Rev. John Crom.
Martin Overholt and Barbara Erford, Dec. 2, 1828, by Rev. John Crom.
Beal Mackinzie Owings and Miranda Young, Sept. 21, 1824, by Robert Orr, J. P.
Isaac Packer and Rebecca Allen, Sept. 5, 1833, by William Arnold. J. P.
William Pain and Eleanor Figley, March 31, 1838, by George Nichols, J. P.
David Palmer and Mary Magdalena Teniper, Jan. 31, 1839, by C. E. Weirick.
George Palmer and Abigail Wood, May 19, 1818, by James Roberts.
Hiram Palmer and Mary Birney, Oct. 12, 1830, by John McArthur, V. D. M.
John Palmer and Sarah Shirey, March 27, 1838, by Robert P. Simpson, J. P.
Alexander Parker and Elizabeth Gilmore, March 29, 1830, by Alexander Simpson, J. P.
David Parker and Nancy Derry, Sept. 22, 1831, by Thomas P. Jenkins.
Harmon Parker and Barbara Shoemaker, April 13, 1837, by John M. Brown, J. P.
Harris Parker and Mary Hutchinson, Aug. 8, 1839, by Samuel Lewis, J. P.
James Parker and Eleanor Smith, Feb. 5, 1831, by George W. Bell, J. P.
Lewis Parker and Elizabeth Hutchinson, Dec. 23, 1830, by Edward Talbott, J. P.
Richard Parker and Catherine Sherow, Jan. 1, 1835, by John McArthur, V. D. M.
Richard Parker and Isabella Gibson, April 10, 1839, by Robert Given, J. P.
Samuel Parker and Elizabeth Parks, Sept. 20, 1832, by John McArthur, V. D. M.
Thomas Parker and Martha Gudgeon, July 22, 1828, by Thomas R. Ruckle.
David Parkhill and Margaret Davidson, July 5, 1832, by William Taggart, V. D. M.
Andrew Parks and Susan Thumaker, June 10, 1825, by James Smith.
Hiram Parks and Mary May, June 29, 1830, by Thomas P. Jenkins, J. P.
John Parks and Ann Firthey, Dec. 26, 1813, by John Rea, V. D. M.
John Parks and Deulah Messenger, Nov. 23, 1820, by Joseph Fry, J. P.
Laben Parks and Rachel Dicks, Feb. 20, 1819, by William Wyckoff, J. P.
Matthew Park and Elizabeth Walker, May 6, 1825, by Alexander Moore, J. P.
William Parks and Eliza Gross, Oct. 2, 1823, by Joseph Fry, J. P.
Henry Parmer and Ruth Hedge, March 27, 1827, by Samuel Hitchcock, J. P.
Nicholas Parmer and Jane Maxwell, Oct. 27, 1836, by David Brown, J. P.
William Parmer and Margaret Naragong, Dec. 25, 1823, by William Holmes, J. P.
Abraham Parrish and Mary Kent, Nov. 27, 1834, by William Arnold, J. P.
Abraham Parrish and Rachel Keesey, Aug. 2, 1837, by Thomas Wilson, J. P.
Garret Parrish and Mary English, June 5, 1818, by Thomas Dickerson, J. P.
John Parrish and Sarah Anderson, Nov. 10, 1835, by Cornelius D. Battelle.
Leonard Parrish and Sophia Forney, Feb. 22, 1816, by Charles Chapman, J. P.
Peter Parish and Peggy McIntire, Nov. 9, 1820, by Thomas Dickerson, J. P.

Tolbert Parrish and Rachel Kent, Nov. 1, 1833, by William Arnold, J. P.
Samuel Parr and Nancy Carruck, Feb. 29, 1816, by John Rea, V. D. M.
Benjamin L. Parson and Susan Norris, Sept. 5, 1830, by Rev. Jacob Lemmon.
Charles Parsons and Hannah Chilcoat, Oct. 7, 1813, by Rev. James Roberts.
Israel Parsons and Hannah Cope, Jan. 18, 1834, by George Brown, J. P.
John Pasley and Dienna Auld, May 9, 1817, by John Crawford, J. P.
Andrew Patterson and Rebecca Craig, Oct. 27, 1835, by Rev. Thomas Hanna.
David Patterson and Catherine Spiker, Jan. 8, 1835, by John McArthur, V. D. M.
George Patterson and Elizabeth Nolan, Aug. 16, 1829, by John G. Houston, J. P.
John Patterson and Mary Delany, March 23, 1824, by William Holmes, J. P.
John Patterson and Jane Graham, March 2, 1826, by Michael Conaway, J. P.
Joseph Patterson and Mary Hays, June 8, 1834, by Samuel Lewis, J. P.
Samuel Patterson and Jane Davis, March 11, 1830, by Rev. Thomas M. Hudson.
William Patterson and Sally Spiker, Oct. 25, 1832, by Michael Conaway, J. P.
William M. Patterson and Susan Amspoker, Dec. 22, 1834, by John McArthur, V. D. M.
John L. Patton and Margaret Johnson, July 15, 1830, by John Rea, V. D. M.
Joseph Patton and Jemima Hogland, Feb. 14, 1822, by Michael Conaway, J. P.
Eli Peacock and Mary Moore, July 24, 1828, by William Wallace, V. D. M.
Eli Peacock and Sarah Hicks, Oct. 11, 1838, by Thomas Phillips, J. P.
John Piers and Jane Singer, Feb. 11, 1821, by Phineas Inskeep, J. P.
James Pierce and Mary Morton, Feb. 11, 1830, by John Heberling, J. P.
John Pearce and Sarah Maholm, July 16, 1840, by Rev. William Knox.
John Pedan and Catherine Slika, Sept. 10, 1822, by Thomas Hanna, V. D. M.
Levi Peddycoart and Lydia Worth, Feb. 23, 1822, by Thomas Patton, J. P.
Joseph Penn and Jane Hamilton, Nov. 6, 1834, by John McArthur, V. D. M.
Thomas Penn and Susana Craig, Oct. 10, 1840, by Rev. E. Smith.
Hugh Pennel and Rachel Abdil, Oct. 16, 1828, by John Rea, V. D. M.
William D. Pennell and Isabella Rea, March 10, 1818, by Thomas B. Clark, V. D. M.
Thomas Pennington and Sarah Randolph, June 19, 1826, by Rev. Simon Lauck.
Jonathan Peoples and Mahalah Norris, Oct. 19, 1826, by Thomas Lakin.
Jonathan Peoples and Easter Galbraith, Dec. 27, 1836, by David Finnicum, J. P.
Isaac Pepper and Anne Cramp, April 22, 1831, by John McArthur.
Henry Peppers and Mary Mullen, Oct. 23, 1828, by George Brown, J. P.
John Peregory and Ann Webb, April 12, 1832, by Rev. William Knox.
James Perry and Jane Smiley, Nov. 19, 1840, by James Kerr, V. D. M.
John G. Parry and Aurela Belknap, June 9, 1839, by C. E. Weirick.
Martin Perry and Margaret Wilkin, Feb. 21, 1833, by John Rea, V. D. M.
Thomas Perry and Sarah Chew, April 18, 1816, by Thomas Dickerson, J. P.
Robert Pervines and Esther Jenkins, Sept. 11, 1823, by Joseph Johnson, J. P.
Isaac Peterson and Mary Bush, Dec. 24, 1829, by Edward Talbott, J. P.
Leroy Petty and Keziah Tipton, Nov. 16, 1830, by Jesse Hooper, J. P.
Peter Petty and Betsey Heathe, Feb. 27, 1834, by George W. Bell, J. P.
Rhodun Petty and Hester Ann R. Fry, Aug. 21, 1838, by Rev. Robert Cook.
William Petty and Adeline Amelia Snider, Sept. 25, 1836, by Joseph Fry, J. P.
Jacob Pfouts and Anna W. Waters, March 10, 1835, by Lot Deming, J. P.
George K. Phillips and Mary Moodey, July 24, 1823, by Michael Conaway.
John Phillips and Eliza Gilmore, May 6, 1828, by William Taggart, V. D. M.

EARLY MARRIAGES

John Phillips and Eleanor Johnson, Nov. 19, 1831, by Rev. Jacob Lemmon.
Joseph Phillips and Jemima Johnson, May 9, 1833, by Rev. Jacob Lennaon.
Lewis Phillips and Matilda Ann Steel, May 9, 1837, by Rev. Jacob Lemmon.
Matthew H. Phillips and Susanna Dickerson, Dec. 11, 1828, by Salmon Cowles, V. D. M.
Richard Phillips and Nancy Davidson, Sept. 24, 1836, by John M. Brown, J. P.
Alexander Picken and Rachel Conaway, April 17, 1834, by William Arnold, J. P.
Alpha Pickens and Jane Anderson, Nov. 27, 1827, by Thomas Hanna, V. D. M.
William Picken and Fanny Overholts, Oct. 15, 1840, by Robert P. Simpson.
Abel Pickering and Susanna Nichols, July 15, 1833, by John Bethel, J. P.
Absalom Pickering and Susan Leinard, Feb. 24, 1831, by Lentulus Kirk, J. P.
Enis Pickering and Susanna New, Oct. 18, 1816, by John Crawford, J. P.
Evan Pickering and Nancy Lewis, Dec. 2, 1819, by Rev. James Roberts.
Jacob Pickering and Mary Nichols, March 16, 1826, by James Clements, J. P.
James Pickering and Nancy Middleton, Oct. 13, 1836, by William Taggart, V. D. M.
Joseph Pickering and Priscilla Ruby, June 10, 1815, by Rev. William Knox.
Israel Picket and Lydia Goodwin, Aug. 25, 1836, by Samuel Lewis, J. P.
Peter Picket and Elizabeth Mills, Nov. 10, 1819, by John Crawford, J. P.
Samuel Pilinger and Jane Lemastress, Jan. 14, 1819, by Robert McKee, J. P.
Samuel Pillars and Charlotte Potts, March 14, 1816, by Alexander Lee, J. P.
Thomas Pinkerton and Jane L. Price, Jan. 6, 1836, by Rev Robert Cook.
Isaac Pittinger and Harriet Myers, June 12, 1832, by Rev. D. C. Merryman.
Peter Pittinger and Jane Buchanan, July 7, 1825, by Robert Maxwell, J. P.
John Pittis and Ann Clark, June 11, 1839, by Thomas Phillips, J. P.
Tobias A. Plants and Mary E. Goodwin, July 30, 1837, by Rev. Jacob Lemmon.
William Pleasants and Margaret Alford, April 25, 1823, by John Russel, J. P.
David Paulin and Arminta Barkhurst, Feb. 3, 1825, by Rev. James Roberts.
Elias Poland and Susan Ann Ford, March 14, 1832, by John Wagner, J. P.
George Poland and Mary Gutshall, Dec. 25, 1831, by John Wagner, J. P.
George Polen and Margaret Walters, July 14, 1836, by John Gruber, J. P.
James Poland and Eliza Perry, Oct. 7, 1830, by Thomas Parkinson, J. P.
John Poland and Polly Hutchinson, July 9, 1829, by Joseph Johnson, J. P.
Jonathan Poland and Catherine Hillicosts, June 15, 1826, by Rev. Simon Lauck.
Nathaniel Polen and Margaret Cutschall, April 15, 1824, by Rev. Daniel Rahauser.
Peter Poland and Sarah Hilligas, May 10, 1830, by Thomas Phillips, J. P.
Samuel M. Poland and Unity Wilkin, May 11, 1830, by John Rea, V. D. M.
William Poland and Ann Wheeler, March 10, 1816, by Rev. M. Cole.
William Poland and Mary Stephens, Dec. 14, 1824, by Rev. James Roberts.
William Poland and Sarah Wallace, Sept. 13, 1838, by Charles Thorn.
William Pollard and Mary Miller, July 29, 1839, by Samuel Lewis, J. P.
Benjamin Pollock and Ann Norman, Jan. 28, 1838, by John Caldwell, J. P.
James Pollock and Margaret Brokaw, July 20, 1826, by George Brown, J. P.
Samuel Pollock and Fanny Wilkins, Feb. 5, 1818, by William Carrothers, J. P.
Thomas Polleck and Elizabeth Hammond, Aug. 9, 1832, by John Walker, V. D. M.
William Pollock and Frances S. Reed Thompson, May 1, 1827, by William Taggart, V. D. M.
David Porter and Terressa Stone, April 28, 1837, by William Arnold, J. P.

James Porter and Sarah Steen, Nov. 10, 1828, by William Taggart, V. D. M.
Joseph Porter and Margaret Walker, June 30, 1836, by William Arnold, J. P.
Joshua Porter and Elizabeth Rankin, May 3, 1822, by George Brown, J. P.
Nathan Porter and Susanna Nofsker, March 17, 1835, by John Gruber, J. P.
Otho Porter and Elizabeth Dusenberry, Aug. 29, 1833, by Rev. John Moffit.
Samuel Porter and Rebecca Dickerson, April 5, 1827, by Rev. James Roberts.
Samuel Porter and Eliza Cox, April 30, 1832, by Thomas Phillips, J. P.
Zachariah Porter and Mary Fivecoat, Jan. 1, 1839, by Richard Hammond, J. P.
Cornelius Post and Rachel Richison, June 11, 1816, by Martin Guilinger, J. P.
James Post and Rachel Moore, Nov. 19, 1837, by William Wyckoff, J. P.
Andrew Poulson and Martha Hines, March 24, 1819, by James McMahon.
Andrew Poulson and Susanna Garner, Dec. 24, 1840, by Rev. Jacob Lemmon.
Charles H. Paulson and Narcissa A. Kilgore, May 1, 1839, by William Taggart, V. D. M.
James J. Poulson and Mary Harrison, July 30, 1829, by John Carson, J. P.
Jehu Poulson and Elizabeth Cox, Aug. 13, 1833, by William Arnold, J. P.
John Poulson and Rachel Rogers, April 9, 1835, by Thomas Phillips, J. P.
John Powell and Mary Scoles, Nov. 16, 1820, by John Graham.
Joseph Powell and Mary Heller, April 10, 1816, by William Wyckoff, J. P.
William H. Powers and Tabitha Boles, June 8, 1840, by Joseph Clokey, V. D. M.
James Prather and Barbara Young, March 26, 1834, by John McArthur, V. D. M.
Oliver Preston and Sally Temple, June 30, 1819, by William Anderson, J. P.
Francis Price and Rosannah McGee, Dec. 30, 1840, by William Wallace, V. D. M.
Garred Price and Susannah Smith, Dec. 25, 1818, by Robert McKee, J. P.
Henry Price and Anna Hoffzgar, Feb. 16, 1837, by Rev. Alexander Biddle.
John Price and Elizabeth Heastand, Aug. 7, 1834, by Alexander Biddle.
Thomas Price and Levina Norman, March 2, 1837, by George Atkinson, J. P.
Jesse Pritchard and Jane Lacey, Oct. 9, 1825, by Donald McIntosh, V. D. M.
Thomas Pritchard and Elizabeth Spring, April 27, 1820, by John Russel, J. P.
Aaron Pugh and Mary Gear, Feb. 10, 1820, by Robert McLaughlin, J. P.
Amos Pugh and Anne Brown, Feb. 21, 1833, by Rev. Moses Scott.
Benjamin Pugh and Jane Shivers, Nov. 1, 1832, by Thomas Phillips, J. P.
Jesse Pugh and Angeline Haines, Dec. 11, 1838, by John Selby, J. P.
John Pugh and Elizabeth Crabtree, Aug. 19, 1830, by Thomas Phillips, J. P.
Ulysses Pugh and Frances Ann Suddith, May 10, 1838, by R. H. Ledwick, V. D. M.
Harlon Pyle and Eliza Sinclear, Sept. 21, 1835, by John L. Layport.
James Quinn and Rachel Moody, Dec. 21, 1824, by Robert Maxwell, J. P.
Elihu Quillen and Sarah Cree, April 28, 1836, by Rev. Robert Cook.
Joshua Quillin and Rebecca Bowles, March 8, 1827, by Thomas Lakin.
Andrew Ralston and Eleanor Paxton, Dec. 11, 1827, by William McMillen, V. D. M.
Lewis W. Ralston and Anna Darr, April 22, 1828, by John Graham.
John Ramage and Elizabeth Lafferty, Feb. 13, 1821, by Joseph Anderson.
Henry Ramer and Catherine Jones, Jan. 4, 1819, by Charles Chapman, J. P.
Benjamin Ramsey and Isabella Hanna, Feb. 1, 1821, by John Rea, V. D. M.
George Ramsey and Margaret Kyle, Oct. 13, 1825, by Thomas Hanna, V. D. M.
Hugh Ramsey and Jane Kyle, Nov. 7, 1826, by Thomas Hanna, V. D. M.
Samuel Ramsey and Lydia Barcroft, March 6, 1833, by John Rea, V. D. M.

William Ramsey and Susanna Ruby, Nov. 1, 1838, by William Knox, V. D. M.
Elias G. Randall and Margaret House, Dec. 20, 1838, by John Selby, J. P.
Enoch Randels and Peggy Williams, Oct. 10, 1816, by Charles Chapman, J. P.
Ephram Randals and Mary Swayne, April 8, 1836, by George Atkinson, J. P.
Jonathan Randolph and Isabel Cady, July 15, 1830, by John McArthur, V. D. M.
Peter Randolph and Ann Atkinson, April 3, 1836, by Thomas Parkinson, J. P.
Josiah D. Raney and Jane Clark, Feb. 1, 1815, by John Rea, V. D. M.
David Rankin and Sarah Porter, March 20, 1819, by William Wyckoff, J. P.
John Rankin and Nancy Smith, March 6, 1834, by Rev. Jacob Coon.
Thomas Rankin and Jane E. Ellis, Sept. 26, 1833, by Rev. Jacob Lemmon.
William Rankin and Christena Knight, April 22, 1813, by Archibald McElroy.
William Raredon and Elmira Gitchell, Dec. 16, 1830, by Philip Fulton, J. P.
Moses Ratlidge and Catherine Patterson, Feb. 14, 1839, by Rev. Dyas Neil.
Thomas Rathrock and Delila Luke, Aug. 21, 1840, by Samuel Lewis, J. P.
James Ravenscroft and Betsey Shuck, Dec. 31, 1816, by Thomas Fisher, J. P.
James Rea and Jane Chambers, Dec. 1, 1835, by John Rea, V. D. M.
John Rea and Sarah Daniels, May 12, 1830, by Thomas Phillips, J. P.
John Rea, and Elizabeth Hamilton, April 9, 1840, by Rev. Alexander Wilson.
Jonathan Ray and Sarah Merryman, Nov. 2, 1839, by M. F. Burkhead, J. P.
Joseph Rea and Jane McConnel Sept. 22. 1818, by Thomas B. Clark, J. P.
Levi Ray and Eliza Merryman, Feb. 27, 1840, by M. F. Burkhead, J. P.
Samuel Rea and Ruth Robinson, Jan. 2, 1823, by Rev. Salmon Cowles.
Samuel Rea and Rachel Chaney, April 11, 1840, by Isaac Crawford, J. P.
William Rea and Jane Hanna, May 23, 1837, by John Rea, V. D. M.
Henry Redick and Eleanor Stroad, Aug. 7, 1828, by Edward Talbott, J. P.
Jonathan Redick and Sarah Fulton, Feb. 23, 1819, by Desberry Johnson, J. P.
William Redick and Matilda Mintier, Feb. 11, 1819, by John Rea, V. D. M.
Andrew Reed and Jane Reed, Oct. 11, 1821, by John Rea, V. D. M.
Benjamin Reed and Rebecca Sellers, Oct. 31, 1824, by Rev. John Wagenhals.
Cyrus Reed and Lavina Kail, Nov. 2, 1837, by John Gruber, J. P.
Daniel Reed and Mary Tipton, April 20, 1829, by John Gruber, J. P.
Francis Reed and Nancy F. Farmer, April 2, 1818, by William Wyckoff, J. P.
Frederick Reed and Rachel Tedrow, Dec. 28, 1817, by Henry Kail, J. P.
George Reed and Susan Swarts, April 10, 1823, by Rev. James Roberts.
Hugh Reed and Margaret Fulton, June 10, 1830, by John McArthur, V. D. M
Jacob Reed and Christianna Shoos, April 20, 1815, by Rev. John Rinehart.
James Reed and Mary McCormick, Oct. 20, 1825, by John Rea, V. D. M.
John Read and Ellen Cunningham, Sept. 10, 1816, by John Crawford, J. P.
John Reed and Fanny Waters, Jan. 17, 1817, by Walter B. Beebe, J. P.
John Reed and Nancy Phillips, Dec. 30, 1824, by Rev. Elijah C. Stone.
John Reed and Motelena Wyant, Feb. 16, 1826, by Samuel Dunlap, J. P.
John Reed and Margaret Milligan, Feb. 16, 1832, by John McArthur, V. D. M.
Quinton Reed and Susanna West, Aug. 11, 1835, by William Arnold, J. P.
William Reed and Jane Gibson, May 15, 1823, by John Rea, V. D. M.
William Reed and Eleanor Tipton, Oct. 20, 1829, by John Gruber, J. P.
William Reed and Sarah McDowell, Sept. 22, 1836, by William Wallace.
V. D. M.
William Reed and Susanna Porter, Oct. 22, 1839, by Thomas Thompson
Amos Rees and Mary Hillis, Jan. 13. 1820, by H. H. Leavitt, J. P.
John Reeves and Henrietta Gardner, Sept. 29, 1829, by Rev. Jacob Lemmon.

John Reeves and Cela Harris, Oct. 19, 1834, by Rev. Jacob Lemmon.
Richard Reaves and Eleanor Persons, Dec. 13, 1822, by Joseph Fry, J. P.
Michael Reniker and Peggy Steffy, Aug. 28, 1821, by John Wagner, J. P.
Isaac Reynolds and Polly Chaney, Sept. 18, 1819, by Thomas Dickerson, J. P.
Joseph Rhodes and Louisa Larry, Nov. 1, 1838, by George Atkinson, J. P.
James Rice and Sarah Dehuff, Dec. 18, 1828, by Rev. Elijah C. Stone.
Stephen G. Rice and Hannah Shuck, Dec. 29, 1832, by Joseph Wolff, J. P.
John Richards and Betsey Fitzsimmons, April 5, 1836, by George W. Bell, J. P.
Edward Richardson and Catherine Wiant, Aug. 4, 1825, by John Hurless, J. P.
John Richardson and Ann Henry, April 30, 1818, by Martha Guilinger, J. P.
David Ritchey and Susan Dausey, Feb. 19, 1840, by Jacob Coon.
John Richey and Margaret McComb, June 20, 1820, by William Anderson, J. P.
Samuel Richey and Elizabeth McGee, June 21, 1832, by William Wallace, V. D. M.
Benjamin Rickey and Susan Williams, Oct. 24, 1833, by Robert Maxwell, J. P.
Daniel Rickey and Providence Shimer, Sept. 21, 1826, by Alexander Moore, J. P.
Henry Ricthard and Tena Dewalt, March 23, 1826, by John Busby, J. P.
Daniel Ridenower and Susanna Shawber, March 2, 1820, by Rev. Josomun Vinnson.
David Ridenower and Sally Shawver, April 15, 1824, by Rev. Daniel Rahauser.
James Rider and Jane Hidey, April 10, 1832, by Thomas Day, J. P.
John Ridgway and Sarah Underwood, Sept. 5, 1833, by Edward Talbott, J. P.
Paul Ridgway and Catherine Harmon, Dec. 16, 1835, by Thomas Foster.
George Rife and Sally Crosky, Oct. 29, 1829, by Rev. Elijah C. Stone.
Augustus Rigby and Catherine Tope, March 5, 1826, by John C. Huston, J. P.
George Rigg and Margaret Greenland, April 2, 1829, by Archibald McGrew, J. P.
John Rigg and Anna Fissel, Oct. 23, 1828, by Michael Conaway, J. P.
Robert Rigg and Loveice Fessel, Sept. 23, 1824, by Michael Conaway, J. P.
Robert Rigg and Margaret Moore, Aug. 25, 1829, by Michael Conaway, J. P.
George Rigel and Susanna Thomas, Feb. 13, 1817, by James Roberts.
George Riggle and Betsey Riggle, April 18, 1838, by John Wagner, J. P.
Jacob Riggle and Nancy Angel, Sept. 25, 1821, by John Wagner, J. P.
John Rigel and Sarah Miller, March 13, 1824, by Rev. John McMahon.
Abraham Riley and Jemima Hinton, March 4, 1823, by Benjamin S. Cowen, J. P.
Harrison Riley and Sarah Ann Luttle, Dec. 17, 1829, by George Brown, J. P.
John Riley and Elizabeth Faucett, Dec. 27, 1827, by Rev. William Knox.
Moses Riley and Nancy Moore, April 27, 1820, by John Russel, J. P.
Peter Riley and Sally Hevenor, April 16, 1818, by Elijah C. Stone.
William Riley and Rachel Phelps, Oct. 13, 1830, by Rev. Benjamin Wood.
Andrew S. Ripley and Eliza Jane Crosby, Oct. 25, 1832, by Thomas P. Jenkins, J. P.
Jacob Ripley and Mary Dixson, Dec. 9, 1820, by Joseph Fry, J. P.
John Ripley and Unity McBride, Feb. 22, 1821, by William Wyckoff, J. P.
William T. Ripley and Margaret Cosgrove, Dec. 8, 1831, by Thomas P. Jenkins, J. P.
Andrew Robb and Margaret McCullough, Aug. 28, 1828, by Salmon Cowles, V. D. M.
James Roberts and Elizabeth Atkinson, Feb. 28, 1833, by John McArthur, V. D. M.

John Roberts and Catherine Goodman, July 5, 1838, by John Knox, J. P.
Jonathan Roberts and Miriam Walker, July 17, 1831, by Edward Talbott, J. P.
Joseph Roberts and Mary Ann Brown, May 13, 1827, by Joseph Rea, J. P.
Joseph Robertson and Esther Crouch, Sept. 16, 1835, by John L. Grubb, J. P.
Joshua Robey and Elizabeth Powlan, March 9, 1831, by John Wagner, J. P.
Anthony Robison and Dianna Cooke, Jan. 27, 1820, by Joseph Fry, J. P.
Benjamin Robinson and Rachel Martin, May 11, 1826, by John Wagner, J. P.
Charles Robinson and Martha Denning, Jan. 9, 1818, by William Wyckoff, J. P.
Christopher Robinson and Susan Kirby, Feb. 10, 1831, by Thomas Day, J. P.
George Robison and Sally Heffling, Jan. 12, 1839, by Rev. Robert Cook.
James Robison and Mary Ann Wallace, June 9, 1836, by Rev. James Taylor.
James Robison and Jane Strong, March 16, 1837, by Rev. Richard Brown.
James Robinson and Rebecca Overhultzer, March 8, 1838, by Rev. Adam Hetsler.
John Robinson and Susan Lemaster, Jan. 1, 1829, by Rev. William Tipton.
John Robison and Jane Brown, Dec. 9, 1830, by John Russell, J. P.
Thomas Robinson and Ann Busket, Sept. 20, 1827, by John Wagner, J. P.
William L. Robinson and Prudence Huff, Feb. 6, 1822, by William Cunningham.
William Robison and Jane Dickey, April 9, 1835, by Thomas M. Granfell, J. P.
Warner Rodgers and Eliza Gregory, Sept. 26, 1816, by William Haverfield, J. P.
Barrett Rogers and Nancy Carson, May 1, 1823, by Hugh Shotwell.
Elijah Rogers and Mary Ann Poulson, Oct. 22, 1833, by Rev. William Tipton.
John Rogers and Lydia Lamaster, Sept. 28, 1815, by Charles Chapman, J. P.
Lewis Rogers and Sarah Ann Hilton, June 25, 1835, by Thomas Philips, J. P.
Lorendo D. Rogers and Jane Amanda Suddeth, May 20, 1828, by Samuel Hitchcock, J. P.
Nelson Rogers and Sarah Barcroft, Oct. 19, 1837, by John Selby, J. P.
Osbun Rogers and Mary Mehaffee, May 12, 1831, by Peter Barger, J. P.
Rowland Rogers and Mary Cummins, March 24, 1836, by Thomas Phillips, J. P.
Thomas Rogers and Anna Wilson, Nov. 2, 1826, by William Taggart, V. D. M.
William Rogers and Hannah Waters, Nov. 2, 1820, by Thomas B. Carter, J. P.
William Rogers and Nancy Burkhead, Dec. 13, 1823, by Hugh Shotwell, J. P.
William Rogers and Susan Carson, Feb. 20, 1823, by Hugh Shotwell, J. P.
William Rogers and Isabella Kelly, Feb. 19, 1835, by William Taggart, V. D. M.
William Rogers and Miriah Adams, June 21, 1838, by John Selby, J. P.
Elisha Romans and Elizabeth Knight, Dec. 10, 1840, by Thomas Phillips, J. P.
Evan Romans and Julian Adams, Nov. 18, 1833, by Alexander Clark, J. P.
Edward Romig and Elizabeth Auld, Dec. 16, 1839, by Rev. Herman J. Titze.
John Romick and Martha Ann Bonsall, Nov. 7, 1837, by Rev. Z. Ragan.
Jonas Romich and Nancy McGonagle, May 13, 1839, by Rev. John Wilson.
Gardner Rose and Ruth Coleman, Jan. 2, 1827, by John Rea, V. D. M.
Henry Rose and Rebecca Kent, Oct. 12, 1820, by Williamson Carruthers, J. P.
Hugh Rose and Julian Garner, July 1, 1828, by Jesse Hooper, J. P.
Jacob Rose and Elizabeth Throckmorton, Aug. 12, 1824, by John Rea, V. D. M.
James Rose and Lucinda Farringsworth, May, 31, 1832, by John Rea, V. D. M.
John J. Rose and Elizabeth Caves, March 14, 1839, by Samuel Skinner, J. P.
Jacob Roser and Margaret Anget, June 13, 1839, by Andrew Lynch, J. P.
Daniel Ross and Barbara Hospelhorn, Sept. 12, 1837, by Rev. James L. Russell.
Ichabod Ross and Margaret Worley, Jan. 9, 1840, by Rev. Parden Cook.
James Ross and Ann Hukill, Feb. 7, 1828, by John Rea, V. D. M.

James Ross and Jemima Hines, Jan. 8, 1839, by Charles Thorn.
John Ross and Mary Tipton, Nov. 13, 1828, by Rev. William Tipton.
Kins Ross and Nancy McMillan, Dec. 25, 1828, by Jesse Hooper, J. P.
Nathan Ross and Sophia Arnold, Oct. 18, 1815, by John Busby, J. P.
David Rouse and Agness Brown, Feb. 3, 1813, by Samuel Dunlap, J. P.
George Roush and Anna Springer, July 6, 1826, by Robert Orr, J. P.
William Rowan and Lydia Ann Bell, Sept. 7, 1837, by Levi Peddycoart, J. P.
James Rowland and Elizabeth Leinard, Feb. 5, 1829, by William Wallace, V. D. M.
John Rowland and Martha Harrison, Dec. 27, 1827, by John Carson, J. P.
John Rowlands and Ann Marshall, June 15, 1837, by Samuel Skinner, J. P.
Levi Rowlands and Mary Shivers, April 22, 1830, by Samuel Hitchcock, J. P.
William Rowland and Jane Fulton, Dec. 28, 1820, by William Wyckoff, J. P.
Hezekiah Rowles and Elizabeth Guynn, Feb. 4, 1819, by Charles Chapman, J. P.
Eli Rozin and Sarah Wardell, May 26, 1832, by Rev. William Knox.
Ezekiel Rubicam and Olive Smith, Jan. 17, 1826, by Joseph Fry, J P.
Henry Ruby and Sarah Earley, Aug. 20, 1835, by Rev. Jacob Lemmon.
Isaac Ruby and Mary Smith, Nov. 9, 1825, by Elder Daniel Limerick.
John M. Ruby and Elizabeth House, April 11, 1826, by Daniel Limerick, Elder M. E. Church.
Lewis Ruby and Sarah Johnson, July 16, 1818, by Rev. Cornelius Springer.
Thomas Ruby and Mary Gibson, July 7, 1831, by James McCullough, J. P.
William B. Ruby and Susan Landis, Dec. 19, 1831, by Rev. Jacob Lemmon.
James Rusk and Sarah McKibbon, Dec. 24, 1818, by John Rea, V. D. M.
John Russell and Matilda Ferguson, Aug. 25, 1831, by William L. Robison, J. P.
Samuel A. Russell and Mary Ann Crawford, June 12, 1839, by Rev. Thomas Hanna.
William Russell and Charlotte Waller, March 10, 1834, by Rev. William Tipton.
Daniel Rutan and Margaret Carr, Jan. 4, 1827, by Thomas Hanna, V. D. M.
John Reutan and Hannah Shivers, June 8, 1820, by B. W. Viers, J. P.
Peter Rutan and Catherine Shriver, Dec. 15, 1831, by Thomas Day, J. P.
John E. Ruth and Catherine Shaffer, April 11, 1820, by John Hurless, J. P.
William Ruth and Peggy Hurless, Oct. 5, 1837, by Robert P. Simpson, J. P.
Jacob Sadler and Mary Wilkison, March 28, 1822, by John Wagner, J. P.
Samuel Salisbury and Margaret Devenbaugh, May 7, 1818, by John Wagner, J. P.
William Saltkele and Sarah Wright, Dec. 31, 1834, by George W. Bell, J. P.
John Saltsgiver and Mary Capper, April 14, 1831, by John C. Huston, J. P.
Joseph Saltsgiver and Rebecca Elliot, Dec. 15, 1831, by Thomas Ford.
Joseph Saltsgiver and Maria Davis, April 26, 1836, by Richard Lyons, J. P.
James Sample and Cassey Britt, Aug. 23, 1827, by Rev. W. B. Evans.
Samuel Sample and Nancy Hanshier, March 16, 1831, by Edward Talbott, J. P.
William Sample and Juliana O'Rourke, Aug. 4, 1831, by Edward Talbott, J. P.
Cornelius Sanders and Ann Reynolds, Aug. 12, 1819, by Archibald McGrew, J. P.
Ezekiel Sankey and Mary McCullough, Feb. 3, 1824, by Salmon Cowles, V. D. M.
Samuel Sankey and Hannah Faroner, June 12, 1834, by Rev. Thomas Hanna.
Rugler Sargent and Sarah Beams, Jan. 2, 1840, by William Arnold, J. P.
Jacob Sarkey and Mary Yarnall, Aug. 3, 1826, by Rev. William B. Evans.
Jerry Sawyer and Dolly Simpson, Nov. 28, 1822, by Jesse Hooper, J. P.

EARLY MARRIAGES

George Sayers and Rachel Barrett, Oct. 10, 1833, by Rev. Jacob Lemmon.
John Sayler and Catherine Benedict, May 29, 1827, by John Wagner, J. P.
William Scales and Elizabeth Elliott, Nov. 23, 1826, by Joseph Rea, J. P.
Richard Scarlet and Jane Birney, Aug. 30, 1832, by William Tipton.
Alexander Schee and Alice Brindley, March 2, 1840, by Rev. William Knox.
Abraham Schoonover and Nancy Rymer, Nov. 1, 1832, by James McCollough.
Kinsey Schooley and Lydia Wright, June 1, 1837, by Rev. James C. Merriman.
Samuel Schooley and Ann Gardner, Aug. 19, 1817, by James Roberts.
Curtis W. Scoles and Elizabeth Simpson, Aug. 16, 1830, by Rev. William Knox.
Samuel Scoles and Rebecca James, Aug. 24, 1824, by George Brown, J. P.
Andrew Scott and Miche Anne Treacle, Sept. 3, 1835, by Joseph Johnson, J. P.
Charles Scott and Margaret Dodds, April 20, 1830, by Jacob Cozad, J. P.
George W. Scott and Ann Hoops, Aug. 22, 1839, by Rev. John Burns.
Jacob Scott and Hannah Wortman, Jan. 12, 1836, by David McGuire.
James Scott and Mary Foster, June 3, 1828, by John Rea, V. D. M.
James Scott and Jane Scott, May 24, 1830, by Thomas Phillips, J. P.
John Scott and Eliza Skelly, April 3, 1821, by John Rea, V. D. M.
John W. Scott and Jane Pittis, Aug. 22, 1839, by Rev. Thomas West.
Joseph Scott and Mary Croskey, Feb. 7, 1822, by John Walker, V. D. M.
Josiah Scott and Mary Lloyd, Aug. 2, 1830, by Rev. James Robertson.
Josiah Scott and Mary Jane Bingham, Nov. 26, 1833, by William Taggart, V. D. M.
Robert Scott and Catherine Scott, Oct. 11, 1839, by Rev. G. D. Kinner.
George Scripper and Jean Ferrier, Feb. 26, 1818, by William Slemmons, J. P.
Ebenezer Scroggs and Sarah Smilie, Sept. 19, 1839, by Rev. Thomas Hanna.
Enoch Sears and Sarah McMillan, Dec. 27, 1839, by Samuel Ramsey, J. P.
Ephriam Sears and Charlotte Shotwell, Nov. 23, 1815, by Charles Chapman, J. P.
Samuel Seers and Jane Pugh, Nov. 19, 1816, by James Roberts.
John W. Selby and Betsy Lion, Dec. 3, 1818, by Thomas Parkinson, J. P.
John Selby and Jane Rogers, Oct. 8, 1840, by Rev. Jacob Lemmon.
Nicholas Selby and Evelina Pugh, Nov. 9, 1837, by Thomas Phillips, J. P.
Benjamin Sell and Mary Fowler, Feb. 20, 1817, by Thomas Fisher, J. P.
Joseph Seton and Lucy Williams, Sept. 24, 1815, by Charles Chapman, J. P.
James Settle and Lydia Hancher, Dec. 11, 1835, by William Boggs, J. P.
Lemuel F. Settle and Eleanor Dewitt, May 7, 1835, by Joseph Fry, J. P.
Asa Sewell and Margaret Evans, Dec. 19, 1833, by George W. Bell, J. P.
Greenberry Sewell and Nancy Gracer, April 27, 1837, by M. F. Burkhead, J. P.
John Sewell and Jane Gilmore, Oct. 10, 1824, by Joseph Fry, J. P.
Abraham Shaffer and Margaret Blagher, May 7, 1835, by Rev. Adam Hetzler.
George Shaeffer and Margaret Saltzgiver, Nov. 25, 1823, by Rev. J. Wagenhals.
Philip Shafer and Sarah Angel, Dec. 2, 1819, by John Wagner, J. P.
Edward Shallcross and Sarah Packer, March 15, 1838, by Samuel Lewis, J. P.
George Shambaugh and Matilda Hazlett, Jan. 24, 1839, by Rev. Adam Hetzler.
Philip Shambaugh and Catherine Albaugh, Jan. 7, 1833, by Dewalt Rothacker.
John Shamel and Rachel Grewell, Aug. 19, 1836, by Thomas P. Jenkins, J. P.
Samuel Shank and Elizabeth Snedeker, Feb. 23, 1816, by Walter B. Beebe, J. P.
Stephen Shanks and Mary Ann Moore, May 24, 1827, by Rev. William B. Evans.
Ebenezer L. Shannon and Elizabeth Butler, Dec. 13, 1832, by Edward Talbott, J. P.

Isaac Shannon and Isabella Hagerty, Sept. 27, 1821, by John Rea, V. D. M.
Isaac Shannon and Sarah Stone, Jan 12, 1826, by Rev. John Rea, V. D. M.
Isaac Shannon and Rachel Reed, June 30, 1837, by Rev. Joseph Clokey.
Nathan Shannon and Martha Hagerty, Dec. 12, 1816, by John Rea, V. D. M.
Nathan Shannon and Mary Endsley, April 27, 1820, by John Rea, V. D. M.
Newton Shannon and Abigail Titus, March 19, 1816, by John Rea, V. D. M.
Wilson Shannon and Sarah Osburn, Nov. 27, 1832, by John McArthur.
Zacheus Shannon and Jemima Huff, June 16, 1822, by William Cunningham.
Benjamin Sharfick and Sarah Blue, Sept. 6, 1821, by John Wagner, J. P.
John Sharon and Matilda Havenor, Dec. 16, 1824, by Robert Orr, J. P.
William Sheren and Rachel Griffin, Dec. 28, 1826, by Robert Orr, J. P.
William Sharon and Esther Barcroft, March 3, 1835, by John Rea, V. D. M.
John Sharp and Catherine Thompson, May 15, 1832, by William Taggart, V. D. M.
Thomas Sharp and Margaret Stine, Aug. 12, 1828, by Morris Allbaugh.
William Sharpe and Elizabeth Goriet, July 14, 1836, by Rev. John Walker.
Thomas M. Shaw and Jane M. Pritchard, June 11, 1839, by Thomas Phillips, J. P.
Abraham Shawver and Caty Wilson, June 24, 1831, by John Wagner, J. P.
Jacob Shawber and Catherine Beckly, March 6, 1814, by Rev. John Rinehart.
Jacob Shawber and Barbara Harner, Dec. 22, 1816, by Rev. John Rinehart.
John Shawver and Elizabeth Shearer, Jan. 14, 1836, by D. Rothacker.
Robert Sheets and Jane C. Carson, Dec. 5, 1839, by Rev. Thomas Hanna.
James Shelby and Mary Ann Rogers, March 15, 1836, by R. Hammond, J. P.
John Shelby and Prudence Poulson, Oct. 28, 1813, by Rev. James Roberts.
Jacob Shepler and Delila Everhart, Jan. 10, 1828, by John Wagner, J. P.
Andrew Sheridan and Margaret Pillars, May 31, 1828, by Rev. Jacob Cozad.
Joshua Sheridan and Mary Dillon, Aug. 13, 1829, by Rev. Jacob Cozad.
Caleb Sherman and Mary Forkner, April 10, 1832, by Thomas Day, J. P.
Hudson Sherrow and Eleanor Mercer, Jan. 26, 1825, by Rev. Jacob Roberts.
Joel Sherwood and Mary A. Cook, Jan. 22, 1835, by George Brown, J. P.
William Sherwood and Jane McCullough, May 22, 1835, by Rev. Jacob Coon.
James Shields and Elizabeth Everhart, May 23, 1826, by William Holmes, J. P.
John Shield and Sarah Turner, Dec. 27, 1816, by William Haverfield, J. P.
William Shields and Anne Thompson, Aug. 18, 1831, by Edward Talbott, J. P.
George Shildts and Margaret Webster, July 2, 1835, by John McArthur, V. D. M.
Jacob Shiltz and Hannah Fisher, Aug. 20, 1840, by John Gruber, J. P.
John Shildtz and Mary Ann Firebaugh, Aug. 10, 1834, by Alexander Biddle.
Wesley W. Shimer and Elizabeth Wilson, Sept. 11, 1834, by Thomas Phillips, J. P.
Wesley Shimer and Sarah Bufton, Feb. 13, 1839, by John Knox, J. P.
William Shimer and Martha Bufkin, June 19, 1839, by Joseph Fry, J. P.
Thomas Shipton and Elice Crossen, April 9, 1839, by W. D. McCartney, V. D. M.
Richard Shivers and Margaret King, April 20, 1826, by Alexander Moore, J. P.
Samuel Shivers and Catherine Brown, April 11, 1833, by George W. Bell, J. P.
Thomas Shivers and Mary Morris, April 20, 1837, by Rev. Jacob Coon.
Arrison Shotwell and Mary Dickerson, Oct. 1, 1835, by William Wyckoff, J. P.
William Shotwell and Rhoda Beebe, Feb. 24, 1819, by H. H. Carith, J. P.
Barnard Shouse and Rachel Parmer, Sept. 14, 1820, by Jacob Tope, J. P.

EARLY MARRIAGES

Isaac Shover and Sally Myers, Nov. 18, 1830, by Morris Allbaugh, J. P.
Jonas Shrieve and Matilda Campbell, April 13, 1826, by Alexander Moore, J. P.
George Shriver and Catherine Harman, June 16, 1831, by Van Brown, J. P.
George Shuck and Isabila Webster, June 26, 1819, by Martin Guilinger, J. P.
John Shook and Betsey Busler, Dec. 8, 1831, by Lot Deming, J. P.
Solomon Shultz and Rachel Kenouve, Aug. 19, 1823, by John Wagner, J. P.
Daniel Shuman and Hetty Pillars, April 11, 1832, by John Huston, J. P.
George Simmons and Elizabeth Stall, April 19, 1833, by John Busby, J. P.
Henderson Simmons and Cena Mills, May 23, 1833, by William Arnold, J. P.
Isaiah Simmons and Rachel Arbaugh, March 3, 1826, by James Manning.
John Simmons and Anne Longshore, Jan. 7, 1830, by Rev. Jacob Lemmon.
John Simmons and Sarah Chaney Feb. 16, 1832, by Thomas Phillips, J. P.
William Simmons and Elizabeth Allbaugh, March 13, 1820, by B. W. Viers, J. P.
George Simonton and Lydia Laymaster, July 4, 1818, by Robert McKee, J. P.
Alexander Simpson and Eliza Evans, April 4, 1826, by James Smith, J. P.
James Simpson and Mary Noble, June 26, 1836, by James Evans, J. P.
John Simpson and Margaret Law, Dec. 26, 1839, by Rev. J. K. McCue.
Matthew Simpson and Anna Wright, Sept. 12, 1820, by John Conaway, J. P.
Matthew Simpson and Susan Orr, April 19, 1827, by Rev. William Knox.
Robert P. Simpson and Asenath Fowler, Aug. 9, 1832, by Elijah C. Stone.
Thomas Simpson and Nancy McIlroy, Nov. 25, 1819, by Michael Conaway, J. P.
Thomas Simpson and Rosanna McMullans, Dec. 24, 1835, by William Wallace, V. D. M.
James Singer and Tacy Goodwin, July 29, 1838, by Samuel Lewis, J. P.
John Singer and Hannah Goodwin, Feb. 27, 1833, by Edward Talbott, J. P.
Thomas Singer and Nancy Woolcord, Nov. 3, 1836, by Samuel Lewis, J. P.
Albert Singhaus and Deborah Busby, Feb. 6, 1838, by William Arnold, J. P.
John Sisler and Elizabeth Hendricks, April 28, 1835, by Richard Lyons, J. P.
Isaac Skeels and Harriett Belknap, May 13, 1817, by William Dixon.
John Skelly and Esther Hanna, Dec. 23, 1834, by John Rea, V. D. M.
Philip Skinner and Mary Ann Collins, March 2, 1826, by Benjamin S. Cowan, J. P.
John Slemmons and Ruth Merrel, June 11, 1840, by Rev. Robert Brown.
Samuel Slemmons and Susanna Osburn, Jan. 21, 1829, by John McArthur, V. D. M.
Matthew Sloan and Eliza Grimes, June 24, 1830, by Rev. Thomas Hanna.
Jacob Smidley and Lydia Shook, Oct. 27, 1831, by Lot Deming, J. P.
James Smiley and Margaret Cone, Oct. 2, 1837, by William Taggart, V. D. M.
Aaron Smith and Margaret House, May 14, 1823, by Rev. Curtis Goddard.
Alexander Smith and Jane Lyons, Jan. 13, 1813, by John Rea, V. D. M.
Alexander Smith and Rebecca Smith, March 5, 1837, by Rev. Benjamin Wood.
Amos Smith and Mary Ann Ford, Oct. 22, 1839, by John Knox, J. P.
Benjamin C. Smith and Jane B. Cartnell, Jan. 11, 1820, by Rev. James Roberts.
Culbert Smith and Jane Anderson, Nov. 13, 1834, by John McArthur, V. D. M.
Culbert Smith and Jane Anderson, Nov. 22, 1834, by Joseph Johnson, J. P.
Daniel Smith and Ziporah Orr, Nov. 23, 1837, by William Taggart, V. D. M.
David Smith and Rachel Busby, May 21, 1818, by Robert McKee, J. P.
Enoch Smith and Damaris Edwards, Aug. 14, 1828, by Thomas P. Jenkins, J. P.
Ephriam Smith and Elizabeth Parkison, Nov. 24, 1818, by John Rea, V. D. M.
Francis Smith and Edith Markee, Aug. 5, 1824, by Thomas Hurless, J. P.

George Smith and Susanna Baker, Feb. 12, 1818, by Walter B. Beebe, J. P.
George Smith and Elizabeth Groves, Dec. 24, 1818, by John Crawford, J. P.
George Smith and Pratty Dodds, Nov. 16, 1820, by Thomas Patton, J. P.
George Smith and Rachel Eaton, Aug. 21, 1823, by Archibald McElroy.
George B. Smith and Mary Emline Pritchard, March 3, 1836, by Samuel Skinner, J. P.
Henry Smith and Elizabeth Keefer, Oct. 18, 1815, by John Busby, J. P.
Henry K. Smith and Elizabeth Dorsey, April 10, 1836, by Rev. Cornelius D. Battelle.
Isaiah Smith and Elizabeth McLenahan, Jan. 14, 1830, by George Brown, J. P.
Jacob Smith and Elizabeth Guttery, Sept. 23, 1824, by Rev. John Crom.
James Smith and Mary Brown, Nov. 21, 1817, by Thomas B. Clark, J. P.
James Smith and Elizabeth Cook, Feb. 23, 1832, by George W. Bell, J. P.
James Smith and Elizabeth Braden, March 10, 1835, by Rev. Edward H. Taylor.
Jesse Smith and Susanna Tipton, May 11, 1825, by Joseph Fry, J. P.
Joel Smith and Susan Conaway, Dec. 31, 1835, by John McArthur, V. D. M.
John Smith and Sarah McFee, March 12, 1821, by Rev. James Roberts.
John Smith and Caty Bair, Oct. 15, 1821, by Rev. Michael Harmon.
John Smith and Sarah Beall, April 24, 1834, by John McArthur, V. D. M.
Joseph Smith and Rebecca Murry, May 14, 1816, by William Haverfield, J. P.
Joseph D. Smith and Louisa Hefling, March 26, 1818, by Rev. Cornelius Springer.
Joseph Smith and Lydia Reeves, Dec. 1, 1825, by Joseph Fry, J. P.
Martin B. Smith and Rebecca Welling, Feb. 8, 1838, by Rev. James Drummond.
Nathan W. Smith and Maria Waits, Nov. 15, 1825, by John Rea, V. D. M.
Nathaniel Smith and Abiah W. Merrill, Aug. 11, 1831, by Rev. Jacob Lemmon.
Samuel Smith and Ruth Ford, Oct. 18, 1838, by David G. McGuire, J. P.
Samuel Smith and Mary Gibson, Oct. 28, 1838, by Aaron Conaway, J. P.
Silas Smith and Nancy Jones, May 26, 1831, by Samuel Skinner, J. P.
Thomas J. Smith and Dorcas Welling, Jan. 19, 1830, by Thomas M. Hudson.
Washington Smith and Hannah Ramage, Feb. 18, 1839, by William Wallace, V. D. M.
William Smith and Sarah Salsbuary, May 2, 1824, by John Wagner, J. P.
William Smith and Nancy Burwell, Aug. 11, 1825, by Rev. William Wallace.
William P. Smith and Margaret Parker, Aug. 31, 1826, by Alexander Moore, J. P.
William Smith and Susanna Huff, Sept. 17, 1829, by Rev. Adam Hetzler.
William Smith and Catherine Naragon, Feb. 16, 1832, by John Wagner, J. P.
Philip Smithley and Polly Cook, Oct. 24, 1833, by David Bower, J. P.
Barton Smoot and Hannah Doney, Dec. 31, 1829, by George Brown, J. P.
John Smoot and Elizabeth Hendershott, Nov. 17, 1825, by George Brown, J. P.
Nathan Smoot and Elizabeth Helm, Oct. 8, 1822, by George Brown, J. P.
Henry S. Sneary and Susanna Minnick, April 13, 1837, by Adam Hetzler.
Jacob Sneary and Mary Turney, Aug. 3, 1830, by John Gruber, J. P.
William Snee and Ann Spirtchel July 3, 1839, by C. E. Weirick.
Adam Snider and Catherine Shuess, June 20, 1822, by John Wagner, J. P.
Adam Snider and Margaret Harner, April 24, 1823, by John Wagner, J. P.
Adam Snider and Polly Angle, Dec. 20, 1838, by Andrew Lynch, J. P.
Henry Snider and Hannah Miller, March 26, 1820, by John Wagner, J. P.
John Snider and Lydia Bennett, Feb. 8, 1818, by Walter B. Beebe, J. P.

EARLY MARRIAGES

John A. Snyder and Christina Copeland, Jan. 22, 1835, by John McArthur, V. D. M.
Samuel Snider and Rachel Moore, Oct. 30, 1838, by Rev. Thomas Hanna.
David Snodgrass and Catherine Phillips, Dec. 20, 1838, by Rev. Thomas Hanna.
George Snoutagle and Peggy Mundole, March 17, 1825, by Donald McIntosh, V. D. M.
John Sparks and Mary Bair, Dec. 2, 1830, by Morris Allbaugh, J. P.
John Speck and Margaret Spiker, June 8, 1837, by Rev. James Merryman.
John Speedy and Christena Ann McMasters, Nov. 1, 1832, by Rev. James Robertson.
John Speer and Mary Crozier, June 7, 1827, by Jacob Tope, J. P.
David E. Spencer and Margaret Ferrell, Oct. 1, 1840, by Rev. William Knox.
James Spencer and Susan Shivers, April 2, 1820, by Thomas C. Carter, J. P.
Joel Spencer and Michael Ridgway, June 16, 1832, by Rev. Jacob Lemmon.
Joseph Spencer and Biddy Archbold, Nov. 18, 1817, by William Anderson, J. P.
Joseph G. Spencer and Mary Bryan, Jan. 17, 1833, by Philip Fulton, J. P.
Christopher Spiker and Ary Carens, Feb. 24, 1825, by Alexander Moore, J. P.
Christopher Spiker and Nancy Lukens, Jan. 1, 1832, by Robert Pittis, J. P.
Jacob Spiker and Juliann Hanna, May 1, 1830, by Thomas McCleary.
Philip Spiker and Rebeckah Makee, Oct. 27, 1814, by William Knox.
Jesse Sponsler and Betsey Rymer, Dec. 29, 1836, by John M. Brown, J. P.
John Spray and Betsey Fowler, Dec. 12, 1822, by Rev. Elijah C. Stone.
Charles Sprenkel and Sarah Neff, Sept. 19, 1826, by John Wagner, J. P.
Frederick Spring and Rachel Horn, Oct. 11, 1838, by Samuel Skinner, J. P.
John Spring and Margaret Williams, Aug. 27, 1818, by James Roberts.
John Spring and Nancy Ferguson, Sept. 7, 1834, by William Wyckoff, J. P.
Jacob Springer and Peggy Albaugh, Jan. 24, 1816, by Martin Guilinger.
John Springer and Margaret Salmons, Aug. 19, 1830, by John Gruber, J. P.
Levi Springer and Mary Hendricks, Dec. 11, 1828, by Robert Orr, J. P.
Samuel Springer and Elizabeth Kennedy, Nov. 29, 1832, by Elder James Garrison.
William Springer and Sarah Dewel, Aug. 1, 1815, by Martin Guilinger, J. P.
John Sproul and Susan Geary, July 10, 1832, by William Wallace, V. D. M.
William Sproul and Mary Young, April 30, 1840, by James Kerr, V. D. M.
Richard Spurrier and Amy Barret, Oct. 20, 1831, by William Arnold, J. P.
Samuel Spurrier and Mary Worrall, March 13, 1828, by Rev. James Roberts.
Warner Spurrier and Mary Hoops, Oct. 11, 1827, by Rev. James Roberts.
Elijah Staats and Ann Baker, Sept 12, 1836, by Rev. Jacob Lemmon.
Abraham Stall and Elizabeth Grove, March 14, 1828, by John Wagner, J. P.
John Stall and Mary Ann Condo, March 29, 1832, by William Arnold, J. P.
William Stall and Susa Firebaugh, Sept. 15, 1816, by Martin Guilinger, J. P.
William Stall and Susanna Knagey, Feb. 10, 1829, by Isaac Allen, J. P.
George Stallsmith and Elizabeth Springer, Nov. 6, 1832, by John Gruber, J. P.
Charles Staples and Margaret Truzle, May 4, 1819, by Michael Harmon.
Charles H. Staples and Mary Suck, April 14, 1836, by Rev. Adam Hetzler.
Horatio St. Clair and Ann Hickey, Oct. 29, 1828, by Rev. Jacob Lemmon.
Israel St. Clair and Hannah Morris, Oct. 12, 1837, by Samuel Lewis, J. P.
Andrew S. Steel and Elizabeth Wellis, May 10, 1835, by Joseph Fry, J. P.
Jacob Steel and Mary Ann Kirby, Sept. 27, 1835, by George Brown, J. P.
James Steel and Susanna Norman, Nov. 25, 1824, by Isaac Allen, J. P.

James Steel and Susannah Tayson, March 7, 1837, by John Rea, V. D. M.
Samuel Steel and Rebecca Kirby, Sept. 20, 1838, by Matthew H. Phillips, J. P.
Elias Steffy and Susanna Wiand, March 5, 1839, by John Gruber, J. P.
George Steffy and Sary Wagner, March 27, 1827, by Rev. Jacob Winters.
Jacob Steinman and Susanna Muntz, July 5, 1821, by John Wagner, J. P.
William Steen and Mary Gibney, Dec. 11, 1823, by Hugh Shotwell, J. P.
John Steeves and Eliza Girt, May 2, 1839, by Rev. Adam Hetzler.
David Stephens and Elizabeth Delany, June 15, 1813, by John Wiley, J. P.
Hezekiah Stephens and Elizabeth Clow, Nov. 13, 1815, by James Roberts.
Jonathan Stephen and Betsey Salmon, Feb. 24, 1825, by J. R. Kirkpatrick, J. P.
Owen Stevens and Anne Chambers, Nov. 15, 1838, by Charles Thorn.
Robert Stephens and Ann Walker, Feb. 22, 1821, by Rev. James Roberts.
John Stevenson and Mary Ann Kinney, Dec. 30, 1829, by Edward Talbott, J. P.
Andrew Stewart and Mary Ann Snider, May 31, 1840, by Rev. Robert Cook.
Christopher Stewart and Magdalene Fulk, May 17, 1832, by Rev. Adam Hetzler.
Ephron P. Stewart and Mary Ann Rigg, April 5, 1832, by Lot Deming, J. P.
George Stewart and Mary Berrick, May 16, 1822, by John Wagner, J. P.
James Stewart and Jane Patterson, Feb. 6, 1834, by John McArthur, V. D. M.
Jesse Stewart and Rebecca Haines, Oct. 7, 1831, by William Arnold, J. P.
Joseph Stewart and Jane Thompson, June 19, 1837, by John McArthur, V. D. M.
William Stewart and Mary Sche, April 18, 1837, by John Graham.
John Stiers and Cinthia Holmes, Jan. 11, 1821, by John Graham.
Andrew Stinson and Elizabeth Moorehead, Aug. 30, 1821, by John Rea, V. D. M.
Elias W. Stone and Tabitha Garven, March 31, 1831, by Rev. William Wallace.
Elijah C. Stone and Mary Suddeth, Dec. 12, 1822, by John Graham.
Lemuel Stone and Catherine McCormick, March 20, 1838, by William Wallace, V. D. M.
Samuel R. Stone and Mary Hanna, March 1, 1831, by John Rea, V. D. M.
Solomon Stone and Catherine Albaugh, Aug. 10, 1819, by B. W. Veirs, J. P.
Frederick Stonebreaker and Fanny Bair, Dec. 5, 1819, by Rev. John Brown.
Jacob Stonebrook and Agnes Markley, Aug. 25, 1825, by John Wagner, J. P.
Jacob Stoner and Honor Snider, April 26, 1838, by David Power, J. P.
John Stracher and Hannah England, Sept. 27, 1818, by Archibald McGrew, J. P.
John Stradling and Sarah Gray, Jan. 12, 1832, by Edward Talbott, J. P.
George Straughsbaugh and Mary Elizabeth Smith, Aug. 22, 1839, by James Kerr, V. D. M.
Peter Strausbaugh and Sophia Grim, April 4, 1833, by Dewalt Rothacker.
William Strawsbaugh and Jane Busby, March 6, 1840, by William Arnold, J. P.
Daniel Strayer and Anna Knagey, May 14, 1823, by Rev. John Crom.
John Striker and Eliza Beadle, Sept. 4, 1832, by Charles Fawcett, J. P.
Richard Stringer and Elizabeth Caren, July 14, 1829, by Rev. John Crom.
William Stringer and Isabella Ferguson, March 27, 1839, by John Rea, V. D. M.
James Stroad and Sarah Parks, April 21, 1825, by Joseph Fry, J. P.
James Strong and Elizabeth Wilkin, Nov. 1, 1832, by John Rea, V. D. M.
John Strong and Sarah Thompson Jan. 24, 1833, by Samuel Skinner, J. P.
William Stroud and Warnetta Houser, March 5, 1836, by John McArthur, V. D. M.
Mordecai Stubbins and Mary Spear, Nov. 21, 1833, by Thomas Phillips, J. P.
George Stull and Mary Albaugh, Aug. 10, 1815, by Martin Guilinger, J. P.

Philip Stull and Catherine Fisher, Feb. 10, 1831, by John Gruber, J. P.
Elias Sudduth and Margaret Garrett, Aug. 15, 1832, by Rev. Benjamin Wood.
Elias Sudduth and Nancy Mills, Aug. 21, 1838, by Samuel Skinner, J. P.
John Summers and Rosanna Turner, April 19, 1838, by William Arnold, J. P.
Isaac Suthard and Agnes Lee, Dec. 16, 1830, by Jesse Hooper, J. P.
Joseph Swallow and Mary Johnson, Nov. 15, 1838, by Charles Thorn.
John Swany and Julia Ann Harris, July 16, 1818, by Daniel David, J. P.
Timothy Swaney and Susan P. Fry, Feb. 17, 1820, by Joseph Fry, J. P.
William Swaney and Margaret Denning, Feb. 18, 1826, by Joseph Fry, J. P.
Johan C. Swangel and Elizabeth Stroup, Jan. 3, 1833, by Joseph Wolff, J. P.
John Swanzel and Agnes Sudduth, Nov. 21, 1839, by John Selby, J. P.
Burd Swagirt and Rachel Brannon, Oct. 30, 1822, by John McMahon.
Elisha Swiger and Mary Eames, June 14, 1820, by William Carrothers, J. P.
Lewis Swigert and Sarah Ames, Jan. 1, 1824, by John Wagner, J. P.
Joseph Swigerts and Caty Eames, Aug. 2, 1821, by Williamson Carrothers, J. P.
Jacob Swolley and Catherine Smith, Aug. 5 1827, by James Manning.
Elijah Swords and Elizabeth Ross, Jan. 10, 1821, by Joseph Fry, J. P,
David Taggart and Mary Bradford, Dec. 29, 1840, by Rev. Thomas Hanna.
James Taggart and Eliza Kernaghan, April 10, 1832, by William Taggart, V. D. M.
James Taggart and Anne Craig, March 12, 1835, by John McArthur, V. D. M.
John Taggart and Margaret Gray, Jan. 8, 1835, by John McArthur, V. D. M.
William Taggart and Betsey Kyle, April 22, 1835, by Rev. Thomas Hanna.
James Tallman and Julian Cooper, Dec. 27, 1836, by Rev. C. D. Battelle.
Dr. Benjamin Tappan and Vella Stanton, June 8, 1838, by William Taggart, V. D. M.
John Tarbert and Sarah Ann Dugan, Jan. 12, 1837, by William Wallace, V. D. M.
Peter Tarbert and Margaret Sands, April 27, 1837, by John Chalfan, J. P.
Robert Tarbut and Marie Lazure, July 6, 1832, by Rev. Jacob Coon.
Daniel Taw and Delila Shilts, Feb. 13, 1840, by David Bowers, J. P.
Abraham Taylor and Mary Warner, June 22, 1833, by Rev. Adam Hetzler.
John Taylor and Isabel Ferrell, June 9, 1830, by John Graham.
Robert Taylor and Ann Ferrell, Feb. 12, 1829, by Samuel Hitchcock, J. P.
Thomas Taylor and Agness Haverfield, Feb. 10, 1834, by William Taggart, V. D. M.
William P. S. Taylor and Sarah Barr, March 17, 1822, by James McMahon.
Curtis W. Teator and Mary Essford, Sept. 5, 1830, by Robert Pittis, J. P.
Enoch Tedrow and Julian Bricker, Nov. 10, 1836, by John Wagner, J. P.
George Tedrow and Betsey Hardsock, Nov. 4, 1826, by John Wagner, J. P.
Jacob Teets and Margaret McMillan, Sept. 19, 1839, by Samuel Ramsey, J. P.
Peter Teet and Margaret Milliken, March 25, 1830, by George Brown, J. P.
Stephen Teets and Jane McMullen, April 12, 1838, by Samuel Ramsey, J. P.
Nathaniel Templeton and Nancy Parker, March 23, 1837, by John M. Brown, J. P.
Simon Tewalt and Elizabeth Lewis, June 15, 1818, by William Carrothers, J. P.
Isaac Thomas, Jr., and Elizabeth Dickerson, Dec. 20, 1822, by Rev. James Roberts
John Thomas and Eliza Jane Turner, Jan. 23, 1836, by Rev. Benjamin Wood.
Joseph S. Thomas and Martha B. Olmsted, March 12, 1840, by James Kerr, V. D. M.

Liverton Thomas and Mary Ann Glendon, Nov. 25, 1834, by William Wallace, V. D. M.
Miller Thomas and Mary Maffit, March 4, 1836, by Rev. James C. Taylor.
Thomas Thomas and Mary Doney, Sept. 24, 1835, by Rev. Benjamin Wood.
Andrew Thompson and Jane Sloan, April 11, 1832, by John McArthur, V. D. M.
David Thompson and Sarah Rea, Feb. 21, 1832, by Rev. John C. Tidball.
Eli Thompson and Sally Sell, Feb. 12, 1829, by Morris Albaugh, J. P.
George W. Thompson and Eliza Huffman, March 31, 1836, by Robert Simpson, J. P.
James Thompson and Mary Koker, Sept. 25, 1823, by John Hurless, J. P.
John Thompson and Mary Devenbaugh, April 28, 1825, by J. R. Kirkpatrick, J. P.
John Thompson and Elizabeth Baker, Sept. 27, 1831, by Rev. David Merryman.
John G. Thompson and Mary Dunlap, March 23, 1837, by John McArthur, V. D. M.
Joseph Thompson and Elizabeth Manly, July 5, 1831, by John Rea, V. D. M.
Richard Thompson and Jane Polen, March 20, 1832, by John Wagner, J. P.
Samuel Thompson and Mary Valentine, March 16, 1824, by Rev. John McMahon.
Thomas Thompson and Rebecca Brown, Dec. 31, 1838, by Rev. James Drummond.
Thomas Thompson and Isabell Edie, July 16, 1840, by W. D. McCartney, V. D. M.
William Thompson and Mary Shields, Dec. 30, 1830, by William Arnold, J. P.
Zachariah Thompson and Priscilla Albaugh, Jan. 15, 1822, by B. W. Viers, J. P.
Jodiah Thorn and Rachel White, Oct. 25, 1825, by Silvanus Lamb, J. P.
John Tice and Polly Merrill, Nov. 1, 1827, by Rev. Jacob Lemmon.
Abraham Timmons and Martha Dent, April 18, 1816, by Charles Chapman, J. P.
Forney Timmons and Elizabeth Lacy, June 11, 1839, by William Arnold, J. P.
Frederick Timmons and Eliza Lacy, Dec. 16, 1828, by Rev. William Knox.
Joseph Tingley and Hannah Neill, Aug. 11, 1816, by Paul Preston.
Henry Tipton and Miscinda Kail, Nov. 6, 1834, by John Gruber, J. P.
John Tipton and Christianna Tanner, April 8, 1818, by William Wyckoff, J. P.
Joshua Tipton and Jane McConkey, Oct. 13, 1836, by James Endsley, J. P.
Josiah Tipton and Catherine Norris, April 1, 1817, by Williamson Carrothers.
Miles Tipton and Susan Ross, March 24, 1831, by John McArthur, V. D. M.
Shadrach Tipton and Mehala Petty, Oct. 20, 1829, by Jesse Hooper, J. P.
Sylvester Tipton and Mary Bliss, June 29, 1830, by Thomas McCleary.
Sylvester Tipton and Naomi Hanna, Dec. 8, 1836, by M. B. Lukins, J. P.
William Tipton and Patience Pugh, Feb. 24, 1818, by James Roberts.
William Tipton and Amelia Thompson, March 23, 1826, by Rev. William Tipton.
William Tipton and Catherine Gregory, Dec. 17, 1829, by Joseph Johnson, J. P.
William Tipton and Orpah Bond, Nov. 20, 1834, by William Arnold, J. P.
William Tipton and Jane McKiterick, March 26, 1839, by W. D. McCartney, V. D. M.
John Titus and Letty Baxter, Sept. 12, 1815, by Charles Chapman, J. P.
Uriah Titus and Eliza Kidwell, May 16, 1833, by Rev. Moses Scott.
George Todd and Jane Williamson, Nov. 15, 1827, by William Wallace, V. D. M.
James Todd and Jane Smith, Nov. 14, 1822, by John Rea, V. D. M.
John A. Todd and Mary Love, Aug. 16, 1830, by William Wallace, V. D. M.

EARLY MARRIAGES

Robert Todd and Martha Auld, Aug. 31, 1824, by Thomas Hanna, V. D. M.
Cornelius Toland and Sarah Crumby, Jan. 24, 1832, by Edward Talbott, J. P.
James Tomlinson and Mary Poulson, Jan. 10, 1825, by John Graham.
James Tomlinson and Margaret Cope, Sept. 30, 1830, by Edward Talbott, J. P.
Charles Toner and Martha Riley, Dec. 29, 1819, by Peter Johnson, J. P.
John Tool and Priscilla Gregory, June 14, 1824, by Thomas R. Ruckle.
Thomas Tool and Matilda Parmer, April 7, 1831, by Philip Fulton, J. P.
Jacob Tope and Catherine Kail, Oct. 17, 1822, by Jacob Tope, J. P.
John Tope and Mary Everly, Nov. 24, 1821, by Robert McLaughlin, J. P.
Stephen Tope and Jemima Kail, Sept. 19, 1824, by Jacob Tope, J. P.
Matthew Torrence and Judia Hess, Dec. 11, 1821, by B. W. Veirs, J. P.
James Townsend and Mary Allen Trover, July 2, 1837, by Samuel Lewis, J. P.
Seneca Townsend and Eliza Downey, Oct. 28, 1830, by Philip Fulton, J. P.
Edward Treakle and Eleanor Hinton Dec. 22, 1831, by James Miller, J. P.
James Treacle and Lina Anders, Aug. 3, 1826, by Alexander Moore, J. P.
Nathan Treacle and Polly Auld, March 27, 1818, by William Wyckoff, J. P.
Samuel Tribby and Fanney Yost, June 22, 1818, by James Roberts.
Philip Trine and Jane Knox, Oct. 15, 1833, by Rev. Aurora Callender.
Alexander Trotter and Elizabeth Shriver, Jan. 17, 1839, by Andrew Lynch, J. P.
John True and Jane Dalby, Dec. 25, 1836, by David Bower, J. P.
John Trusal and Fanny Little, Dec. 26, 1826, by Rev. Samuel Briggs.
Abisha Turner and Priscilla Pickering, Aug. 27, 1825, by John Russel, J. P.
Allen G. Turner and Margaret T. Kennedy, Sept. 7, 1837, by John Rea, V. D. M.
Daniel Turner and Jane Hogg, Nov. 20, 1817, by Daniel David, J. P.
Ellbridge Turner and Elizabeth Johnson, Nov. 1, 1821, by George Brown, J. P.
Henry L. Turner and Julian Sharp, July 26, 1835, by Rev. Benjamin Wood.
Isaac Turner and Rachel Poulson, Oct. 6, 1833, by Rev. Jacob Lemmon.
James Turner and Jane Holmes, Aug. 23, 1834, by Thomas McClintock, J. P.
Joab Turner and Ary Johnson, April 4, 1822, by George Brown, J. P.
Otho Williams Turner and Mary Scott, Dec. 31, 1835, by William Wallace, V. D. M.
Solomon Turner and Elizabeth Porter, Jan. 12, 1832, by Rev. John Moffit.
Sterling Turner and Rebecca Turner, Aug. 24, 1819, by Abriam Johnson, J. P.
Jacob Turney and Rachel Lyle, May 28, 1835, by David Finnicum, J. P.
Jonas Turney and Elizabeth Carpenter, May 8, 1836, by John Gruber, J. P.
Solomon Turney and Barbara Ann Zollars, June 3, 1831, by John Gruber, J. P.
John Turnpaugh and Maria Rogers, Aug. 12, 1824, by Isaac Allen, J. P.
John Tweedy and Elizabeth Bosley, Dec. 29, 1836, by John Wagner, J. P.
Lewis Twigg and Susan Lindsey, June 23, 1831, by George Brown, J. P.
John Twinam and Hannah Whann, June 5, 1828, by Salmon Cowles, V. D. M.
Thomas Underhill and Elizabeth Wright, June 15, 1826, by Michael Conaway, J. P.
James Updegraff and Motlena Manneck, Nov. 16, 1821, by B. W. Veirs, J. P.
John Updegraff and Magdeleny Smithly, Aug. 8, 1833, by Rev. Adam Hetzler.
Henry Urick and Nancy Carpenter, Jan. 6, 1831, by John Gruber, J. P.
John Urquhart, and Mary Holmes, Feb. 18, 1819, by Thomas Dickerson, J. P.
Moses Urquehart and Ann Hanna, July 17, 1823, by John Rea, V. D. M.
Harrison Utterback and Harriet Fincer, Nov. 26, 1833, by George W. Bell, J. P.
James Utterback and Leana Blackwell, Dec. 31, 1835, by M. F. Burkhead.
Robert Utterback and Matilda Hilton, Nov. 7, 1837, by M. F. Burkhead, J. P.

Isaac Vail and Mary Fulton, Nov. 14, 1833, by Rev. Jacob Coon.
Absalom Valentine and Susanna Worley, July 1, 1830, by William Tipton.
Elijah Van Buskirk and Margaret Lyons, Nov. 26, 1840, by Richard Brown.
John Vanceler and Elizabeth Swegirt, April 4, 1822, by John Wagner, J. P.
Jacob Vandegraff and Betsey Hucle, Aug. 15, 1816, by Walter B. Beebe, J. P.
Rezin Vandegraft and Abagail Tedrow, Nov. 14, 1833, by William Arnold, J. P.
Jesse Vandergrifft and Sophia Bricker, March 17, 1836, by John Gruber, J. P.
Bethuel Vandike and Hannah Vankirk, April 21, 1831, by Jacob Tope, J. P.
Peter Vandoluh and Nancy Shotwell, Sept. 28, 1815, by Samuel G. B. Berryhill, J. P.
Azariah Vanhorn and Elizabeth McClary, March 16, 1818, by Thomas Parkinson, J. P.
Isaac Vanhorn and Elizabeth Gilbert, Nov. 27, 1817, by Walter B. Beebe, J. P.
Jacob Vanhorn and Casander Batty, Feb. 8, 1830, by Rev. James Robertson.
John Vanhorn and Mary Rose, March 22, 1821, by John Rea, V. D. M.
Samuel Vanhorn and Elizabeth Minord, Sept. 2, 1823, by Rev. John Crom.
Samuel Vanhorn and Sophia Minard, Oct. 19, 1824, by John Hurless. J. P.
Thomas Vanhorn and Harriet Richards, Nov. 24, 1821, by Robert McLaughlin, J. P.
Henry Vansickle and Mary Dewitt, Sept. 29, 1832, by Thomas P. Jenkins, J. P.
Levi Vansickle and Sarah Lawyers, Sept. 15, 1831, by Thomas P. Jenkins, J. P.

Samuel Vansickle and Elizabeth Reeves, Sept. 12, 1833, by Rev. Jacob Lemmon.
Michael Vanvleara and Phebe Crom, Oct. 15, 1820, by William Haverfield, J. P.
Ephriam Vasbinder and Maria Buchanan, Sept. 17, 1833, by John McArthur, V. D. M.
George H. Veirs and Margaret Robison, April 13, 1832, by Rev. Jacob Coon.
John Veirs and Rebecca Salsbury, Sept. 23, 1824, by John Wagner, J. P.
Edward Veneman and Fanny Switezer, Jan. 26, 1835, by George W. Bell, J. P.
George C. Vincent and Margaret Walker, Sept. 10, 1838, by Rev. Thomas Hanna.
James Vincent and Eliza Jane Cranch, Sept. 19, 1839, by John Rea, V. D. M.
Thomas C. Vincent and Jane Macurdy, Aug. 24, 1820, by John Rea, V. D. M.
Archibald Virtue and Elizabeth Conaway, Feb. 1, 1821, by Robert Maxwell, J. P.
D. Jacob Vorhes and Miss Mary Welch, Dec. 24, 1829, by John Rea, V. D. M.
John Voshel and Nancy Roby, Feb. 11, 1840, by Levi Peddycoart, J. P.
David Waddle and Uthamia Garret, Jan. 12, 1832, by Rev. Benjamin Wood.
Robert Wade and Elizabeth McCarty, Sept. 21, 1840, by Rev. William L. Baldwin.
Nimrod Wagers and Sarah Richey, July 5, 1832, by William Wallace, V. D. M.
Richard Wagers and Sarah Mayes, Aug. 30, 1832, by George W. Bell, J. P.
Daniel Wagner and Polly Brecker, June 14, 1835, by John Gruber, J. P.
George Wagner and Christiana Hiseler, March 29, 1821, by John Wagner, J. P.
Henry Wagner and Susanna Able, Aug. 11, 1829, by John Gruber, J. P.
John Wagner and Peggy Hosterman, Aug. 7, 1823, by William Holmes, J. P.
John Wagner and Molly Saylor, April 27, 1827, by Rev. Jacob Winters.
John Wagner and Anna Johnson, March 18, 1830, by Robert Pittis, J. P.
James Wagstaff and Eve Ross, Sept. 23, 1817, by William Taggart, V. D. M.
John Wagstaff and Isabella Turner, Jan. 17, 1828, by Samuel Hitchcock, J. P.

Joseph Wagstaff and Elizabeth Williams, March 12, 1818, by William Taggart.
Robert Wagstaff and Sarah Duncan, March 15, 1831, by William Taggart, V. D. M.
Robert R. Wait and Sally Staats, March 12, 1822, by Joseph Fry, J. P.
William Wallcutt and Anna Aimes, Sept. 2, 1832, by John Wagner, J. P.
George Walker and Ruth Park, Dec. 26, 1822, by Rev. Elijah C. Stone.
Jacob Walker and Nancy Norman, March 13, 1821, by Rev. James Roberts.
John Walker and Agnes Walker, Jan. 28, 1819, by John Walker, J. P.
John Walker and Margaret Lion, April 18, 1822, by Rev. Elijah C. Stone.
Lorenzo D. Walker and Eliza Matilda Forney, Oct. 29, 1840, by Rev. G. D. Skinner.
Thomas Walker and Esther Barcroft, Jan. 10, 1838, by John Caldwell, J. P.
Wesley Walker and Susanna Forney, Sept. 19, 1833, by Rev. William Tipton.
William Walker and Jane McKinney, June 10, 1834, by Rev. Thomas Hanna.
William Walker and Mary Jane Lightner, Oct. 24, 1839, by Rev. William Taggart.
James Wallace and Jane McFadden, March 11, 1832, by William Taggart, V. D. M.
James B. Wallace and Mary Ann Peterson, Nov. 12, 1839, by Rev. Lewis Janney.
Joseph W. Wallis and Harriet Worster, Sept. 14, 1837, by Samuel Lewis, J. P.
Nathaniel A. Wallace and Jane Watson, March 6, 1834, by Rev. Jacob Coon.
Robert Wallace and Albina Wilson, Jan. 16, 1833, by William Taggart, V. D. M.
Robert Wallace and Rachel Dugan, June 20, 1833, by Thomas Phillips, J. P.
William Wallace and Nancy Muncy, Feb. 17, 1819, by James Roberts.
William Wallace and Elizabeth McCague, June 22, 1835, by Rev. D. C. Merryman.
Verden Wallar and Edith Layport, April 12, 1825, by Michael Conaway, J. P.
William Waller and Sarah Jane M. Rose, Oct. 24, 1839, by Thomas Phillips, J. P.
William Walraven and Polly Ross, Dec. 24, 1818, by James Roberts.
Henry Walters and Catherine Myers, Dec. 12, 1822, by B. W. Veirs, J. P.
Henry Walters and Elizabeth Laughridge, March 9, 1837, by David G. McGuire, J. P.
Jacob Walter and Susanna Manganett, March 26, 1820, by Rev. Michael Herman.
Jacob Walters and Elizabeth Crom, Feb. 20, 1823, by Rev. John Crom.
Jacob Walters and Elizabeth Hogland, May 9, 1833, by George W. Bell, J. P.
Jacob Walters and Clemmy Thompson, May 5, 1839, by John Gruber, J. P.
Samuel Walters and Elizabeth Smith, Nov. 13, 1827, by Rev. John Crom.
James Ward and Martha Thompson, Nov. 4, 1819, by B. W. Veirs, J. P.
John Ward and Nancy McFee, April 13, 1822, by Rev. James Roberts.
Charles Warfel and Mary Boyd, May 7, 1833, by Rev. Thomas Hanna.
George Warfel and Elizabeth Helbert, March 21, 1816, by Charles Chapman, J. P.
Daniel Warner and Sophia Smith, Feb. 23, 1837, by David Bower, J. P.
John Warner and Margaret Chinneth, Oct. 8, 1835, by Rev Adam Webster.
Thomas Warnick and Rachel Thompson, Jan. 17, 1832, by George W. Bell, J. P.
Allen Waters and Mary Ann Haxton, July 17, 1821, by Thomas Patton, J. P.
Allen Watters and Caroline Garret, July 6, 1837, by Rev. Richard Brown.
John Waters and Sarah Kirkpatrick, April 9, 1816, by Charles Chapman, J. P.

John Waters and Mary Johnston, May 23, 1816, by John Rea, V. D. M.
John Watters and Elizabeth Snider, June 26, 1838, by Robert Simpson, J. P.
Joseph Waters and Rebecca Merryman, May 13, 1829, by John Secrest.
Nathan Watters and Catherine Foutz, May 18, 1837, by Robert P. Simpson, J. P.
William Watters and Anne McAdoo, April 19, 1831, by Philip Fulton, J. P.
Andrew Watkins and Hannah Moore, Nov. 1, 1821, by Rev. James Roberts.
James Watkins and Mary Dolvin, June 6, 1839, by John Wilson, Minister.
Elijah Watlin and Eunice Jolly, April 15, 1825, by J. R. Kirkpatrick.
Benjamin Watson and Sarah Norris, March 29, 1821, by Robert McLaughlin.
Daniel Watson and Mary Furbay, June 5, 1824, by Isaac Allen, J. P.
John Watson and Lynna Ann Harris, Jan. 31, 1833, by Rev. William Tipton.
John Watson and Julia Barricklow, April 19, 1838, by Rev. William Wallace.
Joseph Watson and Jane Richey, Sept. 27, 1825, by Donald McIntosh, V. D. M.
David Watt and Ann Gallaher, March 11, 1834, by John McArthur, V. D. M.
John Watts and Eve Shumaker, Jan. 9, 1831, by James McCullough, J. P.
Lemuel Watt and Sarah Johnson, March 4, 1831, by Thomas P. Jenkins, J. P.
Samuel Watt and Anna Stone, July 15, 1820, by Rev. Elijah C. Stone.
Jacob Way and Elizabeth Chaney, Oct. 17, 1839, by Rev. Adam Hetzler.
John Weaver and Mariah Hitchcock, May 28, 1840, by Rev. Richard Brown.
Thomas Weaver and Mary Neel, May 30, 1818, by Robert McLaughlin, J. P.
Ezekiel Webb and Mary Corbin, May 19, 1836, by William Arnold, J. P.
Isaac Webb and Jane McCowley, Feb. 20, 1823, by Joseph Fry, J. P.
Jacob Webb and Mary Ann Walker, Jan. 8, 1833, by William Arnold, J. P.
Jesse Webb and Cassandra Hinton, Jan. 12, 1826, by Isaac Fordyce, J. P.
John Webb and Martha Holmes, Nov. 11, 1830, by Rev. Thomas J. Taylor.
Jonathan Webb and Mary Hinton, April 9, 1826, by George Brown, J. P.
Sarah Webb and George Penn, Dec. 1, 1836, by Thomas Phillips, J. P.
George Webster and Sarah Hendricks, March 16, 1826, by J. R. Kirkpatrick, J. P.
John Webster and Margaret Buchanan, Nov. 13, 1832, by John McArthur, V. D. M.
Peter Weddle and Margaret Hill, Oct. 16, 1828, by Van Brown, J. P.
Ezekiel Weeks and Elizabeth McFadden, Dec. 30, 1819, by John Conaway, J. P.
William M. Weeks and Elizabeth Spiker, Dec. 27, 1825, by Michael Conaway, J. P.
Daniel Welch and Mary Gray, May 5, 1834, by Rev. Thomas Hanna.
George Welch and Margaret Alderman, May 3, 1838, by Levi Peddycoart, J. P.
James Welch and Jane Wagstaff, Dec. 23, 1824, by Donald McIntosh, V. D. M.
James Welch and Martha Slemmons, April 5, 1833, by John McArthur, V. D. M.
John Welch and Elizabeth Hosplehorn, March 27, 1817, by Thomas Fisher, J. P.
John Welch and Margaret Gilmore, April 3, 1833, by John McArthur, V. D. M.
Michael Welch and Mary Fisher, Dec. 0, 1819, by D. W. Veirs, J. P.
Timothy Welch and Octavia Suddith, Sept. 18, 1834, by Rev. Thomas Cook.
William Welch and Adeline Phillips, April 23, 1835, by John McArthur, V. D. M.
William Welsh and Agness Fisher, Oct. 22, 1840, by William D. McCartney, V. D. M.
John Weldon and Ruhamah McKee, Jan. 16, 1823, by John Rea, V. D. M.
Jacob Weldy and Jane McGrue, Dec. 17, 1839, by Rev. Parden Cook.

EARLY MARRIAGES

David Welling and Jane Sharp, Nov. 4, 1834, by John McArthur, V. D. M.
Hamilton Welling and Rachel Corbin, Feb. 8, 1838, by Rev. James Drummond.
Isaac Welling and Ruth Welling, March 21, 1840, by Joseph Fry, J. P.
John Welling and Polly McCullough, June 5, 1821, by Joseph Anderson.
William Welling and Margaret Davis, May 14, 1830, by Rev. Thomas M. Hudson.
Samuel Wellman and Jane Coffee, Sept. 23, 1829, by George Brown, J. P.
Alexander Wells and Mary Ann King, March 31, 1825, by John Conaway, J. P.
Charles Wells and Mary Day, May 23, 1838, by Rev. James Drummond.
David Wells and Mary Delany, April 14, 1818, by Elijah C. Stone.
David Wells and Mary Ann Reed, June 8, 1837, by Samuel Skinner, J. P.
Edwards Wels and Nancy Treacle, Jan. 2, 1819, by William Anderson, J. P.
Francis Wells and Nancy Maffit, Jan. 8, 1816, by William Haverfield.
James Wells and Mary Shimer, Nov. 12, 1840, by John Selby, J. P.
John Wells and Nancy McFadden, Dec. 20, 1822, by John Conaway, J. P.
Joseph Wells and Providence Shimer, March 11, 1825, by Alexander Moore, J. P.
Lakin Wells and Cyntha Maffet, Feb. 4, 1813, by Andrew McNeely, J. P.
Nathaniel Wells and Jane Gilmore, Sept. 25, 1817, by William Taggart, V. D. M.
Richard Wells and Maria Chalk, Dec. 20, 1827, by Michael Conaway, J. P.
William Wells and Mary Townsend, May 29, 1838, by B. Mitchel, V. D. M.
Albert West and Mary Plummer, Jan. 1, 1840, by Aaron Conaway, J. P.
Amos West and Margaret Baker, July 5, 1831, by William Arnold, J. P.
Augustus B. West and Nancy Brindley, April 10, 1834, by Rev. William Tipton.
Elias West and Esther McQueen, Aug. 9, 1827, by John Huston, J. P.
James West and Elizabeth Campbell, Aug. 17, 1826, by Jacob Tope, J. P.
Moris West and Nancy Hudson, March 2, 1819, by Elias Crane.
Robert West and Amelia Cook, June 24, 1813, by John Wiley, J. P.
Thomas West and Mary Ann Tipton, April 7, 1816, by Robert Orr, J. P.
Thomas West and Eliza Tipton, Oct. 23, 1831, by John Busby, J. P.
William West and Mary Allbaugh, Feb. 10, 1825, by Jacob Tope, J. P.
William West and Elizabeth Martin, Jan. 17, 1838, by Samuel Lewis, J. P.
David Wiand and Mary Fisher, Dec. 24, 1833, by John Wagner, J. P.
George Wiant and Catherine Poslan, April 29, 1830, by Rev. H. E. F. Voigt.
John Wyant and Eliza Gance, Jan. 13, 1830, by John C. Huston, J. P.
John Weyant and Nancy Carr, Nov. 15, 1837, by Rev. Thomas Foster.
Samuel Wyant and Eliza McCombs, Sept. 2, 1832, by Charles Faucett, J. P.
Daniel Wharton and Martha Strade, Dec. 26, 1833, by Silvanus Lamb, J. P.
Linton Wharton and Sarah Ann Turner, March 12, 1835, by Samuel Lewis, J. P.
Isaac Whealdon and Mary Ann Grewell, Dec. 29, 1831, by Thomas P. Jenkins, J. P.
John M. Whealdon and Tracy Hibbs, Jan. 15, 1829, by Thomas P. Jenkins, J. P.
Caleb Wheeler and Rebecca Rogers, Aug. 31, 1837, by Rev. Elijah C. Stone.
Christopher Wheeler and Rebecca Arnold, April 13, 1837, by John Wagner, J. P.
Ezekiel Wheeler and Nancy Roberts, Dec. 9, 1824, by Rev. John Waterman.
James Wheeler and Jane Stiers, June 15, 1824, by John Walker, J. P.
Nicholas Wheeler and Hannah Poland, Nov. 3, 1819, by Elijah C. Stone.
Parkinson Wheeler and Jane Carrel, June 8, 1832, by Thomas Phillips, J. P.
Joseph P. Wherry and Emily Johnson, April 7, 1836, by Rev. Robert Cook.
Joshua Whitcomb and Miranda McIntire, Oct. 20, 1822, by Silvanus Lamb, J. P.

Alexander White and Mary Jenkins, Oct. 10, 1838, by Samuel Lewis, J. P.
Charles White and Matilda Cecil, July 23, 1833, by John C. Auld, J. P.
George White and Nancy Knox, March 10, 1829, by Rev. William Tipton.
James White and Rebecca Dorson, Dec. 23, 1824, by Silvanus Lamb, J. P.
James White and Patience Harrison, Oct. 13, 1836, by George Atkinson, J. P.
Joseph White and Elizabeth Friers, Oct. 9, 1823, by Rev. James Roberts.
Joseph White and Hannah Rogers, April 12, 1828, by John Carson, J. P.
William White and Mary Kerr, Aug. 25, 1831, by John Rea, V. D. M.
William White and Mary Ann Barrett, April 23, 1838, by James M. Piper.
Isaac Whitecraft and Ruth Atkinson, Dec. 21, 1826, by William Wallace, V. D. M
Abel Whitten and Amelia Ann Watts, Nov. 26, 1836, by M. B. Lukins, J. P.
Findley Whitten and Eleanor Harding, Oct. 27, 1839, by M. B. Lukins, J. P,
Nelson Whitten and Laney Dunham, Sept. 9, 1833, by Thomas M. Granfel, J. P.
John Whittington and Elizabeth Hollett, Jan. 2, 1840, by John Knox, J. P.
Isaac Whitman and Barbary Tope, April 29, 1824, by Jacob Tope, J. P.
Benjamin Whitmore and Anne Tollars, Dec. 30, 1824, by John Wagner, J. P.
Amos Whitney and Matilda Wright, Feb 11, 1834, by Cornelius Crabtree, J. P.
Isaac Wickersham and Eliza Lister, April 29, 1830, by Alexander Simpson, J. P.
Malen Finley Wiggens and Hannah Johnson, July 5, 1836, by William Taggart, V. D. M.
Joseph Wilcox and Mary Jane McClenahan, May 14, 1834, by Rev. Richard Campbell.
John Wilden and Mary West, Oct. 29, 1818, by Martin Guilinger, J. P.
Joseph Wiley and Anna Roberts, Feb. 25, 1817, by William Dixon.
John Wilkin and Elizabeth Leech, June 12, 1834, by Rev. Thomas Hanna
Robert Wilkins and Elizabeth Holmes, Oct. 11, 1817, by Elijah C. Stone.
Robert Wilkin and Jane Wiley, Aug. 19, 1819, by John Rea, V. D. M.
Samuel Wilkin and Jane Paisley, March 8, 1827, by Daniel McLane.
Henry Willgus and Elizabeth Robinson, Sept. 29, 1831, by Thomas Day, J. P.
Humphrey Williams and Priscilla Mackey, July 2, 1840, by George Clancey.
John Williams and Margaret Crawford, March 22, 1814, by Rev. Thomas B. Clark, V. D. M.
John Williams and Eveline Anderson, Aug. 6, 1835, by Joseph Johnson, J. P.
Noah Willams and Arksey Randels, Feb. 29, 1816, by Charles Chapman, J. P.
Samuel Williams and Rachel Cox, Dec. 1, 1831, by John Gruber, J. P.
Henry Williamson and Rebecca Graham, Feb. 14, 1823, by John Rea, V. D. M.
Henry Williamson and Phebe Haxton, March 6, 1828, by John Rea, J. P.
Isaac Willis and Jane David Sept. 13, 1832, by Joseph Fry, J. P.
James Willis and Mariah Smith, Dec. 19, 1840, by Rev. William Deveny.
Amos Willison and Anne McMillan, Dec. 13, 1836, by William Wallace, V. D. M.
Elijah Willison and Mary Wilson, June 28, 1832, by William Wyckoff, J. P.
Henry Willoby and Susan Ferrier, Feb. 25, 1823, by Rev. Elijah C. Stone.
James Wiliby and Margaret Patterson, Sept. 4, 1818, by William Anderson, J. P.
Arthur Wilson and Sarah Selby, Jan. 3, 1837, by Samuel Skinner, J. P.
Benjamin Wilson and Catherine Crabtree, April 12, 1832, by William Wyckoff, J. P.
Charles Wilson and Eliza Norris, April 11, 1833, by Edward Talbott, J. P.
Daniel Wilson and Agness Johnson, Jan. 9, 1838, by William Taggart, V. D. M.
David Wilson and Elizabeth Ferrier, Nov. 13, 1818, by William Slemmons, J. P.

EARLY MARRIAGES

Hugh B. Wilson and Catherine Runey, Feb. 11, 1819, by Thomas Dickerson, J. P.
Isaac Wilson and Elizabeth Brickles, Dec. 24, 1821, by William Anderson, J. P.
James Wilson and Jane Moody, July 6, 1817, by William Slemmons, J. P.
James Wilson and Gracey All, Oct. 9, 1830, by Rev. Jacob Cozad.
John Wilson and Elizabeth Palmer, Nov. 18, 1819, by Williamson Carrothers, J. P.
John I. Wilson and Ann Humphries, April 20, 1821, by Joseph Fry, J. P.
John Wilson and Rachel Gwynn, Nov. 24, 1835, by William Arnold, J. P.
John Wilson and Jane Crawford, May 4, 1837, by William Wallace, V. D. M.
John Wilson and Leticia Jones, Feb. 13, 1840, by Aaron Conaway, J. P.
Joseph Wilson and Elizabeth Stone, Aug. 19, 1819, by William Wyckoff, J. P.
Robert Wilson and Margaret Arnold, Feb. 16, 1838, by Samuel Lewis, J. P.
Samuel H. Wilson and Sarah L. Auld, Dec. 15, 1831, by Rev. Jacob Cozad.
Samuel H. Wilson and Mary McGill, March 7, 1837, by W. Lukins, J. P.
William Wilson and Sophia Randolph, May 28, 1829, by Archibald McGrew, J. P.
William Wilson and Mary Cox, Jan. 5, 1837, by John McArthur, V. D. M.
William M. Wilson and Elizabeth McConnell, May 7, 1837, by John M. Brown, J. P.
John Winings and Mary Snider, Nov. 12, 1818, by John Wagner, J. P.
Daniel Winshel and Catherine Dewel, Aug. 12, 1824, by Samuel Dunlap, J. P.
Abner Winter and Christena Tingley, June 15, 1813, by James Roberts.
William Winters and Nancy Lisle, Aug. 16, 1821, by John Rea, V. D. M.
George Wise and Sarah Hay, April 19, 1838, by John Wagner, J. P.
Samuel Witmer and Elizabeth Shoos, Sept. 15, 1816, by Rev. John Rinehart.
Thomas Wolf and Mary Kelby, March 8, 1821, by Thomas Patton, J. P.
Anthony Wood and Jane Petty, Oct. 23, 1839, by Rev. Robert Cook.
Benjamin Wood and Levinah Lees, Aug. 16, 1821, by Thomas Parkinson, J. P.
Benjamin Wood and Martha Arskins, Nov. 6, 1828, by Rev. Elijah C. Stone.
Frederick J. Wood and Jane Brown, Jan. 7, 1840, by Rev. Benjamin Wood.
Hugh Wood and Sally Spicer, Oct. 4, 1821, by John Conaway, J. P.
James Wood and Elizabeth Shouse, Feb. 2, 1832, by Rev. Benjamin Wood.
Joseph Wood and Mary Chandler, Oct. 10, 1818, by Thomas Parkinson.
Joshua Wood and Elizabeth Hudson, March 2, 1819, by Robert McKee, J. P.
Reuben B. Wood and Sarah Ann Ferguson, March 29, 1838, by Rev. Benjamin Wood.
Sylvanus Wood and Amanda Tingley, Sept. 8, 1836, by Rev. James C. Taylor
Thomas Wood and Latetia Stackhouse, Feb. 2, 1818, by James Roberts.
Thomas Wood and Margaret Cope, Feb. 28, 1828, by John Carson, J. P.
Jeremiah Woodford and Sarah Ann Wherry, June 26, 1834, by Rev. Jacob Lemmon.
James Works and Ann G. Cunningham, June 18, 1838, by William Colledge.
John Work and Margaret Gallher, March 15, 1836, by John Rea, V. D. M.
Daniel Worley and Sarah Peregory, Jan. 2, 1834, by Rev. Aurora Callender.
David Wourley and Mary Jane Luke, Oct. 6, 1836, by Samuel Lewis, J. P.
Josiah Worley and Mary Ann Minor, Sept. 17, 1833, by Thomas Phillips, J. P.
Michael Worley and Eve Ann Markley, Aug. 21, 1828, by John Wagner, J. P.
Wesley Worley and Jane Virtue, May 8, 1823, by Rev. James Roberts.
George Worrell and Sarah Barnett, Oct. 14, 1830, by John Heberling, J. P.

Nathaniel Worrall and Ann Barnett, Jan. 18, 1827, by Rev. James Roberts.
Norman Worstall and Rebecca Ann Lake, Dec. 21, 1826, by Rev. James Roberts.
James Worth and Nancy Sherron, Oct 5, 1826, by Robert Orr, J. P.
John Worth and Sarah Kent, Dec. 4, 1823, by Robert Orr, J. P.
David Wortman and Elizabeth Reddin, Jan. 12, 1826, by Henry Ford, J. P.
Isaac Wright and Hannah Smith, May 31, 1821, by Joseph Johnson, J. P.
Nathan Wright and Elizabeth Ripley, Aug. 22, 1822, by Rev. Curtis Goddard.
Sylvanus Wright and Desire Hays, Aug. 14, 1828, by George W. Bell, J. P.
Thomas Wright and Mary Cellar, Jan. 28, 1823, by Rev. Salmon Cowles.
Thomas W. Wright and Sally Gardner, Jan. 23, 1827, by Rev. William Knox.
Thomas Wright and Margaret Ann Bear, Sept. 14, 1837, by Rev. Jacob Lemmon.
William Wright and Caty Nevit, Oct. 27, 1816, by William Wyckoff, J. P.
William Wright and Polly Blair, May 15, 1821, by Curtis Goddard.
Thomas C. Wicoff and Sarah Coleman, Dec. 5, 1838, by Rev. Jacob Lemmon.
William Wyckoff and Freelove Crabtree, Nov. 22, 1814, by William Knox.
John Wymer and Fanny Firebaugh, Sept. 14, 1837, by Adam Hetzler.
Aaron Yarnell and Harriet Poulson, Sept. 8, 1836, by Rev. James C. Taylor.
Eli Yarnold and Rebecca Burton, May 24, 1839 by C. E. Weirick.
Mordecai Yarnell and Providence Walraven, Nov. 4, 1824, by Rev. James Roberts.
William Yarnell and Sarah Spencer, Jan. 27, 1833, by William Wyckoff, J. P.
Ziba Yarnall and Jane Bowlen, Aug. 22, 1833, by Rev. Jacob Lemmon.
David Yarrington and Susanna Clark, Sept. 10, 1829, by Samuel Dunlap, J. P.
Ephraim Yarrington and Rebecca Simon, Jan. 19, 1826, by Samuel Dunlap, J. P.
William Yarrington and Susanna Watson, Sept. 21, 1827, by Samuel Dunlap,
Joseph Yingling and Mary Ann Able, Jan. 15, 1835, by John Wagner, J. P.
John Yost and Mary Wilson, Jan. 9, 1834, by Samuel Lewis, J. P.
Benjamin Young and Eve Ann Fisher, Jan. 8, 1829, by Michael Conaway, J. P.
Denton Young and Melida Baker, Jan. 26, 1836, by John Gruber, J. P.
George Young and Mary Ann Burkhead, March 16, 1826, by John Busby, J. P.
Henry Young and Nancy Burkhead, July 6, 1815, by John Busby, J. P.
John Young and Sarah Barkhurst, Feb. 5, 1815, by Paul Preston.
John Young and Sally James, April 1, 1821, by Charles Chapman, J. P.
John Young and Anna Kelly, March 6, 1823, by Rev. Thomas Hunt.
McKinzee Young and Sarah Northamer, Feb. 15, 1820, by William Carrothers, J. P.
Michael Young and Mary Shaeffer, May 4, 1820, by John Hurless, J. P.
William Young and Elizabeth Michals, Aug. 15, 1839, by Joseph Cloakey, V. D. M.
John Zimmerman and Catherine Pardon, Aug. 20, 1831, by John McArthur, V. D. M.
Frederick Zollars and Ann Whitmore, Nov. 27, 1823, by Robert Orr, J. P.
Jacob Zollars and Elizabeth Porter, July 18, 1837, by John Wagner, J. P.
John Zollars and Sarah Wallcutt, Nov. 19, 1835, by John Wagner, J. P.
Zepheniah Zollars and Catherine Shilling, June 2, 1836, by John Gruber, J. P.

SOME HARRISON COUNTY BURIALS.

The following records have been gathered from tombstones standing in the principal cemeteries of Harrison county, particularly, the older cemeteries. The records have been collected at various times during the past five years. In the case of the graveyards of Beech Spring, Crabapple, Unity, Nottingham, Dickerson, Cadiz, and Ridge, all the tombstones standing at the dates the lists were made, have been examined, and their records are here given, without regard to the date of birth of the decedents In all other cases, only those burials are recorded of those who were born prior to 1830, with a view to including only the pioneers of the county. A complete list of all the burials in the graveyards herein given in part, would make a record beyond the limits of one volume.

The location of many of the various graveyards not within the limits of the villages of the county may not be out of place in this connection: Beech Spring graveyard is situated at Beech Spring Church, on the southwest corner of section one, in Green township, about two miles southeast from Hopedale. Dickerson graveyard is situated near the center of section thirty-two, in Cadiz township, about half-way between Cadiz and New Athens. Crabapple and Unity graveyards are situated in Wheeling township, Belmont county, the former about two, and the latter about three miles southeast of New Athens. Bethel graveyard is situated in the southeast quarter of section twenty-eight, in Green township, about half a mile north of Folks' Station. Ridge graveyard is situated in the southwest quarter of section twenty-three, in Archer township, about a mile southeast from Hanover. Nottingham and Rankin graveyards are both in Moorefield township, the former in section six, and about a mile southwest of Rankin, which is in section thirty-one, one mile south of Cassville.

BURIALS IN BEECH SPRING GRAVEYARD.

To July 14, 1896.

Amanda Jane Aikin, daughter of Joseph and Elizabeth, d. Oct. 1, 1864; 7y. 9m.
Joseph Aikin, d. Dec. 27, 1868; 52y.
Isabella Allison, daughter of J. and M., d. July 30, 1830; 2y. 9d.
James Allison, b. 1790; d. Nov 18, 1881; 92y.
James Allison, Jr., d. May, 1859; 33y.
Margaret Allison, wife of James, d. Oct. 28, 1837; 41y. 3m. 9d.
Mary Allison, wife of David, d. Feb. 23, 1865; 40y. 1m. 20d.
Eleanor Barnhouse, wife of William, d. July 8, 1838; 31y. 7m. 18d.
Elizabeth Bell, daughter of J. and N., d. Nov. 15, 1838; 1y. 3m. 6d.
John Bell, d. July 25, 1822; 59y.
John H. Bell, son of J. and N., d. March 13, 1844; 10m.
Margaret Bell, wife of John, d. May 10, 1861; 87y.
Nancy Bell, d. March 31, 1823; 80y.
John Benedict, d. Oct. 11, 1890; 57y. 1m. 11d.
Nancy Benedict, d. Oct. 11, 1890; 56y.
H. Stewart Black, d. Jan. 22, 1890; 70y. 2m.
Isabella Black, wife of James, d. Dec. 30, 1865; 80y.
James Black, Sr., d. Dec. 13, 1846; 90y.
Jane Black, wife of James, Sr., d. Aug. 22, 1835; 82y.
J. H. Black, d. March 26, 1885; 72y.
Mary K. Black, wife of J. H., d. May 11, 1894; 78y. 5m. 25d.
Rachel Bowls, d. Jan. 22, 1845; 9y.
Isabel Brown, wife of Robert, d. April 23, 1871; 92y.
Robert Brown, d. May 18, 1850; 71y.
E. Caldwell, d. Sept. 4, 1831;———
James Carrick, d. Aug., 1820; 76y.
John Carrick, d. Feb. 1, 1854; 74y. 2m. 16d.
Martha Carrick, wife of James W., d. Jan. 8, 1833; 30y. 11m. 8d.
Mary Carrick, wife of James., d. Oct. 31, 1833; 74y.
Andrew Clark, d. Nov. 6, 1848; 60y.
A. F. Clark, d. April 28, 1862; 22y.
James Clark, d. Sept. 3, 1833; 80y.
James Clark, d. Nov. 28, 1847; 36y.
James Clark, son of Francis and Nancy; ....
Jane Clark, wife of James, d. May 17, 1832; 78y.
John G. Clark, son of Andrew M., d. Aug. 15, 1851; 21y.
Joseph Clark, b. Feb. 12, 1778; d. Oct. 3, 1861.
Margaret Clark, wife of Andrew, d. May 20, 1835; 49y.
Margaret Clark, daughter of Andrew, d. March 10, 1846; 19y.
Rachel Clark, wife of Joseph, d. Sept. 3, 1854; 60y. 9m. 4d.
James R. Coulter, d. Oct. 18, 1852; 24y. 6m. 29d.
Mary E. Coulter, daughter of J. R. and Rhoda, d. Sep. 8, 1855; 3y. 9m. 10d.
Carlisle Crawford, son of W. and E., d. Feb., 1847; 6y. 5m.
Eliza Crawford, d. Nov. 3, 1837; 9y.
Elizabeth Crawford, wife of Walter, d. May 27, 1879; 79y. 3m. 22d.
George Crawford, d. Nov. 12, 1835; 13y.
Hannah Crawford, daughter of W. and E., d. June 29, 1851; 14y. 9m. 17d.
Hannah Crawford, d. Nov. 15, 1872; 57y. 10m. 20d.
John M. Crawford, son of J. and H., d. July 31, 1864; 21y. 4m.
John N. Crawford, son of W. and E., d. May 7, 1843; 23y. 6m. 10d.
Samuel Crawford, d. March 23, 1837; 17y.
Walter Crawford, ———, 74y.
Levi Crouch, d. Sep. 6, 1861; 77y.
Mary Crouch, wife of Levi, d. April 22, 1853; 62y.
William H. Crouch, d. Murfeesboro, Tenn., March 19, 1863; 33y. 5m. 29d.
Mary A. Davis, wife of Jesse, d. Sep. 26, 1853; 41y. 5m. 14d.
Elizabeth Delaney, wife of Philip, d. Jan. 17, 1849; 80y.
John Clark Delaney, born in Fayette county, Pa., d. Jan. 8, 1820 27y. 10m. 20d.
Philip Delaney, d. Nov. 21, 1852; 86y.

BEECH SPRING BURIALS

William B. Delaney, d. April 19, 1846; 40y.
Johnnie T. Dickerson, son of J. H. and E. R., d. Aug. 23, 1884; 7m. 25d.
John Reed Dool, son of Rev. Wm. S. and Ann, d. March 26, 1852; 1y. 7m.
Robert Henry Dool, son of Rev. Wm. S. and Ann, d. March 23, 1852; 4y. 27d.
John L. Dunning, d. Sep. 28, 1853; 23y.
John L. Dunning, Jr., d. Oct. 1, 1874; 21y.
Andrew Eagleson, d. March 7, 1836, 58y.
Andrew Eagleson, d. April 11, 1818; 2y.
Hannah Eagleson, d. Dec. 17, 1811; —— 8m.
Israel Eagleson, d. March ——, 1839; 21y.
James Eagleson, d. Dec. 9, 1823; ——
James Eagleson, d. June 20, 1837; 17y.
Jane Eagleson, wife of William, d. Sep. 27, 1852; 41y.
Jane Eagleson, wife of Andrew, d. June 3, 1861; 82y.
Jane C. Eagleson, d. Sep. 27, 1852; 40y. 10m.
John Calvin Eagleson, son of Henry and Eliza, d. Sep. 26, 1841; 3y. 1m. 5d.
Lucinda M. Eagleson, d. July 1, 1893; 73y. 10m.
Margaret Eagleson, d. June 5, 1814; 12y.
Margaret C. Eagleson, daughter of W. and J., d. Sep. 18, 1841; 5y. 4m.
William Eagleson, d. Nov. 15, 1877; 72y. 10m. 7d.
John Eakin, son of John and Mary, d. Dec. 12, 1836; 21y.
John Eakin, d. Feb. 6, 1862; 83y.
Mary Eakin, daughter of John and Mary, d. Oct. 8, 1844; 25y.
Mary Eakin, wife of John, d. March 8, 1861; 84y.
Alfonso T. Ely, son of D. C. and I. L., b. June 15, 1880; d. Dec. 1, 1886.
Odessa M. Ely, daughter of D. C. and I. L., 1m. 5d.
Mary Endsley, d. March, 1826; 85y.
Alex. Foster, d. Feb. 14, 1845; 74y.
James Foster, d. April 4, 1828; 22y.
Martha Foster, d. Aug. 7, 1839; 24y.

Celia France, daughter of J. and R., d. June 15, 1820; 4y 8m. 23d.
John France, d. Dec. 11, 1825; 86y. 6m. 10d.
Rebecca France, wife of John, d. March 29, 1868; 76y. 4m.
Ann Francis, wife of James, d. July 16, 1828; 48y.
James Francis, d. Aug. 17, 1859; 84y.
John Fulton, d. Oct. 2, 1856; 53y.
William Gallagher, d. Oct. 16, 1832; 53y.
Lettissia Gibson, wife of Hugh; d. June 4, 1814; 35y.
George Gourley, d. July 22, 1868; 91y. 3m. 7d.
John Gourley, d. Feb. 6, 1857; 85y.
John G. Gourley, d. June 4, 1870; 45y.
Margaret Gourley, wife of George, d. Nov. 26, 1863; 75y.
Ann Hanna, wife of James, d. April 27, 1833; 73y.
Elizabeth Hanna, wife of Ezekiel, d. Jan. 24, 1845; 48y. 3m.
Ezekiel Hanna, d. May 10, 1861; 61y. 11m. 9d.
James A. Hanna, son of E. and E., d. Jan., 1849; 16y.
James Boggs Hanna, son of Samuel and Doche, d. Oct. 21, 1872; 22y.
Louisa Hanna, daughter of William and Mary, d. April 27, 1834; 11y.
Margaret Hanna, d. April 17, 1853; 57y.
Martha L. Hanna, daughter of John M. and L., d. June 15, 1845; 4m. 7d.
Mary Hanna, daughter of John M. and L. Hanna, d. Jan. 8, 1848; 4y. 6m. 15d.
Mary Hanna, wife of William, d. Nov. 19, 1853; 71y.
Samuel Hanna, son of William and Mary, d. May 6, 1834; 10y.
Sarah Hanna, daughter of William and Mary, d. Jan. 13, 1842; 26y.
William Hanna, d. April 6, 1830; 50y.
William Hanna, son of William and Mary, d. Jan. 8, 1839; 27y.
David T. Harrah, d. Oct. 26, 1886; 75y. 3m. 24d.
James Harrah, d. Sep. 15, 1846; 3y. 9m. 19d.
James C. Harrah, d. Dec. 2, 1871; 92y. 4m. 25d.

James N. Harrah, d. Aug. 2, 1881; 36y. 2m. 1d.
John T. Harrah, son of John and Jane, d. Nov. 10, 1863; 10y. 11m. 15d.
Margaret Harrah, wife of James C., d. Dec. 7, 1834; 58y. 2m. 13d.
Milton A. Harrah, son of John and Jane, d. April 12, 1863; 12y. 8m. 5d.
Nancy Harrah, wife of Adam, d. Aug. 19, 1874; 60y. 5m. 24d.
Martha Eliza Harrison, daughter of W. and S., d. Oct. 27. 1846; 16y. 2m. 27d.
John Harvey, son of H. and M., d. Jan. 16, 1836; 77y. (Henry Harvey buried at Lower Buffalo Graveyard, Va.).
Mary Harvey, daughter of H. and M., d. April 2, 1809; ——
Elizabeth Haslett, d. July 21, 1838; 84y.
Elizabeth Holmes, wife of William, d. May 8, 1849; 59y.
Eliza Jane Holmes, daughter of I. and J., d. Sep. 23, 1856; 18y.
Francis Holmes, d. Aug. 6, 1825; 86y.
Jane Holmes, wife of Francis, d. March 19, 1834; 90y.
Martha Holmes, daughter of I. and J., d. July 29, 1862; 18y. 2m.
William Holmes, d. Jan. 22, 1861; 78y.
Jane Hope, daughter of W. and E., d. Dec. 24, 1848; 17y. 11d.
Maria Hope, daughter of W. and E., d. Nov. 7, 1841; 1y 2m. 4d.
Rebecca Hope, daughter of W. and E., d. Sep. 24, 1839; 7m.
Boyd Houston, son of James and Mary, d. March 12, 1832; 1y. 1d.
Elijah Howell, d. June 27, 1871; 89y.
Mary Howell, wife of Elijah, d. Sep. 11, 1863; 68y.
Eliza Hunter, wife of James, d. April 19, 1853; 33y. 7m. 27d.
George M. Hunter, son of J. and Eliza, d. April 30, 1864; 18y. 8d.
Allen Jamison, d. March 12, 1846; 62y.
Mary Jamison, wife of John, d. April 17, 1828; 48y. 5m. 1d.
Sarah Jamison, wife of Allen, d. Feb. 26, 1858; 65y.
Samuel Jeffers, d. June 8, 1847; 70y.
Eleanor Jelley, daughter of J. and M., d. Nov. 7, 1834; 23y.
James Jelley, d. Aug. 2, 1839; 55y.
Mary Jelley, wife of James, d. Nov. 24, 1863; 79y. 9m. 22d.
Nancy Jelley, d. April 13, 1852; 32y. 7m. 26d.
Elizabeth Johnson, d. Jan. 10, ——; 58y.
Ephraim Johnson, d. Dec. 23, 1833; 59y.
James Johnson, son of E. and M., ——
Joseph B. Johnson, son of J. J. and H. J., d. Feb. 18, 1845; 3y. 11m. 14d.
James Johnston, d. Nov. 9, 1863; 70y. 6m. 27d.
Mary Johnston, wife of James, d. Jan. 25, 1881; 86y. 7m. 27d.
Rachel Karr, wife of John, d. Aug. 8, 1830; 49y.
Infant Son of T. L. and M. L. Kerr, d. Sep. 20, 1851; 4m. 15d.
Agnes Kerr, wife of James, d. June 18, 1836; 85y.
Ann Kerr, wife of Samuel, d. July 1, 1835; 40y.
Betsey Kerr, wife of William, d. Jan. 20, 1823; 35y.
James Kerr, d. June 2, 1825; 74y.
Joseph Kerr, d. Jan. 1, 1850; 28y.
Katharine Kerr, wife of James, d. Sep. 12, 1827; 41y.
Margaret Ann Kerr, d. July 4, 1835; 18y.
Mary J. Leech, daughter of B. and R., d. Aug. 25, 1851; 17y. 6m. 6d.
John Long, d. Aug. 4, 1822; 31y. 2m.
James H. Loughrey, son of J. and M., Aug. 14, 1827; 6y.
Margaret Loughrey, wife of John, of Columbus, Ohio; d. Sep. 6, 1827; 39y.
Mary J. Loughrey, daughter of John and Margaret, d. Dec. 20, 1827; 10y.
Margaret Ann Lowry, daughter of John and Nancy, d. Oct. 19, 1836; 6m. 1d.
David Lyons, d. July 23, 1826; 26y.
Jane Smith Lyons. daughter of E. and J., d. Sep. 8, 1829; 36y.
John Lyons, d. Aug. 3, 1829; 80y. [the adjoining tomb-stone, probably that of his wife, is entirely obliterated].
Sarah McCollough, wife of Joseph, b. Sep. 27, 1795; d. March 24, 1836.
Esther McCrea, wife of Robert, d. May 17, 1834; 83y.
Margaret McCrea, d. June 7, 1823; 47y.

27d.
Margaret McGrew, wife of Archibald, d. April 29, 1828; 49y.
Sarah McKeever, wife of Thomas, d. July 25, 1849; 30y. 9m. 10d.
Eliza Isabella Matthews, b. March 12, 1826; d. June 22, 1846.
William Matthews, Esq., b. Dec. 25, 1787; d. April 17, 1833.
Joseph Mayes, d. Dec. 29, 1845; 60y. 7m.
Elizabeth Melroy, d. May 5, 1815; 41y.
George Melroy, d. Jan. 2, 1829; 58y.
Samuel Melroy, d. Aug. 23, 1825; 65y.
Charles Merryman, d. Aug. 14, 1833; 28y.
John B. Merryman, son of W. and N., d. June 27, 1850; 7y. 5m. 27d.
Kasiah Margaret Merryman, daughter of W. and N., and neice of Elizabeth Merryman, d. Oct. 13, 1857; 89y.
Margaret Merryman, daughter of Charles and M., d. Sep., 1841; 10y.
Nancy Merriman, wife of William, d. Feb. 13, 1849; 30y. 9m. 19d.
Eliza Mil——
John Miller, d. May 12, 1826; 78y.
George Mills, d. Sep., 1820; 57y.
George C. Mills, son of J. and E., b. Aug. 8, 1860; d. Aug. 29, 1890.
Elizabeth Mills, wife of George, d. Jan. 25, 1852; 65y.
Elizabeth A. Mills, daughter of J. and E., b. April 1, 1855; d. April 22, 1883.
George Mills, d. Dec. 29, 1862; 52y. 20d.
John Mills, b. Feb. 23, 1816; d. Oct. 19, 1885.
Martha A. Mills, daughter of J. and E., b. April 1, 1865; d. Nov. 24, 1883.
Mary E. Mills, daughter of J. and E., b. Sep. 25, 1857; d. May 6, 1883.
Nancy J. Mills, daughter of J. and E., b. March 2, 1851; d. Oct. 11, 1882.
William B. Mills, d. Oct. 9, 1888; 28y.
John Moffatt, d. April 6, 1866; 74y.
Nancy Moffat, wife of John, d. Jan. 11, 1845; 69y.
Ellen J. Moore, b. May 27, 1806; d. Feb. 16, 1846.
Fanny Moore, wife of Alex., d. Jan. 18, 1836; 63y.
James M. Moore, b. June 25, 1808; d. Feb. 16, 1884.
Jane Moore, daughter of James M. and E. J., b. May 23, 1832; d. Dec. 18, 1846.
John A. Moore, son of J. M. and E. T., d. Dec. 5, 1835.
Mary Moore, d. Dec. 15, 1832; 47y.
Rebecca A. Moore, b. May 5, 1809; d. April 30, 1879.
Ann Moorehead, wife of James, d. Aug. 15, 1824; 35y.
John Moorehead, d. May 10, 1847; 86y.
Mary Moorehead, d. March 1, 1832; 74y. 3m. 26d.
Sarah Moorehead, d. Sep. 30, 1833; 34y.
Sarah Moorehead, wife of John, d. April 28, 1838; 77y.
James A. Muncy, d. Aug. 23, 1822; 2y.
Eliza M. Neely, daughter of J. and H., d. July 3, 1851; 3y.
Mary J. Neely, wife of John, d. Dec. 28, 1844.
Mary J. Neely, daughter of J. and M., d. Oct. 2, 1851; 6y.
Eliza Jane Newlon, daughter of E. and P., d. Jan. 8, 1834; 7m.
James Newlon, son of Elijah and Phoebe, d. June 6, 1834; 2y. 11m. 10d.
Phoebe Newlon, wife of Elijah, d. Dec. 25, 1833; 28y.
Sarah Newton, wife of Joshua, d. Jan. 25, 1832; 51y.
Elizabeth Ogden, b. May 27, 1814; d. Dec. 28, 1889.
Martha Ogden, wife of Robert, d. April 2, 1866; 85y.
Martha Ogden, daughter of R. and M., d. Nov. 4, 1868; 51y. 6m. 8d.
Mary Ogden, b. Aug. 10, 1815; d. July 18, 1887.
Robert Ogden, d. April 14, 1848; 56y.
Kesiah Emily Paxton, daughter of W. and R., d. June 10, 1852; 3y. 7m.
Lydia Rebecca Paxton, daughter of W. and R., d. Oct. 4, 1838; 1y. 1m.
——— Pennel, ———; 83y.
Eliza J. Pennel, daugher of H. and R., d. Sep. 22, 1832; 2y. 11m. 7d.
Rachel Ann Pennel, daughter of Hugh and Rachel, d. 1838; 3y 11m. 4d.
Sarah J. Perry, daughter of Henry and Sarah, d. Aug. 17, 1828; 2y 7m. 23d.
Rebecca Ramsey, wife of John, d. Feb.

12, 1833; 29y.
William Rankin, d. May 1, 1853; 60y.
Mrs. Elizabeth Rea, wife of Rev. John, d. Aug. 16, 1854; 82y.
Rev. John Rea, D. D., d. Feb. 12, 1855; 83y.
William P. Rea, son of Dr. John; d. June 11, 1846; 36y. 8d.
Isaac Reed, d. April 13, 1846; 15y.
Jane Reed, d. Nov. 8, 1878; 82y.
Mary Jerusha Reed, daughter of M. and S., d. Oct. 31, 1851; 3y. 5m. 8d.
Lavinah Reed, daughter of M. and S., d. Oct. 28, 1853; 10m. 10d.
William Reed, b. Aug. 15, 1800; d. Feb. 27, 1872.
Mary Scott, wife of James, d. May 8, 1850; 44y. 9m. 3d.
Isaac Shannon, d. Sep. 20, 1848; 83y.
Jane Shannon, wife of Isaac, d. June 18, 1820; 51y.
James Sherrard, son of Sarah and John, d. April, 15, 1851; 20y. 6m. 21d.
John Sherrard, d. July 14, 1860; 72y. 8m. 16d.
Sarah Sherrard, wife of John, d. Oct. 15, 1861; 56y. 6m.
A. S. Simpson, d. Nov. 3, 1884; 63y. 10m.
James Simpson, b. July 14, 1791; d. Dec. 8, 1871.
Violet Simpson, wife of James, d. June 30, 1855; 58y.
William S. Simpson, d. March 9, 1891; 65y. 10m. 9d.
Esther Skelley, wife of John, d. Jan. 1, 1860; 56y. 11m. 23d.
John Skelley, d. Nov. 7, 1847; 66y.
Margaret Skelley, wife of John, d. Oct. 11, 1834; 53y.
William Skelley, d. Nov. 2, 1836; 27y.
Catharine Slemons, wife of James, d. July 17, 1851; 62 y. 8m. 25d.
Deborah M. Slemons, daughter of S. and E., d. Aug. 26, 1851; 2y. 3m. 12d.
Ann Smith, wife of John V., d. Dec. 27, 1873; 37y. 2d.
Esther Smith, wife of James, d. July 9, 1832; 36y.
James Smith, d. June 12, 1833; 33y.
Rosannah Stirling, [dates obliterated].
Jane Stringer, wife of William, d. June 15, 1837; 33y.
John Stringer, d. July 17, 1845; 69y.
1m. 7d.
John M. Stringer, d. May. 4, 1889; 57y. 2m.
William Stringer, d. Aug. 16, 1859; 55y. 11m. 28d.
Infant son of George and Maria Taggart, b. Jan. 21, 1844; d. Jan. 30, 1844.
Infant son of J. and A. Taggart, d. Oct. 26, 1842; 3m. 7d.
Alexander W. Taggart, d. June 19, 1858; 38y. 2m.
Anne Craig Taggart, wife of James, b. Feb. 22, 1811; d. Feb. 24, 1887.
David Taggart, d. Dec. 17, 1844; 27y.
David Bayless Taggart, b. Feb. 28, 1846; d. April 7, 1874.
David Welch Taggart, b. Nov. 9, 1850; d. Feb. 17, 1854.
Elizabeth Taggart, wife of William, d. Sep. 25, 1845; 40y. 2m. 9d.
George Taggart, b. Aug. 3, 1814; d. Sep. 18, 1879.
James Taggart, b. July 22, 1806; d. Oct. 15, 1890.
James A. Taggart, son of J. and A., d. May 7, 1849; 1y. 4m.
John Taggart, d. June 4, 1843; 65y.
John C. Taggart, son of J. and A., d. Dec. 1, 1842; 3y. 7m. 3d.
Margaret Taggart, wife of John, d. Aug. 31, 1861; 82y. 5m. 19d.
Maria B. Taggart, wife of George, b. June 27, 1822; d. March 14, 1893.
Orrin G. Taggart, d. April 20, 1887; 31y.
Sarah J. Taggart, d. Jan. 24, 1886; 62y. 10m. 22d.
Eliza Jane Trainer, daughter of J. and C., d. Jan. 26, 1865; 3y 11m. 12d.
William Tweed, d. May 29, 1853; 53y. 6m. 13d.
Jane Vincent, wife of Dr. Thomas, d. Oct. 11, 1858; 75y.
Mary Vincent, daughter of Dr. Thomas and Mary; d. April 13, 1829; 13y.
Mary Vincent, daughter of Thomas and Mary; d. April 3, 1846; 8y.
Dr. Thomas Vincent, d. Aug. 31, 1841; 87y.
Abraham Wallace, son of J. and E., b. Aug. 24, 1813; d. Aug. 18, 1846.
Elizabeth Wallace, wife of John, b. Sep. 23, 1776; d. Feb. 19, 1855.
Jane Wallace, wife of N. A., d. Feb.

9. 1868; 52y. 7m. 8d.
John Wallace, b. May 8, 1774; d. June 4, 1863.
Margaret Wallace, daughter of J. and E., b. July 16, 1806; d. Sep. 26, 1831.
Nathaniel A. Wallace, d. Dec. 28, 1892; 82y.
Esther Watt, wife of William, d. April 24, 1834; 54y.
Samuel Watt, d. Feb. 28, 1818; 76y.
John Waugh, son of J. and S., d. Feb. 17, 1848; 3y. 11m. 25d.
Daniel Welch, Sr., d. Sep. 7, 1819; 56y.
Daniel Welch, d. Aug. 9, 1868; 78y.
Daniel P. Welch, d. May 6, 1864; 24y. 6m. 8d.
Elizabeth Welch, wife of Daniel, d. March 29, 1844; 74y.
Elizabeth Welch, daughter of Daniel and Margaret; 15y.
E. Gray Welch, son of D. and M., d. Nov. 30, 1877; 35y.
John P. Welch, d. July 31, 1867; 31y. 11m. 22d.
Margaret Welch, wife of Daniel, d. Sep. 9, 1833; 37y.
Martha Welch, wife of Samuel, d. April 13, 1836; 21y.
Mary Welch, wife of Daniel, d. Feb. 5, 1848; 41y. 2m. 1d.
Samuel Welch, d. Feb. 22, 1865; 20y. 1m. 1d.
Mary White, wife of William, d. April 4, 1835; 25y.
Anne Wiley, wife of J., d. April 15, 1836; 39y.
Matilda Wiley, daughter of Joseph and Anne; d. April 6, 1832; 5m.
Rebecca L. Wiley, daughter of Joseph and Anne, d. March 17, 1820; 11y.
James Wilkin, d. April 7, 1815; 80y.
James Wilkin, d. Aug. 15, 1822; 19y. 11m. 7d.
William Wilkin, ———— 1808; ————
Infant daughter of A. and L. Work, d. June 10, 1862; 6d.
Alex. Work, d. May 7, 1851; 70y.
Alexander Work, son of Dr. G. L. and S. B., d. May 9, 1862; 19y. 10m. 8d.
Alexander Work, d. Jan. 16, 1883; 55y. 5m. 12d.
David C. Work, son of Dr. G. L. and S. B., d. July 19, 1863; 18y. 5m.
Jane Work, wife of A., d. April 9, 1851; 65y.
John B. Work, son of Dr. G. L. and S. B., d. April 16, 1864; 18y. 1m. 24d.
Nevin Craig Work, son of A. and J., d. Jan. 4, 1854; 1y. 11m. 13d.
Robert A. Work, son of A. and L., d. March 26, 1862; 4y. 13d.
Adam Wylie, d. June 1, 1827; 78y.
John Wylie, d. April 6, 1816; 40y.
Mary P. Wylie, wife of William, d. March 10, 1888; 85y.
William Wylie, d. Nov. 19, 1871; 69y. 9m. 5d.
Agnes Young, consort of Jacob; ————
Jacob Young, ————
Nancy Young, d. Feb. 28, 1827; 49y.

BURIALS IN THE OLD GRAVEYARD AT CADIZ.

To June 22, 1896.

Katharine ———— d. Feb. 12, 1844; 71y.
———— ————son, d. July 2, 1843; 27y. 11m.
Sarah Adams, d. March 25, 1854.
Margaret Alexander, d. July 22, 18—2; 30y. 6m. 27d.
Nancy Alexander, d. Jan. 24, 1855; 55y. 2m. 5d.
Samuel Alexander, d. Feb. 16, 1873; 84y. 21d.
Mary Allen, d. Jan. 7, 1837.
Jane Amspoker, wife of Samuel, d. June 27, 1859; 26y.
William Anderson, son of Hugh and Margaret, d. July 25, 1821; 2y. 3m.
Ruth Andrews, formerly widow of George McFadden, d. May 22, 1871.
Anna Arnold, wife of Rezin, d. Feb. 16, 1825; 29y. 7m. 3d.
John Arnold, son of Rezin and Anna, d. Feb. 27, 1823; 4m. 27d.
Emily Barcroft, daughter of John and Elizabeth, d. May 31, 1834.
James Bernard Barcroft, son of J. and E., d. April 7, 1832; 7y. 10m. 21d.
Martha Ann Barcroft, daughter of John and Elizabeth, d. May 26, 1835; 2y. 9m. 16d.
Sarah Barcroft, daughter of Ralph L. and M., d. Oct. 8, 1824; 4y. 8m. 5d.

Jane Barger, wife of Valentine, d. Sep. 12, 1853; 69y. 11m. 28d.
Jane Barger, daughter of H. and B., d. July 10, 1848; 11y. 28d.
Nancy Barger, daughter of H. and B., d. July 12, 1848; 3y. 8m. 9d.
Peter Bargar, d. Jan. 30, 1860: 71y.
Valentine Bargar, d. Sep. 27, 1851; 68y. 11m. 22d.
Mary Barnett, wife of James, d. Jan. 21, 1838; 67y.
Samuel Barnett, son of William and Phebe, d. March 22, 1842; 1y. 1m.
Mary Ann Beale, consort of John, d. March 2, 1842; 25y.
Robert Beatty, d. Nov. 15, 1849; 34y. 7m. 7d.
Nancy Beebe, wife of Gen. W. B., d. Oct. 13, 1856; 77y.
Gen. Walter B. Beebe, d. Jan. 24, 1836; 50y.
Mary Ellen Bennett, daughter of Willis W. and Mary, d. Aug. 21, 1836; 1y. 1m. 8d.
Lucinda Bingham, wife of Thomas, Sen., d. Nov. 6, 1844.
Hamilton Birch, d. March 27, 1847; 60y.
Isabella Birch, wife of Thomas L., d. Nov. 25, 1836; 77y.
Elizabeth Blackford, wife of Samuel, d. Oct. 4, 1846; 26y. 3m. 26d.
Mary Bostwick, daughter of S. W. and Ann P.———
Virginia Bostwick, daughter of S. W. and Ann P., d. Sept. 6, 1831.
Adaline Boyd, daughter of J. and M., d. June 21, 1851; 18y. 2m. 22d.
Alice C. Boyd, daughter of J. and M., d. Oct. 28, 1847; 9y.
Eliza A. Boyd, daughter of J. and M., d. March 5, 1856; 21y. 16d.
James Boyd, d. Dec. 25, 1851; 46y.
Margaret Boyd, consort of Thomas, d. May 8, 1831; 37y. 1m. 26d.
Mary Jane Boyd, daughter of James and Maria, d. April 19, 1832; 7m. 19d.
Crissinda Braden, daughter of J. B. and J., d. May 8, 1842; 1y. 10m. 2d.
John H. Braden, d. April 24, 1841; 24y.
Robert Braden, d. March 21, 1839; 65y.
Susanna Braden, wife of James, d. Dec. 22, 1857; 31y. 5m. 2d.

Nancy Brothers, d. Oct. 19, 1845; 2y. 26d.
Sara M. Brothers, daughter of J. and N., d. July 3, 1851; 1y. 8m. 6d.
Rosannah Moore Burney, daughter of William and Sarah Moore, and consort of Hugh Burney; [dates gone].
Walter F. Burwell, son of Joseph and Elizabeth, b. March 4, 1865; d. Jan. 10. 1823.
William Bushfield, son of George and Mary, d. Aug. 7, 1828; 10m. 29d.
Caroline T. Cady, daughter of J. and C. T., d. Feb. 15, 1845; 2y. 1m. 10d.
Elizabeth Cady, daughter of J. and C. T., d. Feb. 22, 1848; 1y. 5d.
John Caldwell, b. June 11, 1780; d. Dec. 10, 1859.
William T. Campbell, d. Jan. 26, 1855; 35y. 9m. 23d.
Elizabeth Carnahan, daughter of S. and S., d. Oct. 22, 1847; 8y. 7m. 5d.
George Carahan,———
Joseph Carnahan, son of Samuel and Sarah, d. Dec. 24, 1855; 21y. 11m. 23d.
Joseph Carnahan, d. Feb. 21, 1852, 82y.
Samuel Carnahan, d. Oct. 13, 1851; 87y.
Sarah Carnahan, consort of Samuel, d. Oct. 14, 1841; 34y.
Eliza J. Putnam Brister, daughter of M. P. and C. P., 11 weeks.
David Chambers, son of William and Ann, d. Sep. 13, 1821; 2y. 7m. 10d.
James W. Christy, son of W. and M., d. Nov. 12, 1849; 20y.
Martha Christy, wife of William, d. June 16, 1859: 65y.
William Christy, d. April 23, 1856; 63y.
Agnes Clandon, wife of James M., d. Nov. 20, 1853; 42y. 1d.
George G. Clandon, son of James M. and A., d. June 24, 1844; 1y. 14d.
George S. Clark, d. June 19, 1853; 41y. 27d.
Hannah J. Clark, daughter of Joseph and S., d. May 14, 1855; 3y. 11m.
Jane Clark, wife of Joseph, d. July 12, 1844; 37y.
Mary Clark, daughter of Samuel and Jane, d. Dec. 18, 1857; 1y. 5m.
Matthew Clark, d. May 18, 1852; 53y. 1m. 22d.
Samuel O. Clark, son of Joseph and

CADIZ BURIALS.

S., d. March 8, 1855; 7y. 3m. 6d.
John B. Clifford, son of J. and M. A., d. Oct. 14, 1852; 19y.
Ann Collins, d. Oct. 17, 1828;——
Jeremiah Cox, d. May 17, 1825; 11y. 2d.
Jonathan Cox, d. Aug. 25, 1817; 3y. 9m. 23d.
Ann Crabb, d. June 10, 1844; 13d.
Elizabeth Craig, wife of John, b. in Washington County, Pa., June 23, 1781; came to Ohio, Oct., 1803; d. Feb. 28, 1864.
John Craig, d. Aug. 22, 1825; 50y. 22d.
John Craig, Jr., d. Sep. 16, 1825; 3y. 1m. 16d.
Johnson Craig, son of Johnson and Martha, d. Oct. 1, 1837; 1y. 4m. 14d.
Rachel Craig, d. Aug. 22, 1825; 19y. 11m. 5d.
Rebecca Craig, daughter of Roland and Susanna, d. Feb. 15, 1832.
Roland Craig, d. August 24, 1824; 48y. 11m. 21d.
Susanna Craig, relict of Roland, d. July 13, 1826; 48y. 8m. 20d.
Thomas Craig, son of Walter and Elizabeth, d. Jan. 22, 1838; 18y. 6d.
Jane Crawford, consort of Thomas, d. July 26, 1836; 27y. 11m. 9d.
Myra M. Crawford, wife of J. R., b. May 6, 1811; d. Nov. 4, 1853.
Jane Croiser, consort of John, d. Sep. 15, 1839; 39y.
John W. Culbertson, son of R. and E., d. Dec. 12, 1849; 1m. 12d.
Sara Dawson, d. Jan. 20, 1858; 78y.
Thomas Dawson, d. Jan. 31, 1860; 89y.
E. H. Ditmars, d. May 22, 1852; 22y.
Esther B. Doig, wife of Rev. James R., d. July 6, 1851; 35y.
Isabella Douglass, wife of Samuel, d. July 3, 1849; 32y.
Sara Hull Douglass, daughter of Samuel and Isabella, d. July 17, 1846; 8y.
Ann Drummond, wife of Samuel, d. July 25, 1844; 44y.
James Drummond, Sr., d. March 13, 1830; 83y.
Margaret Drummond, d. July 7, 1839; 70y.
William H. Duncan, son of Richard and M., d. Oct. 1. 1859; 14d.
Sarah Dunlap, wife of Joseph, d. May 18, 1837; 37y. 4m. 4d.
Ezariah Edwards, d. Oct. 5, 1858; 90y.
Henrietta Edwards, wife of Ezariah, d. March 20, 1850; 75y.
Nancy Farrell, wife of Peter, d. May 12, 1845; 82y.
Peter Farrell, d. July 10, 1851; 105y. 1m.
Edward G. Ferguson, son of S. and H. J., d. June 9, 1852; 4 m. 9d.
Lucy M. Ferguson, daughter of S. and H. J., d. Aug. 26, 1853; 7y. 25d.
Robert Ferguson, d. Feb. 25, 1852; 70y.
William Ferguson, d. Dec. 15, 1832; 84y.
Thomas Findley, d. Jan. 11, 1847; 40y.
Julia Jenette Forbes, wife of J. S., d. Nov. 22, 1844; 23y.
Sara Jenette Forbes, daughter of J. and S. N., d. July 20, 1848; 9m.
Sara N. Forbes, wife of J. S., d. June 25, 1848; 22y.
S. J. Forbes, d. April 23, 1848; 21y.
Rebecca Ford, wife of John G., d. April 10, 1846; 19y.
Mary Ann Francis, consort of William, d. Feb. 6, 1833; 27y.
Mary Fryer, wife of Robert, d. May 30, 1837; 45y.
Robert Fryer, d. Jan. 28, 1857; 66y.
Robert Fulton, son of W. and M., d. April 6, 1850; 21y. 9m. 12d.
Thomas Fulton, d. May 26, 1827; 31y.
Abraham Furney, d. August 27, 1842; 84y.
Susanna Furney, d. May 28, 1842; 90y.
Margaret G——vin, d. 18—4; 80y.
Mary Gallagher, daughter of James and Elizabeth, d. Jan. 25, 1828.
Albert J. Gillespie, son of J. W. and C. A., d. July 15, 1853; 5y. 8m. 1c.
James P. Gillespie, son of J. W. and C. A., d. May 4, 1852; 6y. 6m. 3d.
Little Netty Gillespie, d. July 6, 1852; 2y. 9m. 4d.
—— Gilmore, d. March 20, 1840; 18y.
Elizabeth Buchanan Gilmore, consort of Samuel, d. April 16, 1829; 52y.
Francis Gilmore, d. July 8, 1846; 65y.
Rachel Gilmore, daughter of Nathaniel and Mary, d. Jan. 5, 1838; 4y. 3m. 5d.
Samuel Gilmore, d. Sept. 8, 1814; 44y.

"A soldier of the war of 1812."
Mary Katherine Glass, daughter of S. and N., d. Nov. 7, 1846; 1y. 7m. 22d.
Nancy Glass, wife of S., d. Feb. 11, 1858; 41y. 9m. 11d.
Marthas Glassgow, daughter of John W. and Sara W., d. Aug. 18, 1830; 1y. 1m. 6d.
Maryanna Glassgow, daughter of William and Mary, d. June 12, 1830; 16y. 8m. 26d.
Elizabeth Jane Gordon, neice of Dr. M. L. and Elizabeth Wilson, d. March 25, 1842; 18y. 7d.
Ebenezer Gray, Sr., d. Jan. 18, 1861; 38y. 2m. 18d.
Margaret Gray, wife of Ebenezer, d. July 5, 1852; 75y.
Mary Moore Gray, daughter of George and Ann Jane Moore, and wife of John P. Gray; d. Feb. 23, 1836; 22y.
James Grimes, son of William and Rebecca, d. July 10, 1841; 24y.
Francis Grove, d. March 9, 1844; 62y. 7m. 26d.
James Harper Guthrie, son of J. W. and E. S., d. June 12, 1853; 2y. 2m.
Infant son of S. and M. Hamilton.
Elizabeth Hamilton, consort of William, d. Feb. 1, 1829; 51y. 12d.
Francis Hamilton, d. March 1, 1844; 77y.
Joshua Hamilton, son of G. and M., d. Nov. 4, 1853; 6m. 11d.
Margaret Hamilton, daughter of William and Elizabeth, d. March 15, 1830; 35y. 7d.
Margaret Hamilton, wife of Francis, d. Feb. 6, 1857; 30y. 5m. 27d.
Ruth Hamilton, wife of Francis, d. Oct. 22, 1842; 52y. 7m.
Susanna Hamilton, daughter of William and Elizabeth, d. Jan. 8, 1837; 36y. 9m. 3d.
Andrew Finley Hanna, d. April 12, 1847; 34y.
Ann Leonard Hanna, consort of John; d. March 23, 1818; 45y.
George Hanna, son of A. F. and S., d. July 4, 1842; 1y. 5m.
James L. Hanna, d. June 11, 1820; 22y. 8m. 10d.
Jamima Hanna, wife of Rev. Thomas, d. July 14, 1847; 41y. 9m. 15d.
Jane Hanna, daughter of John, d. April 13, 1833; 22y.
John Hanna, d. June 2, 1847; 73y. 5m. 10d.
Mary Hanna, daughter of John, d. Sep. 11, 1820; 20y.
Mary Hanna, daughter of A. and S., d. Nov. 13, 1840; 2y. 6m.
Thomas Hanna, son of R. P. and J. E., d. Sep. 17, 1848; 1y. 10m. 17d.
Cassandria Harper, d. July 23, 1852; 48y.
James Harper, d. June 4, 1853; 60y. 6m. 16d.
Jane S. Harper, daughter of James and Sarah; d. Nov. 19, 1854; 33y. 8m. 1d.
Samuel Harper, d. July 30, 1849; 51y. 10m. 5d.
Sarah Harper, d. Dec. 20, 1837; 64y. 8m. 1d.
Infant daughter of W. and C. Harshe, d. May 10, 1850; 4d.
Eliza Hogg Hatcher, d. June 18, 1860; 57y. 9m. 25d.
Infant daughter of John and Nancy Haverfield, d. Aug. 1, 1849; 5d.
Agnes S. Haverfield, wife of John, d. Oct. 28, 1848; 77y.
Alvan Haverfield, son of John and Nancy, d. Aug. 11, 1844; 2y.
Catharine Haverfield, wife of Joseph, d. Aug. 20, 1852; 65y.
Elizabeth Haverfield, wife of W., d. Dec. 23, 1855; 84y.
Isabella Haverfield, daughter of James and Martha, d. Jan. 3, 1855; 1y. 3m. 19d.
John Haverfield, d. Aug. 23, 1855; 77y.
Joseph Haverfield, d. March 31, 1852; 61y. 11m. 3d.
Martha Haverfield, wife of James N., d. Jan. 28, 1857; 29y. 11m. 1d.
Mary Haverfield, daughter of John and Nancy, d. Oct. 4, 1845; 1y.
William Haverfield, d. June 14, 1859.
Ellen Healea, consort of Thomas, d. April 20, 1840; 20y.
Prudence Hedges, daughter of Samuel and Prudence, d. Oct. 21, 1840; 17y. 11m. 12d.
Alexander Henderson, d. Oct. 24, 1842; 55y.

CADIZ BURIALS.

Mary Ann Henderson, wife of John N., d. Sep. 30, 1854; 50y. 36d.
Mary E. Henderson, wife of John N., d. May 29, 1859; 24y. 4m.
Thomas Henderson, d. June 9, 1852; 70y.
Elizabeth Hitchcock, daughter of Samuel and Isabella, d. Jan. 17, 1832; 17y. 10m. 12d.
Isabella Hitchcock, wife of Samuel, d. Feb. 24, 1851; 63y.
Emley Hohman, daughter of J. and S., d. Dec. 22, 1850, 18y. 1m. 12d.
Percival Thomas Hogg, son of Thomas and E., d. Aug. 16, 1825; 1y. 1m. 9d.
Thomas Hogg, d. April 14, 1853; 55y. 7m. 14d.
William Henry Hogg, son of Thomas and E., d. Oct. 29, 1837; 8y. 2m. 27d.
Infant daughters of J. and E. Howard, d. Aug. 2, 1852, and Aug. 3, 1852.
Joshua Howard, d. July 31, 1859; 32y. 10m. 5d.
Martha Howard, wife of Joshua, d. July 8, 1860; 33y. 11m. 12d.
Mary Howard, daughter of Joshua and Martha, d. Aug. 4, 1853; 4y. 11m. 23d.
Henry Houser, d. Sep. 23, 1855; 69y.
Lydia Houser, wife of Gasaway, d. March 28, 1844; 37y.
Susanna Houser, wife of Henry, d. March 11, 1867; 76y.
Susan Hoyt, d. Feb. 6, 1843; 29y. 11m. 6d.
Clarissa D. Hull, consort of John, d. Dec. 13, 1837; 18y. 1m. 3d.
Daniel K. Hull, son of John S. and Mary Ann, d. Aug. 27, 1843; 6m. 19d.
John R. Hull, son of John and Clarissa D., d. March 13, 1838; 3m. 10d.
John C. Hunter, son of J. S., d. Dec. 26, 1849; 21y. 1d.
Andrew Jamison, d. April 27, 1854; 66y.
Ann Jamison, wife of John, Sen., d. Aug. 30, 1847; 67y.
Barclay Jamison, son of A. and A., d. Oct. 13, 1857; 1y. 5m. 2d.
John Jamison, Sen., d. Oct. 16, 1848; 74y.
Martha Jamison, consort of Walter, d. Nov. 23, 1856; 28y.
Mary Jamison, daughter of Joseph and C., d. Sep. 8, 1858; 7m. 8d.
Nancy Jamison, daughter of A. and M., d. Oct. 14, 1852; 19y.
Oliver Jamison, son of Andrew and A., d. Sep. 30, 1857; 3y. 8m. 20d.
Walter Jamison, son of Walter and Martha, d. March 1, 1835; 8m. 3d.
Willard G. Jamison, son of James B. and E., d. Nov. 23, 1856; 1m. 7d.
William R. Jamison, son of J. and S., d. August 17, 1849; 5y. 10m. 11d.
Martha Jewett, daughter of Thomas L. and Anne, 6y. 7m.
Briceland Johnson, son of James and Ann, d. Dec. 27, 1832; 5y. 3m. 14d.
Edward Johnson, son of W. and S., d. Feb. 6, 1854; 5y. 1m. 7d.
George H. Johnston, son of John and Eleanor, d. May 16, 1834; 21y.
Margaret Johnson, wife of Nicholas, d. Oct. 2, 1837; 68y. 8m. 2d.
Rebecca F. Johnson, daughter of Westcomb, d. Oct. 27, 1860; 4y. 8m. 5d.
Westcomb Johnson, d. August 10, 1859, 47y.
Dr. William Johnson, d. Dec. 27, 1838; 37y.
Calvin Jones, d. Dec., 1836; 37y.
Actia Junkins, consort of Adam, d. Jan. 8, 1829; 39y. 25d.
Mary J. Junkins, daughter of Adam and Actia, d. Nov. 6, 1828; 11m. 2d.
M. E. Junkins, d. April 2, 1826; 3m. 27d.
Samuel P. Junkins, son of Adam and Actia, d. May 6, 1825; 4y. 8d.
Henaby Kerr, a native of Dumfries, Scotland; d. July 12, 1857; 36y.
Mary Kilgore, consort of Daniel, b. May 18, 1800; d. Feb. 3, 1825; 24y. 8m. 16d.
Mary Kilgore, b. Jan. 16, 1852; d. May 19, 1857.
Mary Pritchard Kilgore, daughter of Daniel and Mary, b. Jan. 23, 1825; d. April 25, 1827.
William Philander Kilgore, son of Daniel and Mary, b. March 2, 1820; d. Sep. 30, 1821.
Catherine Kimble, d. July 31, 1830; 63y.
Munson King, son of Job and E., d. July 13, 1830; 1y. 2m. 8d.
Solomon King, son of Job and E., d. Sep. 28, 1833; 3y. 1m. 3d.

Amanda Knox, d. May 9, 1856.
Arthur Knox, d. Aug. 23. 1857.
Esther Knox, d. June 27, 1836.
Esther Knox, wife of William, d. March 2, 1863; 78y.
Margaret Knox, daughter of James and Sarah, d. June 11, 1830; 2y. 3m.
Rev. William Knox, d. June 16, 1851; 84y.
Elizabeth Lacey, daughter of Anna and John, d. Feb. 15, 1823; 1y. 2m. —d.
William Lacey, d. May 17, 1828; 64y.
Edward Lafferty, d. Nov. 8, 1836; 47y.
Jane Lafferty, daughter of Edward and Margaret, d. Jan. 21, 1835; 11y. 3m. 21d.
Samuel Lafferty, d. Aug. 26, 1828; 9y. 9m. 21d.
Robert Laughlin, d. Dec. 11, 1860; 18y. 5m. 6d.
Mary G. Leacock, wife of D. W., d. April 23, 1856; 28y. 1m. 27d.
James Lee, d. Oct. 3, 1845; 59y.
Jesse P. Lee, ———
John Basken Crouch Lee, son of James and Ruth, d. Dec. 3, 1857; 14y. 9m. 5d.
Marie Lee, ———
Martha Lee, daughter of Thomas and Nancy W., d. ———; 6m. 27d.
Martha C. Lee, daughter of Thomas and Nancy W., d. ———; 1y. 5m. 7d.
Thomas Lee, d. Nov. 1, 1854; 51y. 10m.
Jane Williams Lee, daughter of Thomas and Nancy, d. May 19, 1823; 2y. 8m. 28d.
Infant daughter of J. and S. J. Lofland; d. Oct. 9, 1852.
James Love, son of William and Nancy, d. Sep. 9, 1835; 2y.
Ann E. Lyons, d. April 23, 1844; 11m. 18d.
Ann W. Lyons, d. May 16, 1844; 34y.
John McAdams, d. Aug. 28, 1833; 73y. 9d.
Sarah Ann McClellan, wife of James, d. May 31, 1854; 37y. 9m. 26d.
Edward G. McCoy, son of M. and H., d. March 30, 1855; 5m. 7d.
Jane McCoy, wife of Matthew, d. Sep. 18, 1855; 73y. 2m. 29d.
Margaret J. McCoy, d. Jan. 17, 1822; 11y. 3m. 13d.
Martha J. McCoy, daughter of M. and H., d. Oct. 6, 1851; 9m. 24d.
Mary T. McCoy, d. Jan. 8, 1825; 10m. 21d.
Matthew McCoy, d. Oct. 10, 1855; 72y. 2m. 2d.
Amanda Jane McCue, daughter of Thomas and Mary, d. Oct. 16, 1846; 5y. 1m.
William H. H. McCue, son of Thomas and Mary, d. Feb. 12, 1849; 4m. 1d.
Infant daughter of S. B. and S. McFadden.
Elizabeth McFadden, wife of Samuel, d. Dec. 24, 1857; 72y.
Elizabeth McFadden, daughter of J. and M., d. April 19, 1837; 19y.
George McFadden, son of Samuel and Mary, d. Oct. 22, 1832; 8y. 26d.
George S. McFadden, d. Feb. 21, 1844; 60y.
James McFadden, son of Alexander and Margaret, d. August 23, 1839; 32y.
Jane McFadden, consort of Joseph, d. May 5, 1827; 67y.
John McFadden, d. April 13, 1835; 89y.
John McFadden, d. Aug. 30, 1857; 67y.
John McFadden, son of J. and M., d. Sep. 20, 1840; 3y. 4m.
John McFadden, son of S. B. and S., d. Nov. 13, 1840; 10m. 20d.
Joseph McFadden, d. Nov. 17, 1835; 78y.
Joseph McFadden, d. Feb. 26, 1859; 65y.
Margaret McFadden, consort of John, d. April 26, 1826; 75y.
Margaret McFadden, wife of Alexander, d. April 3, 1850; 66y.
Mary McFadden, wife of John, d. March 22, 1858; 70y.
Mary McFadden, wife of Joseph, d. March 2, 1844; 37y.
Mary McFadden, daughter of Samuel and Mary, d. July 1, 1832; 10y. 2m. 8d.
Nancy J. McFadden, d. April 5, 1845; 5y. 1d.
Rebecca McFadden, daughter of John and Mary, d. June 7, 1859; 42y. 2m. 16d.
Robert McFadden, son of Samuel and M., d. March 8, 1857; 21y. 7m. 8d.

CADIZ BURIALS.

Dr. Samuel McFadden, d. April 26, 1834; 77y.
Samuel McFadden, d. July 2, 1837; 59y.
Samuel McFadden, son of S. B. and S., d. Sep. 15, 1847; 6y. 2m.
Samuel McFadden, son of J. and M., d. July 25, 1853; 16y. 7m. 4d.
Samuel McFadden, d. March 26, 1854; 24y. 4m. 21d.
Samuel McFadden, Jr., d. May 5, 1847; 37y.
Samuel B. McFadden, d. March 19, 1855; 76y.
Samuel D. McFadden, son of N. and E., d. Feb. 17, 1860; 24y. 10m. 27d.
Sarah McFadden, daughter of S. and L., d. Feb. 2, 1847; 40y.
John B. McGrew, Jr. b. Nov. 30, 1844; d. Sep. 30, 1845.
Benezer McKinnia, d. June 12, 1847; 31y.
Hester Maholm, wife of Samuel. d. Sep. 22, 1856; 53y.
John Maholm, d. Sep. 9, 1854; 59y.
Margaret Maholm, d. Aug. 18, 1858; 68y.
Martha Maholm, daughter of Samuel and H., d. Aug. 19, 1830; 1y. 20d.
Sarah Maholm, d. July, 1848; 45y.
Sarah Maish, wife of Joseph, d. Nov. 21, 1849; 24y.
George Mahood, d. Dec. 17, 1831; 52y.
Nancy Mahood, wife of James, d. June 24, 1844; 24y.
Lorenzo Marker, son of Samuel and Ciscelia, d. Feb. 6, 1831; 3m. 18d.
Anna Martin, d. April 3, 1856; 56y.
Agnes J. Maxwell, daughter of J. C. and M., d. Dec. 21, 1852; 3y.
Rebecca Mayes, consort of John, d. Feb. 24, 1817; 29y. 8m. 24d.
Samuel Mealey, d. Nov. 25, 1850; 49y. 6m. 6d.
Samuel T. Mealey, son of S. and A., d. Dec. 22, 1850; 18y. 5m. 15d.
William C. Mealey, son of S. and A., d. Nov. 4, 1850; 20y. 7m. 13d.
Margaret Means, wife of James, Jr., d. Feb. 4, 1816; 25y. 2m. 14d.
James D. Meek, d. May 22, 1835; 4y.
Joseph Meek, d. July 23, 1833; 34y. 10m. 29d.
Alfred P. Meeks, d. May. 5, 1835; 8y. 10m.
Joseph Mehollin, d. March 14, 1853; 60y.
Jane Miller, wife of William, d. Jan. 8, 1855; 21y. 4m.
John Miller, d. Feb. 5, 1838; 76y. 4m. 9d.
Margaret Miller, d. Sep. 14, 1856; 27y.
Margaret Miller, daughter of James and Susan, d. March 17, 1832; 2m. 13d.
Mary Miller, wife of John, Sr., d. Sep. 23, 1850; 97y.
Mary Miller, daughter of J. and S., d. March 15, 1832; 4y. 10m. 1d.
Rebecca J. Miller, daughter of James and Susan, d. March 19, 1832; 10m. 16d.
Samuel Miller, son of S. and S., d. Sep. 12, 1828; 7m. 13d.
Sarah Miller, daughter of J. and S., d. Dec. 15, 1830; 4y. 11m. 11d.
Thomas Miller, d. July 25, 1841; 3Cy. 4m. 16d.
Infant daughter of William and Lydia Milligan, d. May 11, 1827.
Alexander Milligan, d. Jan. 29, 1828; 39y. 8m. 20d.
David Milligan, Sr., d. Dec. 8, 1833; 84y.
Lydia Milligan, d. Feb. 11, 1838; 38y. 11m. 7d.
Mary Milligan, daughter of William and Lydia, d. Dec. 14, 1837; 3m. 15d.
Hannah Mitchell, consort of James, d. May 6, 1824; 38y.
Ann Jane Moore, wife of George, d. August 10, 1839; 59y.
Elizabeth Moore, wife of John, d. Sep. 9, 1856; 38y.
Elizabeth Moore, daughter of William and Sarah, d. Sep. 22, 1825; 18y.
George Moore, d. May 19, 1875; 62y.
Hans W. Moore, son of Hans and Caroline, d. May 25, 1845; 6m. 2d.
Mary E. Moore, daughter of A. F. and S., d. March 25, 1852; 1y. 1m. 4d.
Robert Moore, d. Nov. 16, 1837; 30y.
Sarah C. Moore, wife of A. F., b. Sep. 12, 1823; d. March, 25, 1852.
William Moore, d. ———— 1847; 68y.
George Oglevee, son of J. and E. A., d. April 3, 1857; 11y.
Elousia Olmstead, daughter of Plat-

Bennett, b. Dec. 16, 1793; d. Feb. 17, 1856.
Jesse Olmstead, son of John and Elousia, d. April 21, 1837; 21y. 2m. 21d.
John Olmstead, b. Feb. 18, 1782; d. June 11, 1856.
Ziva Bennett Olmstead, son of Elousia, d. Oct. 23, 1823; 3y. 8m.
Charlotte Osborn, daughter of Samuel and C., d. August 6, 1828; 6m. 16d.
Hannah Osborn, wife of Samuel, d. Nov. 15, 1828; 41y. 7m. 10d.
James Osborn, son of Samuel and Hannah, d. May 22, 1823; 8m. 6d.
John Osburn, son of J. and C. d. Nov. 22, 1831; 19y. 11m. 8d.
Samuel Osborn, b. Feb., 1781, d. Feb. 26, 1846.
L—— Parr, daughter of Thomas and Sara, d. Dec. 10, 1825; 11m. 1d.
Elizabeth J. Parrish, daughter of Benjamin and Katharine, d. April 30, 1832; 5y.
Charlotte Patton, wife of Dr. R. W., d. Sep. 26, 1848; 34y. 2m.
John S. Patton, son of J. and N.. d. Nov. 9, 1841; 1y. 10m.
Martha A. Patton, Daughter of J. and N., d. Sep. 2, 1841; 4y. 8m.
Thomas Patton, d. Feb. 28, 1832; 63y. 3m. 22d.
Sarah Paxton, wife of R., daughter of Richard McCullough, d. Jan. 3, 1855; 27y.
John A. Peppard, son of S. G. and S. C.. b. March 14, 1853; d. Nov. 28, 1853.
Samuel G. Peppard, Esq., b. Dec. 29, 1817; d. Dec. 5, 1855:
Elizabeth Pepper, consort of Henry, d. Dec. 11, 1851; 57y. 3m. 20d.
Ada W. Phillips, daughter of B. W. and M., d. Oct. 9, 1854; 2y. 11m. 14d.
Sarah Phillips, daughter of John and Eliza, d. May 31, 1835; 10m. 11d.
James Porter, d. March 20, 1842; 37y.
James Porter, son of D. and T., d. Sep. 21, 1847; 1y. 9m. 14d.
Samuel Porter, son of James, d. Jan. 11, 1835; 10y. 19d.
C. S. Price, wife of B. W., d. May 30, 1857; 40y. 1d.
Jessie Pritchard, d. Jan. 6, 1835; 32y. 6m. 3d.
Sarah Pritchard, daughter of John and Sarah, b. Aug. 11, 1814; d. June 4, 1820; 5y. 9m. 24d.
William T. Pugh, son of E. M. and M. A., d. May 21, 1854; 5y. 9m. 9d.
Elizabeth Rabe, consort of John, d. July 30, 1820; 72y. 2m. 4d.
Isabella Ramsey, wife of Benjamin, d. March 31, 1846; 49y.
Sarah Ramsey, daughter of J. and S., d. Dec. 29, 1851; 29y. 7m. 28d.
Sarah Ann Ramsey, daughter of J. and N., d. July 26, 1850; 8m. 14d.
James Rankin, d. Sep. 23, 1823; 76y.
Infant son of John S. and Sara Rea.—
Adaline Rea, daughter of John and Sarah, d. May 24, 1835; 2y. 6m. 27d.
Mary Richey, wife of Thomas, d. Aug. 2, 1823; 52y.
Thomas Richey, d. Sep. 29, 1824; 55y.
George W. Riley, d. June 8, 1835; 21y. 9m. 29d.
N. Riley, Sr., d. July 18, 1852; 83y.
Nancy Riley, wife of Nathan, d. Feb. 13, 1860; 76y.
Margaret Ritchie, wife of John, d. Dec. 29, 1853; 63y.
John Robinson, d. Jan. 26, 1838; 44y. 5m. 13d.
Mary Jane Robinson, daughter of John and Susanna, d. Jan. 30, 1823; 2y. 2m. 11d.
Mary J. Robinson, daughter of J. and S., d. April 7, 1832; 9y. 8m. 27d.
Infant daughter of J. J. and E. A. Rose, d. Dec. 2, 1854; 1m. 9d.
John M. Rose, son of J. J. and E. A., d. April 16, 1857; 8m. 24d.
James Ross, d. May 7, 1832; 27y. 8m. 5d.
John Ross, d. Sep. 8, 1833; 82y. 11m. 25d.
John Sankey, d. April 17, 1821; 4m. 17d.
Robert Sankey, d. Nov. 18, 1820; 19y. 11m. 24d.
Elizabeth Scoles, wife of Curtis W., d. July 18, 1833; 24y. 5m. 16d.
Eleanor Scott, daughter of James and Harriet, d. Sep. 3, 1823; 10m.
James Sharp, d. Jan. 6, 1838; 5y. 3m.
Jane Sharp, wife of Thomas, **d.** April 24, 1859; 93y. 3m. 24d.

CADIZ BURIALS.

John C. Sharp, son of William and M., d. Nov. 25, 1851; 14y. 3m. 13d.
Joseph Sharp, son of T. and J., d. May 13, 1833; 17y. 8m. 21d.
Joseph Sharp,———
Sarah Sharp, daughter of Thomas and J., d. Sep. 4, 1831; 18y. 8m. 3d.
Thomas Sharp, d. Dec. 29, 1825, 57y. 5m. 11d.
Mary Shotwell, daughter of S. B. and N. G., d. March 2, 1854; 10m.
Walter B. Shotwell, d. May 21, 1847; 16y.
William Shotwell, d. Dec. 1, 1849; 25y.
William Shotwell, d. Jan. 21, 1857; 57y.
Ann Slemmons, wife of M. G., d. March 26, 1857; 39y.
John Slemmons, d. Feb. 23, 1840; 25y.
John D. Slemmons, son of William R. and Nancy, d. Aug. 31, 1821; 13y. 9m. 27d.
William Slemmons, son of M. G., d. May 23, 1846; 1y. 3m. 20d.
William Slemmons, son of B. and S., d. Aug. 19, 1848; 19y.
William R. Slemmons, d. Dec. 6, 1841; 61y.
Elizabeth J. Sloan, daughter of Matthew and Elizabeth, d. March 23, 1842; 3y. 6m. 5d.
Samuel Smiley, son of J. V. and J.
Sarah M. Smiley, daughter of J. V. and J., d. April 23, 1851; 3y. 11m.
William Smiley, son of J. V. and J., d. May 10, 1854; 24y.
Rosswell C. Smith, son of J. M. and R., d. July 29, 1850; 9y. 7m. 2d.
Samuel Smith,———
Rachel Snider, wife of Samuel, daughter of W. and S. Moore, b. March 13, 1819, d. Oct. 18, 1847.
Samuel Snider, d. Dec. 18, 1854; 45y.
Mary Spear, consort of John, d. June 1, 1826; 45y.
John Steward, d. Feb. 13, 1826; 29y. 5m. 5d.
John Steward, d. August 28, 1835; 74y.
Margaret Strausbaugh, daughter of V. and B., d. July 19, 1848; 27y. 25d.
Joseph Wilson Stubbins, son of Henry and Urith, d. May 7, 1830; 30d.
Alexander Taggart, d. Aug. 13, 1836; 32y.

Mary Eliza Taggart, daughter of Alexander and C. H., d. July 24, 1836; 2y.
Samuel David Taggart, son of A. and C. H., d. July 31, 1836; 4y.
Infant daughter of J. and E. Thompson.
David Thompson, d. June 16, 1855; 49y. 8m. 13d.
Frank S. Thompson, son of S. and S. J., d. Sep. 10, 1856; 1y. 7m. 3d.
Jane Thompson, wife of James W., d. May 14, 1829; 52y.
Charles Timmons, d. ———
Eli Timmons, d. April 27, 1829; 33y. 3m. 21d.
Eliza Timmons, daughter of Eli and Naomi, and niece of John S. Lacey, d. July 16, 1832; 19y.
Frederick Timmons, d. Dec. 6, 1837; 32y. 4m. 21d.
Katherine Timmons, daughter of Charles and Mary, d. Jan. 31, 1831; 28y. 5m. 4d.
Mary Timmons, wife of Charles, d. Aug. 5, 1850; 75y.
Mary Ann Timmons, wife of Eli, d. Dec. 17, 1848; 26y.
Anna Mary Tipton, daughter of W. and M. E., d. Feb. 13, 1859; 17d.
Elizabeth Tipton, daughter of J. and R., d. May 24, 1846; 5y. 6m. 3d.
John Tipton, d. Jan. 11, 1845; 30y. 10d.
Ruth Tipton, wife of John, d. March 22, 1849; 38y. 20d.
Elizabeth Vandergraft, daughter of Jacob and Elizabeth, d. Feb. 10, 1838; 5y. 1m. 26d.
Mary Matilda H. Vandolah, daughter of Peter and Nancy, d. May 18, 1824; 1y. 6m. 28d.
Nimrod Wagers, d. July 29, 1841; 32y. 12d.
James Walker, d. April 18, 1852; 73y.
Sara Walker, wife of James, d. Dec. 28, 1858; 79y.
Jamima Wallace, daughter of Robert and Albina, d. June 17, 1860.
J. R. Wallace, b. May. 1, 1809; d. Oct. 29, 1846.
Mary Wallace, consort of John R., d. July 17, 1834; 29y.
William Wallace, d. May 28, 1840; 88y. 2m. 14d.
Sarah T. Waller, daughter of Samuel

and Amy Rose, d. June 13, 1848. Also son, Feb. 7, 1850.
Butler J. Ward, d. Dec. 1, 1844; 22y.

Maria Weaver, consort of John, d. Aug. 8, 1841; 20y. 1m. 28d.
Eliza Welch, wife of Rezin, d. Aug. 6, 1842; 41y.
James Welch, son of B. and J., d. May 27, 1849; 27y.
Rev. Johnson Welch, d. April 7, 1837; 27y. 7m. 2d.
Jane Welling, wife of D., d. June 26, 1844; 32y.
Margaret Welling, wife of David,———
Joseph Wells, son of Thomas W. and Eleanor, d. Jan. 19, 1832; 5m. 19d.
Hannah White, d. Jan. 1. 1849; 75y.
Eleanor Wilkin, d. June 24, 1817.
Matthew Wilkin, d. Aug. 15, 1835; 64y.
Mary Williams, wife of J., d. April 27, 1848; 29y. 3m. 26d.
Infant son of T. A., and S. A. Wilson, d. April 23, 1869.
David Wilson, son of William and Lydia, d. Oct. 1, 1837; 4y. 2m. 4d.
Elizabeth Wilson, wife of Dr. M. L., d. Aug. 10, 1858; 74y.
James Wilson, d. Dec. 6, 1839; 62y. 2m. 6d.
Jane Wilson, wife of James, d. March 31, 1833; 56y. 6m.
Dr. Martin L. Wilson, b. May 15, 1785; d. Jan. 10, 1872; 87y.
Thomas L. Birch Wilson, son of Dr. Martin L. and Elizabeth, d. July 25, 1825; 6 weeks, 2d.
Lucilla Caroline Young, d. April 29, 1834; 33y.

BURIALS IN THE NEW GRAVEYARD AT CADIZ.

[So Far as the Graves are Marked.]

Frank S. Adams, b. March 13, 1867; d. June 30, 1891.
Mary Adams, daughter of William and Matilda, d. Feb. 23, 1862; 22y.
Matilda Adams, wife of William, d. Dec. 17, 1868; 67y.
Elizabeth Allen, wife of C. N., d. Nov. 4, 1863; 36y. 6m.
Teresa J. Allen, daughter of C. N. and E., d. March 16, 1857; 5y. 2m. 7d.
Virginia Allen, daughter of C. N., d. ———, 18—; 2y. 23d.
Alexander M. Amspoker, d. Nov. 20, 1889; 83y.
Mary Amspoker, wife of Alexander, d. April 6, 1867; 65y.
Samuel Wilmer Atkinson, son of B. F. and Eliza A., d. July 27, 1862; 13y. 6m. 27d.
Stella Auld, daughter of E. M. and S. J., d. Sep. 18, 1877; 1y. 1m. 19d.
Mary Barr, wife of W. A., b. Oct. 2, 1844; d. May 9, 1879.
Henry Barricklow, d. Feb. 28, 1873; 36y.
John Barricklow, d. July 21, 1875; 71y. 9m. 3d.
Mary Ann Barricklow, wife of John, d. July 21, 1875; 74y. 5m. 14d.
Richard P. Barricklow, son of G. W. and R. E., b. July 23, 1871; d. Oct. 8, 1890.
Jane Ann Bayless, d. Nov. 24, 1864; 19y. 4m. 17d.
Arter Beatty, b. Jan. 25, 1827; d. Feb. 11, 1894.
Kate Beatty, daughter of Arter and Susan, b. Nov. 16, 1873; d. April 1, 1877.
Lizzie M. Beatty, daughter of Arter and Susan, b. Nov. 12, 1865; d. April 11, 1877.
Maria B. Beebe, d. Aug. 10, 1891; 69y.
Rezin Welch Beebe, son of Stuart and Anjanett; d. Dec. 31, 1874; 2y. 8m.
George S. Bell, d. Aug. 3, 1897; 23y. 6m 15d.
Jennie L. Bigger, wife of John, d. June 30, 1871; 25y. 8m.
Joseph C. Bigger, d. Dec. 4, 1870; 29y. 5m. 13d.
Sarah H. Bigger, b. Dec. 22, 1809; d. Oct. 7, 1875.
Robert Birney, born Sep. 9, 1811; d. Dec. 4, 1884.
Albion W. Bostwick, Captain of Company G, 74th O. V. I., d. Dec. 10, 1862; 35y. 10m. 10d.
Clarence E. Bostwick, son of Albion and Mary, d. Oct. 15, 1861; 7y. 1m. 5d.
Samuel W. Bostwick, d. Oct. 6, 1867;

CADIZ BURIALS.

69y.
Robert Bowland, b. 1798; d. 1880.
Frank Boyles, b. July 6, 1851; d. Sep. 1, 1856.
Henry Boyles, b. Jan. 5, 1814; d. July 8, 1892.
Martha Boyles, wife of Henry, b. May 12, 1826; d. April 4, 1874.
Martha Boyles, b. Aug. 22, 1853; d. May 3, 1874.
William H. Boyles, b. July 6, 1849; d. April 18, 1897.
Isabell N. Braden, daughter of R. L. and L. E., d. Oct. 26, 1894; 6y. 1m. 7d.
James Braden, b. July 3, 1802; d. June 28, 1878.
Melissa Braden, wife of D. B., d. May 14, 1889; 46y.
S. M. Braden, wife of D. B., b. July 2, 1812; d. April 19, 1895.
Elijah B. Brenan, d. March 15, 1876; 52y.
David Bricker, son of John and Anna, d. June 27, 1878; 44y. 6m. 26d.
John Bricker, d. March 27, 1861; 67y. 10m. 19d.
Lucinda Bricker, daughter of Henry and Mary A., and wife of John Bricker, d. May 24, 1871; 86y. 1m. 11d.
Lydia Bricker, wife of Henry, d. Jan. 9, 1865; 68y. 8m. 21d.
Ann Brindley, d. May 27, 1810; d. Oct. 6, 1889.
John Brindley, Jr., b. Feb. 5, 1844; d. Oct. 14, 1880.
Laura E. Brothers, daughter of John and Nancy, d. Sep. 19, 1861; 1y. 7m. 15d.
Mary E. Brothers, daughter of J. and N., d. Sep. 22, 1861; 5y. 6m. 13d.
Ida F. R. Brown, wife of Dr. S. H., and daughter of F. and M. Hamilton, d. Feb. 17, 1871; 21y. 10m. 23d.
Dr. S. H. Brown, b. July 4, 1840; d. March 27, 1882.
Louisa Bryan, wife of William H., d. May 4, 1866; 28y.
Mattie M. Bryan, daughter of Richard and Ella C., b. Oct. 20, 1865; d. Dec. 21, 1865.
Sarah A. Bryan, daughter of G. W. and S., b. Dec. 15, 1834; d. Nov. 27, 1881.
Susanna Bryan, wife of G. W., b. March 18, 1811; d. Jan. 15, 1882.
William H. Bryan, son of G. W. and S., b. Feb. 7, 1836; d. April 14, 1873.
Wilmer E. Bryan, son of R. and E., b. Feb. 23, 1870; d. Aug. 19, 1872.
Enoch Bulger, b. July 2, 1816; d. May 2, 1881.
Susanna Bulger, b. Oct. 19, 1828; d. May 8, 1887.
Annie L. Busby, wife of G. W., d. Aug. 17, 1890; 26y. 8m. 14d.
C. S. Cady. [No dates].
J. Cady. [No dates].
J. R. Cady. [No dates].
Margaret Cady, wife of John, d. May 18, 1864; 99y.
Thomas Cady, son of William and Rachel, d. Aug. 27, 1864; 9y. 4m.
Anna E. W. Campbell, first wife of S. S., d. April 1, 1872; 37y.
Mary L. Campbell, second wife of S. S., d. June 3, 1886; 43y.
S. S. Campbell, d. Jan. 4, 1895; 71y.
George D. Carnahan, d. May 14, 1845; 2y. 11d.
David S. Carrick, b. April 1, 1782; d. Dec. 25, 1863.
Elizabeth Carrick, wife of David S., b. Aug. 26, 1794; d. Nov. 15, 1873.
Rebecca Carrick, wife of William, d. July 3, 1872; 46y. 8m. 25d.
Elijah Carson, d. Nov. 21, 1887; 77y. 7m. 9d.
James N. Carson, b. 1849; d. 1883.
Margaret M. Carson, wife of Elijah, d. Nov. 8, 1884; 81y. 9m. 18d.
Margaret Carson, wife of W. N., b. 1824; d. 1885.
William J. Carson, son of E. and M., d. at Dist. San Vincenti Mineral San Rafael, State of Sinaloa, Republic of Mexico, Dec. 10, 1872; 40y. 8m. 8d; his remains were taken up by his brother, A. W. Carson, and brought to the United States and interred here, Sep. 20, 1876.
Elizabeth Cassell, wife of Jacob, d. April 18, 1867; 63y. 3d.
Jacob Cassell, d. June 7, 1881; 81y. 8m. 22d.
Jennie M. Chaney, daughter of N. and J. M., d. May 17, 1878; 12y. 7m. 3d.

J. W. Chaney, Company C, 5th Ohio Cavalry.

Jane Clark, wife of Matthew, d. Oct. 5, 1869; 70y.

Clara Cochran Clark, wife of Oliver, b. April 3, 1850; d. Jan. 20, 1878.

Ephraim Clark b. Feb. 19, 1826; d. Oct. 10, 1886.

John M. Clark, b. April 12, 1849; d. April 24, 1871.

John B. Clark, b. Oct. 9, 1827; d. Jan. 13, 1872; Colonel of the 126th and 193rd Pennsylvania Volunteers from 1863 to 1864.

Oliver Clark, b. Dec. 9, 1847; d. March 3, 1894.

Retta A. Clark, b. May 10, 1842; d. April 22, 1866.

William James Clark, b. March, 1855; d. Aug. 4, 1882.

John Clifford, son of J. and M. A., d. Sep. 1, 1863; 9m.

John C. Clifford, d. June 13, 1896; 27y. 10m. 22d.

Mary Ann Clifford, wife of John, Jr., d. Sep. 2, 1863; 84y.

Mary Clifford, wife of John, Sr., d. March 24, 1865; 74y.

Mary Clifford, daughter of J. and M. A., d. July 30, 1875; 20y. 4m. 6d.

J. F. Clokey, Company F, 7th Mo. Cavalry.

Eleanor Cochran, daughter of Robert and Sarah, b. Feb. 11, 1808; d. Sep. 17, 1867.

Robert Cochran, b. Sep. 15, 1771; d. Feb. 1, 1862.

Sarah Cochran, wife of Robert, b. Jan. 8, 1787; d. April 4, 1867.

Abraham Coleman, Company C, 13th Q. V. I.

Fanny Bell Conwell, daughter of J. and M. J., d. June 9, 1857; 4y. 3m. 6d.

Rebecca Conwell, b. March 16, 1814; d. June 7, 1886.

William H. Conwell, d. Dec. 7, 1861; 5y. 10m. 2d.

Frank G. Corbly, b. Feb. 8, 1871; d. Jan. 6, 1875.

George D. Corbly, b. Sep. 19, 1872; d. Aug. 27, 1873.

Nettie B. Corbly, b. Feb. 22, 1874; d. Sep. 6, 1892.

Elizabeth Cox, b. Jan. 1, 1801; d. Jan. 31, 1879.

Jacob Crabb, b. April 18, 1815; d. April 24, 1872.

Jane D. Crabb, wife of Jacob, d. Dec. 9, 1889.

Hannah H. Craig, wife of Walter, b. March 10, 1826; d. July 27, 1879.

Jane Craig, wife of Walter, d. July 12, 1859; 36y. 6m. 10d.

Johnson Craig, b. Dec. 3, 1803; d. July 14, 1888.

Martha Craig, wife of Johnson, b. Dec. 26, 1810; d. July 16, 1890.

Nannie N. Craig, daughter of Walter and Hannah H., d. July 20, 1863; 1y. 25d.

Sarah J. Craig, daughter of Walter and Jane, d. Dec. 5, 1857; 13y. 1m. 10d.

Eleanor Crawford, wife of Thomas, d. Nov. 16, 1889; 83y. 11m. 8d.

Elizabeth Crawford, wife of John, b. Dec. 2, 1827; d. Aug. 11, 1877.

Elizabeth J. Crawford, daughter of T. and E., d. March 27, 1864; 21y. 8m. 1d.

Hattie R. Crawford, daughter of J. and E., b. May 16, 1860; d. March 12, 1878.

Thomas Crawford, d. Sep. 23, 1893; 88y. 9m. 20d.

William Croskey, d. July 3, 1872; 79y.

Rebecca Crumley, wife of John, d. June 30, 1870; 48y. 4m. 27d.

David Cummins, b. March 9, 1822; d. July 12, 1894.

Bessie C. Cunningham, daughter of David and Laura, b. May 8, 1873; d. Feb. 17, 1885.

John Cunningham, son of David and Mary McLaughlin Cunningham, b. Oct. 29, 1808; d. Aug. 18, 1870.

Nancy Sharp Cunningham, wife of John, d. Oct. 10, 1875; 65y.

William S. Cunningham, son of David and Laura, d. Aug. 4, 1865; 9m. 12d.

Anne Curtis, wife of Alexander, b. April 11, 1831; d. July 9, 1875.

Henry G. Dallas, b. May 21, 1835; d. March 22, 1875.

Elizabeth Davenport, wife of John S., d. Dec. 18, 1880.

John S. Davenport, a native of Stock-

CADIZ BURIALS.

port, England; d. Nov. 23, 1870; 59y. 10m. 8d.
Elizabeth Davidson, wife of Robert, d. Nov. 26, 1855; 74y.
Robert Davidson, d. Dec. 20, 1805; 88y. 10m. 24d.
Henry S. Davis, son of Henry and Eliza, d. Nov. 6, 1861; 3y. 3m. 10d.
Martha E. Denny, wife of Henry W., d. Feb. 12, 1882; 24y. 3m. 12d.
Alfred W. Dent, b. March 11, 1823; d. Sep. 2, 1880.
Sarah Dent, wife of Alfred W., b. July 26, 1817; d. Oct. 14, 1868.
Margaret Devine, d. Aug. 26, 1865; 69y.
Charles Edward Dewey, b. Dec. 19, 1875; d. Aug. 5, 1876.
Chauncey Dewey, b. March 27, 1796; d. Feb. 5, 1880.
Eliphalet C. Dewey, b. Dec. 16, 1823; d. Feb. 28, 1889.
Nancy Prichard Dewey, wife of Chauncey, b. Oct. 27, 1804; d. Sep. 6, 1897.
Sarah Knox Dewey, wife of E. C., b. July 10, 1823; d. Jan. 15, 1876.
Anna M. Dickerson, daughter of G. M. and L. B., b. March 21, 1882; d. July 8, 1893.
Catherine Dickerson, b. Feb. 1, 1851; d. July 14, 1859.
Granville M. Dickerson, d. Feb. 13, 1882; 26y. 10m. 16d.
Maggie E. Dickerson, daughter of Rev. S. R. and J. J., b. Nov. 22, 1857; d. Nov. 15, 1872.
George Downard, Company C, 126th Ohio Infantry.
Catheran Drummond, wife of Rev. J., b. Jan. 27, 1805; d. Sep. 2, 1883.
James Drummond, M. D., D. D., d. May 10, 1888; 80y.; was a physician 10 years, a minister 52 years.
Hugh Dunlap, b. Oct. 17, 1822; d. March 29, 1894.
Isaac Eddy, Company B, 126th Ohio Infantry.
Rev. Edward Ellison, D. D., d. March 10, 1883; 53y. 1m. 19d.
Amanda J. Estep, wife of Josiah, b. Sep. 23, 1837; d. March 23, 1898.
Clara Estep, b. May 26, 1862; d. Aug. 11, 1863.
Emma F. Estep, b. Oct. 22, 1879; d. July 21, 1880.
Josiah M. Estep, b. Feb. 19, 1826; d. May 5, 1888.
Hannah Farr, daughter of J. and R., d. May 26, 1878; 16y. 11m. 21d.
Rachel Farr, wife of John H.; d. Nov. 30, 1873; 35y. 8m. 12d.
Charles Ferguson, son of S. and H. J., b. March 17, 1856; d. Feb. 21, 1880.
Edwin G. Ferguson, son of S. and H. J., b. Feb. 1, 1852; d. June 9, 1852.
Lucy May Ferguson, daughter of S. and H. J., b. Dec. 31, 1848; d. Aug. 26, 1853.
H. J. Ferguson, wife of Samuel, b. April 4, 1819; d. Oct. 26, 1890.
Robert Ferguson, d. Feb. 25, 1852; 70y.
Samuel Ferguson, b. Sep. 6, 1823; d. Oct. 29, 1895.
Turner Ferguson, son of S. and H. J., b. May 18, 1854; d. Oct. 5, 1861.
Margaret Finney, wife of R. T., d. Jan. 23, 1865; 81y.
Robert Finnical, b. April 4, 1818; d. Dec. 22, 1896.
John Fogle, Sergeant Company B, 30th Ohio Infantry.
H. G. Forker, b. Nov. 19, 1838; d. Jan. 25, 1896.
Mary Forker, d. July 8, 1865; 73y.
Elias Foust, b. Sep., 1826; d. April 5, 1873; 46y. 6m. 9d.
William E. Fulton, son of J. C. and S. C., d. Feb. 25, 1882; 17y. 1Cm. 24d.
Reese Furbay, b. June 20, 1847; d. Nov. 47y. 8m. 26d.; a member of Companies Y and H, 170th O. V. I.
John W. P. Gallagher, d. Aug. 10, 1892; 47y. 8m. 26d.; a member of Companies Y and H, 170th O. V. I.
Joseph Gambs, d. July 1, 1884; 58y. 3m. 5d.
Millie E. Gambs, daughter of J. and L. T., d. Oct. 25, 1876; 9y. 7m. 23d.
Anna L. Garvin, wife of J. M., b. March 6, 1846; d. May 21, 1889.
Helen M. Garvin, daughter of J. M. and A. L., b. Feb. 10, 1872; d. April 10, 1872.
John M. Garvin, b. May 16, 1845; d. July 4, 1897.
Albert George, killed at the Battle of Antietam, Sep. 17, 1862; 21y.

Harry George, son of Thomas and Mira, d. June 8, 1862; 8y. 3m. 8d.
Turner George, b. Dec. 27, 1862; d. Aug. 11, 1863.
Albert J. Gillespie, d. July 15, 1853; 5y.
Cornelia Gillespie, wife of J. W., b. Nov. 27, 1823; d. May 7, 1878.
James P. Gillespie, d. May 4, 1852; 6y.
John W. Gillespie, b. 1819; d. 1885.
Nettie Gillespie, d. July 6, 1853; 2y.
Wayne Gillespie, b. Nov. 11, 1858; d. June 7, 1895.
Bell Glandon, niece of John and Martha Carnahan, d. July 6, 1863; 13y. 10m. 13d.
Jane Glenn, d. Nov. 5, 1886; 82y.
John Q. Glover, d. May 5, 1890; 38y.
Willie J. Glover, son of J. C. and C. J., d. Aug. 24, 1878; 9y. 10m. 7d.
Amanda Gray, b. Jan. 2, 1840; d. Nov. 4, 1877.
Benoni Gray, d. Nov. 26, 1865; 46y. 3m. 16d.
Emma Gray, b. Aug. 23, 1854; d. Jan. 27, 1870.
John Milton Gray, b. May 20, 1849; d. Jan. 10, 1893.
Johathan Gray, b. Jan. 27, 1807; d. July 14, 1873.
Lizzie Gray, b. Aug. 3, 1843; d. Dec. 25, 1881.
Maggie P. Gray, b. Nov. 2, 1841; d. March 27, 1880.
Maria Gray, wife of Jonathan, b. Jan. 13, 1813; d. Aug. 25, 1875.
Mary E. Gray, b. Sep. 7, 1847; d. April 17, 1881.
Mattie J. Gray, b. Sep. 5, 1857; d. Aug. 15, 1881.
Samuel T. Gray, b. May 25, 1838; killed at the battle of Bentonville, Johnson Co., N. C., March 19, 1865; was a member of Co. C, 98th O. V. I.
Mary Green, wife of Allen, d. April 8, 1862; 66y.
Eliza A. Grimes, daughter of T. D. and E., d. Nov. 28, 1861; 15y. 6m. 3d.
Jesse C. Grimes, son of L. B. and M. H., b. Nov. 28, 1880; d. Sept. 20, 1884.
T. D. Grimes, d. Jan. 8, 1861; 45y. 11m. 24d.
William Grimes, Jr., son of W. and R. d. April 30, 1850; 28y.
Jennette Grove, wife of Francis, d. March 24, 1873; 84y.
Joseph Gutshall, b. Feb. 27, 1810; d. Dec. 3, 1880.
Malissa Gutshall, b. Sep. 5, 1842; d. Nov. 22, 1879.
Mary Gutshall, wife of Joseph, b. Nov. 8, 1817; d. March 8, 1884.
Samuel Gutshall, b. Sep. 11, 1839; d. Feb. 2, 1886.
Craig Hamilton, b. April 16, 1825; d. Oct., 1880.
Dr. David Hamilton, d. Jan. 23, 1872; 61y. 6m. 21d.
Francis Hamilton, b. Dec. 13, 1815; d. Jan. 28, 1887.
James Hamilton, d. Jan. 20, 1879; 77y.
Isabella Hamilton, wife of Levi, d. Feb. 25, 1889; 82y.
Levi Hamilton, d. April 6, 1881; 76y.
Matilda Hamilton, wife of Francis, b. Aug. 24, 1813; d. March 5, 1888.
Sadie R. Hamilton, daughter of W. and M., d. Oct. 25, 1868; 16y. 19d.
William Hamilton, d. June 16, 1875; 72y.
William Hamilton, b. Sep. 29, 1818; d. Nov. 14, 1892.
William B. Hamilton, son of W. and E., b. Oct. 29, 1865; d. Nov. 15, 1881.
Alexander Hanna, d. April 9, 1863; 33y. 1m. 13d.
Anna M. Hanna, wife of William, d. Sep. 15, 1885; 72y.
Jane Cowden Hanna, wife of Thomas, d. April 9, 1839; 79y.
J. J. Hanna, b. Oct. 7, 1839; d. Aug. 31, 1890.
Margaret A. Hanna, wife of John A., d. March 27, 1871; 34y. 7m. 4d.
Mary H. Hanna, d. Aug. 17, 1864; 27y. 1m. 9d.
Thomas Hanna, son of Thomas and Elizabeth Henderson Hanna, d. April 9, 1839; 79y.
William Hanna, d. July 22, 1885; 80y.
William F. Hanna, son of A. F. and S., d. Aug. 1, 1864; 18y. 4m. 8d.
Elizabeth Handy, wife of J. B., d. Aug. 27, 1867; 32y. 5m. 9d.
J. B. Handy, b. Sep. 15, 1853; d. July 30, 1880.
Mary M. Handy, daughter of John and

CADIZ BURIALS.   333

Elizabeth, d. Sep. 9, 1865; 5y. 1m. 7d.
Mary T. Handy, d. May 23, 1875; 9y. 6m.
George Harper, drowned near Leesburg, June 27, 1861; 16y. 7m. 23d.
Ruth E. Harper, d. April 29, 1875; 31y. 9m. 1d.
Hannah Harrison, d. May 30, 1890; 70y.
Hezekiah Harrison, d. June 3, 1877; 72y.
John Harrison, d. Sep. 25, 1878; 78y.
Lydia Harrison, wife of Hezekiah, d. May 28, 1869; 55y.
Harris Hatton, Company I, 13th O. V. I.
Margaret Hatton, b. June 10, 1878; d. March 31, 1885.
Richard Hatton, d. Nov. 7, 1869; 61y. 8m. 2d.
Alexander Haverfield, d. Jan. 24, 1875; 70y.
Harriet Haverfield, b. Feb. 8, 1798; d. March 19, 1884.
J. N. Haverfield, b. Sep. 22, 1809; d. May 9, 1873.
Jimmie Haverfield, son of J. N. and J., d. Dec. 12, 1887; 8y.
John N. Haverfield, b. May 17, 1820; d. April 10, 1894.
Mattie E. Haverfield, daughter of N. T. and I., b. Aug. 18, 1879; d. July 14, 1882.
Nancy Haverfield, wife of J. N., b. Jan. 20, 1817; d. March 24, 1895.
Nathan Haverfield, b. Oct. 25, 1796; d. Jan. 26, 1875.
Ora Bell Haverfield, daughter of N. T. and I., b. March 1, 1884; d. Dec. 1, 1887.
S. P. Haverfield, d. Dec. 28, 1885; 49y.
Frances J. Havner, daughter of Joseph and Rebecca, d. April 19, 1869; 12y. 6m.
Eliza B. Hays, d. July 11, 1879; 37y.
Clara Hedge, d. Oct. 25, 1864; 3y. 5m. 11d.
Cora Hedge, d. June 13, 1867; 2y. 11m. 10d.
Ellen M. Hedge, d. Nov. 7, 1864; 9y. 1m. 12d.
Frances Hedge, d. Dec. 9, 1870; 3y. 4m. 13d.

John V. Hedges, d. March 20, 1868; 6m. 23d.
Luther Hedges, b. March 2, 1854; d. Nov. 19, 1896.
Prudence Hedges, wife of Samuel, d. Jan. 15, 1850; 66y. 25d.
Rachel Hedges, d. Jan. 28, 1897; 79y. 3m. 18d.
Samuel Hedges, Sr., d. Dec. 17, 1865; 81y. 11m. 21d.
Samuel Hedges, Jr., b. Jan. 20, 1825; d. May 29, 1886.
William D. Hedge, d. June 4, 1867; 54y. 5m. 22d.
Alexander Henderson, d. Oct. 24, 1842; 55y.
Hannah Henderson, wife of Alexander, d. Sep. 2, 1875; 85y.
Ruth J. Herriman, b. Aug. 22, 1852; d. April 9, 1880.
William C. Hesford, b. Sep. 9, 1858; d. Dec. 27, 1881.
Margaret Highlands, d. Nov. 22, 1876; 36y. 3m. 9d.
David Hilbert, d. Feb. 23, 1863; 53y. 7m. 5d.
Eli Hill, b. April 12, 1815; d. Dec. 7, 1890.
T. B. Hill, Company I, 69th Ohio Infantry.
Lorella Hilligas, wife of David C., d. April 28, 1872; 20y. 3m. 7d.
Nancy T. Lacy Hilligas, wife of T. N., d. June 14, 1870; 60y.
Samuel Hilligas, d. Dec. 12, 1863; 21y. 11m. 9d.; was a member of Company C, 98th O. V. I.
Tunice Hilligas, d. April 22, 1885; 85y.
Kate Drummond Hinton, wife of J. M., d. Sep. 3, 1882; 29y. 2m.
Margaret Hitchcock, wife of Samuel, d. March 12, 1862; 51y. 11m. 26d.
Samuel Hitchcock, b. Aug. 18, 1819; d. Feb. 3, 1879.
John M. Hoffman, d. April 26, 1880; 80y. 4m. 3d.
Sarah Hoffman, wife of John M., d. Dec. 26, 1876; 75y. 5m.
Albert Holbrook, d. Feb. 3, 1882; 51y.
Esther Holland, wife of John, d. April 13, 1889; 68y. 6m. 21d.
David L. Hughes, b. in Berks County, Pa., April 21, 1827; d. March 26, 1891.
Mary Hughes, wife of David L., b.

Dec. 25, 1825; d. July 31, 1886.
Jane Humphreys, wife of William, d. March 1, 1813.
William Humphreys, b. June 24, 1812; d. Aug. 24, 1884.
Joseph R. Hunter, son of James and Nancy Sloan Hunter, b. in Westmoreland county, Pa., May, 1804; d. April 4, 1886.
Letitia McFadden Hunter, wife of Joseph R., d. April 13, 1883; 71y.
Mary Hunter, d. Jan. 30, 1858; 17y. 5m.
Mary B. Hunter, daughter of J. W. and A. M., d. Feb. 28, 1886; 5y. 4m.
Joseph Hurford, b. Oct. 5, 1809; d. July 7, 1897.
Laura L. Hurford, b. April 2, 1847; d. Dec. 23, 1857.
Rebecca A. Hurford, b. Jan. 31, 1824; d. May 15, 1875.
William E. Hurford, b. Jan. 27, 1857; d. Oct. 28, 1865.
Samuel Jackson, d. April 6, 1862; 76y.
Agnes Jamison, b. April 16, 1836; d. Aug. 21, 1891.
Andrew Jam'son, d. Nov. 3, 1895; 61y.
Anna M. Jamison, daughter of J. and C., d. Aug. 6, 1863; 1y. 10m. 5d.
Barklay Jamison, d. Oct. 23, 1869; 74y.
Joseph Jamison, d. Oct. 23, 1872; 46v.
Margaret Jamison, b. ———, 1830; d. May 13, 1875.
M. Belle Jamison, d.———, 18—; 20y. 6m.
Mary Jamison, wife of Andrew, d. Jan. 8, 1867; 78y.
Walter Jamison, d. July 2, 1883; 82y.
Walter C. Jamison, son of Andrew, d. March 2, 1861; 3y. 2m. 15d.
Eliza H. Johnson, daughter of J. R. and I., d. Jan. 3, 1874; 26y.
Hannah Johnson, d. Sep. 1, 1882; 53y. 4m. 18d.
Isabel Johnson, wife of J. R., d. June 25, 1883; 67y.
Joseph R. Johnson, b. Feb. 20, 1814; d. Sep. 23, 1888.
Laura Belle Johnson, daughter of E. H. and I., d. Jan. 3, 1874; 3y.
Margaret J. Johnson, daughter of Newton and Laura, d. Sep. 8, 1891; 1y. 4m.
Mary Belle Johnson, daughter of J. R. and I., d. Jan. 19, 1882; 24y.
Robert E. Jones, son of R. J. and S. J., d. Sep. 29, 1884; 14y. 11m. 18d.
John H. Jumps, b. June 22, 1836; d. April 10, 1895; member of Co. G, 98th O. V. I.
Susannah Jumps, wife of J. H., b. Dec. 25, 1835.
Anna G. Kennedy, daughter of Martin and Martha M., d. Nov. 12, 1876; 1y. 5m. 28d.
Frances Isabella Kennedy, daughter of M. and M. M., d. Oct. 15, 1872; 12y. 10m. 2d.
Martha McKee Kennedy, wife of Martin, d. July 3, 1882; 42y. 7m. 19d.
Margaret Kent, wife of Absalom, b. Oct. 14, 1815; d. March 28, 1892.
Susan Kent, wife of S. H., d. March 25, 1886; 28y.
David Kerr, son of Rev. James and Margaret, d. March 1, 1849; 5m. 10d.
Ellen Kerr, b. Nov. 21, 1831; d. July 8, 1891.
Rev. James Kerr, a native of Scotland, pastor of Presbyterian Church, Cadiz; d. April 9, 1855; 42y.
James Kerr, b. April 19, 1818; d. Jan. 21, 1886.
Joseph S. Kerr, son of Rev. James and Margaret, d. May 29, 1864; 7m.
Julia C. Kerr, b. Jan. 1, 1825; d. May 24, 1891.
M. C. Kerr, daughter of John S. and Ora E., d. Feb. 1, 1871; 1m.
Margaret McWhirter Kerr, wife of Rev. James, a native of Scotland, b. 1816; d. Nov. 1, 1890.
Mary Kerr, daughter of Rev. James and M., d. May 25, 1842; 2y. 10m.
Sarah Kerr, wife of J. C., d. Sep. 5, 1863; 42y.
Laura Kilbreath, wife of J. C., b. March 4, 1854; d. July 28, 1893.
Sarah J. Kinsey, wife of K. W., d. Feb. 7, 1864; 35y. 10m. 5d.
Sarah A. Knox, wife of James, and daughter of William and Jane Arnold, d. April 11, 1869; 34y.
Jane Kyle, wife of Thomas, d. Oct. 4, 1884; 78y.
Kate J. Kyle, daughter of Thomas and Jane, d. Dec. 12, 1866; 24y.
Mary Lacey, wife of J. M., d. April

CADIZ BURIALS. 335

16, 1833; 4Cy.
Elijah Laizure, b. July 20, 1811; d. Feb. 9, 1888.
Eliza M. Laizure, wife of Elijah, b. Sep. 21, 1817; d. May 9, 1887.
James A. Laizure, son of Elijah and Eliza, b. June 23, 1839; Quartermaster 13th O. V. I.; d. at Parkersburg, Va., Oct. 18, 1861.
Alice R. Laughlin, d. Feb. 22, 1899; 48y. 5m. 1d.
Elizabeth Laughlin, daughter of R. and K., d. Jan. 6, 1873; 39y. 1m.
Rachel Laughlin, d. May 2, 1895; 72y.
Jacob Lemmon, d. May 24, 1874; 84y. 6m. 5d.
Rebecca Lemmon, d. Aug. 19, 1872; 58y. 3m. 19d.
Catherine M. Lewis, b. Dec. 31, 1815; d. March 4, 1886.
Charity Lewis, d. Nov. 9, 1866; 84y. 5m. 2d.
Elisha S. Lewis, d. Aug. 17, 1862; 40y. 6m.
Jane Lewis, wife of Joseph, d. April 29, 1883; 73y.
Rachel C. B. Lewis, daughter of E. and C., d. Aug. 8, 1868; 1y. 6m. 7d.
Sarah Lewis, wife of Jacob, Sr., b. Nov. 2, 1802; d. March 1, 1884.
Anna Bell Lewton, d. Dec. 22, 1853; 2y. 3m.
John A. Lewton, d. Oct. 16, 1861; 7y. 6m. 22d.
Eliza Ann Lisle, wife of John, b. Sep. 2, 1811; d. March 20, 1889.
John Lisle, b. Dec. 5, 1803; d. Oct. 3, 1890.
John A. Lisle, b. May 17, 1837; d. Aug. 6, 1890.
Mary P. Lisle, wife of Hamilton, d. March 29, 1875; 24y. 3m. 20d.
Rachel Lisle, wife of William, b. Jan. 14, 1852; d. June 24, 1889.
John Loofborrow, d. March 15, 1872; 38y. 6m. 21d.
Lea Roy Loofborrow, son of J. S. and E., d. April 21, 1872; 13y. 9m. 26d.
James C. Love, d. July 12, 1876; 62y. 5m. 3d.
James H. Lynch, son of E. and P., d. Jan. 23, 1861; 3m. 10d.
Ann B. Lyons, second wife of Robert, b. Aug. 31, 1799; d. Aug. 8, 1884.
Ann Eliza Lyons, daughter of Robert and Ann W., b. May 5, 1843; d. April 23, 1844.
Anna W. Lyons, first wife of Robert, b. April 18, 1810; d. May 16, 1844.
Nancey Lyons, daughter of Robert and Ann W., b. Feb. 27, 1835, d. Oct. 9, 1837.
Robert Lyons, b. Dec. 14, 1803; d. Aug. 17, 1887.
Sallie G. Lyons, wife of J. B., b. April 4, 1838; d. April 21, 1871.
Hannah Jane McAdoo, second wife of William, d. March 19, 1883; 40y. 3m. 21d.
Martha McAdoo, first wife of William, d. Feb. 6, 1864; 45y. 8m. 21d.
Georgia Scott McBean, b. 1849; d. 1873.
Henry McBean, b. July 5, 1848; d. Aug. 2, 1875.
Dr. John McBean, b. Oct. 22, 1797; d. Jan. 7, 1875.
William McBean, b. 1833; d. 1884.
Thomas J. McBride, d. June 15, 1877; 35y.
J. E. McCarty. [No dates].
R. J. McCarty. [No dates].
Samuel L. McClelland, b. Jan. 29, 1831; d. July 19, 1894.
John McCullough, d. May 22, 1868; 70y. 6m. 11d.
Mary McCullough, wife of Robert, d. Dec. 8, 1868; 72y.
Robert McCullough, d. Aug. 15, 1868; 82y.
Mary Quest McConnell, wife of John, A., b. in Hummelstown, Pa., April 5, 1822; d. in Charlestown, Ill., March 14, 1883.
Michael McConnell, b. July 19, 1801; d. July 17, 1872.
Samuel McCormick, b. Feb. 8, 1793; d. Feb. 3, 1875.
Harriett C. McCoy, b. May 28, 1820; d. Feb. 12, 1898.
Matthew McCoy, b. April 4, 1815; d. March 27, 1889.
William H. McCoy, b. Aug. 22, 1832; d. Sep. 27, 1881.
Martha McCrea, d. Jan. 14, 1885; 93y. 9m. 20d.
Rev. J. S. McCready, d. Sep. 7, 1834; 39y.; was captain of Company H, 126th O. V. I., and died from wounds

received at the Battle of the Wilderness.
Charles P. McFadden, son of H. S. and F. J., b. Oct. 20, 1843; d. Oct. 7, 1866.
Elizabeth McFadden, wife of Nathaniel, d. Aug. 18, 1885; 65y.
H. S. McFadden, d. July 4, 1888; 75y.
J. L. McFadden, b. July 16, 1851; d. Nov. 18, 1887.
James McFadden, b. Jan. 5, 1805; d. June 15, 1874.
Jennie McFadden, d. July 17, 1873; 57y. 9m. 22d.
John McFadden, b. Oct. 10, 1810; d. July 4, 1881.
John D. McFadden, b. June 20, 1842; d. Nov. 20, 1866.
Lydia McFadden, wife of Samuel, d. March 22, 1866; 83y.
Mary A. McFadden, b. Nov. 19, 1808.
Mary McFadden, b. June 24, 1838; d. June 4, 1881.
Mary McFadden, wife of Samuel, daughter of J. M. and A. Richey; b. July 7, 1835; d. Feb. 24, 1872.
Nathaniel McFadden, d. Nov. 14, 1892; 82y.
Samuel McFadden, a native of Ireland, d. April 16, 1861; 80y.
Samuel L. McFadden, d. April 1, 1863; 48y.
Ross Leslie McFadden, son of William A. and E. L., d. Nov. 20, 1876; 6y. 8m. 8d.
Winfield McFadden, son of William and Elizabeth, d. March 6, 1861; 9y. 2m. 22d.
James McKee, d. May 6, 1887; 76y. 3m.
James McKee, d. Nov. 19, 1882; 1y. 15d.
John McKee, Company C, 98th O. V. I.; d. Sept. 11, 1864; 23y. 2m. 14d.
Rebecca E. McKee, b. Dec. 1, 1855; d. Jan. 3, 1892.
Robert McKee, d. June 15, 1880; 64y. 6m.
Jessie M. McMath, daughter of Jesse H. and Kate L., d. April 22, 1862; 3y. 8m. 19d.
Margaret Jane McMath, daughter of J. and E. A., d. Jan. 9, 1854; 1m. 19d.
Margaret McMillan, d. March 16, 1890; 64y.
Arthur P. McNutt, d. Dec. 15, 1895; 74y.
George W. McPherson, d. Jan. 10, 1880; 68y. 10m. 23d.
David McWhirter, b. in Scotland, 1788; d. in Cadiz, Sep. 18, 1873; 86y.
Jennette McWhirter, b. in Scotland in 1818; d. in Pittsburg, June 8, 1825; 7y.
John McWhirter, b. in 1824; d. Nov., 1827; 3y.
Mary McWhirter, wife of David, b. in Scotland in 1787; d. in Cadiz, Jan., 1860; 74y.
Alexander A. Manner, lost on the Steamboat Sultanna, April 27, 1865; 25y. 7m. 23d.
Joseph G. Manner, d. Aug. 4, 1870; 33y. 5d.
E. A. Marsh, Company G, 98th Ohio Infantry.
Edward Martin, son of John and Mary, d. Oct. 18, 1879; 11y. 2m. 23d.
Harriet Martin, wife of J. H. [No dates].
John Martin, d. April 17, 1872; 81y. 10m.
Maria Martin, wife of John, a native of Ireland, d. Nov. 21, 1864; 50y.
Samuel Martin, d. Feb. 5, 1873; 73y.
Sarah Ann Martin, wife of John, d. May 2, 1870; 49y. 3m.
Susanna Martin, wife of Samuel, d. Aug. 26, 1884; 84y.
Euphema H. Maxwell, d. Feb. 3, 1866; 57y.
Agnes Mealy, d. Nov. 22, 1896; 93y. 1m. 4d.
Willie Mealy, son of F. K. and H., d. Dec. 3, 1876; 3y. 5m. 4d.
James Means, d. Nov. 3, 1871; 73y. 10m. 12d.
Elizabeth Megaw, wife of James, d. April 1, 1883; 69y.
Jane Megaw, wife of Samuel, d. July 2, 1885; 76y.
Samuel Megaw, d. May. 10, 1881; 78y.
Sarah Jane Megaw, b. May 14, 1824; d. April 16, 1897.
Harry Mercer, son of G. W., b. May 1, 1873; d. Feb. 11, 1887.
Sadie H. Millekin, daughter of John and Mary H., d. April 27, 1892; 12y.

Mary A. Miller, wife of Obadiah. [No dates].
Obadiah Miller. [No dates].
Sarah Miller, d. March 2, 1870; 72y.
James Mitchell, a native of Ireland, d. Oct. 17, 1866; 81y. 7m. 13d.
James T. Mitchell, son of Joseph and Susan, d. Nov. 12, 1878; 27y. 13d.
Joseph Mitchell, son of J. and S., d. Dec. 25, 1875; 18y. 7m. 23d.
Mary Mitchell, daughter of J. and M., d. July 4, 1866; 52y. 6m. 22d.
Thomas S. Mitchell, b. May 2, 1816; d. June 11, 1888.
William Mitchell, d. April 24, 1880; 68y. 6m. 17d.
Edward Fulton Moffett, b. June 3, 1831; d. Jan. 25, 1870.
Mary Moffett, wife of E. F., b. March 6, 1836; d. April 7, 1869.
Annie E. Moore, wife of I. C., and daughter of D. B. and Martha Lyons Welch, b. Jan. 15, 1857; d. Feb. 16, 1895.
David Moore, b. March 8, 1817; d. March 24, 1870; 53y. 16d.
Jane Moore, wife of David, b. Sep. 26, 1818; d. June 23, 1879.
John Moore, b. July 27, 1813; d. Feb. 2, 1883.
Maranda P. Moore, wife of D. B., d. July 8, 1887; 46y.
Myra L. Moore, daughter of D. B. and M. P., d. Feb. 18, 1867; 19d.
Sarah Moore, wife of William, b. in New Jersey, Jan. 12, 1783; came to Ohio in April, 1808; d. March 16, 1863; 80y. 2m. 4d.
Sarah J. Moore, wife of John, b. July 3, 1827; d. June 14, 1874.
Samuel Moorehead, d. Sep. 24, 1879; 83y. 8m. 16d.
J. W. Morgan, Company A, 66th Ohio Infantry.
John P. Morgan, son of J. W. and Hannah, d. Aug. 12, 1872; 4m. 1d.
Alice Neville, b. Nov. 1, 1880; d. July 20, 1884.
Margaret Niblick, wife of John, d. Sep. 14, 1892; 50y. 4m. 8d.
James K. Nicholas, d. April 5, 1888; 27y. 8m. 20d.
John A. Nicholas, d. March 3, 1885; 25y. 5m.

John A. Norris, Major of the 98th O. V. I., d. Jan. 19, 1877; 41y.
Nancy Orr, b. July 8, 1810; d. Sep. 28, 1882.
Alexander Osburn, b. May 17, 1838; d. July 25, 1875.
Mary A. Oglevee Osborn, wife of S. A., d. July 21, 1874; 37y. 2m. 4d.
Mary Louise Osborn, daughter of J. J. and C. M., b. March 14, 1887; d. May 30, 1890.
Samuel A. Osborn, d. July 19, 1872, 32y. 9m. 25d.
Benjamin Parrish, d. March 6, 1865; 85y. 27d.
Charles Parish, d. Jan. 12, 1863; 48y. 11m. 28d.
Mary Patterson, d. May 21, 1875.
Amanda E. Peacock, d. Feb. 17, 1899; 81y. 9m. 23d.
Eli Peacock, d. Feb. 6, 1886; 79y. 4m. 18d.
Sarah Peacock, wife of Eli, d. Jan. 8, 1866; 61y.
John Penn, Company G, 98th Ohio Infantry.
Eliza Phillips, wife of John, and daughter of Samuel and Elizabeth Buchanan Gilmore, b. Feb. 2, 1807; d. Jan. 4, 1873.
Elizabeth Williams Phillips, wife of Thomas, b. in Cecil County, Md., July 11, 1792; d. May 22, 1867.
John Phillips, son of William and Rachel Hamilton Phillips, b. in West Nottingham township, Chester County, Pa., June, 1797; d. May 5, 1859.
Martha Phillips, daughter of John and Eliza, b. Nov. 17, 1832; d. Feb. 21, 1863.
Rachel Phillips, daughter of Thomas and Elizabeth, d. Aug. 14, 1853; 34y. 2m. 6d.
Rachel Ann Phillips, daughter of John and Eliza, b. March 15, 1839; d. July 10, 1863.
Samuel Phillips, sn of John and Eliza, d. May 24, 1860; 23y. 11m.
Thomas Phillips, son of William and Rachel Hamilton Phillips, b. in West Nottingham township, Chester county, Pa., 1792; d. Nov. 23, 1871.
Augustus Porter, b. Feb. 18, 1822; d. March 25, 1893.

Irwin Porter, Sr., b. 1814; d. 1897.
James Porter, b. Aug. 29, 1818; d. Sep. 4, 1898.
Jane Porter, d. Dec. 25, 1848; 47y. 9m. 21d.
Joseph E. Porter, son of S. B. and M., d. April 19, 1884; 4y. 14d.
Mary Porter, d. Oct. 21, 1884; 79y.
Mary Porter, d. July 30, 1881; 68y. 6m. 14d.
Samuel T. Porter, d. April 25, 1897; 75y. 4m. 22d.
Elizabeth Poulson, b. March 15, 1808; d. Oct. 6, 1897.
John Poulson, b. July 14, 1792; d. Nov. 5, 1878.
Samuel Poulson, Company C, 69th Ohio Infantry.
John Prichard, d. June 28, 1844; 69y.
Sarah Prichard, b. Jan. 7, 1782; d. Sep. 15, 1877.
S. Purdy. [No dates].
Adam J. Quigley, b. Sep. 7, 1828; d. Jan. 18, 1863.
John Quigley, b. Jan. 8, 1795; d. Oct. 22, 1867.
Mary Quigley, wife of John, b. Jan. 7, 1798; d. March 1, 1876.
Ada J. Rea, wife of William P., d. April 30, 1875; 19y. 7d.
Isabell C. Rea, wife of John J., b. April 20, 1825; d. Oct. 12, 1879.
Ann W. Richey, wife of John M., b. April 16, 1817; d. Oct. 30, 1889.
Elizabeth Richey, wife of Thomas, b. Aug. 5, 1826; d. July 29, 1889.
Harvey W. Richey, son of T. and E., b. March 21, 1849; d. July 3, 1888.
John M. Richey, b. Nov. 2, 1808; d. Jan. 30, 1897.
Thomas Richey, b. May 27, 1814; d. April 11, 1883.
Craig Robb, son of Joseph and Mary, d. Feb. 28, 1865; 7y. 2m.
James Robb, b. June 2, 1843; d. May 24, 1876.
James Robb, d. May 24, 1870; 22y. 9d.
John Robb, b. March 1, 1844; d. 1880.
Mary Robb, b. Dec. 1815; d. April 3, 1893.
Edward F. Roche, son of J. F. and C. T., d. Sep. 5, 1881; 22y. 10m. 13d.
Ellie Ward Roche, daughter of James F. and Caroline T., d. April 28, 1866; 1y. 4m. 26d.
Samuel Rutan, d. Sep. 15, 1874; 73y. 14d.
Alexander T. Scott, d. Nov. 25, 1865; 46y. 8m. 14d.
David M. Scott, d. Sep. 17, 1872; 16y. 1m.
Eleanor Scott, wife of Alexander T., d. Sep. 10, 1894; 68y. 9d.
John W. Scott, b. in Yorkshire, England, Sep., 1811; d. in Cadiz, Sep., 1886; 75y.
Emaline Shank, daughter of S. and Elizabeth, d. March 25, 1850; 32y. 5m. 10d.
Caroline T. Sharp, d. Dec. 24, 1881; 43y. 5m. 14d.
George Sharp, b. July 9, 1795; d. June 25, 1877.
John Sharp, d. March 16, 1878; 77y.
Nancy Sharp, wife of George, b. April 21, 1807; d. Dec. 13, 1877.
Edward Sheets, d. Oct. 1, 1892; 28y. 7m.
Fleming Sheets, d. March 25, 1871; 49y. 6m. 22d.
Jane Sheets, wife of Robert, d. Oct. 6, 1868; 68y.
Robert Sheets, d. Jan. 15, 1865; 65y.
Elizabeth Sheldon, d. Nov. 27, 1882; 50y.
Stuart B. Shotwell, b. Nov. 1819; d. Dec. 3, 1890.
William J. Shotwell, b. May 15, 1863; d. Sep. 2, 1865.
James Simeral, d. Sep. 21, 1849; 57y.
Mary Ann Simeral, wife of James, b. June 11, 1790; d. April 16, 1866.
Robert V. Simeral, b. July 26, 1822; d. April 15, 1852.
Eliza Slemmons, second wife of Samuel, b. Feb. 22, 1829; d. Feb. 25, 1879.
Mary Jane Slemmons, daughter of S. and S., d. April 7, 1838; 6y. 7m. 23d.
Minnie Slemmons, daughter of Obediah, b. 1862; d. 1879; 17y.
Samuel Slemmons, d. July 26, 1867; 59y.
Susanna Slemmons, first wife of Samuel, d. Oct. 22, 1851; 41y.
Belle S. Smyley, wife of John, b. April 18, 1864; d. July 6, 1883.
Isabella Smiley, wife of J. V., b. June 24, 1806; d. Sep. 10, 1876.

Isabella Smiley, daughter of J. V. and I., b. Dec. 15, 1841; d. May 28, 1876.
James V. Smiley, b. Nov. 15, 1805; d. Jan. 29, 1877.
Matthew Smyley, d. Sep. 15, 1887; 54y. 8m. 20d.
Carl Specht, d. Sep. 19, 1892; 27v.
Susan D. Stoops, b. May 15, 1803; d. May 8, 1897.
Mary Stubbins, wife of Mordecai; b. Oct. 15, 1805; d. Nov. 26, 1869.
Mordecai Stubbins, b. Jan. 3, 1812; d. Oct. 9, 1893.
Thomas J. Swan, b. July 1, 1823; d. Aug. 17, 1882.
David Thompson, d. May 2, 1869; 95y. 2m. 1d.
Elizabeth Thompson, wife of Samuel, d. Aug. 29, 1873; 87y. 9m. 15d.
Elizabeth Thompson, wife of James, d. April 17, 1880; 80y.
J. H. Thompson. [No dates].
James Thompson, d. July 11, 1896; 79y.
Josie B. Timmons, b. Nov. 24, 1850; d. June 4, 1874.
Samuel Thompson, d. June 6, 1886; 84y. 7m.
Martha Thompson, wife of David, d. March 10, 1844; 62y. 3m. 2d.
B. C. Turner, 13th O. V. I., d. at Bowling Green, Ky., March 16, 1862.
Sarah Vanfossan, wife of D. D., d. Nov. 9, 1889; 36y.
Margaret Vasbinder, wife of Jacob, d. Feb. 2, 1873; 90y.
William Voshall, b. July 21, 1840; d. Jan. 7, 1879.
Ephraim Walker, d. April 29, 18—; 63y. 4m. 6d.
John Walker, d. March 23, 1865; 33y. 4m. 6d.
Butler J. Ward, son of W. G. and E., d. Aug. 15, 1868; 9y. 3m. 26d.
Eleanor Ward, wife of John, b. Oct. 31, 1800; d. Sep. 26, 1873; 72y. 10m. 26d.
John Ward, b. Oct. 24, 1798; d. April 12, 1869; 70y. 5m. 20d.
Charles Warfel, b. Oct. 18, 1807; d. Feb. 3, 1871.
Mary Jane Watkinson, wife of Benjamin, d. May 24, 1865; 33y. 2m. 28d.
Etta Kerr Watson, wife of T. S., b. March 22, 1863; d. April 17, 1892.
Sylvester Waters, son of Robert T. and Anna R., d. Sep. 20, 1867; 2y. 4m. 24d.
Martha C. Weir, b. July 23, 1820; d. Sep. 19, 1880.
Eliza Welch, first wife of Rezin, b. Dec. 4, 1801; d. Aug. 6, 1842.
John Welch, b. Nov. 20, 1808; d. Nov. 10, 1881
Maria B. Welch, second wife of Rezin, b. Sep. 12, 1807; d. Aug. 19, 18:6.
Rezin Welch, b. April 28, 1795; d. Nov. 24, 1881.
Rezin Welch, Jr., son of D. B. and Martha, b. at Cadiz, Ohio, Sep. 27, 1867; d. at Lincoln, Neb., Dec. 6, 1895.
Jacob Werner, Company C. 74th Ohio Infantry.
Albert West, son of J. and J., d. Sep. 1, 1873; 19y. 2m. 4d.
Comfort West, wife of Jonathan, d. March 15, 1857; 65y. 8m. 26d.
Jonathan West, Sr., d. Nov. 27, 1862; 75y. 2m. 13d.
Jonathan West, Jr., d. Sep. 11, 1861; 45y. 7m. 13d.
Samuel West, d. April 4, 1871; 56y. 11m. 6d.
Sarah West, b. July 28, 1838; d. June 20, 1861; 28y. 1m.
Eliza Wilkin, wife of Robert, d. Sep. 27, 1863; 33y.
Mary Williams, b. May 24, 1853; d. Jan. 15, 1861.
Dr. J. D. Wortman, b. June 8, 1824; d. Dec. 28, 1898
Nancy Wosley, wife of William, d. March 22, 1877; 44y.

BURIALS IN CRABAPPLE GRAVEYARD.
To August 27, 1896.

Elizabeth Abel, wife of G. W., d. Sep. 22, 1879; 31y. 2d.
Aaron Allen, d. April 13, 1871; 48y. 2m. 2d.
Ann Allen, wife of Aaron, d. March 15, 1873; 50y. 10m. 8d.
Catharine Allen, wife of Moses, d.

April 30, 1857;———
Margaret A. Riddell Allen, wife of J. M. Allen, d. Feb. 28, 1856;———
Rev. Moses Allen, d. Jan. 16, 1846; 60y. pastor of Crabapple congregation.
Oscar G. Allen, d. Nov. 9, 1886; 26y.
William Anderson, d. Nov. 30, 1821; 37y.
Anna Armor, wife of Samuel, d. Sep. 21, 1878; 81y.
Elizabeth B. Armor, daughter of S. and A., d. April 10, 1844; 2y. 6d.
James Armor, son of Samuel and Ann; d. Aug. 27, 1831; 21y. 22d.
Martha A. Armor, daughter of S. and A., d. Oct. 8, 1839; 4y.
Samuel Armor, b. April 19, 1796, d. ———; 72y.
David Armstrong, b. Jan. 27, 1838; d. Oct. 18, 1879.
Eliza Armstrong, wife of Warden, d. July 9, 1885; 69y. 9m. 15d.
George Armstrong, d. Oct. 3, 1849; 75y.
George Armstrong, son of W. and E., d. May 19, 1858; 19y. 20d.
Lydia Heath Armstrong, wife of Rev. Robert, d. Dec. 3, 1875; 53y.
Mary Armstrong, wife of George, d. Aug. 27, 1868; 88y.
Mary Azubah Armstrong, daughter of Rev. R. T. and L. H.,———
Warden Armstrong, d. Aug. 31, 1877; 77y. 7m. 2d.
Putnam Arnold, d. Dec. 21, 1872; 68y.
Sarah Arnold, d. Oct. 12, 1876; 73y.
Marion Bartholomew, son of Samuel and Mary; d. April 21, 1852; 3m. 15d.
James Beall, d. Dec. 29, 1834; 57y.
Jane Beall, d. Nov. 11, 1883; 100y.
Mary Beall, b. Dec. 8, 1823; d. May 15, 1889.
William Beall, b. Aug. 23, 1822; d. Oct. 4, 1856.
David Beatty, son of S. and M., d. Sep. 24, 1814; 13m.
David R. Beatty, d. Sep. 4, 1825; 10y. 10m.
James Beatty, Sr., d. Jan. 3, 1834; 59y.
James Beatty, Jr., son of James and Jane, d. June 18, 1834; 20y.
Jane Beatty, wife of James, d. Dec. 16, 1850; 72y. 21d.
Jesse Beatty, son of S. and M., d. Nov. 5, 1820; 5y.
John Beatty, son of J. and J., d. July 19, 1829; 9y.
Joseph Beatty, d. March 29, 1834; 29y.
Margaret Beatty, daughter of J. and J., d. Oct. 1, 1832; 20y.
Mary Beatty, wife of Samuel; d. Nov. 19, 1828; 48y.
Mary Ann Beatty, daughter of J. and J., d. March 30, 1831; 13y.
Samuel Beatty, d. Jan. 20, 1829: 49y.
Thomas Beatty, son of James and Jane, d. Dec. 5, 1832; 24y.
Thomas Beatty, son of S. and M.———
William Beatty, son of J. and J., d. Jan. 2, 1822; 18y.
William Beatty, son of Samuel and M., d. Jan. 7, 1829; 24y.
Infant child of John and Margaret Bell.
Ann Bell, wife of Joseph, d. Aug. 29, 1832; 73y.
John Bell, d. Aug. 5, 1852; 67y.
Joseph Bell, d. Sep. 26, 1843; 86y.
Joseph Bell, b. June 21, 1817; d. Oct. 23, 1890.
Margaret Bell, wife of John, d. March 21, 1874; 80y.
Martha Bell, b. Nov. 2, 1834; d. Jan. 25, 1887.
Mary Blackburn, wife of William, d. April 29, 1867; 77y. 10m. 7d.
Charlie W. Boggs, son of S. M. and M. P., d. March 3, 1870; 4y. 19d.
Doche Jane Boggs, daughter of Wm. and M..———
James Boggs, d. March 4, 1826; 26y.
James Boggs, b. July 25, 1828; d. Feb. 23, 1840.
John Boggs, b. June 28, 1782; d. Dec. 21, 1848.
Laura S. Boggs, daughter of S. M., and M. P., d. March 29, 1875; 13y. 4m. 27d.
Mary Boggs, daughter of W. and M., d. Aug. 30, 1834; 1y.
Samuel B. Boggs, son of W. and Martha, d. Dec. 16, 1828; 7m.
Samuel M. Boggs, b. Dec. 6, 1820; d. April 30, 1894.
Sarah Boggs, b. Dec. 10, 1787; d. Jan. 6, 1849.
Daniel Brewer, d. March 27, 1865; 51y.
Sarah Rosalie Brewer, daughter of D. and M., d. Sep. 25, 1865; 6m. 19d.

CRABAPPLE BURIALS

Infant daughter of Abram and Mary Brokaw, d. May 12, 1859; 7m. 28d.
Infant daughter of J. and M. Brokaw; d. April 7, 1857; 14d.
Abraham Brokaw, d. May 25, 1825; 69y.
Anna B. Brokaw, daughter of John M. and E., d. Oct. 26, 1877; 17y. 2m. 22d.
Anna Eliza Brokaw, daughter of J. A. and S. J., d. Sep. 12, 1875; 1y. 9m. 21d.
Edward L. Brokaw, son of J. P. and Mary, d. Nov. 3, 1875; 1y. 11d.
Elizabeth Brokaw, wife of John, b. Feb. 4, 1824; d. May 15, 1848.
Elizabeth J. Brokaw, wife of Benjamin, b. May 2, 1822; d. Sep. 3, 1891.
Elizabeth M. Brokaw, daughter of John and Eliza, d. Feb. 6, 1861; 12y. 9m. 6d.
Ella F. Brokaw, daughter of J. A. and S. J., d. Sep. 23, 1882; 10y. 11m. 19d.
Ellen Brokaw, wife of William; d. July 1, 1867; 62y.
George Brokaw, d. June 27, 1842; 87y. 2m. 29d.
George Brokaw, d. Nov. 27, 1880; 97y.
George Brokaw, son of J. and M., d. July 28, 1845; 11m. 16d.
George Brokaw, son of W. and E., d. Aug. 23, 1851; 17y. 1m. 4d.
George M. Brokaw, son of A. and M., d. June 11, 1854; d. June 14, 1890.
Isabella Brokaw, daughter of George and Mary, d. May 4, 1834; 10y. 10d.
James H. Brokaw, son of John M. and E., d. Feb. 24, 1888; 2y. 1m. 1d.
Jane Brokaw, wife of George, d. Oct. 7, 1850; 98y. 5m. 6d.
John Brokaw, b. Dec. 23, 1793; d. March 25, 1876; a soldier of the War of 1812.
John Galvin Brokaw, son of John and Maria, d. July 17, 1875; 4y. 10m. 26d.
John L. Brokaw, son of J. and M., d. July 24, 1845; 2y. 6m. 1d.
Lizzie Bokaw, daughter of John and Maria; d. June 30, 1882; 17y. 9m.
Lyle A. Brokaw, son of William and E., d. March 25, 1858; 22y.
Mary Brokaw, daughter of William and E., d. Jan. 14, 1844; 1y. 11m. 27d.
Mary Brokaw, wife of George, d. July 15, 1851; 69y.
Mary Brokaw, wife of Jacob, d. Sep. 21, 1880; 63y.
Mary A. Brokaw, daughter of J. and M.. d. Nov. 26, 1860; 11y. 4m. 26d.
Nancy Brokaw, d. Jan. 20, 1853; 21y. 2m. 29d.
Nancy Brokaw, wife of George, d. April 13, 1861; 75y. 6m. 10d.
Nancy Brokaw, wife of George, d. Sep. 16, 1876; 76y.
Samuel D. Brokaw, son of William and E., d. March 8, 1859; 20y.
Sarah Brokaw, wife of John, b. Sep. 19, 1802; d. April 15, 1883.
William Brokaw, d. Sep. 1, 1850; 40y. 5m. 26d.
Margaret Brown, wife of William, d. Sep. 14, 1871; 55y.
Fannie E. Caldwell, b. April 6, 1845; d. April 27, 1894.
Rev. John P. Caldwell, d. Jan. 30, 1872; 54y.
Alcinda Campbell, daughter of Richard and Rebecca, b. June 27, 1834; d. Jan. 27, 1835.
Clarissa M. Campbell, b. July 16, 1826; d. March 28, 1893.
Cyrus Campbell, b. May 31, 1820; d. Oct. 15, 1889.
Eleanor Campbell, wife of William, d. Aug. 2, 1842; 61y.
Eleanor Campbell, daughter of J. and M. L., d. Oct. 15, 1843; 9y.
James Campbell, d. July 17, 1842; 60y. 7m. 19d.
James Cambell, b. March 7, 1815; d. Feb. 22, 1858.
Jane Campbell, b. June 25, 1808; d. June 10, 1883.
Jane E. Campbell, daughter of John and Cynthia; d. Sep. 21, 1853; 12y.
John Campbell, d. July 24, 1844; 69y. 6m. 2d.
John Campbell, d. Sep. 14, 1863; 53y. 11m. 20d.
Dr. John Campbell, b. Nov. 21, 1804; d. Sep. 17, 1832.
John A. Campbell, son of Thomas and Nancy; d. May 28, 1828; 1y. 4m. 2=d.
John B. Campbell, son of J. and C., d. Sep. 26, 1865; 7y. 6m. 5d.

Joseph Campbell, d. Dec. 4, 1829; 22y.
Joseph K. Campbell, b. Jan. 21, 1860; d. Sep. 5, 1886.
Julia Ann Campbell, wife of William; d. March 16, 1884; 76y.
J. L. Campbell, son of W. and N. L., d. Jan. 1, 1861; 2y. 10m. 23d.
Lizzie C. Campbell, b. April 17, 1855; d. April 29, 1881.
L. D. Campbell, wife of William M., d. July 19, 1889; 54y. 2m. 11d.
Maggie C. Campbell, d. Oct. 17, 1877; 9y. 8m. 16d.
Margaret Campbell, d. Oct. 8, 1878; 93y. 11m. 22d.
Margaret J. Campbell, wife of Robert, b. March 13, 1830; d. April 7, 1877.
Maria L. Campbell, wife of J., d. Jan. 23, 1847; 30y.
Mary Campbell, wife of John, d. Sep. 28, 1853; 69y.
Mary Campbell, eldest daughter of Dr. J. and Jane, b. Jan. 24, 1833; d. Feb. 15, 1856.
Mary Campbell, wife of William M., d. Dec. 13, 1874; 54y.
Mary A. Campbell, b. Sep. 17, 1859; d. Sep. 13, 1885.
M. J. Campbell, daughter of W. and N. L., d. Dec. 18, 1860; 4y. 6m. 23d.
Peggy Ann Campbell, wife of William, d. Aug. 11, 1842; 22y.
Rachel Campbell, wife of Cyrus, b. Feb. 10, 1826; d. June 20, 1886.
Rev. Richard Campbell, A. M., b. Jan. 4, 1796; d. Nov. 17, 1835.
Robert Campbell, b. April 8, 1809; d. Sep. 27, 1886.
Ruth Ann Campbell, wife of James,—
William Campbell, d. Oct. 28, 1845; 84y.
Caroline Matilda Canon, daughter of Buel and Julia, d. June 28, 1834; 2m. 17d.
Obadiah Franklin Canon, son of Julia and Buel, d. Feb. 26, 1840; 1y. 10m. 29d.
Martha Carrithers, daughter of John and Elisa; d. Feb. 25, 1832; 16y.
Sarah Christy, wife of R. R., d. April 19, 1872; 56y. 9m. 28d.
James Clements, son of J. and P., d. May 14, 1833; 1y. 9m. 18d.
James Clements, d. March 10, 1860; 70y.
Josiah Clements, son of J. and P., d. Jan. 5, 1831; 14y. 9m. 26d.
Merrit G. Clements, son of J. and P., b. Oct. 14, 1837; d. Nov. 25, 1852.
Pleasant Clements, wife of J., d. Oct. 12, 1862; 67y. 6m. 7d.
David Cook, son of J. and W., d. June 22, 1849; 4y. 4m.
Susan M. Coon, daughter of Jacob and Mary, b. Feb. 26, 1837; d. Aug. 1, 1837.
George E. Coup, son of G. W. and E., d. Oct. 28, 1880; 4y. 18d.
Ada Zillah Covert, daughter of B. and C., d. Feb. 8, 1867; 6y. 6m. 24d.
Nona May Covert, granddaughter of B. and C., d. July 21, 1887; 15y. 3m. 26d.
Ora Elme Covert, daughter of B. and C., d. Oct. 15, 1836; 24y. 5m. 14d.
William D. Covert, son of B. and C., d. March 11, 1866; 2m 9d.
Isabella Cowan, d. Nov. 28, 1836; 67y.
Jane Cowles, wife of S. M., d. Jan. 17, 1849; 33y.
Henry Cramblett, son of E. and H., d. Aug. 14, 1857; 21y. 11d.
Nancy J. Cramblett, daughter of E. and H., d. April 1, 1857; 10y. 9m. 16d.
Jane Crawford, wife of Thomas, d. Sep. 4, 1829; 76y.
Thomas Crawford, d. July 17, 1826; 78y.
William Crawford, d. Sep. 1, 1850; 73y. 4m. 3d.
Alvin C. Culbertson, son of S. H. and E. J., d. April 23, 1861; 9y. 4m. 17d.
Esther J. Culbertson, wife of S. H., d. March 13, 1885; 58y. 6m. 29d.
Martha J. Culbertson, daughter of S. H. and E. J., d. May. 4, 1861; 2y. 3m. 1d.
Mary Culbertson, d. Dec. 4, 1886; 56y. 7m. 16d.
Samuel Culbertson, d. Jan. 22, 1871; 91y.
Sarah Culbertson, wife of Samuel, d. July 20, 1856; 64y. 1m. 11d.
S. H. Culbertson, d. Jan. 28, 1893; 69y. 5m. 12d.
Elenor Davis, wife of Nicholas, d. March 6, 1842; 57y. 10m. 2d.

CRABAPPLE BURIALS 343

Ollie Davis, daughter of H. and C. D., d. Sep. 23, 1863; 1y. 7m. 15d.
Martha Ann Dayton, daughter of James and R., d. March 14, 1885; 7y. 4m. 14d.
William Dinsmore, d. Aug. 24, 1870; 59y.
Sarah Doak, daughter of William N., d. Feb. 11, 1853; 5y. 7m. 2d.
Infant son of J. and E. Downing, d. May 27, 1832; 11d.
Alexander Downing, d. April 28, 1872; 69y.
Jane Downing, daughter of J. and Eleanor, d. April 11, 1863; 19y. 5m. 6d.
Margaret A. C. Downing, b. March 15, 1833; d. Oct. 12, 1875.
Mary Downing, daughter of J. and E., d. April 16, 1838; 9y. 5m. 23d.
Sarah G. Downing, wife of Alexander, d. Nov. 14, 1866; 56y.
William Downing, son of A. and S. G., d. Dec. 25, 1834; 3y. 27d.
Hugh Allen Dunlap, son of J. G. and C. E., d. April, 1883; 2m. 25d.
Margaret Dunn, wife of James, d. Oct. 21, 1834; 51y. 5m. 11d.
William Eagelson, d. June 29, 1829; 55y.
Henry Easter, d. June 12, 1842; 55y.
Mary C. Easter, daughter of Henry and Maria, d. Nov. 3, 1858; 19y. 3m. 10d.
Martha Edzinger, wife of A., d. March 1, 1885; 39y. 6m.
Infant daughter of J. W. and A. A. Ferguson, d. June 6, 1880.
Elmira Ferguson, wife of Joseph W., d. Oct. 2, 1877; 40y. 9m. 11d.
Hugh Ferguson, d. Sep. 28, 1878; 78y. 11m.
Margaret Ferguson, wife of H., and daughter of G. and M. Armstrong, d. Nov. 19, 1850; 41y. 15d.
Margaret Ferguson, wife of H. W., d. Sep. 9, 1863; 58y.
Mary Finley, wife of James, d. Jan. 6, 1879; 78y.
Catharine Gallagher, d. Oct. 17, 1881; 81y.
John Gallagher, d. March 3, 1861; 53y.
Nancy Gallagher, Feb. 5, 1858; 84y.
Nancy Gallagher, d. Sep. 26, 1888; 83y.

John Garven, d. Jan. 28, 1863; 75y.
Jane Gilcrest, wife of William, d. Dec. 21, 1827; 53y.
Carrie M. Gordon, d. March 13, 1892; 7y. 1m.
Pleasy H. Gordon, d. Oct. 22, 1891; 37y. 5m. 15d.
David O. Grimes, son of G. D. and J., d. April 5, 1849; 3y. 5m. 11d.
Elizabeth Grimes, wife of Joseph; d. Sep. 12, 1819; 38y.
George D. Grimes, d. Nov. 20, 1875; 67y. 7m. 7d.
Jane Grimes, wife of George D., d. Nov. 3, 1890; 77y. 7m. 14d.
Joseph Grimes, d. Jan. 2, 1840; 57y. 2m.
Martha E. Grimes, d. July 5, 1851; 66y. 6m. 22d.
Mary Halinda Grimes, daughter of George D. and J., d. Aug. 18, 1851; 2y. 5m. 13d.
Nancy E. Grimes, d. March 30, 1838; 84y.
Sarah Grimes, daughter of George D. and Jane, d. April 15, 1860; 8y. 8m.
Sarah B. Grimes, daughter of John L., and M. J., d. Sep. 11, 1867; 1y. 9m. 8d.
Ellen G. Grooms, daughter of William and Delilah, d. Oct. 2, 1859; 9m. 17d.
Infant son of Samuel and E. Guthrie, d. Sep. 24, 1824; 7d.
Elizabeth Guthrie, wife of Samuel, d. Jan. 21, 1868; 85y.
Elizabeth A. Guthrie, daughter of G. and J. D., d. Sep. 26, 1837; 4m.
Jane B. J. Guthrie, d. April 26, 1881; 49y.
Jane D. Guthrie, wife of Dr. G. S., d. July 17, 1837; 23y. 3m.
Robert Guthrie, son of Samuel and E., d. May 2, 1827; 8m.
Samuel Guthrie, d. Sep. 17, 1851; 63y.
Infant son of J. and M. Hanna, ——
Elizabeth Hanna, wife of Samuel, d. March 11, 1829; 62y.
James Hanna, d. Aug. 25, 1859; 56y. 5m. 7d.
John Hanna, Sr., d. Aug. 12, 1849; 63y.
Margaret Hanna, d. Aug. 10, 1859; 65y. 10m.
Mary Hanna, wife of John, d. May 31, 1824; 34y. 6m. 12d.

Rachel J. Hanna, daughter of J. and M., d. Oct. 15, 1857; 31y. 9m. 7d.
Samuel Hanna, son of J. and M., b. May 4, 1828; d. March 24, 1848.
Samuel Hanna, d. May. 8, 1842; 78y. 5m. 9d.
Alex. Harrah, d. July 15, 1831; 81y.
Charles Harrah, d. Jan. 22, 1881; 73y. 2m. 21d.
Jane Harrah, wife of Alex., d. March 7, 1861; 81y.
Rachel Harrah, wife of Charles, d. Dec. 20, 1877; 70y.
Tabitha J. Harrah, daughter of A. and J., d. June 17, 1836; 14y. 4m.
William McAlvin Harrah, son of A. and J., d. April 13, 1831; 7y. 2m. 5d.
Barton Harris, d. June 9, 1842; 10y.
Henderson Hays, b. March 29, 1821; d. Jan. 1. 1890.
Olivia Hays, wife of Henderson and daughter of G. Y. and W. Coulter, b. Nov. 23, 1825; d. Sep. 18, 1852.
William R. Heald, d. Oct. 28, 1847; 27y. 8m. 11d.
Maria M. Henderson, wife of T. A., b. Jan. 12, 1844; d. Dec. 10, 1887.
Elizabeth Henry, d. Nov. 1, 1881; 84y.
James Henry, d. Dec. 15, 1860;———
Jane Henry, d. March 10, 1857; ———
Margaret Henry, d. March 19, 1845;———
Margaret Henry, d. June 10, 1858; ———
Mary Henry, b. Feb. 9th, 1817; d. Nov. 3, 1883.
Mary Henry, d. April 11, ———
Nicholas S. Henry, b. May 10, 1814; d. Oct. 31, 1885.
Samuel Henry, d. May 13, 1871; 70y.
Elizabeth Hillis, wife of Matthew, d. Nov. 6, 1820; 78y.
Tamzen L. Hoge, wife of Byron M., b. May 9, 1847; d. Oct. 15, 1889.
Catharine Irwin, wife of Dr. Thomas, d. June 18. 1848; 26y.
Mary Irwin, wife of Samuel, Sr., d. July 15, 1848; 64y.
Samuel Irwin, Sr., d. April 28, 1836; 63y.
Samuel Irwin, son of James and Rebecca, d. Sep. 25, 1841; 1y. 1m. 25d.
William Irwin. son of S. and Mary, d. Sep. 30, 1827; 7y. 3m.
Lydia Ann Jewell, daughter of R. and M., d. July 28, 1844; 1y.

Sarah Jewell, daughter of R. and M., d. April 7, 1844; 14d.
Abirath Johnson, son of William and Agnes, d. June, 6, 1831; 9y. 3m. 2d.
Abram Johnson, d. Dec. 22, 1863; 69y.
Agnes Johnson, wife of William, d. Feb. 4, 1864; 83y.
Albert Johnson, d. Dec. 10, 1886; 63y. 10d.
Cornelia Ann Johnson, daughter of A. and M. A., d. Feb. 3, 1848; 17y. 6m. 3d.
Elizabeth Johnson d. Sep. 5, 1871; 75y.
John Johnson, d. Sep. 28, 1876; 71y.
Margaret J. Johnson, daughter of William and A., d. Sep. 23, 1832; 9y. 9m.
Mary Johnson, d. April 24, 1886; 85y.
Rebecca Johnson, daughter of W. and Agnes, d. June 5, 1851; 32y. 10d.
William Johnson, d. June 7, 1855; 79y. 9d.
Mary Kerr, wife of J. C., b. March 5, 1813; d. March 22, 1847.
Mary Lawson, wife of Thomas, d. March 25, 1833; 48y.
Thomas Lawson, died June 3, 1845; 72y. 1m. 15d.
Maggie Layport, b. June 2, 1853; d. Feb. 10, 1888.
Willie H. Layport, son of R. B. and M. J., d. Dec. 3, 1883; 1y. 16d.
John Leamon, d. Aug. 27, 1866; 58y. 1m. 27d.
Mary T. Leamon, wife of John, d. March 15, 1863; 49y. 4m. 2d.
Nancy E. Leamon, daughter of G. D. and H. F., d. Feb. 3, 1861; 4y 1m. 9d.
Elvira Lee, d. May 2, 1887; 41y.
James Lee, d. March 10. 1876; 58y.
John Lee, d. March 1, 1813; 33y.
Joseph Lee, b. Oct. 5, 1819; d. June 4, 1888.
Joseph V. Lee. son of R. and M., d. Dec. 19, 1811:———
Mary Lee, wife of Robert, d. Aug. 15, 1859; 83y.
Mary A. Lee, daughter of William and Mary, d. Jan. 2, 1860; 17y. 8m. 1d.
Otilla Lee, daughter of William and Mary; d. Oct. 23, 1864; 14y. 1m. 17d.
Robert Lee, d. Sep. 18, 1838; 23y.
Robert Lee, d. May 12, 1861; 85y.
Rose Lee, b. Aug. 21, 1832; d. March

2, 1892.
Vance Lee, son of J. and C., d. March 16, 1860; 21d.
Anna E. Lewis, daughter of W. H. and R. K., d. July 31, 1863; 20y. 2m.
Thomas M. Lewis, son of W. H. and R. K., d. July 28, 1863; 17y. 9m.
Elizabeth Legrand, daughter of Demarkus L. and Margaret, d. June 19, 1858; 4m. 6d.
Infant daughter of L. H. and E. Lindsay, d. June 4, 1888.
Eliza M. Lindsay, wife of L. H., d. June 12, 1862; 31y. 8m. 16d.
Ella Snedeker Lindsay, wife or L. H., d. June 9, 1888; 29y. 8m. 18d.
James Lindsay, d. July 30, 1829; 33y.
James Lindsay, son of J. and S., d. Dec. 20, 1838; 18y. 8m.
Lewis H. Lindsay, d. March 1, 1877; 46y. 9d.
Martha Lindsay, daughter of James and Susan, d. Jan. 11, 1823; 6m.
William Lindsay, son of J. and S., d. Aug. 4, 1823; 6y. 6m.
Abner L. Lodge, son of T. and R., d. Jan. 10, 1852; 2y. 9m. 27d.
Emmet L. Lodge, son of Thomas and Rebecca, d. Oct. 30, 1859; 2y. 25d.
Hazel Lodge, daughter of J. S. and M. V., d. Aug. 28, 1889; 2y. 8d.
John M. Lodge, b. Aug. 28, 1862; d. April 9, 1882.
Nancy Ellen Lodge, wife of Thomas and daughter of John and Sarah Merritt, d. Aug. 17, 1851; 25y. 2m. 26d.
George Love, d. April 23, 1821; 76y.
George Love, Jr., d. Sep. 21, 1829; 42y.
Eliza Lyle, wife of Robert, d. Sep. 26, 1894; 71y.
Elizabeth Parry Lyle, daughter of William and Isabel, d. April 20, 1840; 11y. 2m. 18d.
Flora J. Lyle, daughter of D. and M., d. May 15, 1861; 1y. 5m. 2d.
Frank M. Lyle, b. March 22, 1892; d. Jan. 4, 1893.
Isabella Lyle, wife of John, b. Oct. 28, 1789; d. July 28, 1858.
Isabell Lyle, wife of William, b. July 7, 1804; d. Jan. 7, 1854.
John Lyle, son of Robert and Eliza, d. Jan. 28, 1840; 1y. 8m. 28d.
John Lyle, d. April 17, 1872; 47y.
John Lyle, b. July 17, 1787; d. June 5, 1851.
Linnie Lyle, daughter of John and Jane, d. Oct. 9, 1885; 26y.
Mary Eleanor Lyle, daughter of G. L. and N. J., b. Feb. 27, 1887; d. March 22, 1892.
Robert Lyle, b. April 28, 1811; d. Nov. 23, 1895.
Rosannah Lyle, daughter of John and Isabella, d. Aug. 1, 1821; 1y. 2m.
William Lyle, b. Sep. 5, 1789; d. Feb. 19, 1854.
Isabella Lyon, wife of John, d. Nov. 1, 1850; 79y.
James Woods Lyon, son of James and Nancy, d. Jan. 5, 1863; 3y. 20d.
Sarah Margaret Lyon, daughter of J. and N., d. Nov. 18, 1838; 11m. 4d.
Benjamin McCann, d. Jan. 28, 1842; 61y. 2m.
Margaret Ann McClelland, daughter of William and C., d. Feb. 11, 1849; 3y. 18d.
John T. McConaughey, son of D. and R. E., d. Aug. 18, 1869; 4y. 10m. 15d.
Maggie M. McConaughey, daughter of D. and R. E., d. Aug. 14, 1869; 6y. 4m. 5d.
Sarah A. McConaughey, d. Dec. 16, 1856; 39y. 10m. 8d.
Elizabeth McConnell, d. April 19, 1857; 92y. 3m. 7d.
Francis Marion McConnell, son of J. and J., d. June 22, 1862; 22y. 9d.
James McConnell, son of John and Jane, d. Jan. 16, 1830; 2y. 3m. 5d.
John McConnell, d. Oct. 16, 1831; 61y.
John McConnell, d. June 22, 1856; 22y. 8m. 19d.
John McConnell, d. Aug. 18, 1878; 82y. 3m. 15d.
Martha McConnell, daughter of John and Jane; d. Sep. 26, 1876; 28y. 8m.
Mary McConnell, wife of John; d.———
William McConnell, d. April 14, 1856; 30y. 8m. 2d.
John G. McCracken, son of Dr. John and Martha, d. July 27, 1819; 5hrs.
Elmira McCullough, d. ———, 1835; —y. 1m. —d.
Esther McCullough, d. Aug. 8, 1841; 86y.

Esther J. McCullough, d. March 12, 1837; 17y. 3m.
George McCullough, b. May 10, 1803; d. April 3, 1845.
Isabella McCullough, wife of William; d. May 23, 1832; 81y.
Isabell McCullough, wife of J. G., d. Aug. 23, 1839; 50y.
Jane McCullough, wife of Robert, d. Oct. 15, 1835; 70y.
Jane McCullough, d. June 13, 1878; 83y.
John McCullough, ——[old sandstone].
John McCullough, son of Samuel and Eliza, d. Jan. 14, 1837; 6y. 4m. 6d.
John McCullough, b. April 29, 1834; d. Sep. 15, 1855.
Lonazelah Jane McCullough, d. Jan. 10, 1841; 10y. 6m. 17d.
Peter John McCullough, d. —— 16, 1841; 9y. 8m. 8d.
Robert McCullough, d. June 17, 1823; 67y.
Rev. Robert McCullough, d. Aug. 13, 1858; 38y.
Samuel McCullough, d. June 28, 1859; 71y.
Samuel I. McCullough, d. April 8, 1884; 56y.
Sarah McCullough, b. Jan. 7, 1807; d. Dec. 9, 1875.
William McCullough, d. March 18, 1831; 83y. [a soldier of the Revolution].
William McCullough, d. Nov., 1834; 18y. 1m. 25d.
Daniel McElhatten, d. Feb. 17, 1843; 65y.
Nancy McElhatten, d. Dec. 29, 186·; 78y. 4d.
Cynthia McGrew, wife of William, d. Jan. 2, 1885; 62y.
Emma F. McGrew, daughter of Wm. and C., d. Oct. 12, 1876; 21y. 10m. 12d.
Charles McGroarty, d. Sep. 30, 1866; 70y.
Mary McKibben, wife of George, d. May 30, 1834; 26y. 5m. 11d.
Sarah McKibben, wife of John, b. 1730; d. June 9, 1812; 82y.
Ann McLaughlin, wife of Edward, d. Sep. 1, 1851; 38y.
Hugh Kelly McMillan, d. Dec. 26, 1852; 22y. 9m. 23d.
Rev. William McMillan, D. D., d. April 11, 1832; 52y.
Alexander McPherson, ——
Catharine McPherson, ——
Rebecca McPherson, ——
Richard Mansfield, d. Sep. 24, 1881; 85y.
Thomas Marshall, d. March 23, 1839; 96y.
Anna Merritt, daughter of J. and S., d. Oct. 3, 1832; 8y. 6m. 29d.
Christina L. Merritt, b. Aug. 22, 1825; d. March 5, 1890.
George M. Merritt, son of A. and I., d. Aug. 15, 1845; 1y. 9m. 17d.
James F. Merritt, b. Feb. 18, 1820; d. March 18, 1859.
John Merritt, d. Jan. 11, 1841; 43y. 9m. 4d.
Josiah S. Merritt, b. May 5, 1811; d. April 14, 1814.
Mary E. Merritt, daughter of Aaron and Isabella; d. March 27, 1852; 1m. 23d.
Sarah Merritt, wife of John, d. Oct. 7, 1834; 34y. 9m. 24d.
William L. Merritt, d. April 20, 1873; 21y. 2m. 20d.
Joanna Milburn, daughter of Jonathan and S. E., b. June 16, 1861; d. Aug. 26, 1876.
Joseph Miller, d. Sep. 16, 1841; 21y. 10m. 25d.
Mary Miller, wife of Robert, d. Aug. 20, 1881; 91y. 7d.
Willie M. Moffatt, son of W. S. and M. J., d. Jan. 15, 1871; 2y.
Albert Moore, b. Dec. 28, 1852; d. Feb. 28, 1854.
Hugh Moore, b. Aug. 9, 1829; d. April 19, 1856.
Joseph Moore, d. May 16, 1875; 76y.
Martin Moore, d. March 30, 1865; 26y. 10d.
Mary Moore, wife of John, d. Aug. 25, 1854; 77y. 8m.
Sarah Moore, b. July 28, 1811; d. April 7, 1895.
William Moore, d. March 11, 1865; 62y.
Thomas Morgan, d. Oct. 18, 1867; 57y.
Elizabeth Morris, wife of John, d. July 11, 1852; 27y. 5m. 10d.
James Noling, d. Sep. 12, 1861; 43y.

CRABAPPLE BURIALS

2m. 14d.
Martha Osborn, daughter of Alex. and Mary, d. July 7, 1822; 34y. 22d.
Mary Osborn, wife of Alex., d. Jan. 5, 1842; 43y.
James Parr, d. Sep. 3, 1853; 95y.
Jane Patton, wife of Samuel, d. April 23, 1841; 85y.
John Patton, son of Samuel and Jane, d. April 15, 1814; 17y.
Samuel Patton, d. Oct. 15, 1828; 67y.
Lorenza Dow Pearse, son of Isaac and May, d. Jan. 9, 1839; 33y. [sandstone near this, marked M. P.].
Elizabeth Pearse, d. April 28, 1822; ———.
Margaret E. Peterson, wife of P. G., d. Aug. 15, 1885; 28y. 11m. 4d.
Infant daughter of J. D. and E. Phillips, d. Oct. 25, 1864; 1m.
Infant son of M. and S. Phillips, d. April 30, 1853; 1m.
Mary Phillips, wife of James, d. May 5, 1838; 59y.
Mary Jane Phillips, daughter of M. and S., d. June 9, 1830; 4m. 21d.
Matthew H. Phillips, d. Sep. 26, 1864; 59y.
Rebecca Phillips, daughter of M. and S., d. March 30, 1842; 10m.
Sarah J. Phillips, daughter of M. and S., d. March 4, 1840; 5y. 2m. 20d.
Mary J. Pollack, wife of R. J., d. Oct. 24, 1882; 55y. 8m. 10d.
Elizabeth Porter, wife of James, d. May 4, 1863; 69y. 1m. 3d.
Margaret Porter, wife of James, d. May 25, 1851; 75y.
Margaret Josephine Porter, wife of Josiah, d. March 25, 1854; 28y.
Rebecca Porter, daughter of James and Elizabeth, d. April 11, 1863; 30y. 1m. 3d.
Samuel Porter, Sr., d. Aug. 2, 1869; 104y.
Terrissa Porter, wife of David, d. Oct. 24, 1862; 51y. 11m. 22d.
Sarah Rainey, d. Aug. 30, 1876; 80y.
William Rainey, d. Oct. 20, 1847; 51y.
William Rainey, son of W. and S., d. Sep. 21, 1829; 8m. 4d.
Isabella Ralston, daughter of R. and M., d. April 16, 1852; 1y. 4m. 5d.
Joseph Ralston, d. April 9, 1828; 60y.

Samuel Rhea, son of John and Mary, d. June 14, 1838; 10m. 6d.
William M. Rhea, son of John and Mary, d. Feb. 29, 1840; 7y. 4m. 3d.
George Richner, son of John and Susanna, d. Sep. 4, 1861; 8y. 1m. 1d.
Isaac Richner, son of J. and S., d. May 18, 1840; 2m 13d.
Sarah A. Richner, daughter of John and Susanna, d. July 16, 1861; 11y. 10m. 20d.
Susanna Richner, wife of John, d. Nov. 2, 1865; 54y.
Susanna R. Richner, daughter of J. and S., d. June 7, 1868; 21y.
Infant son of Andrew and Margaret Richey, d. May 2, 1822;———
Infant son of J. B. and M. A. Richey, d. Feb. 28, 1858; 3m. 16d.
Andrew Ritchey, d. May 30, 1859; 80y. 7m. 28d.
Andrew Richey, son of A. and M., d. Dec. 13, 1828; 2m. 20d.
Ann Ritchey, daughter of A. and M., d. Nov. 9, 1810; 4m.
David Ritchie, d. June 21, 1856; 82y.
Esther Ritchey, d. Sep. 14, 1879; 54y. 9m. 19d.
James Ritchey, son of A. and M., d. Aug. 1, 1813; 9y.
Jane Ritchey, daughter of Andrew and Nancy, d. Sep. 9, 1864; 52y. 7m.
Margaret Ritchey, wife of Andrew, d. Jan. 20, 1861; 66y. 7m.
Martha Agnes Ritchey, daughter of A. and M., d. Aug. 5, 1855; 14y. 5m. 17d.
Mary Ritchie, wife of David, d. ———
Nancy Ritchey, wife of Andrew, d. Aug. 2, 1814; 34y.
Nancy Ritchey, daughter of A. and M. Ritchey; d. Jan. 2, 1815; 5m.
Robert C. Ritchie, son of J. B. and M. A., d. July 30, 1857; 6y. 11m.
Sarah Ritchey, d. Feb. 15, 1829; 20y.
William Richey, son of A. and M., d. May 28, 1833; 1y. 5m. 11d.
Margaret Robb, wife of Andrew, d. March 21, 1845; 47y.
Samuel Rogers, son of Michael and Rachel, d. July 13, 1824; 10m. 2d.
Mariah Scott, wife of Josiah, d. Sep. 30, 1831; 20y. 27d.
Infant son of G. A. and M. Skadden;

d. March 25, 1873; 1m. 14d.

Mary J. Smith, daughter of W. and J., d. June 3, 1846; 14y.

Nicholas Smith, d. Jan., 1826; ——

Anne Snedeker, wife of W. R., b. Sep. 27, 1819; d. Nov. 9, 1881.

Elizabeth Snedeker, d. Oct. 15, 1847; 72y. 5m. 11d.

Elizabeth S. Snedeker, daughter of N. and H., d. June 13, 1827; 18y.

Hannah Snedeker, d. Nov. 24, 1829; 44y.

James W. Snedeker, son of W. R. and A., d. March 16, 1852; 1y. 3m. 17d.

Marion Ross Snedeker, son of Peter and Mary E., d. May 24, 1875; 1m. 7d.

Mary Ann Snedeker, daughter of Josiah and Sarah; d. Dec. 9, 1843; 1y. 1m. 9d.

Mary A. Snedeker, daughter of William R. and Anne, d. Nov. 17, 1857; 11y. 10m. 11d.

Mary F. Ross Snedeker, wife of Peter, d. April 27, 1875; 24y. 3m. 7d.

Nancy Snedeker, d. Aug. 22, 1838; 35y.

Nicholas Snedeker, d. July 28, 1844; 66y.

Peter Snedeker, d. Feb. 29, 1856; 82y.

Sarah Snedeker, wife of Josiah, d. April 20, 1848; 34y. 6m. 11d.

Sarah J. Snedeker, daughter of W. R. and A., d. Aug. 7, 1849; 8y. 6m. 3d.

Candace C. Tannehill, d. Jan. 7, 1849; 3y. 3m. 9d.

Caroline Tannehill, b. Dec. 18, 1817; d. May 12, 1891.

Hannah P. Tannehill, d. Jan. 27, 1849; 5y.

Isaiah Tannehill, Jan. 26, 1817; July 29, 1843.

James Tannehill, d. Sep. 30, 1873; 83y.

Jane Tannehill, wife of James, d. Aug. 24, 1851; 65y. 8m. 14d.

Margaret Tannehill daughter of William and Mary, d. March 16, 1875; 78y.

William Tannehill, d. Oct. 28, 1845; 84y. 1m.

Andrew Thompson, d. May 19, 1877; 77y.

Jane Thompson, wife of Joseph, d. Aug. 26, 1843; 78y.

Joseph Thompson, d. March 22, 1835; 81y. 11d.

Martha P. Thompson, d. March 18, 1883; 76y.

Rachel Ann Thompson, wife of Addison, and daughter of Samuel and Ann Armor; d. April 24, 1855; 24y.

Anne E. Troutman, daughter of Henry and Jane, d. Oct. 28, 1860; 21y. 9m. 26d.

Robert Twigg, son of L. and S., d. March 15, 1836; 3y. 10m. 1d.

William T. Lindsay Twigg, son of Lewis and Susan, d. April 14, 1852; 16y. 1m. 18d.

Ann Vanhorn, daughter of Edward and Margaret, d. Oct. 19, 1815; 12y.

Edward Vanhorn, d. Aug. 19, 1855; 78y.

Jane Vanhorn, b. Feb. 6, 1809; d. Feb. 29, 1888.

Margaret Vanhorn, wife of Edward, d. Oct. 14, 1839; 63y.

Martha Vanhorn, b. April 20, 1805; d. Jan. 27, 1869.

Samuel R. Vincent, son of W. R. and E. J., d. Feb. 22, 1863; 1y. 3m. 28d.

Sarah J. Webb, wife of John W., b. July 22, 1858; d. Jan. 24, 1883.

Mary Welling, b. Feb. 6, 1872; d. Feb. 26, 1872.

Agnes Wellman, wife of Rudolph, d. June 17, 1834; 74y.

Rudolph Wellman, d. Dec. 27, 1836; 78y. 1m. 26d.

Hannah E. Whan, daughter of J. B. and M., d. July 19, 1851; 3m. 13d.

James B. Whan, d. Sep. 19, 1856; 40y. 8m. 10d.

John W. Whan, son of John and Margaret, d. July 19, 1849; 28y. 3m. 9d.

Margaret Whan, wife of James B., d. May 8, 1857; 30y. 4m. 19d.

Mary Whan, daughter of John and Margaret, d. Aug. 6, 1851; 41y.

Jane White, ——

Betsey Wiley, wife of William, d. Sep. 10, 1849; 66y.

Eddie Wiley, son of J. and H. E., d. Oct. 22, 1861; 1y. 9m. 14d.

Joseph Wiley, d. Aug. 20, 1873; 68y. 11m. 2d.

Margaret Wiley, wife of John, d. Aug. 11, 1823; 46y.

Mary Wiley, d. Oct. 6, 1862; 78y.

Rolin P. Wiley, son of J. and H. E., d. Oct. 20, 1857.
William Wiley, d. Sep. 13, 1853; 78y.
Jane Wood Williamson, wife of Rev. MacKnight Williamson, b. March 5, 1801; d. July 24, 1849.
Sarah H. Williamson, daughter of P. and H., d. June 7, 1848; 1y. 8m. 1d.

BURIALS IN UNITY GRAVEYARD.
To August 30, 1896.

James Alexander, b. July 7, 1807; d. Oct. 22, 1887.
Andrew Anderson, d. Dec. 19, 1831; 63y.
Elizabeth Anderson, wife of James, d. June 14, 1842; 25y. 10m. 22d.
Sarah Anderson, wife of J., d. April 6, 1849; 38y. 6m. 29d.
Anna Eleanor Armstrong, daughter of John and Mary, b. in Pittsburg, Pa., Dec. 26, 1814; d. in New Athens, Ohio, Jan. 13, 1831.
Charles Bamford, d. Nov. 15, 1863; 100y. 6m.
Andrew H. Barnes, d. March 24, 1845; 23y.
Thomas Barr, d. May 8, 1848; 27y. 5m. 22d.
Eliza Black, d. Dec. 28, 1842; 24y.
Martha M. Cobbs, wife of Dr. G., d. Oct. 10, 1874; 43y. 20d.
Mattie Cobbs, twin daughter of Dr. G. and M. M., d. April 29, 1871; 2y. 6m. 26d.
Vangeline Cobbs, wife of Dr. Charles, b. April 17, 1845; d. June 8, 1880.
Martin Cochran, d. March 26, 1823; 35y.
George Cook, b. May 5, 1804; d. Sep. 20, 1892.
George Cook, son of George and M., d. Aug. 24, 1851; 17y. 2d.
James Cook, d. Feb. 28, 1815; 60y.
John Cook, d. June 21, 1843; 44y.
Margaret Cook, wife of John, d. Aug. 28, 1839; 35y.
Nancy Cook, wife of James, d. Jan. 20, 1829; 69y.
Nancy Cook, wife of George, d. Jan. 9, 1888; 78y. 14d.
Polly Cook, daughter of John and Margaret, d. April 19, 1835; 2y. 23d.
Rebecca Cook, wife of William, d. 1818; 24y.
Thomas Cooke, b. Jan. 9, 1843; d. May 21, 1872.
William Cook, d. May 8, 1838; 46y.
Elizabeth Craig, d. Jan. 27, 1823; 67y.
James Craig, son of Joseph and Jane, d. June 12, 1839; 7y. 4m. 15d.
Jane Craig, d. May 28, 1864; 75y.
John Craig, son of L. and J. C., d. Dec. 12, 1866; 15d.
Joseph Craig, d. May 28, 1864; 75y.
Nancy Craig, d. July 6, 1852; 74y.
William Craig, minister of the Gospel, son of James and E., d. July 10, 1818; 29y.
Agnes Crawford, wife of Isaac, d. Jan. 8, 1833; 32y. 1m. 10d.
Infant son of J. and S. Culbertson, d. Sep., 1846.
Dorcas Culbertson, d. Aug. 15, 1865; 47y. 5m.
Gillespie Culbertson, d. Sep. 11, 1890; 74y.
Infant son of J. and S. Culbertson, d. June 16, 1887.
Mary Culbertson, wife of Robert, d. July 13, 1886; 67y.
Mary B. Culbertson, daughter of R. and M., d. Oct. 21, 1863; 3y. 8m. 24d.
Robert C. Culbertson, d. Dec. 26, 1880; 87y.
Sarah J. Culbertson, wife of John, b. Aug. 1, 1846; d. Sep. 19, 1890.
Sarah M. Culbertson, daughter of R. and M., d. Oct. 2, 1863; 5y. 4m. 18d.
Thomas Culbertson, d. Aug. 13, 1841; 40y. 6m.
Lizzie Davis, daughter of J. W. and S. J., d. Oct. 24, 1877; 11y. 4m. 15d.
Sarah Davis, wife of J. W., d. Nov. 14, 1875; 35y. 3m.
Samantha Dunbar, d. Sep. 8, 1823; d. May 3, 1890.
William Dunbar, b. April 19, 1810; d. Sep. 6, 1891.
William Dunbar, b. April 13, 1851; d. Aug. 3, 1874.
Jennie Dysart, wife of B. W., d. Nov. 16, 1873; 28y. 1m. 20d.
Lucinda Caroline Dysart, daughter of William and L., d. Nov. 14, 1862; 8y.

6m.
Mary E. Dysart, daughter of William and Lucinda, d. Feb. 9, 1840; 2y. 5m.
Mary M. Ferguson, wife of Malcolm, d. Oct. 5, 1845; 32y. 5m. 11d.
Nancy J. Ferguson, daughter of M., and J. A., d. Nov. 29, 1860; 8y. 4m. 18d.
Agnes Finley, d. Oct. 15, 1843; 47y.
Elizabeth Finley, d. May 8, 1833; 42y.
Emma Eliza Finney, daughter of Thomas and E. [No dates].
Margaret Ann Finney, daughter of Thomas and E. [No dates].
Infant son of Thomas and E. Finney. [No dates].
George Frater, d. July 9, 1877; 78y. 6m. 18d.
George W. Frater, son of J. D. and S. J., d. Sep. 19, 1861; 9m. 29d.
Henry O. Frater, b. Feb. 17, 1858; d. July 17, 1868.
Lillie Frater, daughter of M. O. and J. K., d. Aug. 11, 1889; 4y. 7d.
Luretta Jessie Frater, daughter of W. A. and B. H., d. March 11, 1867; 2m. 2d.
R. F. Frater, b. Feb. 16, 1833; d. Dec. 25, 1881.
Susanna Frater, d. Aug. 19, 1874; 78y. 6m. 18d.
Susanna Frater, b. Oct. 30, 1831; d. Sep. 11, 1891.
Homer Richey Gaston, son of Joseph and Mary, d. Oct. 3, 1885; d. Feb. 19, 1886.
David Givney, d. Feb. 26, 1859; 85y. 11m.
James Gibney, son of D. and M., d. Feb. 14, 1846; 29y. 5m. 21d.
Martha Gibney, daughter of D. and M., d. Dec. 22, 1853; 31y.
Mary J. Gibney, daughter of J. and E., d. Oct. 4, 1856; 9y. 10m. 5d.
Agnes Gillespie, wife of James, d. Sep. 24, 1873; 85y. 8m. 24d.
Eleanor Gillespie, wife of Robert, d. March 28, 1859; 34y.
Joseph H. Gillespie, son of R. and E., b. March 12, 1849; d. Nov. 12, 1861.
Sarah Gillespie, wife of J. T., d. Nov. 2, 1873; 26y. 1m. 14d.
Levi Graham, d. Feb. 26, 1845; 29y. 11m. 10d.
Mary Graham, d. March 5, 1885; 78y.
Agnes Gray, d. Feb. 3, 1879; 72y. 26d.
Benjamin M. Gray, son of Robert and Ann, d. April 7, 1841; 5m. 2d.
Catharine Hammond, wife of Robert, d. July 5, 1846; 32y.
David Hammond, d. Sep. 22, 1826; 63y.
David Hammond, d. July 13, 1836; 30y. 2m. 6d.
Ellen F. Hammond, daughter of J. and S., d. Dec. 14, 1863; 8y. 7m. 15d.
Garrett Hammon, son of William and Jane, d. Feb. 20, 1839; ——
Grizzilla Hammond, daughter of J. and M., d. Dec. 6, 1849; 17y.
Hannah H. Hammond, wife of R., and daughter of Alex. and Eleanor Clark; d. Sep. 15, 1843; 35y.
Infant son of J. and J. Hammond, d. April 21, 1834.
Infant son of J. and J. Hammond, d. April 24, 1838.
Infant daughter of J. and J. Hammond, d. Feb. 28, 1847.
James Hammond, b. May 13, 1808; d. July 9, 1880.
Jane Hammond, wife of Robert, d. Feb. 23, 1852; 88y.
Jane Hammon, wife of William, d. Dec. 16, 1837; 29y. 11m.
Jane Hammond, wife of James, d. May 1, 1850; 37y. 6m.
John Hammond, d. Aug. 6, 1874; 72y.
John G. Hammond, son of J. and J., d. Oct. 15, 1846; 1y. 17d.
Joseph F. Hammond, son of J. and S., d. Dec. 21, 1862; 7y. 2m. 16d.
Martha Ellen Hammond, daughter of J. and M., d. Feb. 18, 1862; 20y.
Robert Hammond, d. Jan. 15, 1845; 81y.
Robert Hammond, d. Aug. 10, 1847; 43y.
Robert Hammond, son of John and M., d. March 17, 1831; 1y. 4m.
Sarah J. Hammond, wife of James, b. Aug. 27, 1832; d. Aug. 4, 1858.
Sarah M. Hammond, daughter of J. and S., d. Dec. 14, 1861; 3y. 11d.
W. Lee Hammond, son of M., d. Aug. 23, 1883; 8m.
Thomas B. Hanna, son of R. P. and J. E., d. June 9, 1860; 5y. 9m. 19d.

UNITY BURIALS

Walter Phillips Hanna, son of J. E. and Belle, d. June 5, 1889; 4m.
David B. Hawthorne, b. March 27, 1875; d. Jan. 9, 1882.
James Hawthorne, d. Oct. 24, 1844; 56y.
Maggie J. Hawthorne, b. Aug. 2, 1862; d. Feb. 16, 1893.
Margaret E. Hawthorne, b. July 1, 1853; d. June 5, 1887.
Martha Venia Hawthorne, b. June 2, 1887; d. Jan. 9, 1882.
Robert G. Hawthorne, d. April 19, 1864; 41y. 6m. 14d.
Rosanna S. Hawthorne, daughter of J. and R., Feb. 14, 1831; 2m.
Willis Lemoin Hawthorne, b. July 27, 1873; d. Dec. 25, 1881.
Sarah A. Trimble Hays, wife of D. J., d. April 26, 1873; 37y. 7m. 6d.
Alex. M. Henderson, son of M. and M. O., d. May 19, 1849; 1y. 11m.
Andrew Henderson, b. April 10, 1798; d. July 1, 1860.
Andrew J. Henderson, b. July 20, 1828; d. April 20, 1830.
David Henderson, d. June 11, 1870; 53y.
Edward Henderson, son of Matthew and Miranda, d. Aug. 16, 1840; 20y. 5d.
George H. Henderson, d. Oct. 30, 1889; 69y. 4m. 20d.
George S. Henderson, son of G. S. and M. A., d. Oct. 14, 1853; 2y. 6m. 29d.
George S. Henderson, son of G. S. and M. A., d. Dec. 12, 1860; 7y. 9m. 28d.
Infant son of G. S. and M. A. Henderson, d. Feb. 28, 1855; 29d.
James C. Henderson, d. Dec. 12, 1870; 61y.
Jane Henderson, wife of William T., d. April 26, 1822; 61y. 11m. 7d.
Jane Henderson, daughter of A. and M., d. June 21, 1825; 10y.
Janet Nichol Henderson, wife of Andrew, b. Jan. 29, 1801; d. Sep. 18, 1891.
Jennie W. Henderson, d. July 12, 1883; 10y. 10m. 20d.
John Henderson, son of Alex. and H., d. Dec. 13, 1842; 5y.
John N. Henderson, b. Sep. 8, 1821; d. March 13, 1882.
Leander Henderson, son of M. and M., d. April 22, 1840; 2y.
Margaret Henderson, daughter of A. and H., d. Dec. 17, 1843; 10y.
Margaret Ann Henderson, d. June 7, 1873; 53y. 10m. 5d.
Martha Henderson, wife of Andrew, d. April 11, 1858; 86y.
Martha M. Henderson, daughter of D. and M., d. Sep. 29, 1863; 8y. 3m. 8d.
Mary Henderson, wife of David, d. July 27, 1874; 58y. 9m. 19d.
Mary J. Henderson, wife of John, b. Dec. 22, 1826; d. June 29, 1847.
Musetta Mary Maud Henderson, daughter of M. H. and M. J., d. Sep. 24, 1875; 1y. 8m. 25d.
Nancy J. Henderson, daughter of G. S. and M. A., d. Oct. 14, 1853; 2y. 6m. 29d.
Nathaniel T. Henderson, b. Dec. 15, 1814; d. Sep. 3, 1888.
Rebecca Jane Henderson, daughter of James and Barbara, d. Jan. 18, 1886; 33y. 2m. 11d.
Samuel Henderson, son of Alex. and Mary, d. Dec. 25, 1815; 7y.
Samuel Henderson, d. Aug. 5, 1833; 2y. 1m. 21d.
William Henderson, son of G. S. and M. A.
William T. Henderson, d. Aug. 25, 1861; 46y.
William T. Henderson, b. May 1, 1838; d. Dec. 18, 1862.
James Henry, d. Sep. 11, 1856; 37y.
Thomas Henry, son of James and Rebecca, d. May 21, 1834; 21y.
Maggie J. McNary Kasley, wife of Samuel H., d. Feb. 3, 1874; 34y. 2m. 26d.
Infant of David and Jane Kilgore.
Elizabeth K. Gilgore, d. March 26, 1877; 57y.
Jeremiah Kilgore, d. April 12, 1868; 56y.
Sarah E. Kilgore, wife of William M., d. July 29, 1871; 24y. 9m.
Tacie Kilgore, wife of William M., b. Sep. 7, 1855; d. Jan. 3, 1894.
Andrew M. King, d. Feb. 12, 1844; 30y.
Griffith Lemmon, d. Nov. 12, 1879; 84y.
Mary Lemmon, wife of Griffith, d. Oct.

20, 1834; 30y.

Margaret Dunbar Lodge, wife of William, d. July 5, 1881; 33y. 1m. 10d.

Caroline J. Love, daughter of G. and J., d. May 28, 1853; 2y. 11m. 11d.

George Love, d. Dec. 20, 1880; 70y. 6m. 21d.

George Love, son of R. M. and S. H., b. Jan. 10, 1867; d. Feb. 24, 1867.

Jane Love, wife of George, d. Feb. 21, 1891; 72y. 3m. 4d.

John Love, d. March 28, 1862; 88y.

Joseph McFadden Love, son of Robert and Sarah H., d. April 15, 1872; 11y. 8m. 12d.

Mary Love, wife of John, d. Dec. 16, 1830; 44y.

Mary Love, wife of John, b. Sep. 11, 1877; 76y.

Nancy Love, daughter of G. and J., d. March 3, 1842; 3y. 5m. 25d.

Nancy J. Love, daughter of G. and J., d. March 19, 1849; 4y. 6m. 6d.

Jane Lumsdon, wife of Thomas, daughter of William and Jane Hindmarsh; born in England, May 15, 1831; d. Jan. 29, 1859.

Emily Lyle, wife of George A., d. April 7, 1879; 21y. 6m.

Carrie Patton Lyle, wife of Addison, d. May 1, 1864; 24y.

Jane L. McBratney, wife of Robert, d. Sep. 15, 1830; 84y. 7m.

Elizabeth McBurney, d. June 9, 1849; 90y.

Alex. McCall, d. Nov. 10, 1833; 64y. 22d.

Alex. McCall, son of T. and M., d. Oct. 22, 1840; 1y. 1m.

Elizabeth McCall, wife of Thomas, d. Dec. 20, 1840; 39y. 2m. 14d.

George S. McCall, son of T. and M., d. Sep. 5, 1849; 6y.

Hugh F. McCall, son of Thomas and Miriam, d. July 22, 1848; 1y. 1m. 20d.

Rev. J. A. McCall, d. July 15, 1860; 56y. Erected by congregation of U. P. Church, Cedarville, O.

Jane McCall, daughter of M. and N., d. Sep. 3, 1872; 68y.

John McCall, b. Aug. 22, 1808; d. Oct. 13, 1883.

Margaret McCall, wife of Alex., d. Dec. 5, 1844; 61y.

Margaret McCall, wife of John, d. May 7, 1839; 20y. 5m. 26d.

Margaret J. McCall, daughter of Thomas and Miriam, d. May 9, 1867; 15y. 5m. 12d.

Matthew McCall, d. April 17, 1838; 65y.

Miriam Alma McCall, daughter of T. and M., d. Feb. 12, 1863; 27y. 6m. 9d.

Nancy McCall, wife of Matthew, d. Oct. 2, 1864; 83y. 2m. 24d.

Thomas McCall, son of M. and N., d. Aug. 26, 1842; 20y. 11m. 20d.

Infant son of T. and M. McCall; d. Feb. 14, 1838.

Margaret McCracken, wife of William, d. June 11, 1832; 29y. 10m. 1d.

Martha McCracken, wife of R., d. Oct. 9, 1850; 82y.

Martha McCracken, d. Jan. 29, 1854; 51y. 3m. 17d.

Martha A. McCracken, daughter of William and Margaret, d. Nov. 22, 1844; 17y. 4m. 13d.

Mary McCracken, wife of William, d. Jan. 21, 1879; 78y. 10m. 21d.

Nancy McCracken, b. Aug. 12, 1804; d. Sep. 10, 1885.

Robert McCracken, d. June 18, 1846; 78y.

William McCracken, b. March 4, 1797; d. June 6, 1884.

Elizabeth McFarland, d. Feb. 5, 1875; 77y.

Margaret A. McFarland, wife of Andrew, d. May 27, 1872; 35y. 6m. 16d.

Mary McFarland, d. Aug. 22, 1883; 87y.

Robert McFarland, d. Nov. 26, 1842; 91y.

William McFarland, d. May. 14, 1877; 84y.

Ann McGaskey, d. Jan. 26, 1850; 67y. 5m. 15d.

James McGaskey, b. May 10, 1797; d. and J. M., b. July 8, 1830; d. June Jan. 9, 1853.

Jane McGaskey, wife of James, b. May 31, 1804; d. Feb. 17, 1831.

Jane McGaskey, b. Oct. 1, 1804; d. Sep. 20, 1884.

Jane McGaskey, daughter of H. M. and R., d. Nov. 20, 1822; 7y. 3m. 17d.

John McGaskey, d. Oct. 11, 1833; 74y.

UNITY BURIALS

John McGaskey, d. May 10, 1872; 78y.
Sarah McGaskey, daughter of H. M. and R., d. July 7, 1847;
Sarah J. McGaskey, daughter of J. and J. M., b. July 8, 1830; d. June 28, 1837.
William McGaskey, b. Nov. 7, 1799; d. May 8, 1855.
Mary T. McHenderson, wife of John, b. Dec. 25, 1837; d. April 12, 1889.
David McKee, d. Sep. 17, 1863; 44y.
Infant daughter of D. and M. A. McKee, d. Aug. 4, 1853; 14d.
Joseph R. McKee, son of D. and M., b. Dec. 3, 1849; d. April 4, 1851.
Elizabeth McMillan, d. [no dates]; 68y.
Nancy McMillan, d. Dec. 26, 1856; 48y.
Robert McMillan, d. Aug. 14, 1887; 83y.
Alex. McNary, d. Aug. 30, 1827; 47y. 10d.
Hannah E. McNary, daughter of J. and M., b. Dec. 3, 1854; d. July 6, 1855.
James McNary, b. March 2, 1810; d. March 2, 1881.
John McNary, b. Oct. 21, 1801; d. Feb. 7, 1890.
Margaret McNary, b. Dec. 11, 1780; d. March 31, 1855.
Martha E. McNary, daughter of J. and M., b. Jan. 5, 1852; d. May 15, 1853.
William McNary, died at Soldiers' Home, Pittsburg, Pa., Sep. 2, 1864; 18y. 1m. 23d.
John Major, d. Dec. 12, 1858; 59y. 9m. 22d.
J. Thomas Marrow, b. July 26, 1829; d. Nov. 26, 1886.
Margaret E. Miller, daughter of W. and M., d. Oct. 10, 1855; 2y. 8m. 8d.
Mary Miller, wife of William, b. Feb. 23, 1830; d. Dec. 23, 1861.
Infant daughter of W. and M. Miller, d. Oct. 12, 1855; 15d.
Alvina Minteer, daughter of J. and E..
Eleanor Minteer, wife of Joseph, d. July 6, 1853; 31y.
Eliza Minteer, wife of Joseph, d. May 26, 1866; 54y. 9m. 15d.
Eliza Ann Minteer, wife of James, d. June 28, 1855; 22y. 3m. 19d.
Elizabeth Minteer, wife of R., d. Oct. 5, 1863; 67y.

Elmer Minteer, son of James and Mary, d. July 2, 1865; 4y. 3m. 25d.
Infant daughter of J. and M. Minteer, d. Jan. 1, 1860; 2d.
Joseph Minteer, d. March 16, 1871; 72y. 8m. 7d.
Joseph C. Minteer, d. Jan. 21, 1863; 28y. 7d.
Lavina A. Minteer, daughter of J. and E., d. Aug. 31, 1849; 3y.
Lillie G. Minteer, daughter of G. and M. J., d. Feb. 9, 1872; 4m. 22d.
Martha Minteer, daughter of R. and E., d. April 20, 1850; 19y.
Mary Minteer, wife of James, d. July 14, 1865; 26y. 9m. 9d.
R. G. Minteer, b. March 31, 1853; d. May 10, 1883.
Robert Minteer, d. Feb. 16, 1870; 78y.
William Vincent Minteer, d. Oct. 18, 1871; 31y. 2m. 13d.
Elizabeth Moore, daughter of J. and M., d. May 22, 1827; 15y.
Gilespie Moore, d. Jan. 4, 1874; 53y. 7m. 28d.
James Moore, d. Aug. 1, 1817; 45y.
James Moore, son of J. and M., d. March 13, 1837; 17y.
James Moore, d. Sep. 22, 1828; 9y. 9m.
Sarah R. Moore, wife of J. W., d. April 5, 1894; 42y. 2m. 21d.
William M. Moore, son of G. and E. A., d. March 3, 1876; 20y. 5m. 11d.
Sarah R. Nichols, wife of M. H., b. Nov. 8, 1839; d. May 5, 1896.
Mary J. Parr, daughter of T. and N., d. Sep. 7, 1842; 1y.
Annie C. Patton, d. June 5, 1885; 75y.
Annie W. Patton, d. Dec. 16, 1891; 67y. 8m. 19d.
Elizabeth Patton, wife of J. B., b. Feb. 2, 1845; d. Sep. 30, 1889.
Harriet Dunbar Patton, wife of Calvin, d. April 6, 1873; 25y.
James H. Patton, d. Oct. 3, 1860; 75y.
Jane Patton, wife of James, b. Sep. 13, 1789; d. June 6, 1880; 91y.
Rachel S. Patton, daughter of J. and J., d. Nov. 20, 1845; 19y.
Ray Jewel Patton, son of C. D. and Jane, b. Sep. 9, 1893; d. Sep. 8, 1894.
Rev. Samuel Patton, d. Nov. 15, 1857; 28y; Pastor of First Associate Presbyterian Church, Detroit, Mich.

Sarah Patton, wife of Dr. R. W., d. Jan. 18, 1876; 59y.
Sylvanus Patton, son of William and A., d. Sep. 29, 1863; 12y.
William Patton, d. May 2, 1873; 74y.
William Patton, son of James and Jane, d. Dec. 8, 1841; 10y. 11m. 2d.
Alex. Pollock, b. March 25, ———; d. Aug. 5, 1821.
James Pollock, b. Sep. 4, 1821; d. Jan. 9, 1823.
James W. Pollock, son of J. and N., d. June 28, 1851; 18y. 9m.
John Pollock, d. April 24, 1853; 82y.
John Pollock, Sr., d. Feb. 26, 1861; 65y. 11m. 23d.
John Pollock, member of Company B, 98th Regiment O. V. I., wounded at Chickamauga, Sep. 20; died at Chattanooga, Tenn., Oct. 17, 1863; 33y. 9d.
Mary Pollock, wife of John, d. April 16, 1856; 78y.
Nancy Pollock, d. Sep. 7, 1879; 81y. 5m. 12d.
Nancy R. Pollock, daughter of Samuel and Jane, d. Sep. 17, 1861; 1y. 10m. 17d.
Rebecca J. Pollock, b. July 7, 1852; d. Feb. 26, 1893.
Samuel Pollock, b. Jan. 11, 1818; d. March 29, 1892.
Margaret D. Porterfield, d. March 19, 1887; 75y.
Sarah Potter, wife of James, d. June 5, 1851; 80y.
Elizabeth Ritchey, wife of John, b. Jan. 8, 1781; d. Nov. 11, 1859.
James Ritchey, son of John and Eleanor, d. Dec. 12, 1839; 15y. 8m. 8d.
John Ritchey, b. Dec. 8, 1776; d. March 24, 1852.
Mary Ann Ritchey, daughter of J. and S., d. Aug. 1, 1844; 3y. 7m. 10d.
Abigail Robb, d. Nov. 17, 1863; 67y.
William Robb, d. Jan. 21, 1858; 72y.
Mary Ellen Rogers, daughter of J. and S., d. Jan. 3, 1863; 14y. 2m. 1d.
James H. Rogers, son of J. and S., d. Dec. 31, 1862; 62y. 4m. 15d.
Joseph Rogers, son of J. and S., d. Jan. 17, 1863; 6y. 2m. 10d.
Robert F. Rogers, son of J. and S., d. Dec. 31, 1862; 7y. 5m.
William James Rogers, son of J. and S., d. April 10, 1831; 31y. 9m. 13d.
Mary M. Cook Rourk, wife of J. H., b. April 11, 1845; d. March 30, 1879.
Jane Scroggs, daughter of J. G. and M. P., d. June 11, 1854; 44y.
John C. Scroggs, d. Feb. 20, 1855; 77y.
Caroline Sharp, d. Oct. 20, 1886; 72y. 8m. 28d.
William Sharp, d. May 18, 1859; 50y. 3m. 8d.
Rachel Jane Shearer, daughter of J. and M., d. Sep. 5, 1849; 1y. 5m. 22d.
E. J. Ferguson Sloan, wife of William, d. Jan. 17, 1867; 52y.
Agnes Smith, d. Nov. 26, 1842; 2m. 2d.
Eliza S. Smith, wife of Joseph B., d. March 12, 1887; 78y.
Joseph Smith, d. Feb. 24, 1878; 86y.
M. J. Smith, d. April 27, 1845; 13y. 27d.
Silas Smith, son of J. and E., d. Nov. 20, 1850; 76y.
Samuel Steen, son of John and Catharine, d. Aug. 18, 1822; 10m. 12d.
Anna A. Stevenson, daughter of Rev. J. and E., d. June 5, 1864; 1y. 9m.
Agnes Stewart, wife of John, d. Oct. 11, 1856; 84y.
Elizabeth Stewart, d. Dec. 25, 1840; 31y.
Elizabeth Stewart, daughter of J. and A., d. Nov. 7, 1831; 2y. 2m.
Esther Stewart, wife of William, d. Oct. 25, 1843; 28y.
Harry A. Stewart, son of J. E. and M. J., d. July 31, 1862; 10m.
James S. Stewart, d. July 1, 1842; 1y. 11m.
Jane Stewart, wife of Edie, d. Feb. 11, 1847; 68y.
Matthew C. Stewart, son of J. S. and J., d. Nov. 8, 1849; 9y. 9m.
Robert Stewart, d. July 30, 1889; 33y.
William Stewart, son of J. and A., d. Nov. 4, 18—; 3y. 11m. 3d.
Martha J. Stiles, wife of W. H., b. Sep. 1, 1857; d. March 28, 1889. [Also infant].
Sarah J. Taggart, daughter of H. and E., d. Feb. 25, 1847; 14y. 6m.
William Taylor, b. Aug. 18, 1849; d.

Sep. 20, 1885.
John G. Thompson, son of S. and M. A., d. Sep. 26, 1849. [No age].
John Trimble, Sr., d. Sep. 14, 1843; 67y.
Mary Trimble, d. Sep. 8, 1825; 40y.
Thomas Trimble, d. Aug. 11, 1876; 62y. 10m.
James Trusdall, son of L. and E., d. June 4, 1847; 21y. 5m.
Margaret G. Vincent, wife of Rev. G. C., d. June 24, 1841; 30y.
James Walker, son of Rev. J. and R., b. Aug. 15, 1813; d. April 12, 1853.
Rev. John Walker, d. March 8, 1845; in the 30th year of his ministry, having been pastor of Unity Church 31 years.
Joseph Hanna Walker, infant son of Rev. J. and R., d. April 7, 1829; 14d.
Margaretha R. Walker, daughter of Rev. J. and R., d. March 15, 1845; 7m. 28d.
Mary Walker, wife of Robert, d. Feb. 27, 1825; 75y.
Nancy M. Walker, daughter of William and Martha M., d. July 9, 1871; 4m. 7d.
Rachel S. Walker, wife of Rev. John, d. Nov. 10, 1830; 43y.
William Houston Walker, Pastor of Associate Ohio Congregation, Beaver Co., Pa., d. June 26, 1841; 26y; in the 4th year of his ministry.
Mary E. Wallace, daughter of T. and M., d. March 6, 1857; 1m. 11d.
Jane Watson, wife of William H.; daughter of J. and M. Hammond, d. July 31, 1854; 26y.
William Watson, b. March 20, 1822; d. June 19, 1889.
Esther White, daughter of Paul and Mary, d. Oct. 20, 1826; 3y. 8m.
Paul White, d. May 25, 1827; 43y.
Henry H. Wilson, son of Mordecai and Hester, d. Sep. 22, 1864; 5y. 11m. 26d.
James Wishart, son of Rev. William and Sarah, d. April 19, 1863; 1y. 2m. 16d.
Samuel Wishart, son of W. and S., d. Dec. 31, 1852; 6 weeks.
Mary M. Yoshall, and infant, wife and daughter of William, d. April 15, 1877; 32y. 11m. 25d.

BURIALS IN NOTTINGHAM GRAVEYARD.

To May 16, 1898.

Elizabeth Alexander, wife of B., d. Sep. 30, 1866; 74y. 8d.
Robert Alexander, d. Feb. 1, 1856; 61y. 11m. 24d.
Jane Barclay, daughter of A. and E., d. Nov. 11, 1854; 11y. 4m. 23d.
Elizabeth Bargar, wife of Alex., d. May 5, 1854; 39y. 8m. 5d.
Jane Bargar, daughter of D. and E., d. Nov. 11, 1854; 11y. 4m. 23d.
Nancy Barricklow, wife of Frederick, d. Oct. 17, 1881; 81y. 8m. 4d.
Frederick Barricklow, d. May 1, 1858; 63y. 5m. 28d.
Henry Barricklow, d. April 27, 1851; 80y.
Meriba Barricklow, wife of Henry, d. May 15, 1848; 75y.
Rachel Barricklow, wife of John, d. March 20, 1839; 20y. 1m. 20d.
Mary J. Belknap, d. Aug. 24, 1854; 39y. 20d.
Elizabeth Bethel, wife of John, d. Dec. 18, 1872; 77y. 10m. 1d.
Frances Bethel, wife of Simpson, d. Oct. 26, 1882; 52y. 5m. 13d.
John Bethel, b. June 29, 1806; d. April 4, 1887.
Allec Carrothers, son of James and Elizabeth, d. Aug. 27, 1873; 1y. 10m. 17d.
Anne Carrothers, wife of George, a native of Ireland, b. May 1, 1798; d. Jan. 14, 1886.
Elizabeth Carrothers, wife of J., d. March 8, 1864; 42y. 4m.
George Carrothers, a native of Ireland and E., d. May 23, 1875; 11y. 2m. 19d.
Hiram D. Carrothers, son of J. and E., d. Jan. 22, 1846; 5y.
Mary Carrothers, daughter of George and Anne, d. Aug. 8, 1864; 29y.
Mary E. Carrothers, daughter of J. and E., d. Jan. 14, 1846; 9y.
Daniel Clements, b. Dec. 24, 1819; d. Sep. 1, 1872.
Elizabeth Clements, b. Nov. 25, 1822;

d. Jan. 22, 1888.
Eliza Clemens, wife of John, d. July 14, 1886; 56y. 3. 14d.
Gillespie Clemens, son of J. and M., d. March 30, 1871; 27y. 11m. 20d.
James Clemens, d. Nov. 20, 1872; 72y.
John Clemens, d. July 28, 1880; 53y. 1m.
Louisa E. Clements, daughter of Daniel and Elizabeth, d. Jan. 10, 1876; 19y.
Lucinda J. Clemens, daughter of J. and E., d. May 23, 1875; 11y. 2m. 19d.
Mary Clemens, wife of James, d. June 10, 1868; 68y.
Rebecca Clemens, daughter of J. and M., d. March 10, 1866; 26y. 7m.
Samuel A. Clements, son of Daniel and Elizabeth, d. March 9, 1876; 26y.
Agness Clifford, daughter of S. M. and M., d. Dec. 2, 1852; 1y. 11m.
David Clifford, d. Sep. 17, 1852; 21y. 3m. 3d.
James W. Clifford, son of S. and N., d. Feb. 14, 1847; 22y. 8m. 7d.
James Clifford, son of E. and R., d. Oct. 27, 1847; 1y. 27d.
Margaret Clifford, daughter of S. M. and M., d. March 26, 1856; 1y. 8m. 12d.
Maria Clifford, wife of S. N., d. April 26, 1856; 27y. 7m. 2d.
Nancy Clifford, wife of Samuel, d. May 3, 1864; 80y.
Samuel Clifford, d. April 22, 1850; 70y.
Compher, see also Gompher.
Charles S. Compher, son of G. W. and M. E., d. Feb. 1, 1892; 5y. 4m. 20d.
Mary Compher, wife of Jacob, d. Nov. 17, 1877; 44y. 22d.
Sarah J. Compher, daughter of J. and M., d. Oct. 26, 1864; 8y. 8m. 2d.
William Bingham Compher, son of S. and J., d. Sep. 6, 1864; 2y 8m. 21d.
Lizzie Crawford, d. April 27, 1876; 23y.
David Cunningham, d. May 27, 1849; 58y.
Mary McLaughlin Cunningham, wife of David, d. April 6, 1829; 46y. 6m. 9d.
Beligah Dickerson, d. Aug. 11, 1887; 80y.
Clara J. Dickerson, daughter of J. and R., d. Jan. 11, 1888; 22y. 22d.

Courtland B. Dickerson, son of J. B. and M., d. Jan. 25, 1878; 1y. 2m. 14d.
Edward Dickerson, son of William and Jane, d. July 18, 1864; 8y. 9m. 19d.
Eliza Dickerson, d. March 20, 1887; 75y.
Elizabeth P. Dickerson, wife of Joshua T., d. July 11, 1876; 42y. 5m. 24d.
Hannah L. Dickerson, wife of M. V., d. June 16, 1895; 37y. 8m. 11d.
Jane Dickerson, wife of William, d. Sep. 11, 1864; 46y. 10m. 7d.
Jane Dickerson, wife of Samuel, d. June 9, 1889; 45y.
John Dickerson, d. Feb. 20, 1878; 68y. 5m. 19d.
John F. Dickerson, son of J. K. P. and H. W., d. April 10, 1889; 3y. 5m. 21d.
Joshua Dickeson, d. April 12, 1850; 50y. 3d.
Joshua Dickerson, d. Oct. 6, 1872; 69y.
Joshua Dickerson, son of Joshua and Beligah, d. Dec. 29, 1848; 7y. 5m. 24d.
Louisa Dickerson, daughter of Joshua and Beligah, d. Dec. 31, 1848; 5y. 3m. 4d.
Mary Dickerson, wife of William, d. May 9, 1877; 50m. 5m. 12d.
Mary Dickerson, daughter of Joshua and Beligah, d. Dec. 31, 1848; 9y. 9m. 16d.
Mary Dickerson, wife of Joseph B., d. April 4. 1878; 26y. 9m. 28d.
Mary E. Dickerson, daughter of J. and R., d. Jan. 25, 1891; 20y. 3m. 19d.
Rebecca Dickerson, daughter of Joshua, d. Dec. 28, 1888; 45y. 1m. 7d.
Rebecca Dickerson, daughter of Joshua and Beligah, d. May 22, 1851; 1m. 9d.
Sarah Dickerson, wife of Joshua, d. Feb. 25, 1871; 91y. 1m. 25d.
Robert Dool, d. Sep. 23, 1829; 42y.
Catherine Dougan, d. Aug. 25, 1851; 85y.
Adam Dunlap, d. Jan. 10, 1830; 77y.
Adam Dunlap, d. Sep. 20, 1863; 73y. 5d.
Adam Dunlap, d. Feb. 20, 1883; 77y. 10m. 12d.
Adam Dunlap, son of John and Nancy, d. April 24, 1849; 36y. 7m. 7d.
Adam Dunlap, d. Feb. 11, 1895; 74y. 1m. 9d.

NOTTINGHAM BURIALS

Adam C. Dunlap, b. June 3, 1851; d. April 18, 1881.
Clara B. Dunlap, daughter of Adam and E. J., d. March 15, 1881; 10y. 11m.
Elizabeth Dunlap, wife of Adam, d. May 15, 1871; 42y.
Evora Jane Dunlap, daughter of J. A. and S., d. Oct. 24, 1885; 6y. 4m. 20d.
James R. Dunlap, d. Dec. 20, 1885; 22y. 10m. 28d.
Jane Dunlap, wife of Adam, d. April 24, 1849; 36y. 7m. 7d.
John Dunlap, d. Feb. 24, 1874; 87y. 27d.
John Dunlap, son of Adam and Jane, d. Dec. 18, 1872; 34y. 4m. 27d.
John A. Dunlap, son of H. P. and S. J., d. June 6, 1865; 12y. 9m. 28d.
Joseph Dunlap, d. March 23, 1878; 85y. 5m. 11d.
Joshua Dunlap, d. Sep. 4, 1879; 57y.
Julia Ann Dunlap, wife of Joseph, d. Sep. 3, 1878; 55y. 1m. 28d.
Lizzie Dunlap, daughter of Adam and Margaret, d. Feb. 26, 1873; 18y. 5m. 25d.
Margaret Dunlap, wife of William, d. May 19, 1838; 51y.
Margaret Dunlap, wife of Adam, d. March 14, 1863; 38y. 9m. 20d.
Martha Dunlap, wife of Adam, d. Feb. 8, 1848; 34y. 2m. 5d.
Mary Dunlap, wife of Robert, d. Sep. 29, 1852; 55y. 11m. 19d.
Mary Dunlap, daughter of Adam and Margaret, d. June 3, 1872; 22y. 7d.
Nancy Dunlap, wife of John, d. Nov. 23, 1870; 80y. 3m. 8d.
Nancy G. Dunlap, d. April 3, 1884; 62y.
Nancy Dunlap, d. Aug. 29, 1885; 61y. 10m. 24d.
Nancy Galaher Dunlap, daughter of Robert and Mary, d. Oct. 16, 1869; 11y. 5m. 12d.
Rebecca Dunlap, d. March 9, 1846; 90y. 4m.
Robert Dunlap, d. March 2, 1860; 65y. 10m. 22d.
Robert Dunlap, son of Robert and Mary, d. Dec. 13, 1848; 11y. 6m. 13d.
Samuel Dunlap, d. Oct. 2, 1839; 66y. 21d.
Samuel Dunlap, b. May 20, 1820; d. Oct. 19, 1889.
Samuel Dunlap, d. June 28, 1882; 53y. 6m. 5d.
William Dunlap, d. Feb. 24, 1865; 85y.
Evalina M. Familton, daughter of Nicholas and M., d. May 24, 1865; 19y. 2m. 9d.
Margaret Familton, wife of Nicholas H., d. May 22, 1847; 25y. 2m. 7d.
Benjamin Ferrel, son of B. and S., d. Dec. 13, 1864; 11y. 8m. 10d.
Adam Figley, d. Aug. 12, 1822; 28y.
Adam Figley, d. March 9, 1850; 50y.
Jacob Figley, d. Sep. 13, 1844; 34y. 8m.
Jane Figley, daughter of A. and E., d. June, 1831; 23y. 8m.
Samuel G. Figley, son of J. and S., d. Nov. 23, 1855; 6y. 10m. 17d.
Sarah A. Fulton, daughter of A. and S., d. Sep. 15, 1852; 2y. 2m. 12d.
Gompher, see also Compher.
J. Lafayette Gompher, son of S. and J., d. July 23, 1879; 26y. 2m. 6d.
Mary Gompher, wife of William Gompher, d. Aug. 27, 1877; 83y. 11m. 8d.
Mary Gompher, wife of Samuel, d. July 11, 1866; 28y. 7d.
William Gompher, d. April 4, 1872; 75y. 8m. 22d.
John Gordon, son of T. A. and M. J., d. Oct. 6, 1865; 8y. 6m.
Mary Gordon, wife of John, d. Dec. 16, 1876; 76y.
Samuel C. Gordon, d. Jan. 17, 1863; 33y.
Thomas A. Gordon, d. March 15, 1879; 45y.
William Gordon, son of T. A. and M. J., d. Sep. 21, 1865; 1y. 5m.
Alfred Gregg, son of Presley and Sarah, d. May 9, 1846; 20y. 5m. 1d.
Henry Gregg, son of Presley and Sarah, d. Jan. 14, 1847; 19y. 9m. 24d.
John Gregg, son of Presley and Sarah, d. Oct. 13, 1837; 1y. 2m. 8d.
Presley Gregg, d. Oct. 1, 1849; 61y.
Sarah Jane Gregg, daughter of Presley and Sarah, d. Sep. 9, 1846; 4y. 5m. 16d.
Jane Guttery, wife of Robert, d. May 31, 1815; 54y.
Robert Guttery, d. May 6, 1815; 63y.
Alexander Hamilton, d. Aug. 17, 1866;

62y.
Andrew Hamilton, d. Sep. 5, 1865; 41y. 11m. 23d.
Rebecca Hamilton, wife of Alex. d. March 24, 1864; 76y. 11m. 24d.
Mary Haverfield, wife of Gillespie, d. April 25, 1859; 40y.
Alex. Hayes, d. April 5, 1852; 34y.
Hannah Hays, wife of John, d. June 10, 1855; 60y. 1m. 18d.
Harriet Hayes, d. July 29, 1845; 7y. 6m.
John Hays, d. Feb. 20, 1842; 52y. 11m. 17d.
John Hays, Jr., d. Oct. 24, 1887; 68y. 29d.
Joseph Hays, d. July 27, 1845; 24y.
Agnes Hilton, wife of Thomas, d. Oct. 5, 1863; 72y.
Margaret Hilton, daughter of T. and A., d. July 5, 1850; 28y. 3m. 18d.
Matthew H. Hilton, d. Oct. 9, 1891; 37y.
Robert Hilton, son of T. and A., d. May 2, 1842: 16y. 8m. 3d.
Thomas Hilton, d. Sep. 4, 1865; 75y. 1m. 17d.
Calvin C. Holliday, son of G. W. and M. E., d. Dec. 30, 1886; 11m. 2d.
Ellen Johnson, wife of Thomas, d. Feb. 20, 1869; 73y.
Margaret J. Johnson, wife of William L., d. June 5, 1873; 23y.
Angeline Kennedy, daughter of J. and E., d. Nov. 1, 1871; 11y. 8m. 24d.
Eliza Kennedy, wife of Jackson, d Sep. 4, 1876; 41y.
Lydia M. Kennedy, daughter of R M. and M., d. Nov. 9, 1876; 6y. 3m.
Maranda A. Kennedy, daughter of Ahio and Sophia, d. Dec. 6, 1871; 9y 6m. 2d.
Martha Kennedy, b. Dec. 13, 1825; d May 1, 1891.
Alvira Kirkpatrick, wife of Robert, d May 27, 1891; 66y.
Anne E. Kirkpatrick, daughter of H and M., d. Sep. 7, 1876; 1y. 3m. 5d
Bell C. Kirkpatrick, d. March 21 1893; 30y. 6m.
Clara A. Kirkpatrick, daughter of E K. and E. S., b. Feb. 22, 1875; d July 16, 1893.
Clara Etta Kirkpatrick, d. July 16, 1891; 20y.
Ellen Sutton Kirkpatrick, wife of James, d. July 25, 1836; 65y. 5m. 25d.
Hannah N. Kirkpatrick, d. July 12, 1888; 78y.
James Kirkpatrick, d. May 16, 1840; 69y. 11m. 5d.
John Kirkpatrick, d. Dec. 26, 1879; 71y.
John W. Kirkpatrick, d. Dec. 23, 1887; 36y. 6m.
Mary Kirkpatrick, b. May 4, 1804; d. Oct. 9, 1891; 84y.
R. M. Kirkpatrick, d. March 22, 1893; 32y. 3m.
Sarah Kirkpatrick, wife of William, d. May 1, 1888; 87y.
W. S. Kirkpatrick, d. Dec. 20, 1893; 30y.
Eleanor Knox, wife of Thomas, d. Jan. 12, 1850; 41y. 3m.
Eliza J. Knox, daughter of Thomas and E., d. July 26, 1847; 12y. 17d.
Samuel Knox, d. Jan. 23, 1845; 81y.
Thomas Knox, d. Jan. 12, 1850; 73y. 2m. 17d.
Allen S. Lafferty, son of H. and J., d. Oct. 17, 1865; 1y. 4m. 2d.
Edward Lafferty, d. Oct. 12, 1851; 39y. 6m. 28d.
Edward Lafferty, d. April 21, 1886; 59y. 4m. 26d.
Elizabeth Lafferty, wife of Edward, d. Aug. 22, 1844; 111y.
Eliza Caroline Lafferty, daughter of J. and E., d. Feb. 21, 1853; 2y. 5m. 4d.
George Lafferty, d. June 25, 1860; 35y. 9m. 5d.
Hiram Lafferty, d. Aug. 30, 1875; 44y. 4m. 25d.
Joseph Lafferty, son of J. and E., d. Aug. 23, 1876; 33y. 5m. 7d.
Margaret Lafferty, wife of Samuel, d. April 4, 1842; 60y.
Margaret Lafferty, wife of Edward, d. Sep. 14, 1864; 75y.
Michael Lafferty, wife of S., d. Dec. 1, 1855; 58y.
Samuel Lafferty, d. Nov. 29, 1857; 75y. 7m. 15d.
Susannah Lafferty, wife of Edward, d. Jan. 5, 1868; 58y. 2d.
William Rea Lafferty, son of J. and

E., d. March 7, 1853; 4y. 9m. 7d.
Amos Laizure, d. Sep. 17, 1881; 76y. 6m. 5d.
Maria Laizure, daughter of A. and M., d. Aug. 17, 1869; 37y. 10m. 11d.
Martha Laizure, wife of Amos, d. May 15, 1878; 81y. 8m. 18d.
Martha J. Leizure, daughter of W. and J., d. July 17, 1854; 27y.
Mary A. Laizure, daughter of H. N. and S., d. Feb. 18, 1856; 2m. 18d.
William McG. Laizure, son of A. and M., d. April 15, 1861; 23y. 5m. 26d.
Eliza E. Lantz, d. Feb. 8, 1887; 72y.
J. N. Lantz, d. Jan. 1, 1891; 48y.
John Lantz, d. Nov. 7, 1859; 71y.
Emma E. Lee, daughter of R. and N., d. May 21, 1861; 11m. 13d.
William Rheuben Lee, son of J. V. and E. J., d. April 1, 1883.
Christeney Leinard, daughter of H. and M., d. Aug. 23, 1830; 4y.
Samuel Leinard, son of H. and M., d. April 14, 1826; 6m. 10d.
Yost Linard, d. Nov. 30, 1856; 93y. 5m. 19d.
Sarah Jane Logan, wife of J., d. July 23, 1848; 30y. 8m. 18d.
Eliza McAdams, daughter of John and S., d. Jan. 23, 1846; 14y. 10m. 12d.
Eliza McAdams, daughter of George and Eliza, d. Oct. 6, 1854; 19y. 9m.
George McAdams, d. Oct. 24, 1848; 78y.
Harriet McAdams, wife of John, d. March 11, 1861; 56y. 1m.
Nancy McAdams, daughter of John and S., d. Aug. 17, 1844; 14y. 2m. 20d.
Sarah McAdams, d. June 24, 1856; 44y. 2m. 15d.
Thomas McAdams, d. March 24, 1885; 56y. 11m. 24d.
William McCullough, d. Sep. 18, 1863; 69y.
Francis McDowell, d. Nov. 7, 1865; 8y. 8m. 8d.
Hannah McDowell, wife of William, d. June 12, 1892; 69y. 9m. 19d.
Jane McDowell, wife of Samuel, d. Dec. 22, 1864; 83y. 4m. 23d.
Jane McDowell, b. Feb. 23, 1805; d. June 22, 1886.
Samuel McDowell, d. April 26, 1852; 76y. 1m. 28d.
Samuel McDowell, d. May 13, 1878; 71y. 11m. 18d.
William McDowell, d. May 21, 1869; 60y. 6m. 16d.
Mable Grace McFadden, daughter of O. R. and S. S., d. Sep. 1, 1884; 10m.
Martha A. McKibben, d. Feb. 23, 1849; 5y. 8d.
Martha McKibben, daughter of G. B. and S., d. Aug. 21, 1884; 24y.
Mary McKibben, wife of George B., d. July 18, 1871; 47y.
Susannah McKibbens, wife of George B., d. June 29, 1863; 33y. 6m.
Theodore McKibben, son of John and Isabella, d. May 26, 1877; 10y. 1m. 29d.
James McMillen, d. Sep. 20, 1861; 68y.
Mary McMillen, wife of James, d. Aug. 20, 1858; 56y.
Robert McMillen, d. April 10, 1854; 74y. 9m. 6d.
Hannah Rosaltha McWalty, daughter of James and Jane, d. Aug. 28, 1863; 1y. 2m. 14d.
Elizabeth Maxwell, wife of James, d. Aug. 26, 1865; 35y. 2m. 21d.
Agnes Mitchell, daughter of J. and M., d. April 4, 1837; 19y. 8m. 15d.
George Mitchell, d. Jan. 10, 1853; 24y.
Rebecca Mitchell, wife of J. D., d. Sep. 15, 1865; 34y. 3m. 13d.
Rebecca H. Mitchell, daughter of J. D. and R., d. Oct. 3, 1865; 19d.
Alexander Moore, d. Feb. 9, 1844; 67y. 11m. 4d.
Ann Christina Moore, wife of Samuel, d. June 24, 1886; 84y. 4m. 23d.
Eliza Moore, wife of John, d. July 4, 1864; 44y. 6d.
Elizabeth Moore, daughter of J. W. and E., d. April 10, 1882; 36y. 5m. 17d.
George Moore, d. Aug. 24, 1864; 28y. 10m. 4d.
James Moore, son of R. and E. J., d. Sep. 13, 1861; 10m. 6d.
James Moore, son of J. W. and E., d. Aug. 29, 1852; 5m.
James Everett Moore, son of S. A. and M. J., d. Sep. 13, 1876; 9m. 12d.
John W. Moore, d. Aug. 3, 1883; 72y.
John Moore, d. Sep. 20, 1857; 33y. 1m.
John Moore, son of J. and E., d. July

2, 1845; 1y. 7m. 11d.
Leona Dell Moore, daughter of W. G. and R. J., d. Sep. 20, 1875; 9m. 12d.
Linard Moore, d. Jan. 18, 1888; 60y. 3m. 18d.
Lucinda Moore, daughter of S. and G., d. Jan. 30, 1870; 28y. 1m. 24d.
Lydia B. Moore, daughter of B. and E. J., d. Nov. 21, 1864; 1y. 5m. 27d.
Margaret Moore, wife of Samuel, d. Oct. 5, 1865; 75y.
Mary Moore, wife of Robert, d. March 22, 1851; 80y.
Mary Moore, wife of R. A., d. Sep. 7, 1864; 60y. 11m. 18d.
Mary E. Moore, daughter of Uriah and Mary A., d. Dec. 12, 1871; 10y. 1m.
Mary E. Moore, daughter of W. G. and R. J., d. Sep. 26, 1881; 19y. 6m. 22d.
Mary F. Moore, daughter of Albert and Sarah, d. May 31, 1870; 6m.
Robert Moore, d. Feb. 1, 1835; 66y.
Robert A. Moore, d. Sep. 3, 1878; 75y. 6m. 25d.
Ruth Moore, d. Jan. 4, 1849; 68y.
Ruth Moore, d. Aug. 21, 1842; 39y. 10m.
Salathiel Elmer Moore, son of W. M. and L. A., d. Feb. 20, 1877; 4y. 1m. 27d.
Samuel Moore, d. April 27, 1856; 76y.
Samuel Moore, son of Linard and Mary, d. Jan. 27, 1867; 11y. 9m. 5d.
Thompson Moore, d. Oct. 5, 1848; 26y. 9m. 4d.
Uriah Moore, b. March 4, 1814; d. Jan. 20, 1893.
Ann J. O'Garner, wife of James, d. July 31, 1856; 28y. 3m. 4d.
Agnes Oglevee, d. Aug. 11, 1853; 82y.
George Oglevee, d. July 25, 1873; 40y.
James Oglevee, d. Oct. 10, 1879; 33y. 3m. 13d.
James Elmer Oglevee, son of George and Eliza, d. Dec. 6, 1876; 13y. 4m. 15d.
Susanna Oglevee, wife of William, d. May 26, 1879; 68y. 23d.
William Oglevee, d. July 6, 1884; 76y.
James Floyd Porter, son of S. M. and M., d. Nov. 26, 1880; 11m. 17d.
Rebecca Porter, d. Dec. 23, 1869; 69y. 3m. 6d.

David Price, son of John and Elizabeth, d. March 8, 1827; 10y.
David Ramsey, d. July 31, 1852; 60y. 6m. 25d.
Jane Ramsey, wife of Charles, d. June 21, 1854; 29y. 2m. 26d.
Mary Ann Ramsey, d. Aug. 17, 1875; 78y. 3m. 24d.
Jane Rea, wife of Joseph, d. May 21, 1859; 58y. 8m. 17d.
Joseph Rea, d. April 19, 1862; 65y. 6m. 29d.
Joseph Rea, son of Joseph and Jane, d. Aug. 13, 1845; 5y. 2m. 27d.
John Reed, d. Nov. 30, 1828; 21y. 3m. 12d.
Matthias Reed, d. March 14, 1864; 57y.
Eliza Roberts, wife of George A., b. July 12, 1831; d. July 23, 1868.
Mary Ann Robinson, wife of David A., d. Sep. 6, 1875; 78y. 3m. 24d.
Julia Ann Ross, d. Dec. 10, 1893; 93y.
Elizabeth Russell, d. Nov. 28, 1878; 73y. 28d.
Anna C. Elise Schreiber, daughter of C. L., d. July 27, 1859.
Anne E. Schreiber, daughter of A. J. and M., b. Dec. 30, 1850; d. Feb. 14, 1873.
C. L. Schreiber, d. Jan. 8, 1856; 67y.
Conrad L. Schreiber, son of A. J. and M., b. March 25, 1855; d. May 2, 1876.
Mary Emma Schreiber, daughter of A. J. and M., b. Nov. 5, 1862; d. Oct. 10, 1863.
Ann Eliza Scott, wife of James, daughter of William and Susanna Oglevee, d. Nov. 10, 1874; 24y. 4m. 2d.
Eleanor Scott, daughter of Thomas and Sarah, d. Feb. 14, 1861; 27y.
James Scott, son of Thomas and Sarah, d. Feb. 8, 1859; 22y.
Jane Scott, wife of William, d. Aug. 25, 1831; 30y.
John Scott, son of Thomas and Sarah, d. Sep. 27, 1865; 25y.
Margaret Scott, wife of John, d. Sep. 23, 1861; 26y.
Margaret E. Scott, daughter of William and Margaret, d. Sep. 16, 1863; 3y. 8m. 18d.
Martha Scott, daughter of Thomas and Sarah, d. July 14, 1858; 15y.
Mary Jane Scott, wife of John, d. Oct.

5, 1865; 26y.
Sarah Scott, wife of Thomas, d. Aug. 26, 1875; 73y.
Thomas Scott, d. Jan. 16, 1875; 82y.
William Scott, d. Oct. 6, 1863; 68y.
Andrew G. Sharp, d. Sep. 22, 1874; 50y.
Elizabeth Shaw, wife of James, d. July 6, 1846; 46y. 1m. 4d.
Henrietta Shaw, wife of James, d. Feb. 28, 1848; 67y. 22d.
James Shaw, d. Sep. 4, 1865; 66y. 2m. 11d.
James W. Slater, d. Aug. 9, 1875; 59y. 3m. 5d.
Margaret J. Slater, d. Dec. 6, 1876; 58y. 6d.
Francis Sloan, d. Nov. 26, 1840; 49y. 7m. 11d.
Jane Sloan, wife of John, d. Sep. 28, 1844; 40y.
Alexander A. Snyder, son of I. and R., d. March 21, 1857; 3y. 6m. 22d.
Rhoda Snyder, wife of Levi, d. Oct. 11, 1873; 39y. 13d.
Elizabeth Sproull, wife of Thomas, d. Feb. 15, 1882; 82y.
Hugh Sproull, son of T. and E., d. Oct. 16, 1855; 11y.
James Sproul, d. Aug. 21, 1856; 39y. 9m. 13d.
Jane A. Sproul, daughter of J. and E., d. April 8, 1874; 20y. 2m. 24d.
John Sproul, son of Francis and Margaret, d. May 21, 1881; 25y. 10d.
Margaret Sproul, wife of Francis, d. Nov. 16, 1840; 49y. 8m. 10d.
Thomas Sproull, Sr., d. April 19, 1872; 83y.
Thomas Sproull, son of T. and E., d. July 7, 1867; 18y. 10m. 11d.
Robert Steel, d. July 20, 1831; 66y. 3m.
Harriett M. Tarbert, daughter of J. and E., d. June 7, 1866; 3y. 13d.
James Tarbert, d. May 31, 1867; 83y. 1m. 27d.
James Tarbert, d. Jan. 28, 1881; 66y. 3m. 14d.
James E. Tarbert, d. June 13, 1865; 23y. 1m. 17d.
Joseph A. Tarbert, d. May 30, 1860; 38y. 10m. 3d.
Josiah Tarbert, d. Nov. 28, 1870; 51y. 7m. 3d.
Margaret Jane Tarbert, wife of Anderson, d. Oct. 14, 1885; 59y.
Maggie Tarbert, daughter of Albert and Mary, d. March 22, 1883; 6m. 2d.
Mary Bell Tarbert, daughter of James and E., d. May 1, 1883; 17y. 8m. 2d.
Salina J. Tarbert, daughter of J. and E., d. Sep. 24, 1884; 15y. 7m. 1d.
Sarah Tarbert, daughter of J. A. and M., d. April 19, 1849; 1m. 2d.
William Tarbert, d. July 27, 1873; 61y.
William Tarbert, b. July 2, 1855; d. July 22, 1893.
Archabold Todd, d. Feb. 19, 1852; 89y. 1m. 7d.
Margaret Ann Todd, wife of William, d. Jan. 18, 1858; 25y. 10m. 18d.
James Walker, d. May 5, 1862; 83y.
James Walker, d. April 22, 1859; 4y.
Margaret Walker, wife of James, d. Aug. 21, 1849; 61y. 6m. 8d.
Bell Wallace, wife of S. M., d. July 17, 1888; 51y.
Allen Wallace, d. Feb. 21, 1880; 86y. 10m. 6d.
John Wallace, d. May 1, 1832; 72y.
Julia Barricklow Watson, wife of John M., d. Feb. 24, 1859; 24y.
Margaret Wallace, wife of John, d. March 25, 1848; 81y.
Mary Wallace, wife of Rev. William, d. Dec. 21, 1869; 72y. 9m. 4d.
Mary Wallace, wife of Allen, d. April 12, 1874; 84y. 3m. 11d.
Nathaniel A. Wallace, d. March 22, 1855; 35y.
Rev. William Wallace, pastor of the Presbyterian Church, Nottingham, d. Dec. 13, 1841; 54y. 7m. 26d.
Wilson E. Wallace, b. May 6, 1836; d. Aug. 18, 1895; 59y.
John W. Watson, d. July 22, 1859; 45y. 5m. 15d.
Mary Jane Watson, daughter of John and Julia, d. Aug. 16, 1848; 10y. 8m. 9d.
Rachel Watson, wife of R. S., d. May 18, 1866; 85y. 5m.
Robert Talbert Watson, son of John and Rebecca, d. Aug. 28, 1849; 3m. 21d.
Robert R. Watson, d. Nov. 19, 1872;

86y. 8m. 16d.
S. R. Watson, d. April 30, 1877; 55y. 6m. 18d.
Martha A. Bell Weaver, daughter of John and Susanna, d. Dec. 24, 1873; 5y. 28d.
Wilson Dunlap Webb, son of John and Louisa, d. Oct. 29, 1880; 1y. 5m. 7d.
David Welling, d. June 19, 1864; 85y. 4m. 18d.
Nancy E. Welling, wife of David, d. Feb. 18, 1873; 50y.
Samuel West, d. Oct. 6, 1864; 12y. 10m. 5d.
George Wibble, d. April 17, 1884; 65y. 10m. 21d.
Nancy Wible, wife of G., d. Oct. 28, 1864; 41y.
Sarah E. Wilaby, daughter of S. and R., d. Sep. 19, 1864; 5y. 7d.
Jane Williamson, wife of John, d. Aug. 8, 1845; 71y.
John Williamson, d. Jan. 25, 1847; 78y.
James Wilson, d. Aug. 4, 1873; 53y. 1m.
Nancy J. Wilson, wife of James, d. Feb. 23, 1858; 34y. 5m. 9d.
Sarah Jane Wilson, wife of James Wilson, daughter of George and Ann Carrothers, d. Feb. 23, 1864; 35y.
William T. Wilson, son of J. and N., d. Sep. 8, 1854; 5m. 8d.
Mary C. Winning, niece of J. W. and S. Milligan, d. June 18, 1845; 11m. 18d.

BURIALS IN RIDGE GRAVE-YARD.

To May 30, 1898.

Ellen Adams, daughter of William and Mary, b. Nov. 10, 1819; d. Aug. 16, 1843.
Jane Adams, d. March 12, 1892; 80y. 4m. 20d.
Mary Adams, wife of William, d. July 24, 1850; 74y.
Samuel Adams, d. June 13, 1874; 66y. 4m. 23d.
William Adams, d. July 28, 1836; 66y.
Catherine Anderson, wife of Samuel, d. Oct. 16, 1847; 50y. 10m. 5d.
Esther McCollough Anderson, wife of Robert, d. Sep. 24, 1892; 73y.
John Anderson, d. April 28, 1855; 26y. 9m. 4d.
John E. Anderson, son of Robert and Esther, d. March 25, 1864; 1y. 7m. 10d.
Robert Anderson, d. April 25, 1891; 76y.
Samuel Anderson, d. Feb. 22, 1866; 83y. 11m. 4d.
John Archabald, d. May 21, 1826; 66y.
Sarah Archabald, wife of John, d. Sep. 30, 1835; 83y.
Elizabeth Osburn Atkison, daughter of J. and M., d. Jan. 17, 1860; 26y. 10m. 12d.
Harriett Atkison, wife of Levi, d. March 26, 1849; 25y. 2m. 20d.
James Atkison, Jr., son of John and Ann, d. at Fredericksburg, Va., May 12, 1864, of wounds received in the Battle of The Wilderness; 27y. 3m. 6d.
Jane Atkison, wife of James, d. Aug. 1, 1862; 70y. 9m. 18d.
Mary Atkison, wife of John, d. Jan. 31, 1835; 21y. 10m. 15d.
Ruth Atkison, daughter of J. and J., d. Feb. 15, 1835; 1y.
Ora Beall, daughter of J. T. and B. A., d. Dec. 28, 1884; 2y. 11m. 2d.
Annie R. Braden, daughter of J. G. and Rachel, d. Sep. 23, 1867; 21y. 9m. 25d.
William Brown, d. Feb., 1829; 60y.
Albert Buchanan, son of Joseph and E., d. Sep. 16, 1861; 2y. 4m. 16d.
Elizabeth Buchanan, wife of J. N., b. Jan. 20, 1819; d. Jan. 6, 1883.
Elizabeth Buchanan, daughter of Joseph and E., d. Oct. 15, 1862; 16d.
James Buchanan, son of Joseph and E., d. Dec. 11, 1857; 1y. 2m. 6d.
John Ross Buchanan, son of T. N. and S. J., b. Oct. 25, 1889; d. May 22, 1890.
Joseph N. Buchanan, b. April 23, 1814; d. July 11, 1883.
Mary Buchanan, wife of Samuel, d. Jan. 21, 1838; 60y.
Samuel Buchanan, d. March 23, 1858; 82y.
Samuel Buchanan, son of Joseph and

E., d. Sep. 5, 1863; 19y. 10m. 10d.
Elizabeth C. Carr, wife of John, d. Feb. 24, 1837; 67y.
Ellen Carr, daughter of J. and S., b. Nov. 29, 1846; d. March 11, 1877.
Isabella Carr, daughter of J. and S., b. Jan. 8, 1849; d. May 8, 1879.
John Carr, d. Aug. 7, 1863; 55y. 8m. 27d.
Sarah Carr, wife of John, d. Oct. 19, 1867; 58y. 1m. 5d.
Sarah Jane Carr, daughter of John, d. May 15, 1836; 1y. 4d.
W. W. Carr, son of J. and S., d. Nov. 21, 1875; 23y. 1m. 18d.
William Carr, d. March 6, 1871; 75y.
Elizabeth Cavan, wife of Hugh, d. Sep. 21, 1878; 68y.
Hugh Cavan, d. Nov. 25, 1855; 56y.
William Cavan, d. Nov. 3, 1862; 22y. 6m. 7d.
Elizabeth Cole, daughter of R. and M., d. May 27, 1852; 4m. 27d.
James Cole, son of R. and M., d. May 9, 1834; 5y. 6m. 16d.
John Cole, son of M. and R., d. Feb. 18, 1863; 20y. 10m. 11d.
Mary Cole, d. Oct. 1, 1875; 19y. 9m. 27d.
Moses Cole, d. Jan. 6, 1865; 49y. 10m. 10d.
Jesse H. Cook, b. Feb. 6, 1847; d. May 27, 1886.
Joann Cook, d. March 13, 1843; 82y.
George Cox, d. Sep. 12, 1849; 65y. 2m. 9d.
Sarah Cox, wife of George, d. Sep. 9, 1877; 90y. 11m. 16d.
Jane Cramer, wife of Joseph, and daughter of William and Mary Adams, d. May 17, 1836; 30y. 2m. 7d.
Nathaniel Crawford, d. April 9, 1895; 56y.
Elizabeth Curry, wife of Samuel, d. Oct. 10, 1849; 62y. 6m. 26d.
Elizal Curry, d. May 23, 1875; 57y. 1d.
Lettice Ann Curry, d. July 18, 1870; 55y. 6m. 9d.
Mary Curry, daughter of E. and S., d. Feb. 24, 1882; 60y. 11m. 12d.
Rosan Curry, daughter of S. and E., d. Feb. 28, 1874; 51y. 2m. 16d.

Samuel Curry, d. May 18, 1866; 71y. 6m. 26d.
Albert Custer, son of W. W. and F., b. April 19, 1850; d. April 1, 1870.
James H. Custer, b. Nov. 26, 1847; d. June 9, 1864.
John A. Custer, son of E. H. and Matilda, d. July 29, 1836; 3y. 3m. 7d.
Matilda P. Custer, wife of E. H. and daughter of B. W. and Hannah Veirs, b. March 4, 1804; d. July 18, 1835.
W. W. Custer, M. D., b. July 1, 1816; d. June 13, 1892.
Alexander Denny, d. Nov. 21, 1886; 75y.
Ellinor Denny, daughter of A. and J., d. Aug. 27, 1859; 12y. 4m. 2d.
Jane Denny, wife of Alexander, d. March 31, 1887; 70y.
William Denny, son of A. and J., d. Oct. 30, 1855; 1y. 2m. 19d.
Ellaburg Donaldson, daughter of W. and N., d. Nov. 9, 1865; 4y. 3m. 27d.
Nancy Donaldson, wife of William, d. March 9, 1866; 34y. 9m. 21d.
Cyrus H. Easlick, d. Jan. 13, 1881; 27y. 7m. 21d.
Elizabeth Easlick, wife of Henry, d. July 1, 1874; 91y.
Harriett Ellen Easlick, daughter of J. and E., d. July 17, 1866; 6y. 11m. 28d.
Harvey A. Easlick, d. Nov. 13, 1879; 22y. 9m. 12d.
Henry Easlick, d. Jan. 6, 1859; 75y. 6m. 6d.
Martha Ann Easlick, daughter of J. and E., d. July 3, 1866; 1y. 10m. 6d.
Melissa Endsley, daughter of R. W. and E., b. April 1, 1847; d. Oct. 9, 1869.
Nancy Easlick, d. Oct. 6, 1880; 56y. 6m. 7d.
Susanna Easlick, d. June 4, 1880; 32y. 1m. 4d.
Elizabeth Edie, daughter of M. C. and E., d. Sep. 19, 1869; 1y. 11m. 4d.
Joseph B. Edie, d. Nov. 14, 1847; 18y. 11m. 24d.
Elizabeth Endsley, wife of James, d. May 25, 1864; 90y. 12d.
Elizabeth Endsley, wife of Robert W.,

b. March 3, 1820; d. March 28, 1897.
James Endsley, d. Jan. 4, 1866; 87y. 9d.
Jane Blair Endsley, wife of John, d. Jan. 29, 1848; 75y.
John Endsley, d. April 29, 1835; 59y.
John Endsley, d. Jan. 23, 1850; 31y.
Robert Endsley, b. Jan. 11, 1813; d. June 6, 1869.
Ann English, d. Oct. 17, 1884; 75y. 8m. 12d.
James English, b. Oct. 27, 1791; d. June 6, 1869.
Jane English, b. Jan. 9, 1797; d. Sep. 30, 1843.
Maggy H. English, wife of George, d. June 13, 1872; 21y. 4m. 15d.
George E. Finnicum, son of A. W. and S. M., d. Jan. 22, 1878; 4y. 5m. 29d.
Emma J. Fisher, daughter of John, d. Jan. 16, 1879; 17y. 1m. 10d.
George Fisher, d. Aug. 13, 1872; 79y. 10m. 26d.
Jacob Fisher, son of G. and M., d. Nov. 3, 1843; 2y. 14d.
James Fisher, b. Nov. 24, 1819; d. Jan. 7, 1882.
Mary Fisher, wife of George, d. Dec. 15, 1844; 33y.
Mary A. Fisher, wife of John, d. May 27, 1895; 55y. 7m. 12d.
Rebecca Fisher, wife of George, d. Sep. 25, 1858; 47y. 4m. 15d.
Robert Maxwell Fisher, son of Eli and Elizabeth, d. Oct. 17, 1843; 3y. 9m. 1d.
Samuel Fisher, son of G. and M., d. Aug. 8, 1836; 1y. 7m. 19d.
Sarah Fisher, wife of George, d. Oct. 25, 1844; 35y.
Susanna A. Fisher, wife of George, d. Sep. 25, 1838; 39y.
William Fisher, b. Sep. 4, 1826; d. April 29, 1855.
Jane Graham, wife of J., d. Aug. 28, 1868; 79y.
Joseph Graham, d. March 13, 1877; 75y. 11m. 26d.
Thomas Gutshall, son of S. and H., d. April 20, 1875; 11m.
Charles W. T. Hamilton, son of James and Mary, d. Aug. 21, 1863; 9y. 4m. 27d.
James S. Hamilton, d. Aug. 8, 1878; 32y.
Mary Hamilton, wife of James, d. March 10, 1877; 64y.
James Henderson, d. Feb. 22, 1862; 82y.
James A. Henderson, son of A. and E. B., d. Nov. 10, 1865; 11m. 24d.
Susanna Henderson, d. Nov. 18, 1892; 73y. 9m.
Winona Henderson, daughter of G. F. and Julia, d. Jan. 28, 1885; 3y. 3m. 4d.
Jane Herron, wife of Rev. Robert, d. March 26, 1859; 29y.
John E. Herron, son of S. and S., d. Jan. 2, 1874; 19y. 5m. 18d.
Rev. Robert Herron, Pastor of Ridge Church 26 years, b. April 10, 1817; d. June 17, 1884.
Amos Hines, son of J. and S., d. July 14, 1857; 24y. 10m. 23d.
George Hines, d. May 18, 1861; 41y. 6m. 29d.
Jacob Hines, d. Dec. 20, 1848; 54y. 9m. 7d.
Martha Hines, wife of John, d. April 5, 1872; 26y. 3m.
Susanna Hines, wife of Jacob, d. Sep. 27, 1885; 87y.
George Hospelhorn, d. Jan. 5, 1835; 76y.
Margaret Hospelhorn, d. Sep. 17, 1834; 75y.
Margaret Hospelhorn, d. June 17, 1836; 3y. 10m.
Mary Huston, daughter of J. and M., d. Feb. 12, 1878; 11m. 28d.
Mary Jane Huston, b. Oct. 25, 1834; d. July 31, 1879.
M. Karr, d. March 25, 1832; 23y. 4m. 24d.
Mary Lee, wife of T. M., d. Jan. 16, 1893; 68y. 2m. 10d.
Archabald Leeper, d. April, 1826; 70y.
Charles Lewton, son of J. and N. A., d. Aug. 20, 1865; 5y. 5m. 28d.
Jacob Lewton, d. Nov. 21, 1877; 87y.
William Lisle, d. July 21, 1837; 74y.
James Newton Lyons, son of J. and M., d. April 27, 1842; 15y. 5d.
John Lyons, d. April 23, 1875; 80y. 7m. 22d.
Malicha J. Lyons, son of R. M. and M., d. Aug. 5, 1861; 9m. 25d.

Martha Lyons, daughter of J. and M., d. July 17, 1838; 14y. 3m. 4d.
Mary Lyons, wife of John, d. March 19, 1875; 80y. 7m. 4d.
Mary Lyons, wife of R. M., d. June 11, 1859.
Nancy Lyons, wife of Richard, b. May 5, 1813; d. June 14, 1835.
Capt. R. M. Lyons, fell at the Battle of The Wilderness, May 6, 1864; 33y.; his remains were never recovered, as they were burned with many others.
McClain, see also McLean.
James McClain, d. June 7, 1852; 49y. 8m. 6d.
Jane McClean, daughter of James L. and Sarah, d. Sep. 29, 1835; 10y.
Joseph McClain, son of S. and J., d. Oct. 9, 1855; 1y. 11m.
Martha McClain, daughter of J. L. and S., d. April 18, 1866; 21y. 6m. 16d.
Nathan S. McClain, d. Aug. 10, 1893; 46y. 10m. 12d.
Sarah McClain, wife of J. L., d. Nov. and Sarah, d. Feb. 22, 1863; 22y. 7m. 26, 1882; 79y. 2m. 6d.
Thomas Endsley McClain, son of J. L. 16d.
William McClain, son of J. L. and S., d. Nov. 26, 1867; 24y. 11m. 27d.
Eleanor McClintock, wife of N. W., d. July 14, 1866; 80y.
Eliza McClintock, d. Aug. 23, 1888; 85y.
Elizabeth McCollough, wife of Joseph, d. April 15, 1884; 83y.
Jane McCollough, wife of John, d. June 3, 1864; 37y. 27d.
John W. McCollough, son of J. and J., d. Feb. 26, 1860; 2y. 11m.
Joseph McCollough, d. Jan. 31, 1870; 74y. 11m. 24d.
Joseph McCombs, d. Aug. 12, 1886; 66y. 10m. 27d.
Ellen McIlravy, wife of Hugh, d. March 28, 1857; 63y. 11m. 9d.
Samuel McIlravy, son of H. and E., d. Oct. 2, 1843; 8y. 7m. 1d.
Catherine McKittrick, d. Sep. 4, 1890; 76y. 8m.
McLean, see also McClain.
Elizabeth McLean, wife of Samuel, d. Jan. 15, 1883; 75y. 6m. 20d.
Emma McLean, d. Oct. 6, 1876; 25y. 11d.

Samuel McLean, d. Aug. 17, 1876; 74y. 2m. 24d.
Samuel H. McLean, d. March 25, 1847; 2m. 21d.
Catherine McMillan, wife of Thomas, d. Oct. 24, 1881; 65y. 10m. 21d.
Thomas McMillan, d. Aug. 27, 1875; 80y.
Barbara McPeck, widow of John Endsley, and second wife of George McPeck, d. Dec. 1, 1855; 34y. 10m. 8d.
Catherine Lyons McPeck, wife of George, b. March 28, 1822; d. July 10, 1883.
David Blair McPeck, son of G. and J., d. Jan. 6, 1845; 21d.
George McPeck, b. Oct., 1808; d. March 24, 1886.
George McKenney McPeck, son of George and Jane, d. Jan. 30, 1874; 27y. 9m. 7d.
Jane Endsley McPeck, wife of George, b. Feb. 10, 1810; d. Aug. 22, 1851.
Willie McPeck, son of George and Catherine, d. July 24, 1875; 16y. 4m. 10d.
Agness D. Maxwell, daughter of William and A., d. July 7, 1853; 13y. 11m. 12d.
Henry Maxwell, d. Oct. 28, 1863; 21y. 10m. 14d.
James Maxwell, son of R. and M. A., d. June 4, 1840; 7y. 3m. 4d.
Jane Maxwell, daughter of Robert and M. A., b. April 11, 1822; d. June 10, 1847.
John Maxwell, son of William and S., b. March 2, 1842; d. Sep. 27, 1846.
John McGaw Maxwell, son of W. and S., b. Nov. 21, 1846; d. Jan. 21, 1854.
Mary Maxwell, wife of Walter C., d. July 21, 1855; 33y. 1m. 25d.
Robert G. Maxwell, d. Jan. 29, 1865; 22y. 1m. 21d.
Catherine Megaw, wife of John, d. Sep. 9, 1847; 58y. 7m. 10d.
James Megaw, d. Oct. 24, 1851; 58y. 1m. 9d.
Mary E. Megaw, daughter of J. and M. E., d. May 28, 1858; 2y. 2m. 13d.
James Melaney, d. May 15, 1888; 75y. 3m. 7d.
Jane Melaney, d. April 21, 1870; 58y. 10m. 3d.

John Melaney, d. Jan. 20, 1863; 76y. 11m. 27d.
Jane Miller, wife of Rozeld, d. March 30, 1849; 36y. 6m. 9d.
Anna Martha Moore, daughter of W. J. and N., d. Sep. 2, 1869; 10y. 8m. 4d.
Margaret Moore, wife of John, d. June 5, 1888; 70y.
William H. Moorhead, son of Samuel and Sarah, d. Feb. 1, 1863; 29y. 4m. 16d.
Alexander Osburn, d. Aug. 17, 1867; 82y. 4m. 3d.
Elizabeth Osburn, wife of James D., d. Jan. 17, 1860; 27y.
Lucinda J. Osburn, daughter of J. D. and E., d. Oct. 18, 1863; 7y. 4m. 16d.
Martha Osburn, wife of Alexander, d. Dec. 25, 1848; 60y.
Mary Palmer Osburn, wife of James D., d. Oct. 14, 1862; 27y.
Isabella Patterson, wife of John, d. Nov. 17, 1846; 37y. 8m. 8d.
Isabella Patterson, daughter of J. and J., d. June 29, 1857; 2y. 2m. 10d.
Jane Patterson, daughter of J. and C., d. Aug. 3, 1840; 11d.
Jean Patterson, daughter of J. and C., d. March 15, 1854; 2y. 2m. 26d.
John Patterson, d. Sep. 13, 1859; 68y.
John Patterson, son of J. and C., d. Aug. 6, 1846; 1y. 7m. 15d.
Maria Patterson, daughter of J. and J., d. July 26, 1865; 2y. 6m.
Mary Ann Patterson, wife of James H., b. Oct. 2, 1832; d. Oct. 24, 1859.
Mary M. Patterson, daughter of J. and J., d. July 23, 1865; 4y. 4m.
Thomas Patterson, son of J. and C., d. Aug. 2, 1840; 10d.
Fremont Patton, son of M. M. and S. J., d. March 5, 1858; 1y. 6m. 6d.
Joseph Patton, son of M. M. and S. J., d. Aug. 22, 1851; 3y. 3m. 15d.
Samuel Patton, son of M. M. and S. J., d. Aug. 31, 1851; 1y. 4m. 19d.
Sarah Jane Patton, d. June 13, 1878; 57y. 8m. 12d.
William Patton, son of M. M. and S. J., d. Feb. 27, 1850; 3y. 6m. 10d.
Matthew Picken, d. March 20, 1849;

June 3, 1845; 74y.
Elizabeth Richey, wife of Jacob, d. Jan. 24, 1845; 58y. 5m. 24d.
Jacob Richey, d. April 25, 1836; 80y. 10m.
Jacob Ritchey, d. Feb. 5, 1845; 55y. 1m. 1d.
Jacob Richey, d. Nov. 4, 1864; 35y. 10m. 13d.
Jane Richey, d. Jan. 13, 1845; 22y. 6m. 27d.
Mary Ann Richey, wife of Jacob, d. June 24, 1835; 75y.
Mary A. Richey, d. Nov. 8, 1873; 53y. 9m. 18d.
William Richey, d. April 24, 1884; 67y. 4d.
Caroline Roberson, wife of William G., d. May 15, 1852; 48y. 3m. 22d.
Elizabeth Roberts, daughter of J. and E., d. Feb. 15, 1855; 1y. 11m. 11d.
John E. Roberts, son of J. and E., d. May 11, 1855; 4y. 3m. 2d.
James S. Robinson, b. April 11, 1808; d. March 1, 1892.
Mary Robison, daughter of J. and M., b. Dec. 1, 1838; d. Dec. 20, 1854.
Hannah Ross, daughter of William M. A., d. April 17, 1840; 4y. 5m. 24d.
Mary A. Ross, d. Feb. 26, 1891; 33y. 6m. 29d.
James C. Scott, son of R. and N., d. Sep. 16, 1851; 3y. 11m.
Lucy Scott, daughter of R. and N., d. Sep. 6, 1848; 3y. 10m. 18d.
Nancy A. Scott, daughter of R. and N., d. Sep. 12, 1848; 5y. 10m. 21d.
Samuel Shaffer, d. Feb. 27, 1854; 49y. 9m. 26d.
Mary Shipman, wife of William, d. July 1, 1827; 37y.
William Shipman, d. April 25, 1854; 73y.
Mary Jane Shipman, daughter of W. and M., d. March 15, 1827; 7y. 2m.
Baty D. Shuse, son of J. and M., d. May 16, 1862; 2y. 9m. 17d.
Mary Jane Simpson, wife of Isaac, d. April 6, 1854; 34y. 6m. 17d.
William H. Simpson, d. Aug. 16, 1858; 2y. 6m. 19d.

RIDGE BURIALS

Sarah J. Skipper, d. March 7, 1891; 68y.
William Skipper, d. April 12, 1891; 85y.
Charles M. Slemmons, son of A. and S., d. May 22, 1849; 6m.
Jane Slemmons, wife of William, d. July 4, 1851; 76y.
Joseph D. Slemmons, d. May 31, 1859; 24y. 7m. 13d.
Joseph J. Slemmons, d. Dec. 4, 1868; 82y.
Susanna Slemmons, wife of Joseph, d. Oct. 29, 1862; 61y.
Susanna Slemmons, d. Feb. 23, 1885; 50y.
William Slemmons, d. Jan. 27, 1827; 66y.
William J. Slemmons, d. April 19, 1859; 21y. 7m. 18d.
Elizabeth Sloan, b. April 5, 1810; d. Jan. 20, 1885.
John Sloan, d. Nov. 12, 1882; 69y. 1m. 4d.
Mary Sloan, wife of William, d. Feb. 10, 1853; 82y.
Robert Sloan, d. April 5, 1880; 72y. 4m. 10d.
William Sloan, d. Feb. 14, 1864; 93y.
Joseph Smith, d. June 28, 1890; 89y. 5m.
David Smylie, d. Sep. 13, 1843; 72y.
David Smylie, son of William and Rachel, d. Oct. 4, 1843; 1y. 7m. 17d.
Jane Smylie, wife of David, d. Oct. 11, 1843; 75y.
Margaret Smylie, daughter of William and Rachel, d. Oct. 7, 1843; 19y. 5m. 21d.
Sarah J. Smylie, daughter of William and Rachel, d. June 24, 1850; 14y. 2m. 24d.
Thomas Smylie, son of William and Rachel, d. Sep. 25, 1843; 12y. 4m. 18d.
Franie Snyder, daughter of D. J. and M. E., d. Feb. 24, 1871; 3y. 1m. 8d.
Willie Snyder, son of D. J. and M. E., d. Aug. 26, 1877; 3y. 23d.
James Stewart, d. Dec. 27, 1878; 68y. 11m. 7d.
Jane Stewart, d. March 24, 1881; 67y. 7m,
Andrew Thompson, d. July 12, 1881; 82y. 3m. 25d.
Andrew Wilson Thompson, son of A. and J., d. Oct. 24, 1870; 20y. 9m. 8d.
Jane Thompson, wife of Andrew, d. Dec. 22, 1889; 85y.
Sarah Thompson, daughter of A. and J., d. Aug. 17, 1845; 8y.
Sarah Toland, daughter of J. S. and J., d. Sep. 15, 1851; 10m. 10d.
Ephraim Vasbinder, d. June 21, 1849; 40y. 1m. 17d.
Mariah Vasbinder, wife of E., d. Aug. 26, 1847; 42y. 26d.
Hannah Viers, wife of B. W., b. Sep. 18, 1885; d. Sep. 5, 1827.
Ann Webster, wife of John, d. March 11, 1894; 68y. 3d.
Florence Webster, daughter of J. and A., d. Aug. 27, 1881; 22y. 7m. 26d.
Ira B. Webster, son of John and Ann, d. Aug. 6, 1893; 20y. 2m. 16d.
John Webster, d. Oct. 28, 1876; 65y. 7m. 8d.
Margaret Webster, wife of John, d. Aug. 22, 1841; 30y. 2m. 6d.
Mary Webster, wife of John, d. March 1, 1848; 72y. 11m. 1d.
Sarah A. Webster, d. March 19, 1888; 50y. 2m. 16d.
Agness Welsh, wife of William, d. Feb. 14, 1845; 24y. 7m. 16d.
Ella J. Welsh, daughter of D. and S., d. Aug. 26, 1865; 2y. 10m.
Emma V. Welsh, daughter of D. and S., d. March 21, 1889; 13y. 6m. 29d.
George Welsh, son of W. and A., d. Aug. 8, 1845; 6m.
Jane Welsh, wife of John, d. Feb. 17, 1872; 79y.
John Welsh, d. Dec. 30, 1871; 89y.
John V. Welsh, son of D. and S., d. Sep. 1, 1865; 1y. 8m. 9d.
Martha S. Welsh, wife of James, d. June 15, 1845; 32y. 9m. 8d.
Samuel Welsh, d. March 30, 1850; 78y.
Martha F Whittaker, d. Feb. 17, 1888; 31y.
Elizabeth Williams, wife of Thomas, d. Feb. 7, 1850; 78y. 8m. 8d.

Note.—The foregoing list of burials is from the present Ridge Graveyard, located on section 23 in Archer township, about a mile southeast from Hanover.

BURIALS IN DICKERSON GRAVEYARD.

To Aug. 3, 1896.

George Allen, d. March 11, 1831; [age gone].
John Allen, d. June 27, 1833; 27y.
Joshua Allen, d. Jan. 22, 1835; 22y.
Josiah Allen, Sr., d. Dec. 28, 1842; 81y.
Nancy Allen, d. July 31, 1835; 33y.
Susanna Allen, wife of Josiah, d. March 14, 1835; 59y.
Susanna Allen, d. Sep. 6, 1832; 33y.
Wilbert Anderson, son of C. and M., d. Dec. 18, 1874; 4y. 19d.
Elisha Buxton, d. May 4, 1838; 66y. 3m.
Mary Buxton, wife of Elisha. d. Nov. 16, 1849; 79y.
William Buxton, d. Aug. 8, 1834; 25y. 6m. 2d.
John Chaney, d. May 9, 1873; 36y.
Thomas Chaney, b. Oct. 28, 1803; d. July 1, 1890.
William V. Cheny, son of S. V. and Clara, b. April 10, 1885; d. May 4, 1885.
Margaret Jane Christy, daughter of Richard B. and Sarah, d. Sep. 1, 1863; 5y. 5m. 1d.
Amanda E. Crumley, daughter of J. and M., July 23, 1845; 8m. 26d.
Caroline Elizabeth Crumley, daughter of D. M. and S., d. April 17, 1854; 3y. 8m. 7d.
Elizabeth Crumley, wife of Thomas, b. Oct. 1, 1780; d. May 15, 1857.
Emily Crumley, daughter of J. and M., b. Dec. 28, 1846; 7m. 2d.
Emma Crumley, daughter of Wilson and Sarah H., d. Sep. 9, 1862; 5y. 1m. 4d.
Hannah Crumley, daughter of J. and M., d. Sep. 14,1849; 1y. 7m. 26d.
James Crumley, d. Jan. 28, 1864; 46y. 7m. 9d. Member of Co. I, 13th O. V. I.
John Crumley, d. April 18, 1865; 52y. 12d.
Joseph Crumley, son of J. and M., d. June, 1851; 1m. 1d.
Margaret Crumley, wife of James, d. Feb. 23, 1854; 37y. 8m. 26d.
Samuel Crumley, d. June 16, 1830; 29y. 8d.
Susanna Moore Crumley, wife of David, b. Feb. 17, 1878; 51y. 4m. 15d.
Thomas Crumley, d. July 3, 1861; 84y. 6m. 3d.
William Crumley, son of J. and M., d. June 28, 1850; 2d.
John Davis, d. Oct. 12, 1876; 69y. 8m. 22d.
Adam Dickerson, d. Feb. 26, 1878; 71y. 2m. 15d.
Adam D. Dickerson, d. April 16, 1875; 27y. 1m. 6d.
Alfred Dickerson, son of William and Gabriella, d. Feb. 21, 1866; 24d.
Aaron M. Dickerson, son of J. and M. J., d. Aug. 30, 1875; 30y.
Barbruch Dickerson, son of J. and M. J., d. Nov. 6, 1864.
Baruch Dickerson, d. Oct. 2, 1824; 38y. 4m. 12d.
Baruch Dickerson, son of Joseph and Mary, d. Sep. 6, 1827; 2d.
Baruch Dickerson, son of William W. and S., d. Feb. 18, 1843; 1y. 7m. 3d.
Bertha Wiley Dickerson, d. May 6, 1886; 6y. 8m. 5d.
Eli Dickerson, d. Nov. 24, 1834; 66y. 10m. 9d.
Elizabeth Dickerson, wife of Joshua, d. July 30, 1842; 31y. 1m. 5d.
James B. Dickerson, son of John and C. A., d. Sep. 30, 1858; 2y. 9m. 22d.
James White Dickerson, d. May 30, 1869; 38y.
Jay Toland Dickerson, son of W. H. and Lizzie, b. March 22, 1891; d. May 3, 1891.
John A. Dickerson, son of Joseph and Mary, d. June 2, 1841; 2y. 23d.
Joseph Dickerson, d. May 10, 1877; 81y.
Joshua Dickerson, son of Thomas and Mary, d. April 17, 1847; 19y. 3m. 22d.
Maria J. Dickerson, daughter of Hiram and Mary, d. July 20, 1850; 10y. 17d.
Mary Dickerson, wife of Thomas, d. March 30, 1853; 87y. 2m. 14d.
Mary Dickerson, wife of Eli, d. April 28, 1831; 55y. 2m. 12d.
Mary Dickerson, wife of Joseph, d.

DICKERSON BURIALS

March 10, 1877; 55y.
Samuel E. Dickerson, son of Joshua and N. A., d. Oct. 9, 1857; 12y. 6m. 3d.
Samuel L. Dickerson, d. July 3, 1880; 39y. 10m. 17d.
Sarah Dickerson, wife of Eli, d. May 8, 1830; 27y. 4m. 16d.
Sarah Dickerson, daughter of Joshua and Sarah, d. Oct. 16, 1823; 10y. 3m. 10d.
Thomas Dickerson, d. Dec. 24, 1852; 88y. 7m. 5d.
Thomas Dickerson, son of William W. and S., d. June 29, 1845; 2m. 20d.
William Jamison Dickerson, son of A. and J., d. Jan. 12, 1878; 27y. 6m. 12d.
Elizabeth C. Dunlap, wife of John, Jr., d. Sep. 6, 1886; 50y. 8m. 27d.
Susan Dunlap, wife of Joseph, d. Aug. 4, 1878; 58y. 5m. 15d.
Argulas W. Edwards, son of J. and E. J., d. Aug. 12, 1863; 2y. 8m. 19d.
Henry Edwards, b. May 15, 1809; d. March 19, 1890.
Maggie M. Edwards, daughter of J. and E. J., d. Sep. 9, 1874; 3y. 8m. 15d.
Willis M. Edwards, son of J. and E. J., d. Nov. 28, 1886; 22y. 2m. 14d.
Jacob Glasener, d. Jan. 14, 1853; 91y.
Ruth Glasener, wife of Jacob, d. March 28, 1846; 77y.
William Glasener, d. May 9, 1863; 34y. 9m. 2d.
Catherine Griffith, wife of R. L., d. March 14, 1890; 57y.
R. L. Griffith, d. Dec. 22, 1890; 62y.
Margaret Hamilton, daughter of Eli and Mary, d. Nov. 3, 1861; 13y.
James C. Harrison, son of G. W. and H., d. March 31, 1852; 3y. 4m. 8d.
Peter Harrison, d. April 20, 1854; 88y.
Emma Laura Hinkle, daughter of J. N. and M. J., d. Feb. 21, 1864; 2m. 14d.
William J. Hinkle, son of W. and E., d. Sep. 20, 1861; 29d.
William O. Hinkle, son of W. and E., d. July 28, 1860; 16d.
Abraham Holmes, d. May 3, 1880; 71y. 5m. 2d.
George H. Holmes, d. June 29, 1886; 86y. 8m. 5d.

John H. Holmes, son of G. B. and A., d. April 27, 1884; 1y. 1m. 20d.
Joseph Holmes, d. April 20, 1868; 97y. 2m. 24d
Joseph Holmes, b. Oct. 24, 1825; d. Nov. 26, 1889.
Mary A. Holmes, daughter of A. and R., d. Feb. 20, 1853; 9m. 6d.
Mary A. Holmes, daughter of J. and M., d. Oct. 20, 1862; 8y. 1m. 8d.
Mary J. Holmes, wife of Joseph, d. March 16, 1856; 34y. 6m. 1d.
Rachel Holmes, wife of Abraham, d. Feb. 12, 1854; 39y. 10m. 28d.
Sarah Holmes, wife of Joseph, d. March 5, 1862; 78y. 6m. 9d.
William A. Holmes, member of Company C, 98th O. V. I., d. Jan. 19, 1872; 26y. 11m. 13d.
William W. Holmes, son of G. B. and A., d. Oct. 16, 1881; 10m. 10d.
Emily C. Howell, daughter of J. and M., d. June 10, 1850; 1y. 7m. 12d.
Thomas McBride, d. Feb. 23, 1867; 56y.
William McBride, member of Company C, 98th O. V. I., d. Feb. 14, 1863; 27y
Albert M. McCoy, son of J. and E., d. April 2, 1875; 23y. 9m. 7d.
Eliza McCoy, b. March 30, 1819; d. July 22, 1890.
Bennett McCoy, d. Dec. 9, 1889; 64y. 4m. 7d.
John McCoy, b. Sep. 23, 1816; d. Dec. 3, 1890.
Mary E. McCoy, daughter of Ebenezer and Hannah, d. May 13, 1859; 8m. 21.
Mary E. McFadden, wife of John, d. Nov. 28, 1890; 36y. 10m. 2d.
Isabella McFarland, daughter of R. P. and E., d. Jan. 10, 1854; 10y 6m. 13d.
William McFarland, son of R. P. and E., Oct. 25, 1852; 7y. 2m. 27d.
Daniel McIlravy, d. April 28, 1860; 62y. 24d.
John W. McIlravy, son of Daniel, d. April 24, 1851; 29y. 3m. 20d.
Maria J. McIlravy, wife of George, d. April 28, 1869; 49y. 9m. 6d.
Ann Mercer, daughter of A. and J., d. July 17, 1822; 1y. 6m.
Susannah Mercer, daughter of Aaron

and Jane, d. Feb. 13, 1830; 7y. 5m. 20d.
Calanthia A. Burdette Minard, wife of H. F., b. Jan. 1, 1865; d. Aug. 6, 1887.
Daniel Mitchell, d. Aug. 11, 1876; 68y.
Elizabeth Mitchell, wife of Daniel, d. Oct. 13, 1844; 37y. 4d.
Elizabeth Mitchell, daughter of D. and E., d. March 3, 1845; 2y. 2m. 2d.
John L. Mitchell, member of Capt. McCready's Company, 126th O. V. I., d. Aug. 10, 1863; 25y. 11m. 10d.
Mary J. Mitchell, daughter of Daniel and Elizabeth, d. Nov. 10, 1849; 17y. 1d.
Reedie Mitchell, son of J. D. and E. E., b. March 20, 1888, d. May 18, 1889.
Sarah Mitchell, d. March 10, 1863; 52y.
Sarah Mitchell, wife of Daniel, d. Aug. 10, 1865; 42y.
Alexander Morris, son of J. and C., d. May 18, 1824; 4y. 10m. 4d.
Eliza Ann Hanna Oglevee, b. June 31, 1808; d. March 31, 1863.
James Wilson Oglevee, member of Capt. McCready's Company, 126th O. V. I., b. May 11, 1842; d. May 23, 1863.
John Oglevee, b. Dec. 14, 1810; d. March 12, 1865.
Nancy Jane Oglevee, b. Feb., 1849; d. June 25, 1865.
Susanna Elizabeth Oglevee, b. July 23, 1852; d. Feb. 10, 1880.
John Pennock, Member of Company C, 98th O. V. L., d. at Camp Dennison, Ohio, June 29, 1863; 32y.
Richard Pennock, d. Jan. 29, 1853; 60y.
Henry Perry, b. March 15, 1774; d. May 21, 1865.
Samuel C. Perry, son of William and E., d. Aug. 5, 1851; 3y. 1m. 12d.
Sarah Perry, b. Jan. 11, 1784; d. April 7, 1866.
William W. Perry, d. Aug. 26, 1865; 42y.
John Ryburn, d. Oct. 5, 1847; 17y. 20d.
Jane Sharp, wife of Joseph, d. July 3, 1844; 34y.
John Smith, d. July 24, 1856. [no age].
Margaret Vertue Smith, sister of John, d. May 11, 1831; 6y.

Margaret A. Shearer, wife of Rev. J. R., d. Oct. 16, 1854; 25y.
Infant daughter of E. and S. Timmons, d. Sept. 17, 1851.
Joseph O. Tucker, son of H. O. and N. M., d. Nov. 12, 1864; 1m. 12d.
George Weaver, d. Sep. 27, 1851; 30y.
Dorcas Welling wife of William, d. April 24, 1848; 69y. 8m. 9d.
Eliza A. Wooley, daughter of W. and E., d. Nov. 4, 1860; 12y.
James Wooley, d. April 7, 1857; 74y. 11m.
Jane Wooley, wife of Wesley J., d. March 18, 1857; 53y. 2m 5d.
Maria B. Wooley, daughter of W. and J., d. Aug. 19, 1854; 18y.
Marion H. Wooley, son of J. and J., d. Jan. 19, 1877; 1y. 8m. 2d.
Martha Wooley, daughter of W. and J., d. Sep. 22, 1839; 6m.
Mary E. Wooley, daughter of W. and J., d. April 9, 1853.
Susanna Wooley, wife of J., d. Feb. 4, 1839; 73y.
Susannah Wooley, daughter of W. and J., d. Oct. 10, 1850; 19y.

BURIALS IN RANKIN GRAVEYARD.

(Those Born Before 1830.)

Albina Barrett, b. Nov. 10, 1827; d. Feb. 13, 1891.
Elizabeth Barrett, wife of Arthur, d. April 11, 1874; 45y.
Joseph Barricklow, d. April 13, 1875; 69y. 10m. 1d.
Elijah Bartow, d. June 22, 1870; 48y. 9m. 22d.
Zenas Beall, d. April 17, 1852; 33y. 8m. 15d.
John P. Cope, d. April 20, 1890; 65y. 8m. 5d.
Rebecca Early, d. May 19, 1831; 22y.
Christinia Fulton, b. July 28, 1825; d. Dec. 2, 1893.
John Hastings, d. Dec. 6, 1840; 80y.
Elizabeth Johnson, d. July 30, 1871; 57y.
John W. Johnson, b. May 29, 1823; d. Nov. 30, 1889.
Mary Johnson, wife of R., d. Dec. 8, 1877; 74y.

William Johnson, Sr., d. Nov. 30, 1889; 79y. 1m. 4d.
Jonathan Jones, d. April 1, 1884; 88y.
Josiah Kidwell, d. Feb. 23, 1846; 72y. 5m. 16d.
William Kidwell, b. Oct. 19, 1814; d. Dec. 22, 1885.
Charles McMillin, d. Aug. 1, 1867; 87y.
Rosanna McMillin, wife of Charles, d. Nov. 27, 1856; 29y. 9m. 7d.
John Morris, b. May 4, 1816; d. Jan. 20, 1894.
Thomas B. Morris, d. April 15, 1890; 68y.
Jane Porter, wife of John, d. Nov. 8, 1837; 25y. 8m. 26d.
James Rankin, d. July 5, 1858; 73y. 6m. 13d.
Kester Rankin, wife of James, d. March 29, 1874; 81y.
Nancy Rankin, daughter of David and Sarah, d. Sept. 28, 1842; 19y. 7m. 19d.
Sarah Rankin, wife of David, d. May 5, 1852; 55y. 4m. 14d.
Thomas Rankin, d. May 12, 1832; 71y. 8m.
William Rankin, d. Jan. 3, 1864; 41y. 9m. 21d.
Cyrus P. Rowland, b. May 28, 1817; d. July 5, 1898.
Elizabeth Rowland, wife of James, d. March 4, 1884; 75y. 10m. 17d.
James Rowland, d. July 31, 1890; 85y. 5m. 7d.
John Rowland, d. April 20, 1855; 96y.
Rachel Rowland, wife of John, d. May 4, 1863; 85y.
Susanna Rowland, wife of Cyrus P. b. April 8, 1818; d. Sept. 12, 1884.
Elizabeth Ruby, wife of John, d. Jan. 28, 1845; 62y.
John Ruby, d. Nov. 6, 1849; 72y.
Ammon Shannon, d. Jan. 23, 1892; 64y. 9m. 6d.
Alexander Simpson, b. March 4, 1771; d. March 22, 1841.
Sarah G. Simpson, d. Dec. 15, 1858; 34y.
Thomas Simpson, d. Aug. 7, 1896; 87y.
Mary Sproul, daughter of John and Jane Hastings, d. Oct. 13, 1836; 44y. 1m.
Mary Stewart, d. April 16, 1845; 20y.
Matilda Toole, wife of Thomas, d. Oct. 10, 1883; 86y.
Thomas Toole, d. May 9, 1864; 70y. 2m. 2d.
Joseph White, d. Dec. 17, 1874; 43y. 10m. 7d.
Sarah White, wife of Joseph, d. Dec. 10, 1865; 38y.
Joseph Wineman, d. Jan. 30, 1872; 79y.

BURIALS IN CORINTH GRAVEYARD.

(Those Born Before 1830.)

Corinth Graveyard is situated in the northwest corner of section 14, town. 12, range 7, in Washington township, about three miles southeast from Tippecanoe.

Rebecca Crabtree, wife of Gabriel, d. Oct. 31, 1869; 74y. 9d.
Jesse Forsythe, d. Nov. 5, 1857; 87y.
John Forsythe, b. June 15, 1818; d. April 3; 26y. 10m. 2d.
Joseph D. Forsythe, d. Nov. 12, 1859; 44y. 10m. 20d.
Levi G. Forsythe, d. Jan. 20, 1854; 31y. 5m. 18d.
Sarah Forsythe, wife of Jesse, d. June 24, 1854; 62y.
James B. Jenkins, d. Nov. 16, 1883; 63y. 11m. 1d.
Frances Kerby, wife of James, d. June 6, 1874; 89y.
John Knox, d. May 21, 1863; 68y. 4m. 23d.
Mary Knox, wife of John, d. April 12, 1887; 85y. 5m. 27d.
Sarah J. Knox, d. May 4, 1848; 18y. 6m.
Hannah Layport, d. May 6, 1880; 80y. 7m. 20d.
Elizabeth Miller, wife of Richard, d. March 16, 1849; 79y. 1m. 21d.
Richard Phillips, d. Dec. 4, 1856; 84y.
Hugh Shotwell, d. March 17, 1854; 90y.
Betsy Slonecker, wife of John, d. Oct. 16, 1855; 49y. 7m. 10d.
John Slonecker, d. May 12, 1862; 67y. 2m. 6d.
James Wright, d. Oct. 29, 1878; 106y.

BURIALS IN MINKSVILLE GRAVEYARD.

(Those Born Before 1830.)

Minksville Graveyard is situated near the southeast corner of section 10, town. 11, range 6, Nottingham township.

Jacob Bargar, d. July 29, 1891; 68y. 11d.
James Campbell, d. May 10, 1846; 55y. 3m. 24d.
Samuel L. Carpenter, b. June 5, 1827; d. March 8, 1885.
Franklin Carson, d. June 16, 1874; 65y. 11m. 2d.
Hannah Carson, wife of John Carson, Sr., d. Nov. 2, 1852; 74y. 11m. 11d.
John Carson, Sr., d. May 13, 1858; 77y. 6m. 27d.
Sarah Carson, wife of Franklin, b. Feb. 10, 1807; d. Feb. 22, 1844.
Tabitha Carson, wife of Franklin, d. Aug. 10, 1869; 58y. 5m. 20d.
Lydia Cash, wife of William, d. May 9, 1837; 23y. 4m. 1d.
Robert Cook, d. Sept. 12, 1845; 41y.
Jacob Cope, b. Oct. 7, 1822; d. April 22, 1897.
Jane Cope, wife of Samuel, d. Aug 7, 1855; 68y. 2m. 17d.
Martha Cope, daughter of Samuel and Jane Cope, d. June 2, 1841; 22y. 9m. 29d.
Martha A. Cope, wife of Jacob, d. April 10, 1869; 37y. 10m. 18d.
Samuel Cope, d. Oct. 19, 1865; 73y. 2m. 17d.
Benjamin Ford, d. Jan. 19, 1855; 33y. 6m. 17d.
Rebecca Ford, wife of Lewis, d. Feb. 23, 1845; 52y.
Deborah Furney, wife of Frederick, d. June 19, 1872; 84y. 3m. 22d.
Frederick Furney, d. Oct. 26, 1855; 68y. 1m. 28d.
Abraham Hillis, d. March 26, 1836; 31y. 1m. 21d.
Elder Abiram Johnson, d. May 5, 1873; 73y. 5m. 11d.
Elizabeth Johnson, wife of Samuel, d. Oct. 22, 1844; 39y. 8m. 14d.
Joelm Johnson, b. June 1, 1822; d. Dec. 22, 1881.
Lydia Johnson, wife of Abiram, d. April 23, 1858; 54y. 4m. 11d.
Mary Ann Johnson, wife of L., d. Oct. 29, 1890; 61y. 3m. 17d.
Nancy Johnson, wife of Ephraim, d. April 3, 1860; 62y. 7m. 7d.
Ellen Mallernee, wife of Levi, d. Dec. 23, 1863; 43y. 10m. 26d.
Emanuel Mallernee, d. Feb. 23, 1839; 60y. 3m. 20d.
Levi Mallernee, b. Feb. 12, 1816; d. June 1, 1880.
Lewis C. Mallernee, b. May 12, 1823; d. Sept. 11, 1892.
James Maxwell, d. April 19, 1870; 80y.
Hannah Milliken, wife of J. Milliken, d. Feb 3, 1842; 63y.
Jonah H. Nichols, d. Aug. 19, 1868; 70y. 6m. 29d.
Martha Nichols, wife of Jonah, d. April 21, 1889; 84y. 7m.
Jonathan Perrin, d. Jan. 2, 1852; 82y.
Arthur Pugh, son of Daniel and Susannah Pugh, d. April 29, 1855; 28y. 6m. 9d.
Emily Ramsay, wife of John C., d. Dec. 1, 1880; 56y. 4m. 27d.
Mary Richardson, wife of William, b. April 7, 1811; d. Feb. 1, 1897.
William Richardson, d. Aug. 20, 1854; 66y. 3m. 3d.
Jane Rowland, wife of William, b. Dec. 15, 1801; d. Nov. 17, 1881.
Piety Ann Rowland, d. Sept. 5, 1865; 35y. 5m. 13d.
William Rowland, b. May 19, 1796; d. Jan. 13, 1873.
James Shields, d. Sept. 21, 1882; 90y.
Albert Singhaus, d. Nov. 2, 1851; 41y. 10m. 16d.
Elias Suddith, d. Feb. 5, 1873; 83y.
Ann Wilson, d. Nov. 30, 1854; 85y.

BURIALS IN PLEASANT VALLEY GRAVEYARD.

(Those Born Before 1830.)

Pleasant Valley Graveyard is situated in the east half of section 14, town. 12, range 6, Stock township, one mile west of Laceysville.

Elizabeth Campbell, wife of John L., d. June 29, 1873; 81y. 4m. 20d.

MORAVIAN RIDGE BURIALS 373

William Evans, b. Dec. 22, 1821; d. Feb. 12, 1890.
Benjamin Fowler, d. May 15, 1891; 88y.
Jane Fowler, wife of Benjamin, d. April 20, 1880; 87y.
James Gallaher, d. Sept. 11, 1856; 83y. 7m. 3d.
Patrick Gallaher, b. Dec. 4, 1794; d. May 1, 1877.
Catherine A. Gibson, wife of Edward, b. June 4, 1820; d. July 9, 1885.
Edward Gibson, d. Jan. 16, 1868; 65y.
John Gildea, d. Sept. 12, 1866; 48y. 7m.
Martha Gildea, wife of John, b. Jan. 25, 1809; d. Oct. 20, 1891.
Elizabeth Heavlin, wife of Stephen H., d. June 13, 1894; 74y. 9m. 12d.
Stephen H. Heavlin, d. Dec. 11, 1885; 66y. 3m. 5d.
Phebe Houghland, wife of James, d. Nov. 12, 1882; 68y. 3m. 29d.
Jesse Hoyt, d. Oct. 27, 1856; 81y.
Anna J. Lacy, wife of John S., b. July 21, 1805; d. Sept. 30, 1885.
John S. Lacy, b. Jan. 14, 1793; d. Jan. 16, 1873.
William B. Lacy, b. Dec. 11, 1823; d. Jan. 14, 1867.
Cynthia Layport, wife of Isaac, b. Sept. 4, 1815; d. May 2, 1895.
Isaac Layport, d. Aug. 3, 1882; 67y. 11m. 8d.
William Layport, d. March 20, 1867; 61y. 9m. 8d.
Elizabeth Leggitt, wife of Levi, d. Feb. 19, 1862; 57y. 1m. 12d.
Levi Leggitt, d. June 9, 1868; 68y. 4m. 18d.
Margaret Lewis, wife of Aaron, d. Oct. 2, 1856; 30y.
Robert McFadden, d. March 15, 1876; 63y.
Sarah McFadden, wife of Robert, d. June 21, 1879; 70y. 3m. 15d.
Samuel Miller, d. July 26, 1889; 85y. 1m.
Worley Mummy, d. Aug. 31, 1884; 55y. 4m. 27d.
Hannah Parker, b. Dec. 31, 1809; d. Dec. 27, 1874.
Francis Simpson, d. March 15, 1870; 66y.
John Simpson, b. March 26, 1814; d. Oct. 7, 1877; 63y. 6m. 11d.
Margaret Simpson, wife of Francis, d. Nov. 9, 1884; 83y.
Abraham Singhaus, d. Oct. 12, 1857; 39y. 9m. 12d.
Margaret Smith, wife of William P., d. April 24, 1870; 66y. 3m. 10d.
William P. Smith, d. May 15, 1890; 86y. 7m. 25d.
Ara Spiker, wife of Christopher, d. March 16, 1870; 63y. 8m. 3d.
Christopher Spiker, d. March 13, 1879; 74y.
Elizabeth Tipton, wife of Samuel, d. July 21, 1876; 67y.
Elizabeth Turney, wife of James, d. Feb. 25, 1887; 76y. 2m. 3d.
Albert West, d. July 6, 1891; 72y. 7m. 3d.
Mary West, wife of Albert, d. Oct. 4, 1859; 37y. 10m. 4d.
Margaret Wheeler, d. Nov. 6, 1858; 68y. 10d.

BURIALS IN MORAVIAN RIDGE GRAVEYARD.

(Those Born Before 1830.)

Moravian Ridge Graveyard is situated in the northwest corner of section 23, town. 10, range 5, in Cadiz township, about four miles west of Cadiz.

Percival Adams, b. Sept. 10, 1820; d. Jan. 30, 1898.
Hugh Anderson, d. March 16, 1891; 64y. 9m. 3d.
Isabella Bargar, wife of John G., d. Oct. 18, 1852; 33y. 6m. 14d.
Sarah Blair, wife of William, d. July 24, 1880; 72y. 2m. 28d.
William Blair, d. Jan. 29, 1867; 62y. 10m. 15d.
Margaret Christy, d. Oct. 11, 1862; 26y. 6m. 14d.
Robert Christy, d. Oct. 9, 1853; 54y.
Lydia Conaway, wife of William, d. July 26, 1853; 21y. 14d.
Elizabeth Cope, wife of David, d. Oct. 3, 1851; 31y. 7m. 13d.
George Day, d. May 4, 1855; 66y.
Margaret Day, wife of George, d. Feb. 14, 1859; 81y. 5m.

John Downs, son of R. and E., d. May 31, 1849; 22y. 1m. 22d.
Mary Downs, wife of George, d. Aug. 19, 1855; 28y. 6m. 27d.
John Finnical, b. April 4, 1829; d. Feb. 4, 1899.
Oliver C. Grimes, b. Aug. 7, 1826, d. Feb. 4, 1892; 65y. 5m. 28d.
Gillespie Haverfield, b. Nov. 14, 1818; d. March 17, 1882.
Stephen Heavlin, d. Feb. 3, 1846; 73y.
Alexander Henderson, b. Aug. 9, 1813; d. March 17, 1883.
Mary Henderson, daughter of William and Nancy, d. Feb. 27, 1851; 22y. 11m. 22d.
Nancy Henderson, wife of William, d. Feb. 3, 1844; 54y. 4m. 14d.
Nancy Henderson, d. April 1, 1857; 33y. 1m.
Thomas B. Henderson, son of William and Nancy, d. Aug. 19, 1845; 28y. 6m. 8d.
William Henderson, d. May 9, 1852; 75y.
Daniel Hines, d. Feb. 3, 1861; 65y.
Elizabeth Hines, wife of Samuel, d. Feb. 18, 1875; 83y.
Elizabeth Hines, d. June 22, 1822; 28y. 3m. 10d.
Hannah Hines, wife of James, d. April 10, 1844; 31y. 7m. 5d.
Isaac Hines, d. Oct. 6, 1865; 76v.
Isabella Hines, d. April 15, 1899; 92y. 2m. 21d.
John Hines, son of Samuel and Elizabeth, d. Feb. 7, 1833; 18y. 5m.
John F. Hines, d. June 29, 1851; 29y. 6d.
Joseph Hines, d. Oct. 1, 1823; 71y.
Martha Hines, daughter of Samuel and Elizabeth, d. Aug. 22, 1821; 1y. 2m. 11d.
Rebecca Hines, wife of John, d. Jan. 27, 1859; 75y. 3m. 13d.
Rudolph Hines, d. Jan. 31, 1888; 74y.
Samuel Hines, d. Oct. 22, 1872; 81y.
Sarah Hines, d. Nov. 9, 1865; 76y.
Sarah H. Hines, daughter of Samuel and Elizabeth, d. Sept. 2, 1830; 1y. 1m. 11d.
Susannah Hines, daughter of Samuel and Elizabeth, d. Jan. 30, 1839; 30y. 7m. 19d.
William Hines, d. Sept. 8, 1887; 87y. 5m. 20d.
Mary Johnson, wife of Hugh, d. Nov. 15, 1869; 74y. 9m. 19d.
John Kent, b. March 6, 1812; d. Nov. 29, 1885.
Ruth J. Kent, wife of John, b. Nov. 11, 1818; d. Dec. 14, 1891.
Sarah Kent, wife of Absalom, d. May 25, 1885; 38y. 8m. 2d.
George Kitt, d. Aug. 2, 1830; 33y.
John Lavely, d. Dec. 3, 1841; 54y. 10m. 25d.
Mary Lavely, d. May 26, 1846; 20y. 2m. 18d.
Jacob Marshall, d. May 15, 1824; 80y. 6m. 7d.
Martha Marshall, wife of Jacob, d. Aug. 7, 1844; 31y.
Mary Marshall, wife of Jacob, d. Jan. 29, 1848; 102y. 10m.
Zapporah Marshall, wife of John, d. June 25, 1838; 79y.
Rachel H. Martin, wife of George, b. Feb. 4, 1831; d. Jan. 17, 1881.
Sophia Merryman, wife of Migagah, d. July 26, 1881; 91y. 4m. 10d.
David Mitchell, d. Aug. 15, 1847; 25y. 8m. 4d.
Hugh Mitchell, d. Aug. 27, 1847; 41y. 5m. 1d.
James Mitchell, d. Sept. 12, 1847; 48y. 6m. 8d.
John Mitchell, d. April 12, 1844; 72y.
John H. Mitchell, d. Sept. 21, 1847; 28y.
Mary Mitchell, wife of John, d. Jan. 7, 1850; 67y. 11m. 26d.
Washington Ourant, b. Sept. 15, 1808; d. Sept. 10, 1884; 76y.
Jemima Patterson, wife of Joseph, b. April 11, 1801, d. April 2, 1896; 95y.
Joseph Patterson, b. April, 1799, in County Down, Ireland; d. April 16, 1879; 80y.
Marcia Patterson, b. Nov. 30, 1822; d. April 12, 1896.
Andrew Poulson, son of James and Rachel, d. Jan 28, 1831; 36y. 1m. 6d.
William Ramsey, d. Feb. 18, 1856; 64y.
Parmelia Rickey, wife of H., d. Feb. 14, 1853; 32y. 2m. 2d.
Providence Rickey, wife of Daniel, d. Sept. 6, 1855; 63y.

Caleb Ross, d. June 4, 1864; 55y. 1m. 29d.
Susanna Ross, wife of Adam, d. Jan. 11, 1847; 68y.
Mary A. Shivers, b. Jan. 26, 1831; d. Jan. 18, 1893.
Elizabeth Watters, wife of John, d. Sept. 30, 1852; 33y.
Mary Wells, wife of Charles, d. Jan. 31, 1889; 72y.

BURIALS IN BETHEL GRAVEYARD.

(Those Born Before 1830.)

William Argo, d. Feb. 26, 1846; 82y. 6m. 14d.
Mary Arnold, b. Feb. 25, 1766; d. Jan. 8, 1854.
James Baker, b. Feb. 17, 1804; d. Nov. 30, 1879.
John Baker, d. Feb. 12, 1847; 69y. 10m. 29d.
Lillah Baker, wife of Otho, b. Aug. 30, 1818; d. Nov. 14, 1843.
Mary Baker, wife of Otho, d. Feb. 13, 1870; 74y.
Otho Baker, d. Feb. 24, 1855; 74y.
Rezin Baker, d. May 23, 1876; 65y. 6m. 18d.
Charles Bartley, d. Feb. 16, 1845; 73y.
Margaret Beatty, d. Oct. 6, 1838; 84y.
Rachel Beatty, wife of Sampson, d. Jan. 25, 1850; 49y. 5m. 1d.
Sampson Beatty, d. Nov. 27, 1849; 63y. 5m. 21d.
Wesley Beatty, son of Sampson and Rachel, d. Sept. 7, 1840; 12y. 23d.
Elizabeth Birney, first wife of Hugh, d. Sept. 5, 1828; 40y.
Hugh Birney, d. Sept. 28, 1861; 82y.
John Birney, d. July 6, 1854; 77y.
Margaret Birney, wife of Robert, d. Feb. 2, 1866; 71y.
Nancy Birney, second wife of Hugh, d. Dec. 27, 1854; 60y.
Nelson Birney, d. June 14, 1867; 47y. 9m. 26d.
Rachel Birney, wife of John, d. Nov. 12, 1843; 63y.
Robert Birney, d. Aug. 16, 1871; 86y. 7m. 15d.
Benjamin Brindley, Jr., d. July 12, 1860; 49y. 5m. 10d.

Hugh Brown, d. Nov. 12, 1822; 36y.
Jane Brown, wife of Hugh, d. Sept. 3, 1884; 96y.
William Brown, d. Dec. 20, 1874; 55y. 5m. 8d.
Catherine Busby, second wife of Sheridan, b. Sept. 25, 1836; d. Feb. 25, 1864.
Eliza Busby, first wife of Sheridan, b. June 22, 1822; d. Nov. 14, 1852.
Sheridan Busby, b. July 4, 1817; d. Aug. 31, 1884.
William Chaney, d. July 30, 1839; 65y. 4m. 10d.
Zebadee Cox, d. Nov. 1, 1861; 65y. 6m. 26d.
James Devore, d. June 12, 1851; 79y.
Lydia Devore, wife of James, d. Dec. 25, 1848; 76y.
Mary Devore, wife of Moses, b. March 27, 1818; d. May 25, 1892.
Moses Devore, d. Jan. 20, 1888; 79y
John Fife, d. Oct. 1868; 62y.
Margaret Fogle, wife of George, d. Jan. 22, 1838; 80y.
Lucinda Foreman, wife of Samuel, b. April 21, 1821; d. May 14, 1897.
Martha R. Foreman, wife of Ephra'm, d. Oct. 14, 1844; 30y. 6m. 11d.
Sarah Foreman, wife of William, d. Sept. 13, 1864; 85y. 5m. 7d.
William Foreman, d. June 6, 1845; 70y. 10m. 9d.
Lemuel Green, d. April 10, 1860; 72y.
Mary Green, wife of Lemuel, d. Sept. 9, 1879; 93y.
Elizabeth Guthrie, wife of James W., d. Dec. 16, 1898; 81y. 2m.
James W. Guthrie, d. Dec. 8, 1883; 84y. 4m.
Isabelle Henderson, wife of Matthew, d. Aug. 31, 1898; 78y. 4m. 6d.
Matthew Henderson, d. Feb. 7, 1898; 81y. 4m.
Gabriel Holland, d. Jan. 18, 1871; 81y. 11m.
Susannah Holland, wife of Gabriel, d. Sept. 27, 1861; 73y. 18d.
Margaret Kail, d. June 10, 1850; 28y. 4m. 11d.
William P. Kent, b. Feb. 14, 1798; d. Oct. 11, 1872; 74y. 7m. 27d.
William W. Kent, b. March 7, 1826; d. Feb. 21, 1886.

George Leas, d. March 7, 1870; 76y. 11m. 5d.
Mary Leas, wife of George, b. April 11, 1805; d. June 6, 1883.
Isaac Lemaster, d. April 21, 1844; 70y. 7m. 7d.
Jane Lemaster, wife of Isaac, d. April 27, 1855; 76y. 1m. 20d.
William Lemaster, d. March 8, 1878; 61y. 2m. 8d.
Hannah Lewis, daughter of Joseph, and Rachel, d. March 11, 1897; 82y. 1m. 26d.
Joseph Lewis, d. Sept. 4, 1853; 83y. 10m. 3d.
Joseph Lewis, d. March 1, 1882; 87y. 25d.
Mary Lewis, wife of Joseph, d. April 17, 1850; 48y. 2m. 19d.
Rachel Lewis, wife of Joseph, d. Sept. 1, 1852; 83y. 10m. 12d.
Anne Lindsey, d. March 13, 1830; 52y.
Nancy McGuire, wife of James, d. Dec. 30, 1834; 49y.
Catherine McKee, d. March 26, 1861; 81y.
Rachel McKee, wife of Robert, d. Sept. 29, 1847; 58y. 4m. 6d.
Robert McKee, d. June 3, 1851; 73y. 7m. 24d.
Axie Maholm, wife of James, d. Feb. 9, 1871; 67y.
James Maholm, d. Feb. 23, 1859; 65y.
Abraham Mattern, b. Oct. 22, 1806; d. Feb. 16, 1889.
Mary Mattern, wife of Abraham, b. April 14, 1808; d. Dec. 17, 1890.
Lucy May, wife of Andrew, d. Dec. 30, 1830; 67y. 3m. 10d.
Abraham Pittinger, d. Oct. 6, 1859; 87y. 2m. 15d.
Margaret Pittinger, daughter of S. and J., d. Nov. 16, 1854; 24y. 6m. 27d.
Jane Pittinger, wife of Samuel, d. Feb. 13, 1875; 75y. 11m. 8d.
Samuel Pittinger, d. Aug. 26, 1876; 78y. 1m.
Susannah Pittinger, wife of Abraham, d. May 2, 1847; 69y. 30d.
John Ralston, d. Oct. 24, 1881; 82y. 3m. 11d.
Leusintha Ralston, wife of John, d. Jan. 13, 1846; 38y. 1m. 5d.

Mary Ralston, wife of John, d. July 5, 1897; 92y. 1m. 4d.
Christopher Rankin, son of Henry and Ruth, d. Nov. 26, 1839; 19y. 7m.
Sarah J. Rankin, daughter of Henry and Ruth, d. April 11, 1840; 11y. 10m.
Jane Ryan, d. Sept. 12, 1866; 74y. 6m. 1d.
Melinda Ryan, wife of Lewis G., d. Oct. 4, 1895; 73y.
Jane Scarlet, wife of Richard, d. Feb. 15, 1868; 66y.
Katherine Speer, d. May 9, 1833; 70y.
Rachel Speer, wife of William, d. May 28, 1867; 65y. 28d.
Sophia G. Speer, d. May 11, 1849; 53y. 5m. 5d.
William Speer, d. Dec. 15, 1849; 53y. 1m. 14d.
Netty Thomlinson, wife of Thomas, d. Feb. 24, 1843; 41y. 1m. 25d.
Elizabeth Thompson, wife of John, d. Jan. 30, 1858; 49y. 7m. 8d.
Mary Thompson, wife of Thomas, d. May 29, 1860; 76y.
Thomas Thompson, d. Sept. 29, 1842; 28y. 3m. 9d.
Samuel Tipton, d. March 27, 1859; 45y. 3m. 24d.
Kezia Wheeler, wife of Mordicai, d. June 5, 1873; 77y. 5m. 20d.
Mordicai Wheeler, d. Feb. 6, 1884; 60y.
Soloman Wyant, d. July 24, 1851; 20y. 3m.

BURIALS IN GREENWOOD GRAVEYARD OF GREEN TOWNSHIP.

(Those Born Before 1830.)

Greenwood Graveyard is situated near the centre of the east line of section 20, town. 10, range 4, Green township, two miles southwest of Hopedale.

David Allison, b. April 20, 1820; d. Sept. 1, 1894.
Samuel P. Baxter, d. Sept. 19, 1887; 90y. 1m. 4d.
Nancy Baxter, wife of Samuel P., d. Nov. 28, 1840; 43y. 7m. 18d.

Dr. William Beadle, b. March 29, 1830; d. Oct. 20, 1880.
Ann Bell, wife of Francis, d. Dec. 30, 1873; 71y. 1m. 20d.
Elizabeth Bell, wife of Francis, d. March 29, 1834; 69y. 4m. 17d.
Francis Bell, b. Feb. 12, 1765; d. Sept. 20, 1848.
Francis Bell, d. July 23, 1862; 62y. 6m. 27d.
Jackson Bell, son of Samuel and Rachel, d. Feb. 5, 1835; 7y. 3m. 29d.
Jane Bell, wife of Francis, d. July 18, 1876; 71y. 8m. 21d.
John M. Bell, son of Samuel and and Rachel, d. Feb. 4, 1835; 5y. 3m. 11d.
William Brinkerhoff, L. L. D., b. Aug. 21, 1821; d. Oct. 5, 1885.
Abraham H. Busby, b. Jan. 22, 1814; d. July 11, 1896.
Amanda Busby, wife of Robert, b. May 10, 1807; d. June 20, 1893.
Eleanor Busby, wife of Abraham H., b. Feb. 20, 1820; d. Aug. 19, 1893.
Robert Busby, b. June 19, 1803; d. Feb. 11, 1896.
Ankrum Cardwell, b. July 23, 1823; d. Dec. 7, 1883.
Isaac Case, d. Nov. 29, 1871; 83y. 1m. 26d.
George Chaney, d. May 5, 1888; 82y. 11m. 18d.
Eleanor Cope, wife of James, d. March 14, 1870; 61y. 11m. 25d.
James Cope, d. Jan. 17, 1868; 62y. 2m. 14d.
Jacob S. Copeland, b. Oct. 10, 1818; d. Aug. 7, 1882.
Nancy Copeland, wife of Thomas, d. April 18, 1857; 64y. 7m. 4d.
Nancy M. Copeland, wife of Jacob S., b. Oct. 4, 1821; d. April 29, 1896.
Thomas Copeland, d. March 8, 1879; 83y. 5m. 13d.
Nathan Couch, Sr., d. March 11, 1846; 72y.
Nathan Couch, Jr., d. Nov. 12, 1847; 28y. 8d.
Catherine Croskey, wife of John, d. Jan. 22, 1863; 82y. 6m. 27d.
Elizabeth Croskey, wife of Jackson, d. April 6, 1882; 67y. 7m. 27d.
Esther Croskey, wife of John, d. Sept. 27, 1835; 27y. 3m. 7d.
Jackson Croskey, d. Feb. 7, 1890; 75y. 1d.
John Croskey, d. March 16, 1862; 86y. 5m. 9d.
John Croskey, d. Oct. 20, 1867; 65y. 6m.
Phebe Dowden, wife of Thomas A., b. July 18, 1819; d. Feb. 23, 1892.
Thomas A. Dowden, b. Nov. 16, 1822; d. Aug. 20, 1890.
Elizabeth Fisher, wife of George, d. Oct. 19, 1838; 89y. 7m. 13d.
George Fisher, d. Sept. 11, 1823; 71y.
Hannah Jane Fulton, wife of William, d. April 13, 1886; 73y. 2m. 15d.
Maria Louisa Fulton, wife of James, d. Sept. 30, 1875; 44y. 6m. 10d.
Sophia Fulton, wife of William, d. July 27, 1889; 73y. 4m. 21d.
William Fulton, d. July 30, 1884; 81y. 1d.
Christopher S. Hall, d. July 23, 1878; 85y. 5m. 7d.
Hannah Hall, wife of Christopher S., d. April 6, 1891; 86y.
Mary Handy, daughter of Moses and Nancy, d. Aug. 18, 1826; 17y. 4m. 5d.
Moses Handy, d. March 2, 1871; 81y. 8m. 22d.
Nancy Handy, wife of Moses, d. Oct. 7, 1860; 71y.
John M. Hanna, d. June 20, 1878; 74y.
Susannah Harrson, wife of William, d. Feb. 25, 1863; 53y.
William Harrison, Sr., d. Sept. 19, 1885; 83y.
Isaac Holmes, d. Feb. 12, 1884; 76y.
Jane Holmes, wife of Isaac, d. July 18, 1884; 84y.
Joseph Howell, b. June 24, 1811; d. Sept. 2, 1884.
Mary Howell, wife of Joseph, b. Feb. 20, 1814; d. May 9, 1884.
William Jones, d. Jan. 24, 1839; 26y. 8m. 23d.
Catherine Kennedy, wife of Dr. Moses, b. Aug. 18, 1794; d. Feb. 5, 1869; 74y. 5m. 13d.
Elizabeth Kennedy, daughter of Moses and Catherine, d. July 11, 1830; 7y. 4m. 19d.

Dr. Moses Kennedy, b. Dec. 24, 1797; d. April 7, 1857; 59y. 3m. 14d.
Edward Laughridge, d. June 14, 1889; 87y.
Elizabeth Leech, wife of William, b. 1826; d. 1897.
William Leech, b. 1821; d. 1897.
Rebecca Lindley, d. Feb. 17, 1866; 47y.
Matilda McClain, d. April 13, 1887; 72y.
D. W. Mansfield, b. March 20, 1829; d. April 14, 1883.
Allen Maxwell, d. July 12, 1804; 77y. 2m. 6d.
Mary A. Maxwell, wife of Allen, d. Aug. 14, 1892; 66y. 3m. 8d.
M. Meuhirter, d. Feb. 2, 1372; 97y.
William Narragong, b. June 15, 1811; d. Sept. 30, 1893.
Elizabeth Parkinson, wife of Thomas, d. April 24, 1847; 88y. 10m. 26d.
Thomas Parkinson, d. Nov. 10, 1838; 76y. 12d.
John Ramsay, b. June 23, 1805; d. March 27, 1895.
Mary B. Ramsay, wife of John, b. June 22, 1817; d. Nov. 11, 1889.
Sarah F. Rife, d. Feb. 22, 1870; 59y. 1m. 10d.
Susannah Rogers, wife of J., d. Aug. 6, 1886; 66y. 6m. 16d.
Christena Shepler, wife of Jacob, d. July 19, 1854; 81y. 5m. 14d.
Jacob Shepler, d. June 18, 1841; 68y. 8m. 29d.
Jacob C. Shepler, d. June 13, 1863; 32y. 7m. 26d.
Samuel Shepler, b. April 9, 1799; d. Oct. 11, 1865.
Susannah Shepler, wife of Samuel, d. March 13, 1854; 49y. 5m. 23d.
Mary Jane Snedderker, wife of Samuel, d. June 24, 1896; 73y.
Catherine Snider, b. March 1, 1804; d. Dec. 24, 1886.
Martin Snider, b. Oct., 1805; d. April 5, 1882.
Catherine Snyder, wife of Martin, d. Aug. 29, 1821; 62y.
Christina Snyder, wife of John A., b. April 1, 1815; d. Aug. 15, 1858.
Martin Snyder, d. Nov. 7, 1810; 82y.
Joseph M. Stewart, b. 1822; d. 1890.
Cynthia Swan, wife of Hezekiah, b. Oct. 4, 1820; d. Feb. 25, 1895.
A. B. West, b. Sept. 1, 1800; d. March 19, 1889.
Mary West, wife of A. B., b. June 28, 1818; d. March 2, 1884.

BURIALS IN HOLMES CHURCH GRAVEYARD.

(Those Born Before 1830.)

Holmes Graveyard is situated in Jefferson county, about one mile southeast from Adena.

Elizabeth Barkhurst, wife of Joshua, b. Nov. 2, 1785; d. March 13, 1873.
Jacob A. Barkhurst, b. Dec. 25, 1807; d. Nov. 20, 1891.
Jane Barkhurst, wife of John B., d. Dec. 26, 1879; 69y. 3m. 1d.
John B. Barkhurst, d. Aug. 19, 1891; 78y. 4m. 19d.
Joshua Barkhurst, b. 1774; d. Sept. 12, 1837; 53y.
Joshua D. Barkhurst, son of Joshua and Elizabeth, d. Sept. 15, 1832; 10y. 7m. 19d
Mary Barkhurst, wife of Joshua, d. June 15, 1872; 64y. 5m. 2d.
Mary Barkhurst, daughter of Joshua and Elizabeth, d. Sept. 13, 1832; 21y. 1m. 20d.
Nancy Barkhurst, wife of William, d. Aug. 22, 1842; 57y. 11m. 7d.
William Barkhurst, d. April 18, 1861; 76y. 1d.
F. Rasbury Belknap, d. Nov. 27, 1826; 23y. 3m.
Elihu Carter, d. Oct. 24, 1898; 75y. 7m. 17d.
Mary Carter, wife of Nelson, d. May 11,1875; 45y. 2m. 11d.
William Comley, b. Oct. 6, 1825; d. Oct. 21, 1897.
Rebecca Edwards, d. Aug. 20, 1820; 9y.
Josiah Glover, b. Nov. 13, 1814; d. May 7, 1891.
Mary Glover, wife of Josiah, d. Feb. 10, 1872; 55y. 5m. 11d.
Mary Hammond, wife of John, d. Sept. 15, 1883; 57y. 4m. 5d.

Eliza Hastings, wife of James, d. Feb. 8, 1840.
James Hastings, d. June 4, 1830; 57y. 9m.
John Hastings, son of James and Eliza, d. June 14, 1828; 24y. 5m. 6d.
Joseph Hastings, b. Nov. 20, 1807; d. April 15, 1889.
Ruth Hastings, wife of Joseph, b. Oct 14, 1812; d. Jan. 7, 1893.
Daniel Hayne, d. May 18, 1868; 101y.
Francis Hayne, d. May 5, 1846; 79y.
Joseph Hayne, son of Daniel and Mary, d. Aug. 29, 1844; 23 y. 3m. 19d.
Mary Hayne, wife of Daniel, d. June 6, 1834; 50y.
Mary Hayne, daughter of Daniel and Mary, d. Aug 30, 1831; 20y.
Nathan Hayne, b. April 20, 1809; d. May 30, 1896.
Phoebe Hayne, wife of Nathan, b. May 10, 1816; d. April 9, 1897.
Rachel Hayne, daughter of Daniel and Mary, d. Oct. 5, 1839; 23y.
Ruth Hayne, daughter of Daniel and Mary, d. March 22, 1830; 25y.
Ann Innskeep, wife of Ralph, d. May 30, 1826; 22y. 8m. 15d.
Absalom McCue, b. June 11, 1810; d. Jan. 18, 1898.
Elizabeth McCue, wife of Absalom, b. March 8, 1818; d. March 21, 1898.
William Meek, d. Aug. 12, 1831; 73y. 5m. 26d.
Mary Moore, wife of Richard, d. Oct. 28, 1878; 59y. 4m. 28d.
Silas Moore, b. Aug. 4, 1792; d. Nov. 5, 1872.
Silvanus Moore, b. March 2, 1754; d. March 5, 1840.
Mary Pearce, wife of Isaac, d. Dec. 20, 1822; 35y. 10m. 24d.
Rebecca Pearce, daughter of Isaac and Mary, d. June 15, 1827; 18y 4m.
John Scott, d. Sept. 23, 1860; 51y. 1m. 25d.
William Scott, d. Nov. 9, 1852; 78y.
Jonathan Talbot, d. Dec. 10, 1863; 72y. 9m. 15d.
Susan Talbot, daughter of Jonathan, d. March 4, 1874; 51y. 7m. 21d.
Sarah Webster, wife of N., d. Nov. 21, 1839; 30y.

BURIALS IN BOWERSTOWN GRAVEYARD.

(Those Born Before 1339)

Elizabeth Addleman, wife of George, d. April 8, 1850; 50y. 5m. 20d.
George Addleman, d. June 30, 1886; 96y. 11m. 2d.
Bettie Baker, b. July 4, 1815; d. April 26, 1897.
Samuel Baker, b. Jan. 23, 1818; d. Sept. 25, 1870.
Ann Bower, wife of Caleb, d. Sept. 28, 1865; 25y. 9m. 9d.
Anna Bower, wife of Jacob, d. April 27, 1870; 65y.
Barnhart Bower, d. Dec. 29, 1844; 84y.
Caleb Bower, d. Oct. 6, 1865; 27y. 7m.
David Bower, d. Feb 16, 1858; 54y. 9m. 2d.
Elias Bower, son of John and Margaret, d. Jan. 4, 1830; 3y. 5m. 15d.
Elizabeth Bower, wife of David, d. Jan. 1, 1866; 59y. 5m. 8d.
Esther Bower, wife of N., d. Aug. 16, 1855; 28y. 3m. 1d.
Henry Bower, d. March 9, 1883; 81y. 10m. 11d.
Jacob Bower, d. Aug. 23, 1871; 70y. 7m. 5d.
Jacob Bower, d. March 29, 1883; 61y. 9m. 27d.
John Bower, d. Sept. 7, 1863; 68y. 6m. 16d.
Margaret Bower, wife of John, d. June 23, 1863; 69y. 2m. 26d.
Margaret A. Bower, daughter of Jacob and Ann, d. Jan. 4, 1893; 62y. 5m. 19d.
Mary Bower, wife of Barnhart, d. May 6, 1847; 87y.
Samuel Bower, son of John and Elizabeth, d. Jan. 1, 1838; 13y. 8m. 23d.
Susan Bower, wife of Henry, d. Aug. 5, 1865; 58y. 10m. 6d.
Thomas Bower, d. May 13, 1852; 31y. 6m. 18d.
John T. Boyd, d. Oct. 11, 1893; 91y. 9m. 18d.
Catherine Crumrine, wife of John, d. Jan. 21, 1885; 87y.
John Crumrine, d. Sept. 6, 1852; 55y. 5m. 1d.

Adam Easterday, d. May 2, 1857; 28y. 4m. 2d.
Elizabeth Easterday, wife of Adam, d. June 7, 1898, 75y. 7m. 24d.
Eve Easterday, wife of John, d. Dec. 28, 1880; 80y. 6m. 28d.
Jacob Easterday, d. Dec. 31, 1824; 59y.
John Easterday, d. Nov. 19, 1873; 7y. 10m. 1d.
Magdalan Easterday, wife of Jacob, d. Nov. 18, 1838; 60y.
Catherine Flory, wife of Joseph, d. March 29, 1883; 83y. 5m. 18d.
Joseph Flory, d. Nov. 17, 1875; 81y. 4m. 1d.
Magdalena Grundy, wife of Benjamin, d. Sept. 18, 1847; 56y. 4m. 14d.
Adam Hagey, d. July 12, 1881; 71y. 6m. 12d.
Maria Hagey, wife of John, d. Dec. 23, 1887; 72y. 7m.
Daniel Hess, d. June 9, 1872; 70y.
Elizabeth Hess, wife of Daniel, d. Jan. 2, 1862; 58y. 8m. 4d.
Judeth Hess, wife of William, d. March 29, 1864; 85y.
Catherine Lawler, wife of William, d. April 25, 1858; 40y. 7m. 3d.
William Lawler, d. Aug. 31, 1837; 45y.
Catherine Little, wife of Samuel, d. April 8, 1880; 85y. 2m.
Hannah Long, wife of George, d. June 9, 1853; 33y. 4m. 21d.
Oliver P. Long, d. Dec. 19, 1888; 63y. 11m. 24d.
Mary McCurdy, d. Sept. 10, 1851; 60y.
Catherine Minnick, wife of John, d. Nov. 8, 1845; 65y. 10m. 2d.
John Minnick, Dec. 7, 1848; 76y. 10m. 5d.
Joseph Minnick, d. May 1, 1871; 53y. 3m. 2d.
Mary Murphy, wife of P., d. June 27, 1855; 51y. 4m. 18d.
Peter Sharp, d. March 12, 1889; 8 y. 2m. 28d.
Henry S. Sneary, d. May 28, 1867; 57y. 6m. 24d.
Susan Sneary, wife of Henry S., d. Sept. 22, 1892; 75y. 11m. 5d.
Gabrial Swinehart, b. July 20, 1798; d. Jan. 15, 1878.
Lesla Swinehart, d. Oct. 1, 1898; 73y. 3m. 17d.
Margaret Swinehart, wife of Gabrial, b. July 9, 1802; d. Sept 28, 1883.
Elizabeth Trusell, wife of Solomon, d. Nov. 6, 1845; 72y. 11m. 5d.
Fannie Trushel, wife of John, d. June 12, 1875; 72y. 6m. 10d.
John Trushel, d. March 22, 1885; 82y. 5m. 25d.
Sarah Trushel, second wife of Valentine, d. March 8, 1876; 51y. 1m. 16d.
Solomon Trusell, d. Feb. 9, 1846; 68y. 9m. 17d.
Susanna Trushel, first wife of Valentine, d. Nov. 8, 1845; 33y. 8d.
Valentine Trushel, d. Oct. 6, 1880; 75y. 7m. 23d.

BURIALS IN CASSVILLE GRAVEYARD.

(Those Born Before 1830.)

David Barclay, d. April 9, 1876; 86y.
Elizabeth Barclay, wife of David, d. June 9, 1871; 70y.
James Barclay, b. Sept. 15, 1828; d. April 21, 1885.
Susanna Bargar, wife of Peter, d. July 7, 1862; 65y. 2m. 6d.
David Barrett, d. April 12, 1881; 59y. 7m. 17d.
Winnifred Barrett, b. March 12, 1787; d. June 11, 1867; 80y. 2m. 29d.
Conrad Barricklow, b. Dec. 15, 1814; d. Dec. 8, 1874.
Elizabeth Blair, wife of John, b. Aug. 13, 1815; d. June 20, 1890.
Jane Clark, wife of Samuel, d. Sept. 26, ——; 57y. 18d.
Joseph Clark, d. Jan. 25, 1885; 82y.
Samuel Clark, d. Sept. 28, 1886; 78y. 21d.
Abraham Corban, d. March 24, 1873; 66y.
Jane Corban, wife of Abraham, d. April 17, 1876; 68y. 11m. 14d.
Ann B. Cunningham, wife of David, b. May 8, 1808; d. Aug. 13, 1887.
Asa Dickerson, d. Oct. 26, 1864; 50y. 7m. 3d.
Jane Dickerson, wife of Asa, d. March 31, 1873; 59y. 4m. 29d.
Alexander Fulton, d. March 15, 1881; 77y. 6m. 3d.

Sarah Fulton, wife of Alexander, d. May 20, 1894; 90y. 3m. 8d.
Adam B. Hamilton, d. May 11, 1872; 46y.
Elizabeth J. Haverfield, wife of James, b. June 2, 1830; d. Aug. 6, 1896.
James Haverfield, b. May 5, 1817; d. April 2, 1881.
Nancy Haverfield, d. Aug. 23, 1882; 70y. 4m. 7d.
William James, d. Aug. 23, 1863; 44y.
Margaret Johnson, b. May 27, 1810; d. Oct. 11, 1887.
Mary Johnson, d. Feb. 16, 1873; 71y.
Ellen Knox, d. July 5, 1888; 68y.
Benjamin McFadden, d. Nov. 7, 1880; 85y.
Elizabeth McFadden, b. May 16, 1818; d. May 26, 1893.
Jane McFadden, wife of Samuel, d. Sept. 9, 1884; 85y. 9m. 6d.
Mary McFadden, wife of Benjamin, d. Sept. 9, 1882; 80y. 4m.
Samuel McFadden, d. Nov. 12, 1869; 84y.
Eleanor McKibben, first wife of George, d. Nov. 15, 1866; 58y.
Jane McKibben, second wife of George, d. Feb. 28, 1887; 66y.
George McKibben, b. Sept. 5, 1804; d. Dec. 27. 1891.
Samuel B. McKibben, d. April 7, 1866; 23y.
Margaret Mehollin, wife of Joseph, d. April 14, 1877; 88y.
John Mitchell, d. Sept. 26, 1865; 78y. 5m. 20d.
Mary Moffit, wife of Henry, d. Feb. 19. 1875; 77y.
Jane Moore, wife of Thomas, b. Oct. 3, 1806; d. Oct. 20, 1891.
Thomas Moore, b. Dec. 10, 1800; d. June 8, 1882.
Hannah Nash, wife of William, d. Feb. 15, 1876; 82y. 11m. 7d.
Margaret Ann Nash, wife of John, d. May 25, 1876; 52y. 5m.
Eliza Sloan, wife of John, b. May 15, 1818; d. Oct. 8, 1890.
John Sloan, b. Nov. 24, 1803; d. Sept. 19, 1878.
James Simpson, d. July 29, 1881; 68y. 2m. 18d.

Susanna Sproul, wife of John, d. July 29, 1870; 73y. 6m.
John A. Todd, d. Nov. 21, 1877; 68y. 5m. 4d.
Martha Todd, wife of Robert, d. Aug. 15. 1870; 70y.
Mary Todd, wife of J. A., d. Dec. 9, 1863; 61y.
Robert Todd, d. Oct. 13, 1882; 85y. 20d.

BURIALS IN DEERSVILLE GRAVEYARD.

(Those Born Before 1830.)

James Abraham, d. Nov. 16, 1857; 70y.
Sarah Abraham, wife of James, d. Nov. 11, 1844; 58y.
Hannah Adams, wife of Thomas, d. May 22, 1836; 39y.
Thomas Adams, d. Oct. 20, 1842; 71y. 11m. 19d.
George Baker, d. Jan. 12, 1877; 70y. 9m. 9d.
Jane Baker, wife of George, d. Nov. 10, 1867; 58y. 9m. 7d.
Dr. J. P. Barnes, d. April 6, 1852; 47y.
Jane Billingsley, wife of J. J., d. Oct. 1, 1881; 71y.
Deborah Bartlett, wife of Philip, d. Dec. 7, 1862; 41y.
Elizabeth Birney, wife of William, d. Nov. 3, 1871; 84y. 6m. 12d.
Hannah Birney, wife of John, d. Feb. 13, 1872; 65y. 1m. 28d.
John Birney, b. Sept. 9, 1808; d. Sept. 20, 1882.
Margaret Birney, wife of Wesley, d. Feb. 24, 1877; 63y. 4m. 7d.
Nancy Birney, wife of Letchworth, d. Oct. 4, 1885; 68y. 10m. 16d.
Wesley Birney, d. Feb. 3, 1864; 51y. 4m. 19d.
William Birney, d. Feb. 17, 1865; 83y. 7m. 11d.
Keziah Bliss, wife of Zadock, d. May 31, 1851; 65y. 1m. 17d.
Zadock Bliss, d. July 8, 1853; 65y. 4m. 12d.
Hannah Burcher, wife of Christopher, d. March 17, 1844; 34y. 2m. 3d.

William Cadwell, d. Dec. 27, 1850; 33y. 4m. 26d.
Leonard Carpenter, d. Feb. 11, 1842; 50y. 4m. 3d.
Mary Carpenter, wife of Leonard, d. Nov. 22, 1856; 57y. 7m. 18d.
Wilson Cawood, d. June 3, 1864; 72y.
William Clark, d. Oct. 1, 1847; 66y.
William Clendening, d. Sept. 15, 1867; 78y.
Elizabeth Coleman, wife of John, d. Aug. 1, 1856; 71y. 7m. 29d.
Finley Coleman, d. Dec. 19, 1887; 66y. 1m. 15d.
Ruth Conaway, d. April 16, 1845; 20y. 10m. 21d.
James Connel, d. Nov. 21, 1836; 60y. 5m. 6d.
Jemima Connel, wife of James, d. Oct. 10, 1850; 72y. 15d.
Sophia Crabtree, wife of G., b. July 31, 1828; d. Nov. 27, 1885.
John P. Cramblett, d. Dec. 22, 1858, 59y. 7m. 8d.
Margaret Cramblett, wife of John P., d. April 18, 1882; 81y. 10m. 4d.
Ellenor Crawford, wife of Josiah, d. May 8, 1883; 79y.
Josiah Crawford, d. Dec. 24, 1889; 80y. 8m. 23d.
John H. Curtis, d. March 2, 1880; 51y. 11m. 2d.
Sarah Czatt, wife of John, d. April 30, 1865; 36y. 4d.
Robert Dawson, b. Dec. 28, 1818; d. Dec. 14, 1883.
Thomas Dawson, d. Sept. 24, 1855; 39y.
Mary Dickey, wife of Benjamin, d Sept. 28, 1861; 61y.
Arnetta Donnell, d. June 14, 1878; 75y. 3m.
Biddy Donnell, d. Sept. 6, 1872; 93y.
Lydia Donnell, d. Nov 17, 1886; 79y. 1m. 15d.
Rachel A. Donnell, wife of Zaza, d. Oct. 20, 1864; 44y.
Anne Dunham, wife of Nathaniel, d. Aug. 4, 1896; 78y.
Nathaniel Dunham, d. June 18, 1869; 84y.
Jehile Eaton, d. April 6, 1852; 42y. 7m. 18d.

Sarah Eaton, wife of Jehile, d. Feb. 12, 1893; 75y. 10m. 24d.
Henry J. Edney, son of Robert and Mary, d. Oct. 18, 1845; 24y. 4m. 6d.
Mary Edney, wife of Robert, d. Sept. 6, 1860; 64y. 4m.
Robert J. Edney, d. Sept. 29, 1866; 74y. 2m. 3d.
Elizabeth Erwin, wife of Henry, d. Dec. 20, 1873; 56y. 10m. 25d.
Henry Erwin, d. April 26, 1897; 82y. 17d.
James Erwin, d. Oct. 28, 1845; 68y.
Louise Erwin, second wife of Thomas, d. May 9, 1863; 38y. 6m.
Rebecca Erwin, first wife of Thomas, d. Dec. 9, 1844; 27y.
William Fitzgerald, d. Feb. 8, 1850; 26y. 8m. 15d.
Claton Ford, d. Feb. 12, 1856; 60y. 23d.
Rachel A. Foust, wife of Elias, d. Feb. 21, 1854; 18y. 8m. 9d.
Eliza Jane Gardner, wife of Samuel, d. Jan. 28, 1845; 21y. 2m. 13d.
Elizabeth Garner, wife of James, d. April 15, 1898; 81y. 3m. 3d.
James Garner, d. March 19, 1888; 78y. 12d.
Elizabeth Gladman, wife of David, d. Feb. 22, 1895; 71y. 6m. 8d.
David Gladman, d. Jan. 26, 1888; 77y. 4m. 22d.
Mary J. Goodwin, wife of George, d. July 27, 1863; 43y. 1m. 28d.
Thomas Grandfell, d. April 23, 1845; 51y. 7m. 5d.
Benjamin Guthrie, d. March 9, 1886; 63y. 6m.
Jane Guthrie, second wife of Robert, d. June 3, 1870; 83y. 3m.
Nancy Guthrie, wife of Robert, d. Aug. 10, 1853; 30y. 24d.
Nancy Guthrie, wife of Nathaniel, d. May 21, 1859; 25y. 11m. 25d.
Robert Guthrie, d. Feb. 1, 1854; 68y. 3m. 21d.
Augustus Guyton, d. July 28, 1856; 31y. 10m. 5d.
Benjamin Guyton, b. June 7, 1820; d. April 3, 1896.
Catherine Guyton, wife of Elisha, d. Feb. 26, 1877; 86y. 3m.
Elanor Guyton, wife of Benjamin, b. May 24, 1823; d. March 28, 1896.

DEERSVILLE BURIALS

Elisha Guyton, d. March 25, 1875; 90y. 7m. 30d.
Charles Harding, d. May 7, 1845; 59y. 11m. 8d.
Margaret W. Harding, wife of John D., d. Jan. 16, 1824; 23y.
Levi Hayes, d. Oct. 14, 1884; 84y. 3m. 10d.
Sarah Hays, wife of Levi, d. Dec. 25, 1883; 72y. 8m.
20, 1836; 36y. 6m. 25d.
Edward Heath, d. Jan. 10, 1845; 85y.
Samuel Hedges, d. Aug. 30, 1850; 30y. 8m. 21d.
Harvey Heed, d. Nov. 26, 1898; 77y. 1m. 25d.
Fielding Hefling, son of John and Lousinah, b. Dec. 26, 1799; d. July
John Hefling, d. Jan. 13, 1859; 81y. 1m. 14d.
Lousinah H. Hefling, wife of John, d. Oct. 19, 1845; 72y. 7m.
Martha Hefling, wife of Noah, d. July 3, 1844; 28y. 2m. 9d.
Noah Hefling, d. Dec. 5, 1886; 73y. 10m. 3d.
Sarah Hefling, wife of Wesley, d. Sept. 26, 1856; 47y. 6m. 12d.
Wesley Hefling, d. June 3, 1857; 47y. 6m. 13d.
Ann Hellyer, d. Jan. 22, 1857; 78y.
Henry Hillyer, b. Oct. 7, 1818; d. Sept. 18, 1890.
Jehu W. Hines, d. April 28, 1863; 37y. 5m. 15d.
Joseph Hines, d. Dec. 27, 1866; 71y. 1m. 22d.
R. D. Hines, d. July 7, 1886; 67y.
William Hines, d. Feb. 10, 1845; 72y.
Mary Hitchcock, d. Nov. 14, 1890; 86y. 8m.
Elizabeth Hotz, wife of Adam, d. Oct. 26, 1857; 42y. 11m. 23d.
Matilda Howse, wife of William, d. March 7, 1863; 46y. 11m. 18d.
William Howse, d. Feb. 21, 1864; 54y. 6d.
John W. Iler, d. May 24, 1888; 88y. 8m. 10d.
Levina Iler, wife of John W., d. Nov. 27, 1847; 40y. 9m. 18d.
Elizabeth Irwin, d. Sept. 25, 1885; 60y. 8m. 25d.

Nevian Irwin, b. 1825; d. 1899; 73y. 6m. 6d.
Richard Irwin, d. Sept. 18, 1864; 41y. 10m. 20d.
William Johnson, d. Jan. 6, 1857; 76y. 5m. 17d.
Catherine Jumps, wife of John, d. Feb. 6, 1885; 47y. 6m. 17d.
John Jumps, d. Feb. 13, 1877; 50y.
Margaret Karr, wife of O. C., d. Aug. 5, 1850; 20y. 1m. 15d.
Elizabeth Lee, wife of John, d. May 30, 1869; 71y.
Jonathan Lee, d. April 30, 1885; 60y.
William Linsley, d. July 2, 1834; 43y.
Jacob C. Lukens, b. Jan. 30, 1805; d. May 24, 1884.
Julian Lukens, wife of Eli, d. April 3, 1866; 94y.
Sarah Lukens, wife of Jacob C., d. Feb. 24, 1886; 75y. 10m. 11d.
Margaret McCullough, wife of William, d. Sept. 29, 1845; 68y.
Rebecca McCullough, wife of John, d. Sept. 21, 1840; 28y. 4m. 28d.
William McCullough, d. Aug. 11, 1883; 72y.
Thomas McGonagle, d. June 23, 1860; 57y.
George McIlroy, d. May 28, 1887; 75y. 2m. 19d.
Nancy McIlroy, wife of George, d. April 9, 1893; 87y.
Elizabeth McMillan, wife of John, d. Oct. 24, 1882; 84y. 10m. 9d.
John McMillan, d. April 5, 1881; 81y 2m. 19d.
Joseph M. Marshall, d. Jan. 10, 1845; 35y. 7m. 20d.
Nancy Marshbank, wife of William, d. March 2, 1868; 81y.
Elizabeth Meldrum, daughter of Robert and Eliza, d. Sept. 19, 1836; 20y. 4d.
William Meldrum, d. March 24, 1847; 74y.
Albina Moore, wife of Hillyer, d. Sept. 7, 1856; 39y. 8m. 2d.
Mary J. P. Moore, wife of Silas, d. 1849; 22y.
Nancy Moore, d. Feb. 15, 1887; 59y. 11m. 14d.

Sarah C. Moore, wife of Aaron, d. April 5, 1875; 55y. 7m. 5d.
Nancy Miller, wife of William C., d. Aug 19, 1879; 77y.
William C. Miller, d. Nov. 12, 1872; 72y. 7m. 8d.
Martha Noble, wife of James, d. March 3, 1852; 50y.
Elizabeth Orr, wife of John, b. March, 1782; d. Feb. 25, 1883; 99y. 11m.
John Orr, b. in County Antrim, Ireland; d. Aug. 5, 1845; 70y. 2d.
Hiram Palmer, d. April 12, 1856; 48y. 5m. 11d.
Mary Palmer, wife of Hiram, d. April 23, 1858; 47y. 3d.
David Parmer, d. July 23, 1877; 59y. 9m. 4d.
Mary Petty, wife of Thornton, d. Feb. 11, 1856; 34y. 3m.
Albert Pittis, d. June 26, 1886; 45y. 2m. 6d.
Edward Pittis, d. Feb. 21, 1861; 48y. 17d.
Henry Pittis, d. March 4, 1870; 55y. 10m. 21d.
John Pittis, Sr., d. June 3, 1855; 81y.
Mary D. Pittis, wife of John, Sr., d. Oct. 18, 1860; 88y. 4m. 15d.
Dr. John Pittis, b. April 27, 1793, at Newport, Isle of Wight; d. April 11, 1884.
Nancy G. Pittis, wife of Henry, d. Sept. 23, 1862; 39y. 13d.
Robert Pittis, Sr., d. Dec. 8, 1858; 80y.
Robert Pittis, b. Nov. 24, 1803; d. June 9, 1869.
Sarah Pittis, wife of Robert, b. Oct. 2, 1808; d. May 23, 1887.
Sarah Pittis, wife of George, d. June 4, 1877; 57y. 11m. 2d.
Smith Pittis, b. July 17, 1804; d. Aug. 29, 1886.
John Poulson, d. Feb. 14, 1847; 83y. 10m. 23d.
John Poulson, d. Feb. 19, 1863; 50y. 9m. 26d.
Rachel Poulson, wife of John, d. April 21, 1876; 60y.
Susan Poulson, wife of A. Poulson, d. July 30, 1899; 73y. 8m. 5d.
Susanna Poulson, wife of John, d. Oct. 3, 1865; 83y. 10m. 17d.

Samuel Ramsey, d. June 6, 1881; 53y. 5m. 23d.
Joseph Rogers, d. Nov. 23, 1882; 76y. 10m. 4d.
Mary Rogers, wife of Joseph, d. March 6, 1863; 56y. 6m. 8d.
Amos Ross, d. Nov. 18, 1864; 59y. 11m. 8d.
Elizabeth Ross, wife of Amos, d. Sept. 21, 1868; 56y. 7m. 26d.
Charles Scott, d. April 18, 1864; 59y.
James Scott, b. April 1, 1832; d. March 15, 1893.
Margaret Scott, wife of Charles, d. Aug. 14, 1881; 70y. 11m. 26d.
Martha Simmons, wife of R. H., b. 1825; d. 1892; 67y.
Dr. R. H. Simmons, b. 1818; d. 1892; 74y.
Pleasant Simonton, second wife of R. L. Simonton, d. Jan. 27, 1893; 68y. 2m. 3d.
Sarah Simonton, wife of F. T., d. arch 29, 1881; 57y. 3m. 24d.
Sicily Simonton, wife of Rev. R. T., d. Nov. 25, 1865; 69y. 15d.
Alicia Smith, wife of John, d. April 7, 1860; 76y. 7m. 25d.
Anne Smith, wife of James P., d. June 21, 1876; 47y. 6m. 15d.
Robert Smith, d. Sept. 5, 1868; 54y. 4m. 24d.
W. H. Smith, d. June 1, 1873; 56y. 10m. 20d.
Rebecca Snee, wife of William, d. May 13, 1834; 29y.
John Spertzel, d. Dec. 16, 1867; 84y. 6m. 27d.
Mary Spertzell, wife of John, d. Nov. 7, 1880; 77y. 5m. 16d.
Mary Spiker, wife of William, b. July 17, 1827; d. Jan. 28, 1897.
William Spiker, b. July 27, 1828; d. Aug. 10, 1893.
Sarah Stallers, d. Jan. 25, 1848; 79y.
Martha Stevens, wife of Benjamin, d. June 21, 1871; 73y. 3m. 18d.
John Stewart, d. June 27, 1881; 74y. 5m.
Samuel Stewart, d. March 9, 1882; 72y. 8m. 14d.
Jane Stoneman, wife of John, d. Aug. 18, 1854; 43y. 5m. 3d.

FREEPORT BURIALS

James Strong, d. May 8, 1836; 53y. 6m. 18d.
Cornelius Vickers, d. March 3, 1877; 47y. 2m. 1d.
Harriet Vickers, wife of John, d. Sept. 29, 1856; 56y.
John Vickers, d. Oct. 20, 1868; 80y. 9m. 5d.
Elizabeth Wagers, wife of Joshua, d. June 26, 1845; 30y. 7m. 19d.
Jane Walker, wife of William, d. July 15. 1878; 75y. 1d.
Jane Walker, wife of Robert, d. March 9, 1880; 71y. 2m. 22d.
Robert Walker, d. Dec. 3, 1858; 60y.
William Walker, b. Aug. 20, 1806; d. April 27, 1886.
Bernard Weaver, d. June 24, 1871; 77y.
Gertrude Weaver, wife of Bernard, b. Dec 25, 1800; d. May 1, 1878; 77y. 4m. 6d.
John Weaver, b. Sept. 3, 1815; d. Oct. 2, 1854; 39y. 1m. 29d.
Sarah Weaver, wife of John, d. Nov. 10, 1884; 74y. 24d.
Louisa Welsh, wife of James, b. June 18, 1826; d. July 26, 1891.
Joseph T. White, d. April 23, 1876; 43y. 5m. 22d.
Elizabeth Wilson, wife of John, d. Oct. 27. 1871; 75y. 2m. 27d.
John Wilson, d. June 9, 1864; 67y. 8m. 25d.
James Wright, d. Dec. 25, 1836; 62y. 11m. 21d.
Mary Wright, wife of William, d. Feb. 5, 1851; 59y.
Mary Wyckoff, wife of Thomas, and daughter of John and Elizabeth Coleman, d. Feb. 13, 1886; 71y. 5m. 2d.
Nackey Yarnell, wife of John,, d. Dec. 5, 1862; 32y. 6m. 1d.
Mary J. Young, b. March 12, 1828; d. Jan. 19, 1886.
Mary J. Young, wife of Robert, d. Aug. 3, 1897; 60y.
Robert Young, d. Dec. 2, 1882; 76y. 11m. 20d.
Robert Young, d. Sept. 16, 1884; 62y. 7m. 5d.

BURIALS IN FREEPORT GRAVE-YARD.
(Those Born Before 1830.)

James Boles, d. Sept. 31, 1845; 71y.
James Boals, d. May 30, 1849; 39y.
Mary Boals, d. June 25, 1864; 60y.
Nancy Boles, wife of James, d. Lec. 5, 1862; 92y.
Thomas Brachen, d. July 1, 1876; 79y. 9m. 11d.
Hannah Buchanan, wife of W. L., d. Sept. 27, 1870; 74y. 28d.
Joseph S. Cook, d. April 10, 1857; 93y.
Margaret Cook, wife of Joseph S., d. Feb. 4, 1860; 92y. 1m. 11d.
Martha Dick, d. June 27, 1871; 59y.
Mary Finney, wife of R. P., b. March 28, 1825; d. Oct. 14, 1845.
Elizabeth Gillespie, wife of William, d. June 15, 1850; 62y. 8m. 14d.
Andrew Hoge, d. March 9, 1861; 45y.
Phebe Hoge, wife of Robert, d. Sept. 29, 1860; 93y. 6m.
Robert Hoge, d. Jan. 10, 1853; 52y. 7m. 11d.
Eliza Holliday, wife of Robert, d. Aug. 16, 1872; 71y. 7m. 21d.
Israel A. Holliday, d. May 25, 1878; 75y.
Robert Holliday, d. July 5, 1855; 62y. 11m. 4d.
Susan Holliday, wife of Israel, d. Oct. 28, 1867; 49y. 11m.
Mary Hutchison. wife of William, d. May 24, 1848; 42y. 7m. 10d.
Rebecca Johnson, wife of Thomas, d. Nov. 22, 1858; 56y. 11m. 23d.
Thomas Johnson, d. Nov. 14, 1871; 69y.
Elizabeth Leeper, wife of James, d. Jan. 22, 1860; 80y.
Moses Leeper, b. May 8, 1810; d. Sept. 4, 1880.
Rachel Leeper, wife of Moses, d. May 23, 1869; 68y.
Esther McCormick, wife of John, d. Sept. 30, 1863; 46y. 7d.
Johanna McCormick, wife of H. J., d. Dec. 2, 1863; 36y. 4m.
John McCormick, d. Nov. 10, 1869; 58y. 8m.
Margaret McCormick, wife of Thomas, d. June 25, 1861; 78y. 7m. 8d.

Rose McCormick, d. May 31, 1860; 45y.
Thomas McCormick, d. June 10, 1852; 27y. 9m. 29d.
Abel McCurdy, d. Oct. 26, 1846; 67y. 7m.
George McGee, d. Jan. 3, 1869; 84y.
Jane McGee, wife of George, d. June 21, 1857; 62y. 5m. 28d.
Amy Nash, wife of John, d. March 14, 1855; 85y.
John Palmer, d. May 1, 1869; 77y. 5m.
Rebecca Quillan, wife of Joshua, d. Sept. 4, 1861; 60y.
Christina Sapter, wife of John, d. May 17, 1855; 71y.
Henry Sapter, d. June 28, 1863; 35y. 5m. 8d.
Jacob Sapter, d. Sept. 9, 1846; 23y. 9m. 19d.
John Sapter, d. May 13, 1863; 81y.
Jonathan Thomas, d. Jan. 22, 1837; 52y. 5m. 27d.
Matthew Tennant, d. Jan. 11, 1853; 75y.
John Wilson, d. Dec. 14, 1866; 66y. 11m. 4d.
William Wilson, d. May 19, 1843; 30y.

BURIALS IN GREENMONT GRAVEYARD AT FREEPORT.

(Those Born Before 1830.)

Greenmont Graveyard is situated about half a mile east of Freeport.

William Adams, d. Jan. 8, 1881; 81y. 4m. 3d.
Joseph A. Bevan, d. Sept. 21, 1884; 65y. 7m. 2d.
Rebecca A. D. Black, wife of H. G., b. May 3, 1818; d. Nov. 25, 1881.
John Carruthers, d. June 6, 1872; 53y. 17d.
Nancy Carruthers, wife of John, d. Feb. 25, 1861; 69y. 5m. 15d.
Elijah Carver, d. Jan. 21, 1897; 86y. 6m. 4d.
Harriett Chaney, wife of Jacob, b. Aug. 24, 1824; d. July 22, 1895.
John Clark, d. Dec. 16, 1881; 78y. 11m.
Joshua Clark, Sr., d. Nov. 26, 1867; 88y.
Sally Clark, wife of Joshua, d. July 5, 1887; 57y. 6m.
Elias Cope, b. Sept. 4, 1811; d. Dec. 24, 1893.
Rachel Cope, wife of Elias, b. Jan. 29, 1814; d. May 16, 1891.
Ellen Curtis, b. Feb. 14, 1822; d. Aug. 16, 1896.
Lucinda Davidson, wife of Lewis H., b. Sept. 8, 1810; d. March 17, 1893.
Lewis Decker, d. Feb. 12, 1890; 73y. 5m. 26d.
Susan Ford, wife of James, d. Dec. 3, 1888; 76y.
Eliza Dean Forsythe, wife of Jesse, b. Aug. 25, 1828; d. Jan. 17, 1890.
Jesse Forsythe, b. Nov. 6, 1826; d. May 14, 1896.
Ann Green, wife of Samuel, d. June 14, 1892; 84y. 3d.
John Green, d. July 4, 1884; 92y.
Mary Green, wife of John, d. Feb. 12, 1883; 85y.
Samuel Green, Sr., d. June 2, 1879; 80y.
Thomas Green, b. May 12, 1826; d. April 22, 1894.
Prudence Harding, wife of James, d. Dec. 22, 1893; 85y.
Priscilla Hayes, wife of Thomas C., d. April 22, 1890; 71y. 1m. 27d.
Sophia Hopkins, wife of Thomas, d. Oct. 23, 1879; 52y.
Thomas Hopkins, d. Feb. 28, 1897; 75y. 8m. 7d.
Sarah Hutchinson, wife of William, d. April 3, 1883; 65y. 6m. 21d.
William Hutchinson, d. Sept. 27, 1884; 79y. 10m. 9d.
Caroline Johnson, wife of W. A. B., d. Jan. 18, 1888; 50y. 1d.
Matthew M. Knox, b. Dec. 26, 1826; d. Jan. 16, 1890.
Robert A. Latham, d. Dec. 14, 1865; 58y. 18d.
Susanna Latham, wife of Robert A., d. Dec. 23, 1890; 79y. 8m. 9d.
Mary E. McNamee, wife of Amzi, d. Dec 21, 1887; 61y. 4m. 13d.
Amy Miller, wife of Nathan, d. June 13, 1885; 73y. 5m.
Nathan Miller, d. Dec. 14, 1882; 76y. 10m.

John Niblick, d. Jan. 8, 1893; 85y. 9m. 9d.
Mary Niblick, daughter of John and Sally, d. Sept. 29, 1892; 60y.
Sally Niblick, wife of John, d. March 1, 1840; 32y.
Rebecca Perdue, wife of William, d. Jan. 11, 1892; 84y. 11m. 12d.
William Perdue, d. Jan. 17, 1892; 81y. 8m. 18d.
Adaline Pettay, wife of William C., d. Feb. 1, 1874; 53y.
James Reaves, b. April 18, 1818; d. June 12, 1893.
David Steadman, d. July 6, 1877; 80y.
Jacob Steele, b. Dec. 1, 1811; d. May 31, 1887.
Mary Ann Steele, wife of Jacob, b. Dec. 9, 1817; d. June 29, 1896.
Margaret N. White, b. 1809; d. April 26, 1892.

BURIALS IN METHODIST EPISCOPAL GRAVEYARD AT FREEPORT.

(Those Born Before 1830.)

Joseph Allen, d. April 27, 1863; 63y. 3m.
Rebecca A. F. Allen, wife of Joseph, d. Jan. 9, 1859; 62y. 11m. 14d.
Thomas Barrett, d. Nov. 19, 1874; 60y.
Rebecca Boyer, wife of William, d. April 13, 1850; 45y. 4m. 21d.
William Boyer, d. April 2, 1851; 53y. 1m.
Eliza Carver wife of Abner, d. July 23, 1855; 54y. 10m. 2d.
Samuel Colvin, d. Sept. 5, 1872; 82y.
Elijah W. Cree, son of J. and S., d. Oct. 1, 1843; 17y. 6m. 8d.
Elizabeth Cree, wife of R., d. March 7, 1841; 78y. 5d.
John Dewitt, d. Sept. 13, 1856; 75y.
Ann Hatton, wife of William, d. Aug. 7, 1845; 31y.
Clarissa Hollett, wife of George, d. March 13, 1845; 31y. 1m. 24d.
John J. Hudson, b. Dec. 1, 1822; d. March 4, 1830.
Hannah Kelly, wife of S. W., d. Dec. 31, 1853; 28y. 27d.

Mary Ann Lakin, wife of Thomas N., d. Aug. 19, 1843; 27y. 4m. 3d.
Hannah Maddon, daughter of E. and S., d. April 7, 1835; 5y. 8m. 18d.
Ann Miller, d. Feb. 1, 1852; 32y.
Rachel Miller d. Aug. 13, 1847; 49y.
Thomas P. Moore, b. Feb. 11, 1765; d. Jan. 20, 1844; 78y. 11m. 22d.
Susan Parsons, wife of B. L., d. Oct. 14, 1873; 65y. 5m. 29d.
Comfort Phillips, wife of Richard, d. Oct., 1835; 60y.
Jacob Romans, d. March 6, 1876; 67y.
Priscilla Shugart, wife of J. M., d. Oct. 20, 1879; 53y. 10m. 15d.
Andrew S. Steele, d. Feb. 2, 1887; 73y. 10m. 15d.
Elizabeth Steele, wife of Andrew, d. Nov. 16, 1887; 73y. 1m. 16d.
Susannah F. Swaney, wife of Timothy, d. May 3, 1867; 64y.
Timothy Swaney, d. May 1, 1864; 70y.
Nancy Vallow, daughter of Stephen and Katherine, d. Jan. 16, 1829; 1y. 4m. 1d.
Susannah Vallow, daughter of Stephen and Katherine, d. May 26, 1824; 16y. 6m. 15d.

BURIALS IN GEORGETOWN GRAVEYARD.

(Those Born Before 1830.)

George Eli, b. Feb. 28, 1827; d. Oct. 4, 1885.
Pheobe Eli, wife of George, b. Sept. 7, 1828; d. March 15, 1889.
Beulah Furbay, wife of James, b. June 17, 1814; d. Jan. 8, 1889.
James Furbay, b. June 23, 1805; d. July 5, 1883.
Annie Jackson, wife of Cyrus, d. Sept. 22, 1876; 73y.
Cyrus Jackson, d. Feb. 20, 1876; 76y.
Elizabeth Johnson, wife of Hugh, d. May 27, 1880; 95y.
Hugh Johnson, d. Sept. 5, 1867; 79y. 6m. 17d.
Stewart Johnson, d. July 26, 1871; 58y. 7m. 4d.
Isaac Lewis, d. July 25, 1870; 57y. 8m. 6d.

Lydia Lewis, wife of Isaac, d. Jan. 12, 1880; 65y. 9m. 15d.
Jonathan Martin, b. June 11, 1825; d. May 19, 1886.
James Munts, d. Feb. 3, 1890: 61y.
George Smyth, b. July 5, 1827; d. Sept. 1898.
Sarah Smyth, wife of George, b. Jan. 6, 1831; d. Oct. 12, 1894.
Elizabeth Wright, wife of William, b. Aug. 30, 1822; d. May 20, 1892.
William Wright, d. June 31, 1886; 71y.

BURIALS IN HARRISVILLE GRAVEYARD.

(Those Born Before 1830.)

Joshua Adams, b. Oct. 26, 1813; d. May 2, 1876; 65y. 5m. 6d.
Mary A. Anderson, wife of James, d. Dec. 2, 1861; 37y. 8m. 5d.
Mary Barkhurst, wife of William, d. Jan. 5, 1882; 50y.
Sarah Barkhurst, wife of Benjamin, d. Dec. 31, 1890; 86y. 10m. 25d.
James W. Beck, b. Nov. 22, 1828; d. May 8, 1897.
Martha Beck, b. Sept. 19, 1805; d. July 25, 1892.
Sarah Boals, wife of William, d. April 8. 1887; 61y. 3m. 8d.
Catherine Braden, wife of Robert, d. June 8, 1863; 74y. 7m. 24d.
Eliza Braden, wife of William, d. Aug. 27, 1871; 53y.
John Calderhead, b. Dec. 14, 1805; d. March 28, 1882.
Nancy Calderhead, wife of John, d. April 13, 1882; 82y.
Lavenia Clawson, d. July 25, 1892; 76y.
Mary Ann Coulter, wife of Thomas, d. Dec. 6, 1887; 73y. 5m. 28d.
Margaret Duff, wife of Thomas, b. Feb. 2, 1819; d. Aug. 25, 1890.
Thomas Duff, b. Feb. 20, 1802; d. July 1, 1878.
William L. Duff, d. Feb. 5, 1856; 46y. 5m.
Samuel Elliott, d. Feb. 6, 1884; 67y.
Sarah H. Elliott, wife of Samuel, d. July 3, 1892; 64y.

Dennis Fisher, d. March 5, 1878; 66y. 9m. 17d.
Elizabeth Fisher, d. Oct. 19, 1884; 62y.
Barnard Geesey, b. Feb. 15, 1816; d. Feb. 4, 1896.
Julia Geesey, wife of Barnard, b. May 27, 1818; d. April 23, 1897.
Catherine G. Hawthorn, wife of John, d. Aug. 3, 1873; 60y. 8m. 10d.
David Hawthorn, b. Jan. 24, 1821; d. Aug. 2, 1899.
Jane A. Hawthorn, wife of Samuel, b. June 19, 1822; d. Jan. 19, 1885.
John Hawthorn, b. Feb. 24, 1786; d. Nov. 7, 1874.
Margaret E. Hawthorn, wife of David, b. June 19, 1828; d. Dec. 31, 1892.
Mary A. Hawthorn, wife of William, b. Feb. 15, 1822; d. Dec. 3, 1892.
Samuel Hawthorn, b. April 22, 1797; d. Aug. 16, 1883.
William Hawthorn, b. March, 1817; d. Jan. 20, 1896.
Alexander Henderson, b. July 24, 1797; d. Dec. 30, 1880.
Hannah Henderson, wife of Alexander, b. Dec. 12, 1798; d. June 29, 1881.
James Henderson, d. June 16, 1873; 46y. 9m. 10d.
John Henderson, b. Sept. 14, 1815; d. April 21, 1898.
Marinda Henderson, wife of Matthew, d. March 1, 1887; 75y. 3m. 28d.
Matthew Henderson, d. Sept. 25, 1862; 95y. 9m. 21d.
Samuel Henderson, b. April 25, 1811; d. Feb. 18, 1895.
William Henderson, b. July 14, 1824; d. April 23, 1888.
William H. Henderson, d. Oct. 1, 1878; 57y. 6m. 1d.
William P. Henderson, son of Matthew and Marinda, d. May 16, 1869; 37y. 3m. 23d.
Enoch J. Jones, b. Oct. 25, 1825; d. Nov. 24, 1879.
Martha J. Jones, wife of Enoch, b. Dec. 27, 1826; d. July 14, 1890.
William Kerr, d. Dec. 3, 1866; 50y. 11m. 22d.
Eliza Jane Lemmon, wife of William, d. Dec. 31, 1884; 65y.

Margaret Lemmon, wife of Griffith, d. Dec. 1, 1872; 76y.
Ephraim McCleary, b. Oct. 19, 1810; d. April 28, 1874.
Mary H. McCleary, wife of Ephraim, b. Aug. 22, 1818; d. May 19, 1886.
John McLaughlin, d. April 25, 1874; 55y.
Nancy McLaughlin, wife of John, b. Oct. 2. 1824; d. Nov. 7, 1898.
John A. Major, b. Oct. 3, 1812; d. June 6, 1885.
Elizabeth Miller, wife of John G., b. Jan. 20, 1830; d. Jan. 22, 1892.
John G. Miller, b. June 22, 1822; d. April 12, 1894.
Agnes E. Moore, wife of John, b. 1829; d. 1899; 70y.
John Moore, b. 1818; d. 1886; 68y.
Mary Moore, wife of Samuel, d. April 2, 1863; 62y.
Nancy Moore, d. Jan. 13, 1881; 57y.
Samuel Moore, d. Aug. 16, 1872; 82y.
George G. Morgan, b. May 18, 1831; d. Oct. 9, 1869.
Levi Morgan, b. March 1, 1829; d. April 7, 1892.
Philip Morgan, b. Sept. 22, 1819; d. Feb. 7, 1892.
Margaret J. Morris, wife of Thomas, b. Feb. 10, 1820; d. Nov. 18, 1887.
Elizabeth Newlin, wife of James P., b. Nov. 7, 1820; d. Sept. 7, 1873.
James P. Newlin, b. Dec. 18, 1817; d. Jan. 10, 1882.
Julia A. Nibble, b. Nov. 14, 1830; d. May 7, 1884.
Jane O'Hara, wife of John, d. Oct. 23, 1868; 79y.
Ann B. Patton, wife of John W., b. July 25, 1820; d. Feb. 10, 1883.
Jacob Peterman, b. March 25, 1827; d. May 21, 1890.
Agnes Rea, wife of David, d. Aug. 5, 1875; 60y.
John Robb, d. March 30, 1882; 68y. 3d.
Eli Seebirt, b. 1827; d. 1899; 72y.
Sarah A. Seebirt, wife of Eli, d. Oct. 21, 1876; 48y. 7m. 17d.
Jane Sloan, wife of William, d. Sept. 5, 1854; 69y.
Mary Jane Sloan, wife of Samuel, d. Oct. 11, 1870; 48y.

William Sloan, d. July 8, 1859; 73y.
David Smith, b. June 8, 1819; d. Aug. 22, 1894.
Henry T. Smith, b. Dec. 15, 1828; d. Feb. 21, 1872.
Joshua P. Watson, b. March 21, 1802; d. July 27, 1882.
Jemimia M. Webster, wife of Nayler, b. Jan. 31, 1806; d. Feb., 1883; 77y. 1m. 3d.
Nayler Webster, b. Oct. 4, 1810; d. June 12, 1883; 82y. 8m. 7d.
Andrew Wilkin, b. April 20, 1801; d. May 30, 1884.
Dr. A. B. Wilkin, b. 1826; d. 1894.
Mary Wilkin, wife of Andrew, d. Sept. 20, 1887; 86y.
Elias Yost, d. Dec. 2, 1896; 91y.
Kezia Yost, wife of Elias, d. June 12, 1887; 66y. 1m. 17d
Martha L. Yost, wife of Isaac, b. Sept. 9, 1806; d. April 26, 1891.
Isaac Yost, b. July 5, 1799; d. Feb. 19, 1892.

BURIALS IN HARRISVILLE METHODIST EPISCOPAL GRAVE-YARD.

(Those Born Before 1830.)

Harmon Anderson, d. Aug. 26, 1865; 46y. 1 m. 2 d.
John Anderson, b. Dec. 27, 1815; d. Aug. 29, 1899.
Mary Anderson, wife of John, b. Jan. 19, 1826; d. Sept. 2, 1896.
Charles Barkhurst, d. March 19, 1851; 76y.
Mary G. Comley, wife of Dr. J. W. d. June 27, 1863; 30 y.
Hannah J. Crawford, daughter of J. and R., d. Feb., 1833; 4y. 8m.
Joseph Crawford, d. Sept. 22, 1829; 29 y. 4 m. 28d.
Joseph Crawford, son of J. and R., d. Sept., 1832; 2y. 4m.
John N. Denny, d. March 23, 1880 69 y. 10m. 18d.
James Drummond, d. Jan. 22, 1849; 48y. 2m. 20d.

Lydia A. Drummond, wife of James, d. March 26, 1847; 42y.
John Dunkin, d. Aug. 6, 1829; 51y. 8m. 8d.
Alcinda Dutton, wife of Robert, d. June 21, 1854; 23y. 2m.
John F. Elliott, d. Feb. 20, 1888; 66y. 7m. 9d.
Sarah J. Elliott, wife of John F., d. Feb. 9, 1883; 59y. 5m. 19d.
John Graham, d. March 13, 1865; 83y.
Mary Lovett, wife of George, b. Jan. 30, 1814; d. May 4, 1840.
Benjamin McCabe, d. June 27, 1846; 35y.
Josiah Mercer, d. Sept. 27, 1864; 49y. 7m. 27d.
Rebecca Mercer, wife of Josiah, b. Sept. 4, 1815; d. Jan. 31, 1881.
Catherine Moore, wife of W., b. May 11, 1792; d. Sept. 13, 1846.
Sarah Mowder, wife of Jacob, b. June 24, 1815; d. May 28, 1845.
Margaret W. Naylor, wife of D. K., d. Sept. 21, 1878; 51y. 5m. 15d.
Frances Patterson, d. Oct. 12, 1833; ——y. 11m. 17d.
Mary Ruth, wife of P., d. July 8, 1848; 44y. 8m. 10d.
Mary M. Ruth, b. Dec. 21, 1831; d. Aug. 12, 1854.
Elizabeth Smith, wife of Ephraim, d. Sept. 6, 1872; 75y. 5m. 23d.
Ephraim Smith, d. July 11, 1843; 50y. 6m. 9d.
John Summer, d. Feb. 18, 1856; 66y.
Elizabeth Toland, d. July 5, 1854; 35y. 1m. 13d.
Jane Toland, wife of Joseph S., b. June 20, 1820; d. Dec. 6, 1898.
Joseph S. Toland, b. March 24, 1816; d. March 19, 1893.
Sarah Toland, wife of John, d. May 31, 1846; 60y. 2 d.
Harriet Walker, wife of Richard, d. April 9, 1877; 69y. 2m. 27d.
Elizabeth Weaver, wife of G. M., d. May 27, 1860; 63y.
Charles White, d. Aug. 27, 1888; 76y. 4m. 29d.
Thomas White, d. July 17, 1846; 62y.
James H. Wilson, d. Oct. 5, 1850; 29y. 9m. 19d.

BURIALS IN HOPEDALE GRAVE-YARD.

(Those Born Before 1830.)

Parkinson Betz, b. Jan. 7, 1822; d. March 16, 1898.
Lee S. Burton, d. May 27, 1882; 73y.
Mary Burton, wife of Lee S., d. Oct. 30, 1862; 47y.
Eliza J. Cassel, wife of John W., b. Nov. 20, 1825; d. May 5, 1892.
John W. Cassell, b. Dec. 27, 1821; d. June 29, 1898.
Alexander Denning, b. 1809; d. 1857.
Margaret Denning, wife of Alexander, b. 1808; d. 1878.
Michael Fogle, d. Sept. 17, 1867; 75y. 6m.
Sarah A. Fogle, wife of Michael, d. Feb. 27, 1877; 80y.
John Frazier, b. June 15, 1822; d. March 7, 1895.
Mary Galbraith, b. Nov. 9, 1824; d. May 28, 1885.
Charles Harrah, d. June 29, 1882; 74y.
Mary Harrah, wife of Charles, d. April 23, 1879; 69y.
Joseph Holmes, b. May 12, 1815; d. March 7, 1891.
W. B. Hunt, b. Sept. 12, 1815; d. March 31, 1900; 85y. 5m. 12d.
James Knox, d. April 19, 1870; 79y.
Sarah Knox, wife of James, d. July 31, 1865; 71y.
Andrew McNeely, b. July 10, 1774, in Pa.; d. in Hopedale, Oct. 1, 1858.
Jane Marchbank, b. July 21, 1812; d. Oct. 15, 1891.
William Marchbank, d. Dec. 15, 1886; 65y. 11m. 8d.
Ann Miller, wife of Enogh, d. Dec. 23, 1871; 74y.
Caroline Miller, daughter of Enogh, d. July 5, 1880; 52y.
Enogh Miller, d. Sept. 15, 1874; 85y.
Bethia Paul, wife of Samuel, d. March 6, 1858; 45y. 2m. 18d.
Samuel Paul, d. July 24, 1890; 77y. 1m. 18d.
Hannah Skelly, wife of Robert, b. 1797; d. July 27, 1878; 81y.
Robert Skelly, b. July 4, 1788; d. Aug. 31, 1868.

Eliza J. Watson, wife of John D., b. July 23, 1823; d. March 4, 1893.
Samuel Young, d. Jan. 22, 1882; 66y. 1m.

BURIALS IN MOOREFIELD GRAVEYARD.
(Those Born Before 1830.)

Elizabeth Adams, wife of Samuel,; 77y. 7m. 1d.
John Adams, d. March 1, 1835; 60y.
Rachel Adams, wife of John, d. Aug. 25, 1851; 75y. 3m. 9d.
Samuel Adams, d. Nov. 17, 1880; 74y. 10m. 1d.
Sarah Barlow, wife of Elisha, d. June 17, 1841; 40y. 9m. 23d.
Richard H. Barnes, d. June 5, 1879; 61y.
Susan J. Barnes, wife of Richard H., d. July 21, 1874; 54y.
Hannah J. Brokaw, wife of Jesse, d. June 13, 1877; 47y. 10m. 16d.
Harvey Butler, b. Aug. 27, 1829; d. Sept. 3, 1894.
Mary E. Butler, wife of Harvey, d. Feb. 4, 1892; 59y.
Elizabeth Campbell, wife of William, b. April 28, 1811; d. Sept. 11, 1895.
Frances Caves, wife of John, d. Nov. 28, 1837; 42y. 7m. 8d.
John Caves, d. Sept. 27, 1837; 43y. 5m. 29d.
Samuel Caves, son of John and Frances, d. Dec. 31, 1845; 28y. 8m. 26d.
Peter Conner, d. Dec. 26, 1847; 56y. 7m. 26d.
James Cooper, d. July 29, 1834; 30y.
Leah Christy, wife of Richard B., b. Sept. 17, 1826; d. Dec. 7, 1898.
Richard B. Christy, b. May 30, 1818; d. Dec. 13, 1898.
Asa Crawford, d. Jan. 26, 1852; 48y. 7m. 3d.
Nicholas H. Familton, d. Jan. 2, 1852; 27y.
Isaac Gardner, d. Aug. 20, 1853; 58y.
Nancy Gardner, wife of Isaac, d. April 2, 1838; 38y.

James Harvey, Sr., d. Sept. 28, 1831; 83y. 6m. 28d.
Susanna Harvey, wife of James, Sr., d. Sept. 24, 1863; 71y. 3m. 27d.
Wilton Harvey, b. Jan. 24, 1816; d. Dec. 30, 1885.
Henry Johnson, d. Aug. 23, 1858; 67y.
Catherine Johnson, wife of Henry, d. Aug. 23, 1863; 77y. 7d.
William Johnson, Sr., d. May 1, 1849; 79y.
Absalom Jones, b. March 25, 1807; d. May 8, 1840.
Edward Jones, d. May 22, 1874; 66y.
C. G. Kennedy, b. March 26, 1808; d. Feb. 11, 1886.
Mary Kennedy, wife of C. G., b. May 8, 1812; d. May 11, 1890;
R. M. Kennedy, d. June 8, 1887; 84y. 3m. 3d.
Tabitha Kinsey, wife of Charles, d. March 16, 1841; 34y. 7m. 18d.
Nancey Knight Lamb, wife of John Knight, and later of John Lamb, d. Oct. 17, 1837; 67y.
Anne Latham, b. July 2, 1814; d. Aug. 8, 1894.
Francis Latham, d. March 21, 1853; 36y.
John Latham, d. March 4, 1836; 63y.
Lucy Latham, wife of John, d. Nov. 8, 1876; 100y.
Alexander McBride, d. Feb. 12, 1854; 40y. 20d.
Abigail McCoy, first wife of Francis, b. Oct. 10, 1821; d. Feb. 13, 1877.
Catherine McCoy, second wife of Francis, b. March 4, 1826; d. Dec. 28, 1877.
Francis McCoy, b. Aug. 12, 1813; d. May 12, 1893.
William McGee, d. March 4, 1854; 34y. 11m.
Sarah Mace, wife of John, d April 16, 1832; 33y.
Abraham Mansfield, d. Jan. 10, 1836; 26y. 6m. 6d.
Christopher Mansfield, d. Dec. 3, 1845; 66y.
Sarah Mansfield, wife of Christopher, d. Sept. 24, 1864; 77y. 5m. 21d.
Malinda Martin, daughter of Samuel and Catherine Skinner, b. April 7, 1818; d. Sept. 15, 1864.

Elias J. Mills, d. April 3, 1837; 70y.
Elias Mills, b. June 27, 1812; d. Oct. 18, 1893.
Elizabeth L. Mills, d. Oct. 29, 1871; 49y. 10m. 29d.
Isabel Jane Mills, wife of Elias, d. May 21, 1849; 29y. 9m. 14d.
Mary J. Mills, wife of Elias, b. Oct. 3, 1822; d. June 21, 1895.
Nancy Ann Mills, wife of Elias J.; 86y.
Reuben Mills, d. Aug. 7, 1884; 67y.
John J. Moore, d. July 24, 1836; 26y. 6m. 8d.
John T. Moore, b. 1813; d. Oct. 23, 1898.
Lydia Moore, wife of William, b. June 6, 1813; d. Oct. 13, 1896.
Sarah Moore, wife of John T., b. 1819; d. Sept. 4, 1891.
William Moore, b. Oct. 4, 1811; d. Jan. 4, 1893.
Elizabeth Picket, wife of Peter, d. Oct. 31, 1857; 59y.
Peter Picket, d. Jan. 14, 1854; 66y. 9m. 4d.
Mary Pumphrey, wife of Elijah, d. April 24, 1855; 71y. 9m. 6d.
Abram Riley, d. Dec. 1, 1880; 80y. 3m. 24d.
Gemimah Riley, wife of Abram, d. Sept. 12, 1865; 62y. 5m. 17d.
Mary Riley, wife of John, d. Feb., 1844; 75y.
Nancy Riley, wife of George, d. Sept. 2, 1870; 45y. 3m. 1d.
Rebecca Riley, wife of John C., d. Aug 12, 1869; 43y.
Elizabeth Russell, wife of James, d Dec. 2, 1869; 86y.
Harriett Russell, wife of John, d. June 20, 1880; 68y. 1m. 23d.
James Russell, d. April 21, 1836; 91y.
John Russell, d. Sept. 14, 1846; 65y.
Catherine Skinner, wife of Samuel, b. Aug. 14, 1796; d. April 3, 1885.
Samuel Skinner, b. Jan. 26, 1794; d. June 2, 1860.
Elizabeth Thompson, wife of Robert, d. March 27, 1889; 87y. 10m. 22d.
Robert Thompson, d. March 18, 1876; 37y. 7m. 16d.
Charles Toner, d. Feb. 25, 1862; 64y. 10m.
Martha Toner, wife of Charles, d. July 14, 1874; 83y. 7m. 15d.
Mary L. Umstot, b. Aug. 29, 1811; d. Oct. 11, 1890.
Dr. James W. Wherry, b. May 23, 1821; d. Jan. 30, 1896.
Joseph Wherry, d. Feb. 9, 1862; 47y.
Levi Wherry, d. Aug. 3, 1868; 80y.
Levi D. Wherry, d. Sept. 7, 1849; 24y. 11m. 23d.
Susanna Wherry, wife of Levi, d. Aug. 21, 1854; 64y. 4m. 29d.
Ann Williams, wife of William, d. Feb. 2, 1865; 70y. 8m. 17d.
Benoni Williams, d. Aug. 11, 1863; 57y.
Mary L. Williams, daughter of William and Ann, d. July 1, 1845; 21y. 10m. 23d.
William Williams, d. May 9, 1857; 70y.
Elijah Willison, d. Aug 28, 1884; 73y. 7m. 6d.
Zillah Willison, first wife of Elijah, d. April 24, 1871; 86y.
Mary Willison, second wife of Elijah, d. May 4, 1872; 62y.
James Wilson, Sr., d. Aug. 7, 1850; 66y.
Maria Wilson, b. Aug. 30, 1822; d. June 17, 1897.
Sarah Ann Woodford, wife of J., d. Feb. 23, 1870; 58y. 3m. 28d.

BURIALS IN SCIO GRAVEYARD,

(Those Born Before 1830.)

Marcy A. Beatty, wife of Thomas, d. May 30, 1897; 64y. 11m. 11d.
William Birney, d. July 26, 1890; 82y. 5m. 12d.
J. M. Bradford, b. 1820; d. 1898.
Elizabeth Evans, wife of James, d. Feb. 16, 1890; 87y. 10m. 27d.
James Evans, d. Nov. 2, 1853; 60y. 4m. 26d.
William Givin, b. Aug. 5, 1820; d. May 21, 1898.
Francis Grace, b. Feb. 28, 1818; d. March 3, 1895.
Hetty Grace, wife of Francis, b. Feb. 15, 1825; d. Feb 12, 1892.

SCIO BURIALS

Elizabeth Groghan, wife of Jesse, d. April 12, 1878; 54y. 10m. 4d.
Margaret Heron, wife of William, d. March 24, 1874; 47y. 11m.
William Heron, d. Sept. 27, 1894; 67y. 10m. 19d.
Elizabeth Hines, wife of George, d. July 25, 1891; 70y. 5m. 24d.
George Hines, d. Sept. 4, 1879; 62y. 7m. 15d.
James Houser, b. Jan. 7, 1816; d. Oct. 9, 1889.
Ruth E. Houser, wife of James, b. Sept. 12, 1824; d. July 26, 1893.
Joshua Jackson, d. April 22, 1873; 51y. 1m. 12d.
John McKlveen [McElveen], d. Feb. 26, 1884; 65y. 11m.
Joseph McKlveen, b. 1824; d. April 10, 1887.
Mary McKlveen, b. March 13, 1822; d. Oct. 27, 1897.
Mary J. McKlveen, wife of Joseph, b. Dec. 17, 1830; d. Nov. 9, 1891.
Nancy McKlveen, b. 1828; d. Feb. 28, 1890.
Rachel McKlveen, wife of Thomas, d. March 18, 1856; 68y.
Thomas McKlveen, d. May 4, 1868; 85y.
J. Rumsey, b. March 14, 1825; d. March 28, 1896; 71y. 14d.
Rebecca A. Stephenson, wife of William H. H., d. Dec. 18, 1888; 78y.
William H. H Stephenson, d. March 5, 1896; 82y. 5m. 18d.
Bazil Thompson, b. Aug. 6, 1813; d Aug. 4, 1895.
Peter Trushel, b. Maq 21, 1831; d Aug. 30, 1896.
Susannah Trushel, wife of Peter, b. April 10, 1837; d. April 16, 1897.
Biddy G. Weight, wife of George A., b. Sept. 10, 1821; d. Feb. 11, 1888.
George A. Weight, b. Nov. 25, 1823; d. June 4, 1891.
Arrabella Whittiker, wife of James, d. Jan. 26, 1867; 81y. 8m. 25d.
James Whittiker, d. April 10, 1869; 79y. 6m.
Thomas Whittaker, b. Sept. 20, 1823; d. March 5, 1896.

BURIALS IN SCIO METHODIST EPISCOPAL GRAVEYARD.

(Those Born Before 1830.)

Elizabeth Beadle, wife of John, d. Jan. 15, 1875; 84y. 9m.
John Beadle, d. March 10, 1862; 74y. 9m. 15d.
Rachel Brake, wife of William, d. Aug. 28, 1878; 68y.
William Brake, d. Feb., 1874; 76y.
Ann Catcott, wife of Edward, d. Feb. 26, 1860; 67y. 5d.
Edward Catcott, d. Jan. 21, 1879; 5Cy. 5m. 16d.
Ann M. Creal, wife of John, d. Feb. 21, 1859; 65y. 3m. 21d.
John Creal, d. May 14, 1871; 85y. 13d.
George Foster, b. Sept. 24, 1794; d. June 8, 1849.
Jane Foster, second wife of George, b. Oct. 14, 1809; d. June 16, 1889.
Jerusha Foster, first wife of George, b. Oct. 25, 1797; d. Sept., 1836.
Ellen Harrison, wife of Joseph, d. April 28, 1853; 45y. 4m. 12d.
Joseph Harrison, d. April 13, 1878; 76y. 3m. 12d.
Christopher Hartley, d. Feb. 28, 1864; 86y.
Mary Hartley, wife of Christopher, d. Nov. 1, 1864; 84y.
Elvira Jolley, wife of Philip, d. Aug. 11, 1871; 45y. 10m. 2d.
William McCarroll, d. March 2, 1842; 52y.
John McDonaugh, d. Jan. 10, 1854; 67y. 1m. 4d.
Elizabeth McLandsborough, wife of John, b. in Otley, Yorkshire, Eng., d. Feb. 13. 1839; 39y. 7m. 15d.
John McLandsborough, Sr., b. in Galloway, Scotland; d. March 14, 1857; 74y. 8m. 7d.
Jonathan Markley, d. May 24, 1878; 71y. 3m.
Thomas Moore, d. April 9, 1866; 80y. 9m. 25d.
Mary Ann Neighbors, wife of Henry, d. Jan. 26, 1860; 43y. 6m. 29d.
James M. Patterson, son of J. and M., d. June 18, 1849; 18y. 9m. 28d.
Eunice Scott, wife of James F., d Feb. 28, 1849; 21y. 9m.

Jane Scott, wife of W. H., d. Dec. 18, 1866; 18y. 7m. 12d.
Christopher Somerville, d. Sept. 21, 1863; 50y. 6m.
Jacob Wortman, d. Sept. 8, 1843; 74y. 10m.
Sarah Wortman, wife of Jacob, d. Dec. 15, 1836; 66y. 11m.

BURIALS IN SMYRNA GRAVE-YARD.

(Those Born Before 1830.)

Ann Baker, wife of Christian, d. July 5, 1852; 82y.
Christian Baker, d. Aug. 20, 1832; 66y.
John Baker, b. Sept. 10, 1795; d. July 24, 1835; 39y. 10m. 5d.
Rosanna Baker, wife of Joseph, d. June 1, 1880; 63y. 2m. 13d.
David Bendure, d. Nov. 6, 1886; 72y. 7m. 1d.
Sarah Bendure, wife of David, d. Aug. 28, 1887; 71y. 7m. 7d.
Brandus Beths, d. March 18, 1870; 64y. 24d.
Sarah Beths, wife of Brandus, d. Nov. 27, 1880; 76y.
Mary Brown, wife of John P., d. May 24, 1874; 74y.
Elizabeth Campbell, wife of Robert, d. Nov. 18, 1875; 76y. 10m. 2d.
Hiram Cecil, d. Jan. 25, 1882; 60y. 1m. 13d.
Susanna Cecil, wife of Hiram, d. Sept. 21, 1883; 61y. 8m. 18d.
Israel Chandler, d. Oct. 8, 1872; 58y. 6m. 2d.
Abigail Criringer, wife of J. W., d. Oct. 30, 1873; 61y. 5m. 18d.
Robert Davis, b. Aug. 27, 1830; d. Nov. 5, 1895.
George Gray, d. Sept. 19, 1875; 80y.
Matilda Gray, wife of George, d. Feb. 10, 1867; 70y. 24d.
William Gray, d. Oct. 13, 1853; 35y. 6m. 29d.
Barbara Hall, wife of Hiram, b. Jan. 18, 1824; d. March 21, 1897.
Mary Hall, wife of Thomas, d. Oct. 15, 1872; 67y. 2m. 13d.
Thomas Hall, d. July 21, 1876; 72y. 1m. 14d.
Elizabeth Henry, d. April 5, 1876; 68y.
Catherine Howser, wife of John G., b. 1806; d. Jan. 19, 1875.
John G. Howser, b. 1801; d. Jan. 25, 1873.
Ann Delina Lamb, wife of Lawrence, d. Nov. 21, 1872; 48y. 8m. 8d.
Rachel Larrimore, wife of Warren, d. June 5, 1853; 34y. 5m. 1d.
Warren J. Larrimore, b. Jan. 4, 1816; d. Jan. 20, 1898; 82y.
Jacob Lightell, d. Sept. 29, 1879; 76y. 5m. 4d.
David McClelland, d. Feb. 5, 1872; 61y. 10m. 12d.
Mary A. McClelland, wife of David, d. Jan. 6, 1860; 37y. 10m. 17d.
Isabella McCotter, b. Feb. 1, 1818; d. March 25, 1896.
Sarah McCotter, d. Jan. 20, 1874; 80y. 7m. 2d.
William McCotter, b. April 27, 1820; d. March 17, 1891.
Francis Medley, June 6, 1874; 94y.
Elizabeth Mollett, wife of Joseph, d. May 21, 1857; 36y. 11m. 17d.
Jesse H. Moore, d. Oct. 30, 1890; 70y. 2m. 2d.
Margaret Moore, wife of Jesse H., d. June 18, 1875; 56y.
James Passmore, d. Oct. 12, 1858; 44y. 8m. 2d.
Catherine Phipps, wife of Elias, d. July 5, 1869; 39y. 5m. 24d.
Therine Tipton, wife of William, d. May 29, 1885; 76y. 6m.
William Tipton, d. Sept. 1, 1881; 72y. 10m. 3d.
Isaac Vickers, d. Jan. 4, 1875; 78y.
Mary Vickers, b. Jan. 21, 1808; d. May 23, 1887.
William Vickers, d. June 2, 1868; 72y. 5m. 27d.
Eliza Ann Whitington, wife of Thomas, d. Feb. 28, 1872; 41y. 11m. 24d.
Thomas S. Whitington, d. Feb. 4, 1892; 88y.

NEW ATHENS AND NEW JEFFERSON BURIALS

BURIALS IN NEW ATHENS GRAVEYARD.

(Those Born Before 1830.)

Catherine Brown, wife of George, b. Nov. 1, 1829; d. Aug. 22, 1890.
George Brown, b. Jan. 8, 1827; d. June 6, 1893.
James H. Covert, b. June 1, 1828; d. Jan. 6, 1895.
Isabell Day, d. Jan. 16, 1897; 76y.
Rezin Holmes, d. Nov. 26, 1881; 54y. 2m.
Edward Hughs, b. Oct. 30, 1814; d. April 5, 1889.
Sarah Hughs, wife of Edward, b. July 14, 1824; d. April 2, 1894.
James R. Peregoy, b. Oct. 28, 1822; d. Nov. 15, 1897.
Rebecca Watson, b. Sept. 15, 1817; d. April 3, 1893.
John Webb, Sr., b. Feb. 5, 1806; d. Jan. 15, 1893.
Martha Webb, wife of John, b. Jan. 8, 1811; d. Sept. 9, 1893.
James White, d. April 19, 1890; 73y.
Sarah White, wife of James, d. July 28, 1888; 69y.
Elizabeth Wiley, b. Oct. 29, 1822; d. March 27, 1895.

BURIALS IN NEW JEFFERSON GRAVEYARD.

(Those Born Before 1830.)

James Aiken, d. Aug. 19, 1884; 83y. 6m. 10d.
Jane Aiken, wife of James, d. June 16, 1867; 61y.
Jane Allender, wife of George, d. Sept. 22, 1859; 31y. 11m. 16d.
James Anderson, d. Aug. 23, 1866; 78y.
Margery Anderson, wife of James, b. Dec. 17, 1794; d. May 9, 1886.
Violet Anderson, wife of James, d. Oct. 11, 1879; 68y. 3m.
Mary Bender, wife of Levi, b. Dec. 11, 1823; d. Jan. 12, 1881.
Thomas Brooks, d. May 11, 1859; 57y.
George Burrier, d. Jan. 19, 1892; 78y. 3m. 12d.
Chastina H. Duffield, wife of Dr. G. W., b. Dec. 3, 1804; d. Jan. 21, 1881.
Dr. George W. Duffield, d. April 19, 1879; 87y. 3m. 24d.
Samuel J. Ferguson, d. Nov. 14, 1866; 50y. 2m. 6d.
Wingent Ferguson, b. July 25, 1812; d. April 20, 1876.
Charles Galbraith, d. Oct. 13, 1873; 82y. 8m. 12d.
Isabell Galbraith, wife of Charles, d. Dec. 8, 1871; 73y. 5m.
Isabel Galbraith, wife of Samuel, d. March 29, 1883; 86y.
Samuel Galbraith, d. July 13, 1875; 85y.
Samuel Galbraith, d. May 18, 1891; 66y. 6m. 23d.
William Galbraith, d. Aug. 1, 1879; 61y. 6m. 4d.
James Gotshall, d. Aug. 16, 1890; 68y. 11m. 28d.
Dr. A. W. Guthrie, d. Feb. 21, 1862; 41y.
Rev. J. Heller, b. Oct. 2, 1807; d. Nov. 3, 1876; 69y. 1m.
Alexander Johnston, d. Feb. 10, 1869; 97y. 7m. 17d.
Eleanor Johnston, wife of Alexander, d. Aug. 31, 1863; 80y.
John Johnson, b. July 12, 1814; d. July 2, 1878.
Uriah Kail, d. April 19, 1873; 46y. 9m. 5d.
James S. Kerr, d. March 16, 1880; 76y.
Ruth Lee, wife of James, d. March 19, 1882; 77y. 11m. 2d.
James C. McClure, d. Feb. 2, 1878; 65y. 10m. 13d.
Margaret McClure, d. July 4, 1897; 73y. 9m. 10d.
Margery McCreary, d. May 12, 1875; 73y.
Mary J. E. McElroy, wife of Joseph, d. June 11, 1876; 49y. 25d.
Matthew R. McNary, b. Feb. 14, 1831; d. Dec. 22, 1898.
Sarah J. Mikesell, wife of Samuel, d. Dec. 25, 1867; 39y. 8m. 10d.
Catherine Miller, wife of George, b. Nov. 22, 1820; d. Aug. 23, 1892.
George Miller, b. Jan. 3, 1823; d. May 18, 1888.

Mary Miller, wife of John, d. Feb. 2, 1874; 76y. 7m. 14d.
Martha Moore, d. Sept. 13, 1869; 92y.
Elizabeth A. Orr, wife of John, d. April 4, 1863; 64y.
John Orr, d. June 29, 1864; 63y.
Anne Patton, wife of Joseph, b. Jan. 13, 1802; d. March 23, 1894.
Joseph Patton, b. March 22, 1803; d. Dec. 4, 1887.
Ellen M. Peeples, b. March 7, 1828; d. June 10, 1898; 70y. 3m. 3d.
Enoch W. Phillips, d. Dec. 7, 1881; 62y. 7m. 11d.
Robert L. Plummer, d. March 24, 1878; 54y. 5m. 16d.
Sarah J. Polen, wife of William, d. April 3, 1876; 59y. 8m. 3d.
William Polen, d. Nov. 12, 1876; 61y. 7m. 20d.
Elizabeth Potts, wife of S. L., d. March 17, 1873; 74y.
Samuel L. Potts, d. Aug. 31, 1867; 64y. 4m.
Mary Reed, d. July 7, 1865; 95y.
Margaret M. Reid, d. Dec. 21, 1866; 76y. 11m. 21d.
Catherine Rider, wife of George, d. Oct. 26, 1879; 85y. 3m. 7d.
George Rider, d. May 8, 1880; 86y. 7m. 2d.
Edmund Roberts, d. Feb. 27, 1895; 84y. 1m. 16d.
Lydia Roberts, wife of Edmund, d. July 2, 1895; 84y. 8m. 26d.
John Scott, d. June 22, 1877; 77y. 21m. 14d.
Henry Smith, d. May 25, 1866; 45y. 9m. 27d.
Mary Ann Smith, wife of Samuel, d. April 18, 1899; 75y. 5m. 8d.
Polly Smith, wife of Samuel, d. March 9, 1866; 50y. 1m. 29d.
Samuel Smith, d. June 3, 1895; 80y. 3m. 23d.
Sarah Smith, wife of Henry, d. Nov. 16, 1864; 33y. 1m. 20d.
Barbary Ann Stinger, wife of William, d. May 26, 1872; 48y. 8m. 2d.
Mary P. Thompson, d. April 17, 1899; 62y.
Samuel Thompson, d. Aug. 23, 1885; 74y.
Sarah Thompson, wife of George, d. May 9, 1866; 91y.
Thomas Thompson, b. Sept. 29, 1818; d. Sept. 17, 1888.
Alexander Trotter, d. March 11, 1857; 62y.
Elizabeth Trotter, wife of Alexander, d. Aug. 13, 1890; 86y.
James Wilson, d. April 29, 1888; 59y.
Jane B. Wilson, wife of Rev. T., b. 1806; d. 1861.
Margaret Wilson, wife of W. H., d. March 8, 1884; 72y. 6m. 26d.
Mary Wilson, b. Dec. 27, 1803; d. Nov. 16, 1886.
Jacob H. Winings, b. July 29, 1828; d. Sept. 4, 1894.
W. S. Wininger, d. Feb. 19, 1878; 47y. 8m. 16d.

BURIALS IN UNITED BRETHERN GRAVEYARD, RUMLEY.

(Those Born Before 1830.)

Nancy Ager, d. July 7, 1871; 43y. 8m. 21d.
Sarah Barrett, wife of Edward, b. April 6, 1826; d. July 23, 1885; 59y. 3m. 74d.
Abigail Beck, wife of Leonard, d. Dec. 4, 1855; 72y. 2m. 15d.
Titus Beck, d. Jan. 17, 1880; 78y. 15d.
John Bishop, b. Sept. 11, 1795; d. Sept. 7, 1891.
Naoma Bishop, wife of John, d. May 6, 1868; 68y. 7m. 2d.
Catherine Bradley, d. May 20, 1882; 72y.
Margaret Bradley, d. July 24, 1873; 91y.
Henry Bricker, d. June 22, 1885; 72y. 10m. 18d.
Mary A. Bricker, wife of Henry, d. Oct. 22, 1860; 44y. 24d.
Catherine Burrier, d. Feb. 14, 1886; 84y. 3m. 23d.
Susan Canaga, wife of Jacob, d. Oct. 22, 1888; 82y.
Martha Constantine, wife of Pharer, d. March 11, 1858; 53y. 6m. 1d.
Isaac Daggon, son of L. and S., d. Nov. 1, 1862; 31 y. 7 m. 4d.

RUMLEY BURIALS. 397

Sarah Daggon, wife of Isaac, d. Nov. 6, 1862; 28y. 6m. 16d.
Sarah Dawson, b. March 25, 1822; d. Oct. 9, 1894.
Eliza Devore, wife of Silas R., d. Jan. 22, 1891; 70y. 4m. 2d.
Silas R. Devore, d. May 24, 1891; 64y.
Susanna Graybill, d. March 14, 1851; 67y. 7m.
William Gundy, d. Nov. 21, 1884; 67y. 8m.
Eve A. Gutshall, wife of Joseph, d. Oct. 26, 1871; 65y. 4d.
Michael Gutshall, d. June 24, 1847; 33y. 11m. 16d.
Samuel Heidy, d. June 12, 1864; 44y. 8m. 1d.
Sarah Heidy, wife of Samuel, d. Aug. 20, 1877; 53y. 4m. 13d.
Susan Heidy, wife of Thomas, d. Aug. 26, 1888; 78y. 8m. 6d.
Thomas Heidy, d. May 13, 1894; 83y. 6m. 26d.
L. P. Jolly, d. May 20, 1864; 34y. 4m. 20d.
Thomas Lewis, b. March 27, 1820; d. March 6, 1897.
Julia Ann McGavran, wife of Stephen, b. June 13, 1814; d. July 29, 1887.
Stephen McGavran, b. June 3, 1814; d. Oct. 27, 1874.
Elizabeth Manbeck, wife of John, d. June 26, 1844; 49y. 7m. 17d.
Eve Manbeck, wife of Jacob, d. Nov. 14, 1854; 77 y. 3m. 18d.
Jacob Manbeck, d. Nov. 6, 1853; 80y. 3m. 3d.
John Manbeck, d. July 25, 1876; 75y. 4m. 12d.
Margaret Manbeck, wife of Peter, d. Aug. 30, 1897; 84y. 3m. 13d.
Peter Manbeck, d. March 8, 1898; 95y. 24d.
John Markley, d. Feb. 21, 1896; 74y. 11m. 4d.
Mary Markley, wife of John, d. Dec. 13, 1893; 68y. 2m. 4d.
John Parker, d. May 27, 1850; 48y. 3m. 6d.
Jane Salmon, wife of Lewis, d. Jan. 19, 1892; 71y. 8m. 12d.
Lewis Salmon, d. Dec. 20, 1872; 54y. 6m. 14d.
Catherine Shambaugh, wife of Philip, d. March 24, 1867; 50y. 9m. 10d.
George Shambaugh, b. Oct. 28, 1813; d. July 25, 1894.
Hetta Shambaugh, wife of Michael, b. April 16, 1816; d. Oct. 21, 1884.
Matilda Shambaugh, wife of George, d. Nov. 23, 1862; 43y. 3m. 26d.
Michael Shambaugh, b. June 11, 1811; d. March 20, 1863.
Philip Shambaugh, d. May 28, 1895; 86y. 3m. 8d.
Susanna Shambaugh, second wife of George, b. Feb. 4, 1822; d. May 22, 1894.
Samuel Snyder, d. Nov. 17, 1884; 59y. 6m. 26d.
Nancy Tope, wife of Joseph, d. Aug. 21, 1873; 62y. 7m. 6d.
John West, b. Oct. 12, 1801; d. Dec. 28, 1864.

BURIALS IN LUTHERAN GRAVE-YARD, RUMLEY.

(Those Born Before 1830.)

Tabitha C. Able, wife of A. P., d. Aug. 27, 1880; 50y. 1m. 14d.
Susanna Acker, d. July 1, 1864; 54y. 1m. 17d.
Elizabeth Amos, wife of John S., d. May 10, 1843; 39y. 11m. 12d.
John Anderson, d. Sept. 15, 1845; 57y. 2m.
Daniel Arbaugh, d. Feb. 13, 1835; 46y.
David Arbaugh, d. Sept. 8, 1876; 61y. 11m. 11d.
John Arbaugh, d. July 22, 1848; 56y. 6m. 21d.
Margaret Arbaugh, wife of William, d. April 10, 1848; 90y.
Mary Arbaugh, wife of Daniel, d. Jan. 23, 1864; 60y. 2m. 24d.
Rosana Arbaugh, wife of John, d. March 14, 1864; 74y. 11m. 27d.
William Arbaugh, b. Aug. 26, 1819; d.

July 3, 1892.
Agness Barr, wife of Hugh P., d. Aug. 3, 1836; 38y.
Hugh P. Barr, d. Feb. 1, 1843; 45y.
Rachel Bradley, wife of Thomas, d. March 10, 1842; 23y. 19d.
Virginia S. Buffum, d. April 20, 1880; 71y. 6m.
Sarah Caldwell, wife of John, d. Jan. 11, 1847; 82y.
Catherine Cluts, wife of George, d. Oct. 13, 1875; 71y. 8m. 11d.
George Cluts, d. July 14, 1877; 76y. 3m. 4d.
Charlotte Cummings, wife of Robert, b. 1796; d. 1854.
Robert Cummings, b. 1789; d. 1823.
Nancy Cunningham, wife of William, d. July 14, 1855; 46y. 1m. 9d.
Dr. William Cunningham, d. Feb. 16, 1842; 45y. 5m. 22d.
Jacob Custer, d. March 6, 1862; 71y. 8m. 19d.
Sarah Custer, wife of Jacob, d. April 19, 1835; 37y. 14d.
Margaret Dell, wife of Peter, d. Feb. 14, 1845; 36y. 10m.
Thomas Dowell, d. Feb. 23, 1872; 96y.
James Duswald, d. Nov. 3, 1875; 68y.
Sarah Duswald, wife of James, d. June 30, 1897; 81y.
John Epley, d. Oct. 7, 1887; 64y. 7m. 17d.
Margaret Finnicum, wife of N. P. T., d. Sept. 4, 1876; 56y. 2m. 17d.
N. P. T. Finnicum, d. Oct. 6, 1881; 68y. 6m. 23d.
Elizabeth Galbraith, wife of James, d. Nov. 6, 1848; 24y 8m. 15d.
Elizabeth Gidinger, d. May 31, 1846; 52y.
Rachel Grimm, wife of Jacob, May 5, 1876; 69y. 1m. 5d.
Samuel Guthrie, d. Aug. 5, 1888; 74y. 4m. 25d.
Ann Mary Gutshall, wife of Jonas, d. Jan. 29, 1871; 69y. 9 m. 18d.
Hannah Gutshall, wife of Joseph, d. Feb. 12, 1842; 42y. 6m. 28d.
Jeremiah Gutshall, d. Oct. 21, 1849; 26y. 3m. 24d.
Jonas Gutshall, d. June 1, 1844; 44y. 5m. 29d.

Joseph Gutshall, d. Sept. 30, 1859; 69y.
Ruth Ann Gutshall, wife of Jacob, d. Aug. 28, 1838; 17y. 4m. 24d.
Solomon Gutshall, son of J. and H., d. Jan. 31, 1848; 22y. 20d.
Agness Huey, wife of William, d. Oct. 29, 1859; 69y. 5m.
William Huey, d. April 20, 1846; 77y.
Abraham Kail, d. July 5, 1856; 59y. 20d.
Ann Kail, d. Feb. 24, 1858; 60y. 7m. 28d.
Elizabeth Kail, wife of Gabrial, d. June 2, 1867; 74y. 5m.
Gabrial Kail, d. Jan. 5, 1850; 62y. 8m. 28d.
Rebecca Keplinger, wife of Martin, d. Aug. 23, 1856; 87y. 5m.
Christena Kimmel, wife of Henry, b. March 7, 1794; d. Oct. 3, 1894; 100y. 6m. 26d.
David Kimmel, d. Jan. 12. 1882; 58y.
Elizabeth Kimmel, wife of Frederick, b. April 22, 1808; d. May 22, 1891.
Eunice Kimmel, wife of David, d. Nov. 5, 1874; 56y. 7m. 18d.
Frederick Kimmel, b. Oct. 18, 1800; d. March 24, 1886.
Henry Kimmel, b. 1798; d. 1826.
Jonathan Kimmel, b. July 15, 1815; d. July 7, 1894.
Maria C. Kimmel, wife of Jonathan, b. Feb. 8, 1818; d. Sept. 28, 1896.
Hamilton King, d. July 29, 1880; 73y.
Sarah King, wife of Hamilton, d. March 17, 1881; 74y.
Israel Kirkpatrick, d. March 6, 1835; 39y. 20d.
John Knouff, d. July 14, 1870; 78y.
Susanna Knouff, wife of John, d. Oct. 15, 1843; 47y. 10m. 21d.
Elizabeth Lisle, wife of Robert, d. Sept. 12, 1852; 72y.
Robert Lisle, d. April 3, 1834; 60y.
Ann Mary Long, wife of Samuel, d. March 9, 1867; 75y. 6m. 5d.
Samuel Long, d. Jan. 26, 1858; 77y. 11m. 1d.
Daniel Lucas, d. Feb. 5, 1863; 58y. 2m. 15d.
George Lucas, d. May 18, 1889; 55y. 6m. 22d.
Sarah Magoogan, wife of Samuel, d. Oct. 1, 1842; 33y. 6m.
Catherine Markley, wife of Daniel, d

RUMLEY BURIALS

March 30, 1876; 78y. 9m. 24d.
Daniel Markley, d. March 15, 1842; 46y. 7m. 6d.
Elizabeth Mathias, daughter of James and Eleanor, d. Feb. 2, 1835; 14 y. 1m. 20d.
Catherine Miller, d. March 25, 1883; 90y. 4m. 3d.
Peter Miller, d. May 25, 1821; 38y. 3m.
Daniel Minard, b. April 6, 1820; d. Nov. 2, 1897.
Jacob Minard, b. Oct. 17, 1821; d. Dec. 28, 1885.
John Minard, d. April 12, 1867; 101y.
Mary Minard, wife of John, d. April 26, 1845; 69y.
Nancy Mounts, wife of Joseph, d. March 16, 1846; 33y. 8m. 24d.
David Mull, d. Feb. 25, 1892; 75y. 11m. 16d.
Jane Nixon, wife of John, Feb. 11, 1874; 81y. 2m. 23d.
Mary H. Nixon, daughter of John and Jane, d. July 20, 1835; 18y. 1m. 2d.
Thomas M. Nixon, son of John and Jane, d. Aug. 25, 1845; 16y. 5m.
John P. Nop, d. July 19, 1850; 65y. 3m. 28d.
George Nupp, b. Nov. 22, 1825; d. Aug. 21, 1899.
Margaret Nupp, wife of George, b. Sept. 9, 1825; d. Aug. 30, 1893.
Susanna Nupp, b. Feb. 22, 1802; d. March 30, 1888; 86y. 1m. 8d.
Lovina Orr, wife of Augustus, d. Oct. 7, 1878; 54y. 4m. 10d.
David Patton, b. Sept. 18, 1823; d. Nov. 24, 1897.
James Patton, d. Sept. 25, 1880; 62y. 5m. 15d.
John Patton, son of Joseph and Sarah, d. Sept. 16, 1828; 20y. 9m. 18d.
Joseph Patton, d. Jan. 6, 1850; 66y.
Mary Patton, wife of James, d. Dec. 12, 1852; 40y. 11m. 15d.
Sarah Patton, wife of Joseph, d. Sept. 24, 1842; 54y.
Catherine Pratt, wife of Isaac, d. June 6, 1879; 59y. 9m. 21d.
Isaac Pratt, d. Jan. 27, 1876; 52y. 9m. 19d.
Lydia A. Sauvel, wife of Jonathan, d. May 14, 1863; 30y. 5m. 2d.
Elizabeth Shambaugh, d. March 26, 1841; 67y. 28d.
George Shambaugh, Sr., d. Sept. 4, 1867; 82y. 4m. 12d.
Henry Shawver, d. Dec. 23, 1856; 37y. 6m. 5d.
Lydia Shawver, wife of Henry, d. Jan. 18, 1897; 73y. 11m. 20d.
Elizabeth Shearer, wife of Henry, d. March 13, 1896; 81y. 2m. 2d.
Henry Shearer, d. Dec. 26, 1886; 76y. 3m. 1d.
Joseph Shearer, d. Jan. 7, 1840; 62y. 8m. 24d.
Mary A. Shearer, wife of Joseph, d. March 23, 1852; 63y. 1m. 15d.
Mary Shearer, daughter of J. and C., d. April 1, 1863; 49y. 5m. 1d.
Elizabeth Shilling, wife of William, d. July 3, 1880; 61y. 7m. 18d.
Annie Snuss, wife of George, d. Aug. 10, 1866; 61y. 7m. 16d.
George Snuss, d. Jan. 22, 1877; 70y.
Elizabeth Simmons, wife of George, d. Nov. 27, 1859; 53y. 11m. 26d.
George Simmons, d. Aug. 12, 1882; 72y. 24d.
Rachel Simmons, wife of Isaiah, d. Aug. 16, 1877; 80y. 27d.
Thomas Simmons, d. Oct. 4, 1881; 80y. 9m. 25d.
Elizabeth Smith, wife of Jacob, d. Feb. 9, 1881; 76y. 2m. 1d.
Jacob Smith, d. Sept. 17, 1884; 84y. 6m. 25d.
Catherine Sloan, wife of James, d. Dec. 22, 1840; 58y.
Sarah Thompson, wife of Thomas, d. June 28, 1844; 27y. 3m. 5d.
Catherine Trout, d. Oct. 10, 1864; 54y. 1m. 17d.
Susanna Wallace, d. Feb. 14, 1891; 73y. 3m. 22d.
Mary Ann Wane, wife of John M., d. March 1, 1844; 30y.
Barbara A. Wiles, wife of Peter, d. June 1, 1895; 75y. 8m. 5d.
Moses Wiles, d. March 3, 1865; 52y. 6m. 29d.
Catherine Wood, wife of Joseph, b. June 12, 1810; d. Aug. 1, 1891.
Elizabeth Wood, dau. of William and Rachel, d. Nov. 25, 1860; 26 y. 5m. 16d.

Ellis Wood, d. Oct. 28, 1860; 31y. 7m. 11d.

Joseph Wood, b. July 22, 1802; d. Sept. 13, 1870.

Leah Wood, wife of Henry, d. June 11, 1830; 27y.

Mary A. Wood, wife of William, d. July 14, 1892; 71y. 7m. 3d.

Rachel Wood, wife of William, d. April 26, 1871; 66y. 9d.

ABSTRACTS OF WILLS RECORDED IN HARRISON COUNTY FROM 1813 TO 1860, INCLUSIVE.

The following will abstracts, as well as the preceding list of marriages and most of the tombstone records given herein, have been gathered and arranged by Mr. William P. Hanna. It is to his industry and painstaking care in the preparation of this data that the readers of the present volume are indebted for what it is safe to say, is the largest and most valuable collection of material for family history that has ever been published in any similar single volume work on county history in Ohio or elsewhere.

These will abstracts alone will furnish more information about the families of the early settlers of Harrison county than is contained in a dozen of the usual "Biographical Encyclopedias," which are sold in such large numbers throughout the country. At the same time, there is much information about the membership of a family that is not always to be found in a will. Many of the wills mention but one or two names of the family, when there may be half a dozen members. In examining the following abstracts, therefore, it is not to be taken for granted that they give the exact extent of the family at the time the will is written. In attempting to trace the genealogy of one's family from these will abstracts, the record may be pieced out in many cases by reference to the list of marriages, and to the burial lists given elsewhere.

The thanks of the writer are due for courtesy and assistance rendered by ex-Judge E. B. McNamee and Judge John B. Worley, of the Probate Office; by Benjamin R. Green, county Surveyor; by S. Edwin Thompson, Recorder; and by many others, who have assisted in the collection of the data herein presented:

WILLS PROBATED IN HARRISON COUNTY TO 1861.

CHRISTOPHER ABEL, date of will, March 28, 1859; date of probate, June 13, 1859; wife, Sarah; children, Alexander, George, Margaret, Ann Hiseler, Elizabeth Lavengood; grandchildren, Enoch-W. and Christopher Abel, Alexander Blickenstaffer; execs., George Abel, George Levengood; wits., William K. Beckett, John Gruber.

GEORGE ADAMS, Franklin township; date of will, July 29, 1851; date of probate, Feb. 18, 1852; wife, Mary; exec., Mary Adams; wits., Citizen J. Kennedy, Augustus Watters.

JOHN ADAMS, date of will, May 6, 1834; date of probate, March 30, 1835; wife, Rachel; children, Samuel, Anthony-Q; granddaughter, Elizabeth Lamb; execs., Samuel Adams, Anthony Adams, Alexander Clark, Evan Romans; wits., Cornelius Barber, Asa Holloway.

THOMAS ADAMS, date of will, Aug. 4, 1842; date of probate, Nov. 1, 1847; wife, name not given; children, William, Joseph, George, Joshua, Nimrod, James, John, Elizabeth; execs., names not given; wits., M. B. Lukens, Citizen J. Kennedy.

THOMAS ADAMS, Nottingham township; date of will, May 4, 1852; date of probate, June 30, 1852; wife, Charity; children mentioned, names not given; exec., Matthew Adams; wits., Abriam Johnson, Rowland H. Rogers.

WILLIAM ADAMS, date of will, not given; date of probate, Sept. 20, 1836; wife, Mary; children, Samuel, William, George, John, Margaret, Nancy, Polly, Catherine, Ellen, Jane, Elizabeth; exec., Josiah Scott; wits., Thomas Bingham, Josiah Scott, Mary Jane Scott.

SARAH AFOLT, Fairfield county, Ohio; date of will, Sept. 16, 1839; date of probate, Nov. 19, 1839; niece, Sarah Hukill; legatee, Johnson Hukill; exec., Johnson Hukill; wits., M. Wilson, Josiah Scott, Samuel McFadden.

HENRY AIMES, date of will, March 9, 1840; date of probate, June, 1840; wife, Margaret; children, Catherine Swigert, Elizabeth Cheney, Sarah Swigert, Anne Wolcott, Mary Ann Davis, William, Samuel, Daniel, George, Henry, Elisha; grand-son, James Swigert; execs., Margaret Aimes, William Aimes; wits., Brice Reed, John Gruber.

ROBERT ALEXANDER, Cadiz township; date of will, Jan. 2, 1856; date of probate, Feb. 21, 1856; wife, Elizabeth; children, John-W., J.; exec., Elizabeth Alexander; wits., Thomas Love, Joseph Rea.

ELIZABETH ALLBAUGH, date of will, Jan. 1, 1858; date of probate, Jan. 27, 1858; husband, James; exec., William Beadle; wits., William Curtis, Samuel Allbaugh.

JOSIAH ALLEN, Shortcreek township; date of will, Oct. 6, 1842; date of probate, May ——, 1843; son, David; grandchildren, Margaret Jane Allen, Josiah Allen; execs., Joshua Hamilton, A. F. Hanna; wits., John Hanna, Levi Dickerson.

JAMES ANDERSON, date of will. Sept. 5, 1845; date of probate, Oct. 10, 1845; wife, Violet; children, John, Abraham, Mary, Jane; execs., Jacob Gutshall, Samuel Galbraith; wits., John Anderson, James Anderson.

JOHN ANDERSON, date of will, Nov. 20, 1841; date of probate, May 2, 1842; wife, Margaret; children, Elenor, Margaret, Isabel, Mary, John, James, Andrew, Richard, William; execs., James Anderson, Samuel Gailbraith; wits., James Anderson, James Gailbraith.

RACHEL ANDERSON, date of will, Aug. 20, 1849; date of probate, Sept. 14, 1849; children, James, Matthew, William, Alexander, Thomas, Martha; sons-in-law, Samuel Davis, Alexander Henry; exec., Hamilton McFadden;

HARRISON COUNTY WILLS

wits., William Givin, Michael Vertue.

THOMAS ANDERSON, Shortcreek township; date of will, Feb. 8, 1844; date of probate, May ——, 1844; wife, Nancy; exec., Samuel Anderson; wits., James F. Inskeep, Henry C. Brown, Rachel Anderson.

WILLIAM ANDERSON, Archer township; date of will, May 13, 1822; date of probate, June 7, 1822; wife, Malila; children, Benjamin, James, Thompson, Thomas, William, George, Ruth, Nancy, Jane, Malila; execs., Benjamin Anderson, William Grimes; wits., Walter B. Beebe, Elizabeth Williams, Nancy Anderson.

JOHN ARBAUGH, Rumley township; date of will, July 22, 1848; date of probate, Aug. 21, 1848; wife, Rose Ann; children, James, Levi, John, Catharine, Margaret, Lavina, Lydia-Ann; exec., Philip Shambaugh; wits., Ephron P. Stewart, Samuel Dayhuff.

SARAH ANN ARCHBOLD, date of will, Oct. 27, 1841; date of probate, Oct. —, 1843; grandchildren, Moses T. Spencer, John A. Spencer, John A. Robinson, Betty Gordon; exec., Jacob Richey; wits., J. Archbold, John Pearce.

FRANCINAH ARNOLD, date of will, Nov. 3, 1856; date of probate, Nov. 8, 1856; legatee, Maria Poulson; exec., William Arnold; wits., William Arnold, Sarah Poulson.

GEORGE ATKINSON, Brooke co., Virginia; date of will, March 1, 1822; date of probate, May 28, 1831; wife, name not given; children, Thomas, James, Margaret, Mary, Eleanor, Sarah, Martha, Ruth, Elizabeth; grandson, Richard Atkinson; exec., Jeremiah Browning; wits., Thomas Hattery, William Atkinson.

GEORGE ATKINSON, Shortcreek township; date of will, July 5, 1854; date of probate, Sept. 5, 1854; children, Mary Hilbert, Elizabeth, John, Ella Ross, Rebecca Ross, George-S., Sarah Kennard; nephew, Wilmer Atkinson; niece, Juliett Atkinson; execs., George Atkinson, David Hilbert; wits., Isaac Lewis, Joseph Wiley, Andrew Jamison.

JOHN ATKINSON, Shortcreek township; date of will, March 1, 1861; date of probate, March 25, 1861; wife, Eliza; exec., William McFarland; wits., George Atkinson, George A. Roberts.

JANE W. AULD, Deersville town; date of will, April 1. 1853; date of probate, Sep. 21, 1858; legatee, Edward Pittis; execs., names not given; wits., Lancelot Hearn, William A. Hearn.

JOHN C. AULD, date of will, Jan. 8, 1834; date of probate, March 31, 1834; wife, Jane; son, Albert; brother, Lazarus Auld; exec., Alexander Henderson; wits., Robert Dodds, H. Worstel.

KATHERINE AULD, Franklin township; date of will, June 15, 1840; date of probate, April 12, 1841; brothers and sisters, John, Alexander, Sarah, Katherine; mentions father and mother; exec., Josiah Scott; wits., Zadack Bliss, Josiah Scott.

JOHN BAKER, date of will, Dec. 20, 1841; date of probate March 13, 1847; wife, name not given; children, Rezin, John, George, Samuel, Elizabeth; exec., John Baker; wits., William Cobb, Jacob Dennis.

OTTO BAKER, date of will, Sept. 14, 1848; date of probate, Feb. 27, 1855; wife, Mary; children, Elizabeth, Mary, Sarah Martin, Abraham, Catharine Kent, William, Agnes Cox, Melinda Young, Otto, Evan, Sheridan; execs., Otto Baker, Charles Conaway; wits., William Tingley, Jeremiah Tingley, S. M. Cormick.

MARY BANE, Green township, date of will, Nov. 18, 1828; date of probate, April 3, 1830; children, John, Hugh, William, Henry, Margaret Bane, Tarbet Bane, Isabella, Jane, Elizabeth, Sarah; grandchildren, John McCoy Merideth, William Wallace Merideth, Mary Dawson; execs., Alexander Reid, Tarbet Bane; wits., Nathan Johnson, John Reid.

SAMUEL BARBER, date of will, Nov. 11, 1851; date of probate, April 19, 1852; wife, Ann; children, Dorothy Hathaway, Elizabeth Lukins, Ann Thomas, James; execs., Townsend Thomas, Wilson Maddox; wits., John Cope, William M. Hilligas.

VALENTINE BARGER, date of will, Nov. 7, 1827; date of probate, Nov. 28, 1827; wife, Elizabeth; son, Henry; granddaughter, Mary Smith; execs., Peter Barger, Jacob Barger; wits., William Van Clese, Jr., Henry Barger, George Sipe.

LEWIS BARKHURST, Shortcreek township; date of will, March 13, 1823; date of probate, June 24, 1823; wife, Arminta; children, William, John, Elizabeth, Margaret, Sarah, Mary, Jerminia; exec., Arminta Barkhurst; wits., John Warfield, Charles Barkhurst, Bradway Thompson.

ALEXANDER BARNES, Washington township; date of will, Feb. 11, 1835; date of probate, Sept. 20, 1836; wife, Elizabeth; execs., Robert Clark, Thomas Clark; wits., William Boyd, John Elliot.

JAMES P. BARNES, date of will, March 10, 1852; date of probate, April 13, 1852; wife, name not given; children, names not given; execs., wife, and W. G. Finney; wits., John Smith, S. R. Magee.

MARGARET BARNHILL, date of will, May 21, 1815; date of probate, Aug. 20, 1817; children, Jenny, Mary, Robert, Hugh; execs., names not given. wits., Robert Russel, Elizabeth Russel, Robert Barnhill.

WILLIAM BARR, date of will, Dec. 18, 1817; date of probate, Aug. 6, 1818; wife, Mary; children, Easter, Jane, Agnes, Mary, Isaac, James, Andrew, Silas, William, infant unborn; execs., Mary Barr, Alexander Johnston; wits., Henry Kail, Jacob Meed, Margaret Peoples.

ARTHUR BARRETT, Cadiz township; date of will, Oct. 27, 1842; date of probate, Dec. 19, 1844; wife, Elizabeth; children, Lewis, Meredith, William-H., Aeneas, John-W., Mary-Ann; exec., Meredith Barrett; wits., William Arnold, Thomas Barrett, Aeneas Barrett.

ISAAC BARRETT, Cadiz township; date of will, July 8, 1850; date of probate, Aug. 21, 1858; wife, Hannah; children, Erasmus, Arthur, Hiram, Mary Ann White, Tabetha Ford; execs., Erasmus Barrett, Arthur Barrett; wits., William Arnold, Thomas McCrary.

THOMAS BARRETT, date of will, Sept. 7, 1849; date of probate, Dec. 20, 1849; wife, Alaneda; children, Thomas, Warden, Arthur, Esther Wilson, Emma Spurrier, Balinda Cadwalader, Anna Miller, Rachel Sears; exec., Joseph Rea; wits., Martin Wilson, William McFaddin.

HENRY BARRICKLOW, date of will, Feb. 21, 1851; date of probate, May 24, 1852; wife, name not given; children, John, Joseph, Henry, Conrad, Gregg; legatee, Rachel Ann Watson; execs., Conrad Barricklow, Farrington Barricklow; wits., S. W. Bostwick, Frederick Barricklow.

ELIJAH BARTOW, date of will, March 16, 1837; date of probate, May —, 1844; wife, Sarah; children, Enos, George, Francis, Syrus, Eli, Samuel, Tebee Woods, Charetee Edgar; stepson, William Houser; execs., names not given; wits., Robert Simpson, John McCarroll.

JOHN BAXTER, date of will, July 25, 1815; date of probate, Sept. 2, 1815; wife, Mary; children, James, William, Robert, John, Elizabeth, Mary; execs., sons, James Baxter, William Baxter; wits., Thomas McGonegle, James Drummond.

COLMORE BEALL, West Bethlehem township, Washington co., Pa.; date of will, Dec. 10, 1829; date of probate, May 24, 1840; wife, Rebecca; children, John, Alexander, James, Hilary, Daniel, Colmore, Thomas, Mary Ann Yarnell, Elizabeth McCoy, Rebecca Smith, Casandra Taylor, Sarah, Nancy, Margaret, Eliza, Jane, Minerva; execs., Alexander Beall, James P. Beall; wits., Zepha Parker, Neal Beall.

JAMES BEATTY, date of will, Sept. 7, 1833; date of probate, Jan. 16, 1834; wife, Jane; children, Martha Jamison. Margaret, James, Thomas,; grandson, James Jamison; execs., Walter Jamison, George Atkinson; wits., William Wiley, Samuel Rogers.

JANE BEATTY, date of will, Oct. 20, 1848; date of probate, Dec. 20, 1850; grandchildren, Ann Jamison, James Jamison, John Jamison; legatees, William Beatty, Uphrim Maxwell, American Bible Society; exec., George Atkinson; wits., William Boggs, David Taggart.

JOSEPH BEATTY, date of will, March 25, 1834; date of probate, April 2, 1834; wife, name not given; mother, name not given; sister, Martha; brother, James; aunt, Ruth Wiley; cousins, Joseph Rogers, Rebecca Rogers, James Beatty; legatees, American Bible Society, Board of Home Missions, and Board of Education of the Presbyterian Church; execs., William Lee, William Boggs; wits., William Hanna, Samuel Rogers.

SAMPSON BEATY, Archer township; date of will, July 9, 1849; date of probate, Dec. 20, 1849; wife, Rachel; sons, Arthur, Johnson, Thomas, Jeremiah, John; exec., Arthur Beaty; wits., William Irwin, Josiah Scott.

SAMUEL BECK, Freeport; date of will, March 25, 1821; date of probate, Aug. 3, 1821; wife, Mary; children, William, Presley, Susanna, Rachel, Mary, Hannah, Eliabeth; exec., son, William Beck; wits., Henry David, James Evans.

JACOB BECKLEY, German township; will not dated; date of probate, Jan. 14, 1832; wife, Mary; children, Henry, Jacob, Lydia; granddaughters, Elizabeth Shawver, Susan Wagner, Mary Ann Abel; execs., Jacob Beckley, John Shober; wits., William Gillespie, Charles Gillespie.

WALTER B. BEEBE, date of will, Feb. 25, 1836; date of probate, Feb. 25, 1836; wife, Nancy; sons, Butler, James, Stewart; execs., Nancy Beebe, Chauncey Dewey; wits., William Tingley, John McBean, John Olmstead.

MARY BEEKLEY, date of will, July 5, 1835; date of probate, Oct. 26, 1835; children, Henry, Jacob, John, George, Lydia, Sally Abel, Susanna Burkhouse, Rachel McGee, Betsey Hirshfield; execs., Jacob Beekley, John Wagner; wits., John Wagner, Jacob Wining.

DANIEL BELKNAP, date of will, Oct. 6, 1831; date of probate, March 12, 1832; wife, Jane; children, Ammoret, Orville, Harriet, Horace, David, Sidney, Thomas, Charles; exec., Horace Belknap; wits., Robert Gilbreath, James Davis.

JOSEPH BERNHARD, Harrison co.; date of will, June 28, 1852; date of probate, Oct. 19, 1853; wife, Sarah; children, Lewis, William, Joseph; grand-daughter, Cynthia A. Michaels; legatee, Ruth Ann Parmer; execs., Lewis Bernhard, William Bernhard, Joseph Bernhard; wits., James McMillan, Joshua P. Watson, Samuel H. Watson.

SAMUEL BIGGART, date of will, Dec. 30, 1830; date of probate, Aug. 2, 1831; wife, name not given; children, Robert, Mordica, Samuel; exec., George Brown; wits., George Brown, William Eagleson.

THOMAS BINGHAM, Cadiz; date of will, April 7, 1853; date of probate, April 20, 1853; children, John-A., Emma-C., Martha B. Lee, Mary Jane Scott, Lucinda B. Wood, Amanda, Emma-E., Isabella, Belinda; grandchildren, Thomas Olmstead, Bingham Scott, Thomas Scott, Bingham Wood, Lucy Wood, Lucy Stewart Bingham, Emma Bingham, Thomas Bingham, Hugh Bingham, Lucinda Bingham; execs., Josiah Scott, John A. Bingham;

wits., William Tingley, Josiah Craig.

DAVID BINNS, Fayette county, Pennsylvania; date of will, July 25, 1846; date of probate, May 22, 1849; wife, Mary; children, Jonathan, William, David, Mary, Sarah, Ann; execs., Jonathan Binns, Charles Kinsey; wits., Abraham Stanley, M. O. Jones.

MARGARET BINNS, date of will, Nov. 11, 1853; date of probate, Feb. 25, 1859; children, Jonathan, William, David, Mary Bracken, Sarah B. Kinsey, Ann H. Cook; execs., Jonathan Binns, Charles Kinsey; wits., George R. Jenkins, Joseph Harris.

HUGH BIRNEY, date of will, Sept. 17, 1860; date of probate, Sept. 23, 1861; children, William, Wesley, Asbury, James, Rebecca Law, Martha, Elizabeth Hitchcock, Jane Lease; execs., William Birney, Wesley Birney; wits., James J. Billingsley, John Birney.

JOHN BIRNEY, Harrison co.; date of will, March 15, 1853; date of probate, Aug. 9, 1854; wife, name not given; children, Jane, John, Ann, Robert, Nelson, Eleanor; exec., John Birney; wits., Samuel Foreman, Hugh Birney.

RUNNELL BLAIR, Brook co., Virginia, date of will, April 11, 1813; date of probate, June 15, 1818; wife, Charity; children, John, Daniel, James, Robert, Jennett, Elizabeth, Mary; execs., wife, Charity Blair, sons, James Blair, Robert Blair; wits., James Blair, Isabella Henderson, James Wilson.

DANIEL BLACK, Carroll co., O.: date of will, July 25, 1857; date of probate, July 22, 1859; wife, Mary; children, John, Henry, Daniel, Hatty-Ann, Isabella, Jane, Mary; exec., Robert Cummings; wits., John L. Hunt, J. M. Forrester.

EDITH BLAKE, date of will, March 3, 1856; date of probate, March 17, 1856; brothers, Benjamin Parrish, James Parrish; legatees, Cara Boyd, John Parrish, Elizabeth Davis, Susanna Cloakley; execs., names not given; wits., Eli Peacock, Forney Timmons.

ZADOCK BLISS, date of will, Aug. 26, 1852; date of probate, Dec. 13, 1853; wife, Nancy; children, John-Q.-A.; execs., Nancy Bliss, John Q. A. Bliss; wits., William B. Hunt, David Gladman.

JAMES BOALES, Green township; date of will, July 2, 1836; date of probate, Aug. 16, 1847; wife, Margaret; children, Samuel, William, Robert, Joseph, John, David, James, Margaret, Tabitha, Mary Strand, Nancy Francis, Esther Bell, Isabella McBirney, Fanny Leech, Jane Moore; grandson, James Boales; execs., Samuel McNary, Josiah Scott; wits., Thomas Bingham, Josiah Scott, William H. Forker.

JOHN BOGGS, date of will, Nov. 2, 1848; date of probate, Feb. 13, 1849; wife, Sarah; children, Thomas-M., John-M., Samuel-M., Robert-W., Sarah-Ann; exec., Samuel M. Boggs; wits., William Lee, James Tannehill.

JOHN BOLIN, date of will, Dec. 22, 1843; date of probate, July 10, 1845; wife, Eliza; execs., Oliver Hestings, Neri Longshore; wits., Andrew Martin, Thomas Joice, Sarah Davison, John Graham, Nicholas Myres.

THOMAS BOOTH, Shortcreek township; date of will, Feb. 3, 1841; date of probate, Aug. 1, 1842; wife, Susanna; children, John, Isaac, Aaron, Catherine, Ann; grandchildren, John T. Larkin, and heirs of deceased son, Jacob; execs., John Booth, Isaac Booth, Aaron Booth; wits., Samuel Lewis, Lewis Parker, James McMillan.

BERNHARD BOWER, date of will, Sept. 2, 1843; date of probate, Jan. 18, 1843; wife, Mary; children, Catherine, Henry, John, Jacob, David; grandsons, Ezekiel Bower, Barnard Bower; execs., Jacob Bower, David Bower; wits., Thomas McClintick, William Welch.

FREDERICK BOWERS, Allegheny county, Maryland; date of will, April 3, 1835; date of probate, June 22, 1835; wife, name not given; legatee, Jacob

Winings; exec., Jacob Winings; wits. Jonathan Smith, George W. Duffield, Charles Burchfield.

JOHN BOYD, Freeport township, date of will, Feb. 18, 1835; date of probate, Oct. 26, 1835: wife, Mary; children, Samuel, William, Elizabeth Barnes, Martha Hamilton, Rosanna Allen, Sarah Allen; execs., Robert Clark, James McMath, Jr.; wits., Joseph Fry, Horace Belknap, John H. Clapp.

THOMAS BOYD, date of will, June 30, 1846; date of probate, April 26, 1847; wife, Catherine; sisters, Mary, Margaret McGonagal, Sarah, Eliza, Jane; brothers, Samuel, James, Albert, William; execs., Patrick Archbold, Catherine Boyd; wits., James R. Myres, Catherine Rose.

WILLIAM BOYD, date of will, Sept. 15, 1853; date of probate, Feb. 21, 1854; wife, Rebecca; children, Malinda Braden, Nancy Johnson, Mariah Warfel, Elizabeth Welch, Martha Ferguson, John; exec., Charles Warfel; wits., Nancy A. Reynolds, Thomas Lee.

DAVID BRADEN, Shortcreek township; date of will, April 14, 1814; date of probate, March 28, 1815; wife, Margaret; sons, James, Joseph; execs., Joseph Braden, John Francis; wits., James Fords, John R. Davison, Joseph Burwell.

JOHN H. BRADEN, Shortcreek township; date of will, April 15, 1841; date of probate, May 21, 1841; wife, name not given; brothers and sisters, Robert, David, William, Ann, Mary-Jane; exec., Francis Grove; wits., Thomas Hanna, Charles Warfel.

HENRY BRICKER, date of will, May 26, 1846; date of probate, Aug. —, 1846; wife, Lydia; children, Henry, David, John, Susanna, Sarah, Ann, Margaret; execs., John Bricker, Samuel Bell; wits., Joseph Clark, Samuel Bell.

JOHN BRICKER, Green township; date of will, June 19, 1860; date of probate, April 22, 1861; wife, Anne; children, John, David, Elizabeth, Martha, Ann Beadle; execs., David Bricker, John Bricker; wits., Jesse H. McMath, James Stewart.

BENJAMIN BRINDLEY, date of will, Jan. 24, 1845; date of probate, Feb. 8, 1845; wife, name not given; children, Benjamin, Samuel, Zachariah, William, Nathaniel, Nicholas, John, Sarah Lewis, Elon Hill, Pricilla Low, Nancy West; exec., John Brindley; wits., John McComb, John Smith, Robert McKee.

ABRAHAM BROKAW, Cadiz township; date of will, Sept. 22, 1824; date of probate, June 13, 1825; wife, Margaret; children, Abraham, Jane, Judith, Mary, Margary, Sally; exec., George Brown; wits., Josiah Thompson, James Tarbert, Robert Thompson.

ANN BROWN, date of will, Oct. 29, 1824; date of probate, Feb. 28, 1825; children, Ruth, Mary, Hanna, Elizabeth, Ellonor; grandchildren, Lydia Johnson (and her husband, Abiram), Sophia Turner; son-in-law, Benjamin Johnson; execs., names not given; wits., Alexander McCullough, John McMath.

DANIEL BROWN, date of will, Feb. 16, 1818; date of probate, Nov. 13, 1823; wife, Marium; children, Elizabeth, William, David; execs., sons, William Brown, Isaac Brown; wits., Jonathan Worrall, Benjamin Worrall.

HUGH BROWN, date of will, Oct. 6, 1822; date of probate, Nov. 16, 1822; wife, Jane; children, William, John, Mary, Ann, Rebekah, Elizabeth; execs., John Baker, Hugh Birney; wits., Samuel Amspoker, John Patterson, Thomas Patton.

JAMES BROWN, date of will, Oct. 23, 1856; date of probate, Dec. 24, 1856; wife, Jane; exec., Edward Hughs; wits., William Mills, George Brown.

ROBERT BROWN, Shortcreek township; date of will, Jan. 20, 1849; date of probate, May 28, 1850; wife, Isabella; legatees, Nancy Johnson, Robert

B. Alexander, William Brown, James P. Johnson and wife (Hannah), Rebecca Binns, George Brown, Mary A. Brown; execs., Samuel Reed, Samuel Kerr; wits., William Stringer, James Kerr.

WILLIAM BROWN, North township; date of will, Sept. 4, 1829; date of probate, April 13, 1830; wife, Jane; legatee, Jane Porter; exec., Jane Porter; wits., Walter B. Beebe, John Olmstead, Chauncey Dewey, William Arnold.

WILLIAM BROWN, date of will, May 31, 1836; date of probate, June 28, 1836; wife, Mary; children, Jane, Mary, John; exec., James McGuire; wits., Abner Hitson, James Shimer.

EZEKIEL O. BRYAN, date of will, April 9, 1849; date of probate, Oct. 29, 1852; wife, Mary Patience; children, William-F., Beal-H., Nancy-Jane, Augaline, Hannah, Caroline-Ann, Mary-Ann; execs., wife, Mary Patience Bryan, William F. Bryan, Beal H. Bryan; wits., Joseph R. Fourpaugh, John R. Huffman, Joseph Mead.

SAMUEL BUCHANAN, Rumley township; date of will, Oct. 3, 1854; date of probate, April 1, 1858; wife, name not given; children, John, Joseph, Jacob Vasbinder; exec., Joseph Buchanan; wits., Thomas Finnicum, Jane Pittinger, Samuel, William John Smylie.

ANN BUFFINGTON, date of will, July 7, 1848; date of probate, April 24, 1849; sisters and brothers, Eliza, Veakim, George, Simon: exec., Thomas Davidson; wits., Wesley M. Davidson, William R. Davidson.

BENJAMIN BURROWS, Nottingham township; date of will, March 3, 1822; date of probate, Sept. 30, 1822; wife, name not given; children, Jemima, James, William, Benedict; grandson, Richard Burrows; exec., Benedict Burrows; wits., Daniel Chicken; James McMath.

ABRAHAM BUSBY, Harrison co.; date of will, April 4, 1855; date of probate, July 2, 1855; wife, Deborah; children, Edward, Elizabeth Laymaster, Amanda Wood, Benjamin, Deborah Maxwell, Shadrach, Martin-Van Buren, Sheriden: niece, Elizabeth; execs., Deborah Busby, Sheriden Busby; wits., Lewis Ryan, Thomas S. Adrean.

EDITH BUSBY, Harrison co.; date of will, June 30, 1825; date of probate, Oct. 30, 1830; daughters, Ureth Shepler, Huldah; exec., John Busby; wits., Joseph Thompson, John Mattern, James W. Thompson.

JOHN BUSBY, Archer township; date of will, Oct. 30, 1851; date of probate, Dec. 10, 1853; wife, Agnes; children, Abraham-H., Sarah Healea, Rachel Smith, Belinda, Betsey Ann Baker, Eda Baker, Mary Ann McCombs, Dorcas Conaway, Deborah Singhaus, Jane Strawbaugh, grandchildren, John B. Busby, Nancy Jane Atkinson; exec., Abraham H. Busby; wits., Rudolph Mitchell, John Megaw.

ELISHA BUXTON, date of will, April 28, 1835; date of probate, May 26, 1838; wife, Nancy; legatees, William Buxton, James Buxton, Britain Jones, Sara Fryer, Elizabeth Barger, Mary Davis, William Welling, John Welling, David Welling; execs., William Welling, Sr., Cyrus Holt; wits., Joshua Dickerson, Alexander Bonham, James McMillan.

ISAAC CADWALADER, Nottingham township, Tuscarawas county; date of will, Feb. 19, 1811; date of probate, Aug. 25, 1813; wife, Elizabeth; children, John, Sarah; exec., Israel Wilson; wits., John Calwalader, Jr., Valentine Creamer.

MICHAEL CAIRNS, date of will, Dec. 17, 1844; date of probate, April 30, 1845; wife, Isabella; children, Margaret Thompson, Isabell Johnson, Ellan Gibson, William, Samuel, Moses, Michael-K., John; execs., Samuel Cairns, Moses Cairns; wits., James Slonaker, Alexander Gamble.

MOSES CARINS, date of will, April

1, 1852; date of probate, April 7, 1852; wife, Sarah Jane; sister, Margaret Mack; execs., not given; wits., Kennedy Cairns, Mathias Glass.

SAMUEL CAIRNS, date of will, May 10, 1855; date of probate, June 13, 1855; wife, Mahala; children, Moses, Elizabeth Kennedy, Margaret, Alice; execs., Mahala Cairns, Samuel Mack; wits., Jacob Weyanett, John Cairns.

JOHN CALDWELL, Green township; date of will, Oct. 18, 1859; date of probate, Jan. 9, 1860; wife, Sarah; children, John, Albert, James, Ankrum, William-H., Martha; grandchildren, James, Elizabeth, Sarah Davidson; execs., Sarah Caldwell, Ankrum Caldwell; wits., William Harrison, Rezin B. Handley.

ROBERT CALDWELL, Franklin township; date of will, April 25, 1851; date of probate, June 24, 1851; children, Robert, James, Joseph, John, William, Jane, Hannah, Isabella; grand-daughter, Rebecca Johnson; wits., Guenne Morrison, John Tennor.

ERASMUS CANNON, Shortcreek township; date of will, Sept. 3, 1814; date of probate, 1814-1815; wife, Mary; children, Rachel, Elizabeth, Mariah, Effey, Harriet, Moses, John, Rasmus; exec., Moses Cannon; wits., Edward Vanhorn, Henry Peregoy; Joseph Strahl.

THOMAS CAREN, date of will, March 17, 1826; date of probate, June 5, 1826; wife, Elizabeth; execs., William Dunbar, Elizabeth Caren; wits., James Conel, John Coalman, John Conel.

SAMUEL CARNAHAN, SR., Cadiz township; date of will, July 29, 1812; date of probate, May 28, 1816; wife, name not given; brothers, John, James, Samuel; nephews and nieces, George, James, William, John, Samuel, George (2d) and Agnes; execs., Samuel Gilmore, John McMillen; wits., Samuel McFadden, John McFadden, Thomas Richey.

SAMUEL CARNAHAN, SR., Cadiz township; date of will, Sept. 5, 1851; date of probate, Oct. 15, 1851; wife, Elizabeth; daughter, Nancy; exec., John McFadden; wits., William Arnold, S. McCormick.

JOHN CROTHERS, [Carrothers]; date of will, Oct. 24, 1832; date of probate, April 9, 1833; wife, Elizabeth; legatees, Martha Rea, Mary Rea, Elizabeth Rea, Robert McConnell, William McConnell, Margaret McConnell, Jane McConnell, Robert Henderson, Johnson Dilworth; execs., John Crothers, Robert Kirk; wits., Bazaleel Slemmons; Joseph Harris, I. Watson.

SAMUEL COROTHERS, Harrison co.; date of will, Jan. 8, 1831; date of probate, April 11, 1831; wife, Debora; sons, James, Samuel, John, Jesse; daughters, Margaret Perkins, Elizabeth Oliver, Mary Thompson, Deborah; execs., John Auld, James Smith; wits., James C. Guthre, Robert Auld.

MARY CARPENTER, Franklin township; date of will, Sept. 24, 1856; date of probate, Dec. 1, 1856; children, Fleming, Albert, John, William, Jane Hoobler, May Hilton, Sarah Ann Irwin; exec., Hiram Worstell; wits., H. Worstell, Charles Scott.

JOHN CARRICK, date of will, Aug. 31, 1852; date of probate, Feb. 4, 1854; wife, name not given; brothers and sisters, David Carrick, James Carrick, Laura Andrews, Nancy Carr; legatee, David Andrews; execs., James Adams, Jashead Adams; wits., James Carrick.

JOHN CARSON, SR., Nottingham township; date of will, Dec. 22, 1856; date of probate, May 15, 1858; children, Elijah, Franklin, William, Walter, John; grandchildren, William F. Hannah, Nancy Calvin, Barrett Rogers, and Finley, Lydia, John, Smith, Hannah, Susanna, and Nancy Hines; execs., Franklin Carson; wits., William Blair, Thomas Ramsey.

ROBERT CARSON, date of will, March 13, 1852; date of probate, Nov. 17, 1858; wife, name not given; brothers, James, William, Adam; nieces, Jane Coulter, Margaret Beck; nephew, Robert Beck; legatee, Ebby Carson; exec., William Lemmon; wits., Matthew Henderson, Griffith Lemmon.

HENRY CARVER, Washington township; date of will, Dec. 12, 1840; date of probate, April 12, 1841; wife, Tetitha; children, James, Abner, Eli'ah, Rebecca Thompson, Elizabeth Carrington, Ann Bailey, Mary Cox; execs., Abner Carver, Elijah Carver; wits., Thomas Ridgway, R. K. Price.

THOMAS CARVER, Shortcreek township; date of will, May 7, 1853; date of probate, Oct. 16, 1855; wife, Rebecca; children, Elizabeth Ann Booth, Julia Ann Watson, Emley Roach, Mary Jane Nicholson; exec., Thomas Nicholson; wits., James Nicholson, John P. Reddig.

JOSHUA CECIL, Cadiz township, Jefferson county; date of will, Feb. 28, 1810; date of probate, April 19, 1814; wife, Mary; children, Jeremiah, Joshua, Kinsey, Brice Berry, Levi, Hazel, Adrin, Ann Andrews, Elizabeth Ball, Tappa, Linney Andrews; grand-sons, John and Philip Cecil; execs., wife, Mary Cecil, and son, Brice Berry Cecil; wits., Thomas Dickerson, William Dunlap, Samuel Dunlap.

DAVID CHAMBERS, Green township, date of will, June 8, 1835; date of probate, July 18, 1835; wife, name not given; children, John, William, Polly, Sarah, Nancy, Rachel; exec., William Moore; wits., Walter B. Beebe, William C. Wilson.

ELIZABETH CHANEY, date of will, July 7, 1860; date of probate, March 21, 1861; children, Sarah-Ann, John-L.; exec., John L. Chaney; wits., John C. Plowman, Stephen J. Thompson.

WILLIAM CHANEY, date of will, May 17, 1839; date of probate, Aug. —, 1839; wife, Elizabeth; children, Sally-Ann, Polly, Thomas-A., Nathan; children by first wife, Charles, William B., Nancy Michener, Elsey, Joshua, Nancy Crane; exec., Elizabeth Chaney; wits., Robert McKee, Lemuel Green.

DANIEL CHICKEN, date of will, Oct. 8, 1823; date of probate, April 6, 1824; wife, Elenor; children, John, Daniel, Henry, Mary; execs., wife, Elenor Chicken, and son, John Chicken; wits., Isaac Whealdon, William Wilson.

ANDREW CLARK, Green township; date of will, Sept. 14, 1848; date of probate, Dec. 16, 1848; wife, Mary; exec., Mary Clark; wits., J. H. Black, George Taggart.

JAMES CLARK, date of will, Nov. 5, 1847; date of probate, April 24, 1848; wife, name not given; father mentioned, name not given; legatee, widow of Rev. John Walker; execs., Johnson Clark, Ingram Clark; wits., C. Dewey, Samuel Moorhead.

MATTHEW CLARK, Cadiz village; date of will, May 8, 1852; date of probate, May 29, 1852; wife, Jane; children, John-B., Elenanor M.; exec., John B. Clark, wits., William Arnold, Joseph Clark.

ROBERT CLARK, Washington township; date of will, April 8, 1857; date of probate, June 11, 1860; wife, name not given; children, James, Thomas, William, Robert, Matthew, Nancy McAdoo, Mary, Margaret; exec., Alexander Moore; wits., Samuel Logan, Alexander Moore.

SAMUEL CLIFFORD, will not dated; date of probate, April —, 1850; wife, Nancy; children, Edward, Katherine; grandchildren, Washington and Eliza Jane Clifford; execs., Edward Clifford, Thomas Clifford; wits., John Lafferty, James McAdams.

WILLIAM COALTRAP, Harrison co., date of will, Aug. 25, 1821; date of probate, Oct. 13, 1821; wife, Mary; children, Sarah McGeel, Margaret Hall, Elizabeth Hall, William, Matthew, Henry, David; execs., Matthew Simpson, Joseph Johnson; wits., Richard Wagner, Aquilla Tipton.

ROBERT COCHRAN, Cadiz village; date of will, April 29, 1847; date of probate, March 23, 1861; wife, Sarah; children, Samuel, David, Robert-R., Elenor, Dorcas Whitaker, Sarah-Jane; execs., Samuel Cochran, Robert R. Cochran; wits., Joshua Hamilton, Josiah Scott.

JOSHUA COLE, Jefferson county; date of will, —— 2, 1855; date of probate, Dec. 31, 1856; wife, name not given; children, Thomas R., Joseph, John, William, Mary Copeland, Elizabeth Tipton; exec., William Cole; wits., William Merryman, James Reed.

JOHN COLEMAN, Nottingham township; date of will, May 28, 1852; date of probate, Sept. 9, 1856; wife, Elizabeth; children, Findly, William, John, Mary Wyckoff, Sarah Eaton, Eliza Moore, Nancy Hefling, Margaret Fuller, Elizabeth; exec., Findly Coleman.

WILLIAM COLVIN, SR., Redstone, Fayette co., Pa., date of will, April 2, 1842; date of probate, Sept. 3, 1842; wife, Mary; children, David-C., Samuel, Levi, William, Rebecca Dunn, Hannah Brashear, Mary Sharpless, Harriet Townsend, Sarah Forsythe; grandson, William Colvin; execs., William Colvin, Levi Colvin; wits., John H. Tarr, Isaac Lynn.

JOHN CONAWAY, Stock township; date of will, April 17, 1860; date of probate, Oct. 14, 1861; wife, name not given; children, Elizabeth, Jemima, Susanna, Rachel, Cynthia Layport, Hannah Whitiker, Martha Patterson; exec., Charles Conaway; wits., Aaron Conaway, Joseph Shearer.

CATHERINE CONNELLY, date of will, Feb. 8, 1844; date of probate, Aug. 16, 1847; sister, Margaret; cousins, John Connelly, Patrick Connelly, Devanna, wife of Patrick Devanna; exec., Samuel Thompson; wits., Samuel Thompson, John Cheney, Susan Cowarden.

JAMES COOK, Cadiz, Jefferson co.; date of will, May —, 1809; date of probate, March 28, 1815; wife, Nancy; daughters, Mary Love, Elizabeth; sons mentioned, but names not given; execs., wife, Nancy Cook, son, Robert Cook, and John Patterson; wits., John Love, John Patterson, Samuel G. Berryhill.

MARGARET COOK, will not dated; date of probate, April 25, 1861; sister, Sarah Angus; exec., Sarah Angus; wits., Francis Moffet, Ephriam Lewis.

JAMES COPELAND, date of will, Feb. 28, 1859; date of probate, May 30, 1859; wife, name not given; children, Thomas, John, Leonard, Samuel, Matilda, Rachel, Maria, Amanda, Isabel, Nancy; exec., Thomas Copeland; wits., James J. Billingsley, Alexander Moore.

JOSEPH COOVERT, Harrison co.; date of will, April 18, 1843; date of probate, May 6, 1844; wife, Nancy; children, Harvey, Catherine; execs., wife, Nancy Coovert, and brother, Abraham Coovert; wits., John R. Wallace, Ezra Thompson, James Deusenberry.

DAVID CORBETT, date of will, May 17, 1836; date of probate, Nov. 11, 1836; wife, name not given; daughter, Sarah Bicking; brother, William; nephew, David Corbet; legatees, William Birney, William Fulton, Sarah Donaghey; exec., William Birney; wits., Joseph Wright, John M. Wright, John Birney.

SAMUEL CORBETT, Harrison co.; date of will, April 15, 1841; date of probate, Nov., 1841; wife, Betsey; children, Mary Maxwell, Margaret Henry, Sarah, David; exec., David Corbett; wits., William Boggs, George Holmes.

SARAH CORBETT, Harrison co.; date of will, April 28, 1843; date of probate, Aug. 21, 1843; brother and sister, David Corbett, Mary Maxwell; legatee, David B. Atkinson; exec., William Lee; wits., John G. McCollough, Abram Acres.

WILLIAM CORKHILL, Harrison co.; date of will, March 2, 1849; date of probate, April 26, 1849; wife, name not given; children, Marinee, Elizabeth, William, Thomas; exec., Thomas Corkhill; wits., James Fisher, William Maxwell.

SARAH COUZENS, Harrison co., date of will, Feb. 6, 1820; date of probate, Sept. 30, 1822; daughter, Ann; grandchildren mentioned, but names not given; exec., Bradway Thomson; wits., James Roberts, Aaron Matson, Thomas Thorn.

GEORGE COX, Archer township; date of will, June 19, 1849; date of probate, Nov. 9, 1849; wife, Sarah; children, John, Hiram, Obadiah, George, Martin, Mary Wilson, Rachel Breden, Sarah Cox, Judy Ann Smiley; exec., Josiah Scott; wits., John A. Bingham; Josiah Scott.

JOSHUA COX, Harrison co.; date of will, Feb. 16, 1854; date of probate, March 31, 1854; wife, Editha; children, William, Ebenezer, James, John, Joshua-T., George-W., Rebecca, Sarah-Jane; execs., wife, Editha Cox, and John Bell; wits., John Bell, James Bell, David Hanlin.

ZEBEDIAH COX, date of will, June 12, 1825; date of probate, June 15, 1825; wife, Charlotte; children, Harrison, Elijah, Ziporah, Zebediar; legatee, Gessa Peppers; execs., John Busby, George Skippers; wits., Abner Hixson, Abraham Laport, Francis Gilmore.

PETER CRABTREE, Harrison co.; date of will, March 22, 1821; date of probate, Dec. 7, 1827; wife, Sarah; children, Rohdia Dixon, Rachel House, Sarah, Ann, Amey, Elizabeth, Cornelius, Gabriel, William; exec., Cornelius Crabtree; wits., Abrim Johnson, John Lawrey.

JOHN CRAIG, Harrison Co.; date of will, Aug. 19, 1825; date of probate, Oct. 24, 1825; wife, Betsey; children, Johnson, William, Walter, John, Jane, Rachel, Polly, Ann, Rebecca; execs., brother, Walter Craig, son, Johnson Craig, and William Moore; wits., Chauncey Dewey, William Grimes, John McFadin.

SUSANNA CRAIG, Cadiz township; date of will, May 22, 1826; date of probate, July 15, 1826; children, Rebecca, Susanna, John, George, William, Samuel; execs., sons, John Craig, George Craig; wits., Walter B. Beebe, J. Harris, J. W. Harris.

ASA CRAWFORD, date of will, Dec. 13, 1851; date of probate, May 11, 1852; wife, Elizabeth; children, James, Mary-Jane, Edward, Catherine; exec., Elizabeth Crawford; wits., John Hastings, William Williams.

EDWARD CRAWFORD, date of will, May 26, 1828; date of probate, Oct. 24, 1831; wife, Mary; children, John, Thomas-W., Alexander, Josiah, Elenor, Mary, Isabelle, Nancy, Margaret, Elizabeth, Harriet; exec., Mary Crawford; wits., Abner Hixson, George Bartow.

THOMAS CRAWFORD, Athens township; date of will, June 12, 1826; date of probate, Oct. 17, 1826; wife, Jane; children, John, William, James, Nathaniel, Margaret, Mary, Sarah; execs., Joseph Grimes, Edward Vanhorn; wits., George Welch, James Grimes.

WILLIAM CRAWFORD, Harrison co.; date of will, Aug. 20, 1850; date of probate, Nov. 5, 1850; wife, Jane; children, Rosannah, Jane Wilson, Obira, Mary, Elizabeth, James, John, William, Robert; exec., John Bethel; wits., James Clements, Daniel Clements.

ELIZABETH CREE, Harrison co.; date of will, May 21, 1831; date of probate, April 12, 1841; son, James; exec., James Cree; wits., Moses Wright, Ebenezer A. Gray, Samuel Mossgrove.

JAMES CREE, Harrison co.; date of will, Feb. 8, 1859; date of probate, July 2, 1859; wife, Sarah; children, John-W., William, George-W., Robert, Thomas, Mary-M., Elizabeth-V., Sarah-J.; execs., names not given; wits., John Watts, Bazel Steel.

THOMAS CRUMLEY, date of will,

Dec. 29, 1860; date of probate, Aug. 6, 1861; wife, name not given; children, Mary Dickerson, Hannah Glazener, Emily Barkhurst, Ira, Joseph, David, James, Aaron; grandchildren, Samuel, Baruch, and Thomas Dickerson, and Elizabeth House; execs., Ira Crumley, David M. Crumley; wits., Robert F. Hargrave, Amon Lemmon.

ROBERT CULBERTSON, Harrison co.; date of will, Jan. 13, 1840; date of probate, April 12, 1841; wife, Mary; children, Ann Crawford, George, Gillespie; exec., Gillespie Culbertson; wits., John Webb.

DAVID CUNNINGHAM, date of will, April 21, 1849; date of probate, Aug. —, 1849; wife, Ann; son, John; grandchildren, David and Mary Cunningham; brother, Robert; legatees, Rev. Samuel C. Baldridge, Thomas Hanna; execs., wife, Ann Cunningham, and son, John Cunningham; wits., James McAdams, Jesse K. Thomas.

DR. WILLIAM CUNNINGHAM, date of will, Feb. 15, 1842; date of probate, April 6, 1842; wife, Nancy; children, Thomas-H., William-C., John-W., George-W., William, Elizabeth; father; mother; execs., Nancy Cunningham, Samuel Heidy; wits., Thomas Day; E. H. Custer.

WILLIAM CUNNINGHAM, Washington township; date of will, March 14, 1855; date of probate, Aug. 18, 1855; wife, name not given; children, Mary-Elizabeth, Emma-Jane, Isabella-Frances, Margaret-Ella; exec., Alexander McCullough; wits., S. K. Billingsley, Alexander McCullough.

JOHN CURBAY, Shortcreek township; date of will, Sept. 9, 1839; date of probate, Nov. 18, 1839; wife, name not given; children, James, Mary; execs., James Curbay, Mary Curbay; wits., David Barrett, William Barrett, Josiah Scott.

LEWIS DAVIDSON, date of will, Sept. 1, 1832; date of probate, April 8, 1833; wife, Mary; children, Mary, Jesse, Thomas, Joseph, Jonathan; execs., John L. Grubb, Lewis H. Davidson; wits., Ira Mitchell, L. Sp--, Joseph Fry.

THOMAS DAVIDSON, date of will, Jan. 3, 1856; date of probate, Feb. 13, 1856; wife, name not given; children, Ruth-Ann, Hary-J., Harriett A. Boyer, Isaac-C., William-R., Nelson-R., Wesley-M., Alfred-A.; exec., William R. Davidson; wits., William Wright, Isaac N. Wright.

JAMES DAVIS, Harrison co.; date of will, Jan. 31, 1851; date of probate, May 11, 1852; wife, name not given; children, John, Martin, Ann Cecil, Yorseth Johnson, Ellen Crabtree, Eliza Buckingham, Elizabeth Crumley; legatee, Providence Crabtree; execs., John Davis; wits., Michael Leard, John Poulson.

JOHN F. DAVIS, date of will, Sept. 7, 1827; date of probate, Oct. 15, 1827; wife, Ann; niece, Catherine; children, names not given; execs., Ann Davis, Henry Carver; wits., Richard Price, Thomas P. Jenkins, William Davis.

JOHN DAVIS, German township; date of will, Aug. 24, 1835; date of probate, Oct. 28, 1835; family mentioned, names not given; execs., names not given; wits., A. Patterson, George W. Duffield.

JOHN DAVIS, Harrison co.; date of will, Jun. 2, 1855; date of probate, Dec. 27, 1855; wife, name not given; exec., Joseph Rogers; wits., Alexander Moore, William F. Hines.

NICHOLAS DAVIS, date of will, Nov. 11, 1826; date of probate, Dec. 21, 1826; wife, Elenor; children, David, William, Elijah, George, Robert, Guyan Nicholas, Elenor, Nancy, Eliza, Catherine, Rebecca; execs., Elenor Davis, George Brown; wits., George Cook, Esther Morrison, George Brown.

SAMUEL DAVIS, Harrison co.; date of will, June 14, 1840; date of probate, June —, 1840; wife, Sarah; children, Mary Knox, Sarah Brown, Margaret Welling, Jane Patterson, Elizabeth, Elenor, Barcus, Susan,

Esther-Ann, John, William; execs., John Davis, John Knox; wits, Enoch Thomas, Robert McMillan, William Boggs.

WILLIAM DAVIS, Harrison co.; date of will, April 24, 1829; date of probate, July 29, 1829; wife, Martha; children, John, George, James, Alfred, Polly; exec., Jacob Ream; wits., James Mathias, J. R. Kirkpatrick.

NATHANIEL DAWSON, Jefferson county; date of will, Feb. 22, 1857; date of probate, May 15, 1857; wife, Amelia; children, Joseph, Nathaniel, John, George-W., Rebecca McGrew, Martha Lewis, Eliza Jane Cramblet; exec., John Dawson; wits., James W. Parr, Joseph Meholin.

THOMAS DAWSON, Cadiz; date of will, Feb. 16, 1858; date of probate, Feb. 2, 1860; wife, name not given; sister, Sarah Kerr; nephew, Thomas Dawson; sister-in-law, Rebecca Dawson: legatees, William, James, Sarah, Elizabeth, Margaret, and Mary Stein; children of Margaret Stein; Joseph, Amanda, Salina, and Sarah Sharp; execs., William McFarland, Andrew McFarland; wits., Boid Christy, Samuel Alexander, J. S. McCready.

GEORGE DAY, Harrison co.; date of will, Feb. 24, 1855; date of probate, May 22, 1855; wife, name not given; children, Uriah, Sally Blair, Charity Milligan, Mary Wells; legatees, Louisa-Jepsa, Margaret-Jane, Mandy, George, Mariah Barger; exec., Alexander Moore; wits. Jehu Polson, James Keesy.

JOHN DEWITT, date of will, Aug. 25, 1856; date of probate, Dec. 20, 1856; wife, Mary; childern, Thomas, George, Jacob, William, John, Jonathan, Ellen Suttles, Mary Vansickle, Rachel Cree, Catherine Steel; execs., Mark Hogue, ————; wits., Thomas Ridgeway, John Knox.

JOHN DICK, Washington township, date of will, Dec. 22, 1829; date of probate, March 30, 1830; wife, name not given; children, Mary Purviance, Sarah McGrew, Rachel Parks, Susan Maxson, Joseph, John, James, Samuel; execs., Elijah Covington, John Dick; wits., Isaac Fordice, Stokely Craig, Richard Price.

THOMAS DICKERSON, date of will, Sept. 16, 1851; date of probate, Feb. 19, 1853; wife, Mary; children, Hiram, John, Susanna Jones, Barrick, Thomas, Levi, Eli, Joseph; exec., Joseph Dickerson; wits., Eli Dickerson, Levi Dickerson.

JOHN DICKEY, Harrison co.; date of will, Jan. 15, 1847; date of probate, Aug. 16, 1847; wife, name not given; brother, Samuel; legatee, Benjamin Dickey; exec., Samuel Dickey; wits., Hiram Worstell, John S. McGill.

MARGARET DICKEY, Harrison co.; date of will, July 3, 1844; date of probate, Nov. 9, 1846; legatee, Samuel Dickey; exec., Samuel Dickey; wits., Stewart Auld, John S. McGill.

JAMES DONAHEY, date of will, April 12, 1843; date of probate, May —, 1846; wife, name not given; children, John, James, Jesse, Margaret Killbreath; execs., John Donahey, James Donahey, Jesse Donahey; wits., Robert Pittis, Sr., Robert Pittis, Jr.

THOMAS DRUMMOND, date of will, Feb. 1, 1838; date of probate, May 21, 1838; wife, name not given; children, Robert, James, Catherine, Mary, grandson, Thomas; execs., John T. Cramblet, William McCullough; wits., James P. Barnes, John T. Cramblet.

JOHN DRYDEN, Freeport township; date of will, Oct. 9, 1832; date of probate, April 8, 1833; wife, Katherine; children, James, John, Samuel, Robert-C., William-K., Jane, Mary, Elizabeth, Martha; execs., Hugh McCullough, Andrew Isaac; wits., Robert Paisley, James McCullough.

ADAM DUNLAP, Harrison co.; date of will, Oct. 24, 1829; date of probate, March 30, 1830; wife, Rebecca; children, Samuel, Joseph, William, John, Robert, Sarah, Esther, Rebecca, Mary, Rachel; execs., Samuel Dunlap,

Henry Barricklow; wits., Uriah McMillen, William Jones, Edward Lafferty.

ADAM DUNLAP, Harrison co.; date of will, April 16, 1849; date of probate, May 22, 1849; wife, name not given: father, John Dunlap; execs., John Dunlap, John Watts; wits., Matthew H. Phillips, William Rankin.

ROBERT DUNLAP, Harrison co.; date of will, Feb. 29, 1860; date of probate, March 13, 1860; wife, name not given; children, Adam, Hugh, Samuel, Nancy, Rebecca McFadden; exec., Samuel Dunlap; wits., John Dickerson, William Rankin.

SAMUEL DUNLAP, date of will, Sept. 21, 1839; date of probate, Nov. 18, 1839; wife, Sarah; children, Rachel, Elizabeth, Susan, Rebecca, Polly, Sarah, Jane, Adam; execs., Adam Dunlap, Edward Clifford; wits., Joshua Dickerson, Thomas Clifford.

DAVID DUTTON, date of will, ——, 1836; date of probate, Dec. 5, 1836; wife, Hannah; children, William, Robert, David, Francis, Asa, Sarah Matson, Hannah Hensall, Susan Cowardan, Anna Mills; execs., Robert Dutton, John Heberling; wits., Thomas Carver, John Stradling, James McMillan.

ROBERT DUTTON, date of will March 16, 1845; date of probate, April —, 1845; wife, Anna; children, Martha-Ann, Scynthia, Hannah, Ezra; execs., Samuel Griffith, David Dutton; wits., William Dutton, Levi Beck, James McMillan.

WILLIAM EAGELSON, Shortcreek township; date of will, June 20, 1829; date of porbate, July 28, 1829; wife, Margaret; children, William, John, Jane; execs., wife, Margaret Eagleson, son, William Eagleson; wits., Joseph Cellar, Samuel Davis.

MAGDALENE EASTERDAY, date of will, Jan. 20, 1838; date of probate, Dec. 17, 1838; nephew, David Bowers; niece, Catherine Shiets; sister, Barbary Bowers: exec., Samuel Gonff; wits., Joseph Flory, Solomon Miner.

HENRY EASTLICK, Archer township; date of will, Oct. 28, 1853; date of probate, Feb. 26, 1859; wife, Elizabeth; children, James, Henry, John, Paseo, Nancy, Rebecca, Jane, Polly Baker, Elizabeth Canaga; execs., James Eastlick, John Atkinson; wits., Josiah Scott, Lawson Scott.

JEHIAL E. EATON, Franklin township; date of will, March 31, 1852; date of probate, May 17, 1852; wife, name not given; children, Mary, Elizabeth-Ann; execs., wife, and Findly Coleman; wits., Robert Pittis, Daniel Palmer.

MARY ECKLEY, Harrison co.; date of will, Nov. 11, 1825; date of probate, Jan. 28, 1826; sister, Ann Clark; nephew, Lewis; nieces, Mary-Ann, Hannah E. Clark, Sarah Williams, Ann Grey; wits., Jonathan Worrell, Eleanor Worrell, Lewis Bernhard.

ADAM EDGAR, date of will, Oct. 16, 1848; date of probate, April 25, 1849; wife, name not given; sister, Elizabeth Edgar; exec., George Kidwell; wits., M. Crowl, Frederick Furney.

HENRY J. EDNEY, date of will, Oct. 17, 1845; date of probate, Nov. —, 1845; wife, name not given; mother, name not given; brother, Robert; sisters, Isabel, Louisa, Mary, Jane, Elizabeth, Adalade, Herriatta; exec., Robert Pittis, Jr.; wits., M. F. Mallernee, Isaac Talbott.

AZARIAH EDWARDS, Cadiz township; date of will, May 14, 1849; date of probate, May 6, 1859; wife, Henrietta; children, Azariah, William, Nancy, Mary; execs., Robert Lyons, Josiah Scott; wits., A. C. Turner, H. H. Paxton.

HENRIETTA EDWARDS, Cadiz village; date of will, Feb. 6, 1859; date of probate, March 21, ——; brothers, Samuel Moore, Hezekiah Moore; exec., Josiah Scott; wits., W. G. Finney, H. G. Forker, Josiah Scott.

JOHN ENDSLEY, date of will, Jan. 18, 1850; date of probate, Feb. 1, 1850;

wife, Barbara; brothers and sisters, Thomas, James, Mary Shannon, Sarah McClain, Jane McPeck; exec., George McPeck; wits.,William Smylie, Robert Maxwell.

ALEXANDER EVANS, date of will, June 4, 1830; date of probate, Aug. 4, 1831; wife, Jane; children, James, William, Rebekah Givin; grandchildren, Alexander Evans, John Evans, Margaret Evans, Caroline Evans; execs., William Evans, Michael Conaway; wits., Alexander Simpson, Robert Simpson.

MARY EVANS, date of will, March 16, 1830; date of probate, Aug. 3, 1830; children, Alexander, John, Margaret; exec., William Evans; wits., Michael Conaway, Francis Grace, John Simpson, Robert Simpson, Alexander Simpson, Robert Given.

ROBERT EYRE, date of will, April 26, 1826; date of probate, July 28, 1828; wife, Jemima; children, Ann, Hannah; exec., John Grubb; wits., J. Harris, Charles Holt, Cyrus Holt.

HENRY FEISTER, Nottingham township; date of will, March 19, 1836; date of probate, Sept. 20, 1836; wife, Margaret; children, John, Charles, Henry, Robert, Levi, Margaret, Hannah, Charlotte, Sarah; execs., Margaret Feister, Charles Feister; wits., Philip Fulton, James Garner.

CHARLES FERRELL, date of will, March 30, 1849; date of probate, March 10, 1852; wife, Mary; children, Isaac, William, James, Thomas, Charles, Isabella, Margaret, Jane, Mary Eleanor, Milly-Maria; wits., Jacob Lewis, James Ferrell.

ADAM FIGLEY, date of will, March 9, 1847; date of probate, April 2, 1850; wife, name not given; children, Deliha Dickson, Joseph, Jacob; exec., Joseph Figley; wits., James Kirkpatrick; George Nickels.

JAMES FINNEY, date of will, Jan. 7, 1822; date of probate, Oct. 19, 1829; wife, Rebecah; children, Robert, John, Walter-B., Thomas, Martha, Francis, Elizabeth McMillen; legatee, Robert Braden; execs., William Hamilton, Baruch Dickerson; wits., Robert Hamilton, James Hamilton.

PHEBE FINNEY, Harrison co.; date of will, Nov. 27, 1820; date of probate, March 19, 1820; daughter, Sarah Gillespie; friend, Amey Brown; legatee, Benjamin Brown; execs., names not given; wits., William Baldwin, John Dunlap.

ELIZABETH FISHER, date of will, Sept. 9, 1827; date of probate, April 1, 1828; sister and brother, Sarah Everett, Joel Hancock; exec., John Everett; wits., Jonathan Worrall, Isaac Ady.

GEORGE FISHER, date of will, March 15, 1821; date of probate, July 31, 1821; wife, Esther; children mentioned, no names given; execs., Samuel Buchanan, Thomas A. Beatty; wits., James Ferrell, John Archbold, Henry Easlick.

GEORGE FISHER, date of will, Aug. 30, 1823 ;date of probate, Aug. 18, 1823; wife, Elizabeth; children, James, Thomas, Eva Gordon, Gracy Snyder, Matilda Rouse, Elizabeth Custard, Susanna Lee, May Welch, Harriett Shrayer; grandchildren, George Fisher, George Custard, Elizabeth Lee, Elizabeth Shrayer; execs., Elizabeth Fisher, Thomas Fisher; wits., George Shrier, Thomas Patton.

JOHN FISHER, Harrison co.; date of will, April 17, 1815; date of probate, July 4, 1815; wife, Sarah; children mentioned, names not given; execs., Samuel Faucet, Joseph Faucet; wits., James Campbell, Jonathan Marsh Ellis.

ANTHONY FISSEL, Harrison co.; date of will, Feb. 26, 1828; date of probate, March 31, 1825; wife, name not given; brothers, John, Jacob; father, John; mother, Ann; exec., Abner Hixon; wits., Abner Hixon, Jacob Polmore.

CHARLES FITZSIMMONS, date of will, May 18, 1830; date of probate,

HARRISON COUNTY WILLS

Aug. 3, 1830; wife, Susanna-Catherine; children, Jacob, Charles, Elizabeth, Katy, Ann; exec., George W. Bell; wits., James Orr, Samuel McCollough.

WILLIAM FOOS, date of will, May 23, 1831; date of probate, Aug. 1, 1831; wife, Catherine; son, John; execs., Catherine Foos, Peter Himebaugh wits., George Himebaugh, John Gruber.

JOSIAH FORBES, Harrison co.; date of will, July 11, 1836; date of probate, Feb. 8, 1837; wife, Ellen; legatees, Church of Christ, Foreign Missionary Society, Domestic Missionary Society; execs., names not given; wits., Samuel Dunlap, Sr., John Moore.

ANN FORD, date of will, Dec. 26, 1820; date of probate, Aug. 3, 1821; children, Eleanor Chicken, Nancy Bricker, Henry David, Daniel David, Sarah Kinsey; grandchildren, Sarah Grewell, David Grewell, Mary Ann Grewell, Rachel Grewell, Thomas Grewell; exec., Henry David; wits., Jonathan Sayrs, Isaac Whealdon.

ISAAC FORD, date of will, Dec. 27; 1830; date of probate, Oct. 27, 1831; wife, Rachel; children, Claton, John, Lewis, Benjamin, Isaac, Nancy, Rachel; granddaughter, Rachel Barber; legatee, Matilda Franks; exec., John Ford; wits., Joseph Meek, John Coalman.

SAMUEL FORDYCE, date of will, Aug. 28, 1850; date of probate, May 2, 1851; wife, Zelpah; legatees, Thomas Crago, Mary Ann Rogers; [a boy and girl that he raised]; exec., Thomas Crago; wits., John M. Brown, Moses Riley.

ABRAHAM FORNEY, Cadiz township; date of will, July 26, 1822; date of probate, Oct. 11, 1824; wife, Susan; children, John, Abraham, Frederick, Catherine, Polly, Susan, Sophia; execs., sons, John Forney, Abraham Forney; wits., Walter B. Beebe, John Pritchard, J. Harris.

SUSANNA FORNEY, Harrison co.; date of will, July 14, 1834; date of probate, June 28, 1842; children, Polly Timmons, Susannah Rabe; friend, John Maholm; exec., John Maholm; wits., Walter B. Beebe, James Smylie.

GEORGE FOSTER, date of will, April 20, 1849; date of probate, Aug. —, 1849; wife, Jane; children, George, Joseph, William, Madison, David, Jane Cummins, Jerusa Custard, Sarah Reed, Elizabeth Kent, Levina; exec., Malachi Jolly; wits., A. F. Croskey, James Veirs.

THOMAS FOSTER, Harrison co.; date of will, Feb. 23, 1856; date of probate, March 13, 1856; wife, Mary; children, Ann Barto, Sally Brumston, John; execs., names not given; wits., Luther Rowley, Charles A. Scott.

FRANCIS FOWLER, date of will, April 2, 1838; wife, Mary; 1 gatee, Francis Fowler, Jr.; exec., Mary Fowler; wits., Thomas McClintock; John Fowler.

JOHN FOWLER, date of will, Dec. 3, 1838; date of probate, April 26, 1847; wife, Elizabeth; children, Andrew, James, John, Mary Cells, Sally Testers, Nancy, Hannah; execs., Elizabeth Fowler, John Fowler; wits., Daniel Conaway, John Gruber, H. H. Beckett.

JOHN FRANCE, date of will, Dec. 9, 1825; date of probate, March 7, 1826; wife, Rebeckah; children, mentioned, names not given; execs., Alexander Foster, William Holmes; wits., William Holmes, John Davis, Alexander Foster.

JOHN FRANCIS, Shortcreek township; date of will, March 24, 1813; date of probate; Aug. 24, 1813; wife, name not given; children, Mary, Ann, Elizabeth Diddle; John; execs., George Diddle, John Clark; wits., John Smith, Michael Yost, John Buss.

ELIZABETH JANE FRY, Cadiz village; date of will, May 17, 1856; date of probate, June 19, 1856; brother, William J.; exec., William J. Fry; wits., Lewis Lewton, Thomas Phillips.

JAMES FULTON, Shortcreek township; date of will, Sept. 6. 1824; date of probate, Oct. 24, 1825; wife, name not given; children David, Hugh, Susanna, Polly; grandson, James Redick; execs., Hugh Fulton, David Fulton; wits., Robert Thompson, John McConnell, Sr., Adam Robison.

JOHN FULTON, Harrison co.; date of will, Sept. 27, 1824; date of probate, Sept. 2, 1825; wife, name not given; children, Nancy, Rachel, Mary, Cynthia, Sarah, Thomas, Alexander, Robert; execs., John Gallagher, John M. Cannon; wits., Samuel Grabel, Rachel Grabel.

PHILIP FULTON, date of will, Sept. 7, 1841; date of probate, Nov. —, 1841; wife, Sarah; children, John, Alexander, William, Philip, Jane, Rowland, Hannah Kirkpatrick, Eliza Lantz, Sara-Ann, Mary-Ann, Juliana; grandson, Philip Fulton; exec., Alexander Fulton; wits., Samuel Rowland, Franklin Carson.

WILLIAM GALLAHER, Harrison co.; date of will, June 16, 1831; date of probate, Nov. 8, 1832; wife, Jane; children, James, Thomas-B., William, John, Margaret, Julyan; execs., Jane Gallaher, James Gallaher; wits., William Holmes, Allen Jamison.

SOLOMON GAMBLE, Archer township; date of will Feb. 4, 1852; date of probate, Nov. 1, 1852; wife, name not given; brother, John; legatees, Elizabeth Calwell, Clarissa Gamble, Solomon Gamble; execs., James S. McCoy, Alexander Holland; wits., William Arnold, James S. McCoy, Jacob Lewis.

JOB GATCHEL, Cadiz township; date of will, Feb. 10, 1815; date of probate, March 28, 1815; wife, name not given; sisters, Ester Pugh, Rachel Perry; brothers, Thomas, Jacob and Joseph; mother, Sarah Gatchel; execs., Sarah Gatchel, John Perry; wits., John Carson, William Rogers.

JAMES GEARY, date of will, Jan. 23, 1816; date of probate, Oct. 17, 1820; father, William Geary; wits., William Wickoff, Abijah Robinett, Thomas Crabtree.

THOMAS GIBBONS, Green township; date of will, Feb. 24, 1834; date of probate, May 28, 1838; wife, Sarah; niece, Eleanor Parry; brother, Joshua; exec., Sarah Gibbons; wits., James Hamilton, Eli Hamilton, Alex. Hamilton.

JOSEPH GILBERT, date of will, Feb. 27, 1832; date of probate, June 11, 1832; wife, name not given; cousins, Gorden R. Hosy, Eli Hosy, John Hosy, Levi Hosy, John Warfel, Joseph Wells, Joseph G. Atkinson, Bazaleel Wells, Ester Warfel, Jane Wells, Mary Warfel, Susanna Warfel, Margaret Wells, Harriet Bell, Mary Jane Atkinson; exec., Samuel Warfel; wits., Joseph Braden, Walter Braden.

THOMAS GILHAM, date of will, July 21, 1856; date of probate, Aug. 7, 1856; wife, Dolly; nephew, William Reese Burr; execs., wife, Dolly Gilham, and Ellsey Moor; wits., J. W. Wherry, Isaac Clevenger, Thomas Jones.

WILLIAM GILMORE, date of will, July 15, 1832; date of probate, Oct. 24, 1833; wife, Rose; children, Nathaniel, Francis, John, James, William, Goron, Jane, Rose; granddaughter, Ester; legatee, Jane McMulen; execs., James McAdams, Joshua Dickerson; wits., Mathew Steen, Samuel Dunlap, James Porter.

JOHN GILLESPIE, Stock township; date of will, Dec. 29, 1831; date of probate, April 2, 1834; wife, Jane; children, John, Thompson, James, Maria Linsiey, Nancy, Margaret, Elizabeth, Sarah; exec., Jane Gillespie; wits., Richard Wagers, Henry Green.

JOHN GILLIS, date of will, Jan. 12, 1832; date of probate, March 31, 1834; wife, name not given; children, James Elizabeth; exec., daughter, Elizabeth McCamess; wits., James Robertson. John Speedy, Samuel Kelly.

JACOB GLASENER, Harrison co.; date of will, Feb. 2, 1839; date of probate, March 9, 1852; wife, Ruth; children, Mary, Jacob, Hannah Hays, Nicholas, Prudence McBride, Nancy Dickerson; execs., Thomas Crumoley, Thomas Hogg; wits., Isaac Lews, William Wiley, George Atkinson.

JOHN GLASENOR, date of will, Aug. 7, 1831; date of probate, June 13, 1833; wife, Mary; children, James, Eli, Garret, Absalom, Jacob, Elizabeth, Eleanor, Rebecca, Hannah; execs., James Glasenor, Eli Glasenor, John Walraven; wits., Thomas Gibbons, Peter Thomas, Ann Griffith.

JACOB GOODSON, date of will, Feb. 1, 1815; date of probate, March 8, 1815; wife, name not given; legatees, Gorden Parker, Jacob Parker; exec., Jacob Parker; wits., James Judkins, James Judkin, Jr., Thomas Ross.

JESSE GOODWIN, Harrison co.: date of will, April 11, 1854; date of probate, Oct. 9, 1856; wife, Ruth; children, Kinsey, Wilson, Abi, Lydia Pickett, Hannah Singer, Lacy Singer, Mary Worley, Martha; execs., Wilson Goodwin, Daniel Worley; wits., Isaac Lewis, Joshua Adams, William Thompson.

JOHN GOURLAY, date of will, Aug. 13, 1830; date of probate, Feb. 18, 1857; wife, name not given; brother, George Courley; exec., George Gourley; wits., Thomas Parkinson, James Johnson, James Leech.

MICHAEL GRABLE, Harrison co.; date of will, April 29, 1850; date of probate, Aug. 15, 1850; wife, Susan; children, William, Thomas, James, John, Phebe, Mary, Martha, Jane, Susan; exec., William Fulton; wits., Alexander Patterson, William Tweed.

THOMAS GRACE, date of will, April 28, 1839; date of probate, Nov. 18, 1839; wife, name not given; children, George, Francis, John, Matthew, Thomas, Jane; son-in-law, John Crawford; execs., John Grace, John Crawford; wits., John Leeper, Charles McDivit.

EBENEZER GRAY, Green township, date of will, Feb. 4, 1850; date of probate, Feb. 16, 1861; wife, Margaret; children, William, Jonathan, John-P., Samuel-R., Benoni, Rezin. Phebe; exec., Jonathan Gray.

SAMUEL GREEN, Franklin township; date of will, Feb. 14, 1859; date of probate, April 30, 1860; wife, Mary; children, Nathan, John, Thomas, Robert, Joseph, Ellen Gallaher, Sarah Myers, Elizabeth, Ann, Ruth Work, Mary Jane Green; execs., Cunningham Gallaher, Samuel Work; wits., Dr. J. B. Ong, Josiah Scott.

VALENTINE GREER, date of will, Feb. 18, 1827; date of probate, Sept. 3, 1827; wife, Belinda; children, Mary Pugh, Rebecca Elliott, Nancy Dunlap, Hannah Dunlap, Actions, William, John, George; exec., William Greer; wits., Van Brown, Robert Burnhill, James Brown.

MARY GREGG, date of will, April 18, 1847; date of probate, April 26, 1847; sisters, Hannah Gregg, Lydia Gregg; exec., Joseph Holloway; wits., Brandus Bethel, Aaron Holloway.

PRESLEY GREGG, Ohio co.; date of will, Sept. 16, 1849; date of probate, Nov. 17, 1849; wife, Sarah; son, Presley, and four other children, names not given; execs., Sarah Gregg, Henry Barricklow; wits., Elizabeth W. Parks, Ann Cunningham.

JOSEPH GRIMES, Wheeling township, Belmont co., O.; date of will, Jan. 11, 1837; date of probate, Feb. 29, 1840; wife, Martha-E.; children, William, Joseph, George-D., John, Lucinda, Isabella, Juliann Campbell; execs., Martha E. Grimes, William Grimes; wits., William Boggs, John Lyle.

WILLIAM GRIMES, Cadiz township; date of will, May 18, 1840; date of probate, Aug. 27, 1840; wife, Rebecca; children, William, Anderson, Thomas, Eliza Sloan, Nancy, Martha-Jane; sister, Jane; exec., Anderson Grimes; wits., Charles Patterson, Thomas C. Vincent.

ABRAHAM GRINE, date of will, March 19, 1842; date of probate, Aug.

18, 1842; wife, Catherine, children, Daniel, Jacob, John, Sophia Strausbaugh, Hannah, Catherine; grandchildren, George, Sophia, Catherine, Abraham, and Daniel Riggles; execs., Jacob Grine, Peter Strausbaugh; wits., Jacob Kail, Robert Orr.

JAMES McC. GALBRAITH, Harrison co.; date of will June 11, 1857; date of probate, Aug. 1, 1857; wife, name not given; children, John-D., Elizabeth Moorehead, Mary, Nancy Paxton, Deborah, Sarah, Jane, Tabitha Baldwin; wits., Samuel Foreman, Samuel Paul.

JOSEPH GUNDY, date of will, June 28, 1820; date of probate, March 18, 1823; wife, name not given; children, Rebeckah, Christina, Mary, Reginah, Magdalena, Framia, Benjamin, Joseph; exec., John Heastand; wits., John Crom, Jacob Crom.

ALEXANDER GUNNING, date of will, Feb. 2, 1859; date of probate, Nov. 16, 1859; wife, name not given; son, John; exec., John Gunning; wits., S. R. Magee, Robert Hillis.

SAMUEL GUTHENE, date of will, Sept. 16, 1851; date of probate, Oct. 10, 1851; wife, Elizabeth; daughter, Jane; execs., names not given; wits., M. R. Williamson, Daniel Garven.

ROBERT GUTHRY, Cadiz township; date of will, May 2, 1815; date of probate, July 5, 1815; wife, name not given; children, Robert, Nathaniel, John, Josiah, Samuel, William, David, James, Joseph, Jane, Nancy, Sally, Martha; execs., William Guthry, Robert Guthry; wits., George S. Broche, Charles Robison.

ROBERT GUTHRIE, Harrison co.; date of will, Aug. 4, 1852; date of probate, May 8, 1854; wife, Jane; children, Lidia, William, Margaret, Sarah, Mary, Rebecca, Elizabeth, Isabella, Sophia-M., Nathaniel-F., Robert-C.; exec., Robert Pittis; wits., James C. Guthrie, Robert Pittis.

JONAS GUTSHALL, Harrison co.; date of will, Oct. 9, 1843; date of probate, Aug. 12, 1844; wife, Mary; execs., brother, Joseph Gutshall, and wife, Mary Gutshall; wits., George Shaffer, Benjamin Manbeck.

HUGH GWYNN, date of will, Nov. 8, 1858; date of probate, Nov. 9, 1861; wife, name not given; children, Hugh, Thomas, William, John, Mary Carter, Margaret Barcroft, Elizabeth Rowles, Susan Madden, Rachel Wilson, Sarah Ann Cope, Hannah Neely; execs., Ralph Barcroft, Hezekiah Rowles; wits., William Arnold, Jesse Arnold, W. H. Arnold.

THOMAS HALEY, Cadiz village; date of will, Feb. 21, 1832; date of probate, March 15, 1832; wife, name not given; grandsons, Joseph S. Healy, Harrison Griffith; legatees, Henry Pepper, Mary Ann Pepper; execs. Thomas Bingham; wits., Nathan Reiley, Casper Singhaus.

JAMES HAMMOND, date of will, Aug. 22, 1850; date of probate, March 25, 1851; wife, name not given; children, Harvey, George, William, Samuel, Mary Ann Fowler, Deborah Ruby; execs., George Hammond, William Hammond; wits., H. Worstell, Joseph McGonagle.

JOHN HANES, Harrison co.: date of will, Sept. 13, 1824; date of probate, Nov. —, 1824; wife, Rachel; children, Sarah, Lewiza, Samuel, Israel; execs., Israel Hanes; wits., Joseph Fry, Benjamin Paisley, Robert Paisley.

JOHN HAUN, German township; date of will, Feb. 20, 1827; date of probate, March 31, 1828; wife, Elizabeth; children, Betsy, Polly, Catherine, Fanny, Susanna; exec., John Wagner; wits., Frederick Zollars, Benjamin Whitmore.

ANN HANNA, German township; date of will, March 23, 1833; date of probate, July 23, 1833; daughters Ann, Prudence; exec., Joseph McCollough; wits., Joseph McCollough, John G. McCollough.

JAMES HANNA, Washington co.; Pa.; probate, May 4, 1813; wife, Anne;

children, Moses, Matthew, William, Joseph, Robert, Samuel, Prudence, Jean, Anne, Martha; execs., James McNary, Robert Hanna; wits, Moses McWhirter, John Smith.

JOHN HANNA, Harrison co.; date of will, May 13, 1847; date of probate, Aug. 16, 1847; wife, name not given; son, John-E.; son-in-law, John Oglevee; nephews, John-Rowland, James, and William Finley Hanna; granddaughter, Mary Ann Small; execs., John Oglevee, Thomas L. Jewett; wits., M. Wilson, R. Teat.

JOHN HANNA, Shortcreek township; date of will, July 19, 1849; date of probate, Aug. ---, 1849; wife, Rachel; brothers, William, James, Ezekiel, Samuel, Archibald; grandsons, Samuel and John Hanna, and John H. Hammond; legatee, Levi Dickerson, execs., James Hanna, Alexander Hammond; wits., George Atkinson, Peter Thomas.

MARY HANNA, Green township; date of will, June 21, 1853; date of probate, Nov. 29, 1853; daughter, Prudence, and other children, not named; legatees, Foreign Missionary Society, American Bible Society, and Educational Society of the Presbyterian Church; exec., James Hanna; wits., James Taggart, James Simpson.

ROBERT HANNA, Mercer, Mercer county, Pa.; date of will, June 21, 1854; date of probate, Nov. 29, 1854; wife, Mary; grandchildren, Mary Hanna Small, Jennette Small, Robert Wilson Hanna Small, and Elizabeth Ann Small, all children of Edward and Mary Ann Hanna Small; nephews and nieces, John Rowland Hanna, Henry James, William, and Thomas Hanna, Jane Auld (wife of John), and Mary Teachener (wife of Mathias), all children of brother, William Hanna; also Robert Paxton, son of sister, Margaret Paxton, Mary Ann Alexander and Rachel Jourdan (wife of J.-P.), both children of sister, Jane Alexander; James and Sarah Gray, children of sister, Elenor Gray; legatees, Robert Hanna Pollock, son of William Pollock; Mercer Female Institute; and American Missionary Association of the Associate Presbyterian Synod of North America; execs., Mary Hanna, William M. Stephenson, Thomas Lee; wits., Joseph Sykes, John Moore.

ROBERT HANNA, Green township; date of will, Aug. 3, 1856; date of probate, Sept. 3, 1856; wife, Sarah; execs., Lewis W. Ralston, James Hanna, Alexander Hanna; wits., Thomas A. Purviance, William Hanna.

THOMAS HANNA, Cadiz township; date of will, March 2, 1839; date of probate, March ---, 1839; wife, Jane; children, John, James, Thomas Elizabeth McKune, Mary Scroggs; execs., sons, John Hanna, James Hanna, and Thomas Hanna; wits., M. Wilson, Francis Grove.

WILLIAM HANNA, Green township; date of will, April 4, 1830; date of probate, Aug. 3, 1830; wife, Mary; children, Esther, Ann, Prudence, Mary, Jane, Martha, Margaret, Sarah, Louisa, James, William, Robert, John, Samuel; execs., Mary Hanna, John Taggart; wits., John McCullough, Samuel Moorehead, Daniel Welch.

WILLIAM HANNA, Green township; date of will, Dec. 29, 1838; date of probate, May ---, 1839; wife, name not given; legatee, William Stone; brothers, sisters, and mother; exec., Robert Hanna; wits., Moses Keneday, James Hanna.

SAMUEL HARGRAVE, Harrison co.; date of will, Nov. 30, 1828; date of probate, Aug. ---, 1839; children, Lemuel, Charles, Martha, Jane, Anna Creem, Mary Bates; exec., Charles Hargrave; wits., Robert Ladd, Thomas Ladd, Benjamin Hunniecutt.

JOHN HARMAN, Harrison co.; date of will, Sept. 28, 1828; date of probate, March 30, 1830; wife, Caty; son, Jacob; exec., Van Brown; wits., Van Brown, J. B. Emery.

JOHN HARMON, date of will, Feb. 20, 1834; date of probate, April 1, 1834;

wife, Magdalena; children, Michael, George, Jacob, Sally Benedick; execs., Magdalina Herman, David Miller; wits., John Wagner, Henry Snyder.

PETER HARRISON, Harrison co.; date of will, May 15, 1847; date of probate, Nov. 8, 1855; wife, name not given; children, El'sha, John, William, Richard, Barzebai, Enoch, Daniel, George, Unity Pallot, Hannah Davidson, Patience Wright, Lydia Ann James; execs., Elisha Harrison, John Harrison; wits., Thomas Lewis, James Romick, George Atkinson.

ELIAS HART, Frederick county, Md.; date of will, March —, 1852; date of probate, June 28, 1852; wife, Margaret; exec., Margaret Hart; wits., Lloyd Dorsen, William H. Albaugh, H. C. Steinor.

JOHN HASTINGS, date of will, Dec. 24, 1839; date of probate, Dec. 7, 1840; wife, Jane; children, William, James, John; grandson, James Hastings; execs., William Hastings, John Hastings; wits., Adam Dickerson, John Dickerson, Benjamin F. Gudgeon.

ELIZA H. HATCHER, Cadiz township; date of will, June 8, 1860; date of probate, June 19, 1860; husband, Mahlon-B.; brothers, Alfred, Robinson, and Fleming Pumphrey; aunt, Sopiah Boone; sisters, Emily Ellen Holmes, Susanna Pumphrey; nieces, Eliza A. Holmes, Eliza Hogg Pumphrey, and Eliza Ann H. Pumphrey; nephew, Thomas Hogg Pumphrey; cousins, Elizabeth Compher, Wesley Boone, legatees, Cyrus McNeely, Jane McNeely, Lidia Talbott; exec., Cyrus McNeely; wits., Thomas Phillips, F. Hamilton.

JOHN HAVERFIELD, Cadiz township; date of will, Aug. 18, 1851; date of probate, Dec. 11, 1856; wife, name not given; children, James, Nancy; nephew, John Clark; execs., names not given; wits., William Arnold, John Barcroft.

JOSEPH HAVERFIELD, Cadiz township; date of will, Dec. 1 1851; date of April 5, 1852; wife, Catherine; children, Gillespie, George, Mary-Ann; exec., James H. Haverfield; wits., William Arnold, Thomas Love.

WILLIAM HAVERFIELD, Cadiz township; date of will, Oct. 18, 1858; date of probate, June 21, 1859; wife, name not given; son, John; exec., John Haverfield; wits., John A. Bingham, James H. Haverfield, John Robb.

JAMES HAWTHORN, date of will, April 11, 1844; date of probate, Nov. 16, 1844; wife, Rosanna; children, Hannah Maxwell, Margaret Ann McNary, Nancy, Jane, Arabella, Robert, William, Samuel-E.; execs., Robert C. Hawthorn, John McNary, William Stewart; wits., Alexander Hammond, Reuben Brennan.

JAMES HAZLETT, date of will, Jan. 23, 1837; date of probate, April —. 1845; wife, Mary; children, John Hazlett, and others, not named; execs., John Wagner, James Hazlett; wits., John Gruber, Lewis Ralston.

MARY HAZELETT, date of will, April 27, 1859; date of probate, Aug. 2. 1861; daughter. Nancy Tope; exec., George Shambaugh; wits., Samuel Foreman, Lucinda Foreman.

EDWARD HEATH, date of will, March 25, 1842; date of probate, April, 1845; wife, Mary; children, Nancy, Sarah, Mary Johnson, Elizabeth Petty, John, Edward, Benjamin; execs., John Cramblett; wits., Richard Parker, Joel Cramblett.

STEPHEN HEAVLIN, Cadiz township; date of will, May 18, 1839; date of probate, March 13, 1847; wife, name not given; children, John, Samuel, Stephen, George, Adam, Alexander, Mary, Phenei, Sally, Cecil, Jane, Bell, Nancy; execs., names not given; wits., Thomas Bingham, Josiah Scott.

SOLOMON HEDGE, date of will, Aug. 16, 1814; date of probate, May 25, 1815; sisters, Catherine, Jamima; exec., King Cash; wits., Walter B. Beck, Andrew McNeely, Phineas Inskeep.

JOHN HEFLING, Washington township; date of will, July 2, 1855; date of probate, Feb. 9, 1859; wife, name not given; children, Nestley, Noah, John, Louisa Smith; execs., Noah Hefling, Joseph D. Smith; wits., Hillery Moore, S. R. Magee, William Griffith.

JOHN HEMRY, North township, will, not dated; date of probate, Sept. 3, 1827; wife, Catherine; children, John, Henry, Isaac, George, Abraham, Elizabeth, Magdalin, Mary, Sarah, Anna; execs., Henry Hemry, Isaac Hemry; wits., Maholm Stewart, John Hagey.

JOHN HENDERSHOT, date of will, July 27, 1857; date of probate, June 17, 1859; wife, Elizabeth; exec., Elizabeth Hendershot; wits., Thomas Phillips, Lewis Lewton.

THOMAS HENDERSON, date of will, May 25, 1852; date of probate, June 21, 1852; wife, name not given; nephews and nieces mentioned, no names given; execs., Alexander Haverfield; wits., William H. Watson, A. H. Burtch.

ANDREW HENDRICK, date of will, Feb. 25, 1835; date of probate, March 30, 1835; wife, Elizabeth; children, Andrew, John, Jacob, James, George, Margaret Sickles, Susanna Ferrier, Mary Spangar, Rachel Hendricks; execs., Elizabeth Hendricks; David G. Meguire; wits., George Roush, Richard Lyons.

JOHN HENDRICKS, Archer township; date of will, May 29, 1818; date of probate, Aug. 4, 1818; wife, Margaret; children, Peter, Andrew, John, Jacob, Joseph, Mary Picaly, Eve Gailiger, Sarah Leiser; execs., Margaret Hendricks, Peter Hendricks; wits., John Forsyth, Abraham Kail.

JAMES HENRY, will, not dated; date of probate, Dec. 11, 1860; wife, name not given; brother, Samuel; sister, Elizabeth Henry; nephew, Nicholas S. Henry; execs., James Kirkpatrick; wits., John Beall, J. M. Estep.

JANE HENRY, date of will, Nov.—, 1845; date of probate, May 19, 1857; sisters, Margaret, Elizabeth; execs., Margaret Henry, Elizabeth Henry; wits., William Boggs, James Simeral.

MARGARET HENRY, date of will, Feb. 20, 1858; date of probate, June 30, 1858; legatee, Elizabeth Henry; execs., Elizabeth Henry; wits., Charles Cobbs, Hiram Lafferty.

VALENTINE HIBBS, date of will, April 17, 1845; date of probate, Aug. —, 1845; wife, name not given; children mentioned, names not given; execs., William Hibbs, Amos Smith; wits., William C. Johnson, R. S. Hallaway;

JOHN HILBERT, date of will, Feb. 25, 1838; date of probate, Dec. 7, 1840; wife, Elizabeth; children, Daniel, Henry, Jacob, Peter, John, Catherine, Lydia, Sally, Mary, Elizabeth, Sophia; execs., Peter Hilbert, Daniel Hilbert; wits., Nathan Adams, John Wagner.

PETER HILBERT, Shortcreek township; date of will, April 2, 1815; date of probate, April 28, 1815; wife, Elizabeth; children, Susannah, Lydia, David; exec., brother, Daniel Hilbert; wits., James McNutt, Martin Snyder, Ebenezer Gray.

LITTLETON HILL, Cadiz township; date of will, Oct. 10, 1845; date of probate, Nov. —, 1845; wife, Elizabeth; children, Sarah, Elenor, Saloame, Mary, Roland, Littleton, William-H.; execs., Thomas Hogg, John Bricker, Zepheniah Bayless; wits., H. S. McFadden, William J. Fry.

ANTHONY HILLER, date of will, June 14, 1849; date of probate, June 13, 1853; wife, name not given; children, Peter, Daniel, Bowen, Louisa; execs., names not given; wits., Daniel Black, Robert McCauley.

PETER HIMEBAUGH, Rumley township; date of will, April 21, 1848; date of probate, Sept. 4, 1855; wife, name not given; children, George, Margaret Gillespie, Peter, Daniel, William, Joseph; execs., Daniel Himebaugh, Joseph Himebaugh; wits., John Gruber, Franklin M. Gruber.

JACOB HINES, Archer township; date of will, Dec. 17, 1848; date of probate, Jan. 3, 1849; wife, Susannah; children, Jacob, Peter, Amos, John, George, Elizabeth Buchanan, Margaret, Abigail; execs., George Hines, Joseph Buchanan; wits., Samuel Shaffer, William Wilson, Hugh Cavan.

RUDOLPH HINES, date of will, Sept. 4, 1823; date of probate, Nov. 11, 1823; wife, Sarah; children, Daniel, William, James, John, Isaac, Samuel, Joseph, Mary, Martha; execs., John Hines, John Mitchell; wits., Thomas Christy, William Henderson, J. Harris.

WILLIAM HINES, date of will, Feb. 4, 1845; date of probate, April —, 1845; wife, Sarah; children, Christopher, John, David, and two daughters, not named; exec., John Hines; wits., John Cramblett, William Lyport.

FREDERICK HISELER, German township; date of will, Oct. 2, 1849; date of probate, Dec. 17, 1849; wife, name not given; children, Henry, Solomon, Frederick, John, Samuel, David, Catherine, Rachel, Susanna, Elizabeth, Nancy, Charlotte, Sarah; execs., David Easterday; wits., Frederick Abel, John Gruber.

THOMAS HITCHCOCK, date of will, Oct. 23, 1823; date of probate, March 31, 1829; wife, Isabella; children, John, Samuel, Isaac, Naomie Ferrell, Jane Hill, Amelia Mahon, Nancy Ferrell, Ann Leara; exec., John Hitchcock; wits., William Tingley, William Cavanee, William Lowery.

ANDREW HOGGE, date of will, Feb. 12, 1861; date of probate, March 26, 1861; sister, Phebe Hogge; nephew, Martin Van Buren Hogge; exec., Mark Wilkin.

JOHN HOGG, Mount Pleasant, Jefferson co., O.; date of will, Oct. 5, 1855; date of probate, Oct. 20, 1857; wife, Miriam; children, William, George-T., Timothy-K., Sarah Ann Simeral, Mary Tipton, Ann, Elizabeth, Caroline; grand-children, Mary-Ann, George-H., James-V., and Ann Elizabeth Simeral; William-B., and John Hogg Tipton; John-T., Nancy-M., and Rachel Jane Mitchell; sons-in-law, Robert C. Kir , George W. Dilworth, Joseph S. Chandler; niece, Hannah Brown; execs , William Hogg, George T. Hogg; wits., J. M. Estep, Jonathan Binns.

PHEBE HOGGE, Washington township, date of will, Sept. 7, 1844; date of probate, Nov. 9, 1860; children, Andrew, Phebe; execs., Mark Hogge, Thomas Holliday; wits., Thomas J. Holliday, Nancy Holliday.

ROBERT HOGGE, date of will, May 2, 1827; date of probate, Sept. 4, 1827; wife, Pheby; children, Robert, Mark, Matthew, James, William, Andrew, Jane, Polly, Pheby; execs., Robert Hogge, Mark Hogge; wits., Joseph Fry, Bazaleel Steel, Joseph Bigley.

WILLIAM HOGG, Fayette county, Pa.; date of will, Sept. 5, 1839; date of probate, Feb. 8, 1841; wife, Mary; nephews, George, John, and Thomas Hogg, George Familton; niece, Dorothy Wilson; legatee, Timothy Rogers; execs., George Hogg, John Hogg; wits., James L. Bowman, James Veech.

JOHN HOLLETT, date of will, Sept. 7, 1859; date of probate, Oct. 1, 1859; wife, Elizabeth; children, William, George, Joseph, Benjamin, John, Hannah Hibbs, Sarah Hibbs, Elizabeth Whitington; execs., Joseph Hollett, Jonathan Hollett; wits., Thomas Wilson, John Knox.

ROBERT HOLLIDAY, Freeport township; date of will, June 18, 1855; date of probate, July 16, 1855; wife, name not given; execs., R. K. Price, Eldred G. Holliday; wits., John Greewalt, Valentine H. Romans, R. K. Price.

JOSEPH HOLLIER, date of will, March 8, 1858; date of probate, March 17, 1858; wife, name not given; legatees, Robert Pittis, Amelia Hazlet; exec., Dr. S. R. Magee; wits., Robert Pittis, Henry Hillyer.

DANIEL HOLLOWAY, date of will, June 24, 1836; date of probate, March 27, 1837; wife, Mary; children, Jonas, John, Mary; execs., wife, Mary Holloway, and Jonas Holloway; wits., Isaac Jones, Enoch Jones, Zachariah Lowden.

JACOB HOLLOWAY, date of will, May 1, 1848; date of probate, June 6, 1851; wife, Martha; children, Daniel, William, Jacob, Sarah; stepson, John Warfield; nieces, Ann Branson, Eliza Wilson, Nancy Faucett; execs, Daniel Holloway, William Holloway, and Jacob Holloway; wits., Asa Branson, Caleb Brockee.

JONAS HOLLOWAY, date of will, Jan. 24, 1857; date of probate, March 11, 1857; wife, name not given; children, William-J., Daniel, John-F., Isaac-J., Mahalah-A., Sarah-M.; exec., John Green; wits., James J. Billingsley, Henry J. Randall.

CHARLES HOLT, Athens township, date of will, June 7, 1841; date of probate, March 2, 1842; wife, name not given; children, Samuel, Cyrus, Thomas, Amy; grand-daughter, Elizabeth Holt; exec., William McFarland; wits., William Arnold, S. McCormick, James Boyd.

ELIZABETH HOOPS, date of will, Feb. 20, 1834; date of probate, Oct. 20, 1834; children, James, Joseph, Thomas, Sarah, Ann; exec., Thomas Hoops; wits., Samuel Barber, Ann Barber, James R. Hague.

GEORGE HOSPELHORN, date of will, April 26, 1832; date of probate, Feb. 11, 1835; wife, Margaret; children, Henry, Jacob, John, Elizabeth Welsh, Hannah Dayhuff, Mary Gottschall; execs., John Hospelhorn, George Fisher; wits., John Shober, Phillip Dotts, Jr.

BENJAMIN HOUSE, date of will, July 16, 1847; date of probate, March 21, 1848; wife, name not given; children, Hillery, William, Robert, Matilda Clark, Polly, Sally, Clarissa Endsley, Peggy Randal; legatees, John, William, David, and Mary Jane Riddle; execs., William House, Robert House; wits., David Lewis, William Ramsey, B. S. Ford.

JOHN HOVEY, date of will, Aug. 29, 1822; date of probate, Sept. 22, 1822; wife, Mary; children, Isabella, Sally, Margaret, Elizabeth, Jane, Nancy, Esther, John; grandson, Joseph Gilbert; exec., David Thompson; wits., John Maholm, Thomas Bingham, J. Harris.

JOSHUA HOWARD, Cadiz township; date of will, June —, 1859; date of probate, Nov. 25, 1859; wife, name not given; children mentioned, names not given; exec., Obadiah Slemmons; wits., Alexander Cessna, O. Slemmons.

WILLIAM HUEY, date of will, April 13, 1846; date of probate, April —, 1846; wife, Agnes; daughter, Jane; nephew, Hamilton King; step-son, Isaac Pratt; sister, Elizabeth Irwin; execs., Agnes Huey, Gideon Seymore; wits., James Cameron, Samuel Cummings. Jr.

JAMES HUMPHREY, date of will, Oct. 4, 1826; date of probate, Nov. 3, 1826; brothers, David, George; sisters, Nancy, Betsy, Polly, Agnes; execs., John Pollock, Sr., Joseph McKee; wits., Thomas Johnson, Joseph McKee.

JOSEPH HUNT, Freeport township; date of will, Sept. 5, 1853; date of probate, Dec. 13, 1853; wife, Salina; grand-sons, Albert James Hunt, and Joseph Hunt; exec., Samuel Mahaffey; wits., Samuel Mahaffey, Thomas Johnson.

GEORGE HURLESS, date of will, June 17, 1826; date of probate, Oct. 19, 1826; wife, Mary; exec., Samuel Hurless; wits., John Crom, John Firebaugh.

SARAH HURLESS, date of will, Dec. 18, 1850; date of probate, March 31, 1851; children, Mary, Magdeline, Christina, John; exec., John Hestand;

wits., Thomas McClintock; Isaac Alexander.

JOHN INSKEEP, date of will, April 29, 1822; date of probate, Sept. 14, 1822; wife, Hannah; sons, Phineas, John; daughters-in-law, Olive and Mary Inskeep; execs., Joseph Larkins, Sr., Phineas Inskeep, John Evans; wits., Joseph Larkins, John Evans, Rees Larkins.

ROBERT IRWIN, Franklin township; date of will, Oct. 27, 1858; date of probate, Feb. 8, 1859; wife, Mary; children, Richard, Ninian, Mary, Ann, Catherine Dickey; execs., Richard Irwin, Hiram Worstell; wits., H. Worstell; James C. Guthrie.

ALLEN JAMISON, German township; date of will, March 11 ,1843;date of probate, April —, 1846; wife, Sarah; execs., Sarah Jamison, Archibald Jamison; wits., A. Work, John A. Work, Archibald Jamison.

JOHN JAMISON, Cadiz township; date of will, Oct. 14, 1848; date of probate, Oct. 20, 1848; wife, name not given; son, Walter; grandsons, James, John, Martin; grand-daughters, Ann, Jane; legatee, Levina Gallaher; exec., Walter Jamison; wits., William Arnold, Samuel McFaddin, Johnson Craig.

JOHN JEFFER, date of will, Dec. 18, 1819; date of probate, Dec. 22, 1819; wife, name not given; children, Joseph, Sarah; execs., John Baker, Sarah Biddinger; wits., John Baker, Sarah Biddinger.

ARCHIBALD JOHNSON, date of will, Feb. 20, 1837; date of probate, March 27, 1837; wife, Christann; exec., Christann Johnson; wits., James Scott, Thomas Baird.

BENJAMIN JOHNSON, Nottingham township; date of will, Nov. 4, 1841; date of probate, May 2, 1842; wife, Sarah; children, Abiram, Enoch, Joseph, Lemuel, Ephriam, Gabriel, Benjamin, Bershebas, Ellen, Druzilla; grand-daughter, Nancy Suddith; execs., Abiram Johnson, Ephriam Johnson; wits., William Arnold, William Barrett, Thomas Phillips.

EPHRIAM JOHNSON, date of will, Sept. 7, 1833; date of probate, March 31, 1834; wife, Mary; children, Ephriam, Jane, Margaret, Eliza, Ann; exec., Mary Johnson; wits., Archibald McGrew, Ezekiel Hanna.

HENRY JOHNSON, Moorefield township; date of will, Jan. 25, 1850; date of probate, Nov. —, 1850; wife, name not given; children, William-C., Henry-M., Wesley, Astory-F., Balinda McBean, Juliann Tallman, Harriet McPherson, Catherine Price; execs., wife, and son, Henry Johnson; wits., John Hastings, John Beale.

JOHN B. JOHNSON, Green township; date of will, Jan. 21, 1845; date of probate, Aug. —, 1845; wife, name not given; uncle, Benjamin Johnson; exec., Henry Eagleson; wits., John Richardson, Lemuel Louden.

NATHAN JOHNSON, Nottingham township; date of will, Oct. 17, 1844; date of probate, Oct. 29, 1844; wife, Mary; children, John-C., William-H., Nathan, Elizabeth Perrine, Margaret, Jane, Emeline, Nancy, Rachel, Cinthia, Harriett, Mary Johnson, widow of John, (his father); legatee, Wesleyan Church; exec., Abiram Johnson; wits., Archibald Blair, Jonathan Perrin.

NATHAN JOHNSON, Green township, date of will, Oct. 1, 1825; date of probate, April —, 1845; wife, Mary; children, John-B., James-S., Samuel-P., Mary-Jane; execs., James Black, Samuel Johnson; wits., Moses Urquhart, Mary Black.

WILLIAM JOHNSON, date of will, May 17, 1855; date of probate, June 15, 1855; wife, Agnes; children, Mary-E., Susanna Fisher, Matthew, Bazzel, Temperance Neal, William, Elizabeth Arnell, Agnes Wilson; execs., James Neal, Albert Johnson; wits., John Davis, Robert McMillen, Samuel M. Boggs.

BENJAMIN JONES, date of will,

Aug. 3, 1851; date of probate, June 5, 1852; wife, name not given; brothers, Isaac, Thomas, John, and Marshal Jones; sisters, Caroline Holloway, Malinda Sudduth, Lydia Lacy; exec., Jonas Holloway; wits., Nimrod Hutson, John Barger, Lewis Jones.

JOHN JONES, date of will, Nov. 12, 1837; date of probate, Aug. 20, 1838; wife, name not given; children, Isaac, Benjamin, Alfred, Thomas, John, Cyrus, Marshall, William, Caroline, Malinda, Lydia; execs., Prettyman Conwell, Michael Brown; wits., Prettyman Conwell, Michael Brown;

GABRIEL KAIL, date of will, Jan. 4, 1850; date of probate, Jan. 17, 1850; wife, Elizabeth; children, Jesse, Joseph, Cridah, Gabrial, Hyrum, Stephen, Sarah, Felicia, Terbitha; exec., Titus Beck; wits., Titus Beck, Joseph Buchanan.

JOHN KAIL, date of will, March 1, 1821; date of probate, May 9, 1821; wife, Catharine; children, Henry, George, John, Jacob, Frederick, Betsy, Polly, Peggy, Nancy, Anny; execs., Henry Kail, Jacob Kail; wits., John Zellars, Solomon Arnold.

WILLIAM KEEPERS, date of will May 11, 1842; date of probate, May —, 1843; wife, Elizabeth; children, Casander Fowler, Elizabeth Orr, Nancy Hogland, Jamima Maxwell, William, Isaac; grandson, William K. Maxwell; execs., wife, Elizabeth Keepers, and son, William Keepers; wits., James Evans, Abraham Barger, Michael Conoway.

DANIEL KELLY, Union township, ——— county; date of will, April 28, 1830; date of probate, Aug. 1, 1831; wife, name not given; children, William, Isaac, David, Jonathan, Anne, Charlotte, Mary, Elizabeth; execs., William Champer, Jacob Hing; wits., William Champer, John S. McClean.

JOHN S. KELLY, date of will, Nov. 5, 1847; date of probate, Nov. 11, 1847; wife, Esther; children, Alexander, Joseph, Mary Jane, and children of deceased daughter, Martha; exec., Samuel Moorehad; wits., C. Dewey, John McCrea, William Eagleson.

WILLIAM KELLY, date of will, Jan. 9, 1849; date of probate, March —, 1854; wife, Sally; children, Daniel, Mary Woolf, Nancy Barnhouse, Sally Barnhouse, Elizabeth Sarbough, Philip, Christina; execs., Philip Kelly, Daniel Kelly; wits., Thomas Tomlinson, James Hanna.

MOSES KENNEDY, Green township; date of will, Oct. 26, 1855; date of probate, April 25, 1857; wife, Catherine; children, Martin-S., Benjamin-F.-M.-B., Caroline-M., Martha-A., Margaret F. Turner, Isabella Clark; execs., Martin S. Kennedy, Benjamin F. Kennedy; wits., Jacob Snider, Ingram Clark.

ABSALOM KENT, will, not dated; date of probate, Aug. 31, 1839; wife, name not given; children, Elizabeth, Nancy, Sarah, John, Joseph, Absalom, William; grandsons, Absalom, John, Jacob; execs., Michael Conaway, Aaron Conaway; wits., William Walker, John H. Kent.

JOSEPH KENT, date of will, Aug. 25, 1824; date of probate, Oct. 30, 1829; wife, Ann; children, William, Absalom, Sarah Worth, Mariam; grandsons, Richard Worth, and William Worth; execs., William Kent, Absalom Kent; wits., Thomas Patton, John Baker.

JOSEPH KENT, Cadiz township; date of will, Oct. —, 1829; date of probate, Dec. 12, 1829; wife, Esther; children, Joseph, Absalom, Esther, Sarah, Kit; execs., father, Absalom Kent, John Poulson; wits., Martin Wilson, Rachel, Mary, Jane Green, Elizabeth Hezekiah Rowles, J. Harris.

JAMES KERR, Shortcreek township; date of will, Sept. 8, 1824; date of probate, June 13, 1825; wife, Nancy; children, John, James, William, Samuel, Mary, Jane, Betsey; grand-children, Alexander Morrow, Nancy Ann

Morrow; execs., James Kerr, William Kerr; wits., Isaac M. Wallace, Thompson Rea.

HENRY KIMMEL, Rumley township; date of will, Oct. 23, 1826; date of probate, Nov. 11, 1826; wife, Christena; children mentioned, no names given; exec., John Kimmel; wits., J. R. Kirkpatrick, Andrew Hendrick, Samuel Gutery.

LENARD KIMMEL, date of will, April 9, 1823; date of probate, March 7, 1826; wife, Susannah; children, Frederick, John, Henry, Adam, Lenard, Nancy Harman, Susan Guttery; execs., names not given; wits., Jacob Mowrey, John Summerman, James G. Ward.

JOHN KING, date of will, April 13, 1836; date of probate, Oct. 31, 1842; wife, name not given; grand-son, Isaac Keepers; daughter, Nancy Barnes; son-in-law, William Keepers; exec., William Keepers; wits., Matthias Lane, Jr., Michael Conaway, Thomas Moody.

HANNAH KINSEY, Columbiana county; date of will, March 8, 1843; date of probate, May —, 1843; nieces, Aseneth Mendinhall, Hannah Singer, sisters, Alice McMillan, Jane Matthews, Ann Goodwin; brother, John Michner; sister-in-law, Mary Michner; execs., John C. Michner, Jesse Goodwin; wits., Joshua Shinn, Robert Jordan, John Santee.

JAMES KIRKPATRICK, date of will, April 1, 1840; date of probate, June —, 1840; wife, name not given; children, Hugh, Robert, James, John, William, Elizabeth McCollough, Polly; exec., John Kirkpatrick; wits., William Wallace, William Scott.

JOHN KNIGHT, Nottingham township; date of will, Nov. 21, 1829; date of probate, June 12, 1837; wife, Catherine; son, Hiram; exec., Catherine Knight; wits., Benjamin Johnson, Joseph Rogers, John Carson.

ARTHUR KNOX, Cadiz township; date of will, Nov. 20, 1856; date of probate, Aug. 31, 1857; wife, name not given; children, William, Clara; exec., Jeremiah Knox; wits., Rachel Saxton, John A. Bingham.

WILLIAM KNOX, Cadiz township; date of will, Jan. 8, 1850; date of probate, Oct. 18, 1851; wife, Hetty; children, David, James, Jeremiah, John, William, Arthur, Sarah, Nancy; grandson, James Allen; legatee, Matthew McCohn; execs., names not given; wits., S. McCormick, William Arnold, S. V. Smiley.

WILLIAM KYLE, date of will, Oct. 17, 1855; date of probate, Aug. 15, 1859; wife, Mary; children, William, Thomas, Margaret Ramsey, Mary Atkinson, Martha Hobes, Jemima H. Taggart; exec., William Reed; wits., W. N. Harrah, C. W. Reed.

ROBERT LADD, date of will, Jan. 30, 1852; date of probate, Nov. 30, 1858; wife, Mary; grand-children, Mary Hardgraves, Mary, Elizabeth, Sarah-Ann, and Robert P. Ladd; execs., Wilson Madox; wits., James Adams, Nathan Lupton, Joshua Adams.

EDWARD LAFFERTY, date of will, Nov. 4, 1836; date of probate, Nov. 23, 1836; wife, Margaret; children, Edward, John, George, Joseph, Hiram, Finley, Elizabeth Grimes, Margaret, Mary-Jane, execs., Margaret Lafferty, John Lafferty; wits., William Taggart, James Miller.

SAMUEL LAFFERTY, Moorefield township; date of will, Dec. 3, 1836; date of probate, Jan. 13, 1858; wife, name not given; children, Jacob, Joseph, Jane Dickerson, Beliiah Dickerson; grand-daughters, Eveline Famelton, Sarah Dickerson; execs., names not given; wits., T. R. Crawford, G. S. Rice.

LAIZURE, see Lezear.

THOMAS LAKIN, Freeport township; date of will, Feb. 21, 1835; date of probate, March 7, 1835; wife, name not given; daughter, Rebecca Robinson; grand-sons, William and Samuel

W. Lakin; execs., Thomas Lakin, William Lakin; wits., Benjamin P. Ferguson, Caleb Hibbard.

JOHN LAMB, date of will, March 18, 1840; date of probate, April —, 1840; wife, name not given; children, Laurence, Timothy, Jacob, Elizabeth, Mary, Christina, Nancy, Hannah, Margaret, Catherine, Rachel, Sarah; execs., names not given; wits., John M. Umstot, Samuel Skinner, Elias Gotshel.

JOHN LAVELY, date of will, Nov. 6, 1841; date of probate, Dec. 25, 1841; wife, name not given; children, Nathan, Henry, Elias, John, Sally, Caroline, Mary, Rachel, Eliza; execs., Henry Lavely; wits., James Hines, Edward Martin, Thomas Wilson.

ABRAHAM LAYPORT, date of will, Sept. 12, 1850; date of probate, Nov. 5, 1850; wife, Sarah; exec. Sarah Layport; wits., Hamilton McFadd.n, William Layport.

GEORGE LEEPORT, date of will, Sept. 11, 1814; date of probate, Nov. 29, 1814; wife, Nancy; children, Margaret Hevlin, Mary Hevlin, Dianna Spiker, Nancy Wilson, Susannah Babb; grand-daughter, Jane Wilson; execs., Rudolph Hines, Samuel Hev.in; wits., William Hall, Peter Moor.

ISAAC LAYPORT, date of will, Aug. 8, 1825; date of probate, Oct. 24, 1825; wife, Sarah; children, mentioned, no names given; execs., Sarah Layport, Alexander Henderson; wits., James Shimer, George Waller.

JOHN LAYPORT, date of will, Feb. 11, 1839; date of probate, May —, 1839; wife, name not given; children, William, Abraham, Isaac; execs., William Layport, George W. Bell; wits., John Tipton, John Hines.

JOHN LEE, Jefferson county; date of will, Jan. 4, 1813; date of probate, Aug. 24, 1813; wife, Hannah; brothers, Hugh, Robert, William, and one other, not named; three sisters, not named; nephews, John, son of William, and John, son of Robert; mother mentioned, but not named; execs., brothers, William Lee, Hugh Lee; wits., John Timmerson, Nathaniel Crawford.

REUBEN LEE, date of will, Oct. 2, 1844; date of probate, Oct. 28, 1844; wife, Elizabeth; son, John; execs., names not given; wits., David Lewis, Washington Ourant.

THOMAS LEE, date of will, Oct. 28, 1854; date of probate, Nov. 7, 1854; wife, Nancy; children, Elizabeth Black, Mary E. Clark, Jane W. Patton, Henrietta M. Lee, Hans-W., James, Thomas; grandson, Thomas L. Moore; execs., wife, Nancy Lee, Alexander Clark; wits., John Carnahan, W. Wilson, J. T. Thomas.

JAMES LEECH, date of will, Aug. 27, 1859; date of probate, Jan. 25, 1861; wife, name not given; children, Robert, John, Elizabeth Wilkins, Mary Jane Parkinson, Margaret Host; exec., John Leech, wits., John Parkinson, Thomas Parkinson, John C. Gouray.

JOHN LEGGIT, date of will, Sept. 29, 1855; date of probate, Aug. 25, 1857; wife, Sophia; children, John, Levi, Jesse, William-A.-D., Sarah; execs., Sophia Leggit, Jesse Leggit; wits, Jacob W. Grisinger, Lewis Leggit.

ISAAC LEMASTER, date of will, March 30, 1844; date of probate, May —, 1844; wife, Jane; children, Nancy Rogers, Liddy Sammonton, Jenny Pittinger, Margaret Ferrell, Susanna Roberson, Elizabeth, Abraham, Isaac, John, Ebenezer, William; execs., wife, Jane Lemaster, William Lemaster; wits., William Smylie, Abraham Busby.

JOSEPH LEWIS, Archer township; date of will, Dec. 18, 1851; date of probate, Sept. 8, 1852; wife, Rachel; daughter, Hannah; grand-daughter, Mary E. Foulks; wits., Jonathan Gray, James McKee.

MOSES LEWIS, North township; date of will, June 3, 1837; date of probate, June 16, 1837; wife, Ann; execs., Ann Lewis, George Foster; wits., Caleb Sherman, Thomas Tomlinson.

JONATHAN LEZEAR, Nottingham township; date of will, Jan. 20, 1819; date of probate, July 5, 1819; wife, Jane; children, William, Amos, Reily, Elijah, Isaac, Julianne, Betsy, Mirah, Amelia; exec., Jane Lezear; wits., John Foote, Benjamin Ruby, Edward Ruby.

ELIZA LINDSEY, Sandusky co., O.; date of will, Dec. 5, 1848; date of probate, Aug. —, 1849; children, Eliza-M., Levina-J., Margaret-A., Christina R. Gibbs. Eluthrous-C., James-M., William H.; exec., William H. Duffield; wits., George W. Duffield, Andrew Lynch.

SUSAN LINDSEY, date of will, March 10, 1860; date of probate, Oct. 19, 1861; children, Eliza Jane Malcom, Ann Culbertson; exec., Eliza Jane Malcom; wits., George Cook, Abram C. Dony.

WILLIAM LISLE, Archer township; date of will, Dec. 8, 1837; date of probate, Aug. 20, 1838; wife, Jane; children, James, John, William, Mary Bartow, Anna Edie, Hannah Winters, Isabella McGonagle, Elizabeth McConkey; exec., James Devore; wits., Robert Maxwell, James Devore.

JOSEPH LOWDEN, date of will, Sept. 18, 1828; date of probate, March 12, 1832; wife, Ruth; wife, sole heir; exec., Ruth Lowden; wits., William Wyckoff, Jonathan Crossley, Philip Crabtree.

JOHN LOWMILLER, date of will, July 8, 1853; date of probate, Jan. 12, 1858; wife, Mary; sons, Manasse, John, Joshua, Baalam, Henry; exec., Andrew Mikesell; wits., John Gruber, Samuel L. Potts.

THOMAS LUKE, date of will, May 15, 1832; date of probate, May — 1839; wife, Martha; children, Rebecca Ann Worstel, Mary, Martha, Delila, Betsey, Fanny; exec., Martha Luke: wits., Morgan Lewis, James Adams, William Kerr.

ANDREW LYNCH, Jefferson township; date of will, April 17, 1860; date of probate, May 26, 1860; wife, Isabella; children, William-C., James-A., Mary, Ellen; exec., Isabella Lynch; wits., John Miller, John Wilkin.

JOHN LYNN, Cadiz, Jefferson county; date of will, Nov. 4, 1814; date of probate, Nov. 29, 1814; wife, Mary; children, James, Hannah; exec., John McConnell; wits., John McConnell, Robert Eyre, Robert Eyre, Jr.

MARY LYNN, date of will, March 20, 1846; date of probate, June 21, 1852; children, Taylor, William, James, Joseph, Eliza Shepard; exec., Taylor Lynn; wits., Hugh B. Hawthorn, William McCracken.

GEORGE McADAMS, date of will, April 21, 1848; date of probate, Nov. 6, 1848; wife, name not given; children, Thomas, James, John, George, William, Sarah, Margaret Burnside, Maria Campbell; execs., James McAdams, George McAdams; wits., Allan Wallace; John Kirkpatrick.

JOHN McADAMS, Lee county, Iowa; date of will, Sept. 8, 1848; date of probate, Nov. 2, 1848; wife, Harriett; execs., wife, Harriett McAdams, and brother, James McAdams; wits., Solomon Jackson; Solomon Cowles, Jr.

DENNIS McBARRON, date of will, April 10, 1844; date of probate, Aug. —, 1846; wife, Polly; children, Rosannah, Betsey, John, Samuel, Dennis, Andrew; exec., John Hitchcock; wits., Thomas Bingham, Josiah Scott.

THOMAS McCALL, Washington county, Penn.; date of will, March 31, 1849; date of probate, May 19, 1851; wife, Mary; nephews, David Stewart, Adams, John, Thomas, James, Alexander, and Marshall McCall; sisters, Jane Walker; legatees, Betsey and Polly Ralston, Thomas Trimble, Mary McCall Stewart, Elizabeth Stewart, Elizabeth Boon, Thomas McCall Penticost, Thomas McCall Pat'erson, Thomas McCall Miller, Thomas McCall Adams, Thomas Tigner, and Jane, Clarissa, and Nancy McFadden; execs., James Thompson, Galbreath

Stewart; wits., T. J. Odenbaugh, John Sampson.

WILLIAM McCARROL, date of will, June 28, 1844; date of probate, August —, 1844; children, Flemming, George, John, Seatt, Ann, Margaret, Catherine Firebaugh, Elizabeth Leeper, Margaret Houser, Martha Houser; exec., James Evans; wits., Robert Hanlin, James J. Maclean.

DARCUS McCLEARY, date of will, March 24, 1819; date of probate, July 6, 1819; children, Polly, John, Jein McCaslin, Roberts; grand-children James and Jane McCleary; execs., William Kelly, William McCaslin; wits., Robert Orr, William Kelly.

WILLIAM McCLELLAND, Monroe township; date of will, Dec. 29, 1849; date of probate, Aug. —, 1850; brother, Andrew; sister, Martha; exec., Andrew McClelland; wits., Robert Henderson, Joshua Brown.

NOBLE W. McCLINTOCK, Stock township; date of will, April 8, 1848; date of probate, Feb. 13, 1849; wife, name not given; daughters, Margaret, Eliza; exec., Josiah Scott; wits., Aaron Conaway, William Walker.

JOHN McCONNEL, date of will, Sept. 7, 1831; date of probate, Oct. 24, 1831; wife, Mary; children, John, Mary, Margaret, Elizabeth; sister, Elizabeth McConnell; exec., Joseph Rea; wits., William L. Robison, William Kincaid.

ROBERT McCONNELL, date of will, July 20, 1845; date of probate, Nov. 6, 1850; wife, Prudence; children, Alexander, Wilson, Robert, John, James, Susanna Lee, Martha, Mary Vance, Hannah Coleman, Margaret Ann Farnsworth, Elizabeth Wilson; execs., John McConnell, Alexander McConnell; wits., Eli Smith, Lemuel Billingsley, Jonas Holloway.

JOHN McCOY, date of will, March 1, 1820; date of probate, Dec. 14, 1820; wife, Susanna; children, Joseph, John, Thomas, Samuel, Susanna Robinson, Sidney Counsel; execs., Thomas Robinson, Thomas Farquher; wits., John Byland, Ebenezer Major, Aaron Yarwell.

MATTHEW McCOY, Archer township; date of will, Dec. 28, 1854; date of probate, Oct. 27, 1855; wife, Jane; children, Matthew, Thomas-M., James-S., William-M.; exec., Matthew McCoy; wits., William Arnold, S. McCormick.

MARTHA McCRACKEN, date of will, March 22, 1847; date of probate, Nov. —, 1850; daughters, Martha, Nancy; execs., names not given; wits., John McConnell, John Brokaw.

MARTHA McCRACKEN, Athens township; date of will, Jan. 25, 1850; date of probate, Feb. 13, 1854; sister, Nancy McCracken; mother, Martha McCracken; exec., William McCracken; wits., John McConnell, John Brokaw.

ROBERT McCRACKEN, date of will, Feb. 1, 1841; date of probate, Aug. —, 1846; wife, Martha; children, John, William, Robert, Margaret Sleeth, Mary White, Jane Love, Martha, Nancy; execs., William McCracken, Robert McCracken; wits., Peter Perrine, Ira T. McMillan, James McMillan.

JOHN McCREA, Cadiz township; date of will, Nov. 21, 1855; date of probate, Aug. 10, 1858; wife, Martha; legatees, Board of Foreign Missions, Board of Domestic Missions, and Board of Education of the Presbyterian Church; execs., James Taggart, John Kerr; wits., Robert Lyons, Josiah Scott.

ALEXANDER McCULLOUGH, date of will, May 19, 1852; date of probate, July 3, 1852; wife, Jane; children, David, John, Leslie, Alexander, Elleanor, Jane Cunningham, Susanna, Mozena, Rebecca; execs., Jane McCullough, David McCullough; wits., Martha Milligan, Thomas S. Milligan.

ALEXANDER McCULLOUGH, Monroe township; date of will, Oct. 11, 1857; date of probate, Nov. 19, 1857; wife, name not given; children, Hugh,

Harriet, Rebecca, Elizabeth; wits., John C. Plowman, James Long.

JOHN McCULLOUGH, date of will, Feb. 7, 1840; date of probate, April 2, 1842; wife, Esther; children, Esther, Hanna, William, John, Joseph, Samuel, Alexander, James, George; execs., sons, William McCullough, John McCullough; wits., John Walker, William McFarland.

ROBERT McCULLOCH, date of will, May 16, 1823; date of probate, June 24, 1823; wife, Jane; children, Margaret, Mary, Robert, William, Alexander, James, John, Peter, George, Samuel; exec., Joseph Grimes; wits., James Grimes, William McCulloch.

WILLIAM McCULLOUGH, date of will, Oct. 29, 1823; date of probate, April 11, 12, 13, 1831; wife, Isabella; sons-in-law, George Brokaw, Joseph Grimes; brother, Peter; two daughters mentioned, names not given; execs., Isabella McCullough, Joseph Grimes; wits., Alexander McWilliams, Samuel Welch.

GEORGE McDIVITT, North township; date of will, July 30, 1837; date of probate, Dec. 13, 1837; wife, Rachel; sons, Charles, George, Lyle, John, Samuel, Andrew; exec., Charles McDivitt; wits., James Evans, James Hoagland.

LYLE McDIVIT, North township, date of will, Jan. 23, 1838; date of probate, March 13, 1838; wife, Nancy; children, William-E., Mary, Jane; exec., James Evans; wits., Charles McDivit, Robert Givin.

HUGH McDONOUGH, date of will, Nov. 29, 1826; date of probate, Dec. 4, 1833; children, Jane, Elizabeth Eslick, Mary Queen, Helen Moony, Edward; grand-daughter, Isabelle; exec., Robert Maxwell; wits., Robert Maxwell, Mary Maxwell, Jane Maxwell.

JOHN McDONOUGH, date of will, March 19, 1853; date of probate, Feb. 18, 1854; wife, Mary; children, Matilda, Susan, Jane, Sally Sproul, Obediah, Aden, Jane, Mary McLandsborough; exec., Joseph Harrison; wits., A. F. Croskey, J. Veirs.

JAMES McDOWELL, Cadiz township; date of will, June 2, 1815; date of probate, April 9, 1815; wife, name not given; sister, Susan McDowell; brothers, Samuel, John, and William McDowell; nephew, James McDowell; execs., Samuel McDowell, William McDowell; wits., Robert M. Burney, Joseph Cox, John Work.

SAMUEL McDOWELL, date of will, Sept. 2, 1850; date of probate, May 4, 1852; wife, Jane; children, William, Susan-J., John, Samuel; legatee, Smith R. Watson; exec., John McDowell; wits., C. Dewey, William Knox, Jr.

GEORGE McFADDIN, date of will, not given; date of probate, March 2, 1844; wife, Ruth; legatee, John M. Richey; exec., John M. Richey; wits., David Braden, S. B. Shotwell, C. Dewey.

JOHN McFADDIN, date of will, June 23, 1829; date of probate, May 28, 1833; wife, name not given; children, Samuel, George-W., John, Joseph, Margaret Lafferty; grand-sons, John Lafferty, John Sharp, John McFadden; execs., Samuel McFaddin, Joseph McFaddin; wits., Asa McMillan, James McMillan.

JOHN McFADDEN, Cadiz township; date of will, Oct. 23, 1854; date of probate, Sept. 22, 1857; wife, name not given; children, Adam, John, Samuel, George, Margaret, Mary, Esther, Rebecca, Rachel, Sarah, Jane; execs., Adam McFadden, John McFadden; wits., James McFadden, Samuel Cockran.

SAMUEL McFADDIN, date of will, Feb. 26, 1837; date of probate, July 20, 1837; wife, Elizabeth; children, James, John, Samuel, Alexander, Sally Kernahan, Jane Dickerson, Margaret; execs., James McFaddin, John McFaddin; wits., John Hanna, Alexander McFaddin, James Miller.

SAMUEL McFADDEN, Cadiz township; date of will, April 21, 1857; date of probate, April 22, 1862; wife, name not given; children, George, Henry S., Isabella Sharp, Jane Johnson, Leticia Hunter, Margaret Craig, Mary Forsythe; servant, Ellen Smith; execs., George McFadden, Henry S. McFadden; wits., William Arnold, Alexander Wilson.

WILLIAM McKAIN, date of will, June 13, 1828; date of probate, July 28, 1828; children, William, James, Natty, Brice, Elisha, John, Polly, Nancy; execs., William McKain, James Clements; wits., Israel Barnes, James Moffit.

ROBERT McKEE, date of will, Jan. 15, 1851; date of probate, June 24, 1851; wife, name not given; children, Thomas, George, Archibald, James, John, Robert, Rebecca, Elizabeth, Hannah Birney, Rachel Birney, Catherine Reynolds, Margaret Strong, Jane McCann; exec., James McKee; wits., Rudolph Mitchell, Samuel Megaw.

ALEXANDER McKEOWN, date of will, Feb. 8, 1852; date of probate, June 1, 1852; wife, name not given; children, Alexander, Arthur, Adam, William, Mary, Jane, Lavina, Margaret, Rosanna; exec., wife; wits., Lewis B. Kingsbury, William L. Packer.

GEORGE McKINNEY, date of will, July 2, 1845; date of probate, Feb. 13, 1849; wife, Mary; children, William, John, James, George, Mary, Elizabeth Downs, Jane Walker, Peggy Marshall, Nancy Gault; grand-children, George Downs, Mary Downs, George Marshall, George Gault, George McKinney, Mary McKinney, and Agnes McKinney; execs., William Henderson, Michael Conaway; wits., Evan L. Crawford, Hamilton McFaddin, William Ramsey.

JOHN McKINNEY, Stock township; date of will, Jan. 6, 1850; date of probate, Feb. 1, 1850; wife, Nancy; daughters, Elizabeth Heavilin, Mary J. Rogers, Agnes Adams, Matilda, Margaret, Lydia, Sarah; father mentioned, name not given; exec., Aaron Conaway; wits., Richard Downs, William Walker.

ELIZABETH McLANSBOROUGH, date of will, Nov. 24, 1839; date of probate, May —, 1839; husband mentioned, name not given; wits., Joseph Harrison, Lot Demming.

JOHN McLANDSBOROUGH, date of will, March —, 1853; date of probate, March 18, 1857; wife, name not given; children, Andrew, John, James, Janet; exec., John McLandsborough; wits., Jonathan Markley, Lot Deming.

JOSEPH McLEAN, Westmoreland co., Pa.; date of will, July 11, 1828; date of probate, March 11, 1835; wife, name not given; children, Fanny, Ann, Betsey, Margaret, Catherine, Samuel, John, Joseph; execs., Joseph McLean, John McLean; wits., Andrew Johnston, James Alexander.

JOHN McMILLAN, Shortcreek township; date of will, Feb. 25, 1838; date of probate, March 20, 1838; wife, Alice; children, Jane, Joanna Allen, Maria Kirby, Amos, Griffith; grandchildren, Ruth, John, Esther, Maria, Allen, Albert and Joseph Dew, and John McMillan; execs., Amos McMillan, Griffith McMillan; wits., Jesse Goodwin, Elias Dew, Wilson Goodwin.

PATRICK McMILLAN, date of will, May 30, 1843; date of probate, Oct. —, 1843; wife, name not given; children, John, Martha, Eliza, Susanna; execs., Henry Lane, Ri'ey Ma'any; wits., William McBeath, Samuel Baker, Samuel R. Johnston.

ROBERT McMILLAN, date of will, Sept. 13, 1851; date of probate, May 9, 1854; wife, name not given; children, William, John, Margaret Crabtree, Nancy Ross, Mary Johnson; exec., John McMillan; wits., Samuel Skinner, Return M. Kennedy.

JAMES McNUTT, Green township; date of will, Jan. 29, 1822; date of probate, May 6, 1822; wife, Jane; children, Benjamin, James, Joseph, Sophia; execs., wife, Jane McNutt, and son, James McNutt; wits., Ebenezer Gray, James Cobean, John McCrea.

JAMES McNUTT, Cadiz township; date of will, May 4, 1855; date of probate, May 21, 1855; wife, name not given; children, John, Arthur; execs., John McNutt, Arthur McNutt; wits., H. S. McFadden, William Arnold, Thomas C. Vincent.

JANE MADDOX, date of will, Aug. 7, 1857; date of probate, May 6, 1859; grand-children, Eliza and Thomas Maddox, William Anderson Wallace, Margaret Patterson; exec., Wilson Maddox; wits., Townsend Thomas, David S. Reppart.

HENRY MAFFET, date of will, March 30, 1836; date of probate, June 28, 1836; wife, Ann; exec., James Lee; wits., William Haverfield, James Miller.

JOHN MAFFET, date of will, Oct. 11, 1830; date of probate, Oct. 22, 1830; wife, Elizabeth; children mentioned, names not given; exec., Francis Gilmore; wits., Henry Maffet, William McFadden, James Miller.

JOHN MAHOLM, Cadiz township; date of will, Sept. 2, 1854; date of probate, Oct. 2, 1854; wife, name not given; sister, Margaret Maholm; wits., William Arnold, J. B. McGrew, Samuel McCormick.

MARTHA MAHOLM, Cadiz township; date of will, Nov. 30, 1847; date of probate, Sept. 2, 1847; daughter, Eliza-Jane; granddaughter, Martha Lyons; exec., John Ritchey; wits., C. Dewey, John McBean.

SAMUEL MAHOLM, Cadiz township; date of will, Jan. 25, 1832; date of probate, Nov. —, 1838; wife, Jane; children, Sarah, Margaret, Jane Wilson, Elizabeth McNutt, Nancy Beebe, Hannah Philips, Polly Lysle, Elenor, Dorcas Bleaks, John; grand-sons, Walter B. Beebe, Jr., John McNutt; exec., James McNutt; wits., Thomas Thompson, Joshua Hamilton.

CHRISTOPHER MANSFIELD, date of will, Nov. 25, 1845; date of probate, April —, 1846; wife, Sarah; children, John, Louiza; execs., Sarah Mansfield, John Mansfield, Milton Harvey; wits., Joseph Romans, James Hastings, Jr.

DANIEL MARCKLEY, date of will, March 29, 1839; date of probate, May 2, 1842; wife, Catherine; children, David, John, Matthias, Mary, Eve-Ann, Sarah, Eliza, Elizabeth; exec., Catherine Marckley; wits., Thomas Day, Hugh Barr.

JACOB MARSHALL, date of will, May 10, 1824; date of probate, Aug. 3, 1824; wife, Mary; children, Elleanor, Penelope; grand-son, Garrett Marshall; exec., John Marshall; wits., Elisha Nelson, William Marshall.

WILLIAM MARSHALL, Cadiz township; date of will, April 10, 1816; date of probate, May 21, 1816; wife, Mary; son, James; brothers, Thomas, John, James; exec., Mary Marshall; wits., James McMillan, Joseph Tingley, Thomas Pugh.

ELLEN MARTIN, Green township; date of will, March 10, 1858; date of probate, March 18, 1858; legatees, William C. Mitchell, Elizabeth Thompson, Eliza Braden; execs., names not given; wits., Joseph Havner, Nancy Thompson.

ELENOR MARTIN, date of will, —, —, 1848; date of probate, Dec. 20, 1858; legatees, Elizabeth Braden, Board of Missions; exec., Matthew M. Sloan; wits., Thomas L. Jewett, Ann H. Jewett.

JAMES MARTIN, date of will, Dec. 3, 1852; date of probate, Jan. 12, 1853; wife, Jane; execs., Andrew Martin, Ezra Brainerd; wits., Joseph Phillips, Lemuel Carruthers.

JOHN MATSON, Shortcreek township; date of will, April 16, 1857; date of probate, May 14, 1857; wife, Perthenia; children, Thomas, Nehemiah, Rachel, Prudence; execs., Thomas Matson, William Binns; wits., Isaac Lewis, Joshua Adams, Asa Holmes, Henry Heberling.

NEHEMIAH MATSON, date of will,

Nov. 5, 1827; date of probate, Oct. 27, 1835; wife, Mary; children, William, Enos, John, Peter, Abigail, Rachel; grand-daughter, Rachel Matson; execs., John Matson, Robert Dutton; wits., Harmon Rhodes, Joseph Rhodes.

WILLIAM MATSON, date of will, May 4, 1846; date of probate, Aug. —, 1846; wife, Sarah; sons, John, Nehemiah; execs., names not given; wits., Thomas Hirst, Samuel Thompson, David Dutton.

JONATHAN MAXSON, date of will, Feb. 26, 1825; date of probate, Oct. 24, 1825; wife, Mary; children, David, Nathan, William, Mary; execs., David Maxson, John Calwalader; wits., John Calwalader, Jacob Milleson.

JOHN MATTERN, Archer township, date of will, Sept. 23, 1850; date of probate, June 15, 1861; wife, Nancy; children, Abraham, John, Jule Ann Smith, Anna Mariah Hanna; exec., Abraham Mattern; wits., John Rea, A. C. Turner.

HENRY MAXWELL, Archer township; date of will, April 14, 1829; date of probate, July 1, 1836; wife, name not given; children, Samuel, Agnes, Euphemy; exec., Henry Maxwell; wits., Robert Maxwell, Sr., Agnes Maxwell.

THOMAS MAXWELL, date of will, Jan. 19, 1832; date of probate, April 25, 1832; wife, Jane; brother, Walter; exec., Henry Maxwell; wits., William Shipton, James Maxwell.

JOSEPH MEEK, date of will, July 20, 1833; date of probate, July 25, 1833; wife, Rachel; children, Joshua, Alfred, James, Mary-Ann; exec., William Tingley; wits., Walter B. Beebe, M. Simpson, Jr., John Christy.

JOSHUA MEEK, Cadiz township; date of will, April 12, 1847; date of probate, May 1, 1847; wife, name not given; sister, Mary-Ann; legatees, Mary Forker; John Conwell; exec., Mary Ann Meek; wits., Josiah Scott, J. P. Wood.

RACHEL MEEKS, Cadiz township; date of will, Aug. 23, 1843; date of probate, Oct. —, 1843; children, Joshua, Mary-Ann; exec., Thomas Lee; wits., William Tingley, Wesley Smith, Thomas Lee.

JAMES MEGAW, date of will, Sept. 23, 1851; date of probate, Nov. 11, 1851; children, John, James-G., George-T., Martha-Matilda, Eliza-Jane, Eleanor, Sarah Ann Paterson; execs., Elizabeth Gutherie, James H. Patton.

WILLIAM MELDRUM, Washington township; date of will, Sept. 30, 1853; date of probate, April 11, 1854; wife, name not given; legatees, James and Jane Billingsly, Thomas Meldrum, Robert Meldrum, Jane Carson; execs., James Billingsly, John Burny; wits., Samuel Logan, John Burney.

WILLIAM MELTON, Freeport township; date of will, Aug. 2, 1820; date of probate, Dec. 20, 1820; wife, Sarah; son, Moses; grand-daughter, Fanny Holliday; step-daughters, Mary Kinsey, Ruth Calwalader; exec., Moses Melton; wits., John Calwalader, John Kinsey.

ISRAEL MENDENHALL, date of will, May 18, 1837; date of probate, May 21, 1838; wife, Sarah; children, Phebe, Hannah, Isaac, Seneth, Milton, Israel, John; execs., Sarah Mendenhall, Robert Dutton; wits., John Worstell, Edward Morris, Jr.

CALEB MERRYMAN, date of will, May 24, 1824; date of probate, Jan. 17, 1825; wife, name not given; son, John; exec., John Merryman; wits., Henry Wilkins, John Merryman, John Wilkins.

BARR MEUHIRTER, date of will, May 10, 1826; date of probate, June 5, 1826; wife, Mary; execs., names not given; wits., Garret Teatsorth, Daniel Grim, Robert Orr.

GEORGE MIKESELL, date of will, Jan. 14, 1854; date of probate, Jan. 28, 1854; wife, Mehala; children, Mary Jane; execs., Andrew Mikesell, Joseph

Mikesell; wits., Abraham Busby, Samuel Guthrie.

PETER MIKESELL, Rumley township; date of will, June 24, 1846; date of probate, Aug. —, 1846; wife, Susan; children, Jesse, David, Samuel, Joseph, Andrew, George, Susey; execs., Joseph, Mikesell, Andrew Mikesell; wits., Jacob Kail, George Tedrow.

ANDERSON MILLER, date of will, April 19, 1839; date of probate, May —, 1839; wife, Margaret; exec., Margaret Miller; wits., William Young, William Martin.

DANIEL MILLER, German township; date of will, July 28, 1854; date of probate, Aug. 26, 1854; wife, Susanna; children, Henry, John, Rebecca, Susan, Margaret, Eliza-Jane, Jane Hoobler; grand-daughter, Sarah Jane Latimore; execs., John Miller, Henry Miller; wits., Daniel Lynch, William S. Winings.

ELI MILLER, Washington township; date of will, March 27, 1850; date of probate, May 21, 1852; wife, name not given; legatees, William Miller, Elwood and Levi Hollingsworth, Sarah Hollingsworth; execs., names not given; wits., James Wherry, Samuel Heston, James Taggart.

HANNAH MILLER, Cadiz township; date of will, Oct. 20, 1816; date of probate, March 10, 1817; children, Abner, Joseph; legatees, Methodist Church, Burying Ground Cadiz; exec., Matthew Simpson; wits., William Tingley, David Chambers, Joseph Tingley.

JOHN MILLER, Green township; date of will, March 19, 1824; date of probate, Oct. 17, 1826; wife, Sarah; children, John, Samuel, Elizabeth, Catharine, Mary, Sarah, Esther, Hannah; execs., John Taggart, Andrew Eagleson; wits., Thomas Rea, John Rea, Andrew Rea.

JOHN MILLER, date of will, Feb. 4, 1832; date of probate, March 13, 1832; wife, name not given; children, Nancy, Jane, Charles, William, John; execs., son, John Miller, and Moses Louthan; wits., George McKinney; Samuel Love.

JOHN MILLER, date of will, July 25, 1834; date of probate, Oct. 20, 1834; wife, Catherine; children, Joseph, David, Daniel, John, Mary Miller, Elizabeth Noftsher, Catherine Arnold, Hannah; execs., grand-children, John and Catherine Lowmiller; execs., David Miller, Daniel Miller; wits., Martin Benedick, John Gruber.

JOHN MILLER, date of will, Jan. 18, 1837; date of probate, March 27, 1837; wife, Margaret; children, Mary-Ann, Susan, Isabella, Elizabeth, Jacob, Daniel; execs., David Mills, David Finnicum; wits., Daniel Miller, Philip Benedick.

JOHN MILLER, date of will, June 5, 1854; date of probate, Aug. 25, 1854, wife, Elizabeth; children, Daniel, Mary-Jane; exec., Joseph Dunlap; wits., John Brokaw, William Miller.

JOHN MILLER, date of will, Jan. 11, 1858; date of probate, Feb. 27, 1858; wife, Mary; children, Albert-B., William; John, Thomas, Daniel-K., Sarah-Jane, Mary; execs., Mary Miller, William Miller; wits., George Cook, William-D. Hedge.

DAVID MILLIGAN, date of will. June —, 1830; date of probate, April 1, 1834; children, David, Joseph, John, William, Sarah, Jane, Mary; exec., Abraham Layport; wits., Alexander Henderson, Thomas Henderson.

JANE MILLIKIN, Cadiz township; date of will, Nov. 11, 1830; date of probate, Aug. 1, 1831; children, John, Mary McFadden, Jane Barger; grand-children, John and Maria Jane Millikin; exec., Samuel McFadden; wits., John Haverfield, Peter Barger.

ELISHA MILLISON, Freeport township; date of will, April 3, 1835; date of probate, June 22, 1835; wife, Hannah; wife sole heir; exec., Hannah Millison; wits., Benjamin Ferguson, Peter Stevenson.

ELIAS J. MILLS, Moorefield township; date of will, March 13, 1837; date of probate, June 13, 1837; wife, Nancy; children, Joseph, Benjamin, William, Matthew, Elias, Reuben, Lener Simmons, Mary Ann Elliott, Rachel, Elizabeth Picket; grand-daughters, Charlotte, Irena; exec., Nancy Mills; wits., Samuel Skinner, James Crawford.

ANDREW MISER, date of will, June 29, 1838; date of probate, Aug. 20, 1838; wife, name not given; children, Margaret, Sarah, Mary, John; exec., Josiah Scott; wits., John Wagner, John Gruber.

HUGH MITCHELL, Archer township; date of will, Aug. 25, 1847; date of probate, Aug. 30, 1847; wife, Elzabeth; exec., Elizabeth Mitchell; wits., William Arnold, William Christy, David H. Henry.

WILLIAM MITCHELL, Green township; date of will, April 6, 1830; date of probate, Oct. 27, 1835; wife, Mary; son, James; exec., James Mitchel; wits., Thomas Gibbens, William Moore.

JAMES MOFFIT, Athens township, date of will, Aug. 12, 1834; date of probate, Oct. 20, 1834; wife, name not given; children, Allen, Mary Ann Ellis, Hannah Kirk, Susanna; exec., Allen S. Moffit; wits., William Heastings, James Heastings.

ALEXANDER MOORE, date of will, Jan. 16, 1841; date of probate, May —, 1844; wife, Ruth; children, James, Alexander, John, George, Thomas, Thompson, Ruth, Nancy Culberson, Melila; grand-daughter, Meriah Moore; execs., wife, Ruth Moore, and Thomas Moore; wits., David Cunningham, John Cunningham.

ANN JANE MOORE, Green township; will not dated; date of probate, Aug. —, 1839; children, Ruth, Ann-Jane, Nancy Bradford, Ruth Moore, John; exec., William Moore; wits., Josiah Scott, William Moore.

DAVIS MOORE, date of will, Aug. 3, 1840; date of probate, Sept. 9, 1840; wife, Sarah; daughter, Maria; exec., Edward Clifford; wits., Alexander Moore, James Miller.

ROBERT MOORE, date of will, Oct. 15, 1837; date of probate, Nov. 18, 1837; wife, name not given; brother, John Moore; exec., brother, John Moore; wits., William Moore, John Moore.

THOMPSON MOORE, date of will, Aug. 20, 1848; date of probate, Nov. 8, 1848; brother, Thomas; sister, Melila Moore: exec., John Cunningham; wits., David Cunningham, Ann Cunningham.

WILLIAM MOORE, date of will, May 23, 1846; date of probate, Nov. —, 1846; wife, Sarah; children, William, Samuel, Alexander, David, Hannah; execs., Samuel Moore, Johnson Craig; wits., H. S. McFadden, Thomas C. Vincent.

JOHN MOOREHEAD, Green township; date of will, Feb. 16, 1847; date of probate, June 23, 1847; wife, name not given; children, James, William, Mary, Elizabeth Stinson, Martha Fletcher; grand-daughter, Mary Moorehead; execs., Joseph Lewis, Mary Moorehead; wits., Henry Barger, Joseph Lewis, Josiah Scott.

ALEXANDER MORGAN, North township; date of will, March —, 1856; date of probate, Dec. 3, 1858; wife, name not given; children, Mary-Ann, Martha-Jane; exec., Jarrard Morgan; wits., Wesley McKean, William Allbaugh.

MICHAEL MORGAN, date of will, Feb. 11, 1829; date of probate, March 31, 1829; wife, Sara; children, George, John, Jacob, James, Catherine Read, Elizabeth Harrison, Polly; grandchildren, heirs of Christina Hurless;exec., John Crom. Sr.; wits., Joseph Norick, Daniel Norick.

JOHN NICHOL, Belmont co.; date of will, Oct. 19, 1825; date of probate, June 17, 1829; wife, Anne; children, Thomas, Matthew, William, John, Anne Drennon, Mary Parks, Martha

Gordon, Margaret Bently, Isabella Drennon, Nancy Jackson, Jane Henderson; execs., John Parke, William Nichol; wits., Moses Given, William Neil.

ANN NICHOLSON, date of will, Oct. 3, 1859; date of probate, Oct. 4, 1860; brothers, Thomas, Augustine, James; sister, Sarah N. Smith; mother, Hannah Nicholson; exec., James Nicholson; wits., A. B. Wilkin, George Cattell.

JOHN NIXON, Archer township; date of will, March 24, 1860; date of probate, Feb. 27, 1861; wife, Jane; children, Anthony-C., James-W., Rebecca-D., Emily-Jane; execs., Anthony C. Nixon; James W. Nixon; wits., Samuel Moorehead, Samuel McClean.

JACOB NOFTSKER, date of will, May 30, 1850; date of probate, June 24, 1850; wife, name not given; children, David, Jacob, Sampson, Daniel, Sarah Biddle, Catherine Kail; exec., John Gruber; wits., Lewis W. Ralston, James Hazlett.

JAMES NOLEN, Belmont co.; date of will, Aug. 23, 1861; date of probate, Dec. 31, 1861; wife, Hester-Ann; two children, names not mentioned; execs., names not given; wits., William H. Watson, Henderson Hays.

PETER NOP, date of will, May 4. 1849; date of probate, Aug. 13, 1850; wife, Susanna; children, George, Henry, Simon, Jacob, Meriah Kimmell, Eliza Reneker, Sarah Kimmell, Su-anna, Mary; exec., George Shambaugh; wits., George Shambaugh, Thomas Finnicum.

JOHN OGLIVEE, Cadiz township; date of will, Aug. 15, 1815; date of probate, Sept. 9, 1815; wife, Agnes; stepdaughters, Jane and Mary Patterson; sons, Barruch, Hugh, William, John; execs., John McConnell, Jacob Webb; wits., Solomon Smoot, James Cornwell.

JOHN OLDSHOE, Fayette county, Penn.; date of will, Jan. 7, 1822; date of probate, Jan. 26, 1822; wife, Sophia; children, George, Daniel, Catherine, Margaret; niece, Margaret Barnes; execs., John McDole, John Hamilton; wits., Samuel Shull, David Wheeler, John Brown.

PETER OLER, date of will, May 14, 1832; date of probate, June 11, 1832; wife, Elizabeth; son, William; execs., Elizabeth Oler, Samuel Bosland; wits., Lot Demming, Henry S. Snerry.

JOHN OLMSTEAD, Cadiz township; date of will, May 16, 1856; date of probate, June 23, 1856; wife, name not given; grand-children, Thomas, Elousia, John, and Henry Olmstead, and Jesse, Mary, Henry, and Martha Thomas; execs., John McBean, Joseph S. Thomas, Martha B. Thomas; wits., William G. Finney, John W. Gillespie.

ROBERT ORR, will, not dated; date of probate, Nov. 20, 1857; wife, name not given; daughters, Martha Lindsey, Esther Maxwell, Jane Maxwell, Mary Ann Hanna, Zaporah Smith, Dorcus Reed, Elizabeth Baker; execs., Daniel Smith, John Reed; wits., Jacob Dennis, John Fife.

HIRAM PALMER, date of will. March 17, 1856; date of probate, April 8, 1856; wife, Mary; brothers, Daniel-B., Henry-H., Lewis-S., John-W.; sisters, Elizabeth Wilson, Sarah Curtis; niece, Elizabeth Simpson; nephew, Hiram Palmer; execs., Mary Palmer, Israel Birney; wits., Aquilla Tipton, Nathan Wright.

JAMES PALMER, Buchanan county, Iowa; date of will, June 23, 1856; date of probate, Dec. 19, 1861; wife, name not given; children, Mariah Edie, Levina Edie, Elizabeth Ramsey, Margaret Rankin; grand-son, Palmer Ramsey; exec., John Edie; wits., James Clark, William Logan.

JOHN PARKER, Fairview, York co., Pa.; date of will, June 12, 1843; date of probate, Aug. 21, 1850; wife, Susannah; exec,. Rudolph Graybill; wits., John Hursh, Jacob Kirk, Jr.

THOMAS PARKINSON, date of will, March 22, 1838; date of probate, November, 1838; wife, Elizabeth; children, John, Jacob, Edward, Margaret Miller, Elizabeth Smith, Mary Michael; execs., Jacob Parkinson, James Leech; wits., George Gourley, James Johnston, Michael A. Dowden.

MORDECI PARRISH, date of will, Aug. 27, 1826; date of probate, Nov. 2, 1826; wife, Rachel; children, Edith Blake, Uareth Stubbens, Leonard, Mordecai, Benjamin, Peter, Jarett; grand-sons, Samuel Swan, John Parrish, (son of Benjamin), John Parrish, (son of Leonard), Mordecai Stubbins; exec., Benjamin Parrish, Mordecai Parrish; wits., James McMillan, Benjamin Michener, William P. L. Taylor.

ARTHUR PATTERSON, Franklin township; date of will, Aug. 30, 1858; date of probate, Oct. 11, 1858; wife, Rebecca; children, Samuel, Obadiah, Arthur, William, Mary A. Gilmore, Catherine Rutledge; execs., Rebecca Patterson, William Patterson; wits., John Markle, Lewis Lewton.

JOSEPH PATTON, date of will, Dec. 21, 1849; date of probate, June 17, 1850; wife, name not given; children. Margaret. Polly Anderson, Ann Webster, Cintha-Jane, Matthew-M., James, David; execs., Matthew M. Patton. James Patton; wits., George McCullough, Robert Scott.

THOMAS PATTON, date of will. Feb. 16, 1832; date of probate, March 26, 1832; wife, Jane; children, Elizabeth, Sarah, Mariah, David, James Joseph; exec., James Lee; wits., John Baker, David Parkhill.

JOHN PAXTON, Cadiz township; date of will, April 1; 1840; date of probate. Nov. 11, 1851; wife, Margaret; children. Henry, Robert, Mary-S., Jane, Nancy. Sarah. Rebecca, Eleanor Rallson, Margaret Johnson; execs., Robert Paxton, Henry Paxton, Allen C. Turner; wits., Thomas Lee, John McBean.

HANNAH PEARSON, Bucks co., Pa.; date of will, Aug. 8, 1848; date of probate, Nov. 6, 1848; sister, Adah P. Lewis; brothers, Albert and Hiram Pearson; execs., Adah P. Lewis, Hiram H. Pearson; wits., Aaron Packer, Margaret L. Packer.

JOHN PEEPLES, date of will, Sept. 6, 1854; date of probate, April 8, 1856; wife, Margaret; children, James, Mary, John, Rebecca McCally, Robert; legatees, American Bible Society, Presbyterian Foreign Missions, Presbyterian Home Missionary Society; execs., John Ramsey, James Peeples; wits., Uriah Kail, Andrew Lynch.

MARY PEOPLES, date of will, May 9, 1856; date of probate, May 22, 1853; brothers, James, Robert, John; sisters, Rebecca McColly, Mariah Linzy, Andrew Lynch; execs., John Wilkin, William Stinger; wits., John Wilkin, William Stinger.

SAMUEL G. PEPPARD, date of will, Dec. 1, 1855; date of probate, Jan. 30, 1856; sister, Margaret; execs., George W. McCook, Josiah M. Estep; wits., Samuel McCormick, William Barrett.

HENRY PERREGOY, date of will. Nov. 6, 1844; date of probate, March 29, 1851; wife, Elizabeth; children, George, John, David, James, Sarah Worley, Rebecca Green, Elizabeth; execs., David Perregoy, James Perregoy; wits., Joshua P. Watson, George Kerr, James McMillan.

JONATHAN PERRIN, date of will, Dec. 9, 1851; date of probate, June 9, 1852; wife, name not given; legatees, Ephraim and Nancy Johnson; exec., Abriam Johnson; wits., John Sloan, Joseph P. Wherry.

SIMON PETERSON, date of will, Jan. 27, 1852; date of probate, April 6, 1852; son, Temple; grandsons, Fleming Peterson, John H. Peterson; wits., John Cramble, Edward Gibson.

GEORGE PFAFF, date of will, Jan. 9, 1845; date of probate, April —, 1846; wife, Rebecca; daughters, Lucy-Ann,

Dilli-Ann; exec., Rebecca Pfaff; wits., Andrew Lynch, Josiah Crawford.

MICHAEL PFOUTS, date of will, Nov. 2, 1849; date of probate, May 17, 1851; wife, name not given; children, Mary Hurless, Elizabeth, Catherine Waters, Michael, Jonathan, John, Jacob, Gideon; execs., Jonathan Pfouts, John Pfouts; wits., Jacob Bowers, David Bowers.

JOHN PHILLIPS, date of will, March 14, 1857; date of probate, March 24, 1857; wife, Rachel-M.; children, James, William, David, Ruth, Matilda, Martha, Jane, Margaret Dayhoff, Pricilla Stonebrook, Mariah Hagey, Elizabeth Palmer, Rebecca Champer, Lydia Laughbridge, Sarah Sawvel; execs., Rachel M. Phillips, Joseph Harrison; wits., Emanuel Hendricks, Magery J. Hudson.

JOHN PHILLIPS, Cadiz township; date of will, March 8, 1859; date of probate, May 17, 1859; wife, Eliza; children, Eliza Jane Hanna, Martha, Rachel-Ann, Samuel, William, Thomas; execs., Eliza Phillips, Samuel Phillips; wits., W. G. Finney, J. P. Hunter.

RICHARD PHILLIPS, Washington township: date of will, April 1, 1846; date of probate, Jan. 1, 1857; wife, Nancy; children, John, Joseph, Lewis, Hannah Horn, Margaret Coruthers, Elenor A. Quillan; execs., Joseph Phillips, John Phillips; wits., James McMath, J. H. McMath.

WILLIAM PHILLIPS, date of will, Sept. 29, 1816; date of probate, Oct. 9, 1816; wife, Fanny; children, Alexander, Reizen, Maria; execs., John Pritchard, Robert Cochran, James Cobean; wits., John Phillips, George Cox, Andrew McNeely, Walter B. Beebe.

EDWARD PITTIS, date of will, Feb. 16, 1861; date of probate, Feb. 26, 1861; wife, Naomi; brothers, John, Thomas, Robert, Henry; sisters, Julia Reynard, Ann Worstell; exec., Henry Pittis; wits., Jacob C. Lukens, Nicholas Merryman.

JOHN PITTIS, Franklin township; date of will, Feb. 9, 1954; date of probate, Nov. 22, 1855; wife, Mary; children, Edward, Henry, Mary Edney, Ann Worstale. Julia Reynolds, John, Thomas, Robert; execs., Robert Pittis, Edward Pittis; wits., W. B. Hunt, S. R. Magee.

ROBERT PITTIS, Deersville village; date of will, Sept. 25, 1847; date of probate, Jan. 21, 1859; wife, name not given; children, Robert, George, Jane Scott; execs., Robert Pittis, George Pittis, John Pittis; wits., Joshua Wagner, S. R. Magee.

JOHN POLLOCK, Green township; date of will, March 29, 1819; date of probate, March 20, 1820; wife. Sarah; children, John, Samuel, Clement, Hugh, Ann Adrain, Elizabeth, Jane; exec., son, John Pollock; wits., Alexander Matthews, Alexander Laughlin.

JOHN PORTER, date of will, Oct. 8, 1830; date of probate, Oct. 24, 1831; wife, name not given; brothers, Samuel, David, James, Smily, Arvis; sisters, Mary, Sarah; grand-son, John Porter; execs., names not given; wits., Joshua Dickerson, Sr., John Dickerson.

MARGARET PORTER, date of will, July 1, 1842; date of probate, Sept. 14, 1852; children, James, Augustus; exec., James Porter; wits., George A. Winson, Samuel Porter, David Porter.

JAMES PAULSON, date of will, Jan. 22, 1816; date of probate, April 9. 1816; wife, Rachel; children, John, Samuel, James, Jehu, Andrew, Ruthy, Mary, Rachel, Prudy, Anne; exec., Rachel Paulson; wits., Rudolph Hines, Isaac Hines, William Phillips.

SAMUEL POULSON, date of will, April 15, 1831; date of probate, Aug. 1, 1831; wife. Polly; children, James, Joshua, J.-W., Thomas-J., Allen, Samuel, Sarah H. Baxter, Rachel-D. Susan-J., Polly; execs., Polly J. Poulson, John Poulson; wits., Abiram Johnson, James Poulson, Rachel Poulson.

CHARLES PRATHER, Brooke county, Va.; date of will, Aug. 2, 1809; date of probate, Oct. 15, 1838; wife, name not given; children, Elizabeth Wells, Henry, John; exec., John Prather; wits., James McGruder, George Hartford, S. Connell.

JOHN PRATHER, Brooke county, Va.; date of will, Nov. 27, 1836; date of probate, Nov. 27, 1837; wife, Mary; execs., John C. Campbell, Adam Ruhic; wits., Campbell Parr, Robert Moore. P. Rattenburg.

JOHN PRITCHARD, Cadiz township; date of will, June 26, 1844; date of probate, Aug. —, 1844; wife, Sarah; children, Rebecca, Mary, Nancy Dewey, Maria Lee, Eliza Houston, Isabella Douglas, Jane Anderson, Benjamin, Jesse; exec., Sarah Pritchard; wits., S. W. Bostwick, James Kerr, S. B. Shotwell.

MATTHEW PROVINES, Washington county, Pa.; date of will, Jan. 25, 1821; date of probate, Sept. 5, 1821; wife, name not given; children, Nancy, Peggy, Jane, Charles, Matthew, Robert; execs., son, Charles Provines, Henry Crooks, Jr.; wits., Andrew Clendenning, Moses Allen.

JOHN PUGH, Nottingham township; date of will, May 17, 1828; date of probate, June —, 1840; children, Jesse, Thomas, John, David, Mary Cope, Hannah Hamett; grand-daughter, Evalena Pugh; exec., David Pugh; wits., John Heavilin, Philip Fulton.

JOSEPH PUGH, date of will, Dec. 4, 1839; date of probate, April 29, 1849; wife, name not given; children, Levi, Ellis, Amos, Patience Tipton, Ann; execs., Thomas Crumley, Robert Harryman; wits., William Boggs, Mary Brown.

G. R. PUMPHREY, Moorefield township; date of will, Jan. 11, 1851; date of probate, March 25, 1851; wife, name not given; sole heir, wife, name not given; exec., William Cogill; wits., Samuel Skinner, James Wood, Brandis Bethel.

JOHN RAMAGE, date of will, March 1, 1849; date of probate, April 24, 1849; wife, Elizabeth; children, William, John-C.; Samuel, Louisa-Jane; execs., Dr. Benjamin F. Bethel, William Ramage; wits., James W. Slater, Joseph Lafferty.

DAVID RAMSEY, Cadiz township; date of will, March 16, 1852; date of probate, Aug. 1, 1852; wife, Mary-Ann; children, Matthew-J., David, William-L., Moses; execs., wife, Mary Ann Ramsey, son, William L. Ramsey; wits., John Mitchell, Thomas Love, Joseph Rea.

WILLIAM RAMSEY, Nottingham township; date of will, Jan. 10, 185=; date of probate, March 11, 1856; wife, Mary; children, Samuel, Robert, Mary Mahanna, Margaret Ford, Jane House, William; execs., William Ramsey, Samuel Ramsey; wits., Aaron Conaway, George McKinney.

JAMES RANKIN, date of will, Jan. 21, 1857; date of probate, Aug. 18, 1858; wife, Hester; children, Thomas, William, Israel, Margaret Jones, Nancy Early, Sarah Gray; execs., William Rankin, James Kirkpatrick; wits., William Kirkpatrick, Hugh Kirkpatrick.

THOMAS RANKIN, date of will, Aug. 2, 1828; date of probate, March 12, 1832; wife, Mary; children, James, William, David, Elizabeth Porter, Nancy Matthews; execs., names not given; wits., Alexander Moore, John A. Guttery, Benjamin S. Cowen.

JOSIAH RATCLIFF, date of will, Nov. 21, 1836; date of probate, Dec. 5, 1836; wife, Mary; children, Robert, John, Martha; execs., Mary Ratcliff, William Ratcliff; wits., Nathan Hale, Thomas Wallace, James McMillan.

JAMES REA, Cadiz township; date of will, Jan. 19, 1845; date of probate, Jan. 28, 1845; wife, Jane; children, Isabella, Sarah, Hellen, Albert; exec., William Knox, Jr.; wits., John W. Scott, Josiah Scott.

JOHN REA, Green township, date of

will, Jan. 9, 1855; date of probate, March 13, 1855; wife, name not given; children, Joseph, John; nephews, William Purdy Rea, John Rea. John M. Rea, Joseph Rea; niece, Elizabeth Rea; Board of Foreign Missions; exec., Joseph Rea; wits., Thomas Jamison, S. R. Watson.

WILLIAM P. REA, Green township; date of will, May 30, 1846; date of probate, Aug. —, 1846; wife, name not given; brothers, John, Joseph; sister, Sarah Thompson; nephews, John M. and Samuel J. Rea; execs., brother, Joseph Rea, and Josiah Scott; wits., Nathaniel A. Wallace, William Porter, Josiah Scott.

MATTHEW REAVES, date of will, Nov. 5, 1857; date of probate, Nov. 18, 1857; wife, name not given; stepmother, Celia Reaves; exec., R. K. Price.

HENRY REDDIG, Shortcreek township; date of will, Sept. 3, 1843; date of probate, May —, 1844; wife, Elenor; execs., wife, Elenor Reddig, and brother, John P. Reddig; wits., Thomas Carver, Jedediah Thorn.

JOSEPH RHODES, date of will, May 5, 1836; date of probate, Oct. 31, 1842; wife, Mary; children, Harman, Moses, Amy Timberlake, Lydia Johnston; sister, Elizabeth Reed; execs., wife, Mary Rhodes, and son, Harman Rhodes; wits., Robert Sutton, James Anderson, James McMillan.

MARY ANN RICHARDSON, date of will, Oct. 9, 1856; date of probate, Oct. 9, 1856; adopted son, Theodore F. Richardson; execs., names not given; wits., M. F. Mallernee, Amon Lemmon, A. C. Turner.

ANDREW RICHEY, date of will. April 20, 1859; date of probate, June 3, 1859; wife, Margaret; children, Alexander, Jane, Gussy Ann Hawthorn, Hannah Bell, Elizabeth, Hester, Abigail, Catherine Beaty, Margaret; exec., Andrew Richey; wits., John Campbell, William Dunbar.

JACOB RICHEY, date of will, June 18, 1836; date of probate, May —, 1839; wife, name not given; children, Ann, John, Jacob, Samuel; execs., Jacob Richey, James Devore; wits., James Devore, Samuel Gamble, John Ross.

RICHARD RIDGWAY, Berklay co., Va.; date of will, March 24, 1806; date of probate, July 22, 1847; wife, name not given; children, David, Hannah Wright, Patience Beeson, Sally Ross, Buly Clevenger; son-in-law, Jonathan Wright; execs., David Ridgway, Jonathan Wright; wits., J. Stephenson, Joel Ward, Robert Wilson.

JOHN RILEY, date of will, March 19, 1819; date of probate, Nov. 11, 1823; wife, Mary; children, Moses, Abram, William, Mary; exec., Joseph Johnson; wits., Abiram Johnson, Jonathan Perrin.

WILLIAM ROBB, Athens township; date of will, Jan. 8, 1858; date of probate, Feb. 25, 1858; wife, Abigail; execs., names not given; wits., William McCall, Thomas B. Morris.

JAMES ROBERTS, Shortcreek township; date of will, Aug. 19, 1828; date of probate, Oct. 27, 1828; wife, Rachel; children, William, James, Anna Wiley, Nancy Wheeler, Matilda Gorsuch; grand-daughter, Rachel Armstrong; exec., William Roberts; wits., John Warfield, Eli Matson.

JOSEPH ROBERTS, Athens township; date of will, March 15, 1833; date of probate, April 8, 1833; wife, Mary-Ann; exec., William McFarland; wits., William McFarland, George Brown.

ROBERT ROBERTS, date of will, April 4, 1836; date of probate, June 28, 1836; wife, Ruth; children, William, George, Ross, John, Mary, Elenor, Caroline; execs., Ruth Roberts, John Gruber; wits., William R. Lloyd, Joseph Smith.

ELIZABETH ROBINSON, date of will, Aug. 29, 1837; date of probate, Feb. 2, 1838; children, Brooks, Thomas, Christopher, Joseph, Elizabeth Willgus,

Hannah, Jane; exec., Brooks Robinson; wits., Michael Miller, David G. Meguire.

JOHN ROBINSON, Cadiz township; date of will, Jan. 11, 1838; date of probate, Feb. 2, 1838; wife, Susan; four children mentioned, names not given; exec., Thomas Lee; wits., Josiah Scott, Andrew Taggart.

WILLIAM ROBINSON, date of will, Feb. 9, 1840; date of probate, April —, 1840; wife, Mary; children, William, Jane Marshall, Polly; grand-daughter, Polly Marshall; exec., William Robinson; wits., Solomon Gamble, Elenor Adams, Margaret Adams.

LESLY ROBY, Monroe township; date of will, Jan. 16, 1835; date of probate, Nov. —, 1838; wife, Lenne; children, John, Elizabeth; exec. Benoni Roby; wits., James Stonaker, Joshua Cheaney.

MOSES ROMANS, date of will, April 8, 1849; date of probate, May 22, 1849; wife, name not given; children, Elisha, Robert, Moses, Lydia; execs., Joseph Romans, Elisha Romans; wits., Job Briggs, Josiah Brown.

CHARLES ROSS, Archer township; date of will, Feb. 18, 1836; date of probate, Aug. —, 1845; wife, name not given; children, William, Natheher, John, Eva Wagstaff, Susan Tipton; exec., William Arnold; wits., George McPeck, William McConkey, John Heiss, William Arnold.

ROBERT ROSE, Washington township; date of will, March 16, 1840; date of probate, Dec. 7, 1840; wife, name not given; children, Amos, Hugh Henry, Jacob, James, Gardner, John Susanna Strahan, Martha Stephens Mary Vanhorn, Nancy Ankrim; exec., Amos Rose; wits., John Auld, William Griffith, Thomas Griffith.

JOHN ROWLAND, Moorefield township; date of will, Feb. 26, 1851; date of probate, June 15, 1855; wife, Rachel; son, Cyrus; exec., James Rowland; wits., Anthony Wood, Benjamin Ruby.

JOHN RUBY, Franklin township; date of will, Feb. 7, 1834; date of probate, June 23, 1834; wife, name not given; children, Benjamin, Thomas, Betsy; exec., John Auld, Jr.; wits., Stewart Auld, Samuel H. Wilson, S. B. Scoles.

JAMES RUSSELL, date of will, Feb. 11, 1833; date of probate, June 28, 1836; wife, name not given; children, James, John, Elizabeth Carney, Mary Anderson, Nancy, Dorcas; grand-son, Riley Muskelly; son-in-law, Christopher; exec., William Henderson; wits., Samuel Skinner, Michael Moore, J. J. Moore.

ADAM SABLE, Green township; date of will, May 12, 1821; date of probate, March 9, 1826; wife, Catherine; children, Michael, Jacob, Anna, Mary Schmick, Christinna Miller; exec., John Shober; wits., Thomas Fisher, Frederick Rohdes.

JONATHAN SAYRS, date of will, Sept. 4, 1839; date of probate, Nov. 19, 1839; wife, Susannah; children, Hannah, Susannah, David, Jonathan; execs., wife, Susannah Sayrs, and son, Jonathan Sayrs; wits., Jacob Lemmon, John Knox, Moses Lemmon.

CHARLES SCOTT, date of will, June 10, 1845; date of probate, Aug. —, 1845; wife, name not given; daughter, Susanna; exec., William Pollock; wits., Isaac Sabbath, Zadoc Bliss.

JOHN SCOTT, date of will, Aug. 23, 1830; date of probate, Oct. 19, 1830; wife, name not given; children, Jane, Steward, Thomas; sisters, Mary, and Eleanor; exec., William Scott; wits., John Watters, Bazzel Watters, Henry Barricklow.

REBECCA SCOTT, Wells township, Jefferson co., O.; date of will, Feb. 26, 1849; date of probate, July 25, 1855; wife, name not given; children, Violet Simpson, Abraham-P., Samuel, Alexander-F., Nancy Marshall; execs., James Simpson, William Marshall; wits., John Daugherty, John V. McCulley.

SAMUEL SHAFFER, Archer township; date of will, Feb. 17, 1854; date of probate, March 31, 1854; wife, Christina; execs., wife, Christina Shaffer, and Samuel Moorehead; wits., William McKittrick, Robert Johnson.

SAMUEL SHANK, Cadiz township; will, not dated; date of probate, July 16, 1860; wife, name not given; sons, George, John, Garrett; execs., names not given; wits., T. Phillips, W. M. Grimes, Dr. John Pearce.

ISAAC SHANNON, date of will, March 20, 1845; date of probate, April 24, 1849; wife, name not given; children, Mary Clark, Jane Reed, Leslie; execs., William Reed, James Taggart; wits., William Paxton, Henry Eagleson.

THOMAS SHARP, date of will, Oct. 15, 1825; date of probate, March 6, 1826; wife, Jane; children, George, John, Joseph, Margaret, Rachel, Jane, Sarah; execs., George Sharp, John Sharp; wits., Charles Hirsey, Thomas B. Carter, James McMillan.

CHRISTOPHER SHAWVER, Green township; date of will, March 22, 1818; date of probate, Aug. 4, 1818; wife, Margaret; sons, John, Samuel, Jonathan, Elias, Jacob; execs., John Shawver, Jacob Shawver; wits., Christopher Shawver, Jacob Beckley, John Wagner, Christopher Able.

JOSEPH SHEARER, date of will, Sept. 21, 1835; date of probate, Dec. 7, 1840; wife, Mary; children, John, Samuel, Benjamin, Henry, Joseph, Elias, Dewitt, Elizabeth, Mary, Catherine, Susanna, Ann, Margaret, Lydia; execs., John Shearer, Samuel Shearer; wits., Jacob Ream, Richard Lyons.

WILLIAM SHIPTON, Archer township; date of will, March 4, 1854; date of probate, June 12, 1854; wife, name not given; children, Eliza, George, Sarah, John, Susanna, Mariah; exec., Hugh Cavan; wits., Samuel Adams, Hugh Cavan.

HUGH SHOTWELL, date of will, Jan. 3, 1840; date of probate, April 18, 1854; children, Arrison, Esther, Susanna, Nancy, John, William, Joseph; grand-children, Nancy Sears, John Vendolah; exec., Arrison Shotwell; wits., John McBean, William Jones.

GEORGE SHUAF, Rumley township; date of will, Nov. 8, 1842; date of probate, April —, 1845; wife, name not given; children, Margaret Cando, Polly Miller, heirs of deceased daughter, Catherine, Sarah Mikesel, Betsey Whitmore, George; son-in-law, Jacob Reed; execs., John Gruber, George Sharp; wits., Andrew Lynch, Samuel Anspoker.

GEORGE SHULTZ, Green township; date of will, April 3, 1824; date of probate, March 31, 1828; wife, Elizabeth; son, Solomon; execs., Jacob Winings, John Shober; wits., John Wagner, Adam Hoobler, Jacob Hosterman.

JAMES SIMERAL, Green township; date of will, May 31, 1849; date of probate, Nov. 6, 1849; wife, Mary-Anne; children, Martha, Amanda, Matilda, Robert; execs., Robert V. Simeral, George Atkinson; wits., Josiah Scott, John Neely.

ROBERT VINCENT SIMERAL, date of will, Jan. 1, 1851; date of probate, April 22, 1852; wife Sarah-Ann; children, George, Mary-Ann; mother, Mary Ann Simeral; legatee, Vincent Boggs; exec., William Boggs; wits., John Beall, W. Welch.

ALEXANDER SIMPSON, Athens township; date of will, March 10, 1841; date of probate, April 12, 1841; wife, Jane; children, Thomas, James, Polly Gilmore, Betsy McCune, Eleoner Nox, Jane; exec., John McAdams; wits., Nathan Tannehill, John McAdams.

JAMES SIMPSON, Cadiz township; date of will, June 8, 1812; date of probate, (in Allegheny county, Penn.), June 28, 1815; wife, Sarah; brother, Matthew Simpson; wits., George Boggs, James Beaumont, Robert McElhinney.

HARRISON COUNTY WILLS

NANCY SIMPSON, Athens township; date of will, Oct. 3, 1839; date of probate, April —, 1840; sister, Jane Simpson; execs., names not given; wits., John Newell, Nathan Tannehill.

JOHN SINGER, Shortcreek township; date of will, July 18, 1840; date of probate, Aug. 1, 1842; wife, Elizabeth; children, Mariah, Jane, James, Lard, John; grand-son, George Nownan; exec., Samuel Lewis; wits., Samuel Bonsall, Talason G. Elliott, Lewis Parker, John Ramick.

SAMUEL SKINNER, Moorefield township; date of will, April 21, 1860; date of probate, Nov. 15, 1860; wife, Catherine; children, C.-Adolphus, Melinda Martin; exec., C. Adolphus Skinner; wits., James Sloan, Benjamin Wood.

JANE SLEMMONS, date of will, March 12, 1851; date of probate, July 8, 1851; children, Matthew, Alexander, Jane Almspoker, Susanna Lyle; stepdaughter, Margaret Vasbinder; stepson, Thomas Slemmons; exec., Matthew Slemmons; wits., John Carnahan, A. H. Carnahan.

WILLIAM R. SLEMMONS, date of will, Nov. 21, 1844; date of probate, Jan. 28, 1845; wife, Nancy; daughter, Henrietta; execs., Nancy Slemmons, Andrew F. Hanna; wits., Eli Peacock, C. Dewey, S. B. Shotwell.

JAMES SLONAKER, date of will, April 27, 1853; date of probate, June 13, 1853; wife, Nancy; children, Mary-Ann, Elizabeth, Jane, Rebecca, Sally, Matilda, Louisa, Susanna; grand-children, David and John Wesley Slonaker; exec., Nancy Slonaker; wits., Alexander Gamble.

CAROLINE SMITH, Moorefield township; date of will, Nov. 20, 1851; date of probate, March 29, 1852; husband, Thomas H. Smith; legatee, Mary Jane Mouser; exec., John Parrish; wits. William G. Smith, James Wood.

JOHN W. SMITH, Shortcreek township; date of will, Oct. 12, 1852; date of probate, Oct. 19, 1852; wife, Margaret; children, Ellis; exec., father, John Smith; wits., Milton Mendenhall, Joseph Townsend, James McMillan.

JOHN SMITH, Athens township; date of will, Dec. 4, 1854; date of probate, July 29, 1856; wife, name not given; niece, Jane Worley, and her children, Robert-W., James-T., Smith, Isabella, Sara-Ann, and Martha Worley; exec., William McFarland; wits., Robert S. Watson, John W. Watson, William McFarland.

JOSEPH SMITH, date of will, Sept. 11, 1857; date of probate, Nov. 19, 1858; wife, name not given; father and mother mentioned, names not given; brother, Pleasant; relatives, Adeline Smith, Samuel Smith, Perry Smith, Lucy Christian, Elizabeth Eps, Michael M. Smith, Frederick D. Smith; exec., brother, Pleasant Smith; wits., William Beadle, Samuel Christian.

NANCY SMITH, date of will, Feb. 26, 1847; date of probate, Nov. 8, 1848; children, Mary Jane Cooper, John; execs., names not given; wits., Joan Cramblett, Thomas Peterson.

WILLIAM SMITH, date of will, Feb. 10, 1820; date of probate, July 31, 1820; wife, Olife; children mentioned, names not given; exec., Olife Smith; wits., Joseph Fry, John Lyons, Polly Lyons.

WILLIAM SMITH, Brooks co., Va.; date of will, Aug. 20, 1846; date of probate, July 31, 1855; wife, name not given; children, Andrew, Catherine Hunter; legatees, John and Sally Estep; exec., Andrew Smith.

WILLIAM SMITH, Stock township; date of will, Aug. 13, 1858; date of probate, Sept. 11, 1858; wife, name not given; sons, James, George; execs., William Givin, Andrew Crawford; wits., George A. Givin, Jonas Turner.

SOLOMON SMOOT, date of will, Feb. 20, 1828; date of probate, March 8, 1828; children, Betsy, John, Barton; grand-son, Solomon Burke; exec.,

Henry Barricklow; wits., George W. Craner, Isaac Helems.

JOHN SNEDAKER, date of will, May 16, 1816; date of probate, July 4, 1816; wife, Elizabeth; children, Rebeckah, Samuel, Garret; exec., Thomas Ford; wits., John Wilson, John France.

ADAM SNIDER, Green township; date of will, Nov. 9, 1848; date of probate, Nov. 13, 1848; wife, Margaret; daughter, Katherine Lewis; exec., Samuel Moorehead; wits., John Thompson, Jesse Lewis.

SAMUEL SNIDER, date of will, Dec. 11, 1854; date of probate, Dec. 25, 1854; wife, name not given; execs., Daniel Moore, Walter Jamison; wits., William G. Finney, Joshua Cope.

GEORGE SNODIGLE, date of will, Jan. 5, 1837; date of probate, March 27, 1837; wife, Margaret; daughter, Catherine; exec., James Cummings; wits., James Crumley, John Ford.

JOHN SPEER, date of will, July 29, 1831; date of probate, Oct. 24, 1831; wife, Mary; children, John, William, Samuel, Robert, Sarah, Elizabeth; exec., Mary Speer; wits., Walter B. Beebe, David Smylie, John M. Lacey.

ROBERT SPEAR, date of will, April 15, 1850; date of probate, June 27, 1853; mother, Mary Stubens; sister, Elizabeth Spear; exec., William Fry; wits., Samuel G. Sheppard, Matthais Bartelson.

WILLIAM J. SPENCER, Nottingham township; date of will, Sept. 3, 1855; date of probate, Jan. 4, 1858; wife, name not given; children, Lorenzo, Martha, Sarah, Hannah; exec., Abiram Johnson; wits., C. Dewey, William Arnold.

JOSEPH SPIDEL, Tuscarawas co., O.; date of will, Oct. 11, 1841; date of probate, Nov. —, 1845; wife, name not given; legatees, Thomas and John Wilson; execs., names not given; wits., John Gruber, Jacob Matterman.

CHRISTIAN SPIKER, date of will, Dec. 9, 1820; date of probate, Jan. 6, 1821; wife, Diana; children, Christian, John, Joseph; execs., Henry Spiker, Joseph Johnson; wits., George Waller, Edward Moore, Malaslin Layport.

ISAAC SPIKER, Stork township; date of will, July 26, 1855; date of probate, Sept. 1, 1855; wife, name not given; mother, Sarah Ann Spiker; nephews and nieces, Henry M. Wells, William M. Spiker; Sarah-Ann, Emma, Virginia Spiker; and Abraham, John, Catherine, Isaac, Mary, Margaret, and Elizabeth Patterson; execs., names not given; wits., James Keesy, J. C. Wells.

JOHN W. SPIKER, Stock township; date of will, April 24, 1854; date of probate, May 3, 1854; wife, name not given; nieces, Sara Ann Spiker, Emma Spiker, Virginia Spiker; nephew, William M. Spiker; legatees, Isaac Spiker, John-C., and Catherine Wells, William and Mary Patterson, David and Catherine Patterson. Samuel Gilbert; exec., Alexander Henderson; wits., James Kelly, Hester Ann Kent.

SARAH A. SPIKER, date of will, Aug. 27, 1858; date of probate, Jan. 25, 1861; grand-children, Absolom, Joseph-B., John, Catherine, Isaac, Mary-M., Elizabeth, Isaac, William, John, Amanda, Absolom, Joseph-B., Isaac, and John Patterson; legatees, Mary and Catherine Patterson; exec., Joseph P. Patterson; wits., A. C. Nixon, Fryer McKinney.

WILLIAM SPIKER, Stock township; date of will, July 3, 1853; date of probate, Sept. 5, 1853; wife, Elizabeth; children, William-M., Emma, Virginia; execs., John W. Spiker, Alexander Henderson; wits., Aaron Conaway, William Walker.

FRANCIS SPRAUL, date of will, Nov. 25, 1840; date of probate, April 12, 1841; wife, name not given; sons, James, Hugh; execs., James Spraul, Hugh Spraul; wits., James Miller, John Wilson, Thomas Miller.

JAMES SPROUL, Moorefield township; date of will, July 31, 1856; date of probate, Nov. 24, 1856; wife, Elizabeth; execs., Hugh Sproul, Peter Compher.

JOHN SPROUL, Nottingham township; date of will, April 23, 1846; date of probate, April 27, 1846; wife, name not given; brothers and sisters mentioned, names not given; exec., Ephraim Johnson; wits., John Hastings, J. T. Conn.

RALPH SPURRIER, date of will, Nov. 30, 1838; date of probate, April 25, 1848; wife, Eleanor; children, John, Samuel, Warner, William, Richard, Sarah, Matilda, Elizabeth, Mary-Ann, Aseneth; execs., Warner Spurrier, Richard Spurrier; wits., John Heberling, Nathan Williams, Evan Hurford.

JACOB STALL, date of will, Sept. 8, 1845; date of probate, Oct. 10, 1845; wife, Elizabeth; children, James, William, John, Elizabeth, Margaret, Mary, Catherine, Susie; grand-children, John, Jacob, Samuel, Margaret; execs., John Stall, Jeremiah Condo; wits., David Finicum, George Tedrow.

BAZALEEL STEEL, date of will, May 11, 1853; date of probate, Oct. 22, 1857; wife, Rachel; children, Andrew, Bazaleel, Daniel,'David, William, Jane Hoge, Mary Batton, Matilda Phillip, Nancy Sparling; exec., Rachel Steel; wits., Jacob Lemmon, John Knox.

HESTER STEPHEN, date of will, Jan. 27, 1830; date of probate, March 30, 1830; wife, name not given; sisters, Elizabeth Harmon, Mary Polar, Ann Walker, Vila Chance, Ellener Stephanes; mother, Catherine Stephen; brother, Jonathan; exec., John Mercer; wits., William Stephen, Phebe Stephen.

BENJAMIN STEVENS, date of will, July 9, 1843; date of probate, —— —, 1845; wife, Martha; children, Ruth Irwin, Sophiah Barkas, Rachel Henry, David, Gardner, Benjamin-K.; exec., Jonas Holloway; wits., Ely Smith, Amos Rose.

ARCHIBALD STEWART, date of will, Feb. 4, 1854; date of probate, April 11, 1854; wife, name not given; children, Isabel, Mary Ann Guthrie, James, Samuel; grand-sons, James and William Hefling; exec., Samuel Stewart; wits., James Billingsly, Jacob Cox,

JAMES STEWART, date of will, Oct. 7, 1835; date of probate, April 4, 1836; wife, name not given; children, James, Erasmus, William, Robert, Charles, Thomas, Jane, Mary; execs., John Smith, William Stewart; wits., Josiah Scott, Robert Erwin.

JAMES STEWART, Archer township; date of will, Aug. 5, 1836; date of probate, March 27, 1837; wife, name not given; legatee, Samuel McKitterick; exec., William Ross; wits., Robert Maxwell, James G. Maxwell.

LYDIA STRATTON, date of will, Oct. 29, 1860; date of probate, May 28, 1861; mother, Hannah T. Stratton; exec., Hannah T. Stratton; wits., W. H. McGavran, William T. Deming.

MARTHA STRATTON, date of will, Oct. 29, 1860; date of probate, May 28, 1861; mother, Hannah T. Stratton; exec., Hannah T. Stratton; wits., W. H. McGaran, W. T. Deming.

MICHAEL STULL, date of will, Oct. 8, 1842; date of probate, Nov. 2, 1842; wife, Peggy; children, mentioned, names not given; execs., Peggy Stull, George Stull, Samuel Berrier; wits., John Wagner, Daniel Hilbert, George Miller.

JOHN T. SUMMERS, date of will, March 14, 1837, date of probate, July 4, 1837; wife, Jane; children, Andrew-J., John, Nancy Bishop, Taras Muckelroy, Rebecca; grand-son, John W. Bishop; grand-daughter, Rebecca Summers; exec., Ebenezer A. Gray; wits., James Carruthers, William Maxson.

JOHN SUMMERS, Shortcreek township; date of will, Nov. 27, 1855; date of probate, Feb. 23, 1856; wife, Elizabeth; children, Amy Estep, Reuben-P.; grand-children, John, Hester, Ann-Eliza, Benjamin, Abraham, and Cyrus

Soper; legatee, Adolphus DeWitt; exec., Reuben Summers; wits., William Buchanan, William Carns, Robert Wade.

JOSHUA SWAYNE, date of will, Feb. 28, 1830; date of probate, Sept. 10, 1832; wife, Mary; execs., Mary Swayne, James Kinsey; wits., Thomas Hall, William Matson, Nathan P. Hall.

JOHN TAGGART, date of will, June 21, 1839; date of probate, Aug. 14, 1843; wife, Margaret; children, James, John, George, Alexander, David, Margaret, Mary, Jane; exec., James Taggart; wits., John H. Jelly, C. Dewey.

WILLIAM TARBET, Belmont co.; date of will, Sept. 20, 1817; date of probate, March 27, 1818; wife, name not given; cousins, James Tarbet, Martha Tarbet; aunt, Insey Gordon; exec., James Tarbet; wits., Alexander Buchanan, Benjamin Wilson, Samuel Wilson.

JONATHAN TAYLOR, Mt. Pleasant, Jefferson county; date of will, April 1, 1831; date of probate, May 4, 1832; wife, Ann; daughter, Rebecca; grand-sons, Jonathan T. Updegraff, David Updegraff; son-in-law, David Updegraff; execs., David Updegraff, Benjamin Wright; wits., L. Walker, Samuel Steer, Lemuel Jones.

MARGARET TAYLOR, Cadiz township; date of will, March 7, 1856; date of probate, Nov. 16, 1859; daughters, Margaret, Jane; execs., Margaret Taylor, Jane Taylor; wits., Sarah Mills, Josiah Scott.

THOMAS TAYLOR, SR., Cadiz township; date of will, Oct. 23, 1845; date of probate, Dec. 4, 1845; wife, Margaret; children, Josiah, Thomas, Urijah, Peggy, Jane; exec., Thomas Taylor; wits., William Tingley, Samuel Amspoker, Jr.

ENOCH TEDROW, German township; date of will, March 24, 1857; date of probate, July 28, 1857; wife, July-Ann; niece, Christeny Ann Tedrow; exec., July Ann Tedrow; wits., John R. Kail, Andrew Lynch.

GEORGE TEDROW, date of will, Sept. 15, 1815; date of probate, March 22, 1819; wife, Rachel; children, Margaret, Rachel, George, Isaac, Washington, Enoch; execs., wife, Rachel Tedrow, and brother, John Tedrow; wits., Nicholas Wheeler, John Heridy, Philip Biddinger.

WASHINGTON R. TEDROW, German township; date of will, Sept. 27, 1849; date of probate, Dec. 17, 1849; wife, name not given; son, Reuben; legatee, servant, Elizabeth Ann Little; exec., John Gruber; wits., Michael Miller, Peter R. Miller.

HUGH TEES, date of will, July 23, 1827; date of probate, April 1, 1828; wife, Mary; execs., names not given; wits., Archibald McGrew, Walter B. Beebe, John Maurdy.

MATTHEW TENANT, date of will, Dec. 28, 1852; date of probate, Jan. 29, 1853; wife, name not given; children, Robert, William, George, David, Isabelle; execs., John Long, Samuel Richey; wits., John S. Vandolah, John Long.

ISAAC THOMAS, Shortcreek township; date of will, Aug. 14, 1824; date of probate, Jan. 28, 1826; wife, Susanna; children, Isaac, Peter, Hannah, Sarah, Rheuanna; execs., Peter Thomas, Jonathan Taylor; wits., Thomas Gibbons, Nathaniel Worrall, Isaac Cope.

DANIEL THOMPSON, date of will, March 20, 1816; date of probate, April 11, 1816; wife, name not given; sisters, Anne W. Kenny, Jane Wilson, Margaret Burns; nephews, Samuel Burns, Matthew Thompson; execs., Samuel Thompson, John Burns; wits., Natcher Ross, Jonathan West.

JOHN THOMPSON, date of will, Oct. 22, 1830; date of probate, April 11, 1831; wife, Nancy; children, George, William, David, Elizabeth; execs., Nancy Thompson, James Evans; wits., John Leeper, Andrew Thompson, Alexander Simpson, William Evans.

HARRISON COUNTY WILLS

JOSIAH THOMPSON, Athenstownship; date of will, March 7, 1826; date of probate, June 6, 1826; wife, Elizabeth; daughters, Margaret, Jane, Eliza; exec., John Lyle; wits., John Tarbert, John W. Kibbens, James Hood.

REBECCA THOMPSON, date of will, March 30, 1854; date of probate, Aug. 5, 1854; children, Mary-Ann, Hugh; exec., John Brindly, wits., Hugh Birney, John L. Brown.

ELI TIMMONS, Cadiz town; date of will, December 10, 1828; date of probate, July 28, 1829; wife, name not given; brothers, Benjamin, Forney, Samuel; mother, Mary Timmons; execs., Samuel Leach, Adam Junkins; wits., Henry Stubbins, Chauncey Dewey.

MARY TIMMONS, Cadiz township; date of will, Nov. 15, 1845; date of probate, Aug. 13, 1850; children, Furney, William, Samuel, Abraham, Benjamin, Catherine; grand-children, heirs of deceased son, Frederick; exec., Benjamin Timmons; wits., William Arnold, Samuel Bell.

AQUILLA TIPTON, date of will, Aug. 14, 1826; date of probate, Oct. 17, 1826; children, Rebecca Wollan, Charity Gugan, Nancy, Keziah, Ketura Cox, William, Shederick, Samuel, John; execs., John Tipton, Joseph Johnson; wits., George W. Wallar, Aquilla Tipton.

JOHN TIPTON, date of will, Aug. 5, 1823; date of probate, June 11, 1832; wife, Keturah; legatee, William Tipton; exec., William Tipton; wits., George McCollough, William Tingley.

MARY TIPTON, date of will, Nov. 7, 1825; date of probate, Sept. 3, 1827; children, John McGuire, Patience, Sarah; grand-daughter, Jerity Tipton; exec., John Dugan; wits., James Worth, Sr., Thomas Patton.

RACHEL TITUS, date of will, June 20, 1860; date of probate, Jan. 21, 1861; sisters., Abigail Hooper, Sarah Cox; exec., Salathael J. Hooper; wits., William Johnson, J. M. Johnson.

TIMOTHY TITUS, date of will, June 2, 1857; date of probate, Jan. 19, 1859; wife, name not given; children, Uriah, William-L., Samuel, Jonathan, Eliza, Timothy, Jane Irons, Susanna Middleton, Mary Ann Wallace; wits., W. S. Granfell, Amon Lemmon.

SOLOMON TRUSHEL, date of will, Dec. 3, 1845; date of probate, Feb. 28, 1846; wife, name not given; children, Mary Homerichouser, Susanna Guthry, Elizabeth Bearer, John, Valentine, Peter; grand-children, Solomon, David, Mary-O., Delila, and Zebadee Staples. execs., Robert P. Simpson, William Guthry; wits., W. H. McGavran, Joseph Masters.

CHRISTOPHER TUCKER, date of will, Feb. 12, 1842; date of probate, May 4, 1842; wife, Rachel; children, James-W., Greenberry-W., Levi-J., William-W., Christopher, Stephen, Rebecca, Rachel, Eliza, Sarah, Edgamanan; exec., Rachel Tucker; wits., John Knox, Jacob Lemmon.

NATHAN R. TURNER, date of will, March 7, 1845; date of probate, April —, 1845; wife, name not given; children, John, Nancy; exec., Thomas Merchant; wits., Gideon Seymour, Andrew Lynch.

ALEXANDER URQUEHART, date of will, Jan. 17, 1814; date of probate, June 28, 1814; wife, Frances; sons, Syrus, John, Moses; exec., Thomas Dickerson; wits., Samuel Paulson, Isaac Allen, Baruch Dickerson.

EDWARD VANHORN, New Athens township; date of will, Dec. 30, 1844; date of probate, July 12, 1856; wife, name not given; daughters, Martha, Jane, Jermima Downey; execs., names not given; wits., Alexander Nelson, James Wilson.

ROBERT VINCENT, date of will, Jan. 14, 1828; date of probate, Aug. 18, 1841; wife, name not given; children, Thomas-C., Jane Chambers; exec., Thomas Vincent; wits., Walter B. Beebe, John Maholm, George Mehood.

THOMAS VINCENT, date of will, Feb. 27, 1840; date of probate, Nov. —, 1841; wife, Jane; children, Joseph, Thomas-W., Robert, James, Amanda, Sarah, Martha Milligan, Jane Holmes; execs., Jane Vincent, Joseph Vincent; wits., William Holmes, William Smiley.

JOHN WAGNER, Jefferson township; date of will, Oct. 10, 1857; date of probate, Feb. 17, 1858; wife, name not given; children, George, John, Levi, Daniel, Henry, Catherine, Sarah, Rachel, Polly, Susanna, Drusilla; execs., John Winings, Jr., Samuel Smith; wits., John Gruber, Milton Burchfield.

WILLIAM WAGSTAFF, date of will, Dec. 22, 1838; date of probate, June —, 1840; wife, Charity; children, James, Joseph, William, Daniel, John, Robert, Elizabeth, Edie, Matilda Anderson; execs., James Wagstaff, Robert Wagstaff; wits., John Beal, Henry Maxwell.

JAMES WALKER, Cadiz township; date of will, Dec. 27, 1858; date of probate, May 30, 1859; wife, Margaret; niece, Margaret McKitrick; sister, Martha Hutchison; legatees, Isaac Lawrence, John Rolston; execs., names not given; wits., Samuel N. Clifford, Samuel Nash.

JOSEPH WALKER, Stock township; date of will, Feb. 18, 1839; date of probate, April 12, 1841; children, William, John, George, James, Elizabeth Parker, Mary Kent; exec., Samuel McFadden; wits., Jacob Wright, John McKenney.

ROBERT WALKER, date of will, Nov. 8, 1858; date of probate, Jan. 22, 1859; wife, name not given; children, James, Charles, John-W., David-A., William-M., Robert-A., Margaret-J.; exec., Wesley Birney; wits., James Billingsley, Alexander Moore.

ROBERT WALKER, date of will, March 12, 1855; date of probate, April 29, 1859; children, Nelson, Lorenzo, Nancy Davis; exec., Nelson Walker; wits., Alexander Moore, John Poulson.

JOHN R. WALLACE, date of will, June 10, 1846; date of probate, April 26, 1847; wife, Elizabeth; children, Amanda, John, William; exec., Robert Davidson; wits., Samuel Kincaid, William Buchanan.

NATHANIEL A. WALLACE Moorefield township; date of will, March 20, 1855; date of probate, April 5, 1855; wife, Juliann; children, Mary-Mc., Thomas-C.; wits., T. R. Crawford, James Kirkpatrick.

WILLIAM WALLACE, Moorefield township; date of will, Aug. 23, 1841; date of probate, May 2, 1842; wife, Polly-W.; children, John, Nathaniel-S., William-A., Samuel-M., Wilson-E., Sarah-Ann, Elenor-S., Margaret-J.; execs., Polly W. Wallace, Thomas J. Holliday; wits., Thomas J. Holliday, John W. Milligan.

WILLIAM WALRAVEN, Jefferson county; date of will, Sept. 25, 1810; date of probate, May 3, 1813; wife, name not given; children, William, Elias, John, Hester, Harriett, and five other daughters, not named; sisters, Sarah, Mary, and Susannah Walraven, and Margaret Guyton; execs., son, John Walraven, and Joseph Holmes; wts., Richard Jones, Andrew Eagleson, Thomas Dickerson.

JACOB WALTERS, date of will, Jan. 25, 1849; date of probate, June 21, 1854; children, Jacob, John, Samuel, George, Martin, David, Joseph, Abraham, Elizabeth; exec., Abraham Walters; wits., Lot Deming, William Deming, Thomas Lyons.

ISAAC WARNER, Moreland, Montgomery co., Pa.; date of will, Feb. 3, 1824; date of probate, Dec. 25, 1829; wife, name not given; children, Isaac, Thomas, Joseph, Ruth, Martha, Mary; grand-son, Isaac Jeams; execs., Thomas Warner, Isaac Warner, Joseph Warner; wits., Elias Booskirk, Sr., Benjamin Briggs.

ANN WATERMAN, Short Creek township; date of will, Nov. 16, 1855;

date of probate, Dec. 15, 1855; children, Leona Dickey, Rebecca Jane Chamberlain; execs., Milton R. Pettot, Ezra Cattell; wits., John Nicholson, John S. Reddig.

JOHN WATKINS, date of will, Nov. 23, 1847; date of probate, Dec. 16, 1847; wife, Margaret; legatees, Silas H. Amos, and children of his brothers and sisters, names not given; exec., Spencer Webb; wits., Joseph Harrison, John Creal.

JOHN W. WATSON, date of will, July 17, 1859; date of probate, July 29, 1859; wife, Rebecca; children, Rachel-Ann, Nancy-A., Adam-D.; exec., S. R. Watson; wits., John Webb, Joseph Dunlap.

ALLEN WATTERS, date of will, July 1, 1821; date of probate, March 18, 1823; wife, Jane; children, John, Allen, William, Anna, Fanny, Elizabeth; exec., John Watters; wits., Thomas Graham, James C. Hutchinson, Michael Grable.

THOMAS WEAVER, date of will, Oct. 25, 1822; date of probate, April 3, 1827; wife, Mary; nephews, James and Thomas Weaver; Jane Beeabout, and Thomas Weaver; brother, Robert; sister-in-law, Betsey; legatees, Jane Beeabout, Jane Wilson; execs., brother, Robert Weaver, and nephew, James Weaver; wits., S. Connell, James Burson, Isaac Jones.

JACOB WEBB, date of will, Feb. 5, 1834; date of probate, April 12, 1834; wife, Hannah; children, Robert, Ezekiel, Joseph, Jacob, Hannah, Ann, Sarah, Esther, Edith, Mary; execs., John Webb, Sirus Holt; wits., Robert McCracken, William McFarland, James McMillan.

JOSEPH WEBB, Athens township; date of will, Feb. 7, 1850; date of probate, Oct. 22, 1850; wife, Susan: exec., Smith R. Watson; wits., William Boyer, S. B. Shotwell.

DANIEL WELCH, Green township; date of will, Sept. 3, 1819; date of probate, Nov. 15, 1819; wife, Elizabeth; children, Daniel, Reasin, Benjamin, Jacob, William, Cyrus, Rodey; grand-daughters, Elizabeth and Rachel Welch; execs., sons, Daniel and Reasin Welch, and daughter, Rodey Welch; wits., William Kyle, James Cobean.

SAMUEL WELCH, date of will, May 4, 1849; date of probate, April 5, 1850; wife, name not given; children, John, James, William, Nancy Johnson, Ellenor Dunbar; grand-daughters, Elizabeth Fisher, Catherine Welch; execs., John Welch, James Welch; wits., Fryer McKinney, Michael Conaway.

WILLIAM WELCH, date of will, Feb. 9, 1856; date of probate, March 11, 1856; wife, Isabelle; children, George, Thomas; exec., Isabelle Welch; wits., John W. McClaren, Steward Price.

JOHN WELLING, date of will, ——, 1818; date of probate, Jan. 22, 1821; wife, Mima; children, William, John, David, Thomas, Henry, Nancy, Polly, Elizabeth; execs., William Welling, John Welling; wits., John Maholm, Connel Abdit, J. Harris.

JOHN WELLS, date of will, Aug. 15, 1824; date of probate, June 5, 1826; wife, Catherine; children, Isiah, Elizabeth, Susannah Gray; grand-son, John Morris; execs., Isiah Wells, William Lewis; wits., Joseph Rhodes, Samuel Lewis, Edwin Patterson.

JOHN WEYANDT, date of will, July 19, 1845; date of probate, April 24, 1848; wife, Motlena; children, Daniel, Jacob, Abraham, Polly Heller, Teny Warner; daughter-in-law, Nancy; execs., Jacob Weyandt, Daniel Weyandt, Abraham Weyandt; wits., Thomas McClintock, John Plowman.

JOHN WHAN, Shortcreek township; date of will, Oct. 25, 1855; date of probate, April 9, 1859; wife, Margaret; children, James-B., Sarah, Ellen, Hannah; grand-children, Martha Stewart, William Twinnam, Mary Twinnam, William McCollough, Mary Bell, William Morgan; execs., James

B. Whan, Marshal Morgan; wits., James Hanna, John Hanna.

ISAAC WHEALDON, date of will, April 16, 1836; date of probate, May 21, 1841; wife, Elizabeth; children, Ann, and others, names not given; execs., wife, Elizabeth Whealdon, Joseph Whealdon; wits., Abel Pickering, Jonathan Sayers.

BENJAMIN WHEELER, Baltimore co., Md.; date of will, Jan. 25, 1806; date of probate, Aug. 22, 1807; wife, name not given; children, Nicholas, William, Benjamin, Mordicai, James, Richard, Rachel, Elizabeth, Keziah, Isabella; exec., William Wheeler; wits., Samuel Price, Daniel Basley, John Price.

JOHN WHITE, Shortcreek township; date of will, Jan. 1, 1835; date of probate, Dec. 7, 1840; wife, Jane; children, Ann Tribby, Rachel Thorn, James; grand-son, John McMillan; execs., John Tribby, James White; wits., John Howard, John C. Thompson, Thomas Hirst.

ANDREW WYLIE, Green township; date of will, June 2, 1832; date of probate, Oct. 25, 1833; wife, name not given; brothers, Samuel, William; sisters, Jane Wilkin, Elizabeth, and Nancy; execs., David Watts, William Wylie; wits., William Watts, William Fulton.

JOHN WILEY, Green township; date of will, April 3, 1816; date of probate, April 10, 1816; wife, Margaret; children, Elizabeth, Nancy, Jean, William, John, Samuel, Andrew; execs., Daniel Welch, William Watts, Margaret Wiley; wits., John Miller, James Black, William Waddle.

MATTHEW WILKIN, date of will, April 10, 1830; date of probate, Aug. 24, 1833; wife, Jane; children, John, Matthew, Robert, Betsy, Fanny Pollock, Peggy Day, Jane Orr; exec., John Patterson; wits., Thomas Patton, Edward Fletcher.

ELIZABETH WILLIAMS, date of will, Dec. 2, 1847; date of probate, Feb. 26, 1850; children, Rachel Warwick, Elizabeth Wagstaff, Mary Henry, Jane McKinney, Susanna Reckey, Martha Brown, William, Samuel; exec., William Williams; wits., Daniel McIlrevy, Charles Conaway.

NATHAN WILLIAMS, date of will, May 19, 1841; date of probate, Aug. 16, 1841; wife, Sarah; execs., Wilson Maddox; wits., Evan Hurford, Asenath Spurrier, Amelia Stephens.

THOMAS WILLIAMS, Archer township; date of will, April 13, 1816; date of probate, Nov. 27, 1816; wife, Betsey; children mentioned, names not given; execs., Robert Maxwell, Thomas Maxwell; wits., Robert Maxwell, Thomas Maxwell.

WILLIAM WILLIAMS, Moorefield township; date of will, May 2, 1857; date of probate, Aug. 8, 1857; wife, Ann; sons, Isaac-W., James-A.; exec., Ann Williams; wits., John Sloan, Robert C. McConnell.

JANE WILLIAMSON, date of will, July 4, 1849; date of probate, Aug. —, 1849; children, Frances-T., Phebe-M., Lusia, Mary-J.-G., William McKnight; exec., Robert Woods; wits., David T. Robe, John Campbell.

CHARLES WILLISON, Moorefield township; date of will, Aug. 14, 1830; date of probate, Oct. 19, 1830; wife, Zillah; children, Elijah, Amos, Jeremiah, Charles, Gerusha, Abijah, Anne, Rosilla; exec., Zillah Willison; wits., William Wyckoff, Ephriam Johnson, Benjamin S. Cowen.

JANE WILSON, date of will, Feb. 12, 1831; date of probate, June 23, 1834; children, Sarah Crain, Joseph, Robert; wits., William L. Robison, William Russel.

JOHN WILSON, date of will, Oct. 27, 1810; date of probate, Nov. 15, 1819; wife, Hannah; children, mentioned, names not given; execs., Hannah Wilson, Jacob Kiser; wits., John Wagner, John Waind, John Winings.

HARRISON COUNTY WILLS

SAMUEL WILSON, Freeport township; will, not dated; date of probate, April 24, 1850; wife, name not given; children, William-P., Samuel-C., Lydia Halliday; grand-daughters, Ann-Eliza and Eveline Wilson; legatees, Sarah A. Irvin, Sarah A. Wilson; exec., William P. Wilson; wits., R. K. Price, Joseph Whealdon.

THOMAS WILSON, Cadiz township; date of will, Nov. 30, 1829; date of probate, March 30, 1830; wife, Levinah; children, John, William, Isaac, Thomas, Levinah, Rebecca, Mary, Elizabeth, Rachel; execs., John Wilson, Thomas Wilson; wits., Alexander Henderson, Joseph Burwell, William Crom.

JACOB WININGS, date of will, June 28, 1843; date of probate, Oct. —, 1844; wife, Elizabeth; children, John, Jacob, Catherine; son-in-law, James McClure; legatee, W. D. Stringer; exec., John Winings; wits., Alexander Patterson, Samuel S. Winings.

JOHN WININGS, German township; date of will, June 19, 1829; date of probate, April 8, 1833; wife, Barbara; children, Margaret, Elizabeth, Catherine, Mary; execs., Jacob Winings, John Winings; wits., John Shober, John Coyl.

LOVINA WINROD, date of will, Nov. 7, 1861; date of probate, Nov. 18, 1861; children, Rachel-E., Lewis-D.; exec., Milton Harvey; wits., John Winrod, James W. Wherry.

WILLIAM WOOD, date of will, Jan. 13, 1830; date of probate, April 11, 1831; wife, Margaret; children, Hugh, Thomas, John, William, Jane Pool, Margaret Chance, Effey Chance, Marget Prane, Mary Beall; exec., Margaret Wood; wits., Samuel Cope, John Suddith.

ZACHARIAH WOOD, North township; date of will, Sept. 9, 1831; date of probate, Oct. 24, 1831; wife, Mary; children, Charles, John, Isaac, Lisha, Zachariah, Benjamin, Joseph, Henry, William, Nancy Lowry, Salle Low; execs., names not given; wits., Peter Rutan, Jonas Gutshall, John Creal, Jonathan Shotwell.

ALEXANDER WORK, date of will, Jan. 25, 1845; date of probate, Aug. 27, 1861; wife, Jane-T.; children, Anderson-D., Alexander-T.; adopted daugter, E. W. Wilcott; execs., John A. Work, James T. Work; wits., John Adams, Anderson D. Work.

THOMAS WORLEY, date of will, July 3, 1834; date of probate, May —, 1859; wife, Mary; children, David, Thomas, Daniel, James, Susanna Martin, Julianna Bonum, Margaret, Elizabeth; execs., Thomas Worley, James Worley; wits., Benjamin Gudgen, David Worley, James McMillan.

ISAAC WRIGHT, date of will, March 27, 1852; date of probate, July 31, 1852; wife, Hannah; children, Mary-Jane; legatee, Hannah Jane Hurles; execs., Hannah Wright, Jacob Reigal; wits., Thomas Underhill, Robert Wright.

JAMES WRIGHT, date of will, Sept. 10, 1836; date of probate, Nov. 4, 1842; wife, Barbary; children, Jacob, Thomas, Eliza, Metilda Whitney; execs., names not given; wits., Peter Crabtree, Cornelius Crabtree.

JONATHAN WRIGHT, Frederick co., Va.; date of will, Jan. 28, 1819; date of probate, March 5, 1838; wife, Hannah; children, Richard, Thomas, David, Esther Lupton, Margaret Cattle, Sally Smith, Bulah, Ruth, Tacy; execs., wife, Hannah Wright, and son, David Wright; wits., William W. Hutt, Martha A. Lupton, Micagah Beeson, Margaret Wolf, Jonathan Pickering.

MOSES WRIGHT, date of will, April 11, 1854; date of probate, June 14, 1854; wife, Ann; children, Isaac, John-C., Thomas, Nathan, Benjamin, William, Moses, Nathan, Pricilla Stugert; execs., Nathan Wright, William Wright; wits., Isaac Cope, John Knox.

AARON YARNELL, Nottingham township, date of will, June 15, 1851;

date of probate, Nov. 18, 1853; wife, Mary Ann; children, no names given; exec., Michael Crowl; wits., William Johnson, M. Crowl.

MARY ANN YARNELL, Nottingham township; date of will, May 2, 1855; date of probate, Oct. 2, 1856; children, Zeba, William, Aaron, Colmer, John, Nelson, Lydia, Mary-Ann; exec., M. Crowl; wits., M. Crowl, Cyrus Rowland.

HENRY YEISALY, date of will, Oct. 18, 1828; date of probate, April 12, 1841; wife, Barbary; son, John; exec., Adam Hubler; wits., Christopher Able, William Abaugh, Frederick Able.

DENTON YOUNG, date of will, July 22, 1831; date of probate, Jan. 4, 1831; wife, name not given; children, Denton, Mark, John, McKinzie, Marandie, Manervy; exec., Andrew Keys; wits., Thomas Patton, Hugh Birney.

JOHN YOUNG, date of will, March 14, 1861; date of probate, June 19, 1861; wife, name not given; children, Mary Sproul, Jane Moore, Sarah Ann Wages, Elizabeth McIlroy, William, Jared, Robert-G.; execs., names not given; wits., R. M. Coultrap, G. W. Spiker.

WILLIAM YOUNG, Brooks county, Va.; date of will, May 18, 1812; date of probate, Aug. 24, 1813; wife, name not given; children, Jean Eagleson; nephews, William Hervey (and his daughter, Margaret) James Hervey, David Hervey, Henry Hervey; sisters, Jean Young, Agnes Young; legatees, Andrew Eagleson, Isabella Hervey; execs., William Hervey, Andrew Eagleson; wits., John McComb, John Henry.

MATTHIAS ZIMMERLY, date of will, Aug. 24, 1839; date of probate, Nov. —, 1847; wife, name not given; children, Jacob, John, George, Catherine Kaylor; execs., names not given; wits., William L. Packer, Thomas Davidson.

PART THIRD

HARRISON COUNTY GENEALOGIES

PART THIRD

HARRISON COUNTY GENEALOGIES*

JOHN ADAMS, a native of Ireland, settled in Short Creek township, Harrison county, Ohio, about 1805, where he d. 1812; m. ———, d. 1846; had issue: 1. William; 2. James; 3. Samuel, b. Dec. 1, 1809; m. (1st) 1842, Sarah Chambers, d. February 7, 1851, daughter of David Chambers, of Green township; m. (2d) April 2, 1857, Mary Clark, daughter of James Clark, of Athens township (had issue by first wife: i. Joshua, b. August 2, 1842; ii. Rachel, b. September 3, 1844; iii. John, b. December 11, 1850; d. April 27, 1882; had issue by second wife: iv. Clark, m. November 26, 1884, Dora Copeland, daughter of Henry Copeland, of Green township; v. Sarah-Elizabeth); 4. Hannah; 5. Joshua; 6. John.

JOHN ADAMS, a native of Pennsylvania, b. November 13, 1774; settled in Freeport township, Harrison county, Ohio, about 1807, where he d. 1835; m. May 2, 1799, Rachel Asher; b. in Pennsylvania May 16, 1776; d. August 25, 1851; had issue:
I. Rebecca, b. February 29, 1800. II. Elizabeth, b. April 16, 1801. III. Rachel, b. December 18, 1803. IV. Samuel, b. January 16, 1806, in Erie county, Penn.; came with his parents to Ohio; settled in Moorefield township, Harrison county, 1828, where he d. November 17, 1880; m. January 24, 1828, Elizabeth Johnson, d. May 19, 1883, daughter of William and Nancy Stalson Johnson, early settlers in Moorefield township; had issue: 1. John, b. January 17, 1831, in Moorefield township; m. January 13, 1853, Mary E. Swearingen, b. December 30, 1835, daughter of John and Nancy Pumphrey Swearingen, natives of Virginia (had issue: i. Henry-T.; ii. Annie-E.; iii. Albert-D.; settled in Chicago, Ill.; iv. W.-S.; v. Emma-V.; vi. Sadie; vii. Mary-E.); 2. Rachel-A., m. ——— Romans; 3. Mary, m. ——— Johnson; settled in Washington, Davis county, Ind.; 4. William; 5. Samuel, d. young; 6. Rebecca, m. J. Moore. V. John, b. June 20, 1808. VI. Julia-A., b. December 13, 1811. VII. Anthony, b. October 4, 1815.

THOMAS ADAMS, b. in Pennsylvania, about 1790; removed to Cadiz township, Harrison county, Ohio, 1815; settled in Nottingham township, in 1846, where he d. 1855; m. Charity Blair, a native of Ohio, b. 1792, d. 1866, daughter of John Blair; had issue: 1. John, d. in infancy; 2. Maria-Rogers; 3. Percival, b. September 10, 1820, in Cadiz township; m. March 27, 1845, Mary J. Downs, b. August 26, 1822, daughter of Richard and Elizabeth McKinney Downs (the former b. 1797, in Carroll county, Ohio; the latter b. January 22, 1797, in Lancaster county, Penn.); (had issue: i. John-F., b. March 20, 1846; ii. Albert-B., b. May 23,

---

* In the family records given in the following pages, the names of the children of the first one of the family to settle in Harrison county are usually preceded by roman capital numerals (I., II., III., IV., etc.); the names of the grandchildren, by arabic numerals (1, 2, 3, 4, etc.); and the names of the great-grandchildren by roman lower-case numerals (i., ii., iii., iv., etc.).

1849; iii. Eliza-J., b. March 14, 1851, d. November 14, 1887; iv. Richard-M., b. August 27, 1853; v. Thomas-P., b. December 3, 1857; vi. James-B., b. July 12, 1860; vii. Margaret-B., b. December 13, 1865); 4. James, d. in Nottingham township, October 8, 1888; 5. Matthew, settled in Cadiz; 6. Albert, settled in Missouri; 7. Isabelle, m. Thomas Rogers, settled in Crawford county, Ohio; 8. William, settled in Cadiz; 9. John, settled in Uhrichsville, Tuscarawas county, Ohio; 10. Sarah-E.

WILLIAM ADAMS, a native of Pennsylvania, of Scotch-Irish descent, m. Mary ———, b. in Pennsylvania; settled in Archer township, Harrison county, Ohio, 1819; had issue, among others: 1. Samuel, b. January 20, 1808; d. June 13, 1874, in Archer township; m. 1833, Jane C. Stewart, b. in Pennsylvania, daughter of James Stewart, a native of Ireland who settled in Philadelphia July 4, 1811, thence removing to Washington county, Penn. (had issue, among others: 1. Samuel-W., b. November 18, 1839, m. Flora J. Gray, daughter of Samuel and Eliza Gray, residents of Findlay).

WILLIAM ADAMS, b. September 5, 1799, in Fayette county, Penn.; resided in Short Creek township, Harrison county, Ohio, until 1880; thence removed to Freeport township; d. January 8, 1881; m. in Pennsylvania, Elizabeth Clark, d. December 10, 1869, daughter of Joshua Clark; had issue: 1. David, settled in Short Creek township; m. (1st) November 10, 1855, Lucinda Marsh, of Iowa, d. December 9, 1865; m. (2d) March 14, 1867, Mary Ann Moore (had issue by second wife: i. ———, d. in infancy; ii. William-Moore; iii. Robert-C.).

JAMES AIKEN, a native of Ireland, emigrated to America and settled, about 1803, near Hickory, in Washington county, Penn.; had issue: 1. James, b. 1802, in Ireland; came to Washington county, Penn., with his parents; removed in 1826, to Jefferson, German township, Harrison county, Ohio, and in 1870 to Jewett, Rumley township, where he d. 1885; m. in Jefferson, 1829, Jane Scott, b. 1806 in Washington county, Penn., d. 1867, daughter of Josiah Scott (had issue: i. Elizabeth; ii. John, a minister, settled in Wayne county, Ind.; iii. Martha; iv. Jane, m. John Roberts; v. Annie, m. James Dennis, settled at Wellsville, Ohio; vi. Robert, settled in Amsterdam, Jefferson county, Ohio; vii. James, b. June 19, 1840; m. March 11, 1865, Maria Mikesell, daughter of Joseph and Magdalene Hoobler Mikesell; viii. Samuel-B.; ix. Josiah; x. Alexander, served in the Civil War; xi. Benjamin; xii. George); 2. John, settled in Chester county, Penn.; 3. William, settled in Baltimore, Md.; 4. Alexander, settled in Pittsburg, Penn.; 5. David, settled in Washington, D. C.; 6. Margaret, m. ——— Agnew, settled in Washington county, Penn.

JOHN ALEXANDER, a native of County Antrim, Ireland, emigrated to America and, about 1826, settled in Pennsylvania; two years later removed to Freeport township, Harrison county, Ohio, where he d. June, 1869; m. in Ireland Mary Allen; d. 1838; had issue: 1. Eleanor; 2. Thomas; 3. Jesse; 4. Mary-Ann; 5. John, settled in Kansas; 6. James, b. March 8, 1829; m. May 27, 1852, Margaret Forsythe, daughter of Matthew Forsythe, of Freeport (had issue: i. Matthew, settled in Freeport township; m. November 20, 1888, Nancy Harbison; ii. Mary; iii. John; iv. Maggie-E.); 7. Hannah-J.; 8. Elizabeth, settled in Kansas.

JAMES ALLEN, a native of Maryland, d. 1792; m. Rebecca Miller; had issue, among others: I. Reuben, b. in Maryland, 1783; removed in 1812 to Cadiz township, Harrison county, Ohio, where he d. July 8, 1875; m. 1812, Johanna McMillan, d. 1869, daughter of John McMillan, a resident of Harrison county; had issue: 1. Isaac, b. September 16, 1813; m. 1841, Sarah Barrett, daughter of David Barrett, of Cadiz township (had issue: i. Reuben; ii. Rebecca-J., m. R. M. Black; iii. Albert; iv. Winifred); 2. Rebecca; 3. Esther; 4. Amos; 5. Mary-Jane; 6. Ruthann; 7. Johanna; 8. James.

JAMES ALLISON, a native of Ireland, b. 1790; d. at Hopedale, Ohio, 1881; emigrated to America and first settled in Philadelphia, Penn., about 1805; removed to Pittsburg, Penn., and thence to Cadiz, Harrison county, Ohio, where he resided until about 1818; removing thence to Stark county, where he resided until about 1825; m. in Cadiz, Margaret Hervey, d. 1837; daughter of

HARRISON COUNTY GENEALOGIES

William and Margaret Hervey; had issue: 1. Margaret, m. John Galbraith; 2. John-Rea; 3. David, b. in Stark county, Ohio, April 20, 1820; m. (1st) 1854, Mary Crouch, d. 1865, daughter of Levi Crouch, who settled in Green township before 1817, where he d. 1862; m. (2d) 1867, Martha-E. Smith, daughter of Joel Smith (had issue: i. Henry-F.; ii. Willard-R.; iii. Howard-Smith); 4. Henry; 5. Sarah; 6. James, d. 1859; 7. Mary-Jane, m. John Hammond; settled in Athens township, Harrison county; 8. Joseph; 9. Elizabeth, m. Daniel Eaton; settled in Jefferson county, Ohio; 10. Isabella, d. 1830.

SAMUEL AMSPOKER, see Family of Henry Ferguson.

ROBERT ANDERSON, b. in Ireland, 1753; d. September 2, 1838, in Claysville, Washington county, Penn.; emigrated to America and first settled in Maryland about 1780, where he remained until 1786, and then removed to Washington county, Penn.; m. 1781, in Maryland, Margaret Johnson, b. in Ireland, 1760; d. September 13, 1827; had issue:
I. Samuel, b. 1783, in Maryland; d. February 22, 1866; removed to the Stillwater Valley, in Stock township, Harrison county, Ohio, about 1838, locating seven miles west from Cadiz; m. 1813, Catherine Forbes, daughter of John Forbes, of Scotch-Irish ancestry; had issue: 1. Robert, b. in Claysville, Penn., October 11, 1815; came with his father to Harrison county, in 1838; located in North township; m. July 1, 1840, Esther McCollough, a native of Archer township, of Scotch descent (had issue: i. Sarah-A., b. May 23, 1842; m. Thomas McDivitt; ii. William-B., b. in Stock township, Dec. 29, 1843; served in the Civil War; m. Sept. 6, 1870, Mary Buchanan, b. near Jewett, Ohio, Dec. 19, 1845; of Scotch-Irish descent, daughter of Joseph and Elizabeth Hines Buchanan; iii. Samuel-L., b. in Harrison county, January 22, 1846; iv. Isabel-J., b. in Harrison county, January 12, 1848; m. S. J. Rippeth, who d. Dec. 19, 1883; v. Joseph-M., b. in Carroll county, Feb. 20, 1850; a Presbyterian minister; settled in Cincinnati; vi. Mary-E., b. in Carroll county, March 5, 1852; m. Thomas Brough; vii. Thomas-H., b. in Carroll county, August 23, 1854; viii. Martha-F., b. in Carroll county, December 30, 1856, d. Feb. 17, 1888; m. Thomas Whittaker; ix. John-E., b. August 15, 1862; d. March 25, 1864); 2. John; 3. James; 4. Samuel; 5. Hugh; 6. William; 7. Jane; 8. Thomas.
II. Richard, b. in Maryland; III. John, b. in Washington county, Penn., as were also his younger brothers and sisters; IV. William; V. Robert; VI. Mary; VII. Hugh; VIII. James; IX. Jane; X. Margaret; XI. Thomas; XII. ———, d. in infancy.

WILLIAM ARBAUGH, a native of Maryland, of German descent, and a soldier of the Revolution, had issue: I. Jacob; II. Daniel; III. Rachel; IV. Margaret; V. John, b. in Maryland, where he m. Rosanna Wentz, a native of that State; removed to Rumley township, Harrison county, Ohio, about 1820; had issue: 1. Sarah; 2. Margaret; 3. Lavina; 4. Lydia; 5. John; 6. James; 7. Adam; 8. Levi, b. October 28, 1825; m. (1st) December 23, 1858, Elizabeth Reid, d. 1885; daughter of Hugh and Margaret Fulton Reid, pioneers of Archer township, Harrison county; m. (2d) April, 1889, Louisa Hilbert, of Defiance, Ohio.

JONATHAN ARNOLD, of Welsh descent, removed probably from Virginia to Luzerne township, Fayette county, Penn., before 1786, there settling "at a place called the West Bend of the Monongahela River, six or seven miles above Redstone Old Fort (now Brownsville);" d. 1799 (before July 5th); m. Sarah Scott; had issue: I. Jonathan; II. Benjamin, d. about 1804; m. Comfort (or Mary) Cullum (her father of Scotch-English descent; her mother, Dutch), b. about 1758; d. in Archer township, Harrison county, Ohio, 1856, having removed there with her children from Fayette county about 1810; had issue: 1. Rezin, b. in Luzerne township, Fayette county, Penn., Feb. 25, 1786; d. at Manhattan, Kan., Nov. 23, 1858; served in the War of 1812; m. (1st), Dec. 24, 1821, Anna Arrison, b. July, 1794; d. Feb. 16, 1823; m. (2d) at Cadiz, Dec. 9, 1824, Maria Eleanor Robertson, b. Aug. 25, 1802; d. Nov. 15, 1869; daughter of Robert and Beulah Stanley Robertson (the latter descended from George Maris, a Quaker preacher who emigrated to Pennsylvania in 1683; the former, son of John and Eleanor Dick Robertson); (had issue: i. Josephine-A., b. Sept. 30, 1825; m. J. H. Brouse; ii. Marion, b. April 25, 1827; m. Mary O. Borden; iii. William-Stanley, b. March 16, 1829; d. at Los Angeles, Cal., Sept. 7, 1870; m. Katharine Davidson; iv. Maria-Louisa, b. May 3, 1831; m. Dr. S. Whitehouse; v. Laura-Anna, b. June 19, 1833; m. D. W. Lane; vi. Benton, b. March 7, 1835; vii. Amanda-Tingley, b. March 18, 1837; viii. Robert-Robertson, b. in Morgan county, Ohio, Feb. 15, 1839; d. March 5, 1863; ix. John-Hanna, b. July 18, 1841; d. Nov. 7, 1862; x. James-D., b. May 5, 1844; d. Jan. 8, 1891; xi. Charles-Robertson, b. Aug. 15, 1846); 2. Jonathan; 3. James; 4. Comfort, m. Jonathan West, (see West Family); 5. Aneka (Axie), m. James Mehollin; 6. Sophia, m. 1815, Nathan Ross, of Richland; 7. Frances, m. 1819, Charles Conaway; 8. William, b. 1798; d. at Cadiz, 1874; m. May 17, 1831, Jane C. Hoyt, b. 1806; d. 1872; daughter of Jesse and Sarah Hoyt, natives of New York (descendants of Simon Hoyt, who emigrated from England to Massachusetts about 1638); (had issue: i. John, d. in Kansas, 1855, while serving as a Government Surveyor; ii. Mary-A., m. John W. Simmons; iii. Sarah, d. in Washington, Guernsey county, Ohio, 1869; m. James Knox, of Cadiz; iv. Jesse, settled in Washington, D. C.; v. William-H., m. (1st) 1866, Lydia Hunter, d. Feb. 28, 1886, daughter of Judge Joseph R. Hunter, of Cadiz; m. (2d) Caroline Thompson, daughter of James Thompson, of Cadiz township; vi. George, settled at Columbus, Ohio; vii. Jane, settled at Portland, Oregon). III. Levi. IV. William. V. Jemima, m. Rezin (?) Virgin. VI. Rachel, m. William (?) Hammond. VII. Hannah. VIII. Sarah.

GAVIN ARTHURS, see Family of Jonathan West.

THOMAS ATKINSON, d. in Amwell (now Franklin) township, Washington county, Penn., June-September, 1784, leaving children: Mercy, m. ——— Ellet; Eleanor, m. Charles (?) Cracraft; Elizabeth, m. ——— Ellet; Jean, m. ——— Sargent; William; George; Thomas; and (probably) John. George Atkinson, probably the son of Thomas Atkinson first named above, died in Brooke county, West Virginia, 1824; leaving children: Thomas, Mary, Margaret, Eleanor, Sarah, Martha, Ruth, and Elizabeth. Of these: George, b. May 1, 1778; d. Aug. 27, 1854; m. Sarah Snodgrass, b. Dec. 1, 1786; d. Dec. 23, 1854; had issue: 1. Mary, b. Oct. 7, 1812; m. David Hilbert; 2. Elizabeth, b. Dec. 12, 1813; m. 1833, James Roberts; 3. Elenora, b. March 5, 1816; m. James Ross; 4. Samuel, b. Nov. 30, 1817; d. Oct. 30, 1821; 5. Rebecca, b. Oct. 17, 1818; d. March 17, 1860; m. Andrew Finley Ross, son of Reynolds and Martha Finley Ross, of Westmoreland county, Penn.; 6. George-S., b. Nov. 14, 1819; m. Matilda Simeral, b. Dec. 25, 1818; daughter of James and Mary Ann Vincent Simeral (had issue: i. James-S., b. Aug. 8, 1845; d. March 11, 1895; ii. Frank-H., b. Oct. 12, 1847; m. Mary Bell Shauf; iii. Charles-D., b. Jan. 24, 1851; d. June 18, 1885; iv. Anna-Amanda, b. Nov. 5, 1853; d. Nov. 16, 1855; v. Emma-Caroline, b. Nov. 5, 1853; d. Sept. 24, 1855); 7. Sarah, b. March 1, 1823; m. Levi J. Kennard; 8. Francis, b. June 28, 1825; d. April 11, 1854; m. Eliza Bostwick; 9. Leann, b. Feb. 1, 1827; d. Oct. 1, 1840.

SAMUEL AULD, see Family of Archibald Stewart.

JOHN BAKER (son of John Baker), b. in Pennsylvania, 1777; came with his parents to Green township, Harrison county, Ohio, in 1802; d. Feb. 12, 1847; m. Margaret Buchanan; d. 1829; had issue: 1. Delilah, d. in infancy; 2. John; 3. George; 4. Elizabeth; 5. Rezin, b. November 10, 1810; d. May 26, 1876; m. February 13, 1835, Sarah Thompson, daughter of Thomas Thompson, of Cadiz township (had issue: i. John-L., b. November 20, 1836; ii. Thomas-J., b. January 9, 1838; iii. Weston, b. November 17, 1841; iv. ———, d. aged twenty-two months; v. Elijah-W., b. January 4, 1847); 6. Samuel; 7. William, d. in infancy.

DAVID BARCLAY, b. May 18, 1790, in county Derry, Ireland; emigrated to Baltimore, Md., in 1826, thence removed to Pittsburg, Penn., where he remained two years, and came to Nottingham township, Harrison county, Ohio, where he d. April 9, 1876; m. in Ireland, September 26, 1822, Elizabeth Kissick, b. in County Derry, March 17, 1801; d. January 9, 1871; had issue: 1. James, b. in Ireland; 2. William, b. in Ireland; 3. Barbara, m. ——— Love; 4. Eleanor, m. ——— McAdams; 5. David;

settled in Allegheny County, Penn.; 6. John; 7. Joseph, b. September 3, 1846, in Nottingham township, where he settled; m. April 30, 1872, Sarah Scott, b. December 28, 1846, in Athens township, Harrison county, daughter of Thomas and Sarah Hogg Scott; 7. Elizabeth, b. Feb. 18, 1841; m. Joseph M. Easter, b. 1841; d. 1871; son of James and Sarah Mehollin Easter; 8. Ann, m. ——— Lee; settled in Jefferson county, Ohio; 9. Jane, d. in childhood.

ARTHUR BARRETT, a native of West Virginia, b. 1743; removed to Harrison county, Ohio, in 1803, settling on Brushy Fork Creek, in Cadiz township, where he d. 1828; had issue: I. Nancy. II. Susan. III. Hannah. IV. Rachel. V. Sarah. VI. Thomas, d. Sept.-Dec., 1849; m. Alaneda ———; had issue: 1. Thomas; 2. Warden; 3. Arthur; 4. Esther, m. ——— Wilson; 5. Emma, m. ——— Spurrier; 6. Belinda, m. ——— Cadwalader; 7. Anna, m. ——— Miller; 8. Rachel, m. ——— Sears. VII. Arthur, b. in Virginia, 1780; came to Ohio with his father; settled in Cadiz township, where he d. 1845; m. (1st) Mary Huff, d. 1814; daughter of William Huff, a famous Indian scout and fighter, who was a pioneer in Ohio; m. (2d) Elizabeth Wolf, d. 1887; had issue by first wife: 1. Meredith; 2. Lewis; 3. William-H., b. June 10, 1812; m. May 25, 1837, Eliza V. Betz, of Jefferson county, Ohio, b. 1817, daughter of William and Elizabeth Betz (had issue: i. Meredith-Mc.; ii. Marion-B.; iii. Brice-W., a Methodist Episcopal minister, d. 1866, in Mount Union, Ohio; iv. Mary-E., m. Henry Haverfield; v. Margaret-E., m. William Birney; vi. Emma-E., m. Samuel Crawford; vii. William-F.; settled at Martin's Ferry, Ohio; viii. Flora-M.); 4. Mary; had issue by second wife: 5. Louisa; 6. Aeneas; 7. John; 8. David. VIII. David. IX. Aeneas. X. Isaac, d. before Aug. 21, 1858; m. Hannah ———; had issue: 1. Erasmus, m. ——— Keesey; 2. Arthur; 3. Hiram; 4. Mary-Ann, m. ——— White; 5. Tabitha, m. ——— Ford.

CONRAD BARRICKLOW, b. in New Jersey, where his emigrant ancestor, a native of Holland, had settled before 1671, emigrating with a brother, who located on Long Island; d. in Franklin township, Fayette county, Penn., 1802, where he had settled about 1790; served in the Revolutionary War; m. Sarah Farrington; had issue: I. Henry, b. 1771; d. April 27, 1851; m. about 1802, Meriba Oglevee, b. 1773; d. May 15, 1848; removed to Harrison county about 1809; had issue, among others: 1. John, b. in Fayette county, Penn., Oct. 18, 1803; d. July 21, 1875; m. (1st) 1836, Rachel Watson, b. 1819; d. 1839; daughter of Robert S. and Rachel Wilson Watson; m. (2d), 1853, Ann Johnston, d. 1875; daughter of Nicholas Johnston (had issue by first wife: i. Henry, b. March 2, 1837; d. Feb. 28, 1873; served in the Civil War; m. 1869, Rebecca J. McFadden, daughter of Samuel McFadden); ii. Robert-Watson, b. March 6, 1839; m. Aug. 20, 1867, Isabella Alice Mocre, daughter of John Moore, of Cadiz); 2. Sarah; 3. Joseph, b. in Fayette county, Penn.; d. April 13, 1875; m. 1846, Phœbe Bartow, b. May 21, 1813 (had issue: i. Henry-S., b. Dec. 10, 1847; m. Oct. 11, 1883, Elizabeth B. Haverfield, d. Sept. 13, 1884, daughter of James and Elizabeth Haverfield; ii. Maribah-Anne, b. April 22, 1849; iii. Joseph-E., b. July 1, 1855; m. Oct. 10, 1883, Mary L. Walker, daughter of Isaac and Angeline Walker); 4. Anna; 5. Henry; 6. Julia; 7. Conrad; 8. Farrington, b. in Athens township, June 6, 1817. II. Daniel. III. John. IV. Farrington. V. Anne ("Nancy"), b. 1778; d. Oct. 16, 1845; m. 1790, Joseph Oglevee, a native of Cecil county, Maryland, who had settled in Franklin township, Fayette county, Penn., about 1788-89; b. 1760; d. Sept. 14, 1835; had issue: 1. Jesse, b. 1804; d. Jan. 26, 1876; m. 1826, Elizabeth Galley, b. 1807; d. 1858; daughter of Philip Galley (had issue, eight children, of whom: i. Joseph, b. June 2, 1827; m. 1850, Rebecca Stoner; ii. John; iii. Philip); 2. John; 3. Farrington.

William Hoese von Barkeloo and his brother, Harman Jansen von Barkeloo, with his wife and two children, landed in New York, where Harman died before 1671. William m. Elizabeth Jane Cloessen in 1666, and d. in 1683. His son, Direk, m. Jamelia (or Janetjie) Van Arsdale, Sept. 17, 1709, and settled at Freehold, Monmouth county, N. J. Conrad, b. Dec. 4, 1680; d. 1714; settled at Raritan, and m. a daughter of Jacob Loes, of Monmouth county. Their son, Conrad, removed to Bucks county, and was the ancestor of the Barkalows there. The family came from Borkelo, in Zutphen, Province of Guilderland, Holland. The name is variously spelled in America, Barkalow, Barcalow, Baricklo, Barricklow, Borcelo, etc.

FREDERICK BARRICKLOW, son of Henry, b. Dec. 3, 1794; d. May 1, 1858; m., 1826, Nancy Dugan, b. 1800; d. Oct. 17, 1881; daughter of John and Catherine McClelland Dugan, of Fayette county, Penn.; removed to Harrison county in 1832; had issue: 1. John-D., b. Nov. 6, 1828; m. Mary Dunlap, daughter of Adam and Martha Thompson Dunlap; served in the Civil War; 2. Henry, b. March 10, 1829; m., October, 1878, Mary Henderson, of Jefferson county, Ohio; 3. Alexander; 4. Margaret-A.; 5. George-W., b. Aug. 7, 1837; m. 1869, Ruth Emily Gregg, daughter of Presley and Sarah Gregg, of Indiana.

JAMES BEALL, b. 1778; d. Dec. 29, 1834; removed from Washington (?) county, Penn., to Wheeling township, Belmont county, Ohio; m. Jane Baird, b. 1783; d. Nov. 11, 1883; had issue: 1. John, m. (1st) Mary A. Hield, b. 1817; d. March 2, 1842; m. (2d) Agnes T. Vincent, daughter of Thomas C. and Jane McCurdy Vincent, of Green township (had issue by first wife: i. Amanda-M., m. James Paul; ii. William-R., m. Laura Clark; had issue by second wife: iii. Jane-C., m. Wesley B. Hearn; iv. Mary-Q., m. Jesse W. Grimes; v. Thomas; vi. Ida-F.; vii. Laura-A.; viii. Emma-A., m. Henry H. McFadden; ix. Anna, m. R. N. Dodds, and settled at Springfield, Ill.; x. John-A., a physician, m. Ocena Billinghurst; settled at Detroit, Mich.); 2. Isabel; 3. James, m. Sarah Jamison; 4. Eleanor, m. John McDowell; 5. William, b. 1822; d. Oct. 4, 1856; m. Mary Culbertson, b. 1823; d. May 15, 1889; 6. Jane, m. George McKibbon; 7. Mary-A., b. Dec. 19, 1807; d. May 30, 1834; m. George McKibbon; 8. Josiah, m. Martha Anderson.

JAMES P. BEALL, a native of Pennsylvania, removed before 1826 to Nottingham township, Harrison county, Ohio, where he resided until 1857; thence settled in Crawford county, Ohio, where he d. February 24, 1869; m. (1st) ———; m. (2d) Minerva Huff, d. January 14, 1875. daughter of William Huff (whose sons William, Reuben, Jackson, and Johnson Huff were Indian scouts in eastern Ohio, Jackson being killed by the Indians); had issue by first wife: 1. Jane, settled in Crawford county; 2. Zenas; had issue by second wife: 3. Elizabeth; 4. Cassandra; 5. Colmore-C., b. June 5, 1826, in Nottingham township; d. March 15, 1880; m. January 24, 1850, Hannah Rogers, b. in Nottingham township, August 19, 1830, daughter of Barrett and Nancy Carson Rogers, natives of Ohio; 6. James-P.; 7. Cyrus; 8. John (Cyrus and John served in the Civil War, dying in the service); 9. Rebecca; 10. Susan; 11. Minerva; 12. Zephaniah.

SAMPSON BEATTY, a native of Ireland, b. 1786; d. November 27, 1849, in Archer township, Harrison county, where he had settled in 1826; m. April 20, 1826, Rachel Johnson, d. June 25, 1850, daughter of Samuel Johnson, a resident of Pennsylvania; had issue, among others: 1. Arthur, b. January 25, 1827, in Archer township; m. March 27, 1851, Susan McDivitt, daughter of Samuel McDivitt, of Stock township, Harrison county; 2. John served in the Civil War; d. 1862, in Knoxville, Tenn.; 3. Jeremiah, served in the Civil War.

STEWART BEEBE, whose paternal ancestor came from England to Massachusetts about 1623, d. at Wilbraham, Hampden county, Mass., 1825; m. Huldah ———; d. 1803; had issue, among others:

I. Walter-Butler, b. at Wilbraham, Mass., 1785-86; d. at Cadiz, Jan. 24, 1836; m. Nancy Maholm, b. 1779-80; d. Oct. 13, 1856; daughter of Samuel and Jane Maholm, of Cadiz; had issue: 1. Walter-Butler, m. 1841, Maria Bayless Welch, b. 1812; d. Aug. 10, 1891; daughter of Rezin and Eliza Bayless Welch, of Cadiz (had issue: i. Eliza-Bayless, m. E. Z. Hays; ii. Nancy-Jeanette, m. John A. Norris, and settled at Columbus; iii. Stuart; settled at Columbus); 2. Stewart, removed to Iowa; 3. James, removed to Coshocton, Ohio (had issue, among others: i. James; ii. Stacy).

II. Rhoda, b. in Hampden county, Mass., June 19, 1792; d. at Cadiz, March, 1876; m. 1819, William Shotwell, son of Hugh and Rosetta Arrison Shotwell (see Shotwell Family).

EDWARD BETHEL, a native of Virginia, removed in 1813 from Loudoun county, that State, to Flushing township, Belmont county, Ohio; had issue:

I. Simpson, a native of Loudoun county, Va.; removed to Athens township, Harrison county, Ohio, about 1810, where he died; m. in Virginia, Nancy Holloway; d. in Harrison county; had issue: 1. John, b. June 29, 1806, in Loudoun county, Va.; removed with his parents to Athens township, Harrison county, where he d. April 4, 1887; m. in Harrison county, Elizabeth Oglevee, a native of that county, b. 1804; d. December 5, 1881; daughter of John and Agnes Passmore Oglevee (had issue: i. Simpson, b. Dec. 29, 1828, in Athens township; m. September 23, 1858, Frances Clemens, d. October 26, 1884, daughter of James Clemens, a resident of Athens township; ii. Agnes, m. John Price; iii. John-H.; iv. Sarah-Jane, m. Monroe Dunn; v. Mary-E., m. Samuel Dunlap; vi. Caroline, m. Samuel Compher; vii. Hiram; viii. Isaac-H., b. in Athens township; ix. Elizabeth, m. W. J. Dunlap); 2. Mary; 3. James; 4. Caroline; 5. Hiram. II. James, b. in Virginia about 1795; m. Mary Brock; had issue: 1. Edward; 2. Benjamin; 3. Alfred, m. Margaret McCall (had issue: i. John-A.); ii. James-O., b. December 19, 1848; removed to Moorefield township, Harrison county, 1869; m. June 30, 1870, Nancy M. Slater, b. October 1, 1846, daughter of James Wells and Margaret Dunlap Slater; iii. Jesse-B.; iv. Franklin; v. Mary; vi. Jane; vii. ———, d. in infancy; viii. ———, d. in infancy); 4. Abner; 5. Marion; 6. James-S., settled in Belmont county; 7. Sarah; 8. Lucinda, settled in Kansas; 9. Elizabeth-A.; 10. Mary, b. April 25, 1826; m. August 18, 1844, Joseph Lafferty, b. October 26, 1819, in Virginia; d. March 29, 1886, in Moorefield township, son of Samuel and Margaret Figley Lafferty (had issue: i. ———, d. in infancy; ii. ———, d. in infancy; iii. James; iv. Elizabeth; v. Mary-E.; vi. Sarah-E.; vii. Laura-L.; viii. George-F.); 11. Mary; 12. Eliza-J.; 13. Quintery. III. Anne-Katherine. IV. William V. Henry, had issue, among others: 1. Broudus, b. in Loudoun county, Va.; removed from Belmont county to Harrison county; d. March 17, 1870; m. June 14, 1827, Sarah Smith, d. November 28, 1876, daughter of William Smith (had issue: i. James; ii. Anna; iii. Mary-E.; iv. Henry-Matthess; settled in Moorefield township; v. William-S., b. September 3, 1834; settled in Freeport township, Harrison county, where he m. October 19, 1858, Phebe Ann Price, d. December 11, 1890, daughter of Reynolds K. and Mary Michnor Price, residents of Harrison county; vi. Louis-B.; vii. Sarah-E., m. W. C. Smith; viii. Barnett; ix. David-R., settled in Freeport; x. Ruth-Ann; xi. Celinda, m. ——— Niblock). VI. Thompson. VII. John-Thornton, b. in Virginia, February 11, 1802; removed about 1834 from Belmont county to Harrison county, and settled four miles from Freeport, in Freeport township, Harrison county, where he d. March 1, 1877; m. September 14, 1824, Mary Jackson Billingsby, a native of Virginia; d. August 15, 1870; had issue: 1. Lorinda; 2. Vitura; 3. Celestine; 4. Melinda; 5. Ruth; 6. George-W., b. February 21, 1833, in Belmont county; removed to Harrison county with his parents; settled in Freeport, Harrison county. VIII. Elizabeth.

JOHN, HUGH, ROBERT, and WILLIAM BINGHAM (Hugh and Robert, at least, brothers, and thought to be the sons of Richard Bingham, of Scottish descent), emigrated to America between 1736 and 1760, and before 1774 settled in the Manor of Maske, now Cumberland, Liberty, and Hamiltonban townships in Adams (formerly York) county, Penn.; John Bingham died there Dec. 18, 1739, aged twenty-six years; William Bingham's name appears on a petition from the settlers in Cumberland township in 1755; the names of Hugh and Robert Bingham appear on the tax-list of Hamiltonban township for 1767 (the earliest one now extant), together with the names of Samuel and Thomas Bingham, in the same year. It is possible that John or William Bingham, first named above, may have been the father of Samuel, Thomas, Hugh, and Robert, the last three of whom, at least, were brothers; of these:

A. Samuel, may have been a brother to Hugh, Robert, and Thomas above; or, possibly, the son of Hugh above (see IV. below).

B. Thomas, see below.

C. Robert, probably the same who died in Hamiltonban township, November-December, 1798, and who had issue: 1. Samuel; 2. Abraham; 3. Eve; the executors mentioned in his will were William Bingham, James Agnew, and

Barnabas McSherry; the name of Catharine Bingham appears as witness to will of Barnabas McSherry in 1823.

D. Hugh, d. in Hamiltonban township, September-October, 1777; m. Martha Armor, daughter of Thomas (?) and —— McKinley Armor, and probably sister or aunt to Thomas Armor, an active Revolutionary patriot, who died in Yorktown, Penn., February-March, 1785 (he mentions in his will "cousins" Robert and Thomas Bingham); had issue:

I. Samuel; settled in Metal township, Franklin county, Penn., where he d. September, 1801; m. Mary ——; had issue: 1. Elizabeth; 2. Jean; 3. Mary; 4. Catharine, m. —— Anderson; 5. John, possibly the same who d. in Green township, Franklin county, Penn., August, 1818 (leaving a wife, Hannah, and children: i. Elizabeth; ii. Eleanor, m. —— Furrey; iii. David; iv. John; v. James; vi. Samuel); 6. Hugh, m. his cousin, Jean Bingham, daughter of Hugh (IV. below); 7. Samuel; 8. Thomas.

II. William, b. 1748; d. Feb. 2, 1816; m. (probably) Ann ——, b. 1760; d. April 9, 1838; had issue: 1. James; 2. Thomas; 3. Hugh; 4. Charles-W., served as an officer in the War of 1812; m. Margaret Agnew, of Emmitsburg, Md. (had issue: i. Sophia; ii. William; iii. Agnew; iv. Albert; v. Martha; vi. Margaret, m. 1866, Samuel McFarland, of Smith township, Washington county, b. June 11, 1812; d. June 29, 1829; vii. James, a physician, settled at Clinton, Allegheny county; viii. Emma, m. Dr. W. V. Riddle; ix. Mary; x. Charles-Carroll); 5. John; 6. Armor; 7. Anna-Eliza; 8. William.

III. Robert, possibly the Robert who d. in 1798, whose will is given in connection with his uncle, Robert (C, above); but more probably the Robert Bingham who died in Hopewell township, Washington county, June, 1804; m. Mary ——; had issue: 1. Hugh; 2. James; 3. Robert; 4. John; 5. Joseph; 6. Elizabeth; 7. Jane; 8. Mary; 9. Phebe.

IV. Hugh, d. in Hamiltonban township, May 11-15, 1793; had issue: 1. John-Armor, d. at Natchez, Miss., 1824; 2. Jean, d. at Freeport, Penn., 1857; m. her cousin, Hugh, son of Samuel (I. above); 3. Hugh, d. at New Wilmington, Lawrence county, Penn., 1865; m. (1st) Oct. 13, 1807, Esther Bailey, daughter of Captain William and Mary Ann Duncan Bailey, of York, Penn.; m. (2d) Ellen Junkin Galloway; settled in Mercer, Penn., soon after 1800 (had issue by first wife: i. John-Armor, b. at Mercer, Penn., Jan. 21, 1815; settled in Ohio about 1841, and later, at Cadiz; served as a representative in Congress from 1854 to 1873, with the exception of one term; served as United States Minister to Japan from May, 1873, to 1885; d. at Cadiz, March 19, 1900; m. 1844, at Cadiz, his cousin, Amanda Bingham, daughter of Judge Thomas and Lucinda Stuart Bingham [had issue: Lucinda-Stuart, m. 1869, Rev. Samuel Robinson Frazier; Emma; Marie-Scott, m. at Tokio, Japan, 1876, James Robert Wasson]; ii. Marian; iii. William, a Baptist minister; iv. Martha, m. —— Patterson, and settled at Pittsburgh; v. Hugh-Mason; had issue by second wife: vi. Thomas, settled in California; vii. Ellen-Mary, settled at Canton, Ohio).

William Bailey, father of Esther Bailey Bingham, served, in 1775, as second lieutenant of the Independent Light Infantry Company of the first battalion of York county (Penn.) Militia, formed in Yorktown, December, 1775; the company was commanded in 1776 by William Bailey as captain, and was captured by the British at the fall of Fort Washington; settled in Yorktown after the Revolution; m. Mary Ann Duncan, probably daughter of —— and Margaret Mason Duncan, the latter a native of Scotland, who d. Nov. 16, 1802, leaving funds with which to build the second United Presbyterian Church of Philadelphia;

4. Thomas, d. at Cadiz, April, 1853; m. Lucinda Stuart, d. at Cadiz, Nov. 6, 1844; daughter of James and Mary Ann McIlvaine (or McElwain) Stuart, of Newville, Cumberland county, Penn. (had issue: i. Martha-Armor, m. [1st] 1832, Henry Olmstead; m. [2d] Van Rensselaer Lee; settled at Cincinnati; ii. Lucinda, m. Joseph P. Wood; settled at Omaha, Neb.; iii. Mary-Jane, m. 1833, Josiah Scott; iv. Thomas-M., m. 1844, Rachel Sheets; v. John-Stuart, d. at Shippensburg, Penn., 1891; vi. Amanda, d. 1891; m. 1844, John Armor Bingham, her cousin, son of Hugh and Esther Bailey Bingham; vii. Emma-E., m. 1870, Judge John Stoneman Pearce, of Cadiz; viii. Isabella; ix. Belinda).

James Stuart (or Stewart), father of Lucinda Stuart Bingham, m. near Newville, Penn., Mary Ann McIlvaine (or McElwain); he was probably son of Alexander or Archibald Stewart, of Cumberland county; had issue: 1. Lucinda, m. Thomas Bingham, as above; 2. Mary, m. Samuel Patterson, of Newville, and settled at Cincinnati. V. Elizabeth.
VI. Mary, m. ——— McKinley; had issue: 1. Mary; 2. John; 3. Hugh.

Thomas Bingham, a soldier of the Revolution, lived in Mercer county, Penn., as late as 1816; probably brother or son to Hugh, who d. 1777, although not mentioned in his will; but described in will of Thomas Armor, of Yorktown, who died 1785, as his "cousin," and brother to Robert.

Patrick Bingham, d. in Mount Joy township, Adams county, 1796, leaving a wife, Mary, and children: 1. Samuel; 2. Hugh; 3. Bryan; 4. Eleanor; 5. Agnes.

Agnes Bingham, d. in Manor of Maske, Adams county, Dec. 18, 1749, aged fourteen years.

Margaret Bingham is mentioned by her father, Alexander McVear, of Hamiltonban township, Adams county, in his will, dated April 13, 1799.

HUGH BIRNEY, a native of Ireland, son of John Birney, emigrated to America and settled in Chester county, Penn., in 1815; removed in 1819 to Green township, Harrison county, Ohio, where he d. September, 1862; m. 1800, ——— Brown, a native of Ireland; had issue: 1. William, settled in Rumley township; 2. Wesley; 3. Rebecca; 4. Martha, m. Samuel Hitchcock; settled in Indiana; 5. Jane, m. George Leese; settled in Coshocton, Ohio; 6. James, settled in Nebraska; 7. Elizabeth, m. Jacob Hitchcock; settled in Iowa; 8. Samuel, settled in Colorado; 9. Asbury, b. March 15, 1815; m. April 23, 1840, Ellen McCollough, b. May 29, 1821, daughter of Hugh and Isabella Cunningham McCollough, natives of Ireland, who settled in Jefferson county, Ohio, in 1810 (had issue: i. Isabella, d. May 22, 1863; ii. Oliver, settled in German township, Labette county, Kan.; iv. Hugh-W., b. March 17, 1849; m. (1st) June 15, 1883, Estella Montgomery, d. 1884; m. (2d) February 9, 1886, Hadassah Jackman, a native of Washington county, Penn., daughter of Andrew and Elizabeth Gaddis Jackman, natives of Ireland; v. Elizabeth, m. Joseph McCollough; settled in Archer township; vi. Rebecca-J., m. Henry K. Ford; settled in Salem township, Jefferson county).

ISRAEL BIRNEY, a native of German township, Harrison county, Ohio, removed to Nottingham township, where he d. May 11, 1862; m. in Franklin township, Martha Hedges, d. August 30, 1870, daughter of Samuel Hedges, of Cadiz township; had issue: 1. Samuel-H., b. October 28, 1838; m. March 3, 1863, Cynthia Johnson, daughter of Nathan Johnson, of Nottingham township; 2. Prudence, m. Slemmons Welsh; 3. William; 4. Elizabeth; 5. Israel.

JOHN BIRNEY, b. in Green township, Harrison county, Ohio; d. in Washington township, September 9, 1885; m. (1st) in Green township, Hannah McKee, d. 1872, daughter of Robert McKee; m. (2d) Sarah Eaton; had issue by first wife: 1. Rachel, m. Henry Pittis; 2. Nelson; 3. Robert-M.; 4. James-N., b. in Washington township, August 27, 1847; m. 1869, Anna R. McFadden, daughter of Robert McFadden, of Harrison county; 5. Rebecca-J., m. Matthew Simpson; 6. John-T.

ROBERT BIRNEY, b. in Ireland, about 1787; emigrated to America and about 1801 settled in Chester county, Penn.; removed with his family in 1807 to German township, Harrison county, Ohio, where he d. 1874; m. in Chester county, Penn., Margaret Northhammer, b. 1795, d. 1871; had issue: 1. Mary; 2. Zilla; 3. Wesley; 4. John; 5. Asbury; 6. Lot, settled in Washington county, Iowa; 7. Elizabeth, b. March 3, 1822; m. December 26, 1843, Robert W. Endsley, b. 1813, son of James and Elizabeth Walker Endsley; settled in Jewett, in Rumley township, Harrison county (had issue: i. Mary-M., m. William C. Adams; settled in Archer township; ii. Melissa; iii. Lucinda-J., m. Eli Caven; iv. Elizabeth-A., m. R. H. Freshwater, a minister, of Steubenville, Ohio; v. Rebecca-Frances, m. Charles A. Naylor, a minister); 8. Rebecca, settled in Washington county, Iowa; 9. J.-S., b. May 23, 1824; m. March 10, 1847, Susan Mummey, daughter of Charles and Rebecca Hedges Mummey, of Cadiz township (had issue: i. Margaret; ii. Mary, m. John B. Busby; iii. William-Asbury, settled in Cadiz; iv. Robert-M.; v. Charles-R., a minister, settled in New Philadelphia, Ohio; vi. Maria-B., m. Goliath Tedrow).

James Endsley, father of James Endsley, who married Elizabeth Birney, was a son of James Endsley, a native of Lancaster county, Penn., where he died; the son came with his widowed mother to Archer township before 1817, where he d. 1869; m. in Pennsylvania about 1815, Elizabeth Walker, d. 1865, a native of Columbiana county, Ohio; they were the parents of four children, three sons and one daughter, of whom: 1. Robert-W., b. 1813, m. Elizabeth Birney; 2. James, b. Sept. 7, 1817.

JANET BLAIR, see Family of Thomas Phillips.

JOHN BLAIR, a native of Ireland, emigrated to America, and d. about 1840, in Cadiz township, Harrison county, Ohio, where he had settled before 1804; had issue: I. John. II. Daniel. III. James. IV. Charity. V. William, b. March 14, 1804; d. January 29, 1867; m. Sarah Day, b. April 26, 1808; daughter of George and Margaret Moore Day, natives of eastern Pennsylvania, who were early settlers in Cadiz township; had issue: 1. George; 2. John-W., b. May 15, 1831, in Cadiz township; settled in Stock township; m. January 19, 1853, Melissa A. Carson, b. June 19, 1831, daughter of Elijah and Catherine Knight Carson; 3. Albert; 4. Mary.

JAMES BLACK, a native of Ireland, b. 1756; emigrated to America and first settled in Pennsylvania; removed to Green township, Harrison county, Ohio, about 1806, where he d. 1846; served in the Revolutionary War; m. about 1783, Jane Stewart, b. 1753; d. Aug. 22, 1835; had issue: 1. James, b. in Adams county, Penn., 1785; m. 1812, Isabella Hervey, b. 1785; d. Dec. 30, 1865; daughter of Margaret Hervey, an early settler in Harrison county, coming there after death of her husband (had issue: i. John-Hervey, b. in Green township, 1813; d. March 26, 1885; m. Feb. 22, 1838, Mary K. Work, daughter of Alexander Work, a resident of Green township; ii. James-S., b. June 20, 1816; iii. H.-Stewart, b. Nov. 22, 1819; d. Jan. 22, 1890; m. Oct. 31, 1843, Jane Thompson, daughter of Samuel Thompson, of Green township; iv. Margaret-J., b. March 21, 1845; m. William Dunlap); 2. Mary; 3. Elizabeth; 4. Margaret; 5. Jane.

WILLIAM BOGGS, b. in the North of Ireland, 1716; removed to America about 1728, and afterward settled in Chester county, Penn., where he died; m. Jane Stein, a native of Ireland; had issue: James, b. July 21, 1735; John, b. February 19, 1737; Margaret, b. February 23, 1739; Robert, b. April 9, 1741; William, b. March 14, 1743; Jane, b. April 10, 1745; Elizabeth, b. July 31, 1747; Rebecca, b. January 31, 1749; Agnes, b. February 17, 1752; Mary, b. May 24, 1753; Joseph, b. October 1, 1754; Moses, b. May 6, 1757.

James Boggs (b.1735) settled in Newcastle county, Del.; served in the Revolutionary War; removed about 1790 to Washington county, Penn., settling near the present site of Cross Creek Village; m. (1st) in Newcastle county, Del., Hannah Rice; m. (2d) Sarah Brown; had issue by first wife: 1. William; 2. Rice, 3. Jane; had issue by second wife: 4. James, b. April 27, 1778; 5. Margaret; 6. Robert (twin brother to Margaret), b. November 17, 1779; 7. John, b. June 28, 1782; 8. Rebecca; 9. Mary (twin sister to Rebecca), b. February 15, 1784; 10. Sarah, b. April 21, 1786.

John Boggs (b. 1782), son of James, in 1839 removed from Washington county, Penn., to Harrison county, Ohio, where he d. December 21, 1848; m. September 17, 1812, Sarah Marshall, d. January 6, 1849; had issue: 1. Thomas-Marshall, b. June 26, 1813, in Washington county, Penn.; a Presbyterian minister; removed to Marietta, Lancaster county, Penn., thence to Mount Joy, in the same county, where he d. 1850; m. A. J. Cunningham, of Chester county, Penn.; d. January 6, 1849 (had issue: i. Elizabeth, m. Rev. Edgar, President of the Wilson College for women, in Chambersburg, Penn.; ii. John-C.; iii. William-M., settled in Chicago); 2. James-Brown, b. January 20, 1815; d. in infancy; 3. William, b. November 5, 1816; d. 1836; 4. John-M., b. October 20, 1818; a Presbyterian minister; served Paxtang and Derry congregations, near Harrisburg, Penn., thence removed to Millersburg, Ohio, and from there to Independence, Iowa, where he d. September 1, 1872; 5. Samuel-M., b. December 6, 1820, removed to Short Creek township, Harrison county, where he remained until 1884, when he settled in Athens; m. September 1, 1854, Margaret Parks; 6. Sarah-Ann, b. February 3, 1823; m. William H. Watson; settled in Belmont county (had issue: seven children); 7. Robert-W., b. August 1, 1825; removed to Short Creek township, where he remained until 1884, then settled in Athens; 8. James, b. July 23, 1828; d. February 13, 1840.

WILLIAM BOGGS, see Family of James Simeral.

SAMUEL BORLAND, a native of Ireland, emigrated to America and before 1785 settled near the present Manor Station, in Westmoreland county, Penn., where he m. Lydia Cary; both died in Pennsylvania; had issue:
I. Samuel, b. in Westmoreland county, 1785; d. 1862, in North township, Harrison county; m. (1st) Mary Little; m. (2d) Elizabeth Hevlin, daughter of Samuel and Elizabeth Hevlin; had issue, by first wife: 1. William, settled in Tuscarawas county, Ohio; 2. Washington, settled in Carroll county, Ohio; 3. Lydia, m. James Waddington, of Nebraska; had issue by second wife: 4. Mary, m. James Mackey; her family settled in Dennison, Ohio; 5. David, b. January 27, 1831, in North township; m. December 24, 1857, Ann Havnar, b. 1833; d. October 26, 1890; daughter of Dominick and Elizabeth Havnar, both of whom died in Monroe township.

JOHN BOYD, b. in Ireland; d. 1832; m. (2d) ——— McMillan; emigrated to America about 1812 and settled in Freeport township, Harrison county, Ohio; had issue: 1. Samuel; 2. William, b. 1798; d. April 21, 1867; m. about 1864, Anne White, b. in Ireland, 1802; d. at Freeport, Jan. 7, 1879 (had issue: i. John, m. Sarah Fulton; ii. Hannah, m. William Williams; iii. George, b. 1827; m. Eliza Vail Markee, daughter of William and Hannah Norris Vail; iv. Sarah, d. young; v. Eliza, m. William Fulton; vi. Mary, m. James Fulton; vii. Margaret, m. ——— Likes; viii. Belinda, m. James Carr; ix. William, m. Mary Phillips; x. Martha, m. R. Niblick; xi. Melancthon, d. young).

HENRY BOYLES, b. 1770; d. 1834; removed from New Jersey to Virginia, where he m. (1st) Rachel Barkhurst; m. (2d) in Chester county, Penn., Jane Filson, d. 1854; daughter of Robert Filson; removed to Bedford county, Penn., and thence, in 1821, to Steubenville, Ohio; had issue by first wife, three children; had issue by second wife: 4. John; 5. Samuel; 6. Elisha; 7. Margaret; 8. Henry, b. in Lancaster county, Penn., Jan. 5, 1814; d. July 8, 1892; removed to Harrison county, 1843; m. at Cadiz, Martha Grimes, b. May 12, 1826; d. April 4, 1874; daughter of William and Rebecca Grimes (who had settled in Harrison county about 1802), and both died at Cadiz, 1840; 8. Joseph-Filson, d. at Rockport, Ind., 1889.

GETTYS BRADEN, see Family of Jacob Stahl.

ROBERT BRADEN, of Irish descent, b. 1773, in Pennsylvania, of which State his paternal grandfather was a native, removed in 1800 to Short Creek township, Harrison county, Ohio, where he d. 1837; m. (1st) in Pennsylvania, ——— Finney, daughter of James Finney, who settled in Short Creek township 1800; m. (2d) 1815, Catherine Hay, b. about 1775; d. 1845; had issue by first wife: 1. ———; 2. ———; had issue by second wife: 3. John, d. aged twenty-four years; 4. David-B., b. August 21, 1818, in Short Creek township; m. (1st) November 5, 1851, Susannah M. Groves, b. 1813; d. October 19, 1885, daughter of Francis and Jeanette Groves, of Cadiz township; m. (2d) in Canonsburg, Penn., September 2, 1886, Melissa Donnell, a native of that place; d. May 14, 1889; 4. Anna, m. Walker Patton; 5. Robert, settled in Washington, Iowa; 6. William, settled in Iowa; 7. Elizabeth, d. aged eight years; 8. Mary-Jane, m. Casper Devilbiss, and settled in Iowa.

JAMES BRADFORD, of Scottish descent, b. in Washington county, Penn., 1790, a son of James Bradford, a native of Lancaster county, Penn.; removed about 1800 to Cadiz, Harrison county, Ohio, where he d. 1830; m. Mary Morrison, who after her first husband's death returned to Washington county, Penn., where she m. (2d) David Watson, of Pennsylvania; she d. aged eighty-one years; daughter of James Morrison, of Washington county, Penn.; had issue (surname Bradford): 1.

James-M., b. February 28, 1821, in Cadiz; settled in Scio, about 1874; m. 1844, Julia Ann Lewis, of Jefferson county, Ohio, daughter of William and Mary Lewis (had issue: i. Ann-Eliza, m. (1st) Dr. Kennedy; m. (2d) Marian Coates; settled in Pratt county, Kan.); 2. David, settled in Washington county, Penn.; 3. Eliza, settled at Scio.

ABRAHAM BRANSON, a native of Virginia, of English descent, removed from near the vicinity of Winchester to central Ohio, about 1800; had issue: I. Reese, located in St. Clairsville, Belmont county, Ohio, where he died; had issue: 1. Abraham-Dow, b. June 13, 1806, in Belmont county, Ohio; located, 1831, at Kinsey's Mills, Belmont county, on the National Pike; settled near Georgetown, in Short Creek township, Harrison county, Ohio, about 1833, where he d. January 16, 1867; m. June 2, 1831, in Jefferson county, Ohio, Ann W. Wilson, b. 1806, near Mount Pleasant, Ohio; d. February 3, 1888, daughter of Jonathan and Hannah Wilson, pioneers of Jefferson county (had issue: i. Lindley-M., b. September 26, 1832, at Kinsey's Mills, Belmont county, Ohio; m. May 7, 1874, Anna M. Fox, daughter of Charles J. and Esther Cooper Fox, of Harrison county; ii. Elizabeth-S., m. Isaac Thomas; iii. Abraham-Wilson, b. December 9, 1846, in Short Creek township; m. May 25, 1875, Lucy Thomas, daughter of Isaac and Annie Ladd Thomas; iv. Rachel, settled in Iowa; v. William, settled in Kansas; vi. Jonathan, d. in infancy; vii. John-C., d. young); 2. William; 3. Maria; 4. Eliza.

Isaac Thomas, father of Annie L. Branson, was b. June 1, 1813; settled in Short Creek township; afterward removed to Mount Pleasant, Jefferson county, Ohio; m. January 1, 1834, Mary Ladd. b. near Richmond, Va., August 14, 1812; d. 1872; daughter of Robert and Mary Ladd.

ANTHONY BRICKER, of German ancestry, removed from Pennsylvania to Green township, Harrison county, about 1804, where he d. 1813; m. Margaret ———; had issue: 1. Henry; 2. George; 3. John, b. May 9, 1793; d. March, 1861; m. Anna Busby, b. 1812 (had issue: i. David; ii. John, m. ——— Holmes; iii. Elizabeth, m. Dr. William Beadle); 4. David; 5. Elizabeth, m. (1st) ——— Hilbert; m. (2d) ——— Warfel.

JESSE BRINDLEY, a native of Germany, settled in Maryland about 1775, where he died; m. (1st) in Germany, ———; m. (2d) Julia Kent; had issue, among others:
I. Benjamin, b. in Maryland; removed from Harford county, that State, to Archer township, Harrison county, Ohio, in 1825; afterward settled in Green township, where he died; m. in Maryland, Ellen Cooper, b. about 1759; d. 1824; had issue, ten children, of whom: 1. Priscilla, m. Caleb Low; settled in Steubenville, Ohio; 2. John, b. in Harford county, Md., March 16, 1806, came to Harrison county with his parents; settled in Cadiz, about 1873; m. 1830, Ann Brown, b. 1809; d. October 6, 1889; daughter of Hugh and Jane Brown, residents of Archer township (had issue: i. Hugh, settled in Kansas; ii. Benjamin; iii. Ellen, m. James Crawford; iv. Frank; v. Albert; vi. David; vii. Nathaniel; viii. Wesley; ix. Sarah, m. J. Rea Finney; x. John; xi. ———, d. in infancy; xii. ———, d. in infancy; xiii. Thomas, b. March 16, 1846; m. November 11, 1869, Hester A. Birney, daughter of Hamilton Birney, a resident of Archer township).

GEORGE BROKAW, of Huguenot descent, emigrated to America before 1775, with his brother, John, both of whom served in the Revolutionary War; located in Pennsylvania; removed about 1802 to Green township, Harrison county, Ohio, and afterwards settled in Athens township; m. about 1777 (?), Jane Custard (or Custer); had issue: 1. Abraham, b. April 8, 1778; 2. Benjamin, b. Sept. 28, 1779; 3. Sarah, b. Feb. 20, 1782; 4. George, b. March 27, 1784; 5. William, b. Feb. 10, 1786; 6. Judah, b. March 19, 1788; 7. Jane, b. July 15, 1790; 8. John, b. Sept. 23, 1793; settled in Athens township, where he d. March 25, 1876; m. July 10, 1823, Sarah Burwell, b. 1802; d. April 5, 1883, daughter of Job Burwell, a resident of Harrison county (had issue: i. Catherine, b. April 18, 1824; m. Benjamin Covert; ii. Jane, b. August 22, 1825; m. William Smith; iii. Mary, b. November 29, 1827; m. Isaac Fitch; iv. Margaret, b. November 19, 1829; m. William Price; v. Nancy, b. October 21, 1831; vi. George, b. Decem-

HARRISON COUNTY GENEALOGIES

ber 5, 1833; settled in Iowa; vii. John-P., b. April 25, 1836; m. December 25, 1867, Mary E. McGrew, daughter of William McGrew, a resident of Green township; viii. Sarah, b. July 29, 1843; m. Wesley Van Horn; ix. Martha, b. September 1, 1845; m. Abraham Atzinger); 9. Mary, b. February 14, 1796; 10. Isaac, b. April 30, 1798; 11. Jacob, b. October 31, 1800; 12. Peter, b. December 25, 1802.

Some families of the name of Brocaw are found in the early records of Somerset county, N. J., and Adams county, Penn.

BASIL BROWN and THOMAS BROWN, two brothers, settled in Luzerne (then Springhill) township, Fayette county, Penn., about 1768. Thomas, b. about 1746, settled on the site of the present town of Brownsville about 1776, and began to lay out town-lots in 1785; he died in 1797, before March 27th, leaving issue: Ignatius, Thomas, Levi, Zachariah, Simeon, Elizabeth (m. —— Cox), Eleanor, Ann, and Ruth; two of his daughters married William Crawford and —— Ewing. Basil left issue: Thomas, m. (1st) Dorcas Goe, daughter of William Goe; m. (2d) Mrs. Philip Worley; Basil, d. unm.; Sarah, d. unm. Possibly descended from one of the above was Basil Brown, said to have been a native of England, who resided in Brownsville before 1800; had issue, among others: 1. Basil, b. at Brownsville, 1801; d. at Cambridge, Ohio, 1851, where he had settled in 1844; m. Nancy Johnson, b. 1809, d. 1888, a native of Pennsylvania (had issue, seven children, among whom: i. Turner, m. Mary E. Price; ii. Melford-J., b. in Brownsville, Jan. 16, 1832; removed to Ohio about 1850, and in 1853 settled at Cadiz; m. 1855, Martha Robinson, daughter of John Robinson, an early settler, who came from Pennsylvania).

JOHN BUCHANAN, a native of Londonderry, Ireland, settled in Carlisle, Penn., before 1776; served in the Revolutionary War, and after the close of that war located in Washington county, Penn.; m. —— Ross; had issue: I. John. II. Jonathan. III. Mary. IV. Ross. V. Samuel, b. in Maryland, March 4, 1773; d. March 23, 1858; removed to the Connotton Valley, Harrison county, Ohio, before 1806; m. (1st) in Washington county, Penn., 1799, Mary Neiper, a native of that county; d. July 15, 1818; m. (2d) Mrs. Mary Stanley Buchanan, b. 1778; d. January 21, 1838; of Mt. Pleasant, Ohio, widow of John Buchanan, who was a second cousin to Samuel Buchanan; had issue by first wife: 1. Jane; 2. Maria; 3. John, b. 1807; 4. Margaret; 5. Joseph, b. April 23, 1814; d. July 11, 1883; m. February 8, 1838, Elizabeth Hines, b. 1819; d. Jan. 5, 1883; daughter of Jacob and Susanna Brough Hines, of Archer township (had issue: i. Margaret, b. October 28, 1839; m. Johnson Montgomery; settled in Jefferson county, Ohio; ii. Susan, b. October 9, 1841; m. John Stringer; settled in Harrison county; iii. Samuel, b. October 25, 1843; d. September 5, 1863; iv. Mary, b. Dec. 19, 1845; m. William B. Anderson; v. John, b. March 11, 1848; settled in Pueblo, Colo.; vi. Thomas, b. November 8, 1850; a Presbyterian minister; settled at Ida Grove, Iowa; vii. Malinda, b. April 6, 1854; m. John Patterson; settled in Archer township; viii. James, b. October 5, 1856; d. December 11, 1857; ix. Albert, b. May 1, 1859; d. in infancy; x. Elizabeth, b. 1861; d. in infancy); 6. Nancy. VI. Thomas. VII. Joseph. VIII. George. IX. Margaret. X. Mary. XI. ——, m. —— Harvey.

WILLIAM BUCHANAN, b. in Pennsylvania, 1790, of Scotch descent; served in the War of 1812; settled in Harrisville, Harrison county, Ohio, before 1853; m. in Ohio, Abigail Mercer, d. May 30, 1857, a descendant of Edward Mercer, of Anglo-Irish descent, who settled in America about 1720; had issue: 1. David; 2. Wilson; 3. William, b. May 1, 1853; settled in Hopedale, Harrison county; m. June 29, 1880, Virginia W. Maddox, a native of Short Creek township, daughter of Wilson and Mary Ladd Maddox.

Wilson Maddox, father of Virginia Maddox Buchanan, came to Harrison county in 1826, where he d. April 30, 1859; his wife d. January 17, 1875; came from Virginia and settled in Harrison county in 1833.

JOHN BUSBY, a native of Maryland; settled in Archer township, Harrison county, Ohio, in 1805; m. Agnes Wisner; had issue, fourteen children, among whom: 1. Abraham-H., b. in Archer township, Jan. 18, 1814; m. May 18,

1848, ―― Marshall, daughter of James and Elizabeth Marshall, natives of Pennsylvania, of Irish descent (had issue: i. John-B.; ii. Nancy-Jane, d. March 5, 1885; iii. Isaac-Jackson; iv. William-R.; v. James-W.; vi. Anna-Mary, m. Delmar Robinson); 2. Sarah, m. ―― Healea; 3. Rachel, m. David Smith; 4. Belinda, m. 1819, Nathaniel Baker; 5. Elizabeth-Ann; 6. Eda, m. Zachariah Baker; 7. Mary-Ann, m. 1834, John McCombs; 8. Dorcas, m. 1833, Aaron Conaway; 9. Deborah, m. 1838, Albert Singhaus; 10. Jane, m. 1840, William Strawsbaugh.

JOHN CADY, a native of county Tyrone, Ireland (son of Joseph Cady, who settled in Reading, Penn., in 1783), settled in Washington county, Penn., and thence removed to Cadiz township, where he died, 1824; m. Margaret Parr; had issue, among others: 1. James, b. in Washington county, Penn., March 2, 1812; removed to Virginia in 1832, and thence to Flemingsburg, Ky., in 1838; returned to Cadiz, 1842, and settled at Cadiz Junction, 1856; m. October 2, 1834, Caroline T. Purdy, a native of New York City (had issue: i. Isabel; ii. William-H.; settled in Dennison, Ohio; iii. Dorcas-C., m. William H. Randall, of Southern California; iv. Adaline-E.; v. Caroline-T.; vi. Elizabeth-A.; vii. Ella, m. R. J. McCarty; viii. Lucinda-M., m. John S. McKay; settled in Memphis, Tenn.; ix. John-E., settled at Cadiz Junction; x. James-R.); 2. Mary, b. 1790; d. July 8, 1865; m. Hiram Conwell; 3. William, settled at Cadiz (had issue, among others: i. James; ii. Isabel, m. ―― Lupton; iii. Ida).

JOHN CALDWELL, b. near Redstone Creek, Fayette county, Penn., 1781, of Scotch-Irish descent; in 1808 removed to Green township, Harrison county, Ohio, where he d. Dec. 10, 1859; m. (1st) in Pennsylvania, Elizabeth Birney; d. in Harrison county; m. (2d) Sarah Reed, b. 1791; d. Feb. 16, 1871; daughter of Robert Reed, a pioneer in Harrison county; had issue by first wife: 1. Robert-Reed, settled in Wood county, Ohio, where he died aged seventy-five years; had issue by second wife: 2. Samuel-Mitchell, settled in Clarke county, Ohio; 3. Elizabeth-Rea, m. James Davidson; 4. Ankrum; 5. William-H., b. Aug. 22, 1825; settled in Cadiz township; m. 1856, Mary-Ann Cochran, daughter of Robert and Sarah Cochran, of Harrison county; 6. John, settled in Marshall, Kan.; 7. Isaac-Shannon; 8. Martha-McCrea, m. James English; 9. James, settled in Fort Wayne, Ind.; 10. David-Hilbert; 11. Albert-Hamilton. David and Albert Caldwell settled in Guernsey county, Ohio.

JOHN CAMPBELL, see Family of Samuel Patton.

JOHN CAMPBELL, a native of Scotland, had issue, among others:
I. John, probably b. in Pennsylvania; removed to Guernsey county, Ohio, before 1818, where he resided for four years; then settled in Green township, Harrison county, where he died; m. (1st) Margaret Fogle; d. 1844; m. (2d) ――, of Tuscarawas county; had issue by first wife: 1. George; 2. Nathaniel; 3. Andrew; 4. Elizabeth; 5. Margaret; 6. Abraham; 7. Frederick; 8. John, b. Feb. 26, 1822; m. Malinda Dennis, daughter of Jacob Dennis, a resident of Green township (had issue: i. William; ii. Rebecca, m. William Ford; iii. Jennie, m. James Rutledge; iv. Margaret, m. Merchant Ault; v. John; vi. Laura, m. William Abraham; vii. Edward; viii. Josiah-P.-Scott; ix. ――, d. in infancy; x. James; xi. Nellie); 9. Hester; 10. Robert; 11. Henry.

JOHN CAMPBELL, d. in Windsor township, York county, Penn., 1775 (before Sept. 18), leaving a wife, Anna, and children, William, John, James, Charles, and Ann; of these:

John Campbell, b. 1744; d. Aug. 13, 1807; served in the Revolutionary War (probably as a militia lieutenant); removed with his family to Washington county, about 1780, and settled in Cross Creek township, where he died; m. March 31, 1772, Mary Hammond, of York county, b. 1752-53; d. March 18, 1817; had issue:

I. Ann, b. March 27, 1773; probably d. young.

II. Griselda ("Gracie") b. Feb. 19, 1775; m. Major Benjamin Bay, and removed to Belmont county, Ohio, about 1812.

III. John, b. Jan. 22, 1775; d. July 24, 1844; m. Elizabeth Lyle, and removed to Wheeling township, Belmont county, Ohio.

IV. William, b. Aug. 11, 1779; m.

Eleanor (?) Smith, and removed to Wheeling township,· Belmont county, Ohio.

V. James, b. Dec. 29, 1781; d. July 17, 1842; m. Margaret Smith, b. Oct. 16, 1784; d. Oct. 8, 1878; removed to Wheeling township, Belmont county, Ohio, in 1803; served as a captain in the War of 1812; had issue, among others: 1. John, a physician, b. Nov. 21, 1804; d. Sept. 17, 1882; m. May 11, 1830, Jane Irwin, b. 1808; d. 1883 (had issue: i. Mary, b. Jan. 24, 1833; ii. Margaret-A., b. Feb. 17, 1836; iii. James-B., b. Nov. 14, 1839; iv. Rachel-J., b. April 14, 1842; v. Maria-L., b. March 29, 1848; vi. Martha-E., b. Jan. 18, 1852); 2. William-M., b. 1808; m. (1st) Mary Kerr, b. 1820; d. Dec. 13, 1874; m. (2d) Louisa Dixon, b. May 8, 1835; d. July 19, 1889.

VI. David, b. March 25, 1784; m. Ann Rea, daughter of William and Jane Mason Rea, of Lower Mount Bethel township, Northampton county, Penn. (the former b. Sept. 13, 1762; d. in Cross Creek township, Washington county, Penn., Sept. 28, 1835; son of the Revolutionary Col. Samuel [b. 1732; d. 1813] and Ann McCracken Rea).

VII. Charles, b. Oct. 31, 1786; d. June 4, 1832; m. Feb. 22, 1810, Esther Mason, of Cross Creek township; had issue: 1. Lucinda, b. 1811; 2. Mary, b. 1812; 3. Elizabeth, b. 1813; 4. John, b. 1815; 5. William-Mason, b. Nov. 10, 1816; m. (1st) 1841, Isabella Ramsey; m. (2d) 1856, Anna E. McIlvaine; 6. Louisa, b. 1818; 7. David, b. 1820; 8. Hannah, b. 1822; 9. Esther, b. 1824.

VIII. George-H., b. June 5, 1789; m. Elizabeth Rea, sister to Ann Rea; had issue: 1. Jane, m. John Wilson, of Noble county, Ohio; 2. John, m. Eliza Moore, of Hickory, Penn.; 3. Mary, m. John Graham, of Knox county, Ohio; 4. William, m. Elizabeth Nichols, of Greene county, Penn.; 5. Elizabeth, d. unm., aged fifty-eight; 6. Samuel-Scott, b. 1822; d. 1895; removed to Harrison county, Ohio; m. (1st) —— Wright; m. (2d) Ann E. Wallace, of Washington, Penn.; m. (3d) Mrs. Mary Law Long, of Harrison county; 7. George-W., b. 1826; d. 1885; 8. Esther-I., removed to Cadiz, Ohio (three other children died young).

IX. Mary, b. Feb. 4, 1792; m. William Fulton, of Mount Pleasant township, Washington county.

X. Elizabeth, b. Oct. 9, 1793; m. William Mason Rea, brother to Ann and Elizabeth Rea.

CHRISTIAN CANAGA (originally spelled Gnaegi), emigrated from Berne province, Switzerland, to America before the Revolution (1750-70), and afterwards settled in Somerset county, Penn., whence he removed to North township, Harrison county, Ohio, about 1807, where he died 1812; had issue, among others: I. Jacob, b. Feb. 23, 1780; d. 1872; m. 1804, Susanna Livingstone, d. 1830, daughter of Christian and Anna Livingstone, of Somerset county; removed to North township, Harrison county, about 1806; had issue: 1. Anne-D., b. May 19, 1805; d. 1889; m. 1823, Rev. D. Strayer; 2. Catharina, b. May 23, 1807; m. Michael Firebaugh; 3. Levi, b. Aug. 29, 1809; 4. Joseph, b. Feb. 21, 1811; 5. Jacob, b. Jan. 15, 1813; d. 1837; m. Sarah Fisher; 6. Salome, b. Aug. 10, 1814; 7. Elias-Greene, b. April 23, 1816; d. Sept. 4, 1888; m. June 27, 1844, Jane McClintock, b. 1818; d. 1894; daughter of Thomas and Elizabeth McClintock, of Carroll county (had issue: i. Silas-Wright, b. June 2, 1845; m. 1868, Elizabeth Wight, daughter of George Adam and Biddy Gordon Wight; ii. Orlando-Loomis, b. July 11, 1846; iii. Milton-Addison, b. 1848; d. young; iv. Alfred-Bruce, b. Nov. 2, 1850; v. Elizabeth-Ellen, b. June 21, 1852; vi. Melissa-Anna, b. Feb. 18, 1854; vii. Josephine, b. Dec. 14, 1855; viii. Emma-Jane, b. June 9, 1857; ix. Heber-Edson, b. Jan. 3, 1860; x. Thomas-McClintock, b. March 12, 1863; xi. Barton Livingston, b. Dec. 19, 1865; xii. Ira-Atilla, b. Jan. 31, 1867; xiii. b. Sept. 25, 1870); 8. Lydia, b. Aug. 1, 1819; m. Napoleon B. Fisher; 9. Manassas, b. May 17, 1821; 10. Susanna, b. June 5, 1823; 11. Mary, b. 1825; 12. John, b. Feb. 10, 1830.

ERASMUS CANNON, b. in Maryland, March 3, 1763; settled about 1815, in Athens township, Harrison county, Ohio, where he died; m. Mary Bowman, d. aged ninety years, a native of Maryland; had issue: I. Mary. II. Rachel. III. Maria. IV. Euphemia. V. Harriet. VI. Moses, b. in Maryland, Oct. 15, 1794; settled in Athens township, where he d. Aug. 26, 1851; m. October 15, 1819, Rachel Turner, d. December 11, 1864, daughter of Joshua and Priscilla

Turner, of Moorefield; had issue: 1. Sarah-Ann, m. Joseph Dickerson, and settled in New Athens; 2. William, settled in Cadiz; 3. James, b. March 31, 1824; m. Oct. 21, 1848, Mary Trimble (daughter of John Trimble, whose father was killed while serving in the Revolutionary War; his mother, Eliza McCall Trimble, settled in Belmont county, Ohio, in 1805); (had issue: i. Mary-E.; ii. Sarah-T.; iii. Rett-A.; iv. John-A.; v. Hayes, settled in Butte City, Mont.; vi. Jeanette; vii. A.-A.); 4. John; 5. Rachel-Jane; 6. Thomas; 7. Moses; 8. Allen; 9. Caroline, m. Basil Bowers; settled in New Martinsville, W. Va. VII. Ewell. VIII. John. IX. Erasmus. X. Thomas.

JOHN CARNAHAN, a native of the North of Ireland, d. at Cadiz, May 20, 1806, being the fourth person buried in the old graveyard at that place; had issue, among others: I. George. II. Samuel, b. 1764; d. Oct. 13, 1851; m. Sarah ———. III. Joseph, b. 1770; d. Feb. 21, 1852; m. ——— Slater; had issue: 1. Joseph; 2. Samuel; 3. James; 4. John, b. 1806; d. 1882; m. 1831, Martha Henderson, b. 1800; d. 1880, daughter of Alexander and Mary Bell Henderson (had issue: i. Mary-Belle, m. Lawson Scott; ii. Andrew-Henderson, m. 1860, Elizabeth Wood, daughter of Sylvanus and Amanda Tingley Wood; iii. Elizabeth, m. Dr. William T. Sharp; iv. Thomas-Lee, m. Sarah Emerson; v. Martha, m. George Black); 5. Margaret; 6. Sarah; 7. Isabel, d. May, 1816. IV. John. V. James.

JAMES CARRICK, a native of Adams county, Penn., of Scotch-Irish descent, removed to Harrison County, Ohio, about 1811, settling in Short Creek township, where he d. 1820; m. in Adams county, Penn., 1775; his wife d. 1833; had issue, among others: 1. David, b. April 1, 1782; d. Dec. 25, 1863; served in the War of 1812; m. Elizabeth ———, b. 1794; d. Nov. 15, 1873 (had issue, among others: i. Agnes-E., m. 1845, John Hanna Hammond); 2. John, d. 1854; 3. Laura, m. ——— Andrews; 4. Nancy, m. ——— Carr; 5. James-W., b. October 14, 1799; removed with his parents to Short Creek township, where he d. March 10, 1885; m. (1st) 1825, Martha Pennel, d. Jan. 7, 1833; m. (2d) 1834, Mrs. Sarah Campbell Boggs, a native of Belmont county, Ohio, d. 1870, daughter of William Campbell, an early pioneer of Belmont county (had issue by first wife, three children; had issue by second wife, eight children, of whom: i. Ezra-L., b. December 15, 1843; served in the Civil War; m. 1872, Martha Jamison, daughter of Andrew Jamison).

GEORGE CARROTHERS, b. in Ireland, 1784; emigrated to America and first located in Washington county, Penn., 1803; removed, about 1813, to Nottingham township, Harrison county, Ohio, and in 1836 to Moorefield township, where he d. December 4, 1863; m. (1st) in Pennsylvania about 1810, Jane Hall, b. in Ireland, February 2, 1791; d. February 2, 1828; m. (2d) 1828, Ann Hastings, a native of county Fermanagh, Ireland, b. May 1, 1798; d. January 14, 1886; had issue by first wife: 1. James; 2. John; 3. George; 4. William; 5. Margaret; had issue by second wife: 6. Sarah, m. James Wilson; 7. Beatty, b. March 14, 1832, in Nottingham township; settled in Moorefield township; m. (1st) Nov. 26, 1856, Martha J. McClintock; d. March 26, 1859; m. (2d) June 21, 1860, Elsie Johnson, b. July 10, 1839; 8. Eliza, m. Jackson Kennedy; 9. Mary, 10. Christopher; went to Japan as a missionary in 1869.

JOHN CARSON, a native of Maryland, b. 1780; d. May 13, 1858; settled in Nottingham township, Harrison county, Ohio, about 1800; m. Hannah Rogers, also a native of Maryland, b. 1777; d. Nov. 2, 1852; had issue, among others:

I. Franklin, b. July 8, 1808; d. June 16, 1874; m. (1st) Oct. 20, 1829, Sarah Hines; d. 1844; daughter of John and Rebecca Deacon Hines, who were among the early settlers in Harrison country, coming from Westmoreland county, Penn.; m. (2d) Nov. 25, 1852, Tabitha Hines, sister of his first wife; had issue by first wife: 1. Louisa-A., b. September 2, 1830; 2. John, b. November 2, 1831; settled in Lucas county, Iowa; 3. Hannah, b. December 6, 1833; 4. William-F., b. August 4, 1835; settled in Lucas county, Iowa; 5. Elijah-R., b. June 13, 1837; m. Drucilla P. Johnson, b. Sept. 13, 1840, daughter of Abiram and Lydia Turner Johnson, pioneers of Nottingham township; 6. Walter-B., b. August 20, 1838; 7. Rebecca, b. December 8, 1839; 8. Harvey-L., b. September

19, 1841; served in the Civil War and died in that service; 9. Isaac, b. February 15, 1844; settled in Lucas county, Iowa.

II. Elijah, b. 1810; d. November, 1887; m. 1832, Margaret Mahaffey, b. in Washington county, Penn., 1803; d. 1884; had issue, among others: 1. ———, m. Joseph G. Rogers; 2. Elmira-J., m. James M. Hines; 3. ———, m. Thomas Benton Huffman. III. William. IV. Walter. V. John.

JOHN CARSON, see also Family of Rudolph Hines.

WILLIAM CARSON, b. in Ireland, 1803; d. there, 1865; m. Jane Noble, b. 1792; d. 1812; had issue, among others: 1. William-N., b. 1822; d. 1899; m. in Ireland, 1845, Margaret Tiernan, b. 1821, d. 1885, daughter of Henry and Jane Abram Tiernan.

JOHN HENRY CARVER, b. in Germany; came to America as a drummer boy with a regiment of Hessian soldiers who served on the British side in the Revolutionary War; about 1779 m. Talitha Mitchell, d. March 14, 1845, a native of North Carolina; he settled in Mt. Pleasant, Jefferson county, Ohio, about 1798, removing thence to Flushing township, Belmont county, where he resided until 1812, and then located at Freeport, Harrison county, where he died March 15, 1841; had issue: I. John. II. Rebecca, m. ——— Thompson. III. Henry. IV. Elizabeth, m. ——— Carrington. V. Jane. VI. Ann, m. ——— Bailey. VII. Abner, b. Jan. 23, 1805; d. May 13, 1884; m. (1st) 1829, Eliza Norris, d. July 23, 1855, daughter of Thomas Norris, of Freeport; m. (2d) Rachel Cullen, d. Aug. 14, 1882; had issue, among others: 1. Thomas-P., b. Sept. 19, 1843; served in the Civil War; m. November 15, 1868, Mary A. Johnson, daughter of William Johnson, of Smyrna. VIII. Mary, m. ——— Cox, and settled in Iowa. IX. Elijah, b. July 17, 1810, in Belmont county; settled in Freeport; m. (1st) Nov. 26, 1835, Nancy Boals, d. Jan. 24, 1854; dau. of James Boals, of Freeport; m. (2d) April 25, 1871, Narcissa E. Bevan, daughter of Joseph Bevan; had issue by first wife: 1. Henry-B., b. October 17, 1836; d. June 25, 1890; settled in Washington township; m. (1st) April 8, 1858, Sarah Phillips; d. Aug. 20, 1876; daughter of John Phillips, of Washington township; m. (2d) March 20, 1878, Nancy E. McCullough, daughter of Jonathan McCullough, of Tippecanoe; 2. Mary-J., m. Thomas Sloan. Elijah Carver had issue by second wife: 3. Anna; 4. Thaddeus.

JOHN CASSELL, a native of Germany, emigrated to America and settled in Frederick county, Maryland, where he married and died; had issue, among others: 1. Jacob, b. April 15, 1799 d. near Hopedale, 1881; m. in Maryland, 1821, and removed from Unionville, that State, to Green township, Harrison county, about 1835 (had issue: i. John-Wesley, m. 1893, Elizabeth Jones; ii. Chelnissa, d. 1888; m. ——— Decker; iii. Mary, d. young).

PHILIP CECIL, born in Maryland, son of Kingsbury Cecil, also a native of Maryland, who afterward settled in Kentucky, where he died; the son removed to Harrison county, Ohio, before 1823, where he died in 1850; m. Mary Logan; d. 1845; daughter of John Logan; had issue: 1. Richard, b. in Harrison county, May 23, 1823; m. Feb. 25, 1847, Jane E. Bliss, daughter of Zadoc Bliss, of Franklin township (had issue: i. Sarah-Jane, b. April 16, 1848; m. A. Oliphant; ii. George, b. July 17, 1850; iii. Mary-K., b. May 19, 1853; iv. Emma-L., b. April 9, 1856; v. John-B., b. Dec. 11, 1858; vi. Jesse-F., b. March 21, 1861; vii. Clara, b. Sept. 10, 1863; viii. ———, d. in infancy; ix. Clarence-A., b. June 8, 1867; x. Merritt-R., b. March 31, 1870); 2. John, m. Dec. 10, 1846, Susanna Donahey; 3. William; 4. Kingsbury; 5. Margaret; 6. Jesse, m. 1838, Elizabeth Goddard; 7. Wesley.

Zadoc Bliss, father of Jane E. Cecil, was a native of Connecticut, b. Feb. 26, 1788; d. July 8, 1850; settled in Franklin township, about 1826, having removed thither from Columbiana county, Ohio; m. Keziah Hoskins, b. April 4, 1786; d. May 31, 1851; had issue: 1. Ralph; 2. Sarah-C.; 3. Mary; 4. Emily; 5. James; 6. George-W.; 7. Zebulon; 8. John; 9. Keziah; 10. Jane-E., m. Richard Cecil.

NATHAN CHANEY, d. 1827: a native of Maryland; removed from Virginia to Cadiz township, Harrison county, Ohio, about 1805; m. in Virginia, Sarah Mansfield; d. 1847; had issue, among others:

I. Thomas, b. Oct. 28, 1803, in Virginia; d. July 1, 1890, in Archer township; served in the War of 1812; m. Sept. 25, 1836, Elizabeth Clark, had issue: 1. James; 2. John; 3. William; 4. Sarah; 5. Martha; 6. Samuel, b. Dec. 14, 1846; m. Aug. 5, 1875, Clarinda Edwards, daughter of John Edwards, of New Athens, Harrison county; 7. Mary-Ann; 8. Elizabeth-Ann; 9. Mary-Ellen; 10. Thomas-W.; 11. Hannah; 12. Nancy.

James Clark, father of Elizabeth Chaney, was a native of Fayette county, Penn., where he married Sarah Watson; served in the War of 1812; had issue: 1. Martha; 2. Elizabeth, m. Thomas Chaney; 3. Mary; 4. John; 5. William.

ROBERT CHRISTY, of Scottish descent, b. about 1732-35; emigrated to America and first settled in New York City; removed to Jefferson county, Ohio, before 1800, and later located in Archer township, Harrison county, Ohio, where he d. 1830; served in the Indian wars; m. Margaret Marshall, a resident of New York; had issue: 1. George, d. aged eighty-four years; served in the War of 1812; 2. William; 3. Robert, b. in Jefferson county, 1799; settled in Nottingham township, Harrison county, about 1832, where he d. Oct. 9, 1853; m. 1831, Jane M. McCleary, b. 1812, daughter of Andrew McCleary (d. in Jefferson county, 1812) and sister to James McCleary (b. 1809) (had issue: 1. David, b. Nov. 12, 1832; settled in Stock township; m. April 7, 1864, Elizabeth Spiker, daughter of Christopher Spiker; ii. Elizabeth, m. John R. Hines; iii. Margaret; iv. James; v. Sarah-A., m. Meredith Barrett; vi. George; served in the Civil War; vii. Jane-Anne; viii. Mary, m. George Garver; ix. Lydia-C., m. Elias Hines; x. Joanna-Matilda, m. Pinckney Moore); 4. David; 5. John; 6. Sarah, d. aged eighty-three years; 7. Nancy, d. aged over eighty years; 8. Margaret.

JAMES CLARK, b. probably in Virginia; d. in Pennsylvania; m. Margaret Trimble; had issue: 1. James; 2. Matthew, b. 1800, in Virginia or Pennsylvania; d. in Cadiz township, 1852; m. in Washington county, Penn., Jane Barr, b. 1801; d. Oct. 5, 1865; daughter of John and Sarah Gailey Barr, of Scotch-Irish descent (had issue: i. John-Barr, b. Oct. 9, 1827; d. Jan. 13, 1872; a United Presbyterian minister; served as colonel of the 193d Pennsylvania Volunteer Infantry in the Civil War; m. (1st) Lydia Collins; m. (2d) Frances Florence; ii. Eleanor-Margaret, m. John C. Jamison, of Cadiz, Ohio); 3. Samuel, m. Jane Hawthorne; 5. John; 6. Thomas, m. Ellen Barr; 7. Sarah, m. James Hunter; 8. Elizabeth, m. James Carnahan; 9. Rebecca, d. young; 10. Anne, d. young.

JOSHUA CLARK, a native of Fayette county, Penn., of the family of Walter Clark; removed, in 1804, to Belmont county, Ohio, and in 1808 to Short Creek township, Harrison county, thence to Freeport, in the year 1839, where he d. Jan. 17, 1868; m. in Pennsylvania, Susannah Flaugh, of English descent; d. July 6, 1853; had issue: 1. Elizabeth; 2. John; 3. Abisha, settled in Maynard, Ohio; 4. Mary; 5. James; 6. Hannah; 7. Margaret, m. Augustus Harris; 8. Susan, m. James Reeves, and settled in Washington township; 9. Joshua, b. April 9, 1823; settled in Freeport; m. Feb. 28, 1862, Sarah Covington; d. July 5, 1887; daughter of Elijah Covington.

ROGER CLARK, b. 1726, in Ireland; d. 1765; settled in Cumberland county, Penn.; m. (1st) in Pennsylvania, —— Agnew; m. (2d) ————; had issue by first wife: Elizabeth, James, Nancy, and Jane; had issue by second wife: Joseph and John.

James Clark, the second child by the first wife, was b. 1751, in Cumberland county, Penn., removed to Westmoreland county, Penn., 1776; settled in Jefferson county, Ohio, in 1810, where he died, in 1833; served in the Indian and Revolutionary Wars; m. 1775, Jane Jack, a native of Cumberland county, b. 1753; had issue:

I. John. II. Joseph, b. in Westmoreland county, Penn., Feb. 12, 1778; removed to Jefferson (now Harrison) county, Ohio, in 1808, and settled in Green township, where he d. Oct. 3, 1861; m. March 4, 1811, Rachel Johnson; b. Dec. 31, 1793; d. Sept. 3, 1854; had issue: 1. James, b. 1812; d. 1847; removed to New Philadelphia; 2. Mary, b. Aug. 22, 1813; 3. Johnson, b. Aug. 31, 1814; settled in Cadiz; 4. Ingram, b. Sept. 21, 1816; d. Feb. 18, 1876; served in the Ohio Legislature, 1866-68; m. Feb. 16, 1842, Sarah Moore, daughter of William Moore, a resident of Green township (had issue: i. Rachel, b. Nov. 10, 1842; d. April 22, 1865; ii. Alfred-W., b. Aug. 27, 1845; settled in Nebraska; iii. John, b. April, 1849; d. April 12, 1871; iv. Joseph-A., b. Nov. 16, 1852; settled in Nebraska; v. Clara-J., b. Feb. 27, 1855; d. April 22, 1880; m. Lee Johnson; vi. Charles-G., b. July 10, 1860; settled in Nebraska; vii. Ella-B., b. December 5, 1862; m. George Mills); 5. Jane, b. Sept. 26, 1818; m. David Moore (had issue: i. James-Clark, settled in Cadiz); 6. Rachel, b. March 4, 1824; 7. Ephraim, b. Feb. 19, 1826; d. at Cadiz, Oct. 10, 1885; served in the Ohio Legislature, 1855-57; m. Isabella Kennedy, daughter of Dr. Moses and Catherine Snyder Kennedy (had issue: i. Oliver, removed with his parents to Cadiz, in 1871; m. (1st) Sept. 13, 1871, Clara S. Cochran; d. Jan. 20, 1878; daughter of Samuel Cochran; m. (2d) March 20, 1879, Elizabeth Agnes Kerr, daughter of James Kerr, of Cadiz; ii. Frances, d. aged six years; iii. Ida, m. George D. McFadden, of Cadiz; iv. Cora-V., d. aged seven years); 8. Joseph, b. June 4, 1830; settled in Cadiz; 9. Oscar, b. March 10, 1833; m. Margaret Hamilton; settled in Walton, Kan.; 10. Albert, b. Jan. 16, 1836; m. Amanda Kerr, daughter of John C. Kerr, of Harrison county; settled in Nebraska. III. William. IV. Mary. V. James. VI. Andrew. VII. Thomas. VIII. Robert. IX. Francis.

Samuel Kerr, grandfather of Elizabeth Kerr Clark, was b. Oct. 25, 1792; d. in Short Creek township, Harrison county, where he was among the pioneers; served in the War of 1812; m. (1st) Sept. 28, 1815, Annie Smith; m. (2d) September 8, 1835, Agnes Hamilton; had issue by first wife: 1. Sarah-J., m. James McLaughlin; 2. James, b. April 19, 1818; d. in Cadiz, Jan. 21, 1886; m. Julia Ann Carrick (had issue: i. Samuel-Mason; ii. David-Ramsey, a minister; iii. Elizabeth-Agnes, m. Oliver Clark; iv. James-A.; v. Adda-Zilla, m. Charles G. Clark, and settled in Nebraska; vi. Mary-M.; vii. Julia-Ella, m. —— Matson, and settled in Short Creek township); 3. Mary, m. William Campbell, of Belmont county, Ohio; 4. Joseph-S.; 5. Ellen, m. Stewart Carrick; 6. Robert, a Presbyterian minister; had issue by second wife: 7. Thomas-H.; 8. Samuel-C., a Presbyterian minister; 9. Margaret-Ann, m. John Calderhead; 10. William-J.; 11. Effie-J.

JAMES CLEMENTS, a native of Maryland, settled in Cadiz township, Harrison county, Ohio, before 1819; later removing to Athens township, where he died; m. Plessey Merritt, a resident of Belmont county, Ohio; had issue: 1. Nancy; 2. Josiah; 3. Daniel, b. in Athens township, Dec. 24, 1819; d. Sept. 1, 1872; m. 1842, Elizabeth Dickerson; d. Jan. 22, 1888; daughter of Baruch Dickerson, a resident of Cadiz township (had issue: i. Thomas-W., b. June 14, 1846; m. June 19, 1883, Josephine Smith, a resident of Harrison county; ii. John-M., b. June 4, 1848; m. June 20, 1888, Mary Sloan, daughter of John Sloan, a resident of Moorefield township; iii. Samuel; iv. Jane-Elizabeth, m. Robert Bartow; v. Josiah; vi. Louisa; vii. Clara-P., m. —— Dunlap; settled in Belmont county, Ohio); 4. John; 5. Esther; 6. Eliza; 7. Mary; 8. Merritt; 9. James.

JOHN CLEMENS, a native of county Tyrone, Ireland, died aged one hundred years, his wife also having attained the same age when she died; first settled in Eastern Pennsylvania; removed from Raccoon Creek, Washington county, Penn., to Harrison county, Ohio, about 1837, and later to Tuscarawas county, where he died; m. in Ireland, Frances Scott, a sister of Alexander Scott, later of Scott's Mills, Tuscarawas county, Ohio; had issue: 1. David; 2. John; 3. Joseph; 4. William; 5. James, d. aged seventy-two; first located in Washington county, Pennsylvania; removed to Harrison county, Ohio, in 1836, and subsequently settled in Athens township; m. in Pennsylvania, Mary Campbell, a native of that State, d. aged seventy years, daughter of James Campbell and wife, of Scotch descent, who died in Pennsylvania (had issue: i. John, m. Elizabeth Moore; ii. Eliza-Jane; iii. Frances, m. Simpson Bethel; iv. Samuel-C., b. June 28, 1833, in Washington county, Penn.; removed to Athens township, Harrison county, Ohio, and later to Cadiz township; m. May 12, 1864, Sarah J. Dunlap, daughter of Hugh B. Dunlap, of Athens township; v. Mary-J., m. Thomas Furbay, of New Athens, Ohio; vi. Alexander-S., settled in Newport, Tuscarawas county; vii. Rebecca; viii. Gillespie); 6. Samuel, d. 1887, in Iowa; 7. Elizabeth; 8. Mary; 9. Frances; 10. Rebecca.

SAMUEL COCHRAN, of Scotch-Irish descent, b. in Lancaster (now Dauphin) county, Penn., 1738; d. 1818; served in the Revolutionary War; located on the Monongahela River, ten miles above Pittsburgh, before 1800; m. 1770, Mary Shearer, b. 1754; d. 1805; had issue, among others:
I. Robert, b. in Lancaster (now Dauphin) county, Penn., Sept. 15, 1771; d. Feb. 1, 1861; settled near Cadiz, Ohio, about 1801; m. (1st) 1800, in Pennsylvania, Dorcas Neal, d. 1801; m. (2d) 1807, in Allegheny county, Penn., Sarah Calhoun, b. Jan. 8, 1787; d. April 4, 1867; daughter of David and Eleanor King Calhoun; had issue by first wife: 1. Dorcas, b. 1801; d. 1853; m. Isaac Whittaker; had issue by second wife; 2. Eleanor, b. Feb. 11, 1808; d. Sept. 17, 1867; 3. Samuel, b. March 30, 1811; d. September, 1899; m. (1st) 1839, Sarah J. Hedges, d. 1841; m. (2d) 1849, Margaret Thompson, b. July 11, 1820, daughter of Samuel Thompson, of Green township (had issue by first wife: i. an infant, d. 1841; had issue by second wife: ii. Clara-S., d. 1878; m. Oliver Clark, of Cadiz; iii. Robert-Byron, m. 1886, Flora Morgan, daughter of M. Morgan, of Short Creek township; iv. Belle, m. William Morgan, of Cadiz township; v. Martha); 4. David, a United Presbyterian minister; b. Aug. 1, 1814; d. Oct. 30, 1883, in Leavenworth, Kan.; m. Martha Shearer (had issue, three sons and six daughters, of whom: i. William; ii. Martha—both removed from Leavenworth with their mother to San Jose, Cal., after 1883; iii. James, settled in Oregon; iv. ——, m. —— Shearer, and settled in Kansas City, Mo.; v. ——, m. —— Bissett, and settled in Leavenworth, Kan.; vi. George; settled in Kansas City, Mo.; vii. ——, m. —— Pierson, and settled in Tonganoxie, Kan.; viii. ——, m. —— Monks, and settled in Chicago; ix. Elizabeth, settled in Lawrence, Kan.); 5. Mary, b. Dec. 11, 1817; d. July, 1899; m. W. Harvey Caldwell, and settled near Cadiz; 6. Robert-Reed, b. Sept. 14, 1822; m. Oct. 10, 1867, Rachel Hedges, daughter of William and Mary Jane McClellan Hedges, of Cadiz township (had issue: i. John-William; ii. Robert-Emmett; iii. Mary-Eleanor; iv. Frank McClellan; v. Rees-Burchfield); 7. Sarah-Jane, b. Oct. 9, 1825.

DAVID COLLINS, m. Mrs. Ann Workman Glasgow; had issue: 1. John, m. Ellen Patterson (had issue: i. Patterson; ii. David; iii. Jane; iv. Elizabeth; v. Ellen); 2. Martha, d. 1847; m. (1st) James Bowland; m. (2d) 1822, John Maholm (had issue, by first husband, surname Bowland: i. Robert, b. 1798; d. 1880; ii. Anna, b. April 18, 1810; d. May 16, 1844; m. Robert Lyons; had issue by second husband, surname Maholm; iii. Eliza-Jane, m. 1848, Joseph Sharon; iv. Martha-Matilda, m. 1845, Rezin J. Bennett; v. James-B.); 3. Elizabeth, m. Robert Gilmore (had issue: i. Ephraim, m. Julianna Dennison; ii. John; iii. Arabella, m. Theodore Jennings; iv. Joseph, m. Letitia A. Brady; v. Ann-W., b. April 16, 1817; d. Oct. 30, 1880; m. John M. Richey; b. Nov. 2, 1808; d. Jan. 30, 1897); 4. Ruth, m. George McFadden.

GEORGE COLLINS, b. in Maryland, about 1796; d. in Moorefield township, Harrison county, Jan. 1, 1870, where he had settled in 1832; m. in Frederick county, Maryland, Eliza Johnson, b. 1803; d. 1890, daughter of Joseph and —— Bain Johnson; had issue: 1. Elizabeth; 2. Israel; 3. William; 4. Amanda; 5. Mary; 6. Zachariah, b. in Maryland, 1828; d. 1884; m. Rachel Willoughby (daughter of Henry Willoughby), b. in Knox county, Ohio, 1831 (had issue: i. George-H., m. Elizabeth A. Hilbert; ii. William; iii. Nicholas-B.; iv. Elizabeth, d. young; v. Ann-Eliza, m. David N. Reynolds; vi. Parley-A., m. Frank J. Mead); 7. Catharine; 8. George-P.; 9. Nicholas; 10. Battelle; 11. John-W.; 12 Cyrena; 13. Eliza; 14. Thomas-L.

DAVID COMLY, b. in Washington county, Penn., Aug. 8, 1798; removed in 1814 to what is now Carroll county, Ohio; settled near Mount Pleasant, Jefferson county, about 1817, where he d. 1886; m. 1821, Sarah Whinnery, a native of Pennsylvania; had issue, among others: 1. John-W., a physician; b. June 24, 1823; settled in Harrisville, Harrison county; m. 1849, Mary C. Armstrong, a native of Ohio, of Scotch-Irish descent; d. 1863; daughter of Charles and Sarah Armstrong (had issue: i. Sarah-J., m. Dr. N. R. Coleman,

HARRISON COUNTY GENEALOGIES

and settled in Columbus; ii. Marietta; iii. William-J., d. in infancy).

CHARLES CONAWAY, see also Family of William Johnson.

MICHAEL CONAWAY (brother to Charles [1751-1837] and Samuel Conaway) b. 1737, near Baltimore, Md., of Scotch-Irish descent; m. 1779, Elizabeth Davis, a native of Scotland; had issue: I. Michael-C., b. near Baltimore, Md., 1780; removed about 1800 to Pennsylvania; in 1805 settled with his parents in what is now Stock township, Harrison county, Ohio; m. in Pennsylvania, 1805, Martha Hoagland, daughter of James and Mary Hooey Hoagland; had issue: 1. Eli, b. 1806; d. 1832; 2. Aaron, b. Oct. 13, 1807; settled in Archer township; m. March 28, 1833, Dorcas Busby, daughter of John Busby, of Archer township (had issue, fourteen children, of whom: i. Michael; ii. ———; killed in the Civil War; iii. ———; iv. John-B., settled in York, Neb.; v. Henry-O., settled in Omaha, Neb.; vi. Alpheus-B., settled in New Sharon, Iowa; vii. ———, m. R. M. Welch; viii. ———, m. C. B. Burrier); 3. Elizabeth, m. 1828, George McKinny (had issue, five children); 4. Henry, m. Rosanna Mosholder (had issue, three children); 5. Susanna, m. Joel Smith (had issue, three children); 6. Rachel, m. Alexander Picken (had issue, seven children); 7. Enoch, d. 1861, in West Virginia; m. (1st) Amanda Granfel; m. (2d) Charlotte Loman (had issue by both wives); 8. Mary, d. 1855; 9. Moses-H., b. Aug. 6, 1817; d. Oct. 3, 1890; m. (1st) July 15, 1856, Mary J. Crozier, b. Feb. 15, 1829; d. Nov. 19, 1862; m. (2d) Sept. 13, 1883, Kate Gallaher, b. Sept. 28, 1843. II. John, b. 1790, in Kent county, Md.; came with his parents to Stock township, Harrison county, where he d. 1861; served in the War of 1812; m. Elizabeth Hoagland, b. 1797, in Pennsylvania; d. 1886, in Stock township; had issue, nine children, of whom: 1. Charles, b. Sept. 12, 1819; m. April 1, 1847, Mary Given, b. Sept. 1822, daughter of Robert and Rebecca Evans Given, pioneers of Harrison county (had issue: i. Rebecca-J., d. aged fourteen years; ii. Robert, settled in Conneaut, Ohio: iii. John-W.; iv. Ella-E., m. Samuel Milliken, and settled in Tuscarawas county, Ohio; v. Mary-Martha); 2. Elizabeth; 3. Jemima; 4. Susanna; 5. Rachel; 6. Cynthia, m.

——— Layport; 7. Hannah, m. ——— Whitaker; 8. Martha, m. ——— Patterson. III. Charles, m. Frances Arnold; had issue, nine children. IV. Catharine, m. Henry Barnes. V. Susan, m. Gabriel Holland (see Holland Family). VI. Elizabeth, m. Archibald Virtue.

James Hoagland, father of Martha Conaway, was of Dutch descent; settled in Harrison county; his wife, Mary Hooey, was of Irish descent; had issue, among others: 1. Martha, m. Michael Conaway (b. 1780); 2. Mary, m. Harvey Tumbleson; 3. Jane, settled in the South; 4. Ann, m. Piatt Martin. James Hoagland's brother, Aaron Hoagland, settled in Ashland county, Ohio; another brother, Moses, settled in Holmes county, Ohio.

PATRICK CONNOR, b. in Ireland, 1807; d. in Pennsylvania, 1890; m. Margaret Gallagher, b. 1813; d. 1889; had issue: 1. Bryan, b. 1835; settled at Salineville, Ohio, 1871; m. in England, Mary Morris, daughter of James Morris (had issue: i. James-V.); 2. Mary, m. ——— Cordy; 3. Margaret, m. ——— Whalen; 4. John, m. Mary McCann.

HIRAM CONWELL, a native of Virginia, of Scotch descent; settled in Harrison county before 1816; about 1830 he went to New Orleans, and never returned, having died, it is thought, of cholera, which was epidemic at that time; in Ohio he had married Mary Cady (b. 1790; d. July 8, 1865), a daughter of John and Margaret Parr (1761-1864) Cady; had issue, among others: 1. John, b. 1827, in Cadiz; served as an officer in both the Mexican and Civil Wars; he was one of a party that went to the gold fields of California in 1849, returning to Cadiz in 1851; m. (1st) October, 1848, Mary J. Gordon, a native of Ireland (had issue: i. Jesse-L.; ii. Frances-May; iii. William-Henry, who died in infancy; iv. Charles-Emmett; v. Minnesota, m. Wesley Holmes, of Harrison county; vi. Caroline, m. John F. Kennedy; vii. Ella, m. (1st) Charles B. Pearce; m. (2d) Dr. Campbell); John Conwell m. (2d) Elizabeth McConnell, of Cadiz. Mrs. Mary Cady Conwell married (2d) Joseph Forker, by whom she had issue, surnamed Forker: 1. Isabella-Belinda, m. John Shauff; 2. Henry-G., settled in Cadiz; 3. Mary-Jane, m. Dr. C. Thomas; settled in Des Moines, Iowa.

JAMES COOKE, a native of Ireland (son of Robert Cooke, a native of Scotland, who removed to Ireland), emigrated to America and, about 1788, settled in Washington county, Penn., thence removed to Athens township, Harrison county, Ohio, about 1805; d. 1815; m. in Ireland, Nancy Moore, d. 1829; had issue: I. Mary, m. John Love. II. Elizabeth, m. John Henderson. III. Robert. IV. William. V. James. VI. John. VII. Thomas. VIII. George, b. in Washington county, Penn., May 5, 1804; settled in Athens township; m. July 10, 1824, Nancy Anderson, daughter of Col. William Anderson, an early settler in Cadiz township; had issue: 1. Nancy, m. William Gillespie, and settled in Guernsey county; 2. Melila, m. James Crossan; 3. Ruth-E., m. David McConaughey; 4. Mary; 5. Jane, m. Thomas Morrow; 6. James, b. Dec. 28, 1835; m. March 4, 1858, Jane McCracken, daughter of William McCracken, of Belmont county; 7. William; 8. George; 9. John, settled in Bridgeport, Ohio; 10. Thomas, twin brother to John; 11. Mary-N., m. John H. Rourk; 12. Matilda, m. William Walker.

JOSEPH COOK, b. in Pennsylvania; settled in Freeport township about 1820; had issue: 1. Jesse, b. 1810; d. 1898; m. 1825, at Westchester, Ohio, Susanna Wilson, b. 1814; d. 1896; daughter of James Wilson (had issue: i. William, b. 1837; removed to Bloomington, Ill.; m. Temperance Peregoy; ii. T.-H.; settled in Scio); 2. Joseph, b. 1812; 3. David, b. 1815; 4. Jane.

WILLIAM C. COOPER, a native of England, emigrated to America and first settled in Pennsylvania; later removed to near Deesville, Harrison county, Ohio, where he died; his widow d. in Cadiz township; had issue: 1. Sarah, m. ——— Lafferty, and settled in Cadiz township; 2. William, settled in Carrollton, Ohio; 3. Benjamin; 4. Stephen, settled in Oregon; 5. John, settled in Rising Sun, Ohio; 6. Thomas, d. in the army; 7. Michael, removed to Indiana; 8. Louisa, m. John S. Clevender, and settled in Dakota; 9. Mary.

JOHN COPE, a native of Virginia (great grandson of Oliver Cope, who emigrated from Wiltshire, England, to Pennsylvania, 1687, and d. 1701), removed from Virginia to Belmont county, Ohio, in 1812; located in Short Creek township, Harrison county, in 1813, where he died; m. in Virginia, Grace Steer, b. 1763; d. March 30, 1885; had issue:
I. William, b. Aug. 1, 1796; d. in Iowa, Sept. 27, 1869. II. Joseph, b. in Virginia, Jan. 9, 1799; d. April 22, 1885; m. in Fayette county, Penn., 1825, Ruth Griffith, of Welsh descent, b. in Westmoreland county, Penn., Jan. 1, 1801; daughter of William and Sarah Cooke Griffith; had issue: 1. Amos-A., settled in Powesheik county, Iowa; 2. Benjamin-T., b. May 15, 1828; m. 1855, Rachel Lukens, b. 1834, in Guernsey county, Ohio, daughter of Moses and Elizabeth Barber Lukens; 3. Israel, d. in infancy; 4. Oliver-G., b. Aug. 11, 1830; served in the Ohio Legislature, 1880-1881; m. March 6, 1856, Sarah Williams, d. May 19, 1859, daughter of Nathan and Sarah Williams, of Harrison county; 5.———, d. in infancy. III. Isaac, b. Feb. 1, 1801; d. Dec. 19, 1883. IV. John, b. in Virginia, April 25, 1803; m. 1832, Mary Lukens, b. in Pennsylvania, Nov. 4, 1804; d. July 19, 1876; daughter of Moses and Sarah Lukens; had issue: 1. Sarah-T., b. June 2, 1833; 2. Lemuel, d. young; 3. Hiram, b. Dec. 16, 1843; m. 1872, Martha Thomas, daughter of Isaac and Anna Thomas, early settlers in Harrison county. V. James, b. Nov. 9, 1806; d. in Hopedale, Jan. 17, 1868.

Moses and Elizabeth Lukens, parents of Rachel Cope, removed to Harrison county from Guernsey county, in 1838. The father of Elizabeth Lukens was Samuel Barber, b. 1777; d. in Harrison county, in January, 1851; m. Ann Schooley, b. 1766; d. Oct. 1, 1863.

SAMUEL COPE, b. in Frederick county, Va., 1762; d. November, 1854; settled in Green township, 1823; m. in Frederick county, Va., 1797, Sarah Steer, b. Feb. 27, 1778; d. 1828; daughter of James and Abigal Steer; had issue: 1. John, b. 1799; 2. Elizabeth, b. 1801; 3. Susannah, b. 1803; m. 1830, Lloyd Case of Pennsylvania (had issue: i. James; ii. William; iii. Thomas; iv. Sarah-Elizabeth; v. Rhoda-Jane); 4. Abigail, b. 1805; 5. Joshua, b. 1808; 6. Jane, b. 1811; 7. Sarah, b. 1814; 8. Anna, b. 1816; 9. Mary, b. 1819; 10. Rachel, b. 1823.

JAMES COPELAND, a native of Ireland, emigrated to Pennsylvania and settled in Westmoreland county, thence

removing to Wayne township, Jefferson county, Ohio, in 1800; had issue:
I. Thomas, b. in Westmoreland county, Penn., 1795; settled in Green township, Harrison county, Ohio, in 1814, where he d. 1879; m. Nancy Shepler; had issue: 1. Christina; 2. Mary; 3. Jacob; 4. Lucinda; 5. James, b. Sept. 4, 1823; settled in German township; m. 1846, Margaret Gutshall, daughter of Daniel and Mary Hospelhorn Gutshall, who settled in Harrison county, in 1800—the father served in the War of 1812—(had issue: i. Mary-M.; ii. Thomas-D.; iii. Nancy-J.; iv. Elizabeth-A.; v. Christina-L.; vi. Rebecca-S.; vii. Sarah-S.; viii. James-A.; ix. Emma-A.; x. Adaline; xi. Evaline, twin sister to Adaline last named; xii. Laura-B.; xiii. Samantha-M.); 6. Samuel; 7. Peter; 8. Joseph-L.; 9. John-M.; 10. Henry; 11. Thomas-F.; 12. George. II. James. III. Susan. IV. Samuel. V. Mary. VI. Jennie. VII. Joseph. VIII. Nancy. IX. John. X. Iba.

JOHN COPELAND, a native of Ireland, emigrated to America and settled in Maryland or Pennsylvania, whence, in 1805, he removed to Jefferson county, Ohio; d. 1840; m. Isabelle Leach, a native of Pennsylvania; had issue: 1. Samuel; 2. Thomas, b. in Jefferson county, Ohio; removed to Franklin township, Harrison county, Ohio, before 1837, where he d. July 4, 1877; m. in Harrison county, Nancy A. Dick; d. April 1, 1880, daughter of William Dick, a resident of Harrison county (had issue: i. Jane, m. John Hilton; ii. Isabelle, m. Nathaniel Lukens; iii. John; iv. Mary; v. William, b. Sept. 4, 1837; m. 1863, Mary Cruin, daughter of George Cruin, of Franklin township); 3. Joseph; 4. James, b. in Maryland, Aug. 7, 1801; settled in Washington township, where he d. April 30, 1859; m. 1837, Mary A. Walters, daughter of Leonard and Rachel Ruby Walters, of Jefferson county (had issue: i. Thomas-W., b. in Franklin township, Aug. 25, 1838; settled in Washington township; served in the Civil War; was a prisoner at Andersonville; m. Aug. 29, 1869, Mary E. Ramsey, of Washington township; ii. Matilda; iii. Rachel; iv. Amanda; v. Isabelle; vi. Leonard; vii. S.-S.; viii. Nannie-E.; ix. John, served in the Civil War; d. about 1865); 5. David; 6. William, settled in Franklin township, where he d. 1870; m. 1833, in Harrison county, Mary Dempster, daughter of Robert and Elizabeth Hunter Dempster, of Jefferson county (the former a native of Pensylvania; the latter a daughter of John Hunter, who settled in Jefferson county in 1820); (had issue: i. John-W.; ii. William-D., b. Jan. 8, 1836; m. March 10, 1867, Lucy Burns, daughter of John M. and Elizabeth Hilbert Burns; iii. Joseph; iv. Albert; v. Elizabeth; vi. Isabelle; vii. Mary-M.; viii. Margaret-J.); 7. Archibald.

John M. Burns, father of Lucy Burns Copeland, was a native of Westmoreland county, Penn.; removed to Smithfield, Jefferson county, Ohio; afterward settled in German township, Harrison county; m. Elizabeth Hilbert, daughter of John Hilbert; had issue: 1. Frances-Samantha, m. Alexander Henderson; 2. Letitia, m. Joseph Courtright; 3. Lomida, m. Henry Taylor; 4. Lucy, m. William D. Copeland.

Leonard Walters, father of Mary Walters Copeland, was an early settler in Jefferson county; m. Rachel Ruby; had issue: 1. Thomas; 2. Joseph; 3. Mary-A., m. James Copeland; 4. Catharine; 5. Martha; 6. Maria.

ROBERT COULTER, a native of county Antrim, Ireland; emigrated to America and settled with three brothers in Chester county, Penn., 1780-1790; thence removed to Lancaster county, Penn.; m. Isabella Mayes, a native of the North of Ireland, daughter of Joseph Mayes, who after the death of her first husband, m. Robert McCoy; removed in 1816 to Jefferson county, Ohio; thence in 1828 to Perry township, Tuscarawas county, Ohio, where she d. June, 1849; had issue: 1. Andrew, b. June 14, 1796, in Lancaster county, Penn.; d. Sept. 30, 1872, at Smithfield, Ohio; removed in 1816 to Jefferson county, Ohio; m. (1st) Jane Reed, a native of Jefferson county; m. (2d) June 9, 1844, Nancy Mayes, b. Sept. 15, 1815; d. June 17, 1859; had issue, among others: 1. Robert-McCoy, b. March 19, 1849, near Bethel, Ohio; a Presbyterian minister; m. Sept. 27, 1881, Janet E. McCoy, daughter of Matthew McCoy, of Archer township, Harrison county.

Joseph Mayes, father of Nancy Mayes Coulter, was b. June 6, 1785, in Washington county, Penn., of Scotch-Irish descent; settled near Folks' Station,

Green township, Harrison county, where he d. Dec. 29, 1845; m. Sarah Miller, daughter of John Miller, of Beech Spring, Ohio.

WILLIAM COULTRAP, a native of Virginia, of Scottish descent, settled in Stock township, Harrison county, Ohio, in 1816, where he d. 1845; m. in Virginia, Mary Woods; d. 1842; had issue: 1. William, b. in Virginia, 1800; d. 1845; m. in Jefferson county, Sarah Moore; b. 1796; d. Sept. 8, 1889 (had issue: i. Nathaniel; ii. Nancy; iii. Mary; iv. Richard-M., b. 1840; m. Mary E. Moore; v. David; vi. Ruth; vii. Oliver; viii. Nathan; ix. William; x. Susannah; xi. Margaret; xii. Charles); 2. Henry; 3. David; 4. Matthew; 5. Elizabeth, m. —— Hall; 6. Sarah, m. —— McGeel; 7. Margaret, m. —— Hall.

JOHN COURTRIGHT, b. in New Jersey, Sept. 7, 1774; removed to Washington county, Penn., and thence to near the present site of Salineville, Columbiana county, Ohio, before 1809; had issue:
I. Jacob-V. II. James. III. Samuel, b. April 30, 1809; removed in 1829 to Carrollton, Ohio, later to Short Creek township, Harrison county, and in 1856 to Smithfield, Jefferson county; m. (1st) 1829, Frances Zollars; d. 1862; daughter of Frederick Zollars, of Harrison county; m. (2d) 1867, Mary E. Stonebraker; had issue by first wife: 1. James; 2. Franklin; 3. Z.-Z., b. July 12, 1832; settled in Freeport in 1875; m. 1858, Mary A. Crew; 4. Vail, settled in Illinois; 5. Mary-Jane, m. George D. Walcott; 6. Charles; 7. Ann-Rebecca, m. Thomas Penny; 8. John; 9. Sarah, m. William Carrick; 10. William, settled in Franklin; 11. Joseph-W., b. Jan. 6, 1847, in Short Creek township; settled in Freeport township; served in the Civil War; m. (1st) Sept. 28, 1866, Letitia Burns; d. Aug. 17, 1875; daughter of John M. Burns; m. (2d) Oct. 15, 1881, Laura Steadman, of Freeport; 12. Melissa, m. Wilson Lugar. IV. Isaac. V. William. VI. Milo. VII. Judith. VIII. Rebecca.

GEORGE COX, see Family of David Smylie.

PETER CRABTREE, a native of England, emigrated to America and first settled in western Pennsylvania; removed to Rush Creek, Jefferson county, Ohio, where he remained until about 1812, and then settled in Nottingham township, Harrison county, Ohio, where he d. 1829; had issue:
I. Rhoda. II. Sarah. III. Rachel. IV. Ann. V. Amy. VI. Cornelius. VII. Gabriel. VIII. William, b. in Pennsylvania, about 1795; m. Rachel Moore, b. about 1811; daughter of Loami Moore, who served in the Revolutionary War; had issue: 1. Sarah; 2. Keziah; 3. John-D., b. June 12, 1825; m. May 27, 1847, Elizabeth Moore, b. Feb. 6, 1829, in Moorefield township, Harrison county, daughter of David and Sarah Kidwell Moore (had issue: i. William; ii. Sarah; iii. Martha; iv. Gabriel; v. Mary; vi. Edmond; vii. Elmer); 4. Loami; 5. Gabriel; 6. Shepard; 7. James, served in the Civil War; 8. William, served in the Civil War; 9. Peter; 10. Mary-A.

WALTER CRAIG, a native of Ireland, of Scotch descent, settled at West Middletown, Washington county, Penn., about 1791; m. in Ireland, Jane McCleon; had issue:
I. David. II. Thomas. III. Ann, b. 1780; d. Aug. 30, 1847; m. John Jamison (see Jamison Family). IV. Rebecca. V. William. VI. John, b. in Ireland, Aug. 1, 1775; emigrated to America with his parents, and afterwards settled at Hardscrabble (now West Alexander), Penn., removed in 1803 to Green township, Harrison county, Ohio, where he d. Aug. 22, 1825; m. in Pennsylvania, Elizabeth Johnson, b. June 23, 1781; d. Feb. 28, 1864; had issue: 1. Jane, b. June 14, 1802; d. 1890; m. Joshua Hamilton; 2. Johnson, b. in Green township, Dec. 19, 1803; d. 1888; m. 1834, Martha Thompson, b. 1810; d. July 16, 1890; a daughter of Samuel Thompson of Green township (had issue: i. John, d. in infancy; ii. Thompson, settled in Nebraska; iii. Rachel-A., m. George W. Brown; settled in Nebraska; iv. Eliza-J., m. M. K. Turner, and settled in Nebraska; v. William-S.; settled in Nebraska; vi. John-A., b. May 6, 1852; m. Oct. 20, 1881, Elizabeth J. Mills, daughter of James and Nancy Davis Mills); 3. Rachel, b. Sept. 16, 1805; d. Aug. 22, 1825; 4. Mary, b. July 16, 1808; m. Nathaniel Gilmore; settled in Ford county, Ill.; 5. Ann, b. Feb. 22, 1811; d. Feb. 27, 1887; m. James Tag-

HARRISON COUNTY GENEALOGIES 481

gart; 6. Rebecca, b. July 27, 1813; m. Andrew Patterson, of Pickaway county, Ohio; 7. William, b. March 15, 1816; d. Feb. 8, 1872, in Fulton county, Illinois; 8. Walter, b. July 4, 1819; m. (1st) 1844, Jane Moore, b. 1824; d. 1859; daughter of William and Sarah Moore, of Green township; m. (2d) 1860, Hannah Henderson, d. 1879; m. (3d) Florence Welch, daughter of William Welch (had issue by first wife: i. Sarah-Jane, d. aged thirteen years; ii. Amanda, m. Cassius M. Nichols; iii. John, settled in Nebraska; iv. Elizabeth, m. W. H. Oglevee, and settled in Illinois; had issue by second wife: v. William; vi. ———, d. in infancy); 9. John, b. July 31, 1822; d. Sept. 16, 1825. VII. Walter. VIII. Jane. IX. Susan.

EDWARD CRAWFORD, b. in Virginia, about 1760; d. in Archer township, Harrison county, 1831; removed there from Brooke county, West Virginia, in March, 1806; m. Mary Wiggins, b. 1770; d. 1864; daughter of Edward and Charity Wiggins, of Brooke county; had issue: 1. Ellen, m. James Hagerty; 2. Mary, m. James Harper; 3. Alexander, d. in Carroll county; 4. Thomas, b. Dec. 3, 1804, in Brooke county, Va.; removed with his parents to Archer township; m. (1st) 1829, Jane Kelly, daughter of Hugh and Mary Kelly, residents of Cadiz; m. (2d) March 5, 1839, Mrs. Eleanor Forbes, widow of Joseph Forbes, a former resident of Harrison county (had issue by first wife: i. Hugh; ii. Edward; iii. Isabella; iv. Thomas; had issue by second wife: v. John-A.; vi. Elizabeth; vii. Jane; viii. Robert; ix. James-F.; x. Jason); 5. Isabella, m. William Welch; 6. Charlotta; 7. Josiah; 8. Nancy, m. William Lewis; settled in Holmes county; 9. Margaret; 10. Elizabeth, m. Joseph McGonigal; 11. John, b. in Archer township, Nov. 29, 1816; m. in 1849, Elizabeth Hedges, b. 1827; d. 1877; daughter of Samuel and Prudy Hedges (had issue: i. Mary, m. Hamilton Lisle, of Archer township; ii. Samuel-E., b. in Archer township, 1853; settled in Cadiz township; m. 1874, Emma E. Barrett, a native of Nottingham township, daughter of William H. Barrett; iii. Alexander; settled in Archer township; iv. Harriet, d. 1878; v. Martha, m. John Holland, of Cadiz; vi. Margaret); 12. Harriet, m. Matthew McCoy, of Archer township. Alexander Wiggins, the father of Edward Wiggins, was of Scotch descent, having come to America from the North of Ireland a short time before Edward was born. Edward Wiggins died in Virginia.

ROBERT CREE, a native of Pennsylvania, m. Elizabeth Villars, b. in Pennsylvania, Oct. 12, 1763; daughter of John and Mary Villars; had issue:
I. Ann, b. Nov. 13, 1788.
II. Mary, b. Dec. 17, 1789.
III. Janet, b. Feb. 5, 1790.
IV. Robert, b. April 12, 1791.
V. George, b. Dec. 28, 1793.
VI. Eleanor, b. April 20, 1795.
VII. John, b. Sept. 18, 1796.
VIII. James, b. in Pennsylvania, May 12, 1798; d. May 16, 1859; removed to Freeport township, Harrison county, Ohio, about 1817; m. Dec. 27, 1817, Sarah Woods, b. March 10, 1803; d. Sept. 23, 1860; had issue: 1. William-A., b. Dec. 31, 1818; d. Oct. 17, 1881; 2. Elijah-W., b. April 22, 1826; d. Oct. 17, 1843; 3. James-H., b. Aug. 29, 1829; d. Dec. 6, 1855; 4. John-W., b. Jan. 30, 1832; 5. ———, b. April 24, 1833; d. in infancy; 6. Thomas-M., b. April 24, 1835; m. March 6, 1859, Caroline A. Grant, b. Nov. 20, 1839; daughter of Mead and Elizabeth Grant, of Carroll county, Ohio; the former d. June 7, 1883; the latter d. Feb. 8, 1886; 7. Sarah-J., b. May 20, 1837; 8. George-W., b. April 4, 1839; 9. Robert-B., b. Nov. 5, 1841; served in the Civil War; d. May 10, 1863, in the army; 10. Mary-M., b. Sept. 7, 1844; 11. Elizabeth-V., b. June 16, 1847.

ROBERT CROSKEY, a native of Ireland, emigrated to America and later, in 1802, removed to Green township, Harrison county, Ohio; had issue:
I. William. II. John, b. in New Jersey, Oct. 7, 1775; d. March 16, 1862; m. in Pennsylvania, Feb. 9, 1801, Catherine Fry, b. June 25, 1781; d. in Iowa, Jan. 22, 1863; daughter of Samuel Fry, a resident of Pennsylvania; had issue: 1. John, b. April 19, 1802; d. Oct. 20, 1867; m. Esther ———; 2. Christina, b. Feb. 13, 1804; 3. Rachel, b. Feb. 22, 1806; 4. Samuel-F., b. Dec. 11, 1808; 5. Sarah, b. Jan. 12, 1811; 6. Jackson, b. Feb. 6, 1815; d. Feb. 7, 1890; 7. William, b. Oct. 11, 1817; m. Jan. 16, 1840, Susan Baxter, b. May 11, 1822, daughter of Samuel P. Baxter, a pioneer of Green township

(had issue: i. Nancy-Jane, b. June 25, 1841; m. Edward Hall; ii. Clarinda, b. Oct. 9, 1846; m. Rezin B. Mansfield; iii. Louisa-Caroline, b. Sept. 9, 1848; d. June 28, 1869; iv. Susan-Amanda, b. Feb. 7, 1856; m. William F. Houser); 8. Abraham, b. Jan. 24, 1820; settled in Chicago; m. Mary Phillips, daughter of Thomas and Elizabeth William Phillips (had issue: i. Thomas, m. Martha Osburn).

WILLIAM CROSKEY, b. in Ireland, 1795; d. 1873; son of Robert Croskey, who emigrated to Maryland, in 1775; removed to Washington county, Penn., and thence, in 1812, to Green township, Harrison county, Ohio; m. 1848, Margaret Crabb, of Jefferson county, Ohio; had issue: 1. Robert; 2. Margaret, m. James Thompson; 3. Henry, settled in McLean county, Ill.; 4. Anna, m. John Clifford, and settled in Green township; 5. Mary, m. George McFadden; 6. Sarah, m. Thomas Groves, of Jefferson county; 7. John, died in infancy; 8. ———; 9. ———.

THOMAS CRUMLEY, a native of Virginia, b. Dec. 31, 1776; d. July 3, 1861; settled near what is now the village of Harrisville, Harrison county, Ohio, in 1802, coming into Ohio with the Dickersons and Dunlaps; m. in West Virginia, Elizabeth Gardner, of English descent; d. 1856; had issue: 1. Samuel; 2. Sarah; 3. Mary, m. Joshua Dickerson; 4. William; 5. Thomas; 6. Ira, b. Oct. 7, 1809; settled near Freeport, in Washington township; m. Jan. 31, 1840, Jane Dickerson (had issue: i. Mary-E., m. David McFadden, and settled in Iowa; ii. Sarah, m. William Wilson, and settled in Freeport, Harrison county; iii. Hiram; iv. Clara; v. Thomas, m. Oct. 9, 1888, Abbie Kirkpatrick, daughter of G. W. Kirkpatrick, of Moorefield township, Harrison county); 7. Elizabeth; 8. John; 9. Hannah, m. ——— Glazener; 10. James; 11. Aaron-W.; 12. Emily, m. ——— Barkhurst; 13. Joseph; 14. David.

ROBERT CULBERTSON, b. in Ireland, 1743; emigrated to Ohio in 1811, and settled one mile northeast of New Athens, in what is now Harrison county, Ohio, where he died Dec. 22-24, 1840; m. (1st) in Ireland, ———; m. (2d) in Ireland, ———; d. aged sixty-seven; had issue by first wife:
I. James. II. John. III. Samuel. IV. Ezekiel; had issue by second wife: V. Thomas. VI. Robert. VII. Benjamin. VIII. William. IX. Hugh. X. Joseph. XI. George, settled in Muskingum county, Ohio. XII. Annie, m. Thomas Pollock, and settled in Guernsey county, Ohio. XIII. Mary, d. aged eight. XIV. Gillespie, b. in Athens township, October, 1816; m. (1st) Dec. 17, 1840, Dorcas Holt, of Guernsey county, b. 1818; d. Aug. 15, 1865; m. (2d) Nov. 8, 1866, Eliza J. Duncan, a native of Guernsey county, daughter of James Duncan (d. 1835), and Elizabeth McKinney Duncan (d. 1861); had issue by first wife: 1. John, b. Sept. 20, 1841, in Athens township; m. Nov. 8, 1866, Sarah Jane McDowell, b. 1845; d. 1890; daughter of William and Hannah Watters McDowell, early settlers in Athens township; 2. Mary, m. Jeremiah Brown, of Monroe township; 3. Sarah-Ann, m. F. M. Cooper, and settled in New Athens; 4. Robert, d. aged seventeen; had issue by second wife: 5. Dorcas-Eliza, m. Samuel A. Kirkland.

JOHN CUNNINGHAM, a native of Ireland, of Scottish descent, emigrated to America, and first settled at Baltimore; thence removed to Fayette and Westmoreland counties, Penn.; d. in Westmoreland county, April 19, 1797; m. Elizabeth ———, d. in Westmoreland county, March 2, 1816; had issue: I. James, b. 1780; d. at Mansfield, Ohio, 1870; served as a captain in the War of 1812. II. Ezekiel, m. Feb. 25, 1813, Mary Dregoo; settled near Chillicothe, Ross county, Ohio. III. David, b. May 6, 1783; d. May 27, 1849; m. (1st) Dec. 23, 1806, in Fayette county. Penn., Mary McLaughlin, b. Sept. 28, 1782; d. April 6, 1829; daughter of John and Elizabeth McLaughlin; m. (2d) Ann Barricklow, b. May 8, 1808; d. Aug. 13, 1887; had issue by first wife: 1. John, b. Oct. 29, 1808; d. Aug. 18, 1870; m. Feb. 3, 1829, Nancy Sharp, b. 1810; d. Oct. 10, 1875; daughter of William (d. 1835) and Mary McFadden Sharp, who removed from Hopewell township (?), Washington county, Penn., to Harrison county (had issue: i. Mary, m. 1850, Eldred Glencairn Holliday, son of Robert and Eliza White Holliday; ii. David, b. March 1, 1837; m. 1859, Laura Phillips, daughter of Thomas and Elizabeth Williams Phillips, natives of Chester county, Penn., who settled at Cadiz about 1820-25. IV. Joseph, d. May 18, 1807. V. Robert, d. in West Virginia.

EMANUEL CUSTER, d. at Jessups, Maryland, of which State he was a native, aged over one hundred years; removed to Harrison county, Ohio, early in the century, afterwards returning to Maryland; had issue:
I. John, a native of Frederick county, Md., d. at Cresaptown, Allegany county, that State, 1830; had issue, among others: 1. Emanuel-H., b. at Cresaptown, Dec. 10, 1806; removed to Rumley, Harrison county, Ohio, about 1824, and later, to Monroe, Mich.; m. (1st) Aug. 7, 1828, Matilda Viers, d. July 18, 1834; m. (2d) Feb. 23, 1836, Mrs. Mary Ward Kirkpatrick, b. near Burgettstown, Washington county, Penn., May 31, 1807; daughter of Thomas and Sarah Ward, of Cross Creek township (she m. 1st, Israel R. Kirkpatrick, and by him had issue: i. David; settled in Wood county, Ohio; ii. Lydia-A., m. David Reed, and settled at Monroe, Mich.) (had issue by first wife, three children, of whom: i. Brice-V., settled at Columbus, Ohio; had issue by second wife: iv. George-Armstrong, b. Dec. 5, 1839; served as general in the Civil War, and afterwards killed by the Indians at the battle of the Little Big Horn, June 25, 1876; m. Feb. 9, 1864, Elizabeth Bacon, daughter of Judge Daniel S. Bacon, of Monroe, Mich.; v. Nevin, b. July 29, 1842; settled near Monroe, Mich.; vi. Thomas-Ward, b. March 15, 1845; lieutenant U. S. A.; killed at battle of the Little Big Horn, June 25, 1876; vii. Boston, b. Oct. 31, 1848; killed at the battle of the Little Big Horn, June 25, 1876; viii. Margaret-Emma, b. June 5, 1852; m. Lieut. ——— Calhoun, killed at the battle of the Little Big Horn, June 25, 1876).
II. Jacob, b. 1790, at Jessups, Md.; d. 1862, in Rumley township, Harrison county, where he had settled before 1816; m. Sarah Webster, b. 1798; d. 1835; daughter of William Webster, a pioneer of Ohio; had issue: 1. William-Webster, b. in New Rumley, July 1, 1816; settled at Scio, about 1850; m. in New Hagerstown, Frances Amelia Phelps, b. in Massachusetts, daughter of Eben and Mary Kibbee Phelps, who settled in Franklin (now Kent), Portage county, Ohio, when Frances was five years old; (had issue: i. Mary-E., m. Dr. D. J. Snyder; ii. Caroline-A., m. W. N. McCormick; settled in Florida; iii. James-A., served in Civil War; killed at Mount Sterling, Ky.; iv. Albert-O., b. 1850; d. April 1, 1870, in Steubenville, Ohio; v. Clarence-P.); 2. Alexander, d. aged four years; 3. Stewart-F., settled in Connotton, Harrison county; 4. John; 5. Henry-L., settled in New Philadelphia; 6. Robert, settled in Scio; 7. Isaac, settled in Westerville, Ohio; 8. Vincent, d. in infancy.
III. Emanuel, d. in Maryland.
IV. Charlotte, b. 1796; d. 1854; m. Robert Cummings, b. 1789; d. 1823.
V. Susan, m. John Hendricks.
VI. Mary, m. Joseph Cummings.

ROBERT DAVIDSON, a native of Pennsylvania, removed to Green township, Harrison county, in 1802; m. about 1804, ——— Croskey, sister of John Croskey, with whom he came to Ohio; had issue: 1. Margaret; 2. Elizabeth; 3. Robert; 4. James; 5. Rachel; 6. William, b. 1822; removed to Iowa in 1877; m. Oct. 10, 1849, Christian Shepler, daughter of Samuel Shepler, of Green township (had issue: i. Samuel-F., b. March 19, 1850; m. Nov. 18, 1869, Caroline M. Bell, daughter of Francis Bell, a resident of Wayne township, Jefferson county, Ohio; ii. James-H.); 7. Mary.

SAMUEL DAVIDSON, b. in Allegany county, Md., 1771; was one of a family of thirteen children; his father was a native of Ireland, who emigrated to Maryland; settled in Washington township, Harrison county, Ohio, in 1812, where a cousin had preceded him; m. Mary Drake, a native of Pennsylvania; had issue:
I. Lewis. II. Jesse. III. Jonah, b. in Allegany county, Md., July 4, 1804; d. June 16, 1889; m. 1829, Sarah Joice, d. 1859; had issue: 1. Eliza, b. in Washington township, Oct. 26, 1832; m. Aug. 4, 1864, James Wilson; d. 1873; son of James and Sarah Brock Wilson, natives of Virginia, who were among the early settlers of Moorefield township. IV. Mary. V. Hannah. VI. Nancy.

WILLIAM DAVIDSON, b. Nov. 20, 1747, son of William Davidson, a native of Ireland, who settled in Pennsylvania before the Revolutionary War; m. (1st) Rosanna Hutchinson, a native of

Wales; m. (2d) Barbara McDale (by whom he had issue, five sons and three daughters); had issue by first wife, three sons and two daughters, of whom:
I. Lewis, b. March 23, 1773, in Fayette county, Penn.; removed in 1801 to the present site of Catlettsburg, Kentucky; a year later located on the French grant, in Scio county, Ohio, where he remained until 1809, and thence removed to Freeport, Harrison county, Ohio; served in the War of 1812; m. his cousin, Mary Davidson, b. in Allegany county, Md., Sept. 23, 1778, daughter of Lewis and Nancy Todd Davidson; the former was a brother of William Davidson, Jr.; the latter a native of England. Lewis and Mary Davidson were m. in Fayette county, Penn., in July, 1798; had issue: 1. William; 2. Nancy, d. in Scioto county, Ohio; 3. Rosanna, d. in Scioto county; 4. John-S.; 5. Mordecai-W.; 6. Lewis-H., b. 1809, in Scioto county; removed with his parents to Harrison county; settled in Freeport township, Harrison county; was licensed to preach Feb. 8, 1845; m. Jan. 7, 1830, near Moorefield, Harrison county, Lucinda Latham, b. Sept. 18, 1810, in Fauquier county, Va. (had issue: i. Isaiah, d. in infancy; ii. Lucy, d. in infancy; iii. Sarah, d. in infancy; iv. James-M., killed Sept. 20, 1863, in the battle of Chickamauga; v. Mary, m. —— McPeck, and settled near Jewett, Harrison county; vi. Latham-A., settled in West Milford, Harrison county, W. Va.; vii. Alexander-J., settled in Tucson, Ariz.); 7. Susanna; 8. Mary; 9. Jesse; 10. Thomas-L.; 11. Joseph-C.; 12. Jonathan-S.

JESSE DE LONG (son of Solomon De Long), of French descent, b. about 1776, on Short Creek, Jefferson county, Ohio, where his parents came from Pennsylvania; d. near Dennison, Ohio, May 8, 1882; his family served in the Revolutionary War and the War of 1812; removed to Tuscarawas county, Ohio, where he m. Nancy Wagner; afterward settled near Dennison; had issue, among others: 1. Espy, b. May 11, 1832; removed to Monroe township, Harrison county, Ohio, 1872; served in the Civil War; m. March 6, 1864, Sarah A. Carmack, b. May 1, 1847, in Canal Dover, Ohio, daughter of Jacob and Clarissa Carmack, natives of Maryland.

DANIEL DEWEY, b. in Lebanon, Conn., June 19, 1731; d. March 9, 1816; served as ensign, lieutenant, and captain in Company 4, Twelfth Connecticut Militia, 1767 to 1772; a personal friend of "Brother Jonathan" Trumbull (Governor of Connecticut); m. Feb. 22, 1753, Temperance Bailey, b. Feb. 2, 1731; d. March 31, 1795; daughter of Isaac and Abigail Hunt Bailey; had issue, nine children (Temperance, Esther, Daniel, Eliphalet, Philena, Ebenezer, Joshua, Experience, and Anna), of whom:
I. Eliphalet, b. at Lebanon, Conn., Dec. 13, 1762; d. at Cadiz, 1838; removed to Hartwick, Conn, 1798, where he was instrumental in building Hartwick Seminary; emigrated to Ohio in 1835, where he joined his son, Chauncey, who had preceded him; m. at Lebanon, Conn., Aug. 25, 1793, Rachel Ann Hyde, b. Dec. 3, 1761, at Norwich West Farms, Conn.; d. at Cadiz, 1847; daughter of Silas and Martha Waterman Hyde; had issue, nine children (Eliphalet, Susan, Lucy-Williams, Martha, Chauncey, Josiah, Henry, Harriet and Silas), of whom: 1. Chauncey, b. March 27, 1796, at Norwich West Farms, d. Feb. 15, 1880; removed to Cadiz, September, 1821; m. Feb. 11, 1823, Nancy Pritchard, b. Oct. 27, 1804, at Uniontown, Pa.; d. Sept. 6, 1897; daughter of John and Sarah Bromfield Pritchard (the former a native of Wales, b. 1775; d. 1844; the latter b. 1782); (had issue: i. Eliphalet-C., b. Dec. 16, 1823; d. 1886; m. 1845, Virginia Affleck; ii. Harriet-Eliza, b. 1825; d. 1831; iii. Henry, b. 1828; d. 1830; iv. John-Henry, b. 1830; d. 1848; v. Orville-C., b. Nov. 12, 1833; m. 1868, Elizabeth Good Tingle; vi. Mary-Pritchard, b. March 6, 1836; d. 1869; m. 1857, Edward Fulton Moffett; vii. Martha, b. 1839; d. 1840; viii. Charles-Paulson, b. Oct. 24, 1843; m. (1st) Emma Scott; m. (2d) Mrs. Gertrude Osborne Jewett; ix. Albert-B., b. 1846; m. 1880, Louise Shufeldt, of Chatham, N. Y.; x. Clara-Hyde, m. Charles Mather Hogg. Daniel Dewey (1731-1816) was the son of John (b. 1700; d. at Lebanon, Conn., 1774) and Experience Woodward Dewey (m. 1726); grandson of Josiah (b. 1666 at Northampton, Mass.) and Mehitable Miller Dewey (m. 1691); and great-grandson of Josiah (b. at Windsor, Conn., 1641, where he was a fellow-townsman of President Grant's

immigrant ancestor, Matthew Grant) and Hepzibah Lyman (daughter of Richard and Hepzibah Ford Lyman) Dewey. Josiah Dewey, last named, was the son of Thomas Dewey (b. about 1597, at Sandwich, Kent county, England) who immigrated to Dorchester (now South Boston), Mass., in 1630, on the vessel, "Mary and John," with Matthew Grant and others, whence he removed to Connecticut, in 1635, and helped to found the town of Windsor.

ASA DICKERSON, b. 1814; d. 1864; a native of Washington county, Penn., probably of the immediate family of John or Henry Dickerson; removed to Harrison county, Ohio, where he m. Jane Dunlap, b. in Harrison county, 1814; d. 1873; had issue: 1. Samuel-D.; settled at Peabody, Kan.; 2. William-H.; 3. Sarah-J., m. Adam Dunlap; 4. Lydia-E., m. J. E. Carnahan, and settled in Pawnee county, Neb.; 5. Dunlap, d. in the army during the Civil War; 6. Granville, settled at Maryville, Mo.; 7. Rebecca-Caroline, m. Joseph McFadden Hamilton; 8. Adam-J., settled in Lyons, Kan.

JOHN DICKERSON and HENRY DICKERSON settled in Amwell (now Franklin) township, Washington county, before 1780, John apparently having come from Dunbar (now Tyrone) township, Fayette county, where his name appears on the tax-list in 1772, and where Joshua Dickerson (1740-1827) had settled about 1770; Joshua and John were doubtless brothers, and Henry may have been a third brother, although more probably the son of John.

John Dickerson d. in Washington county in 1785 (before March), leaving a widow, Ruth (d. before December, 1807), and children, of whom the following were mentioned in his will, written more than seven years before his death: 1. Susannah; 2. Henry (may have been the Henry mentioned below); 3. Gideon, d. unm. September-November, 1789; 4. Baruch; 5. Asa, d. January, 1794; m. Lydia ———— (had issue: i. John; ii. William, d. 1860; m. (1st) Sarah Jolly; m. (2d) Martha Clark); 6. Drusilla.

Henry Dickerson, of Morris township, d. before Aug. 13, 1825; m. Ann ————; had issue: 1. Joshua, b. in Washington county, May 3, 1781; d. April 30, 1853; m. (1st) Margaret McPherson; m. (2d) Cornelia Craig (had issue: i. Joshua-D.; ii. Nancy; iii. Alexander; iv. John, b. April 13, 1810; d. April 10, 1865; m. [1st] Mary Adams, daughter of Robert; m. [2d] Mary Johnson; v. Jane, m. Samuel Walters; vi. Ruth, m. Lewis Barker; vii. Henry; viii. Lydia, m. Howard Trusell; ix. Margaret, m. William Hazlett; x. Matilda); 2. George; 3. Gideon, m. Eliza Gunn, and removed to Ohio; 4. Henry, m. Catharine Beck, and removed to Illinois; 5. Leonard, m. Susan Wolf, and removed to Ohio; 6. Asa; 7. Margaret, m. ———— McLaughlin; 8. Ruth, m. ———— Reynolds.

JOSHUA DICKERSON, b. 1740; d. in Fayette county, Penn., Oct. 10, 1827; came from New Jersey; settled on what is now called Dickerson's Run, in Dunbar township, near East Liberty, Fayette county, Penn., about 1770; here, in 1780, he built a grist-mill on the site of the mill now owned by the Oglevee brothers; from this settlement and its vicinity emigrated to Harrison county the families of Dunlap, Oglevee, Barricklow, Rankin, and others; Joshua Dickerson had six sons, Thomas, William, John, Joshua, Levi, and Eli, all of whom removed to Ohio near the beginning of the present century. Joshua Dickerson also had, among other daughters, one, Sarah, who m. Samuel Dunlap; of the sons:

Eli, b. 1768; d. in Harrison county, Nov. 24, 1834; m. Mary ————, b. 1776; d. April 28, 1831.

Thomas, b. May 19, 1764; d. Dec. 24, 1852; m. in Fayette county, Mary Curry, b. Jan. 16, 1766; d. March 30, 1853; emigrated to Harrison county about 1802, and settled at the present site of Dickerson's church; had issue:

I. Baruch, b. May 21, 1786; d. Oct. 2, 1824; m. in Harrison county, Elizabeth Holmes, b. near Wellsburg, W. Va., daughter of William Holmes and sister of Joseph Holmes; served as a captain in the War of 1812; had issue: 1. Joshua, b. Nov. 9, 1808; m. (1st) 1834, Elizabeth Crumley (d. 1839), whose parents removed from Western Virginia to Harrison county early in the century; m. (2d) Mary Elliott, b. Dec. 10, 1820, daughter of Samuel (d. 1828) and Nancy Grimes (d. 1830) Elliott, of Belmont county (had issue by second wife: i. Aaron-M., b. 1845; d. 1875; ii.

Baruch, b. 1846; d. 1864; iii. Thomas; settled near Flushing, Ohio; iv. Sarah; v. Elizabeth; vi. Theodore; vii. Samuel, d. in infancy; viii. Hiram, settled near New Athens; ix. Charles, settled in Colorado); 2. Susanna, m. Edward Lafferty; 3. Mary, d. in infancy; 4. Thomas; 5. Mary, m. Arrison Shotwell, and settled at Glenville, Ohio; 6. Jane, m. Ira Crumley, and settled in Washington township; 7. William-Wilson, b. April 12, 1818; settled in Athens township; m. Oct. 17, 1839, Susan McCoy, daughter of Thomas McCoy, of Athens township (had issue: i. Baruch, d. in infancy; ii. Thomas, d. in infancy; iii. Hannah; iv. Granville; v. Winfield; vi. William; vii. Elizabeth; viii. Clara; ix. Alvin); 8. Elizabeth, m. Daniel Clemens; 9. Baruch, d. in infancy.

II. Joshua, b. in Fayette county, Penn.; d. April 12, 1850; m. Sarah Dunlap, b. 1779; d. Feb. 25, 1871; had issue: 1. Rebecca, m. Samuel Porter; 2. Joshua; 3. Adam; 4. John, b. Aug. 10, 1810; d. Feb. 20, 1878; m. Elizabeth McFadden, d. March 21, 1887, daughter of Samuel McFadden of Cadiz township (had issue: i. Joshua; b. Dec. 15, 1832; ii. Elizabeth, b. March 2, 1834; m. Thompson McFadden; iii. Sarah, b. Sept. 24, 1836; m. Jacob Webb; iv. Jane, b. April 24, 1838; m. Hiram Lafferty; v. Samuel-C., b. May 19, 1840; vi. John-J., b. April 29, 1842; vii. Rebecca, b. Nov. 16, 1843; m. Joshua Dickerson; viii. Margaret, b. March 20, 1845; m. Samuel B. Porter; ix. William-N., b. Dec. 3, 1846; settled near New Athens; m. Oct. 14, 1880, Mary B. McFadden, b. July 19, 1857, daughter of Robert and Rebecca Dunlap McFadden; x. James-M., b. Dec. 2, 1848; xi. Susan-C., b. Dec. 26, 1851; m. Gilmer Richey; xii. Mary-A., b. May 2, 1853; m. Watson Dunlap); 5. Susan; 6. Sarah; 7. William, b. Oct. 7, 1815; m. (1st) 1838, Jane Lafferty, b. 1817; d. Sept. 11, 1864; daughter of Samuel Lafferty, of Moorefield township; m. (2d) Mary McMillan; m. (3d) 1881, Margaret Bartow (had issue by first wife: i. Samuel; ii. Joshua, b. Sept. 2, 1842; m. 1864, Rebecca Dickerson, daughter of John and Elizabeth McFadden Dickerson; iii. William, settled in Moorefield township; iv. John, settled in Illinois; v. Joseph-B., b. Oct. 30, 1848; m. 1874, Mary Barrett, daughter of Erasmus Barrett, of Cadiz township; vi. Margaret, m. John Dickerson, and settled in Kansas; vii. Sarah, m. ——— Scott; viii. Mary, m. John Lafferty; ix. Edward); 8. Mary, m. William Knee; 9. Jane, twin sister to Mary.

III. Thomas, settled in Harrison county.
IV. John.
V. Joseph, b. 1796; d. in New Athens, 1877; m. (2d) Mrs. Sarah Ann Cannon Mills, b. July 27, 1820.
VI. Eli.
VII. Levi.
VIII. Hiram.
IX. Jane.
X. Susan.

JOHN DOWNS, a native of Ireland; settled in Pennsylvania before 1800; removed to Carroll county, Ohio, where he died; has issue, among others: 1. Richard, b. in Pennsylvania, 1800; d. 1860, in Stock township, Harrison county, where he came from Carroll county, before 1832; m. in Stock township, Elizabeth McKinney, b. in Ireland; d. Jan. 19, 1886; daughter of George McKinney (had issue: i. Mary-J., m. Percival Adams; ii. George-M.; iii. John; iv. James; v. John-F., b. March 2, 1832; m. Nov. 9, 1860, Sarah West; d. May 18, 1879; daughter of Amos West; vi. Richard; vii. Margaret).

George McKinney, father of Elizabeth McKinney Downs, was a native of Ireland; settled in Stock township, Harrison county, before 1832, where he d. 1845; his wife d. 1841; had issue: Elizabeth, John, Nancy, Jane, George, Fryer, James.

ADAM DUNLAP, b. 1752; d. Jan. 10, 1830; removed from Dunbar township, Fayette county, Penn., to Athens township, Harrison county, before 1809; m. Rebecca Work, b. Dec., 1745; d. March 9, 1846; had issue:

I. Samuel, b. Sept. 11, 1772; d. Oct. 2, 1839; settled in Athens township, Harrison county, Ohio, before 1805; m. about 1800, Sarah Dickerson, a native of Fayette county, Pa.; d. Nov. 11, 1858; daughter of Joshua Dickerson; had issue, among others: 1. ———, m. Nelson Pearce, and settled in Cadiz township; 2. Adam, b. April 8, 1805; d. Feb. 20, 1883; m. (1st) Margaret Thompson; b. 1824; d. 1863; daughter of David Thompson; m. (2d) Elizabeth J. Sprott, b. 1829; d. 1871 (had issue by first wife: i. Sarah, m. John Porter; ii. Martha, m. Samuel Porter; iii. Mary,

m. J. D. Barricklow; had issue by second wife: iv. Nancy, m. A. Farrell, and removed to West Virginia; v. Samuel, d. Jan. 4, 1859; vi. Elizabeth-J., m. Robert Holliday, and settled in Moorefield township; vii. Amanda-Adaline, m. Henry Barto; viii. John-A., b. Dec. 11, 1859; m. Mary H. Chaney, daughter of James and Margaret Chaney; ix. William-S.; x. Clara-B., d. young).

II. William, b. 1780; d. Feb. 24, 1865; settled on the Brushy Fork of Stillwater Creek about 1812-13, later returning to Fayette county, Penn., and thence removing to Belmont county, Ohio; m. Margaret Rankin, b. in Fayette county, Penn., 1787; d. May 19, 1838; had issue: 1. Adam, settled in Missouri; 2. James; 3. William, settled in Missouri; 4. Samuel, b. June 25, 1825; removed to Belmont county, Ohio; m. (1st) 1844, Elizabeth Jane Bethel, b. 1827; d. 1858; daughter of James and Mary Brock Bethel; m. (2d) 1859, Mary E. Bethel; d. 1872; daughter of John and Elizabeth Oglevee Bethel (had issue by first wife: i. William-J.; ii. Margaret, m. A. Dunlap; iii. Lycurgus-M.; iv. Thomas-A.; v. Joseph-C.; had issue by second wife: vi. O.-E.; vii. Eliza-J., m. ——— Compher; viii. Isaac-E.; ix. Samuel-A.; x. Cora-B.); 4 Margaret; 5. Rebecca.

III. John, b. Jan. 28, 1787; d. Feb. 24, 1874; m. Nancy Dickerson, a native of Fayette county, Penn.; had issue: 1. Adam; 2. Susan; 3. Mary; 4. Rebecca; 5. Joshua, b. 1822; d. Sept. 4, 1879; m. 1847, Nancy G. Watson; d. 1884; daughter of Robert S. Watson (had issue: i. Watson, b. Oct. 13, 1849; m. Sept. 4, 1874, Mary A. Dickerson; ii. Adam-C.; iii. Rachel-A., m. J. L. Scott, and removed to Missouri; iv. Mary-J., m. Winfield Scott, and removed to Missouri; v. Louisa-B., m. John Webb; vi. Susan, m. John P. Dunlap); 6. John.

IV. Adam, b. Sept. 15, 1790; d. Sept. 20, 1863; m. 1817, Jane Patterson; had issue: 1. Joseph, b. June 29, 1818; m. February, 1846, Julia Ann Hayes, d. Sept. 3, 1878; daughter of John and Hannah Hayes, natives of Pennsylvania (had issue: i. Adam-B.; ii. John-A.; iii. Harriet-J., m. Israel Howells; iv. Patterson; v. William-H.; vi. Harriet-F., m. Israel Shepard; vii. Mary, m. John Stephenson; viii. A.-M., b. 1860; m. Laura J. Moore, daughter of R. L. and Sophia Moore; ix. James-V.; x. Cora-B.; xi. Robert-S.; xii. LeGrand-E.); 2. Hugh-B., b. Feb. 15, 1820; m. Feb. 15, 1844, Elizabeth Dunlap, daughter of Joseph and Sarah Gilmore Dunlap (had issue: i. Sarah-J., m. Samuel Clemens; ii. Joseph-G.; iii. Mary-E.; iv. William-A.; v. John-P.); 3. Rebecca, d. in infancy; 4. Nancy; 5. Mary-J.; 6. Sarah-A., b. 1828; 7. Adam, b. 1834; 8. Patterson; 9. Samuel; 10. John; 11. Robert; 12. William.

V. Joseph, b. in Fayette county, Penn., Oct. 12, 1792; d. March 23, 1878; m. (1st) 1819, Sarah Gilmore, b. Jan. 14, 1800; d. May 18, 1837; daughter of Samuel and Elizabeth Buchanan Gilmore; m. (2d) Mary Anne Roberts, d. 1856; m. (3d) 1859, Susan Webb; had issue by first wife: 1. Samuel, b. May 20, 1820; d. Oct. 19, 1889; m. Oct. 22, 1844, Mary Rea, b. Dec. 14, 1821, daughter of Joseph and Jane McConnell Rea, of Green township (had issue: i. Martha, m. J. McKibben; ii. Sarah, m. ——— Dickerson; iii. Mary, m. H. Dunlap, of Athens township; iv. Clara-B.); 2. Joseph, b. May 30, 1834; m. 1855, Elizabeth Dickerson, daughter of Adam Dickerson (had issue: i. Sarah, b. 1856; ii. Jane, b. 1858; iii. Lee-D., b. 1861; iv. Crittenden, b. 1862).

VI. Robert, b. May 11, 1794; d. March 2, 1860; m. 1819, Mary Patterson, d. Sept. 29, 1852; daughter of Hugh and Nancy Patterson, natives of Ireland, who emigrated to Pennsylvania, where the father died; had issue: 1. Adam, b. Oct. 2, 1820; d. 1895; m. (1st) 1845, Margaret McFadden, d. 1863, daughter of Samuel McFadden; m. (2d) 1874, Sarah Jane Dickerson, d. 1875 (had issue by first wife: i. Robert, b. Nov. 14, 1845; m. April 20, 1871, Margaret McFadden, daughter of John J. McFadden, of Athens township; ii. Samuel, b. Nov. 13, 1847; m. March 16, 1876, Annie R. McFadden, daughter of John J. McFadden; iii. Mary; iv. Elizabeth; v. A.-J., b. June 14, 1859; m. June 9, 1887, Annie McAdam); 2. Hugh-Patterson, b. Oct 17, 1822; d. March 29, 1894; m. 1856, Sarah Jane Kennedy, b. 1832; daughter of Napoleon B. and Mary Gilmore Kennedy (had issue: i. Robert-Kennedy; ii. Mary, m. William B. Scott, and removed to Missouri; iii. John-A., d. young; iv. Joseph-B.; v. Amanda-B; vi. Samuel-P.; vii. Albert-C.); 3. Samuel, b. Dec. 24, 1825; d. June 29, 1882; m. 1857, Mary J. Dunlap; d. 1900; daughter of Adam Dunlap (had issue: i. William-F., b. Aug. 2, 1858; m. Oct. 29, 1885, Mary H. Dunlap, daughter of Samuel Dunlap, of Nottingham township; ii. Emily-J.; iii. James-P.); 4. Nancy; 5. Rebecca; 6. Mary; 7. Robert.

VII. Mary, b. 1788; d. March 22, 1858; m. John McFadden, son of John and Margaret Sharp McFadden (see McFadden Family).

VIII. Sarah, b. Dec. 31, 1779; d. Feb. 25, 1871; m. Joshua Dickerson (see Family of Joshua Dickerson).

IX. Esther, m. ——— Rankin.

X. Rebecca, b. March 31, 1786; d. March 24, 1864; m. (1st) ——— Rankin; m. (2d) Alexander (?) Hamilton.

XI. Rachel, m. Baruch Oglevee.

JAMES EDGAR, of Scotch-Irish descent; removed from Washington county, Penn., to Wellsburg, Va., and thence to Nottingham township, Harrison county, Ohio, where he died in 1845; had issue:

I. James, b. in Washington county, Penn., Feb. 22, 1794; d. March 16, 1882; m. Charity Bartow, b. in Washington county, N. Y., July 24, 1798; d. March 16, 1882; daughter of Zenas and Elizabeth Carpenter Bartow (the former born about 1750, was an officer in the Revolutionary War, and settled about 1809 at Connotton, Harrison county, Ohio); had issue: 1. ———, d. in infancy; 2. Elizabeth; 3. Adam; 4. Cyrus, settled in Monroe county; 5. Margaret; 6. James, killed in the Civil War; 7. Phœbe, m. ——— Petty; 8. Francis; 9. Matilda, m. ——— Kidwell; 10. Elijah-G.; 11. Charity, m. ——— Hanlon; 12. Samuel-D., b. Aug. 30, 1842, in Monroe county, Ohio; settled in Nottingham township, Harrison county; served in the Civil War; m. Jan. 14, 1869, Susan Poulson, b. March 14, 1852, in Nottingham township, daughter of John and Rachel Rogers Poulson.

II. Jane. III. William. IV. Adam. V. Elizabeth. VI. Nancy.

ANDREW EKEY, see Family of Obediah Holmes.

JOHN ELDER, see Family of William Scott.

SAMUEL ELLIOTT, a native of Ireland, emigrated to America, and, about 1800, settled in Belmont county, Ohio; m. (1st) Mary Grimes; m. (2d) ———; had issue by first wife: 1. Joseph, settled in New Athens, Harrison county; 2. Samuel, b. in Belmont county, about 1817; settled in Short Creek township, Harrison county, in 1847, where he died Jan. 15, 1884; m. 1845, Sarah Thomas, b. Oct. 28, 1828 (had issue: i. Mary-Elizabeth, settled in Guernsey county, Ohio; ii. Hameline, settled near Cadiz, Ohio; iii. Martha-J., m. ——— Thomas, and settled near Mount Pleasant, Jefferson county; iv. Susann-A., m. ——— Anderson, and settled in Short Creek township; v. Reason-Wilson, settled near Harrisville, Ohio; vi. Malinda, m. Samuel Brokaw, and settled in Belmont county; vii. Aaron, settled in Short Creek township; viii. Harvey, b. 1864; d. 1883; ix. Taylor); 3. James; 4. Mary, m. Joshua Dickerson; 5. Nancy, m. Joshua B. Dickerson, and settled in Short Creek township.

Isaac Thomas, a native of Virginia, father of Sarah Thomas Elliott, was one of the first settlers of Short Creek township, Harrison county, Ohio, locating there in the early part of the century; had issue: 1. Peter; 2. Isaac, b. 1785; d. 1867, in Washington county, Iowa, where he had settled in 1843; m. Elizabeth Holmes, b. 1800; d. 1852 (had issue: i. Aaron; ii. Asa; iii. Abram, a Methodist Episcopal minister; iv. John, settled in Iowa; v. Taylor; vi. William, settled in Colorado; vii. Sarah, b. Oct. 28, 1828; m. Samuel Elliott; viii. Susan, m. David Twinand); 3. Susan; 4. Ruth; 5. Anna; 6. Sarah; 7. Aaron.

JOHN ENDSLEY, see Family of George McPeck.

PATRICK ENGLISH, a native of Great Britain, served in the Revolutionary War, and afterwards settled at Redstone, Fayette county, Penn.; thence removed to Cadiz, Harrison county, Ohio; from there he went to Coshocton county, where he died; had issue, among others:

I. James, b. Oct. 17, 1791, either in Virginia, or Baltimore county, Md.; d. in North township, Harrison county, Ohio, June 6, 1869; m. (1st) Jane Pickens, d. 1842; m. (2d) Ann McCarroll, b. Jan. 25, 1809; d. Oct. 17, 1884 (daughter of John McCarroll, a native of Scotland, who died in Harrison county); had issue by first wife: 1. Talitha; 2. John, settled in Tuscarawas county, Ohio; 3.

HARRISON COUNTY GENEALOGIES 489

James, d. aged seventeen; 4. Matthew, settled in New Philadelphia, Ohio; 5. Thomas, served in the Civil War; d. at Nashville, Tenn; 6. Susannah; 7. Alpha, settled in Iowa; 8. Nelson, d. in Iowa; 9. Nancy, m. William Donaldson, and settled in North township; 10. William, settled in Kansas; 11. Jane, m. Samuel McLean, and settled in Iowa; 12. Alexander, settled in Harrison county; 13. James (second), settled in Brilliant, Ohio; 14. Mary-E., m. John Morgan, and settled in Iowa; had issue by second wife; 15. Martha, b. July 2, 1845; m. James Price; settled in Leesville, Carroll county, Ohio; 16. George, b. Feb. 11, 1847, settled near Scio; m. Sept. 4, 1877, Julia A. Lewis, daughter of Griffin Lewis, of Jefferson county, Ohio; 17. Isaiah, b. Dec. 5, 1848; settled in North township; 18. Malida, b. Aug. 17, 1850; m. T. W. Smith, and settled in North township; 19. Scott, b. Aug. 13, 1852, in North township, where he settled; m. Oct. 29, 1879, Ida Masters, daughter of Isaac and Ann Overholtz Masters.

JAMES ERVIN, a native of Maryland, settled in Short Creek township, Harrison county, Ohio, about 1812; afterward removing to Franklin township, Harrison county, where he d. 1850; m. in Maryland, Elizabeth Bann, d. 1870; had issue: 1. William; 2. James; 3. John; 4. Henry, b. April 6, 1815; settled in Washington township; m. 1840, Elizabeth Watts, of Harrison county (had issue: i. James; ii. John; iii. Mahala; iv. Ann; v. Margaret-H.; vi. Sarah-J.; vii. Isabelle; viii. Thomas; ix. Actia-A.); 5. Phœbe; 6. Isaac; 7. Nancy.

JOHN ESTEP, d. aged about eighty-four years; removed from Pennsylvania to Short Creek township, Harrison county, Ohio, before 1826; m. in Pennsylvania, Sarah Smith; d. aged about eighty-four years; daughter of Edward Smith; had issue: 1. Harrison, settled at Lloydsville, Ohio; 2. William, a physician, settled in Lloydsville; 3. Robert; 4. Harriet, m. Taylor Lynn; 5. Andrew, b. 1826; settled in Kansas City, Mo., where he d. 1884; m. 1850, Sarah Henderson, daughter of Andrew and Martha Nichol Henderson.

The Nichol family was of Scotch origin; during the religious persecution in Scotland they passed from Scotland to county Derry, Ireland, thence emigrated and settled in Cumberland county, Penn., 1789; afterward located in Westmoreland county, Penn.; and about 1800 removed to Colerain township, Belmont county, Ohio; the parents of Martha Nichol Henderson were Andrew (1798-1861) and Jeanette (b. 1801) Nichol. Andrew and Martha Nichol Henderson had issue: 1. Martha; 2. John-N.; 3. Anna; 4. Agnes, m. Thomas Love, and settled at Aledo, Ill.; 5. Margaret, m. Robert C. McConnell, and settled at Brady, Ohio; 6. Mary-J., m. John Mintier, and settled at Shepherdstown, Ohio; 7. Andrew-Jackson; 8. Sarah, m. Andrew Estep; 9. Isabelle, m. John Anderson, and settled in Iowa; 10. Andrew, settled at Hardy, Neb.; 11. Elizabeth, m. R. W. Castle, and settled in Iowa; 12. Harriet, m. John Sweeney, and settled in Iowa; 13. William-T.; 14. Thomas-Jefferson; 15. M.-N.

ROBERT ESTEP, a native of New Jersey, settled in Peters (now Union) township, Washington county, Penn., before 1784; had issue, thirteen children, among whom: 1. Nathan, died without issue; 2. William (had issue, among others: i. Joseph); 3. Ephraim (had issue: i. Elmira); 4. James-S., a Baptist minister; m. Sarah Gaston (see Gaston Family), b. about 1808; d. 1875; daughter of Samuel and Margaret Penny Gaston, of Peters township (Samuel, b. 1772; d. 1853; son of John and Charity Cheeseman Gaston, who removed to Washington county from Upper Freehold township, Monmouth county, N. J., before 1783); (had issue, at least six children, of whom: i. Josiah-Morgan, b. Feb. 19, 1826; d. May 5, 1888; settled in Cadiz, Ohio, about 1853; m. 1857, Amanda J. Crabb, b. September, 1837; d. March 23, 1898; daughter of Jacob and Jane D. Crabb; ii. Harrison, removed to Marion, Ind.; iii. James, removed to Marion, Ind.).

ISAAC FINICAL, a native of Pennsylvania, of German descent, b. 1779; removed from Washington county and settled in Cadiz township, Harrison county, Ohio, in 1831; afterwards removed to Short Creek township, where he d. 1854; m. in Pennsylvania, Margaret Anderson, b. 1797; d. 1885; daughter of Robert Anderson, of Washington county, who served in the Revolutionary War; had issue: 1. Eliza-May, m. William Spiker; 2. Margaret, m. Alexander Henderson; 3. Jane, m. William Miller; 4. Frances-C., m. David Stewart; 5. Mary-E., m. Calvin Rodgers; 6. Rachel-A., d. in infancy; 7. Robert; 8. John, b. in Washington county, Penn., April 4, 1829; m. April, 1856, Martha Irwin, daughter of William Irwin, who afterwards removed to Iowa (her mother was a native of Ireland, her family having settled in Harrison county when she was six years of age); 9. Thomas.

MICHAEL FINLEY, b. in Scotland or Ireland about 1680-90; emigrated from county Armagh, Ireland, to America, landing at Philadelphia Sept. 28, 1734, with his wife and seven or eight sons; first settled on Neshaminy Creek in Bucks county, Penn., afterwards in New Jersey, and later in Sadsbury township, Chester county, Penn., where he lived from 1737 to 1747 or later; had issue, among others:

1. John, b. in county Armagh, Ireland, killed by Indians about 1757-59, in Lurgan township, Cumberland county, Penn., where he had settled near Middle Spring Church before 1744; m. Martha Berkley; had issue: 1. James, settled in upper South Carolina; 2. Mary, m. (1st) John Thompson; m. (2d) James Leonard, d. in South Huntingdon township, Westmoreland county, Penn.,1791; (had issue by first husband: i. Martha, d. unm., aged twenty-eight years; ii. Anthony, m. Rachel Henley, d. in Davis county, Ky., aged seventy-five years; iii. Jane, m. Charles Foster, and both d. 1796 in Cincinnati; iv. Mary, d. 1806; m. Adam Carnahan; had issue by second husband; v. Catharine, m. ——— Williams; vi. Elizabeth, b. March 4, 1772; d. June 25, 1863; m. (1st) March 3, 1796, Capt. Alexander Buchanan, b. 1760; d. May 8, 1810; m. (2d) Nov. 19, 1811, David Compton, of Meadville, Penn., had issue by first husband: Robert; James; Mary; Thomas; Alexander; Sarah; John; and by second husband: Rebecca and Nancy-Hanna; vii. Ann, or Nancy, b. June 7, 1775; d. at Cadiz, Ohio, March 23, 1818; m. Dec. 6, 1796, John Hanna, of Greensburgh, Penn., son of John Hanna, and had issue: James-Leonard, 1797-1820; Catharine, 1799-1801; Mary Leonard, 1800-1820; John-Evans, 1805-1894; Jane-Finley, 1811-1833; Andrew-Finley, 1813-1847, and David-Wilson, 1843; viii. John-Berkley (or Barclay), b. 1777; m. ——— Austin, and removed South; ix. James-Finley, m. Sarah Barber, and settled at Bath, Summit county, Ohio); 3. Michael, b. about 1747; d. near Chillicothe, Ohio; 4. Ann, m. Thomas Johnston, who lived in Westmoreland county, Penn., in 1775; 5. Elizabeth, b. about 1748; m. (1st) John Prebles (or Peebles), m. (2d) William McCracken; m. (3) Capt. William Rippey, of Shippensburg, Penn.; 6. Andrew, b. 1750; d. July 5, 1829, in South Huntingdon township, Westmoreland county, Penn.; served as first lieutenant in the Revolution (8th Pennsylvania, 1777); m. Jane Jack, daughter of John and Eleanor Jack, of Westmoreland county (had issue: i. John, m. Mary Stokeley, daughter of Nehemiah Stokely, of Westmoreland county, and had issue: Nehemiah and Stokeley; ii. Andrew, removed to Indiana; iii. Mary, m. ——— Bell; iv. Nancy, m. ——— Bell; v. Jane); 7. Samuel, b. April 15, 1752; d. April 2, 1829; served as major of a Virginia Cavalry regiment during the Revolution, and as a brigadier-general in the War of 1812; m. May 5, 1789, at Newville, Cumberland county, Penn., Mary Brown, daughter of James Brown (had issue: i. Martha, b. March 16, 1792; m. Rev. W. L. McCalla, of Philadelphia; ii. James-Brown, b. June 7, 1794; d. May 14, 1851; m. (1st) Mary Theresa Brown; m. (2d) Mary E. Moore; lived in Chillicothe, Ohio, until 1829, and at South Bend, Ind., in 1836; iii. Clement-Alexander, b. May 11, 1797, at Newville, Penn.; d. Sept. 8, 1879, at Philadelphia; surgeon-general U. S. A., 1861, and brigadier-general, 1876; m. (1st) Elizabeth Moore, daughter of Samuel Moore, of Philadelphia; iv. Samuel-Berkley, b. Feb. 10, 1800; d. about 1877; thrice married; v. John-Knox, b. Jan. 13, 1806; d. about 1885; m. Margaret Nevin); 8. John, b. 1754; d. 1837 or 1838, in Fleming county, Ky.; served as lieutenant and captain in the Revolution (Pennsylvania Line, 2d, 5th, and 8th regiments, and as major in Wayne's army, 1793); settled at Upper Blue Lick, Ky., before 1800; m. Hannah Duncan, daughter of David Duncan, of Ft. Pitt (had issue: i. David-Duncan, lived in Nicholas county, Ky., as late

as 1871); 9. Clements; settled in South Carolina (?). (See Clements, VI.)

II. Samuel; a minister; b. in county Armagh, Ireland, 1715; d. in Philadelphia, July 17, 1766; m. (1st), Sept. 26, 1744, Sarah Hall, b. 1728; d. July 30, 1760; m. (2d), Ann Clarkson, daughter of Matthew Clarkson, of Philadelphia; President of Princeton College, 1761 to 1766; had issue: 1. Rebecca, b. about 1743; m. about 1760, Samuel Breese of New Jersey (had issue, among others: Elizabeth-Ann., b. Sept. 29, 1766; m. May 14, 1789, Rev. Jedediah Morse, of Connecticut, and among their children was Samuel Finley Breese Morse, of Connecticut, the inventor of the telegraph); 2. Joseph, b. about 1745; d. unm.; 3. Sarah, b. about 1747; m. Isaac Snowden, of Philadelphia; 4. Samuel, b. about 1748; d. unm.; served as surgeon in the Revolution (Massachusetts Line); 5. John-Hall, b. about 1750; served as first lieutenant in the Revolution (Fifth Pennsylvania Battalion, 1776); 6. Ebenezer, b. about 1754; served as captain in the Revolution (on staff of General Smallwood, Maryland Line, 1777); 7. James-Edwards-Burr, b. May 15, 1758; d. June 3, 1819; served as surgeon in the Revolution (Massachusetts Line, 4th, 5th, and 15th regiments), m. Jan. 2, 1798, Mary Peronneau, daughter of Arthur Peronneau, of Charleston, S. C. (had issue: i. Samuel-Benjamin-Rush, a physician; b. Dec. 13, 1801; d. without issue, 1833; m. Mary Ancrum; ii. William-Peronneau, b. Jan. 3, 1803; d. April 9, 1876; m. (1st) Nov. 14, 1833, Clelia Peronneau; m. (2d) Anna M. Harris Gibson; iii. Mary-Hutson, d. young; iv. Sarah-Anna, d. young; v. James-Edwards-Burr, a physician; b. June 28, 1808; d. May 11, 1844; m. Feb. 14, 1832, Maria Ancrum); 8. ——, d. in infancy.

III. William, d. 1800; lived in Sadsbury township, Chester county, 1737 to 1747, in West Caln township, 1750 to 1764, or later; removed from Chester to York (now Adams) county, Penn., after 1764, and thence to Augusta county, Va.; m. (1st) ———; m. (2d) Catharine Culbertson (mother of William and Michael Finley), daughter of Samuel Culbertson, of Londongrove township, Chester county; m. (3d) Ann Cowan, daughter of David Cowan, of Lancaster county; m. (4th) Eleanor ———; had issue by first three wives: 1. William, lived in York county (now Adams county) in 1771; 2. Michael, b. 1744; d. Aug. 13, 1821; m. Nov. 29, 1772, Mary Waugh, daughter of William and Mary Waugh, and removed to Rockbridge county, Va. (had issue: i. William, b. Oct. 4, 1773; m. (1st) June 28, 1796, Margaret Horner; m. (2d) Elizabeth Christian, and had issue: David-Horner; John-Horner; Matilda, m. Rev. James Paine; Drusilla, m. John S. Leech; Elizabeth, m. James Johnston, and Margaret, m. Joseph Bell; ii. Samuel, b. June 9, 1775; m. Sept. 22, 1796, Mary Tate, daughter of John Tate, of Virginia, and had issue: Maria-Waugh, 1779-1849, m. Rev. Isaac Jones; John-T., 1801-1848; Jane-Tate, 1803-1854, m. John B. Christian; George-W., 1806-1834; Nancy McClung, b. 1807; William, 1812-1871; Lavinia, 1812-18; Caroline-Ellen, m. James Harper; Samuel-B., 1818-1874; and Mary McClung, d. 1829; iii. John, b. Sept. 2, 1778; m. April 21, 1807, Ellen Tate, and had issue: Clarinda-J.; Eliza, d. 1856; m. Dr. Thomas S. Bouchelle; Augustus-Washington, 1813-1889; William-Waugh, 1815-1874, and John Tate, b. 1817; iv. Mary, b. Sept. 2, 1778; d. Dec. 29, 1804; m. Aug. 22, 1797, Samuel Patterson, of Rockbridge county, Va.; v. Elizabeth, m. Jesse Scott, and removed to Indiana; vi. Esther, b. Sept. 30, 1780; d. unm., July 26, 1804; vii. Catharine, b. Sept. 30, 1780; d. in infancy; viii. Michael, b. March, 1783; d. June 6, 1823; m. April 26, 1808, Ruth Irvine, and had issue: Augustus-C., 1809-1858; Maria-Waugh, 1812-1891; m. Jonathan Brooks; Caroline-E., 1812-1832, m. Samuel Patterson; and Harriet-Newell, 1822-1842, m. David C. Gilkeson); 3. Aaron, d. before 1794; m. Margaret Withrow; 4. Andrew, b. Feb., 1764; d. May 8, 1844; m. (1st) Ann McClain, of Pennsylvania; m. (2d) Jane Lyle, of Virginia; 5. James, d. young; 6. Samuel, d. young; 7. ——— (a daughter), m. ——— Morrow (?); 8. Margaret, m. 1770, D. C. Humphreys, and settled in Augusta county, Va.; 9. Elizabeth, m. David Blythe, of York county, Penn.; 10. Anna, d. before 1794; m. Robert Campbell, of Berkeley county, West Va.; 11. Susan, m. Robert Rowan, and removed to Ohio; 12. Mary, living in 1794; m. John Martin.

IV. Michael, of Chester county, lived in Sadsbury and West Caln townships about 1737-1758, and in Londonderry township, 1764; m. Ann Lewis, of Chester county; had issue: 1. Joseph-Lewis, b. 1760 (?); d. May 23, 1839; served as lieutenant, captain, and major in the Revolution (Miles' Rifle Battalion, and 13th, 8th, and 2d regiments, Pennsylvania Line); lived in Adams county, Ohio, in 1833 (had issue: i. John-Blair, lived in Lewis county, Ky., in 1841); 2. Ebenezer; a merchant of Baltimore; m. (1st) Jane, daughter of Rev. John McKnight, of Franklin county; m. (2d) Mrs. Catharine (Allen) Marshall, of Kentucky.

V. James, a minister; b. in county Armagh, Ireland, February, 1725; d. in Rostraver township, Westmoreland county, Penn., Jan. 6, 1795; minister of Rock or East Nottingham Church, Cecil county, Md., 1752 to 1783; and of Rehoboth and Roundhill churches, Westmoreland county, Penn., 1783 to 1795; m. 1752, Hannah Evans, b. 1715; d. April 1, 1795; daughter of Robert Evans; had issue: 1. John-Evans, a minister; b. July 6, 1753; d. in Ohio after 1813; pastor of Fagg's Manor church, 1781 to 1793, when he removed to Bracken, Mason county, Ky., and thence to Red Oak, Ohio; m. —— Ruston, daughter of Job Ruston, of Londonderry township, Chester county, Penn.; 2. Samuel-Robert, b. Dec. 19, 1758; d. Oct. 25, 1839; 3. Margaret, b. Sept. 5, 1756; d. May 10, 1836; m. Col. John Power, of Westmoreland county, Penn., b. 1757; d. July 29, 1805; 4. Ebenezer, b. Dec. 30, 1758; d. Jan. 18, 1849; settled on Dunlap's Creek, Fayette county, Penn., in 1772; m. (1st) Jane Kinkaid, b. 1762-4; d. June 5, 1793; m. (2d) Violet Lowrey, d. Nov. 11, 1804; m. (3d) Margery Cunningham, b. 1770; d. Jan. 27, 1822; m. (4th) Mrs. Sarah Jones, b. Sept. 14, 1769; d. Jan. 24, 1848 (had issue: i. John-Evans, b. November, 1783; d. March, 1793; ii. James, b. November, 1784; d. 1861; iii. Elizabeth, b. December, 1786; d. July, 1860; iv. Joseph, b. March, 1788; d. December, 1848; v. Hannah, b. October, 1791; d. March, 1793; vi. Rebecca, b. October, 1795; vii. Hannah, 2d, b. Oct. 10, 1796; viii. William, b. August, 1798; d. January, 1865; m. Rhoda Harris; ix. Samuel, b. July, 1800; d. in Ohio; x. Jane, b. 1802; d. August, 1890; m. —— Hibbs; xi. Ebenezer, b. Oct. 24, 1804; d. Dec. 28, 1891; m. Feb. 9, 1826, Phœbe Woodward; xii. Eli-H., b. April 6, 1807; d. Jan. 7, 1892; xiii. Robert, b. April 1809; d. October, 1874; m. Ann ——; xiv. Margaret, b. Nov. 29, 1810); 5. Hannah, b. June 20, 1764; d. before 1820; m. John Robinson; 6. Joseph, b. Dec. 13, 1766; d. June 3, 1860; m. (1st) —— Veech; m. (2d) Frances Moore; 7. James, b. Jan. 14, 1769; d. Nov. 17, 1772; 8. William, b. June 10, 1772; d. Aug. 20, 1857; m. (1st) Sarah Patterson; m. (2d) Margaret Wilson; 9. Michael, b. March 24, 1774; d. July 29, 1850; m. (1st) Eleanor Elliott, daughter of William Elliott; m. (2d) Mrs. Mary Plumer Smith.

VI. Clements, b. March, 1735; d. Aug. 11, 1775, in South Huntingdon township, Westmoreland county, Penn.; m. Jan. 12, 1761, Elizabeth Carnahan (sister of John Carnahan); had issue: 1. Elizabeth, b. April 9, 176—; 2. John, b. May 18, 1766 (had issue: i. James-Power, b. Aug. 6, 1792; ii. Jane, b. July 16, 1794; iii. Clements, b. Nov. 17, 1796; iv. Mary, b. Jan. 28, 1799); 3. Martha, b. June 12, 1775; d. May 27, 1847; m. 1793, Reynolds Ross, of Westmoreland county; b. in Ireland, April 2, 1755; d. Feb. 11, 1847 (had issue: i. Clements, b. June 6, 1795; ii. John, b. Aug. 31, 1797; iii. Elizabeth, b. Feb. 21, 1800; m. —— Boyd; iv. William, b. Aug. 15, 1803; v. Samuel, b. Sept. 11, 1805; vi. Mary, b. Nov. 29, 1807; m. —— McCurdy; vii. Jane, b. April 5, 1809; viii. Martha, b. March 12, 1811; m. —— Wallace; ix. Andrew-Finley, b. June 4, 1813; d.——; x. James, b. Jan. 27, 1816). It is possible that this Clements Finley was a son and not a brother of John Finley (I.), who married Martha Berkley. John's son removed to South Carolina, but there are many circumstances leading to the conclusion that he may afterwards have settled in Westmoreland county, Penn., and died there in 1775.

HENRY FERGUSON, of Scotch-Irish descent, settled in Indiana county, Penn., about 1778; removed in 1802 to Green township, one mile west from Hopedale, in Harrison county, Ohio; had issue: I. Samuel. II. John. III. Joseph. IV. Thomas. V. Henry, b. in Indiana county, Penn., 1788; d. in Green township, 1863; served in the War of 1812; m. 1810, Elizabeth Johnson; d. 1856; had issue: 1. Vincent, b. July 12, 1812; d. May 20, 1876; removed to Germano, Harrison county, in 1835; m.

March 19, 1835, Mary Amspoker, b. Dec. 21, 1816; daughter of Samuel and Mary Norris Amspoker (had issue: i. Amelia; ii. John-H., b. Jan. 20, 1838, in Germano; served in the Civil War; m. Oct. 6, 1881, Addie Plummer, b. July 18, 1849, in Washington county, Ohio; daughter of Robert L. and Charlotte Faires Plummer; iii. Elizabeth, m. Martin Overholt; settled in Custer county, Neb.; iv. Samuel-J.; v. Mary-Jane; vi. Rebecca-A.; vii. Susan-P., m. Henry Redman; settled in Iowa; viii. Mary-I.; ix. Margaret-A., settled in Iowa; x. Henry-W., settled in Colorado; xi. Sarah-C.; xii. Etta-R.); 2. Samuel; 3. John, settled in Kansas; 4. Isabelle; 5. Mary; 6. Eliza-A., m. ——— Ferguson, and settled in Archer township.

Samuel Amspoker, father of Mary Amspoker Ferguson, settled in Harrison county, Ohio, in 1803, locating five miles north from Cadiz; had issue: 1. John; 2. Alexander; 3. Samuel; 4. Elizabeth; 5. Susan; 6. Mary, m. Vincent Ferguson; 7. Sarah; 8. Charles-N.; 9. James.

DANIEL FIERBAUGH, a native of Germany, settled in Pennsylvania about 1779; removed to what is now North township, Harrison county, Ohio, but afterward returned to Pennsylvania, where he died, his widow settling in Ohio after his death; had issue, among others:

I. David, b. either in Pennsylvania or Maryland, 1787; settled in North township, where he d. June 14, 1864; m. in Harrison county, Magdalena Gundy, b. 1797; d. 1878; daughter of Rev. Joseph and Fannie Coffman Gundy (the former a Mennonite minister, who settled in Harrison county, in 1804); had issue: 1. Frances, m. John Weimer, and settled in Austin, Neb.; 2. Daniel, b. April 27, 1817; d. Oct. 14, 1885; m. 1841, Elizabeth Boor, daughter of Michael and Caroline L. Barence Boor (the former came to Harrison county with his parents in 1838; d. in Defiance, Ohio) (had issue: i. Caroline-L., d. Jan. 26, 1866; m. Rev. B. F. Rinehart; ii. Mary-M., m. Ebenezer W. Laughridge; iii. Michael-B., b. Aug. 7, 1845; served in the Civil War; m. Nov. 18, 1869, Sarah E. Smith, b. 1852; d. Feb. 10, 1890; daughter of Thomas and Mary Smith; the former b. 1809; d. February, 1881; the latter b. 1813; d. 1882; iv. David-G., d. April 13, 1870; v. Clara-E., d. Oct. 27, 1879).

JOHN FIREBAUGH, a native of Pennsylvania, of German descent, b. 1786; d. April 8, 1872, in North township, Harrison county, Ohio, where he had settled before 1825; served in the War of 1812; m. Elizabeth Friend, b. 1793; d. Feb. 19, 1872; daughter of Jacob and ——— Bowers Friend; had issue: 1. Mary, m. John Shiltz; 2. Jacob, m. Catherine McCarroll, and settled on the Kanawha River, Virginia; 3. John, m. (1st) Nancy Capper, a native of Ohio; m. (2d) Amanda Rippeth, also of Ohio; 4. Elizabeth; 5. Catherine, m. (1st) Joseph Heaston; m. (2d) J. Overholtz; 6. Margaret, m. Isaac Heaston; 7. David, b. March 11, 1825; served in the Civil War; m. 1854, Christina Heaston, b. in Monroe township, daughter of John and Christina Heaston, pioneers of Harrison county, both having died in Monroe township (the former a native of Maryland; the latter born in what is now a part of Philadelphia); 8. Samuel, settled in Southern Kansas; m. (1st) Julia True, of Ohio; m. (2d) Jemima Schooly, of Iowa; m. (3d) Emily Tucker, of Kansas; 9. Susan, m. David Addleman; 10. Frances, m. John Heaston; 11. Elias, settled in Nebraska; m. Mary Boor, of Ohio; 12. Sarah, m. Andrew Hale, of Carroll county, Ohio; 13. Joseph, b. 1838; d. Jan. 26, 1879, in Uhrichsville, Tuscarawas county, Ohio.

JOHN FORD, removed from Redstone, Fayette county, Penn., and settled in Nottingham township, Harrison county, Ohio, before 1827; had issue, among others: 1. Lewis, b. in Washington or Fayette county, Penn., 1794; d. in Nottingham township about 1846; m. Rebecca Dodd, b. about 1795 (had issue: i. Slemmons; ii. William; iii. Lewis; iv. Emily; v. Piety-A.; vi. Ruth; vii. John-E., b. in April, about 1832; m. Dec. 2, 1870, Viney R. Hudson, b. in Indiana, June 3, 1843.

ADAM FORKER, b. in Scotland, 1793; d. in Mercer, Penn., 1837; m. Jane Green, d. 1836; had issue: 1. Jacob. b. 1786; d. July 19, 1842; 2. George, b. 1788; 3. Hannah, b. Oct. 21, 1791; 4. Joseph, b. Dec. 30, 1799; d. at Cadiz, 1841; m. Mrs. Mary Cady Conwell, b. in Reading, Penn., 1792; d. 1865; daughter of John and Margaret Parr Cady (had issue: i.

Belinda, m. John Shauf; ii. Mary-Jane, m. Dr. Chalkley Thomas, and settled in Des Moines, Iowa; iii. Henry-G., b. Nov. 19, 1838; d. Jan. 25, 1896); 5. Samuel, b. 1805; d. Sept. 5, 1866; 6. James, d. July 18, 1852; 7. John, d. Jan. 17, 1865; 8. Mary, d. June 14, 1856; m. ——— Harris; 9. Israel, d. April 28, 1866; 10. William, d. April 6, 1871.

ABRAHAM FORNEY, b. 1740; d. Aug. 27, 1824; a native of Germany; m. Susanna ———, b. 1752; d. May 28, 1842; emigrated to America about 1798, and in 1801 settled in Cadiz township, Harrison county, Ohio; had issue: I. John. II. Abraham. III. Catharine. IV. Mary, b. 1775; d. Aug. 5, 1850; m. about 1793, probably near Martinsburg, West Va., Charles Timmons, b. 1751; d. 1820 (see Timmons Family). V. Susanna, m. ——— Rabe. VI. Frederick, b. Aug. 28, 1787, in Germany; removed to Nottingham township, 1827, where he d. 1854; served in the War of 1812; m. Oct. 29, 1812, Deborah Harris, d. June 21, 1873, whose parents were pioneers in Harrison county; had issue: 1. Sophia, b. Sept. 6, 1813; 2. Susanna, b. Nov. 3, 1814; 3. Mary-Ann, b. Aug. 6, 1817; 4. John, b. Nov. 29, 1820; settled at Deersville; m. Nancy Johnson, daughter of Ephraim Johnson, of Moorefield; 5. Eliza-M., b. July 6, 1825; 6. Catherine, b. July 8, 1827; 7. Alice, b. July 4, 1829. VII. Sophia.

JOHN FORSYTHE, a native of Ireland, of Scotch descent, emigrated with his wife and settled in Fayette county, Penn., before 1800; had issue:
I. John. II. Robert. III. Jesse, b. in Fayette county, Penn.; d. in Washington township, Harrison county, Ohio, Nov. 5, 1857; m. (1st) Mahala Patterson, in Pennsylvania, where all his children but the youngest one, were born; m. (2d) 1811, Sarah Colvin, d. June 24, 1854; had issue by first wife: 1. William, b. March 10, 1800; 2. Maria, b. Sept. 25, 1801; 3. Elizabeth, b. Sept. 21, 1803; 4. Matilda, b. Sept. 21, 1805; had issue by second wife: 5. Samuel, b. Jan. 19, 1812; 6. Harrison, b. Jan. 15, 1813; 7. Joseph, b. Dec. 22, 1814; 8. Nancy, b. Nov. 19, 1816; 9. John, b. June 15, 1818; 10. Benjamin-F., b. March 15, 1820; 11. Levi-C., b. Aug. 2, 1822; 12. Rebecca, b. Dec. 1, 1824; d. Aug. 19, 1872; m. Judge Amon Lemmon; 13. Jesse, b. Nov. 6, 1826, in Washington township, Harrison county, Ohio; served in the Civil War; served as a member of the Ohio Legislature, 1877; m. Oct. 26, 1854, Eliza Dean, b. 1829; d. Jan. 17, 1890; daughter of Samuel and Mary Dean, of Cross Creek township, Jefferson county, Ohio. IV. Mary, b. V. Nancy. VI. Elizabeth.

GEORGE FOSTER, a native of England, b. Sept. 24, 1794; settled near Scio, Harrison county, Ohio, 1816, where he d. June 8, 1849; m. (1st) Jerusha Wortman; m. (2d) 1837, Jane Shouse, a native of Pennsylvania, of German descent, b. 1810; d. June 16, 1889; had issue by first wife: 1. George; 2. Jane, m. Joseph Cummings; 3. Jerusha, m. ——— Custer; 4. Sarah, m. ——— Reed; 5. Elizabeth, m. ——— Kent; 6. Lavina; had issue by second wife: 7. Joseph-B., d. Aug. 18, 1889; 8. William, settled in Superior, Neb.; 9. Madison-J., b. June 22, 1842; settled in North township; m. July 9, 1863, Margaret J. Somerville, daughter of Christopher and Jane L. Somerville; 10. John, d. in infancy; 11. David-C., settled at Uhrichsville, Ohio.

JOHN FOWLER, a native of Maryland, whose father was killed in the Revolutionary War, removed to West Virginia in 1800, settling opposite Steubenville, Ohio; afterward located near Hopedale, Harrison county, Ohio, and, before 1819, settled near Hanover, where he died about 1840; m. in Maryland, Mary Huff; had issue, among others:
I. Garrett, b. in Maryland, Feb. 28, 1799; settled in Monroe township, Harrison county, Feb. 15, 1828, where he d. March 21, 1867; m. April 23, 1819, Hannah H. Eagleson, b. near Waterford, Erie county, Penn., March 21, 1805; daughter of John and Mary Simpson Eagleson (the former a native of Maryland; served in the War of 1812, settling near Cadiz, in Harrison county, in 1813; the latter a native of Ireland, her parents having settled in Allegheny City, Penn., where she was married); Garrett and Hannah Fowler had issue: 1. Mary-Ann, m. Joel Cramblet, and settled in Franklin township, Harrison county; 2. John-E., settled in Columbus, Ohio; 3. Asenath-T.; 4. Thomas-E., b. Dec. 6, 1830; served in the Civil War; m. Nov. 27, 1856, Maria McBeth, a native of Harrison county,

daughter of John and Mary McBeth (had issue, seven children); 5. Richard-P., settled in California; 6. Isaiah, settled in Brown county, Neb.; 7. Jeremiah, b. July 10, 1837; m. 1859, Catherine Auld, of Franklin township, daughter of Stewart (b. in Pennsylvania, 1792; d. September, 1883) and Sarah McConnell (d. 1844) Auld; settled in Scio; 8. Joseph-C., b. Aug. 30, 1841; served as an officer in the Civil War; m. Oct. 14, 1869, Maria C. Simmons, daughter of George and Sophia Simmons (had issue, nine children); 9. Malachi, d. in infancy; 10. Joel-C., d. aged four years; 11. Garrett-H., settled in Dennison, Ohio; 12. Clarissa, m. John Spray, and settled in Franklin township.

II. John, d. April, 1847; m. Elizabeth ———; had issue: 1. Andrew; 2. James; 3. John; 4. Mary, m. ——— Cells; 5. Sarah, m. ——— Leaters; 6. Nancy; 7. Hannah.

III. Benjamin, b. in Pennsylvania, Oct. 31, 1802; d. May 15, 1891; settled in Monroe township; m. Jane Whittaker; b. 1793; d. April 20, 1880; had issue: 1. Mary; 2. Jane; 3. John; 4. James-W., b. Oct. 12, 1829; settled in Stock township; m. June 7, 1852, Elizabeth Crawford, daughter of Andrew Crawford, of North township (had issue, nine children); 5. Rebecca; 6. Francis; 7. Benjamin-B.; 8. William; 9. Arabella.

IV. Francis, d. 1838; m. 1830, Mary Giles; had issue: 1. Francis.

V. Joel, m. 1836, Esther Fisher.

VI. Jeremiah.

VII. Cena.

JOSIAH FOX, b. at Falmouth, England, 1763, son of John and Rebecca Steevens Fox; d. in Colerain township, Belmont county, Ohio, 1847, where he had settled in 1814; m. at Philadelphia, 1794, Anna Miller, b. 1768; d. 1841; of German descent; daughter of Peter Miller; had issue: 1. Charles-James, b. in Washington, D. C., 1805; d. 1895; settled in Short Creek township, Harrison county, Ohio, about 1839; m. Feb. 7, 1837, at Flushing, Ohio, Esther Cooper, b. near Baltimore, April 10, 1810; d. 1896; daughter of Nicholas and Sarah Balderson Cooper· (had issue: i. Anna-Miller, m. Lindley M. Branson; ii. William-Spicer, b. 1839; m. 1876, Esther J. Moore, daughter of Jeremiah and Sarah Moore; iii. Sarah-C.; iv. Francis-C.); 2. John, d. young; 3. Elizabeth-Miller, m. Moses Chapline; 4. Anna-Applebee, m. Robert I. Curtis; 5. Rebecca-Steevens, m. Elijah Pickering; 6. John-Charles, d. young; 7. Sarah-Scantlebury, m. B. E. Dungan; 8. Francis-Drake.

JOHN FULTON, b. Aug. 26, 1777, near Havre de Grace, Maryland, of which place his parents were residents, removed in 1816 to Green township, Harrison county, where he d. Oct. 2, 1856; m. Dec. 12, 1799, Lydia Mitchell, b. Aug. 26, 1777; d. July 18, 1844; daughter of Samuel Mitchell, a resident of Maryland; had issue: 1. Mary, b. Sept. 13, 1800; 2. Margaret, b. Feb. 21, 1802; 3. William, b. July 29, 1803; d. July 30, 1884; 4. John, b. Nov. 26, 1805; 5. Elizabeth, b. Dec. 2, 1808; 6. Susannah, b. Jan. 1, 1811; 7. Miriam-Jane, b. Jan. 29, 1813; d. April 13, 1886; 8. Sophia, b. March 6, 1816; d. July 27, 1889; 9. Phœbe, b. July 13, 1819; 10. James, b. Jan. 25, 1825; m. (1st) April 4, 1855, Maria Louisa Simpson Gibson; d. Sept. 30, 1875; daughter of William Gibson, a resident of Holmes county, Ohio; m. (2d) Oct. 12, 1889, Charlotte Branson Pittis, daughter of George Pittis, of Scio (had issue by first wife, eight children).

PHILIP FULTON, b. in Cecil county, Md., June 24, 1777; d. Sept. 14, 1841 (his father, of Scottish descent, had settled in Maryland before the Revolution); about 1805 he removed to Washington county, Penn., thence to Steubenville, Ohio, in 1810, and in 1814 settled in the southeastern part of Nottingham township, Harrison county; served in the War of 1812; m. in Maryland, April 2, 1801, Sarah Hanna, b. in Harford county, Md., May 8, 1782; d. Sept. 3, 1845; had issue: 1. Jane-S., b. Dec. 15, 1801; 2. Alexander, b. in Maryland, Sept. 12, 1803; d. March 15, 1881; m. Nov. 2, 1826, Sarah Ramsay, b. in Maryland, Feb. 12, 1804, only child of Samuel and Elizabeth Cochrane Ramsey (had issue: i. Samuel, b. Aug. 17, 1827; m. March 13, 1860, Caroline Watson, b. Oct. 11, 1838, in Marion county, Ohio, daughter of William and Sarah Kennedy Watson [the former born in Ireland, 1798; d. in Illinois, 1870]; ii. Elizabeth, m. ——— Yarnall, and settled in Moorefield township; iii. Alexander; iv. Albert; v. Philip, settled in Nottingham township; vi. Mary-J.; vii. Sarah-A.); 3. William, b. April 28, 1806; 4. Philip-S., b. July 10, 1808; 5. Hannah, b. Feb. 4, 1811; m. —— Kirkpatrick; 6. Harrison, b. May 11, 1813; 7. Elizabeth, b. Feb. 9, 1815; m. —— Lantz; 8. Sarah-Anne, b. July 20, 1818; m. —— Davison, and settled in Freeport township; 9. Mary-Ann, b. April 14, 1821; m. —— Moore, and settled in Moorefield township; 10. Julianna, b. May 3, 1823; m. —— Pickering, and settled in Moorefield township; 11. John, b. March 2, 1827; settled in Nottingham township; 12. Calvin, b. Aug. 19, 1833.

Samuel Ramsey, father of Sarah Ramsey Fulton, was a son of Charles Ramsey; b. in Chester county, Penn., May 23, 1780; d. in Harrison county, Ohio, March 14, 1858; m. 1802, Elizabeth Cochrane, b. in Chester county, Penn., Oct. 28, 1768; d. Nov. 18, 1857; in 1804 the Ramsey family removed to Allegheny county, Penn., remaining there until 1814, when they settled in Harrison county, Ohio.

JOHN GASTON, b. about 1600, in Scotland (or France), of Huguenot descent; m. in Scotland, and had, among others, three sons: John, William, and Alexander, who emigrated to county Antrim, Ireland, about 1660-1668; of these, probably John (whose name appears on hearth-money rate list for Ireland in 1669, is of Magheragall, county Antrim) had issue, among others, several sons, some of whom remained in Ireland, and some emigrated to America, as did also the sons of other brothers; of the emigrants of that generation the names of eight are known (and the children of William, son of John last named), viz., Hugh of New Jersey, Joseph of New Jersey, Joseph of Pennsylvania (probably a son of Hugh), William of Pennsylvania (probably a son of Hugh), John of New Jersey (probably a son of Hugh), James of New Jersey (probably a son of Hugh). John of Connecticut, Alexander of Massachusetts. Of these, the last two were brothers, and are said by Marshall Gaston's account to have first landed in New Jersey, with one or more other brothers, who remained there; it is probable that they may have been brothers of Hugh and Joseph of New Jersey; they have also been identified in part as brothers of the William who remained at home, his residence being Caranleagh (Carnlough?), Cloughwater, county Antrim (near Ballymena), Ireland. In the account given below, these nine progenitors of the Gaston family in America will be designated as follows:

William Gaston of Antrim (whose children emigrated to South Carolina).
Hugh Gaston (1st).
William Gaston (1st).
Joseph Gaston of Pennsylvania (1st).
John Gaston of New Jersey (1st).
James Gaston (1st).
Joseph Gaston of New Jersey (1st).
John Gaston of Connecticut (1st).
Alexander Gaston (1st).

Another of the Gastons who remained in Ireland (living at Gastontown, Killycowan, county Antrim), had a daughter, who m. Gavin MacArthur; their son, William, b. 1796, emigrated to America after 1818, settling in Vermont; m. Malvina Stone (had issue, among others: i. Chester Alan Arthur, twenty-first President of the United States).

First will be given the family of William Gaston of Antrim, who remained in Ireland, but whose children all emigrated to America and eventually settled in South Carolina.

William Gaston of Antrim, b. at Caranleagh, Cloughwater, county Antrim, Ireland, about 1680-90; d. about 1770; m. —— Lemon; had issue:
I. John, d. 1782; m. Esther Waugh, d. 1789; emigrated to Pennsylvania, and thence removed about 1751-52 to Chester District, South Carolina, settling on Fishing Creek; served as King's Justice before 1776; and as leader of the patriots of his vicinity during the British incursion, 1780-81; had issue: 1. Margaret, b. Aug. 29, 1739; m. James McCreary (had issue: i. John, served in the Revolutionary War, and as a member of Congress; ii. Samuel; served in the Revolutionary War; became a Baptist minister); 2. Martha, b. June 11, 1741; m. her kinsman, Joseph Gaston, great-grandson of the first Irish William (had issue, among others: i. Alexander, m. Mary Blair); 3. William, b. June 5, 1743; served as a captain in the Revolutionary War (had issue: i. William; ii. James); 4. John, b. June 24, 1745; d. about 1806, leaving

descendants, who emigrated to Illinois (had issue, among others: i. William); 5. James, b. April 15, 1747 (had issue: i. Stephen; and several daughters, who removed to Ohio about 1801-02); 6. Robert, b. March 11, 1749; served in the Revolutionary War; killed at the battle of Hanging Rock (S. C.), Aug. 6, 1780; 7. Hugh, b. March 12, 1751; m. his cousin, Martha McLure; removed to Wilcox county, Ala., 1826, and thence to Mississippi (had issue: i. John; ii. Ebenezer; iii. James; iv. William; v. Hugh; vi. Mary; vii. Martha; viii. Esther; ix. Margaret); 8. Alexander, b. Aug. 24, 1753; killed at the battle of Hanging Rock; 9. David, b. July 7, 1755; killed at the battle of Hanging Rock; 10. Ebenezer, b. Sept. 15, 1757; killed at the battle of Hanging Rock; 11. Esther, b. Oct. 18, 1760; m. her kinsman, Alexander Walker, son of ——— and Jane Gaston Walker (the latter a great-granddaughter of the first Irish William); (had issue: i. John-Gaston); 12. Joseph, b. Feb. 22, 1763; d. Oct. 10, 1836; m. 1790, Jane Brown, b. 1768; d. 1858; served in the Revolutionary War, and wounded at the battle of Hanging Rock (had issue: i. John-Brown, b. Jan. 23, 1791; m. Mary Beaufort McFadden; ii. Narcissa, b. Nov. 17, 1792; m. ——— Lewis; iii. Eliza, b. Sept. 20, 1794; m. ——— Neely; iv. Esther, b. Dec. 4, 1796; m. D. G. Stinson; v. Margaret, b. April 29, 1798; vi. Jane, b. Aug. 17, 1800; m. ——— Crawford; vii. James-A.-H., b. Oct. 17, 1801; viii. Robert, b. Jan. 1, 1808).

II. Elizabeth, m. John Knox; settled in South Carolina; had issue: 1. William, a minister, b. 1768; 2. James, a physician (had issue, among others: i. Jane, probably the same who m. Samuel Polk, of Mecklenburg county, N. C., and who became the mother of James Knox Polk, eleventh President of the United States); 3. John; 4. Hugh; 5. Sarah, m. John Johnston.

III. Hugh, d. Oct. 20, 1766, a minister; emigrated to America about 1766, and died at the house of his brother, John, shortly after landing; had issue: 1. William; a physician; b. Feb. 6, 1749; 2. Alecia, b. Feb. 16, 1750; d. 1825; m. ——— Nelson; 3. Martha, b. June 11, 1752; m. James Ross (had issue: i. James, emigrated to America, but returned to Ireland, and settled at Londonderry; ii. ——— (a daughter), m. ——— and had issue, who settled at Baltimore; iii. Hugh-Gaston, emigrated to America, and served in the War of 1812; iv. Rebecca, m. ——— Latimer, of New Jersey); 4. James, b. Oct. 6, 1754 (had issue, eight children); 5. Mary, b. Dec. 7, 1756; d. young; 6. Elizabeth, b. June 16, 1759; m. ——— Rogan, a physician, of the North of Ireland; 7. Thomas, emigrated to America, and settled in New York (had issue, two daughters, of whom: i. ———, m. ——— Lindsay, and settled at Orange, N. J.); 8. Mary, b. April 4, 1763; d. unm.; 9. Hugh, b. April 27, 1765.

IV. Mary, m. James McLure; emigrated to America, and settled in South Carolina; had issue: 1. John; served as a captain in the Revolutionary War; killed at the battle of Hanging Rock (S. C.), Aug. 6, 1780; 2. William; a physician (had issue: i. Hannah, d. 1813; m. 1805, Judge William Gaston, son of Dr. Alexander Gaston); 6. Mary, m. Samuel Lowry; 7. ———, m. Edward Martin.

V. Robert, emigrated to America, and settled on Lynch's Creek, Lancaster county, S. C.; had issue: 1. William, b. July 23, 1755; d. 1838; served in the Revolutionary War; removed to Kentucky, and thence to Walnut Hill, Marion county, Ill. (had issue, four sons and five daughters, of whom: i. Samuel, b. 1826; settled in Marion county, Ill., 1819; ii. William; served in the War of 1812; iii. John, settled in Bond county, Ill.; iv. Robert, settled in Bond county, Ill., 1822; v. Margaret, m. Thomas Kell, and removed to Marion county, Ill., 1822); 2. James; 3. John; 4. Hugh; 5. Joseph; 6. Margaret, d. 1816; m. her second cousin, John McCreary.

VI. Janet, m. Charles Strong; emigrated to America, and settled in South Carolina; had issue: 1. William; served in the Revolutionary War, and killed in that service; 2. Christopher; 3. Letitia, m. her cousin, James Strong; 4. Margaret, m. John Simonton (had issue: i. Charles-H.); 5. Janet, m. ——— Gladney.

VII. William, drowned at Kell's Ford, Chester county, S. C.; m. after his fortieth year, ——— Harbison, sister of James Harbison; had issue: 1. Hugh (had issue: i. William); 2. William, m. ——— Beaufort; removed to Corinth, Miss., and thence to Memphis, Tenn.

(had issue: i. Leroy, a Presbyterian minister).

VIII. Martha, m. Alexander Rosbrough; emigrated to America, and settled in South Carolina; had issue: 1. William-Gaston, a minister; d. unm.; 2. Joseph, removed to Indiana about 1800; 3. Alexander, a physician, m. (1st) Mary Hemphill; m. (2d) Janet Porter (had issue by first wife: i. Mary-Martha; ii. William-Andrew; had issue by second wife, six sons and two daughters, of whom: iii. Alexander-M., removed to California in 1848, and became a judge at Eureka, that State; iv. Joseph-Brown, removed to California in 1848, and thence to Salt Lake City; v. David, settled in Texas; vi. John, settled in Tennessee; vii. Maclin, settled in Tennessee); 4. John, b. 1776; d. 1854; m. Eleanor Key (had issue, four sons and six daughters, of whom: i. John, killed in the Civil War; ii. William; settled at Sardis, Miss.); 5. ———, m. Rev. J. Bowman, and settled in Tennessee.

IX. Alexander, a physician, emigrated to America, and settled at Newberne, N. C., where he was killed by the British and Tories, Aug. 20, 1781; had issue: 1. Jane, m. Chief Justice John L. Taylor, of North Carolina (had issue: i. ———, m. David E. Sumner, of Gates county, Tenn.); 2. William, b. Sept. 19, 1778; d. Jan. 23, 1844; served in Congress, 1813-15; and as chief justice of North Carolina, 1834-44; m. (1st) 1803, Susan Hay, daughter of John Hay; m. (2d) 1805, Hannah McLure; m. (3d) 1816, Eliza Ann Worthington, daughter of Dr. Charles Worthington, of Georgetown, D. C. (had issue by first wife: i. Alexander; ii. Susan, m. Robert Donaldson, of New York; had issue by second wife: iii. Hannah, m. Judge Mathias E. Manley, of North Carolina; had issue by third wife: iv. Eliza, m. ——— Graham, of Maryland; v. Catherine, d. unm.).

Three brothers, Joseph, Robert, and Matthew Gaston, said to be great-grandsons of the first Irish William, emigrated to South Carolina, with their sister, Jane Gaston Walker, leaving a fourth brother, Alexander, in Ireland, b. about 1750; d. about 1840; of these Joseph Gaston m. Martha Gaston, daughter of Justice John (above).

The name of John Gaston appears on the tax-list of Lurgan township, Cumberland (now Franklin) county, Penn., in 1751, and the name of Robert Gaston on the tax-list of Sadsbury township, Lancaster county, 1754 to 1759. These may have been two of the brothers (sons of William of Antrim) recorded above.

———

Hugh Gaston (1st), b. in county Antrim, Ireland, 1687; d. in Bedminster township, Somerset county, N. J. (buried in Lamington graveyard), Dec. 23, 1772; m. Jennet ———, b. 1698; d. Aug. 1, 1777 (buried at Lamington); took up land in Mount Bethel township, Bucks (now Northampton) county, Penn., Feb. 10, 1746, and June 20, 1751; had probably a sister, Mary, m. to James Cauldwell (who emigrated to New Jersey from the North of Ireland about 1732, and settled on Long Hill addition to Elizabethtown); Hugh Gaston was probably the brother of Joseph Gaston, of New Jersey (1st), and the father of William and Joseph of Pennsylvania, of James and John of New Jersey, and of Margaret, who m. Nov. 8, 1750, Thomas Moffat (d. 1770), of Middlesex county, or one or more of them; also, either the father or grandfather of Hugh Gaston, Jr. (below), and of his sisters, Elizabeth Kirkpatrick and Mrs. William Logan; of these:

William Gaston (1st), took up land in (Upper) Mount Bethel township, Bucks (now Northampton) county, Penn., Feb. 20, 1751, on the same date as an entry made by Hugh (1st) above, of whom he was probably the son or possibly a brother; b. probably 1715-20; killed by the Indians in December, 1755, leaving a widow, who d. before September, 1762, and five children, as follows:

I. John, b. May, 1740; d. Sept. 10, 1823; m. in Monmouth county, N. J., Feb. 4, 1760, Charity Cheeseman, b. March 13, 1734; d. Feb. 15, 1821 (both buried at Mingo graveyard, Union township, Washington county, Penn.; Charity Gaston being the daughter of Joseph Cheeseman of Upper Freehold (now Millstone) township, Monmouth county, N. J., who d. 1783; and probably a descendant of the William Cheeseman who settled at Middletown, Monmouth county, 1667); removed from Monmouth county, N. J., after 1767, to Mount Bethel township, Northampton county, Penn., where he took up 275 acres of land in February, 1772; served as a major in the Revolutionary War; removed, about 1780-82, to Rostraver township, Westmoreland county, Penn., and thence, about 1790, to Peters (now Union) township, Washington county, his wife's sister, Elizabeth Cheeseman, accompanying them; had issue: 1. William, b. July 15, 1761; removed to Ohio; 2. Joseph, b. April 25, 1763; d. Nov. 21, 1821; removed to Abbeville District, South Carolina; served as captain and major of the Savannah regiment in the Revolutionary War, 1782; m. Martha Hutton, and thence, about 1807, removed to Butler county, Ohio (had issue: i. Rebecca, b. Feb. 20, 1784; m. John Kerr; ii. Ann, b. Dec. 16, 1785; iii. Margaret, b. March 17, 1788; m. Ezekiel McConnell; iv. John, b. June 17, 1790; v. Mary, b. Sept. 23, 1792; vi. William, b. April 20, 1795; vii. Joseph, b. Oct. 9, 1796; viii. Matta-Ann, b. Feb. 6, 1799; m. William Hayden; ix. Lydia, b. July 22, 1801; m. Ebenezer Wilson; x. Lucinda, b. May 9, 1804; m. Daniel Symmes; xi. Eliza, b. Feb. 16, 1807; m. Benjamin R. Symmes); 3. John, b. Jan. 7, 1765; 4. Samuel, b. Feb. 18, 1767; d. in infancy; 5. James, b. Feb. 18, 1767; d. April 13, 1813; m. Mary Estep, b. Oct. 10, 1773, daughter of Robert and Dorcas Estep; removed to Hamilton county, Ohio (had issue: i. Nancy, b. March 25, 1794; m. ——— Spencer; ii. Dorcas, b. Aug. 19, 1796; m. David Figley, and settled in Scott county, Iowa; iii. Charity, b. Dec. 1, 1798; m. Enoch King, and settled in Clark county, Ohio; iv. Joseph; a minister; b. March 25, 1801; d. Dec. 6, 1834; settled in Carroll county, Ohio; v. Maria, b. April 6, 1803; d. Oct. 20, 1803; vi. Martha, b. Jan. 20, 1805; m. Enoch King (his second wife), and settled in Clark county, Ohio; vii. Rachel, b. March 18, 1807; d. Oct. 7, 1862; m. William S. Manfull, and settled at Steubenville, Ohio; viii. James-Estep; a minister; b. April 14, 1809; d. at Des Moines, Iowa, 1888-89; removed from Warren, Trumbull county, Ohio, about 1850, to Monmouth, Ill., and thence to Davenport, Iowa, later settling at Des Moines [had issue: Thomas-Kirk; William-Henry; Mary; Joseph-James; John; Sarah-Kirk]; ix. Robert, b. July 25, 1811); 6. Samuel, b. Oct. 10, 1772; d. Feb. 21, 1853; m. Margaret Penny, of Allegheny county, b. 1776; d. Aug. 14, 1841 (had issue: i. John, b. 1800; m. Patience Morrison; ii. Charity, b. 1802; m. Robert Donaldson; iii. Margaret, b. 1803; m. Thomas Perry; removed to near Burlington, Iowa, 1844; iv. Nancy, b. 1805; m. William Peppard, and removed to Ohio about 1837; v. William, b. 1807; d. 1880; m. Eliza Morrison; vi. Sarah, b. 1808; d. 1875; m. Dr. James Estep—afterwards a Baptist minister—d. Feb. 26, 1861; son of Robert and Dorcas Estep, who came from New Jersey [had issue, six children, among whom: Harrison, settled at Marion, Ind.; James, settled at Marion, Ind.; Josiah-Morgan, b. Feb. 19, 1829; d. at Cadiz, May 5, 1888; m. 1857, Amanda J. Crabb]; vii. Eliza, b. 1810; m. Samuel Morgan; viii. Joseph-Smith, b. 1811; d. 1870; m. Jane Hindman; d. 1879 [had issue, among others: Samuel, b. 1831; m. 1st, Martha A. McClure; m. 2d, Amanda M. Way]; ix. Samuel, b. 1814; d. un-m., 1839); 7. Elizabeth, b. May 8, 1778; d. Feb. 28, 1858; 8. Margaret, m. Samuel McClain, a native of New Jersey; settled in Nottingham township, Washington county, Penn., where they d. without issue.

II. William, b. 1742-48; d. in Upper Mount Bethel township, Northampton county, Penn., April-May, 1801; m. Elizabeth ———; had issue: 1. Alexander, m. Huldah ———; resided at Richmond, Lower Mount Bethel township, until after 1811; 2. William; 3. Charles; 4. Margaret, m. before 1806, Elisha Everitt; 5. Elizabeth, m. 1806-07, Simeon Hart.

III. Hugh, b. 1743-48; served in the Revolutionary War from Mount Bethel township; resided in Allegheny county, Penn., in 1795.

IV. Jennet, b. 1744-48; m. Moses Phenix.

V. James, b. 1748-55; lived in Mount Bethel township in 1773.

Joseph Gaston of Pennsylvania (1st), probably a brother of William Gaston (1st) and perhaps a son of Hugh Gaston (1st), d. in Mount Bethel township, Northampton county, Penn., October, 1775, where he had taken up land in January, 1765; served as a King's Justice from 1766 to 1775; m. Isabel ———, d. after 1775; had issue, five children, Hugh, James, Elizabeth, John, and Alexander, who were probably those given below, although it is possible these are not the same (Joseph Gaston's will names his "trusty friends, Hugh Gaston of East Jersey, Samuel Rea, and Major John Gaston of Mount Bethel township" [designated Major John Gaston in executors' deed made in 1779] as his executors, and makes provision for giving his five children an education):

I. Hugh, b. Jan. 18, 1764; d. in Columbiana county, Ohio, June 24, 1839; lived in Bedminster township, Somerset county, N. J., 1787; removed to Washington county, Lycoming county, about 1795-99, and thence to western Pennsylvania and Ohio; m. March 14, 1789, Grace Gaston, his cousin, b. Nov. 25, 1764; d. March 14, 1838; daughter of Robert (II. below) and Rosanna Cooper Gaston (had issue: i. Joseph, b. Dec. 24, 1789; m. Elizabeth Conkle [had issue: Samuel, Hamilton, Martin, Watson, Hugh, Jacob, Elizabeth]; ii. James, b. Jan. 20, 1793; d. March 13, 1872; m. Elizabeth Kilgore, sister to Daniel Kilgore, of Cadiz [had issue: William-Kilgore, m. (1st) Martha Graham; m. (2d) Andora Waage; Hugh-F., m. Elizabeth Stokes; Nancy, m. Stuart B. Shotwell, of Cadiz; Mary, m. her father's cousin, James W. Gaston, son of James Gaston, brother to Hugh (3d); Elizabeth, m. Joseph Lyons; Philander, m. (1st) Lucinda Conkle; m. (2d) Charity Moore; Narcissa, m. Albert Brockway; Daniel-O., d. unm.; Eleanor-Jane, m. John Geeting; John, d. unm.]; iii. Robert, b. Feb. 23, 1794; d. June 4, 1801; iv. Elizabeth, b. Sept. 7, 1797; d. Jan. 14, 1816; v. Hugh, b. April 9, 1804; d. March 27, 1854 [had issue: Hamilton, Martha, Elizabeth, Mary].

II. James, d. in Smith township, Washington county, Penn., May-June, 1813, where he had settled about 1788, having removed from Lower Mount Bethel township, Northampton county, m. Jane —— (she m. 2d —— Stewart) (had issue: i. William. d. unm., in Brooke county, West Va., 1830; ii. Mary, m. —— Anderson; iii. Jane, m. —— Gordon; iv. Eleanor, m. —— Moore; v. James-W., m. his cousin, Mary Gaston, daughter of Hugh (3d) above; vi. John; vii. —— m. Mr. Moore [had issue, William]). The name of the mother of Hugh and James Gaston last given was Simanton (probably a sister of the Robert Simanton, who settled in Bedminster township, Somerset county, N. J., before 1754; whose land at that date adjoined the land of Hugh Gaston; and who removed to Pennsylvania and d. in Mount Bethel township, Northampton county, 1786, leaving children: James, Ephraim, Robert, Peter, Benjamin, Margaret Nelson, Jean Britton, and Esther Ross, of whom James and Peter settled in Washington county, Penn. The Simantons were closely connected with the family of Ephraim McDowell, who d. in Bedminster township, 1763, leaving, among other children, five sons, John, Matthew, Ephraim, Peter, and Benjamin).

III. Elizabeth.

IV. John, probably settled in Indiana.

V. Alexander, a physician, b. July 22, 1769; d. July 9, 1825; possibly the Alexander whose name appears in connection with that of John Gaston (son of William, 1st) as a taxpayer in Rostraver township, Westmoreland county, Penn. (that part now contained in Washington township, Fayette county), in 1783, when his household contained five persons; settled with his mother in Canton township, Washington county, about 1792; m. Rachel Perry, b. Sept. 1, 1773; d. Sept. 14, 1833; daughter of John and Jane McMillan Perry, who removed from West Nottingham township, Chester county, Penn., to Washington county, about 1787-99, settling in Buffalo township in 1799, and removing thence to Belmont county, Ohio, about 1800 (John, b. 1752; d. 1825; served in the Revolutionary War; Jane, b. 1744; d. 1819); removed to Brooke county, West Va., thence, about 1800, to near St. Clairsville, Ohio; and from there to Morristown, Ohio, 1811 (had issue: i. John-Perry, b. April 24, 1793; ii. Jane, b. April 10, 1795; d. Nov. 4, 1796; iii. Robert, b. Jan. 17, 1797; d. Sept. 27, 1834; m. Martha McClure; iv. Ephraim; a physician; b. June 26, 1799; d. May 30, 1868; m. (1st) Mary Wilson; m. (2d) Agnes Vance; v. Mary, b. May 20, 1801; d. Dec. 20, 1846; m. —— Tracy, and settled at McConnellsville, Ohio; vi. Charity, b. at St. Clairsville, July 27, 1803; d. 1887; m. John Lippincott, of Morristown; vii. Joseph, b. May 14, 1805; d. July 9, 1833; m. Nancy Fowler; viii. Alexander, b. Aug. 4, 1807; ix. Matthew, b. July 9, 1809; d. March 17, 1878; m. Drusilla Bute; settled at Plattsmouth, Neb.; x. Isaac, b. Sept. 16, 1811; d. at Colonna, Iowa, April 30,

1881; xi. James, b. Nov. 1, 1813). One account of Alexander Gaston (b. 1769) states that he was the son of Ephraim Gaston, who was the son of Ebenezer Gaston, who emigrated from Ireland to America in company with his brother, Matthew (d. unm.); and that Alexander Gaston had a brother, Joseph, who settled in southern Indiana; and another brother who settled in West Virginia. This account probably assumes Joseph, son of John, who married in South Carolina and settled in Butler county, Ohio, to have been the brother of Alexander.

Hugh Gaston, Jr., probably a son (or grandson) of Hugh Gaston (1st), b. 1734; d. June 25, 1808; m. (1st) Mary Sloan, b. 1742; d. Aug. 14, 1766; daughter of William and Mary Sloan, of Bedminster (?) township; m. (2d) Mary Adams, b. 1741; d. Feb. 16, 1793; daughter of John and Agnes Adams; m. (3d) Mary Kirkpatrick, b. in Bedminster township, Nov. 23, 1761; d. July 1, 1842; daughter of David and Mary McEowen Kirkpatrick (the former b. at Wattiesneach, Dumfriesshire, Scotland, Feb. 17, 1724; son of Alexander and Elizabeth Kirkpatrick, who emigrated to America with his family in 1736, and m. March 31, 1748, Mary McEowen); Hugh Gaston had issue by first wife: 1. William, b. April 12, 1763; d. Dec. 15, 1763; 2. Joseph, b. Dec. 18, 1765; d. Aug. 14, 1777; had issue by third wife: 3. Samuel Kirkpatrick, a physician; m. Nancy T. Cooper, daughter of Henry Cooper, of Chester, Morris county (had issue: i. Henrietta); 4. John, b. 1796; d. Feb. 17, 1800. Hugh Gaston, Jr., of Bedminster, had sisters: Elizabeth, b. 1737; m. Thomas Kirkpatrick; and ———, m. Captain William Logan, of Peapack; had issue, among others: 1. John.

Elizabeth Gaston, b. 1737, sister to Hugh Gaston, Jr., and probably daughter of Hugh Gaston (1st), m. Thomas Kirkpatrick, who settled near Liberty Corners, Bernard township, Somerset county, N. J.; had issue: 1. John, m. Anne Coriell, daughter of Elias Coriell (had issue: i. Sarah, m. John Layton, and settled at Plainfield; ii. Elizabeth, m. John King, son of John King, of Liberty Corners; iii. Thomas, m. Maria Hurd; iv. Elias, m. Jane Squier, daughter of Ludlow Squier, and settled at Plainfield; v. James, m. (1st) Aletta Van Arsdale, daughter of Philip Van Arsdale; m. (2d) Mary Stout; vi. Lydia, m. Stephen Woodard, son of Samuel Woodard, and removed to Chicago; vii. Jane, m. David Kline; viii. Mary, m. Tunis Van Nest; ix. John, d. at Newark, unm., aged thirty; x. Ann, m. Philip Van Arsdale, son of Peter Van Arsdale; xi. Hugh, m. Elizabeth King, of Belleville); 2. Jane, d. unm., aged about sixty.

——— Gaston, sister to Hugh Gaston, Jr., and probably daughter to Hugh Gaston (1st), m. Captain William Logan, of Somerset county, N. J.

Margaret Gaston, probably daughter of Hugh Gaston (1st), m. 1750, Thomas Moffat, who d. 1770, Hugh Gaston serving as administrator of his estate.

John Gaston of New Jersey (1st), settled in Upper Freehold (now Millstone) township, Monmouth county, N. J., about 1741, where, in 1758, he was owner of a grist and fulling mill; a member of Dr. William Tennent's Freehold Presbyterian congregation; subscriber in 1758 to the fund for a parsonage for Allentown Church; deeded a tract of land to his son, Hugh Gaston, in 1793; probably the son of Hugh Gaston (1st) and brother of William (1st) who was killed by the Indians (as John Gaston, Jr., the son of the latter, made his home in Upper Freehold township from before 1760 until after 1767, marrying there); had issue, as shown by the records of Tennent Church, Freehold: I. Mary, baptized Dec. 9, 1739. II. James, baptized March 28, 1742; probably the same who m. April 20, 1773, Lydia Tapscott; and who contributed to fund for repair of Cranbury Church in 1785; had issue, probably, among others: 1. William, served in the Revolutionary War; m. Catharine English, daughter of Dr. James English, of New Brunswick (had issue, as shown by baptismal records of Cranbury Church: i. Lydia-Tapscott, b. Dec. 4, 1804; m. Aaron Allen; ii. John-Baird, b. May 25, 1806; iii. Mary-Ann, b. March 20, 1810; m., probably, John Perrine, Jr., also, iv. Letitia; v. Hannah). III. Hugh, bap. July 15, 1744; lived in Millstone township, Monmouth county, N. J., until after 1801. IV. Mary (2d), bap. March 8, 1747. V. Elizabeth, twin sister to Mary, bap. March 8, 1747. VI. Daniel, bap. April 3, 1749; served in the Revolutionary War; lived in Millstone township, Monmouth county, during the Revolution; had issue, among others: 1. John, bap. April 14, 1776. VII. Catharine, bap. June 2, 1751. VIII. John, bap. Jan. 20, 1754. IX. William, bap. July 18, 1756. X. Jane, bap. March 25, 1759.

James Gaston (1st), probably a brother to John Gaston of New Jersey (1st), his name appears as a subscriber to the fund for building Allentown Church parsonage, 1758, in connection with that of John Gaston of Upper Freehold (1st, above); possibly, he may have been the son of that John—whose oldest son, James, was baptized at Tennent Church, March 28, 1742. The name of James Gaston also appears as a member of the congregation of Lamington Church, in Bedminster township, Somerset county, N. J., during the pastorate of Rev. James McCrea, which terminated in 1766. A James Gaston also took up land in Mount Bethel township, Northampton county, Penn., in 1773 (probably son of William, 1st), and the name of James Gaston appears on tax-list of Cecil township, Washington county, Penn., 1787 and 1788; and on that of Rostraver township, Westmoreland county, Penn., 1789.

Joseph Gaston of New Jersey (1st), d. in Bernard township, Somerset county, N. J., shortly after March 31, 1777; member of Baskinridge Presbyterian congregation; m. Margaret ———, who survived him (probably his second wife, as a Joseph Gaston and Margaret Lines were married in Somerset county, about Nov. 2, 1772); emigrated from Ireland to New Jersey about 1720; probably a brother to Hugh Gaston (1st); had issue:

I. Margaret, m. Andrew Kirkpatrick, of Bernard township, Somerset county, N. J., son of Alexander and Elizabeth Kirkpatrick (the former of whom d. at Mine Brook, N. J., June 3, 1758); removed to Redstone, Fayette county, Penn.; had issue: 1. Alexander; 2. Jennet, m. Abner Johnson; 3. Elizabeth. m. Hugh Barclay (or Bartley); 4. Margaret, m. Joseph McMartin; 5. Mary; 6. Sarah; 7. Anne; 8. Hannah.

II. John, b. Nov. 10, 1730; d. Oct. 3, 1776; m. (1st) June 27, 1758, Elizabeth Ker, b. March 19, 1738; d. May 6, 1765; daughter of William and Catherine Ker, natives of Scotland (the former b. 1700; d. July 4, 1777; buried at Lamington graveyard, Somerset county, N. J., son of Walter [1656-1748] and Margaret [1661-1734] Ker, who were exiled from Scotland about 1685, and settled at Freehold, N. J.); m. (2d) Sarah Ogden; had issue by first wife: 1. Catherine, b. May 12, 1759; d. April 14, 1762; 2. William, b. Jan. 13, 1761; d. Feb. 13, 1809; m. Dec. 10, 1782, Naomi Teeple, daughter of John and Margaret Teeple (had issue): i. John-W., b. Sept. 26, 1783; d. June 19, 1859; m. 1805, Sarah Castner; ii. Walter, d. in infancy; iii. William, b. Sept. 26, 1787; d. in New York City, Sept. 12, 1837; resided in Savannah, Georgia; iv. Margaret, b. Oct. 30, 1789; d. Nov. 3, 1827; m. 1819, John McCowen; v. Joseph, b. Feb. 13, 1792; d. April 5, 1814; vi. James, b. Jan. 8, 1795; d. March, 1820; vii. Oliver, b. Jan. 8, 1795; d. Jan. 21, 1823; viii. Abraham, b. April 25, 1797; d. Jan. 21, 1823; ix. Hugh, b. Aug. 27, 1800; d. March 30, 1821); 3. Joseph, b. May 2, 1763; d. Oct. 16, 1796; m. March 1, 1781, Ida Van Arsdale, b. April 28, 1762; daughter of Philip and Margaret Stryker Van Arsdale (the former b. 1734; d. 1776; the latter b. 1741; d. 1819) (had issue: i. Elizabeth, b. Nov. 17, 1782; d. Nov. 11, 1857; ii. Isaac-V., b. Sept. 9, 1784; d. February, 1811; iii. John-I., b. Feb. 14, 1787; d. March 23, 1846; iv. Margaret-B., b. Feb. 21, 1789; d. July 9, 1804; v. William-B., b. Aug. 9, 1791; vi. Sarah-E., b. Dec. 9, 1793; d. 1885; vii. Lydia, b. 1795; d. 1800); had issue by second wife: 4. John, m. ———Lansing, and settled at Lansingburgh, N. Y.; 5. Stephen, settled in New York State; 6. Elizabeth, m. Elias Hodges, and settled at Colerain, Hamilton county, Ohio; 7. Isaac. b. March 25, 1773; m. March 17, 1803, Anna Hedges; settled near Morristown, N. J. (had issue, among others: i. Augustus-L., b. May 15, 1806; d. 1841; settled at Reily, Butler county, Ohio, in 1828; ii. E.-H., settled at Reily, Butler county, Ohio); 8. Margaret. m. Smith Scudder, of Elizabethtown, N. J. (had issue, two sons, of whom: i. Mansfield).

III. Robert, b. Jan. 23, 1732; d. in Turbut (now Delaware) township, Northumberland county, Penn. (buried in Warrior's Run graveyard), Sept. 2, 1793; m. May 15, 1762, in Bedminster township, Somerset county, N. J., Rosanna Cooper, b. March 23, 1742; d. Jan. 14, 1817; daughter of Daniel Cooper (b. at sea during the emigration of his parents from Holland to New York, May 1, 1695; d. May 2, 1795; m. six times, 1st, April 17, 1726, to Grace Runyon, b. January, 1706; d. November, 1755; lived at Piscataway; settled in Morris county, N. J., about 1732; had issue, ten children). Robert and Rosanna Cooper Gaston resided in Bernard township, Somerset county, until about 1770; then in Pequannock township, Morris county, from before 1771 to 1777, returning thence to Bedminster township, Somerset county, and removing to Northumberland county about May, 1792; served in the Revolution as captain and lieutenant-colonel of New Jersey militia, and as captain in the Continental Line; had issue: 1. Joseph, b. Nov. 19, 1766; d. April 18, 1831; m. 1789, Margaret Melick, b. Dec. 22, 1767; d. Feb. 5, 1838; daughter of Aaron and Catherine Miller Moelich (had issue: i. Robert, b. March 30, 1790; d. Sept. 22, 1854; m. April 8, 1824, Eleanor Shannon, b. 1795; d. Oct. 12, 1867 [had issue: Martha-J.; Margaret-M.; Solomon-P.; Mary-E.; Charlotte-A.; Sarah-Ann; Sarah]; ii. Charlotte, b. Sept. 22, 1792; d. Aug. 13, 1824; m. James Durham; iii. Rosanna, b. June 7, 1795; d. Nov. 19, 1845; iv. Aaron, b. April 25, 1799; d. Oct. 24, 1868; m. [1st] Sarah Ann Clarke; m. [2d] Rosanna Camp; v. Daniel; a Presbyterian minister; who settled in Philadelphia; b. July 26, 1801; d. April 28, 1860; m. 1839, Rosa Morris, b. 1803; d. 1873; vi. Mary, b. May 14, 1804; d. July 11. 1880; vii. Anne, b. Dec. 20, 1808; m. William Sample); 2. Margaret, b. Dec. 17, 1768; d. Sept. 10, 1807; m. 1785, Daniel Melick, son of Aaron and Catherine Miller Moelich, of Bedminster township (had issue: i. Aaron; ii. Elizabeth; iii. Charlotte; iv. Rosanna; v. John; vi. Mary; vii. David; viii. William; ix. Daniel; x. Catherine); 3. Mary, b. Feb. 12, 1770; 4. Daniel, b. April 5, 1773; 5. Anne, b. March 25, 1774; 6. George-W., b. April 2, 1777; 7. John, b. Feb. 8, 1780.

IV. Joseph, b. 1738-39; d. 1803-04; served as paymaster of New Jersey militia from Somerset and Sussex counties, in the Revolution; named as executor of his father's will (dated March 31, 1777); settled in Hardwick township, Sussex county, N. J., about 1783; m. —— Linn, daughter of Joseph and Martha Kirkpatrick Linn (who removed from Bernard township, Somerset county, to Hunterdon county, thence to Hardwick township, Sussex county, and later to Hardyston township, Sussex county; he b. 1725; d. 1800; she b. 1723; d. 1791); had issue: 1. —— m. Dr. Elijah Everitt, b. in Kingwood township, Hunterdon county, 1770-80; d. Jan. 11, 1850; settled in Sparta township, Sussex county; 2. —— m. Rev. John Boyd.
V. Martha, m. —— Patterson.
VI. Priscilla, m. about Sept. 24, 1771, David McCain.
VII. ——, m. David Chambers; had issue: 1. Joseph; 2. William; 3. John.

John Gaston, of Connecticut (1st), b. in county Antrim, Ireland, probably near Ballymena (or, possibly, Ballymoney), 1703-04; emigrated to America, 1720-26, with his brother Alexander and perhaps a third brother, who settled in New Jersey; settled at Voluntown, Conn., 1726-27, where he d. March 29, 1783; m. about 1735, Janet Thomson b. in Scotland, 1711; d. at Killingly, Conn., Nov. 3, 1806; daughter of Rev. Alexander Thomson, a native of Scotland, who lived for a time at Andover, Mass., and afterwards at Stonington, Conn.; had issue:

I. Margaret, b. 1734; d. Feb. 5, 1811; m. James Dickson, b. 1728; d. 1815; had issue: 1. James; 2. John; 3. Alexander; 4. Joseph ; 5. Nancy, m. William Church; 6. Phebe, m. Uriah Church (had issue: i. Andrew, m. Ruth Hall [their daughter, Clara, m. 1831, Horace White, of Syracuse, N. Y., and was the mother of Andrew Dickson White, b. at Homer, N. Y.. Nov. 7, 1832]; ii. Gaston; iii. John; iv. Vesta; v. Nelson; vi. Diodata).
II. Alexander, b. 1739; served in the French and Indian War, and died, 1760, of disease contracted in that service.
III. John, b. at Voluntown, 1750; d. there Oct. 26, 1805; served in the Connecticut Legislature; m. about 1770, Ruth Miller, b. at Plainfield, Conn.,

1750; d. at Killingly, May 10, 1825; daughter of Rev. Alexander and Esther Miller (the former a Presbyterian minister, who settled at Plainfield, called to the Separatist Church at Voluntown, 1751, and imprisoned in the Windham county jail for a long time for refusing to pay the Established [Congregational] Church rates); had issue: 1. Alexander, b. at Voluntown, Aug. 2, 1772; d. at Roxbury, Mass., Feb. 11, 1856; where he had settled 1838; served in the Connecticut Legislature; m. (1st) April 1, 1803, Olive Dunlap, b. at Plainfield, 1769; d. at Killingly, Sept. 7, 1814; daughter of Joshua Dunlap; m. (2d) April, 1816, Kezia Arnold, b. at Burrillville, R. I., November. 1779; d. at Roxbury, Mass., Jan. 30, 1856; daughter of Aaron and Rhoda Hunt Arnold (the former a descendant of Thomas Arnold, b. 1599) (had issue by first wife: i. Esther, b. 1804; d. 1860; ii. John, b. 1806; d. 1824; had issue by second wife: iii. William, b. at Killingly, Oct. 3, 1820; d. Jan. 19, 1894; served as member of the Massachusetts Legislature; as mayor of Boston; and as governor of Massachusetts; m. May 27, 1852, Louisa A. Beecher, b. at Boston, Dec. 27, 1830; daughter of Laban S. and Frances Lines Beecher, natives of New Haven—the former a descendant of John Beecher, who emigrated probably from Kent, England, and d. at New Haven, 1637-38 [had issue: Sarah Howard, b. April 23, 1853; William-Alexander, b. May 1, 1859; m. 1892, May D. Lockwood; and Theodore-Beecher, b. Feb. 8, 1861; d. July 16, 1869]; 2. Margaret, b. Dec. 13, 1781; d. young.

Alexander Gaston (1st), b. 1714; m. Mary Wilson, b. 1716; emigrated to America with his brother John about 1720-26; said to have had a third brother in New Jersey; settled at Richmond, Mass.; had issue: I. William, b. Aug. 9, 1744. II. John, b. March 3, 1746. III. Robert, b. Dec. 28, 1747. IV. Mary, b. Sept. 20, 1749. V. Janet, b. Dec. 27, 1750; m. Robert Kasson. VI. Margaret, b. Jan. 5, 1753. VII. Alexander, b. Oct. 28, 1754; had issue, among others: 1. John, b. 1746, d. at Stockbridge, Mass., Sept. 6, 1834 (had issue, among others: i. John, b. 1786; d. March, 1873). VIII. David, b. Jan. 13, 1757. IX. Thomas, b. March 16, 1759. X. Phebe, b. April 22, 1765; m. —— Bacon. (Mr. Marshall Gaston, of Oberlin, Ohio, made, before 1892, a nearly complete record of the descendants of the children of Alexander Gaston (1st) down to his own generation.)

JOHN WALLACE GILLESPIE, a native of Ohio, b. 1819; d. 1885; m. (1st) Nov. 29, 1842, Cordelia Anderson, b. in Wheeling, West Virginia, 1827; d. May 7, 1877; m. (2d) 1879, Mrs. Jane Dallas, widow of Henry Dallas; had issue by first wife: 1. Albert; 2. James; 3. Nettie; 4. Elosia, m. William McFadden; 5. Laura, m. John C. Spencer, and settled in Chicago; 6. John-W., b. May 1, 1857; m. April 15, 1890, Agnes Sheriff, daughter of Adam N. and Mary Vickery Sheriff; 7. Wayne.

FRANCIS GILMORE, a native of Ireland, settled in Archer township, Harrison county, Ohio, before 1815; m. in Harrison county, Sarah McBride, a native of Ireland, b. about 1790; d. March 30, 1840; had issue: 1. William; 2. Margaret, b. in Archer township, Jan. —, 1816; m. in 1833 John Welsh, b. in Pennsylvania, Nov. 20, 1808; d. Nov. 10, 1881 (son of Samuel and Catherine Welsh, natives of Ireland, who settled in Archer township before 1814); removed to Cadiz in 1874, where he died (had issue: i. Samuel, settled in Missouri; ii. Jason, settled in Iowa; iii. Sarah-Jane, m. John Adams, and settled in Archer township; iv. Amanda, m. Samuel F. Ross, a Methodist Episcopal minister, and settled in New Philadelphia, Ohio); 3. John, settled in Oskaloosa, Iowa; 4. Thomas, settled in Iowa; 5. Samuel, settled in Iowa.

NATHANIEL GILMORE, of county Cavan, Ireland; d. about 1771; m. Sarah McFadden, b. about 1748, at Coote Hill, county Cavan, Ireland; d. Dec. 29, 1835, near West Middletown, Penn. (Sarah McFadden Gilmore m. [2d] John Jamison, and emigrated to America about 1780-83, first settling in Shearman's Valley, Cumberland [now Perry] county, (?) Penn., thence removing to Independence township, Washington county, Penn.); had issue: 1. Jane, b. 1768; m. John Parr; removed first to Jefferson county, Ohio, and later to Illinois (had issue: i. John, m. —— Wheeler; ii. Mary; iii. Elizabeth, m. John Leech); 2. Samuel, b. 1770; d. Sept. 8, 1814; served as ensign in the War of 1812 (Capt. Baruch Dickerson's company, 2d Ohio Militia); m. Elizabeth Buchanan, b. 1777; d. Sept. 16, 1829; daughter of William (and Nancy?) Buchanan, of Washington county, Penn.; removed to Cadiz township, Harrison county, Ohio, about 1800-1 (had issue: i. Sarah, b. Jan. 14, 1801; d. May 18, 1837; m. Joseph Dunlap; ii. Samuel; iii. Nathaniel, m. Mary Craig; iv. Cyrus, b. 1811; d. April 14, 1883; m. Hannah Moore; v. William; vi. Mary, m. Napoleon B. Kennedy; vii. Eliza, b. Feb. 2, 1807; d. Jan. 14, 1873; m. May 1, 1828, John Phillips, b. June, 1797; d. at Cadiz, Ohio, May 5, 1859; son of William and Rachel Hamilton Phillips, of West Nottingham township, Chester county, Penn.

JOSIAH GLOVER, b. in Baltimore, Md.; removed to Smithfield, Jefferson county, Ohio; had issue: I. Josiah, m. 1833, Mary Barkhurst, a native of Maryland, b. 1817-18; d. February, 1872; had issue: 1. Sarah, m. Augustus Carter, of Jefferson county; 2. Nancy; 3. Susan, m. William Comly; 4. George-W.; 5. Josephine, m. John C. Brown; 6. Jefferson-C., b. March 3, 1845; m. 1869, Caroline I. Snyder, daughter of Samuel Snyder; 7. Elizabeth, m. Milton Hall, of Jefferson county; 8. Esther; 9. Quincy; 10. Leonora, m. John C. Brown (his second wife); 11. William-L.

JONAS GOTSHALL, emigrated from Perry county, Penn., to Harrison county before 1823; m. Mary Laler; had issue: 1. Jeremiah, m. Mary Long; 2. John; 3. Anna, m. William Arbaugh; 4. Jacob; m. (1st) Eliza Long; m. (2d) Ruth Hendrix; 5. Daniel, b. in Rumley township, 1831; m. (1st) Amanda Wortman, b. 1835; d. 1869; daughter of John and Rebecca Wortman; m. (2d) Eliza Wood; 6. Samuel, m. (1st) Margaret Carr; m. (2d) Harriet McClain; 7. Matilda, m. Alpheus Lowmiller; 8. Elizabeth, m. John Wood; 9. Katharine, d. young.

ALEXANDER GREEN, a native of Ireland, settled in Belmont county, Ohio, 1808; m. (1st) in Ireland, Eleanor Chambers; m. (2d) Mary Bell; had issue by first wife: 1. Thomas; 2. John; 3. Samuel, b. in Ireland, Dec. 5, 1799; came to Ohio with his parents; settled in Washington township, Harrison county about 1829, where he d. June 2, 1879; m. Oct. 29, 1829, Ann Thompson, b. in Jefferson county, June 13, 1808; daughter of Aaron and Sarah Balderson Thompson (had issue: i. William, b. Oct. 29, 1830; ii. James, b. in Washington township, Sept. 16, 1833; m. March 20, 1881, Clara M. Pittis, daughter of George Pittis, of Harrison county; iii. Aaron, b. May 6, 1836; iv. Sarah, b. Oct. 31, 1838; d. Sept. 16, 1844; v. Samuel-H., b. Dec. 5, 1840; d. Feb. 2, 1869; vi. Ruth-T., b. June 18, 1843; vii. Israel-J., b. Nov. 11, 1845); 4. James; 5. Elizabeth; 6. Abbie; had issue by second wife: 7. Isaac; 8. Alexander; 9. Sampson; 10. William; 11. Sarah; 12. Ellen; 13. Mary-Ann; 14. Maria; 15. Ruth.

Aaron Thompson, father of Ann T. Green, was a native of Ireland, b. Jan. 26, 1775; d. June 22, 1838; first settled in Chester county, Penn., 1790; removed to Jefferson county, Ohio, in 1802; son of William Thompson and Esther Chalfant; the former b. in Ireland, March 26, 1747; d. in Chester county, Penn., July 7, 1806; Aaron Thompson, m. in Chester county, Penn., 1797, Sarah Balderson, b. March 5, 1778; d. Sept. 26, 1846; had issue: 1. Esther, b. Nov. 19, 1798; 2. William, b. Jan. 3, 1801; 3. John, b. June 28, 1803; 4. Aaron, b. Sept. 13, 1805; 5. Ann, b. June 13, 1808; m. Samuel Green; 6. Ruth, b. Oct. 4, 1810; 7. Lewis, b. Nov. 21, 1813; 8. Israel, b. Jan. 4, 1818.

JOSEPH GRIMES, see Family of William McCullough.

WILLIAM GRIMES, removed from Washington (?) county, Penn., to Harrison county, Ohio, before 1805, and about 1810 settled at Cadiz, where he d. May-August, 1840; m. Rebecca ———, d. about 1840; had issue: 1. James, b. 1817; d. July 10, 1841; 2. William, b. 1822; d. April 30, 1850; 3. Thomas-D., m. 1835, Margaret Lafferty (?); 4. Martha, b. May 12, 1826; d. April 4, 1874; m. Henry Boyles; 5. Elizabeth, m. 1830, Matthew M. Slcan (had issue, among others: i. William-Grimes, settled at Omaha; ii. Rebecca, m. Asbury F. Johnson, son of Henry and Catherine Johnson, of Moorefield township; settled at Laramie, Wyoming; iii. Elizabeth-J., b. 1838; d. 1843); 6. Nancy; 7. Anderson.

EDWARD HALL, b. March 4, 1760; son of Joshua Hall, of Howard Hill, Baltimore, Md.; an English sea-captain who served on the American side in the Revolutionary War; removed to

Jefferson county, Ohio, about 1803, settling near Smithfield; had issue: 1. Richard; 2. Harry; 3. Christopher-S.; 4. Edward-Thomas, b. Dec. 25, 1795, in Hallsboro, Baltimore county, Md.; settled with his parents near Smithfield, Jefferson county, Ohio; afterwards located in Washington, Guernsey county, Ohio, where he d. March 9, 1891; m. at York Haven, Penn., Dec. 20, 1827, Henrietta Catherine Roberts, b. April 12, 1804, at Fells Point, Baltimore, Md., daughter of Francis Cateby Roberts, an English sea-captain, who was drowned 1803, and Elizabeth Snyder Karg, a native of Baltimore (Edward and Henrietta Roberts Hall had issue: i. Francis-Spry, b. Oct. 3, 1828; settled in Washington, Guernsey county, Ohio; ii. Charles-Grafton, b. July 24, 1830; d. in California, Dec. 8, 1859; iii. Wilson-Roberts, b. July 8, 1832; d. March 16, 1849; iv. Thomas-Henry, d. in infancy; v. Sarah-Virginia, b. Oct. 6, 1835; m. William L. Houser; vi. Eliza-Jane, b. Feb. 9, 1838; d. Jan. 12, 1865, in Harrisburg, Penn.; vii. Edward-Harrison, b. April 12, 1840; served in the Civil War; d. Sept. 26, 1878; viii. Richard-Montgomery, b. Jan. 27, 1842; settled in Washington, Guernsey county; ix. George-Alfred, b. Dec. 9, 1843; d. March 31, 1849; x. Henrietta-Frances, b. Oct. 28, 1852; m. Dr. H. H. Harrison; settled in Wheeling, W. Va.).

After the death of her first husband, Elizabeth Snyder Karg Roberts, mother of Henrietta Hall, m. 1808, Charles Merrill Poor, a native of Greenland, N. H., of Puritan ancestry, son of John Poor; had issue, among others: Sarah-Ann, b. 1814; d. 1892; m. Robert Jackson Fleming, of Harrisburg, Penn.; George-A., settled in Vallejo, Cal.; Frances-Isabella, m. Henry S. McFadden, of Cadiz.

JOSEPH HALL, settled in the western part of Jefferson county, Ohio, about 1802, having come from North Carolina; d. 1825, in Jefferson county; m. in North Carolina, 1773, Christiana Peel; d. 1803; had issue, ten children, among whom:

I. Jesse, d. in Jefferson county, 1806; his wife died the same year; had issue, among others: 1. William, b. in Jefferson county, 1804; d. Dec. 14, 1883; m. April, 1826, Hannah Wharton, b. in Bucks county, Penn., 1807, daughter of Ezra and Martha Terry Wharton (who settled in 1818 on the present site of Harrisville, Harrison county, Ohio, where they died; the former b. Aug. 26, 1773; d. May, 1847; the latter b. May 19, 1778; d. Dec. 19, 1866; they were m. April 19, 1797); (William and Hannah Hall had issue: i. Ezra, d. 1852 in Minnesota; ii. Nathan-L.; iii. Penina; iv. Parker, b. June 6, 1829; settled in Short Creek township, Harrison county, Ohio, in 1853; m. [1st] August, 1853, Rebecca Hobson, a native of Belmont county, Ohio; d. 1866; m. [2d] 1872, Mrs. Tabitha D. Bundy, a native of Belmont county; v. Tilman, settled in Mahoning county; vi. Linton, settled in Columbiana county; vii. Martha, m. Thomas Dewees; settled in Morgan county, Ohio).

SAMUEL W. HAMILL, b. in county Antrim, Ireland, about 1787; d. in Monroe township, Harrison county, Ohio, Sept. 20, 1870; emigrated to America about 1820, first settling in New York City, where he remained for seven years; in 1824 m. Eliza Graham, b. in New York City, 1803; d. 1876; daughter of George and Rebecca Graham (the former a native of New York, the latter a native of Ireland); removed to Leesville, Carroll county, Ohio, in 1827, and located in Monroe township, Harrison county, in the spring of the following year; had issue: 1. Rebecca-J., m. William B. Edwards, of Plymouth, Ill.; 2. Catherine-A., m. Edward Greenlus, of Tuscarawas county, Ohio; 3. Samuel-S., b. June 22, 1840; settled in Monroe township; served in the Civil War, and as sheriff of Harrison county; m. March 21, 1872, Mary E. Heller, a native of Monroe township, daughter of Henry B. and Mary-A. Heller, early settlers in Harrison county; 3. Lindley-M., settled in Monroe township; served as an officer in the Civil War; 4. Wallace-S., served in the Civil War, and died in service August, 1861; 5. Robert-Emmet, served in the Civil War; d. in Sibley, Kan., Nov. 9, 1884; 6. Benjamin-G., settled in Kentucky; served as an officer in the Civil War.

FRANCIS H. HAMILTON, b. in Ireland, 1766; d. 1844; emigrated to America and first settled in Noblestown, Penn., about 1800; removed to Canonsburg, and afterwards to Mercer, where he remained until 1820, and then settled in Cadiz, Ohio; served in the War of 1812; m. 1806, Ruth Williams, b. 1788; d. 1842; of Scotch descent; had issue: 1. John, d. in Pennsylvania; 2. James, d. in Illinois; 3. David; 4. Jane; 5. Francis, b. Dec. 13, 1815; d. Jan. 28, 1887; m. Matilda ———, b. 1813; d. 1888; 6. William, b. Sept. 29, 1818; d. Nov. 14, 1892; 7. Samuel, b. in Cadiz, April 19, 1821; m. (1st) Aug. 6, 1843, Margaret J. Miller, of German descent, b. Aug. 10, 1826; d. Feb. 7, 1857; daughter of Michael Miller, of Harrison county; m. (2d) Bridget Downey, b. in Ireland, 1839 (her parents came to Vermont about 1842; her father d. in Kansas City, Mo., 1889); (had issue by first wife: i. ———, d. in infancy; ii. Samuel-D., settled in Harrisville, Ohio; iii. Henry-C., b. Dec. 29,1850; iv.Eloisa-B.; had issue by second wife: v. Emma-Frances, m. William C. Leslie); 8. Sarah; 9. Mary, m. Jacob H. Herdman, and settled in New Concord, Muskingum county, Ohio; 10. Thomas.

JOSHUA HAMILTON, a native of Pennsylvania, of Scotch-Irish descent; settled in Harrison county, Ohio, before 1825; d. in Springfield, Ohio, Dec. 17, 1870; m. in Harrison county, Jane Craig, d. Nov. 9, 1889; had issue, eleven children, among whom: 1. Craig, b. April 16, 1825; d. in Cadiz township, Oct. 5, 1880; m. (1st) Feb. 21, 1850, Margaret McFadden, b. 1825; d. 1853, in McLean county, Ill., daughter of Joseph McFadden, of Harrison county; m. (2d) Jan. 28, 1858, Elizabeth McFadden, b. Oct. 29, 1836, daughter of Samuel and Margaret Rankin McFadden, of Cadiz township (had issue by first wife: i. Joshua, d. in infancy; ii. Joseph-McFadden, b. March 8, 1851; m. Dec. 25, 1873, Rebecca Caroline Dickerson, daughter of Asa and Jane Dunlap Dickerson; had issue by second wife: iii. Margaret-Jane, b. March 5, 1859; m. Eugene Watson, and settled in Belmont county; iv. Samuel-Rankin, b. March 17, 1863; m. Sept. 1, 1886, Georgianna Dickerson, a native of Noble county, Ohio, daughter of John and Catherine Lowe Dickerson; v. William-Sherman, b. Sept. 1, 1865).

The father of Craig Hamilton's second wife. Samuel McFadden, was b. 1815; d. 1863; his father, Samuel McFadden, was a native of Ireland, who settled in Harrison county, where he d. 1837; Margaret Rankin McFadden, the mother of Elizabeth McFadden Hamilton, b. 1813; d. July 5, 1890, was a daughter of Robert Rankin, a native of Pennsylvania; the children of Samuel and Margaret Rankin McFadden were: 1. Robert; 2. Rebecca-J., m. Henry Barricklow; 3. Elizabeth, m. Craig Hamilton; 4. Sarah, m. Albert Moore; 5. Margaret, m. Thomas Richey; 6. Samuel.

ROBERT HAMILTON, d. before 1790; m. in West Nottingham township, Chester county, Penn., before 1770, Martha McMillan, b. 1748-49; d. March 18, 1831; daughter of John and Rachel McMillan; his widow removed with her four children to Buffalo township, Washington county, Penn., about 1795-98, in company with her brother-in-law and sister (John and Jane McMillan Perry), and, about 1803, settled at St. Clairsville, removing thence to Morristown, both in Belmont county, Ohio, where she died; had issue: 1. Rachel, d. 182—; m. about 1787, William Phillips, d. July 18, 1854; son of Thomas and Jane Blair Phillips, of West Nottingham township (had issue: i. Robert; ii. Martha, m. James Ross; iii. Thomas; iv. Jane, m. Samuel Lee; v. John; vi. William; vii. Mary, m. Jacob Grist; viii. Margaret, m. John Johns; ix. Eliza, m. ——— Keatley); 2. Margaret, b. Nov. 26, 1776; d. Oct. 14, 1839; m. Edward Van Horn, b. 1777; d. Aug. 19, 1855; settled at New Athens, Harrison county, Ohio (had issue: i. Anne, b. 1803; d. 1815; ii. Martha, b. 1805; d. 1869; iii. Jemima; iv. Robert, d. 1895; v. Jane, b. 1809; d. 1888); 3. Martha, m. Alexander Morrison, and settled at Morristown, Ohio (had issue, among others: i. Robert, b. 1802; d. July 9, 1895); 4. John-Blair, d. about 1806; m. Mary Perry, b. ———; d. ———; daughter of John and Jane McMillan Perry (had issue, among others: i. Robert; a physician: b. Nov. 14, 1803; m. 1836, Margaret Wilson); 5. Jane, d. 1798; m. ——— McClure (had issue, among others: i. Martha, b. Dec. 23, 1795; d. April 15, 1870; m. June 6, 1819, Robert Gaston, b. Jan. 10, 1797; d. Sept. 23, 1834; removed to Morgan county, Ohio, 1828, and thence to Knox county in 1831.

ROBERT HAMMOND, b. in county Tyrone, Ireland, 1765; d. in Belmont county, Ohio, 1845; m. Jane Cassell, b. in county Down, Ireland, 1764; d. 1852; emigrated to America and first settled in Pennsylvania, removing to Belmont county before 1809; both were members of the Seceder Church; had issue:

I. Mary, b. July 30, 1788.
II. Alexander, b. May 16, 1790; d. in Harrison county, 1874, where he had settled in 1809; in 1812 he located in Short Creek township, subsequently removing to Harrisville; was a member of the Seceder Church, and his house was a station on the "underground railroad,", many slaves having been given shelter in his home before being taken to Canada; m. in 1812, Elizabeth Hanna, b. 1793; d. 1886; daughter of Samuel (b. in Cumberland county, Penn. 1763) and Elizabeth Duncan (b. in Scotland, 1766) Hanna, of Short Creek township; had issue, among others: 1. Esther, m. Robert Porter Hanna; 2. Margaret, m. S. J. Hawthorne, of Harrisville; 3. John-Hanna, b. in Harrison county, Ohio; settled in Cadiz in 1872; served as an officer in the Civil War; m. 1845, Agnes E. Carrick, daughter of David and Elizabeth Carrick, early settlers of Harrison county, the former having served in the War of 1812 (had issue: i. Alexander-James, b. Aug. 14, 1846; served in the Civil War; settled in Cadiz in 1878; m. in Cadiz, 1870, Charlotte Hunter, daughter of Joseph and Letitia McFadden Hunter; ii. Anderson-N., b. in Short Creek township, Harrison county, Ohio, 1848; settled in Cadiz, 1866; m. in Cadiz, 1870, Nancy Jane Moore, daughter of John Moore; removed to Chicago).
III. David, b. June 26, 1792.
IV. William, b. Aug. 2, 1794.
V. Margaret, b. July 8, 1795.
VI. Elizabeth, b. Oct. 24, 1797.
VII. Esther, b. Feb. 1. 1801.
VIII. John, b. March 10, 1803.
IX. Robert, b. March 20, 1805.
X. James, b. May 13, 1808.

ALEXANDER HANNA, b. in Ireland, 1737; d. in Somerset county, Penn., 1809; his son, James, b. in Ireland, 1770; emigrated to America when young; d. in Somerset county, 1819; served in the Pennsylvania Legislature; m. Ann Leech; had issue: 1. John, served in the Pennsylvania Legislature; 2. Mary; 3. Thomas; 4. James; 5. Alexander, b. 1802; d. 1881; 6. William; 7. Philo; 8. Jane; 9. Martha; 10. Anna.

ANDREW HANNA, settled in Paxtang township, Lancaster (now Dauphin) county, Penn., before 1737; d. in Hanover township, 1766; had issue: 1. Samuel, b..in mid-ocean; probably settled in Hopewell township, Cumberland county, see Samuel Hanna below; 2. Andrew, settled in Hopewell township, Cumberland county, Penn., about 1766; removing thence, 1772-75, to Guilford county, N. C.; m. Mary ———; 3. Margaret; 4. Isaac, b. 1743; d. in Aron, Livingston county, N. Y., 1816; m. April 15, 1766, Martha Bell, b. August, 1746; d. 1811; sister of Thomas, Lucy, Anna, and Walter Bell; removed from Dry Valley, Union county, Penn., to Livingston county, N. Y., about 1810 (had issue: i. Andrew, b. 1769; d. at Aronsburg, Centre county, Penn., Jan 24, 1835; m. Margaret Cook, b. 1776; d. 1841; their son Andrew settled in Canal township, Venango county, Penn.; ii. Samuel, m. ——— McPherson; iii. Elizabeth, m. Levi Van Fossen; iv. Matthew, b. 1780; d. at Aron, N. Y., Nov. 12, 1813; m. July 23, 1807, Catharine Pearson, b. Feb. 19, 1791; d. Sept. 9, 1882; v. Thomas, settled in Chautauqua county, N. Y.; m. Nancy Pearson, sister of Catharine, b. Feb. 11, 1797; d. May 8, 1817; vi. John, removed to Livingston county, N. Y.; vii. Anna, m. Alexander (or James) Beatty; viii. Martha, m. (1st) ——— McPherson; m. (2d) ——— Briggs; removed to Livingston county, N. Y.; and from there to Hyattsville, Ohio; ix. Isaac, m. Sarah ———); 5. Mary, m. William Woods; 6. John, removed to South Carolina; 7. Elizabeth, m. Moses Carson; 8. Matthew, settled in Hopewell township, Cumberland county, before 1771, where he resided as late as 1781.

JAMES HANNA, settled in Little Britain township, Lancaster county, Penn., before 1738, where he was living after 1769; had issue, among others: 1. James.

JAMES HANNA and his wife, Martha, emigrated from the North of Ireland, and settled in Pennsylvania; removed thence to Berkeley county, West Va., and from there to Mercer county, Ky., where he d. about 1798; had issue, six sons and six daughters, four of whom were born in Ireland; among others were: 1. Stephen; 2. James; 3. Adam, removed to Shelby county, Ky.; 4. Hannah, m. John Myles; 5. Thomas, m. Margaret Smith; removed to Shelby county, Ky. (had issue, among others: i. John-Smith, b. in Mercer county, Ky., March 27, 1798; d. ———; m. Aug. 11, 1825, Jane A. King, b. Oct. 10, 1805, daughter of Thomas and Anna McAfee King).

JAMES HANNA, b. in Washington county, Penn., 1792; settled in German township, Harrison county, Ohio, 1816, where he d. Jan. 14, 1877; m. in Pennsylvania, 1816, Mary McCleary, b. 1793; d. Oct. 31, 1872; had issue: 1. Mary, m. Robert Herron, a minister, and settled in Scio; 2. Esther, m. Robert Smiley, and settled in Archer township, Harrison county; 3. Tabitha-Jane, m. James Lawthers, of Bowerstown, and settled in German township; 4. Jerusha-Elizabeth, m. Wesley Brindley, and settled in Green township; 5. Ann, b. Aug. 27, 1818; settled in Jewett, 1877; 6. Alexander; 7. William-J.; 8. Sarah; 9. Dorcas.

JOHN HANNA and WILLIAM HANNA, probably brothers, emigrated from the North of Ireland, about 1731, and settled in East Fallowfield township, Chester county, Penn., about 1733, John first having located on Neshaminy Creek, in Bucks county, and about 1739, removed from Fallowfield township to West Nantmeal (now Honeybrook) township; of these two:

John Hanna, b. about 1700; d. March 8-13, 1770; m. Jane Andre, d. December, 1774; had issue:

I. John, a physician and minister, b. in mid-ocean, 1731; d. Nov. 4, 1801; m. about 1760, Mary McCrea, daughter of Rev. James and Mary Graham McCrea; served as minister of the Presbyterian churches of Bethlehem. Kingwood, and Alexandria, N. J., 1761-1801: had issue. thirteen children, six of whom died in infancy: 1. James, settled at Newtown, Bucks county; removed to Frankfort. Ky., after 1793; m. Mary Harris, of Newtown, daughter of John and Hannah Stewart Harris (had issue: i. John-Harris; ii. Sophia; iii. Charles-Stewart; iv. A daughter; one of the daughters m. John J. Crittenden, of Kentucky); 2. John-Andre, b. 1761; d. at Harrisburg, Penn., July 23, 1805; m. Mary Read Harris, b. Oct. 1, 1770; d. Aug. 20, 1851; daughter of John Harris, the founder of Harrisburg (had issue: i. Mary-Read, b. April 30, 1788; d. March 14, 1826; m. April 29, 1817, John Tod, of Bedford; ii. Juliana-Catharine, b. Nov. 8, 1789; d. without issue, April, 1861; m. Jan. 14, 1812, John Fisher; iii. Frances, b. April 27, 1791; d. 1868; m. Oct. 27, 1812, John Carson McAllister; iv. Caroline-Elizabeth, b. Feb. 5, 1794; d. Jan. 29, 1872; m. Dec. 8, 1812, Joseph Briggs, of Silvers' Spring, Cumberland county; v. Henrietta, b. Aug. 23, 1796; d. unm., Nov. 18, 1840; vi. Sarah-Elder, b. June 20, 1798; d. April 2, 1829; m. April 18, 1820, Richard Templin; vii. Eleanor, b. Feb. 22, 1800; d. 1802; viii. Esther, b. July, 1801; d. 1801); 3. Catharine, m. Dr. Samuel Tolbert, of New York (had issue: i. Catharine, m. ——— Brooks; ii. Jane, m. ——— Sanford); 4. Mary, m. Dr. ——— Holmes, of Mansfield, Sussex county, N. J.; 5. William-R.; 6. Sarah, m. ——— Payne, of Mansfield, N. J.; 7. Jane.

II. William, a minister, settled at Albany, N. Y., about 1765, where he served as the first pastor of the Presbyterian Church of that place; became an Episcopalian clergyman and settled in Culpeper county, Va., about 1774, from whence, on account of his Toryism, he was obliged to remove to Montreal, Canada, at the breaking out of the Revolutionary War.

III. James, b. 1722; d. Jan. 21, 1807; m. Elizabeth ———, b. 1740; d. Dec. 12, 1821; had issue: 1. John, m. probably, Jane Guthrie, daughter of Adam Guthrie; 2. William, resided in Huntingdon county, Penn., in 1805; 3. Mary, m. ——— Gault; 4. Jane, m. William Irwin: 5. James; 6. Agnes.

IV. Robert.

V. Agnes. m. ——— Culbertson.

VI. Elizabeth, m. ——— McCool.

VII. Margaret. d. November, 1802; m. James Galt, of Salisbury township, Lancaster county; d. June, 1773.

William Hanna, d. after Sept. 22, 1766; had issue:

I. John. d. March-April. 1784; m. Abigail Wilson. b. 1739; d. 1833: daughter of Thomas Wilson. of Newlin township: had issue: 1. Elizabeth; 2. Mary, b. after 1766; 3. John, b. after 1763; 4.

Abigail, b. after 1766; 5. Margaret, b. after 1766; 6. Phœbe, b. after 1766; 7. Jacob, b. 1771; d. Aug. 13, 1839.

II. William, m. Esther Wilson, daughter of Thomas Wilson, of Newlin township; settled in Newlin township, about 1776.

JOHN HANNA, b. in county Derry, Ireland, 1752; d. in South Huntingdon township, Westmoreland county, Penn., June 9, 1832; m. 1789, Elizabeth Miller, b. 1762; d. Oct. 4, 1835; daughter of John and Elizabeth Lindsey Miller; had issue: 1. Thomas, b. March 6, 1790; d. Dec. 29, 1855; m. Feb. 29, 1816, Esther Trout, b. Nov. 13, 1796; d. Oct. 24, 1876; daughter of Henry and Catharine Bossart Trout; 2. Martha, b. 1791; d. Sept. 18, 1862; m. 1817, Henry Lake, b. 1777; d. Jan. 10, 1839; 3. Alexander, b. Feb. 15, 1796; d. Jan. 4, 1883; m. May, 1824, Eliza Hamilton; 4. John; 5. Elizabeth, m. Peter Broadsword; 6. James, b. 1800; d. 1829; 7. Margaret, b. May, 1803; d. Feb. 7, 1866; m. Dec. 30, 1830, John Hanna (a cousin); 8. Robert, b. 1806; m. 1833, Priscilla Hamilton.

JOHN HANNA, of Hopewell township, Cumberland county, Penn., d. after probably 1809; had issue:

I. John, d. Oct. 10, 1792 (or 1802).

II. Samuel, b. Nov. 29, 1763; m. Elizabeth Duncan, b. July 27, 1766; removed to Canton township, Washington county, Penn., about 1785; thence to Warren county, Ohio, about 1799-1800, and from there to Short Creek township, Harrison county, Ohio, 1801; had issue: 1. Jeanette, b. Feb. 22, 1786; d. young; 2. John, b. June 26, 1787; d. in Harrison county, Ohio, Aug. 12, 1849; m. 1826, Rachel Fulton; 3. Archibald, a minister; b. Feb. 12, 1790; d. in Wayne county, Ohio, June 9, 1875; m. April 4, 1816, Mary Ramage, daughter of William and Mary Ramage; 4. Elizabeth, b. Jan. 26, 1792; d. April 24, 1884; m. 1812, Alexander Hammond; 5. Samuel, b. Sept. 2, 1795; d. in Richland county, Ohio, June 2, 1862; 6. Isabella. b. June 25, 1797; d. 1846; m. Benjamin Ramsey; 7. Ezekiel, b. June 1, 1799; d. near Beech Spring, Harrison county, Ohio, May 10, 1861; m. Aug. 30, 1821, Elizabeth Anderson, b. Oct. 21, 1796; d. Jan. 24, 1845; 8. Robert, b. April 26, 1801; d. in Mansfield, Ohio, Dec. 2, 1886; 9. James, b. March 13, 1803; d. Harrison county, Ohio, Aug. 25, 1859; m. 1824, Margaret Fulton, b. in Fayette county, Penn., 1803; d. Aug. 10, 1859 (had issue, among others: i. John-Newton, settled in Short Cheek; m. [1st] 1861, Margaret A. Finley; d. March, 1871; daughter of Dr. Robert Finley, of Mount Pleasant, Ohio; m. [2d] 1878, Mahala Narragan, a native of Ohio); 10. William, b. Feb. 24, 1805; d. in Savannah, Ohio, Dec. 19, 1886; 11. Margaret, b. April 27, 1807; d. June 3, 1888; m. Levi Dickerson; settled near Malta, Ohio; 12. ———; 13.———.

III. Ann, m. Hugh Wylie.

IV. Esther, m. James Pitts.

V. Ezekiel, d. in Indiana county, Penn., 1817.

JOHN HANNA, removed from eastern Pennsylvania (probably from Cumberland county) and settled on Hendricks' Run, Fairfield township, Westmoreland county, before 1772; d. about September, 1788; had issue, among others: 1. John, b. in Fairfield township, Dec. 23, 1773; d. near Cadiz, Ohio, June 2, 1847; removed to Harrison county about 1814; m. (1st) Dec. 6, 1796, Ann (or Nancy) Leonard, b. June 7, 1775; d. March 23, 1818; daughter of James and Mary Finley Leonard (the last named a daughter of John and Martha Berkley Finley, of Lurgan township, Franklin county); m. (2d) Mrs. Margaret Wylie; had issue by first wife: 1. James-Leonard, b. Oct. 5, 1797; d. June 11, 1820; m. June, 1819, Mary Craig (had issue: i. Mary-Ann, m. 1839, Rev. Edward Small, of Mercer, Penn.); 2. Catharine, b. March 6, 1799; d. June 5, 1801; 3. Mary-Leonard, b. Feb. 5, 1800; d. unm. Sept. 11, 1820; 4. John-Evans, b. Dec. 19, 1805; d. Aug. 30, 1894; m. (1st) June 8, 1826, Susanna Robertson, b. March 9, 1804; d. April 15, 1865; daughter of Robert and Beulah Stanley Robertson, of Loudoun county, Virginia; m. (2d) Sarah E. Swayze, b. Sept. 4, 1819; daughter of Rev. William and Frances Peck Swayze (had issue: i. Neri-Augustus, b. April 3, 1827; m. June 7, 1849, Eliza Jane Phillips, b. Feb. 22, 1829; daughter of John and Eliza Gilmore Phillips; ii. James-Leonard, b. Aug. 25, 1829; m. Dec. 22, 1853, Harriet N. Wood; iii. Maria-Eliza, b. March 9, 1832; d. March 2, 1898; m. July 1, 1857, Sharon S. Heskett; iv. John-Edward, b. Aug. 12, 1834; d. Aug. 11, 1892; m. [1st] May 12, 1860, Harriet E. Perkins; m.

[2d] Elizabeth ———; m. [3d] Alice Hill; v. Finley Robertson, b. Feb. 3, 1837; m. June 18, 1871, Ada M. Develing; m. [2d] Mrs. Mary Hyatt; vi. Mary-Ann, b. March 26, 1839; d. Aug. 26, 1840); 5. Eliza-Ann, b. Jan. 8, 1808; d. March 31, 1863; m. 183—, John Oglevee, b. in Cadiz township, Harrison county, Dec. 14, 1810; d. March 12, 1865; son of John and Agnes Oglevee, of Fayette county, Penn., who emigrated to Harrison county, the father dying in 1815 (had issue: i. Mary-Ann, b. May 16, 1837; d. July 21, 1874; m. S. A. Osburn; ii. William-Hamilton, b. Sept. 10, 1838; m. June 20, 1867, Elizabeth A. Craig, daughter of Walter and Jane Moore Craig; iii. John-Finley, b. May 16, 1840; m. [1st] Jean Eagleson; m. [2d] Euphemia [Effie] Eagleson, sister of Jean; iv. Baruch-Francis, b. June, 1842; d. June 12, 1844; v. James-Wilson, b. May 11, 1842; d. May 23, 1863; served in the Civil War, and died from disease contracted in that service; vi. George-Hopkins, b. February, 1847; d. April 12, 1857; vii. Nancy-Jane, b. February, 1849; d. June 25, 1865; viii. Susanna-Elizabeth, b. July 23, 1858; d. Feb. 10, 1880); 6. Jane-Finley, b. June 2, 1811; d. April 13, 1833; 7. Andrew-Finley, b. Feb. 21, 1813; d. April 12, 1847; m. Jan. 13, 1835, Susanna Craig (had issue: i. John-Rowland, b. Oct. 17, 1836; m. June 13, 1861, Ione Theresa Munger; ii. James-Wilson, b. April 13, 1843; m. May 30, 1867, Anna E. Carter; iii. William-Finley, b. March 23, 1846; d. Aug. 1, 1864; iv. Mary-Ann, d. in infancy; v. George-Edward, d. in infancy); 8. David-Wilson, b. Aug. 22, 1815; d. July 2, 1843).

JAMES HANNA, of Washington county, Penn. (probably of Hopewell or Strabane township), b. 1749; d. near Canonsburg, April 6, 1813; m. Anne ———, b. 1760; d. in German township, Harrison county, April 27, 1833; had issue: I. Moses. II. Matthew. III. William, b. 1780; d. April 6, 1830; settled in Green township, Harrison county, Ohió, about 1805; m. Mary ———, b. 1782; d. Nov. 19, 1853; had issue: 1. Robert; 2. John; 3. Esther; 4. Anne; 5. James, settled in German township, where he remained until 1858, thence removed to Monroe county, Ind., where he d. Oct. 12. 1886; m. 1835, Cynthia Shannon, daughter of William Shannon, of Jefferson county, Ohio (had issue: i. William, served in the Civil War; ii. Isaac; iii. James, served in the Civil War; iv. Robert-Porter, served in the Civil War; d. 1863, near Atlanta; v. John-N., b. about 1845; resided in Indiana until 1875, and then returned to Hopedale, Harrison county, where he settled; served in the Civil War; m. Dec. 30, 1872, Nancy J. Copeland, daughter of Jacob Copeland, of Hopedale; vi. Samuel-T.; vii. Moses-K.; viii. Delmar-H.; ix. James-S.; x. Mary; xi. Jennie); 6. Martha; 7. Margaret; 8. William, b. 1812; d. Jan. 8, 1839; 9. Sarah, b. 1822; d. Jan. 13, 1842; 10. Louisa, b. 1823; d. April 27, 1834; 11. Samuel, b. 1824; d. May 6, 1834; 12. Prudence; 13. Mary; 14. Jane. IV. Joseph. V. Robert. VI. Samuel. VII. Prudence. VIII. Jean. IX. Anne. X. Martha. XI. John. XII. James.

PATRICK HANNA, of Hopewell township, Cumberland county, Penn., d. in Monaghan township, York county, about November, 1758; probably the same whose name occurs on tax-list of New Garden township, Chester county, Penn., 1739; had issue: 1. John (probably one of the two Johns last named above); 2. Joshua; 3. Samuel, d. in Hopewell township, about April, 1789; m. Mary Brady, daughter of Hugh and Hannah Brady; after his death, his widow removed, about 1790, with her family to Fairfield township, Westmoreland county, settling near her brother-in-law and sister, Archibald and Margaret Brady Hanna (had issue: i. Joseph; ii. Margaret; iii. Samuel; iv. Elizabeth; v. Mary; vi. Ebenezer, b. after 1770; vii. [a daughter], b. about May, 1785); 4. Archibald, d. in Fairfield township, Westmoreland county, June, 1794; m. Margaret Brady, daughter of Hugh and Hannah Brady (had issue: i. Hugh; ii. William; iii. Mary, m. Robert Williams; iv. Hannah); 5. Martha; 6. Rosanna; 7. William; 8. ———, m. Moses Stuart, son of Andrew and Mary Stuart, of Hopewell township; removed to Peters township, Franklin county, before 1763.

ROBERT HANNA, died in Hempfield township, Westmoreland county, Penn., about April-May, 1786; m. Elizabeth Kelly, daughter of John Kelly, of Donegal township, Lancaster county; settled in Hempfield township, about

1769-70, and founded Hannastown (which was attacked and burned by the Indians and British, July 13, 1782; when some of the inhabitants were killed and many carried to Canada as prisoners, among the latter being Elizabeth Hanna and her daughter, Jane, who were released at Montreal and returned home the following December; had issue: 1. Jane, b. May 13, 1764; d. June 11, 1816; m. Lieut. David Hammond, an officer in the Revolution; b. about 1749; d. April 27, 1801 (had issue: i. Elizabeth, b. June 21, 1786; d. May 5, 1822; m. John Watson, of Watsontown, Pa., b. Dec. 13, 1779; d. Jan. 13, 1856; ii. Mary, m. John Montgomery, and settled at Muncy, Penn.; iii. Grace, m. ——— Montgomery, of Paradise, Penn.; d. without issue: iv. Robert-Hanna, b. 1791; d. 1848; major and paymaster, U. S. A., m. Elizabeth Clark Gloninger; v. Jane); 2. Elizabeth, b. about 1773; m. about 1797, her cousin, James Kelly, b. 1776, son of Col. John and Sarah Polk Kelly, of Buffalo Valley, Union county. Pa. (had issue: i. Eliza, m. John Bates; removed to Perrysburg, Wood county, Ohio; ii. John-Robinson, d. young; iii. Robert-H., d. unm.; iv. James-Andrew, d. unm.; v. Susan-Robinson, d. without issue; vi. Jane, d. unm.; vii. Maria (or Margaret), m. ——— Hutchison, and settled in Huntingdon county, near Altoona, Penn.); 3. Susanna, m. William Robinson; d. without issue; 4. Margaret, d. young.

ROBERT HANNA, of Westmoreland county, Penn. (probably of Fairfield township); had issue: 1. William, settled on Chartiers Creek, three miles north of Canonsburgh, Washington county, before 1800; removed to Ohio, 1802 (had issue, among others: i. John; ii. Thomas; iii. Isaac).

ROBERT HANNA, settled in Lower Smithfield township, Northampton (now Monroe) county, Penn., before 1748, where he d. June-July, 1777; m. Margaret ———; had issue, among others: 1. Benjamin. Robert Hanna mentions in his will grandchildren, Robert Hanna and John and Eleanor Sealy.

ROBERT HANNA, b. about 1754; settled in what is now Greene county, Penn., before 1780, with his brother, Benjamin; had issue. among others: 1. Joseph, b. about 1786; m. Elizabeth Hammer; removed about 1818-19, to Greene county, Ohio; and in 1820 to Jackson county, Indiana; 2. John; 3. Samuel; 4. Robert.

SAMUEL HANNA, probably son of Andrew Hanna, of Paxtang (above), d. in Hopewell township, August-September, 1808; m. Agnes ———; had issue: 1. Samuel; 2. Jean, m. ——— White; 3. Martha, m. James Sharp; 4. Mary, m. James Sterret, son of James Sterret, of Donegal township, Lancaster county (had issue: i. James; ii. Samuel); 5. Elizabeth, m. ——— Sterrett; 6. Rachel, m. ——— Trimble; 7. Nancy, m. ——— Williamson; 8. Sarah, m. ——— White.

THOMAS HANNA, of county Monaghan, Ireland (probably from Ballybay), m. Elizabeth Henderson, and emigrated to America about 1763, supposed to have settled in Pennsylvania; d. about 1764-5; had issue:

I. John, b. about 1763; when the family reached Newcastle, Del.

II. James (twin), b. March 7, 1753; d. Oct. 31, 1827; m. (1st) in Maysville, Ky., Hannah Bayless, b. Aug. 13, 1761; d. Aug. 14, 1804; m. (2d) in Dayton, Ohio, Elizabeth ———; removed from Pennsylvania to Georgetown, Scott county, Ky., and about 1803 settled near Dayton, Ohio; had issue by first wife: 1. Thomas, d. in Massachusetts, without issue; m. three times; 2. James; a minister; settled in Crawfordsville, Ind. (had issue, among others: i. Bayless-W., U. S. Minister to Argentina,1884-89); 3. Samuel, b. in Scott county, Ky., Oct. 18, 1797; d. at Ft. Wayne, Ind., June 11, 1866; m. Eliza Taylor, b. Feb. 2, 1803; d. Jan. 12, 1888; in 1819, settled at Ft. Wayne, Ind.; 4. Hugh, b. July 24, 1799; settled in Ft. Wayne, 1824, and, in 1835, laid off the town of Wabash, Ind.; 5. Elizabeth, m. (1st) John Johnson; m. (2d) ——— McCorkle; settled at Thorntown, Ind.; 6. Martha, m. Andrew Telford (or Tilford), and settled in Troy, Ohio; 7. Sarah, m. Harvey Ward, and settled in Lafayette, Ind.; 8. Nancy-W., m. James Barnett, and settled in Ft. Wayne, Ind.; 9. Joseph-S., b. in Dayton, Ohio, Dec. 7, 1803; d. Aug. 4, 1864; m. (1st) ———; m. (2d) Hester Ann Sumwalt. James Hanna had issue by second wife: 10. Amos; 11. Harriet. m. ——— McClure; 12. Benjamin; 13. Deborah.

HARRISON COUNTY GENEALOGIES

III. Robert (twin), b. March 7, 1753; d. at New Lisbon, Ohio, July 17, 1837; m. Jan. 31, 1776, Catherine Jones, b. Aug. 27, 1754; d. Sept. 28, 1835; dau. of Benjamin Jones (b. in the Great Valley, Chester county, Pa., d. 1754) and his wife Esther Evans Jones, b. in Chester county about 1734; d. about 1816 (m. 2d, John Jones). Robert Hanna and his wife became Quakers about 1780; removed from Pennsylvania to Lynchburg, Va., and about 1802-10 to Columbiana county, Ohio; had issue: 1. Thomas, b. May 2, 1777; d. Sept. 17, 1828; m. Anna ———; 2. Benjamin, b. June 14, 1779; d. July 16, 1853; m. (1st) Dec. 15, 1803, Rachel Dixon, b. July 19, 1785; d. Feb. 28, 1851; m. (2d) 1851-2. Hannah Kersey, (had issue by first wife: i. Joshua, b. Nov. 8, 1804; d. July 7, 1881; m. Feb. 3, 1830, Susan R. Lathrop, b. June 24, 1803; d. Dec. 17, 1875; ii. Leonard, b. March 4, 1806; d. Dec. 15, 1862; m. Sept. 10, 1835, Samantha M. Converse, b. April 3, 1813 [and had issue, among others: Marcus-A., b. July 11, 1838]; iii. Levi, b. Feb. 7, 1808; m. March 21, 1833, Nancy Watson, b. July 11, 1808; d. April 1, 1879; settled at Greeley, Col.; iv. Zalinda, b. Feb. 23, 1810; d. Dec. 4, 1854; m. Feb. 28, 1828, Charles D. Hostettor, b. April 29, 1802; d. Aug. 26, 1872; v. Robert, b. Aug. 15, 1812; d. April 3, 1882; m. March 16, 1837, Harriet A. Brooks, b. March 8, 1815; d. July 27, 1882; vi. Tryphena, b. June 12, 1814; d. Dec. 28, 1893; m. Sept. 4, 1833, Samuel Nicols, b. Jan. 21, 1807; d. May 23 1873; vii. Rebecca, b. Sept. 21, 1816; d. Oct. 15, 1847; m. May 31, 1837, Jesse Holmes; viii. Thomas-B., b. May 22, 1818; d. Nov. 9, 1885; m. March 2, 1843, Sophia T. Tabor, b. May 24, 1822; d. Oct. 20, 1895; ix. Anna, b. March 3, 1821; d. Jan. 26, 1846; m. March 27, 1845, Hiram T. Cleaver; x. Benjamin, b. March 14, 1823; d. April 3, 1881; m. March 26, 1845, Catherine M. McCook, b. Nov. 24, 1823; xi. Kersey, b. Oct. 6, 1824; m. March 15, 1849, Mary A. McCook, b. Jan. 7, 1826; d. Feb. 7, 1891); 3. Esther, b. Aug. 6, 1781; d. Nov. 3, 1791; buried in South River graveyard, Va.; 4. David, b. Jan. 9, 1784; d. Oct. 24, 1791; 5. Caleb, b. Sept. 4, 1786; d. July 15, 1790; 6. Robert, a portrait painter of Virginia; b. June 28, 1789; m. Roxanna ——— (had issue: i. Raphael; ii. Fletcher); 7. Esther (2d), b. April 10, 1792; d. Dec. 6. 1849; m. Charles Hole, a Quaker minister; (had issue, nine children); 8. Catherine, b. Nov. 25, 1794; d. May 3, 1881; m. John Hole (had issue, eight children); 9. Ann, b. July 30, 1797; d. 187—; m. Benjamin Hambleton (had issue, living in Iowa); 10. Joshua, b. Feb. 16, 1802; d. Sept. 11, 1834.

IV. Hugh, d. August, 1820; m. Rebecca ———, and settled on Ten Mile creek, Morris township, Washington county, Pa., about 1790; had issue: 1. John-Vance, m. Lydia McCollum (had issue: i. Thomas; ii. Matilda, m. John Braden, and settled at Rankinville; iii. Margaret, m. Mathias Minton, and settled in the village of Prosperity; iv. ———; v. ———; vi. ———); 2. James, m. Phoebe, daughter of Benjamin Day; removed to Carrollton, Ohio; 3. Elizabeth, m. Samuel Clutter; 4. Rebecca, d. unm.; 5. Nancy, m. Jacob Hathaway; 6. Eleanor; 7. Martha, m. Dr. Spencer Blachly, of Waynesburg, Pa.; Hugh, settled at Connellsville, Fayette county; 9. Thomas, d. young.

V. Martha, b. Jan. 7, 1758; m. ——— Saunders, and settled on Ten Mile Creek, Washington county, Pa.

VI. Thomas, b. 1760; d. April 9, 1839; m. Jane Cowden, b. 1759; d. near Cadiz, Ohio, April 4, 1839; settled in Buffalo township, Washington county, Pa., before 1793; removed to Harrison county, Ohio, 1835; had issue: 1. John-C., d. Sept. 13, 1865 (had issue: i. James-Rankin; ii. Maria, m. W. G. Maxwell and settled in Buffalo township; iii. Elizabeth-M., m. ——— Leiper, and settled in Denver, Col.; iv. Thomas, d. young; v. Thomas-H., a minister; settled in Monmouth, Ill.; vi. Margaret-M.; vii. Jane-C.; viii. James-M.; ix. Hugh-Allison; x. ———, died in infancy); 2. James, settled near Cadiz, Ohio (had issue: i. Martha, m. Rev. George C. Vincent); 3. Thomas, d. young; 4. Thomas, a minister; d. Feb. 9, 1864; settled in Cadiz, Ohio, about 1821; removed to Washington, Pa., about 1848; m. (1st) Jemima ———, b. Oct. 30, 1805; d. at Cadiz, July 14, 1847; m. (2d) Sept., 1848, Sarah R. Foster, of Washington, Pa., b. in Hebron, Washington county, N. Y., Nov. 10, 1802 (had issue by first wife: i. Robert-P.; m. Esther Hammond, and settled at New Athens, Ohio; ii. Thomas-B.; a minister; d. 1850-60; iii. Sarah-J., settled at Salem, Washington county, N. Y.; iv. Mary, m. Dr. J. B. McMichael, of Monmouth, Ill.; v. Maria, m. Andrew J. Sweeney, of Wheeling, West Va.; vi. Martha, m. Dr. W. A. McKenzie; settled at Salem, N. Y.; vii. Joseph, d. young); 5. Elizabeth, m. ——— McCune; 6. Mary, d. July 29, 1848; m. Rev. Joseph Scroggs, b. near Newville, Pa., March 1, 1793; d. in Fairfield township, Westmoreland county, Pa., April 21, 1873 (had issue, ten children, among whom: i. Joseph, a United Presbyterian minister, b. July 28, 1836).

WILLIAM HANNA, b. 1720; d. in Frankford township, Cumberland county, Penn., Oct. 3, 1807, where he had settled before 1764; had issue: I. John, d. June, 1824; had issue: 1. William; 2. John, d. October, 1839; m. Jane ——— (had issue: i. William, d. August, 1861; ii. Eliza); 3. Mary, m. ——— Mitchell; 4. Eliza. II. (possibly) Samuel.

WILLIAM HANNA, settled in Antrim township, Franklin county, Penn., before 1762, where he d. November, 1785; m. Elizabeth ———; had issue: 1. John; 2. ———, m. James Morrow; 3. ———, m. Henry Morrow; 4. ———, m. John Wherry; 5. ———, m. Samuel Adams.

HEZEKIAH HARRISON, of English descent, b. in Maryland, 1804; d. June 3, 1877; settled in Green township, Harrison county, Ohio, about 1820; m. 1829, Lydia Hilbert, b. 1813; d. May 28, 1869; daughter of David Hilbert; had issue: 1. David, settled in Marion county, Kan.; 2. Albert-J., d. May, 1889; served in the Civil War; m. Susanna Holmes, daughter of Asa and Mary McCoy Holmes; 3. Henry-H., m. (1st) ———; m. (2d) Henrietta F. Hall; settled in Wheeling, W. Va.; 4. William, b. in Short Creek township, Nov. 21, 1842; served in the Civil War; m. 1867, Sarah A. Hargrave, daughter of Joseph and Margaret Hargrave, of Harrison county; 5. Milton, d. in infancy; 6. Arabella.

JAMES HARRISON, b. in Ireland; m. Elizabeth Addy; d. 1872; had issue: 1. James; 2. Hugh; 3. Matilda, m. Seth Munn; 4. Sarah, m. Samuel Poulson; 5. Margaret, m. Richard Duncan; 6. Elizabeth, m. 1856, Patrick Lynch, b. in Ireland, 1833; d. 1887; settled in Cadiz, Ohio, 1856.

JOHN HARRISON, a native of England, b. 1758, emigrated to America and first settled in Pittsburg, Penn., about 1814; settled in North township, Harrison county, Ohio, about 1816; d. in England, 1833; his wife also d. in England; had issue: I. Joseph, b. near Otley, Yorkshire, England, 1800; came to Ohio with his parents in 1816, and settled in North township, where he died April 13, 1878; m. (1st) 1828, Ellen Hartley, a native of Carlton, England, b. 1806; d. 1853; daughter of Christopher and Mary Hartley, also natives of England (the former b. 1778; d. 1864; the latter b. 1789; d. 1867); m. (2d) 1857, Sarah Herron, b. 1813; d. 1890; had issue by first wife: 1. John, b. July 10, 1830; m. April 22, 1852, Euphemia Patterson, daughter of John and Isabella McMillan Patterson, early settlers of Carroll county, Ohio, who were m. 1824 (the former d. 1859; the latter, who was a daughter of Robenia McKelvey, and a granddaughter of Ann Shearer, a native of Scotland, d. 1846); (had issue, eight sons and four daughters); 2. William, b. Oct. 29, 1837; settled near Scio, m. 1860, Elizabeth Waddington, a native of Harrison county, daughter of William and Ann Wallace Waddington (had issue, ten children); 3. Joseph, b. 1840; d. 1847.

William Waddington, father of Elizabeth Harrison, was a native of Yorkshire, England, b. 1815; settled in Harrison county about 1835, where he m. 1839, Ann Wallace, a native of Pennsylvania who had settled in Harrison county; later they removed to Tuscarawas county, Ohio; had issue: 1. James; settled in Christian county, Ill.; 2. Elizabeth, m. William Harrison; 3. John; 4. William; 5. Henry; 6. Mary-Jane; 7. Sarah; 8. Amos; 9. Isaac; 10. David.

JAMES HAVERFIELD, of Scotch-Irish descent, emigrated to America and settled in Huntingdon county, Penn.; located in what is now Harrison county after 1800; m. Nancy ———; had issue:

I. William, b. in Pennsylvania, 1774; d. in Harrison county, June 14, 1859; m. in Pennsylvania, Elizabeth Stitt, a native of that State; d. 1858; served in the War of 1812; had issue, ten children, among whom: 1. John, b. 1811; d. May 9, 1873; settled in Cadiz township; m. 1836, Nancy Richey, daughter of Thomas Richey, a native of Ireland, who had located in Harrison county (had issue: i. William-S., b. in Cadiz township, Oct. 2, 1838; served in the Civil War; m. 1865, Mary Haverfield, daughter of Alexander Haverfield, d. in Harrison county; ii. Eliza-Jane, m. R. A. McCormick, of Cadiz; iii. Alvin; iv. John; v. Mary; vi. Jessie, m. John S. Thompson; settled in Carroll county, Ohio).

II. John, b.1788; d. 1855; served in the War of 1812; m. Agnes Henderson, b. 1771; d. 1848; settled in Harrison county, Ohio; had issue: 1. Alexander, b. 1805; settled 1825, in Cadiz township, where he d. in January, 1875; m. Catherine Shimer, b. in Ohio, 1813; of Scotch descent; d. May, 1879 (had issue: i. Eliza, m. James M. McGaw; ii. James-H., killed at the battle of Snicker's Gap; iii. J. Calvin, b. March 12, 1842, in Cadiz township; served in the Civil War; m. 1870, Martha G. Thompson, daughter of R. G. and Jane Thompson, residents of Carroll county, Ohio; iv. Mary-H., m. W. S. Haverfield; v. Clarence-H.); 2. Jane, m. —— Clark; 3. Nancy; 4. James, b. 1814; d. April 2, 1880; m. Elizabeth Barr, b. 1829; d. Aug. 6, 1895; daughter of Hugh and Agnes Henderson Barr (had issue: i. Agnes, m. B. F. Oglevee; ii. Hugh; iii. Martha-Jane; iv. Caroline, m. C. O. Hines; v. Elizabeth-B., m. Henry S. Barricklow; vi. Ella; vii. John-Harvey; viii. Rheta-May; ix. Lulu-Irene).

III. Joseph, b. April 28, 1790; d. March 31, 1852; served in the War of 1812; had issue: 1. Gillespie, b. 1820; d. near Cadiz, March 17, 1882; m. May —, 1860, Sarah J. Hines, b. Oct. 29, 1830, daughter of William and Isabella Hitchcock Hines, of Cadiz township; (had issue: i. William-H., a minister, b. near Cadiz, March 14, 1861); ii. Mary-Belle, m. John Keesey; iii. Catherine-May, m. John Barger; iv. Gillespie-Sherman; v. Ida-Alice; vi. Melissa-Jennette; vii. Martha-Alberta); 2. George-L.; 3. Mary-Ann.

IV. James, served in the War of 1812.

V. Nathan, b. 1797; d. 1873, near Wheeling, W. Va.; came with his father to Harrison county, Ohio; m. in Pennsylvania, Harriett Barnett, d. 1877; had issue: 1. John-N., b. May 17, 1820, in Cadiz township; settled in Stock township, 1861; m. Oct. 27, 1842, Emeline Laveley, b. April 30, 1822; daughter of John and Annie Gorsuch Laveley, natives of Maryland (had issue: i. Henry-L., b. July 29, 1843, in Cadiz township; served in the Civil War; m. April 17, 1866, Mary Elizabeth Barrett, a native of Harrison county, Ohio, daughter of William H. and Eliza Barrett; ii. Harriet-A., m. —— Birney; removed to Tuscarawas county; iii. William-Kinsey, b. Jan. 23, 1854; m. 1875, Anna Humphrey, daughter of William and Jane Law Humphrey; settled in Jewett; iv. Emmet-N., b. December, 1859; settled in Cadiz; m. 1875, Mary A. Finical, daughter of Robert Finical); 2. James-Nathan, b. Oct. 14, 1821, in Cadiz township; m. (1st) 1844, Martha Hitchcock, d. 1856; daughter of Samuel and Isabella Moore Hitchcock, of Harrison county; m. (2d) 1857, Eliza McDougall, born in Harrison county, daughter of Moses McDougall, who had married in Ireland before emigrating to Harrison county (had issue by first wife: i. Nathan; had issue by second wife: ii. Sarah-Alma, m. George F. Hanna; iii. Amanda, m. William H. Wiley; iv. Nancy-Estelle; v. James-Lloyd); 3. William-B.; 4. Thomas-H.; settled in Indiana; 5. Sarah-Jane; 6. Jemima-H., m. Jeremiah Weaver; settled in Franklin township, Harrison county; 7. Joseph, b. Nov. 15, 1832, in Cadiz township; m. March 15, 1855, Mary Jane Johnston, daughter of Samuel Johnston, of Harrison county (had issue: i. Harriet-Elizabeth, m. James A. Mitchell, of Cadiz township; ii. Kersey-Wood; iii. Bertha-Virginia); 8. Nathan-B., b. Jan. 29, 1835, in Cadiz township; served in the Civil War; m. Nov. 15, 1865, Mary A. Harper, daughter of Samuel and Cassandra Harper, who were among the early settlers of Harrison county; 9. Samuel-Patterson; 10. George-A., served in the Civil War; 11. Nancy-E., m. Neal McCaffrey; settled in Iowa.

JAMES HAWTHORNE. b. in Ireland, 1788; settled in Harrison county, Ohio, before 1819, where he d. 1844; two of his brothers settled in Jefferson county, Ohio; m. Rosanna Stewart, d. aged ninety-two years, daughter of Robert Stewart; had issue: 1. Hannah, m. —— McIlroy, and settled in Washington county, Iowa; 2. Margaret-Ann, m. John McNary, and settled near New

Athens, Harrison county; 3. Nancy-Jane; 4. Arabella, d. aged twelve years; 5. Robert-Creighton, b. Oct. 5, 1819; removed to Muskingum county, Ohio, in 1861, where he d. 1864; m. 1842, Margaret J. Grove, b. in York county, Penn., Aug. 26, 1817, daughter of Francis and Jeanette Grove (had issue: i. Arthur-Allison, b. Feb. 27, 1845; m. Jan. 3, 1878, Jane Eliza Maxwell, a native of Jefferson county, daughter of Samuel and Isabella McMillan Maxwell; ii. Francis-Grove, b. Jan. 25, 1847; iii. Emily-Arabella, b. Oct. 20, 1849; m. James Holmes; settled in Greene county, Ohio; iv. James-Stewart, b. Aug. 2, 1852; settled in Adena, Jefferson county); 6. Samuel-E.; 7. William; 8. Rosanna.

The parents of Margaret J. Hawthorne, Francis and Jeanette Grove, settled in Cadiz township, Harrison county, in 1833, where they resided until the time of their death; the former b. 1782; d. March, 1844; the latter b. 1789; d. 1873; had issue: 1. Emily; 2. Susan; 3. Maria; 4. Charlotta; 5. Margaret-Jane, m. Robert C. Hawthorne; 6. Eleanor-R., m. Oliver R. McNary, and settled in Leavenworth, Kan.; 7. Thomas-Cross, settled in Jefferson county, Ohio; 8. Sarah-Elizabeth, m. Samuel Kyle, and settled in Muskingum county, Ohio; 9. Francis-Pringle, settled in Cadiz township; 10. William-Scott, settled in Kansas.

LANCELOT HEARN, b. in Baltimore, Md., 1794, of Scotch-English descent; removed to eastern Ohio in 1815; settled in Cadiz, Harrison county, Ohio, about 1849; m. Barbara Sutherland Urquhart, daughter of Alexander and Francis Tucker Urquhart, who had settled near Cadiz in 1813 (the former was a native of Scotland, and served in the Revolutionary War; the latter, a native of West Virginia); had issue: 1. Eliza, b. 1829; d. Feb. 25, 1879; m. Samuel Slemmons; 2. Wesley-Browning, b. in Jefferson county, Oct. 6, 1840; settled in Cadiz; served in the Ohio Legislature, 1890-92; m. 1868, Jane C. Beall, daughter of John and Agnes Vincent Beall, of Cadiz; 3. Albert, settled at Dodgeville, Wis.

JOHN HEASTAN, a native of Somerset county, Penn.; removed to Harrison county before 1827 and settled in Monroe township; m. 1833, Mary Hines, a native of Westmoreland county, Penn., daughter of Christopher and Jane Jeffers Hines, who settled near Cadiz; had issue, among others: 1. John-Wesley, b. Jan. 8, 1840; m. 1863, Mary J. Bower, daughter of Jacob and Anne Bower.

JOHN HEBERLING, b. 1777; d. in Short Creek township, Harrison county, Ohio, 1864, where he had settled in 1823; served in the War of 1812; son of Andrew Heberling, a native of Germany, who settled in Virginia before 1784; m. in Virginia, Mary Crumley, b. 1780-83; d. 1864-67; had issue:

I. Henry, d. in Jefferson county, Ohio. II. Eliza, m. James Ady, and settled in Muscatine county, Iowa. III. John, settled in Miles, Jackson county, Iowa. IV. Hiram, settled in Osage county, Kan. V. William, settled in Greene county, Ill. VI. George-H., b. in Berkeley county, West Va., Feb. 6, 1814; settled in Short Creek township; m. 1835, Matilda Spurrier, a native of Maryland, d. Dec. 23, 1890; daughter of Ralph and Eleanor Cleary Spurrier; had issue: 1. Thomas; 2. William, served in the Civil War; killed at the battle of Perryville, Ky.; 3. Mary-Ellen, m. J. R. Watkins; 4. John; 5. Warner, m. Rosanna Hagan, d. 1881; 6. Andrew, settled in California; 7. Henry, m. Mary J. Stevens, of Short Creek township; 8. Hazlett; 9. Martha. VII. James, settled in Howard county, Mo. VIII. Andrew, settled in Iowa. IX. Rebecca, m. Thomas Lewis, and settled in Dubuque, Iowa. X. Mary, m. Joseph Holmes.

Ralph Spurrier, father of Matilda Heberling, was a native of Maryland, b. 1773; d. April 2, 1848, in Short Creek township, having settled there in 1801; m. March 3, 1801, Eleanor Cleary, b. Dec. 18, 1784; d. June 2, 1869; had issue: 1. John, b. April 3, 1802; 2. Samuel, b. Feb. 21, 1805; 3. Warner, b. Aug. 19, 1807; 4. Sarah, b. Nov. 10, 1809; 5. Richard, b. Sept. 5, 1812; 6. Ruth, b. March 24, 1815; 7. Matilda, b. Sept. 15, 1817; 8. Elizabeth, b. March 7, 1820; 9. Mary-Ann, b. Dec. 5, 1822; 10. Asenath, b. Sept. 20, 1824; 11. William, b. March 22, 1827.

SAMUEL HEDGES, b. in Virginia, Dec. 26, 1783; d. 1865; settled in Cadiz township about 1805; m. in Virginia, 1789, Prudence Dunlap, b. at West Liberty, (West) Virginia, Dec. 20, 1873; d.

Jan. 15, 1850; had issue: 1. Abraham, b. June 30, 1811; d. young; 2. William-Dunlap, b. 1812; d. June, 1867; m. Mary Jane McClelland, b. at Ballanahinch, Ireland, 1824; d. 1897; daughter of John and Jane Beatty McClelland (had issue: i. Rachel, b. 1844; m. Robert Reid Cochran; ii. Norwood, b. 1849; d. 1896; iii. Sarah-Jane, b. 1851; m. Alexander Osburn; iv. Margaret-Anne, b. 1854; v. Samuel-Beatty, b. 1857; vi. Martha-Ellen, d. 1864; vii. Clara, d. 1864; viii. Cora, d. 1867; ix. Mary-Emma, m. Beatty Osburn; x. Infant; xi. William-Francis, b. 1867; d. 1870); 3. Sarah, b. Oct. 14, 1814; d. young; 4. Martha, b. April 27, 1816; d.1854; m.Israel Birney; 5. Rachel, b. Oct. 10, 1817; d. 1896; 6. Sarah, b. 1819; d. 1839; m. Samuel Cochran; 7. Margaret, b. January, 1820; d. young; 8. Prudence, b. Nov. 9, 1822; d. 1840; 9. Samuel, b. Jan. 20, 1825; d. 1886; m. 1851, Mrs. Sarah Rowley Welsh, b. in Carroll county, 1827; daughter of Luther Rowley (had issue: i. Martha, m. Samuel Richey; ii. Luther-R.; iii. William-P., b. 1858; m. 1879, Susan Ross, daughter of Aaron Ross; iv. Mary-E., m. William Boyles).

JOHN HENDERSON, a native of Ireland, d. February, 1862, in Rumley township, Harrison county, Ohio, where he had settled in 1817; after emigrating to America, first settled in Maryland, thence removed to Indiana county, Penn., and afterwards located in Harrison county; m. in Hagerstown, Md., —— Henderson, d. May 13, 1877; daughter of George Henderson; had issue, among others: 1. James, b. in Indiana county, Penn., Sept. 10, 1813; d. Nov. 1, 1889; m. October, 1838, Susanna McClintock, a native of Monroe township, daughter of Thomas and Elizabeth Fisher McClintock (had issue, among others: i. John-C., b. July 21, 1839; m. (1st) 1862, Hester Fisher, of North township, d. Jan. 4, 1865; m. (2d) April 2, 1866, Mahala P. Fisher, sister of his first wife, d. Oct. 8, 1877; m. (3d) March 27, 1879, Sarah McPeck, daughter of George McPeck, a resident of Archer township; ii. Thomas; iii. Alexander; iv. Elizabeth-Jane; v. George; vi. Lavina; vii. Barbara; viii. Henry; ix. Walter; x. William-Homer).

WILLIAM HENDERSON, a native of Pennsylvania, removed to Ohio, and, before 1813, settled in Cadiz township, Harrison county, where he died; m. Nancy Wilkins, a resident of what is now Carroll county, Ohio; had issue, among others: 1. Sarah, m. —— Love; 2. Jane, m. —— Patterson; 3. Catherine, m. —— Trimbull; these three sisters settled near New Athens, Harrison county; 4. Alexander, b. Aug. 9, 1813; settled in Cadiz township; d. March 17, 1883; m. 1843, Margaret Finical, a native of Washington county, Penn., daughter of Isaac and Margaret Finical, who were early settlers in Harrison county (had issue: i. William, b. May 11, 1844; served in the Civil War; m. Dec. 7, 1871, Rachel H. Robison, daughter of James and Mary Barnes Robison, of Archer township, Harrison county; ii. Alvin, a physician, settled in New York; iii. James-O., b. Feb. 26, 1847; m. 1874, Belle Wells, daughter of Charles Wells, of Cadiz township).

JOHN HILBERT, emigrated from Adams county, Penn., to German township, Harrison county, Ohio, about 1833; had issue: 1. Peter; 2. John; 3. Daniel; 4. Henry, b. in Adams county, Penn., 1819; m. (1st) 1845, Anne Waddington; m. (2d) 1853, Margaret Finnicum, daughter of David and Elizabeth Lowmiller Finnicum; 5. Jacob, m. Mary Lowmiller; 6. Elizabeth, m. John Burns; 7. Mary, m. Frederick Trump; 8. Sarah, m. Jacob Bosley; 9. Lydia, m. Edwin Robinson; 10. Katharine, m. Jacob Unger; 11. Sophia, m. Edwin Robinson.

JOHN HINES, see Family of James Ramsey.

RUDOLPH HINES, b. in Germany; d. September-November, 1823, aged ninety; son of John Hines, who came to America before the Revolutionary War; removed to Steubenville, Ohio, in 1796, thence to Virginia in 1806; settled in Harrison county, Ohio, 1814; served in the Revolutionary War; m. Sarah Huff; had issue, twelve children, among whom:

I. William, b. in Allegany county, Md., March 19, 1800; d. September, 1887; m. Feb. 15, 1827, Isabella Hitchcock, b. Jan. 24, 1806; daughter of John and Jane McMahon Hitchcock (the former a native of Maryland, of Irish descent; the latter born in Ireland); had issue: 1. John-R., settled in Clark county, Iowa, 1879; m. 1853, Elizabeth Christy, d. at Murray, Iowa, 1880;

daughter of Robert and Jane Christy, natives of Harrison county; 2. Sarah-Jane, m. Gillespie Haverfield; 3. ———, d. in infancy; 4. Lemuel-Browning, settled in Redfield, Cal.; 5. William-Fletcher, b. February, 1839; served in the Civil War; m. Feb. 7, 1867, Christina Spiker, a native of Harrison county, daughter of Christopher and Ara Carnes Spiker, early settlers in Harrison county (the former d. 1879; the latter 1870); 6. Mary-Ellen, m. Joseph McBeth, and settled in Deersville; 7. Samuel-Montgomery, settled in Nottingham township; 8. James-McMahon, b. March 5, 1844; settled in Cadiz township; served in the Civil War; m. Nov. 3, 1868, Elmira J. Carson, a native of Harrison county, daughter of Elijah and Margaret Mahaffey Carson; 9. Thomas-Hogg, d. in infancy; 10. Ezra-Lawson, d. aged fourteen years.

II. Daniel. III. James. IV. John. V. Isaac. VI. Samuel. VII. Joseph. VIII. Mary. IX. Martha.

John Carson, d. in Nottingham township, was among the early settlers of Harrison county; Elijah, his son, father of Elmira Hines, was b. 1810; d. November, 1887; m. Margaret Mahaffey, b. in Washington county, Penn., 1803; d. 1884; her mother was a native of Maryland, of Welsh descent; had issue, seven children, of whom: 1. ———, m. Joseph G. Rogers; 2. Elmira-J., m. James M. Hines; 3. ———, m. T. B. Huffman.

THOMAS HITCHCOCK, a native of Maryland, removed to Jefferson county, Ohio, about 1792; settled in Archer township, Harrison county, after 1800; had issue, among others:

I. Samuel, b. in Maryland, 1787; removed to Cadiz township before 1812, where he d. Feb. 3, 1879; m. Isabella Moore; had issue: 1. Margaret; 2. Jane; 3. Isabella; 4. Harriet; 5. Maria; 6. Elizabeth; 7. Mary; 8. Martha; 9. John, b. March 12, 1812; settled in Franklin township, 1841; m. Jan. 8, 1835, Sarah Kelly, d. Sept. 10, 1889; daughter of Hugh and Mary Kelly, of Short Creek township (had issue: i. Isabella, m. Sept. 24, 1862, S. M. Birney; ii. John-A., settled in Cleveland, Ohio; iii. Mary-E., m. A. J. Lever, a minister; iv. Johnson, settled in Washington township; v. Mary; vi. Samuel, twin brother to Mary, m. 1875, Nancy McGill, daughter of John McGill, of Franklin township); 10. Thomas.

JAMES HOAGLAND, see account of Michael Conaway.

GABRIEL HOLLAND, a native of Maryland, of English descent, settled in Archer township, Harrison county, Ohio, before 1814; m. in Maryland, Sarah Harriman; had issue, eight children, of whom:

I. Gabriel, b. in Maryland, 1789; d. in Archer township, 1871; m. Susannah Conaway; b. 1784; d. 1861; daughter of Michael and Elizabeth Conaway, of Archer township, pioneers of Harrison county; had issue: 1. John, b. September, 1814; he settled in Cadiz township; m. 1840, Esther West, of Cadiz township, b. 1820; d. April 13, 1889; daughter of Jonathan and Mary Comfort West (had issue: i. Sarah-Jane, m. J. Welling, and settled in Guernsey county, Ohio; ii. Samuel; iii. Elizabeth, m. D. B. Harrison, and settled in Iowa; iv. Martha; v. Susan, b. 1854; d. Feb. 22, 1889; m. C. McCune; vi. Gabriel, d. 1889; vii. Jonathan; viii. Amanda); 2. Sarah; 3. Elizabeth, m. A. Pickens, and settled in Iowa; 4. Mary-Jane; 5. Ellen; 6. Nancy, m. Martin Maholm, and settled in Archer township; 7. Harriet, m. ——— Lewis, and settled in Archer township; 8. Samuel, settled in Archer township.

ROBERT HOLLIDAY, son of Arthur Holliday, b. in the North of Ireland, 1758; d. at Martin's Ferry, Ohio, 1851; emigrated to America about 1793, first settling in the Cumberland Valley, and thence removing to Westmoreland county, Penn.; located in the western part of Harrison county, Ohio, about 1815; m. in Ireland, Rebecca Ramsey, d. 1826; had issue, nine children, of whom: 1. Nancy, m. ——— Cooper, and settled in Henry county, Indiana; 2. Robert, b. Aug. 1, 1792; d. July 5, 1885; served in the War of 1812; settled in Freeport about 1830; m. (1st) March 25, 1817, Frances Melton, b. Nov. 22, 1795; d. Dec. 22, 1818; m. (2d) March 29, 1821, Elizabeth White, b. Dec. 25, 1800; d. Aug. 16, 1872 (had issue by first wife: i. Frances-Melton, b. Nov. 28, 1818; had issue by second wife, thirteen children, of whom: ii. Theodore-Oscar, m. Susan Reaves; iii. Anne, m. 1846, David Winder; iv. Eldred-Glencairn, b. Jan. 19, 1822; m. Jan. 10, 1850, Mary Cunningham, daughter of John and Nancy Sharp Cunningham).

LEVI HOLLINGSWORTH, a Quaker, great-great-grandson (through three ancestors, each named Thomas Hollingsworth) of Valentine Hollingsworth, who emigrated from Belfast, Ireland, to Pennsylvania, about 1683; removed to Flushing township, Belmont county, in 1804; had issue: 1. Elihu, b. in Belmont county, 1813; m. 1839, Lydia Ann Fisher, daughter of Barrack Fisher, of Pughtown, Va. (had issue: i. David, b. at Flushing, Ohio, Nov. 21, 1844; m. April, 1875, Belinda McBean, daughter of Dr. John McBean).

REV. OBADIAH HOLMES, b. in Manchester, England, about 1606; m. 1636; emigrated with his wife, Catharine, from Preston, Lancashire, and settled at Salem, Mass., 21st of 11th month, 1638; removed about 1643-44 to Rehoboth, R. I., as he was a Baptist and not allowed to live in the Puritan colony; publicly whipped by the Puritans at Boston, in September, 1651, on account of his religious opinions, and "for holding meetings on Lord's Day from house to house;" served as minister of the Baptist Church at Newport, R. I., from 1652 to 1682; d. Oct. 15, 1682; had issue: 1. Jonathan, b. about 1637; 2. John, b. about 1639; 3. Martha, b. 1640; 4. Samuel, b. 1642; 5. Obadiah, b. 1644; 6. Hope, m. —— Taylor; 7. Mary, m. John Browne; 8. Lydia, m. Captain John Browne. Of these, Jonathan, d. 1713; m. Sarah Borden; settled at Middletown, Monmouth county, N. J., 1667 (had issue: i. Obadjah; ii. Jonathan; iii. Samuel; iv. Joseph; v. Sarah, m. —— Oulde (?); vi. Mary, m. —— Easton; vii. Catharine, m. —— Whitman; viii. Martha, m. —— Tillinghast). Obadiah m. —— Cole; settled at Middletown, N. J., 1663 (had issue, two sons and two daughters, of whom: i. Samuel, d. young; ii. Jonathan, d. Sept. 8. 1715). Rev. Obadiah Holmes, the emigrant, had about 5,000 descendants living in America as early as 1790.

Descended from one of the above was, Obadiah Holmes, b. at Trenton, N. J., 1721; settled in the Virginia Valley; living in Rockingham county, Va., about 1768; in Jefferson county, West Va., about 1771; in Bedford county, Penn., about the time of the Revolution; in Strabane township, Washington county, Penn., 1784-85; and later in Brooke county, West Va., where he d. about 1796; m. in New Jersey, Mary Clum, d. in York township, Jefferson county, Ohio, 1812; had issue:
I. John; served in the Revolutionary War; was taken a prisoner and died in service.
II. William.
III. Obadiah.
IV. Isaac, b. in New Jersey, April 29, 1764; removed with his parents to Virginia; served in the War of 1812; settled in what is now Carroll county, Ohio, 1814, where he d. June 9, 1851; m. in Virginia, 1794, Elizabeth McNabb, b. July 24, 1772, in Shepherdstown, Va.; daughter of George and Martha McNabb and sister to Sarah McNabb; had issue: 1. Martha, d. in Kenton, Ohio, aged eighty-seven years; m. (1st) Joseph Wilson; m. (2d) William Leaper; 2. Clum, d. aged twenty-three years; 3. Sarah, d. in Ottumwa, Iowa, aged eighty-five years; m. Jacob Millisack; 4. Nancy, d. in infancy; 5. Mary, m. James Price, and settled at Leesville, Carroll county, Ohio; 6. Susannah, m. Joseph Masters, and settled at Connotton, Harrison county; 7. George-Washington, b. Dec. 30, 1807; settled in North township, 1843, where he d. June 26, 1887; m. (1st) 1837, in North township, Mary Cripliver; m. (2d) Amanda Jenkins; m. (3d) Emily Stratton (had issue: i. Jacob-M.; ii. Isaac-C., settled in Columbus, Ohio; iii. Samuel-W., settled in Kansas; iv. John-D.; v. Luther-L.; vi. Edward-S.; vii. Martha-E.; viii. Phœbe-A.; ix. Mary-Alice; x. Ora-A., m. J. M. Harrison, and settled in Washington State; xi. Emma, m. Charles Crawford; settled in New Philadelphia, Ohio); 8. Samuel, settled in Leesville, Carroll county; 9. Elizabeth, m. Sampson Jenkins, and settled near Salem, Jefferson county, Ohio; 10. John-McNabb, d. in Connotton, aged sixty-five years; m. Emily ——, who settled near Des Moines, Iowa.
V. Jacob, b. in Rockingham county, Virginia, Dec. 8, 1768; d. at Kenton, Ohio, Oct. 14, 1841; m. on Buffalo Creek, Brooke county, West Va., 1791, Elizabeth Huff, b. May 22, 1772; d. Jan. 27, 1857; shortly after his marriage he was

employed by the Government as an Indian scout, and in company with his brother-in-law, Kinsey Dickerson, and another man, was thus employed for three years, receiving for his services a section of land in Short Creek township, Jefferson county, near Mt. Pleasant; here he settled in 1796; had issue, among others: 1. (a daughter), m. —— Wilkin; 2. ——, m. Augustine Bickerstaff, of Steubenville, Ohio; 3. ——, m. Nathaniel Moore, of Little York, Jefferson county.

VI. Joseph, b. in Shepherdstown, Jefferson county, West Va., Jan. 27, 1771; removed to what is now Jefferson county, Ohio, before 1799; settled in Short Creek township, Harrison county, about 1800, where he d. April 20, 1868; served in the Indian Wars, and as an officer in the War of 1812; served in the Ohio Senate, 1832-34; m. in Jefferson county, Sarah McNabb, b. 1783; d. Feb. 10, 1862; sister to Elizabeth McNabb and daughter of George and Martha McNabb, of Scotch descent, early settlers near Mount Pleasant, Ohio; had issue: 1. George, b. 1799; d. 1886; m. (1st) Hannah Lynn; m. (2d) 1824, Tacy Thompson; m. (3d) 183—, Hannah Mansfield, daughter of Thomas and Mary Hill Mansfield (the former a native of England, b. 1757; d. 1844; the latter b. 1767; d. 1854) (had issue by first wife: i. Joseph, b. 1825; d. 1889; m. Mary McConnell; ii. Rezin, b. 1827; m. Emeline Mansfield; had issue by second wife: iii. Emma, m. 1864, Kersey Wood Kinsey); 2. Mary, m. John Glazner; 3. Elizabeth, m. (1st) William Dickerson; m. (2d) Isaac Thomas; 4. Cynthia, m. John Styres; 5. Asa, b. in Short Creek township, Dec. 4, 1806; d. Jan. 3, 1891; m. 1837, Mary McCoy, daughter of Thomas and Hannah McCoy, of Athens township, Harrison county (had issue: i. James-Taylor, served in the Civil War; settled in Columbus, Ohio; ii. Susanna, m. Albert Harrison, and settled in Cadiz; iii. Abram, served in the Civil War; settled in New Philadelphia; iv. Emeline; v. Sarah-Elizabeth, m. Henry Stringer, of Short Creek township; vi. Wilson; settled near Smithfield, Jefferson county; vii. Mary-Ellen, m. Samuel Dickerson, and settled in Athens township; viii. Henrietta, m. C. A. McCleary, and settled at Cadiz; ix. Oliver-Wendell, a Methodist Episcopal minister, settled in Kent, Ohio; ix. Clifton-A.); 6. Abraham, b. in Short Creek township, Dec. 1, 1808; d. May 3, 1880; m. (1st) 1836, Rachel Mansfield, b. 1814; d. Feb. 12, 1854; daughter of Thomas Mansfield, of Jefferson county; m. (2d) 1856, Phœbe Ann Ekey, a native of Jefferson county, daughter of Andrew and Ann Howden Ekey (had issue by first wife: i. Joseph-M., b. 1847; d. 1871; m. 1870, Chloe A. McCleary, b. 1850, daughter of Ephraim and Mary A. Gillespie McCleary; ii. William; had issue by second wife: iii. ——, d. in infancy; iv. Wesley-A., b. in Short Creek township, Aug. 19, 1859; m. 1884, Minerva Conwell, daughter of John and Mary Conwell, of Cadiz); 7. Martha, m. John Webb, and settled at New Athens; 8. Joseph, m. Sarah Moore, and settled at Hopedale; 9. Sarah, m. James Haverfield; 10. Susan, m. (1st) Joseph Webb; m. (2d) Joseph Dunlap; 11. John, d. aged eight years.

VII. Samuel.
VIII. Elizabeth.
IX. Margaret.

Andrew Ekey, father of Phœbe Ekey Holmes, was b. in Pennsylvania, 1791; d. 1873; was of Irish descent; settled in Jefferson county, Ohio, 1801; m. Ann Howden, b. 1799; d. Feb. 5, 1870; had issue: 1. Andrew; 2. Margaret; 3. Mary-Ann, m. Benjamin Barkhurst, and settled in St. Clairsville, Ohio; 4. Phœbe-Ann, m. Abraham Holmes; 5. David; 6. Edward, settled in Jefferson county; 7. John-H.; 8. James, settled in Jefferson county; 9. Wesley.

WILLIAM HOLMES, b. 1782, son of William Francis Holmes, a native of Ireland, who settled in Pennsylvania, removed to Green township, Harrison county, Ohio, about 1802, where he d. Jan. 22, 1861; m. (1st) in Pennsylvania, Elizabeth Crouch, b. 1790; d. 1849; m. (2d) Matilda Thaker, d. in Mount Pleasant, Jefferson county; had issue by first wife: 1. Isaac, b. in Green township, where he d. Feb. 12, 1884; m. 1833, Jane Vincent; d. July 17, 1884; daughter of Dr. Thomas Vincent, of Green township (had issue: i. Sarah; ii. William-F., b. Dec. 25, 1836; m. (1st) Oct. 10, 1860, Amanda S. Baxter, b. April 25, 1836; d. Oct. 13, 1881; daughter of Samuel Baxter, of Green township; m. (2d) Dec. 24, 1884, Hannah J. Starr, daughter of William Starr, of Wayne

HARRISON COUNTY GENEALOGIES

township, Jefferson county, Ohio; iii. Thomas-V., b. March 14, 1840; m. Oct. 21, 1869, Melissa Jane Harrah, b. Feb. 13, 1847, daughter of John Harrah, of Jefferson county; iv. Eliza-Jane; v. Martha; vi. Matilda; vii. Mary; viii. Josephine; ix. Amanda; x. ———, d. in infancy; xi. ———, d. in infancy; xii. Winfield-S.); 2. Susan; 3. Sarah; 4. Elizabeth.

HARVEY HOST, a native of Germany, emigrated, before 1800, to Pennsylvania, where he died; m. Nancy Fulton (b. 1776; d. Jan. 11, 1845), who after the death of her husband, married (2d) John Moffat, and removed to Harrison county, Ohio; had issue by first husband (surname Host): 1. Harvey; 2. Samuel, b. in Pennsylvania, Dec. 20, 1801; settled in Green township, Harrison county, where he died Nov. 2, 1889; m. (1st) Aug. 27, 1825, Louisa Oxley; d. June 12, 1834; m. (2d) April 5, 1838, Jane Hines, a daughter of William Hines, of Harrison county (had issue by first wife: i. Henry; ii. James; iii. Mary-Ann; iv. John, b. in Jefferson county, Sept. 27, 1831; m. April 22, 1858, Ruth A. McMillan, b. Aug. 31, 1835; a daughter of John McMillan, of Carroll county, Ohio; v. Louisa; had issue by second wife; vi. William-H.; vii. Sarah; viii. David; ix. Amos; x. Eliza-Jane); 3. James; 4. John; 5. William; 6. Eliza.

HENRY HOUSER, b. in Kentucky, 1786; settled in Cadiz, Harrison county, Ohio, before 1825; d. Sept. 23, 1855; served in the War of 1812; m. at Bennett's Creek, Frederick county, Maryland, 1824, Susannah Ramsower, b. 1791; d. 1867; had issue: 1. William-Lambdin, b. June 17, 1825; m. Sept. 24, 1857, Sarah Virginia Hall, of Washington, Guernsey county, Ohio, daughter of Edward and Henrietta Catherine Roberts Hall (had issue: Francis-E., Mary-Virginia, Ellsworth-Wilson, William-Henry, Thomas-Edward, Isabel-McFadden, and Henrietta-Katharine); 2. Wilson- Lee, b. April 1, 1828; 3. Warnetta, m. William Stroud.

MICHAEL HUFF, of Brooke county, Va., m. Hannah Doddridge; had issue: 1. Joseph, an early Indian scout and fighter of Harrison county, d. in Short Creek township; 2. Michael, killed by the Indians on the Mississippi; 3. Elizabeth, b. May 22, 1772; d. at Kenton, Ohio, Jan. 27, 1857; m. 1791, Jacob Holmes, b. in Rockingham county, Va., Dec. 8, 1768; d. at Kenton, Ohio, Oct. 14, 1841; 4. William, an early Indian scout and fighter of Harrison county, d. in Short Creek township; 5. John, m. Sarah Johnson; d. at Columbia, near Cincinnati, Ohio, 1842; 6. Samuel, d. in Highland county, Ohio, about 1846; 7. Eleazer, d. in Highland county, Ohio, about 1833.

EDWARD HUGHES, of Scotch-Irish descent, settled before 1800 near Rising Sun, in Cecil county, Md., where he died; had issue: 1. Robert-M.; 2. Sarah, m. ——— Smith; 3. Rebecca, m. ——— Poole; 4. Edward, b. Oct. 30, 1814; removed about 1834 to Port Deposit, Md., thence to Philadelphia; located in Cadiz, Harrison county, Ohio, in 1839; afterwards settling in New Athens, where he d. April 5, 1889; m. in New Athens, Sarah Ann Brown, daughter of James and Jane Welch Brown (had issue: i. Hester-A.; ii. Eliza-Jane, m. Prof. Thomas M. Sewell, of New Athens; iii. Oliver-P.; iv. John-W., settled in Springfield, Ohio; v. George-W., settled in Hopkins, Mo.; vi. Mary-E., m. Rev. Oliver Holmes, and settled in Kent, Ohio; vii. James-C.; viii. Edgar; ix. Theodore, settled in Iowa; x. Vandorn; xi. and xii. Twins, d. in infancy.

James Brown, father of Sarah Ann Hughes, was b. in county Derry, Ireland, in 1785; settled near New Athens, Harrison county, about 1814; d. 1860; his wife was b. 1788; d. 1865; had issue: 1. George, settled in St. Clairsville, Ohio; 2. Joseph, settled near Flushing, Belmont county, Ohio; 3. Mary-Ann; 4. Jane; 5. Margaret, m. James Rankin, and settled in Missouri; 6. Sarah-Ann, m. Edward Hughes.

THOMAS HUNTER, d. in Newberry township, York county, Penn., before Nov. 19, 1777; m. Mary Canon; had issue, Nancy, James, Ephraim, Jane, Mary, of whom:

James, b. Dec. 6, 1738; d. Jan. 27, 1809; settled on Fourteen Mile Run, Unity township, Westmoreland county, Penn., about 1768-70; served in the Revolutionary War, and was one of the founders of Unity Presbyterian Church; m. Elizabeth McDonald; had issue: I. Ephraim. II. Joseph. III. Sarah. IV. William. V. Mary. VI. James, b. in

Westmoreland county, Penn., Feb. 4, 1777; d. in Wayne county, Ohio, Sept. 16, 1829; m. Agnes (Nancy) Sloan, b. March 28, 1777; d. Aug. 15, 1858; daughter of —— Sloan; had issue: 1. Elizabeth; 2. Samuel; 3. Joseph-R., b. in Westmoreland county, Penn., May 26, 1804; d. at Cadiz, April 4, 1886; m. March 16, 1835, Letitia McFadden, b. 1812; d. April 13, 1883; daughter of Samuel and Lydia Stafford McFadden, of Cadiz (had issue: i. Cyrus-James; a Presbyterian minister; settled in Uhrichsville, Ohio; ii. Samuel-McFadden; settled at Newark, Ohio, where he became a judge; iii. Mary, b. 1840; d. 1858; iv. Lydia, d. Feb. 28, 1886; m. William H. Arnold, of Cadiz; v. Charlotte, m. Alexander J. Hammond, of Cadiz; vi. William-Henry; settled at Chillicothe, Ohio; vii. George-Frederick; settled at Chillicothe, Ohio); 4. Isaac; 5. John-Sloan; 6. James; 7. Nancy-Sloan. VII. Thomas. VIII. Samuel. IX. Ralph.

JOHN HURFORD, b. in Culpepper county, Virginia, son of Samuel Hurford, whose father, John Hurford, was an English Quaker; m. in Virginia, Sarah Hayes, a native of that State; removed to Harrison county while it was still a part of Jefferson; had issue: 1. Evan, b. in Virginia; m. in Jefferson county, Sarah Hall, a native of North Carolina, who was a member of the Friends' Church; settled about five and one-half miles southeast of Cadiz, where they died, both in their ninety-first years (had issue: i. Aquila; ii. Joseph, b. in Cadiz township, 1809; m. Rebecca Ann Welsh, of Washington county, Penn.; d. in New Brighton, 1885; settled in Pittsburgh; had issue, one daughter and one son, both of whom died in infancy; iii. Mary-Ann; iv. Christian; v. Sarah; vi. John; vii. Hannah; viii. Rachel); 2. John; 3. Samuel; 4. Rachel; 5. Sarah; 6. Mary; 7. Ann.

SOLOMON INSLEY, b. in Maryland about 1770; d. in Guernsey county, Ohio; m. Britannia Dean, b. in Maryland; had issue:
I. Jemima.
II. Sarah.
III. Rebecca.
IV. Eunice.
V. Hudson.
VI. Micajah, b. in Maryland, 1791; d. 1845, in Nottingham township, Harrison county, Ohio; came to Ohio with his parents; m. Clarissa Hawse, b. in Maryland, 1801; d. 1885; had issue: 1. Asbury; 2. Eunice; 3. Sarah, b. March 18, 1829; m. Jan. 1, 1857, James Barclay, b. in county Derry, Ireland, Sept. 23, 1823; d. April 21, 1885 (had issue: i. Joseph; ii. David, settled at Dennison, Ohio; iii. John; iv. Clara; v. William; vi. Benjamin, settled at Poughkeepsie, N. Y.; vii. James; viii. Annie); 4. Maria, m. —— Kennedy, of Tuscarawas county, Ohio; 5. Robert, settled in Kansas; 6. John, settled in Uhrichsville, Ohio; 7. Rachel, settled in Tuscarawas county; 8. Benjamin, served in the Civil War; killed at the battle of Petersburg, August, 1864.

JOHN JAMISON, b. in Ematris Parish, near Coote Hill, county Cavan, Ireland, 1743; d. near West Middletown, Washington county, Penn., Jan. 28, 1811; m. (1st) about 1765, —— ——; d. before 1772; m. (2d) about 1772, Sarah McFadden Gilmore, d. Dec. 29, 1835 (widow of Nathaniel Gilmore), of Coote Hill, county Cavan, Ireland; emigrated to America with his family and his wife's two children by her first marriage (see Family of Nathaniel Gilmore, p. 504) about 1773 (?), first locating in Shearman's Valley, near Newport, Perry county, Penn.; removed to Washington county and located in Chartiers Creek about 1782, afterwards settling near Buffalo Creek in Independence township, three miles southwest of West Middletown; with his second wife; buried in Mt. Hope graveyard, near West Middletown; had issue by first wife:

1. Andrew, b. 1766; d. at Cadiz, Ohio, March 30, 1859; m. about 1792, Nancy McKee, b. 1775; d. at Cadiz, Ohio, April 18, 1855; removed from Washington county, Penn., to Harrison county, Ohio, about 1830 (had issue: i. John, d. in Huron county, Ohio; m. Sarah Mulholm; ii. Barkley, b. 1795; d. Oct. 23, 1869; m. Margaret Patterson, d. 1875; iii. Elizabeth, d. about 1861; m. John Forbes and removed to Illinois; iv. Isabel, m. Levi Hamilton, b. 1805; d. April 6, 1881; v. Mary, d. about 1860; m. James Hutchison, and removed to Illinois; vi. Samuel, d. about 1825; vii. Isaac, b. 1808; d. Jan. 7, 1840; viii. Alexander, d. in Belmont county,

Ohio, March 18, 1856; m. Mary McConahy).

2. Samuel, b. 1768; d. Nov. 4, 1855; m. (1st) about 1797, Martha Barber, d. about 1823; emigrated to America about 1801; m. (2d) Mrs. Sarah Cope, d. about 1850, all buried at West Middletown (had issue by first wife: i. John, b. 1798; d. Feb. 14, 1875; m. [1st] about 1819, Mary Nealy, m. [2d] Ann Smith; ii. Elizabeth, m. John Dinsmore, and settled in Jefferson county, Ohio, near Steubenville).

John Jamison had issue by second wife:

3. Mary, b. 1773; d. 1850; m. about 1793, Robert Law, b. 1771; d. 1860; settled at New Lexington, Perry county, Ohio, about 1835, where they are buried (had issue: i. Thomas, b. 1794; d. 1878; m. Mary Buchanan, and removed to Iowa; ii. Sarah, b. 1795; m. about 1812, Aaron Johnson; settled in Perry county, Ohio; iii. John, m. Mary Perry, settled in Perry county, Ohio; iv. Jane, b. 1797; d. March 16, 1882; m. Robert Welch, b. Feb. 26, 1787; d. Aug. 21, 1866; settled at Bloomfield, Muskingum county, Ohio; v. Robert, d. about 1825; vi. William, d. 1883; m. Sarah Dodan; settled at Xenia, Ohio; vii. Mary, m. about May, 1829, James McFadden, b. 1804; settled near Cadiz, Ohio; viii. James, b. 1809; d. May, 1884; m. [1st] Rebecca Patterson; m. [2d] ——— Skinner; settled at Monmouth, Ill.; ix. Samuel, m. Hannah Brown; settled in Iowa; x. Andrew, b. June 16, 1816; m. [1st] ——— Hull; m.[2d] ——— Smith, d. 1895; settled in Perry county, Ohio).

4. John, b. 1774; d. Oct. 16, 1848; settled near Cadiz, Ohio, about 1801; a soldier of the War of 1812; m. about 1800, Ann Craig, b. 1780; d. Aug. 30, 1847, both buried at Cadiz (had issue: i. Walter, b. Feb. 24, 1801; d. at Cadiz, Ohio, 1883; m. [1st] 1828, Martha Beattie, daughter of James and Jane Reynolds Beattie, of Short Creek township, b. 1807-8; d. Jan. 21, 1835; m. [2d] 1837, Mary Snyder, daughter of Martin Snyder).

5. Margaret, b. 1775; d. July 17, 1873; m. about 1792, Thomas McKeaver, b. 1768; d. June 27, 1861; removed from Washington county, Penn., to Perry county, Ohio, 1834; both buried at Iliff's M. E. Church, Perry county, Ohio (had issue: i. Thomas, d. young; ii. Sarah, b. 1798; m. about 1815, John Dodds; iii. John, m. [1st] Elizabeth Rogers; m. [2d] Emily Rogers, sister of Elizabeth; settled near Morristown, Belmont county, Ohio; iv. Ann, b. 1793; m. Lewis Lunsford; settled near Wheeling, West Va.; v. Mary, m. George Bushfield; settled in Illinois; vi. Margaret, d. 1873; m. Joseph Lane; vii. Barbara, b. 1817; d. Dec. 13, 1876; m. Jeremiah Driggs, b. 1804; d. May 25, 1867; both buried at Iliff's Church, Perry county, Ohio; viii. Nancy, b. 1806; m. about 1831, Robert Scott; settled in Iowa; ix. Eliza, d. Nov. 5, 1885; m. Ephraim Knoowy; settled in Perry county, Ohio; x. Martha, m. ——— DeLong; xi. Joseph, m. ——— Alexander; settled at Olathe, Kan.; xii. Samuel, m. ——— Wylie; settled in Perry county, Ohio; xiii. William, m. ——— Hollenbach; xiv. Jane, m. John Yost).

6. Nancy, d. 1862; m. about 1798, Robert McBroom, d. 1856; both buried at Lower Buffalo, Brooke county, West Va. (had issue: i. John, b. March, 1799; d. Feb. 25, 1895; m. [1st] about 1827, Elizabeth Griffa, d. Sept. 21, 1858; m. [2d] 1860, Margaret Moore, b. 1808; d. August, 1866; all three buried at Iliff's Church, Perry county, Ohio; ii. Mary, m. John Dickey; iii. William, d. in Ohio; iv. Andrew, d. in Brooke county, West Va., about 1850; v. Thomas, m. [1st] Margaret Anderson; m. [2d] ——— Griffa; vi. Samuel, m. about 1834, ——— Henry; vii. Sarah, m. about 1835, Christopher Hootman, d. in Brooke county, West Va.; viii. Jane, d. about 1838; ix. Nancy, d. 1863; x. Robert, m. about 1846, Rebecca Haggarty; xi. David).

7. William, b. 1782; d. unm., May 26, 1860; buried in Mt. Hope graveyard.

8. Elizabeth, b. 1785; d. Dec. 24, 1857; m. 1803, Samuel McFadden, b. 1778; d. July 2, 1837; settled near Cadiz, Ohio, where both are buried (had issue i. James, b. 1804; d. June, 1874; m. May, 1829, Mary Law; ii. Sarah, b. 1807; d. Oct. 14, 1841; m. Samuel Carnahan; iii. Eliza, m. John Dickerson; iv. John, d. July 4, 1881; m. about 1835, Margaret McFadden; v. Samuel, d. March, 1863; m. about 1834, Margaret Rankin; vi. Jane, m. Adam Dickerson; vii. Alexander, d. in California; m. about 1342, Mary McFadden; viii. Margaret, m. ——— Dunlap).

9. Robert, b. 1788; d. Aug. 3, 1832; m. (1st) 1812, Jane Hill, b. 1787; d. March

26, 1829; m. (2d) Dec. 3, 1830, Margaret Anderson, b. 1798; d. May 25, 1871; all buried at Mt. Hope graveyard, Washington county (had issue: i. John, b. April 8, 1813; d. Sept. 23, 1872; m. Feb. 8, 1840, Sarah Ralston; b. May 22, 1812; d. May 25, 1881; settled at Bloomfield, Muskingum county, Ohio; ii. Thomas, b. Aug. 31, 1815; m. April 18, 1848, Nancy Moore, b. Feb. 9, 1819; iii. Sarah, b. May 13, 1819; d. Sept. 15, 1893; iv. Samuel, b. Dec. 11, 1822; m. [1st] August, 1846, Susannah Herron, d. September, 1850; m. [2d] March 5, 1863, Mrs. Nancy [Lawrence] Patterson; v. William, b. Oct. 22, 1824; d. Jan. 26, 1893; m. [1st] Oct. 8, 1851, Mary Stewart; m. [2d] Margaret Anderson, b. 1798; d. 1871; settled at Keokuk, Iowa; vi. Robert, b. June 14, 1832; m. March, 1858, Elizabeth Hutchinson).

10. Sarah, b. 1789; d. June 25, 1880; m. 1813, Robert Graham, b. 1773; d. December, 1863; both buried in South Buffalo graveyard (had issue: i. John, b. May, 1814; ii. Robert, b. July, 1815; d. May 18, 1878; iii. Mary, d. November, 1887; m. about 1850, Robert Noble; iv. William, m. April, 1846, Susannah Jamison; settled at Indianola, Iowa; v. Sarah, m. —— Buchanan; settled near West Alexander, Penn.; vi. Margaret, m. about 1860, —— Chambers; vii. Jane, d. young; viii. Samuel, d. young).

PHILIP JARVIS, of German descent, b. in Baltimore county, Md., 1785; d. in Harrison county, Ohio, 1866; settled in Belmont county, Ohio, about 1811; m. in Baltimore county, Md., Mary Barnett, b. 1789; d. 1855; had issue: 1. Jacob, b. January, 1815; settled in Moorefield township, Harrison county, 1845; m. Oct. 6, 1842, Eliza M. O'Brien, b. 1814; daughter of Ezekiel O'Brien (had issue: i. Frank; ii. Mary, m. Samuel McConnell; iii. Jane, m. Albert Quigley; iv. Eliza-A., m. John Perry).

ALEXANDER JOHNSON, b. in county Tyrone, Ireland, 1772; emigrated to America and settled at Wilmington, Del., in 1783, thence removed to Butler county, Penn., and in 1814 settled near Jefferson, German township, Harrison county, where he d. 1869; m. in Pittsburg, Mrs. Eleanor Brown Work (widow of William Work), b. 1787, in Baltimore, Md.; d. 1862; had issue: 1. Andrew, d. in Sparta, Ill.; 2. John, b. 1814; d. 1875; 3. Nancy; 4. Alexander, b. Aug. 18, 1818; settled in Rumley township about 1883; m. Dec. 7, 1852, Margaret Galbraith, daughter of Samuel Galbraith, who with his wife, was a native of Ireland, and who removed from Pennsylvania to Harrison county (had issue: i. John; ii. Samuel; iii. Alexander, settled in Columbus, Ohio; iv. Ellen-Jane; v. Isabella-Ann, m. Michael Finical); 5. Mary, m. Joseph Hamilton.

HENRY JOHNSON, b. ——; d. 1850; removed from Allegheny county, Penn., to Harrison county, Ohio, before 1812, and settled in Moorefield township; m. Catherine ——, b. ——; d. ——; had issue: 1. Henry-M., m. 1824, Margaret Gibson (?); 2. William-C.; a physician; m. 1836, Jane McFadden, daughter of Samuel and Lydia Stafford McFadden; 3. Wesley; 4. Asbury-F., m. Rebecca Sloan, daughter of Matthew M. and Elizabeth Grimes Sloan; removed to Laramie, Wyoming; 5. Belinda, m. 1829, Dr. John McBean, of Cadiz, b. 1797; d. Jan. 7, 1875; 6. Julianna (?), m. James Tallman; 7. Harriet, m. 1836, George W. McPherson, b. 1811; d. Jan. 10, 1880; 8. Catherine, m. —— Price.

WILLIAM JOHNSON, b. in Pennsylvania, May 26, 1776; removed, 1804, to Short Creek township, Harrison county, Ohio, where he d. Jan. 7, 1855; m. Agnes Pickens, b. in Pennsylvania, May 15, 1781; d. Feb. 24, 1864; had issue: 1. Susanna, m. —— Fisher; 2. Mary-L.; 3. Margaret; 4. John; 5. Martha; 6. Josiah; 7. Basil; 8. Temperance, m. —— Neal; 9. William; 10. Elizabeth, m. —— Arnold; 11. Agnes, m. —— Wilson; 12. Rebecca; 13. Abram; 14. Albert, b. Nov. 30, 1823; d. Dec. 10, 1886; m. 1861, Rachel Conaway, daughter of Charles and Frances Arnold Conaway.

Charles Conaway, father of Rachel Conaway Johnson, removed from Maryland and located in Archer township, Harrison county, about 1805; removed with his wife to Richland county, Ohio, 1861, where he d. 1870; m. Dec. 17, 1819, Frances Arnold, d. 1872, daughter of Benjamin and Comfort Arnold, residents of Maryland; had issue: 1. Benjamin; 2. John; 3. Sophia; 4. Ann; 5. William; 6. Elizabeth; 7. Michael; 8. Mary; 9. Charles; 10.

HARRISON COUNTY GENEALOGIES

Rachel, m. Albert Anderson; 11. Susannah; 12. Frances-Jane; 13. Enoch-W., served in the Civil War; killed August, 1862, in the battle of Perryville.

WILLIAM JOHNSON, a native of Ireland, d. June 4, 1829; removed from Washington county, Penn., to Short Creek township, Harrison county, Ohio, about 1814, where his son, John, had settled in 1802; m. in Westmoreland county, Penn., Elizabeth Laughlin, d. Jan. 10, 1816; had issue:
I. John, settled in Harrison county, in 1802. II. William. III. Richard. IV. Alexander. V. Robert. VI. James, b. in Washington county, Penn., April 12, 1793; d. Nov. 9, 1863; m. March 19, 1818, Mary Simpson, b. May 28, 1794; d. Jan. 25, 1881; daughter of James Simpson; had issue: 1. Margaret, b. Oct. 6, 1819; m. Sept. 18, 1845, Samuel Muchmore, d. Aug. 21, 1889 (had issue: i. Albert, b. Nov. 6, 1847; d. Dec. 28, 1878; ii. Martha, b. July 29, 1850; m. Dec. 3, 1868, John Tallman; iii. William, b. June 29, 1853; m. March 11, 1886, Anna Tidball); 2. Elizabeth-J., b. Feb. 12, 1821; 3. Mary-Simpson, b. July 5, 1823; m. June 28, 1854, John Dickerson, d. April 12, 1865 (had issue: i. James-H., b. May 3, 1855; m. Oct. 1, 1879, Eva Parkinson; ii. Anna-M., b. Nov. 16, 1856; m. Feb. 1, 1882, William H. Hunter; iii. Ruth, b. Dec. 11, 1857; d. April 19, 1887; iv. Lewis, b. Jan. 16, 1859; d. Feb. 4, 1864; v. Flora-Bell, b. Oct. 15, 1865; m. Jan. 1, 1890, Isaac B. Scott); 4. Sarah, b. Dec. 30, 1825; d. April 8, 1887; m. Oct. 8, 1846, William Boals (had issue: i. James, b. April 24, 1848; m. Aug. 11, 1876, Mary Walker); 5. Catherine, b. Oct. 15, 1830; 6. William-H., b. May 4, 1833; m. Oct. 11, 1877, Mary Ann Parkinson, daughter of Thomas Parkinson, of Green township, Harrison county. VII. Samuel. VIII. Ann. IX. Catherine. X. Mary. XI. Elizabeth.

SAMUEL R. JOHNSTON, of Scotch-Irish descent, b. in Baltimore, Md., Dec. 3, 1798; removed with his mother to Charleston, S. C., about 1800, where he remained until 1824, and then located in Monroe township, Harrison county, Ohio; d. Nov. 10, 1883; m. July 20, 1826, Rebecca Barnhill, b. 1807, in Harrison county; d. Aug. 23, 1873; daughter of William and Mary Barnhill, natives of Ireland, who settled in Harrison county; had issue, eleven children, of whom: 1. William-B., settled at Connotton, Ohio; 2. Mary, m. Joseph McKelveen, and settled in Scio, Harrison county; 3. Joseph-E., b. Aug. 11, 1832; served in the Civil War; m. Jan. 26, 1865, Hannah S. Smith, b. near Laceysville, daughter of William P. and Margaret Smith, early settlers in Harrison county; 4. Margaret, m. Jacob Norrick; settled in Nodaway county, Mo.; 5. Rebecca, m. Simeon Smith, and settled at Tappan, Ohio; 6. Elizabeth, m. Daniel Smith, and settled at Laceysville; 7. Cecilia, m. Jonathan Manbeck, and settled at Des Moines, Iowa; 8. Samuel-R., served in the Civil War.

JOHN KAIL, b. in Pennsylvania about 1775, son of John Kail; d. March-May, 1821; settled in German township, Harrison county, Ohio, 1800; m. Catherine Rouch, b. in Pennsylvania about 1775-85; d. 1870; had issue:
I. Henry. II. Frederick. III. John. IV. Mary. V. Margaret. VI. Nancy. VII. Anna. VIII. Elizabeth. IX. George. X. Jacob, b. in Pennsylvania, 1798; d. in German township, Harrison county, Ohio, 1874; served in the War of 1812; m. Mary Whitmore, b. 1798; d. 1852; had issue: 1. Elizabeth, m. Jacob Bosley; 2. George; 3. Lucinda, settled in the West; 4. Samuel; 5. John-R., b. Jan. 13, 1826; d. September, 1890; m. Nov. 1, 1853, Elizabeth Tedrow, of Rumley township, Harrison county, daughter of George and Elizabeth Hardsock Tedrow; 6. Lavina, settled in Kansas; 7. Hance-W., b. March 11, 1829; settled in Rumley township, 1857; m. August, 1854, Elizabeth Bricker, b. May 2, 1838; d. Oct. 1, 1889, daughter of Henry and Mary Ann Smith Bricker; 8. Enoch, settled at Conrad Grove, Grundy county, Iowa.

JAMES KANE, b. in Ireland; d. in Zanesville, Ohio, about 1818; m. in Cadiz township, Anne Porter, whose parents were natives of Pennsylvania; had issue: 1. William, b. 1813; d. 1895; m. 1839, Mary Minerva Gray, b. 1823; d. 1882; daughter of Jeremiah and Margaretta Taylor Gray (the former from Long Island, the latter from Wales); (had issue: i. Rebecca, m. 1879, George Marple; ii. William-Henry-Harrison, m. Mary Kennedy; iii. James-Jeremiah, m. Ida McMillan; iv. Margaretta; v. Elizabeth-Phillips, m. 1888, Frederick

Carmen; vi. Mary-Maritia, m. William McGrew; vii. Jessie-Lee); 2. Hugh; 3. Margaret, m. Josiah Craig; 4. Martha-Anne, b. 1817; d. 1897.

MATTHEW KENNEDY, b. in Scotland, 1765-67; d. 1847; emigrated to America, and settled in Georgetown, D. C., before 1802, where he m. Christina Hines, d. 1836; removed to Harrison county about 1811; had issue: 1. William-C., m. Sarah Wyckoff; 2. Citizen-J., m. Maria Moore; 3. John-L., m. Matilda Ourant; 4. Mary-A., d. young; 5. Napoleon-Bonaparte, b. November, 1801; d. 1889; m. 1826, at Cadiz, Mary Gilmore, b. 1805; d. 1873; daughter of Samuel and Elizabeth Buchanan Gilmore (had issue: i. Samuel-Gilmore, b. 1827; m. Mary Ensley; ii. Elizabeth, b. 1829; d. 1851; m. Levi Morris; iii. Sarah-Jane, b. 1832; m. Hugh Patterson Dunlap; iv. Christina, b. 1834; d. 1883; m. Levi Morris (his second wife); v. Martha-A., b. 1836; m. John Heller; vi. Matthew-L., b. 1839; m. (1st) ——— Haley; m. (2d) Mrs. ——— Kramer; vii. Mary-F., b. 1844; d. 1863); 6. Return-Matthew, b. March 15, 1803; d. June 16, 1888; m. Feb. 19, 1824, Jane Moore, b. Sept. 20, 1792; d. Sept. 25, 1866; daughter of Robert and Margaret Armstrong Moore (had issue: i. Mary-A.; ii. Howard; iii. Robert; iv. Jackson, b. June 18, 1828; m. (1st) April 3, 1851, Eliza Carrothers, b. March 2, 1835; d. Sept. 4, 1876; daughter of George Carrothers; m. [2d] June 21, 1877, Mrs. Lucy Kennedy Heffling, widow of Walker Heffling, and daughter of Carroll and Mary Latham Kennedy; v. Maria; vi. Salathiel); 7. David-W., m. (1st) ——— Buckington; m. (2d) ——— Gibson; 8. Ahio-F., m. Elizabeth Harvey; 9. Thomas-J.; 10. Elizabeth, d. young; 11. Philip-H., m. Susan Jones; 12. Jacob-J., m. Matilda Smith; 13. Abraham-H.; 14. Christian-H., m. Matilda Todd; 15. Daniel, m. Mary Jane Johnson; 16 and 17. died in infancy.

ABSALOM KENT, b. in Virginia, 1777; son of Absalom Kent, a native of that State; removed to Stock township, Harrison county, Ohio, before 1810; d. in Illinois, 1875, where he had settled; had issue:
I. Absalom, b. in Stock township, 1810; d. 1876; m. (1st) Mary Walker, d. 1848; m. (2d) Sarah Traub; m. (3d) Margaret Worman; had issue by first wife: 1. Absalom, settled in Nottingham township; m. Jane A. Lee, b. July 17, 1837, daughter of Jesse and Harriet Mason Lee, natives of Virginia; 2. John-H.; 3. Joseph-W.; 4. Stewart; 5. William; 6. Tabitha; had issue by second wife: 7. Sarah-J., m. ——— Toole; had issue by third wife: 8. Mary, m. ——— Grimes, and settled in Cadiz. II. Abner. III. John. IV. Jacob. V. Jane. VI. Mary.

AARON KERR, see Family of William Scott.

JAMES KERR, see Family of Roger Clark.

JAMES KERR, b. 1751; d. June 2, 1825; emigrated from Adams and Westmoreland counties, Penn., settling in Short Creek township, Harrison county, Ohio, in 1805; m. Agnes (Nancy) ———, b. 1751; d. June 18, 1836; had issue, eight children, among whom:
I. James, b. 1787, in Adams county, Penn.; d. 1846, in Bellefontaine, Ohio; m. (1st) 1807, Catherine Duff; d. September 21, 1827; m. (2d) 1829, Martha Morrison, of Belmont county, Ohio; had issue by first wife: 1. John-C., b. April 15, 1811, in Short Creek township; settled in Belmont county; from whence he served as a member of the Legislature in 1846; m. (1st) March 23, 1836, Mary Henderson; d. 1847; m. (2d) Jan. 14, 1854, Sarah Newell; d. 1862; m. (3d) Nov. 3, 1863, Grizelle Taggart, daughter of Rev. William Taggart, of Cadiz, Harrison county (had issue by first wife: i. Martha-A.; ii. Amanda-K.; iii. James-H.-H.; had issue by second wife: iv. George; v. John; vi. Gilland; vii. Bentley; viii. Thomas-Corwin; ix. Vance-C.); 2. James; 3. William; 4. George; 5. Margaret-Ann; 6. Joseph; 7. Thomas-L.
II. Samuel, b. in York, now Adams county, Penn., Oct. 25, 1792; d. Feb. 27, 1882, in Short Creek township, where he had settled; served in the War of 1812; m. (1st) Sept. 8, 1815, Anne Smyth, d. 1833; m. (2d) September, 1835, Agnes Hamilton, a native of Ohio; d. March 28, 1885; had issue by first wife, seven children; had issue by second wife: 8. ———, d. in infancy; 9. ———, d. in infancy; 10. Thomas-H., b. Aug. 15, 1836, in Short Creek township, where he settled; m. Nov. 7, 1861, Letitia A. Calderhead, a native of Har-

HARRISON COUNTY GENEALOGIES

rison county, daughter of William and Nancy McLaughlin Calderhead 11. Samuel-C., a Presbyterian minister, b. in Short Creek township, Sept. 9, 1838; settled in Franklin county, Kan., 1889; m. March 11, 1871, Elizabeth N. Rowley, daughter of Luther Rowley, of Bowerston, Harrison county; 12. Margaret-A., m. ——— Calderhead Hanna.
III. John. IV. William. V. Mary. VI. Jane. VII. Elizabeth.

JOHN KERR, d. in Wigtonshire, Scotland, at the age of ninety-four; m. Grace McCracken, who d. aged ninety-six; had issue: 1. James, a Presbyterian minister, b. at Kirkcolm, Scotland, 1805; d. April 9, 1855; emigrated to America and first settled at Winchester, Virginia, removing to Cadiz, Ohio, in 1839; m. 1837, at Pittsburg, Margaret McWhirter, b. in Scotland, 1816; d. Nov. 1, 1890; daughter of David and Mary Fleming McWhirter, of Whithorn, Scotland (had issue: i. Mary; ii. Joseph; iii. David; iv. William; v. John, m. Ora Price; vi. James-W., b. 1850; m. 1881, Martha Lewis; vii. Eliza, m. Rev. Cyrus J. Hunter; viii. Agnes, m. J. W. Slemmons); 2. Grace; 3. Agnes; 4. Mary; 5. John; 6. Stair.

CONRAD KEESEY, b. in Pennsylvania, 1790; d. in Harrison county, Ohio, 1874, where he had settled 1816; m. (1st) in Pennsylvania, ——— Burkett; m. (2d) in White Cloud, Iowa, Ellen Brooks; had issue, among others: 1. ———, m. Erasmus Barrett, of Cadiz township; 2. James, b. 1821, in Harrison county; d. Jan. 6, 1884; settled about five miles northwest of Cadiz, Ohio; m. May 30, 1846, Margaret Layport, b. Dec. 22, 1826, daughter of John L. and Verlinda Harrison Layport (had issue: i. Jane-Ann; ii. Conrad, settled in Uhrichsville, Ohio; iii. Mary-Verlinda; iv. Amanda-V., m. (1st) A. Johnson; m. (2d) D. D. Bowman; v. John-L., b. Oct. 23, 1852; settled four and one-half miles from Cadiz; m. Nov. 24, 1881, Mary Belle Haverfield, daughter of Gillespie and Sarah J. Hines Haverfield; vi. Susan-H., m. James Milliken; settled in Cadiz; vii. Charles-W., settled in Peabody, Kan.; viii. Ella, m. Edward Trenner; settled in Arcola, Ill.; ix. Frankie, d. in infancy; x. Jessie-F., m. Elmer Bowers; settled in Arcola, Ill.; xi. Margaret-B.; xii. Bert-Q.).

DANIEL KILGORE, see Family of John Pritchard.

LEONARD KIMMEL, b. in Germany, 1741; d. in Rumley township, Harrison county, Ohio, 1825; emigrated to America, 1758, and later settled at The Glades, Somerset county, Penn., thence removed to the Cheat River, West Virginia about 1800, and settled in Rumley township a short time afterward; m. Susan Zimmerman, of The Glades, Penn., b. 1748; d. 1828; had issue:
I. John, emigrated from Somerset county, Penn., and settled in Rumley township, Harrison county, Ohio before 1814; m. Eve Turney, of Stone Creek, Penn.; had issue: 1. Susan, m. ——— Wallace; 2. Mary; 3. Sophia; 4. David, b. 1816; d. 1882; m. 1839, Eunice Belle Moore, b. March 17, 1818; d. Nov. 5, 1874; daughter of Thomas and ——— Bonnell Moore, of Pennsylvania (had issue: i. Maria, b. 1840; d. 1873; m. Frank Jamison; ii. John, b. 1842; d. 1863; iii. Daniel-Moore, b. 1843; d. 1865; iv. Royal, b. 1845; d. 1875; v. Thomas-Moore, b. 1848; m. 1872, Sarah Gotshall; vi. Steven, b. 1850; d. 1850; vii. Eunice-Mehitabel, b. 1851; d. 1852; viii. David-Patton, b. 1854; m. 1881, Sarah Schultz); 5. Adam; 6. Claytus; 7. Katharine.
II. Adam.
III. Henry, b. in Pennsylvania, 1789; settled in Rumley township; m. 1814, Christina Gidinger, b. at The Glades, Somerset county, Penn., 1794; daughter of Martin and Elizabeth B. Gidinger, natives of Germany, who settled in Harrison county, in 1808; had issue: 1. Susan; 2. Jonathan, b. July 15, 1815, in Rumley township; m. January, 1836, Mariah Catharine Nupp, daughter of John P. and Catharine Wolf Nupp, natives of Gettysburg, Adams county, Penn. (had issue: i. Sarah-Jane, m. Jacob Condo, of Germano, Ohio; ii. Elizabeth, m. Jacob Stall, and settled in Jewett, Ohio; iii. Nimrod, served in the Civil War; killed at the battle of Fisher's Hill; iv. Christina; v. Titus; vi. Simon-P.; vii. Jonathan; viii. George; ix. Isaac; x. Mary-Magdalena; xi. Martin).
IV. Leonard.
V. Frederick, b. in West Virginia, 1800; d. in Rumley township, March 24,

1885; m. 1826, Elizabeth Yingling; had issue: 1. Sarah, m. John Knoff, of North township; 2. Mary-Ann; 3. Rebecca; 4. Joseph, settled in North township; 5. Lydia-Ann, m. Jacob Binker, and settled in North township; 6. Henry; 7. William, b. Feb. 11, 1838; settled near Scio; m. Feb. 16, 1860, Louisa Sneary, b. May, 1844, daughter of Jacob and Mary Turney Sneary; 8. John; 9. Barbara; 10. Mahala; 11. Delila, m. Samuel Webb, and settled in Cleveland, Ohio; 12. Amos; 13. Joshua.
VI. Nancy, m. —— Harmon.
VII. Mary.
VIII. Susanna, m. 1819, Samuel Guthrey.

JOHN KINSEY, an English Quaker, native of London, emigrated to America, arriving at New Castle, Delaware, in the ship "Kent," June 16, 1677; one of the Commissioners for the settlement of New Jersey, under the purchase by Edward Byllinge; made selection and bargain with Peter Cock, the Swedish deputy, for purchase of 300 acres of land. situated above the mouth of the Schuylkill, near the place which afterwards became known as the site of Penn's Treaty and of the city of Philadelphia. John Kinsey, Jr., came to America in 1678, and settled on the tract of land purchased by his father, where he reared a family; his son John, was Chief Justice of Pennsylvania; Edmund Kinsey, another of his sons, removed in 1715 to Buckingham township, Bucks county, Penn., where he settled; was one of the founders of the Buckingham Monthly Meeting in 1720; m. Nov. 21, 1708, Sarah Osburn; his children were Samuel, David, Mary, Elizabeth, John, Joseph, Sarah, Benjamin, Jonathan. Of these, Benjamin, b. Oct. 22, 1727; m. (1st) 1749, Susanna Brown; m. (2d) 1776, Martha White; had issue, among others:

I. George, m. Dec. 22, 1773, Mary Gillingham; had issue: 1. Sarah; 2. Susanna; 3. Edmund; 4. James; 5. Aaron; 6. John; 7. George; 8. Charles, b. in Bucks county, Penn., May 19, 1786; removed with his parents to Mount Pleasant, Ohio, in 1798; located in the western part of Cadiz township, Harrison county, about 1815, thence, in 1832, removed to Moorefield; afterwards settling in Flushing, Belmont county, where he d. Feb. 11, 1884; m. (1st) in Philadelphia, June 1, 1815, Ann Worrall, b. 1793; d. Oct. 26, 1832; m. (2d) in Moorfield, Talitha Gatchel; d. about 1838; m. (3d) 1842, Rhoda Boone, of Kentucky (had issue by first wife: i. Gillingham, d. aged twenty-two years; ii. Kersey-Wood, b. in Cadiz township, Nov. 2, 1823; settled at Cadiz, in 1847; m. (1st) May 6, 1847, Sarah Jane Haverfield; d. February, 1864; daughter of Nathan Haverfield; m. (2d) Nov. 9, 1864, Emma Holmes, b. Jan. 20, 1835, daughter of George and Hannah Mansfield Holmes; iii. Sarah-Jane, d. in infancy; had issue by second wife: iv. ——, m. David Comly, and settled in Adena; v. ——; vi. ——; had issue by third wife: vii. Emily, m. Eli Davis, and settled in Pittsburg; viii. Charles-Wesley, m. Isabel McFadden, daughter of Henry S. and Isabel Poor McFadden; settled in Oakland, Cal.); 9. Ann.

George Holmes Kinsey, father of Mrs. Emma Holmes Kinsey, was a son of Col. Joseph Holmes, a pioneer of Harrison county; m. (1st) Hannah Linn; m. (2d) Tacy Thompson; m. (3d) Jan. 7, 1834, Hannah Mansfield, daughter of Thomas Mansfield, of Jefferson county, Ohio; had issue by second wife: Joseph and Rezin, and two others; had issue by third wife: William, d. aged six years; Mary, d. aged three years; Emma, m. Kersey Wood Kinsey.

JAMES KIRKPATRICK, b. in Cecil county, Maryland, June 14, 1770; removed in 1801 to Washington county, Penn., where he remained until 1821, and then settled in Athens township, Harrison county, Ohio; settled, 1823, in Moorefield township, Harrison county, where he d. May 26, 1840; m. in Maryland, Mary Cochran, a native of Cecil county, b. Jan. 31, 1771; d. July 25, 1836; had issue: 1. Hugh, b. Sept. 21, 1795; 2. Robert, b. April 29, 1797; 3. Elizabeth, b. July 26, 1799; 4. William, b. in Cecil county, Dec. 11, 1801; d. in Moorefield township, May 1, 1888; m. Dec. 25, 1823, Sarah Guthrie; d. Jan. 14, 1885 (had issue: i. James, b. Nov. 21, 1824; m. (1st) Feb. 25. 1847. Ellen S. Wallace, b. June 17, 1827; d. Nov. 8, 1882; daughter of Rev. William and Mary McWilliams Wallace [natives of Pennsylvania, who settled in Ohio about 1817]; m. (2d) Oct. 12, 1886, Belle Guthrie, b. Dec. 10, 1835; daughter of Robert and Jane Cunningham Guthrie; ii. Robert-G.; iii. Joseph-C., b. Jan. 6,

1828; settled in Moorefield township; m. March 7, 1854, Margaret J. Wallace, b. Dec. 23, 1834, daughter of Rev. William and Mary McWilliams Wallace; iv. Hugh; settled in Iowa; v. Mary-J.; vi. Adeline, m. ——— Kirk, and settled at Flushing, Ohio; vii. Sarah, m. ——— Hays; viii. Elizabeth, m. W. E. Wallace; ix. John, b. 1839; d. 1845; x. Nancy; xi. Margaret, m. ——— Hays); 5. Mary, b. March 4, 1804 (had issue: i. Mary, m. ——— Douglas); 6. James, b. Jan. 10, 1807; 7. John, b. June 11, 1809.

WILLIAM KNOX, a Methodist minister, probably born in Ireland, 1767, of Scottish descent, settled in Maryland, about 1790; removed after 1800 to Harrison county, Ohio, where he d. June 16, 1851; m. Esther ———, b. 1785; d. March 2, 1863; had issue: 1. Jeremiah; 2. William; 3. David; 4. Sarah; 5. John, b. in Maryland; settled in Freeport; served in the War of 1812; d. May 16, 1863; m. about 1815, Mary Davis, a native of Ireland; d. April 12, 1887, daughter of Samuel Davis, who settled in Athens township (had issue: i. William; ii. Samuel; iii. Margaret; iv. Ann; v. Matthew-M.; vi. John-D.; vii. Sarah-J.; viii. James; ix. George-M.; x. E.-M., b. Aug. 16, 1840; settled in Freeport; m. (1st) Nov. 20, 1862, Abbie H. Bendore; d. April 25, 1884; daughter of John and Nancy Bendore, of Smyrna. Ohio; m. (2d) July 24, 1889, Mrs. Elizabeth Tipton Robinson; xi. Theodore); 6. James; 7. Arthur, d. Aug. 23, 1857 (had issue: i. William; ii. Clara); 8. Nancy.

WILLIAM LACEY, b. in Sussex county, Del., 1764; d. May 17, 1828; m. Elizabeth Stinson; removed to Ross county, Ohio, and thence to Harrison county; had issue: I. Robert, d. 1812; a soldier of the War of 1812. II. Anderson, removed West; had issue: 1. Joseph. III. John-Stinson. b. 1793; d. Jan. 16, 1873; m. Dec. 31, 1820, Anna Jeanette Hoyt, b. in New York City, July 21, 1802; d. Sept. 29, 1885; daughter of Jesse and Anna Hoyt; settled at Cadiz, Ohio, about 1816; had issue: 1. Elizabeth. b. Nov. 22, 1821; d. Feb. 16, 1823; 2. William-B., b. Dec. 11, 1820; d. Jan. 14, 1867; 3. Jesse-Hoyt. b. July 8, 1826; d. Sept. 29, 1899; 4. Henry-Brush, b. Nov. 11, 1828; m. (1st) Oct. 4, 1855, Frances Rebecca Stuart; m. (2d) Oct. 5, 1865, Mary Ann Beardsley; 5. John-S., b. July, 1831; d. Dec. 22, 1832; 6. Robert-S., b. Sept. 22, 1833; 7. Anderson-Parker, b. Dec. 11, 1835; d. Jan. 21, 1895; 8. Lewis, b. Oct. 2, 1837; d. Jan. 22, 1843; 9. Anna-Jeanette, b. April 5, 1842; d. Jan. 4, 1866; m. Rev. W. B. Watkins.

EDWARD LAFFERTY (originally Lafetra), removed from Washington county, Penn. (probably Peters township), to Moorefield township, Harrison county, Ohio, some years before 1810, where he died; m. Elizabeth Ramage, b. 1733; d. 1844; had issue, among others:

I. Samuel, b. April 14, 1782; d. Nov. 29, 1857; m. Jan. 1, 1807, Margaret Figley, b. 1782; d. April 4, 1842; had issue: 1. Belijah, b. 1807; d. Aug. 11, 1887; m. 1830, Joshua Dickerson; 2. Jacob, b. Dec. 1. 1809; 3. Edward, b. March 14, 1812; 4. Elizabeth, b. Aug. 7, 1814; 5. Jane, b. Dec. 4, 1817; d. Sept. 11, 1864; m. 1839, William Dickerson; 6. Joseph, b. Oct. 26, 1819; 7. Margaret, b. March 15, 1822; d. May 22, 1847; m. Nicholas Familton.

II. Edward, b. in Pennsylvania, 1789; removed to Moorefield township with his parents, and afterward settled in Athens township, where he d. Nov. 8, 1836; m. Margaret McFadden, b. 1789; d. Sept. 14, 1864; sister of Joseph McFadden; had issue: 1. Samuel; 2. John; 3. Elizabeth, d. 1847; m. Thomas Grimes; 4. Margaret, m. Luke Vorhees, and settled at Loraine, Ohio; 5. George, d. 1860; 6. Joseph, settled in Belmont county; 7. Edward, b. Nov. 25, 1826; d. April 2, 1886; m. Sept. 7, 1865, Sarah A. Cooper, daughter of William C. Cooper; 8. Hiram, b. April 15, 1831; d. Aug. 31, 1875; m. 1857, Jane Dickerson, daughter of John Dickerson, of Athens township; 9. Finley, settled in Nebraska; 10. Mary-Jane.

The Laffertys may have removed to Washington county from Bedminster township, Somerset county. N. J., where a number of them lived during the Revolution. Edmund Lafetra, of Huguenot origin, settled in Monmouth county, N. J., in 1667; d. 1687; m. Frances ———; had issue: 1. Edmund; 2. Elizabeth, m. John West.

SYLVANUS LAMB, b. in Massachusetts, removed from Pittsburg, Penn., to Georgetown, Ohio, and thence in 1843 to Athens county, Ohio, where he

d. 1848; m. in Pittsburg, Isabella White, a native of that place, daughter of Samuel White, a native of Ireland, who afterward settled in Short Creek township; had issue, eight children, among whom: 1. Leonard, settled in Adalissa, Iowa; 2. Sylvanus, settled in Shickley; Neb.; 3. L———-B———, b. in Short Creek township, Jan. 27, 1833; removed to Athens county with his parents in 1843; subsequently returned to Short Creek township; served in the Civil War; m. 1854, Catherine Brooke, a native of Martin's Ferry; d. March 15, 1887; daughter of Benjamin and Martha Brooke, early settlers in Belmont county, where they came from Pennsylvania. (Benjamin Brooke served in the War of 1812.)

PETER LANTZ, a native of Pennsylvania, d. in Jefferson county, Ohio, 1821, where he had settled before 1809; m. Mary Patterson, a native of Pennsylvania, of Scotch-Irish descent; had issue: 1. Christopher-P.; 2. William; 3. John, b. May 24, 1809; d. Nov. 7, 1879; settled in Moorefield township, Harrison county, Ohio, about 1822; m. 1837, Eliza Fulton, b. Feb. 9, 1815; d. Feb. 8, 1887 (had issue: i. Dewey-S., settled in Belmont county, Ohio; ii. R.-W.; iii. Jasper-N., b. Jan. 22, 1843; served in the Ohio Legislature from 1883 to 1889; m. April 27, 1871, Sarah Sloan, b. April 20, 1848, daughter of John and Eliza Wherry Sloan; iv. A.-E., killed in the Civil War; v. Samuel-M., settled at Piedmont, Ohio; vi. Albert C.); 4. Abraham; 5. Abigail; 6. Mary, m. ——— Beall, and settled at Coshocton county, Ohio; 7. Sarah, m. ——— Cramer, and settled in Medina county, Ohio.

EDWARD LAUGHRIDGE, a native of Ireland, emigrated to America and settled at Wilmington, Delaware, 1809; removed to Brooke county, Va., and thence to Jefferson county, Ohio; m. in Ireland, Margaret McConnell; had issue: 1. Robert; 2. Edward, b. in county Tyrone, Ireland, Sept. 10, 1803; d. in Green township, Harrison county, Ohio, June 16, 1889; m. (1st) Marjory McConnell, d. Aug. 26, 1868; m. (2d) Susannah Conaway of Stock township, daughter of John Conaway (had issue by first wife: i. Jane, b. Nov. 24, 1824; ii. Joseph, b. Sept. 20, 1826; iii. Margaret, b. Sept. 25, 1828; iv. Thomas, b. Feb. 2, 1831; v. Robert, b. Nov. 21, 1832; vi. Edward, b. Aug. 16, 1834; vii. Elizabeth, b. May 2, 1836; viii. Nancy, b. April 21, 1838; ix. John, b. Sept. 27, 1840; x. William, b. Feb. 28, 1843; xi. Samuel, b. June 7, 1847; had issue by second wife: xii. James-H., b. Dec. 14, 1869; xiii. Susannah, b. Jan. 12, 1872); 3. James; 4. Matthew; 5. Joseph; 6. Jane; 7. Elizabeth; 8. Margaret.

JAMES LAUGHRIDGE, b. in Ireland, 1806, coming the same year with his parents to North township, Harrison county, Ohio, where he d. in 1866; m. Dec. 19, 1836, Anna Henderson, daughter of William and Sarah Henderson, of Harrison county (both of whom died in Tuscarawas county, Ohio, the former in 1852, the latter in 1850); had issue: 1. Sarah-Ann, m. Elias Stonebrook, and settled near Carrollton, Ohio; 2. E.-W., b. February 2, 1840; m. May 2, 1867, Mary M. Fierbaugh, daughter of Daniel and Elizabeth Fierbaugh, of North township; 3. Eliza-Jane, m. Henry Lutz, and settled near Carrollton; 4. James-Wesley, settled in Carroll county.

JOHN LAW, a native of Ireland, of Scotch descent, b. about 1765; d. about 1859; settled in Monroe township, Harrison county, Ohio, about 1826; m. in Ireland, Elizabeth Lynn, b. about 1781; d. about 1860; had issue, among others:

I. Matthew, b. in Ireland, 1806-8; d. in Monroe township, Sept. 9, 1878-79; m. March 31, 1836, Rebecca Birney, of Green township, b. 1816; d. September, 1864; had issue: 1. John, b. Aug. 26, 1837; m. Feb. 26, 1862, Sarah Jane Trimble, daughter of Robert and Sarah Evans Trimble; 2. William-B., b. Feb. 22, 1841; settled in North township; m. (1st) October, 1862, Rebecca J. Forbes; m. (2d) 1888, Florence Donaldson, daughter of William and Nancy English Donaldson; 3. Robert-B., settled in North township; 4. Jane, d. in infancy.

II. Jane, b. in Ireland, March 1, 1813; came to Harrison county with her parents; m. April 10, 1834, William Humphrey, b. in Ireland, June, 1812; settled with his mother and sister in Stock township, Harrison county, in 1832, where he d. 1884; had issue: 1. Elizabeth; 2. Thomas, d. March 31, 1886, in Saline county, Mo., where he had settled in 1865; 3. Margaret, m. Joseph Patterson, and settled in Mis-

souri; 4. Mary-J., m. William Patterson, and settled in Greenwood county, Kan.; 5. Catherine, m. William Foster, a physician, and settled in Superior, Neb.; 6. John, settled in Labette, Kan.; 7. Ellen, m. Almond Birney, and settled in Labette, Kan.; 8. Martha, m. Marion Spiker, and settled at Cadiz; 9. Rebecca-Anne, m. W. K. Haverfield, and settled at Jewett.
III. Henry. IV. Charlotte, m. William Beatty, and settled in Licking county, Ohio. V. Frances, m. John McMillan, and settled in Washington township. VI. Rebecca, m. Robert Irvine. VII. Margaret, m. John Simpson, and settled in Stock township. VIII. Mary, m. ——— Simpson; d. in Illinois. IX. Elizabeth, m. Robert Birney.

Robert Trimble, father of Sarah Trimble Law, settled in Monroe township, about 1833; m. Aug. 7, 1825, Sarah Evans, of Jefferson county, Ohio; had issue: 1. Mary; 2. Ann; 3. Lucy; 4. John, settled in Union county, Ohio; 5. Martha; 6. George; 7. Rebecca, m. Frank Courtwright; settled in Franklin; 8. Sarah-Jane, m. John Law.

GEORGE LAYPORT (or Leporth, as originally spelled), of French Huguenot descent, emigrated from Maryland to the Beech Flats, near Steubenville, Ohio, before 1800; thence removed to Cadiz township, Harrison county, before 1806, settling on the farm now used as the county infirmary; his settlement at the first was on the frontier, and during the border wars with the Indians, his cabin was burned by them, and his son Thomas, aged eighteen, killed; after peace was declared, one of the Indians who had taken part in this attack, boasted of it in the presence of John Layport (Thomas's brother), during a general muster held in New Philadelphia. The brother attempted to kill the Indian on the spot, but was restrained. He afterwards followed him from New Philadelphia across Harrison county, to Salt Run in Jefferson county, and then despatched him while the Indian was stooping down to take a drink (from account of Rev. E. Layport; see also page 54, for a similar incident). George Leporth was one of the famous hunters of Harrison county in pioneer days, all kinds of wild game, turkeys, deer, wolves, and bears then being plentiful in his neighborhood. He was also a skilled trapper; and set large steel traps for bear. "On one occasion," says Howe, in his "History of Ohio," "two of his sons, having trapped a wolf, skinned it alive, and then turned it loose," as an awful example to its fellows of what was in store for them in case they molested the settler's fold. George Leporth once set a trap for a bear, which was accustomed to follow a certain trail; and placed it by a log which the bear would have to step over, expecting it to step into the trap. But it happened that a Methodist missionary came along the trail that day on his way to a preaching station, near what is now Asbury chapel; and his horse stepped into the trap intended for the bear. Not being strong enough to release the trap by himself, the minister was obliged to wait until Leporth came along before he could proceed. George Leporth, or Layport, d. before Nov. 29, 1814, leaving a wife, Nancy, and children, John, Margaret Hevlin, Mary Hevlin, Dianna Spiker, Nancy Wilson, Isaac, and Susanna Babb; of these: 1. John, d. February-May, 1839; settled in Stock township (had issue: i. William, b. June 12, 1805; d. March 20, 1867; ii. Abraham, d. September-November, 1850; m. Sarah ———; iii. Isaac, b. Aug. 26, 1814; d. Aug. 3, 1882; m. Cynthia ———, b. 1815; d. May 2, 1895); 2. Isaac, d. August-October, 1825; m. Sarah ——— (left issue).

JACOB LEMMON, a Methodist Episcopal minister, b. 1789; d. May 24, 1874; removed with his parents from Maryland, and settled in Freeport township, Harrison county, before 1821; m. Sarah Bosley; had issue: 1. Bosley; 2. Amon, m. 1852, Rebecca Forsythe, b. 1824; d. Aug. 19, 1872; daughter of Jesse and Sarah Colvin Forsythe, of Freeport township; 3. Moses, m. Mary Allen; 4. Sarah, m. ——— Allen; 5. Rebecca; 6. Rachel; 7. Eliza.

ISAAC LEMASTERS, d. in Archer township, Harrison county, March, 1844; m. Jane ———; had issue: I. Nancy, m. 1815, John Rogers. II. Lydia, m. 1818, George Simonton. III. Jane, m. 1819, Samuel Pittinger. IV. Margaret, m. ——— Ferrell. V. Susannah, m. 1829, John Robinson. VI. Elizabeth. VII. Abraham, m. 1824, Nancy Barnes. VIII. Isaac. IX. John, m. 1833, Mercy

Johnson. X. Ebenezer, m. 1840, Rebecca D. Nixon. XI. William, b. in Ohio, Dec. 20, 1816; removed from Short Creek to Archer township, Harrison county, where he d. March 8, 1877; m. 1839, Elizabeth Busby, daughter of Abraham Busby, of Archer township; had issue: 1. Abram-R., b. Sept. 7, 1840; d. Sept. 13, 1843; 2. Deborah-J., b. April 13, 1842; d. April 27, 1855; 3. Amanda-A., b. May 12, 1845; d. Oct. 11, 1854; 4. Isaac-K., b. Sept. 8, 1846; m. 1869, Elizabeth Devore, b. Aug. 9, 1850, daughter of Moses Devore, of Harrison county; 5. Melinda, b. Aug. 29, 1848; 6. ———, b. Feb. 12, 1850; 7. Mary, b. Aug. 23, 1853; d. Nov. 1, 1854; 8. John, b. May 1, 1855; 9. William-Jacob, b. Aug. 29, 1856; 10. Joshua-Ellsworth, b. Dec. 28, 1861; d. July 21, 1883.

ROBERT LISLE, b. 1774, a native of Pennsylvania, of Scotch-Irish descent, removed to Jefferson county, Ohio, before 1803, where he died, April 3, 1834; m. in Pennsylvania, Elizabeth ———, b. 1780; d. Sept. 12, 1852; had issue: 1. William; 2. Nancy; 3. Hannah; 4. Robert; 5. Jane; 6. Rachel; 7. Mary; 8. Eliza; 9. John, b. in Jefferson county, Ohio, Dec. 5, 1803; settled in Archer township, Harrison county, 1839, where he d. Oct. 30, 1890; m. in Jefferson county, 1829, Eliza A. Johnston, daughter of Robert Johnston (had issue: i. Johnston; ii. William, b. May 6, 1833; served in the Civil War; m. 1878, Rachel Beatty, daughter of Arthur Beatty, of Archer township; iii. Elizabeth; iv. Mary-Jane; v. John, b. Feb. 27, 1842; served in the Civil War; m. Nov. 6, 1873, Jennie Henderson, daughter of James Henderson, a resident of North township; vi. Hamilton, b. May 12, 1844; m. (1st) Nov. 11, 1869, Mary Crawford. d. March 29, 1875, daughter of John Crawford, a resident of Archer township; m. (2d) Oct. 2, 1882, Mrs. Elizabeth Haverfield, of Cadiz township; vii. Martha).

LISLE, see also Lyle.

SAMUEL LONG, of German descent, b. in Frederick county, Md., 1780; d. January, 1858; settled in Rumley township, Harrison county, about 1827; m. Anna Mary Myers, b. 1791; d. 1866; daughter of Jacob Myers; had issue: 1. Elizabeth, b. 1816; d. 1900; 2. Susanna, b. 1817; 3. Katharine, b. 1819; 4. Mary, b. 1820; d. 1892; m. (1st) ——— Gotshall; m. (2d) ——— Wood; 5. Jacob, b. 1822; d. 1899; 6. Rebecca, b. 1823; 7. Sarah, d. 1859; m. Joseph Graybill; 8. Eliza, b. 1829; d. 1876; m. Jacob Gotshall; 9. Joseph; a minister; b. 1832; m. Margaret Smith, daughter of Samuel and Margaret Axline Smith; 10. William, b. 1832; d. 1886; m. (1st) Sarah Nicholson; m. (2d) Celestia Redmond.

GEORGE LOVE, emigrated from county Tyrone, Ireland, to New York, 1791, and about 1792 settled in Washington county, Penn.; removed in 1800 to Wheeling township, Belmont county, Ohio, where he died; m. in Ireland, Isabella Smith; had issue:

I. John, b. in county Tyrone, Ireland, about 1770, came with his parents to Belmont county; removed in 1808 to Athens township, Harrison county, Ohio, where he d. March, 1860; m. about 1807, Mary Cooke, d. Dec. 16, 1830, daughter of James Cooke; had issue: 1. George, b. March 29, 1810, in Athens township, where he d. Dec. 20, 1880; m. March 17, 1830, Jane McCracken, d. Feb. 21, 1879, daughter of Robert McCracken (had issue: i. Robert-M., b. Dec. 21, 1830, in Athens township; m. June 3, 1854, Sarah Henderson, daughter of William Henderson, of Cadiz township; ii. Mary, b. Sept. 20, 1832; m. David Lyle; settled in Uniontown, Belmont county; iii. John, b. Sept. 16, 1834; m. (1st) Eliza Taylor, d. Jan. 28, 1869; m. (2d) Mary J. Mundell; iv. Martha, b. Dec. 24, 1836; v. James, b. Aug. 22, 1840; killed in the Civil War; d. Sept. 3, 1864, in Frederick City; vi. Nancy, b. Sept. 8, 1838; d. March 3, 1842; vii. George, b. Sept. 9, 1842; m. Dec. 6, 1865, Eleanor Haley, daughter of Samuel Haley, who removed from Belmont county to McLean county, Ill.; viii. Nancy-Jane, b. Sept. 13, 1844; d. March 19, 1849; ix. Margaret. b. Sept. 19, 1847; m. Dec. 15, 1870, Robert Henderson, b. Jan. 8, 1845; d. Feb. 14, 1887; son of William Henderson; x. Caroline-Jane, b. June 17, 1850; d. May 28, 1853); 2. James-C., b. Feb. 9, 1814, in Athens township, Harrison county, where he d. July 12, 1876; m. April 10, 1839, Jane McFadden, daughter of Samuel McFadden, a native of Ireland, who settled in Cadiz township (had issue: i. ———; served in the Civil War; d. in hospital in Fredericksburg, Va.; ii. John; iii. James; iv. Mary, m. ——— McCracken;

settled in Stearns county, Minn.; v. Elizabeth, m. —— McFadden; settled in Marion county, Kan.; vi. George, settled in Scio, Ohio; vii. Jennie; viii. Alexander, b. Nov. 21, 1846, in Archer township, where he settled; m. Nov. 16, 1876, Jennie L. Devore, a daughter of Andrew Devore, of Archer township); 3. Thomas, b. Jan. 31, 1820; settled in Aledo, Ill.; m. Agnes Henderson; 4. Mary, b. Feb. 15, 1825; d. Oct. 27, 1886; m. Joseph Wallace; 5. John, b. July 22, 1827; settled in Arkansas City, Kan.; m. Nancy Downing; 6. Nancy.

II. Thomas, engaged in river traffic on the Mississippi; place of death unknown.

III. George, b. about 1784, in county Tyrone, Ireland; came to Belmont county with his parents, where he d. Feb. 21, 1829; served as an officer in the War of 1812; m. Mary Moore, b. 1801, in county Tyrone, Ireland; daughter of John and Mary Smith Moore (she m. 2d, John A. Todd, of Nottingham township); had issue: 1. Thomas, settled in Madison county, Iowa; 2. John; 3. George, b. Aug. 14, 1827, in Belmont county; removed 1831, to Nottingham township, Harrison county; m. November 21, 1854, Barbara Barclay, daughter of David and Elizabeth Kissick Barclay, natives of Ireland.

IV. William.

V. Jane, m. Thomas Gillespie.

VI. Catherine, m. Joseph Haverfield.

VII. Mary, m. Jacob Morgan.

JACOB LUKENS, of Dutch descent, settled in York county, Penn., about 1780; later removed to near Havre de Grace, Maryland, where he died; had issue, among others: I. Eli, b. in York county, Penn., 1783; removed to Baltimore, Md., before 1804; afterward located in Bel Air, Harford county, Md.; in 1828, settled near Fairview, Guernsey county, Ohio, where he d. 1842; m. in Baltimore, 1804, Juliana Tollinger, of Dutch descent, b. 1765; d. in Franklin, Ohio, 1866; had issue: 1. Jacob, b. at Bel Air, Md., 1805; settled near Deersville, Ohio, where he d. May 27, 1884; m. 1830, Sarah C. Bliss, b. 1810; d. Feb. 21, 1886; daughter of Zadoc Bliss, of Hartford, Conn., who had settled in Ohio, in 1816 (had issue: i. Joseph-G., settled at Tippecanoe, Ohio; ii. Merriken-B., a physician, settled at Dalton, Ga.; iii. Benjamin-F., a physician, settled at Philadelphia, Penn.; iv. William-H., b. Oct. 22, 1838; settled at Deersville; m. September, 1867, Rosa McKinney Clark, daughter of William and Louisa Clark; v. Charles-M., a physician, settled at Syracuse, N. Y.; vi. Thomas-J., b. May 1, 1843; served in the Civil War; m. Oct. 1, 1873, Jennie Thompson, daughter of James F. Thompson, of Montgomery county); 2. Naomi; 3. Elizabeth; 4. Eli; 5. George; 6. William; 7. Alexander; 8. Nathaniel.

MOSES LUKENS, see Family of John Cope.

ROBERT LYLE, b. 1698, a native of Ireland (son of John Lyle, who removed from Scotland to county Antrim, Ireland in 1681), in 1742, accompanied by his brother John. came to America; first settling in New York; John removed to New Jersey, near the present site of New Brunswick, where he died; Robert m. 1747, Mary Gilleland, thence removed to Northampton county, Penn., where he d. Dec. 9, 1765; had issue (all the sons but David serving in the Revolutionary War): I. John, d. April 17, 1826. II. Robert, b. 1753; d. Nov. 17, 1843. III. Moses. IV. Aaron, b. Nov. 17, 1759; d. in Washington county, Penn., Sept. 24, 1825, where he had settled in 1784; served in the Revolutionary War, in the Pennsylvania Legislature, 1797-1801, and in Congress, 1808 to 1816; m. 1782, Eleanor Moore, daughter of John Moore, of Northampton county Penn.; had issue: 1. Moses, b. 1783; d. 1840; m. Sarah Kerr; 2. James, b. 1785; d. 1860; m. Mary Campbell; 3. Mary, b. May 31, 1787; d. Sept. 25, 1853; m. John Campbell, of Washington county, Penn., b. 1775; d. July 24, 1844 (see Family of John Campbell); 4. Agnes, b. 1789; d. 1790; 5. Robert, b. 1791; d. 1820; 6. Jane, b. 1793; d. 1845; m. Samuel Ewing; 7. Margaret, b. 1798; d. 1883; m. William Patterson; 8. Aaron; 9. ——; 10. ——, b. 1805; d. 1807. V. David. VI. Jane. VII. Elizabeth. VIII. Rosannah. IX. Eleanor. X. Mary.

WILLIAM LYLE, of Scotch-Irish descent, m. Mary Maholm; had issue, among others: 1. William, b. Jan. 15, 1812; d. near Rumley, in Harrison county, 1861; m. July, 1836, Jane Lewis, b. near Manchester, England. March 1, 1817, daughter of George and Elizabeth

Powell Lewis (the former of whom emigrated to Harrison county in 1818); (had issue: i. Rosanna, m. George Schultz; ii. George, settled in Scio, Harrison county; iii. Elizabeth, m. Thomas McChannel; settled in Kearney, Neb.; iv. Mary, m. James McNab; settled in Jackson county, Wis.; v. Martha; vi. Sarah-E., m. Albert D. Finnicum; vii. Amanda, m. Edward L. Moore; settled in Cheyenne county, Neb.; viii. Emma-M., settled in Palestine, Texas).

Thomas and Elizabeth Smith Powell, parents of Elizabeth Powell Lewis, had issue: 1. James, b. March 17, 1785; 2. Jane, b. May 20, 1786; 3. Elizabeth; 4. Richard, b. Dec. 30, 1789.

LYLE, see also Lisle.

SAMUEL LYON, a native of Great Britain, emigrated to America about 1800, and first settled in Maryland; removed to Jefferson county, Ohio, about 1818, and afterward located in Harrison county; had issue, among others: 1. Samuel, b. in Jefferson county, 1818; d. in Washington township, Harrison county, Jan. 1, 1871; m. 1840, Catherine Hedges, b. 1811; d. Aug. 8, 1884 (had issue: i. Harriet, m. Leander Cramblett; ii. Aaron; iii. John-H.; iv. Elizabeth; v. Reuben-P., b. Nov. 8, 1847; m. Feb. 10, 1870, Eliza Jane Wiley, of Coshocton county, Ohio; vi. Jemima, m. David Meeks; vii. Robert-P.).

ROBERT LYONS, b. in Pennsylvania, Dec. 14, 1803; d. in Cadiz, Ohio, Aug. 17, 1887, where he had settled about 1818; m. (1st) 1832, Anne Bowland; b. April 10, 1810; d. May 16, 1844; m. (2d) Mrs. Anne Bowland Allison, of Washington county, Penn.; had issue by first wife: 1. James-Bowland, m. (1st) Sarah G .Thomas, b. April 4, 1838; d. April 21, 1871; 2. Nancy, b. 1835; d. 1837; 3. Richard, b. Aug. 21, 1840; d. Martha-Collins, m. 1857, David Barclay Welch, son of Rezin and Eliza Bayless Welch; b. 1843; d. 1844.

WILLIAM LYONS, a native of Ireland, emigrated to America before 1776; served in the Revolutionary War, receiving a wound which caused his death some years later in Morgan county, Ohio, whence he had removed from Harrison county; had issue: I. Thomas, b. in Pennsylvania; settled in Butler county, that State; removed to Ohio in 1820, first locating near the present site of Tippecanoe; later settled in Carroll county, where he died; m. Menie Lowrie, a native of Scotland, whose parents came to America when she was a child; sister of Walter Lowrie; had issue, ten children, among whom: 1. John-C., b. in Butler county, Penn.; settled in Bowerstown, Ohio; m. Susanna Forbes, d. Feb. 3, 1883 (had issue, four children, of whom: i. John-F., served in the Civil War and died at Resaca, Ga., 1865).

JAMES McAFEE, a native of Ireland, d. about 1795; emigrated to America, and about 1780 settled in Westmoreland (or Washington) county, Penn.; had issue: 1. Matthew; 2. James, b. in Washington county, Penn., 1785, where he m. Mary Wible, b. 1790; d. 1777; dau. of George and Mary Rummel Wible (natives of Germany, who removed from Pennsylvania to Ohio); settled in Rumley township, Harrison county, about 1823-28, where he d. 1876 (had issue, among others: i. Sarah; ii. Mary; iii. George, b. in Westmoreland county, Penn., Jan. 27, 1813; settled in Archer township, Harrison county; d. Nov. 20, 1889; m. June, 1835, Jane Hixon, daughter of Abner Hixon, a resident of Hanover; iv. James, b. in Washington county, Penn., 1817; settled in Rumley township; m. (1st) 1840, Letta Gordon; d. 1846, daughter of David and Elizabeth Archibald Gordon; m. (2d) 1849, Margaret Hendricks, b. Aug. 6, 1823; d. September, 1878, daughter of Peter and Catherine Webster Hendricks; m. (3d) 1880, Sarah Jane Gundy, daughter of William and Susanna Gatchell Gundy; v. John; vi. Matilda; vii. Hannah; viii. Rachel); 3 .John; 4. Mary; 5. Martha; 6. Jane; 7.―――― (a daughter).

JOHN McBEAN, a physician, b. in Scotland, Oct. 22, 1797; d. at Cadiz, Jan. 7, 1875; m. March 18, 1829, Belinda Johnson, daughter of Henry and Catherine Johnson, of Moorefield township, both natives of Pennsylvania; had issue: 1. Jane, m. Armistead T. Ready, and settled at New Philadelphia; 2. William, b. 1833; d. 1884; 3. Catherine-L., m. Jesse H. McMath, and settled at Cleveland; 4. John-S.; a physician; b. 1840; m. (1st) 1876, Georgia Scott, b. 1849; d. 1883; daughter of George W. and Anna Scott, of Columbus; m. (2d) 1886, Alice Kennedy, daughter of Martin S. and Martha

HARRISON COUNTY GENEALOGIES

McKee Kennedy; 5. Mary, m. Albert Lakin; 6. Harriet, m. Col. James M. Steele; 7. Julia, m. Dr. Milton Hoge, of Cambridge, Ohio; 8. Belinda, m. David A. Hollingsworth; 9. Laura, m. William S. Cessna; 10. Henry, b. 1848; d. Aug. 2, 1875.

JOSEPH McBETH, a native of Scotland, settled with his wife, Elizabeth, at Bolivar, Westmoreland county, Penn., before 1808, where he died; had issue, twelve children, among whom: 1. John, b. in Bolivar, Penn., Sept. 7, 1808; removed to Monroe township, Harrison county, Ohio, 1829, where he d. July 22, 1863; m. April 18, 1833, Mary Webster, b. in Harrison county, 1811; d. July 27, 1858; daughter of John and Katherine Webster, early settlers in Harrison county, where they came from Pennsylvania (had issue: i. Nancy, m. J. M. Ferrell, of Orrville, Ohio; ii. Mariah, m. Thomas E. Fowler; iii. Robert-C., settled in Clinton, Henry county, Mo.; iv. David-J., b. June 10, 1841; served in the Civil War; and a prisoner at Andersonville; m. June 22, 1871, Elmira Crim, a native of Franklin township, Harrison county, daughter of George and Catherine Crim, natives of West Virginia; v. William, d. in the Army Hospital, at Nashville, November, 1862; vi. Margaret-Ann, m. Garrett Fowler, and settled in Dennison, Ohio; vii. John; viii. Amanda, m. Thomas Bower, and settled in Bowerston, Ohio; ix. Mary, m. William J. Albaugh).

JOSEPH McCLAIN, removed from Westmoreland county, Penn., to North township, Harrison county, Ohio, in 1823; had issue: 1. James, b. 1801; d. 1851; m. Sarah Endsley, b. 1801; d. 1881; daughter of John Endsley, an early settler in Archer township (had issue: i. Jane; ii. Joseph, settled in Oregon; iii. John-E.; iv. Mary-Ann; v. Samuel, settled in Iowa; vi. James-Alexander, settled in Archer township; vii. Sarah, m. Edward Smith; viii. Harriet, m. Samuel Cutshall, and settled in Carroll county, Ohio; ix. Thomas-E., served in the Civil War and died in service, 1863; x. William; xi. Martha-Jane; xii. Nathan-S., b. 1848).

JOHN McCONNELL, of Scottish descent, emigrated from the North of Ireland, and probably before the Revolution settled in Pennsylvania; had issue:
I. James, settled in Athens township, Harrison county, Ohio; afterward removed to Louisville, Ky.
II. Elizabeth, settled in Athens township.
III. John, b. probably in the North of Ireland; came to Pennsylvania with his parents; probably settled in Washington county; removed to Athens township, 1801, where he was one of the first white settlers, and built one of the first horse-mills in that township; d. September-October, 1831; m. in Pennsylvania, Mary Morton, daughter of Edward Morton; had issue: 1. James; 2. William; 3. Margaret; 4. Elizabeth; 5. John, b. in Pennsylvania, May 5, 1796; settled in Athens township, where he d. Aug. 18, 1878; m. Oct. 20, 1823, Jane Robinson, d. April 10, 1887, daughter of Adam and Elizabeth Robinson, of Irish and German descent, who lived near Wilmington, Delaware (had issue: i. Robert, settled in Guernsey county, Ohio; ii. William; iii. James; iv. Margaret, m. William Howell; v. Mary, m. Joseph Holmes; vi. John; vii. Edward-S., b. April 3, 1836; m. Dec. 29, 1859, Cynthia Styers, daughter of John Styers, of Coshocton county, Ohio [a native of Pennsylvania, of German descent, whose parents were among the early settlers in Northwestern Pennsylvania]; viii. Elizabeth, m. John Cook, and settled at Bridgeport, Ohio; ix. Francis-M.; x. Adam, b. June 3, 1842; m. Oct. 3, 1865, Mary McFadden, daughter of John J. and Esther Clifford McFadden; xi. La Fayette; xii. Martha); 6. Jane.

ROBERT McCONNELL, a native of Pennsylvania, removed probably from Washington county, that State, to Belmont county, Ohio, 1807; and thence in 1814 to Washington township, Harrison county, Ohio, where he d. Aug. 22, 1850; served in the War of 1812; m. (1st) in Pennsylvania, Mary Caldwell; m. (2d) Prudence Coleman, d. 1867; had issue by first wife: 1. James, b. 1790; 2. Susan, b. 1793; m. ——— Lee; 3. David, b. 1795; 4. Alexander, b. 1796; 5. Martha, b. 1797; 6. Mary, b. 1800; m. ——— Vance; had issue by second wife: 7. Robert, b. Nov. 21, 1802; 8. Hannah, b. Sept. 30, 1804; m. ——— Coleman; 9. John-C., b. in Belmont county, Jan. 1, 1807; settled in Washington township with his parents; d. July 18, 1873; m. (1st) Jane Boles; d. May 29, 1841; daughter of James Boles; m. (2d) April 9, 1848, Rachel Browning, b. Jan. 25, 1825; daughter of Samuel Browning; 10. William, b. Jan. 6, 1809; 11. Wilson, b. April 13, 1811; 12. Prudence, b. March 22, 1813; 13. Margaret-Ann, b. Sept. 21, 1815; m. —— Farnsworth; 14. Sarah, b. Nov. 18, 1817; 15. Elizabeth, b. Nov. 6, 1819; m. —— Wilson; 16. Alexander-S., b. March 25, 1822; 17. David, b. Sept. 4, 1824.

Samuel Browning, father of Rachel McConnell, d. in Athens township, 1864; served in the War of 1812; m. Margaret Markee, whose parents were natives of England; had issue: 1. Julia-A.; 2. Elias; 3. Samuel; 4. Absalom; 5. Rachel; 6. Margaret; 7. Sarah; 8. Asbury-T.; 9. Susanna; 10. Wesley; 11. Zara; 12. Edward.

JOHN McCORMICK, b. in Pennsylvania, 1810; d. near Freeport, Ohio, Nov. 9, 1869; served as sheriff of Harrison county, 1846-48; m. Esther Allen, d. aged forty-seven; daughter of Reuben and Joanna McMillan Allen (both of Quaker origin, and both died in Washington township, aged respectively ninety-three and seventy-eight); had issue: 1. Reuben-Allen, b. in Washington township, June 19, 1839; served as an officer in the Civil War, as auditor of Harrison county, and as doorkeeper of the House of Representatives at Washington, D. C.; settled in Cadiz; m. 1863, Eliza Haverfield, a native of Cadiz township, daughter of John and Nancy Haverfield, of Cadiz township; 2. James-B., settled at Sidney, Neb.; 3. Henry-Clay, served in the Civil War, dying in the army; 4. John-T., settled at Columbus Junction, Iowa; 5. William-M., settled at Columbus Junction, Iowa.

JOHN and JOSEPH McCORMICK, brothers, emigrated from County Tyrone, Ireland, and probably first settled in Cumberland county, Penn.; removed about 1788, to North Huntingdon township, Westmoreland county; Joseph died unmarried, at the age of eighty-seven; John m. in Ireland, Sarah Sloan, sister to Dr. William Sloan; had issue, the first four of whom were born in Ireland: 1. William; 2. Andrew; 3. Jane, d. without issue; m. (1st) Robert Donaldson; m. (2d) —— McDonald; m. (3d) Daniel Hellman; 4. Joseph; 5. John, b. Aug. 22, 1789; m. Esther Sowash, of Huguenot descent (had issue: i. William, d. in infancy; ii. Eli, b. May, 1820; iii. John-Calvin; iv. Sarah, d. young; v. George; vi. James-Irwin; a physician; vii. Silas; viii. Samuel; ix. Mary-Elizabeth, d. in infancy; x. Albert, d. young; xi. Rachel, m. John George; xii. Henry-H., speaker of the Pennsylvania House of Representatives in 1874; m. Martha Sharon, daughter of Joseph and Eliza Maholm Sharon; xiii. Horace-Greeley); 6. David; 7. Sarah, d. unm.; 8. Samuel, b. Feb. 8, 1793; d. Feb. 3, 1875; m. Margaret Kemerer; settled at Cadiz, Ohio (had issue: i. Albert-G.; ii. John, settled at Omaha; iii. Josiah-S.; iv. Finley; v. Hannah-J., m. Henry J. Dobbins; vi. Lucretia-S., m. James Barlow; vii. Mary-Belle, m. Benjamin Linton; viii. Adaline, m. George Elliott; ix. Sarah, m. Samuel Burns, and settled at Omaha; x. Clarissa); 9. Thomas; 10. Elizabeth, m. Samuel Osborne, and settled at Stewartsville (had issue, eight children).

JOHN McCOY, emigrated from Washington county, Penn., and settled in the northeastern corner of Athens township before 1806; d. 1820; m. Susanna ——; had issue: I. Joseph. II. John. III. Samuel. IV. Susanna, m. —— Robinson. V. Sidney, m. —— Counsel. VI. Thomas, m. Hannah Major; had issue: 1. John, b. Sept. 23, 1816; d. Dec. 3, 1890; m. about 1839, Eliza Walker, b. March 30, 1819; d. July 22, 1890 (had issue: i. Margaret-Jane, b. 1840; d. 1849; ii. Amanda, m. John Dickerson; iii. Thomas; iv. Mary, b. 1847; m. 1867, Davis Garvin; v. John; vi. Martin-J., b. Nov. 25, 1853; m. 1878, Isabella De Armond, daughter of David and Isabella De Armond; vii. Albert; viii. William, m. Alice McCoy; ix. Vincent-W., m. Ida Worstell, and settled in Morgan county, Ohio; x. Laura, m. John Anderson; xi. Olive, m. John McManus; xii. Isabel, m. Idelbert Burdette); 2. Thomas; 3. Ebenezer; 4. Susan, m. Wilson Dickerson; 5. Mary, m. Asa Holmes; 6. Lorilla, m. —— Dickerson; 7. Elizabeth, m. —— Anderson.

MATTHEW McCOY, b. Aug. 8, 1783; removed from Pennsylvania to Archer township, Harrison county, before 1820, where he d. Oct. 10, 1855; m. Jane ———, b. June, 1782; d. Sept. 18, 1855; had issue, among others: 1. Matthew, b. April 4, 1815; d. March 27, 1889; m. Harriet C. ———, b. May 28, 1820; d. Feb. 12, 1898 (had issue, among others: i. Edward-G., b. 1850; d. 1855; ii. Martha-J., b. 1851; d. 1851); 2. Thomas-M.; 3. James-S.; 4. William-M.

WILLIAM McCOY, removed from Washington county, Penn., to Carroll county, Ohio, about 1835; m. Jane ———; had issue: 1. William-H., b. in Canonsburg, Aug. 22, 1832; d. Sept. 19, 1884; settled in Cadiz, in 1857; served as an officer in the Civil War; m. March 24, 1857, Margaret A. Welling, b. in New Rumley, Harrison county, daughter of William and Margaret Welling.

JOHN McCULLOUGH, d. 1842, probably the son of William McCullough, who settled in Hopewell township, Washington county, Penn., before 1780; m. in Washington county, 1785, Esther Gamble, b. 1755; d. Aug. 8, 1841; removed to Wheeling township, Belmont county, Ohio, and, about 1813, settled near New Athens; had issue: 1. Esther; 2. William; 3. Alexander; 4. Margaret; 5. Joseph, b. Feb. 7, 1795; d. in Archer township, Harrison county, Jan. 31, 1870; m. (1st) 1817, Sarah Lyons, b. Sept. 27, 1797; d. March 24,1836; daughter of John and Elizabeth Beatty Lyons; m. (2d) Elizabeth ———, b. 1801; d. April 15, 1884 (had issue by first wife: i. Elizabeth, b. 1818; d. 1856; m. 1836, John Moore; ii. Esther, b. 1820; d. Sept. 24, 1892; m. 1841, Robert Anderson, b. near Claysville, Washington county, Penn., Oct. 11, 1815; d. April 25, 1891; son of Samuel and Catharine Forbes Anderson; iii. John, b. 1822; m. 1848, Jane Welch; iv. Mary, b. 1824; d. 1890; m. 1847, Martin Lee; v. Sarah-Jane, b. 1827; d. 1874; m. 1857, John Moore, husband of her deceased sister, Elizabeth; vi. Isabel, b. 1829; m. 1856, Daniel Mikesell; vii. James-Beatty; a physician; b. 1831; d. 1897; m. 1855, Martha Megaw; viii. Martha); 6. Samuel, twin brother to Joseph; 7. Martha; 8. James; 9. George; 10. Hannah; 11. John.

Three McCullough families seem to have settled in the vicinity of Crabapple Church near the beginning of the century, and the heads of the three families were either brothers, or very closely related. In addition to John McCullough, whose family is given above, Robert and William McCullough settled in Wheeling township, Belmont county, just south of New Athens, and were among the organizers of Crabapple Church, both appearing among the first bench of elders. They both also appear to have come from Hopewell township, Washington county, Penn., within the bounds of Upper Buffalo Presbyterian Church. In the call extended by the united congregations of Cross Creek and Upper Buffalo Churches to Rev. Joseph Smith, in 1779, are to be found the names of George, Robert, and William McCullough. William McCullough, of whom some account is given below, mentions in his will a brother, Peter.

ROBERT McCULLOUGH, b. 1756-57; d. June 17, 1823; removed from Hopewell township, Washington county, Penn., to Wheeling township, Belmont county, Ohio, before 1800; m. Jane ———, b. 1765; d. Oct. 15, 1835; had issue: 1. Margaret; 2. Mary; 3. Robert; 4. William; 5. Alexander; 6. James; 7. John; 8. Peter; 9. George; 10. Samuel.

WILLIAM McCULLOUGH, b. 1748; d. March 18, 1831; probably removed from York or Cumberland county to Hopewell township, Washington county, Penn., about 1779, where he (or possibly his father of the same name) appears as an elder of Upper Buffalo Presbyterian Church as late as 1793; served in the Revolutionary War; removed before 1800 to Wheeling township, Belmont county, Ohio, where, with Robert McCullough, he helped to organize Crabapple Church; m. Isabella ———, b. 1751; d. May 23, 1832; had issue, among others: 1. Mary, b. 1782; d. July 15, 1851; m. George Brokaw, b. March 27, 1784; d. Nov. 27, 1880; 2. Martha-E., b. Dec. 14, 1784; d. July 5, 1851; m. Nov. 2, 1820, Joseph Grimes (his second wife), b. November, 1782; d. Jan. 2, 1840 (had issue: i. George-D., b. April 13, 1808; d. Nov. 20, 1875; m. Jane ———, b. March 27, 1812; d. Nov. 3, 1890; ii. Julia-Ann, b. 1809; d. March 16, 1884; m. William Campbell; iii. Joseph, a minister, removed to Independence, Kan.; iv. William-M., a minister; b. Sept. 23, 1821; d. Nov. 23, 1886; m. March 5, 1857,

Amanda S. Simeral; v. John; vi. Lucinda; vii. Isabella).

GEORGE McDIVITT, removed from Pennsylvania to North township, Harrison county, before 1817; d. 1837; m. Rachel ——— (possibly his second wife); had issue: 1. Charles, m. 1823, Frances Fisher; 2. George, b. 1797; d. February, 1869; m. (1st) 1817, Mary Johnston (?); m. (2d) Mrs. Susan Rutter Scott, of Leesville, Ohio (had issue by first wife, eight children; had issue by second wife: ix. Mary; x. Martha; xi. Eliza, m. Isaiah English; xii. Thursby, m. John Miner, of Pittsburg; xiii. John, settled in Stock township; xiv. Thomas-R., b. Dec. 8, 1837; served in the Civil War; m. 1865, Sarah Anderson, daughter of Robert and Hester Anderson; xv. Samuel; xvi. Lyle, b. October, 1846; m. 1869, Elizabeth Buxton, daughter of Haddon Buxton); 3. Lyle, d. March, 1838; m. Nancy ——— (had issue: i. William-E.; ii. Mary; iii. Jane); 4. John, m. 1827, Susanna Simpson (?); 5. Samuel; 6. Andrew, m. 1831, Jane Moody (?).

JAMES McDIVITT, removed from Westmoreland county, Penn., to North township, Harrison county, Ohio, about 1820; had issue, five sons, of whom the youngest: James, b. in Westmoreland county, Penn., Dec. 25, 1810; settled in North township, Harrison county, where he d. March 19, 1874; m. about 1830, Anna Birney, b. in Green township, 1808; d. Oct. 15, 1862; daughter of John Birney (had issue, ten children, of whom five died in infancy, of the others: i. Margaret, m. James Nixon; ii. Elizabeth, m. William Nixon, and settled in Stock township; iii. John, b. March 10, 1845; settled in Monroe township; m. June 24, 1875, Martha M. Easterday, a native of Harrison county, daughter of David and Mary Easterday; iv. Nancy, m. Thomas Cummings, and settled at Topeka, Kan.; v. ———).

SAMUEL McDOWELL, probably b. in Ireland, 1769; emigrated to America and settled in Washington county, Penn.; removed before 1808 to Athens township, Harrison county, Ohio, where he died; m. in Pennsylvania, Jane Moreland; had issue: 1. Nancy, m. James McAdams; 2. Samuel; 3. William, b. Nov. 6, 1808; d. May 21, 1869; m. Sept. 19, 1842, Hannah Watters, daughter of John W. Watters, a resident of Delaware county, Ohio (had issue: i. Sarah-J., m. John Culbertson; ii. Mary-A., m. T. E. Johnson; iii. Samuel-Madison, b. March 6, 1851; iv. Emma, m. Dr. Thompson; v. Frances-A.; vi. Florence-A., twin sister to Frances); 4. James; 5. John; 6. Sarah, m. William Reed; 7. Susan-J., m. Smith Watson.

——— McFADDEN, of Coote Hill, county Cavan, Ireland, of Scottish descent; had issue:
I. John, b. about 1746; d. near Cadiz, Ohio, April 13, 1835; emigrated to America about 1774, and settled near West Middletown, Hopewell township, Washington county, Penn.; m. Margaret Sharp, b. 1751; d. April 26, 1826; daughter of John and Agnes Sharp, of Washington county, Penn. (or of George Sharp, who served from Washington county as a captain in the Revolution); removed to Cadiz township, Harrison county, Ohio, 1800; had issue: 1. Samuel-B., b. 1779; d. March 19, 1855; m. 1836, Sarah McFadden, daughter of Dr. Samuel and Nancy Logan McFadden; 2. George-S., b. 1784; d. Feb. 21, 1844; m. Ruth Collins, daughter of David and Ann Workman Collins; 3. John, b. 1789-90; d. Aug. 30, 1857; m. 1815, Mary Dunlap, b. in Maryland or in Fayette county, Penn., 1788-89; d. March 22, 1858; daughter of Adam and Rebecca Work Dunlap (had issue: i. Adam, b. 1815; d. July 17, 1873; ii. John-J., b. Oct. 21, 1820; settled in Athens township; m. Feb. 28, 1844, Esther Clifford, daughter of John Clifford, a native of Ireland [had issue: Mary, m. Adam McConnell; Margaret-Jane, b. July 12, 1846; m. Robert Dunlap; Rebecca-Ann, m. Samuel Dunlap; John-C.; George-D.; Edwin-Stanton; Sarah, m. Samuel McFadden; Adam; and Samuel-W.]; iii. Samuel-R., b. Oct. 10, 1825; m. May 7, 1851, Martha Robb, daughter of William and ——— Warnick Robb; iv. George; settled in Cadiz township; m. 1860, Mary Croskey, daughter of William and Mary Croskey, of Green township; v. Margaret, m. John McFadden, b. Oct. 10, 1810; d. in Cadiz, July 4, 1881; vi. Rebecca; vii. Mary, m. William Hamilton, and settled at Cadiz; viii. Sarah, m. John Porterfield, and settled at St. Clairsville; ix. Jane; x. Esther, m. ———

Phillips, and settled in Nebraska; xi. Rachel, m. William Hamilton, and settled in Belmont county; xii. Elizabeth, b. 1818; d. April 19, 1837); 4. Joseph, b. 1793; d. Feb. 26, 1859; m. (1st) 1826, Mary Thompson, d. March 2, 1844; daughter of David Thompson; m. (2d) Oct. 11, 1855, Catharine Henderson (had issue by first wife: i. Thompson, b. June 7, 1830; m. Nov. 23, 1854, Elizabeth Dickerson, daughter of John and Eliza McFadden Dickerson; ii. Joseph; settled in Cadiz township; iii. Mary, m. ——— Fitch, and settled in California); 5. Mary, m. James Sharp, of Cadiz township (had issue: i. John, b. 1801; d. March 16, 1878); 6. Margaret, b. 1789; d. Nov. 29, 1857; m. 1813, Edward Lafferty, b. 1789; d. Nov. 8, 1836; son of Edward and Elizabeth Ramage Lafferty (had issue: i. Edward; ii. John; iii. Joseph; iv. George; v. Hiram; vi. Finley; vii. Elizabeth; viii. Margaret, m. 1835, Thomas D. Grimes; ix. Mary-Jane).

II. Sarah, b. 1748; d. near West Middletown, Pa., Dec. 29, 1835; m. (1st) Nathaniel Gilmore; d. in Ireland, about 1770-71; m. (2d) John Jamison, b. 1743; d. near West Middletown, Pa., Jan. 28, 1811; emigrated to America with her husband and children about 1773-83, and first settled near Newport, Perry county, Penn., afterwards removing to Independence township, Washington county; had issue by first husband: 1. Jane, b. 1768; m. John Parr; 2. Samuel, b. 1770; d. Sept. 8, 1814; a soldier of the War of 1812; removed to Harrison county, Ohio, about 1800-3; m. Elizabeth Buchanan (had issue: i. Sarah, m. Joseph Dunlap; ii. Samuel; iii. Nathaniel; iv. Cyrus; v. William; vi. Mary, m. Napoleon B. Kennedy; vii. Eliza, m. John Phillips); had issue by second husband: 3. John, m. Anne Craig, and settled in Harrison county, Ohio (had issue: i. Walter); 4. William; 5. Robert; 6. Margaret, m. ——— McKeever; 7. Elizabeth, m. Samuel McFadden (had issue: i. John); 8. Nancy, m. ——— McBroom; 9. Mary, m. ——— Law; 10. Sarah, m. ——— Graham.

III. Joseph, b. 1757; d. near Cadiz, Ohio, Nov. 17, 1835; settled near West Middletown, Penn., about 1774; and thence removed to Harrison county, 1800-03; m. Jane ———, b. 1760; d. May 5, 1827; had issue: 1. Samuel, b. in county Cavan, Ireland. 1785; d. near Cassville, Nov. 12, 1869; m. (1st) Mary Milligan, b. 1775; d. 1842; a native of Adams county, Penn.; m. (2d) Jane ———, b. Jan. 3, 1799; d. Sept. 9, 1884 (had issue by first wife: i. Jane, m. James Love, and settled in Archer township; ii. Elizabeth, m. ——— Mehollin; iii. Alexander, b. Sept. 19, 1818; settled at Cadiz; m. June 29, 1846, Elizabeth Barger, daughter of Valentine Barger [had issue: Joseph; Mary-Jane; Martha-A., m. J.-Law McFadden; and Elza]; iv. Mary; v. George; vi. Joseph); 2. Joseph; 3. George; 4. Margaret; 5. Jane.

IV. Samuel, a physician, b. 1757; d. April 26, 1834; m. Nancy Logan; emigrated to America before 1795, and first settled in Philadelphia; removing thence to West Middletown, Hopewell township, Washington county, Penn., and from there, soon after 1800, to Cadiz township, Harrison county, Ohio; had issue: 1. Sarah, d. at sea; 2. Margaret, m. ——— Moore; 3. Mary, m. ——— Wallace; 4. Thomas; 5. Benjamin, b. in 1795; d. Nov. 7, 1880; m. 1821, Mary Wilson, b. 1802; d. Sept. 9, 1882; 6. William; 7. Elizabeth, m. 1827, Robert McGonagle; 8. Sarah, m. 1836, Samuel B. McFadden; 9. Samuel; 10. Jane, m. ——— Welling; 11. Nathaniel, b. October, 1811; m. 1833, Eliza Green; daughter of John and Mary Green, Pennsylvania Quakers (had issue: i. Samuel; ii. John; settled in Archer township; iii. William; settled in Kansas; iv. Hezekiah; v. George; settled in Archer township; vi. Mary, m. F. Crawford; vii. Henry; settled in Kansas; viii. Nancy-J.; ix. Elizabeth); 12. Nancy, m. ——— Brothers; 13. Joseph; settled near Pittsburg.

V. ———, emigrated to America, and settled in Philadelphia, where he died, leaving among others, two sons, John and George, who both left issue.

VI. George, of Coote Hill, county Cavan, Ireland, m. Isabella McIntosh; d. in Cadiz; daughter of James McIntosh; had issue, among others: Samuel, b. 1782; d. 1861; m. Lydia Stafford, b. 1783; d. March 22, 1866; emigrated to America about 1820, and first settled at Philadelphia, removing thence to Cadiz, Ohio, 1831; had issue: 1. George, d. 1868; m. Charlotte Elliott; 2. Sarah, d. 1847; 3. Henry-Stafford, b. 1813; d. July 4, 1888; m. Dec. 6, 1842, Frances Isabella Poore, daughter of Charles M.

and Elizabeth Karg Poore (the latter a native of York county, Penn., whose parents had come from Brunswick, Germany; the former a descendant of John Poore, of Newburyport, who emigrated from England to Massachusetts, in 1635); (had issue: i. Charles-Poore, b. 1843; d. Oct. 7, 1866; ii. Henry-Hunter, m. [1st] Sarah Craig; m. [2d] Emma Beall; iii. Frances, m. John J. Hanna; iv. Isabelle, m. Charles W. Kinsey, and settled at Oakland, Cal.; v. Elizabeth-T.; vi. John-F., m. Laura Samson; settled at Columbus; vii. George-E., m. Iona Huffman; settled at Fresno, Cal.; viii. Samuel-Fleming); 3. Isabella, d. 1883; m. William L. Sharp, and settled at Steubenville; 4. Letitia, b. 1812; d. April 13, 1883; m. Joseph R. Hunter (see Hunter Family); 5. Jane, d. 1895; m. 1836, Dr. William C. Johnson, and settled at Marion, Ohio; 7. Margaret, d. 1895; m. 1838, Samuel Craig, and settled at Cambridge, Ohio; 8. Mary, d. 186—; m. Rev. Hugh Forsythe.

VII. ———, had issue, who came to America: 1. Alexander; 2. Samuel, b. 1778; d. July 2, 1837; m. near Middletown, Washington county, Penn., Elizabeth Jamison, b. 1785-86; d. Dec. 24, 1837; daughter of John and Sarah McFadden (II) Jamison; removed to Harrison county, Ohio, before 1815 (had issue: i. Alexander; settled in Kansas; ii. Elizabeth, m. John Dickerson, of Athens township; iii. Jane, m. Adam Dickerson, and settled in Athens township; iv. Margaret, m. Adam Dunlap, and settled in Athens township; v. Sarah, m. 1829, Samuel Carnahan, of Cadiz township; vi. James, b. Jan. 5, 1805; d. June 15, 1874; m. in Washington county, Penn., Mary Law, b. Nov. 19, 1808; daughter of Robert and Mary Jamison Law, the former a native of Scotland [had issue: Samuel, b. Oct. 12, 1830; m. (1st) 1854, Mary Richey, b. 1835; d. Feb. 24, 1872; daughter of John M. Richey; m. (2d) 1876, Eliza J. Richey, sister of Mary Richey: Mary; Robert; settled in Logan county, Ohio; William; James. b. Sept. 20, 1841; m. 1866, Arabella Richey, daughter of John M. and Ann Collins Richey; John, b. March 18, 1845; m. 1870, Margaret E. Morgan, daughter of Marshall and Ellen Morgan; Jamison-Law, b. July 16, 1851; d. Nov. 18, 1887; m. Aug. 26, 1874, Elizabeth Barger]; vii. John; viii. Samuel); 3. Mary, m. Andrew Jamison.

John McFadden, probably a connection of the above family, m. Mary ———, and settled in Washington county, Penn.; their daughter, Mary, m. William Sharp; had issue: 1 ———, b. in Harrison county, 1807; d. at Millersburg, Holmes county, Ohio, 1893 (see William Sharp Family); 2. Nancy, b. 1810; d. Oct. 10, 1875; m. 1829, John Cunningham, son of David and Mary McLaughlin Cunningham.

SAMUEL McFADDEN, see also Family of Joshua Hamilton.

ROBERT McFARLAND, a native of Ireland, of Scottish descent, emigrated to America, and settled near Taylorstown, Washington county, Penn., in 1794, removing to Ohio some years later; m. Elizabeth Ferguson; had issue, among others: 1. William, b. 1795; d. 1878, near New Athens, Ohio, where he had located in 1824; served as a member of the Ohio Legislature; m. in Belmont county 1823, Elizabeth Henderson, b. 1800; d. 1867; daughter of Andrew and Martha Henderson, of Pennsylvania (had issue: i. Andrew; ii. Mary; iii. Martha; iv. Elizabeth, v. James; vi. William-Henderson, a United Presbyterian minister, b. June 14, 1832; settled at Cambridge, Ohio; m. ——— Hanna; vii. Margaret, b. near New Athens; m. 1856, Rev. Jonathan Sharp McCready, b. near New Galilee, Beaver county, Penn., April 15, 1828; d. Sept. 7, 1864, from wounds received in the battle of the Wilderness, where he served as captain of Company H, 126th O. V. I.; son of Hugh McCready, of Pennsylvania; settled in Cadiz, Ohio, where he first served as minister in the Seceder (or Associate Presbyterian) Church, and later in the United Presbyterian Church; viii. Robert; ix. Nancy; x. Sarah); 2. Mary, died in Harrison county, in her eighty-seventh year; 3. ——— (a daughter), d. in infancy.

JOHN McGAVRAN, a native of Ireland, b. 1737; d. 1770; emigrated to America and settled in Maryland about 1755-60; m. Margaret Hill (m. 2d, ——— O'Daniel), d. in Fayette county, Penn.; had issue:

I. Mary. II. Margaret. III. Mark. IV. William, b. 1767, in Harford county, Md.; d. 1853; removed to Springfield

HARRISON COUNTY GENEALOGIES

township, Jefferson county (now Lee township, Carroll county, Ohio) in 1818; m. March 17, 1791, Ann Thompson, b. in Harford county, Md., 1772; d. in Columbiana county, Ohio, 1863; daughter of Thomas Thompson; had issue: 1. Elizabeth, d. aged ninety-six; m. (1st) Thomas Magattogan; m. (2d) Benjamin Toland; 2. Mary, d. in Schuyler county, Ill., aged seventy-five; m. Charles Lucy; 3. Sarah, d. in Morgan county, Ohio; m. Samuel Hill; 4. John, d. in Columbiana county, Ohio; 5. Martha, d. in Illinois; m. John Mayes; 6. Margaret, d. in Kentucky; m. George Lucy, brother to Charles Lucy; 7. Thomas, d. in Colorado; m. Margaret Brown; 8. "Dillie"-Ann. d. aged twenty-two; 9. Mark, d. in Minneapolis, Minn., m. Louisa Daniels; 10. Stephen, d. in Harrison county, Ohio; 11. William-H., b. March 3, 1812, in Harford county, Md.; removed first to Jefferson county, and in 1843 to North township, Harrison county, Ohio; served as a member of the Ohio Legislature; m. in Stark county, Ohio. Elizabeth Brown, a native of Kentucky, of Scotch-Irish descent, daughter of James Brown (had issue: i. James-B.; ii. Henrietta, m. William H. H. Masters, of Scio; iii. George-W.; iv. Samuel-B., b. near Connotton, Harrison county, Nov. 25, 1847; settled in Cadiz; served in the Ohio Legislature; m. August. 1872, Jennie E. Johnson, of Carroll county; v. Elizabeth-Margaret, m. W. E. Clendenning, of Harrison county; vi. William-Thomas).

JAMES McGREW, a native of Western Virginia, settled in Jefferson county, Ohio, about 1832; m. April 26, 1824, Mary Pentecost, a native of West Virginia. d. in Harrison county, Ohio, 1840; had issue: 1. Alexander; 2. Murray; 3. William. b. in Hancock county, West Va., April 6, 1828; settled in Green township, Harrison county; m. (1st) Oct. 26, 1848. Cynthia Corbin. d. Jan. 26, 1885; m. (2d) March 31, 1887, Martha Kane, daughter of William Kane, of Cadiz; 4. James; 5. Joseph.

ROBERT McKEE, of Scotch-Irish descent, was a native of Redstone, Fayette county, Pennsylvania, where he m., 1806, Rachel Wills; was one of twelve children; settled in Archer township, Harrison county, Ohio, about 1807; had issue, among others: 1. James, b. Feb. 11, 1811; settled in Green township, where he d. May 8, 1886; m. Nov. 24, 1834, Sarah Lewis, daughter of Joseph Lewis (had issue: i. Mary, b. Aug. 25, 1835; ii. Hannah, b. Nov. 20, 1836; d. Sept. 19, 1843; iii. Rachel, b. March 23, 1838; iv. Martha, b. Nov. 4, 1839; d. July 3, 1882; v. John, b. June 27, 1841; d. Sept. 11, 1864; vi. Henry, b. Feb. 16, 1843; vii. Joseph, b. July 17, 1845; viii. Amanda, b. Oct. 14, 1847; ix. Robert-M., b. March 17, 1849; d. June 24, 1857; x. Eliza, b. March 30, 1851; d. May 17, 1854; xi. Adeline, b. June 29, 1853; xii. Anna-Rebecca, b. Dec. 1, 1855).

Joseph Lewis, father of Sarah Lewis McKee, was born in New Jersey, Oct. 31, 1769; settled in Pennsylvania, where he died Sept. 4, 1853; was a Quaker, as was also his wife, Rachel Canby, b. in Pennsylvania; d. Sept. 1, 1852; removed from Chester county, Penn., and first settled in Harrison county, Ohio, about 1829, but afterward returning to Pennsylvania; had issue: 1. Jesse, b. June 30, 1792; settled in Harrison county, 1817; 2. Jacob, b. Aug. 14, 1793; d. Feb. 5, 1883; removed to Harrison county with his brother Jesse; 3. Joseph, b. Jan. 5, 1795; d. March 1, 1882; settled in Harrison county in 1829; 4. Elizabeth, b. May 11, 1796; 5. David, b. Oct. 20, 1797; 6. Vernon, b. Oct. 23, 1798; d. April 5, 1882; 7. Lydia, b. March 10, 1800; 8. Rebecca, b. April 18, 1802; d. April 20, 1802; 9. Esther, b. April 21, 1804; 10 William, b. May 15, 1806; 11. Rachel. b. April 26, 1810; 12. Sarah, b. Nov. 24, 1812; m. James McKee; 13. Hannah, b. July 20, 1815.

RICHARD McKIBBEN, a native of Pennsylvania, of Irish descent; settled at Warrentown, Jefferson county, Ohio, about 1790; a short time afterward removed to Belmont county, Ohio; thence to Moorefield township, Harrison county, Ohio, and finally removed to Morgan county, Ohio, where he d. 1827; m. (1st) _____ Coulter; m. (2d) _____ Robison; m. (3d) Sarah Brokaw; had issue by third wife: 1. Richard; 2. Joseph; 3. Samuel; 4. Thomas; 5. William; 6. Rebecca; 7. Jane; 8. George, b. in Jefferson county, Ohio, Sept. 15, 1804; settled in Moorefield township, Harrison county; m. (1st) 1828, _____ Brashers; m. (2d) 1830, Martha Brokaw; m. (3d) Eleanor Morrison; m.

(4th) Jane Beall; d. 1887 (had issue by first wife: i. Jesse, settled in Illinois; had issue by second wife: ii. George, settled in Nottingham township, Harrison county; iii. John, b. Jan. 27, 1833; settled in Moorefield township; m. Jan. 3, 1856, Isabelle McMillan, b. Oct. 6, 1829; daughter of Charles and Rosanna Gilmore McMillan, natives of Ireland, who came to Harrison county from New York; had issue by third wife: iv. William; v. Eleanor; vi. Richard).

JOHN McLAUGHLIN, b. in Washington county, Penn., Nov. 4. 1774; d. at Adena, Jefferson county, Ohio, Nov. 10, 1860; settled in Ohio in 1801, removing to Adena the following year; served as a spy from Pittsburg to Wheeling, W. Va., during the Indian Wars; served in the Ohio Legislature for eight consecutive years, and in the State Senate the same length of time; m. about 1799, Anna Johnstone, d. June 6, 1849; had issue, thirteen children, among whom: 1. James, b. 1814; d. Aug. 25, 1865; m. Sarah J. Kerr, a native of Harrison county, daughter of Samuel and Annie Smith Kerr (had issue: i. William-B.; settled in Adena; ii. Ann-E., m. Lewis Bernhard, and settled in Harrison county; iii. Mary-E., m. William Courtright, and settled in Franklintown, Ohio; iv. Nancy-J., m. J. C. McNary, and settled in Unionport, Ohio; v. Samuel-K., b. in Adena, Sept. 12. 1846; m. May 22, 1872, Mary Belle Snider, a native of Green township. daughter of Samuel and Hannah Snider; settled in Harrison county, 1875; served in the Ohio Legislature, 1894-98); 7. Sarah-A., m. H. W. Parks, of Hopedale; 8. Joseph-S., settled in Jefferson county; 9. Mary-Emma, m. R. G. Dean, and settled in Omaha, Neb.

ROBERT McMILLAN, a native of Pennsylvania, removed to Jefferson county, Ohio, 1816, and in 1818 to Nottingham township, Harrison county, where he d. 1854; m. (1st) in Pennsylvania, Nancy Mitchell, d. 1840; m. (2d) Mary Boyd, d. 1844; m. (3d) Ellen Moore; had issue by first wife: 1. John, b. 1800; d. in Nottingham township, April 5, 1881; m. 1822, Elizabeth Peacock; d. Oct. 4. 1882; daughter of Eli Peacock (had issue: i. Robert-N.; ii. Thomas. b. June 9, 1826; settled at Deersville, in 1865; m. Dec. 23, 1852, Martha Ross, daughter of James and John Endsley), b. 1821; d. Nov. 1, 1854; Martha Phillips Ross; iii. Susan, d. Aug. 3, 1890; iv. Nancy, d. 1865; m. John Black); 2. Jane; 3. Nancy; 4. Margaret; 5. Mary; 6. Ann; 7. Robert; 8. Matthew.

ELIAS McNAMEE, of Scotch-Irish descent; emigrated from Pennsylvania, and settled in Freeport, Ohio; m. Mary Delaney, of French descent; had issue: 1. Amzi, b. Dec. 25, 1825; m. Mary Ellen Harvey, whose parents came from Maryland; b. 1823; d. 1886 (had issue: i. John; ii. Elias-B., m. Eva May Weeks).

ANDREW McNEELY (whose father emigrated from Ireland to America before the Revolution), b. in Berks county, Penn., 1772; d. in Cadiz township, Harrison county, Ohio, 1858, where he had settled in 1802; served as a member of the Ohio Legislature four years; m. in Philadelphia, 1800, Sarah Bettle, b. 1772; d. 1852, a native of that city; had issue, among others: 1. Cyrus, b. in Cadiz township, Harrison county, May 27, 1809; laid out the town of Hopedale, Harrison county, 1849, where he settled in that year; m. May 19, 1837, Jane Donaldson, b. 1807; d. 1887; a native of Cincinnati (had issue: i. Lorenzo; ii. Bryant; both died young).

JAMES McNUTT, d. in Green township, about May, 1822; m. Jane ———; had issue: 1. Benjamin; 2. James, d. 1855; m. Elizabeth Maholm, daughter of Samuel and Jane Maholm, of Cadiz (had issue: i. John; ii. Arthur-P., b. 1821; d. Dec. 15, 1895); 3. Joseph; 4. Sophia.

GEORGE McPECK, b. 1778; d. April 20, 1858; removed from Westmoreland county, Penn., to Harrison county, Ohio, in 1844; his wife b. 1785; d. April 27, 1869; they were m. Sept. 6, 1803; had issue, six sons and three daughters, of whom: I. William, settled in Union county, Ohio. II. George. b. in Westmoreland county, Penn., Oct. 24, 1808; came to Harrison county, Ohio, in November, 1829, and settled at Hanover, thence removed to Archer township, where he d. March 24, 1886; m. (1st) d. 6. 1831, Jane Endsley, d. Aug. 22, 1852. daughter of John and Jane Blaine Endsley; m. (2d) Oct. 6, 1853. Mrs. Barbara Endsley (widow of m. (3d) Mrs. Catherine A. Lyons Cald-

HARRISON COUNTY GENEALOGIES

well, b. March 28, 1822; d. July 10, 1883; had issue, nine children, of whom: 1. John-Endsley, b. at Hanover, Aug. 1, 1832; settled in Archer township; served as an officer in the Civil War; m. Sept. 8, 1858, Mary Davidson, daughter of Rev. Lewis H. Davidson, of Washington township; 2. George-McKenney, b. 1836; d. Jan. 30, 1874; 3. David-Blair, b. 1845; d. in infancy; 4. William, b. 1859; d. July 24, 1875.

John Endsley, father of Jane Endsley McPeck, was b. 1776; first settled in Cumberland county, Penn., where he m. Jane Blaine, b. in Ireland, 1773; d. Jan. 29, 1848; removed to Pittsburg, Penn., and thence, in 1808, to Archer township, Harrison county, Ohio, where he died April 29, 1835; had issue: 1. John, m. Barbara ———; 2. Jane, m. George McPeck; 3. Thomas; 4. James; 5. Mary, m. Nathan Shannon; 6. Sarah, m. Joseph McClain.

THOMAS MADDOX, b. in Virginia, 1778; son of Wilson Maddox, a native of Virginia; removed to Short Creek township, Harrison county, Ohio, about 1825, where he d. 1838; m. Jane Freeman, b. 1774; d. 1858; had issue: 1. Eliza, d. in Virginia, March 11, 1824; 2. Wilson, b. in Caroline county, Va., July 24, 1813; d. 1860; m. Nov. 30, 1836, Mary T. Ladd, b. in Virginia, 1818; d. 1874 (her parents were Robert and Mary T. Ladd, who came to Harrison county, about 1831, where they both died); (had issue: i. Eliza, m. G. B. Coutant; ii. Thomas, b. June 22, 1841; m. 1869, Henrietta T. Hague, d. Jan. 13, 1886; daughter of Henry and Sarah A. Thompson Woodward Hague, of Short Creek township; iii. Mary-Jane, m. Benjamin Chambers; iv. Virginia-W., m. William Buchanan, and settled at Hopedale, Harrison county).

SAMUEL MAHOLM, d. at Cadiz, November, 1838; m. Jane ———; had issue: 1. Jane, b. 1776; d. March 31, 1833; m. James Wilson, b. 1777; d. Dec. 6, 1839; 2. Nancy, b. 1779-80; d. Oct. 13, 1856; m. Walter B. Beebe, b. 1786; d. Jan. 24, 1836 (had issue: i. Walter-Butler, m. Maria B. Welch, b. 1822-23; d. Aug. 10, 1891; daughter of Rezin and Eliza Bayless Welch; ii. James); 3. Elizabeth, m. James McNutt, of Cadiz, d. May 1855, son of James and Jane McNutt (had issue: i. John; ii. Arthur-P., b. 1821; d. Dec. 15, 1895); 4. Margaret, b. 1790; d. 1858; 5. Hannah, m. ——— Phillips; 6. Mary, m. William Lyle; 7. Dorcas, m. John Bleaks; 8. Eleanor; 9. John, b. 1795; d. Sept. 9, 1854; m. April 4, 1822, Mrs. Martha Collins Bowland, daughter of David and Ann Workman Collins (had issue: i. Eliza-Jane, m. Joseph Sharon; ii. Martha-M., m. Rezin Bennett; iii. James-Bowland); 10. Sarah, b. 1803; d. 1848.

WILLIAM MALLERNEE, a native of Maryland, settled in Jefferson county, Ohio, 1809; m. Sarah ———; had issue:

I. Emanuel, b. in Maryland, Nov. 3, 1779; removed to Nottingham township, Harrison county, Ohio, about 1829, where he d. Feb. 23, 1839; m. (1st) Rachel Matthews, b. in Maryland, Nov. 3, 1788; d. June 24, 1828; daughter of Francis and Mary Karr Matthews, natives of Maryland who settled in Ohio in 1809; m. (2d) Hannah Eaton; had issue by first wife: 1. William, b. March 30, 1807; 2. Aquila, b. Jan. 6, 1809; 3. Mary-A., b. Aug. 17, 1811; 4. Matthew-F., b. Oct. 12, 1813; 5. Levi, b. Feb. 12, 1816; settled at Deersville, Harrison county, where he d. June 1, 1880; m. (1st) Dec. 6, 1838, Eleanor Johnson, b. Jan. 27, 1820; d. Dec. 23, 1863; daughter of Benjamin and Eleanor Johnson; m. (2d) Mrs. Jemima Garner Hines; m. (3d) June 1, 1879, Rachel Crabtree (had issue by first wife: i. David Turner, b. Nov. 18, 1839; ii. Emanuel, b. March 22, 1843; iii. Mary-A., b. March 25, 1846; m. J. H. Kent, and settled in Illinois; iv. Benjamin-J., b. Feb. 10, 1849; m. Jan. 17, 1872, Margaret Warman, b. in Illinois, March 15, 1850; daughter of William and Margaret Hoffman Warman; v. Lemuel, b. July 5, 1851; vi. Lydia-A., b. Aug. 3, 1854; vii. Caroline-L., b. Aug. 26, 1857; viii. Eleanor-J., b. July 18, 1860; m. L. D. Wells, and settled in Illinois); ix. Kinsey-C., b. Dec. 20, 1863; had issue by second wife: x. James-G., b. Oct. 10, 1866; xi. Levi-E., b. Oct. 20, 1868; xii. Ruth-J., b. Jan. 6, 1871); 6. Emanuel, b. Nov. 3, 1818; 7. Lewis, b. May 18, 1822; 8. Elizabeth, b. May 25, 1825; had issue by second wife: 9. Benjamin, b. Oct. 4, 1830; 10. Rachel, b. Aug. 13, 1832; 11. Jared, b. Sept. 10, 1834.

II. Mary.

III. Jared.

THOMAS MANSFIELD, a native of England, b. 1757; emigrated to America, and settled in Maryland before the Revolution; removed to Westmoreland county, Penn., and in 1797 settled on what was known as the Dorsey Flats, in Jefferson county, Ohio, where he d. June, 1844 (his two elder brothers served in the Revolutionary War; his brother Samuel served in the War of 1812); m. Mary Hill, b. 1767; d. 1854; had issue, among others: 1. William-L., b. in Jefferson county, November, 1810; settled in Green township, Harrison county, in 1866; m. 1840, Harriet Harrah, daughter of James G. Harrah (had issue: i. Margaret-J., m. A. Moore; ii. Thomas-B., served in the Civil War; settled in Iowa; iii. James-Harvey, d. 1876; iv. Mary-Ellis, m. Alonzo Hoobler; v. Nettie, m. John Mansfield, and settled in Steubenville; vi. Addie-R., m. William Hall).

ARTHUR MARTIN, b. in Ireland, 1771; emigrated to America and first settled in Lancaster county, Penn.; removed to Harrison county, Ohio, about 1817, locating in Cadiz township, where he d.. 1826; m. in Lancaster county, Margaret Urey, a native of Pennsylvania, b. 1773; d. 1856; her grandfather, George Urey, served in the Revolutionary War; had issue: 1. Ann; 2. Mary, m. Washington Ourant, and settled in Cadiz township; 3. Edward; 4. John-H., b. in Pennsylvania; m. 1840, Harriet Hitchcock, b. in Harrison county, Nov. 6, 1819, daughter of Samuel and Isabella Moore Hitchcock (had issue: i. Albert, served in the Civil War; settled in Jay county, Md.; ii. Margaret; iii. Samuel; iv. Edward; v. John; vi. George; vii. Belle, m. John F. Mehollin; viii. Jane, m. John Jamison; ix. James, settled in Athens township; x. Mary, m. Joseph D. Clark; settled in Colorado); 5. George, b. in Harrison county, Ohio, March 1, 1817; m. Jan. 3, 1853, Rachel H. Kennedy, b. 1831, in Tuscarawas county, Ohio; d. 1881; a daughter of John and Matilda Kennedy.

Samuel Hitchcock, father of Harriet Martin, was b. 1788; d. Feb. 7, 1879, in Harrison county, where he had settled 1808; m. Isabella Moore, b. 1788; d. Feb. 2, 1851; they had twelve children, among whom were John and Harriet.

PETER MARTIN, a native of New Jersey, b. 1764; m. in Virginia, Elizabeth Heberling, a native of Maryland, b. 1770; removed to Short Creek township, Harrison county, Ohio, about 1822, where they died, the former in 1837, the latter in 1854; had issue: 1. Luther; 2. Nancy; 3. Sarah; 4. John, b. in Jefferson county, Va., Nov. 5, 1805; 5. Elizabeth; 6. Jacob; 7. Susan; 8. William; 9. George, settled near Zanesville; 10. Jesse, b. July 29, 1819; settled in Green township; m. Oct. 18, 1853, Elizabeth Scarborough, daughter of Thomas and Sarah Harris Scarborough, of Green township.

Thomas Scarborough, father of Elizabeth Martin, was b. in Pennsylvania, Feb. 1, 1796; d. in Green township, Harrison county, Sept. 4, 1867; m. Sarah Harris, d. July 6, 1855; had issue: 1. Charles, b. Oct. 5, 1824; 2. Mary-E., b. Feb. 5, 1828; 3. Elizabeth, b. Oct. 22, 1830, m. Jesse Martin; 4. Margaret, b. Nov. 21, 1832; 5. William, b. July 4, 1835; 6. Thomas, b. Dec. 12, 1839; 7. Asbury, b. Oct. 24, 1841.

JOHN MATTERN, removed from Westmoreland county, Penn., to Archer township, Harrison county, where he died June, 1861; m. Nancy ———; had issue: 1. Abraham, b. in Westmoreland county, Penn., Oct. 22, 1806; removed with his parents to Archer township, Harrison county, Ohio; located in Green township, April, 1837, where he d. Feb. 16, 1889; m. 1833, Mary Brown, b. April 14, 1808; d. Dec. 17, 1890; had issue: 1. Jane; 2. John; 3. Nancy-Ann; 4. Hugh-B.; 5. Wesley; 6. Alfred-S., b. Feb. 18, 1853; settled at Folks' Station, Green township; m. Sept. 14, 1881, Jennie R. Pry, daughter of Robert Pry, a resident of Pennsylvania, who afterward settled in Wellsburg, W. Va. II. John. III. Julia-Ann, m. ——— Smith. IV. Anna-Maria, m. ——— Hanna.

JAMES MAXWELL, a native of Ireland or Scotland, emigrated to America and settled near Baltimore, Md.; had issue: John, James, Hugh, George, Robert. Of these children, James Maxwell removed to Pennsylvania, where he was married; had issue:
I. John. II. Robert, b. July 30, 1769; settled near Bloomfield, Jefferson county, Ohio, 1798; m. in Pennsylvania, Deborah Wierman; had issue: 1. Robert, b. Jan. 20, 1794; d. Jan. 8, 1866; m. June 18, 1823; 2. Susannah, b. Aug. 5, 1795; d. Nov. 7, 1840; m. Oct. 13, 1813;

3. James, b. April 5, 1797; d. Jan. 13, 1860; m. June 27, 1822; 4. William, b. March 14, 1799; d. Oct. 5, 1884; m. Sept. 10, 1828; 5. John, b. Nov. 5, 1800; d. Oct. 3, 1821; 6. Mary, b. June 28, 1802; d. March 3, 1864; 7. Harmon, b. Feb. 1, 1804; m. May 23, 1833; 8. Thomas, b. May 20, 1805; m. Aug. 14, 1828; 9. Archibald, b. Dec. 2, 1806; d. Oct. 27, 1882; m. Feb. 7, 1832; 10. David, b. Nov. 19, 1808; d. Oct. 20, 1842; m. April 27, 1837; 11. Isabella, b. Sept. 15, 1810; d. June 21, 1872; m. July 10, 1835; 12. Matilda, b. June 15, 1812; d. July 5, 1813; 13. Hiram, b. Nov. 13, 1813; d. Aug. 8. 1852; m. Nov. 13, 1834; 14. Hezekiah, b. Aug. 21, 1815; d. Oct. 4, 1885; m. Oct. 5, 1843; 15. Allen, b. in Jefferson county, Ohio, May 7, 1817; settled in Harrison county, Ohio, 1856; m. 1843, Mary Ann Bell (had issue: i. Francis-B., b. April 25, 1845; d. June 26, 1845; ii. Martha-J., b. May 13, 1846; d. Dec. 21, 1870; m. Dec. 15, 1864, Henry Copeland; iii. Jackson-B., b. Sept. 4, 1849; m. Sept. 22, 1875, Esther Devore; iv. Elizabeth-D., b. July 13, 1852; d. Feb. 14, 1855; v. Nancy-A., b. July 10, 1855; m. Sept. 28, 1876, Emanuel Howard; vi. Mary-Belle, b. Dec. 2, 1857; d. Aug. 15, 1888; m. Sept. 23, 1887, J. F. Mattern; vii. Caroline-S., b. May 25, 1860; d. Jan. 21, 1863; viii. Vall-A., b. April 22, 1863; d. Nov. 27, 1886; ix. ———, b. and d. Dec. 11, 1865; x. Orpha, b. Jan. 22, 1873); 16. Margaret. b. July 5, 1819; d. June 28, 1841. III. Mary. IV. Margaret. V. Jane.

WILLIAM MAXWELL, a native of Ireland, as was also his wife, emigrated to America, and settled in Virginia before the Revolutionary War; had issue: 1. James, b. in Virginia; d. in Nottingham township, Harrison county, Ohio, 1868; settled in Jefferson county, before 1838, and thence removed to Harrison; m. in Virginia, Hannah Pollock, d. July 23, 1886 (had issue: i. David; ii. Mary-Jane; iii. Walker; iv. John; v. Elizabeth; vi. Margaret; vii. Henry; viii. James, b. in Nottingham township, April 26, 1838; m. (1st) Dec. 14, 1859, Elizabeth McCullough, of Nottingham township; m. (2d) Sarah Willison, of Washington township, Harrison county; ix. William; x. Rachel); 2. William; 3. Henry; 4. Alexander; 5. John; 6. Margaret; 7. Elizabeth.

JOSEPH MAYES, see Family of Robert Coulter.

SAMUEL MEARS, b. in Ireland, May 13, 1777, where he m. Leah Serges, b. May 8, 1786; emigrated to America and about 1790 settled at Baltimore, Md.; removed in 1818, to Perry township, Tuscarawas county, Ohio, where he died; had issue: 1. John, b. Nov. 2, 1805; 2. Alexander, b. Jan. 1, 1807; 3. William, b. April 1, 1809; d. Aug. 3, 1879; 4. Catherine, b. Nov. 23, 1810; 5. Jane, b. Oct. 2, 1811; d. March, 1879; 6. Robert, b. Oct. 26, 1813; settled at West Chester, Tuscarawas county, 1842, where he d. July 21, 1890; m. (1st) 1842, Anna Eliza Thompson, b. June 7, 1819; d. Sept. 28, 1861, daughter of Thomas and Mary Amelia Mitchell Thompson; m. (2d) Mary McCord (had issue by first wife: i. Elizabeth-Jane, b. July 29, 1843; d. Aug. 31, 1871; ii. Samuel-T., b. Oct. 1, 1845; settled in Freeport, Harrison county, 1882; m. Dec. 25, 1866, Sarah Arminda Stewart, of Freeport, daughter of Andrew and Mary A. Snider Stewart; iii. Robert-T., b. Nov. 24, 1848; iv. Mary-L., b. Oct. 20, 1851; d. July 17, 1873; v. Nathan-H., b. Cct. 19, 1856; vi. Harriet-A., b. Oct. 25, 1859); 7. Samuel, b. Sept. 28, 1815; 8. Rachel, b. Jan. 20, 1818; 9. Nathan, b. Sept. 27, 1820.

The parents of Ann Eliza Mears, Thomas and Mary Amelia Mitchell Thompson, were natives of county Down, Ireland, where they were m. 1816; emigrating to America and settling in New York the same year; removed to Harrison county, Ohio, 1820, locating three miles west of Freeport; the former was b. 1782; d. Sept. 12, 1828; the latter was b. Dec. 20, 1780; d. Aug. 17, 1865; had issue: 1. Ann-Eliza, b. June 7, 1819; d. Sept. 28, 1861; m. Robert Mears; 2. Robert, b. 1821; d. March 15, 1885; m. Louisa Carruthers; 3. James, b. 1823; m. Margaret Boles; 4. Harriet, b. 1825; m. Siles Stephens; 5. Julia, b. 1827; m. John R. Frazier.

JOHN MEGAW, a native of Ireland, emigrated to America about 1775; served in the Revolutionary War. entering the American army immediately after his arrival; removed from Westmoreland county, Penn.,to North township, Harrison county, Ohio, about 1814; m. Jane Hamilton; had issue:
I. John, b. in Pennsylvania, Feb. 18,

1784; came to Harrison county with his parents; settled in Archer township, 1822, where he d. March 9, 1865; m. in Westmoreland county, Penn., 1812, Catherine Best; b. in Pennsylvania, Jan. 31, 1789; d. Sept. 9, 1847; daughter of James Best; had issue: 1. Samuel, b. in Westmoreland county, Penn., Feb. 25, 1813; settled in Archer township; m. Nov. 13, 1834, Jane McCombs, d. July 2, 1885; daughter of James McCombs, a resident of Pennsylvania (had issue: i. Catherine-A., b. Oct. 9, 1835; ii. Margaret-M., b. Feb. 26, 1837; iii. John-C., b. May 20, 1838; d. May 30, 1864; iv. James-R., b. May 1, 1840; v. Samuel, b. Nov. 10, 1841; d. Sept. 30, 1845; vi. Mary-Jane, b. Aug. 19, 1843; vii. Eleanor, b. Dec. 24, 1845; viii. Sarah-E., b. Oct. 31, 1848); 2. Jane; 3. Sarah, b. in North township, Oct. 17, 1817; m. Dec. 31, 1843, William Maxwell, of North township, removed to Washington county, Iowa, in 1848 (had issue: i. Robert, d. near Hanover; ii. John; d. in Harrison county; iii. William-James; iv. Catherine-Jane; v. Nathaniel-McDowell; vi. ——, d. in infancy); 4. John; 5. James, b. in Archer township, Nov. 11, 1823; m. (1st) Oct. 5, 1851, Elizabeth Mitchell, d. April 7, 1880; daughter of John Mitchell, of Archer township; m. (2d) Oct. 30, 1884, Eliza Haverfield, daughter of Alexander Haverfield, of Cadiz township, Harrison county (had issue by first wife: i. J.-M., b. March 9, 1857); 6. John, b. in Archer township, Aug. 14, 1826; removed to Cadiz township, in 1856; m. 1852, Sarah Jane Christy, daughter of William Christy, who with his wife, was an early settler in Harrison county (had issue: i. John, d. 1866; ii. Martha-Ann d. 1866; iii. Margaret-Jane, d. 1866; iv. Clara-Catherine; v. Everett-Grimes); 7. Jacob, b. Aug. 21, 1829; d. Feb. 15, 1888; m. June 22, 1867. Eleanor Robinson, d. May 21, 1882, daughter of James Robinson (had issue: i. James-R., b. May 4, 1865; ii. Minerva-R., b. Feb. 6. 1868; iii. John-B., b. May 17, 1871; iv. Catherine, b. Aug. 9, 1873; v. Lawson-E., b. Dec. 24, 1880).
II. Rebecca.
III. Jane.
IV. Samuel.
V. Sarah.
VI. James, b. Sept. 15, 1793; d. Oct. 24, 1851; had issue: 1. John: 2. James-G.; 3. George-T.; 4. Martha-Matilda; 5. Eliza-Jane; 6. Eleanor; 7. Sarah-Ann, m. ——— Patterson.

JOSEPH MEHOLLIN, a native of Ireland, of Scottish descent; settled at Smithfield, Jefferson county, Ohio, before 1800, where he died; had issue: I. Joseph, d. aged sixty-five years; settled in Cadiz township; m. Margaret McFadden, b. 1789; d. 1877; had issue, among others: 1. John, b. in Cadiz township, 1818; d. 1900; m. Elizabeth McFadden (had issue: i. Samuel, b. Sept. 28, 1846; m. (1st) 1871, Mary Nash, b. 1853; d. 1879; daughter of Samuel Nash, of Cassville; m. (2d) Belle Smith, daughter of Archibald Smith, of Dickerson's Mills, Harrison county; ii. Joseph; iii. Mary-Margaret, m. Leonard Rowland, of Cadiz township; iv. John-Findley, b. in Cadiz township, March 17, 1856; m. 1878, Belle Martin, daughter of John and Harriet Martin, of Cadiz township); 2. Sarah, m. William Jamison, and settled in Cadiz township; 3. Margaret, m. George Tarbot, and settled near Moorefield.

MICAJAH MERRYMAN, of German descent, b. in Maryland, April 25, 1775; removed to Smithfield, Jefferson county, Ohio, about 1815; later settled in Archer township, Harrison county, and subsequently removed to Tuscarawas county, Ohio, where he d. 1847; served in the War of 1812; m. 1811, ——— Snyder, b. in Maryland, March, 1795, daughter of Martin and Mary Ann Snyder, natives of that State; had issue, among others: 1. John, b. in Cadiz township, July 26, 1823; settled in Archer township; m. Mary Shivers, b. in Nottingham township. Aug. 22, 1824, daughter of John and Elizabeth Shivers, pioneers of Harrison county, whence they came from Maryland (had issue: i. Martha, m. James B. Rogers, and settled at Cadiz; ii. Caroline; iii. Alexander; iv. Hannah, m. George English; v. Jackson; vi. Elizabeth. m. Lincoln Blair, and settled in Stock township; vii. Jeremiah-C., settled in Nottingham township; viii. Lafayette; ix. Sarah-M., m. James Love, and settled in Sauk Centre, Minn.; x. John).

JOHN PETER MIKESELL, a native of Frederick (now Carroll) county, Md.; d. in Rumley township, Harrison county, July 15, 1846, where he had settled in 1816; son of John Mikesell, a native of Germany; m. Mary Ann Long, b. in Maryland; had issue: 1. Joseph, b. March 25, 1811; settled at Jewett, Harrison county; m. Oct. 22, 1839, Magdaline Hoobler, b. Feb. 17, 1821; daughter of Adam and Elizabeth Lawyer Hoobler (had issue: i. Maria, b. May 6, 1843; m. James Aiken, of Jewett); 2. Andrew; 3. George; 4. Jesse, b. Dec. 11, 1819; d. Feb. 23, 1887; m. 1847, Mary E. Roby, daughter of John H. and Sophia Roby (both b. in Maryland, 1800); 5. Daniel; 6. Susanna; 7. Samuel.

JOHN MILLER, a native of Frederick county, Md.; removed to Rumley township, Harrison county, Ohio, about 1806, where he d. 1836; had issue:

I. Daniel, b. in Frederick county, Md., 1788; came with his parents to Harrison county; settled in German township, where he d. 1854; m. 1817, Susannah Lowmiller, b. in Dauphin county, Penn., 1796; daughter of John and Catherine Lowmiller, who settled in Harrison county before 1810; had issue: 1. Catherine; 2. Elizabeth; 3. Sarah; 4. John, b. Feb. 22, 1822; m. May 1, 1849, Susannah Mikesell, b. in Rumley township, Feb. 15, 1824, daughter of Peter and Mary A. Long Mikesell, who removed from Frederick county, Md., to Harrison county, before 1810 (had issue: i. O.-B.; settled at Germano, Harrison county; ii.Rebecca-Margaret; iii. H.-A., b. March 8, 1851; m. 1874, Sarah C. Wood, b. Sept. 22, 1852, daughter of Ellis and Elizabeth Shearer Wood, of Carroll county; iv. Andrew-B., settled in Rumley township; v. Daniel-D., a minister, settled at Parker's Landing, Penn.; vi. Samuel-H., settled in Greensville, Penn.; vii. John-O.; viii. Joseph-M., settled in Washington county, Penn.; ix. Clement-E.; x. Clayton-L.; xi. Jesse-L.); 5. Henry, b. Aug. 27, 1824; served in the Civil War; m. May 20, 1856, E. W. Gault, b. Feb. 28, 1831, daughter of John and Nancy McKinsey Gault, who settled in Harrison county, in 1839; 6. Susannah; 7. Rebecca; 8. Margaret; 9. Abigail; 10. Eliza-J. II. David. III. John, b. 1801; settled in Rumley township before 1828, where he d. 1836; m. Margaret Lowmiller, b. 1805; d. 1876; daughter of John and Susannah Ulerich Lowmiller; had issue: 1. Mary-Ann; 2. Susanna, b. in Rumley township, Oct. 11, 1828; m.

May, 1847, Thomas W. Ramsouer, b. in Rumley township, 1820; d. in Jewett, 1880; son of John and Catherine H. Ramsouer (had issue: i. Josiah-A.; ii. John-William; iii. Margaret-C.; iv. Sabella-J.; v. Harden-Miller, settled in Massillon, Ohio; vi. Daniel-D.; vii. Hester-A., m. Wm. Custer Edwards; settled in Dennison, Ohio; viii. Lauretta-F.; ix. Susan-Maria, m. Richey Osborn); 3. Isabella, m. William Manbeck; 4. Elizabeth, m. Isaac McCloud, and settled in Kansas; 5. Jacob; settled in Jefferson county, Ohio; 6. Daniel. IV. Jacob. V. Joseph. VI. Catherine. VII. Hannah. VIII. Mary. IX. Sarah.

WILLIAM MILLER, born in the North of Ireland; emigrated to America, and settled in Huntingdon county, Penn., about 1789; m. Rebecca Wylie; had issue: 1. James; 2. Samuel; 3. Joseph; 4. Benson; 5. Margaret; 6. Isabel; 7. Martha, d. 1873; m. John L. Martin, son of John and Elizabeth Livingston Martin, of Mifflin county, Penn. (had issue: i. Rebecca-Jane, m. 1861, Lyons F. Grider; ii. John, m. Jane Johnson; iii. Samuel; iv. William; v. Joseph); 8. Hester; 9. Rebecca.

ALEXANDER MILLS (whose father d. Feb. 10, 1776), was b. in county Down, Ireland, Dec. 11, 1738; d. Dec. 4, 1815; had issue:

I. John, b. in county Down, Ireland, Nov. 18, 1766; emigrated to America and before 1811 settled in Jefferson county, Ohio, removing thence to Carroll county, where he d. April 29, 1853; had issue, among others: 1. William, b. Sept. 1, 1811; removed to New Athens, where he d. 1864; m. 1844, Sarah Ann Cannon, b. July 27, 1820 (had issue: i. Rachel-Jane; ii. James-Allen; iii. Moses-Cannon; iv. John-Sullivan; v. Jesse-Lewis; settled in Kansas; vi. Mary-E., m. Dr. J. H. Irwin; settled in Oregon; vii. Nancy-Priscilla, m. Dr. James A. Calhoon, and settled at Pittsburg; viii. Robert-Emmett); 2. Alexander, settled in Carroll county (had issue, among others: i. Thomas; ii. Shane).

GEORGE MILLS, a native of Ireland or Scotland, emigrated to America and first settled in Pennsylvania, where he m. Elizabeth Caldwell, a native of Ireland; removed to Jefferson county, Ohio, before 1816; had issue: 1. George; 2. William; 3. John, b. Feb. 23, 1816; m.

March 21, 1850, Eliza J. Henderson, b. Aug. 28, 1827; daughter of John Henderson, of Jefferson county; 4. James; 5. Jane; 6. Nancy; 7. Eliza.

ROBERT MINTIER, b. in Pennsylvania, 1791, of Scotch-Irish descent; removed to Belmont county, Ohio, before 1819, where several of his children were born; located in Short Creek township, Harrison county, about 1831, where he d. 1870; m. in Belmont county, 1819, Elizabeth Hammond, b. 1798; d. 1863; daughter of Robert and Jane Hammond; had issue: 1. Alexander; 2. Joseph, b. in Jefferson county, Oct. 25, 1822; in 1854 located in Bureau county; settled in Short Creek township in 1862; m. (1st) 1846, Eleanor Campbell, d. 1853; daughter of William and Ellen Campbell, of Belmont county, Ohio (who had removed there from Washington county, Penn.); m. (2d) 1854, Eliza Jane Carrick, b. in Short Creek township; daughter of James (d. 1885) and Martha Pennell Carrick (the former having come to Ohio from Pennsylvania); (had issue by first wife: i. Elizabeth; ii. Martha, settled in Leavenworth, Kan.; iii. Robert; had issue by second wife: iv. Sarah-Belle; v. James-C., settled at Oberlin, Decatur county, Kan.; vi. Josephine, m. Alonzo Eli, and settled in Athens township; vii. Milton-S.; viii. Minerva-Jeanette; ix. Oscar-Glenn); 3. Thomas, settled in Muskingum county, Ohio; 4. William, d. in infancy; 5. John, settled in Belmont county; 6. James, b. March 9, 1829; served in the Civil War; settled in Short Creek township, in 1859; m. (1st) Oct. 26, 1854, Eliza Ann Kibble, d. 1855; m. (2d) Oct. 27, 1858, Mary Barnett, of Guernsey county, Ohio; d. 1865; m.(3d) Aug. 16, 1866, Elizabeth A. Davis, b. in Belmont county; daughter of John and Eleanor J. Israel Davis (the former d. in Jefferson county, in October, 1884; the latter also died in 1884; the maternal grandparents of Elizabeth Davis were Germans; her great-grandfather, Robert Israel, was an officer in the Revolutionary War); 7. Mary, m. John Hanna, of New Athens; 8. Martha, twin sister to Mary, d. young; 9. Eliza-Jane, m. James Henderson, and settled at Harrisville, Ohio; 10. Robert-Johnson, settled in Kansas; 11. Esther, m. Joseph Shepard, and settled in Iowa; 12. David, b. Feb. 3, 1841, settled in Short Creek township; served in the Civil War; m. Sept. 26, 1867, Margaret Jane Richey, daughter of Alexander and Eliza Haneway (b. 1810; d. 1839) Richey (the former d. in Muskingum county, Ohio, March, 1867; the grandfather of Margaret Jane Richey, Andrew Richey, was one of the first settlers in Harrison county, and died there.

JOHN MITCHELL, b. 1774; a native of Ireland or Scotland; emigrated to America and first settled in Maryland; removed to Steubenville, Ohio, before 1816, and later located in Archer township, Harrison county, where he d. April 12, 1844; m. Mary Hines, b. 1782; d. 1850; daughter of Rudolph Hines, of Cadiz township, Harrison county; had issue, among others: 1. Robert, b. in Archer township, Jan. 5, 1816; m. Jan. 2, 1845, Eliza Jane Atkinson, b. June 16, 1823; daughter of James Atkinson, of Archer township (had issue: i. Jane, b. Oct. 31, 1845; d. June 30, 1871; m. Feb. 2, 1865, John Biggar; ii. John-R., b. March 11, 1847; iii. James-A., b. March 13, 1851; iv. William, b. Aug. 19, 1853; v. Mary-E., b. Sept. 2, 1855; m. (1st) Clarence Haverfield; m. (2d) Hamilton Lisle).

MATTHEW MITCHELL, b. in Ireland, where he m. Jennie McDill; emigrated to America, and, about 1785, settled in Washington county, Penn.; removed to Harrison county, Ohio, before 1806, subsequently returning to Pennsylvania, where both himself and wife died; had issue, among others: I. John, b. April 6, 1787, in Washington county, Penn.; d. 1865, in Harrison county, where he had settled in 1816; m. Margaret McGee, b. about 1790; d. 1875; had issue: 1. Jane, m. Abraham Corban, and settled near Cassville; 2. Matthew, settled in Noble county, Ohio; 3. Nancy; 4. Rose-Ann, m. John Chamberlain, and settled in Poweshiek county, Iowa; 5. Morris, settled in Knox county, Illinois; 6. Elizabeth; 7. Margaret-Ann, m. John Nash; settled near Cassville. Ohio (had issue, six sons); 8. John-D., b. Nov. 22, 1825, near Cadiz; m. (1st) 1852, Rebecca Hammond, d. about 1865; m. (2d) Nov. 5, 1868, Elizabeth A. Kyle, daughter of Thomas and Jane McNary Kyle, of German township, Harrison county Ohio; 9. George; 10. Sarah, m. John

Houser, and settled in Mercer county, Ill., where she died, leaving six children; 11. Mary, m. Welling Calhoon, and settled in Crawfordsville, Ind.

AMMI MOORE, b. in New Jersey, 1767; removed to Greene county, Penn., about 1795, and in 1817 to Moorefield township, Harrison county, Ohio, where he d. 1823; m. Sarah Shepard, b. in Pennsylvania, 1777; d. 1841; daughter of William Shepard, a native of Pennsylvania, who had settled in the eastern part of Greene county; had issue: 1. Rebecca; 2. Mary; 3. Rachel; 4. Elizabeth; 5. Shepard; 6. John; 7. Uriah, b. in Greene county, Penn., March 4, 1814; m. Oct. 13, 1842, Mary Ann Fulton, b. April 14, 1821; daughter of Philip and Sarah Hanna Fulton, natives of Maryland, who settled in Harrison county, about 1819 (had issue: i. Sarah-A., m. ——— Corbin; ii. John-F.; iii. William-A.; iv. Hannah-M., m. ——— Dickerson; v. Albert-D., settled in Nottingham township; vi. Zephaniah; vii. Anderson-W.; viii. Vincent-C.; ix. Elliott-D.; x. Mary-E.).

ROBERT MOORE, b. in Ireland, 1771; emigrated to America and first settled in New York City, 1793, thence removed to eastern Pennsylvania, and in 1795, to Jefferson county, Ohio, locating ten miles west from Steubenville; about 1800 settled in Moorefield township, Harrison county, where he d. Feb. 1, 1835; m. Mary Armstrong, b. in Ireland, 1771; d. March 22, 1851; had issue: 1. Samuel; 2. Robert-A., b. in Jefferson county, about 1800; d. in Nottingham township, 1877; m. Elizabeth Peacock, d. 1864 (had issue: i. Mary-A., m. ——— Adams, and settled in Freeport, Harrison county; ii. Susannah; iii. Eli-Peacock, settled in Freeport township; iv. William-C., b. April 20, 1836; settled in Moorefield township; m. March 21, 1861, Rebecca J. Adams, b. Jan. 21, 1842, daughter of Samuel and Elizabeth Johnson Adams; v. Eliza-J., m. ——— Bartlett, and settled in Iowa; vi. Robert-B.; vii. Julia-A., m. ——— Snyder; viii. Thomas-A.); 3. John, b. in Jefferson county, Aug. 4, 1809; d. May 14, 1874; settled in Moorefield township, Harrison county; m. Elsie Johnson, b. Oct. 6, 1811; daughter of William Johnson, an early settler of Moorefield township (had issue:

i. Mary, m. Jackson Rea, of Cadiz township; ii. Johnson, settled in Moorefield township; iii. Albert, b. July 7, 1841; m. June 13, 1867, Sarah McFadden, b. May 13, 1844, daughter of Samuel and Margaret Rankin McFadden); 4. William, b. Oct. 4, 1811; settled in Moorefield township; m. March 15, 1837, Lydia Delaney, b. June 7, 1820; daughter of John and Rachel Delaney, natives of Delaware, who were early settlers in Harrison county (had issue: i. Robert; ii. Sophia, m. Robert Moore; iii. Allen-D.; iv. Stewart; v. William, settled in Missouri; vi. Howard, settled in Cadiz; vii. Lucinda; viii. Lydia, m. Linard Fulton, settled in Missouri); 5. Jane; 6. Margaret; 7. Mary.

WILLIAM MOORE, b. 1779; d. at Cadiz, 1847; removed from Westmoreland county, Penn., to Harrison county, Ohio, about 1808; m. in Westmoreland county, 1802, Sarah Corey, b. in New Jersey, Jan. 12, 1783; d. at Cadiz, March 16, 1863; had issue: 1. Mary, b. 1803; d. 1882; m. William Fulton; 2. Rosanna, b. 1805; d. young; 3. Elizabeth, b. 1807; d. 1825; 4. Nancy, b. 1809; d. 1881; m. William Birney; 5. Samuel, b. 1811; d. 1880; m. Isabel Birney; 6. John, b. July 27, 1813; d. Feb. 2, 1883; m. (1st) 1836, Elizabeth McCullough, b. 1818; d. Sept. 9, 1858; daughter of Joseph and Elizabeth Lyons McCullough, of Archer township; m. (2d) Sarah J. McCullough, b. 1827; d. June 14, 1874; m. (3d) Phebe Gray (had issue by first wife: i. Sarah; ii. David-O., a physician, removed to Bloomington, Ill.; iii. William-A.; iv. Beatty; v. Mary, m. Thompson Craig; vi. Alice, m. Robert Watson Barricklow; vii. Nancy, m. Anderson N. Hammond, and removed to Chicago; viii. Joseph, a physician, removed to Omaha, Neb.; ix. Ingram-Craig); 7. Hannah, b. 1815; m. 1834, Cyrus Gilmore, son of Samuel and Elizabeth Buchanan Gilmore; 8. David, b. 1817; d. 1870; m. Jane Clark, b. 1818; d. June 23, 1879; 9. Rachel, b. 1819; d. 1845; m. Samuel Snyder; 10. Sarah, b. 1822; m. Ingram Clark (see Family of Roger Clark); 11. Alexander, b. 1824; d. 1885; m. Mrs. Susan Craig Hanna, widow of Andrew Finley Hanna, of Cadiz; 12. Jane, b. 1827; d. 1858; m. Walter Craig; 13. William, b. 1829; d. 1885; m. (1st) ——— Saunders; m. (2d) ——— Hurford; m. (3d) ——— Purviance.

JAMES MORRIS, a native of Virginia or Maryland (whose grandparents are said to have come from England to Virginia before 1750), removed from Maryland to West Virginia with his family; had issue:
I. Daniel.
II. Thomas.
III. James.
IV. Zachariah.
V. John, b. in West Virginia, opposite the city of Marietta, Ohio, April 4, 1785; removed in 1813 to Cadiz, Ohio, and, in 1816, located at New Athens, where he d. April 4, 1865; m. in New Athens, Jan. 8, 1816, Charlotte Huff, daughter of Joseph and —— Doddridge Huff (the former was a celebrated Indian scout and fighter during and after the Revolutionary War, and was also one of the first white settlers in Short Creek township, Harrison county; he was given a section of land in Athens township by the United States Government for services rendered in Indian wars; his wife was of the well-known Doddridge family, of Hopewell township, Washington county, Penn., where during Indian attacks she had molded bullets in the block-houses of the settlements); John and Charlotte Morris had issue: 1. ——, d. in infancy, Nov. 26, 1817; 2. Alexander, b. July 14, 1819; d. May 18, 1824; 3. Joseph, b. March 16, 1822; settled in German township; m. (1st) March 9, 1843, Mary Brock, d. Oct. 28, 1873, daughter of George S. Brock, of Belmont county; m. (2d) Feb. 17, 1875, Emma Moore, daughter of Cyrus Moore, of Jefferson county, Ohio (had issue by first wife: i. John-A., b. Jan. 11, 1844; ii. Mary-E.-C., b. June 27, 1847; iii. George-S., b. Oct. 21, 1850; iv. L.-V., b. June 12, 1854; d. Feb. 2, 1885); 4. Margaret, b. March 21, 1824; d. Sept. 25, 1846; 5. John, b. May 10, 1826; 6. Mary-Ann, b. May 26, 1828; 7. Prudence, b. July 23, 1830; d. March 2, 1838; 8. Philip-D., b. May 21, 1833; d. Oct. 28, 1865; 9. Charlotte, b. May 16, 1835; d. March 9, 1838; 10. Elizabeth, b. Jan. 12, 1840; d. Jan. 1, 1866.
VI. Elizabeth.
VII. Morgan, b. in Maryland; removed first to West Virginia, and thence to Jefferson county, Ohio, before 1812, where he d. June 4, 1864; served in the War of 1812; m. (1st) in West Virginia, Elizabeth Wood, d. 1837; daughter of Edward Wood, a pioneer; m. (2d) Ellen Smith, of Harrison county; had issue by first wife: 1. Nancy; 2. Mary; 3. Phœbe; 4. John, b. May 4, 1816; settled in Athens township, about 1850; m. (1st) March 20, 1846, Elizabeth Porter; d. July 11, 1852; daughter of James T. Porter; m. (2d) April 29, 1859, Elizabeth Maxwell, daughter of James Maxwell (had issue by first wife: i. James; ii. Elizabeth, m. Johnson Hughes; iii. Rebecca-Jane; iv. William; v. Margaret; had issue by second wife: vi. Alonzo, b. Jan. 12, 1860; m. June 13, 1881, Laura E. Dickerson, daughter of J. T. Dickerson, of New Athens; vii. John-O.; viii. Thomas-M., b. Feb. 1, 1862; settled in Belmont county; m. 1888, Mary E. Monahan; ix. Mary-Alice; x. Morgan; xi. Sarah-J.; xii. Charles); 5. Elizabeth; 6. Thomas; 7. Hannah; 8. William; 9. Morgan; 10. Eliza-Jane; had issue by second wife: 11. Rebecca-Ann; 12. James-S.
VIII. Phœbe.

MICHAEL MYERS, see Family of Ezra Wharton.

ANDREW NICHOL, see Family of John Estep.

JAMES OGLEVEE, emigrated from the North of Ireland and settled in East Nottingham township, Chester county, Penn. (now Cecil county, Md.) before 1722 (probably a son or brother of John Oglevee, who died in Cecil county, January, 1744, leaving a wife, Rachel, and children, James, Dorcas, and Jean); d. 1751-53; m. Sarah ——; d. May, 1753; had issue: John, Sarah, Jean, Margaret (m. —— Boggs), and Violet (m. —— Porter, and had two sons, James and John); his son, grandson, or nephew, John Oglevee, died in Cecil county, January, 1797, leaving children, John, Joseph, Mary, Sarah, Margaret, and Anne, of whom:
I. John, removed from Cecil county, Maryland, to Fayette county. Penn., and thence, soon after 1800, to Harrison county, Ohio, and settled on Boggs' Fork of Stillwater Creek, where he d. 1815; served in the War of 1812; m. Mrs. Agnes Passmore Patterson, b. 1771-72; d. Aug. 11, 1853 (she had issue by her first husband, —— Patterson: 1. Jane, m. Adam Dunlap, and settled in Harrison county; 2. Mary, m. Robert Dunlap, and settled in Harrison county); John and Agnes Oglevee had is-

sue: 1. Elizabeth, b. 1804; d. Dec. 5, 1881; m. 1827, John Bethel, son of Simpson and Nancy Holloway Bethel; 2. William, b. 1808; d. July 6, 1884; settled in Moorefield township; m. 1830, Susanna Price, b. near Stillwater, Belmont county, 1811; d. May 26, 1879; daughter of John Price, of English descent (a pioneer, who served in the War of 1812; his wife, of Scottish descent); (had issue: i. John; settled in Morgan county, Ohio; ii. George; iii. Agnes, m. Archibald Hammond, of New Athens; iv. David, b. May 10, 1837; settled at Cadiz, 1889; m. October, 1866, Jane Ramsey, daughter of William and Mary Ramsey [the former a son of John Ramsey, one of the early settlers of Harrison county; the latter, daughter of John Hines, also an early settler]; v. Hugh, b. in Moorefield township, Aug. 1, 1839; settled at New Athens; served in the Civil War; m. in Belmont county, Aug. 16, 1866, Mary Brock Morris, native of Harrison county; vi. Elizabeth-Ann, m. Dewey Lantz, and settled in Belmont county; vii. Jane; viii. James; ix. Baruch-Francis, b. March 3, 1848; settled in Cadiz township; m. 1885, Agnes Haverfield, daughter of James and Elizabeth Haverfield, of Cadiz township; x. Anna-E.; xi. Sarah-S., m. Oscar McFadden, and settled in Athens township); 3. Hugh; 4. John, b. Dec. 10, 1810; d. March 12. 1865; m. Eliza Ann Hanna, b. Jan. 8, 1808; d. March 31, 1863; daughter of John and Ann Leonard Hanna (who removed from Rostraver township, Westmoreland county, to Cadiz, in 1814); (had issue: i. Mary-Ann, b. May 17, 1837; d. July 21, 1874; m. Samuel A. Osburn; ii. William-Hamilton, b. Sept. 10. 1838; settled at Clinton, Ill.; m. 1867, Elizabeth A. Craig, daughter of Walter and Jane Moore Craig; iii. John-Finley, b. May 16, 1840; m. (1st) Jeanette Eagleson; m. (2d) Euphemia Eagleson; served as an officer in the Civil War, and as Auditor of the State of Ohio; settled in Chicago; iv. James Wilson, b. May 12, 1842; d. May 23, 1863; served in the Civil War, and died from disease contracted in that service; v. Baruch-Francis, b. May 20, 1844; d. June 12, 1845; vi. George-Hopkins, b. April 17, 1846; d. April 10, 1857; vii. Nancy-Jane, b. Feb. 8, 1849; d. June 25, 1866; viii. Susanna-Elizabeth, b. June 28, 1852; d. Feb. 10, 1880); 5. Nancy 6. Baruch.

II. Joseph, b. in Cecil county, Md., 1765; d. in Franklin township, Fayette county, Penn., Sept. 14, 1835; m. Ann Barricklow, b. 1768; d. Oct. 16, 1845; daughter of Conrad and Sarah Farrington Barricklow (see Barricklow Family); had issue: 1. Jesse, b. 1804; d. Jan. 26, 1876; m. 1826, Elizabeth Galley, b. 1807; d. 1858; daughter of Philip Galley (had issue: i. Joseph; June 2, 1827; m. 1850, Rebecca Stoner; settled at East Liberty, Dunbar township, Fayette county; ii. John; iii. Philip); 2. John; 3. Farrington.

III. Margaret, b. 1776; d. May 25, 1851; m. James Porter, son of John Porter, of Pennsylvania; settled in Cadiz township, Harrison county: had issue: 1. Joseph; 2. Elizabeth; 3. John; 4. Ann; 5. James, b. Aug. 29, 1818; d. unm., Sept. 4, 1898; 6. Augustus, b. Feb. 18, 1822; d. unm., March 25, 1893.

ROBERT ORR, a native of county Tyrone, Ireland, b. 1769; d. Nov. 4, 1857; son of Andrew Orr; emigrated to America, and in 1795 settled in Westmoreland county, Penn.; removed to Green township, Harrison county, Ohio, 1802; m. Ann Huston, a native of Ireland; had issue: 1. Martha, b. May 23, 1801; m. David Lindsay; 2. Esther, b. Aug. 15, 1802; m. Henry Maxwell; 3. Jean, b. April 1, 1804; m. John Maxwell; 4. Mary-Ann, b. Sept. 6, 1806; m. Matthew Hanna; 5. Miriam, b. Aug. 13, 1808; 6. Ziporah, b. March 13, 1809; m. 1837, Daniel Smith; 7. Bathsheba, b. April 2, 1810; 8. Dorcas, b. June 4, 1812; d. Oct. 8, 1866; m. 1846, John Reed (see Reed Family); 9. Elizabeth, b. July 7, 1814; m. Samuel Baker.

SAMUEL OSBURN, a native of county Derry, Ireland, of Scotch descent, emigrated to America, and settled in Westmoreland county, Penn.; served in the Indian wars; m. in Ireland, Susanna Garven; had issue, among others:

I. Alexander, b. May 14, 1785; removed to Athens township, Harrison county, Ohio, 1816; settled in Archer township, Harrison county, 1829, where he died Aug. 17, 1867; served in the War of 1812; m. (1st) in Pennsylvania, May 10, 1808, Mary Barnes, b. 1780; d. in Athens township, Jan. 5, 1824; daughter of James and Mary Barnes, natives of Ireland, who had settled in Pennsylvania; m. (2d) Martha Rankin, of Washington county, Penn., d. Dec. 25, 1848; had issue by first wife, among others: 1. Samuel, b. in Westmoreland county, Penn., April 4, 1813; settled in Archer township, Harrison county, Ohio; m. 1835, Elizabeth Welsh, daughter of John and Jane Welsh, of Scotch-Irish descent, who had removed from Lancaster county, Penn., to Archer township, in 1822 (had issue: i. Alexander, b. 1841; d. July 24, 1875; settled in Archer township; m. 1868, Sarah Hedges, daughter of William P. Hedges, of Cadiz township; ii. John-W., served in the Civil War; settled in Cadiz township; iii. Jane, m. Morrison Moorehead, and settled in Green township; iv. Martha, m. Granville Dickerson, and settled in Nodaway county, Mo.; v. Amanda, m. L. A. Welsh, and settled in Archer township; vi. Matthew-Beatty); 2. John; 3. Mary, m. William C. Mason; a Presbyterian minister; and settled in Illinois; had issue by second wife: 4. James-D., settled in Carroll county, Ohio; 5. Rebecca, m. —— Ramsey, of Scio, Ohio.

JOHN OURANT, settled in Columbiana county, Ohio, before 1808; m. Rachel Hewett; had issue: 1. Obadiah; 2. Matilda; 3. Harriet; 4. Washington, b. in Columbiana county, Sept. 15, 1808; removed to Moorefield, Harrison county, about 1822, and later settled in Nottingham township, where he d. Sept. 13, 1884; m. (1st) Jan. 22, 1830, Mary Martin, b. April 5, 1808; d. March 20, 1866; daughter of Arthur Martin; m. (2d) Ann Horn, b. March 21, 1813 (had issue by first wife: i. John-M., b. in Nottingham township, June 27, 1831; m. 1852, Harriet Kennedy, b. June 1, 1834, daughter of John L. and Matilda Ourant Kennedy; ii. James-K., b. Dec. 19, 1833; settled in Cadiz township; iii. Eliza-A., b. Feb. 20, 1836; iv. William-G., b. Oct. 11, 1839; settled in Cadiz township; v. George-W., b. June 10, 1842; vi. Enos-B., b. Sept. 5, 1844; settled at Omaha, Neb.; vii. Joseph-R.-T., b. Oct. 5, 1847; settled at Freeport; viii. Mary-M., b. Oct. 24, 1851; settled in Minnesota).

THOMAS PARKINSON, a native of Frederick, Md., b. 1762; removed to Green township, Harrison county, Ohio, where he d. 1838; served in the Revolutionary War; m. in Maryland, Elizabeth Schleiff, b. 1758; d. 1847; had issue, four sons and three daughters, of whom:
I. John.
II. Jacob, b. in Maryland, 1787; removed, 1814, to Smithfield township, Jefferson county, Ohio, where he d. 1865; served in the War of 1812; m. in Maryland, 1810, Mary Kellar; d. 1876; had issue: 1. John; 2. Thomas, b. in Jefferson county, Feb. 19, 1818; removed to Green township, Harrison county, 1844; m. Oct. 1, 1844, Caroline C. Cuppy, daughter of Abraham Cuppy, a resident of Jefferson county (had issue: i. Mary-Ann, b. Aug. 6, 1845; m. William H. Johnson; ii. Susanna, b. Feb. 7, 1847; d. June 17, 1870; iii. Evaline-R., b. Aug. 25, 1853; m. James Dickerson); 3. Joseph; 4. William; 5. David; 6. Louisa; 7. Elizabeth; 8. Nancy; 9. Edward.
III. Edward.
IV. Margaret, m. —— Miller.
V. Elizabeth, m. 1818, Ephraim Smith.
VI. Mary, m. —— Michael.

JOSEPH PATTERSON, b. 1791; d. 1859; removed from Pennsylvania to Carroll county, Ohio, in 1825; m. (1st) at Harper's Mills, Pennsylvania, Isabella McMillan, b. in Scotland, 1809; d. Nov. 17, 1846; m. (2d) March 27, 1849, Catherine Adams, d. 1882; had issue by first wife: 1. James, settled in Linn county, Kansas; 2. Margaret, m. Matthew Nickle, of Beaver county, Penn. (had issue: i. William-P., settled at Scio); 3. Robenia, m. William Rutan, of Ashland county, Ohio; 4. Euphemia, m. John Harrison, of Harrison county, Ohio; 5. William, settled in Morgan county, Illinois; 6. Mary, b. in Carroll county; m. Aug. 25, 1853, Alexander M. Scott, b. 1826; d. Jan. 8, 1878; son of Benjamin and Susannah Scott, of Washington county, Penn., who came to Carroll county in 1851; his widow settled in Scio; 7. Isabella, m. William Hogue, and settled in Carroll county; 8. Adam, served in Civil War; killed in battle; 9. Thomas, d. in infancy; 10. Jane, d. in infancy; 11. Martha, m. Joseph Doty, of Richland county, Ohio; 12. John, d. in infancy; 13. Alexander; settled in Morgan county, Ill.; had issue by second wife: 14. Elizabeth, m. Dr. Cook, of Scio; 15. Jane, d. in infancy; 16. Samuel, settled in the West; 17. John, settled in Carroll county.

JOSEPH PATTERSON, of Scotch descent, b. in county Down, Ireland, April, 1799; emigrated with his parents to New York in 1811, thence removed to Pittsburg, Penn., and later to Harrison county, Ohio, settling in Cadiz township, 1852, where he d. 1879; m. Feb. 14, 1822, Jemima Hoagland, daughter of James Hoagland, of Stock township (had issue, eleven children, of whom: i. J.-C., b. Aug. 30, 1835; served as an officer in the Civil War; m. Sept. 7, 1865, Mary Ann Simpson, daughter of John and Margaret Simpson; ii. James-H., settled in Cadiz township).

JAMES H. PATTON, a native of Pennsylvania, b. 1785-6; d. Oct. 3, 1860; served in the War of 1812; settled in Short Creek township, Harrison county, Ohio, in 1816; m. Jane Walker, b. in Pennsylvania, Sept. 13, 1789; d. June 6, 1880; had issue, among others: 1. John-Walker, b. 1818; d. Sept. 7, 1890; m. Dec. 30, 1846, Anna Braden, b. near Cadiz, July 25, 1820; d. Feb. 10, 1883 (her parents were pioneers in Harrison county); (had issue: i. Robert-B., a United Presbyterian minister, settled in Columbus, Ohio; ii. Esther-M.); 2. Rachel-S., b. 1826; d. Nov. 20, 1845; 3. William, b. 1831; d. 1841.

JOSEPH PATTON, a native of Pennsylvania, removed to Rumley township, Harrison county, Ohio, 1816, where he d. 1851; m. in Fayette county, Penn., Sarah Burns, d. September, 1842, daughter of John Burns, a resident of Pennsylvania; had issue: 1. John; 2. Sarah; 3. Joseph; 4. Margaret (all born in Pennsylvania); 5. Matthew M., b. in Fayette county, Penn., Sept. 3, 1815; m. March 3, 1844, Sarah Jane McCullough, d. June 13, 1878, daughter of Samuel McCullough, of Carroll county, Ohio (had issue: i. Sarah-Margaret, b. Jan. 19, 1843; m. Adam Miller, and settled in German township; ii. James, b. Oct. 23, 1844; iii. John-H., b. Aug. 25, 1846; iv. Joseph, b. May 7, 1848; d. Aug. 22, 1851; v. Samuel-M., b. April 12, 1850; d. Aug. 31, 1857; vi. Addison, b. May 25, 1852; vii. William, b. Aug. 17, 1854; d. Feb. 27, 1858; viii. Fremont, b. Aug. 29, 1856; d. March 5, 1858; ix. ———, b. March 12, 1859; d. March 17, 1859; x. Ida, b. Feb. 9, 1860; xi. Fremont (2d), b. April 12, 1862; xii. Thomas-B., b. Dec. 8, 1863; m. March 20, 1888, Harriet E. Finnicum, daughter of John Finaicum, of Rumley township); 6. James; 7. Mary; 8. Cynthia-J.; 9. David; 10. Ann.

SAMUEL PATTON, a native of county Down, Ireland, b. 1761; d. Oct. 15, 1828; emigrated to America, but returned to county Down in 1798, where he m. Jane Friar, of Scotch descent, b. 1756; d. April 23, 1841; settled at Wheeling, F. Va., in 1803, and the following spring settled in Belmont county, Ohio, near the junction of Wheeling and Crabapple Creeks; had issue: 1. James, d. in Ireland, in infancy; 2. William, b. in Ireland, 1799; d. May 2, 1873; m. Anna Clark, b. 1810; d. 1885; daughter of Alexander Clark, of Belmont county (had issue: i. Samuel, a Presbyterian minister; d. in Detroit, Mich.; ii. Margaret, m. Rev. J. P. Robb, and settled at Iberia, Morrow county, Ohio; iii. John, settled in Arkansas City, Kansas; iv. Ellen, m. Rev. Josiah Stephenson, and settled at Olathe, Kan.; v. Alexander-C., settled at Springfield, Ohio; vi. Caroline, m. Addison Lyle, and settled at Pittsburg, Penn.; vii. James-B., settled at Shepherdstown, Belmont county; viii. George-M., b. April 9, 1844; settled near New Athens; served in the Civil War; m. Jan. 1, 1868, M. Louise Campbell, daughter of Dr. John Campbell, of Uniontown, Ohio; ix. Calvin-W., settled at St. Clairsville; x. William-L., settled at Fairpoint, Belmont county; xi. Sylvanus; xii. Thomas-L., settled at Fairpoint); 3. John, d. in Cambridge, aged seventeen years.

Dr. John Campbell, father of Mrs. M. Louise Campbell Patton, was b. in Belmont county, Nov. 21, 1804 (his father, James Campbell, an officer of the War of 1812, came from Cross Creek township, Washington county, Penn, and settled at Uniontown, Belmont county); d. September, 1882; m. May 11, 1830, Jane Irwin, b. 1808; d. June, 1883; had issue: 1. Mary; 2. Margaret-A.; 3. James-B.; 4. Rachel-J.; 5. M.-Louise, m. George M. Patton; 6. Martha-E.

JOSEPH H. PENN, b. in England, April 25, 1813, son of Thomas and Hannah Penn, who emigrated to America and located at Cadiz, Harrison county, Ohio; settled in German township, where he d. Sept. 21, 1881; m. Nov. 6, 1834, Jane Hamilton, b. June 28, 1813; d. Feb. 8, 1878; daughter of Francis and Ruth Hamilton; had issue: 1. Florella; 2. Thomas; 3. Francis-Hamilton; 4. Hannah-Mary; 5. Joseph-Rollins; 6. William-Boyce, b. April 9, 1849; settled at Bowerston; m. May 29, 1870, Martha Ann Weyandt, daughter of Abraham Weyandt; 7. Chastina-Ann.

HENRY PERRY, b. in the Wyoming Valley, Penn., about 1774; d. at New Athens, 1865; when about three years old, his parents were massacred by the Indians and himself carried off captive; afterwards liberated, and settled at Pittsburg; m. Sarah Franks, b. 1786; d. 1866, of Fayette county, Penn., of German descent; removed to Cadiz; had issue: 1. Martin, d. in Indiana; 2. Henry, d. young; 3. Adam, d. young; 4. Eliza, m. James Polen, and settled in Guernsey county; 5. John, d. young; 6. Thomas, d. young; 7. William-W., b. Dec. 18, 1823; d. Aug. 26, 1865; served in the Civil War, and died of disease contracted in that service; m. Dec. 18, 1845, Elizabeth Kelley, b. Oct. 14, 1816; daughter of James and Jane Kelley; settled in Short Creek township (had issue: i. John-H., b. Dec. 22, 1846; served in the Civil War; m. Sept. 9, 1871, Eliza Ann Jarvis, daughter of Jacob and Eliza O'Brien Jarvis; ii. James-A., b. May 3. 1849; m. 1881, Anna Norman, daughter of Daniel and Elizabeth Norman; iii. Albert-K., b. Nov. 14, 1852; m. Rebecca Riley, of Clermont county; iv. Samuel-L., b. 1855; d. 1858; v. William-T., b. Sept. 28, 1858; m. Sept. 5, 1878, Josephine M. Blackburn, daughter of John and Margaret Blackburn, of Franklin township; served as prosecuting attorney for Harrison county; vi. Joseph-D., b. Sept. 16, 1861; m. 1884, Lillian Walker); 8. James, removed to Illinois, where he d. 1882; 9. Mary, m. Joseph Howell, and settled at Hopedale; 10. Sarah-J., d. young; 11. Susan.

LEROY PETTY, of English descent; settled in Washington township, Harrison county, Ohio, before 1830, where he d. Aug. 31, 1882; m. (1st) Keziah Tipton; d. 1853; m. (2d) Hannah Hogue; had issue by first wife: 1. Henry, b. Nov. 11, 1835; d. Feb. 27, 1881; m. Nov. 23, 1858, Sarah J. Cree, daughter of James Cree; 2. John; 3. Mary-Ann; 4. Elizabeth; 5. Martha; had issue by second wife: 6. Levi; 7. Harriet.

RICHARD PHILIPS, b. in Pennsylvania, 1772, where his parents had settled, having come from England before the Revolutionary War; removed to Jefferson county, Ohio, in 1803, where he remained until 1815, and then settled in Washington township, Harrison county, Ohio, where he d. December, 1856; m. Comfort Davidson, d. 1835; had issue: 1. Joseph, b. Jan. 14, 1803; d. April 19, 1886; m. May 9, 1833, Jemima Johnson, d. Sept. 3, 1888, daughter of Griffin Johnson (see below) (had issue: i. Comfort-Ann, b. Aug. 24, 1834; m. Warner Rogers; ii. Sophia, b. Sept. 10, 1836; iii. Amasa, b. Sept. 22, 1838; m. (1st) June 5, 1862, Elizabeth Hogue, d. May 30, 1880; m. (2d) Feb. 19, 1885, Mary Ellen Crouch; d. Aug. 30, 1885; m. (3d) May 26, 1886, Elizabeth Mears, daughter of William Mears; iv. Almeda, b. May 9, 1841; d. Sept. 9, 1844; v. John, b. June 14, 1843; vi. Elihu, b. Sept. 26, 1846; vii. Margaret, b. June 11, 1849; d. April 12, 1878; viii. Joseph, b. Aug. 19, 1851; d. Dec. 31, 1875; ix. Jemima, b. March 23, 1858); 2. John, b. near Smithfield, Jefferson county, Dec. 19, 1804, where he d. July 1, 1886; m. 1831, Eleanor Johnson, b. at Wheeling, West Virginia, Sept. 5, 1804, daughter of Griffin Johnson (had issue: i. Richard, b. Aug. 14, 1832; m. (1st) Oct. 1, 1862, Sarah Jane Jenkins, of West Chester, Tuscarawas county; d. June 16, 1878; m. (2d) Sept. 18, 1879, Nancy Carruthers, of Harrison county; d. April 10, 1888; ii. Mary, m. William Boyd; iii. Alfred, b. Dec. 26, 1835, in Washington township; removed, 1873, to Freeport township, Harrison county; m. Sept. 1, 1863, Rachel A. Mears, daughter of William Mears, of Tuscarawas county, Ohio; iv. Sarah, m. ─── Carver; v. Nancy); 3. Margaret; 4. Hannah; 5. Lewis; 6. Eleanor-Ann.

James Johnson, father of Griffin Johnson, and grandfather of Mrs. Jemima Johnson Phillips and Mrs. Eleanor Johnson Phillips, was a resident of Ohio (now Brooke) county, West Virginia, where some time between 1776 and 1790, he was captured by the Indians while in camp on McIntyre's Creek, in Jefferson county, in company with two neighbors, McIntyre and Layport, who were killed. James Johnson was carried to Sandusky as a prisoner, but afterwards released and returned home. Later he settled in Warren township, Jefferson county, Ohio, where, in October, 1788, his two sons, John, aged thirteen, and Henry, aged eleven, while searching in the forest for their cows, were captured by two Indians. When night came, the two boys arose, one of them secured possession of his captor's rifle, and the other, a tomahawk, with which they killed the two Indians while they slept. The two boys were afterwards donated a section of land by the Government for their bravery, it being located in Wells township, Jefferson county, the supposed scene of their adventure. James Johnson had several children, of whom: 1. John, b. 1775; 2. Henry, b. Jan. 4, 1777, settled in Monroe county, Ohio; 3. Griffin, removed from Wheeling to Washington township, about 1805 (had issue, twelve children, of whom: i. Eleanor, b. 1804; ii. 1831, John Phillips; ii. Jemima, b. 1810; d. 1888; m. Joseph Phillips; iii. Nancy, m. Zera Davidson).

THOMAS PHILLIPS, d. October, 1790, in West Nottingham township, Chester county, Pa., where about 1763-5 he m. Jane Blair, dau. of —— and Janet Blair; served in the Revolution in Capt. Ephraim Blackburn's company of Col. Evan Evans's Battalion of Chester county militia; took up land in Nottingham township, Harrison county, Ohio, before 1809; had issue: William, John, Sarah, Mary, and Rachel, of whom:

William Phillips, b. about 1765-67; d. July 18, 1854; m. before 1787, Rachel Hamilton, d. 182—. daughter of Robert and Martha McMillan Hamilton (the latter born 1748; d. at Morristown, Belmont county, Ohio, March 18, 1831; daughter of John [d. 1778] and Rachel McMil'an, of West Nottingham township, Chester county, Penn.); had issue:

I. Robert, b. about 1787; d. April 20, 1850; m. 1814, Rosanna Mullen; had issue: 1. Rachel, b. Oct. 16, 1815; m. Morris Melrath (had issue: i. William-H., m. (1st) Thirza Chapman; m. (2d) Ella Oviatt; ii. Mary-E.; iii. Rosanna-J.; iv. Joseph-L., m. Emma Opdyke; v. Robert-A., m. Emma Reynolds; vi. Sarah-M.; vii. Thomas-M., m. Ella Fitzgerald; viii. Martha-E.); 2. John-Arthur, b. Dec. 17, 1817; d. Oct. 22, 1819; 3. William, b. March 1, 1820; m. Martha Maria Lee, daughter of Samuel and Jane Phillips Lee (had issue: i. Samuel-Lee, m. Margaret Rissler; ii. Robert-Lee, m. Gertrude Rissler; iii. Oscar-Miles, m. Elizabeth Stacey; iv. William-Brummel, m. Luella Kelso; v. Edward-Wilson, m. Hannah Deal; vi. Charles-Hilbert; vii. Jane-Hamilton; viii. Thomas-Newton; ix. Emma-Bolton; x. Rosella); 4. Mary-Ann, b. Oct. 16, 1822; m. Josiah Brown (had issue: i. Sarah, m. Charles S. Jacobs); 5. Sarah, b. Nov. 19, 1825, m. Milton Brown (had issue: i. John-Milton, m. Rachel Ann Anderson; ii. Martha-Ann, m. Reed W. Anderson; iii. Henry-Clay, m. Sarah Martha Webb; iv. Thomas-Wood, m. Hannah Riley Jones); 6. Martha-J., b. Oct. 17, 1828; m. Montillion Brown (died without issue); 7. Rosanna-Rebecca, b. Oct. 17, 1831; m. William Phillips, grandson of John Phillips, Sr. (had issue: i. Joseph, m. Sarah Hilaman; ii. Mary, m. Harry Goodwin; iii. John).

II. Martha, b. 179—; d. December, 1836; m. James Ross, b. 1797; d. 1878; removed to Nottingham township, Harrison county, 1827; had issue: 1. Rachel, m. Immer Knight; 2. Deborah, m. William Poulson; 3. Jane, m. Isaac Drummond; 4. William-Phillips, d. young; 5. Mary-Eliza, d. young; 6. Thomas-Hamilton, m. Eliza Fulton; 7. Martha, m. Thomas McMillan, and settled at Deersville; 8. Barbara, m. Beall Pumphrey.

III. Thomas, b. 1792; d. Nov. 23, 1871; m. Elizabeth Williams, b. July 11, 1792; d. May 22, 1867; removed to Cadiz, Ohio, before 1820; had issue: 1. Adaline, m. William Welch, son of Daniel and Elizabeth Waits Welch, of Green township; removed to Mount Pleasant, Iowa, and thence, after the death of her husband, to Osceola, Neb. (had issue: i. William; ii. Thomas; iii. Daniel; iv. Ross, m. Anna Sherwood; also, four other children, who died in infancy); 2. Rachel, d. unm.; 3. Martha, d. in infancy; 4. Mary, m. Abraham Croskey, and settled at Chicago (had issue: i. Thomas, m. Martha Osburn); 5. Basil-Lee-Williams, b. Aug. 19, 1824; m. Feb. 25, 1846, Mary Pritchard, d. Nov. 27, 1896; daughter of John and Sarah

Bromfield Pritchard (had issue: i. Sarah; ii. Mary-Isabella, m. May 12, 1869, William Moseback, of Chicago; iii. Ada-Welch, d. young; iv. Virginia-Anderson, d. young; v. Clara-Anderson, m. H. G. Cass); 6. William, m. (1st) Elizabeth Anderson; m. (2d) Sarah Lord, daughter of William Lord; m. (3d) Mrs. Lucretia Hilts (had issue, by second wife: i. Marcia); 7. John, m. Sarah Hilligas (had issue: i. Mary, m. Henry Cruse, Jr.; ii. Jessica, d. young; iii. Thomas; iv. Elizabeth; v. Katharine; vi. George; vii. John); 8. Caroline; 9. Laura, m. David Cunningham (had issue: i. Mary, m. John Maholm Sharon; ii. John, m. Mary Day Welch; iii. Ralph; iv. Elizabeth, d. young; v. Helen); 10. Caroline.

IV. John, d. young.

V. Jane, b. April 26, 1794; d. April 1, 1870; m. Samuel Lee; had issue: 1. Martha-Maria, m. William Phillips, son of Robert and Rosanna Mullen Phillips, and settled at Charlestown, West Va.; 2. Esther-Ann, m. William Pennell (died without issue); 3. Josiah-Parker, m. Sarah-Wilson (had issue: i. Edwin-Kirk; ii. Addison, m. Ella McCann; iii. Rosella, m. James Kehoe; iv. Isaac, m. Sarah Kehoe); 4. Jane, m. Taylor Janney (died without issue); 5. Rachel-Hamilton, b. May 5, 1831; 6. Philena-Rebecca, m. Joseph Lincoln Stephens (had issue: i. Emma, m. Edward Haines; ii. Mary-Lincoln, m. Norville C. Brown; iii. Lydia-W., m. Elmer Vanneman; iv. Jane-Lee, m. Charles M. Riesler; v. Elizabeth-Rutledge; vi. John-Lincoln); 7. Samuel-Thomas, m. Anne Wilson (had issue: i. Leonard-W., m. Lydia Tollinger; ii. Frances, m. Francis Russell; iii. Charlotte, m. Joseph Brown; iv. Emma, m. William Steele; v. Rachel, m. Ellis Nelson; vi. Samuel; vii. Charlotte; vii. Minerva; ix. Anna); 8. Charlotte, m. Caleb Conner (had issue: i. Samuel-Lee, m. Emma Stoner; ii. Mary-Susan; iii. T.-Eugene).

VI. John (2d), b. June, 1797; d. May 5, 1859; m. May 6, 1828, Eliza Gilmore, b. Feb. 2, 1807; d. Jan. 14, 1873; daughter of Samuel and Elizabeth Buchanan Gilmore; had issue: 1. Eliza-Jane, b. Feb. 22, 1829; m. 1849, Neri A. Hanna, b. April 7, 1827, son of John-Evans and Susan Robertson Hanna, of McConnellsville, Ohio (had issue: i. Mary-Eliza; ii. William-Phillips; iii. George-Finley, m. Alma S. Haverfield; iv. John; v. Charles-A.; vi. Harry-Gilmore, m. Alice Anderson; vii. Samuel-Edward, m. Katharine Jones); 2. William, d. young; 3. Martha, d. unm.; 4. Sarah, d. young; 5. Samuel, d. unm.; 6. Rachel-Anne, d. unm.; 7. William-Welch, m. Mary E. Craig, and settled at Lincoln, Neb. (had issue: i. William-Craig, m. Ada Guthridge; ii. John, d. unm.; iii. Lucy, died young; iv. Charles-Frederick, m. Miriam A. Parks; v. Francis); 8. Thomas, m. Frances Flagg, and settled at Chicago (had issue: i. William-Eugene; ii. Sarah).

VII. William, b. 1800; d. Dec. 11, 1884; m. Mary Eliza Smith; had issue: 1. George, m. Hannah Blake, and settled at Berryville, Va. (had issue: i. Nancy); 2. Robert, m. Susan McDonald; 3. William, m. Mary White, and settled at Wilmington, Del. (had issue: i. Ira-May, m. ——— Applebee; ii. Willametta; iii. Roberta; iv. Elizabeth-Thomas); 4. Mary-Eliza, m. Samuel George, of Cadiz, Ohio, and removed to Des Moines, Iowa (had issue: i. Margaret; ii. William; iii. Eliza; iv. Laura; v. Beulah; vi. Murray).

VIII. Margaret, b. 1803; d. April 19, 1872; m. John Johns; had issue: 1. Rachel-Jane, m. Hiram McCrery (had issue: i. Jessie, m. Anna Ross; ii. Hiram-Jackson, m. Jane McVey); 2. Margaret, m. John Morris (had issue: i. John; ii. David; iii. Jane, m. ——— Crompton; iv. Phineas; v. Sarah; vi. Walter-E.); 3. Mary, m. John F. Ferguson (had issue: i. Lydia; ii. Laura, m. Alfred Hannum; iii. James; iv. William; v. Emma; vi. Cleveland).

IX. Mary, b. 1800; d. April, 1878; m. Jacob Griest; died without issue.

X. Eliza, m. Thomas Keatley; had issue: 1. Thomas, m. Emma Magaw (had issue: i. Lydia, m. William Newlin); 2. William, m. Eliza Terry (had issue: i. Mary-Luella; ii. Monroe; iii. George-D.; iv. William-Thomas; v. Helen-Margaret; vi. Jane-C.; vii. Elizabeth-S.).

ABRAHAM PITTENGER, b. in New Jersey, about 1774; d. 1865; removed to Harrison county, Ohio, about 1812, and later settled in Cadiz township; son of Henry Pittenger, a native of New Jersey, of German descent; served in the War of 1812; m. Susanna Osborn, b. 1780; d. 1847; daughter of William Osborn, an early settler near Cadiz, who afterward removed to Richland county, Ohio; had issue: 1. Henry; 2. Samuel, b. 1798; d. Aug. 26, 1875; m. Jan. 10, 1820, Jane Lemasters; d. Feb. 14, 1874; daughter of Isaac Lemasters, of Archer township; had issue, among others: 1. Samuel, b. Aug. 15, 1830; d. Jan. 30, 1880; m. Oct. 11, 1849, Antoinette Thompson, daughter of Gabriel Thompson, of Carroll county, Ohio; 3. Peter; 4. Sarah; 5. Abraham; 6. Isaac-O.; 7. Mary; 8. Jacob, b. near Jewett, Aug. 19, 1812; m. April, 1842. Mary Ann Hendricks, d. 1884, daughter of Peter and Catharine Webster Hendricks, who were of Dutch descent and among the earliest settlers of Rumley township (had issue: i. Isabella, m. O. S. Dutton; ii. John-Wesley, d. 1882); 9. Phœbe, m. Robert Atkinson; 10. John; 11. Nathaniel, settled at Dennison, Ohio; 12. Nancy, m. James Foster, and settled in Jackson county, Ohio.

JAMES POULSON, a native of Maryland, b. about 1781; settled in Cadiz township, Harrison county, Ohio, before 1810; m. twice; had issue by first wife: 1. John, b. in Cadiz township, April 23, 1812; settled in Nottingham township, where he d. Feb. 19, 1863; m. Rachel Rogers, b. April 26, 1816, daughter of Samuel and Sarah Lewis Rogers (had issue: i. Samuel; ii. Elizabeth; iii. Sarah, m. ——— Russell, and settled in Belmont county, Ohio; iv. Thomas; settled in Nottingham township; v. Matilda; vi. Harriet, m. ——— Rogers, and settled in Nottingham township; vii. Susan, m. Samuel D. Edgar; viii. Salina-J.; ix. Evans); 2. James; settled in Jasper county, Iowa; 3. Jacob; 4. Elizabeth; 5. Jehu; settled in Jasper county, Iowa; 6. Wilson; 7. William; settled at Montpelier, Ind.; 8. Harriet; 9. Mary-Ann; had issue by second wife: 10. Samuel; 11. Robert; 12. Maria.

JOHN PORTER, a resident of Nottingham township, Chester county, or of Drumore township, Lancaster county, Penn., had issue, among others, three sons: Robert, Samuel, and James, of whom: Robert, settled in Washington county, and Samuel and James in Harrison county, Ohio. Of these sons:

Robert Porter, served in the Revolutionary War; settled near Canonsburg, Penn.; had issue, among others:
I. John, served in the War of 1812.
II. James-T., b. near Canonsburg, Penn., 1786; d. in Cadiz township, Feb. 24, 1836; m. March 31, 1812, Elizabeth Porter, daughter of Samuel and Sarah Burns Porter; had issue: 1. Mary; 2. Sarah; 3. Elizabeth; 4. Samuel, d. young; 5. Samuel-T.; 6. Robert; 7. Elizabeth (2d); 8. Jane; 9. Rebecca; 10. Margaret.

Samuel Porter, a native of Pennsylvania, b. 1765, of Scotch-Irish descent; removed with his brother, James, to Cadiz township, Harrison county, Ohio, in 1802, where he d. Aug. 2, 1839; m. in Pennsylvania, Sarah Burns, b. Aug. 15, 1786; d. 1830; had issue:
I. John, d. 1831. II. James. III. Elizabeth, b. in Pennsylvania, April 1, 1794; d. in Cadiz township, May 4, 1863; m. 1812, James T. Porter, of Scotch-Irish descent, b. near Canonsburg, Washington county, Penn., 1786; d. in Cadiz township, Feb. 24, 1836, son of Robert Porter, who served in the Revolutionary War, and whose son, John, served in the War of 1812.
IV. David, b. in Washington county, Penn., Feb. 5, 1802; d. Dec. 22, 1885; m. Theresa Stone, b. in Belmont county; d. 1859; had issue: 1. Sarah; 2. John-D., b. Jan. 14, 1839; m. March 7, 1876, Mary Isabelle Porterfield, daughter of Alexander and Sarah Warnock Porterfield, of Belmont county; 3. Mary; 4. James, d. in infancy; 5. Samuel-B., b. in Athens township, Oct. 8, 1843; settled in Green township; m. 1864, Margaret Dickerson, daughter of John and Eliza McFadden Dickerson.
V. Samuel, d. Aug. 2, 1869. VI. Jane. VII. Mary. VIII. Smiley, b. 1807; d. in Morgan county, Ohio, 1865, where he had settled about 1853; m. Margaret Dugan, a native of Pennsylvania, b. 1808; d. 1875; had issue: 1. Caroline; 2. Margaret, d. in infancy; 3. Mary, twin sister to Margaret; settled in Noble county; 4. Catherine, m. Samuel Marquis, of Noble county; 5. Sarah-Jane, m. John Harper, of Morgan county; 6. Samuel, settled in Cadiz township; 7. John, settled in Belmont county; 8. Irwin, b. in Cadiz township, 1854; settled in Cadiz township; m. Dec. 25, 1888, Ida McFarland, a native of Harrison county. IX. Nancy, d. in infancy. X. Irwin, b. March 8. 1814; settled in Cadiz township. XI. Sarah.

James Porter, who came to Ohio with his brother, Samuel, in 1802, was born 1766; d. in Cadiz township, 1836; m.

1807, Margaret Oglevee, b. in Maryland, 1776; d. May 25, 1851; daughter of John Oglevee, of Scotch-Irish descent; had issue: 1. Joseph; 2. Elizabeth; 3. John; 4. Ann; 5. James, b. Aug. 29, 1818; d. unm.; 6. Augustus, b. Feb. 18, 1822, d. unm.

JOSIAH PRICE, a native of Wales, emigrated to America and settled in New Jersey before 1768; m. Mary Frazier; had issue: I. James. II. Benjamin, b. in New Jersey, Dec. 12, 1768; settled in Jefferson county, Ohio, before 1805; d. Sept. 18, 1853; m. Catherine Beebout, b. Sept. 5, 1766; had issue, among others: 1. Joel, b. in Jefferson county, Jan. 9, 1805; removed to Franklin township, Harrison county; m. in Jefferson county, May 24, 1836, Sophia Leas, a native of that county, daughter of Jacob and Elizabeth Zimmerman Leas, of German descent, who removed from Adams county, Penn. (had issue: i. Jacob-Leas, b. Sept. 13, 1837; ii. Catherine, b. Sept. 30, 1839; iii. William-H.-H., b. Oct. 14, 1841; iv. Elizabeth, b. Nov. 4, 1843; v. Sarah-J., b. Oct. 29, 1845; vi. Benjamin-F., b. Oct. 20, 1847; m. 1877, Mary Barkley, daughter of Andrew and Rebecca Welch Barkley; vii. George-W., b. Dec. 3, 1849; d. Oct. 28, 1864; viii. Leonard, b. Aug. 23, 1852; ix. John-L., b. Dec. 30, 1854; m. 1887, Alice Cummings, daughter of Stephen Cummings; x. Mary-M., b. Dec. 28, 1859). III. Josiah. IV. Mary. V. Margaret. VI. Phebe. VII. Jeanette.

JOHN PRITCHARD or PRICHARD, was born in Wales, 1775 (son of Jesse Pritchard, who was born in 1750); emigrated to America with his father, 1785, settling at Frederick, Maryland, whence, in 1795, he removed to Uniontown, Fayette county, Penn., and from there to Cadiz, Ohio, in 1807; d. June 28, 1844; m. Feb. 7, 1798. Sarah Beeson Bromfield, b. Jan. 7, 1782; d. Sept. 15, 1877; daughter of Captain Benjamin (1745-1824) and Mrs. Mary White Bromfield (or Brounfield); had issue: 1. Mary, b. May 18, 1800; d. May 13, 1825; m. 1816, Daniel Kilgore, d. 1850 (had issue: i. Narcissa, m. Charles Paulson, of Pittsburg; ii. John-P.. m. Mary, daughter of Rev. Alexander Wilson, of Cadiz and Philadelphia); 2. Jesse, b. July 3, 1802; d. 1835; m. 1825, Jane S. Lacey (had issue: i. William-Lee, b. 1826; d. unmarried; ii. John, b. 1827; d. 1847; iii. Martha-Jane, b. Sept. 13, 1829; m. Daniel Spencer; iv. Sarah, b. July 29, 1831; m. William V. Keepers, of Uhrichsville, Ohio; v. Jesse, b. Dec. 17, 1830; removed to Gilpin county, Colo., in 1859, and thence to Leavenworth, Kan.; vi. Clara-J., b. December, 1834; m. Thomas J. Forbes, of Coshocton, Ohio); 3. Nancy, b. Oct. 27, 1804; d. Sept. 6, 1897; m. Chauncey Dewey (for issue, see Dewey Family); 4. Maria, b. April 3, 1807; m. William Lee (had issue: i. James; ii. Emma; iii. Albert; iv. William; v. Elizabeth, m. Samuel Hilles, of Barnesville, Ohio); 5. Benjamin, b. Nov. 3, 1809; m. Mary Deardorff (had issue: i. Sarah; ii. John); 6. Eliza, b. Feb. 4, 1812; m. William Houston, of Wheeling, West Va. (had issue: i. Sarah, d. unm.; ii. William, m. ——— Mason); 7. Sarah, b. Aug. 11, 1814; d. 1820; 8. Isabella, b. Jan. 18, 1817; d. 1849; m. Samuel Douglass (had issue, both married, and living in Chicago: i. Sarah; ii. Ella); 9. Clarissa, b. Aug. 10, 1819; d. Dec. 18, 1837; 10. Sarah-Jane, b. Oct. 7, 1821; m. George Anderson, of St. Clairsville, Ohio (had issue: i. William, m. Alice Russell; ii. Clara, m. S. W. Dodds; iii. Margaret); 11. Rebecca, b. March 7, 1825; m. John Hamilton, of Cadiz (had issue: i. Sarah, m. Benjamin Funk; ii. Mary, m. Andrew Wilson; iii. Alice, m. Joseph Dalbey; iv. Eleanor. m. William Anderson; v. Isabella, m. H. V. Moore; vi. Elizabeth, m. Charles H. Pierson; vii. Ernest); 12. Mary, b. Sept. 29, 1827; d. Nov. 27, 1896; m. Basil Lee Williams Phillips, of Cadiz and Chicago (had issue: i. Elizabeth; ii. Adaline; iii. Virginia-Jane-Anderson; iv. Mary-Isabella, m. 1869, William Moseback, of Chicago; v. Clara-Anderson, m. H. G. Cass, of Chicago).

ANDREW RALSTON, b. in Adams county, Penn., 1753, of Scotch-Irish descent; his father, mother, sister, and brother were killed by Indians in Adams county, in 1761, one sister (who afterwards married and settled at Pittsburg) and himself escaping the massacre; served in the Revolutionary War; m. in Adams county, Sophia Waltermeyer, a native of that county; Andrew removed to Jefferson county, Ohio, in 1814, where he d. 1827: had issue, among others: 1. Lewis-W., b. in

Adams county, Nov. 30, 1806; settled in German township, Harrison county, about 1833, where he d. Sept. 6, 1884; m. (1st) 1828, Ann Darr, of Jefferson county; d. 1832; m. (2d) 1832, Eleanor Moorhead, daughter of William and Elizabeth Scott Moorhead (the former a native of Virginia, of Irish descent); (had issue by first wife: i. ———, d. in infancy; ii. ———, d. in infancy; iii. John-N., d. aged eighteen years; had issue by second wife: iv. Andrew, d. in infancy; v. Elizabeth, d. aged twenty-five years; vi. Lewis-B., b. Feb. 16, 1839; m. Jan. 8, 1861, Maria V. Sanders, daughter of Joseph and Elizabeth Oliver Sanders, both of whom settled in Ohio, 1830; the former a native of England, the latter of Scotland; vii. Ruth; viii. Sophia; ix. Mary-E., m. James Bosley, and settled in Springfield, Ohio).

WILLIAM RAMAGE, of Scottish birth or descent; settled on Wheeling Creek, Wheeling township, Belmont county, Ohio, before 1800; had issue:
I. William, settled in Moorefield township, Harrison county.
II. John, b. April 7, 1788; settled in Moorefield township; m. (1st) Esther Bell, d. 1815; m. (2d) Elizabeth Lafferty, b. about 1808; had issue by first wife: 1. William, b. Jan. 8, 1813; d. July 29, 1888; m. Rebecca Smith, b. in Belmont county, April 1, 1816, daughter of William and Rebecca Smith, who settled in Belmont county, in 1805, having come from Allegheny county, Penn. (had issue: i. Thomas-L.; ii. Esther-A., b. July 24, 1837; m. Nov. 3, 1853, Harrison Kirkpatrick, b. in Athens township, Harrison county, Oct. 27, 1822; settled in Moorefield township; iii. John-C.; iv. William-S.; v. Sarah-R.; vi. Mary-M., m. ——— Jackson, and settled at Jackson, Mich.; vii. James-O.; viii. Robert-B.; ix. Joseph-B.); had issue by second wife; 2. Samuel; 3. Louisa; 4. John.
III. James, d. March 11, 1849.
IV. Joseph, settled at St. Clairsville, Belmont county.
V. Samuel.
VI. Archibald-C., b. Oct. 12, 1808; settled in Smith township, Belmont county; served as a member of the Ohio Legislature, and as a member of the State Board of Equalization.
VII. Elizabeth.
VIII. Jane.
IX. Mary.
X. Letitia.
XI. Margaret.
William and Rebecca Smith, parents of Rebecca Smith Ramage, had issue: 1. Sarah, m. ——— Ramage; 2. John; 3. Joseph; 4. James; 5. William; 6. Robert; 7. Steel; 8. Washington; 9. Smiley.

GEORGE RAMSEY, a native of Ireland, emigrated to America and settled in Washington county, Penn.; m. (1st) ———; m. (2d) ——— Leeper, d. aged ninety-nine years; had issue by first wife, six children, among whom:
I. John, b. in Washington county, 1781; removed with his family to Green township; served as Lieutenant of Captain Allen Scroggs's Company of Col. John Andrews' Ohio Militia in the War of 1812, and died in that service, at Lower Sandusky, Ohio, 1812; m. 1800, Nancy McLaughlin (who m., 2d, 1818, James Lyons, a resident of Jefferson county, their daughter, Elizabeth, marrying ——— Gladman, of Franklin township, Harrison county); had issue: 1. Hugh; 2. George; 3. John, b. June 23, 1805; m. (1st) May 24, 1827, Rebecca McCurdy; d. Feb. 12, 1833, daughter of John McCurdy, of Cadiz; m. (2d) Jan. 7, 1839, Mary Barr, b. July 22, 1817; d. Nov. 11, 1889, daughter of John Barr, of Carroll county, Ohio (had issue by first wife: i. Ebenezer, settled in California; ii. Thomas-Vincent, m. Sarah Patrick, and settled at Mount Vernon, Ohio; iii. Samuel, b. July 13, 1832; d. Sept. 18, 1872; a Presbyterian minister; settled at Tarentum, Penn.; m. June 28, 1864, Nancy J. Randolph; had issue by second wife: iv. William-Marshall, m. Mary Elizabeth Howell; v. John-Barr, b. June 20, 1841; served in the Civil War; killed in battle at Perryville, Oct. 8, 1862; m. 1862, Anna Vermillion; vi. Nancy-Elizabeth, m. John Vermillion, and settled in Jefferson county; vii. Margaret-Rebecca, m. John Lease, and settled in Green township; viii. Mary-A.; ix. Jennie, m. Samuel F. Birney); 4. Mary; 5. Nancy; 6. Nancy, d. Nov. 22, 1889, in Colorado, m. ——— Maxwell; George Ramsey had issue by second wife: II. David, b. Jan. 6, 1792; d. July 31, 1852; m. Mary Ann ———, b. April, 1797; d. Aug. 17, 1875; had issue, among others: 1. Matthew-J.; 2. David; 3. William-L.; 4. Moses. III. Nancy. IV. William.

JAMES RAMSEY, b. in Ireland, about 1744; emigrated to America with his parents, and settled in York county, Penn., about 1756; settled in Washington county, 1802, where he d. 1837; served in the Revolutionary War; his wife, whom he m. in York county, was of Scotch-Irish descent; had issue, among others:

I. William, b. in York county, Penn.; removed with his parents to Washington county, in the same State, where he resided until 1837; thence removed to Nottingham township, Harrison county, Ohio, where he d. 1856, aged sixty-six years; served in the War of 1812; m. Mary Anderson, daughter of Robert Anderson, of Washington county, Penn.; had issue: 1. James; 2. Robert, d. in Iowa, 1889; 3. William, b. in Washington county, May 1, 1817; settled at Cadiz, in 1874; m. 1840, Mary Hines, a native of Harrison county, daughter of John and Rebecca Dickens Hines (had issue: i. John, b. 1843; served in the Civil War; killed at the battle of Spottsylvania Court House, 1864; ii. James, settled in Texas; iii. William-Robert, settled in Texas; iv. F.-Marion, settled in Texas; v. Anderson-Deacons, settled in Texas; vi. Jennie, m. David Oglevee; vii. Philene; viii. Mary, d. in infancy); 4. Thomas, settled in Coshocton county, Ohio; 5. John, b. Nov. 4, 1823; m. (1st) March 16, 1847, Sarah J. Hines, a native of Nottingham township, d. 1865; daughter of Isaac and Sarah Patterson Hines, m. (2d) 1865, Emily Ford, b. in Harrison county, 1825; d. about 1880; m. (3d) 1882, Angeline Hines, b. Oct. 31, 1831, daughter of Abraham and Hannah Carson Hines (had issue by first wife: i. Isaac-L.; ii. Mary-E.; iii. William-B., b. March 14, 1852; settled in Williamson county, Tenn.; iv. John-F., b. Dec. 20, 1853; settled in Cadiz township; v. James-P., b. Feb. 5, 1856; settled in Freeport township; vi. Harvey-C., b. April 19, 1859; vii. Robert-F., b. Oct. 6, 1861; viii. Martha-A., b. Nov. 25, 1863); 6. Samuel; 7. Margaret, m. B. S. Ford; 8. Mary, m. John Mahanna; 9. Jane.

John Hines, b. 1778; d. 1871; father of Mary Ramsey, m. 1807, Rebecca Dickens or Deacons, d. 1859; removed from Pennsylvania to Harrison county, settling in Cadiz; had issue, fourteen children, among whom: 1. Jeremiah; 2. David; 3. James, settled in Nottingham township; 4. Abram; 5. Mary, m. William Ramsey.

SAMUEL RAMSEY, see Family of Philip Fulton.

DAVID RANKIN, emigrated from the north of Ireland, and settled in Frederick county, Virginia, about 1738-50; d. near Winchester, Va., 1768; leaving a widow, Jennet, and children, David, William, Hugh, and Barbara; of these: William Rankin, b. about 1720; d. 1793; m. in Virginia, Abigail Tassia; removed to Mount Pleasant township, Washington county, Penn., 1774, and purchased 1,600 acres of land on Raccoon Creek; had issue:

I. David, m. and remained in Virginia.

II. William, m. and remained in Virginia.

III. Zachariah, d. 1785-86, from the bite of a mad wolf; m. Nancy ———; had issue: 1. ———, m. Jesse Woods.

IV. Matthew.

V. John, d. April, 1788; m. Rebecca ———; had issue: 1. James; 2. Mary.

VI. James, killed by the Indians while on a return trip from Kentucky to Pennsylvania.

VII. Thomas, b. in Virginia, 1760; d. May 12, 1832; removed to Moorefield township, Harrison county, about 1805; served in the Indian wars of the border; m. Nancy Foreman; had issue: 1. James, b. in Washington county, Dec. 22, 1784; settled in Athens township, Harrison county; served in the War of 1812; m. Dec. 15, 1809, Hester Early, b. near Chartiers Creek, Washington county, Penn., May 31, 1793; d. March 29, 1874 (had issue: i. Jane; ii. Thomas; iii. Margaret; iv. Nancy; v. Sarah; vi. William, b. in Athens township. March 12, 1822; d. Jan. 3, 1864; m. Nov. 27, 1856, Mary Dunlap, daughter of John Dunlap; vii. Matilda; viii. Israel, b. Nov. 20, 1830; m. Aug. 18, 1870, Sarah Dickerson; d. Aug. 29, 1886; daughter of Adam Dickerson); 2. William; 3. David; 4. Jane; 5. Nancy.

VIII. Mary.

IX. Abigail, m. William Campbell (?)

X. Jesse, d. in Pennsylvania.

XI. Samuel, b. in Winchester, Virginia, July 18, 1769; d. October, 1820; m. Jan. 7, 1796, Jane McConahey, b. Feb. 18, 1775; d. July 20, 1869; had issue: 1. William, b. Nov. 24, 1796; d. Jan. 13, 1884; m. Dec. 16, 1819, Nancy Lyle,

HARRISON COUNTY GENEALOGIES

b. Jan. 22, 1801; d. 1870; daughter of John Lyle (had issue: i. Elizabeth, b. Jan. 21, 1821; d. Feb. 14, 1880; ii. Samuel, b. July 19, 1823; d. September, 1845; iii. John-L., b. Oct. 16, 1826; m. 1849, Elizabeth Campbell; iv. David, b. May 30, 1829; d. September, 1845; v. William, b. April 4, 1832; vi. Jane, b. March 24, 1834; vii. James, b. Sept. 2, 1836; m. (1st) 1864, Elizabeth F. Barnes; d. 1870; m. (2d) 1880, Margaret E. Forsythe, of Burgettstown, Penn.); 2. John, b. April 4, 1798; d. April, 1866; 3. David, b. Feb. 15, 1800; d. July 27, 1858; 4. Matthew, b. Feb. 15, 1802; d. June, 1880; 5. Matilda, b. March 22, 1804; d. February, 1875; 6. Samuel, b. June 3, 1806; d. May 27, 1834; 7. Abigail, b. October, 1808; d. Nov. 17, 1892; 8. James, b. March 24, 1811; d. July 27, 1887; 9. Stephen, b. Aug. 20, 1813; d. February, 1877; 10. Jane, b. Feb. 6, 1817.

JOHN REA, b. 1771-2; d. Feb. 12, 1855; son of Joseph and Isabella Rea, of Tully, Ireland; emigrated to America about 1790, and first settled in Washington county; organized the Presbyterian churches of Beech Spring, Crabapple, Nottingham, and Cadiz; m. 1793, Elizabeth Christy, of Washington county, Penn.; settled in Green township, Harrison county, Ohio, 1803; had issue, nine children, of whom: I. Joseph, b. in Hopewell township, Washington county, Penn., Sept. 20, 1796; d. April —, 1862; m. Sept. 22, 1818, near New Athens, Jane McConnell, b. 1800; d. 1859; daughter of John and Mary McConnell, the former an early settler in Harrison county; had issue: 1. Elizabeth, m. John Lafferty, and settled in Cadiz township; 2. Mary, m. Samuel Dunlap, and settled in Nottingham township; 3. John, settled in Kansas; 4. Andrew-Jackson, b. in Moorefield township, Nov. —, 1826; m. 1856, Mary Moore, daughter of John and Elsie Johnson Moore, who were of Scotch-Irish extraction, coming to Harrison county shortly after 1800; settled in Cadiz township shortly after his marriage (had issue: i. Martha-Elizabeth, m. George Holliday, of Moorefield township; ii. Elsie-J.; iii. Joseph, d. aged fourteen years; iv. Lenora; v. John-M.); 5. Martha: 6. William; 7. Joseph. II. William Purdy, b. 1810; d. 1846; m. Jane Hanna. III. John, m. Sarah Daniels; had issue: 1. Martha; 2. May; 3. William-P. IV. Sarah, m. David Thompson. V. James.

JOHN REAVES, b. in Norfolk county, Va., 1740; had issue:
I. John, settled in Harrison county, Ohio.
II. Richard, settled in Harrison county, Ohio.
III. James, b. in Virginia, Aug. 4, 1776; removed to Harrison county, about 1811, and subsequently settled in Freeport township, where he d. Jan. 3, 1851; m. in Virginia, 1801, Sarah Howell, b. Nov. 20, 1775; d. June 28, 1856; had issue: 1. John, b. Dec. 15, 1802; 2. Nancy, b. Oct. 10, 1804; 3. Lydia, b. Dec. 27, 1805; 4. Jesse, b. April 20, 1807; 5. Winifred, b. May 1, 1809; 6. Elizabeth, b. Nov. 30, 1810; 7. Hallowell, b. April 30, 1813; 8. Sarah, b. Aug. 17, 1815; 9. James, b. April 28, 1818; settled in Washington township; m. July 2, 1841, Susan Clark, of Freeport township (had issue: i. Matthew-C., b. 1842; m. Dec. 31, 1868, Mary E. Rogers, d. April 30, 1874, daughter of Thomas Rogers; ii. Joshua; iii. Harrison; iv. Martha-J.; v. James-F., m. Feb. 3, 1886, Anna Leinard, daughter of Alexander and Mary Leinard, of Washington township, Harrison county).
IV. William, settled in Harrison county, Ohio.
V. Thomas, settled in Harrison county, Ohio.

ARTHUR REED, b. 1791; d. May 12, 1859; a native of Pennsylvania; settled in Archer township, Harrison county, Ohio, 1810; had issue: 1. John, b. June 6, 1818; d. March 18, 1884; settled in Green township; m. March 3, 1846, Dorcas Orr, b. in Green township, June 4, 1812 (had issue: i. Robert-W., b. May 17, 1848; m. Elizabeth McClellan, daughter of William and Eve Rinehart McClellan; ii. Elizabeth-Ann, b. 1850; d. 1853); 2. James; 3. William; 4. Nancy; 5. Ellen; 6. Margaret; 7. Mary-Anne; 8. Catharine; 9. ———, m. Lemuel Hale, of Bloomfield; 10. ———, m. Alexander Dennis, and settled in Indiana.

ADAM RITCHEY, of Scotch-Irish descent, emigrated to America and settled in York county, Pennsylvania, before 1750; m. in Pennsylvania; had issue: John, Thomas, Isaac, William, David, Andrew; the first four named served in the Revolutionary War; Isaac and William died in that service.

Andrew Ritchey, above named, was b. 1758, in York county; removed about 1780 to Washington county, Penn., where he d. 1838; m. in York county, Ann Campbell; d. 1834; had issue:
 I. David.
 II. John, b. in York county, Dec. 8, 1776; removed with his parents to Washington county, Penn.; settled in Short Creek township, Harrison county, Ohio, 1807, where he d. March 24, 1852; m. Jan. 10, 1809, Mrs. Elizabeth Brown Patterson, b. in Pennsylvania, 1781; d. Nov. 11, 1859; had issue: 1. David, b. Aug. 26, 1810; removed to Mercer county, Ill., 1845, where he d. June 19, 1847; m. Feb. 11, 1840, Susan Dossy (had issue: i. Mary-Ann, b. Dec. 22, 1840; ii. John, b. Sept. 15, 1842; iii. George, b. July 28, 1844; iv. Elizabeth-Jane, b. Feb. 28, 1848); 2. Mary-Ann, b. Dec. 11, 1813; d. in Illinois, 1872; m. Jonah Nicholls (had issue, four children); 3. John-P., b. Jan. 7, 1816; 4. William, b. May 24, 1821; m. 1860, Jane Leach, of Green township, Harrison county, Ohio, daughter of James Leach, a pioneer in Harrison county, who d. 1860 (his wife d. 1856).
 III. Andrew, b. Oct. 2, 1778; d. in Short Creek township, May 30, 1859, where he had settled in 1803; m. (1st) Nancy Trinnel, of York county, Penn., b. 1780; d. 1814; m. (2d) June, 1818, Margaret Boggs, of Belmont county, county, Ohio, b. June, 1794; d. Jan. 20, 1861; had issue by first wife, seven children, and by second wife, eleven children, among whom were: 1. Alexander; 2. Jane; 3. Griselda-Ann, m. Hugh B. Hawthorn; 4. Hannah, m. —— Bell; 5. Elizabeth; 6. Hester; 7. Abigail; 8. Catherine, m. —— Beatty; 9. Margaret.
 IV. Charles, removed to Short Creek township, in 1805, where he resided until 1829, thence returned to Washington county, Penn.; settled in Logan county, Ohio, 1835, where he d. 1839; m. Jane McWilliams, of Belmont county, Ohio; had issue, fifteen children, most of whom settled in Logan county.
 V. James.
 VI. Hannah.
 VII. Ann.
 VIII. Catherine.

THOMAS RICHEY, a native of Ireland, b. 1769; d. in Cadiz township, Sept. 29, 1824, where he had settled in 1805; m. Mary Clifford, b. in Ireland, 1771; d. Aug. 12, 1823; emigrated to America, and first settled in New York City about 1795, removing thence to Harrison county; had issue:
 I. Margaret, m. —— Milliken, of Allen county, Ohio.
 II. Mary, m. James Haverfield, of Harrison county.
 III. Jane, m. Joseph Watson, of Harrison county.
 IV. Samuel.
 V. John-M., b. in Cadiz township, Nov. 2, 1808; d. Jan. 30, 1897; m. 1834, Anne Gilmore, b. 1817; d. 1880; daughter of Robert and Elizabeth Collins Gilmore; settled at Cadiz, in 1877; had issue: 1. Mary, m. Samuel McFadden; 2. Ruth, m. Craig Gilmore, and settled in Illinois; 3. George; 4. Eliza-Jane, m. Samuel McFadden, and settled in Cadiz township; 5. Arabella, m. James McFadden, and settled in Cadiz township; 6. Thomas-J., b. July 5, 1845; served in the Civil War; m. 1868, Margaret McFadden, daughter of Samuel McFadden, of Cadiz township (who d. 1863); 7. Robert-Gilmore, m. Susan C. Dickerson, and settled in Missouri; 8. Samuel, settled in Cadiz township; 9. Martha, m. 1876, Charles Osburn, son of John Osburn, of Archer township.
 VI. Sarah, m. (1st) Nimrod Wagers; m. (2d) John Weaver.
 VII. Thomas, settled in Cadiz township.
 VIII. Nancy, m. John Haverfield, and settled in Cadiz township.
 IX. ——, d. in infancy.
 X. ——, d. in infancy.

GEORGE RIFE, b. in Pennsylvania (?), 1801; d. in Cincinnati, 1873; m. in Harrison county, 1829, Sarah Croskey, b. 1811; d. 1870; daughter of John and Catherine Croskey; had issue: 1. John, b. 1830; m. 1853. Anna Smith, daughter of Joseph and Nancy Martin Smith, of Virginia; 2. George-W., b. 1833; m. Rebecca Cartwright; 3. Katharine, b. 1834; m. David Spencer; 4. Jackson, b. 1837; m. —— Hanna; 5. Mary-Jane, b. 1839; m. James Stone; 6. David, b. 1841; m. Emma ——; 7. Rachel, b. 1844; m. William Wallace; 8. Samuel, b. 1847.

WILLIAM ROGERS. b. in Maryland, Aug. 20, 1749; d. in Harrison county,

HARRISON COUNTY GENEALOGIES

Dec. 27, 1830, where he settled 1809; of British descent, his parents having come to America early in the eighteenth century; settled in Jefferson county, in 1808, removing to Lee's Run, in Harrison county, a year later; m. Susanna Barrett, b. in Maryland, July 30, 1752; d. Dec. 27, 1830; had issue, eleven children, the youngest of whom: I. John, b. in Maryland, 1795; d. 1878, in Cadiz township; m. Sept. 28, 1815, Nancy Lemasters, b. near Hopedale; d. 1869; daughter of Isaac and Jane Lemasters, early settlers in Jefferson and Harrison counties; had issue: 1. William, b. in Cadiz township, Dec. 14, 1817; m. June 21, 1838, Maria Adams, d. July 24, 1881, a native of Harrison county, daughter of Thomas and Charity Blair Adams (had issue: i. James-Birney; settled at Cadiz; ii. John-Thomas, settled at Newark, Ohio; iii. Isabella-Jane, m. John Freeburn; iv. William-Pinckney; v. Albert-Lawson; vi. Nancy-Ellen, m. A. B. Cutshall, and settled in Stock township; vii. Bailey-Sumner, settled at Scio).

WILLIAM ROGERS, b. in Maryland, Nov. 30, 1798; son of Joseph Rogers, who settled in Cadiz township, Harrison county, Ohio, 1808; removed to Nottingham township, in 1856, where he d. April 28, 1863; m. Susan Carson, b. Aug. 14, 1803; d. May 25, 1844; had issue: 1. Snydonia, b. Nov. 5, 1823; d. March 12, 1855; 2. John-B., b. May 18, 1825; 3. Jesse-B., b. April 24, 1828; 4. Hannah, b. April 24, 1830; d. Feb. 4, 1871; 5. Nancy-C., b. Sept. 17, 1832; 6. William-F., b. Oct. 28, 1834; 7. Calvin, b. in Cadiz township, Jan. 19, 1837; settled in Nottingham township; m. Sept. 29, 1859, Mary E. Finical, b. in Cadiz township, Nov. 10, 1833, daughter of Isaac and Margaret Anderson Finical; 8. Barrett, b. March 29, 1839; 9. Susanna, b. July 8, 1842; d. March 4, 1847; 10. Lydia, b. May 22, 1844; d. June 9, 1844.

JAMES ROSS. b. in West Nottingham township. Chester county, Penn., 1797; d. in Nottingham township, Harrison county, Ohio, 1878; removed to Harrison county about 1827; m. (1st) Martha Phillips, daughter of William and Rachel Hamilton Phillips, d. 1836; m. (2d) Jemima Hines, d. July 5, 1882; had issue by first wife: 1. Rachel, m. Immer Knight; 2. Deborah, m. William Poulson; 3. Jane, m. Isaac Drummond; 4. William-P.; 5. Mary-E.; 6. Thomas-H.; 7, Martha, m. Thomas McMillan; 8. Barbara, m. Beall Pumphrey; had issue by second wife: 9. Eliza, m. George Oglevee; 10. John-H.; 11. James-N.; 12. Rebecca, m. Anthony Blackburn; 13. Sarah, m. William Nash.

JOHN ROSS, b. in Ireland, Sept. 13, 1750; d. Sept. 8, 1833; emigrated to Pennsylvania, and thence removed to Harrison county, Ohio, about 1804, settling within four miles of Cadiz; m. in Pennsylvania, Charlotte Hatcher, d. in Morgan county, Ohio; had issue:
I. Adam, b. in Pennsylvania; settled in Cadiz township; served in the War of 1812; d. in that service at Sandusky, Ohio; m. in Pennsylvania, Susannah Rowe, b. 1778; d. 1848; had issue: 1. John; 2. Adam; 3. George, twin brother to Adam; settled in Missouri; 4. Caleb; 5. Joseph; 6. Aaron, twin brother to Joseph, b. in Cadiz township, July 3, 1811; m. June 16, 1853, Nancy Harper, a native of Harrison county, daughter of Samuel and Cassandra Cox Harper, both of whom died in Cadiz township.
II. William. III. John. IV. James. V. Hannah. VI. Eve. VII. Susannah, b. 1798; d. Aug. 31, 1889, m. Miles Tipton. VIII. Mary.

ROBERT ROBERTS, b. in Brooke county, West Virginia, 1790; d. in German township, Harrison county, Ohio, 1834, where he had settled in 1827; was one of five children, viz.: Samuel, Alexander, William, Robert, Mary; m. 1817, Ruth Atkinson, d. 1885, daughter of James Atkinson, a resident of German township; had issue: 1. William; 2. Thomas; 3. George; 4. Mary; 5. James-Ross, b. at Annapolis, Ohio, May 20, 1826; settled at Jewett; m. (1st) February, 1851, Dillie Ann Potts. d. 1856, daughter of Samuel and Elizabeth Potts, natives of Ohio; m. (2d) 1858, Margaret Ryder, daughter of George and Catherine Culp Ryder (had issue by first wife: i. Elizabeth, m. Jacob Miller; ii. Samuel, settled at Dennison, Ohio; iii. Richard, d. in infancy; had issue by second wife: iv. Catherine-Bell. m. Minden Hall, and settled at Crafton, Penn.; v. John, settled at Dennison; vi. Thomas; vii. McClellan; viii. William); 6. Ellen; 7. John; 8. Caroline.

ROBERT ROWLAND, a native of

Scotland or Wales, emigrated to America and settled in York county, Penn., about 1750, where he was twice married; had issue:

I. Matthew, settled near Mansfield, Ohio.

II. James, settled near Cincinnati, Ohio.

III. John, b. in York county, Penn., 1758; d. in Moorefield township, Harrison county, Ohio, April 20, 1855; served in the Revolutionary War; was an Indian scout for three years along the Muskingum and Ohio Rivers, from Steubenville, Ohio, to Louisville, Ky.; settled at Steubenville, where he remained until 1815, and then located in Moorefield township, Harrison county; m. Rachel Ingle, of Steubenville, daughter of William and Rachel Edington Ingle, early settlers in that place; had issue, among others: 1. James, b. Feb. 24, 1805; d. July 31, 1890; m. 1829, Elizabeth Leinard, b. April 17, 1808; d. March 4, 1884; daughter of Yost and Elizabeth Leinard (had issue: i. John, settled in Kansas; ii. Matthew, settled in Nottingham township, Harrison county; iii. Henry; iv. James; v. Leinard, b. in Monroe township, March 1, 1848; settled in Cadiz township; m. 1873, Margaret Mehollin, d. Dec. 13, 1890, daughter of John and Elizabeth Mehollin, of Cadiz township; vi. Sarah-Jane; vii. Ann-Christina, m. John Houser, and settled in Mercer county, Ill.; viii. Elizabeth, m. Eli Moore, and settled in Freeport township; ix. Rachel, m. John Mitchell, and settled in Knox county, Ill.; x. Mary; xi. Margaret, m. John F. Poulson, and settled at Allegheny, Penn.; xii. Nancy-Ellen); 2. Sarah; 3. William, b. May 19, 1796; d. Jan. 13, 1873; removed to Maryland; subsequently he returned to Ohio, settling in Nottingham township, Harrison county; m. Jane Fulton, b. Dec. 15, 1801; d. Nov. 17, 1881; daughter of Philip Fulton (had issue: i. John, settled in Freeport; ii. Levi; iii. Philip, b. May 25, 1825, in Nottingham township; m. (1st) August, 1847, Piety Ann Ford, d. 1865, daughter of Lewis and Ann Ford; m. (2d) Julia Hart, daughter of Benjamin and Myrtilla Hart, of Harrison county; iv. James, settled in Freeport; v. Sarah; vi. William, settled in Freeport; vii. Hannah; viii. Rachel; ix. Mary, m. Elihu Petty; x. Alexander); 4. Mary; 5. Rachel; 6. Levi; 7. Elizabeth; 8. Cyrus; 9. Rebecca; 10. John.

CHARLES SAMPSON, b. at Claughter, county Tyrone, Ireland; had issue, among others, John Sampson, who emigrated to America and first settled in York county, Penn.; removed to Stock township, Harrison county, Ohio, about 1827, where he d. April 28, 1841; m. in Ireland, Sarah Gibson; had issue, among others: 1. Francis, b. in county Tyrone, Ireland, 1804; d. March 15, 1870; m. in New York, Aug. 30, 1827, Margaret Evans, a native of Wales, b. 1801; d. Nov. 9, 1884; daughter of Christmas Evans (had issue, among others: i. John-G., b. July 4, 1828; settled at Wichita, Kan.; served in the Civil War; m. Feb. 14, 1850, Elizabeth Birney; ii. Sarah-Ann, d. in infancy; iii. William-E., b. March 20, 1833; settled in Stock township; m. Oct. 25, 1866, Susan M. Welch, daughter of William Welch, of Archer township; iv. Charles-W., b. March 12, 1836; served in the Civil War; m. May 21, 1867, Rachel A. Poulson, daughter of Jehu and Elizabeth Cox Poulson, who came to Ohio from Maryland about 1802; v. Archibald-J., b. June 21, 1839; served as an officer in the Civil War; as United States Consul to Paso del Norte, Mexico; attorney for the State Board of Education of Missouri, etc.; m. 1866, Kate Turner, d. Dec. 15, 1886, daughter of Allen C. Turner, of Cadiz; vi. Francis-A., b. Feb. 6, 1842; m. July 1, 1869, Mrs. Harriet Lacey, a native of England; removed to Sedalia, Mo.).

ADAM SAWVEL, of German descent; came from Pennsylvania and settled in Rumley township, Harrison county, Ohio, 1815; served in the Revolutionary War; had issue:

I. Mary.
II. Christina.
III. Michael.
IV. Jacob, b. in York county, Penn., 1780; resided in Adams county, Penn., where he remained until 1827; thence located in Rumley township; removed to Van Buren county, Iowa, in 1850, where his wife d. 1853; thence removed to Hillsboro, Texas, 1857, where he died; m. Margaret Epley; had issue: 1. Michael, settled in Arkansas; 2. John; 3. Jacob, d. in infancy; 4. Jonathan, b. in Adams county, Penn., Dec. 17, 1826; settled in Rumley township; m. (1st)

Jan. 16, 1851, Lydia A. Arbaugh, d. in Iowa, 1863, daughter of John and Rosanna Wentz Arbaugh; m. (2d) 1863, Sarah Shambaugh, daughter of Philip and Catherine Arbaugh Shambaugh; 5. Emanuel, settled in Iowa; 6. Jeremiah; 7. Johanna, settled in Iowa; 8. Rebecca, m. Joseph Martin, and settled in Vinton county, Ohio; 9. Amy, m. Isaac Kimmel, and settled in Darke county, Ohio; 10. Elizabeth, m. Adam Arbaugh, and settled in Iowa; 11. Lydia, m. —— Dillin, and settled in Iowa; 12. Sarah-Ann, m. —— Marrow, and settled in Iowa; 13. Mary-A., m. —— Reniker, and settled in Iowa.

THOMAS SCARBOROUGH, see Family of Peter Martin.

ABRAHAM SCOTT, b. 1677, son of Hugh Scott, who emigrated from the North of Ireland, and settled in Chester county, Penn., probably before 1700; had issue, among others: 1. Anne, b. October, 1699; d. 1792; m. about 1720, Arthur Patterson, b. about 1700; d. about 1763 (had issue: William, Rebecca, Samuel, Arthur, Ellen, James, Catherine, Elizabeth, and Jane); 2. Samuel, b. about 1705; 3. Rebecca, b. Dec. 17, 1707; m. 1737, James Agnew (had issue: Samuel, Martha, James, David, Margaret, Rebecca, Sarah, Abraham, Anne); 4. Alexander, b. 1716-17; 5. Grace; 6. Hugh, b. 1726; m. 1754, Jennet Agnew, daughter of James Agnew by a former marriage (had issue: Rebecca, Abraham, James, Hugh, John, Elizabeth, Sarah, Margaret, and Josiah); 7. Josiah.

Josiah Scott, last named, son of Abraham Scott (1st), was born in Chester county, Penn., 1735, removed to Washington county, where he d. Feb. 20, 1819; m. (1st) 1760, Violet Foster; m. (2d) Jane ——; had issue by first wife, eight children, of whom:

I. Alexander, m. Rachel McDowell, daughter of John and Agnes Bradford McDowell; had issue, among others: 1. Josiah, settled at Bucyrus, Ohio.

II. Abraham, m. Rebecca McDowell, sister to Rachel McDowell; had issue, among others: 1. Josiah, settled near Cadiz, Ohio (had issue, among others: i. Lawson, settled at Oak Park, a suburb of Chicago, Ill.: ii. J.-Edward, a physician, settled at San Bernardino, Cal.); 2. William, a minister, settled in Guernsey county, Ohio; 3. James, a minister, settled at Mt. Vernon, Ohio; 4. Josiah, settled in Columbiana county, Ohio; 5. Mary, m. William Cotton, of Beaver county, Penn.; 6. Elizabeth, m. Robert Stevenson, of Beaver county, Penn.

Josiah Scott (1st) had issue by second wife:

IX. Robert, m. 1804, Elizabeth Munell; settled in Carroll county, Ohio, 1827, where he d. 1830; had issue, among others: 1. Robert-G., b. in Washington county, Sept. 18, 1813; m. April, 1835, Elizabeth Steeves, b. in New Brunswick, Canada, 1814, daughter of Christian and Olive Lutz Steeves, who removed to Scio, Ohio, in 1829 (had issue: i. Isabelle, m. Jesse Campbell, of Carroll county; ii. Eliza, m. Henry Spence, of Jefferson; iii. Margaret; iv. Josiah-R., d. while in the army, at Jackson, Tenn.; v. Dorinda, m. James McGeary; vi. James; vii. Mary-Jane, m. H. H. Meiser; viii. Robert-C.; ix. Olive-A.; x. Martha; xi. William-W., settled at Jefferson).

X. Hugh, d. in Washington county, Penn.

XI. Samuel.

XII. John, d. in Washington county, Penn.

JAMES SCOTT, a native of Sowerby Bridge, Yorkshire, England; son of Timothy Scott, who died in England; emigrated to America and settled at York (now Toronto), Canada, about 1816, thence removed to New York; located in Cadiz, Harrison county, Ohio, 1819, where he died; m. (1st) —— Howarth, d. in England; m. (2d) Harriet Arnold; had issue by first wife: 1. John-W., b. in Yorkshire, England, September, 1811; d. in Cadiz, Oct. 8, 1886; m. 1839, Jane Pittis, daughter of Robert Pittis, who emigrated with his family from the Isle of Wight and settled at Deersville, Harrison county, Ohio (had issue: i. James, d. young; ii. Albert, d. young; iii. Julia, m. Dr. George W. Woodburne, and settled at Uhrichsville; iv. Cyrus-M., served as an Indian scout in the Indian Territory; settled at Arkansas City, Kan.; m. Margaret Gardner; v. Robert-P., settled at Baltimore; vi. Lanphear; vii. Charles-S.; viii. Thomas-A., m. Susan Pittis, daughter of George Pittis, of Scio; ix. Mary, d. young); 2. William; 3. Eliza; had issue by second wife: 4. Daniel; 5. James, settled at Akron, Ohio; 6. Thomas, settled in Texas (had issue, among others: i. Emma, m. Charles P. Dewey; ii. Edward); 7. Mary, m. ——— McMasters, and settled at Mount Pleasant, Ohio.

WILLIAM SCOTT, a native of county Antrim, Ireland; had issue: 1. Thomas, b. in Ireland, 1793; emigrated to America and in 1822 settled in Harrison county, Ohio; d. in Moorefield township, Jan. 16, 1875; m. Sarah Hogg, b. 1802; d. 1875 (had issue: i. Jane; ii. ———, d. in infancy; iii. Susan; iv. William, b. March 7, 1833; settled in Moorefield township; m. April 9, 1859, Ann Eliza Sloan, daughter of John Sloan, one of the earliest settlers in Moorefield township; v. Eleanor; vi. Mary; vii. ———, d. in infancy; viii. James; ix. John; x. Martha; xi. Sarah; xii. Robert-W., twin brother to Sarah; b. Dec. 28, 1846; m. May 17, 1877, Mary A. Wallace, b. Feb. 23, 1849, daughter of Nathaniel and Julia Fulton Wallace [the former of whom d. March 25, 1855, and his widow m. William Pickering, of Moorefield township]); 2. John; 3. William; 4. Mary; 5. Eleanor.

WILLIAM SCOTT, a native of Ireland; emigrated to America and settled near Pigeon Creek, Somerset township, Washington county, Penn., where he died; m. in Ireland, Rebecca ———; had issue:

I. Joseph.
II. Thomas.
III. Alexander, b. in Ireland, 1775; d. in Tuscarawas county, Nov. 2, 1853; m. in Washington county, 1813, Gertrude Kerr, b. 1790; d. April 5, 1868; daughter of Samuel and Rhoda Byshire Kerr (the former an early settler in Washington county); had issue: 1. William-H., b. Jan. 15, 1814, on Pigeon Creek, Washington county, Penn.; settled at Scio, Harrison county, Ohio, 1840; m. (1st) 1842, Jane Whittaker, b. 1818; d. 1866; daughter of James and Arabell Whittaker; m. (2d) Dec. 10, 1868, Mrs. Sarah J. Kerr Elder, b. in Washington county, Penn., May 24, 1827, widow of John Elder, Jr., and daughter of Aaron and Margaret Nevin Kerr (the latter a daughter of John Nevin, a native of Ireland, who settled in Beaver county, Penn.) (had issue by first wife: i. Alexander, m. Margaret A. Calhoun; ii. James, b. Sept. 30, 1844; settled in North township; m. May 25, 1875, Gelina M. Elder, a native of Carroll county, daughter of John Elder, Jr., and Sarah J. Kerr [second wife of William H. Scott]; iii. Maria; iv. Christian; v. Thomas-W., twin brother to Christian; vi. William; vii. Mary-Arabell; viii. Caroline-G., m. Philip C. Spiker of Tippecanoe); 2. Samuel, settled at Uhrichsville; 3. Robert, d. in Uhrichsville; 4. Albert, settled near New Cumberland, Tuscarawas county; 5. Lewis-L., settled at Waynesburg, Stark county, Ohio; 6. Eliza, m. Joseph Meek, of Washington, Iowa; 7. Maria, m. Rev. Moses M. Bartholomew, of Goshen, Ind.; 8. Sarah, m. John Ralston, of Spencer, Owen county, Ind.; 9. Caroline, m. Dr. John C. McGregor, and settled at Brazil, Clay county, Ind.; 10. Margaret, m. Samuel G. Smith, of Uhrichsville.

Aaron Kerr, father of Sarah J. Scott, was a native of Washington county, Penn.; settled in Carroll county, Ohio, 1831, where he died Sept. 28, 1856; m. Margaret Nevin, daughter of John Nevin, a native of Ireland, who settled in Beaver county, Penn.; had issue: 1. Samuel Lewis, a physician, settled at El Paso, Ill.; 2. John-Jackson, m. Cornelia E. Hutchinson, and settled at Wintersett, Iowa; 3. Sarah-Jane, m. (1st) in Carroll county, July 10, 1857, John Elder, Jr., b. in Washington county, Penn., 1799; d. in Carroll county, Ohio, 1866; m. (2d) Dec. 10, 1868, William H. Scott (had issue by first husband: i. Gelina-M., m. James Scott; ii. John-S., settled in Holmes county; iii. Flora; iv. Lissa; v. Clara-S.); 4. Joseph-Alexander, m. Carrie E. Grizzell, and settled at Salem, Ohio; 5. Margaret-Ann, d. 1869; m. Uriah Coulson, an officer in the Civil War; 6. Aaron-Wylie, d. in Dallas, Tex.; 7. George-Nevin, served in the Civil War; d. at Cottonwood Falls, Kan., Nov. 14, 1890; 8. Robert-Hervey, m. Alice Miller, and settled in Jefferson county; 9. James-McMillan, served in the Civil War; removed to Washington, Iowa, where he m. Mary Young, daughter of Judge ——— Young; afterward settled at Cottonwood Falls, Kan.

John Elder, b. in New York, about 1750; d. Dec. 16, 1840; his parents, who were natives of Ireland, emigrated to America and landed on the date of his birth; removed to near Buffalo, Washington county, Penn.; m. Elizabeth McKinney, who d. aged seventy-five years; had issue: 1. Samuel, b. Jan. 24, 1791; d. Nov. 13, 1826; 2. Mary, b. Feb. 12, 1793; d. Aug. 6, 1877; 3. Jane, b. Oct. 13, 1794; d. Jan. 6, 1830; 4. Sarah, b. May 28, 1797; m. March 4, 1831, Samuel McEldeny (had issue, among others: i. Margaret-A., m. ——— Smith, and settled near Carrollton); 5. Thomas, b. June 23, 1799; d. July 30, 1831; 6. James, b. Oct. 4, 1803; d. Oct. 12, 1829; 7. David, b. Oct. 23, 1805; d. Sept. 2, 1831; 8. John, b. April 4, 1807; d. in Carroll county, 1866; m. July 10, 1857, Jane Kerr.

PETER SEWELL, of German descent; b. in Delaware, 1796; removed to Maryland, and thence to Harrison county, Ohio, in 1828, where he d. 1885; m. 1826, Susan Wiley, of Scotch-Irish descent, b. in Virginia, 1801; d. 1883 (daughter of John Wiley, who served in the War of 1812 and died at Alexandria, Va., from effects of a wound received in that service); had issue: 1. Rebecca; 2. Mary-Ann; 3. Theodore; 4. John-William; 5. Thomas-M., b. in Belmont county, Oct. 29, 1842; settled at New Athens, Ohio; served in the Civil War; m. 1870, Eliza J. Hughes, daughter of Edward and Sarah Hughes, of New Athens; 6. Josephus.

GEORGE SHAMBAUGH, b. in Pennsylvania about 1745; d. in Perry county, that State, 1827, son of George Shambaugh, a native of Germany, who emigrated to Pennsylvania; had issue:
I. George, b. in Perry county, Penn., 1787; removed to Rumley township, Harrison county, Ohio, 1817, where he d. Sept. 4. 1867; served in the War of 1812; m. in Pennsylvania, Mrs. Elizabeth Brown Wirt, a widow, b. 1777; d. about 1863; daughter of Michael Brown, of German descent; had issue: 1. Philip; 2. Michael, b. in Perry county. June 18, 1811; d. March 20, 1863; settled in Rumley township; m. May 31, 1832, Hettie Hazlett, b. April 16, 1816; d. Oct. 22, 1884 (had issue: i. James, b. March 5, 1833; settled near New Rumley; ii. Elizabeth, b. Aug. 1, 1834; d. in Iowa, March, 1864, m. Abraham Fetroe; iii. Mary-A., b. July 27, 1836; m. John W. Finnicum, of Rumley township; iv. Simon-B., b. Sept. 7, 1838; d. Oct. 14, 1873; v. Adam-H., b. Sept. 11, 1841; m. Mary Jane Scott, daughter of Samuel Scott, of Rumley township; vi. Charlotte, b. June 21, 1842; d. January, 1879; m. May, 1873, Peter Overholt, d. February, 1877; vii. Maria, b. Aug. 22, 1844; m. Aug. 3, 1871, Harvey L. Thompson, and settled in Archer township; viii. Jane, b. Nov. 28, 1846; d. Oct. 30, 1867; ix. John, b. Oct. 13, 1848; m. Elizabeth Gutshall, daughter of Jacob Gutshall, and settled near Des Moines, Iowa; x. Philip, b. Feb. 18, 1851; m. March 15, 1881, Eliza Loretta Scott, of New Rumley, daughter of John A. and Eliza Bivington Scott; 3. George; 4. Margaret, m. Samuel Hazlett.
II. Jacob, served in the Revolutionary War.
III. John.
IV. Philip.
V. Mary.
VI. Barbara.
VII. Catherine.

WILLIAM SHARON, of Scotch-Irish descent, removed from Westmoreland county, Penn., to Wells township, Jefferson county, Ohio, about 1802; d. 1809; m. Mrs. Sarah Whitaker; had issue: 1. James, b. 1790; m. about 1815, Martha Eaton (had issue, two sons and two daughters); 2. William, b. 1793; d. April 24, 1875; m. about 1815, Susan Kirk (had issue: i. John, a physician, b. about 1816; d. Sept. 2, 1860; settled at Carrollton, Ill.; ii. Mary-Ann, b. about 1818; m. 1863, Dr. Jacob Hammond, and settled in Steubenville; iii. Sarah, b. 1820; removed to California; iv. William, b. Jan. 9. 1821; d. Nov. 13, 1885; removed to California; represented Nevada in the United States Senate, 1875-81; v. Lewis, b. 1822; m. 1855, Sarah McKim; vi. Susan, b. 1825; m. Isaac M. Davis; vii. Smiley. b. Feb. 14, 1827; m. 1848, Sarah Ann Hurford); 3. Smiley, b. June, 1795; d. Oct. 16, 1876; m. June, 1827, Martha Kithcart (had issue, five sons and three daughters); 4. John, b. September, 1798; d. Oct. 23, 1870; m. February, 1832, Helen Hall (had issue, three sons and six daughters).

GEORGE SHARP, d. in Hopewell township, June, 1812, leaving a wife, Rachel, and children: 1. Joseph (possibly the son-in-law of John Sharp); 2. John; 3. Thomas; 4. Mary.

Joseph and Thomas Sharp, of Washington county, probably the sons of George, or son and son-in-law of John, took up two sections of land in Wheel-

37

ing township, Belmont county, Ohio, in 1806, just south of Athens and Short Creek townships, Harrison county; of these:

I. Thomas, b. 1768; d. Dec. 29, 1825; m. Jane ——, b. Feb. 1, 1766; d. April 24, 1859; had issue, among others: 1. George, b. July 9, 1795; d. June 25, 1877; m. Nancy ——, b. April 21, 1807; d. Dec. 13, 1877; 2. John;'3. Margaret; 4. Rachel; 5. Jane, b. 1812; d. June 6, 1844; m. 1834, David Welling; 6. Sarah, b. Feb. 3, 1813; d. Sept. 4, 1831; 7. Joseph, b. Aug. 23, 1815; d. May 13, 1833.

II. Joseph, d. near Cadiz, and buried in the Old Cemetery; but dates illegible.

Besides the above, the following Sharp families appear on the early records of Harrison county:

Thomas Sharp, m. 1828, Margaret Stine.

William Sharp, b. 1809; d. May 18, 1859; buried at Unity; probably the same who m. 1836, Elizabeth Goriet.

Caroline Sharp, b. Jan. 23, 1814; d. Oct. 20, 1886; buried at Unity.

Caroline T. Sharp, b. July 10, 1838; d. Dec. 24, 1881.

James Sharp, b. 1832; d. 1838.

George Sharp, of Hopewell township, first above named, who died in 1812, was an elder in North Buffalo United Presbyterian Church.

William Sharp, probably closely connected with Thomas or Joseph Sharp; removed from Hopewell (?) township, Washington county, to Wheeling township, Belmont county, Ohio, and d. near Union town, 1835; m. in Washington county, Mary McFadden, daughter of John (?) and Mary McFadden; had issue, among others: 1. John, b. in Harrison or Belmont county, 1807; d. at Millersburg, Holmes county, Ohio, 1893, where he had settled in 1834; m. 1832, Catharine Thompson, b. 1814; d. 1900; daughter of David Thompson, of Cadiz township (had issue: i. William-Thompson, a physician, b. Dec. 16, 1833; d. 1899; served in the Civil War; m. Oct. 12, 1859, Elizabeth Carnahan; ii. David, m. Lydia Armstrong; settled in Holmes county; iii. John; settled at Millersburg, Holmes county; iv. James, a United Presbyterian minister, m. Agnes Ballantine; settled at Sidney, Ohio; v. George, m. Annette Donnan; settled at Millersburg; vi. Samuel, a physician, m. Cordelia Maxwell; settled in Oregon; vii. Martha, m. John T. Maxwell, of Millersburg; viii. Mary, d. young; ix. Margaret; x. Joseph, m. Margaret Maxwell; settled in Holmes county); 2. Nancy, b. 1810; d. Oct. 10, 1875; m. 1829, John Cunningham, son of David and Mary McLaughlin Cunningham.

JOHN SHARP, d. in Hopewell township, Washington county, Penn., 1797; m. Agnes ——; had issue: 1. Mary, m. —— Girvan; 2. Agnes, m. —— Ramsey; 3. John; 4. Margaret; 5. Janet; 6. Thomas; besides these children, John Sharp mentions in his will two sons-in-law, Joseph Sharp and Andrew Garret, probably the husbands of his two daughters, Margaret and Janet. He also mentions as one of his executors, John McFadden.

JOSEPH SHERIFF, b. (probably) in the North of Ireland, 1787; emigrated to America with his parents, and settled in Mercer county, Penn., where he d. 1872; m. at Steubenville, Ohio, Nancy Fulton, b. 1797; d. 1841; daughter of —— and Nancy Liggett Fulton; had issue: 1. Sarah, m. William Weimer; 2. Joseph, m. Nancy Shipler; 3. Martha, m. Alexander Thompson; 4. William, m. Anna Glenn; 5. Ellen, m. John McElheney; 6. Adam-N., b. July 6, 1832; d. 1880; m. 1856, Mary Vickery; 7. Margaret, m. Allen Turner; 8. Thomas, m. Jane Boyd; 9. John, m. —— Hosick; 10. Mary, m. William Fowler.

William Vickery, father of Mary Vickery Sheriff, was born in England, 1791; d. at Steubenville, Ohio, 1856; emigrated to America and first settled in Beaver county, Penn., thence removed, 1839, to Steubenville, Ohio; m. in England, Mary Collings, daughter of —— and Mary Wellington Collings; had issue: 1. Johanna, m. William Johnston; 2. Mary, b. 1831; d. 1896; m. Adam N. Sheriff; 3. Ellen, m. John McMurray.

JOHN SHOTWELL, came from England, Scotland, or New England, to New Jersey, and settled on the road between Scotch Plains and Plainfield; m. (1st) —— Smith, daughter of Shubal Smith; m. (2d) Mary Webster; had issue: John-Smith, Jacob, William, Isaiah, James, Hugh, Mary, m. James Stevens, Sarah, and Martha. Of these: Hugh Shotwell, b. near Plainfield, N. J., March 19, 1764; d. at Freeport,

Ohio, March 17, 1854; removed before 1790 to Franklin township, Fayette county, Penn., thence, about 1808, to Harrison county, Ohio, settling in Washington township about 1828; m. in Sussex county, New Jersey, Feb. 23, 1783, Rosetta Arrison, b. 1764; d. 1836; daughter of John Arrison (who lived at Wyoming, Pa., and was driven thence by the Indians during the Revolutionary War, settling in New Jersey); had issue: I. John, b. 1784; d. 1869; m. (1st) Sarah Shanklin; m. (2d) Hannah Myers. II. Esther, b. 1785; d. 1870; m. (1st) Timothy Smith; m. (2d) Major George Clark Seton. III. Susanna, b. 1789; d. 1874; m. Charles Wintermute. IV. Charlotte, b. 1790; d. 1827; m. Ephraim Sears. V. Nancy, b. 1796; d. 1861; m. (1st) Peter Vandolah; m. (2d) Jacob Ebert. VI. William, b. in Fayette county, Penn., 1798; settled in Cadiz township, about 1837; m. 1819, at Wilbraham, Hampden county, Mass., Rhoda Beebe, b. June 19, 1792; d. March, 1876; daughter of Stuart and Huldah Beebe (see Family of Stewart Beebe); had issue: 1. Stuart-Beebe, b. Nov. 22, 1819; d. Dec. 3, 1890; m. 1851, Nancy Gaston, daughter of James and Elizabeth Kilgore Gaston, of Columbiana county, Ohio (had issue: i. Mary, b. 1853; d. in infancy); ii. Walter-Gaston; a judge; b. Dec. 27, 1856; m. Dec. 24, 1884, Belle McIlvaine, daughter of George W. and Caroline Rinehart McIlvaine; iii. Stuart-Beebe, b. 1867; m. Caroline McIlvaine, sister of Belle McIlvaine; settled at St. Paul, Minn.; iv. Martha; v. William-James, d. in infancy); 2. John, b. 1821; d. young; 3. Samuel, b. 1823; d. young; 4. William, b. 1825; d. Dec. 1, 1849; 5. Theodore, b. March 20, 1828; d. Jan. 28, 1899; m. (1st) Sarah J. Lucas, of Steubenville; m. (2d) Anna G. Seton Beckwith; settled at Minneapolis; 6. Walter-Beebe, b. 1831; d. May 21, 1847; 7. Rhoda-Loretta, b. July 27, 1834; d. August, 1888; m. Smiley Sharon. VII. Joseph, b. 1801; d. 1883; m. Mary Arrison. VIII. Arrison, b. 1812; d. 1893; m. Mary Dickerson.

James Gaston, father of Nancy Gaston Shotwell, was the son of Hugh and grandson of Joseph Gaston, who d. in Mount Bethel township, Northampton county, Penn, 1775; Hugh was b. Jan. 18, 1764; d. June 24, 1839; m. March 14, 1789, Grace Gaston, b. Nov. 25, 1764; d. March 14, 1838. Grace Gaston, wife of Hugh, was the daughter of Robert Gaston, of Somerset county, N. J., b. Jan. 28, 1732; d. near Warrior's Run Presbyterian Church, Northumberland county, Penn., Sept. 2, 1793; served as a colonel in the Revolutionary War, and as a member of the Committee of Safety for Morris county, N. J.; m. May 15, 1762, Rosanna Cooper, b. March 23, 1742; d. Jan. 14, 1817. Robert Gaston, father of Grace Gaston, was the son of Joseph Gaston, of Bernard township, Somerset county, N. J., who d. 1777 (see Gaston Family).

JAMES SIMERAL, b. 1792; d. Sept. 21, 1849; m. Mary Ann Vincent, b. June 11, 1790; d. April 16, 1866; daughter of Robert Vincent; had issue: 1. Jane, b. Nov. 16, 1815; 2. Martha, b. Jan. 3, 1817; m. 1838, William Boggs (had issue i. Vincent-Simeral; ii. William-Edwin; d.1878; m. Adaline Friend, of Wheeling; iii. Oliver-Stevenson, d. 1882; iv. Albert-Whitten; v. Emmet-Addison; vi. Anna-Mary); 3. Matilda, b. Dec. 25, 1818; m. George S. Atkinson (see Atkinson Family); 4. Robert-Vincent b. July 26, 1822; d. April 15, 1852; m. Sarah Ann Hogg, daughter of John and Miriam Hogg, of Mount Pleasant, Jefferson county (had issue: i. Mary-Ann, m. ——— Jenkins; ii. George-H., m. Margaret Kidd, of Bloomington, Ill.; iii. James-V.; iv. Ann-Elizabeth); 5. Amanda, b. July 10, 1826; m. 1857, Rev. William M. Grimes.

The name, Simeral, is a corruption. It was originally Somerville, and was so written many times during the eighteenth century by the ancestors of families now bearing the name, Simeral. The Harrison county Simerals are probably descended from John Simeral, who removed from Adams county and settled in Hempfield (now South Huntingdon) township, Westmoreland county, Penn., before 1772, with his brother, Thomas Simeral (who died there in 1772) and sister, Mary Kincaid (wife of Robert Kincaid). John Simeral established a ferry across the Youghiogheny River at the present town of West Newton (originally called Simeral's Ferry, and later, Robbstown). He died there after 1794, leaving children: Joseph, John, Alexander, Mary, and Elizabeth. Margaret Simeral died in Westmoreland county, 1779, leaving children, Isaac and Martha, and perhaps more, as George Simeral's name appears as a witness to her will. James Simeral died there in 1781; and William Simeral, in 1796, leaving as next of kin, Sarah Simeral, who was appointed administratrix of his estate.

JAMES SIMPSON, b. in Ireland, April 30, 1750; d. Sept. 20, 1819; settled in Washington county, Penn., near the close of the last century; m. in America, Margaret Conner, b. in Ireland, Oct. 25, 1755; d. March 25, 1815; had issue: I. John. II. Margaret. III. William. IV. Elizabeth. V. James, b. in Washington county, Penn., July 14, 1791; d. in Green township. Harrison county, Dec. 8, 1871; first settled in Belmont county, about 1816, removing to Harrison county in 1820; m. in Washington county, 1816, Violet Scott, d. June 30, 1855; daughter of Rev. Abram Scott, a Presbyterian minister, had issue: 1. Margaret-Rebecca, b. Dec. 25, 1818; d. July 26, 1843; 2. Abram-Scott, b. in Belmont county, Jan. 3, 1821; d. Nov. 3, 1884; m. March 26, 1857, Celia Davis, daughter of John Davis, of German township; 3. John-McDowell, b. Oct. 4, 1822; d. April 16, 1825; 4. William, b. April 30, 1825; settled in Green township; 6. Josiah-Marshall, b. Sept. 15, 1828; d. May 30, 1830; 7. Sarah-Mariah, b. Dec. 29, 1833. VI. Mary. VII. Robert. VIII. Sarah.

THOMAS SIMPSON. a native of the North of Ireland, of Scottish descent, emigrated from county Londonderry to Baltimore, Md., in 1793, and thence removed to Jefferson county after 1800; had issue: 1. Andrew. settled at Chillicothe, Ohio; 2. John, a native of county Tyrone, Ireland, emigrated to America. and settled in Washington county, Penn., where he m. Margaret (or Mary) McElroy; removed to Harrison county, Ohio, about 1800, and settled in Stock township, where he d. 1836; had issue, among others: 1. John, b. 1814; d. 1877; m. 1839, Margaret Law, b. in county Tyrone, Ireland, 1820, daughter of John and Bessie Linn Law, who settled in Harrison county. 1830 (had issue: i. Mary-Ann, b. 1841; m. Joseph C. Patterson; ii. Martha, b. 1842. m. Robert Birney; iii. Margaret, b. 1844, m. Francis Welch; iv. Matthew-W., b. Aug. 20, 1846; settled in Washington township; served in the Civil War; m. Sept. 16, 1869, Rebecca Birney, daughter of John Birney of Tippecanoe, Ohio; v. James, b. 1850; vi. Henry, b. 1851; vii. William, twin brother to Henry, b. 1851; viii. Ella, b. 1857; ix. Homer, b. 1860; x. Frank-H., b. 1860; m. Dec. 7, 1883, Phœbe Taylor, b. 1865, daughter of Samuel Taylor, of Tuscarawas county (of English descent), who m. Melissa Laken, and removed to Stock township); 2. William, settled at Watertown, Erie county, Penn., before 1813; 3. Matthew, b. June, 1776; d. in Allegheny, Penn., 1874; emigrated to America, 1793, and settled at Cadiz; served in the Ohio Legislature; 4. James, d. at Pittsburg, June, 1815; emigrated to America, 1793, and settled at Cadiz; m. June 10, 1806, Sarah Tingley, b. in New Jersey, May 23, 1781; daughter of Jeremiah Tingley, who served in the Revolution, and about 1790 removed from South Amboy, N. J., to Winchester, Va., thence to Warren township, Jefferson county, Ohio, about 1801 (had issue: i. Matthew, b. at Cadiz, June 20, 1811; d. at Philadelphia, June 18, 1884, bishop in the Methodist Episcopal Church. m. Ellen H. Verner); 5. Mary, m. John Eagleson, and settled in Harrison county.

WILLIAM SKELLEY, a native of Ireland, emigrated to America and settled in the Ligonier Valley, Westmoreland county, Penn., about 1792; m. in Ireland, —— Ferguson; both died at the place of their first settlement; had issue: 1. John, settled in Green township, Harrison county; 2. William; 3. Robert, b. in Ireland, 1788; d. 1868; removed to Stark county, Ohio, in 1820, and thence to Green township, Harrison county, December, 1842; served in the War of 1812; m. in Pennsylvania (1st), 1816, Elizabeth Creighton; b. in Pennsylvania, about 1796; d. in Stark county, Ohio, 1838; daughter of Patrick and Elizabeth Creighton, who were both born in Ireland; m. (2d) 1845, Hannah Miller (had issue by first wife: i. Sarah; ii. Elizabeth; iii. John; iv. Elinor; v. Elizabeth; vi. Jane; vii. Robert; viii. William, b. in Stark county, Aug. 6, 1831; removed to Green township; served as an officer in the Civil War; m. in Hopedale, 1862, Mary Frances Moore, a native of Harrison county, daughter of James and Ellen

Moore; ix. James, settled at Milford, Kosciusko county, Indiana).

JOSEPH SKINNER, b. in France, June 14, 1766; emigrated to America and first settled near the Natural Bridge in Rockbridge county, Virginia; afterward removed to Morristown, Belmont county, Ohio, where he d. April 18, 1837; his wife was b. in Scotland, Dec. 21, 1770; d. Jan. 5, 1811; had issue: I. William. II. Philip. III. Madison. IV. John. V. Joseph. VI. Samuel, b. in Virginia, Jan. 26, 1794; d. in Moorefield township, Harrison county, June 2, 1860, where he had located in 1820; m. July 22, 1817, Catharine Clements, b. Aug. 14, 1796; d. April 3, 1885; daughter of Abraham Clements, of Guernsey county, Ohio; had issue: 1. Malinda-Martin, b. 1818; d. Sept. 5, 1864; 2. Carleton-Adolphus, b. in Moorefield township, Aug. 18, 1829; m. July 3, 1856, Lucy A. Thompson, b. Jan. 8, 1826, daughter of Robert and Elizabeth Hague Thompson, residents of Moorefield (the former of Scotch-Irish descent; the latter of English). VII. Charles. VIII. Nancy, m. ——— Hull. IX. Lucy, m. ——— Willis.

WILLIAM SLEMMONS, settled in Canton township, Washington county, Penn., about 1786, then well advanced in years, probably removing from Hamiltonban township, York (now Adams) county; died after 1800, leaving two sons, Thomas and William, of whom:
I. Thomas, b. 1748-49; d. April 9, 1826; m. Elizabeth ———, b. 1754-55; d. April 17, 1835; had issue: 1. Samuel; 2. William; 3. Thomas-B., m. Jane Vasbinder, daughter of William and Mary Buchanan Vasbinder, of West Middletown, Hopewell township, Washington county (who had removed from Carlisle, Penn.); 4. John, m. Margaret Vasbinder; 5. James; 6. Susanna; 7. Eliza; 8. Jane; 9. Margaret, m. John Vasbinder; 10. Mary.

II. William (probably the son of William and brother of Thomas above), b. 1761; d. Jan. 27, 1827; m. (1st) ———; m. (2d) Jane Osburn, b. 1775-76; d. July 4, 1851; had issue: 1. William-R. (?), b. 1780; d. Dec. 6, 1844; m. Nancy ——— (had issue: i. John-D., b. 1807; d. 1821; ii. Henrietta); 2. Margaret, b. 1783-84; d. Feb. 2, 1873; m. Jacob Vasbinder; 3. Joseph-J., b. 1786; d. Dec. 4, 1868; m. Susanna ———, b. 1801; d. Oct. 29, 1862; 4. Basil-Lee, m. S. ——— (had issue, among others: i. William, b. 1829; d. 1848; ii. Obediah); 5. Thomas; 6. Samuel, b. 1808-09; d. July 26, 1867; m. (1st) 1829, Susanna Osburn, b. 1810; d. Oct. 22, 1851; m. (2d) Eliza Hearn, b. Feb. 22, 1829; d. Feb. 25, 1879; daughter of Launcelot and Barbara Sutherland Urquhart Hearn; 7. Matthew-G., m. 1842, Ann ——— b. 1818-19; d. March 26, 1857 (had issue, among others: i. William, b. 1845; d. 1846); 8. Alexander; 9. Jane, m. ——— Amspoker; 10. Susanna, m. 1829, John Lyle; 11. Martha, b. Sept. 7, 1812; d. June 15, 1845; m. 1833, James Welsh, son of Samuel and Catherine Coulter Welsh, of Archer township.

MATTHEW M. SLOAN, see Family of William Grimes.

DANIEL SMITH, b. in Maryland, 1774; d. in Stock township, Harrison county, Ohio, July 14, 1856; removed to Huntingdon county, Penn., before 1803, and thence to Jefferson county in 1818, and to Stark township about 1821; m. Elizabeth Perrigo; had issue: I. William-P., b. in Huntingdon county, Sept. 20, 1803; d. May 15, 1890; m. Aug. 31, 1826, Margaret Parker, d. April 24, 1870, daughter of Richard Parker, an early settler in Stock township (had issue: i. James-P., b. June 23, 1827; m. (1st) Sept. 30, 1847, Anna Cramblet, d. June 21, 1876, daughter of John Cramblet, of Stock township; m. (2d) Oct. 18, 1877, Nancy C. Rogers, of Nottingham township; ii. Harriet, m. David Hines; iii. Lina, m. George W. Spiker; iv. Richard-P., b. July 20, 1832; m. Nov. 2, 1853, Mary Jane Miller, daughter of Samuel G. Miller; v. Daniel; vi. Margaret, m. John Miller; vii. David, d. in the army, 1861; viii. Hannah, m. Joseph E. Johnson; ix. Simeon, twin brother to Hannah, b. Jan. 2, 1841, m. Jan. 30, 1870, Rebecca Johnston. daughter of Samuel R. and Rebecca Barnhill Johnston).

JOHN SMITH, a native of Ireland; emigrated to America, and, about 1818, settled in Nottingham township, Harrison county, Ohio, where he died; his widow died in Deersville, aged ninety years; had issue: 1. Thomas, b. in Ireland, May 6, 1809; settled in North township; d. Feb. 23, 1881; m. 1838, in Ireland, Mary Hopkins, b. in Ireland, Aug. 27, 1813; d. in North township,

June 5, 1882, sister of Dr. Abram Hopkins, d. 1882, who settled in Canada (had issue: i. Joseph-J., settled in Cleveland, Ohio; ii. Robert-H., d. in Pittsburgh, Dec. 12, 1885; iii. Edward-A., d. 1861; iv. Theodore-W., b. March 17, 1846; settled in North township; m. Dec. 8, 1870, Malila English, a native of North township, daughter of James and Ann McCarroll English; v. Alice-J., d. in Leesville; vi. Sarah-E., m. M. Friesbaugh); 2. Robert; 3. William; 4. John; 5. Sarah, m. F. T. Simonton, of Deersville.

WILLIAM SMITH, see Family of William Ramage.

DAVID SMYLIE, a native of Ireland, emigrated to America and first settled in Washington county, Penn., before 1794; removed to Westmoreland county, Penn., and in 1815 located at Cadiz, Harrison county, Ohio, where he died Sept. 13, 1843; m. in Ireland, Sarah Jane Coon, d. 1843; had issue, among others: 1. William, b. in Washington county, Penn., 1794; settled in Archer township, Harrison county, 1825, where he remained until 1855, and then located in Washington county, Iowa, dying there February, 1858; m. 1820, Rachel Borland, d. March, 1875, daughter of James Borland, of Butler county, Penn. (had issue: i. David; ii. James; iii. Margaret; iv. John, b. Nov. 9, 1826; m. May 1, 1849, Julia A. Cox, daughter of George and Sarah Titus Cox; v. Samuel; vi. Robert; vii. Matthew; viii. Hugh; ix. Thomas; x. Sarah-Jane; xi. William; xii. Joseph; xiii. Rachel; xiv. David).

George Cox, father of Julia A. Smylie, was b. 1784; d. Sept. 12, 1849; son of Richard Cox, of Dutch descent, who came from New Jersey to Steubenville, Ohio, before 1800, and later settled in Archer township; m. 1808, Sarah Titus, b. 1786; d. 1877, daughter of Jonathan Titus and wife, who were natives of Wales, and settled near Cadiz, before 1812; had issue: 1. Mary; 2. Hiram; 3. Rachel, b. in Steubenville; 4. Jeremiah; 5. George; 6. Jonathan; 7. Sarah; 8. Obediah; 9. John; 10. Julia-A., m. John Smylie; 11. Martin.

GARRETT SNEDEKER, settled in Washington county, Penn., before 1789; removed to Harrison county, Ohio, about 1800; had issue:

I. John, b. in Washington county, 1789; settled in German township, 1816, where he died the same year; m. in German township, Elizabeth Cutshall, b. in Pennsylvania; d. Sept. 19, 1875; daughter of Nicholas Cutshall, who settled in German township, 1800; had issue: 1. Rebecca, m. Jacob Dunmire, and settled in Jasper county, Iowa; 2. Samuel, b. in Wayne township, Jefferson county, Feb. 9, 1812; settled in German township; m. Oct. 30, 1849, Mary J. Glasener, daughter of Garrett and Ann Maholm Glasener, natives of Pennsylvania, who settled at Cadiz, 1800; 3. Garrett, d. in infancy; 4. Elizabeth. II. Jacob. III. Elizabeth. IV. Mary.

MARTIN SNYDER, a native of Germany, b. 1728; d. Nov. 7, 1810; emigrated to America and first settled in Adams county, Penn., before 1775, where he married Catherine Amon, b. in Pennsylvania, 1759; d. Aug. 29, 1821; settled in Green township, Harrison county, Ohio, about 1802; had issue: I. Martin, b. in Adams county, Penn., 1775; d. in Green township, April 12, 1819; m. 1803, Ruth Tipton, b. near Baltimore, 1779; d. Feb. 5, 1850; daughter of Samuel and Nancy Tipton (the former, after the death of his wife, located in Jefferson county, Ohio, about 1802); had issue: 1. Catherine; 2. Martin, b. 1805; d. 1882; 3. Mary, b. in Green township, Sept. 7, 1808; m. July 13, 1837, Walter Jamison (his second wife), b. Feb. 24, 1801; d. July 1, 1883; son of John and Ann Craig Jamison, who settled in Cadiz township, about 1802 (had issue: i. Martin-S., settled in Cadiz; ii. Jane-A., m. George W. Glover; iii. Ruth-Ellen, d. in infancy; iv. William-Walter, b. 1849; d. 189—); 4. Amon; 5. Jacob, b. July 5, 1814; m. June 24, 1847, Elizabeth Bradford, daughter of Thomas Bradford, of Green township (had issue: i. Martin, b. March 7, 1848; m. (1st) Mary J. Carson, d. August, 1857; m. (2d) Nancy Jane McGuire; ii. Mary-Catherine, m. Leander Bigger, of Cadiz; iii. Sarah; iv. Caroline; v. Isabella, m. Finley Mattern); 6. Nancy; 7. Zachariah; 8. Samuel. II. Adam. III. Henry. IV. John. V. Catherine, b. in Ireland, 1794; d. Feb. 5. 1869; m. 1820, Dr. Moses Kennedy, b. Dec. 24, 1797; d. April 7, 1857; son of Michael and Margaret Thompson Kennedy, of the North of Ireland; had issue: 1. Margaret, b. 1821; d. 1871;

m. 1837, Allen G. Turner (had issue, among others: i. Moses-Kennedy, m. Eliza J. Craig, daughter of Johnson and Martha Thompson Craig; settled at Columbus, Neb.); 2. Elizabeth-Ann, b. 1822; d. young; 3. Michael-Butler, m. Lucinda Crossan; 4. Isabella, b. 1837; m. 1847, Ephraim Clark (see Family of Roger Clark); 5. Martin-Snyder, b. 1829; m. Martha McKee; 6. Caroline-M., b. 1832; 7. Martha-A., b. 1834; m. John McConnell; 8. Benjamin-F., b. 1836; m. Mary Jane Harrison. VI. Mary. VII. Eve. VIII. Elizabeth. IX. Magdalene, m. ------ Pumphrey.

CHRISTIAN SPIKER, of Dutch descent, emigrated from Pennsylvania, and settled in Stock township, before 1806; d. December, 1820; m. Diana ------; had issue:
I. Christian, or Christopher, b. in Stock township, Harrison county, Ohio, 1806; d. 1879; m. Aerie Carnes, b. 1804; d. March 1870; had issue: 1. William, b. 1826; settled at Deersville; m. 1845, Mary Cottrell, daughter of Adam Cottrell, a native of Scotland (d. 1842; his wife d. 1886) (had issue, among others: i. George-D., b. Dec. 26, 1846; settled at Scio, Harrison county; m. 1871, Elizabeth Gibson, daughter of Edward and Catherine Gibson (both of whom died in Harrison county); 2. George-W.; 3. Mary-J., m. Cornelius Vickers; 4. John-W., b. July 31, 1833; m. 1859, Nancy Crawford, daughter of Josiah Crawford, of Stock township; 5. Henry-C.; 6. Henry; 7. Elizabeth, m. David Christy; 8. Christiana, m. William Hines; 9. Catherine, m. Samuel Hines; 10. Sarah-Ann.
II. John.
III. Joseph.

THOMAS SPROULL, b. in Ireland, 1799, son of Robert Sproull; emigrated to America, and, about 1819, settled in Short Creek township, Harrison county, Ohio; removed in 1823 to Moorefield township, where he d. April 19, 1872; m. (1st) in Ireland, Mary Hastings; d. about 1822; m. (2d) Elizabeth Caldwell; had issue by first wife: 1. William, settled in Coshocton county, Ohio; had issue by second wife: 2. Andrew; 3. Robert; 4. John, b. Sept. 23, 1842; m. Amanda White, b. July 26, 1854, daughter of Joseph and Sarah Lee White, of Nottingham township; 5. Hugh; 6. Thomas.

RALPH SPURRIER, see Family of John Heberling.

JACOB STAHL, b. in Maryland, Aug. 13, 1784; d. 1845; settled in Rumley township, Harrison county, Ohio, in 1816; had issue: 1. William, b. in Charles county, Md., 1810; d. 1876; m. in Rumley township, Susanna Canaga, b. 1811; d. 1872 (had issue: i. Sarah, m. Abram Busby; ii. Maria, m. James Shambaugh; iii. Elizabeth, m. A. L. Ridenaur; iv. James, b. Oct. 6, 1845; m. Oct. 11, 1866, Sarah Jane Braden, b. Feb. 2, 1844, daughter of Gettys and Rachel Cox Braden); 2. Elizabeth, m. George Simmons; 3. John, b. in Frederick, Md., June 12, 1810; d. Aug. 27, 1881; m. March 18, 1832, Mary Ann Condo, b. in Penn., Feb. 28, 1813; d. Feb. 9, 1896; daughter of Jacob and Mary Ann Shuss Condo (had issue: i. Jacob, b. 1833; d. 1872; m. (1st) Catherine Knauf; m. (2d) Elizabeth Kimmel; ii. Margaret, b. July, 1835; m. Thomas Lucas; iii. Catherine, b. 1837; m. Arnold Wheeler; iv. Mary-Ann, b. 1839; m. David Hazlitt; v. Susan, b. 1841; d. young; vi. Samuel, b. 1846; d. in infancy; vii. Samantha-Jane, b. Jan. 20, 1854; m. Albert Houck); 4. Margaret, m. Peter Manbeck; 5. Catherine, m. Abraham Gotshall, and settled in Meigs county, Ohio; 6. Mary, m. Daniel Hilbert, and settled in Defiance county, Ohio; 7. Matilda, d. young; 8. Susanna, m. Abraham Kimmel; 9. James, m. Elizabeth Shuss; 10. Lydia, m. Jeremiah Condo.

Gettys Braden, d. April 13, 1851, in Crawford county, Ohio, father of Sarah Jane Braden Stahl, was a son of Thomas and Jane Braden, of Gettysburg, Penn., m. May 2, 1842, Rachel Cox, d. at Baxter Springs, Cherokee county, Kan., Feb. 7, 1883, daughter of George and Sarah Cox; had issue: 1. Sarah-Jane; 2. Rachel-Ann, b. 1846; d. 1867; 3. George-Thomas, settled at Caney, Kan.; 4. William-Wilson; settled at Conneaut, Ohio.

JAMES STEEL, a native of Virginia; had issue:
I. John.
II. Basil-E., b. in Berkeley county, West Va.; removed to Pennsylvania, and thence, about 1815, to Washington township, Harrison county, Ohio; d. 1857; m. in Pennsylvania, Rachel Spaulding, d. 1874; had issue: 1. John;

2. Sarah; 3. Mary; 4. Matilda-Jane; 5. Nancy; 6. Andrew; 7. Basil; 8. William; 9. Daniel; 10. David, b. Oct. 31, 1822; m. (1st) April 10, 1845, Elizabeth Vermillion, of Guernsey county, Ohio; d. Dec. 17, 1885; m. (2d) Feb. 11, 1890, Mrs. Comfort Lindsey, of Flushing (had issue by first wife: i. John-B.; ii. Andrew-J.; iii. Joseph-M.; iv. Franklin; v. William; vi. Henry; vii. Spaulding; viii. Amanda; ix. Matilda; x. Olive).

SILAS STEPHEN, settled in Short Creek township, Harrison county, Ohio, about 1808 or 1810; had issue among others: 1. Jonathan, b. June 5, 1799; d. 1880; m. Feb. 24, 1825, Elizabeth Salomons, b. Jan. 22, 1808 (had issue, among others: i. Zachariah, served in the Civil War, and died in that service; ii. Silas, b. Dec. 23, 1841; served in the Civil War; m. May 7, 1889, Sarah R. Barcroft, daughter of Joseph and Elizabeth Hunter Barcroft (the former b. in Jefferson county, 1814; d. in Hopedale, Nov. 6, 1886; the latter, a native of Westmoreland county, Penn., who came with her parents to Ohio in 1835).

ARCHIBALD STEWART, a native of Ireland; emigrated to Pennsylvania with his parents, and about 1816 removed to Harrison county, Ohio, settling near Cadiz, where he d. March 18, 1854; m. in Pennsylvania, 1805, Margaret Donaldson; d. Nov. 13, 1849; had issue: 1. James; 2. Samuel, b. June 25, 1809; settled in Washington township; m. June 2, 1840, Maria Auld, daughter of William and Mary McAdoo Auld (had issue: i. Mary, b. April 6, 1841; ii. Archibald, b. Jan. 10, 1843; iii. William-Alexander, b. Aug. 16, 1845; iv. Margaret, b. Sept. 10, 1847; v. James-M., b. Jan. 25, 1850; vi. Samuel-D.; vii. Thomas-M., b. Nov. 3, 1855); 3. Mary; 4. Isabelle; 5. Margaret.

Samuel Auld, grandfather of Maria Auld, was a native of Ireland; emigrated to Pennsylvania and thence removed to Nottingham township, Harrison county; had issue: 1. John; 2. Samuel; 3. Mary; 4. James; 5. William, 6. Eliza; 7. Diana; 8. Robert; 9. Stewart; 10. Grace; 11. William, d. Jan. 11, 1880; m. (1st) Mary McAdoo; d. 1820; m. (2d) Elizabeth Todd (had issue by first wife: i. Maria, m. Samuel Stewart; had issue by second wife: ii. James; iii. George-T.; iv. Alexander-T.).

JACOB STONER, b. near Hagerstown, Md., Dec. 25, 1815; son of Jacob and Mary Stoner, the former of whom died in Maryland in 1817; settled in Colerain township, Belmont county, Ohio, 1818, thence removed to Deersville, Harrison county, some years afterward, and later located in Monroe township; m. April 26, 1838, Honor Sneider, b. in Washington county, Penn., June 25, 1820, daughter of David and Christina Sneider, of Monroe township; had issue: 1. Mary-E., m. Urias B. Hite, and settled at Dennison, Ohio; 2. Sarah, m. Michael Lynch, and settled at Dennison, Ohio; 3. William, settled in Monroe township; served in the Civil War; 4. David, b. Sept. 23, 1845; served in the Civil War; m. (1st) March 14, 1867, Mary Fowler; d. March 31, 1874; daughter of John E. Fowler; m. (2d) Sept. 26, 1879, Susan Winrod, b. in Belmont county, Ohio; 5. Jacob-S., settled in Franklin township; 6. James-M., settled at Tippecanoe, Ohio; 7. Ella-C., m. James M. Evans, and settled at Auburn, Sangamon county, Ill.; 8. George-W., served in the Civil War; d. March 30, 1865, at Camp Chase.

JOHN STRINGER, b. in Chester county, Penn., 1776; removed to Jefferson county, Ohio, about 1800; settled near York, Ohio, 1811, where he d. July 10, 1845; his wife, whom he had married in Pennsylvania, d. May 12, 1850; had issue: 1. William, b. in Jefferson county, Aug. 19. 1803; d. Aug. 16, 1859; m. (1st) March 19, 1829, Jane Johnston; d. June 5, 1838; daughter of Richard Johnston, a resident of Harrison county, Ohio; m. (2d) 1839, Isabella Ferguson; d. Oct. 15, 1888, daughter of Henry Ferguson (had issue by first wife: i. Jane; ii. John-M., b. March 4, 1832; settled in Green township, where he d. May 4, 1889; m. Sept. 5. 1861, Susanna Buchanan, b. Oct. 9, 1841, daughter of John Buchanan, a pioneer in Harrison county; iii. Johnston; iv. Ann-E.; had issue by second wife: v. Henry; vi. Thomas-J.; vii. Joseph-E.; viii. Frederick-M.; ix. Sarah; x. Maria); 2. James; 3. John; 4. Sarah; 5. Elizabeth; 6. Mary; 7. Rebecca.

JAMES TAGGART, a native of Pennsylvania, m. Mary Ferguson; had issue:

I. John, b. in Washington county, Penn., 1778; d. June 4, 1843; removed to

Green township, Harrison county, Ohio, 1803, where he died; m. in Pennsylvania, Margaret Miller, b. March 12, 1779; d. Aug. 31, 1861; had issue: 1. James, b. July 22, 1806; d. Oct. 15, 1890; m. March 12, 1835, Anne Craig, d. Feb. 24, 1887, daughter of John Craig, an early settler in Ohio (had issue: i. Margaret, b. April 23, 1836; m. Dr. J. B. Crawford, and settled at Gillespie, Ill.; ii. John, b. May 28, 1839; d. Dec. 31, 1842; iii. Milton-J., b. July 19, 1842; served in the Civil War; m. Oct. 25, 1887, Anna Patten, of Sidney, Shelby county, Ohio, daughter of H. T. Patten; iv. Elizabeth-A., b. March 10, 1845; m. J. B. Mansfield, and settled in Jefferson county; v. James-A., b. Jan. 8, 1848; d. May 7, 1849; vi. Mary-R., b. May 27, 1850; vii. Luella-K., b. Oct. 26, 1856; m. W. H. Eagleson, and settled in Green township); 2. Margaret; 3. Mary; 4. John; 5. George; 6. Jane; 7. David; 8. Alexander. II. James. III. Samuel. IV. Robert. V. Jane. VI. Elizabeth.

ISAAC THOMAS, see account of Abraham Branson.

AARON THOMPSON, see account of Alexander Green.

DAVID THOMPSON, a native of county Tyrone, Ireland, b. 1772; d. 1868; son of Joseph Thompson, who emigrated to America and settled near Chambersburg, Penn., in 1792 (Joseph Thompson d. about 1819); David m. in Pennsylvania, Martha Gift, of German parentage, b. 1778; d. 1843; settled about one mile north of Cadiz, Harrison county, Ohio, in 1814; had issue: 1. Joseph; 2. Elizabeth, m. William McFadden, and settled in Iowa; 3. Mary, m. Joseph McFadden, and settled in Cadiz township; 4. David; 5. John, d. in Washington county, Iowa; 6. Katherine, m. John Sharp, of Holmes county, Ohio; 7. Martha, m. Adam Dunlap; 8. Rachel, m. S. Atkinson, and settled in Holmes county, Ohio; 9. James, b. March 3, 1818; m. 1848, Margaret Croskey, daughter of William and Mary Crabb Croskey, of Harrison county; removed to Cadiz, 1889 (had issue: i. Mary-Emma, d. aged sixteen years; ii. Martha-Elizabeth, m. A. W. McDonald, of Pittsburg, Penn.; iii. Anna-Caroline, m. William H. Arnold, of Cadiz; iv. David); 10. Sophia, m. John Hitchcock.

GABRIEL THOMPSON, b. in Harford county, Md.; d. at Jewett, Ohio, February, 1879; m. in Carroll county, 1830, Elizabeth Allen, d. in Carroll county, Aug. 26, 1866; daughter of Joseph and Sarah Allen, of Otsego county, N. Y.; had issue: 1. Gilbert, m. 1854, Elizabeth A. Carr; 2. H————-W., m. 1865, Catherine Kirby; 3. Lydia-A., m. 1848, Henry Pittenger; 4. Antoinette, m. 1848, Samuel Pittenger; 5. Bathsheba, m. 1860, Henry Mook; 6. Harvey-L., b. in Perry township, Carroll county, June 7,1842; settled in Archer township, Harrison county, 1878; m. Aug. 3, 1871, at New Rumley, Maria Shambaugh, b. Aug. 22, 1844; daughter of Michael (b. in Penn., 1811; d. 1863) and Hetta Hazlett (b. in Penn., 1816; d. 1884) Shambaugh; 7. Sarah-A., m. 1873, Josiah Long; 8. Joseph-W.,d. May,1882.

THOMAS THOMPSON, b. in Pennsylvania, 1780; d. Jan. 18, 1875; removed to Harrison county, Ohio, 1816 (his father, who was twice married—Eleanor Lindsey, of Scotch descent, having been his first wife—was a native of Ireland who had settled in Half Moon Valley, Centre county, Penn.); m. May 4, 1803, Catherine Weston, b. 1785; d. May 29, 1860, of German descent, daughter of Thomas Weston, whose family were pioneers in Pennsylvania; had issue: 1. Nancy; 2. John, b. in Half Moon Valley, Penn., Aug. 8, 1808; removed to Green township, Harrison county, about 1831, where he settled; m. (1st) Elizabeth Baker, d. 1851; m. (2d) Sept. 27, 1859, Hannah Lewis, daughter of Joseph Lewis (had issue by first wife: i. Thomas; ii. Margaret; iii. John-B.; iv. Mary; v. Rezin; vi. Joseph-M.; vii. Sarah-C.; viii. Nancy-E.; ix. Elijah); 3. Sarah; 4. Thomas; 5. Mary; 6. Catherine; 7. Elijah; 8. Eleanor; 9. Joseph; 10. Rachel-Jane.

WILLIAM THOMPSON, of Scotch-Irish descent, a native of Franklin county, Penn.; removed from Chambersburg to Westmoreland county, Penn., about 1780, where he died; served in the Revolutionary War; had issue, among others: I. Samuel, b. Nov. 6, 1781; d. June 6, 1866; settled in Harrison county, 1813; m. in Pennsylvania, 1810, Elizabeth Stewart, b. Dec. 14, 1785; d. Aug. 29, 1873; daughter of John Stewart, of Scotch descent, who had settled in Butler county, Penn.; had issue: 1. Samuel, b. Sept. 18, 1822; m. Sept. 18, 1851, Sarah Jane Moorhead, daughter of Judge Moorhead, of Archer township; settled in Green township; 2. Jane, m. H. Stewart Black; settled in Green township; 3. Eliza, m. —— Gray, and settled in Delaware county, Ohio; 4. Ellen, m. —— Moorhead, and settled in Delaware county, Ohio; 5. Martha, b. Dec. 26, 1810; d. July 16, 1890; m. 1834, Johnson Craig, b. Dec. 3, 1803; d. July 14, 1888; 6. Maria, b. Jan. 13, 1813; d. Aug. 25, 1875; m. Jonathan Gray, b. 1807, d. July 14, 1873; 7. Isabel, m. —— Rea; 8. Margaret, b. July 11, 1820; m. Samuel Cochran.

CHARLES TIMMONS, b. 1751; d. 1820; removed from Martinsburg, West Va., to Cadiz, Ohio, about 1812; m., probably in West Virginia, Mary Magdalene Forney, b. 1775; d. 1850; daughter of Abraham (1740-1824) and Susanna (1752-1842) Forney, all of German descent; had issue: 1. Abraham, b. Aug. 11, 1794; m. Martha Dent; 2. Eli, b. Aug. 18, 1796; 3. William, b. June 15, 1798; 4. Charles, b. Sept. 28, 1800; d. 1801; 5. Catherine, b. Oct. 27, 1802; 6. Frederick, b. July 15, 1805; m. Eliza Lacey; 7. Emanuel, b. May 9, 1808; 8. Benjamin, b. at Martinsburg, Nov. 17, 1810; d. June 3, 1898; m. at Mount Pleasant, Ohio, 1854, Mary Ann Meek, daughter of Joseph (1798-1833) and Rachel Cuppy (1784-1843) Meek; 9. Samuel, b. 1813; 10. Forney, b. March 3, 1817; d. 1886; m. at Cadiz, 1839, Elizabeth Stinson Lacey, b. June 8, 1818; d. 1898; daughter of —— and Mary Clifton Lacey (had issue: i. Caroline, b. 1840; m. 1864, Charles N. Allen; ii. Milton-J., b. 1841; served in the Civil War; m. Josephine B. McLean; settled at Peabody, Kan.; iii. Benjamin-F., b. 1844; served in the Civil War; m. Frances Jones; settled at Peabody, Kan.; iv. Robert-Lacey, b. January, 1850; m. 1879, Isabel Amanda Howard, daughter of John M. and Elizabeth Edna Howard, of Barnesville, Ohio).

WILLIAM TINGLEY, b. in New Jersey, 1787; d. at Cadiz, Ohio, 1863; removed to West Virginia, and thence, about 1806, to Cadiz; m. Rachel Paulson, b. in Maryland, 1789; d. 1876; daughter of James and Rachel Durbin Paulson, of Harrison county (the former d. 1816); had issue: 1. Amanda, b. 1816; d. 1888; m. 1836, Sylvanus Wood, b. 1805; d. 1845; son of James and Elizabeth Steel Wood, from Washington county, N. Y. (had issue: i. Elizabeth, m. Andrew Henderson Carnahan; ii. Tingley-Sylvanus, m. Leonora Chestnut, and settled at Leadville, Colo.); 2. Joseph, b. 1822; 3. Jeremiah, b. 1826; 4. Temperance, b. 1830. William Tingley's father (Jeremiah Tingley) and grandfather (Joseph Tingley), both natives of New Jersey, both served in the Revolutionary War.

AQUILA TIPTON, removed from Jefferson county, and settled in Stock township, Harrison county, about 1800, where he died October, 1826; had issue, among others: 1. Aquila, b. June 1, 1800; d. May 30, 1875; m. Nancy Waller, b. in Maryland, Dec. 26, 1802; d. May 4, 1871; daughter of George Waller, a native of Maryland (had issue: i. Benjamin, b. Jan. 5, 1823; ii. Mary-J., b. Aug. 22, 1824; settled in Missouri; iii. Sarah-A., b. Aug. 24, 1826; iv. Ruth, b. Jan. 15, 1829; m. —— Hines; settled in Uhrichsville, Ohio; v. Rachel, b. Aug. 10, 1830, m. —— Abrams, and settled in Oregon; vi. Charlotte-H., b. Aug. 4, 1832; vii. Jared, b. Sept. 4, 1834; viii. Ephraim, b. May 4, 1836; ix. Aquila, b. May 24, 1838; settled in Nottingham township; m. April 28, 1861, Maria Scott, b. July 25, 1840, daughter of Charles and Margaret Dodds Scott [the former a native of Jefferson county, Ohio; the latter a native of Ireland]; x. Martha, b. 1840; xi. Nancy, b. Aug. 31, 1841; xii. George-W., b. Sept. 7, 1844; settled in Archer township; xiii. Thomas-B., b. Sept. 15, 1856; settled in Illinois); 2. Rebecca, m. —— Waller; 3. Charity, m. —— Gugan; 4. Nancy; 5. Keziah; 6. Ketura, m. —— Cox; 7. William; 8. Shadrach; 9. Samuel; 10. John.

DAVID TOWNSEND, d. near Harrisville, 1874, where he had settled in 1812, having removed from Bucks county, Penn., with his father, Joseph Townsend (d. about 1815); m. in Ohio, Catherine Cherry, d. 1872; had issue, among others: I. Joseph, b. June 2, 1818; m. 1842, Albina Strodes, a native of Harrisville, d. 1874; had issue: 1. David-C., b. March 13, 1846; m. 1870, Adeline Morris.

ROBERT TRIMBLE, see Family of John Law.

JOHN TRUSHEL, b. 1802; d. 1884; son of Solomon Trushel, an old settler in Harrison county, Ohio; m. Frances Little, b. 1796; d. 1876; had issue: 1. Solomon; 2. Eli, settled in Tuscarawas county, Ohio; 3. Peter, settled in North township; 4. David, settled in Carroll county; 5. William; 6. Valentine, b. Oct. 17, 1846; settled in North township; m. 1875, Rebecca Stearns, daughter of William and Susan Stearns, of Carroll county, Ohio; 7. Abraham; 8. Joshua; 9. Mahala; 10. Elizabeth, m. James Morgan, of Carroll county; 11. Susanne; 12. Mary, m. Thomas Rea, of Monroe township; 13. Sarah.

ROBERT VINCENT, d. 1841; emigrated from the North of Ireland, and about 1801, settled in Green township, Harrison county, Ohio; had issue, among others: 1. Thomas-C., m. 1820, Jane Macurdy, daughter of John Macurdy (had issue: i. Agnes-T., m. John Beall—see Beall Family; ii. Jane-C., m. James Deary; iii. Thomas-M., m. Laura Lancaster; iv. Albert; v. Mary, m. Thomas Craig; vi. Sarah; vii. Oliver); 2. Jane, m. William Chambers.

THOMAS VINCENT, a physician, b. 1754; d. Aug. 31, 1841; settled in Green township before 1827; m. Jane ———, b. 1783; d. Oct. 11, 1858; had issue: 1. Joseph; 2. Thomas-W.; 3. Robert; 4. James; 5. Amanda; 6. Sarah; 7. Martha, m. 1827, Thomas Milligan; 8. Jane, m. 1834, Isaac Holmes.

JACOB VOORHEES, a native of New Jersey, b. 1767; d. July 4, 1876; son of Jacob Voorhees (of German descent, the family having first settled in America about 1670); removed to Wellsburg, Va., thence to Jefferson county, Ohio, with his father, before 1803; settled in North township, Harrison county, Ohio, 1833, where he died; m. in Fayette county, Penn., Elizabeth Gaskell, b. 1795; d. Jan. 16, 1876; daughter of Budd and Hannah G. Gaskell (the former served in the Revolutionary War, and d. in Crawford county, Penn.); had issue: 1. Samuel-Sickles; 2. Andrew-Linn; 3. Charles-F., settled at Millersburg, Ohio; 4. John-Alexander, b. Oct. 20, 1823, in Jefferson county; settled in North township; m. 1864, Ann Doyle, b. in Ireland, 1842; d. July 2, 1890; daughter of Patrick and Honora Hickey Doyle (the latter d. in Ireland, 1848; the former settled in America, 1853); 5. Crawford-B., settled at Scio; 6. Louise, m. Benjamin Simms, and settled in Missouri; 7. George-W., b. 1830; d. in Coshocton county, Ohio, Nov. 11, 1890; 8. Jacob-Ogden, settled at Uhrichsville; 9. Richard-Marion, settled in Coshocton, Ohio.

WILLIAM WADDINGTON, see Family of John Harrison.

JOSEPH WALKER, b. in county Derry, Ireland, 1757; emigrated to America and settled in New York City, 1813; a short time later removed to Greensburg, Penn., and in 1822 to near Laceysville, Stock township, Harrison county, Ohio, where he d. 1842; m. in Ireland, Constancia Stewart, b. 1755; d. 1846; had issue: 1. John; 2. James; 3. George; 4. William, b. in Ireland, 1806; settled in Stark township, where he d. April 27, 1886; m. June 10, 1834, Jane McKinney, b. in Washington county, Penn., July 14, 1802; d. July 5, 1878; daughter of George and Mary McKinney (had issue: i. Joseph, b. June 24, 1836; m. Feb. 12, 1863, Agnes Gibson, b. Jan. 4, 1843, daughter of James B. and Lillian Maxwell Gibson, natives of Pennsylvania; ii. Mary, m. ——— Anderson, and settled in Auglaize county, Ohio); 5. Mary; 6. Elizabeth.

JOHN WALLACE, a native of York county, Penn., b. 1760; d. May 1, 1832; removed to Washington county, Penn., about 1804, and a year later to Putney township, Belmont county, Ohio; settled in Moorefield township, Harrison county, 1822; m. Margaret Anderson, b. in York county, Penn., 1767; d. March 25, 1848; had issue: 1. William, d. 1842; m. Mary W. ——— (had issue: i. John; ii. Nathaniel-S.; iii. William-A.; iv. Samuel-M.; v. Wilson-E.; vi. Sarah-Ann; vii. Eleanor-S.; viii. Margaret-J.); 2. Allen, b. in York county, Penn., April 15, 1793; settled in Moorefield township, where he d. Feb. 21, 1880; m. in Belmont county, Mary Brown (had issue: i. John; ii. Andrew; iii. William; iv. Mary; v. James; vi. Elijah-R., b. March 16, 1828; m. Jan. 23, 1868, Elizabeth Brokaw, b. March 25, 1842, daughter of Abraham and Mary Guthrie Brokaw, natives of Ohio); vii. Anderson, settled at Wooster, Ohio; viii. Samuel, settled at Wooster, Ohio); 3. Nancy; 4. Jane.

THOMAS WALLACE, of Scotch-Irish descent; resided in York county, Penn., about 1775; had issue, among others: I. John, b. in York county, Penn., May 8, 1774; removed to Warren township, Jefferson county, Ohio, 1796, where he remained until 1804, thence located in Green township, Harrison county, Ohio, where he d. June 4, 1863; m. in York county, Oct. 6, 1795, Elizabeth McCleary, b: Sept. 23, 1776; d. Feb. 19, 1855; daughter of Abel McCleary, a resident of York county; had issue: 1. William, b. Oct. 3, 1796; 2. Isaac, b. Oct. 9, 1798; 3. Thomas, b. Sept. 20, 1800; 4. Robert, b. Oct. 26, 1802; 5. Rebecca, b. June 6, 1804; 6. Margaret, b. July 16, 1806; 7. John, b. May 5, 1809; 8. Nathaniel-Anderson, b. July 16, 1811; d. Dec. 28, 1892; m. (1st) March 4, 1834, Jane Watson; d. Feb. 18, 1868, daughter of Robert Watson, of Athens township, Harrison county; m. (2d) Sept. 2, 1869, Sarah Goodrich; d. Oct. 9, 1873, daughter of George Goodrich, formerly a resident of Carroll county, Ohio; m. (3d) June 24, 1875, Elizabeth Marsh, daughter of Oliver Marsh, a resident of Pennsylvania; 9. Abraham, b. Aug. 24, 1813; 10. Elizabeth, b. March 22, 1821.

JOSHUA P. WATSON, of Scotch-Welsh descent, b. near West Liberty, West Va., March 21, 1802; son of Aaron and Nancy Watson, who settled in West Virginia about 1800; removed, about 1831, to New Athens, Harrison county, Ohio; settled in Harrisville, Harrison county, 1835, where he d. July 27, 1882; m. (1st) in West Virginia, 1823, Martha Humes, b. May 29, 1804; d. Feb. 27, 1836; m. (2d) Sarah M. McMillan, a native of Harrisville, d. Aug. 8, 1844; m. (3d) Louise M. Rimby, had issue by first wife: 1. Samuel-H., settled at Vinton, Iowa; 2. Martha-Ann, m. ——— Collins, and settled at Vacaville, Cal.; 3. Louis-W., b. March 2, 1827; d. May 25, 1861; m. March 16, 1848, Julia Carver, b. Nov. 14, 1830, daughter of Thomas and Tomson Gray Carver, the former b. in Bucks county, Penn., 1788; d. Oct. 13, 1855, having come there from Downingtown, Penn., 1815; the latter b. 1797; d. Feb. 4, 1843; daughter of Thomas Gray, who settled in Harrisville, 1803 (had issue: i. William, b. June 29, 1848; d. in infancy; ii. Albert, b. July 30, 1849; d. in infancy; iii. Thomas-Wesley, b. Sept. 21, 1850; settled in Harrisville; m. Nov. 22, 1876, Nancy J. King, b. Aug. 28, 1848, daughter of Charles Edward and Hannah Mary Hanna King, of Mount Pleasant, Ohio (the former b. near Baltimore, Md., 1808; d. March 27, 1857; the latter a native of Loudoun county, Virginia, b. Sept. 17, 1815; d. Jan. 8, 1872); iv. Florence, b. July 11, 1853; d. Oct. 10, 1873; v. Mary-Narcissa, b. March 25, 1856; m. Aug. 30, 1875, J. W. Adams, and settled in Short Creek township); 4. ———; 5. ———; 6. ———; 7. ———; 8. ———; 9. ———; had issue by second wife: 10. James-M., settled at Vinton, Iowa; 11. ———; 12. ———; had issue by third wife: 13. ———, m. Dr. R. D. Wilkin; settled in Atlantic, Iowa; 14. Charles-N.; 15. George-W.; 16. Frank, settled at Chicago; 17. Harvey, settled at Chicago.

WILLIAM WATSON, emigrated from Scotland and settled at Baltimore; removed to Pennsylvania about 1790; had issue: I. Robert, b. in Scotland or in Baltimore, March 3, 1786; removed to Athens township, Harrison county, Ohio, 1831, where he d. Nov. 19, 1872; m. in Washington county, Penn., Oct. 25, 1810, Rachel Wilson, d. May 18, 1866, daughter of Robert Wilson; had issue: 1. James, b. March 2, 1812; d. Aug. 15, 1815; 2. John-W., b. in Washington county, Feb. 7, 1814; d. July 22, 1859; m. (1st) Julia Barricklow; m. (2d) March 16, 1848, Rebecca Dunlap, daughter of John Dunlap, of Athens township (had issue by first wife: i. Rachel; had issue by second wife: ii. Robert, b. May 7, 1849; d. Aug. 28, 1849; iii. Adam-D., b. March 24, 1850; iv. Nancy-A., b. March 28, 1853); 3. Jane, b. May 1. 1815; d. Feb. 9, 1868, m. N. Anderson Wallace; 4. Alexander, b. July 3, 1817; d. Nov. 7, 1817; 5. Rachel, b. Jan. 30, 1819; d. March 30, 1839; m. John Barricklow; 6. Smith-R., b. Oct. 12, 1821; d. April 30, 1877; served as a member of the Ohio Legislature, 1864; m. Dec. 9, 1847, Susan J. McDowell, daughter of Samuel McDowell, of Athens township; 7. Nancy-G., b. Jan. 30, 1823; m. Joshua Dunlap.

WILLIAM WATTERS, a native of Maryland, of Scotch descent, settled in Harrison county, Ohio, before 1813, where he died; had issue, among others: 1. Nathan, b. in Harrison county, 1813; d. April 29, 1887; m. Catherine Foutz, b. in North township, Harrison county, 1813; d. April 28, 1874; daughter of Michael Foutz, a pioneer of Harrison county (had issue: i. John; ii. Elizabeth; iii. Jonathan; iv. Elijah; v. William, b. Sept. 12, 1848; settled in North township; m. March 23, 1882, Mrs. Sarah A. Clemens, widow of Jephtha Clemens (who d. in Youngstown, Ohio), daughter of George W. and Sophia Simmonds, of Monroe township; vi. Isaiah, settled in Tuscarawas county, Ohio).

JACOB WEBB, a native of Maryland, b. 1773; removed to Brownsville, Penn., before 1800, where he m. Hannah Kirk, b. 1775; d. 1858; daughter of Adam Kirk, a native of Pennsylvania; settled in Athens township, Harrison county, Ohio, 1809, where he d. 1833; had issue: 1. Sarah; 2. Esther, m. Joseph Huff, and settled in Athens township; 3. Edith, m. John Major, and settled in Athens township; 4. Hannah, m. Cyrus Holt; 5. John, b. Feb. 5, 1806; settled in Athens township; m. Nov. 11, 1830, Martha Holmes, b. in Short Creek township, Jan. 8, 1811, daughter of Col. Joseph Holmes (had issue: i. Joseph, b. 1833; ii. Jacob, b. Nov. 8, 1833; m. 1860, Sarah Dickerson, daughter of John Dickerson, of Athens township; settled in Athens township); 6. Mary, m. Robert Eanos, and settled near Columbus, Ohio; 7. Jacob, d. in western Illinois; 8. Ann, m. John Perrego, and settled in Athens township; 9. Ezekiel, m. Mary Corbin (had issue: i. John, settled in Athens township; ii. Rebecca, m. Joseph Figley, and settled in Indiana); 10. Joseph; 11. Robert, settled in Illinois; 12. Phœbe, d. aged seven years.

JOHN WEBSTER, removed from Maryland to Rumley township, Harrison county, Ohio, before 1824; d. before 1824; m. Mary ———, b. April 30, 1775; d. March 1, 1848; had issue, six children, of whom: I. John, b. March 20, 1811; d. Oct. 28, 1876; m. (1st) 1832, Margaret Buchanan, d. 1841, a resident of Rumley township; m. (2d) 1847, Ann Patton, daughter of Joseph Patton, of Rumley township; had issue by first wife: 1. Maria; 2. David, b. Oct. 3, 1836; settled in Archer township; m. (1st) 1870, Susanna Devore, d. Feb. 20, 1875; m. (2d) April 15, 1884, Rosella Work, daughter of Alexander Work, of German township; 3. Sarah; had issue by second wife: 4. John; 5. Joseph; 6. Mary-M.; 7. Catherine-Jane; 8. Matthew; 9. Florence; 10. Robert; 11. Mansfield; 12. Cora; 13. Ira-B.

JOHN WELLING, d. about 1821; m. Mima ———; had issue: 1. William, m. Dorcas ———, b. Aug. 15, 1778; d. April 24, 1848; 2. John; 3. David, b. Feb. 1, 1779; d. June 19, 1864; settled in Athens township before 1817; m. (1st) Margaret ———; m. (2d) Nancy Elizabeth Black, of Guernsey county, b. 1823; d. Feb. 18, 1873 (had issue by first wife, six children; had issue by second wife: vii. Margaret-Jane, m. Finley Butler; viii. William-W.; ix. Nancy-Jane; x. Martha-A., m. Joseph White; xi. George-W., b. June 15, 1855; xii. Harriet-C.; xiii. John); 4. Thomas; 5. Henry; 6. Nancy; 7. Mary; 8. Elizabeth. Other Welling families in Harrison county, are those of the following, most or all of them probably descended from John and Mima:

John Welling, m. 1821, Mary McCullough.

John Welling, b. 1814; d. 1887; m. Jane McFadden.

David Welling, m. 1834, Jane Sharp, b. 1812; d. 1844.

William Welling, m. 1830, Margaret Davis.

DANIEL WELCH, a native of Ireland, of Scottish descent; emigrated to America and probably first settled at Carlisle, in Cumberland county (as the name, Daniel Welch, appears on the Carlisle tax-list from 1767 until after 1776); had issue, among others:

I. Daniel, b. 1763; d. Sept. 7, 1819; settled in Cecil township, Washington county, Penn., as early as 1786 (probably accompanied by his father, for the names of two Daniel Welches appear on the tax-lists of that township for 1787 and 1788); m. Elizabeth Waits, b. 1770; d. March 29, 1844; daughter of John (d. before 1786) and Sarah (d. 1818) Waits; removed to Harrison county, Ohio, about 1801, and settled at Beech Spring, on the head waters of Short Creek, in Green township; established here a horse-mill, probably the first in Harrison county; organized Beech Spring Church; had issue: 1. John, served in Captain John Allen Scroggs' company of Colonel John Andrews' regiment of Ohio Militia in the

War of 1812; died in that service, unmarried; 2. Daniel, b. 1790; d. Aug. 9, 1868; m. (1st) Margaret Bayless, b. 1796; d. Sept. 9, 1833; m. (2d) 1834, Mary Gray, b. 1806; d. Feb. 5. 1848 (had issue, among others, by first wife: i. Elizabeth, d. aged fifteen years; had issue by second wife, among others: ii. E.-Gray, b. 1842; d. Nov. 30, 1877); 3. Rezin, b. in Cecil township, Washington county, Penn., April 27, 1795; d. at Cadiz, Nov. 24, 1881; where he had settled in 1833; m. (1st) at Steubenville, 1818, Eliza Bayless, b. 1801; d. Aug. 6, 1842; daughter of Elias and Margaret Barclay Bayless, natives of Maryland; m. (2d) 1846, Maria Bayless, b. Sept. 12, 1807; d. Aug. 19, 1886; sister to his Eliza Bayless (had issue by first wife: i. Maria-B., b. 1822; d. Aug. 10, 1891; m. Walter Butler Beebe, of Cadiz; ii. Rachel-Anne, m. William R. Allison, and settled at Steubenville; iii. Caroline, m. Thomas C. Rowles, and settled at Topeka, Kan.; iv. David-Barclay, b. at Smithfield, Ohio, Nov. 23, 1830; m. 1857, Martha Collins Lyons. daughter of Robert and Ann Bowland Lyons. of Cadiz; v. Eliza, m. H. Parks MacAdam, and settled at New York Mills, N. Y.); 4. Benjamin; 5. Pressley; 6. William, m. 1835, Adaline Phillips, daughter of Thomas and Elizabeth Williams Phillips, of Cadiz; removed to Mount Pleasant, Iowa, where he died, and his widow removed thence to Osceola, Neb. (had issue, eight children, four of whom died in infancy, of the others: i. William; ii. Thomas; iii. Daniel-P., b. 1839; d. May 6, 1864; served in the Civil War, and died in that service; iv. John-Ross, m. Anna Sherwood; settled near Osceola, Neb.); 7. Jacob, m. Charlotte Pumphrey; 8. Cyrus; 9. Samuel, m. Martha Moore, b. 1815; d. April 13, 1836; 10. Mary, m. 1829, Dr. Jacob Voorhes; 11. Rhoda, m. 1828, John Mansfield.

Elizabeth Waits Welch, wife of Daniel Welch, was the daughter of John Waits, whose name appears on the taxlist of Springhill township. Fayette (then Bedford. and later, Westmoreland) county, Penn., in 1772, the first year after the organization of Bedford county, and in 1783; he settled in Cecil township, Washington county, on the head waters of Chartiers Creek in the spring of 1785: and died before April 5, 1786, at which date his land was patented to his widow, "in trust, for the use of his heirs;" he m. Mrs. Sarah Blair, d. 1818, a widow (who had three grown sons by her first husband living in Cecil township in 1788—Joseph, Samuel, and William—who later removed to Kentucky); had issue: 1. Elizabeth, m. Daniel Welch, and removed to Ohio; 2. Richard; 3. Reuben; 4. Mary, m. ——— Phillips; 5. Sarah; 6. Jacob.

JOHN WELSH, b. in Ireland, 1782-83; d. Dec. 30, 1871; removed to Westmoreland county, Penn., about 1797, and thence to Archer township, Harrison county, Ohio, before 1822, where he remained until 1860, and then settled in Stock township; m. Jane McClellan, b. in Pennsylvania, 1793; d. Feb. 17, 1872; had issue: 1. Mary; 2. Elizabeth; 3. Ann; 4. Samuel; 5. John-K.; 6. Jane; 7. Matthew; 8. James-M., b. Oct. 11, 1832; settled in Stock township; 9. David; 10. William-A., b. April 5, 1835; settled in Washington township; m. April 7, 1859, Margaret McFadden, daughter of Robert McFadden.

SAMUEL WELSH (or Welch), b. in Ireland, 1772; d. March 30, 1850; emigrated to America and settled in Westmoreland county, Penn.; removed before 1814 to Archer township, Harrison county, Ohio; m. (1st) Catherine Coulter, d. 1842; m. (2d) 1846, Mrs. William Keepers, of Stock township; had issue by first wife: 1. John, b. Nov. 20, 1808; settled at Cadiz; d. Nov. 10, 1881; m. 1833, Margaret Gilmore (had issue: i. Samuel, settled in Missouri; ii. Jason, settled in Iowa; iii. Sarah-Jane, m. John Adams, and settled in Archer township; iv. Amanda, m. Samuel F. Ross, a Methodist Episcopal minister, and settled at New Philadelphia); 2. James, b. July 9, 1815; settled at Deersville; m. (1st) March 28, 1833, Martha Slemmons, b. Sept. 7, 1812; d. June 15, 1845, daughter of William and Jane Osburn Slemmons; m. (2d) Nov. 17, 1860, Mrs. Louisa Cope, b. June 18, 1826. daughter of Barrett and Nancy Carson Rogers (had issue by first wife: i. Catherine, settled in Nottingham township; ii. Samuel-S., settled in Franklin township; iii. William-C., settled in Kansas; iv. Martha-J., m. ——— Johnson; settled in Nottingham township; v. John-M., a physician, b. Dec. 19, 1842;

settled in Deersville; m. Aug. 28, 1862, Martha Moore, b. in Nottingham township, Oct. 12, 1841, daughter of Samuel and Margaret Given Moore, natives of Ireland; vi. James-Cameron; had issue by second wife: vii. Flora-J., m. ——— Wagers, of Deersville; viii. Emmet-A., a physician; ix. Bingham, d. in infancy); 3. William, b. in Archer township, Sept. 18, 1818; m. (1st) Oct. 22, 1840, Agnes Fisher, b. 1820; d. Feb. 14, 1845; daughter of George Fisher, of Rumley township; m. (2d) Sept. 18, 1845, Emily Jane Nixon, of Archer township; d. Feb. 28, 1887 (had issue by first wife: i. Susan, m. William Sampson, and settled in Stock township; had issue by second wife: ii. James-W., b. July 1, 1847; m. May 25, 1869, Kate M. Conaway, daughter of Aaron Conaway; iii. Rebecca-Jane, m. A. J. Palmer and settled in Stock township; iv. John-N., settled in North township; v. A.-C., a Methodist Episcopal minister; settled in Youngstown, Ohio); 4. Mary, b. 1811; d. Dec. 15, 1844; m. 1833, George Fisher, b. 1792; d. 1872 (had issue, among others: i. Elizabeth; ii. Samuel, d. in infancy; iii. Jacob, d. in infancy); 5. Eleanor, m. 1839, Joseph Dunbar; 6. Nancy, m. 1840, Matthew Johnson.

Francis Gilmore, father of Margaret Welsh, was a native of Ireland; emigrated to America and settled in Archer township, Harrison county, Ohio, before 1815; m. Sarah McBride, a native of Ireland; d. March 30, 1840; had issue, eight children, of whom: 1. William; 2. Margaret, m. John Welsh; 3. John, settled in Oskaloosa, Iowa; 4. Thomas, settled in Iowa; 5. Samuel, settled in Iowa.

JAMES WEST, b. in Kirkcaldy, Fifeshire, Scotland, June 11, 1791; d. in Fox township, Carroll county, Ohio, 1851, where he had located in 1828; son of John West; emigrated to America, and first settled in Maryland, 1815; removed to Wood county, West Virginia, in 1817, and thence, in 1825, to Summit county, Ohio, whence he came to Carroll county; m. in Wood county, W. Va., 1825, Isabella Douglass, b. Sept. 15, 1802, in Akeld, Northumberland, England, daughter of John and Susan Howey Douglass, natives of Scotland (the latter a daughter of Andrew and Margaret Mitchison Howey; and the former a son of Anna Davidson Douglas); had issue: 1. Susanna, m. Robert Philpot, of Humboldt, Neb.; 2. John-Douglass, a physician, b. in Carroll county, Ohio; settled at Hopedale, Green township, Harrison county, Nov., 1866; m. (1st) 1853, Martha Jane Merrick, b. June 9, 1832; d. April 12, 1884; daughter of Israel J. Merrick, a native of Maryland (b. 1802; d. 1881), and Sarah Arbuckle (b. 1812); m. (2d) November, 1886, Mrs. Josephine M. Mansfield, widow of Thomas Mansfield, and daughter of Isaac Holmes, an early settler in Green township; 3. Katherine, m. John Hunter, of Delroy, Carroll county; 4. Margaret-Ann, m. John Bebout, of Mechanicstown; 5. Isabella, m. William A. Frater, of Douglas county, Oregon; 6. James-D., settled at East Liverpool, Ohio; 7. Mary-Elizabeth, m. (1st) John Smalley; m. (2d) William Kerr; settled near New Lisbon, Ohio; 8. ———, d. in infancy; 9. ———, d. in infancy.

JONATHAN WEST, a native of Pennsylvania, of Scotch-Irish descent, settled in Cadiz township, Harrison county, Ohio, 1811; m. Comfort Arnold, daughter of Benjamin and Comfort Arnold, of Fayette county, Pennsylvania; had issue: 1. Amos, b. in Pennsylvania; settled in Franklin township, Harrison county; m. 1832, Margaret Baker, daughter of Otto Baker, of Archer township (had issue: i. Mary; ii. Samuel; iii. Wilson-S.; b. Aug. 7, 1842; m. 1868, Susannah Renshaw; iv. Sarah; v. Naomi, m. John Renshaw) 2. Rezin, b. April 19, 1812; m. Dec. 10, 1835, Nancy Arthurs, daughter of Gavin Arthurs, of Harrison county (had issue: i. Jonathan; ii. Comfort; iii. Rachel; iv. Amos, m. Melissa Copeland; v. Japheth, m. (1st) Lucinda Yant, of Tuscarawas county, Ohio; d. Sept. 21, 1883; m. (2d) Martha J. Baker; vi. Sarah-E.; vii. William-G., m. April 15, 1881, Rebecca Wright, daughter of Sylvanus Wright; viii. James-M., m. Elizabeth Rinehart, of Franklin township; ix. Esther); 3. Samuel; 4. Jonathan; 5. Mary; 6. Esther; 7. Actia; 8. James; 9. Elizabeth; 10. Comfort; 11. Sarah.

Gavin Arthurs, father of Nancy Arthurs West, was a native of Ireland; settled in Harrison county, where he d. Feb. 1, 1876; m. Rachel Hall, of Maryland; d. 1845; had issue: 1. Robert; 2. William; 3. James; 4. Eliza; 5. Mary-

J.; 6. Amelia; 7. Nancy, m. Rezin West; 8. Sarah; 9. Louisa.

JOHN WEYANDT, of German descent, removed probably from Pennsylvania or Maryland to Monroe township, Harrison county, before 1817; d. 1848; m. Motlena ———; had issue: 1. Daniel; 2. Jacob; 3. Abraham, b. 1821; d. 1899; m. (1st) Roxanna Warner; m. (2d) Margaret Gamble (had issue: i. Amadilla, m. E. M. Long; ii. Eleanor, m. M. Rohan; iii. Martha-Ann, m. William B. Penn; iv. Webster, m. Ruth Myers; v. Olive, m. L. D. Price; vi. Melinda, m. Oscar Price); 4. Mary, m. 1837, Henry B. Heller; 5. Christina, m. ——— Warner.

JOHN WHAN, b. in Chester county, Penn., Sept. 25, 1776; removed to Harrison county, Ohio, 1815; m. Aug. 21, 1804, Margaret Boggs, b. Nov. 17, 1779; had issue: 1. William, b. July 7, 1805; d. March 18, 1833; 2. Sarah, b. Jan. 7, 1807; d. in New Athens, Dec. 9, 1875; m. George McCullough, b. 1803; d. April 3, 1845 (had issue: i. Margaret, m. S. K. Kane, of Darlington, Penn.; d. in Mississippi; ii. Martha, m. James Stewart; d. in Pittsburg, Penn.; iii. John, b. 1834; d. 1855; iv. Robert, settled in Milwaukee, Wis.; v. William, b. 1840; settled in New Athens); 3. Hannah, b. Oct. 16, 1808; 4. Mary, b. Dec. 1, 1810; d. Aug. 6, 1851; 5. Ellen, b. May 13, 1813; m. Michael Morgan, and settled in Short Creek township; 6. James, b. Jan. 9, 1816; d. Sept. 19, 1856; 7. John, b. May 10, 1821; d. July 19, 1849.

EZRA WHARTON, removed from Bucks county, Penn., to Harrison county, Ohio, about 1820, and settled in Short Creek township; had issue, among others: I. Joel, settled in Washington township, before 1833, where he d. 1863; m. about 1822, Abigail Bundy, d. 1874; had issue: 1. Martha; 2. Bethia; 3. Josiah; 4. Rachel; 5. Tabitha-A.; 6. Matilda; 7. Ezra, b. June 21, 1833; m. Feb. 22, 1859, Martha Myers, of Franklin township, daughter of Samuel and Mary Connell Myers (had issue: i. Olive, m. William Laizure; ii. Samuel-M.; iii. David-B.; iv. Oscar-E.; v. Arthur-B.); 8. Abigail; 9. Susannah. II. Anna. III. Hannah. IV. Daniel. V. Lynton. VI. Amos. VII. James. VIII. Silas. IX. Levi.

Michael Myers, a native of Pennsylvania, grandfather of Martha Myers Wharton, settled near Tippecanoe, Harrison county, Ohio, before 1830; m. in Pennsylvania, Martha Huffman; had issue: 1. George; 2. John; 3. Michael; 4. Samuel; 5. Philip; 6. David; 7. Berlin; 8. Eliza; 9. Catherine; 10. Rachel; 11. James. Samuel Myers was b. 1802; d. in Franklin township, June 3, 1879; m. 1830, Mary Connell (had issue: i. Jemima; ii. David; iii. Martha, m. Ezra Wharton; iv. Jonathan; v. Wesley; vi. George; vii. Catherine; viii. Sarah-J.; ix. Amanda; x. Sansom; xi. Mary-J.; xii. Samuel-S.; xiii. John).

JOSEPH WHITE, of Scotch descent; settled in Frederick county, Md., before 1775, where he d. about 1818; served in the Revolutionary War; m. Mary Fulton, of Scotch-Irish descent; b. 1756-1766; d. in Franklin township, Harrison county, Ohio, Feb. 20, 1856; had issue: 1. Catherine; 2. William; 3. Joseph, b. in Frederick, Md., Sept. 12, 1798; removed with his mother to Harrison county in 1819, and first located in Nottingham township; later settled in Franklin township, where he d. Sept. 29, 1877; m. April 12, 1828, Hannah Rogers, d. May 17, 1866, daughter of Joseph and Pamela Rogers, early settlers in Harrison county, who came from Maryland (had issue: i. Jackson-R.; ii. William-P.; iii. Pamela [or Pamalah]; iv. Joseph-T.; v. Benjamin-F.; vi. Warren-R.; vii. Mary-Ann; viii. Joshua-P., b. Nov. 15, 1840; served in the Civil War [as did also three of his brothers]; m. Sept. 29. 1870, Agnes C. Glandon, daughter of William and Mary Glandon, early pioneers in Harrison county; ix. Charles-W.; x. Hannah-E.); 4. Charles.

WILLIAM WILEY, b. in Washington county, Penn., 1776; d. in Short Creek township, Harrison county, Ohio, 1853, where he had settled about 1804; son of Thomas and Rebecca Lytle Wiley, natives of Lancaster county, Penn.; m. in Pennsylvania, 1804, Elizabeth Vance; had issue: 1. Joseph; 2. Thomas. m. Mary Tendeley; 3. Anna, m. Hugh Martin; 4. John; 5. David, m. Laura J. Stanley; 6. James, m. Harriet Wight; 7. William, b. in Short Creek township; m. Nov. 3, 1864, Olive M. Stanley, daughter of Noah Stanley (b. in Trumbull county, Ohio, where he d. 1873), and Sarah Bowman Stanley (b. in Columbiana county, Ohio); 8. Rebecca;

9. Mary-Jane, m. N. W. Shannon; 10. Elizabeth; 11. Clarissa, m. Joseph Jamison; 12. Wilson, m. Eliza McGowan; 13. Priscilla.

ROBERT WILKIN, settled in Pennsylvania, 1770; removed to near the present site of Cadiz, Harrison county, Ohio, about 1802, and a few years later settled at Londonderry, Guernsey county; m. in Pennsylvania, Mary Hyde; had issue: I. Elizabeth. II. Nancy. III. Jane. IV. Rebecca. V. Mary. VI. Samuel. VII. Thomas. IX. Archibald, b. in Pennsylvania; settled in Washington township, Harrison county, before 1818, where he d. 1870; m. Hannah Davidson, d. 1856, daughter of Samuel Davidson, of Washington township; had issue: 1. Samuel, b. in Washington township, May 23, 1818; m. (1st) April 18, 1843, Margaret Foraker, of Guernsey county; d. Oct. 22, 1864; m. (2d) Aug. 6, 1866, Jeanette McCormick, of Guernsey county (had issue by first wife: i. Ellis; ii. Mary-Ann; iii. Archibald; iv. Hannah; v. Samuel; vi. Margaret-S.); 2. Mary-Ann; 3. Jane; 4. Angelina. X. William. XI. James. XII. Robert.

CHARLES WILLISON, settled in Moorefield township, Harrison county, Ohio, before 1818; had issue: 1. Amos; 2. Jeremiah, b. in Moorefield township, where he d. 1850; m. 1847, Rebecca Figley (had issue: i. Rachel-A.; ii. JohnM., b. July 3, 1850; m. Jan. 8, 1879, Julia McCullough, daughter of William and Julia Laizure McCullough); 3. Elijah; 4. Abijah; 5. Charles; 6. Rosilla; 7. Annie; 8. Rusha; 9. Rachel.

JOHN WILSON, a native of Washington county, Penn.; removed to Short Creek township, Harrison county, Ohio, 1806; and in May, 1834, settled in Rumley township; m. in Pennsylvania, Esther Fisher; had issue: 1. WilliamH., b. Sept. 22, 1803; d. in Rumley township, August, 1887; m. Margaret A. McComb, d. March, 1884 (had issue: i. Eliza-J., m. C. N. Coulter, and settled in Michigan; ii. John-A.; iii. Hadassah, m. James V. Thompson, and settled in Richland county, Ohio; iv. R.-M.; v. W.-L., b. Oct. 29, 1841; m. August, 1880, M. A. Mehaffey, of near Mount Hope, Washington county, Penn.; vi. MaryE.; vii. James-R., settled at Arkansas City, Ark.; viii. David-Mc.; ix. T.-H., m. S. G. Phillips, and settled at Arkansas City, Ark.); 2. James; 3. Hugh; 4. John; 5. Samuel; 6. David; 7. Esther; 8. Margaret; 9. Elizabeth, d. in infancy.

GEORGE WORK, a native of Ireland; emigrated to America, and, before 1800, settled in Hopewell township, Washington county, Penn., where he d. 1830; m. in Ireland, Martha Dunlap; had issue, among others: 1. Alexander, b. in Ireland, 1781; settled in Pennsylvania with his parents; removed to German township, Harrison county, Ohio, 1818, where he d. May, 1851; m. in Pennsylvania, April 10, 1809, Jane Taggart, a native of Washington county; d. April, 1851 (had issue: i. George; ii. James; iii. John; iv. Mary-K., m. John Hervey Black; v. Samuel; vi. Anderson-D.; vii. Jane; viii. Margaret; ix. Alexander).

THOMAS WORLEY, b. in Pennsylvania; removed to Harrison county, and settled in Athens township, about 1802, where he d. May, 1859; m. Mary Walker, daughter of Gabriel Walker; had issue: 1. Thomas; 2. Daniel b. 1792; d. 1887; m. 1849, Mary Goodwin, b. 1827; d. daughter of Jesse and Anne Michner Goodwin, of Short Creek township (had issue: i. William, m. Eliza Morrison; ii. Jesse, m. Ella Skouten; iii. Emory, m. Mary Morrison; iv. Martha, m. Samuel Parks; v. Emma; vi. John-Brough, m. Auta Groves; vii. Alice, m. Edwin Aukerman; viii. Lafayette, m. Ella McManus); 3. David, m. 1836, Mary Jane Luke; 4. James, b. May, 1782; d. April 7, 1857; m. Susanna ———, b. 1766; d. Feb. 4, 1839; 5. Susanna, m. 1822, Samuel Martin; 6. Julianna, m. 1827, Smith Bonham; 7. Margaret, m. 1840, Ichabod Ross 8. Elizabeth, m. ——— Yarnell; 9. Mary (?), m. Jacob Figley.

Other Worley families of Harrison county:

Wesley J. Worley, m. 1823, Jane Virtue, b. Jan. 13, 1804; d. March 18, 1857.

Daniel Worley, m. 1834, Sarah Peregoy.

Josiah Worley, m. 1836, Mary Ann Minor.

Michael Worley, m. 1828, Eve Ann Markley.

Mary Goodwin Worley (b. 1827) is the daughter of Jesse Goodwin, b. in Pennsylvania, Oct. 11, 1784; d. in Harrison county, Ohio, Oct. 2, 1856; m. (1st) Anne Michner, b. 1789; d. Feb. 27, 1843; m. (2d) Ruth McMillan; had issue by first wife: 1. Lydia, b. 1810; 2. Hannah, b. 1812; 3. Lewis, b. 1813; 4. Wilson, b. 1816; 5. Elisha, b. 1818; 6. Tace, b. 1820; 7. Alice, b. 1821; 8. Anne, b. 1824; 9. Kinsey, b. 1826; 10. Mary, b. Nov. 27, 1827; m. Daniel Worley; 11. Abi, b. May 22, 1829; m. Jackson Shields; 12. Martha, b. 1830; 13. Jesse, b. 1834.

Anne Michner Goodwin was the daughter of Baruch and Jane Wilson Michner, who were married in Pennsylvania, and removed to Harrison county; had issue: 1. Anne; 2. John; 3. Hannah; 4. Sarah; 5. Alice; 6. Jane.

MATTHEW WORSTELL, b. in Bucks county, Penn.; a descendant of James Worstell, who emigrated before 1700; removed to Philadelphia, before 1804, and in 1805 settled near Steubenville, Ohio; m. Rachel Price; had issue: 1. Ceneath; 2. Hiram, b. in Philadelphia, Sept. 7, 1804; settled in Franklin township, Harrison county, Ohio, where he d. in January, 1884; m. near Steubenville, Ann Pittis, d. 1873, daughter of John Pittis, of Deersville (had issue: i. John; ii. Mary; iii. Thomas; iv. Robert; v. Edward; vi. Elizabeth; vii. Jane; viii. William; ix. Julia; x. Henry-P., b. in Tuscarawas county, May 18, 1836; settled in Franklin township; m. Jan. 5, 1860, Eleanor Scott, daughter of Charles Scott, of Harrison county); 3. Martha; 4. Smith; 5. Matthew; 6. Sarah; 7. John; 8. Rachel; 9. William; 10. James.

LOT WORTMAN, b. in New Jersey, about 1779; d. 1839; probably a descendant of John Wortman, who emigrated from Holland to America in 1750, and settled in Bedminster township, Somerset county, N. J.; m. in Westmoreland county, Penn., Margaret Metzlar, d. 1860; removed to Muskingum county, Ohio, about 1808; had issue, twelve children, of whom: 1. Jesse-David, b. in Muskingum county, 1824; d. Dec. 28, 1898; m. 1860, Jane P. Jamison, daughter of Barkley and Margaret Jamison; 2. Jonathan-Washington, settled in Zanesville; 3. John, settled in Kansas.

AARON YARNALL, son of Thomas Yarnall, b. in Washington county, Penn., about 1783; settled in Nottingham township, Harrison county, Ohio, 1811, where he died 1851; m. Mary A. Bell, of Washington county; d. 1857; had issue: 1. Ziba; 2. William; 3. Aaron; 4. Eli; 5. Colver; 6. John, b. Feb. 27, 1827; m. (1st) April 24, 1850, "Nackkey" Rogers, d. 1861; m. (2d) 1863, Mrs. Elizabeth Ross, b. June 28, 1833, widow of Thomas Ross, and daughter of Alexander and Sarah Ramsey Fulton, of Nottingham township (had issue by first wife: i. Henry-H., settled in Tuscarawas county, Ohio; ii. Sylvester-F., settled at Oberlin, Kan.; iii. Jasper; had issue by second wife: iv. Mary-R.; v. Ida-B.); 7. Nelson; 8. Lydia; 9. Mary-A.

MICHAEL YOST, a native of Virginia, b. Nov. 3, 1766; d. Feb. 2, 1849, of German descent, as was also his wife; the fathers of both having served in the Revolutionary War; removed to Short Creek township, Harrison county, Ohio, 1806; m. Rachel Keckley, b. in Virginia, 1780; d. Feb. 19, 1849; had issue, among others: 1. Elias, b. near Winchester, Frederick county, Va., Dec. 2, 1805; settled in Short Creek township; m. (1st) Dec. 30, 1834, Kezia Kithcart, b. in Pennsylvania, April 25, 1812; d. 1878; daughter of Joseph Kithcart (d. in Pennsylvania; his wife settled in Harrison county, 1824); m. (2d) March 7, 1880, Ann Macklin, b. in county Armagh, Ireland, Dec. 2, 1842, daughter of Samuel and Ann Benson Macklin (both of whom died in Scotland, the former in 1847; the latter in 1858) (had issue by first wife, eleven children).

SUPPLEMENT.

ADDITIONAL HARRISON COUNTY MARRIAGES.

SUPPLEMENT.

ADDITIONAL HARRISON COUNTY MARRIAGES.*

1841 to 1850, Inclusive.

Edward Abraman and Rachel Tipton, Oct. 31, 1850, by Rev. A. Magee.
William Abraham and Maria Arnold, Oct. 7, 1841, by R. Brown.
George Adams and Mary Carothers, April 4, 1848, by Rev. Pardon Cook.
Henry Adams and Sarah Arbaugh, Dec. 2, 1841, by Rev. Benjamin Pope.
James Adams and Rachel Hines, Sept. 15, 1844, by Isaac Talbott, J. P.
James Adams and Nancy McKinney, Jan. 19, 1847, by John Blair, J. P.
John Q. Adams and Chilnissa D. Carrell, March 2, 1847, by Rev. D. S. Welling.
Nathan Adams and Hannah Black, Dec. 31, 1850, by Andrew Lynch, J. P.
Perceival Adams and Mary Jane Downs, March 23, 1845, by John Blair, J. P.
Samuel Adams and Sarah Chambers, May 12, 1842, by Thomas Phillips, J. P.
David Addleman and Susanna Firebaugh, Jan. 24, 1850, by Rev. Eli Slutes.
John Addleman and Charity Jones, Dec. 14, 1843, by David Bower, J. P.
John W. Adron and Nancy Jane Swallow, June 28, 1849, by B. Herron.
Alexander Ager and Susan Bishop, Dec. 26, 1850, by L. B. Lukins.
Elisha Aimes and Agnes Gibson, Oct. 26, 1848, by Rev. D. S. Welling.
Joseph Akin and Elizabeth Baxter, April 10, 1849, by James Kerr, V. D. M.
Jesse Alexander and Jane Forsythe, March 18, 1845, by Rev. James Love.
John Alexander and Esther Alexander, April 8, 1841, by Rev. Thomas Hanna.
John Alexander and Nancy Andrews, Feb. 1, 1848, by Rev. John Marshall.
Aaron Allen and Sarah A. Stephenson, May 27, 1846, by C. C. Riggs.
Isaac Allen and Sarah Barrett, June 24, 1841, by Elijah Carson, J. P.
Isaac Allen and Sarah Ann Lemmon, May 12, 1846, by Rev. J. J. Covert.
William R. Allison and Rachel Ann Welch, Dec. 29, 1842, by James Kerr, V. D. M.
Charles N. Amspoker and Jane Slemmons, April 9, 1846, by Rev. James Cameron.
Andrew Anderson and Mary Patton, March 29, 1849, by Rev. C. C. Riggs.
Elijah Anderson and Mary E. Sparkman, June 16, 1850, by Thomas Phillips, J. P.
James Anderson and Ann P. Johnson, April 30, 1848, by Michael Carrol, J. P.
John S. Anderson and Esther Ann Davis, July 3, 1840, by Wesley Smith.
Richard Anderson and Susan Tedrow, Dec. 10, 1846, by Rev. Thomas Hanna.
Robert Anderson and Esther McCollough, July 1, 1841, by John Rea, V. D. M.
Samuel Anderson and Martha A. Bryant, Dec. 10, 1845, by Rev. Ebenezer Hays.
David Andrews and Ruth McFadden, Oct. 23, 1849, by James Kerr, V. D. M.

* The spelling of the original records has been preserved in most cases.

Thomas Andrews and Nancy Caves, Sept. 12, 1850, by T. R. Crawford, V. D. M.
James Angus and Nancy Stewart, Jan. 13, 1848, by R. K. Price, J. P.
William G. Angus and Margaret A. McConnell, Sept. 15, 1850, by John Knox, J. P.
Samuel Ankrum and Jane Leard, Sept. 17, 1846, by Rev. John Hattery.
John Antibush and Rachel Carpenter, Sept. 25, 1844, by E. H. Custer, J. P.
Adam Arbaugh and Elizabeth Sawvill, Dec. 30, 1841, by Rev. Benjamin Pope.
John Arbaugh and Martha Vasbinder, April 20, 1843, by E. H. Custer, J. P.
William Arbaugh and Dianna Gutshall, Feb. 26, 1846, by Amos Bartholomew.
James Armstrong and Julia Ann Lewis, April 13, 1843, by Thomas Phillips, J. P.
Josiah Armstrong and Rebecca Scott, March 1, 1849, by Joseph Chambers.
John Arneel and Elizabeth Johnson, Nov. 28, 1850, by McKnight Williamson.
John Arnold and Hannah Foos, May 30, 1844, by E. H. Custer, J. P.
John Arnold and Mary Quillan, Aug. 29, 1850, by John Wilkins, J. P.
James Arters and Catharine Septer, March 31, 1844, by Samuel Skinner, J. P.
Andrew M. Atkinson and Eleanor Cusick, April 22, 1847, by Samuel Mahaffy, V. D. M.
Benjamin F. Atkinson and Eliza Ann Bostwick, Aug. 4, 1846, by James Kerr, V. D. M.
George Atkinson and Matilda Simeral, April 29, 1844, by John Rea, V. D. M.
John Atkinson and Eliza Thompson, Dec. 15, 1842, by George Clancy, V. D. M.
Levi Atkinson and Harriett Busby, June 29, 1848, by Rev. Thomas Hanna.
Levi Atkinson and Penelope Heavilin, Jan. 1, 1860, by Aaron Conaway, J. P.
Robert Atkinson and Phœbe Pittinger, March 31, 1845, by Rev. E. Hays.
Samuel Atkinson and Rachel Thompson, Nov. 25, 1847, by James Kerr, V. D. M.
George T. Auld and Martha Ann Maxwell, Sept. 25, 1847, by Rev. Thomas Hanna.
James M. Auld and Caroline Fitzgerald, March 12, 1846, by Rev. Samuel W. Day.
John Avers and Margaret Carothers, Dec. 14, 1843, by Rev. Jacob Lemmon.
William Boals and Margaret C. Donaghey, March 21, 1844, by Rev. Robert Cook.
John Bacher and Phœbe J. Blazer, Nov. 7, 1844, by Rev. J. Nickols.
Michael Backley and Ara Johnson, March 28, 1843, by John Hastings.
John Bair and Lucinda Bethel, April 18, 1850, by Rev. Jacob Lemmon.
Daniel Baird and Margaret France, March 22, 1841, by John R. Dunlap.
James H. Baker and Susanna Barta, June 2, 1842, by Rev. John Moffitt.
James Harvey Baker and Margaret W. Caves, Oct. 12, 1842, by Samuel Skinner.
Otho Baker and Drusilla Birney, June 17, 1841, by Andrew Lynch, J. P.
Otho Baker and Catharine Shanks, Nov. 20, 1845, by John Graham, J. P.
Sheridan Baker and Charlotte Ross, Dec. 17, 1850, by Rev. John Moffitt.
Sylvester Baker and Mary Jane Swallow, July 27, 1848, by Rev. James C. Merryman.
William Baker and Trissa Ann Conner, March 9, 1841, by Samuel Skinner, J. P.
William Baker and Elizabeth Burkhead, July 1, 1850, by James Taggart, J. P.
David Bannister and Mary Jane Dorsey, Feb. 17, 1842, by Rev. Harvey Bradshaw.
David Bannister and Martha Dorsey, Jan. 11, 1844, by Rev. Jacob Lemmon.
James Banister and Nancy Robinson, July 20, 1843, by Rev. Jacob Lemmon.
David Barcus and Eleanor Reddick, Nov. 5, 1845, by N. Linder.
Henry Barger and Lydia Yarnal, July 13, 1841, by James Kerr, V. D. M.
Henry Barger and Mary Ann Cobb, March 11, 1844, by Wesley Smith.
Isaac Bargar and Nancy Baxter, Nov. 8, 1849, by Hugh Parks, V. D. M.
Jacob Barger and Rebecca Jane Miller, May 18, 1844, by John Blair, J. P.
Jacob Barger and Martha Keckler, June 12, 1847, by Elijah Carson, J. P.
Jacob Barger and Abigail Campbell, Dec. 3, 1849, by Elijah Carson, J. P.
Jacob Barger and Catherine Minteer, July 9, 1850, by John Blair, J. P.
John Barger and Elizabeth Beall, May 27, 1841, by Richard Brown.
Samuel Barger and Mary Cusic, Oct. 31, 1844, by James Kerr, J. P.
James Barkhurst and Mary Jane White, Dec. 4, 1844, by Rev. Thomas Cullin.
William Barlow and Catharine E. Smith, Oct. 19, 1850, by Jonas Holloway, J. P.

ADDITIONAL HARRISON COUNTY MARRIAGES

Christopher Barnhouse and Drusilla Wagner, June 27, 1841, by Andrew Lynch, J. P.
Peter Barnhouse and Lydia Wise, Jan. 16, 1845, by Andrew Lynch, J. P.
Samson Barnhouse and Ann Susanna Catharine Able, Jan. 8, 1843, by Andrew Lynch, J. P.
Robert Barns and Lucy Ann Ladd, Feb. 20, 1849, by Thomas Phillips, J. P.
Thomas Barr and Rebecca Patton, April 12, 1848, by William Wishart.
Albert G. Barrett and Mary Ann McKeever, Aug. 2, 1843, by Edwin H. New.
Hiram Barrett and Esther Barr, Aug. 17, 1842, by Rev. Thomas Hanna.
John W. Barrett and Sarah Landy, Nov. 14, 1844, by Rev. Harvey Bradshaw.
Thomas Barrett and Almeda Wilson, Jan. 25, 1846, by Samuel Ramsey, J. P.
Thomas Barrett and Rebecca Annash, April 22, 1850, by Samuel Ramsey, J. P.
Thomas B. Barrett and Rebecca Conwell, Dec. 18, 1845, by Rev. Ebenezer Hays.
Uriah Barrett and Nancy Beall, Sept. 19, 1850, by Rev. D. Neel.
Joseph Barricklow and Phœbe Bartow, Oct. 22, 1847, by B. W. Viers, J. P.
Philip Bartlett and Deborah Birney, June 24, 1841, by Rev. Jacob Lemmon
Beall, see also Bell.
Abriam Beall and Maria Feaster, Feb. 13, 1845, by William Tipton.
Colmore Beall and Hannah Rogers, Jan. 24, 1850, by Rev. A. McGee.
Elias Beall and Martha Jane Cray, June 8, 1848, by T. T. Larkin, J. P.
James Beall and Sarah Jamison, March 16, 1848, by Rev. Alexander Wilson.
James P. Beall and Mary Ann Keckler, Dec. 28, 1848, by R. K. Price, J. P.
John Beall and Agnes Vincent, March 7, 1844, by James Kerr, V. D. M.
Zeneas Beall and Eliza Ann Pugh, Aug. 19, 1841, by R. Brown.
Harvey Bean and Elizabeth Mitchell, April 1, 1847, by Rev. John Hoover.
Reuben Bear and Mary Jane Dougherty, Dec. 16, 1847, by Rev. James Hoover.
James Beatty and Lucinda Graham, June 28, 1849, by Rev. D. Sparks.
Robert Beatty and Mary Ann Gilmore, March 29, 1842, by Rev. Alexander Wilson.
Samuel Beatty and Eliza Jane Gibson, Feb. 14, 1850, by James Kerr, V. D. M.
William Beatty and Charlotte Law, May 23, 1844, by Rev. Dyas Neil.
Arvine P. Beck and Phebe W. Covington, Jan. 28, 1849, by Rev. E. Tipton.
William A. Beck and Sarah Ann Spencer, Sept. 5, 1844, by Rev. Ebenezer Hays.
Frederick L. Beckler and Margaret Miser, June 8, 1843, by John R. Dunlap.
Walter B. Beebe and Maria B. Welch, May 4, 1841, by James Kerr, V. D. M.
Bell, see also Beall.
Colmore Bell and Martha Millener, Oct. 3, 1848, by Rev. Jacob Lemmon.
Edmund E. Bell and Sarah Palen, Dec. 9, 1845, by G. A. Lowman.
Emanuel Bell and Margaret Chaney, Jan. 8, 1847, by Rev. William W. Simpkins.
Elias Benedict and Barbara H. Gutshall, May 28, 1844, by Andrew Lynch, J. P.
Levi Benedick and Mary Roberts, April 25, 1841, by Andrew Lynch, J. P.
Rezin J. Bennett and Martha M. Maholm, May 21, 1844, by James Kerr, V. D. M.
William Bernard and Jane Williams, June 7, 1849, by Rev. John Burns.
Edward Berry and Margaret E. Klingman, July 4, 1850, by Rev. John Moffitt.
Alexander Best and Sarah Jane Poole, April 4, 1849, by Rev. John Burns.
James Best and Alice McDonald, Nov. 19, 1850, by William Buchanan, J. P.
James Bethel and Eleanor Matthews, Dec. 15, 1842, by Rev. Jacob Lemmon.
James Betz and Rebecca M. Tweed, Nov. 7, 1850, by Rev. John Knox.
McCartney Betz and Sarah Jane Jamison, April 16, 1849, by Rev. William Loumes.
Elijah Billingsly and Prudence Strong, Dec. 30, 1841, by William Deveny.
Samuel K. Billingsley and Rebecca F. Knight, April 2, 1843, by Rev. Harvey Bradshaw.
Hiram Bingham and Levina Lamb, Oct. 9, 1845, by N. Linden.
Thomas M. Bingham and Rachel Sheets, Jan. 28, 1844, by James Welsh, J. P.
John Binger and Mary Markley, Sept. 30, 1841, by C. H. Cuter, J. P.
Israel Birkshire and Mariah Kendricks, Dec. 3, 1846, by Rev. A. Magee.
Ebenezer Birney and Elizabeth A. Larkin, Feb. 10, 1846, by G. A. Lowman.
Joseph Birney and Susanna Mummy, March 11, 1847, by Rev. Jacob Lemmon.
Hiram H. Bishop and Mary Ann Gutshall, Jan. 31, 1842, by Samuel Lewis.

Oliver Bishop and Sarah A. Cortright, April 9, 1846, by Rev. Thomas McGaw.
Andrew M. Black and Elizabeth Lee, Jan. 1, 1845, by Rev. Thomas Hanna.
Samuel Blackford and Elizabeth Campbell, Dec. 12, 1844, by Rev. John Walker.
Samuel Blackford and Mahala Sisler, Feb. 9, 1848, by B. W. Viers, J. P.
Michael Blackman and Julian McGrew, Jan. 9, 1841, by Rev. John Mercer.
Isaac H. Blackwell and Margaret Shultz, Feb. 17, 1848, by John Hitchcock, J. P.
James R. Blackwell and Emeline Red, Feb. 4, 1844, by M. F. Burkhead, J. P.
David Bleckenstaffer and Mary Ann Able, June 11, 1843, by Andrew Lynch, J. P.
John Q. A. Bliss and Jane Weaver, Nov. 18, 1847, by Rev. William B. Hunt.
Zebulon H. Bliss and Mary A. Marshall, April 27, 1845, by Isaac Talbott, J. P.
Ralph L. Bliss and Mary Ewin, June 6, 1846.
David Boals and Sarah Lyon, Nov. 19, 1842, by William Cable, J. P.
William Boals and Margaret C. Donaghey, March 21, 1844, by Rev. Robert Cook.
William Boals and Sarah Johnson, Oct. 8, 1846, by John Rea, V. D. M.
William Bond and Elizabeth Williams, Feb. 25, 1846, by James Kerr, V. D. M.
Banks Booher and Sarah Dudgeon, Aug. 19, 1848, by James Skinner, J. P.
Zacharias P. Boone and Marinda Medley, Sept. 7, 1846, by Samuel Skinner, J. P.
Adam Booth and Rachel Matson, May 14, 1843, by George Clancey, V. D. M.
Isaac Booth and Hester Ann Field, March 25, 1841, by Rev. E. Smith.
Washington Borland and Magdalene Esterday, April 27, 1848, by Rev. A. N. Bartholomew.
Samuel Bosley and Sarah Ann Stevens, Dec. 31, 1849, by William Reed, J. P.
Solomon Bower and Susan Lawrence, July 5, 1843, by David Bower, J. P.
Jeremiah Bowers and Lydia Boreland, Feb. 4, 1847, by Rev. Abraham Bartholomew.
Thomas Bowers and Sarah Bell, Nov. 3, 1849, by Rev. A. N. Bartholomew.
Jeremiah Bowman and Nancy Wyckoff, April 11, 1843, by Rev. Jacob Lemmon.
David Boyd and Chilla Conner, Oct. 21, 1841, by Rev. Israel Archbold.
George N. Bodyston and Rebecca Calahan, Oct. 24, 1847, by Rev. Jas. C. Merryman.
Thomas N. Boyer and Harriett N. Davidson, May 20, 1845, by Rev. Jacob Lemmon.
James G. Braden and Rachel Cox, May 3, 1842, by W. D. McCartney, V. D. M.
Robert Braden and Malinda K. Boyd, Oct. 11, 1850, by Samuel McArthur, V. D. M.
Samuel Braden and Mary Merrell, Feb. 8, 1848, by R. Brown.
Thomas W. Bradley and Eliza Jane Bayles, Sept. 6, 1843, by Wesley Smith.
John Branchfield and Mary Rizzle, May 10, 1843, by John L. Layport.
Elijah Brannon and Sarah Hill, May 10, 1847, by Michael Toland, J. P.
Reuben Brenaman and Mary A. Dickerson, Oct. 21, 1846, by James Kerr, V. D. M.
David Bricker and Elizabeth Busby, Oct. 14, 1845, by James Kerr, V. D. M.
Simon Bricker and Rhoda Heavlin, May 23, 1844, by James Kerr, V. D. M.
Charles Bridgman and Mary Harding, Oct. 21, 1847, by Rev. Asbury W. Simpkins.
Thomas Bridgman and Margaret Hardin, Feb. 13, 1845, by Rev. Jacob Brill.
Stapleton C. D. Brock and Catharine Dony, July 21, 1841, by Matthew Phillips, J. P.
Richard Broff and Caroline Mansfield, June 10, 1845, by Rev. Elias Gatchel.
Benjamin Brokaw and Eliza J. McCullough, April 9, 1846, by James Kerr, V. D. M.
John Brokaw and Margaret Morris, March 1, 1842, by Charles Thorn.
Benjamin F. Brook and Catharine Lee, Jan. 10, 1849, by Elijah Carson, J. P.
Edward Brown and Mary Ann Lyttle, Oct. 5, 1848, by Henry Byrnes, J. P.
George Brown and Catharine Mann, July 26, 1849, by Rev. John Moffitt.
James Brown and Elizabeth Wright, April 6, 1846, by Rev. W. R. McGowan.
John Brown and Phebe Crum, Feb. 20, 1844, by Hamilton McFadden, J. P.
John Brown and Jane Simpson, Aug. 9, 1846, by Rev. Elias Gatchel.
John Brown and Mary Quillan, Dec. 1, 1850, by Rev. Jacob Lemmon.
John M. Brown and Sarah B. Foster, Feb. 15, 1844, by Rev. Jacob Lemmon.

ADDITIONAL HARRISON COUNTY MARRIAGES

Joshua Brown and Nancy Cheney, Nov. 10, 1849, by Rev. Jeremiah Phillips.
Norvill H. Brown and Nancy Baird, April 1, 1841, by John R. Dunlap.
Robert Brown and Fanny E. Webber, Aug. 21, 1845, by J. J. Cover.
Samuel Brown and Elizabeth J. Ogden, March 29, 1846, by Rev. Jacob Lemmon.
William Brown and Rebecca Coleman, Sept. 8, 1843, by Rev. A. Bartholemew.
Elias Browning and Elizabeth Crago, Sept. 2, 1847, by Rev. J. McBride.
Rev. John Bryan and Eliza J. Phillips, Dec. 3, 1844, by Rev. Thomas Hanna.
William Buchanan and Abigail Mercer, Jan. 23, 1845, by F. T. Larkin, J. P.
William Buchanan and Jane Sloan, June 6, 1850, by Hugh Parks, V. D. M.
John Buckle and Sophia Kimmell, April 7, 1848, by Rev. A. N. Bartholomew.
John Bucy and Lydia Dorsey, April 3, 1847, by Rev. Elias Gatchel.
Jesse Buffington and Ann Jones, Sept. 9, 1845, by Jonas Holloway, J. P.
John Buffington and Frances Kirbay, Sept. 16, 1841, by Matthew H. Phillips, J. P.
Henry Bumgarner and Massa Teets, June 10, 1841, by Thomas Phillips, J. P.
William Burch and Margaret McKee, April 1, 1846, by Rev. C. C. Riggs.
Abraham H. Busby and Elizabeth Marshall, May 18, 1848, by James Kerr, V. D. M.
Sheridan Busby and Eliza Jane Quigley, Jan. 15, 1845, by James Cameron.
Joseph Butler and Mary Ann Stewart, Nov. 3, 1841, by George Clancy, V. D. M.
Joseph Butler and Phebe Jane Hallowell, Nov. 1, 1847, by T. T. Larkin, J. P.
Samuel Cairns and Mahala Fisher, April 5, 1847, by Robert Henderson, J. P.
Robert Caldwell and Rachel Cramblett, March 20, 1845, by Rev. Robert Cook.
Samuel L. Caldwell and Rachel Davidson, Sept. 9, 1846, by Rev. Alexander Wilson.
William Caldwell and Catharine Ann Lyons, May 11, 1841, by W. D. McCartney, V. D. M.
James H. Calvert and Melissa A. Russell, Aug. 8, 1850, by Rev. Samuel W. Day.
Aaron L. Campbell and Mariah McAdam, Oct. 6, 1842, by Hugh Parks, V. D. M.
Hugh Campbell and Sarah Ann Heavlin, Oct. 28, 1841, by B. W. Veirs, J. P.
Jesse Campbell and Mary Bensall, March 31, 1844, by Asa Holmes, J. P.
John Campbell and Berlinda Dennis, Jan. 18, 1850, by Rev. D. S. Welling.
Samuel S. Campbell and Harriett Williams, June 4, 1846, by John Cramblett, J. P.
William Campbell and Elizabeth Downer, Nov. 26, 1846, by William Arnold, J. P.
Manassas Caneagy and Elizabeth Easlick, Feb. 7, 1845, by James Cameron.
Albert S. Canfield and Louis Copeland, Oct. 14, 1845, by Rev. George Lucy.
Andrew Cannon and Nancy Findley, March 20, 1845, by Cyrus McNeely.
David Capper and Ann Foster, Nov. 19, 1844, by Rev. John M. Trego.
Joseph Capstack and Mary Jane Coleman, July 5, 1849, by Rev. Alexander Wilson.
Joseph Carnahan and Mary Ann Sharp, Oct. 3, 1850, by T. R. Crawford, V. D. M.
Samuel Carnahan and Jane Finney, Jan. 27, 1847, by Rev. John Hattery, J. P.
William Carnahan and Jane McCullough, Nov. 9, 1843, by Rev. Israel Archbold.
Rezin Carnes and Mary Ann Vickers, Feb. 21, 1850, by Rev. A. Magee.
James Carpenter and Nancy Turner, Feb. 19, 1850, by Rev. Jacob Lemmon.
James H. Carpenter and Elizabeth Hilton, March 27, 1842, by M. B. Lukens, J. P.
John B. Carpenter and Rachel Ann Long, March 16, 1848, by James Hoover, J. P.
Peter Carpenter and Mary Geary, Nov. 3, 1849, by Samuel Ramsey, J. P.
Walker Carpenter and Ann Linsey, Oct. 28, 1841, by Rev. Israel Archbold.
William Carpenter and Margaret Antibush, Aug. 14, 1843, by William Arnold, J. P.
John Carson and Mary Dodds, May 20, 1841, by G. D. Kinner, V. D. M.
William Carson and Eliza Mays, March 1, 1842, by John Rea, V. D. M.
William Carter and Nancy Nuby, June 28, 1849, by William Arnold, J. P.
Thomas C. Carthill and Lucinda Crawford, Jan. 8, 1844, by Wesley Smith.
Joseph Carver and Sarah Bashor, Jan. 4, 1842, by Samuel Lewis, J. P.

John Case and Lucy A. Patterson, Aug. 3, 1843, by Asa Holmes, J. P.
Johnson Case and Martha Jane Feigley, Aug. 9, 1849, by James J. McIlgar.
Henry Cash and Eunice Brown, Feb. 17, 1848, by John W. Baker.
Hezekiah Cash and Sarah Ann Jones, Oct. 20, 1842, by Rev. Henry Bradshaw.
Samuel H. Cash and Elizabeth Adams, Feb. 6, 1845, by James Cameron.
Joseph Castell and Eliza Jane Cannon, Feb. 28, 1850, by Rev. D. S. Welling.
David Carnahan and Sarah Gilmore, March 16, 1841, by Rev. Alex. Wilson.
President Carrel and Hannah Fowler, March 13, 1842, by John Gruber, J. P.
John S. Carrick and Eleanor Kerr, Oct. 7, 1847, by Rev. John Rea.
George Caves and Rachel Bartlett, June 24, 1847, by Rev. Elias Gatchel.
Hiram Cecil and Susanna Comfer, Dec. 29, 1842, by Rev. G. M. Hair.
John Cecil and Susanna Donahey, Dec. 10, 1846, by Hamilton McFadden, J. P.
Joshua Cecil and Rebecca Christy, Nov. 12, 1848, by Michael Lard.
Phillip Cecil and Rachel Sinclair, April 24, 1845, by Isaac Talbott, J. P.
Richard Cecil and Jane Bliss, Feb. 25, 1847, by Rev. Job Lisetor.
John Chamberlain and Rosanna Mitchel, March 1, 1843, by Rev. G. M. Hair.
Daniel D. Chicken and Mary Hall, Dec. 13, 1846, by R. K. Price, J. P.
James Christy and Nancy Johnston, Dec. 24, 1846, by James Kerr, V. D. M.
John Christy and Rachel Vanhorn, Dec. 21, 1844, by M. F. Burkhead, J. P.
Rev. A. D. Clark and Mary L. Lee, Oct. 11, 1849, by Rev. A. W. Black.
Arnold Clark and Charity Locks, Sept. 28, 1846, by Thomas Phillips, J. P.
Ephraim Clark and Isabella Kennedy, March 11, 1847, by Rev. John Rea.
John Clark and Amy Humphreys, March 8, 1845, by R. K. Price, J. P.
John Clark and Elizabeth Smith, Oct. 26, 1848, by John Graham, J. P.
John Clark and Mary Jane Legget, July 19, 1847, by David Bower, J. P.
John T. Clark and Sarah Jane Mercer, Oct. 12, 1848, by Michael H. Toland.
Johnson Clark and Mary Ann Gourley, Sept. 15, 1842, by B. Mitchel, V. D. M.
William Clark and Silence Foreman, Dec. 23, 1845, by David Bower, J. P.
Daniel Clements and Elizabeth Dickerson, April 5, 1843, by Rev. G. M. Hair.
John Clements and Malinda Ramage, Jan. 29, 1846, by Rev. Thomas Merrill.
Thomas Clifford and Rachel Dunlap, Nov. 10, 1841, by James Kerr, V. D. M.
John S. Cloakey and Susanna Parrish, May 28, 1850, by Rev. Alexander Wilson.
Abraham Coleman and Rachel Mercer, March 23, 1847, by Thomas Phillips, J. P.
Richard Coleman and Mary Barnhouse, Feb. 24, 1848, by Andrew Lynch, J. P.
William Collans and Sidney Jones, Oct. 11, 1842, by John Hastings, J. P.
Thomas B. Colvin and Lydia Ann Gruble, June 17, 1841, by Joseph Fry, J. P.
William Colvin and Emma L. Carr, Feb. 2, 1843, by Rev. Elias Gatchel.
Dr. John W. Comley and Mary C. Armstrong, Dec. 17, 1850, by Robert Scott.
Adam Compher and Elizabeth Bone, Aug. 28, 1849, by T. R. Crawford, V. D. M.
William Compher and Elizabeth Moore, Feb. 24, 1848, by Rev. Elias Gatchel.
Enoch Conaway and Ruth A. Granfell, June 6, 1844, by Rev. Israel Archbold.
John Conwell and Mary Gordon, Oct. 6, 1848, by Rev. James C. Merryman.
George Cooper and Mary Ann Dickerson, Oct. 24, 1850, by Thomas Phillips, J. P.
Morris Coovert and Catharine Swallow, Nov. 1, 1848, by John W. Baker, J. P.
Joshua Cope and Hanna Dungan, Jan. 3, 1843, by William Arnold, J. P.
Nathan Cope and Jane Black, Sept. 17, 1841, by J. Montgomery.
Samuel Cope and Louisa Rogers, Aug. 17, 1847, by Elijah Carson, J. P.
James Copeland and Margaret Gutshall, March 19, 1846, by Henry H. Beckitt, J. P.
John G. Copeland and Ann Copeland, June 23, 1843, by Rev. Thomas Hanna.
Jonathan Copeland and Isabella Mealy, Feb. 20, 1844, by James Kerr, V. D. M.
David Corbett and Susan Harrison, May 11, 1842, by George Clancy, V. D. M.
Patrick Cosgrove and Elizabeth Doyle, Oct. 17, 1850, by William Arnold, J. P.
Henry Cotton and Eliza Cox, Oct. 8, 1848, by R. K. Price, J. P.
Andrew Coulter and Nancy Mays, Jan. 9, 1844, by John Rea, V. D. M.
John S. Coulter and Mary Tumlinson, Nov. 30, 1843, by E. H. Custer, J. P.
Samuel Cortright and Eleanor Wheeler, April 18, 1850, by George F. Jones.
William Courtright and Mary Sergent, Nov. 17, 1842, by George Atkinson, J. P.
Nelson Cousins and Herilda Singer, Dec. 2, 1847, by John Cheney, J. P.

ADDITIONAL HARRISON COUNTY MARRIAGES

Benjamin Covert and Catharine Brokaw, May 15, 1845, by Rev. Moses Allen.
Joseph Covert and Susan Huston, May 23, 1844, by Rev. Elias Gatchel.
Harrison Cox and Eliza Jane Harper, Aug. 12, 1845, by Rev. Alexander Wilson.
Elisha Cox and Elizabeth Vansickle, Oct. 5, 1845, by J. J. Covert.
John Cox and Easter Caven, Dec. 17, 1850, by R. Herron.
Joshua Cox and Elizabeth Lockman, Aug. 13, 1848, by Rev. Jacob Lemmon.
Isaac Crawford and Louis J. Jackson, March 22, 1845, by T. T. Larkin, J. P.
John Crawford and Elizabeth Hedges, May 17, 1849, by James Kerr, V. D. M.
John Crawford and Sarah Hunt, Nov. 21, 1850, by Rev. J. M. Bray.
John C. Crawford and Catherine Shadran, Aug. 4, 1842, by Robert P. Simpson, J. P.
Lemuel Crawford and Sarah Henderson, March 27, 1850, by R. Herron.
William H. Crawford and Henriette Brown, Jan. 6, 1845, by Robert Wade, J. P.
Washington Crabb and Sarah J. Carnahan, Sept. 8, 1846, by Rev. Thomas Hanna.
Gideon Crabtree and Sarah Jane Carothers, March 14, 1850, by Samuel Skinner, J. P.
Cornelius Crabtree and Sophia Poulson, Nov. 25, 1846, by Rev. Jacob Lemmon.
Samuel Craig and Margaret Ann McFadden, June 14, 1841, by Rev. Alexander Wilson.
William Craig and Elizabeth Wallace, Feb. 9, 1843, by James Kerr, J. P.
Walter Craig and Jane Moore, Jan. 9, 1844, by James Kerr, V. D. M.
Jacob Cramblett and Sarah McClintick, April 25, 1845, by R. Brown.
Joel Cramblett and Mary Ann Fowler, May 30, 1844, by Rev. Benjamin Wood.
Frederick Cramer and Phebe Ann Parker, April 14, 1842, by Reynolds K. Price.
Wesley Creal and Diana Manbeck, March 8, 1849, by Rev. Lemuel B. Perkins.
William Cree and Rachel Jewell, April 2, 1848, by R. K. Price, J. P.
John H. Creger and Margaret Dolby, April 18, 1847, by Rev. A. C. Hunger.
Reuben Creger and Mary Ann Middleton, May 20, 1849, by James Hoover, J. P.
Abraham Croskey and Mary Jane Phillips, Sept. 29, 1842, by James Kerr, V. D. M.
Alexander Crossan and Rebecca Oglevee, May 14, 1846, by James Kerr, V. D. M.
Andrew Crouch and Malinda Crouch, April 24, 1846, by James Kerr, V. D. M.
Samuel Crouch and Susanna J. Harvey, Oct. 18, 1848, by Samuel Cunningham, J. P.
Wilson Crouch and Margaret Campbell, Nov. 22, 1849, by John Wilkin, J. P.
Joseph Crumley and Elizabeth A. Crabtree, Oct. 10, 1850, by Rev. A. Magee.
Solomon Crumrine and Franney Kerr, Sept. 12, 1844, by David Bower, J. P.
William Crumrine and Susan Kimmel, April 4, 1844, by William Arnold, J. P.
Samuel H. Culbertson and Esther J. Clements, Feb. 1, 1849, by Rev. Joseph Gordon.
William T. Cullin and Rachel Grewell, Sept. 27, 1846, by R. K. Price, J. P.
James Cummings and Rebecca Edwards, Oct. 25, 1841, by John Graham.
Samuel Cummings and Margaret Thomas, March 25, 1847, by Rev. D. S. Welling.
Philip Cummins and Mary Ann Trimble, Jan. 12, 1847, by G. A. Lowman.
David Cunningham and Ann Barricklow, March 18, 1841, by Hugh Parks, V. D. M.
John Cunningham and Sarah A. Bone, June 17, 1847, by Rev. Richard Gray.
Samuel Cunningham and Margaret Lewis, May 27, 1846, by James Kerr, V. D. M.
Robert F. Custer and Margaret Baker, Oct. 10, 1850, by Rev. A. Magee.
William Custer and Margaret Welch, Nov. 4, 1847, by Rev. Jacob Lemmon.
Leslie Cutshall and Carolina Gibson, Nov. 28, 1850, by W. D. Webb.
John Czatt and Sarah J. Johnson, Jan. 1, 1846, by Thomas Phillips, J. P.
Bazel Danbow and Ruth Tenner, Jan. 2, 1845, by Rev. Elias Gatchel.
Aaron Davis and Mary Ann Busby, Nov. 29, 1846, by Rev. D. S. Welling.
Henry Davis and Catharine Renniker, Sept. 6, 1848, by John Adams, J. P.
James Davis and Sidney Marshall, Oct. 4, 1843, by Wesley Smith.
James Davis and Elizabeth Parrish, May 29, 1845, by William Tipton.
John Davis and Rhoda Emily Townsend, Oct. 4, 1849, by Cyrus McNeely.

Nicholas Davis and Susannah B. Barrett, Sept. 1, 1848, by Rev. Harvey Bradshaw.
Robert Davis and Nancy Pritchard, Nov. 14, 1850, by Thomas Jones.
Alfred A. Davidson and Catharine A. Covert, Dec. 19, 1850, by Rev. Samuel W. Day.
Faris Davidson and Nancy Myers, April 8, 1841, by Rev. Benjamin Furgason.
Jacob L. Davidson and Dorcas A. Derry, April 19, 1846, by R. K. Price, J. P.
William Davidson and Sarah Petty, April 16, 1846, by Elijah Carson, J. P.
William Davidson and Christina Shepler, Oct. 7, 1849, by Rev. Alexander Wilson.
William R. Davidson and Sarah A. Fulton, Oct. 9, 1847, by Rev. Jacob Lemmon.
Zera Davidson and Nancy Johnson, Jan. 28, 1841, by Rev. Benjamin P. Ferguson.
James Day and Isabella Crabb, Oct. 3, 1841, by James E. Taylor.
James A. Day and Emily Walcutt, Aug. 29, 1850, by R. Herron.
Milton Dearth and Matilda Rankin, May 7, 1846, by Rev. J. J. Covert.
Jesse De Long and Eleanor Watson, Oct. 29, 1841, by Jesse Merrill, J. P.
Albert Demster and Lucy Trimble, April 24, 1849, by Rev. Pardon Cook.
Silvester S. Demuth and Isabella A. Miller, Aug. 25, 1849, by William Reed, J. P.
William T. Demming and Mary Wilson, Dec. 25, 1850, by Rev. J. M. Bray.
Jacob Depue and Rebecca Bishop, March 1, 1849, by Rev. Lemuel B. Perkins.
Lewis Devault and Margaret Straughbaugh, March 23, 1843, by William Cobb, J. P.
Jacob Devault and Margaret Gutshall, April 4, 1844, by Henry H. Beckett, J. P.
Casper Devilbiss and Mary Jane Braden, Jan. 25, 1849, by Cyrus McNeely.
Andrew Devore and Sarah Holland, June 3, 1841, by William Arnold, J. P.
Elisha Devore and Mary Ann Petty, April 6, 1849, by W. C. P. Hamilton.
Jeremiah Devore and Letticia Shimer, July 21, 1842, by James Welsh, J. P.
John Devore and Mariah F. Petty, Nov. 16, 1843, by Rev. Elijah Carson.
Silas Devore and Eliza Bishop, Oct. 10, 1850, by Rev. John Burns.
Elias Dew and Elizabeth Craig, April 15, 1841, by John H. Brown, J. P.
Joseph Dew and Mary Ann Gray, Dec. 12, 1844, by F. T. Larkin, J. P.
John Dewitt and Polly Mountz, July 16, 1849, by James J. McIlgar.
William Dewitt and Nancy Swaney, Aug. 4, 1844, by Reynolds K. Price, J. P.
James H. Dicks and Mary Davis, Jan. 14, 1848, by Rev. Asbury W. Simpkins.
William Dicks and Eliza Cullin, Aug. 24, 1845, by R. K. Price, J. P.
Joshua Dickerson and Nancy Elliott, Dec. 30, 1841, by Rev. William F. Lauck.
Joshua Dickerson and Mary Jane Elliott, Feb. 8, 1844, by Wesley Smith.
Benjamin Dickey and Mary Riley, Dec. 30, 1847, by Rev. Jacob Lemmon.
Samuel Dickey and Catharine Irvin, Jan. 27, 1848, by Isaac Falbeth, J. P.
Frederick Dinger and Margaret Naregong, May 29, 1842, by Henry H. Beckett, J. P.
Sampson Dinger and Mary Ann Stall, Jan. 4, 1849, by Henry H. Beckett, J. P.
Robert Dodds and Rebecca McCartney, Oct. 10, 1842, by Isaac Talbott, J. P.
William Donaldson and Nancy English, Sept. 29, 1848, by Rev. Jeremiah Phillips.
Zaza Donnell and Nancy Boon, Sept. 11, 1845, by James Kerr, V. D. M.
Henry Dool and Mary Clifford, Dec. 16, 1846, by Rev. Alexander Wilson.
James Dooling and Lucinda Davis, May 6, 1841, by Rev. E. Smith.
Samuel Dougan and Ellen Dougan, March 5, 1842, by George Cook, J. P.
Lemuel Dowden and Catharine Monciff, July 31, 1845, by Cyrus McNeely.
Thomas B. Dowden and Elizabeth Drummond, April 14, 1847, by Rev. Alexander Wilson.
George Downs and Mary Jane Anderson, July 1, 1847, by Hamilton McFadden, J. P.
William Drummond and Margaret Fulton, April 15, 1847, by James Kerr, V. D. M.
Robert M. Duncan and Mary Ann Alexander, Oct. 10, 1850, by Rev. John Marshall.
Joshua Dunham and Matilda Nelson, Jan. 15, 1841, by Robert Givin, J. P.

ADDITIONAL HARRISON COUNTY MARRIAGES

Adam Dunlap and Margaret J. Buchanan, Aug. 20, 1845, by Rev. Moses Allen.
Hazard Dunlap and Rebecca Brown, Sept. 28, 1850, by David Hanlin, J. P.
Hugh Dunlap and Elizabeth Dunlap, Feb. 15, 1844, by James Kerr, V. D. M.
Joseph Dunlap and Julia Ann Hays, Feb. 12, 1846, by James Kerr, V. D. M.
Joshua Dunlap and Nancy Watson, Oct. 16, 1847, by Rev. Alexander Wilson.
William Dunlap and Margaret Millikin, Feb. 14, 1850, by James Kerr, V. D. M.
James H. Duswald and Sarah Shook, Dec. 9, 1847, by B. W. Viers, J. P.
George Easterday and Mary M. Warner, April 3, 1848, by Rev. A. N. Bartholomew.
Presley Edwards and Elizabeth Glass, Oct. 18, 1842, by David Bower, J. P.
Richard Edwards and Sarah Ann Quillan, March 7, 1850, by David Hanlin, J. P.
George Eli and Phebe M. Corey, Oct. 28, 1848, by William Arnold, J. P.
George Elliott and Adeline McCormick, April 4, 1849, by Rev. Alexander Wilson.
James Elliot and Sarah Jane Howser, Sept. 5, 1848, by Rev. James C. Merryman.
Joseph Elliott and Amelia Catherine Ely, April 15, 1843, by Wesley Smith.
Samuel Elliott and Sarah H. Thomas, March 4, 1845, by Rev. E. Hays.
Jeremiah Enlowes and Hannah Corbin, July 3, 1840, by Wesley Smith.
John Endsley and Barbara Knouff, June 29, 1848, by James Kerr, J. P.
Robert W. Endsley and Elizabeth Birney, Dec. 26, 1843, by James Kerr, V. D. M.
Alpheus English and Nancy M. McCarroll, Oct. 7, 1847, by Thomas Phillips, J. P.
James English and Ann McCarroll, Aug. 19, 1844, by Rev. James W. Walker.
John Epley and Rebecca Kimmel, Feb. 17, 1848, by Rev. A. Bartholomew.
James Eslick and Eliza Ross, Oct. 8, 1847, by B. W. Viers, J. P.
John Evans and Sarah Stewart, Dec. 22, 1842, by Rev. W. T. Adams.
William Evans and Margaret Brown, Oct. 17, 1844, by Rev. Israel Archbold.
Edward Exbee and Melina Moore, Nov. 6, 1849, by Hugh Parks, V. D. M.
Thomas Familton and Elizabeth Middleton, Aug. 13, 1848, by John Graham, J. P.
David Farmer and Polly Jamison, Dec. 27, 1849, by William Larimer.
John W. Farnsworth and Margaret Jane McConnell, April 2, 1843, by John L. Layport, J. P.
Jackson Fawcett and Mary Guyn, Nov. 9, 1841, by Samuel Lewis, J. P.
Brice Felingberger and Sarah M. Reed, Aug. 9, 1849, by Thomas Finnicum, J. P.
William Fell and Elizabeth A. Fields, May 5, 1847, by Rev. Charles Thorn.
Andrew Ferrell and Mary A. McCurdy, May 18, 1846, by Samuel Skinner, J. P.
Curtis Ferrell and Philand Packer, Nov. 28, 1850, by Rev. John Knox.
Isaac Ferrell and Elizabeth Conaway, Aug. 22, 1844, by Rev. Ebenezer Hays.
John W. Ferrell and Cynthia Burrier, Oct. 3, 1848, by William Arnold, J. P.
Henry Ferrensworth and Susanna Strahan, March 8, 1848, by R. K. Price, J. P.
R. P. Finney and Mary Hitchcock, Dec. 11, 1844, by James Kerr, V. D. M.
Robert P. Finney and Lydia Ann Jenkins, Nov. 8, 1846, by John Graham, J. P.
Thomas Finney and Susanna Cocherel, May 2, 1847, by R. K. Price, J. P.
Thomas Finney and Margaret Nash, May 4, 1848, by John Blair, J. P.
George Finicum and Lydia A. Hilbert, Sept. 6, 1846, by E. H. Custer, J. P.
Robert Finnical and Sarah M. Hines, Nov. 14, 1850, by Rev. John Moffitt.
David Finnicum and Rebecca Gibler, Aug. 19, 1847, by Rev. Thomas N. Megaw.
David Firebaugh and Elizabeth Boor, June 10, 1841, by Rev. Adam Hetzler.
Albert M. Fisher and Nancy McKittrick, June 28, 1846, by James Cameron.
George Fisher and Emily Russel, Sept. 9, 1843, by Rev. Thomas R. Buckle.
John Fisher and Margaret Robison, July 19, 1846, by Andrew Lynch, J. P.
Joseph Fisher and Mary Covert, Oct. 15, 1842, by Wesley Smith.
Wilson Fisher and Catharine A. Middleton, Sept. 7, 1848, by James Moore, J. P.
George Fivecoats and Frances Ann Lee, June 13, 1850, by Samuel Ramsey, J. P.
William Fivecoats and Lucinda Lee, June 24, 1841, by Rev. Elias Gotshall.
George Fogle and Mary A. Mosgrove, Nov. 22, 1849, by Cyrus McNeely.
John M. Folks and Mary E. Taylor, July 4, 1848, by Rev. James Henderson.
Joseph Foot and Catherine Linard, Feb. 15, 1844, by Alexander Barger, J. P.
B. Slemmons Ford and Margaret Ramsey, Jan. 20, 1842, by Robert Clark.

Edward Ford and Catharine Minney, Dec. 11, 1844, by Reynolds K. Price, J. P.
John C. Ford and Rebecca Vasbinder, Feb. 19, 1846, by James Kerr, V. D. M.
Lewis Ford and Mary Matilda Simes, Sept. 6, 1849, by Rev. William P. Hunt.
William Ford and Tabitha Barrett, Sept. 26, 1846, by Rev. Josiah Gibson.
Aaron Forman and Jane Ann Ferry, Sept. 16, 1849, by Rev. John Burns.
Reason Foreman and Sarah Penn, Oct. 7, 1841, by Thomas Phillips, J. P.
Rezin Foreman and Sarah Ann Thompson, May 3, 1849, by Rev. John Burns.
Samuel Foreman and Susanna Copeland, March 24, 1842, by William Argo.
John Forsyth and Eliza Allen, Sept. 10, 1844, by Rev. Jacob Lemmon.
Levi C. Forsythe and Emma Abrams, Dec. 9, 1848, by Rev. E. Vilton.
David Fortner and Margaret Beck, Aug. 18, 1844, by Rev. Elias Gatchel.
Caleb Foster and Malila J. Picken, July 10, 1846, by R. Brown.
Gideon Fouts and Delila Ann Jones, Jan. 18, 1843, by Rev. Jacob Brill.
John Fouts and Margaret Sprowls, Dec. 19, 1850, by Rev. James M. Bray.
Jeremiah Fowler and Mariah Fisher, May 25, 1842, by Rev. Benjamin Wood.
John E. Fowler and Ingalia Spray, Nov. 17, 1844, by Rev. Benjamin Wood.
Thomas Fox and Rebecca Stewart, Jan. 7, 1845, by Nathan Tannahill, J. P.
James B. Frazer and Elizabeth Farmer, April 19, 1847, by Rev. Robert Andrews.
John Frazier and Sarah Ann Ferguson, Oct. 24, 1850, by James Kerr, V. D. M.
Robert Freshwater and Elizabeth Thompson, March 23, 1848, by Samuel Cunningham.
John Fulton and Christianne Leinard, April 27, 1849, by James J. McIlgar.
William Fulton, Jr., and Eliza Boyd, July 4, 1848, by James Kerr, V. D. M.
John Furney and Nancy Johnson, Sept. 26, 1844, by Rev. Robert Cook.
James Galbreath and Agnes M. Stout, June 5, 1850, by McNight Williamson.
John Gilbraith and Margaret Allison, March 20, 1845, by James Kerr, V. D. M.
Joseph Galbraith and Mary Stevens, Aug. 19, 1841, by John Knox, J. P.
Washington Gilbreath and Jemima Stull, Jan. 15, 1850, by Macknight W. Cleaverson.
John Gallagher and Margaret Farmer, Jan. 9, 1845, by Rev. Joseph Cloaky.
Samuel Gambel and Susanna Heavlin, Nov. 25, 1847, by Hamilton McFadden, J. P.
William Gamble and Lecta J. Rowley, Dec. 11, 1845, by Rev. W. R. McGowan.
John Gardener and Maria Jones, Sept. 25, 1850, by William Wilson, J. P.
James Gardner and Jane Scott, Dec. 24, 1846, by Isaac Talbot, J. P.
James Gardner and Tabitha Ann Cox, Oct. 10, 1848, by William Smith.
Samuel Gardner and Mary E. J. Guthrie, Feb. 15, 1844, by R. Brown.
Samuel Gardner and Elizabeth Leard, Jan. 8, 1846, by Samuel W. Day.
Edward Garner and Julia Ann Merryman, Sept. 7, 1848, by Rev. Pardon Cook.
Daniel Garvin and Catherine Davis, Sept. 15, 1842, by Rev. Moses Allen.
William Garven and Martha E. McCullough, Jan. 25, 1849, by James Kerr, V. D. M.
Hiram Gatchel and Sarah Moore, Sept. 5, 1842, by John Blair, J. P.
Jacob Gatchel and Elizabeth Barger, Aug. 1, 1844, by Elijah Carson, J. P.
Jobe W. Gatchell and Frances Norris, July 17, 1844, by Rev. Elias Gatchel.
John Geesey and Nancy Davis, March 28, 1844, by Asa Holmes, J. P.
Jonas Geesy and Elizabeth Moore, Dec. 30, 1841, by Rev. Jacob Lemmon.
Washington C. George and Sarah Currell, Oct. 7, 1848, by James Kerr, V. D. M.
Obediah Gibler and Phebe Finnicum, July 16, 1848, by Rev. Lemuel B. Perkins.
John Gibson and Mary Mills, March 8, 1841, by James Evans, J. P.
John Giles and Charlott Hendrix, Dec. 1, 1842, by E. H. Custer, J. P.
William Giles and Sarah Ann Coleman, Nov. 21, 1850, by Rev. John Burns.
John W. Gillespie and Cornelia Ann Anderson, Nov. 29, 1842, by Wesley Smith.
Thomas Gillespie and Isabella Jane Haverfield, Feb. 9, 1843, by Rev. Thomas Hanna.
William Gillespie and Nancy Cook, June 9, 1846, by William Taggart, V. D. M.
Samuel Gilmore and Elizabeth McMillan, Jan. 2, 1845, by Nathan Tannehill, J. P.
William Gilmore and Margaret Carrothers, March 25, 1841, by James Kerr, V. D. M.

ADDITIONAL HARRISON COUNTY MARRIAGES 597

William C. Glasgow and Eliza Poulson, April 3, 1846, by John Layport, J. P.
Solomon Glass and Nancy Snider, June 30, 1841, by Thomas Phillips, J. P.
Isaac Glazener and Mary Ross, Nov. 22, 1849, by James Kerr, V. D. M.
James C. Gleaves and Elmira A. McDonald, April 6, 1848, by Rev. J. C. Merryman.
John S. Goe and Catherine E. Colvin, Oct. 7, 1847, by Rev. Elias Gatchel.
William Goff and Elizabeth Markley, March 23, 1848, by Andrew Lynch, J. P.
Francis E. Graham and Rose A. Barnhouse, Oct. 20, 1846, by Rev. C. C. Riggs.
John Graham and Sarah Ann Dicks, May 26, 1842, by John Megaw.
Thomas M. Granfell and Jane Shanks, Jan. 30, 1848, by Jonas Holloway, J. P.
Andrew J. Gray and Nancy Brown, Dec. 6, 1849, by Rev. John Moffit.
James A. Gray and Jane E. Junkins, May 17, 1842, by James Kerr, V. D. M.
John Gray and Sarah Mays, June 27, 1849, by James Kerr, V. D. M.
Samuel R. Gray and Eliza E. Moorehead, Feb. 4, 1846, by John Rea, V. D. M.
Silas Gray and Sarah Rankin, June 16, 1842, by Rev. Harvey Bradshaw.
William Gray and Sarah Ann Cartle, March 6, 1845, by F. T. Larkin, J. P.
Jacob Graybill and Elizabeth Megunnell, Jan. 8, 1848, by Rev. Abraham Lemaster.
George Green and Mary Ann Scott, April 7, 1844, by Wesley Smith.
John Green and Sarah Ross, Nov. 30, 1848, by James Kerr, V. D. M.
James Greenfield and Lovenia Hanshaw, April 14, 1842, by George Clancy, V. D. M.
John Oliver Greenwalt and Hannah L. Packer, Dec. 2, 1846, by R. K. Price, J. P.
Joshua C. Greenwalt and Eleanor Grover, Oct. 18, 1849, by James Taggart, J. P.
Isaac Grewell and Eleanor Brown, Feb. 8, 1843, by Mark Hogge, J. P.
William W. Griffin and Meriam Dunlap, Dec. 21, 1849, by Rev. Eli Slutes.
Harrison Griffith and Deborah Carrothers, March 20, 1841, by Cornelius Crabtree, J. P.
Joshua Griffith and Eleanor Ann Oxley, Jan. 26, 1841, by Cornelius Crabtree, J. P.
Thomas G. Grisinger and Sarah Jane Barrier, July 23, 1849, by Rev. Lemuel B. Perkins.
John Grooms and Rachel Mansfield, Dec. 15, 1842, by Matthew H. Phillips, J. P.
William Grubb and Elizabeth Latham, Nov. 24, 1842, by Samuel Skinner, J. P.
John Gruber and Margaret Baird, Nov. 14, 1848, by Rev. C. C. Riggs.
David Gundy and Rachel Hines, March 27, 1845, by Rev. Charles Carter.
Jacob Gundy and Elizabeth Gutshall, April 13, 1843, by Rev. W. Simpkins.
Michael V. Gundy and Christiana Overholtz, Jan. 27, 1848, by Rev. Andrew Klingle.
Robert Grunning and Ann Hutchison, March 23, 1848, by T. T. Larkin, J. P.
Alexander W. Guthrie and Elizabeth Potts, Sept. 5, 1850, by Samuel Langdon.
Benjamin Guthrie and Harriett Fitzgerald, Oct. 28, 1841.
John M. Guthrie and Caroline Crabtree, Feb. 10, 1846, by Samuel W. Day.
William Guthrie and Isabella Leard, June 15, 1843, by Rev. Harvey Bradshaw
Abraham Gutshall and Catherine Stall, May 11, 1843, by Thomas Finnicum, J. P.
Daniel Gutshall and Hannah A. Gibson, June 29, 1843, by Henry F. Brickett, J. P.
Gideon Gutshall and Sarah Jane Welling, March 28, 1850, by Rev. John Hare.
Jacob Gutshall and Mahabeth Snider, May 16, 1843, by E. H. Custer, J. P.
Jacob Gotshall and Eliza Long, Oct. 3, 1850, by Rev. D. Sparks.
James Gutshall and Catharine A. Reecer, July 10, 1844, by James Welsh, J. P.
James Gutshall and Susanna Smith, Aug. 18, 1850, by George T. Jones.
John Gutshall and Rebecca McClintock, Sept. 24, 1846, by R. Brown.
Joseph Gutshall and Eve Manbeck, March 5, 1846, by Thomas Finnicum.
Levi Gutshall and Catharine Kail, May 3, 1849, by Rev. Lemuel B. Perkins.
Samuel Gutshall and Ruth Graham, March 19, 1842, by Thomas McClintock.
Moses C. Guy and Mary Ann Fowler, Jan. 13, 1848, by William Arnold, J. P.
Thomas Guynn and Mary Cope, April 12, 1846, by Thomas Phillips, J. P.
William Guynn and Martha Ramsey, April 30, 1845, by William Arnold, J. P.

Benjamin Guyton and Eleanor Fitzgerald, Oct. 2, 1845, by Rev. Abraham Wheeler.
Francis A. Haines and Arabella Haines, Aug. 5, 1847, by Rev. William Knox.
Hiram Haines and Terza J. Wilson, March 4, 1845, by Samuel Skinner, J. P.
Jesse Hall and Hannah Herford, June 6, 1844, by James Kerr, V. D. M.
John Hall and Elizabeth Richard, Nov. 23, 1848, by John Ross, J. P.
Lewis Hall and Margaret Kent, Dec. 14, 1843, by William Cobb, J. P.
Reuben W. Hall and Sarah Jane Jones, Nov. 2, 1849, by Rev. Jacob Lemmon.
Tipton B. Hall and Rachel Fife, March 24, 1847, by Rev. D. S. Welling.
Henry Hallyer and Matilda Castell, Oct. 9, 1842, by Richard Gray.
Alexander Hamilton and Nancy Hilton, Oct. 28, 1847, by Rev. T. A. Crawford.
Craig Hamilton and Margaret McFadden, Feb. 21, 1850, by Rev. Alexander Wilson.
John Hamilton and Rebecca Pritchard, Aug. 21, 1845, by James Kerr, V. D. M.
Joseph H. Hamilton and Mary Johnson, Dec. 3, 1846, by James Kerr, V. D. M.
William Hamlin and Julia Jackson, Jan. 7, 1845, by Rev. George Coleman.
Harvey Hammond and Margaret A. Feigley, May 27, 1847, by Rev. J. Lester.
John H. Hammond and Nancy Carrick, Nov. 11, 1845, by James Kerr, V. D. M.
John Hancher and Priscilla Batten, June 4, 1843, by Wesley Smith.
Rezin Handley and Calista R. Hurlbert, July 16, 1843, by E. H. Custer, J. P.
Neri A. Hanna and Eliza Jane Phillips, June 7, 1849, by James Kerr, V. D. M.
Samuel Hanna and Docia A. Boggs, March 16, 1847, by Rev. John Rea.
Smith Hanshaw and Sarah Johnson, Feb. 20, 1844, by Asa Holmes, J. P.
John Harbin and Providence Graden, Oct. 9, 1843, by Rev. Jacob Lemmon.
Charles Harding and Pamelia Carnes, June 20, 1849, by Marshall McCall, J. P.
Edward Harding and Sarah Tucker, Dec. 11, 1847, by Rev. J. W. Case.
William Hardisty and Charlotte Hill, Dec. 24, 1847, by T. T. Larkin, J. P.
Thomas Harmony and Sarah A. Neal, July 29, 1847, by John Graham, J. P.
Ebenezer C. Harriett and Eleanora Norris, Oct. 11, 1848, by R. K. Price, J. P.
Augustus C. Harris and Margaret Clark, March 14, 1844, by Reynolds K. Price, J. P.
John Harris and Mary Jane Brown, Feb. 19, 1850, by Rev. John Moffitt.
John Harrison and Rueann Ogden, June 5, 1849, by James Kerr, V. D. M.
Thomas W. Harrison and Mary P. Robertson, Oct. 30, 1848, by Rev. Joseph Gorden.
Walter Harshe and Catharine Carothers, April 5, 1849, by James Kerr, V. D. M.
James Harshee and Maria Carothers, May 22, 1849, by James Kerr, V. D. M.
Thomas Hartley and Lydia Tomlinson, Oct. 11, 1849, by Rev. Lemuel B. Perkins.
William H. Harton and Mary Marris, Dec. 8, 1841, by Rev. L. Janney.
James Harvey and Margaret Clark, March 14, 1850, by Hugh Parks, V. D. M.
Milton Harvey and Elizabeth Bartlett, June 11, 1845, by Samuel Skinner, J. P.
William Harvey and Catherine J. Baxter, Aug. 24, 1848, by John Graham, J. P.
Philip Hatz and Martha McConnell, Jan. 17, 1848, by Rev. John Hattery.
William Hatton and Margaret Rutledge, July 3, 1849, by Rev. John Burns.
Joseph Havener and Rebecca Mitchell, Sept. 3, 1846, by James Kerr, V. D. M.
Gillespie Haverfield and Mary Clifford, Jan. 18, 1844, by Hugh Parks, V. D. M.
James N. Haverfield and Martha Hitchcock, Nov. 28, 1844, by James Kerr, V. D. M.
James N. Haverfield and Sarah Holmes, Nov. 3, 1841, by James C. Taylor.
John Haverfield and Emeline Lavely, Oct. 27, 1842, by Rev. Harvey Bradshaw.
Robert Haverfield and Sarah Moffett, Oct. 16, 1850, by Rev. John Moffitt.
Thomas H. Haverfield and Mary Ann Bell, March 22, 1849, by John Blair, J. P.
William S. Haverfield and Ruhama Nash, March 13, 1842, by Rev. Alexander Wilson.
William Hawthorn and Mary Stires, March 4, 1847, by Rev. Charles Thorn.
Abriam Hayes and Anne De Long, April 8, 1845, by Robert Henderson, J. P.
Daniel Hayne and Lorana Wharton, Sept. 10, 1848, by William Arnold, J. P.
William Haynes and Martha M. Williams, Nov. 24, 1848, by Elijah Carson, J. P.

ADDITIONAL HARRISON COUNTY MARRIAGES

Andrew Hazlett and Margaret Jane Johnson, April 19, 1849, by Rev. John Burns.
Thomas M. Hazlett and Amelia Bone, Aug. 15, 1850, by Rev. A. Magee.
Joseph Healea and Polly Ferrell, April 27, 1843, by Wesley Smith.
Samuel Healea and Sarah Ann Boils, Sept. 2, 1841, by James Kerr, V. D. M.
Thomas Healea and Catharine Thompson, Jan. 21, 1842, by Rev. Wm. F. Lauck.
John Heaston and Frances Firebaugh, Oct. 16, 1850, by Rev. Eli Slutes.
Benjamin Heavlin and Sarah McPeck, Dec. 21, 1847, by James Hoover, J. P.
Isaac Heavlin and Susannah Bricker, Aug. 20, 1846, by James Kerr, V. D. M.
Stephen H. Heavlin and Elizabeth McKinney, Nov. 12, 1846, by Hamilton McFadden, J. P.
Samuel Hedge and Mary Blair, Jan. 29, 1844, by Rev. James W. Walker.
Chalkey Hefflin and Nancy Coleman, Jan. 7, 1847, by G. A. Lowman.
John Hefling and Nancy Gardner, Sept. 12, 1846, by G. A. Lowman.
John W. Hefling and Rachel Middleton, Nov. 11, 1848, by John Graham, J. P.
Lindley Hefling and Elizabeth Gardner, Aug. 20, 1846, by John Graham, J. P.
Samuel Heidy and Jane Hendrix, Jan. 6, 1842, by E. H. Custer, J. P.
Israel Hemery and Eleanor Tomlinson, June 25, 1849, by Rev. Lemuel B. Perkins.
Jacob Hendershot and Mary Welling, March 19, 1844, by Hugh Parks, V. D. M.
Alexander Henderson and Margaret Finical, June 15, 1843, by James Kerr, V. D. M.
Elias Henderson and Sarah Crawford, June 10, 1847, by Rev. Charles H. Peters.
Rev. James Henderson and Eleanor A. Thompson, July 12, 1848, by Rev. James C. Merryman.
John Henderson and Mary J. Hammond, Aug. 27, 1846, by Rev. Thomas Hanna.
John Henderson and Mary Ann Haverfield, March 28, 1850, by Rev. James R. Doig.
Matthew Henderson and Isabella Maxwell, Sept. 3, 1844, by James Thornberg.
William Henderson and Rosanna Dool, Dec. 29, 1842, by Rev. G. M. Hair.
William H. Henderson and Julia Ann Bargar, March 22, 1849, by James Kerr, V. D. M.
Meshec Hendricks and Margaret Darr, May 29, 1845, by Rev. Charles Carter.
Peter Hendricks and Mary Elizabeth Weyant, March 28, 1850, by Abraham Busby, J. P.
Jacob Hennes and Sarah Medley, Sept. 3, 1845, by Samuel Ramsey, J. P.
Andrew Henry and Elizabeth McGuire, April 26, 1850, by Thomas McClintock, J. P.
Thomas Henry and Hannah Chaney, Jan. 27, 1842, by Robert P. Simpson, J. P.
Jacob H. Herdman and Mary E. Hamilton, March 20, 1848, by Rev. Alexander Wilson.
Lemuel Herron and Rachel Ann Lemaster, Sept. 21, 1848, by William Wilson, J. P.
Hiram Herryman and Nancy Jane Bell, Feb. 14, 1849, by Rev. James C. Merryman.
Joseph Hestand and Catharine Firebaugh, Sept. 16, 1841, by Rev. J. Moffitt.
Samuel Heston and Lucinda Holmes, Nov. 24, 1842, by Rev. William Deveney.
Hiram Hibbard and Sarah Hamilton, March 30, 1843, by George Clancey, V. D. M.
Richard R. Higgins and Ann E. Branson, April 21, 1842, by George Atkinson, J. P.
Daniel Hilbert and Mary Stall, March 11, 1841, by Benjamin Pope.
Henry Hilbert and Ann Waddington, Feb. 5, 1846, by Amos Bartholomew.
Reuben Hilbert and Margaret Ann Moore, Feb. 14, 1850, by Andrew W. Lynch, J. P.
Philip Hill and Mary Ann Reed, June 12, 1850, by William Reed.
Robert Hill and Elizabeth Rea, Jan. 8, 1846, by John Rea, V. D. M.
Charles Hilliard and Angeline Andrews, Jan. 2, 1844, by Alexander Bangor, J. P.
Conrad Hilligas and Mary Harris, July 27, 1845, by William Arnold, J. P.

HISTORICAL COLLECTIONS OF HARRISON COUNTY

John Hilton and Nancy Davidson, Sept. 24, 1843, by Isaac Talbott, J. P.
John H. Hilton and Icy Utterback, Oct. 11, 1842, by M. F. Burkhead, J. P.
John W. Hilton and Mary Vasbinder, June 15, 1843, by James Kerr, V. D. M.
Daniel Himebaugh and Charity Dowell, Aug. 1, 1850, by Rev. John Burns.
Joseph Himbaugh and Jane Maynard, June 12, 1849, by B. Herron.
Daniel Hines and Lurana Myres, Sept. 27, 1849, by Rev. Isaac W. Baird.
David Hines and Harriet Smith, Dec. 16, 1847, by Rev. Pardon Cook.
Jeremiah Hines and Elizabeth Irons, Nov. 4, 1847, by Rev. Thomas Guy.
William Hines and Ruth Tipton, Aug. 31, 1847, by Rev. Verdon Waller.
Aaron Hitchcock and Mary Lease, Jan. 15, 1850, by Rev. John Moffitt.
Jacob Hitchcock and Elizabeth Birney, March 22, 1849, by Rev. James C. Merryman.
John Hitchcock and Sophia Thompson, Oct. 6, 1847, by Rev. Alexander Wilson.
Samuel Hitchcock and Christian Kimmel, April 20, 1844, by Thomas Finnicum, J. P.
Amos Hixson and Sibby Palmer, June 21, 1849, by Henry Wisner, J. P.
Henry Hoagland and Charity Moore, Sept. 25, 1847, by Aaron Conaway, J. P.
John Hodgins and Isabella Lucy, May 4, 1843, by Rev. George Lucy.
Joseph Hoffman and Hannah Kaufman, March 16, 1847, by Joseph Masters, J. P.
Lewis Huffman and Catharine Collins, Oct. 10, 1844, by J. W. McAbee.
Robert H. Hoge and Catharine De Witt, Dec. 29, 1842, by Reynolds K. Price.
Alexander Holliday and Susanna Lawrence, Dec. 25, 1843, by John Knox, J. P.
Eldrid G. Holliday and Mary Cunningham, Jan. 10, 1850, by Hugh Parks, V. D. M.
James P. Holliday and Ruth Greenell, March 22, 1842, by Reynolds K. Price.
Robert Holliday and Robert Clark, Dec. 9, 1846, by Rev. John Hattery.
Joseph Holloway and Ann Grigg, April 11, 1841, by John Knox, J. P.
Rev. Charles A. Holmes and Tempe Tingley, Oct. 14, 1850, by Rev. John Moffitt.
Isaac Holmes and Sarah Plummer, Sept. 19, 1844, by Aaron Conaway, J. P.
James Holmes and Eleanor Edwards, Sept. 30, 1841, by Jesse Merrill, J. P.
Joseph Holmes and Mary Jane Heberling, Feb. 10, 1842, by Rev. William F. Lauck.
Joseph Holmes and Mary McConnel, Jan. 7, 1850, by Rev. Charles A. Holmes.
Samuel Holmes and Emily E. Pumphrey, Dec. 8, 1841, by Rev. William Knox.
John Hoobler and Sarah Miller, March 5, 1846, by Rev. Adam Stump.
Thomas N. Hooper and Sarepta Woodruff, Jan. 24, 1847, by Rev. Jacob Lemmon.
Thomas Hoops and Ann Gray, Aug. 4, 1846, by James Kerr, V. D. M.
James Hoover and Parmelia Keys, March 17, 1842, by John Gruber, J. P.
James Hoover and Nancy Sterling, March 10, 1849, by Rev. John D. Rich.
John Hoover and Catharine Ann Hines, Nov. 28, 1848, by Rev. J. Rich.
George Horn and Mariah Saxton, April 14, 1841, by Cyrus McNeely.
George Horn and Sarah Spring, March 19, 1846, by Rev. Elias Gatchel.
George P. Horn and Jane McGonagle, Sept. 2, 1841, by Rev. Jacob Lemmon.
William Horn and Sarah Christy, Dec. 16, 1848, by Rev. Edward Smith.
Jacob Hosterman and Susan Naragong, June 27, 1843, by Henry F. Brickitt, J. P.
Adam Hotz and Elizabeth Guyton, Oct. 2, 1845, by Rev. Abraham Wheeler.
Michael Hotz and Ann Sincleare, June 13, 1850, by Rev. A. Magee.
Robert House and Jane Ramsey, Feb. 23, 1846, by Samuel W. Day.
Jacob Houser and Elizabeth Smith, March 13, 1842, by Alexander Wilson.
Elisha Huston and Rebecca Arnold, Feb. 16, 1849, by Andrew Lynch, J. P.
Robert Houston and Mary Ann Morris, July 21, 1848, by Rev. James C. Merryman.
Joseph Howard and Sarah Jane Moore, Oct. 18, 1849, by Rev. Charles A. Holmes.
James Howell and Margaret Jamison, Dec. 5, 1843, by W. Lorimire.
John Howell and Sarah Crouch, Oct. 12, 1841, by William Cobb, J. P.
Nathan A. Howell and Sarah Smith, Oct. 24, 1848, by A. W. Simpkins.
James Hoy and Margaret Browning, July 10, 1850, by James Taggart, J. P.
John Hoy and Julia Ann Brown, May 21, 1843, by John M. Brown, J. P.
Edward Huebener and Sarah Haines, May 29, 1845, by Elijah Carson, J. P.

ADDITIONAL HARRISON COUNTY MARRIAGES 601

Andrew Huff and Phœbe Smith, Nov. 14, 1844, by David A. Scott, J. P.
James Huff and Abby Weaver, Oct. 11, 1845, by James Holloway, J. P.
Jesse Huff and Susanna Welch, Jan. 29, 1843, by Thomas McClintick, J. P.
Richard Huff and Hester Green, June 13, 1844, by Rev. William Simpkins.
Thomas Huff and Mary Edwards, Jan. 26, 1847, by Thomas McClintock.
Edward Hughs and Sarah Brown, Jan. 21, 1841, by Jacob Coon.
Thomas Hughs and Keziah Wheeler, Sept. 29, 1847, by Rev. D. S. Welling.
John Hull and Elizabeth Straughsbaugh, March 9, 1842, by William Cobb, J. P.
Amblin W. Hunt and Elizabeth Stiles, May 5, 1849, by Rev. Jacob Lemmon.
Charles Hunt and Emilia Hays, Jan. 31, 1841, by John Knox, J. P.
James F. Hunter and Martha Jane Roby, Jan. 25, 1849, by Edward Smith.
James Huntsman and Rebecca Hammond, Jan. 25, 1844, by Isaac Talbott, J. P.
James Huntsman and Mary Jane Granfel, March 2, 1848, by Rev. Pardon Cock.
Belden G. Hurlbert and Caroline Delany, July 4, 1850, by William S. Dool.
Emanuel Hurless and Mary Heaston, Jan. 19, 1848, by Rev. Andrew Klingle.
George Hurless and Elizabeth Palmer, Dec. 1, 1842, by Aaron Conaway, J. P.
John Hurless and Sally Ann Wright, May 14, 1842, by Rev. Benjamin Wood.
John Hurless and Mary Jane Wright, May 11, 1846, by Rev. Elias Gatchel.
Michael Hurless and Hannah Tennar, May 22, 1849, by Rev. Jeremiah Phillips.
Zephus Hurless and Elizabeth Green, Oct. 29, 1841, by Robert P. Simpson, J. P.
Alexander Huston and Amanda M. Collins, May 7, 1843, by Israel Archbold, V. D. M.
Caleb Irwin and Elizabeth Carns, Aug. 23, 1845, by John Cramblett, J. P.
Ninian Irwin and Sarah Ann Carpenter, Sept. 28, 1848, by Isaac Talbot, J. P.
Robert Irwin and Louisa Vickers, Aug. 21, 1845, by Isaac Talbott, J. P.
John Ish and Susanna Dinger, Dec. 18, 1843, by Henry N. Beckett, J. P.
Nathaniel Jenkin and Mehala Smith, Feb. 22, 1849, by John Graham, J. P.
William Jenkins and Mahala Jinkins, Jan. 5, 1843, by Rev. Elias Gatchel.
Joseph E. Junkins and Elizabeth Hanna, June 11, 1846, by James Kerr, V. D. M.
Zachariah Jewell and Mary Dool, Sept. 4, 1848, by T. R. Crawford, V. D. M.
Elias Johnson and Matilda Campbell, Nov. 25, 1841, by Rev. Robert Clark.
Elijah Johnson and Mary Cocherel, Jan. 14, 1847, by Rev. William B. Hunt.
Joseph R. Johnson and Malinda Wright, Feb. 1, 1849, by John Graham, J. P.
Lewis Johnson and Hannah S. West, Oct. 4, 1849, by T. R. Crawford, V. D. M.
Samuel Johnson and Mary Shiery, Sept. 18, 1846, by James Cameron.
Thomas Johnson and Eleanor Scott, Oct. 3, 1843, by James Kerr, V. D. M.
Wesley Johnson and Elizabeth Roby, Dec. 30, 1846, by Rev. B. S. Johnson.
Wesley Y. Johnson and Susanna Hamilton, Dec. 25, 1847, by Samuel Skinner, J. P.
William Johnson and Hannah Dowell, April 1, 1841, by Rev. Elias Gatchel.
William B. Johnson and Mary Gundy, March 16, 1848, by Rev. Andrew Klingle.
William Johnson and Elizabeth Carpenter, Oct. 12, 1848, by Isaac Vallcott, J. P.
Alexander Johnston and Matilda Hendricks, April 26, 1845, by R. Brown.
George Johnston and Isabella Cairns, March 3, 1842, by R. Brown.
John Johnston and Eleanor Cairns, Nov. 23, 1843, by R. Brown.
John Johnson and Mary Hagan, Sept. 9, 1846, by T. T. Larkin, J. P.
Thomas Joice and Elizabeth McCullough, June 22, 1845, by John Graham, J. P.
Alexander Jones and Marinda McKnight, April 28, 1850, by Samuel Skinner, J. P.
David Jones and Margaret Riggle, Aug. 22, 1844, by Rev. A. Bartholomew.
Henry Jones and Ann Jenkins, June 27, 1849, by Rev. Jacob Lemmon.
John Jones and Edith Miller, Oct. 12, 1844, by Jonas Holloway, J. P.
John Jones and Lydia Richards, March 23, 1848, by John Rea, V. D. M.
Lewis Jones and Elizabeth Brown, Nov. 14, 1843, by Wesley Smith.
Samuel Jones and Nancy Quillan, Aug. 9, 1844, by Reynolds K. Price, J. P.
William Jones and Sarah Renicor, April 8, 1849, by William Arnold, J. P.
William M. Jones and Lydia Hallett, Jan. 12, 1845, by John Knox, J. P.
George Joy and Sarah Fisher, July 13, 1841, by Nathan Tannehill, J. P.
Abraham Jackson and Susan Thompson, Dec. 29, 1849, by Joshua Adams.
John Jackson and Margaret Neill, Jan. 24, 1842, by William Ross, V. D. M.

John James and Matilda Holmes, July 29, 1841, by Jesse Merrell, J. P.
Andrew Jamison and Ann Jamison, Sept. 6, 1849, by James Kerr, V. D. M.
Archibold Jamison and Mary E. Martin, Jan. 16, 1845, by James Cameron.
Robert Jamison and Mary Welch, Oct. 25, 1845, by Rev. Alexander Wilson.
William Jamison and Sarah Easter, Jan. 18, 1848, by Hugh Parks, V. D. M.
Jacob Jarvis and Eliza Matilda Bryan, Oct. 6, 1842, by Rev. William Knox.
George Kail and Nancy Curran, Dec. 14, 1843, by Henry H. Beckett, J. P.
Jackson H. Kail and Elizabeth J. Stonaker, June 18, 1847, by Rev. A. C. Hunger.
Samuel Kail and Catharine Nofsinger, May 28, 1846, by Abraham Lemaster, V. D. M.
Isaac B. Keepers and Mary Ann Hickson, Sept. 28, 1843, by Rev. Israel Archbold.
David Keeser and Minerva Ruby, Sept. 23, 1843, by M. Crowl, J. P.
Simon Keeser and Mary Ann Johnson, Sept. 15, 1843, by James McGaw.
Conrad Keesey and Ellen Brooks, Jan. 14, 1841, by John Selby, J. P.
James Keesey and Margaret Layport, April 30, 1846, by Rev. Samuel W. Day.
William Kelly and Margaret Wood, Sept. 5, 1843, by Reynolds K. Price, J. P.
Daniel Kennedy and Mary Ann Johnson, Feb. 14, 1850, by Rev. William B. Hunt.
James Kennedy and Sarah E. Knox, July 23, 1846, by Rev. J. Drummond.
Levi J. Kennard and Sarah Atkinson, Feb. 2, 1847, by James Kerr, V. D. M.
Michael B. Kennedy and Lucinda Crossan, April 25, 1848, by James Kerr, J. P.
Robert Kennedy and Eliza Jane McCullough, Aug. 16, 1848, by Samuel Skinner, J. P.
Absalom Kent and Sarah McColms, Oct. 30, 1849, by M. Crowl, J. P.
Enoch Kent and Margaret Ramsey, April 10, 1848, by Thomas Phillips, J. P.
William Kent and Hannah Lewis, March 30, 1848, by Rev. James Henderson.
James Kerr and Julia A. Carrick, Feb. 25, 1847, by James Kerr, V. D. M.
William Kidwell and Sarah Crabtree, April 5, 1842, by J. Montgomery.
Abraham Kimmell and Susanna Stall, Sept. 19, 1844, by Rev. Amos Bartholomew.
Adam Kimmel and Martha Wallace, March 28, 1849, by Rev. Lemuel B. Perkins, J. P.
Isaac Kimmel and Amanda Sawville, March 24, 1845, by James Cameron.
Samuel Kincaid and Sarah Rea, Feb. 28, 1850, by James Kerr, V. D. M.
John Kinsey and Nancy Strachan, Dec. 30, 1846.
Kersey W. Kinsey and Sarah J. Haverfield, May 6, 1847, by Rev. Thomas Hanna.
Rees Kinsey and Tabitha Whealdon, April 19, 1843, by Reynolds K. Price, J. P.
Reese Kinsey and Eliza Ridgway, Oct. 2, 1845, by Thomas Phillips, J. P.
John Kirk and Mary Ann Nickels, Nov. 29, 1843, by T. M. Erwin, V. D. M.
James Kirkpatrick and Ellen S. Wallace, Feb. 25, 1847, by James Kerr, V. D. M.
Robert G. Kirkpatrick and Elvira Hays, March 13, 1850, by T. R. Crawford, V. D. M.
Joseph Knight and Eliza Ann Jones, Feb. 10, 1842, by John Knox, J. P.
Abraham B. Knittle and Harriet Boar, Jan. 18, 1844, by R. Brown.
John Knoff and Sarah Kimmel, June 4, 1846, by Rev. Amos Bartholomew.
George Knouff and Lettyann McKelveer, Dec. 18, 1844, by John Bryan.
Arthur Knox and Amanda Winter, Aug. 1, 1844, by Wesley Smith.
Robert Knox and Lucy Smith, Aug. 12, 1847, by Rev. Pardon Cook.
Charles Koogler and Mary Welch, June 19, 1849, by Joshua Adams, J. P.
Moses Kraus and Fanny Rothchild, April 14, 1846, by Andrew Lynch, J. P.
George Lafferty and Margaret J. McConnell, April 14, 1847, by H. Parks, V. D. M.
John Lafferty and Elizabeth Rea, March 1, 1842, by James Kerr, V. D. M.
John V. Lafferty and Jane Walters, Sept. 7, 1843, by Rev. Harvey Bradshaw.
Samuel Lafferty and Michael Geary, Jan. 17, 1849, by T. B. Crawford, V. D. M.
Thomas J. Lafferty and Lucy Caves, Sept. 18, 1848, by Samuel Skinner, J. P.
Benjamin Laizure and Mary Ann Laizure, March 29, 1844, by George Cook, J. P.
Moses Lakin and Jane Drydon, Feb. 15, 1842, by John Knox, J. P.

ADDITIONAL HARRISON COUNTY MARRIAGES

Samuel Lakin and Dorcas Colvin, June 22, 1843, by Rev. Elias Gatchel.
Thomas N. Lakin and Mary S. Pickett, Jan. 28, 1847, by John Graham, J. P.
Leonard Lamb and Rebecca Jane Stuart, Aug. 25, 1849, by Joshua Adams, J. P.
John J. Lane and Lucinda Grimes, Oct. 18, 1847, by B. Mitchell, V. D. M.
David Lanning and Mary McMath, Nov. 15, 1846, by R. K. Price, J. P.
John Lathem and Elizabeth Clark, April 18, 1850, by Hugh Parks, V. D. M.
Joseph Laughridge and Lydia A. Phillips, Sept. 19, 1850, by Thomas McClintock, J. P.
George Lavengood and Elizabeth Abel, March 8, 1849, by Andrew Lynch, J. P.
James Law and Eleanor C. Nelson, Feb. 11, 1841, by M. B. Lukins, J. P.
Freeman Lawrence and Emily Mitchell, July 14, 1841, by William Arnold, J. P.
Ezra E. Lawson and Matilda Davis, July 4, 1844, by Daniel Scott, J. P.
Abraham Layport and Sarah Heath, April 30, 1846, by Isaac Talbott, J. P.
Reed Lewis and Maria Ferrell, Nov. 20, 1849, by James Kerr, V. D. M.
William Lewis and Selina Thompson, Feb. 17, 1846, by James Kerr, V. D. M.
William H. Lewis and Harriett Holland, Dec. 14, 1848, by James Kerr, V. D. M.
George Lickey and Phoebe A. Cramer, May 5, 1846, by R. K. Price, J. P.
James Lightner and Elizabeth K. Hoagland, Dec. 23, 1847, by Aaron Conaway, J. P.
Junkins Lightner and Susan Fisher, Nov. 3, 1842, by Hamilton McFadden.
John Lightner and Eliza Jane Dickerson, April 7, 1842, by James Kerr, V. D. M.
Samuel Lightner and Rachel Bingham, Dec. 31, 1846, by Rev. Thomas Hanna.
William Lightner and Sarah A. Shipton, Dec. 21, 1844, by James Kerr, V. D. M.
Joseph Lightell and Ester Morton, April 20, 1848, by Jonas Holloway, J. P.
James Linden and Deborah Davis, March 5, 1841, by John H. Brown, J. P.
James Lindon and Mary Ann Garry, June 31, 1845, by Samuel Ramsey, J. P.
Joseph Lindsey and Hannah Teal, Aug. 10, 1843, by George Clancey, V. D. M.
Francis Lindsley and Elizabeth Cecil, Nov. 16, 1848, by John W. Baker, J. P.
John S. Lisle and Elizabeth J. Lightell, Oct. 11, 1849, by Rev. A. Magee.
Thomas Lock and Mary Skipper, Dec. 29, 1846, by Thomas McClintock, J. P.
Hezekiah Long and Sarah Jane Middleton, May 14, 1843, by Elder Jacob S. Hanger.
James Long and Sarah Dunlap, Feb. 23, 1846, by Richard Brown.
William Long and Mary Ann Stonaker, Dec. 21, 1843, by David Bower, J. P.
John Love and Nancy Downing, Nov. 27, 1850, by McKnight Williamson.
John Lowmiller and Rachel Haun, Oct. 1, 1846, by Andrew Lynch, J. P.
Joshua Lowmiller and Rebecca Sawville, Sept. 11, 1842, by Benjamin Pope.
Aquilla Lukens and Jane Harding, Dec. 26, 1850, by Rev. Thomas Ferrell.
George T. Lukins and Mary Whitten, Feb. 15, 1844, by John L. Layport, J. P.
Nathaniel H. Lukins and Keziah Bliss, May 9, 1844, by Isaac Talbott, J. P.
Francis S. Layport and Rachel L. Ford, April 10, 1845, by Isaac Talbott, J. P.
Isaac Layport and Rachel L. Johnson, Feb. 25, 1841, by Rev. Robert Cook.
Isaac Layport and Cynthia Conaway, June 3, 1847, by Rev. Samuel W. Day.
William Layport and Jane Laughridge, May 10, 1849, by Hamilton McFadden, J. P.
Reuben Lee and Nancy Jane Laizure, Aug. 19, 1847, by Samuel Skinner, J. P.
Thomas Martin Lee and Mary L. McCullough, Feb. 11, 1847, by James Kerr, V. D. M.
George Leece and Jane Birney, Jan. 9, 1849, by Rev. James C. Merryman.
Amon Lemmon and Rebecca Forsythe, Aug. 8, 1850, by Rev. A. Magee.
Moses Lemmon and Mary Ann Allen, Nov. 19, 1846, by Rev. Josiah Gibson.
William Lenheart and Mary Harris, Dec. 22, 1846, by E. P. Jowle.
Elisha Lewis and Catherine Snider, March 18, 1841, by William Arnold, J. P.
Elias Lewis and Mary Trickle, Feb. 2, 1843, by Rev. Harvey Bradshaw.
Jacob Lewis and Catharine Mattern, Aug. 4, 1841, by John Ross.
Jacob Lewis and Sarah Kelly, Sept. 12, 1844, by Rev. Ebenezer Hays.
William Lynn and Mary Butler, Oct. 11, 1842, by Matthew H. Phillips, J. P.
David T. Lyon and Ann B. Miller, Sept. 12, 1850, by Cyrus McNeely.
Ruben Lyon and Eliza Ann Fogle, July 25, 1841, by Cyrus McNeely.

604   HISTORICAL COLLECTIONS OF HARRISON COUNTY

David W. Lyons and Sarah Ann Wallace, March 31, 1842, by James Kerr, V. D. M.
James Lyons and Margaret Crouch, Aug. 31, 1841, by James Kerr, V. D. M.
John G. Lyons and Martha T. Wycoff, April 27, 1847, by Rev. Jacob Lemmon.
Samuel Lyons and Livonia Dunlap, Aug. 23, 1850, by R. Brown.
Alexander Lytle and Maria Sheldz, April 5, 1849, by Michael Oswalt.
John McAdam and Harriett Butler, April 13, 1848, by Rev. Samuel Findley.
Alexander McAdoo and Elizabeth Beck, July 6, 1850, by James Taggart, J. P.
William McAdoo and Nancy Clark, Oct. 10, 1844, by John Graham, J. P.
James McAfee and Margaret Atkinson, April 4, 1846, by Rev. Thomas McGaw.
William Macance and Michel Cramblett, Feb. 24, 1842, by John L. Layport, J. P.
Dennis McBaines and Mary Jane Dickey, Sept. 30, 1847, by Rev. Job Lister.
Andrew McBrean and Elizabeth Starr, July 29, 1846, by John Wallace, J. P.
Robert McBride and Anne Jones, May 18, 1845, by John Knox, J. P.
Thomas McCall and Mary Adams, Oct. 5, 1848, by Rev. Joseph Gorden.
William McCamiss and Melisa Carrol, Jan. 17, 1844, by Rev. A. Bartholomew.
William McCamiss and Barbara Palmer, Feb. 5, 1850, by Rev. C. C. Riggs.
Thomas A. McCann and Jane McKee, April 1, 1845, by Rev. E. Hays.
Isaac McCauley and Rebecca Peoples, May 28, 1850, by Rev. Alexander Swany.
John McCleary and Emely Thompson, Nov. 17, 1842, by Wesley Smith.
James McClintick and Catharine Walters, June 1, 1844, by John L. Layport, J. P.
William McClish and Susanna Bell, Jan. 28, 1848, by James Hoover, J. P.
James McCollam and Sarah Straub, Nov. 30, 1845, by John Ross, J. P.
Matthew McCollom Knox and Hannah H. Romans, May 16, 1848, by Rev. J. C. Merryman.
Johnson G. McCollough and Margery Brokaw, Feb. 21, 1850, by James Kerr, V. D. M.
David McConkey and Margaret Reed, Feb. 22, 1843, by William Cable, J. P.
William McConkey and Nancy Likes, Dec. 13, 1849, by Cyrus McNeely.
John C. McConnell and Rachel Browning, April 9, 1848, by R. K. Price, J. P.
Robert McConnell and Sarah Ann Pickering, May 25, 1843, by Rev. Jacob Lemmon.
Wilson McConnell and Rachel Hooper, April 21, 1842, by M. Crawe, J. P.
Andrew McCormick and Jane Murdock, May 24, 1843, by George Clancey, V. D. M.
John McCormick and Priscilla Purviance, Sept. 3, 1843, by George Clancey, V. D. M.
John W. McCort and Margaret Evans, Oct. 24, 1844, by Rev. Israel Archbold.
Ebenezer McCoy and Hannah Dickerson, March 16, 1848, by Rev. James Henderson.
Francis W. McCoy and Catharine Dudgeon, April 1, 1849, by James J. McIlgar.
Matthew McCoy and Harriett Crawford, Dec. 3, 1847, by James Kerr, V. D. M.
Colmar McCoy and Elizabeth Corbin, Aug. 31, 1843, by James L. Clark.
Thomas McCrary and Elizabeth Chapman, Dec. 25, 1843, by Rev. William Knox.
Alexander G. McCullough and Evaline Tomlinson, Dec. 7, 1848, by James Kerr, V. D. M.
Andrew McCullough and Rebecca McCullough, Dec. 10, 1847, by Rev. Israel Archbold.
James McCullough and Mary Brown, Jan. 9, 1845, by Edwin H. Nevin, V. D. M.
John McCullough and Martha J. Welch, April 26, 1849, by B. Herron.
Jonathan McCullough and Ann E. Hill, Dec. 10, 1845, by John Graham, J. P.
Joseph McCullough and Elizabeth Patton, Sept. 18, 1843, by Rev. Thomas Hanna.
Cyrus McCurdy and Peggy Ann Bowers, Feb. 20, 1849, by Rev. A. N. Bartholomew.
David McCurdy and Mary McNamee, July 13, 1843, by James Simpson, J. P.
Peter McCurdy and Mary Ann Bower, Sept. 6, 1848, by Rev. A. N. Bartholomew.
Martin McDevitt and Jane Scott, May 20, 1847, by E. P. Jacob.
Samuel McDivitt and Isabella Jeffers, Sept. 25, 1841, by James Evans, J. P.

ADDITIONAL HARRISON COUNTY MARRIAGES

James McDonough and Fanny Abbott, July 17, 1847, by Aaron Conaway, J. P.
Obediah McDonough and Mary A. Shaffer, March 13, 1844, by Robert P. Simpson, J. P.
Alexander McFadden and Elizabeth Barger, June 29, 1847, by James Kerr, V. D. M.
Benjamin McFadden and Margaret Cusick, Oct. 4, 1849, by Hugh Parks, V. D. M.
John W. McFadden and Hannah Hillhouse, Oct. 8, 1846, by Thomas Phillips, J. P.
John McFadden and Catherine Haverfield, Dec. 17, 1847, by Rev. Alexander Wilson.
Samuel McFadden and Jane Baxter, July 3, 1845, by Hugh Parks, V. D. M.
Thomas M. McGaw and Emily Ann Dicks, Feb. 10, 1842, by Rev. Samuel Loney.
John McGill and Nancy Auld, Nov. 13, 1844, by Isaac Talbott.
Robert McGill and Rachel Richerson, June 25, 1846, by Isaac Talbott, J. P.
William McGrew and Cynthia Ann Corbin, Oct. 26, 1848, by Rev. James C. Merryman.
Sampson McGuire and Nancy Hoover, Aug. 13, 1846, by Rev. Samuel W. Day.
Joseph McIlroy and Mary Jane E. Lee, Oct. 9, 1850, by William Lowmes.
Joseph McIlveen and Mary Johnston, May 23, 1850, by John Bryan.
David H. Mackey and Margaret Harryman, Nov. 11, 1848, by Rev. James C. Merryman.
Ebenezer McKinney and Ruhamah Drummond, Nov. 18, 1840, by Rev. Thos. Hanna.
John McKinley and Elizabeth Morris, Aug. 8, 1848, by Rev. James C. Merryman.
Andrew McLandsborough and Marcy McDonagh, Nov. 10, 1846, by Joseph Masters, J. P.
John McLandsborough and Catharine Ann Ely, Aug. 16, 1849, by Rev. Lemuel B. Perkins.
James M. McLane and Mary McFarland, April 3, 1850, by Rev. William Wishart.
John McLaughlin and Nancy Kerr, Feb. 8, 1844, by Rev. John Rea.
Goodnow McMillan and Margaret Glass, Dec. 8, 1850, by David Hanlon, J. P.
James B. McMillan and Eva Glass, June 13, 1844, by Rev. Israel Archbold.
Joel McMillan and Sarah M. Morris, Aug. 10, 1848, by Thomas Phillips, J. P.
John McMillan and Jane Moore, Oct. 10, 1850, by T. R. Crawford, V. D. M.
Matthew McMillan and Rosilly Willison, Nov. 22, 1849, by Samuel Skinner, J. P.
Robert McMillan and Mary Boyd, May 19, 1842, by Reynolds K. Price.
Robert McMillan and Eleanor Moore, Aug. 27, 1850, by J. P. Work, J. P.
Amzi McNamee and Mary E. Harvey, April 11, 1846, by Samuel Skinner, J. P.
Oliver McNary and Eleanor Grove, Sept. 16, 1846, by Rev. Thomas Hanna.
Thornton McNight and Charlotte Houston, Nov. 17, 1844, by Samuel Skinner, J. P.
Martin McPeck and Mary Jane Iler, March 22, 1849, by Aaron Conaway, J. P.
Arthur M. Maholm and Nancy Holland, March 23, 1848, by James Kerr, V. D. M.
John Maholm and Elizabeth McFadden, Nov. 27, 1845, by H. Parks, V. D. M.
James Mahood and Nancy Grimes, Nov. 31, 1843, by Rev. Thomas Hanna.
Joseph Maish and Sarah Ritchey, Sept. 18, 1845, by James Kerr, V. D. M.
Archibald R. Major and Francis Lemmon, March 27, 1845, by B. Mitchell, V. D. M.
Joseph Major and Sarah Jane Bell, Feb. 21, 1849, by Rev. James C. Merryman.
Lewis C. Mallernee and Levina McFadden, March 3, 1846, by Michael Leard, J. P.
William Mallernee and Susanna Walker, Nov. 18, 1848, by Michael Lard.
John Manbeck and Phebe Beck, Sept. 18, 1847, by Rev. Abraham Lemaster.
William Manbeck and Isabella Miller, Jan. 25, 1849, by Thomas Finnicum, J. P.
James Manly and Ann Jordon, Aug. 25, 1848, by Rev. Joseph Gorden.
Jerret Manning and Doratha Familton, Dec. 1, 1842, by Rev. Israel Archbold.
Nathaniel Mansfield and Eliza Jane Pearce, July 5, 1849, Joshua Adams, J. P.
James Markee and Eleanor Norris, Jan. 18, 1846, by M. F. Burkhead, J. P.
John Markee and Parmelia Ann Davidson, April 7, 1841, by Rev. Benjamin P. Furgason.

William Markee and Lucinda Smith, April 5, 1842, by J. Montgomery.
David Markley and Eleanor Stevens, Dec. 24, 1846, by Andrew Lynch, J. P.
John Markley and Mary Ann Manbeck, Feb. 20, 1848, by Rev. Abraham Lamaster.
Matthias Markley and Rebecca Staphens, Jan. 24, 1850, by Andrew Lynch, J. P.
Thomas Markley and Mary Henderson, May 21, 1846, by Rev. James Cameron.
Christopher Marshall and Catharine Shiver, March 6, 1845, by John Blair, J. P.
Jacob Marshall and Sarah Jane McFadden, Feb. 12, 1846, by William Arnold, J. P.
John G. Marshall and Nancy Sloan, Feb. 4, 1847, by H. Parks, V. D. M.
John F. Marshbank and Elizabeth Wirick, Jan. 20, 1848, by T. R. Crawford, V. D. M.
Alexander Mason and Nancy Ann Roper, Feb. 8, 1850, by Rev. J. W. Shrewe.
William C. Mason and Mary Osbourne, Sept. 4, 1849, by James Kerr, V. D. M.
Brice Masten and Lydia A. Hilbert, April 8, 1845, by Rev. Amos Bartholomew.
Isaac Masters and Ann Overholtz, March 15, 1849, by Rev. Michael Oswalt.
Morris Matson and Mary Mercer, March 12, 1845, by Robert Wade.
Abijah Matthews and Nancy Ford, June 1, 1842, by John Knox, J. P.
William Matthews and Margaret Ray, Feb. 6, 1845, by John Rea, V. D. M.
William Matthews and Susanna Whitington, Oct. 11, 1849, by John Knox, J. P.
James Maxwell and Mary Robison, Nov. 19, 1846, by Rev. Thomas Hanna.
James Maxwell and Deborah Busby, March 21, 1850, by John Bryant, J. P.
Robert Maxwell and Rachel J. Tompson, March 24, 1847, by James Kerr, V. D. M.
Samuel Maxwell and Elizabeth Hager, April 4, 1844, by George Cook, J. P.
Samuel Maxwell and Mary Ann Howser, Nov. 11, 1847, by James Kerr, V. D. M.
Thomas Maxwell and Sarah Jane Miller, Oct. 6, 1850, by Rev. James R. Leig.
Walter C. Maxwell and Mariah Shipton, Aug. 19, 1841, by W. D. McCartney, V. D. M.
Thomas H. Mazend and Susanna McCullough, Oct. 14, 1845, by Rev. Samuel Langden.
John Means and Mary Wilson, April 19, 1850, by Rev. Alexander Wilson.
Isaac N. Meek and Sarah Foster, March 25, 1841, by Rev. E. Smith.
John Melany and Martha McMullen, Aug. 18, 1843, by R. Brown.
Thomas Meldrum and Rachel Billingsley, Jan. 27, 1848, by Pardon Cook.
Thomas Merchant and Eliza E. Merchant, Oct. 10, 1844, by Rev. John R. Dunlap.
Thomas Merrill and Elizabeth Jackson, Aug. 31, 1842, by James Kerr, V. D. M.
Daniel Merryman and Mary Ann Yarnel, June 15, 1848, by Rev. Pardon Cook.
John Merriman and Mary Shivers, Nov. 14, 1844, by John Blair, J. P.
Henson Merryman and Mary Moore Hill, March 1, 1843, by Rev. Harvey Bradshaw.
Dennis Micheal and Cynthia Barnhart, Aug. 10, 1848, by Rev. J. Burns.
Jesse Middleton and Susan A. Titus, Dec. 24, 1845, by Samuel Ramsey, J. P.
Andrew Mikesell and Sarah Ann Hilbert, June 1, 1843, by Andrew Lynch, J. P.
George Mikesell and Mahala Hoobler, Jan. 9, 1845, by Rev. A. Bartholomew.
Asa Miller and Matilda Wharton, Oct. 20, 1850, by James Taggart, J. P.
Eli Miller and Mary Hollingsworth, March 6, 1846, by Jonas Hollaway, J. P.
Elias Miller and Rebecca Foos, June 17, 1841, by Thomas Finnicum, J. P.
George Miller and Catharine Lowmiller, Nov. 7, 1843, by Thomas Finnicum, J. P.
Jacob Miller and Eleanor Cox, Oct. 7, 1849, by James Taggart, J. P.
James Miller and Delila Cissel, June 30, 1842, by Hamilton McFadden, J. P.
John M. Miller and Hannah Smith, March 28, 1841, by Samuel Lewis, J. P.
John Miller and Jane A. Bryan, Nov. 22, 1844, by J. W. McAbee.
John Miller and Susanna Mikesell, May 1, 1849, by Rev. D. Sparks.
John Miller and Fanny Gordon, Feb. 28, 1850, by Rev. John Moffitt.
John Miller and Elizabeth Shepherd, May 7, 1850, by William Wilson, J. P.
Milton Miller and Jane Blackburn, Aug. 9, 1847, by Rev. D. S. Welling.
Richard Miller and Elizabeth Jenkens, Feb. 6, 1850, by Rev. Jacob Lemmon.

ADDITIONAL HARRISON COUNTY MARRIAGES

Rozel D. Miller and Jane Robison, Feb. 6, 1850, by B. Brown.
Solomon Miller and Elizabeth Long, March 8, 1849, by Rev. D. Sparks.
James Milligan and Elizabeth Hays, May 31, 1845, by Robert Henderson, J. P.
Mark Milligan and Joanna Smith, Feb. 17, 1845, by John Blair, J. P.
Alexander Milliken and Eliza Ann Lee, Dec. 30, 1841, by Rev. Elias Gatchel.
Elias Mills and Mary Brown, July 29, 1850, by Rev. Samuel W. Day.
Reuben Mills and Elizabeth Parks, April 1, 1845, by Rev. Elias Gatchel.
William Mills and Sarah A. Cannon, Sept. 3, 1844, by Rev. Ebenezer Hays.
Harlin Milliner and Nancy Hooper, March 1, 1849, by Rev. Jacob Lemmon.
Jacob Miner and Mary Kimmell, Dec. 9, 1847, by Rev. A. Bartholomew.
John Minor and Catharine Gillespie, July 28, 1841, by E. H. Custer, J. P.
Eli Minteer and Sarah Teel, Sept. 26, 1844, by Rev. Thomas Hanna.
John Minteer and Ann Maffett, July 7, 1846, by James Kerr, V. D. M.
Alexander Miser and Eleanor Roberts, April 9, 1848, by Rev. A. N. Bartholomew.
Hugh Mitchel and Nancy Nash, March 19, 1844, by Hugh Parks, V. D. M.
Joseph Mitchell and Hannah Arthur, April 25, 1849, by Rev. Alexander Wilson.
Joseph Mitchell and Susanna Thompson, Oct. 8, 1850, by James Kerr, V. D. M.
Robert Mitchell and Eliza J. Atkinson, April 1, 1845, by Rev. Thomas Hanna.
Rudolph Mitchell and Nancy Ferrell, Feb. 18, 1841, by James Kerr, V. D. M.
Samuel Mitchel and Mary Marshall, April 21, 1849, by Rev. Alexander Wilson.
Hiram Mitchner and Eliza Long, Oct. 21, 1845, by Robert Henderson, J. P.
Seth Mitchener and Elizabeth Ann Shannon, Sept. 3, 1850, by William Browning.
Adam Moffitt and Eliza Jane Means, Oct. 28, 1845, by Rev. George Lucy.
Andrew Monroe and Loisa Mansfield, May 12, 1841, by Elias Gatchel, V. D. M.
John Monroe and Rachel Mills, Sept. 18, 1842, by Samuel Skinner, J. P.
Abriam Moore and Hannah Shivers, Nov. 13, 1841, by Rev. Robert Cook.
Alexander Moore and Elizabeth Johnson, Nov. 27, 1842, by Rev. Harvey Bradshaw.
Alexander F. Moore and Susanna Hanna, July 26, 1848, by Rev. Joseph Gorden.
Christopher Moore and Margaret Cameron, June 15, 1850, by William Arnold, J. P.
David Moore and Jane Clark, March 11, 1841, by James Kerr, V. D. M.
Elisha Moore and Rebecca Boutel, Dec. 4, 1845, by Nathaniel Linder.
Enos Moore and Hannah Bargar, May 14, 1846, by John Blair, J. P.
George Moore and Eliza Jane Christy, May 11, 1847, by John Graham, J. P.
Gillespy Moore and Eliza Ann Patton, Oct. 5, 1842, by John Walker, V. D. M.
Henry Moore and Mary A. Collins, April 8, 1845, by J. N. McAbee.
Isiah Moore and Henrietta Reynolds, Sept. 25, 1847, by Aaron Conaway, J. P.
James Moore and Julia L. Edney, Feb. 25, 1849, by Rev. Pardon Cook.
Jeremiah Moore and Catharine Davidson, Aug. 22, 1841, by O. N. B. Lukins, J. P.
John Moore and Elizabeth Figley, March 27, 1846, by Rev. J. J. Covert.
John Moore and Ann Chandler, Oct. 12, 1850, by Thomas Phillips, J. P.
Samuel Moore and Isabella Birney, Oct. 22, 1845, by Samuel W. Day.
Thomas Moore and Catherine Kimmell, June 15, 1841, by Rev. Benjamin Pope.
Thomas Moore and Mary Dugan, Dec. 15, 1847, by H. Parks, V. D. M.
Uriah Moore and Mary Ann Fulton, Oct. 13, 1842, by Rev. G. M. Hair.
William Moore and Emelina Brooks, Jan. 14, 1841, by John Selby, J. P.
William Moore and Susanna Carpenter, April 13, 1843, by E. H. Custer, J. P.
William Moore and Harriett Wilson, Sept. 19, 1844, by John Blair, J. P.
William Moore and Hannah Sanders, Dec. 31, 1850, by Rev. John Burns.
John Morris and Lucinda Dowdell, Aug. 8, 1844, by Robert Wade, J. P.
John Morris and Eliza Worley, Dec. 13, 1849, by William Arnold, J. P.
John Morris and Elizabeth Porter, March 20, 1846, by William Arnold, J. P.
Morgan Morris and Eleanor Smith, Dec. 27, 1843, by Matthew H. Phillips, J. P.
Thomas Morris and Jane Maxwell, March 25, 1846, by Matthew H. Phillips, J. P.
Francis Morrison and Permilla Lawver, June 7, 1850, by Henry H. Beckett, J. P.
George Morrow and Nancy Bowland, June 11, 1846, by R. Brown.
William J. Morrow and Joanah Easter, June 30, 1847, by Thomas Merrell.
Jacob Mowder and Martha Gilbert, Aug. 2, 1846, by L. Liender.

Allen T. Musgrove and Mary A. Gotshall, Jan. 6, 1850, by Marshall McCall, J. P.
Daniel W. Mustard and Sarah Jane Young, April 30, 1842, by R. Brown.
Samuel Myers and Sarah Layport, Aug. 5, 1845, by Samuel W. Day.
Alexander Noragong and Delila Waters, Jan. 1, 1846, by Rev. Cyrus Riggs.
Samuel Naragong and Lavina Hoobler, June 22, 1848, by Henry H. Beckett, J. P.
John M. Nash and Margaret Ann Mitchell, Dec. 20, 1849, by Hugh Parks, V. D. M.
Samuel Nash and Easter Ann Clifford, Jan. 25, 1849, by Hugh Parks, V. D. M.
Clark Neely and Sarah Ogdon, Nov. 5, 1844, by John Rea, V. D. M.
John Neely and Mary Jane Skelly, March 22, 1842, by Thomas C. Vincent, J. P.
John Neely and Hannah Guynn, Jan. 27, 1848, by James Kerr, V. D. M.
George C. Nelson and Charlotte Carnes, April 7, 1842, by William Arnold, J. P.
John Nelson and Jane Lawrence, Aug. 31, 1848, by Thomas Phillips, J. P.
Isaac Nichols and Jane Ferrell, Jan. 27, 1842, by Rev. William F. Lauck.
Jonah Nichols and Elizabeth Herriman, March 16, 1843, by Wesley Smith.
Jonah Nichols and Mary Ann Ritchey, Aug. 31, 1848, by A. D. Blank.
William Nichols and Sophia Corbin, Feb. 11, 1845, by John Blair, J. P.
Thomas Nicholson and Mary Jane Carver, June 8, 1848, by Rev. James Henderson.
Anthony C. Nixon and Sarah A. Jones, April 9, 1846, by Rev. Harvey Bradshaw.
Daniel Noftzer and Elizabeth Crumrine, Jan. 20, 1848, by H. H. Becket, J. P.
James Norman and Martha J. Walcutt, Nov. 16, 1848, by James Kerr, V. D. M.
George Norris and Rebecca Tyler, Nov. 19, 1847, by William Smith.
Jeremiah Norris and Ruth Ann Nevett, Oct. 11, 1849, by Rev. James W. Shreaver.
James Norris and Nancy Mills, Feb. 19, 1846, by William Smith.
John Norris and Ruth Rea, April 4, 1843, by Edwin H. Nevin.
Otho Norris and Sarah Brokaw, Oct. 27, 1842, by James Kerr, V. D. M.
George Nup and Margaret Rutan, Feb. 15, 1849, by Thomas Finnicum, J. P.
David O'Donal and Elizabeth A. Lemaster, Aug. 4, 1844, by Joseph W. Spencer, J. P.
Samuel O'Donnel and Jane Forbes, June 3, 1841, by Richard Brown.
Baruch Oglevee and Mary Evans, Sept. 16, 1841, by Rev. Alexander Wilson.
Harry Oliver and Jane Ferrell, Jan. 2, 1845, by James Kerr, V. D. M.
Augustus Orr and Levina Arbaugh, Aug. 30, 1849, by Thomas Finnicum, J. P.
George Osborne and Mary Law, May 12, 1842, by J. Montgomery.
George Palmer and Mary Jane Cox, Dec. 16, 1847, by Aaron Conaway, J. P.
John Palmer and Elizabeth Fry, April 25, 1841, by Rev. Jacob Lemmon.
John W. Palmer and Hester Ann Blair, March 15, 1841, by Rev. William Deveny.
Michael Palmer and Phœbe A. Campbell, Dec. 28, 1845, by Joseph Masters, J. P.
John Pane and Anne B. Yancy, Aug. 1, 1850, by Rev. Alexander Wilson.
James Parker and Matilda Louden, Dec. 26, 1848, by John Graham, J. P.
John W. Parker and Jane Simpson, Feb. 25, 1843, by Thomas Phillips, J. P.
Robert Parker and Margaret Swaney, Dec. 26, 1843, by Reynolds K. Price, J. P.
William H. Parkinson and Mary Jane Leech, Jan. 11, 1842, by Joseph Clokey, V. D. M.
James Parks and Nancy Sudduth, May 13, 1847, by Rev. Elias Gatchal.
Lewis Parmer and Mary Smith, Feb. 7, 1845, by William Tipton.
Joshua Parrish and Rachel Brown, Jan. 30, 1844, by Rev. Jacob Lemmon.
Arthur Patterson and Mary Fowler, Aug. 16, 1844, by Rev. Israel Archbold.
John Patterson and Catharine Adams, March 21, 1849, by James Kerr, V. D. M.
Joseph Patterson and Margaret Patterson, Sept. 19, 1844, by Asa Holmes, J. P.
Obadiah Patterson and Rebecca Smith, May 14, 1850, by H. Worstell, J. P.
Stephen Patterson and Mary Lamver, Nov. 29, 1842, by David Bower, J. P.
William Patterson and Sarah Ann Megaw, Jan. 4, 1849, by R. Brown.
James Patton and Mary Sloan, Aug. 25, 1847, by Rev. Alexander Wilson.
James H. Patton and Mary Megaw, Feb. 17, 1845, by James Cameron.
John W. Patton and Anne Braden, Dec. 31, 1846, by Rev. Thomas Hanna.
Robert Patton and Sarah Porterfield, March 26, 1850, by Rev. James R. Doig.

ADDITIONAL HARRISON COUNTY MARRIAGES

Jacob Pearce and Jane Dickerson, May 11, 1845, by Rev. George Lucy.
John Pearce and Esther Jane Urquhart, Sept. 1, 1848, by Thomas Phillips, J. P.
William Pearce and Sarah Mansfield, July 16, 1844, by Matthew H. Phillips, J. P.
William N. Pearce and Elizabeth Dunlap, Oct. 21, 1844, by Rev. George Lucy.
James Peddicort and Mary Roby, Sept. 5, 1848, by Rev. Edward Smith.
George Penn and Margaret Best, Aug. 27, 1846, by James Kerr, V. D. M.
John Penn and Ellen Mercer, March 21, 1843, by George Clancey, V. D. M.
John W. Penn and Margaret Simmons, Jan. 13, 1846, by John Wilkin.
James Peoples and Ellen M. Hahn, March 10, 1846, by James Cameron.
John Peoples and Eliza Gotschall, Aug. 5, 1847, by Rev. D. S. Welling.
Joseph W. Peoples and Susanna Parmee, Jan. 6, 1847, by H. H. Beckett, J. P.
John Casper Pepper and Mary Fisher, April 11, 1843, by Thomas McClintick, J. P.
Harvey Perry and Rebecca Kincaid, Aug. 15, 1844, by Matthew H. Phillips, J. P.
William Perry and Elbina Pugh, Oct. 11, 1843, by Elijah Carson, J. P.
William Perry and Betsey Kelly, Dec. 18, 1845, by Rev. Thomas Hanna.
James Perrygoy and Lucinda Smith, Nov. 13, 1842, by Matthew H. Phillips, J. P.
Jacob Peterman and Susanna Ramsey, Nov. 14, 1850, by Henry Heberling, J. P.
Arvin Peters and Permelia Swaney, Sept. 28, 1848, by John Adams, J. P.
Alfred Petty and Rebecca Long, Dec. 25, 1845, by Elijah Carson, J. P.
Thornton Petty and Mary Davidson, Oct. 2, 1846, by Elijah Carson, J. P.
Michael Pfauts and Mary Jane Jeffers, Oct. 7, 1847, by Rev. Andrew Klingle.
Bazaleel Phillips and Mary Pritchard, Feb. 25, 1846, by James Kerr, V. D. M.
Enoch W. Phillips and Jane Gallbraith, Feb. 27, 1845, by John Bryan.
Mitton Phipps and Orpha Minster, Aug. 31, 1848, by R. K. Price, J. P.
John Pickering and Nancy Bleak, March 2, 1843, by Rev. William Deveney.
Moses Pickering and Lydia Thornton, Jan. 1, 1846, by John Graham, J. P.
Barton H. Pickett and Eliza A. Norris, Feb. 27, 1846, by Rev. William Smith.
William Pilcher and Mary Jane Hamilton, May 5, 1842, by Rev. G. M. Hair.
William Piles and Phœbe Barkhurst, Sept. 27, 1845, by Rev. Robert Scott.
Jacob Pittinger and Mary Ann Hendricks, April 21, 1842, by Rev. William G. Lauck.
Nathaniel Pittinger and Mariah S. Atkinson, Oct. 28, 1841, by W. M. McCartney.
John Pittis and Asseneth Cottrell, June 3, 1847, by Rev. Samuel W. Day.
John C. Plowman and Mary E. Crawford, Dec. 31, 1850, by Israel Archbold.
James Pogue and Sarah Barkcroft, Jan. 1, 1846, by Rev. George Lucy.
Cyrus Poland and Susanna Petty, Feb. 11, 1841, by Michael Crawl, J. P.
Elias Polen and Mary Hurless, March 22, 1849, by James Hoover, J. P.
Mordicai Poland and Elizabeth Bell, March 16, 1843, by John L. Layport, J. P.
Nathaniel Polan and Mary Swan, Sept. 25, 1843, by Rev. William Knox.
Peter Polen and Ann Maria Graham, Jan. 9, 1849, by Rev. Charles Carter.
William Polen and Elizabeth Crumrine, Feb. 27, 1845, by Robert Henderson, J. P.
David Pool and Martha Gorley, March 19, 1845, by James Kerr, V. D. M.
Hugh Porter and Sarah Irwin, June 23, 1842, by Joseph W. Spencer, J. P.
Johnston Porter and Rachel Anderson, Oct. 18, 1843, by Wesley Smith.
William Porter and Elizabeth Jones, Aug. 12, 1841, by Rev. Jacob Lemmon.
James Poulson and Asneth Spray, March 29, 1849, by E. P. Jacobs.
John Poulson and Mahala Spray, March 25, 1845, by Robert P. Simpson, J. P.
William Poulson and Deborah Ross, Nov. 24, 1842, by Thomas Phillips, J. P.
Norvil Powell and Margaret Jane Crossan, April 20, 1850, by A. D. Clark.
Junias Preston and Elizabeth A. Barcroft, Dec. 12, 1845, by Rev. A. N. Hamlin.
Bazaleel Price and Catharine Johnson, Sept. 17, 1844, by J. W. McAbee.
Ira Price and Belinda Dunlap, May 5, 1842, by R. Brown.
Ira Price and Rachel Arbaugh, April 26, 1849, by Rev. D. Sparks.
James Price and Nancy Williamson, April 4, 1844, by James Kerr, V. D. M.
Stewart Price and Maranda Rowley, Dec. 14, 1843, by R. Brown.
Ellis Pugh and Cassandra Sulfridge, March 31, 1846, by Rev. Elias Gatchel.

Eneas Pugh and Margaret Jane Russell, Oct. 24, 1841, by John Selby, J. P.
Enoch Pugh and Mary Ann Foot, Aug. 5, 1847, by Thomas Phillips, J. P.
Enos Pugh and Hannah Nichols, Nov. 17, 1846, by Elijah Carson, J. P.
Fleming Pumphrey and Mary J. Murry, July 1, 1845, by R. K. Price, J. P.
Harrison R. Pumphrey and Susanna Pumphrey, Nov. 5, 1844, by Rev. Samuel Langdon.
Amos Quillan and Mary Johnston, Dec. 17, 1844, by Rev. George Lucy.
David Quillan and Jane Wilkins, March 13, 1844, by Rev. Jacob Bull.
Elihu Quillan and Eleanor Ann Phillips, Jan. 7, 1841, by Rev. Benjamin P. Ferguson.
Stinson Quillan and Urcellia Milhom, March 8, 1842, by Martz Hoggs, V. D. M.
Thomas J. Quillan and Rachel Dennis, Nov. 25, 1847, by R. K. Price, J. P.
William Quillan and Abby Bell, Aug. 15, 1850, by David Hanlin, J. P.
Thomas Quinn and Mariah Watters, April 30, 1846, by Rev. Samuel W. Day.
Anderson Ralston and Catharine Jane Michael, Oct. 26, 1848, by Rev. J. Burns.
David H. Ralston and Rebecca McCammis, Feb. 11, 1841, by John R. Dunlap.
Ephraim Ralston and Magdalena Hildenbrand, Dec. 16, 1841, by Rev. John P. Dundass.
Lewis W. Ralston and Nancy Sears, Dec. 30, 1847, by Rev. Elias Gatchel.
Hugh Ramsey and Elizabeth Lyons, Jan. 26, 1841, by John Rea, V. D. M.
John Ramsey and Nancy Maffit, May 31, 1844, by James Kerr, V. D. M.
John Ramsey and Sarah Jane Hines, March 16, 1847, by G. A. Lowman.
Samuel T. Ramsey and Mary Barger, Feb. 16, 1843, by James Kerr, V. D. M.
Thomas Ramsey and Louisa Carson, Sept. 8, 1850, by Rev. W. B. Hunt.
William Ramsey and Mary Hines, Feb. 23, 1841, by James Kerr, V. D. M.
William Ramsey and Tabitha Wilson, Oct. 27, 1841, by Rev. Alexander Wilson.
Thomas Ramsour and Susanna Miller, May 14, 1846, Rev. Amos Bartholomew.
Henry J. Randall and Ann Huntsman, Feb. 4, 1849, by Jonas Hollaway, J. P.
Jonathan Randal and Mary Sinclear, Jan. 31, 1846, by Samuel W. Day.
Joshua Randall and Mary Holloway, Feb. 20, 1845, by William Tipton.
James P. Rankin and Margaret Brown, April 14, 1842, by Rev. Jacob Lemmon.
Samuel O. Ray and Mary A. Norfolke, Aug. 26, 1847, by Rev. John Rea.
Joseph Rea and Matilda Russell, March 30, 1848, by Rev. Elias Gatchell.
Ambrose Read and Mary Ann Lewis, May 10, 1848, by Rev. Henry Heberling.
William Readman and Mary Ann Anderson, Feb. 11, 1841, by Thomas Phillips, J. P.
James Reames and Susanna Clark, July 22, 1841, by Rev. Jacob Lemmon.
John P. Redding and Belinda Strode, May 29, 1842, by George Clancey, V. D. M.
Benjamin Reed and Sarah Smith, Aug. 26, 1842, by Cyrus McNeely.
Benjamin Reed and Catharine Shauss, Nov. 15, 1848, by Thomas Finnicum.
Brice Reed and Eady Bishop, June 6, 1844, by Henry H. Beckett, J. P.
David Reed and Lydia Ann Kirkpatrick, Dec. 1, 1846, by Rev. D. S. Welling.
Davis Reed and Susannah Simmons, April 19, 1843, by Thomas Phillips, J. P.
John Reed and Mariah Hilbert, Jan. 8, 1843, by Andrew Lynch, J. P.
Mitchell Reed and Sarah Foster, April 9, 1846, by John Rea, V. D. M.
Andrew Renaker and Catharine Grim, Aug. 19, 1849, by Andrew Lynch, J. P.
Edward Reniker and Elizabeth Nup, Jan. 21, 1841, by Thomas Finicum, J. P.
Jacob Renaker and Susanna Sheldtz, Nov. 16, 1849, by R. Brown.
John Reynard and Julia Pitts, Sept. 9, 1841, by R. Brown.
Alexander Reynolds and Catharine McKee, Feb. 18, 1845, by Rev. E. Hays.
Thomas Rice and Margaret Barcroft, Dec. 25, 1845, by Rev. A. N. Hamlin.
William Richardson and Caroline Fisher, April 18, 1843, by Rev. Thomas Hanna.
Daniel W. Richison and Keziah Barkhurst, April 5, 1843, by George Clancey, V. D. M.
Nathan Rickets and Jane Corban, Feb. 15, 1849, by Rev. James C. Merryman.
Jonathan Ridgeway and Elizabeth Hines, May 9, 1844, by Rev. James W. Walker.
Abraham Riggle and Rachel Branchfield, May 30, 1844, by Isaac Talbot, J. P.
William Rigel and Rachel Ann Willison, Feb. 10, 1846, by William Arnold, J. P.

ADDITIONAL HARRISON COUNTY MARRIAGES

Henry Ripley and Elizabeth E. Rogers, Feb. 18, 1847, by Rev. B. Ragan.
James Roach and Hannah Morris, June 29, 1848, by Rev. James Merryman.
William Roach and Jane Jones, March 30, 1844, by Jonas Halloway, J. P.
John Robb and Elizabeth Miller, March 15, 1842, by Hugh Parks, V. D. M.
George Roberts and Nancy Benedick, Aug. 22, 1841, by Andrew Lynch, J. P.
Hazel Roberts and Sarah H. Spring, March 12, 1846, by Rev. Elias Gatchel.
Charles W. Robinson and Jane Connaugh, Oct. 13, 1842, by W. D. McCartney, V. D. M.
Madison Robinson and Sarah A. Cooper, Oct. 31, 1844, by Asa Holmes, J. P.
Edmund Robison and Sophia Hilbert, Oct. 30, 1841, by John Gruber.
James D. Robison and Sarah Ann Longshore, Feb. 1, 1848, by John Graham, J. P.
John M. Robison and Juliet Bostwick, Aug. 15, 1850, by Rev. J. Moffitt.
William Roby and Pricilla Blair, Oct. 15, 1846, by Rev. A. N. Hamlin.
John Rogers and Catherine Houston, May 21, 1850, by William Kemsburg.
Joseph Rodgers and Susan Frater, Nov. 21, 1844, by Rev. Thomas Hanna.
Rowland Rogers and Mary Jane McKinney, Feb. 27, 1848, by John Blair, J. P.
Thomas Rogers and Isabella Adams, Dec. 3, 1846, by John Blair, J. P.
Thomas Rogers and Lucinda Quillan, Aug. 11, 1850, by William Remsburgh.
Wesley Rogers and Albina Johnson, March 23, 1846, by Rev. J. J. Covert.
Gardner Rose and Elizabeth Adams, Nov. 10, 1848, by Rev. Pardon Cook.
Henry Rose and Ruth Rose, Sept. 28, 1850, by Marshall McCall, J. P.
John Stanley Rose and Betsey Johnson Ford, June 8, 1843, by Rev. Jacob Lemmon.
Thompson Rose and Rebecca Scott, Jan. 1, 1849, by Jonas Hollaway, J. P.
William Rose and Lucinda Rose, June 1, 1848, by Marshall McCall, J. P.
John Ross and Margaret Weaver, Jan. 22, 1848, by Rev. Job Lister.
John Rowland and Rosannah Corban, Oct. 28, 1850, by Hugh Parks, V. D. M.
Philip Rowland and Piety Ann Ford, Aug. 29, 1847, by Rev. Job Lister.
Thomas C. Rowles and Caroline Welch, Nov. 4, 1845, by James Kerr, V. D. M.
James Rozengrant and Lenora Conner, July 23, 1848, by Rev. Samuel Skinner.
Benjamin Ruby and Margaret Nash, Nov. 16, 1848, by Hugh Parks, V. D. M.
Robert M. Ruby and Debora Hammond, Nov. 7, 1849, by Rev. J. Lister.
Samuel Runyon and Sarah J. Moore, June 5, 1845, by Rev. William Argo.
William Runnion and Margaret Elliott, May 2, 1842, by James Kerr, V. D. M.
William A. Runyon and Sarah Foreman, Oct. 27, 1842, by Wesley Smith.
John Russell and Mary Fell, Oct. 14, 1847, by T. F. Lukens, J. P.
William Russell and Maria Wallar, March 10, 1848, by William Arnold, J. P.
Benjamin Rutledge and Susan Lewis, Oct. 30, 1845, by Rev. E. Hays.
Thomas Rutledge and Eleanor Birney, June 19, 1845, by Rev. E. Hays.
Lewis Ryan and Malinda Wheeler, March 16, 1847, by Rev. D. S. Welling.
Calvin Sadler and Rachel Bishop, Nov. 3, 1844, by Thomas Finnicum, J. P.
Lewis Salmons and Jane Pittinger, Feb. 21, 1843, by Thomas Phillips, J. P.
John G. Sampson and Elizabeth Birney, Feb. 14, 1850, by Rev. A. Magee.
Edmund T. Sands and Mary A. McFadden, Oct. 10, 1844, by H. Parks, V. D. M.
David Sayres and Margaret Morton, March 22, 1845, by R. R. Price, J. P.
William Sayres and Hannah Winders, Dec. 14, 1841, by Rev. Jacob Lemmon.
John F. Scarborough and Jane Fowler, April 16, 1848, by G. A. Lowman.
Daniel Schiltz and Maria Heath, Sept. 21, 1849, by Aaron Conaway, J. P.
Adolphus J. Schreiber and Mary Ann Moore, March 19, 1850, by Hugh Parks, V. D. M.
Schulein Schwabacher and Nancy Kraus, May 23, 1847, by Andrew Lynch, J. P.
James F. Scott and Eunice Jolly, June 7, 1848, by Rev. Jeremiah Phillips.
John Scott and Jane Evans, June 22, 1841, by Rev. Moses Allen.
Samuel Scott and Dinah Young, Jan. 5, 1843, by John Knox, J. P.
William Scott and Margaret West, Nov. 19, 1844, by James Kerr, V. D. M.
William H. Scott and Jane Whitaker, Sept. 13, 1842, by J. Montgomery.
John Selfridge and Christina Selfridge, Nov. 4, 1850, by Rev. S. P. Woolf.
Charles Sergent and Tabitha Strode, Aug. 17, 1843, by Rev. John Hantewa.
Andrew Sewell and Priscilla Creggo, Dec. 12, 1844, by John Graham, J. P.

John H. Shaffer and Ida Handly, March 4, 1841, by Cyrus McNeely.
Isaac Shane and Hannah Baird, April 7, 1849, by Rev. C. C. Riggs.
James Shanks to Elizabeth McBarren, Feb. 16, 1843, by Rev. Robert Cook.
William Sharow and Marche Cants, Sept. 5, 1850, by Rev. A. Magee.
William Sharp and Sarah H. Roberts, Nov. 3, 1848, by Samuel Skinner, J. P.
Samuel Shause and Nancy Dudgeon, June 24, 1841, by Rev. Elias Gotshall.
Henry Shawner and Lydia Shearer, May 21, 1841, by Rev. Benjamin Pope.
Joseph Shields and Martha Stiers, Aug. 30, 1849, by Joshua Adams, J. P.
David Shilts and Mary Snider, Dec. 27, 1841, by Robert P. Simpson, J. P.
Henry Shildts and Mary Hauze, June 17, 1841, by David Bower, J. P.
Isaac Shildts and Susan Cessill, June 9, 1844, by Hamilton McFadden, J. P.
John Shilling and Susanna Maynard, Sept. 1, 1844, by Rev. A. Bartholomew.
William Shilling and Elizabeth Kimmel, March 12, 1846, by Thomas Finnicum, J. P.
Samuel Shipman and Margaret Lawson, Nov. 16, 1843, by Thomas Phillips, J. P.
John Shipton and Dorcas Herron, Nov. 16, 1841, by M. F. Burkhead, J. P.
John Shirey and Eliza Queen, Oct. 18, 1841, by W. D. McCartney.
David L. Shisler and Elizabeth Crawford, April 19, 1849, by R. Brown.
Isaac Shissler and Emily Patton, Feb. 1, 1847, by Daniel A. Scott, J. P.
Jacob Shritt and Jane Gamble, April 6, 1843, by Rev. G. M. Hair.
Jacob Shoemaker and Mary Ann McKee, Dec. 15, 1842, by John R. Dundass.
James M. Shugart and Priscilla Wright, Oct. 10, 1850, by Lewis H. Davidson.
Hiram Shultz and Maria Sproals, Jan. 17, 1850, by Rev. A. N. Bartholomew.
Jacob Sidle and Mary Pickering, Aug. 15, 1843, by Alexander Barger, J. P.
Philip Sigars and Melinda Knapp, June 24, 1842, by Rev. William G. Lauck.
Findley T. Simonton and Sarah A. Smith, Oct. 28, 1845, by Rev. A. Wheeler.
John T. Simpson and Nancy H. Livingston, April 4, 1845, by R. Brown.
Thomas E. Simpson and Jane Patterson, Dec. 10, 1850, by Rev. John M. Bray.
Isaac Sinclear and Sarah Ann Tipton, March 27, 1849, by Rev. Jacob Lemmon.
Abraham Singhaus and Rachel Heald, May 27, 1845, by Rev. George Lucy.
Charles Skinner and Julia A. Toombs, Dec. 29, 1845, by Samuel Skinner, J. P.
Abraham Skipper and Lydia Pittinger, July 19, 1849, by Rev. Lemuel B. Perkins.
Robert Sleeth and Sophia Bowman, April 16, 1844, by William Arnold, J. P.
Bazalee Slemmons and Margaret Adams, May 6, 1841, by W. D. McCartney, V. D. M.
James Slemmons and Margaret J. Lemmon, June 18, 1846, by B. Mitchell, V. D. M.
Matthew G. Slemmons and Ann Welch, Jan. 26, 1841, by W. D. McCartney, V. D. M.
Obadiah Slemmons and Eleanor M. Boyles, April 2, 1846, by James Kerr, V. D. M.
John Sloan and Eliza Wherry, June 3, 1847, by Rev. Z. Ragan.
Philip Smick and Sarah Swan, Feb. 6, 1849, by Rev. D. Sparks.
John Smiley and Judy Ann Cox, May 1, 1849, by B. Herron.
Eli Smith and Sarah Molesworth, Sept. 19, 1844, by Rev. William Tipton.
George Smith and Sarah Jane Case, June 28, 1847, by Rev. Alexander Wilson.
George Smith and Sarah Hendershot, April 16, 1843, by Rev. Jacob Brill.
Jacob Smith and Susanna Granfell, Jan. 12, 1843, by Rev. Dyas Neel.
James P. Smith and Ann Cramblet, Oct. 16, 1847, by G. A. Lowman.
James W. Smith and Sarah Jane Bosley, Dec. 31, 1849, by William Reed, J. P.
Jesse P. Smith and Margaret Brown, March 1, 1849, by R. K. Price, J. P.
John Smith and Mary Ann Anderson, Jan. 25, 1843, by Thomas McClintick, J. P.
John F. Smith and Margaret Donnard, Nov. 3, 1846, by Rev. John Marshall.
John P. Smith and Hannah Welch, Feb. 13, 1845, by Rev. Samuel Langdon.
Nathan P. Smith and Keziah Wheeler, Oct. 10, 1844, by Rev. Samuel Langdon.
William Smith and Matilda Ingle, Oct. 5, 1842, by Thomas Phillips, J. P.
William Smith and Eliza Wright, Nov. 16, 1844, by Rev. John M. Trego.

ADDITIONAL HARRISON COUNTY MARRIAGES 613

William Smith and Mary Jane Ellis, March 25, 1847, by Jonas Holloway, J. P.
William Smith and Eliza Lewis, March 7, 1848, by William Arnold, J. P.
William Smith and Jane Brokaw, Nov. 14, 1849, by McKnight Williamson.
William L. Smith and Rebecca Fullerton, July 27, 1842, by George Atkinson, J. P.
William Snee and Emma Wells, July 25, 1841, by M. B. Lukins, J. P.
Jacob Snider and Elizabeth Bradford, June 24, 1847, by Rev. D. S. Welling.
John Snider and Emeline Middleton, Sept. 28, 1841, by David Bower, J. P.
John Snider and Barbara McDivitt, June 6, 1844, by Rev. Israel Archbold.
Samuel Snider and Hannah Hall, Nov. 1, 1849, by Rev. John Burns.
Joseph K. Soneaker and Margaret A. Covington, Aug. 18, 1846, by Rev. Jacob Lemmon.
John Sparrow and Sarah Jane Adams, Aug. 29, 1849, by Thomas Phillips, J. P.
Daniel Spencer and Martha J. Pritchard, Oct. 22, 1846, by James Kerr, V. D. M.
Samuel C. Spencer and Isabella Wood, Oct. 7, 1847, by Rukney Lewis, V. D. M.
George W. Spiker and Sina Smith, Nov. 9, 1848, by Rev. Pardon Cook.
Lorenzo D. Spiker and Rebecca Jane Dicks, Sept. 5, 1850, by Rev. Abraham Lemaster.
William Spiker and Elizabeth Finnical, April 9, 1844, by Rev. Henry Bradshaw.
Hugh Sproul and Jane Shaw, Aug. 18, 1847, by H. Parks, V. D. M.
James Sproul and Elizabeth Compher, Nov. 15, 1847, by Thomas Merrill.
John Sproul and Elizabeth McLandsborough, Aug. 23, 1849, by Rev. Lemuel B. Perkins.
Thomas Sprawl and Elizabeth McDivitt, Aug. 17, 1848, by Rev. Israel Archbold.
Jacob Spring and Mary Jane Brokaw, Oct. 27, 1842, by Rev. Elias Gatchal.
William Spurrier and Mary L. Dungan, March 22, 1849, by Joshua Adams, J. P.
James M. Stanley and Susanna Scott, June 24, 1848, by John Hitchcock, J. P.
Solomon Staples and Elizabeth Clark, March 8, 1842, by Rev. Adam Hetzler.
Adam States and Mary Ann Sawvill, Feb. 2, 1843, by Benjamin Pope.
Henry A. Stealey and Elizabeth Matthews, March 12, 1843, by James T. Larkin, J. P.
Solomon Steffy and Eliza Simonton, May 9, 1844, by James Kerr, V. D. M.
John Steirs and Emily Belknap, Sept. 7, 1847, by Rev. James Henderson.
Thomas Stephens and Catherine Ann Fitzgerald, April 13, 1847, by William Arnold, J. P.
Thomas Stephens and Eleanor Griffith, Aug. 20, 1849, by James Taggart, J. P.
John H. Stephenson and Gertrude Duffield, May 6, 1845, by James Cameron.
James Sterling and Elizabeth Jones, April 2, 1844, by Rev. Dyas Neal.
Robert B. Stevens and Margaret Murdock, Jan. 18, 1849, by J. Adams, J. P.
Andrew Stewart and Henrietta Slemmons, Jan. 4, 1848, by James Kerr, V. D. M.
James Stewart and Margaret McGonagale, Feb. 11, 1841, by George Clarcy, V. D. M.
James Stewart and Elizabeth Palmer, Sept. 2, 1841, by M. B. Lukins, J. P.
Joel Stewart and Rebecca Bell, Jan. 5, 1848, by James Hoover, J. P.
Alexander Stinard and Sarah Ann Bolin, Oct. 31, 1841, by M. Crowl, J. P.
Washington Stinard and Jane Teel, Sept. 11, 1845, by Rev. Thomas Hanna.
William Stinger and Barbary Ann Winings, April 20, 1843, by John Knox.
John Stoneman and Jane Marshal, July 28, 1846, by Rev. Samuel W. Day.
William Stoops and Susan Daugan, Dec. 10, 1845, by William Arnold, J. P.
Benjamin R. Stout and Jane Hilton, March 7, 1843, by James Kerr, V. D. M.
John Stout and Elizabeth Ann Hobb, Dec. 28, 1848, by John W. Baker, J. P.
Robert Strachan and Rachel Ruby, Sept. 8, 1845, by William Wickoff, J. P.
Ephraim Straughsbaugh and Jane Barger, Aug. 22, 1844, by James Kerr, V. D. M.
Joseph Strausbaugh and Rebecca Dewalt, Feb. 26, 1845, by John Wilkin, J. P.
Michael Straughsbaugh and Christina Straughsbaugh, April 8, 1847, by John Wilkin, J. P.
Michael Strawsbaugh and Mary Moorhead, Dec. 9, 1847, by James Kerr, V. D. M.
Peter Strausbaugh and Elizabeth Dewalt, April 15, 1845, by Rev. Amos Bartholomew.

James Strong and Margaret McKee, Feb. 24, 1843, by Wesley Smith.
James Stuart and Martha McCullough, Oct. 9, 1850, by Thomas Merrill.
Elias Sudduth and Malinda Jones, April 15, 1847, by Rev. Elias Gatchel.
John Sudim to Deborah Hale, Aug. 1, 1843, by E. H. Custer, J. P.
William R. Sumption and Rachel Howard, Dec. 5, 1843, by T. L. Larkin, J. P.
Evan Swain and Mary Ellen Sears, Jan. 12, 1843, by George Clancy.
William Swallow and Emily Eneas, Aug. 26, 1841, by Charles Thorn.
Benjamin Swaney and Jane Christian, July 3, 1845, by Thomas Phillips, J. P.
Jacob Swinehart and Juliann Cook, March 5, 1844, by Aaron Conaway, J. P.
George Taggart and Mariah Welch, Dec. 13, 1842, by John Rea, V. D. M.
James S. Taggart and Adaline Hilligas, March 20, 1845, by Cyrus McNeely.
Samuel Taggart and Jemima H. Kyle, April 24, 1849, by Alexander Wilson.
Henry Tailor and Mary Brown, Jan. 2, 1845, by James Simpson, J. P.
Samuel Tannehill and Nancy Oglevee, May 25, 1842, by Rev. George M. Hair.
John Tanner and Elizabeth Adams, May 9, 1844, by Rev. Elias Gatchel.
Joseph A. Tarbert and Margaret Wilson, Feb. 26, 1846, by Samuel Skinner, J. P.
King Taylor and Sarah Jane Hagan, Nov. 30, 1849, by William Buchanan, J. P.
Elias Tedrick and Sarah Ford, July 1, 1847, by R. K. Price, J. P.
Goliah Tedrow and Christina Miller, April 1, 1841, by Andrew Lynch, J. P.
David Tennant and Mary Watson, Nov. 6, 1845, by John Graham, J. P.
Edwin Thomas and Sarah Ann Turney, March 14, 1843, by C. H. Custer, J. P.
Frederick A. Thomman and Harriet Ditmars, May 18, 1850, by Rev. John Moffitt.
Christopher Thompson and Eliza Utterback, March 21, 1847, by N. Linder.
Ezra Thompson and Prudence Matson, March 21, 1850, by Rev. Charles A. Holmes.
John Thompson and Elizabeth Ruby, April 5, 1842, by Samuel Skinner, J. P.
John Thompson and Maria B. Gruber, March 9, 1848, by Rev. D. S. Welling.
Joseph Thompson and Mary Conaway, April 5, 1849, by Rev. James C. Merryman.
Perry Thompson and Mary Jane Miser, April 27, 1848, by Rev. D. S. Welling.
Robert Thompson and Rachel Ann Cox, April 28, 1850, by R. Brown.
Robert B. Thompson and Harriett Bell, March 31, 1842, by Thomas Phillips, J. P.
Thomas C. Thompson and Mary Coulter, Dec. 24, 1842, by John Rea, V. D. M.
Samuel Thrawls and Sarah Huff, Feb. 11, 1845, by Rev. Jacob Brill.
Joseph Tigley and Sarah Guthrie, June 19, 1845, by Rev. Moses Allen.
Eli Timmons and Sarah Dickerson, Sept. 25, 1850, by Rev. John Moffitt.
Albert Tipton and Nockey West, Dec. 30, 1845, by Thomas Phillips, J. P.
Benjamin Tipton and Eleanor Herron, Sept. 7, 1845, by S. W. Day.
John Tipton and Jane West, Sept. 12, 1844, by William Arnold, J. P.
Samuel Tipton and Sarah Richey, Aug. 24, 1848, by James Kerr, V. D. M.
George W. Todd and Eliza Crawford, March 25, 1845, by T. T. Larkin, J. P.
Joseph S. Toland and Jane Slemmons, April 2, 1846, by Joseph Masters, J. P.
Michael H. Toland and Julian Doudle, Oct. 31, 1844, by T. T. Larkin, J. P.
Thomas Tomlinson and Julia Phillips, Aug. 28, 1844, by Rev. Thomas Hanna.
Joseph Toner and Rebecca Geary, Feb. 15, 1848, by Samuel Ramsey, J. P.
Jacob J. Tope and Mary Jane Brown, Aug. 3, 1843, by Rev. Israel Archbold.
Joseph Townsend and Albina Strode, Feb. 24, 1842, by George Clancy, V. D. M.
Valentine Trushel and Sarah Smith, Feb. 26, 1846, by Joseph Masters, J. P.
David Turner and Mary Bell Divine, Sept. 11, 1844, by Rev. Robert Cook.
James Turner and Mary Gladmon, April 26, 1847, by Rev. Job Leister.
James P. Turner and Harriett W. Ankrum, Aug. 20, 1846, by Rev. John Hattery.
George Tyler and Nancy Davidson, March 25, 1849, by Rev. William Smith.
Mathias Ulman and Rebecca Kline, Sept. 9, 1848, by William Wilson, J. P.
Barrett Utterback and Nancy Blackwell, May 24, 1848, by John Hitchcock, J. P.
Elias F. Utterback and Hester A. Sharloat, Sept. 27, 1849, by John Hitchcock, J. P.
Henry C. Utterback and Ruth Simpson, Sept. 13, 1843, by M. F. Burkhead, J. P.
John Utterback and Mary Jenkins, Oct. 15, 1845, by M. F. Burkhead, J. P.

William Utterback and Olive Smith, Sept. 20, 1843, by Rev. M. F. Burkhead.
Edward Vanhorn and Eliza Gilbert, Sept. 11, 1849, by Rev. Charles A. Holmes.
Edward W. Vanhorn and Margaret A. Winner, May 9, 1846, by Townsend T. Larken, J. P.
Joseph Vanwel and Martha Peterson, May 4, 1848, by James Kerr, V. D. M.
Thomas Vasbinder and Rebecca Craig, June 11, 1846, by Rev. Ebenezer Hays.
James Vincent and Elizabeth Merrell, June 14, 1849, by Richard Brown.
Joseph A. Vincent and Levina J. McNulty, Oct. 21, 1845, by James Kerr, J. P.
Archibald Virtue and Anne Simpson, Aug. 5, 1841, by James McClintock, J. P.
Luke Voorhies and Margaret Lafferty, May 1, 1844, by Rev. Thomas Hanna.
Nelson Voshel and Amy Glass, March 1, 1843, by David Bower, J. P.
James Waddington and Lydia Bolen, Feb. 26, 1846, by Andrew Lynch, J. P.
Alexander Waddle and Eliza Swezy, Dec. 23, 1845, by Cyrus McNeely.
Joshua Wagers and Isabella Edney, Nov. 14, 1846, by Rev. Alexander Wilson.
Ephraim Walker and Mary Layport, Oct. 9, 1850, by Rev. John Burns.
John Walker and Fanny Hoffman, Dec. 27, 1842, by James Kerr, V. D. M.
Isaac Walkers and Winnifred Barrett, May 4, 1843, by John Huntsman.
Jesse Wallace and Susanna Kimmell, July 18, 1848, by Rev. A. N. Bartholomew.
John W. Wallace and Mary Guttney, April 1, 1845, by R. Brown.
Joseph Wallace and Mary Love, May 15, 1845, by Rev. William Taggart.
Nathaniel A. Wallace and July A. Fulton, March 12, 1846, by James Kerr, V. D. M.
Samuel Wallace and Nancy Donaghy, Dec. 27, 1845, by William B. Hunt.
William Wallace and Margaret Settle, Aug. 14, 1845, by Thomas Phillips, J. P.
William Wallace and Mary Ann Titus, Jan. 16, 1847, by Samuel Ramsey, J. P.
William L. Wallar and Jane Ross, April 2, 1846, by James Kerr, V. D. M.
William Waller and Penina Rozencrantz, Aug. 16, 1849, by Rev. John Burns.
Robert Wane and Mary Ann Speer, March 20, 1849, by Lemuel B. Perkins.
James Warden and Elizabeth Frost, Sept. 27, 1849, by McKnight Williamson.
Daniel Warner and Mary L. Bowers, Jan. 17, 1848, by Rev. Andrew Klingle.
Josiah Warner and Phebe Rickey, Dec. 12, 1842, by William Arnold, J. P.
Rezin Watkins and Hannah Johnson, Aug. 2, 1849, by Rev. William Knox.
James Watson and Mary McClish, July 28, 1841, by M. F. Burkhead, J. P.
John W. Watson and Rebecca Dunlap, March 16, 1848, by T. R. Crawford.
Joshua P. Watson and Louisa M. Remby, March 4, 1845, by Rev. E. Hays.
Lewis Watson and Julia Ann Carver, March 16, 1848, by T. T. Larkin, J. P.
Smith R. Watson and Susan J. McDowell, Dec. 9, 1847, by T. R. Crawford, V. D. M.
Uriah Watson and Mary Miller, Nov. 26, 1846, by Robert Wade, J. P.
Joseph Walters and Nancy Peddycoart, Jan. 4, 1842, by Thomas McClintock.
Martin Walters and Susannah Hess, Dec. 24, 1846, by Daniel A. Scott, J. P.
William H. Watters and Susan C. Merryman, Dec. 17, 1847, by John Blair, J. P.
James W. Waugh and Ann D. Lewis, Jan. 1, 1850, by Cyrus McNeely.
Jacob Weaver and Elizabeth Hooper, Oct. 29, 1850, by Rev. Samuel W. Day.
Jeremiah Weaver and Isabella Hitchcock, March 10, 1842, by James Kerr, V. D. M.
Robert Webb and Martha Worley, March 11, 1841, by William Arnold, J. P.
Samuel Webb and Mary Goodwin, May 23, 1847, by William Arnold, J. P.
John Webster and Anna Patton, June 12, 1845, by John Knox, J. P.
Andrew Weir and Isabella Crossan, April 30, 1850, by A. D. Clark.
Thomas Weir and Mary Dugan, April 9, 1849, by James Kerr, V. D. M.
Daniel Welch and Mary Dunning, April 10, 1848, by John Rea, V. D. M.
John P. Welch and Sarah Rowley, June 29, 1847, by Richard Brown.
Samuel Welch and Elizabeth Keepers, Oct. 30, 1849, by James Kerr, V. D. M.
David Welling and Sarah Dickerson, Feb. 10, 1842, by James Kerr, V. D. M.
David Welling and Mary A. Black, Aug. 19, 1845, by Hugh Parks, V. D. M.
Alexander S. West and Nancy J. Marshall, Aug. 23, 1845, by Rev. Alexander Wilson.
Augustus B. West and Mary Lewis, April 22, 1841, by William Arnold, J. P.
Jonathan West and Jane Ferrell, Dec. 12, 1844, by Rev. E. Hays.

Morris West and Michal Ann Spencer, Oct. 4, 1846, by Thomas McClintock, J. P.
Samuel West and Mary Ann Goddard, Dec. 15, 1842, by William Arnold, J. P.
Thomas West and Sally Underhill, Dec. 31, 1846, by Thomas McClintock, J. P.
William West and Sophia Keeser, Jan. 10, 1844, by John L. Layport, J. P.
John Whaling and Chastina Dunlap, Aug. 31, 1848, by Richard Brown.
Josiah Wharton and Eliza Jane Norris, Nov. 9, 1847, by James Hoover, J. P.
Silas Wharton and Loranda Sergent, Nov. 3, 1842, by George Atkinson, J. P.
Harrison Wheeler and Mary Watson, Oct. 16, 1848, by James Hoover, J. P.
Joshua Wheeler and Sarah Long, Dec. 30, 1847, by James Hoover, J. P.
Nicholas Wheeler and Margaret De Long, Sept. 28, 1841, by David Bower, J. P.
Joseph Wheldon and Sarah Jane Henderson, April 8, 1841, by Samuel Skinner, J. P.
David White and Nancy Wright, Dec. 30, 1847, by M. Crowl, J. P.
Jackson R. White and Rebecca Delong, Jan. 12, 1846, by John L. Layport, J. P.
Thomas Whitmore and Lucinda Wallace, June 28, 1849, by H. H. Beckett, J. P.
Benoni Whitten and Mariah Dunham, March 28, 1844, by Isaac Talbott, J. P.
Joseph Wileman and Mary Martin, July 25, 1850, by William Buchanan.
Henry Williams and Elizabeth Whittington, Dec. 16, 1841, by John Knox, J. P.
Joseph Williams and Mary Jane Queen, July 6, 1841, by Rev. E. Smith.
Joseph Williams and Elizabeth Speer, June 4, 1850, by Rev. John Burns.
Thomas Williams and Rachel Brokaw, March 27, 1844, by Wesley Smith.
W. H. Williams and Hannah Boyd, Feb. 11, 1847, by John Graham, J. P.
Amos H. Willis and Jane W. Quillan, Aug. 6, 1850, by John Knox, J. P.
George Wilson and Susan Harvey, Oct. 10, 1850, by Samuel Skinner, J. P.
John Wilson and Sophia Cuzick, Oct. 24, 1846, by James Kerr, V. D. M.
John Wilson and Mary Ann Dinger, Jan. 17, 1849, by Rev. D. S. Welling.
John Wilson and Phebe Grable, Nov. 12, 1850, by Rev. John Knox.
Samuel Wilson and Roxanna Wilson, Jan. 30, 1845, by John Blair, J. P.
Samuel H. Wilson and Sarah Guthrie, Dec. 23, 1846.
William Wilson and Martha McGill, Jan. 28, 1841, by M. F. Burkhead, J. P.
William Wilson and Rhoda Pickering, Jan. 31, 1846, by Matthew H. Phillips, J. P.
William W. Wilson and Mary Parrish, Jan. 13, 1848, by Joseph Cloaky. V. D. M.
William Wilson and Ruth Ferguson, April 11, 1850, by James Kerr, V. D. M.
Jesse Winrod and Lavina Medley, April 19, 1849, by James J. McIlgar.
John Winrod and Nancy Mealy, May 3, 1846, by Rev. J. J. Covert.
Abraham Winters and Eliza A. Divine, March 26, 1846, by James Kerr, V. D. M.
Robert Winters and Sarah Berry, Sept. 16, 1841, by Rev. Elias Gatchel.
James Wittington and Sarah Hill, March 3, 1842, by John Knox, J. P.
Hanson Wood and Mary E. Derry, Nov. 3, 1845, by R. K. Price, J. P.
Morris Wood and Bersheba Suddith, April 27, 1843, by Rev. Robert Cady.
William Wood and Amanda Busby, March 25, 1847, by Rev. D. S. Welling.
Lewis Woodman and Sarah Michner, July 9, 1843, by Asa Holmes, J. P.
Peter Woods and Elizabeth Brady, July 4, 1849, by William Arnold, J. P.
Isaac Woodward and Emily Townsend, Nov. 16, 1848, by John Adams, J. P.
Anderson D. Work and Mary Jane Howell, March 1, 1847, by Rev. Charles Thorn.
George L. Work and Sarah Ellen Crouch, Sept. 15, 1841, by John Rea, V. D. M.
Samuel E. F. Work and Ruth Green, May 17, 1843, by Rev. William Knox.
Daniel Worley and Mary Webb, June 29, 1848, by Rev. James Merryman.
Wesley Worley and Elizabeth Worley. Dec. 7, 1843. by William Arnold, J. P.
Daniel Wright and Mary A. Snider, July 1, 1847, by David Bower, J. P.
George Wright and Mariah C. Lucas. Feb. 17, 1848, by Samuel Skinner, J. P.
James D. Wright and Margaret Ann Evans, March 7, 1847, by N. Linder.
John M. Wright and Susanna Brown, Nov. 23, 1843, by Rev. Jacob Lemmon.
Samuel Wright and Margaret Maynard, Oct. 8, 1850. by Rev. John Burns.
William Wright and Mary Cook. Sept. 11. 1844. by Reynolds K. Price, J. P.
Abraham Wyant and Roxrany Dunlap, Dec. 6, 1843. by David Bower, J. P.
David Wiant and Catharine Grundy, May 2, 1844, by Rev. C. Carter.
George Wyant and Margaret Shober, Jan. 13, 1848, by Andrew Lynch, J. P.

ADDITIONAL HARRISON COUNTY MARRIAGES

Henry Wyant and Lydia Shober, Oct. 20, 1846, by Andrew Lynch, J. P.
Solomon Wyandt and Margaret Wyandt, Aug. 20, 1850, by William Arnold, J. P.
Colmer B. Yarnell and Elizabeth Worley, Jan. 21, 1842, by Rev. William F. Lauck.
John Yarnel and Actia Rogers, April 26, 1849, by Rev. Pardon Cook.
William Yarnel and Mary Kelly, Sept. 11, 1850, by William Browning.
John A. Yencel and Mary Ann Faulkner, Feb. 6, 1850, by Lemuel B. Perkins.
Jared Young and Mary Jane Tipton, Jan. 11, 1844, by Isaac Talbott, J. P.

INDEX.

As the family names in Parts II. and III. are arranged in alphabetical order, it has not been deemed necessary to repeat them in this index. For the same reason, the alphabetical lists of names given on pages 82–89, 102–106, 116–127, and 181–182, in Part I., will not be repeated.

Abdill, 80.
Abdill, 82.
Abolitionism, 137, 138, 149.
Ackelson, Andrew, 131.
Adair, 10.
Adams, 30.
Adams, 79.
Adams, 80.
Adams, 181.
Adams, 188.
Adams, 189.
Adams, 190.
Adams, S., 179.
Adams, William C., 113.
Agnew, 7.
Agnew, 10.
Aiken, 7.
Albertson, 31.
Albertson, 187.
Alexander, 7.
Alexander, 107.
Alexander, 148.
Allen, 30.
Allen, Moses, 132, 156.
Allison, 7.
Allison, Thomas, 147.
Almond, 31.
Ames, 107.
American People, 1.
Amspoker, 48.
Anderson, 7.
Anderson, 189.
Anderson, 190.
Anderson, John, 133.
Anderson, Joseph, 93, 95, 96, 128, 130, 156.
Andrews, 30.
Angles, 5.

Anglo-Saxons, 2.
Anthony, 31.
Antrim, 32.
Arbaugh, Thomas, 112.
Archibald, 186.
Armor, 137.
Armstrong, 132.
Armstrong, John, 134, 135.
Armstrong, W. W., 3.
Arnold, 6.
Arnold, 32.
Arnold, 44.
Arnold, 78.
Arnold, 80.
Arnold, 81.
Arnold, 82.
Arnold, 112.
Arnold, 165.
Arnold, 168.
Asbury, Bishop, 176.
Ash, 77.
Ash, 81.
Associate Presbyterian Church, of Cadiz, 145-155.
Associate Reformed Presbyterian Church, of Cadiz, 140-145.
Atkinson, 48.
Atkinson, 187-8.
Atkinson, 190.
Athey, Walter, 180.
Auckerman, 181.

Bailey, 30.
Bailey, 31.
Bailey, 32.
Bailey, 48.
Baker, 31.
Baker, 81.

For additional names, see alphabetical lists on pages 82-89, 102-106, 116-127, 181-182, 202-454, 457-584, and 587-617.

INDEX

Baker, 109.
Baker, 178.
Baker, 179.
Baker, 181.
Ball, 30.
Ballard, 30.
Ballard, 31.
Bamb, 31.
Barclay, 7.
Barcroft, Ralph, 111.
Bargar, 181.
Barger, 160.
Barger, Alexander, 112.
Barnhill, 184.
Barrett, 44.
Barrett, 109.
Barrett, 168.
Barrett, 182.
Barrett, William, 112.
Bartley, Mordecai, 3.
Bartley, Thomas W., 3.
Bates, 30.
Baugham, 32.
Baxter, 79.
Baxter, 168.
Baxter, 169.
Baxter, 171.
Bayless, Zephaniah, 111.
Beall, 7.
Beall, 173.
Beall, James P., 112.
Beard, 32.
Beatty, 78.
Beatty, 181.
Beatty, 189.
Beatty, John, 3.
Beauchamp, 31.
Beebe, 109.
Beebe, Stewart, 108.
Beebe, Walter B., 107, 110, 111, 113.
Beech Spring Burials, 314-319.
Beach Spring Congregation, Extent of 97.
Beech Spring Presbyterian Church, 92-100.
Beek, 31.
Belden, George W., 109.
Bell, Samuel, 113.
Berry, 32.
Bethel Burials, 375-376.
Bethel M. E. Church, 178-182.
Betts, 31.
Bevin, 30.
Biggar, 8.
Biggs, Zachariah, 141.
Biggs and Beatty, 75, 157, 168.
Billingsley, James J., 113.
Binford, 30.

Binford, 31.
Bingham, 136.
Bingham, 141.
Bingham, John A., 3, 113.
Bingham, Thomas, 109.
Birdsall, 30.
Birney, 178, 179.
Birney, 181.
Birnie, 8.
Birney, J. Fletcher, 178.
Bishop, 32.
Black, 44.
Black, Andrew, 136.
Blackburn, 30.
Blackburn, 32.
Blair, 7.
Blair, 14.
Blizzard, 31.
Bloxom, 30.
Boggs, 7.
Boggs, 107.
Boggs, William, 110.
Bogue, 31.
Bond, 30.
Bond, 31.
Bostwick, Samuel W., 110, 111, 113.
Boswell, James, 112.
Bowerstown Burials, 379-380.
Boyce, William, 112.
Boyles, 7.
Boyles, 10.
Boyles, 106.
Boyd, 7.
Boyd, 10.
Boyd, 12.
Boyd, 78.
Boyd, 81.
Boyd, 109.
Boyd, James, 112.
Boyd, Samuel, 109.
Bracken, 137.
Braden, 44.
Braden, 147.
Braden, 181.
Bradfield, 30.
Bradford, 32.
Brady, E. W., 180.
Brannon, 106.
Branson, 30.
Branson, 32.
Branson, Lindley M., 113.
Bray, J. M., 180.
Brereton's Travels, 14.
Brice, John, 93.
Brice, John, 96.
Brice, John, 130.
Brindley, 179.
Brindley, 181.

For additional names, see alphabetical lists on pages 82-89, 102-106, 116-127, 181-182, 202-454, 457-584, and 587-617.

INDEX 623

Brock, 32.
Brockunier, S. R., 176, 180, 181.
Brokaw, 130.
Brokaw, 134.
Brokaw, 167.
Brokaw, 169.
Brokaw, 171.
Brokaw, 173.
Brooks, 31.
Broomhall, 30.
Brown, 6.
Brown, 30.
Brown, 31.
Brown, 44.
Brown, 81.
Brown, 179.
Brown, 181.
Brown, 189.
Brown, W. L., 3.
Browne, 78.
Browning, Wesley, 165.
Browning, W., 180.
Brownson, Alfred, 163.
Bruce, 135.
Bruce, 137.
Bruce, Robert, 5.
Buchanan, 8.
Buchanan, 30.
Buchanan, 48.
Buchanan, 186.
Buchanan, 187-188.
Buchanan, 189.
Buchanan, George, 140, 141.
Bullock, 82.
Bundy, 31.
Bundy, 32.
Bunker, 31.
Burgess, 30.
Burials, 312-400.
Burnet, Jacob, 3.
Burnett, William, 135.
Burnett, William, 143.
Busby, 181.
Buskirk, 161.
Butler, 30.
Butler, 31.

Cadiz in 1847, 79.
Cadiz Burials, 319-339.
Cadiz, Early Churches of, 139.
Cadiz laid out, 75, 77.
Cadwalader, 30.
Cady, William, 112.
Cain, 48.
Calderwood, 10.
Caldwell, 7.
Caldwell, 134.
Caldwell, J. A., 130.

Caldwell, John, 112.
Caldwell, John P., 132.
Caldwell, W. B., 3.
Calhoun, 8.
Cameron, James, 187, 188.
Campbell, 130.
Campbell, 154.
Campbell, 155.
Campbell, 181.
Campbell, Alexander, 133.
Campbell, David, 110.
Campbell, James E., 3.
Campbell, Richard, 135.
Canby, 30.
Cannon, 7.
Carle, 30.
Carle, 32.
Carnahan, 7.
Carnahan, 44.
Carnahan, 79.
Carnahan, 140.
Carnahan, 144.
Carnahan, 151.
Carnahan, 154.
Carothers, 8.
Carpenter, 48.
Carrick, 7.
Carrick, John, 113.
Carson, 7.
Carver, Elijah, 113.
Carver, James C., 111, 112.
Cary, 31.
Cassil, 48.
Cassville Burials, 380-381.
Castleman, 48.
Cavin, 190.
Celt and Teuton, 6.
Chambers, 48.
Chambers, Joseph H., 189.
Chaney, 178.
Chapel, 31.
Chapman, 79.
Chapman, 165.
Chase, Salmon P., 3.
Chew, 31.
Chichester, Arthur, 10.
Church, Thomas, 162.
Clark, 7.
Clark, 31.
Clark, 44.
Clark, 48.
Clark, 94.
Clark, 109.
Clark, 137.
Clark, 149.
Clark, 185, 188.
Clark, Alexander D., 136.
Clark, A. D., 172.

For additional names, see alphabetical lists on pages 82-89, 102-106, 116-127, 181-182, 202-454, 457-584, and 587-617.

INDEX

Clark, Ephraim, 110.
Clark, Ingram, 110.
Clark, John, 3.
Clark, John, 93.
Clark, John B., 155.
Clark, J. L., 180.
Clark, Matthew, 148.
Clark, Thomas B., 132, 170.
Cleaver, 32.
Clendennin, 7.
Clendennin, Nathaniel E., 111.
Close, H. M., 180.
Cobean, James, 112.
Cochran, 7.
Cochran, 44.
Cochran, 79.
Cochran, Robert, 59.
Cockerill, John A., 3.
Coffee, 30.
Coffin, 31.
Cole, 189.
Collier, 31.
Collins, 7.
Colvin, Samuel, 112.
Como, 30.
Compher, 173.
Conaway, 107.
Conaway, 179.
Connard (Kennard), 30.
Conrad, 48.
Conwell, 109.
Cook, 32.
Cook, 133.
Cook, Pardon, 179, 180.
Coon, Jacob, 132.
Coon, Jacob, 135.
Cope, 30.
Cope, Oliver G., 110.
Copeland, 31.
Corinth Burials, 371.
Coulter, 7.
Coulter, R. M., 45.
Cowan, 136.
Cowan, Benjamin, 109.
Cowles, Salmon, 132, 134.
Cox, 30.
Cox, 31.
Cox, W., 181.
Crabapple Burials, 339-349.
Crabapple Presbyterian Church, 128-132.
Craig, 8.
Craig, 30.
Craig, 44.
Craig, 79.
Craig, 137.
Craig, 139.
Craig, 140.
Craig, 145.
Craig, 154.
Craig, 157.
Craig, John, 112.
Craig, Walter, 113.
Cramblett, Jacob, 113.
Crampton, 30.
Crawford, 7.
Crawford, 132.
Crawford, 171.
Crawford, Thomas, 166.
Crawford, Thomas R., 95, 172.
Creek, 30.
Crew, 30.
Crew, 31.
Crew, George A., 111.
Crook, George, 180.
Croskey, 109.
Croskey, Jackson, 113.
Culbertson, 7.
Cunningham, 7.
Cunningham, 10.
Cunningham, 13.
Cunningham, 155.
Cunningham, 166, 167.
Cunningham, David, 110, 111, 113.
Cunningham, Thomas, 144.
Curl, 31.
Currey, 190.
Custer, 48.
Custer, George A., 113.

Danes, 5.
Davidson, 8.
Davidson, 151.
Davidson, W. A., 181.
Davis, 31.
Davis, 32.
Davis, 48.
Davis, 164.
Dawson, 48.
Day, 187.
Day, 188.
Day, 189.
Day, James, 110, 180.
Day, Thomas, 112.
Decker, 48.
Deersville Burials, 381-385.
DeLong, 48.
DeLong, Jesse, 45.
Dennis, 179.
Dennis, 181.
Devinney, W., 180.
Devore, 181.
Dew, 32.
Dewey, 6.
Dewey, Chauncey, 110, 113.
Dewey, Orville, 6.

For additional names, see alphabetical lists on pages 82-89, 102-106, 116-127, 181-182, 202-454, 457-584, and 587-617.

INDEX

Dickerson, 44.
Dickerson, 78.
Dickerson, 107.
Dickerson, 161.
Dickerson, 177.
Dickerson, 178.
Dickerson, 182.
Dickerson, Baruch, 112.
Dickerson Burials, 368-370.
Dickerson Church, 175-178.
Dickerson M. E. Church, 175-178.
Dickson, 8.
Dickson, Robert, 159.
Dillhorn, 32.
Dillon, 30.
Dinmore, James, 94.
Dodd, 31.
Dodd, Thaddeus, 93.
Doig, J. R., 149.
Doudna, 31.
Douglas, 7.
Downing, John, 113.
Doyle, John H., 3.
Draper, 31.
Drummond, James, 164.
Duff, 48.
Dunlap, 7.
Dunlap, 44.
Dunlap, 98.
Dunlap, 109.
Dunlap, 168.
Dunlap, 169.
Dunlap, 171.
Dunlap, 173.
Dunlap, James, 93.
Dunlap, Samuel, 110, 130.
Dunn, 48.

Eagleson, 94.
Early, 30.
Early, 182.
Edgerton, 31.
Edgerton, 48.
Edgington, 98.
Edney, Robert, 111.
Elliott, 8.
Elliott, 31.
Ellis, 30.
Ellis, Michael, 162, 163.
Endsley, 185.
Enoch, George, 180.
Ervin, 7.
Erwin, 32.
Estep, Josiah M., 113.
Evans, 30.
Evans, 32.
Evans, William, 113.

Faucett, 30.
Faulkner, 32.
Ferguson, 7.
Ferguson, 98.
Ferrall, 32.
Ferrell, 30.
Fife, 179.
Fife, 181.
Finch, 32.
Findley, Samuel, 142.
Finley, 8.
Finley, James, 93.
Finley, James B., 161, 163, 176, 178.
Finney, 44.
Finney, 77.
Finney, 80.
Firebaugh, Michael, 113.
First Land-owners, 195-237.
Fisher, 30.
Fisher, 189.
Fitzpatrick, 48.
Flanner, 31.
Fleming, Thornton, 162.
Fogle, John, 112.
Foraker, Joseph B., 3.
Ford, Henry, 112.
Ford, Stephen, 110.
Forker, Henry G., 111.
Forsythe, 8.
Forsythe, 186.
Forsythe, James, 151.
Forsythe, James C., 144, 145.
Forsythe, Jesse, 110.
Ford, Seabury, 3.
Foreman, 178.
Foreman, 181.
Foster, 78.
Foster, Charles, 3.
Foster, Sarah, 148.
Foust, Elias, 111.
Fowler, 136.
Fox, George, 22.
Franklin College, 133-137.
Freeport in 1817, 90.
Freeport Burials, 385-387.
Freeport Presbyterian Church, 174.
French, David, 147.
Froggs, 48.
Fullerton, 7.
Fulton, 7.

Galbreath, 31.
Galloway, 8.
Garfield, James A., 3.
Garvin, Davis, 112.
Garvin, John M., 111, 112.
Gatchell, 79.
Genealogies, 457-584.

For additional names, see alphabetical lists on pages 82-89, 102-106, 116-127, 181-182, 202-454, 457-584, and 587-617.

INDEX

George, 30.
George, 138.
Georgetown Burials, 387-388.
German Emigration, 35, 36, 37.
Germans in Harrison County, 34.
Gilbret, 30.
Giles, Thomas W., 111.
Gillespie, 7.
Gilmore, 8.
Gilmore, 44.
Gilmore, 109.
Gilmore, 139.
Gilmore, H., 180.
Gilmore, Quincy A., 3.
Gilmore, W. J., 3.
Given, John C., 111.
Glazener, Garret, 75, 156.
Glenn, 167.
Glenn, 169.
Glenn, 171.
Glover, George W., 110.
Glover, Jefferson C., 112.
Goddard, 48.
Goodwin, 31.
Gordon, H., 7.
Grace, Frank, 111.
Graham, J., 180.
Graham, John B., 174.
Granfell, William S., 111.
Grant, 8.
Grant, U. S., 3.
Gray, 31.
Graybill, John, 112.
Green, 31.
Green, 178.
Green, 179.
Green, 181.
Green, Benjamin J., 113.
Green, P., 180.
Greenwood Burials, 376-378.
Gregg, 30.
Grimes, 78.
Grimes, 108.
Grimes, 109.
Grimes, 132.
Grimes, 134.
Grimes, 145.
Grimes, Landon B., 112.
Grimes, William M., 159.
Grove, 154.
Grove, Francis, 148.
Gruber, Jacob, 163.
Gruber, John, 110.
Gurrell, 30.
Gwinn, Andrew, 157.

Hackett, George S., 132.
Hackney, 30.
Hadly, 31.
Hague, 30.
Hair, Gilbert M., 172.
Hale, 31.
Haley, 107.
Hall, 31.
Hallock, Jeremiah H., 109.
Hamill, Samuel S., 111, 112.
Hamilton, 7.
Hamilton, 12.
Hamilton, 79.
Hamilton, 109.
Hamilton, 134.
Hamilton, 140-1.
Hamilton, 151.
Hamilton, 153.
Hamilton, 155.
Hamilton, 171.
Hamilton, James, 9.
Hamilton, W. F., 94.
Hammett, J., 180.
Hammond, 7.
Hammond, 133.
Hammond, 134.
Hammond, 138.
Hammond, John, 110.
Hampton, 30.
Hance, Joseph C., 110.
Hank, W., 179.
Hanna, 7.
Hanna, 32.
Hanna, 44.
Hanna, 138.
Hanna, 149.
Hanna, 160.
Hanna, James L., 111.
Hanna, John, 110, 111.
Hanna, Samuel, 130, 131.
Hanna, Thomas, 134, 148.
Hanna, Thomas Beveridge, 155.
Harbison, 48.
Hargrave, 30.
Hargrave, Elisha, 112.
Harlan, 32.
Harrell, 31.
Harris, 31.
Harris, 32.
Harris, 80.
Harris, 81.
Harris, Joseph, 111.
Harris, Joseph, 112.
Harrison, 30.
Harrison, Albert J., 111.
Harrison County Organized, 101.
Harrison County in the War of 1812, 102-106.
Harrison County in 1813, 101.
Harrison County in 1817, 89.

For additional names, see alphabetical lists on pages 82-89, 102-106, 116-127, 181-182, 202-454, 457-584, and 587-617.

INDEX

Harrison County Burials, 312-400.
Harrison County, First Settlements in, 56-58.
Harrison County Genealogies, 457-584.
Harrison County, Indian Trails Through, 76.
Harrison County Land Patents, 195-237.
Harrison County Marriages, 1813-1840, 238-312 (see also Supplement for marriages from 1840 to 1850, 587-617).
Harrison County Pioneers, 54.
Harrison County Pioneers, 59-74.
Harrison County Settlers in 1813, 116-127.
Harrison County Wills, 401-454.
Harrisville Burials, 388-390.
Harvey, 10.
Harvey, 98.
Hasket, 31.
Hatcher, 151.
Hattery, John, 174.
Hatton, 181.
Hatton, Frank, 113.
Haverfield, 7.
Haverfield, 44.
Haverfield, 141.
Haverfield, 151.
Haverfield, 153.
Haverfield, 155.
Haverfield, George A., 111.
Haydock, 31.
Hays, Ebenezer, 180.
Hayes, Rutherford B., 3.
Hayes, William P., 111.
Hearn, 6.
Hearn, 81.
Hearn, Lancelot, 112.
Hearn, Wesley B., 111.
Hearn, William A., 112.
Henderson, 7.
Henderson, 31.
Henderson, 135.
Henderson, 137.
Henderson, 148.
Henderson, 149.
Henderson, Alexander, 109, 113, 157.
Henderson, Elescondo, 112.
Henderson, J., 180.
Henderson, William, 112.
Herron, 7.
Herron, 189.
Herron, 190.
Herron, Robert, 183, 188-190.
Herron, Samuel, 110.
Hervey, Henry, 172.
Hervey, James, 172.
Hiatt, 31.

Hicks, 31.
Hilbert, David, 111, 112.
Hill, 48.
Hilligas, 81.
Hilton, 173.
Hines, 31.
Hines, 78.
Hines, Albert B., 112.
Hitchcock, 44.
Hitchcock, 109.
Hitchcock, Samuel, 113.
Hixon, Abner, 113.
Hoagland, 48.
Hoagland, James, 113.
Hobson, 31.
Hockaday, 30.
Hodge, 32.
Hodgson, 31.
Hogg, 7.
Hogg, 137.
Hogg, Charles M., 110.
Hoggatt, 32.
Holland, 181.
Holland, W. J., 95.
Holliday, 174.
Hollingsworth, 6.
Hollingsworth, 31.
Hollingsworth, David A., 110, 111, 113.
Holloway, 30.
Holloway, 32.
Holloway, Terrell, 32.
Hollowell, 31.
Holmes, 44.
Holmes, 54, 55.
Holmes, 161.
Holmes, 178.
Holmes Burials, 378-379.
Holmes, C. A., 180.
Holmes, Joseph, 110, 112, 175.
Hopedale Burials, 390-391.
Hopkins, R., 180.
Horner, 32.
Hospelhorn, 185.
Host, David P., 112.
Hough, 32.
House, 48.
Houser, 81.
Howard, 32.
Howard, Emanuel, 112.
Howe, Henry, 79.
Howell, 31.
Howells, William Dean, 3.
Hubbard, 32.
Hudson, Thomas, 176.
Huff, 44.
Huff, 175.
Huff, Eleazer, 112.
Hughes, 30.

For additional names, see alphabetical lists on pages 82-89, 102-106, 116-127, 181-182, 202-454, 457-584, and 587-617.

Hughes, 95.
Hughes, James, 93.
Humes, 161.
Humphrey, Caleb, 162.
Hunnicutt, 31.
Hunt, 31.
Hunt, 32.
Hunter, 7.
Hunter, Hocking H., 3.
Hunter, William H., 137.
Hussey, 31.

Ingles, 44.
Ingles, 167.
Ingles, 168.
Inskeep, 163.
Ireland, North of, 4.
Irwin, John, 130.

Jackson, 7.
Jackson, 78.
Jagner, 81.
James, I., 9.
James, I., 11.
James, 31.
James, 32.
James, 130.
Jamison, 7.
Jamison, 44.
Jamison, 79.
Jamison, 80.
Jamison, 82.
Jamison, 139.
Jamison, 140.
Jamison, 151.
Jamison, 154.
Jamison, 155.
Jamison, 157.
Jamison, Andrew, 113.
Jamison, James B., 110.
Jamison, John C., 110.
Jamison, T., 180.
Jamison, Walter, 113.
Janney, 30.
Jarvis, Jacob, 113.
Jay, 31.
Jay, 32.
Jelly, 179.
Jenkins, 30.
Jenkins, 31.
Jenkins, George K., 136.
Jennings, 134.
Jennings, Obediah, 158.
Jessop, 31.
Jewett, Thomas L., 110, 111, 113.
Jinnett, 31.
John, 30.
Johns, 107.

Johnson, 30.
Johnson, 31.
Johnson, 44.
Johnson, 48.
Johnson, 78.
Johnson, 81.
Johnson, 109.
Johnson, 135.
Johnson, 161.
Johnson, 182.
Johnson, J. J., 111.
Johnson, W. W., 3.
Johnson, William, 112.
Johnston, 8.
Jones, 31.
Jones, 32.
Jones, 168.
Jones, 175.
Jones, 178.
Jones, 182.

Kellum, 32.
Kelly, 32.
Kelly, 79.
Kennedy, 7.
Kennon, 136.
Kennon, William, 3, 109, 135.
Kent, 44.
Kent, 178.
Kent, 181.
Kent, J. P., 180.
Kerr, 7.
Kerr, 8.
Kerr, 48.
Kerr, James, 159, 161.
Kersey, 32.
Kilgore, 160.
Kilgore, Daniel, 110, 113.
Killey, 31.
Kincade, 174.
Kinsey, 82.
Kinsey, Kersey W., 111.
Kirby, E. B., 112.
Kirkpatrick, 8.
Kirkpatrick, 173.
Knight, 31.
Knox, 8.
Knox, 181.
Knox, John, 5.
Knox, John D., 177, 180.
Knox, Samuel, 110, 111.
Knox, William, 109, 180.
Kyle, 7.
Kyle, 154.
Kyle, 155.

Lacey, 6.
Lacey, Anderson P., 110.

For additional names, see alphabetical lists on pages 82-89, 102-106, 116-127, 181-182, 202-454, 457-584, and 587-617.

INDEX 629

Lacey, John S., 111, 112.
Lacy, 30.
Lacy, 165.
Ladd, 30.
Ladd, Benjamin, 138.
Lafferty, 168.
Lafferty, 171.
Lafferty, 173.
Laizure, 164.
Lamb, 48.
Lambdin, W., 180.
Lambden, William, 163.
Land Patents in Harrison County, 195-237.
Langagar, 31.
Lantz, Jasper N., 110.
Larkins, 107.
Larow, 31.
Latham, John, 113.
Lauck, Simon, 180.
Lauck, W. F., 180, 181.
Law, Harvey B., 111.
Lawrence, 31.
Lawrence, 136.
Lawton, Henry W., 3.
Layport, 44.
Layport, 167.
Leaper, 174.
Lease, 179.
Lease, 181.
Lea, 30.
Lee, 138.
Lee, 145.
Lee, 148.
Lee, 149.
Lee, Hans W., 155.
Lee, Thomas, 110.
Lemasters, 181.
Lemmon, Amon, 111.
Lemmon, Jacob, 110.
Lewis, 31.
Lewis, 32.
Lewis, 179.
Lewis, 181.
Lewton, Lewis, 110, 111, 113.
Light, 49.
Limerick, D., 180.
Lindley, Jacob, 95.
Lisle, 184.
Lisle, 187.
Little, 30.
Lloyd, 30.
Lloyd, 138.
Logan, 7.
Logan, 170.
Logan, James, 15, 16.
Lorimer, William, 144.
Love, 44.

Love, 133.
Love, 151.
Love, George, 113.
Low, 31.
Lundy, 31.
Lupton, 30.
Lupton, 32.
Lynch, 30.
Lyle, 132.
Lyons, 8.
Lyons, 44.
Lyons, 187.
Lyons, 188.
Lyons, 189.
Lyons, 190.
Lyons, R. M., 112.

McArthur, Duncan, 3.
McArthur, John, 158, 186, 188.
McBean, 8.
McBean, 165.
McBean, John, 110.
McBride, 7.
McCall, 133.
McCall, Marshall, 110.
McCartney, William D., 187.
McCaskey, 133.
McClary, 44.
McCleary, T., 180.
McClellan, 7.
McClintock, 79.
McClintock, 187-8.
McConnell, 7.
McConnell, 44.
McConnell, 109.
McConnell, 165.
McCooks, The Fighting, 3.
McCormick, John, 112.
McCormick, Reuben A., 111.
McCormick, Samuel, 113.
McCormick, Samuel M., 112.
McCoy, 8.
McCoy, 160.
McCoy, 186.
McCoy, Martin J., 112.
McCoy, Matthew, 112, 158.
McCoy, William H., 111.
McCracken, 133.
McCracken, 134.
McCray, 78.
McCrea, 7.
McCrea, 80.
McCrea, 82.
McCready, 7.
McCready, J. S., 150-153.
McCue, P. K., 180.
McCulloch, 7.
McCullough, 44.

For additional names, see alphabetical lists on pages 82-89, 102-106, 116-127, 181-182, 202-454, 457-584, and 587-617.

McCullough, 94.
McCullough, 98.
McCullough, 129.
McCullough, 130.
McCullough, 131.
McCullough, 160.
McCullough, John, 109.
McCune, 94.
McCurdy, John, 109.
McDonald, 7.
McDonald, 49.
McDonald, H. R., 174.
McDowell, Irvin, 3.
McElravy, 178.
McElroy, Archibald, 162, 163.
McElroy, Archibald, 176.
McFadden, 7.
McFadden, 44.
McFadden, 79.
McFadden, 139.
McFadden, 140-1.
McFadden, 144.
McFadden, 151.
McFadden, 157.
McFarland, William, 110.
McGaughy, 78.
McGavran, 81.
McGavran, Samuel B., 110.
McGavran, William H., 110.
McGee, Stephen R., 112.
McGlaughlin, 134.
McGraw, 174.
McIlravy, 188.
McIlravy, 189.
McIlravy, 190.
McIlvaine, George W., 3, 110.
McIntosh, 8.
McIntosh, Donald, 134, 158, 186, 188.
McKay, 8.
McKee, 8.
McKee, 164.
McKee, 165.
McKee, 179.
McKee, 181.
McKendree, Bishop, 176.
McKibben, 94.
McKibben, 109.
McKibben, 130.
McKibbon, 171.
McKie, 12.
McKinley, 8.
McKinley, William, 3.
McKinney, 188.
McKinney, 189.
McKinney, 190.
McKitrick, 154.
McLane, 187.
McLane, 188.

McLean, John, 3.
McLaughlin, Samuel K., 111.
McMath, 7.
McMath, Jesse H., 111, 113.
McMillan, 7.
McMillan, 81.
McMillan, James, 113.
McMillan, John, 93, 128, 130, 132, 169.
McMillan, P., 109.
McMillan, William, 96, 134, 135.
McMillen, 78.
McMillen, Thomas, 113.
McMuir, 31.
McMychen, 7.
McNamee, Elias B., 111, 112.
McNary, 134.
McNeely, 78.
McNeely, 80.
McNeely, 81.
McNeely, 109.
McNeely, 138.
McNeely, Andrew, 110.
McNees, 49.
McNutt, Mrs., 154.
McNutt, James, 111, 112.
McPeck, 185.
McPeck, 187.
McPeck, 189.
McPeck, 190.
McPeck, John E., 112.
McPherson, 8, 30.
McPherson, James B., 3.
McRae, 8.
Macbeth, 5.
MacDonnell, 11.
Mace, 31.
Mace, 32.
Macfarland, 8.
MacLellan, 12.
Macurdy, Elisha, 96, 128, 156.
Macy, 30.
Macy, 31.
Maddox, 30.
Mahaffey, Samuel, 174.
Maholm, 44.
Maholm, 78.
Maholm, 81.
Maholm, 109.
Mann, 49.
Mansfield, John, 110.
Mapins, 49.
Maremoon, 31.
Marine, 31.
Marmaduke, 31.
Marquis, Thomas, 130.
Marriages, 238-312, 587-617.
Martin, Thomas, 112.
Mason's Diary, 90.

For additional names, see alphabetical lists on pages 82-89, 102-106, 116-127, 181-182, 202-454, 457-584, and 587-617.

Masters, Joseph, 113.
Mattern, 179.
Matthews, 49.
Maxwell, 7.
Maxwell, 10.
Maxwell, 44.
Maxwell, 147.
Maxwell, 148.
Maxwell, 149.
Maxwell, 179.
Maxwell, 181.
Maxwell, James, 110.
Maxwell, Robert, 110, 112.
Mead, 30.
Means, 179.
Means, Thomas, 110.
Medary, Samuel, 3.
Medill, 137.
Medill, Joseph, 3.
Medill, William, 3.
Meek, 78.
Meek, Joseph, 111.
Megaw, 154.
Megaw, 160.
Megaw, 187.
Megaw, 188.
Megaw, 189.
Mehollin, 181.
Meigs, Governor, 108.
Meloy, William T., 140, 153, 155.
Melville, Andrew, 5.
Mendenhall, 31.
Mendenhall, 32.
Menser, 49.
Mercer, 109.
Merrill, Jesse, 112.
Merritt, 98.
Merritt, 130.
Merryman, D. C., 180.
Merryman, J. C., 180.
Methodist Episcopal Church of Cadiz, 161-165.
Middie, 109.
Milford, T. J., 132.
Miller, 30.
Miller, 32.
Miller, 98.
Miller, 145.
Miller, 151.
Miller, 187.
Miller, James, 111.
Miller, John, 113.
Miller, John H., 110.
Milligan, 112.
Milligan, 173.
Milligan, William, 111.
Millikan, 32.
Milliner, 30.

Mills, 32.
Minksville Burials, 372.
Minor, J. W., 180.
Minor, S. F., 180.
Mitchell, 7.
Mitchell, 144.
Mitchell, 151.
Mitchell, 153.
Mitchell, 155.
Mitchell, Benjamin, 137.
Mitchell, D. P., 177, 180.
Mitchell, O. M., 3.
Mitchner, 32.
Moffit, 31.
Moffitt, 168.
Moffitt, 182.
Moffitt, John J., 180, 181.
Monroe, J., 179.
Monroe, J., 180.
Montgomery, 7.
Montgomery, 10.
Montgomery, 12.
Montgomery, Hugh, 9.
Montgomery, Thomas, 9.
Moore, 7.
Moore, 31.
Moore, 44.
Moore, 109.
Moore, 179.
Moore, James, 112.
Moore, Robert B., 113.
Moore, Samuel A., 111.
Moore, Samuel B., 112.
Moore, William, 110.
Moorefield Burials, 391-392.
Moorehead, Samuel, 110, 113.
Moormon, 30.
Moormon, 31.
Moravian Ridge Burials, 373-375.
Morgan, 30.
Morlan, 31.
Morlan, 32.
Morris, 31.
Morris, 32.
Morris, Daniel, 113.
Morrison, 7.
Morrow, 171.
Morrow, 173.
Morrow, Jeremiah, 3.
Mt. Pleasant Presbyterian Church, 93-94.
Muir, 10.
Mullen, 32.
Munson, John, 156.
Murray, 10.
Murray, 12.
Myers, 30.
Myers, 80.

For additional names, see alphabetical lists on pages 82-89, 102-106, 116-127, 181-182, 202-45½, 457-584, and 587-617.

INDEX

Myers, 82.
Myers, 101.
Nevin, Edwin H., 136.
New Athens Burials, 395.
Newby, 31.
Newby, 32.
New England, 2, 6.
New Jefferson Burials, 395-396.
Nichols, 30.
Nichols, 138.
Niel, 109.
Nixon, 49.
Nixon, A. C., 110.
Noble, 187.
Norman, 181.
Norse, 5.
Nottingham Burials, 355-362.
Nottingham Presbyterian Church, 166-174.
Nowles, 49.
Noyes, 49.

Ogden, Ephraim, 188.
Ogilvie, 8.
Oglevee, 178.
Ohio Presbytery, 93.
Oliphant, 32.
O'Neal, 32.
O'Neale, Con, 8.
Orr, 78.
Orr, 141.
Orr, 179.
Osburn, 109.
Osburn, 154.
Osburn, 188.
Osburn, 189.
Osburn, 190.
Osburn, Samuel, 111.
Otterburn, Battle of, 5.
Ourant, 78.
Outland, 31.
Ovburn, 44.
Ovburn, 189.

Painter, 32.
Pancoast, 30.
Parker, 107.
Parks, Hugh, 143.
Parremore, 49.
Parsons, 32.
Parsons, 44.
Pastorious, 34.
Pathfinders of Jefferson County, 137.
Patrick, James, 110.
Patterson, 8.
Patterson, 31.
Patterson, 188.
Patterson, Alexander, 110.

Patterson, Charles, 111, 112.
Patterson, John, 110.
Patterson, Joseph, 93, 96, 128.
Patton, 7.
Patton, 141.
Patton, 143.
Patton, 190.
Patton, George M., 111.
Patton, James, 113.
Patton, John C., 113.
Patton, Samuel, 150.
Paul, 49.
Paul, 78.
Paxton, 109.
Paxton, 154.
Peacock, 107.
Pearce, John S., 110, 111, 113.
Pearson, 31.
Peaty, 32.
Peebles, 31.
Peele, 31.
Pegg, 32.
Pennsylvania Dutch, 34.
Penrose, 32.
Peppard, Samuel G., 110, 111, 113.
Pepper, 79.
Pepper, 160.
Perdue, 31.
Perkins, 31.
Perry, 78.
Perry, 81.
Perry, 178.
Perry, William T., 112.
Pettay, L., 180.
Perviance, 32.
Peterson, Daniel, 157.
Phillips, 7.
Phillips, Enoch W., 113.
Phillips, William, 112.
Picts and Scots, 5.
Pickering, 30.
Pidgeon, 30.
Pidgeon, 32.
Pierce, 31.
Pierson, 31.
Piggot, 30.
Pike, 31.
Pike, 32.
Piley, 49.
Pittenger, 179.
Pittenger, 181.
Pittenger, Nicholas, 96.
Pittis, John H., 113.
Platt, 49.
Pleasant Valley Burials, 372-373.
Plumber, 32.
Porter, 7.
Porter, 109.

For additional names, see alphabetical lists on pages 82-89, 102-106, 116-127, 181-182, 202-454, 457-584, and 587-617.

INDEX

Potts, William O., 111.
Poulson, 164.
Poulson, Wesley S., 111.
Powell, 31.
Power, James, 93.
Power, James, 135.
Pratt, 189.
Presbyterian Churches, 92.
Presbyterian Church of Cadiz, 156-161.
Preston, 30.
Price, 31.
Price, 168.
Price, 171.
Price, Reynolds K., 110.
Pritchard, 78.
Pritchard, 80.
Pritchard, 81.
Pugh, 32.
Pugh, 44.
Pugh, 78.
Pugh, 81.
Pugh, John, 112.
Pumphrey, Nimrod B., 111.
Pynnar's Survey, 13.

Quaker Emigration to Ohio and Indiana, 26-29.
Quakers in Harrison County, 22.
Quakers in Pennsylvania, 24.
Quakers Persecuted in New England, 23.
Quakers in the South, 24, 25.
Quigley, Albert, 112.
Quinn, James, 162.
Quinn, James, 163.
Quinn, James, 180.

Ralston, 179.
Ralston, 181.
Ralston, Samuel, 96, 130, 169.
Ramage, John, 112.
Ramsay, 160.
Ramsey, 8.
Ramsey, V., 7.
Rankin, 7.
Rankin, 107.
Rankin, 181.
Rankin, 182.
Rankin Burials, 370-371.
Rankin M. E. Church, 182.
Ranney, Rufus P., 3.
Ratcliff, 30.
Rattekir, 30.
Rawlins, 49.
Ray, Joseph, 135.
Rea, 7.
Rea, 44.
Rea, 81.

Rea, 173.
Rea, Jackson, 113.
Rea, Rev. John, 93, 94, 96, 98, 130, 131, 139, 156, 157, 158, 167, 169, 171, 172, 173, 184, 185.
Rea, Joseph, 110, 112.
Reams, 31.
Reburn, 49.
Redder, 30.
Reece, 32.
Reed, 49.
Reed, 171.
Reed, 184.
Reid, 147.
Reid, Whitelaw, 3.
Reno, 49.
Revolutionary Pensioners, 107.
Rich, A. J., 179, 180.
Richards, 32.
Richardson, 30.
Richardson, 101.
Richey, 7.
Richey, 109.
Richey, 187-8.
Richey, Andrew, 112.
Richey, Samuel, 113.
Richey, Thomas, 111.
Ricks, 30.
Ricks, 31.
Ridge Burials, 362-367.
Ridge Presbyterian Church, 183-191.
Rigdon, 49.
Roberts, 32.
Roberts, 109.
Roberts, Bishop, 176.
Roberts, James, 109, 110.
Roberts, James, 182.
Robertson, James, 186.
Roberts, R. R., 162.
Robinson, 31.
Robinson, 137.
Robinson, 160.
Rodgers, 138.
Rogers, 7.
Romanized Britons, 5.
Ross, 44.
Ross, 49.
Ross, Andrew Finley, 134.
Rowland, 168.
Rowland, Barkley W., 112.
Rowles, Thomas C., 112.
Rowley, Luther, 113.
Ruggles, Benjamin, 109.
Rumley Burials, 396-400.
Russell, 31.
Russell, 173.
Russell, John, 111.

For additional names, see alphabetical lists on pages 82-89, 102-106, 116-127, 181-182, 202-454, 457-584, and 587-617.

Russell, Samuel A., 110, 113.
Rutledge, 181.
Ryder, Thomas H., 113.
Ryan, 179.
Ryan, 181.

Sawhill, B. F., 180.
Scarlot, 179.
Schooley, 32.
Schuley, 30.
Scio Burials, 392-394.
Scoles, 175.
Scoles, 178.
Scoles, Curtis W., 113.
Scooly, C., 31.
Scotch-Irish, 1, 3, 4.
Scotch-Irish Emigration to America, 14, 17, 20.
Scotch-Irish in Pennsylvania, 15, 20.
Scotland, 5.
Scott, 6.
Scott, 31.
Scott, 95.
Scott, 173.
Scott, 188.
Scott, 189.
Scott, Alexander, 180.
Scott, Allen W., 112.
Scott, James M., 111.
Scott, Josiah, 3, 110, 111, 113.
Scott, T. J., 180.
Scroggs, Joseph, 133.
Sears, 90.
Sears, 109.
Sears, Ephraim, 109, 110.
Sears, Joseph J., 111.
Seceder Fever, 146.
Sems, 31.
Settlement at Marietta, 43.
Settlers, First, in Ohio, 43, 47-52.
Shannon, Wilson, 3, 135.
Sharon, 136.
Sharon, Joseph, 113.
Sharp, 30.
Sharp, John, 111, 112.
Shaw, 10.
Shearer, J. W., 180.
Shepler, 44.
Sheridan, Phil., 3.
Sherrard, 78.
Shiff, 49.
Shine, 32.
Shinn, Asa, 161.
Shinn, Asa, 175.
Shirer, J. W., 180.
Shoemaker, 30.
Shotwell, Walter G., 110, 111, 113.
Shrom, William P., 157, 160.

Sidwell, 32.
Simpson, 7.
Simpson, 78.
Simpson, 80.
Simpson, 82.
Simpson, 163.
Simpson, 164.
Simpson, Matthew, 3, 109, 110, 113, 134, 163, 165.
Sinclair, 30.
Sinclair, 32.
Sinsabaugh, Hiram, 180.
Skinner, Carleton A., 113.
Sloan, John, 113.
Sloan, Matthew M., 112.
Smiley, 81.
Smiley, 189.
Smith, 30.
Smith, 31.
Smith, 32.
Smith, 44.
Smith, 109.
Smith, Andrew, 113.
Smith, Edward, 179, 180.
Smith, Joseph, 93, 135.
Smith, Richard, 3.
Smith, Wesley, 180.
Smyrna Burials, 394.
Snedeker, 130.
Snodgrass, 95.
Snodgrass, James, 185.
Snyder, 44.
Snyder, 78.
Snyder, 81.
Snyder, Levi, 113.
Soule, 178.
Spears, 32.
Speer, 101.
Speer, 181.
Speer, Thomas, 143.
Spence, Henry, 111.
Spencer, 30.
Spencer, 32.
Spencer, Daniel, 113.
Spiker, John W., 113.
Spive, 31.
St. Clair, Arthur, 3.
St. Clairsville Presbyterian Church, 93.
Stafford, 31.
Stafford, 32.
Stalker, 31.
Stanley, 30.
Stanton, 30.
Stanton, 31.
Stanton, Edwin B., 111, 113.
Starbuck, 31.
Steadman, James B., 3.
Steer, 30.

For additional names, see alphabetical lists on pages 82-89, 102-106, 116-127, 181-182, 202-454, 457-584, and 587-617.

INDEX

Stephens, 78.
Stevenson, Joseph, 156.
Stewart, 7.
Stewart, 12.
Stewart, Robert, 111.
Stinson, Lared, 111.
Stokes, 32.
Stokes, 108.
Stokes, John, 112.
Stratton, 30.
Stratton, 32.
Suddith, 107.
Sumner, 31.
Swain, 31.
Swan, 81.
Swan, Joseph R., 3.
Swayne, 30.
Swayze, William, 162.

Taggart, 44.
Taggart, 109.
Taggart, William, 141, 142, 143.
Talbott, 30.
Tannehill, 132.
Tannehill, 173.
Tappan, Benjamin, 109.
Taylor, 30.
Taylor, 31.
Taylor, 32.
Taylor, 44.
Taylor, E. H., 180.
Taylor, I. C., 164.
Taylor, J. C., 180-1.
Teas, 44.
Tellus, 32.
Terrell, 30.
Thomas, 31.
Thomas, 178.
Thomas, Abraham, 178.
Thompson, 7.
Thompson, 141.
Thompson, 178.
Thompson, 181.
Thompson, David, 112.
Thompson, Harvey L., 111.
Thompson, S. Edwin, 112.
Thorn, C., 180.
Thorn, Charles, 180.
Thornton, 31.
Tilton, 49.
Tingley, 79.
Tingley, 80.
Tingley, 82.
Tingley, 163.
Tingley, 164.
Tingley, William, 112.
Tipton, 164.
Tipton, 165.

Tipton, 181.
Tipton, William, 163, 176, 179.
Tod, George, 109.
Todd, 107.
Todd, 171.
Todd, 173.
Tomlinson, 32.
Townsend, 30.
Townsend, 32.
Trehern, 30.
Trimble, 133.
Trimble, 134.
Trimble, Allen, 3.
Trine, 164.
Trotter, 31.
Turner, 165.
Turner, Allen C., 111.
Tyrone, Earl of, 11.

Underground Railway, 137.
United Presbyterian Church of Cadiz, 140-155.
Unity Burials, 349-355.
Unity Presbyterian Church, 133-138.
Updegraff, 32.
Updegraff, 137.
Urquhart, 144.

Vallandingham, C. L., 152.
Vance, 7.
Vance, 12.
Vance, Joseph, 3.
Vasbinder, 187-8.
Vaughn, 79.
Via, 32.
Viers, Brice W., 111.
Viers, Brice W., 112.
Vikings, 5.
Villages of Harrison County, 113.
Vimon, 31.
Vincent, 44.
Vincent, Thomas, 112.
Vincent, Thomas C., 110.
Vincent, William R., 132.
Virginians in Harrison County, 37-42.

Waddell, 8.
Waddle, William G., 113, 138.
Wagner, 82.
Walker, John, 133.
Walker, John, 133-38, 147-48.
Walkinshaw, 135.
Wallace, 7.
Wallace, 44.
Wallace, 49.
Wallace, 171.
Wallace, 173.
Wallace, William, 5, 171, 174.

For additional names, see alphabetical lists on pages 82-89, 102-106, 116-127, 181-182, 202-454, 457-584, and 587-617.

INDEX

Walraven, 161.
Walraven, 175.
Walter, 30.
Walters, 107.
Walton, 30.
War of 1812, 102-106
Ward, 31.
Ward, 32.
Ward, 49.
Ward, 138.
Ward, John Q. A., 3.
Warfel, 143.
Warfel, 144.
Warfel, 151.
Warfel, 153.
Warfel, 154.
Warfel, 155.
Warfell, Charles, 110.
Watkins, 31.
Watkins, W. B., 180.
Watson, 7.
Watson, 49.
Watson, Smith R., 110.
Watt, 98.
Watt, James, 161.
Waxler, 44.
Webster, 181.
Weels, 179.
Welch, 7.
Welch, 44.
Welch, Daniel, 95, 98, 110.
Welsh, 137.
Welsh, 186.
Welsh, 187.
Welsh, 189.
Welsh, John, 135.
Welsh, Johnson, 135.
Welling, 175.
Welling, 178.
Welling, David S., 180.
Wells, 32.
Wells, 107.
Wells, Charles, 113.
West, Thomas, 62.
West, 161.
West, 178.
Whan, 134.
Wharton, 32.
Wharton, H., 180.
Wheeler, 181.
White, 30.
White, 32.
White, 164.
White, 165.

Whitaker, 32.
Whiteacre, 30.
Wickersham, 30.
Wildman, 30.
Wildman, 31.
Wiley, 7.
Wiley, William, 110, 112.
Wilkin, 44.
Wilkin, 80.
Wilkin, 82.
Wilkinson, 30.
Williams, 31.
Williams, 32.
Williams, 49.
Williams, John S., 66.
Wills of Harrison County, 451-454.
Wilson, 7.
Wilson, 30.
Wilson, 44.
Wilson, 78.
Wilson, 81.
Wilson, 151.
Wilson, 168.
Wilson, Alexander, 143-144.
Wilson, Job, 180.
Wilson, S. J., 160.
Wishart, William, 138.
Wolf, S. P., 180.
Wood, 6.
Wood, 30.
Wood, 32.
Wood, Reuben, 3.
Woodborne, Edwin S., 112.
Woodborne, George, 112.
Woods, 31.
Worley, 175.
Worley, John B., 111.
Worstell, Henry P., 113.
Wrenn, 31.
Wright, 30.
Wright, 32.
Wright, John C., 3.
Wylie, 134.
Wylie, William, 131.

Yarnell, 32.
Yost, John, 113.
Young, 78.
Young, 80.
Young, 81.
Young, 181.
Young, Isaac, 163.
Young, Jacob, 162, 179.
Young, Thomas L., 3.

For additional names, see alphabetical lists on pages 82-89, 102-106, 116-127, 181-182, 202-454, 457-584, and 587-617.

www.ingramcontent.com/pod-product-compliance
Lightning Source LLC
Chambersburg PA
CBHW070905300426
44113CB00008B/937